Lecture Notes in Computer Science   14004

The series Lecture Notes in Computer Science (LNCS), including its subseries Lecture Notes in Artificial Intelligence (LNAI) and Lecture Notes in Bioinformatics (LNBI), has established itself as a medium for the publication of new developments in computer science and information technology research, teaching, and education.

LNCS enjoys close cooperation with the computer science R & D community, the series counts many renowned academics among its volume editors and paper authors, and collaborates with prestigious societies. Its mission is to serve this international community by providing an invaluable service, mainly focused on the publication of conference and workshop proceedings and postproceedings. LNCS commenced publication in 1973.

Carmit Hazay · Martijn Stam
Editors

Advances in Cryptology – EUROCRYPT 2023

42nd Annual International Conference on the Theory
and Applications of Cryptographic Techniques
Lyon, France, April 23–27, 2023
Proceedings, Part I

 Springer

Editors
Carmit Hazay 🆔
Bar-Ilan University
Ramat Gan, Israel

Martijn Stam 🆔
Simula UiB
Bergen, Norway

ISSN 0302-9743 ISSN 1611-3349 (electronic)
Lecture Notes in Computer Science
ISBN 978-3-031-30544-3 ISBN 978-3-031-30545-0 (eBook)
https://doi.org/10.1007/978-3-031-30545-0

This Springer imprint is published by the registered company Springer Nature Switzerland AG
The registered company address is: Gewerbestrasse 11, 6330 Cham, Switzerland

Preface

The 42nd Annual International Conference on the Theory and Applications of Cryptographic Techniques, Eurocrypt 2023, was held in Lyon, France between April 23–27 under the auspices of the International Association for Cryptologic Research. The conference had a record number of 415 submissions, out of which 109 were accepted.

Preparation for the academic aspects of the conference started in earnest well over a year ago, with the selection of a program committee, consisting of 79 regular members and six area chairs. The area chairs played an important part in enabling a high-quality review process; their role was expanded considerably from last year and, for the first time, properly formalized. Each area chair was in charge of moderating the discussions of the papers assigned under their area, guiding PC members and reviewers to consensus where possible, and helping us in making final decisions. We created six areas and assigned the following area chairs: Ran Canetti for Theoretical Foundations; Rosario Gennaro for Public Key Primitives with Advanced Functionalities; Tibor Jager for Classic Public Key Cryptography; Marc Joye for Secure and Efficient Implementation, Cryptographic Engineering, and Real-World Cryptography; Gregor Leander for Symmetric Cryptology; and finally Arpita Patra for Multi-party Computation and Zero-Knowledge.

Prior to the submission deadline, PC members were introduced to the reviewing process; for this purpose we created a slide deck that explained what we expected from everyone involved in the process and how PC members could use the reviewing system (HotCRP) used by us. An important aspect of the reviewing process is the reviewing form, which we modified based on the Crypto'22 form as designed by Yevgeniy Dodis and Tom Shrimpton. As is customary for IACR general conferences, the reviewing process was two-sided anonymous.

Out of the 415 submissions, four were desk rejected due to violations of the Call for Papers (non-anonymous submission or significant deviations from the submission format). For the remaining submissions, the review process proceeded in two stages. In the first stage, every paper was reviewed by at least three reviewers. For 109 papers a clear, negative consensus emerged and an early reject decision was reached and communicated to the authors on the 8th of December 2022. This initial phase of early rejections allowed the program committee to concentrate on the delicate task of selecting a program amongst the more promising submissions, while simultaneously offering the authors of the rejected papers the opportunity to take advantage of the early, full feedback to improve their work for a future occasion.

The remaining 302 papers progressed to an interactive discussion phase, which was open for two weeks (ending slightly before the Christmas break). During this period, the authors had access to their reviews (apart from some PC only fields) and were asked to address questions and requests for clarifications explicitly formulated in the reviews. It gave authors and reviewers the opportunity to communicate directly (yet anonymously) with each other during several rounds of interaction. For some papers, the multiple rounds helped in clarifying both the reviewers' questions and the authors' responses.

For a smaller subset of papers, a second interactive discussion phase took place in the beginning of January allowing authors to respond to new, relevant insights by the PC. Eventually, 109 papers were selected for the program.

The best paper award was granted to the paper "An Efficient Key Recovery Attack on SIDH" by Wouter Castryck and Thomas Decru for presenting the first efficient key recovery attack against the Supersingular Isogeny Diffie-Hellman (SIDH) problem. Two further, related papers were invited to the Journal of Cryptology: "Breaking SIDH in Polynomial Time" by Damien Robert and "A Direct Key Recovery Attack on SIDH" by Luciano Maino, Chloe Martindale, Lorenz Panny, Giacomo Pope and Benjamin Wesolowski.

Accepted papers written exclusively by researchers who were within four years of PhD graduation at the time of submission were eligible for the Early Career Best Paper Award. There were a number of strong candidates and the paper "Worst-Case Subexponential Attacks on PRGs of Constant Degree or Constant Locality" by Akın Ünal was awarded this honor.

The program further included two invited talks: Guy Rothblum opened the program with his talk on "Indistinguishable Predictions and Multi-group Fair Learning" (an extended abstract of his talk appears in these proceedings) and later during the conference Vadim Lyubashevsky gave a talk on "Lattice Cryptography: What Happened and What's Next".

First and foremost, we would like to thank Kevin McCurley and Kay McKelly for their tireless efforts in the background, making the whole process so much smoother for us to run. Thanks also to our previous co-chairs Orr Dunkelman, Stefan Dziembowski, Yevgeniy Dodis, Thomas Shrimpton, Shweta Agrawal and Dongdai Lin for sharing the lessons they learned and allowing us to build on their foundations. We thank Guy and Vadim for accepting to give two excellent invited talks. Of course, no program can be selected without submissions, so we thank both the authors of accepted papers, as well as those whose papers did not make it (we sincerely hope that, notwithstanding the disappointing outcome, you found the reviews and interaction constructive). The reviewing was led by our PC members, who often engaged expert subreviewers to write high-quality, insightful reviews and engage directly in the discussions, and we are grateful to both our PC members and the subreviewers. As the IACR's general conferences grow from year to year, a very special thank you to our area chairs, our job would frankly not have been possible without Ran, Rosario, Tibor, Marc, Gregor, and Arpita's tireless efforts leading the individual papers' discussions. And, last but not least, we would like to thank the general chairs: Damien Stehlé, Alain Passelègue, and Benjamin Wesolowski who worked very hard to make this conference happen.

April 2023   Carmit Hazay
                                                                                   Martijn Stam

Organization

General Co-chairs

Damien Stehlé — ENS de Lyon and Institut Universitaire de France, France

Alain Passelègue — Inria, France

Benjamin Wesolowski — CNRS and ENS de Lyon, France

Program Co-chairs

Carmit Hazay — Bar-Ilan University, Israel

Martijn Stam — Simula UiB, Norway

Area Chairs

Ran Canetti — Boston University, USA
(for Theoretical Foundations)

Rosario Gennaro — Protocol Labs and CUNY, USA
(for Public Key Primitives with Advanced Functionalities)

Tibor Jager — University of Wuppertal, Germany
(for Classic Public Key Cryptography)

Marc Joye — Zama, France
(for Secure and Efficient Implementation, Cryptographic Engineering, and Real-World Cryptography)

Gregor Leander — Ruhr-Universität Bochum, Germany
(for Symmetric Cryptology)

Arpita Patra — Google and IISc Bangalore, India
(for Multi-party Computation and Zero-Knowledge)

Program Committee

Masayuki Abe	NTT Social Informatics Laboratories and Kyoto University, Japan
Adi Akavia	University of Haifa, Israel
Prabhanjan Ananth	UC Santa Barbara, USA
Gilad Asharov	Bar-Ilan University, Israel
Marshall Ball	New York University, USA
Christof Beierle	Ruhr University Bochum, Germany
Mihir Bellare	UC San Diego, USA
Tim Beyne	KU Leuven, Belgium
Andrej Bogdanov	Chinese University of Hong Kong, China
Xavier Bonnetain	Inria, France
Joppe Bos	NXP Semiconductors, Belgium
Chris Brzuska	Aalto University, Finland
Ignacio Cascudo	IMDEA Software Institute, Spain
Nishanth Chandran	Microsoft Research India, India
Chitchanok Chuengsatiansup	The University of Melbourne, Australia
Michele Ciampi	The University of Edinburgh, UK
Ran Cohen	Reichman University, Israel
Jean-Sébastien Coron	University of Luxembourg, Luxembourg
Bernardo David	IT University of Copenhagen, Denmark
Christoph Dobraunig	Intel Labs, Intel Corporation, Hillsboro, USA
Léo Ducas	CWI Amsterdam and Leiden University, Netherlands
Maria Eichlseder	Graz University of Technology, Austria
Pooya Farshim	IOHK and Durham University, UK
Serge Fehr	CWI Amsterdam and Leiden University, Netherlands
Dario Fiore	IMDEA Software Institute, Spain
Pierre-Alain Fouque	Université Rennes 1 and Institut Universitaire de France, France
Steven Galbraith	University of Auckland, New Zealand
Chaya Ganesh	IISc Bangalore, India
Si Gao	Huawei Technologies Co., Ltd., China
Daniel Genkin	GeorgiaTech, USA
Craig Gentry	TripleBlind, USA
Benedikt Gierlichs	KU Leuven, Belgium
Rishab Goyal	UW-Madison, USA
Vipul Goyal	NTT Research and CMU, USA
Viet Tung Hoang	Florida State University, USA
Andreas Hülsing	Eindhoven University of Technology, Netherlands

Antoine Joux   CISPA, Helmholtz Center for Cybersecurity,
                                      Germany
Karen Klein   ETH Zurich, Switzerland
Markulf Kohlweiss   University of Edinburgh and IOHK, UK
Jooyoung Lee   KAIST, Korea
Gaëtan Leurent   Inria, France
Shengli Liu   Shanghai Jiao Tong University, China
Yunwen Liu   Cryptape Technology Co., Ltd., China
Stefan Lucks   Bauhaus-Universität Weimar, Germany
Hemanta Maji   Purdue, USA
Alexander May   Ruhr University Bochum, Germany
Nele Mentens   Leiden University, Netherlands and KU Leuven,
                                      Belgium
Tal Moran   Reichman University, Israel
Michael Naehrig   Microsoft Research, USA
Ngoc Khanh Nguyen   EPFL, Switzerland
Emmanuela Orsini   Bocconi University, Italy and KU Leuven,
                                      Belgium
Jiaxin Pan   NTNU, Norway
Omkant Pandey   Stony Brook University, USA
Anat Paskin-Cherniavsky   Ariel University, Israel
Chris Peikert   University of Michigan and Algorand, Inc., USA
Léo Perrin   Inria, France
Giuseppe Persiano   Università di Salerno, Italy
Thomas Peters   UCLouvain, Belgium
Christophe Petit   Université libre de Bruxelles, Belgium and
                                      University of Birmingham, UK
Krzysztof Pietrzak   ISTA, Austria
Bertram Poettering   IBM Research Europe – Zurich, Switzerland
Bart Preneel   KU Leuven, Belgium
Divya Ravi   Aarhus University, Denmark
Christian Rechberger   TU Graz, Austria
Ron Rothblum   Technion, Israel
Carla Ràfols   Universitat Pompeu Fabra, Spain
Paul Rösler   FAU Erlangen-Nürnberg, Germany
Yu Sasaki   NTT Social Informatics Laboratories, NIST
                                      Associate, Japan
Dominique Schröder   FAU Erlangen-Nürnberg, Germany
Omri Shmueli   Tel Aviv University, Israel
Janno Siim   Simula UiB, Norway
Daniel Slamanig   AIT Austrian Institute of Technology, Austria
Yifan Song   Tsinghua University, China

Qiang Tang   The University of Sydney, Australia
Serge Vaudenay   EPFL, Switzerland
Fernando Virdia   Intel Labs, Switzerland
Meiqin Wang   Shandong University, China
Mor Weiss   Bar-Ilan University, Israel
David Wu   UT Austin, USA

Additional Reviewers

Behzad Abdolmaleki   Katharina Boudgoust
Damiano Abram   Christina Boura
Hamza Abusalah   Zvika Brakerski
Leo Ackermann   Lennart Braun
Amit Agarwal   Marek Broll
Ghous Amjad   Ileana Buhan
Benny Applebaum   Matteo Campanelli
Gal Arnon   Federico Canale
Thomas Attema   Anne Canteaut
Benedikt Auerbach   Gaëtan Cassiers
Lukas Aumayr   Wouter Castryck
Gennaro Avitabile   Pyrros Chaidos
Melissa Azouaoui   André Chailloux
Saikrishna Badrinarayanan   T.-H. Hubert Chan
Karim Baghery   Anirudh Chandramouli
Kunpeng Bai   Rohit Chatterjee
Shi Bai   Hao Chen
David Balbás   Long Chen
Manuel Barbosa   Mingjie Chen
Khashayar Barooti   Yanbo Chen
James Bartusek   Yanlin Chen
Andrea Basso   Yilei Chen
Balthazar Bauer   Yu Long Chen
Carsten Baum   Wei Cheng
Michiel van Beirendonck   Céline Chevalier
Josh Benaloh   James Chiang
Fabrice Benhamouda   Wonhee Cho
Ward Beullens   Wonseok Choi
Amit Singh Bhati   Wutichai Chongchitmate
Ritam Bhaumik   Hien Chu
Alexander Bienstock   Valerio Cini
Alexander Block   Christine Cloostermans
Jonathan Bootle   Andrea Coladangelo
Cecilia Boschini   Daniel Collins

Sandro Coretti-Drayton
Craig Costello
Elizabeth Crites
Miguel Cueto Noval
Jan-Pieter D'Anvers
Sourav Das
Alex Davidson
Gabrielle De Micheli
Cyprien Delpech de Saint Guilhem
Patrick Derbez
Lalita Devadas
Siemen Dhooghe
Jesus Diaz
Khue Do
Jelle Don
Rafael Dowsley
Avijit Dutta
Sébastien Duval
Christoph Egger
Tariq Elahi
Lynn Engelberts
Felix Engelmann
Muhammed F. Esgin
Thomas Espitau
Andre Esser
Simona Etinski
Prastudy Fauzi
Patrick Felke
Hanwen Feng
Rex Fernando
Tako Boris Fouotsa
Danilo Francati
Sapir Freizeit
Paul Frixons
Rachit Garg
Sanjam Garg
Aymeric Genêt
Marios Georgiou
Satrajit Ghosh
Niv Gilboa
Valerie Gilchrist
Emanuele Giunta
Aarushi Goel
Eli Goldin
Junqing Gong

Alonso González
Lorenzo Grassi
Jiaxin Guan
Zichen Gui
Aurore Guillevic
Aditya Gulati
Aldo Gunsing
Chun Guo
Divya Gupta
Felix Günther
Hosein Hadipour
Mohammad Hajiabadi
Shai Halevi
Peter Hall
Shuai Han
Patrick Harasser
David Heath
Lena Heimberger
Alexandra Henzinger
Julia Hesse
Minki Hhan
Dennis Hofheinz
Maya-Iggy van Hoof
Sam Hopkins
Akinori Hosoyamada
Kristina Hostáková
Martha Norberg Hovd
Yu-Hsuan Huang
Loïs Huguenin-Dumittan
Kathrin Hövelmanns
Yuval Ishai
Muhammad Ishaq
Tetsu Iwata
Michael John Jacobson, Jr.
Aayush Jain
Samuel Jaques
Jinhyuck Jeong
Corentin Jeudy
Ashwin Jha
Mingming Jiang
Zhengzhong Jin
Thomas Johansson
David Joseph
Daniel Jost
Fatih Kaleoglu

Novak Kaluderovic
Chethan Kamath
Shuichi Katsumata
Marcel Keller
John Kelsey
Erin Kenney
Hamidreza Khorasgani
Hamidreza Khoshakhlagh
Seongkwang Kim
Elena Kirshanova
Fuyuki Kitagawa
Bor de Kock
Konrad Kohbrok
Lisa Kohl
Sebastian Kolby
Dimitris Kolonelos
Ilan Komargodski
Yashvanth Kondi
Venkata Koppula
Alexis Korb
Matthias Krause
Hugo Krawczyk
Toomas Krips
Mike Kudinov
Péter Kutas
Thijs Laarhoven
Yi-Fu Lai
Baptiste Lambin
Nathalie Lang
Abel Laval
Laurens Le Jeune
Byeonghak Lee
Changmin Lee
Eysa Lee
Seunghoon Lee
Sihyun Lee
Dominik Leichtle
Jannis Leuther
Shai Levin
Chaoyun Li
Yanan Li
Yiming Li
Xiao Liang
Jyun-Jie Liao
Benoît Libert

Wei-Kai Lin
Yao-Ting Lin
Helger Lipmaa
Eik List
Fukang Liu
Jiahui Liu
Qipeng Liu
Xiangyu Liu
Chen-Da Liu-Zhang
Satya Lokam
Alex Lombardi
Patrick Longa
George Lu
Jinyu Lu
Xianhui Lu
Yuan Lu
Zhenliang Lu
Ji Luo
You Lyu
Reinhard Lüftenegger
Urmila Mahadev
Mohammad Mahmoody
Mohammad Mahzoun
Christian Majenz
Nikolaos Makriyannis
Varun Maram
Laurane Marco
Ange Martinelli
Daniel Masny
Noam Mazor
Matthias Meijers
Fredrik Meisingseth
Florian Mendel
Bart Mennink
Simon-Philipp Merz
Tony Metger
Pierre Meyer
Brice Minaud
Kazuhiko Minematsu
Victor Mollimard
Tomoyuki Morimae
Nicky Mouha
Tamer Mour
Marcel Nageler
Mridul Nandi

María Naya-Plasencia
Patrick Neumann
Hai Nguyen
Ky Nguyen
Phong Q. Nguyen
Ryo Nishimaki
Olga Nissenbaum
Anca Nitulescu
Ariel Nof
Julian Nowakowski
Adam O'Neill
Sai Lakshmi Bhavana Obbattu
Miyako Ohkubo
Eran Omri
Claudio Orlandi
Michele Orrù
Elisabeth Oswald
Omer Paneth
Guillermo Pascual-Perez
Kenneth G. Paterson
Sikhar Patranabis
Alice Pellet-Mary
Maxime Plancon
Antigoni Polychroniadou
Alexander Poremba
Bernardo Portela
Eamonn Postlethwaite
Emmanuel Prouff
Kirthivaasan Puniamurthy
Octavio Pérez Kempner
Luowen Qian
Tian Qiu
Willy Quach
Håvard Raddum
Srinivasan Raghuraman
Justin Raizes
Sebastian Ramacher
Hugues Randriambololona
Shahram Rasoolzadeh
Simon Rastikian
Joost Renes
Nicolas Resch
Alfredo Rial Duran
Doreen Riepel
Silvia Ritsch

Melissa Rossi
Mike Rosulek
Yann Rotella
Lawrence Roy
Roozbeh Sarenche
Amirreza Sarencheh
Pratik Sarkar
Arish Sateesan
Christian Schaffner
Carl Richard Theodor Schneider
Markus Schofnegger
Peter Scholl
André Schrottenloher
Gregor Seiler
Sruthi Sekar
Nicolas Sendrier
Meghna Sengupta
Jinrui Sha
Akash Shah
Siamak Shahandashti
Moni Shahar
Shahed Sharif
Laura Shea
Abhi Shelat
Yaobin Shen
Sina Shiehian
Jad Silbak
Alice Silverberg
Luisa Siniscalchi
Tomer Solomon
Karl Southern
Nicholas Spooner
Sriram Sridhar
Srivatsan Sridhar
Akshayaram Srinivasan
François-Xavier Standaert
Uri Stemmer
Lukas Stennes
Patrick Steuer
Christoph Striecks
Patrick Struck
Chao Sun
Erkan Tairi
Akira Takahashi
Abdullah Talayhan

Titouan Tanguy
Stefano Tessaro
Emmanuel Thomé
Sri AravindaKrishnan Thyagarajan
Yan Bo Ti
Mehdi Tibouchi
Tyge Tiessen
Bénédikt Tran
Andreas Trügler
Daniel Tschudi
Aleksei Udovenko
Jonathan Ullman
Dominique Unruh
Vinod Vaikuntanathan
Daniele Venturi
Michiel Verbauwhede
Javier Verbel
Gilles Villard
Mikhail Volkhov
Satyanarayana Vusirikala
Benedikt Wagner
Roman Walch
Hendrik Waldner
Alexandre Wallet
Michael Walter
Mingyuan Wang
Yuyu Wang
Florian Weber
Hoeteck Wee
Puwen Wei
Charlotte Weitkaemper

Weiqiang Wen
Benjamin Wesolowski
Daniel Wichs
Wessel van Woerden
Ke Wu
Keita Xagawa
Hanshen Xiao
Jiayu Xu
Yingfei Yan
Xiuyu Ye
Kevin Yeo
Eylon Yogev
Albert Yu
Aaram Yun
Alexandros Zacharakis
Thomas Zacharias
Michal Zajac
Greg Zaverucha
Runzhi Zeng
Cong Zhang
Lei Zhang
Ren Zhang
Xinrui Zhang
Yuqing Zhao
Yu Zhou
Dionysis Zindros
Giorgos Zirdelis
Lukas Zobernig
Arne Tobias Ødegaard
Morten Øygarden

Sponsoring Institutions

– Platinum Sponsor: Université Rennes 1 and PEPR Quantique, Zama
– Gold Sponsor: Apple, Cryptolab, ENS de Lyon, ENS PSL, Huawei, Sandbox AQ, Thales, TII
– Silver Sponsor: Algorand Foundation, ANSSI, AWS, PQShield
– Bronze Sponsor: Cosmian, CryptoExperts, CryptoNext Security, IBM, Idemia, Inria, LIP

Contents – Part I

Oblivious Transfer and Data Access

Quantum Cryptography

Invited Talk

Indistinguishable Predictions
and Multi-group Fair Learning

Guy N. Rothblum[(✉)] [iD]

Apple, Cupertino, USA
guy.rothblum@gmail.com

Abstract. Prediction algorithms assign numbers to individuals that are popularly understood as individual "probabilities"—what is the probability that an applicant will repay a loan? Automated predictions increasingly form the basis for life-altering decisions, and this raises a host of concerns. Concerns about the *fairness* of the resulting predictions are particularly alarming: for example, the predictor might perform poorly on a protected minority group. We survey recent developments in formalizing and addressing such concerns.

Inspired by the theory of computational indistinguishability, the recently proposed notion of *Outcome Indistinguishability (OI)* [Dwork *et al.*, STOC 2021] requires that the *predicted* distribution of outcomes cannot be distinguished from the real-world distribution. Outcome Indistinguishability is a strong requirement for obtaining meaningful predictions. Happily, it can be obtained: techniques from the algorithmic fairness literature [Hebert-Johnson *et al.*, ICML 2018] yield algorithms for learning OI predictors from real-world outcome data.

Returning to the motivation of addressing fairness concerns, Outcome Indistinguishability can be used to provide robust and general guarantees for protected demographic groups [Rothblum and Yona, ICML 2021]. This gives algorithms that can learn a single predictor that "performs well" for every group in a given rich collection G of overlapping subgroups. Performance is measured using a loss function, which can be quite general and can itself incorporate fairness concerns.

1 Introduction

Machine learning tools are used to make and inform increasingly consequential decisions about individuals. Examples range from medical risk prediction

This extended abstract overviews the recent developments and contributions in [14,41], and borrows liberally from those works. The research described in this extended abstract was done while the author was at the Weizmann Institute of Science and while visiting Microsoft Research. This project has received funding from the European Research Council (ERC) under the European Union's Horizon 2020 research and innovation programme (grant agreement No. 819702), from the Israel Science Foundation (grant number 5219/17), and from the Simons Foundation Collaboration on the Theory of Algorithmic Fairness.

© International Association for Cryptologic Research 2023
C. Hazay and M. Stam (Eds.): EUROCRYPT 2023, LNCS 14004, pp. 3–21, 2023.
https://doi.org/10.1007/978-3-031-30545-0_1

to hiring decisions and criminal justice. Automated risk prediction comes with benefits, but it also raises substantial societal concerns. First and foremost, how meaningful are the predictions? Another prominent concern is that these algorithms might discriminate against protected and/or disadvantaged groups. In particular, a learned predictor might perform differently on a protected subgroup compared to the general population.

In a sequence of recent works we tackle these concerns with novel tools and perspectives. Our approach is inspired by the cryptographic and complexity-theoretic literature on indistinguishability, as well as the burgeoning literature on algorithmic fairness. This manuscript aims to highlight these developments, focusing on the following contributions:

Outcome Indistinguishability: a new framework for meaningful predictions. Prediction algorithms "score" individuals, mapping them to numbers in $[0, 1]$ that are popularly understood as "probabilities" or "likelihoods" of observable events: the probability of 5-year survival, the chance that the loan will be repaid on schedule, the likelihood that the student will graduate within four years. What do these numbers actually mean? How can we judge a predicted probability when the event (e.g. 5-year survival) is non-repeatable? The question of "individual probabilities" has been studied for decades across many disciplines without clear resolution (see Dawid [9]).

In recent work with Dwork *et al.* [14] we propose *Outcome Indistinguishability (OI)*: a novel framework for guaranteeing meaningful predictions. In a nutshell, the predictions should be *indistinguishable*, given real-world outcomes, from the true probabilities governing reality. We show that Outcome Indistinguishability is feasible: building on a connection to the notion of multi-calibration [30], we construct algorithms for learning OI predictors from outcome data. These contributions are described in Sect. 2.

Multi-group fair learning. The literature on (supervised) learning and loss minimization takes a different approach to predicting outcomes. Given an i.i.d. training set of labeled data, the goal is learning a predictor p that performs well on the underlying distribution. Performance is measured using a *loss function*, such as the squared loss or various other measures. In agnostic learning [35], the loss incurred by the predictor p should be competitive with the best predictor in a benchmark class $\mathcal{H}$. These approaches have enjoyed tremendous success, but they does not resolve basic questions about the meaningfulness of predictions. Given a predictor that achieves a certain loss, how should we judge its performance? Both at an aggregate level, over the entire population (what level of loss is "good"?), at the level of protected subgroups, and at the level of individual predictions. Indeed, it has been demonstrated that standard machine learning tools, when applied to standard data sets, produce predictors whose performance on protected demographic groups is quite poor [4].

Motivated by these concerns, in work with Yona [41] we study *multi-group agnostic learning*. For a rich collection $\mathcal{G}$ of (potentially) overlapping groups, our goal is to learn a single predictor p, such that the loss experienced by every group $g \in \mathcal{G}$ (when classified by p) is not much larger than the loss of the best predictor *for that group* in the class $\mathcal{H}$. This should hold for all groups in $\mathcal{G}$ simultaneously. To capture a wide variety of settings, we aim to be quite general in our treatment of different loss functions. In particular, the loss function itself can also incorporate fairness concerns. We show that this ambitious objective is obtainable! Multi-group fair predictors can be learned for a rich class of loss functions. The learning procedure itself is constructed via a reduction to Outcome Indistinguishability, demonstrating the power and the flexibility of the OI framework. We detail these contributions in Sect. 3.

Further related work and recent developments. We discussed further related work in Sect. 2.3 and before Sect. 3.1. We conclude in Sect. 4 with a brief discussion of more recent developments that build on the contributions described in this extended abstract.

2 Outcome Indistinguishability

The recently-proposed notion of *Outcome Indistinguishability* (OI) [14] proposes and studies novel criteria for significant predictions. The outputs of a prediction algorithm are viewed as defining a generative model for observational outcomes. Ideally, the outcomes from this generative model should "look like" the outcomes produced by Nature (the real world). A predictor satisfying outcome indistinguishability provides a generative model that cannot be efficiently refuted on the basis of the real-life observations produced by Nature. In this sense, the probabilities defined by any OI predictor provide a meaningful model of the "probabilities" assigned by Nature: even granted full access to the predictive model and historical outcomes from Nature, no analyst can invalidate the model's predictions. This provides a computational/cryptographic perspective on the deeper discussion of what we should demand of prediction algorithms–a subject of intense study in the statistics community for over 30 years (see, *e.g.*, the forecasting work in [8, 19, 20, 42, 43])—and how they should be used. For example, the study of Outcome Indistinguishability has led to lower bound results that provide scientific teeth to the political argument that, if risk prediction instruments are to be used by the courts (as they often are in the United States), then at the very least auditors should be given oracle access to the algorithms.

Basic notation. We focus on the fundamental setting of predicting a binary outcome, but note that the OI framework has been extended to deal with more general outcomes [15]. Individuals are represented by a collection of covariates from a discrete domain $\mathcal{X}$, for example, the set of d-bit strings (there might be collisions, or it may be the case that each individual has a unique representation). We model Nature as a joint distribution, denoted $\mathcal{D}^*$, over individuals and outcomes, where $y_x^* \in \{0, 1\}$ represents Nature's choice of outcome for individual $x \in X$. We use $x \sim \mathcal{D}_{\mathcal{X}}$ to denote a sample from Nature's marginal distribution over individuals and denote by $p_x^* \in [0, 1]$ the conditional probability that

Nature assigns to the outcome y_x^*, conditioned on x. We emphasize, however, that Nature may choose $p_x^* \in \{0, 1\}$ to be deterministic; our definitions and constructions are agnostic as to this point.

A *predictor* is a function $\tilde{p} : \mathcal{X} \to [0, 1]$ that maps an individual $x \in \mathcal{X}$ to an estimate $\tilde{p}_x$ of the conditional probability of $y_x^* = 1$. For a predictor $\tilde{p} : \mathcal{X} \to [0, 1]$, we denote by $(x, \tilde{y}_x) \sim \mathcal{D}(\tilde{p})$ the random process of drawing an individual-outcome pair, where $x \sim \mathcal{D}_{\mathcal{X}}$ is sampled from Nature's distribution over individuals, and then the outcome $\tilde{y}_x \sim \mathrm{Ber}(\tilde{p}_x)$ is sampled from the Bernoulli distribution with parameter $\tilde{p}_x$.

Outcome Indistinguishability. Imagine that Nature selects $p_x^* = 1$ for half of the mass of $x \sim \mathcal{D}_{\mathcal{X}}$ and $p_x^* = 0$ for the remainder. If the two sets of individuals are easy to identify then we can potentially recover a close approximation to p^*. Suppose, however, that the sets are *computationally indistinguishable*, in the sense that given $x \sim \mathcal{D}_{\mathcal{X}}$, no efficient observer can guess if $p_x^* = 1$ or $p_x^* = 0$ with probability significantly better than $1/2$. In this case, producing the estimates $\tilde{p}_x = 1/2$ *for every individual* $x \in \mathcal{X}$ captures the best computationally feasible understanding of Nature: given limited computational power, the outcomes produced by Nature may faithfully be modeled as a random. In particular, if Nature were to change the outcome generation probabilities from p^* to $\tilde{p}$ we, as computationally bounded observers, will not notice. In other words, predictors satisfying OI give rise to models of Nature that cannot be falsified based only on observational data.

Definition 1 (Outcome Indistinguishability). *Fix Nature's distribution* $\mathcal{D}^*$*. For a class of distinguishers* $\mathcal{A}$ *and* $\varepsilon > 0$*, a predictor* $\tilde{p} : \mathcal{X} \to [0, 1]$ *satisfies* $(\mathcal{A}, \varepsilon)$*-outcome indistinguishability (OI) if for every* $A \in \mathcal{A}$,

$$\left| \Pr_{(x, y_x^*) \sim \mathcal{D}^*} [\, A(x, y_x^*; \tilde{p}) = 1 \,] - \Pr_{(x, \tilde{y}_x) \sim \mathcal{D}(\tilde{p})} [\, A(x, \tilde{y}_x; \tilde{p}) = 1 \,] \right| \leq \varepsilon.$$

The above definition is purposefully vague about the distinguisher's access to the predictor $\tilde{p}$: we anchor a hierarchy of OI variants around different levels of access to $\tilde{p}$. The definition of Outcome Indistinguishability can be extended in many other ways, for example to distinguishers receive multiple samples from each distribution (this will be used in Lemma 11 below), and to the case of non-Boolean outcomes [15].

In the extreme, when we think of $\mathcal{A}$ as the set of all polynomial-time distinguishers, outcome indistinguishability sets a demanding standard for predictors that model Nature. Given an OI predictor $\tilde{p}$, even the most skeptical scientist—who, for example, does not believe that Nature can be captured by a simple computational model—cannot refute the model's predictions through observation alone. This framing gives a cryptographic or computational perspective on the scientific method, by considering $\tilde{p}$ as expressing a hypothesis that cannot be falsified through observational investigation.

The OI hierarchy. In the most basic variant of the definition, the distinguisher does not get direct access to the predicted probabilities, only to the outcomes (drawn by p^* or by $\tilde{p}$). A predictor $\tilde{p}$ satisfies this most basic notion of OI if for all $A \in \mathcal{A}$, the probability that A accepts the sample (x, y_x) is (nearly) the same for Nature's distribution and the predictor's distribution. The requirement can be strengthened by also giving the distinguisher direct access the predictor $\tilde{p}$ itself: either access to the predicted probability $\tilde{p}_x$ of the sample at hand, oracle access, or even access to the code. We emphasize, however, that the distinguisher never gets access to p^*: Nature's true probabilities are unknowable.

These differing levels of access to the predictor produce a hierarchy of definitions, which we illustrate through an example. Imagine a medical board that wishes to audit the output of a program $\tilde{p}$ used to estimate the chances of five-year survival of patients under a given course of treatment. We can view the medical board as a distinguisher $A \in \mathcal{A}$. To perform the audit, the board receives historical files of patients and their five-year predicted (*i.e.*, drawn from $\mathcal{D}(\tilde{p})$) or actual (drawn from $\mathcal{D}^*$) outcomes. The requirement is that these two cases be indistinguishable to the board.

1. To start, the board is only given samples, and must distinguish Nature's samples $(x, y_x^*) \sim \mathcal{D}^*$ from those sampled according to the predicted distribution $(x, \tilde{y}_x) \sim \mathcal{D}(\tilde{p})$. The board gets no direct access to predictions $\tilde{p}_x$ of the program; we call this variant *no-access-OI*.
2. Naturally, the board may ask to see the predictions $\tilde{p}_x$ for each sampled individual. In this extension—*sample-access-OI*—the board must distinguish samples of the form $(x, y_x^*, \tilde{p}_x)$ and $(x, \tilde{y}_x, \tilde{p}_x)$, again for $(x, y_x^*) \sim \mathcal{D}^*$ and $(x, \tilde{y}_x) \sim \mathcal{D}(\tilde{p})$.
3. *Oracle-access-OI* allows the board to make queries to the program $\tilde{p}$ on arbitrary individuals, perhaps to examine how the algorithm behaves on related (but unsampled) patients.
4. Finally, in *code-access-OI*, the board is allowed to examine not only the predictions from $\tilde{p}$ but also the actual code, *i.e.*, the full implementation details of the program computing $\tilde{p}$.

2.1   Feasibility and Learnability of OI Predictors

Do efficient OI predictors always exist? In particular, *can we bound the complexity of OI predictors, independently of the complexity of Nature's distribution?* The picture here is subtle, and Outcome Indistinguishability differs qualitatively from prior notions of indistinguishability.

Beyond he question of *existence*, it is also important to understand whether it is possible to *learn* OI predictors from outcome data (we focus on the natural setting where outcomes are all we can hope to observe). A learning algorithm receives outcome data drawn from $\mathcal{D}^*$, with the goal of learning a predictor $\tilde{p}$ that satisfies OI w.r.t a given class $\mathcal{A}$ of distinguishers. Happily, OI predictors can be learned from outcome data at all levels of the hierarchy, with *logarithmic* sample complexity in the size of the family of distinguishers.

The first two level of the OI hierarchy. Dwork *et al.* [14] show that no-access-OI and sample-access-OI are closely related to the notions of multi-accuracy and multi-calibration [30], respectively, studied in the algorithmic fairness literature. Very loosely, for a collection $\mathcal{C}$ of subpopulations of individuals, $(\mathcal{C}, \alpha)$-multi-calibration asks that a predictor $\tilde{p}$ be calibrated (up to α error) not just overall, but also when we restrict our attention to subpopulations $S \subseteq \mathcal{X}$ for every set $S \in \mathcal{C}$. Here, calibration over S means that if we restrict our attention to individuals $x \in S$ for which $\tilde{p}_x = v$, then the fraction individuals with positive outcomes (i.e., $x \in S$ such that $y_x^* = 1$) is roughly v. Loosely, by equivalent we mean that each notion can enforce the other, for closely related classes $\mathcal{C}$ and $\mathcal{A}$. Importantly, the relation between the class of distinguishers and collection of subpopulations preserves most natural measures of complexity; in other words, if we take $\mathcal{A}$ to be a class of efficient distinguishers, then evaluating set membership for the populations in $\mathcal{C}$ will be efficient (and vice versa). No-access-OI is similarly equivalent to the weaker notion of multi-accuracy, which requires accurate expectations for each $S \in \mathcal{C}$, rather than calibration.

Leveraging feasibility results for the fairness notions from [30], we can obtain efficient predictors satisfying no-access-OI or sample-access-OI, by reduction to multi-accuracy and multi-calibration. Informally, for each of these levels, we can obtain OI predictors whose complexity scales linearly in the complexity of $\mathcal{A}$ and inverse polynomially in the desired distinguishing advantage ε. The result is quite generic; for concreteness, we state the theorem using circuit size as the complexity measure.

Theorem 2 (Informal [14]). *Let $\mathcal{A}$ be a class of distinguishers implemented by size-s circuits. For any $\mathcal{D}^*$ and $\varepsilon > 0$, there exists a predictor $\tilde{p} : \mathcal{X} \to [0,1]$ satisfying $(\mathcal{A}, \varepsilon)$-sample-access-OI (similarly, no-access-OI) implemented by a circuit of size $O(s/\varepsilon^2)$.*

OI predictors can be learned using only a bounded number of observed outcomes $(x, y_x^*) \sim \mathcal{D}^*$. The learning algorithm, which leverages algorithms for learning multicalibrated predictors, has sample complexity that is logarithmic in the size of the distinguisher class $\mathcal{A}$. The runtime for learning is *linear* in the size of $\mathcal{A}$ and polynomial in $(1/\varepsilon)$. Alternatively, the task of learning an OI predictor can be reduced to an agnostic learning task on a hypothesis class that is related to $\mathcal{A}$. See [14,30] for further details.

The top two layers of the OI hierarchy. There is a general-purpose algorithm for constructing OI predictors, even when the distinguishers are allowed arbitrary access to the predictor in question. This shows the existence and learnability of oracle-access-OI and code-access-OI predictors. This construction of [14] extends the learning algorithm for multi-calibration of [30] to the more general setting of OI. When we allow such powerful distinguishers, the learned predictor $\tilde{p}$ is quantitatively less efficient than in the weaker notions of OI. For the overivew in this manuscript we state the bound informally, assuming the distinguishers are implemented by circuits with oracle gates (see [14] for a full and formal treatment). As an example, if we let $\mathcal{A}$ be the set of oracle-circuits of some fixed polynomial size (in the dimension d of individual's representations), and allow arbitrary oracle queries, then $\tilde{p}$ will be of size $d^{O(1/\varepsilon^2)}$.

Theorem 3 (Informal [14]). *Let $\mathcal{A}$ be a class of oracle-circuit distinguishers implemented by size-s circuits that make at most q oracle calls to the predictor in question. For any $\mathcal{D}^*$ and $\varepsilon > 0$, there exists a predictor $\tilde{p} : \mathcal{X} \to [0,1]$ satisfying $(\mathcal{A}, \varepsilon)$-oracle-access-OI implemented by a (non-oracle) circuit of size $s \cdot q^{O(1/\varepsilon^2)}$.*

We omit a discussion of the complexity of learning oracle-access-OI, as well as the results (and definitional subtleties) of code-access-OI. We refer the interested reader to [14]. We remark that for code-access-OI, the complexity may scale doubly exponentially in poly($1/\varepsilon$).

Hardness via Fine-Grained Complexity. Dwork *et al.* [14] established a connection between the fine-grained complexity of well-studied problems and the complexity of achieving oracle-access-OI. Under the assumption that the (randomized) complexity of counting k-cliques in n-vertex graphs is $n^{\Omega(k)}$, the construction of Theorem 3 is optimal up to polynomial factors. Specifically, they rule out (under this assumption) the possibility that the complexity of a oracle-access-OI predictor can be a fixed polynomial in the complexity of the distinguishers in $\mathcal{A}$ and in the distinguishing advantage ε. Their hardness result holds for constant distinguishing advantage ε and for an efficiently-sampleable distribution $\mathcal{D}^*$. This hardness results are in stark contrast to the state of affairs for sample-access-OI (see Theorem 2). Concretely, in the parameters of the upper bound, the result based on the hardness of clique-counting rules out any predictor $\tilde{p}$ satisfying oracle-access-OI of (uniform) size significantly smaller than $d^{\Omega(1/\epsilon)}$.

Theorem 4 (Informal [14]). *For $k \in \mathbb{N}$, assume there exist $\alpha > 0$ s.t. there is no $o(n^{\alpha \cdot k})$-time randomized algorithm for counting k-cliques. Then, there exist: $\mathcal{X} \subseteq \{0,1\}^{d^2}$, an efficiently-sampleable distribution $\mathcal{D}^*$, and a class $\mathcal{A}$ of distinguishers that run in time $\tilde{O}(d^3)$ and make $\tilde{O}(d)$ oracle queries to $\tilde{p}$, s.t. for $\varepsilon = \frac{1}{100k}$, no predictor $\tilde{p}$ that runs in time $(d^{\alpha \cdot k} \cdot \log^{-\omega(1)}(d))$ can satisfy $(\mathcal{A}, \varepsilon)$-oracle-access-OI.*

This lower bound is robust to the computational model: assuming that clique-counting requires $n^{\Omega(k)}$-sized circuits implies a similar lower bound on the circuit size of oracle-access-OI predictors. The complexity of clique counting has been widely studied and related to other problems in the fine-grained and parameterized complexity literatures, see the discussion in [14]. We note that, under the plausible assumption that the fine-grained complexity of known clique counting algorithms is tight, this result shows that obtaining oracle-access-OI is as hard, up to sub-polynomial factors, as computing p^*. We emphasize that this is the case even though the running time of the distinguishers can be arbitrarily small compared to the running time of p^*.

Dwork *et al.* also show that, under the (milder) assumption that BPP $\neq$ PSPACE, there exists a polynomial collection of distinguishers and a distribution

$\mathcal{D}^*$, for which no polynomial-time predictor $\tilde{p}$ can be OI. The distinction from the fine-grained result (beyond the difference in the assumptions) is that here $\mathcal{D}^*$ is not efficiently sampleable, and the distinguishing advantage for which OI is hard is much smaller.

2.2   Broader Context and Discussion

We highlight a few possible interpretations and insights that stem from the technical results described above. The ability to construct predictors that satisfy outcome indistinguishability can be viewed both positively and negatively. On one hand, the feasibility results demonstrate the possibility of learning generative models of observed phenomena that withstand very powerful scrutiny, even given the complete description of the model. On the other hand, OI does not guarantee statistical closeness to Nature (it need not be the case that $p^* \approx \tilde{p}$). Thus, the feasibility results demonstrate the ability to learn an *incorrect* model that cannot be refuted by efficient inspection. In this sense, attempting to recover the "true" model of Nature based on real-world observations is futile: no efficient analyst can falsify the outcomes of the model defined by $\tilde{p}$, agnostic to the "true" laws of Nature.

The most surprising (and potentially-disturbing) aspect of our results may be the complexity of achieving oracle-access-OI and code-access-OI. In particular, for these levels, we show strong evidence that there exist p^* and $\mathcal{A}$ that do not admit efficient OI predictors $\tilde{p}$, *even when $\mathcal{A}$ is a class of efficient distinguishers!* That is, there are choices of Nature that cannot be modeled simply, even if all we care about is passing simple tests. This stands in stark contrast to the existing literature on indistinguishability in cryptography, where the complexity of the indistinguishable object is usually smaller than the distinguishers' complexity, and in complexity theory, where the object is polynomial in the distinguishers' complexity.

Lessons for auditing predictors. The increased distinguishing power of oracle access to the predictor in oracle-access-OI may have bearing on ongoing societal debates regarding appropriate usage of algorithms when making high-stakes judgments about individuals, e.g. in the context of the criminal justice system. Much of the discussion revolves around the idea of *auditing* the predictions, for accuracy and fairness. The separation between oracle-access-OI and sample-access-OI provides a rigorous foundation for the argument that auditors should at the very least have query access to the prediction algorithms they are auditing: given a fixed computational bound, the auditors with oracle-access may perform significantly stronger tests than those who only receive sample access.

The representation is central. The *representation* of individuals is of central importance to the OI framework. If the representation space $\mathcal{X}$ contains little information that is relevant to the prediction task at hand, then p^* itself will not be very informative, and neither will a predictor $\tilde{p}$ that is OI. It is also important to note that a fixed representation of features may be informative for the general population, but lacking in pertinent information for a protected demographic group. In any setting where automated prediction is considered for deployment, the representation or feature space must be carefully considered.

The OI framework can be extended, allowing for the representation of individuals to be augmented throughout time. Given such an enriched representation, and an enriched class of distinguishers (which take advantage of the new representation), the predictor $\tilde{p}$ can be updated to obtain an improved predictor that fools the new class of distinguishers. A potential argument can be used to show that each such update moves $\tilde{p}$ meaningfully towards the "true" individual probabilities, and thus this representation-augmentation process cannot happen too many times. See [14] and see also the work of [21].

2.3   Further Related Work

The framing of outcome indistinguishability draws directly from the notion of computational indistinguishability, studied extensively in the literature on cryptography, pseudorandomness, and complexity theory (see, e.g., [22–24,45] and references therein).

Outcome Indistinguishability is related to the extensive literature on online *forecast testing*. The latter literature focuses on an online setting where there are two players, Nature and the Algorithm. Nature controls the data generating process (e.g., the weather patterns), while the Algorithm tries to assess, on each Day $t - 1$, the probability of an event on Day t (e.g., will it rain tomorrow?). In the early 1980s,s, [8] proposed that, at the very least, forecasts should be calibrated. Later works considered more stringent requirements. A signal result in the forecasting literature, due to Sandroni [42], applies to a more general notion of *tests*. A test tries to assess whether an algorithm's predictions are "reasonably accurate" with respect to the actual observations. It is required to satisfy a strong completeness property: no matter what Nature's true probabilities are, the test should accept them w.h.p. (indeed, calibration tests have this property). Sandroni's powerful result [42], shows, non-constructively[1], how to generate probability forecasts that fool any such complete test. The computational complexity of forecasting was studied by Fortnow and Vohra [18] and by Chung, Lui and Pass [6]. See [14] for a full comparison between the forecast testing literature and the new notion of Outcome Indistinguishability.

Algorithmic fairness. Tests are also implicit in the literature on algorithmic fairness, where they are sometimes referred to as *auditors*. One line of work, the *evidence-based fairness* framework—initially studied in [13,30,36]—relates directly to outcome indistinguishability and centers around tests that Nature always passes. Broadly, the framework takes the perspective that, first and foremost, predictors should reflect the "evidence" at hand—typically specified through historical outcome data—as well as the statistical and computational resources allow.

---

[1] The result leverages Fan's minimax theorem.

Central to evidence-based fairness is the notion of multi-calibration [30], which was also studied in the context of rankings in [13]. [32] provide algorithms for achieving an extension of multi-calibration that ensures calibration of higher moments of a scoring function, and show how it can be used to provide credible prediction intervals. [44] study multi-calibration from a sample-complexity perspective. In a similar vein, [46] study a notion of individualized calibration and show it can be obtained by randomized forecasters.

Evidence-based fairness is part of a more general paradigm for defining fairness notions, sometimes referred to as "multi-group" notions, which has received considerable interest in recent years [1, 13, 30, 32–34, 36, 39, 44]. This approach to fairness aims to strengthen the guarantees of notoriously-weak group fairness notions, while maintaining their practical appeal. For instance, [33, 34, 39] give notions of multi-group fairness based on parity notions studied in [11, 29]. [1] extend this idea to the online setting. Other approaches to fairness adopt a different perspective, and intentionally audit for properties that Nature does not necessarily pass. Notable examples are group-based notions of parity [29, 33, 34, 40].

3   Multi-PAC Learning

As discussed in the introduction, one prominent concern about predictors obtained via machine learning is that they might discriminate against protected groups. With fairness in mind, the loss minimization paradigm raises a fundamental concern: since the predictor's loss is measured over the entire underlying distribution, it might not reflect the predictor's performance on sub-populations such as protected demographic groups. Indeed, it has been demonstrated that standard machine learning tools, when applied to standard data sets, produce predictors whose performance on protected demographic groups is quite poor [4].

Motivated by these concerns, in work with Yona [41] (and building on earlier work by Blum and Lykouris [1]) we study *multi-group* agnostic learning. For a rich collection $\mathcal{G}$ of (potentially) overlapping groups, the goal is to learn a single predictor p, such that the loss experienced by every group $g \in \mathcal{G}$ (when classified by p) is not much larger than the loss of the best predictor *for that group* in the class $\mathcal{H}$. We emphasize that this should hold for all groups in $\mathcal{G}$ simultaneously. The study of this question also differs from much of the agnostic learning literature in considering quite general loss functions. In particular, the loss function itself may incorporate fairness considerations (see [41]). The question we ask is: *for which loss functions is multi-group agnostic learning possible?*

To see how this objective is different from the standard agnostic PAC learning setting, consider the simple example in which $\mathcal{H}$ is the class of hyperplanes and we have two subgroups $S, T \subseteq \mathcal{X}$. Suppose that the data is generated such that every group g has a hyperplane h_g that has very low error on it (but that these are different, so e.g. h_T has large loss on S and vice versa). This means that there is no classifier $h \in \mathcal{H}$ that perfectly labels the data. If S is small compared to T, then the agnostic learning objective could be satisfied by h_T, the optimal classifier for T. For *multi-group* agnostic PAC, the fact that there is some other classifier in $\mathcal{H}$ that perfectly labels S serves to disqualify h_T (more generally, it could be the case that no $h \in \mathcal{H}$ will be multi-PAC). This also highlights that the multi-group objective becomes challenging when the groups in question are intersecting (if the groups are disjoint, we can combine the optimal classifiers for each group [12]).

Multi-group PAC learning via OI. [41] construct a "multi-PAC" agnostic learning algorithm for any loss function that satisfies: (i) a uniform convergence property: it should be possible to estimate the loss of a predictor (or a whole class) from data sampled i.i.d. from the underlying distribution, and (ii) f-proper: meaning that there should be a rule f for transforming Bayes-optimal predictions (the probabilities p^*) into loss-minimizing predictions. Under these two assumptions, there is an algorithm that, for any specified finite collection $\mathcal{G}$ and finite hypothesis class $\mathcal{H}$, learns a multi-group agnostic predictor from labeled data. The sample complexity is logarithmic in the sizes of $\mathcal{G}$ and $\mathcal{H}$. The algorithm is derived by a reduction to *outcome indistinguishability* (OI), drawing a new connection between OI and loss minimization, and demonstrating the power and the flexibility of the OI framework.

Related work. Blum and Lykouris [1] studied this question in an online setting with sequential predictions. Our focus is on the batch setting. They showed that (for every collection of groups and every benchmark hypothesis class) it is possible to achieve competitive loss for all groups, so long as the loss function is *decomposable*: the loss experienced by each group is an average of losses experienced by its members. On the other hand, they showed a loss function (the average of false negative and false positive rates), for which the objective is infeasible even in the batch setting.

See Sect. 2.3 for a discussion of related work in the algorithmic fairness literature. We briefly discuss the relationship to multi-group fair learning. Many works in the algorithmic fairness literature aim to ensure parity or balance between demographic groups, e.g. similar rates of positive predictions or similar false positive or false negative rates [29,40]. As discussed above, other works consider accuracy guarantees, such as calibration [7] for protected groups. Protections at the level of a single group might be too weak [11], and recent works have studied extending these notions to the setting of multiple overlapping groups [30,33].

3.1   Loss Functions

A loss function L is a mapping from a distribution $\mathcal{D}$ and a predictor p to $[0, 1]$. We use $L_{\mathcal{D}}(p)$ to denote the loss of p w.r.t. a distribution $\mathcal{D}$. For a sample $S = \{(x_i, y_i)\}_{i=1}^{m}$ we use $L_S(p)$ to denote the empirical loss, calculated as $L_{\hat{\mathcal{D}}}(p)$, where $\hat{\mathcal{D}}$ is the empirical distribution defined by the sample S. This setup is extremely general, and assumes nothing about the loss (except that it is bounded and can't depend on what happens outside $\mathcal{D}$). In machine learning it is common to consider more structured losses, in which $L_{\mathcal{D}}(p)$ is the expected loss of p on a random example drawn according to $\mathcal{D}$. We refer to such structured losses as *decomposable* losses.

Definition 5 (Decomposable losses). *A loss function L is* decomposable *if there exists a function $\ell : X \times Y \times [0,1] \to [0,1]$ such that for every distribution $\mathcal{D}$ and predictor p, $L_{\mathcal{D}}(p) = \mathbf{E}_{(x,y)\sim\mathcal{D}}[\ell(x,y,p(x))]$.*

For example, for binary classifiers a standard decomposable loss is the 0–1 loss, in which $\ell(x,y,p(x)) = \mathbf{1}[p(x) \neq y]$. For predictors, an example of a standard decomposable loss is the squared loss, in which $\ell(x,y,p(x)) = (p(x) - y)^2$.

Beyond decomposable losses. While decomposable losses are standard and common, there are many loss functions of interest that don't have this form – especially in the literature on algorithmic fairness. For this reason, we focus on a general notion of loss functions in our exploration of multi-group agnostic PAC learning. Two prominent examples of such losses are:

- **Calibration.** [5,30,40,44] As discussed above, a predictor is *calibrated* if for every value $v \in [0,1]$, conditioned on $p(x) = v$, the true expectation of the label is close to v. This is a fundamental requirement in forecasting [7,19]. This loss is not decomposable because it is a global function of the predictions, not a property of the prediction for a single $x \in \mathcal{X}$.
- **One-sided error rates** [1,2,5,29,33]: The *false positive rate* (similarly, false negative rate) measures the probability of a random example being labeled as $p(x) = 1$, conditioned on the true label being $y = 0$. This isn't a decomposable loss because the exact contribution of a single misclassification depends on the frequency of the negative labels, which is a global property.

See [41] for further examples and discussion. In this manuscript we focus on loss functions with two additional properties: uniform convergence and f-properness.

Uniform Convergence. We begin by recalling uniform convergence for hypotheses classes:

Definition 6 (Uniform Convergence for hypotheses classes). *We say that a hypothesis class $\mathcal{H}$ has the uniform convergence property (w.r.t. a domain $X \times Y$ and a loss function L) if there exists a function $m_{\mathcal{H}}^{UC} : (0,1)^2 \to \mathbb{N}$ such that for every $\varepsilon, \delta \in (0,1)$ and for every probability distribution $\mathcal{D}$ over $X \times Y$, if S is a sample of $m \geq m_{\mathcal{H}}^{UC}(\varepsilon, \delta)$ examples drawn i.i.d. according to $\mathcal{D}$, then, with probability of at least $1 - \delta$, $\forall h \in \mathcal{H}: \quad |L_S(h) - L_{\mathcal{D}}(h)| \leq \varepsilon$.*

In our context, we are interested in uniform convergence as a property of the *loss function*. A loss L has uniform convergence (w.r.t finite classes) with sample complexity $m_L^{UC} : (0,1)^2 \times \mathbb{N} \to \mathbb{N}$ if every finite class $\mathcal{H}$ has the uniform convergence property w.r.t L with sample complexity $m_{\mathcal{H}}^{UC}(\varepsilon, \delta) \leq m_L^{UC}(\varepsilon, \delta, |\mathcal{H}|)$.

Specifically, we will be interested in losses that have the uniform convergence property with sample complexity that depends polynomially on $1/\varepsilon, 1/\delta$ and $\log|\mathcal{H}|$. This gives rise to the following definition:

Definition 7 (Uniform convergence for loss functions). *A loss L has the uniform convergence property (w.r.t finite classes) with sample complexity* $m_L^{UC} : (0,1)^2 \times \mathbb{N} \to \mathbb{N}$ *if there exists a polynomial* $f : \mathbb{R}^3 \to \mathbb{N}$ *such that for every* $\varepsilon, \delta \in (0,1)$ *and* $k \in \mathbb{N}$,

$$m_L^{UC}(\varepsilon, \delta, k) \triangleq \max_{\mathcal{H}:\, |\mathcal{H}|=k} m_{\mathcal{H}}^{UC}(\varepsilon, \delta) \leq f(1/\varepsilon, 1/\delta, \log(k))$$

The uniform convergence property is satisfied by any decomposable loss function. This follows by a combination of Heoffding's bound (for a single h) and a union bound to get a simultaneous guarantee for every $h \in \mathcal{H}$. For calibration, uniform convergence follows as a special case of the bounds in [44]. However, the loss that takes a convex combination of the false positive and the false negative rates does *not* satisfy uniform convergence. See [1, 41]) for further details, examples and discussion.

f-proper loss functions. Recall that proper losses (or proper scoring functions) are losses that are minimized by the Bayes optimal predictor p^*, i.e. conditional expectation predictor $x \mapsto \mathbf{E}_\mathcal{D}[y|x]$ [3]. The f-proper condition is a relaxation: it says that for every distribution, a minimizer can be obtained as some *local* transformation of this predictor (i.e. that does not depend on the rest of the distribution).

Definition 8 (f-proper). *For a function* $f : \mathcal{X} \times [0,1] \to [0,1]$, *we say that a loss L is f-proper if for every distribution $\mathcal{D}$ on $\mathcal{X} \times Y$, the classifier $h_\mathcal{D}$ given by $h_\mathcal{D}(x) = f(x, p^*(x) = \mathbf{E}_\mathcal{D}[y|x])$ minimizes the loss w.r.t $\mathcal{D}$: $h_\mathcal{D} \in \arg\min_h L_\mathcal{D}(h)$.*

The L_2 loss is a well-known example of a proper loss function (f simply outputs its second argument). The 0–1 loss is another well-known example, where the loss is minimized by $f(x, z) = 1\,[z \geq 0.5]$.

3.2   Multigroup PAC Learnability via OI

The objective of agnostic PAC learning is outputting a predictor p that satisfies $L_\mathcal{D}(p) \lesssim L_\mathcal{D}(\mathcal{H})$. Multigroup (agnostic) PAC learning [41] asks for a predictor that satisfies the above, but simultaneously for every group g in a collection $\mathcal{G}$: $L_{\mathcal{D}_g}(p) \lesssim L_{\mathcal{D}_g}(\mathcal{H})$, where $\mathcal{D}_g$ denotes the restriction of $\mathcal{D}$ to samples from g. Moreover, a learning algorithm should be able to find such a solution in sample complexity that is inverse-polynomial in the parameters in question and polylogarithmic in the sizes of $\mathcal{H}$ and $\mathcal{G}$.

Definition 9 (Multi-PAC learnability). *A loss L is* multi-PAC learnable *with sample complexity $m_L^{gPAC} : (0,1)^3 \times \mathbb{N}^2 \to \mathbb{N}$ if there exists a learning algorithm with the following property: For every $\varepsilon, \delta, \gamma \in (0,1)$, for every finite hypothesis class $\mathcal{H}$, for every finite collection of subgroups $G \subseteq 2^{\mathcal{X}}$ and for every distribution $\mathcal{D}$ over $\mathcal{X} \times Y$, when running the learning algorithm on $m \geq m_L^{gPAC}(\varepsilon, \delta, \gamma, |\mathcal{H}|, |\mathcal{G}|)$ i.i.d. examples generated by $\mathcal{D}$, the algorithm returns p such that, with probability at least $1 - \delta$ (over the choice of the m training examples and the coins of the learning algorithm) $g \in \mathcal{G}_\gamma$, $L_{\mathcal{D}_g}(p) \leq L_{\mathcal{D}_g}(\mathcal{H}) + \varepsilon$, where $\mathcal{G}_\gamma \subseteq \mathcal{G}$ is the subset of groups whose mass under $\mathcal{D}$ is at least γ: $\mathcal{G}_\gamma = \{g \in \mathcal{G} : \mathbf{Pr}_{\mathcal{D}}[x \in g] \geq \gamma\}$.*

Additionally, the sample complexity m_L^{gPAC} should be polynomial in $(1/\varepsilon)$, in $(1/\delta)$, in $(1/\gamma)$, in $(\log(|\mathcal{H}|))$, and in $\log(|\mathcal{G}|))$.

When $\mathcal{G}$ consists of intersecting groups, it is not immediately clear that this objective is remotely feasible: it might not be satisfied by *any* predictor $p : \mathcal{X} \to [0,1]$! For a simple (but contrived) example, let h^0, h^1 denote the all-zeroes and all-ones predictors, and consider a loss L that specifies that $L_{\mathcal{D}_S}(h^0) = 0$ and $L_{\mathcal{D}_T}(h^1) = 0$ (and for any other classifier p, the loss of every distribution is always 1). Then the multi-group objective w.r.t $\mathcal{G} = \{S, T\}$ requires that we label the intersection $S \cap T$ as both 1 and 0, which is impossible. See [1,41] for further discussion and natural examples of infeasible loss functions.

Rothblum and Yona [41] show that multi-PAC predictors exist and can be learned for every loss function satistfying the uniform uniform convergence and f-proper conditions.

Theorem 10 (Multi-PAC Learning [41]). *If L is f-proper (Definition 8) and has the uniform convergence property (Definition 7), then L is multi-group learnable (Definition 9).*

The Theorem is proved by a reduction to Outcome Indistinguishability. For a loss function L satisfying the theorem conditions, for and group g and hypothesis h, [41] show how to construct a sample-access-OI distinguisher $A_{L,g,h}$ s.t. if a predictor $\tilde{p}$ is OI w.r.t the distringuisher, then applying f to $\tilde{p}$ gives a predictor whose loss is competitive with h (f is the post-processing function for which L is a proper loss function). This is the crux of the proof of the reduction, and a powerful demonstration of the power of the Outcome Indistinguishability framework. With this reduction in place, multi-PAC learning can be performed using any OI learning algorithm (e.g. the algorithm of Theorem 2): i.e., by learning a predictor $\tilde{p}$ that is OI w.r.t. the class of distinguishers $(A_{L,g,h})_{g \in \mathcal{G}, h \in \mathcal{H}}$. The predictor $\tilde{h}(x) = f(x, \tilde{p}(x))$ will be competitive with $\mathcal{H}$ for all groups $g \in \mathcal{G}$ simultaneously. The heart of the argument is in constructing the distinguishers:

Lemma 11 (Loss Minimization via OI [41]). *Let L be an f-proper loss function that has the uniform convergence property. For a predictor $\tilde{p}$, define the hypothesis $\tilde{h}(x) = f(x, \tilde{p}(x))$.*

Let $\mathcal{D}$ be a distribution, $g \subseteq \mathcal{X}$ a subgroup s.t. $\mathcal{D}_{\mathcal{X}}[g] \geq \gamma$, $h : \mathcal{X} \to [0,1]$ a hypothesis, and $\alpha \in [0,1]$ a desired error parameter. There exists a multi-sample sample-access-OI distinguisher $A_{L,g,h}$ s.t. if $\tilde{p}$ is $(\{A_{L,g,h}\}, \Theta(\alpha))$-sample-access-OI then:

$$L_{\mathcal{D}_g}(\tilde{h}) \leq L_{\mathcal{D}_g}(h) + \alpha.$$

The distinguisher $A_{L,g,h}$ operates on $k = \tilde{O}((m_L^{UC}(\Theta(\alpha), \Theta(\alpha), 1))/\gamma)$ samples (where m_L^{UC} is the sample complexity for uniform convergence). Its complexity is polynomial in k, in the complexity of determining group membership in g, and in the complexity of the classifier h.

Proof. We want to guarantee that the loss of the hypothesis $\tilde{h}(x) = f(x, \tilde{p}(x))$ is competitive with the loss of h, where both losses are measured on the distribution $\mathcal{D}_g$ over members of the group g. We begin by observing that this is true when the labels are drawn by $\tilde{p}(x)$ (as in the distribution $\tilde{\mathcal{D}}$). We will use OI (with an appropriately constructed distinguisher) to ensure that it is also true for the "real" distribution $\mathcal{D}_g$.

In more detail, since L is an f-proper loss function, we have:

$$L_{\tilde{\mathcal{D}}_g}(\tilde{h}) \leq L_{\tilde{\mathcal{D}}_g}(h),$$

because in $\tilde{\mathcal{D}}$ the labels are indeed generated by $\tilde{p}$, i.e. $\tilde{p}(x) = E_{\tilde{\mathcal{D}}}[y|x]$. By uniform convergence, this will remain true—up to an additive $\Theta(\alpha)$ slack—even if we consider the empirical loss over a (sufficiently large) i.i.d. sample from $\tilde{\mathcal{D}}_g$. We now define the distinguisher $A_{L,g,h}$, which takes as input k samples $\{(x_i, y_i, \tilde{p}_i)\}$ and checks whether, for the samples where $x_i \in g$, it is true that the loss obtained by predicting $f(x_i, \tilde{p}_i)$ for each x_i is competitive with the loss obtained by h on those samples (up to an additive factor of $\Theta(\alpha)$). By the above discussion, when the outcomes y_i are drawn by $\text{Ber}(\tilde{p}_i)$, and assuming that there are sufficiently many samples in g to guarantee uniform convergence for the loss L, the distinguisher will accept with high probability.

Now, if $\tilde{p}$ is OI w.r.t. the distinguisher $A_{g,h,\alpha}^k$, then the distinguisher should accept with similar probabilities whether the labeled examples are drawn by $\tilde{\mathcal{D}}$ or by $\mathcal{D}$ (where in both cases the predictions are by $\tilde{p}_i$). I.e., $A_{L,g,h}$ should also accept w.h.p. when the examples are drawn by $\mathcal{D}$. By uniform convergence, this can only happen if the predictor $\tilde{h}$ is competitive with the hypothesis h w.r.t. the distribution $\mathcal{D}_g$: exactly the guarantee we wanted from $\tilde{h}$!

The above reduction, together with the OI learning algorithm of Theorem 2, gives the multi-group agnostic learning algorithm of Theorem 10. The sample complexity of the learning algorithm is governed by the sample complexity of OI learning, which is logarithmic in the number of distinguishers. The reduction includes $|\mathcal{G}| \cdot |\mathcal{H}|$ multi-sample distinguishers. The OI learning algorithm can be modified to handle multi-sample distinguishers, or we can further reduce (a class of) multi-sample distinguishers to (a class of) single-sample distinguishers using a hybrid argument. This all results in sample complexity that is logarithmic in $|\mathcal{G}|$ and in $|\mathcal{H}|$. We note that we need $\mathcal{G}$ and $\mathcal{H}$ to be finite because the known OI learning algorithm works for finite collections of distinguishers.

Even more general losses. Rothblum and Yona [41] separate the questions of multi-group *feasibility*: i.e. does a multi-group predictor always exist for a given loss function, from the question of *learnability*. They show a loose characterization of the loss functions for which multi-PAC learning is feasible, and use the connection to OI to construct a learning algorithm for *any* such loss function that also satisfies uniform convergence.

4   Recent Developments

Several recent works have refined, developed and extended the Outcome Indistinguishability and multi-calibration frameworks. The literature has been growing rapidly—we briefly mention some notable examples. Gupta *et al.* [28] consider real-valued predictions and the meaningfulness of the predictor's confidence intervals and moments. As noted above, the study was extended to large outcome spaces in [15], see also [27]. Dwork *et al.* [16] show connections between the literature on multi-calibration and Outcome Indistinguishability, regularity in graph theory and the leakage simulation lemma in cryptography.

An emerging and exciting body of work shows that multi-calibration and Outcome Indistinguishability open the door to machine learning that is quite flexible and robust. An *omni-predictor*, as proposed and studied by Gopalan *et al.* [26], is a single predictor that can be trained once and then adapted to different loss functions. They show that multi-calibration for a collection of sets implies omni-prediction w.r.t. a hypothesis class that is directly related to the collection of sets, and a broad range of loss functions. A similar statement holds for OI, because of the equivalence between OI and multicalibration. We view this as further demonstration of the power and flexibility of the multi-calibration and Outcome Indistinguishability frameworks. Subsequent works (e.g. [25]) sharpen this connection, and use it in the context of optimization under fairness constraints [31]. At a very high level, these results leverage properties of OI (or multicalibration) that are similar in spirit to the "loss minimization to OI" reduction of Lemma 11. There are differences in the types of loss functions that are considered, but the main difference is on the conceptual level: the focus in omni-prediction is on training a predictor that can later be used to handle many loss functions, whereas [41] only use the reduction in the context of a fixed loss function.

Several other works leverage multi-calibration or OI to achieve robustness or adaptability to changes that might be encountered after training. The work of Kim *et al.* [37] on *universal adaptability* shows this in the context of propensity scoring in statistical analysis, where the goal is adapting an analysis to a new target population. Diana *et al.* [10] show a result of this flavor for downstream post-processing of predictions, whereas Kim and Perdomo [38] consider a prediction setting where individuals might exhibit performative behavior.

Finally, Outcome Indistinguishability aims to obtain predictions that cannot be refuted based on real-world outcome data. The real world itself, however, does not treat all demographic groups similarly. In recent work with Dwork and

Reingold [17], we consider corrective transformations τ that aim to map probabilities p^* in the real world to a better world $\tau(p^*)$. We study the goal of learning a predictor that is indistinguishable from the better world, and characterize the transformations for which this goal is achievable.

Acknowledgements. This overview is based on the works [14,41] and borrows liberally from those works. We are indebted to our co-authors and collaborators Cynthia Dwork, Michael Kim, Omer Reingold and Gal Yona for many wonderful and illuminating discussions.

References

1. Blum, A., Lykouris, T.: Advancing subgroup fairness via sleeping experts. arXiv preprint arXiv:1909.08375 (2019)
2. Blum, A., Stangl, K.: Recovering from biased data: can fairness constraints improve accuracy? arXiv preprint arXiv:1912.01094 (2019)
3. Buja, A., Stuetzle, W., Shen, Y.: Loss functions for binary class probability estimation and classification: Structure and applications. Working draft, 3 November 2005
4. Buolamwini, J., Gebru, T.: Gender shades: intersectional accuracy disparities in commercial gender classification. In: Friedler, S.A., Wilson, C. (eds.) Conference on Fairness, Accountability and Transparency, FAT 2018, 23–24 February 2018, New York, NY, USA. Proceedings of Machine Learning Research, vol. 81, pp. 77–91. PMLR (2018). http://proceedings.mlr.press/v81/buolamwini18a.html
5. Chouldechova, A.: Fair prediction with disparate impact: a study of bias in recidivism prediction instruments. Big Data **5**(2), 153–163 (2017)
6. Chung, K., Lui, E., Pass, R.: Can theories be tested?: a cryptographic treatment of forecast testing. In: Kleinberg, R.D. (ed.) Innovations in Theoretical Computer Science, ITCS 2013, Berkeley, CA, USA, 9–12 January 2013, pp. 47–56. ACM (2013). https://doi.org/10.1145/2422436.2422443
7. Dawid, A.P.: The well-calibrated Bayesian. J. Am. Stat. Assoc. **77**(379), 605–610 (1982)
8. Dawid, A.: Objective probability forecasts'. Technical report, Research Report 14, Department of Statistical Science, University College London (1982)
9. Dawid, P.: On individual risk. Synthese **194**(9), 3445–3474 (2015). https://doi.org/10.1007/s11229-015-0953-4
10. Diana, E., Gill, W., Kearns, M., Kenthapadi, K., Roth, A., Sharifi-Malvajerdi, S.: Multiaccurate proxies for downstream fairness. In: FAccT 2022: 2022 ACM Conference on Fairness, Accountability, and Transparency, Seoul, Republic of Korea, 21–24 June 2022, pp. 1207–1239. ACM (2022). https://doi.org/10.1145/3531146.3533180
11. Dwork, C., Hardt, M., Pitassi, T., Reingold, O., Zemel, R.: Fairness through awareness. In: Proceedings of the 3rd Innovations in Theoretical Computer Science Conference, pp. 214–226 (2012)
12. Dwork, C., Immorlica, N., Kalai, A.T., Leiserson, M.: Decoupled classifiers for fair and efficient machine learning. arXiv preprint arXiv:1707.06613 (2017)
13. Dwork, C., Kim, M.P., Reingold, O., Rothblum, G.N., Yona, G.: Learning from outcomes: evidence-based rankings. In: 2019 IEEE 60th Annual Symposium on Foundations of Computer Science (FOCS), pp. 106–125. IEEE (2019)

14. Dwork, C., Kim, M.P., Reingold, O., Rothblum, G.N., Yona, G.: Outcome indistinguishability. In: Khuller, S., Williams, V.V. (eds.) STOC 2021: 53rd Annual ACM SIGACT Symposium on Theory of Computing, Virtual Event, Italy, 21–25 June 2021, pp. 1095–1108. ACM (2021). https://doi.org/10.1145/3406325.3451064

15. Dwork, C., Kim, M.P., Reingold, O., Rothblum, G.N., Yona, G.: Beyond Bernoulli: generating random outcomes that cannot be distinguished from nature. In: Dasgupta, S., Haghtalab, N. (eds.) International Conference on Algorithmic Learning Theory, 29–1 April 2022, Paris, France. Proceedings of Machine Learning Research, vol. 167, pp. 342–380. PMLR (2022). https://proceedings.mlr.press/v167/dwork22a.html

16. Dwork, C., Lee, D., Lin, H., Tankala, P.: New insights into multi-calibration. CoRR abs/2301.08837 (2023). https://doi.org/10.48550/arXiv.2301.08837

17. Dwork, C., Reingold, O., Rothblum, G.N.: From the real towards the ideal: risk prediction in a better world (2023)

18. Fortnow, L., Vohra, R.V.: The complexity of forecast testing. Econometrica **77**(1), 93–105 (2009). https://doi.org/10.3982/ECTA7163

19. Foster, D.P., Vohra, R.V.: Asymptotic calibration. Biometrika **85**(2), 379–390 (1998)

20. Fudenberg, D., Levine, D.K.: An easier way to calibrate. Games Econom. Behav. **29**(1–2), 131–137 (1999)

21. Globus-Harris, I., Kearns, M., Roth, A.: An algorithmic framework for bias bounties. In: FAccT 2022: 2022 ACM Conference on Fairness, Accountability, and Transparency, Seoul, Republic of Korea, 21–24 June 2022, pp. 1106–1124. ACM (2022). https://doi.org/10.1145/3531146.3533172

22. Goldreich, O.: Foundations of Cryptography: Volume 1, Basic Tools. Cambridge University Press, Cambridge (2006)

23. Goldreich, O.: Computational Complexity: A Conceptual Perspective, 1st edn. Cambridge University Press, Cambridge (2008)

24. Goldreich, O.: Foundations of Cryptography: Volume 2, Basic Applications. Cambridge University Press, Cambridge (2009)

25. Gopalan, P., Hu, L., Kim, M.P., Reingold, O., Wieder, U.: Loss minimization through the lens of outcome indistinguishability. In: Kalai, Y.T. (ed.) 14th Innovations in Theoretical Computer Science Conference, ITCS 2023, 10–13 January 2023, MIT, Cambridge, Massachusetts, USA. LIPIcs, vol. 251, pp. 60:1–60:20. Schloss Dagstuhl - Leibniz-Zentrum für Informatik (2023). https://doi.org/10.4230/LIPIcs.ITCS.2023.60

26. Gopalan, P., Kalai, A.T., Reingold, O., Sharan, V., Wieder, U.: Omnipredictors. In: Braverman, M. (ed.) 13th Innovations in Theoretical Computer Science Conference, ITCS 2022, 31 January–3 February 2022, Berkeley, CA, USA. LIPIcs, vol. 215, pp. 79:1–79:21. Schloss Dagstuhl - Leibniz-Zentrum für Informatik (2022). https://doi.org/10.4230/LIPIcs.ITCS.2022.79

27. Gopalan, P., Kim, M.P., Singhal, M., Zhao, S.: Low-degree multicalibration. In: Loh, P., Raginsky, M. (eds.) Conference on Learning Theory, 2–5 July 2022, London, UK. Proceedings of Machine Learning Research, vol. 178, pp. 3193–3234. PMLR (2022). https://proceedings.mlr.press/v178/gopalan22a.html

28. Gupta, V., Jung, C., Noarov, G., Pai, M.M., Roth, A.: Online multivalid learning: means, moments, and prediction intervals. In: Braverman, M. (ed.) 13th Innovations in Theoretical Computer Science Conference, ITCS 2022, 31 January–3 February 2022, Berkeley, CA, USA. LIPIcs, vol. 215, pp. 82:1–82:24. Schloss Dagstuhl - Leibniz-Zentrum für Informatik (2022). https://doi.org/10.4230/LIPIcs.ITCS.2022.82

29. Hardt, M., Price, E., Srebro, N.: Equality of opportunity in supervised learning. In: Advances in Neural Information Processing Systems, pp. 3315–3323 (2016)

30. Hébert-Johnson, Ú., Kim, M.P., Reingold, O., Rothblum, G.: Multicalibration: calibration for the (computationally-identifiable) masses. In: International Conference on Machine Learning, pp. 1939–1948 (2018)

31. Hu, L., Navon, I.L., Reingold, O., Yang, C.: Omnipredictors for constrained optimization. CoRR abs/2209.07463 (2022). https://doi.org/10.48550/arXiv.2209.07463

32. Jung, C., Lee, C., Pai, M.M., Roth, A., Vohra, R.: Moment multicalibration for uncertainty estimation. arXiv preprint arXiv:2008.08037 (2020)

33. Kearns, M., Neel, S., Roth, A., Wu, Z.S.: Preventing fairness gerrymandering: auditing and learning for subgroup fairness. In: International Conference on Machine Learning, pp. 2564–2572 (2018)

34. Kearns, M., Neel, S., Roth, A., Wu, Z.S.: An empirical study of rich subgroup fairness for machine learning. In: Proceedings of the Conference on Fairness, Accountability, and Transparency, pp. 100–109 (2019)

35. Kearns, M.J., Schapire, R.E., Sellie, L.M.: Toward efficient agnostic learning. Mach. Learn. **17**(2–3), 115–141 (1994)

36. Kim, M.P., Ghorbani, A., Zou, J.: Multiaccuracy: black-box post-processing for fairness in classification. In: Proceedings of the 2019 AAAI/ACM Conference on AI, Ethics, and Society, pp. 247–254 (2019)

37. Kim, M.P., Kern, C., Goldwasser, S., Kreuter, F., Reingold, O.: Universal adaptability: target-independent inference that competes with propensity scoring. Proc. Natl. Acad. Sci. **119**(4), e2108097119 (2022). https://doi.org/10.1073/pnas.2108097119

38. Kim, M.P., Perdomo, J.C.: Making decisions under outcome performativity. In: Kalai, Y.T. (ed.) 14th Innovations in Theoretical Computer Science Conference, ITCS 2023, 10–13 January 2023, MIT, Cambridge, Massachusetts, USA. LIPIcs, vol. 251, pp. 79:1–79:15. Schloss Dagstuhl - Leibniz-Zentrum für Informatik (2023). https://doi.org/10.4230/LIPIcs.ITCS.2023.79

39. Kim, M.P., Reingold, O., Rothblum, G.N.: Fairness through computationally-bounded awareness. In: Advances in Neural Information Processing Systems (2018)

40. Kleinberg, J., Mullainathan, S., Raghavan, M.: Inherent trade-offs in the fair determination of risk scores. arXiv preprint arXiv:1609.05807 (2016)

41. Rothblum, G.N., Yona, G.: Multi-group agnostic PAC learnability. In: Meila, M., Zhang, T. (eds.) Proceedings of the 38th International Conference on Machine Learning, ICML 2021, 18–24 July 2021, Virtual Event. Proceedings of Machine Learning Research, vol. 139, pp. 9107–9115. PMLR (2021). http://proceedings.mlr.press/v139/rothblum21a.html

42. Sandroni, A.: The reproducible properties of correct forecasts. Internat. J. Game Theory **32**(1), 151–159 (2003)

43. Sandroni, A., Smorodinsky, R., Vohra, R.V.: Calibration with many checking rules. Math. Oper. Res. **28**(1), 141–153 (2003)

44. Shabat, E., Cohen, L., Mansour, Y.: Sample complexity of uniform convergence for multicalibration. arXiv preprint arXiv:2005.01757 (2020)

45. Vadhan, S.P.: Pseudorandomness. Now Publishers Inc., Hanover (2012)

46. Zhao, S., Ma, T., Ermon, S.: Individual calibration with randomized forecasting. arXiv preprint arXiv:2006.10288 (2020)

Theoretical Foundations

Worst-Case Subexponential Attacks on PRGs of Constant Degree or Constant Locality

Akın Ünal$^{(\boxtimes)}$ (ORCID)

Department of Computer Science, ETH Zurich, Zurich, Switzerland
akin.uenal@inf.ethz.ch

Abstract. In this work, we will give new attacks on the pseudorandomness of algebraic pseudorandom number generators (PRGs) of polynomial stretch. Our algorithms apply to a broad class of PRGs and are in the case of general local PRGs faster than currently known attacks. At the same time, in contrast to most algebraic attacks, subexponential time and space bounds will be proven for our attacks without making any assumptions of the PRGs or assuming any further conjectures. Therefore, we yield in this text the first subexponential distinguishing attacks on PRGs from constant-degree polynomials and close current gaps in the subexponential cryptoanalysis of lightweight PRGs.

Concretely, against PRGs $F : \mathbb{Z}_q^n \to \mathbb{Z}_q^m$ that are computed by polynomials of degree d over a field $\mathbb{Z}_q$ and have a stretch of $m = n^{1+e}$ we give an attack with space and time complexities $n^{O(n^{1-\frac{e}{d-1}})}$ and noticeable advantage $1 - O(n^{1-\frac{e}{d-1}}/q)$. If q lies in $O(n^{1-\frac{e}{d-1}})$, we give a second attack with the same space and time complexities whose advantage is at least $q^{-O(n^{1-\frac{e}{d-1}})}$. If F is of constant *locality* d and q is constant, we construct a third attack that has a space and time complexity of $\exp(O(n^{1-\frac{e'}{(q-1)d-1}}))$ and noticeable advantage $1 - O(n^{-\frac{e'}{(q-1)d-1}})$ for every constant $e' < e$.

1 Introduction

A pseudorandom number generator (PRG) is a deterministic algorithm $F : \{0,1\}^n \to \{0,1\}^m$ that stretches a given string of bits i.e. $m > n$. We expect a PRG to expand a uniformly drawn string to a longer string of bits that sufficiently simulates randomness. More formally, for a PRG F its output – when evaluated on a short uniformly random string – should be for a certain class of computational models indistinguishable from a longer uniformly random string, even if the algorithm F is publicly known.

PRGs are an important tool in the toolbox of cryptography besides one-way functions [1, 27], pseudorandom permutations and pseudorandom functions. Further, in complexity theory, the existence of PRGs implies the derandomization of certain complexity classes [38]. For example, it is known that the existence of

C. Hazay and M. Stam (Eds.): EUROCRYPT 2023, LNCS 14004, pp. 25–54, 2023.
https://doi.org/10.1007/978-3-031-30545-0_2

so-called *high-end* PRGs implies that **P** equals **BPP** [29]. Additionally, PRGs have the real world task of simulating cryptographic pseudorandomness in deterministic software applications.

Of particular interest are PRGs that can be efficiently evaluated. Very prominent examples are *local* PRGs [26]. Each output bit of a local PRG depends on only a constant number of input bits. Besides their simplicity, local PRGs are an important building block in advanced cryptographic constructions, e.g. two-party protocols for computing circuits with constant overhead [30] or indistinguishability obfuscation [31,32]. Assuming additionally the pseudorandomness of arithmetic PRGs $F : \mathbb{Z}_q^n \to \mathbb{Z}_q^m$ where each output value is computed by a polynomial of constant degree over $\mathbb{Z}_q$ leads to arithmetization of such primitives, like e.g. arithmetic two-party protocols [5].

Since PRGs play such a crucial role in cryptography, cryptoanalysis of PRGs is of general importance. In particular, local PRGs $F : \{0,1\}^n \to \{0,1\}^m$ of poly-stretch, i.e. $m \geq n^{1+e}$ for some constant $e > 0$, have been the subject of various attacks, and it could be shown that such PRGs can be distinguished by subexponential-size[1] circuits, or even poly-size circuits if $e > 0.5$ [3,4,11,18,39, 41].

PRGs of constant degree, i.e. PRGs that can be computed by polynomials of constant degree over some finite field, can be seen as a generalization of local PRGs. However, constant-degree PRGs have received much less attention in cryptoanalytic literature than local PRGs. While there is a huge collection of algebraic attacks on refuting and inverting constant-degree PRGs like F4/F5 and the XL-algorithms [12,16,17,23,24,36,44], we do not know of any attacks whose time-complexity for poly-stretch constant-degree PRGs is guaranteed to be subexponential even in the worst case. We intend to close this gap by introducing a new algebraic attack that is provably subexponential against poly-stretch PRGs of constant degree.

1.1   Contribution

In this text, we will introduce new algebraic attacks on PRGs and prove upper bounds for their complexities and lower bounds for their advantage in the worst case. Let $F : \mathbb{Z}_q^n \to \mathbb{Z}_q^m$ with $m \geq n^{1+e}$. Then, we give the following attacks on the pseudorandomness of F:

- If F is of degree d over $\mathbb{Z}_q$, we have an attack with subexponential space and time complexities $n^{O(n^{1-\frac{e}{d-1}})}$. The advantage of this attack is $1 - O(n^{1-\frac{e}{d-1}}/q)$, which is noticeable if q is large enough.
- If q should be small (e.g. $q \in O(n^{1-\frac{e}{d-1}})$), then we give a second attack in the above case with the same space and time complexities for which we can guarantee a subexponentially small advantage of $q^{-O(n^{1-\frac{e}{d-1}})}$.

---

[1] The notion of *subexponentiality* is ambiguous in literature. Here, we denote by subexponential a function that is contained in $\bigcup_{c<1} 2^{O(n^c)}$.

– If q is constant and F is of *locality* d, we give for each constant $e' \in [0, e)$ a third attack with subexponential space and time complexities $2^{O(n^{1-\frac{e'}{(q-1)d-1}})}$. For this attack, we will prove a noticeable advantage of $1 - O(n^{-\frac{e'}{(q-1)d-1}})$.

To the best of our knowledge, we give the first distinguishing algorithms on constant-degree PRGs that are provably subexponential in the worst case for sufficiently large moduli. Additionally, our second and third attack algorithms are faster than the attacks of Bogdanov & Qiao [11]. Hence, these attacks give new baselines for the cryptoanalysis of local PRGs.

1.2 Technical Overview

We want to motivate and explain here the ideas behind our new attacks. Let q be a prime, $\mathbb{Z}_q$ be the finite field of size q and $F : \mathbb{Z}_q^n \to \mathbb{Z}_q^m$ be a PRG of degree d. I.e., the i-th output value of F is computed by a polynomial $f_i \in \mathbb{Z}_q[X] := \mathbb{Z}_q[X_1, \ldots, X_n]$ of total degree $\leq d$. Now, assume we would know a non-zero polynomial $h \in \mathbb{Z}_q[Y] := \mathbb{Z}_q[Y_1, \ldots, Y_m]$ that vanishes on the image of F i.e.

$$h(F(x)) = 0 \tag{1}$$

for all $x \in k^n$. Let D be the total degree of h. Since h is not the zero polynomial, we have according to the famous Schwartz-Zippel lemma [40]

$$\Pr_{y \leftarrow \mathbb{Z}_q^m}[h(y) = 0] \leq \frac{D}{q}. \tag{2}$$

I.e., while h will always be zero on the image of F, the probability that h vanishes on a random point can be controlled by D/q. If D is sublinear and q is sufficiently large, $q \geq n$ for example, h gives us a strong indicator for distinguishing image points of F from random points of $\mathbb{Z}_q^m$. In fact, by using h we can distinguish the distribution $(F(x))_{x \leftarrow \mathbb{Z}_q^n}$ from $(y)_{y \leftarrow \mathbb{Z}_q^m}$ with advantage at least $1 - \frac{D}{q}$.

However, the following two questions remain:

1. For which degrees D can we guarantee the existence of a non-zero polynomial h of degree D that vanishes on the image of F?
2. Even if we know that such a polynomial h must exist, how can we algorithmically compute it?

Finding Algebraic Relations. The set of polynomials h that vanish on each $F(x)$ has a specific algebraic structure. To explore this structure, we consider the following morphism of $\mathbb{Z}_q$-algebras:

$$\phi : \mathbb{Z}_q[Y_1, \ldots, Y_m] \longrightarrow \mathbb{Z}_q[X_1, \ldots, X_n] \tag{3}$$
$$g(Y_1, \ldots, Y_m) \longmapsto g(f_1(X), \ldots, f_m(X)). \tag{4}$$

ϕ maps polynomials in $\mathbb{Z}_q[Y]$ to polynomials in $\mathbb{Z}_q[X]$ by substituting each variable Y_i by the polynomial $f_i(X)$. Denote by $\ker \phi$ the kernel of ϕ, i.e.

$$\ker \phi = \{g \in \mathbb{Z}_q[Y] \mid \phi(g) = 0\}. \tag{5}$$

If g lies in $\ker \phi$, we have $\phi(g) = g(f_1(X), \ldots, f_m(X)) = 0$. In particular, we have for each $x \in \mathbb{Z}_q^n$ then

$$g(f_1(x), \ldots, f_m(x)) = \phi(g)(x_1, \ldots, x_m) = 0. \tag{6}$$

This means, the kernel of ϕ contains polynomials h that are of interest for us.

Therefore, we can restate our questions as follows:

1. For what D can we guarantee the existence of a non-zero element of $\ker \phi$?
2. How can we compute all elements of $\ker \phi$ up to degree D?

To answer the first question, we define the following $\mathbb{Z}_q$-vector spaces for $\ell \in \mathbb{N}$:

$$\mathbb{Z}_q[X]^{\leq \ell} := \{g \in \mathbb{Z}_q[X] \mid \deg g \leq \ell\}, \tag{7}$$

$$\mathbb{Z}_q[Y]^{\leq \ell} := \{g \in \mathbb{Z}_q[Y] \mid \deg g \leq \ell\}. \tag{8}$$

The vector spaces $\mathbb{Z}_q[X]^{\leq \ell}$ and $\mathbb{Z}_q[Y]^{\leq \ell}$ contain all elements of $\mathbb{Z}_q[X]$ resp. $\mathbb{Z}_q[Y]$ of total degree $\leq \ell$. They are spanned by all monomials in the X-resp. Y-variables of degree $\leq \ell$. Therefore, we have

$$\dim_{\mathbb{Z}_q} \mathbb{Z}_q[X]^{\leq \ell} = \binom{n + \ell}{\ell} \quad \text{and} \quad \dim_{\mathbb{Z}_q} \mathbb{Z}_q[Y]^{\leq \ell} = \binom{m + \ell}{\ell}. \tag{9}$$

Now, we want to restrict ϕ on $\mathbb{Z}_q[Y]^{\leq \ell}$. Remember that F is a PRG of degree d, i.e., each f_i is a polynomial of degree d. It is easy to see that ϕ stretches the degree of each polynomial by at most a factor of d. I.e., we have for each $g \in \mathbb{Z}_q[Y]$

$$\deg \phi(g) = \deg g(f_1(X), \ldots, f_m(X)) \leq d \cdot \deg g. \tag{10}$$

So, by restricting ϕ on $\mathbb{Z}_q[Y]^{\leq \ell}$, we get a linear map

$$\phi^\ell : \mathbb{Z}_q[Y]^{\leq \ell} \longrightarrow \mathbb{Z}_q[X]^{\leq d \cdot \ell} \tag{11}$$

for each ℓ. For linear maps, it is quite easy to guarantee the existence of non-trivial kernel elements. In fact, by dimension formulas, we have

$$\dim_{\mathbb{Z}_q} \ker \phi^\ell \geq \dim_{\mathbb{Z}_q}(\mathbb{Z}_q[Y]^{\leq \ell}) - \dim_{\mathbb{Z}_q}(\mathbb{Z}_q[X]^{\leq d \cdot \ell}) \tag{12}$$

$$= \binom{m + \ell}{\ell} - \binom{n + d \cdot \ell}{d \cdot \ell}. \tag{13}$$

Therefore, it suffices to find the smallest D s.t.

$$\binom{m + D}{D} > \binom{n + d \cdot D}{d \cdot D}. \tag{14}$$

As we already stated, we are interested here in PRGs of poly-stretch, so let $e > 0$ be constant s.t. $m \geq n^{1+e}$. We claim that inequality Eq. (14) holds for $D \in \Omega(n^{1 - \frac{e}{d-1}})$. To see this, note that we have

$$\binom{m + D}{D} > \binom{n + d \cdot D}{d \cdot D} \tag{15}$$

$$\Longleftrightarrow \frac{(m+D)\cdots(m+1)}{D\cdots1} > \frac{(n+dD)\cdots(n+1)}{(dD)\cdots1} \tag{16}$$

$$\Longleftrightarrow (m+D)\cdots(m+1)\cdot(dD)\cdots(D+1) > (n+dD)\cdots(n+1). \tag{17}$$

To show Eq. (17), we lower bound the LHS terms $(dD)\cdots(D+1) > D^{(d-1)D}$ and $(m+D)\cdots(m+1) > m^D$. Further, for the simplicity of this exposition, we approximate $(n+dD)\cdots(n+1)$ by n^{dD}. We then get roughly

$$(m+D)\cdots(m+1)\cdot(dD)\cdots(D+1) \tag{18}$$

$$> m^D \cdot D^{(d-1)D} \tag{19}$$

$$\geq n^{(1+e)D} \cdot n^{(1-\frac{e}{d-1})\cdot(d-1)D} \tag{20}$$

$$= n^{(1+e)D+(d-1-e)D} \tag{21}$$

$$= n^{dD} \approx (n+dD)\cdots(n+1). \tag{22}$$

This shows that the degree $D \in \Omega(n^{1-\frac{e}{d-1}})$ is a plausible bound for non-trivial elements in $\ker \phi$. In Sect. 3, we will show that we can choose any $D \geq c \cdot n^{1-\frac{e}{d-1}}$ for a constant $c \in (2,4]$ that depends on d.

The above considerations also give us a straight-forward algorithm for computing a non-zero element $h \in \ker \phi$: For each $\ell = 1,\ldots,D$, we compute a matrix representation of the linear map

$$\phi^\ell : \mathbb{Z}_q[Y]^{\leq \ell} \longrightarrow \mathbb{Z}_q[X]^{\leq d\cdot\ell}. \tag{23}$$

By using Gaussian elimination, we can then check if this matrix has a non-trivial kernel vector. Such a non-trivial kernel vector corresponds to a non-trivial kernel element $h \in \ker \phi$ of degree ℓ. By our observations above, we know that for $\ell = D = c \cdot n^{1-\frac{e}{d-1}}$, this algorithm must eventually find a non-zero polynomial.

The space and time complexities of this algorithm is in each step dominated by computing the Gaussian elimination of a matrix of shape $M_\ell \times N_\ell$ where $M_\ell = \binom{m+\ell}{\ell} \in O(n^{(1+e)\ell})$ and $N_\ell = \binom{n+d\ell}{d\ell} \in O(n^{d\ell})$. Therefore, we need to store $M_D \cdot N_D \in n^{O(n^{1-\frac{e}{d-1}})}$ field elements and perform $D \cdot M_D \cdot N_D^2 \in n^{O(n^{1-\frac{e}{d-1}})}$ arithmetic operations in $\mathbb{Z}_q$.

Evaluating h on a point $y \in \mathbb{Z}_q^m$ costs $D \cdot M_D \in n^{O(n^{1-\frac{e}{d-1}})}$ field operations. The advantage of using h in distinguishing a random point from an image point of F is at least $1 - D/q$. Hence, for $q \in \omega(n^{1-\frac{e}{d-1}})$ and $m \geq n^{1+e}$, we have an attack algorithm with noticeable advantage, which is subexponential in the worst case.

We give a detailed description of the algorithms sketched here and formal proofs for their correctness in Sect. 3 and Sect. 4.

Handling Small Moduli. Note, that we cannot guarantee any advantage of the above algorithm if $q \leq D = cn^{1-\frac{e}{d-1}}$. In fact, it may be that the above algorithm will retrieve the kernel element $h(Y) = Y_1^q - Y_1 \in \ker \phi$ in this case, which is not helpful since the polynomial $Y_1^q - Y_1$ vanishes on each point $y \in \mathbb{Z}_q^m$.

We can prevent the appearance of trivial polynomials in the kernel of ϕ as follows: instead of $\mathbb{Z}_q[X]$ and $\mathbb{Z}_q[Y]$ we consider the rings

$$R_q[X] := \mathbb{Z}_q[X]/(X_1^q - X_1, \ldots, X_n^q - X_n) \tag{24}$$

$$R_q[Y] := \mathbb{Z}_q[Y]/(Y_1^q - Y_1, \ldots, Y_m^q - Y_m). \tag{25}$$

On these rings, we have a morphism

$$\phi_q : R_q[Y] \longrightarrow R_q[X] \tag{26}$$

$$g(Y_1, \ldots, Y_m) \longmapsto g(f_1(X), \ldots, f_m(X)) \tag{27}$$

that again maps each variable Y_i to the polynomial f_i. The non-zero elements of $\ker \phi_q$ are now exactly the polynomials h that vanish on the image of F, but not everywhere on $\mathbb{Z}_q^m$. If we restrict ϕ_q to $R_q[Y]^{\leq \ell}$ we get again a linear map

$$\phi_q^{\ell} : R_q[Y]^{\leq \ell} \longrightarrow R_q[X]^{\leq d\ell}, \tag{28}$$

and it can be shown again that we have for $D \geq c \cdot n^{1 - \frac{e}{d-1}}$ for some constant c

$$\dim_{\mathbb{Z}_q} R_q[Y]^{\leq D} > \dim_{\mathbb{Z}_q} R_q[X]^{\leq dD}. \tag{29}$$

Therefore, $\ker \phi_q$ must contain a non-zero element h of sublinear degree D that is not contained in the ideal $(Y_1^q - Y_1, \ldots, Y_m^q - Y_m)$. For such an element, it can be shown that its probability to not vanish on a random point can be subexponentially bounded, even if $D > q$. I.e.

$$\Pr_{y \leftarrow \mathbb{Z}_q^m}[h(y) \neq 0] \geq q^{-D}. \tag{30}$$

This gives us an algorithm of subexponential complexity with a subexponentially small advantage in distinguishing between random points and images of the PRG F.

In a multi-challenge setting, where the adversary can query multiple values $y_1, \ldots, y_Q$ that either are all uniformly and independently random or are all values in the image of F, the above attack can be amplified to have a noticeable advantage for a subexponential number $Q \in q^{\Omega(n^{1 - \frac{e}{d-1}})}$ of challenges.

Local PRGs of Constant Moduli. While the advantage of the above attack may be much higher in practice (since the probability that h vanishes on a random point may be higher than q^{-D}), from a theoretical point of view the postulated subexponential advantage is not satisfying.

Fortunately, in the case where the modulus q is constant and F is of constant locality, we can use a little trick to noticeably boost the advantage of our attack. For simplicity, we will assume here that q is 2, however the following approach works for each constant modulus:

Let $F : \mathbb{Z}_2^n \to \mathbb{Z}_2^m$ be of locality d. This means, the i-th bit of the output of F is computed by a function $f_i : \mathbb{Z}_2^n \to \mathbb{Z}_2$ that only depends on d of its inputs. Choose a prime number $p \in [n, 2n]$ and note that – due to the locality of F – for each f_i we can find a polynomial $f_i' \in \mathbb{Z}_p[X]$ of degree d that coincides[2] with f_i on

---

[2] Note, that in the case $q > 2$, the degree of the polynomials f_i' that coincide with f_i on the set $\{0, \ldots, q - 1\}^n$ will be $(q - 1)d$ instead of d.

$\{0,1\}^n$, i.e., we have $f_i'(x) = f_i(x)$ for each $x \in \{0,1\}^n$. So, instead of attacking the pseudorandomness of F, we can focus on the pseudorandomness of the map $F' : \mathbb{Z}_p^n \to \mathbb{Z}_p^m$ of degree d that consists of the polynomials $f_1', \ldots, f_m'$. However, distinguishing a random point $y \leftarrow \mathbb{Z}_p^m$ from $F''(x) = F(x)$, for $x \leftarrow \{0,1\}^n$, is obviously simple, since the latter will always lie in $\{0,1\}^m$. To come up for that, we set $m' := \frac{m}{3 \log p}$ and draw a uniformly random matrix $A \leftarrow \mathbb{Z}_p^{m' \times m}$. According to the Leftover Hash Lemma, the distributions

$$(A, Ay)_{y \leftarrow \{0,1\}^m} \quad \text{and} \quad (A, y')_{y' \leftarrow \mathbb{Z}_p^{m'}} \tag{31}$$

are statistically very close. Therefore, if $F : \mathbb{Z}_2^n \to \mathbb{Z}_2^m$ is pseudorandom, then the map $G : \mathbb{Z}_p^n \to \mathbb{Z}_p^{m'}$ of degree d that maps x to $A \cdot F'(x)$ must be, too. However, we can apply our first attack against G. Since $m \geq n^{1+e}$, we have $m' \geq n^{1+e'}$ for any constant $e' < e$ and therefore an attack of time and space complexity $2^{O(n^{1-\frac{e'}{d-1}})}$ and noticeable advantage $1 - O(n^{1-\frac{e'}{d-1}})/p \geq 1 - O(n^{-\frac{e'}{d-1}})$. Going back to F, we get an algorithm of subexponential complexity that has a noticeable advantage in distinguishing images of F from random bit strings $y \leftarrow \{0,1\}^m$. We detail this attack in Sect. 5.

1.3   Related Work

We try to give here a short survey of the current cryptoanalytic literature on PRGs.

Linear Tests and Low-Degree Correlation. A *linear test* for a PRG $F : \mathbb{Z}_q^n \to \mathbb{Z}_q^m$ is a degree-1 polynomial $L \in \mathbb{Z}_q[Y]$ that has a noticeable advantage

$$\left| \Pr_{x \leftarrow \mathbb{Z}_q^n} [L(F(x)) = 0] - \Pr_{y \leftarrow \mathbb{Z}_q^m} [L(y) = 0] \right| \tag{32}$$

in distinguishing random points from image points of F. While linear tests form a very simple class of attacks against PRGs, it can be shown that they are a good sanity check in the case of local PRGs: a local random PRG that is secure against linear tests also fools other classes of distinguishers like e.g. $\mathbf{AC}^0$, l-wise tests and degree-2 threshold functions [2, Proposition 4.10]. Mossel *et al.* [37] shows that there exist PRGs of constant locality s.t. each linear test only has negligible advantage against those PRGs, even if the PRG is of polynomial stretch $m = n^{1+e}$. Their construction is based on the famous tri-sum-and predicate

$$X_1 X_2 + X_3 + X_4 + X_5 \tag{33}$$

that gets applied on random subsets of the input to compute the output bits of the PRG.

If we allow the degree of L to be greater than 1, we get a polynomial test of higher degree. Viola [43] showed that for each constant d a PRG can be constructed that cannot be distinguished by degree-d tests with noticeable advantage (his constructions allows non-constant values for d, however such d reduce the stretch of the PRG substantially).

Groebner Basis-Based Attacks. A huge class of attacks against PRGs of constant degree constitute of algebraic attacks [12,16,17,23,24,36,44]. These attacks aim to invert the potential image of a PRG by computing a Groebner basis or something similar in the case of XL-algorithms.

These algorithms work well in practice, and it has been suspected that they give subexponential attack algorithms against PRGs of polynomial stretch [9]. However, computing a Groebner basis can be a task of double exponential complexity in the worst case, and therefore those algorithms do not give us provable subexponential attacks.

In the full version [45] of this text, we will give a deeper comparison of our algorithms with Groebner basis-based algorithms, draw new insights for Groebner basis-based algorithms and construct a Macaulay matrix-based algorithm that is provable subexponential in the worst case when distinguishing the images of poly-stretch PRGs.

Random Local Functions. A *random local function* is a PRG $F : \{0,1\}^n \to \{0,1\}^m$ where each output bit is computed by a fixed predicate $P : \{0,1\}^d \to \{0,1\}$ that is applied on a random subset of bits of the input string. The notion of random local functions has been put forth by Goldreich [26] and was the subject of a great body of cryptoanalytic literature. For exhaustive surveys and studies on the security of random local functions, we refer the reader to the works of Applebaum [2] and Couteau *et al.* [18]. We will only review here some attacks on random local functions, which we think are the most relevant for the context of this work:

1. It is known that F can be inverted in polynomial time and with high probability if $m \in \Omega(\log(n) \cdot n^{\frac{\lfloor 2d/3 \rfloor}{2}})$ [2]. First note, that F can be efficiently inverted by linearization of the corresponding polynomial equation system if it is of stretch $m \in \Omega(n^{\deg P})$, where $\deg P$ denotes the degree of P as a polynomial over $\mathbb{Z}_2$.

   This means, the degree of P must be greater than $d/3$ if we want to avoid the above attack for $m \geq n^{\frac{d}{3}}$. However, if $\deg P \geq d/3$, then P is correlated with the sum of $c \leq d - \frac{d}{3}$ of its variables [41]. I.e., P can be written as

$$P(Z_1, \ldots, Z_d) = Z_1 + \ldots + Z_c + N(Z_1, \ldots, Z_d) \qquad (34)$$

   where N is a biased predicate i.e. $\Pr_{z \leftarrow \{0,1\}^d}[N(z) = 0] \neq \frac{1}{2}$. When solving the system $F(x) = y$, one can see the N predicates as dependent noise added to linear equations. This constrained noisy linear equation system can be solved efficiently if $m \in \Omega(n^{c/2})$ [15,25].

2. There is a subexponential inversion attack [2,11] on $F(x)$ that utilizes approximations of the correct inverse and has a runtime complexity of $2^{O(n^{1-\frac{e}{2d}})}$ (if $m \geq n^{1+e}$). The idea is to assign random bits to the first $(1 - 2n^{-\frac{e}{2d}})$ bits of an approximate solution. By iterating over all possible $x' \in \{0,1\}^n$ with the given prefix, one will find an approximation that coincides with x on at least $(\frac{1}{2} + n^{-\frac{e}{2d}})n$ of its bits with probability at least $\frac{1}{2}$. This approximation can now be used to find efficiently and with high probability the correct solution x.

Note, that the time complexity $2^{O(n^{1-\frac{e}{2d}})}$ of this algorithm is worse than the time complexity $2^{O(n^{1-\frac{e'}{d-1}})}$, for any constant $e' < e$, of the algorithm we sketched against d-local PRGs of stretch n^{1+e}.

3. Couteau et $al.$ [18] constructed a guess-and-determine-style attack on PRGs $F : \{0,1\}^n \to \{0,1\}^{n^{1+e}}$ of constant locality. Their attack guesses – in an intelligent way – a portion of the bits of x and tries to extract a linear equation system from the system $F(x) = y$ for the unguessed input bits. If the predicate P for F is of the form

$$P(X_1, \ldots, X_r) = X_1 X_2 + X_3 + \ldots + X_r, \tag{35}$$

they can prove that their attack will succeed in distinguishing random points from images of F and has a time complexity of $2^{O(n^{1-e})}$. Note, that r does not need to be constant.

They even generalize their attack to work with general predicates

$$P(X_1, \ldots, X_r) = M(X_1, \ldots, X_d) + X_{d+1} + \ldots + X_r, \tag{36}$$

for any predicate $M : \{0,1\}^d \to \{0,1\}$ and get an attack algorithm of time complexity $2^{O(n^{1-\frac{e}{d-1}})}$. However, to prove a high success probability of the generalization of their attack they need to assume a special conjecture that depends on M.

4. While there are a lot of efficient attacks against local PRGs of sufficient stretch, it is known that algebraic attacks against d-local PRGs of stretch n^{1+e} will have a time complexity of at least $n^{O(n^{1-32\frac{e}{d-2}})}$ in the worst case [2, Theorem 5.5]. This means, up to some constants in the exponent, the time complexities we achieve with our attacks are optimal for algebraic attacks.

Attacks Based on Sum-of-Squares. Sum-of-Squares attacks are a special class of SDP-based attacks. These attacks were discovered recently and used to refute several candidate light-weight PRGs of polynomial stretch for indistinguishability obfuscation schemes [7,8]. While these attacks are efficient, they need to make special assumptions about the PRGs they attack, which limits the generality of those attacks. We will list below some PRGs for which a sum-of-squares attack can successfully distinguish PRG images from random points:

1. Let $F : \{0,1\}^{nb} \to \{0,1\}^m$ be *two block-local*, i.e., the input is partitioned into n blocks of size b and each output depends on two blocks. If $m \in \Omega(2^{2b} \cdot \log^2(n) \cdot n)$ is big enough, then there is an efficient attack on F [7].

2. Let $c > 0$ be a constant and let Y be a distribution over $\mathbb{R}$ s.t. we have $\Pr_{y \leftarrow Y}[y \notin [a, a + c]] \geq \frac{1}{10}$ for each $a \in \mathbb{R}$. Let $F : \{0,1\}^n \to \mathbb{R}^m$ be a PRG of degree d over the reals s.t. the polynomials in F have at most s monomials. If $m \in \Omega(\log^2(n) \cdot s \cdot n^{\lceil d/2 \rceil})$ is big enough and if we assume a special assumption for the polynomials $f_1, \ldots, f_m$, there is an efficient attack that can successfully distinguish images of F from points $y \leftarrow Y^m$ [7].

3. Let $t \in \text{poly}(n)$ and let Q be a distribution of quadratic polynomials in $\mathbb{R}[X]$ with some special properties. If $m \in \log(n)^{\Omega(1)} \cdot n$ is big enough, there is an efficient algorithm that can extract with high probability the input x from $(F, F(x))$ where we sample $x \leftarrow [-t, t]^n$ and $F \leftarrow Q^m$ [8].

1.4 Organization of this Text

In Sect. 2, we will introduce some algebraic and cryptographic preliminaries. In Sect. 3, we will give an algorithm that finds non-trivial polynomials that vanish on the images of PRGs $F : \mathbb{Z}_q^n \to \mathbb{Z}_q^m$ of constant degree d and prove that one can find such polynomials of sublinear degree if F is of polynomial stretch $m = n^{1+e}$. In Sect. 4, we will give a distinguishing attack on F of time and space complexity $n^{O(n^{1-\frac{e}{d-1}})}$ and prove that it has an advantage of at least $1 - O(n^{1-\frac{e}{d-1}}/q)$. In Sect. 5, we will investigate the case of small constant moduli q. For simplicity, we will only treat the representative case $q = 2$, however all results shown for $q = 2$ can be generalized for any small or constant prime q. We will show in this section, that one can find a polynomial of sublinear degree that vanishes on the image of F, but does not vanish everywhere on $\mathbb{Z}_q^m$. This leads to a second attack on degree-d PRGs $F : \mathbb{Z}_q^n \to \mathbb{Z}_q^m$ of complexity $n^{O(n^{1-\frac{e}{d-1}})}$ and subexponential advantage $q^{-O(n^{1-\frac{e}{d-1}})}$. Additionally, we will in this section give an attack on d-local PRGs $F : \mathbb{Z}_q^n \to \mathbb{Z}_q^m$ that has a time and space complexity of $2^{O(n^{1-\frac{e'}{(q-1)d-1}})}$ and noticeable advantage $O(n^{-\frac{e'}{(q-1)d-1}})$ for every constant $e' < e$. In Sect. 6, we will derive some insights for the design of PRGs that shall be secure against subexponential adversaries.

In the full version of this text [45], we will give an exhaustive comparison between our algorithms and Groebner basis-based algorithms, derive some insights for Groebner basis-based algorithms, give a new attack algorithm against PRGs of constant degree and polynomial stretch, which is also Groebner basis- or rather Macaulay matrix-based, and prove that it is subexponential in the worst case. Additionally, we will formally prove some claims that were only sketched and give some algebraic background.

2 Preliminaries

2.1 Notation

Denote by $\mathbb{N} = \{1, 2, 3, \ldots\}$ the set of natural numbers and by $\mathbb{N}_0 = \mathbb{N} \cup \{0\}$ the set of natural numbers plus zero.

For the rest of this text, by k we will always denote a field and by $k[X_1, \ldots, X_n]$ resp. $k[Y_1, \ldots, Y_m]$ the corresponding polynomial ring, for $n, m \in \mathbb{N}$. Since the numbers of X and Y variables will always be n resp. m, by abuse of notation, we will write $k[X]$ resp. $k[Y]$ instead of $k[X_1, \ldots, X_n]$ resp. $k[Y_1, \ldots, Y_m]$.

Let $f \in k[X]$. When we speak of f's *degree* we always mean its *total degree* that is the minimum number $d \in \mathbb{N}_0$ s.t. f can be written as a k-linear combination of monomials that are the product of $\leq d$ variables.

If S is a finite set, we denote by $x \leftarrow S$ the fact that the random variable x is drawn uniformly and independently at random from S.

For a number $q \in \mathbb{N}$, we define the finite ring $\mathbb{Z}_q := \mathbb{Z}/q\mathbb{Z}$.

We will denote by n the security parameter in this text. The parameter $m = m(n)$ will in most cases be dependent on n. For this to be consistent, we assume in those cases that m is time-constructible.

We call a function $\epsilon : \mathbb{N} \to [0, 1]$ negligible, if we have $\lim_{n \to \infty} \epsilon(n) \cdot n^d =$ for each $d \in \mathbb{N}$. By $\mathrm{poly}(n) := \{f : \mathbb{N} \to \mathbb{N} \mid \exists c, d \in \mathbb{N} : f(n) \le n^d + c\}$ we denote the set self-maps of the natural numbers that are upper-bounded by constant-degree polynomials.

Given two discrete distributions $\mathcal{X}$ and $\mathcal{Y}$, we define their statistical distance as $\Delta(\mathcal{X}, \mathcal{Y}) := \frac{1}{2} \sum_x |\mathcal{X}(x) - \mathcal{Y}(x)|$.

Given two vector spaces V, W over the same field, we denote by $V \oplus W$ their direct sum.

2.2 Mathematical Preliminaries

We will introduce now some basic facts and notions for the polynomial ring $k[X]$:

Remark 1. Let $n \in \mathbb{N}$. Let k be any field and consider the polynomial ring $k[X] = k[X_1, \ldots, X_n]$. The ring $k[X]$ is graded and can be written as

$$k[X] = \bigoplus_{\ell=0}^{\infty} k[X]^{\ell} \tag{37}$$

where $k[X]^{\ell}$ is the finite-dimensional k-vector space generated by all monomials of total degree $= \ell$, i.e.

$$k[X]^{\ell} = \mathrm{span}_k \left\{ X_1^{a_1} \cdots X_n^{a_n} \mid a_1, \ldots, a_n \in \mathbb{N}_0, a_1 + \ldots + a_n = \ell \right\}. \tag{38}$$

By $k[X]^{\le \ell}$ we denote the space generated by all monomials of degree $\le \ell$, i.e.

$$k[X]^{\le \ell} := \bigoplus_{i=0}^{\ell} k[X]^i. \tag{39}$$

The dimensions of $k[X]^{\ell}$ and $k[X]^{\le \ell}$ are given by

$$\dim_k k[X]^{\ell} = \binom{n + \ell - 1}{\ell} \quad \text{and} \quad \dim_k k[X]^{\le \ell} = \binom{n + \ell}{\ell}. \tag{40}$$

Sometimes, we will use the notion $X^{\alpha_1}, X^{\alpha_2}, \ldots$ to denote monomials

$$X_1^{a_{1,1}} \cdots X_n^{a_{1,n}}, X_1^{a_{2,1}} \cdots X_n^{a_{2,n}}, \ldots. \tag{41}$$

In those cases, the $\alpha_1, \alpha_2, \ldots \in \mathbb{N}_0^n$ are multi-indices given by

$$\alpha_i = (a_{i,1}, \ldots, a_{i,n}). \tag{42}$$

In the case of $k = \mathbb{Z}_q$ for a small prime q, it might be necessary to include the field equations $X_1^q - X_1, \ldots, X_n^q - X_n$ when considering $k[X]$. In this text, we will only treat the case $q = 2$, which is representative for all cases of constant moduli q:

Remark 2. Let $k = \mathbb{Z}_2$ and denote by $I \subset \mathbb{Z}_2[X]$ the ideal generated by the field equations of $\mathbb{Z}_2$, i.e.

$$I := (X_1^2 - X_1, \ldots, X_n^2 - X_n). \tag{43}$$

The ring $\mathbb{Z}_2[X]/I$ is not graded any more, since I is not a homogenous ideal. However, it is still filtrated where the filtration steps are given by the vector spaces

$$\mathbb{Z}_2[X]^{\leq \ell}/(I \cap \mathbb{Z}_2[X]^{\leq \ell}). \tag{44}$$

A basis for $\mathbb{Z}_2[X]^{\leq \ell}/(I \cap \mathbb{Z}_2[X]^{\leq \ell})$ is given by the set of all monomials of degree $\leq \ell$ where each variable occurs at most once. Therefore, we have for $\ell \leq n$

$$\dim_{\mathbb{Z}_2}(\mathbb{Z}_2[X]^{\leq \ell}/(I \cap \mathbb{Z}_2[X]^{\leq \ell})) = \sum_{i=0}^{\ell} \binom{n}{i}. \tag{45}$$

In particular, we have for $\ell \leq n$

$$\sum_{i=0}^{\ell} \binom{n}{i} = \dim_{\mathbb{Z}_2}(\mathbb{Z}_2[X]^{\leq \ell}/(I \cap \mathbb{Z}_2[X]^{\leq \ell})) \leq \dim_{\mathbb{Z}_2}(\mathbb{Z}_2[X]^{\leq \ell}) = \binom{n+\ell}{\ell}. \tag{46}$$

Definition 1 (Dual Morphisms). *Let k be any field and $k[X] = k[X_1, \ldots, X_n]$. Let $f_1, \ldots, f_m \in k[X]$ and $k[Y] = k[Y_1, \ldots, Y_m]$. The function*

$$F : k^n \longrightarrow k^m \tag{47}$$
$$x \longrightarrow (f_1(x), \ldots, f_m(x)) \tag{48}$$

*gives us a geometrical map that is continuous in the Zariski topology. It has a **dual morphism** of k-algebras*

$$\phi : k[Y] \longrightarrow k[X] \tag{49}$$
$$Y_i \longrightarrow f_i(X) \tag{50}$$

that maps each polynomial $h \in k[Y]$ to a polynomial $h(f_1(X), \ldots, f_m(X))$ in $k[X]$ by substituting each appearance of Y_i in h by f_i for each $i \in [m]$.

Definition 2 (Algebraic Independence). *In the situation of Definition 1, we call $f_1, \ldots, f_m$ **algebraically independent** if ϕ is injective.*

*If ϕ is not injective, we call a non-zero element $h \in \ker \phi$ of its kernel an **algebraic relation** of the elements $f_1, \ldots, f_m$.*

When working with polynomials over $k = \mathbb{Z}_q$ for q sufficiently large, the Schwartz-Zippel Lemma is a helpful tool to lower bound the probability that a fixed polynomial vanishes on a random point of $\mathbb{Z}_q^m$.

Lemma 1 (Schwartz-Zippel [40]). *Let $q \in \mathbb{N}$ be a prime and let $m, d \in \mathbb{N}$. Let $h \in k[Y]$ be a polynomial of degree d. Then, we can bound the probability of h vanishing on a random point of $\mathbb{Z}_q^m$ by*

$$\Pr_{y \leftarrow \mathbb{Z}_q^m} [h(y) = 0] \leq d/q. \tag{51}$$

2.3   Cryptographic Preliminaries

In this subsection, we will introduce the notion of pseudorandom number generators, and define a simple security game for them.

Definition 3 (Pseudorandom Number Generators). *Let $m : \mathbb{N} \to \mathbb{N}$ be a time-constructible function and let k be any field. A **pseudorandom number generator** (PRG) is a family of functions $F = (F_n)_{n \in \mathbb{N}}$ s.t. each F_n is a deterministic function*

$$F_n : k^n \longrightarrow k^m. \tag{52}$$

*We call m the **stretch** of the PRG. If there is a constant $e > 0$ s.t. $m \geq n^{1+e}$, we say that $(F_n)_{n \in \mathbb{N}}$ is a **poly-stretch** PRG.*

Remark 3. If $F = (F_n)_{n \in \mathbb{N}}$ is a PRG, we will, by abuse of notation, just write

$$F : k^n \to k^m. \tag{53}$$

For a given n, we will further write F when we actually mean F_n.

The adversaries in this text are always given a description of F_n (which we will simply denote by F) that allows the adversary to efficiently evaluate F_n on points of k^n. We assume that this description of F_n always contains binary representations of the numbers n, m and a description of the field k that allows the adversary to perform arithmetic operations over k. Additionally, if F is of locality or degree $d \in \mathbb{N}$ (in the sense of Definition 4), we expect the description of F to contain a binary representation of d.

Definition 4 (Locality and Degree of PRGs). *Let $F = (F_n)_n$ be a PRG of stretch m over k. Let $d \in \mathbb{N}$. For $n \in \mathbb{N}$ and $i \in [m]$, we denote by $f_{n,i} : k^n \to k$ the function of the i-th output of F_n. I.e., $f_{n,1}, \ldots f_{n,m}$ are uniquely determined by*

$$F(x) = (f_{n,1}(x), \ldots, f_{n,m}(x)) \tag{54}$$

for all $x \in k^n$.

1. *We say that F is d-**local** if each of its output values depends on only d input values. I.e. for each $n \in \mathbb{N}$ and $i \in [m]$ there is a function $g : k^d \to k$ and indices $l_1, \ldots, l_d \in [n]$ s.t. we have for each $x \in k^n$*

$$f_{n,i}(x_1, \ldots, x_n) = g(x_{l_1}, \ldots, x_{l_d}).$$

2. *We say that F is of **degree** d if each $f_{n,i}$ can be computed by a polynomial of degree d. I.e., for each $n \in \mathbb{N}$ and $i \in [m]$ the function $f_{n,i} : k^n \to k$ coincides with a polynomial in $k[X]$ of degree $\leq d$. In this case, by abuse of notation, we will directly interpret $f_{n,i}$ as an element of $k[X]^{\leq d}$.*

For a given n, we will simply write $f_1, \ldots, f_m$ instead of $f_{n,1}, \ldots, f_{n,m}$ to denote the partial functions of F. We will usually say in those cases that F is made up of or consists of $f_1, \ldots, f_m$.

Definition 5 (Security Game for PRGs). *Let k be finite now and let $F : k^n \to k^m$ be a PRG. We describe here a non-interactive security game between a probabilistic challenger $\mathcal{C}$ and a (potentially probabilistic) adversary $\mathcal{A}$. The game is parametrized by n and proceeds in the following steps:*

1. *$\mathcal{C}$ draws a bit $b \leftarrow \{0,1\}$. If $b = 0$, it samples a preimage $x \leftarrow k^n$ uniformly at random, computes $F(x)$ and sends $(F, F(x))$ to $\mathcal{A}$. If $b = 1$, it samples $y \leftarrow k^m$ and sends (F, y) to $\mathcal{A}$.*
2. *$\mathcal{A}$ receives (F, y^*) for some $y^* \in k^m$ and must decide which bit b has been drawn by $\mathcal{C}$. It makes some computations on its own without interacting with $\mathcal{C}$ and finally sends a bit b' to $\mathcal{C}$.*

$\mathcal{A}$ wins an instance of this game iff $b = b'$ holds at the end. We define $\mathcal{A}$'s advantage against F by

$$\mathsf{adv}_F(\mathcal{A}) := 2\Pr[\mathcal{A} \text{ wins}] - 1 = \Pr_{x \leftarrow k^n}[\mathcal{A}(F, F(x)) = 0] + \Pr_{y \leftarrow k^m}[\mathcal{A}(F, y) = 1] - 1 \tag{55}$$

where we take the probability over the randomness of $\mathcal{A}$ and $\mathcal{C}$.

We define $\mathcal{A}$'s space complexity to be the number of bits and elements of k it stores simultaneously in step 2, and we define its time complexity by the number of bit-operations and arithmetical operations over k it performs in step 2.

Definition 6. *We say that an algorithm is **subexponential** if there is a constant $e \in [0,1)$ s.t. its time and space complexities lie in $2^{O(n^e)}$.*

Lemma 2 (Leftover Hash Lemma (Matrix Version) [21]). *Let $q \in \mathbb{N}$ be a prime and let $m, m' \in \mathbb{N}$ be natural numbers.*
If we draw $A_1, A_2 \leftarrow \mathbb{Z}_q^{m \times m'}, y_1 \leftarrow \{0,1\}^m, y_2 \leftarrow \mathbb{Z}_q^{m'}$, we have

$$\Delta((A_1, A_1 y_1), (A_2, y_2)) \leq \frac{1}{2}\sqrt{2^{m' \cdot \log q - m}}. \tag{56}$$

3   Finding Algebraic Relations

In this section, we introduce an algorithm $\mathcal{B}1$ that – given a set of polynomials – finds an algebraic relation among these polynomials. Further, we will prove upper bounds for the degree of this relation and for the complexity of the algorithm.

Now, let $n, m, d \in \mathbb{N}$ and let k be any field in this section. Let $F : k^n \to k^m$ be a polynomial mapping of degree $\leq d$ that is given by polynomials $f_1, \ldots, f_m \in k[X]$ of degree $\leq d$.

Denote by $\phi : k[Y] \to k[X]$ the dual morphism to F. Note, that ϕ expands the degrees of its inputs by a factor of at most d, i.e., we have for each $\ell \in \mathbb{N}_0$

$$\phi(k[Y]^{\leq \ell}) \subseteq k[X]^{\leq d \cdot \ell}. \tag{57}$$

Let $\ker \phi = \{h \in k[Y] \mid \phi(h) = 0\}$ be the kernel of ϕ. Our aim is to compute a non-trivial element of $\ker \phi$.

We will propose a straight-forward approach for this task: For $\ell = 1, 2, \ldots$, the algorithm $\mathcal{B}1$ will compute a monomial basis for $k[Y]^{\leq \ell}$ and check – by linear algebra – if the vector space $k[Y]^\ell \cap \ker \phi$ is non-trivial. If $k[Y]^\ell \cap \ker \phi$ contains a non-trivial element eventually, $\mathcal{B}1$ will output it and terminate. Formally, $\mathcal{B}1$ is given by:

Algorithm 1. The algorithm $\mathcal{B}1$ gets as input numbers $n, m, d \in \mathbb{N}$, a description of k and a description of a polynomial map $F : k^n \to k^m$. It has to output a non-zero element of $\ker \phi$.

$\mathcal{B}1$ sets an iteration variable $\ell := 1$ and proceeds in the following steps:

1. $\mathcal{B}1$ computes $N := \binom{n+d\ell}{d\ell}$ and $M := \binom{m+\ell}{\ell}$
2. $\mathcal{B}1$ computes a finite list $(Y_1^{a_1} \cdots Y_m^{a_m} \mid a_1, \ldots, a_m \in \mathbb{N}_0, a_1 + \ldots + a_m \leq \ell) = (Y^{\alpha_1}, \ldots, Y^{\alpha_M})$ of all monomials in $k[Y]$ of degree $\leq \ell$.
3. $\mathcal{B}1$ applies ϕ to each Y^{α_i} and computes a second list $(\phi(Y^{\alpha_1}), \ldots, \phi(Y^{\alpha_M}))$ of polynomials in $k[X]$ of degree $\leq d\ell$.
4. Let $X^{\beta_1}, \ldots, X^{\beta_N}$ be the set of all monomials in $k[X]$ of degree $\leq d\ell$. Then, $X^{\beta_1}, \ldots, X^{\beta_N}$ is a basis of $k[X]^{\leq d\ell}$ and for each $\phi(Y^{\alpha_i})$ there is a unique column-vector $w_i = (w_{i,1}, \ldots, w_{i,N}) \in k^N$ s.t.

$$\phi(Y^{\alpha_i}) = \sum_{j=1}^{N} w_{i,j} \cdot X^{\beta_j}. \tag{58}$$

$\mathcal{B}1$ computes for each Y_{α_i} the corresponding vector w_i and writes down the matrix

$$W_\ell := (w_1 | \ldots | w_M) \in k^{N \times M}. \tag{59}$$

5. $\mathcal{B}1$ uses Gaussian elimination to compute a basis for the vector space

$$K_\ell := \{r \in k^M \mid W_\ell \cdot r = 0\}. \tag{60}$$

6. If K_ℓ is the trivial null-space, $\mathcal{B}1$ increases ℓ by one and goes back to step 2.

7. Otherwise, $\mathcal{B}1$ chooses an arbitrary non-zero vector $r \in K_\ell$, computes the polynomial

$$h := r_1 \cdot Y^{\alpha_1} + \ldots + r_M \cdot Y^{\alpha_M} \in k[Y] \tag{61}$$

of total degree $\leq \ell$ and outputs it.

We will show the following properties for $\mathcal{B}1$:

Lemma 3. *Let $n, m, d \in \mathbb{N}$ s.t. $m > n$. Let $F : k^n \to k^m$ be a polynomial map of degree $\leq d$. Let $y \in k^m$. We have the following:*

1. *On input n, m, d and F, $\mathcal{B}1$ will always terminate after a finite number of steps and output a polynomial h.*
2. *The polynomial h outputted by $\mathcal{B}1$ will always lie in $\ker \phi$ and be non-zero.*

Proof. 1. Note that $m > n$. The first claim of the lemma is equivalent to stating that m elements of $k[X]$ must be algebraically dependent and $\phi : k[Y] \to k[X]$ cannot be injective. This is a well-known fact in algebra and is easy to prove, however writing down a formally correct proof will make the notions of transcendency bases and function fields necessary. A proof of this statement can be found in the full version [45] of this text.
2. Assume that $\mathcal{B}1$ stops after D iterations and outputs h. Then, h is a polynomial in $k[Y]$ of degree D and can be written as

$$h := r_1 \cdot Y^{\alpha_1} + \ldots + r_M \cdot Y^{\alpha_M} \in k[Y] \tag{62}$$

where $M = \binom{m+D}{D}$ and r is a non-zero kernel element of R_D. I.e., we have

$$\sum_{i=1}^{M} r_i \cdot w_i = 0. \tag{63}$$

Since the entries of w_i are exactly the coefficients of $\phi(Y^{\alpha_i})$, we have

$$\phi(h) = \phi\left(\sum_{i=1}^{M} r_i \cdot Y^{\alpha_i}\right) = \sum_{i=1}^{M} r_i \cdot \phi(Y^{\alpha_i}) = 0. \tag{64}$$

Ergo, $h \in \ker \phi$.

Lemma 4. *Assume that $\mathcal{B}1$ terminates after D iterations. Then, its space complexity can be bounded by $O(NM)$ and its time complexity can be bounded by $O(DN^2M)$ for $N = \binom{n+d\cdot D}{d\cdot D}$ and $M = \binom{m+D}{D}$.*

Proof. In each iteration step, $\mathcal{B}1$ computes a matrix of shape at most $N \times M$ over k. Therefore, the number of bits and elements of k it needs to store simultaneously can be bounded by $O(NM)$.

We can bound the time complexity of each iteration step from above by the time complexity of the D-th iteration step. In this step, $\mathcal{B}1$ performs Gaussian elimination on an $N \times M$-matrix which needs $O(N^2M)$ arithmetical operations over k. Therefore, the number of bit-operations and arithmetical operations $\mathcal{B}1$ needs to do in each step can be bounded by $O(N^2M)$, and $\mathcal{B}1$'s total time complexity can be bounded by $O(DN^2M)$.

Note, that $\mathcal{B}1$ starts at $\ell = 1$ and increases ℓ by one subsequently. Since $\mathcal{B}1$ terminates only if it finds a non-trivial element in $k[Y]^\ell \cap \ker \phi$, this means that the number D of iterations $\mathcal{B}1$ has to perform is exactly the lowest total degree of non-zero elements of $\ker \phi$.

Lemma 5. $\mathcal{B}1$ *terminates after D iterations iff $D = \min\{\deg h \mid h \in \ker \phi, h \neq 0\}$.*

3.1 Bounding D for Poly-stretch PRGs

We have seen in the last subsection that the time and space complexity of $\mathcal{B}1$ is substantially influenced by D. Since D is the minimal degree of a non-trivial element of $\ker \phi$, our aim in this subsection is to bound the degree of algebraic relations for all sets of polynomials $f_1, \ldots, f_m$ of degree $\leq d$.

Since we are interested in the case of poly-stretch PRGs, we introduce an additional constant $e > 0$ and assume that m is always larger than n^{1+e}.

Let ϕ_ℓ be the restriction of ϕ on $k[Y]^{\leq \ell}$. Then, each ϕ_ℓ is a linear map of type $k[Y]^{\leq \ell} \rightarrow k[X]^{\leq d \cdot \ell}$. We can guarantee that ϕ_ℓ has a non-trivial kernel, if the dimension of $k[Y]^{\leq \ell}$ exceeds the dimension of $k[X]^{\leq d \cdot \ell}$. Now, the dimensions of $k[Y]^{\leq \ell}$ and $k[X]^{\leq d \cdot \ell}$ are given by

$$\dim_k(k[Y]^{\leq \ell}) = \binom{m + \ell}{\ell} \quad \text{and} \quad \dim_k(k[X]^{\leq d \cdot \ell}) = \binom{n + d \cdot \ell}{d \cdot \ell}. \quad (65)$$

Therefore, we get for algorithm $\mathcal{B}1$:

Lemma 6. *Let D be the number of iterations of $\mathcal{B}1$. Then, we have*

$$D \leq \min \left\{ \ell \in \mathbb{N} \mid \binom{m + \ell}{\ell} > \binom{n + d \cdot \ell}{d \cdot \ell} \right\}. \quad (66)$$

Inequality Eq. (66) gives us a tool to compute a worst-case bound for $\mathcal{B}1$'s complexity for each possible case of polynomials $f_1, \ldots, f_m$. In the next lemma, we will show that we can bound D by $O(n^{1 - \frac{e}{d-1}})$. While $n^{1 - \frac{e}{d-1}}$ is non-constant for $e < d-1$, it implies that we can bound the complexity of $\mathcal{B}1$ subexponentially by $n^{O(n^{1 - \frac{e}{d-1}})}$.

Lemma 7 (Main Inequalities). *Let $d \in \mathbb{N}, d \geq 2$ and $e \in (0, d-1]$. Let $m : \mathbb{N} \rightarrow \mathbb{N}$ be a function with $m(n) \geq n^{1+e}$ and set $c = 2^{\frac{d}{d-1}}$. Then, we have for all integers $n \geq (2dc)^{\frac{d-1}{e}}$*

$$\binom{m(n) + L(n)}{L(n)} > \binom{n + dL(n)}{dL(n)} \quad (67)$$

where $L(n) = \lceil cn^{1 - \frac{e}{d-1}} \rceil$.

Proof. In the proof, by abuse of notation, we write $m = m(n)$ and $L = L(n)$.

We first prove the inequality $dL \leq n$. In fact, we have

$$dL = d \lceil cn^{1 - \frac{e}{d-1}} \rceil \leq d(c \cdot n^{1 - \frac{e}{d-1}} + 1) = dc \cdot n^{1 - \frac{e}{d-1}} + d. \quad (68)$$

Since $n \geq (2dc)^{\frac{d-1}{e}}$, d must be smaller than $n/2$. For $dc \cdot n^{1-\frac{e}{d-1}}$, we have the equivalent inequalities

$$dc \cdot n^{1-\frac{e}{d-1}} \leq \frac{1}{2}n \iff dc \leq \frac{1}{2}n^{\frac{e}{d-1}} \tag{69}$$

$$\iff 2dc \leq n^{\frac{e}{d-1}} \tag{70}$$

$$\iff (2dc)^{\frac{d-1}{e}} \leq n \tag{71}$$

where the last inequality is exactly the requirement in our lemma for n. Therefore, we get

$$dL \leq dcn^{1-\frac{e}{d-1}} + d \leq \frac{n}{2} + \frac{n}{2} = n. \tag{72}$$

Now, for the claimed inequality of the lemma, we have the following chain of equivalent inequalities

$$\binom{m+L}{L} > \binom{n+dL}{dL} \tag{73}$$

$$\iff \frac{(m+L)\cdots(m+1)}{L!} > \frac{(n+dL)\cdots(n+1)}{(dL)!} \tag{74}$$

$$\iff (m+L)\cdots(m+1) \cdot (dL)\cdots(L+1) > (n+dL)\cdots(n+1). \tag{75}$$

Note, that we have for all n the inequalities

$$(m+L)\cdots(m+1) > m^L, \tag{76}$$

$$(dL)\cdots(L+1) > L^{(d-1)L}. \tag{77}$$

For the right-hand side, we have

$$(n+dL)\cdots(n+1) \leq (n+dL)^{dL} \leq (2n)^{dL} = n^{dL} \cdot 2^{dL}. \tag{78}$$

By using the inequalities Eqs. (76) to (78), we see that Eq. (75) is implied by the inequality

$$m^L \cdot L^{(d-1)L} \geq n^{dL} \cdot 2^{dL}. \tag{79}$$

By reducing Eq. (79) to the L-th root, we get the equivalent inequality

$$m \cdot L^{(d-1)} \geq n^d \cdot 2^d. \tag{80}$$

Now, it is easy to show that this inequality holds:

$$m \cdot L^{(d-1)} \geq n^{1+e} \cdot \left(c \cdot n^{1-\frac{e}{d-1}}\right)^{(d-1)} = n^{1+e+(d-1)-e} \cdot c^{d-1} = n^d \cdot 2^d. \tag{81}$$

This completes the proof.

Lemmas 3 to 7 now implies the following theorem:

Theorem 1. *Let $d \in \mathbb{N}$, $e > 0$ be constants and $m \geq n^{1+e}$. Let $f_1, \ldots, f_m \in k[X]$ be polynomials of degree $\leq d$.*
    Then, $\mathcal{B}1$ in Algorithm 1 outputs a non-trivial element of $\ker \phi$ of degree $O(n^{1-\frac{e}{d-1}})$. Its space and time complexities lie in $n^{O(n^{1-\frac{e}{d-1}})}$.

4   Attacks on Constant-Degree PRGs over Large Moduli

In this section, we will focus on the case $k = \mathbb{Z}_q$ for a prime q that is sufficiently high (e.g. $q \in \Omega(n)$). We claim that in this case $\mathcal{B}1$ from Algorithm 1 gives us a subexponential attack on each PRG of constant degree over $\mathbb{Z}_q$ and poly-stretch. In this section, we will prove:

Theorem 2. *Let $d \in \mathbb{N}, e > 0$ be constants. Let $m \geq n^{1+e}$ and let $F : \mathbb{Z}_q^n \to \mathbb{Z}_q^m$ be a PRG of degree d over $\mathbb{Z}_q$.*
  Then, there is an attack algorithm $\mathcal{A}1$ whose time and space complexities are bounded from above by $n^{O(n^{1-\frac{e}{d-1}})}$. Further, there exists a constant $c > 0$ s.t. $\mathcal{A}1$'s advantage in the security game Definition 5 is lower bounded by

$$\mathsf{adv}_F(\mathcal{A}1) \geq 1 - c \cdot n^{1-\frac{e}{d-1}}/q. \tag{82}$$

The attack $\mathcal{A}1$ on F is defined as follows:

Algorithm 2. $\mathcal{A}1$ receives as input a description of F that includes the numbers $n, m, q, d \in \mathbb{N}$ and an element $y^* \in \mathbb{Z}_q^m$. The goal of $\mathcal{A}1$ is to output 0, if y^* lies in the image of F, and 1, otherwise.
  $\mathcal{A}1$ proceeds in two simple steps:

1. $\mathcal{A}1$ executes the algorithm $\mathcal{B}1$ from Algorithm 1 on the input n, m, d, q, F and receives a non-zero polynomial $h \in \mathbb{Z}_q[Y]$ as output.
2. $\mathcal{A}1$ outputs 0 if $h(y^*) = 0$. Otherwise, $\mathcal{A}1$ outputs 1.

The bound on the time and space complexities of $\mathcal{A}1$ follows now from Theorem 1. The advantage of $\mathcal{A}1$ can be bounded as follows:
  If $b = 0$ in the security game of Definition 5, then the challenger $\mathcal{C}$ samples $x \leftarrow \mathbb{Z}_q^n$ and gives the pseudorandom image $y^* = F(x)$ to $\mathcal{A}1$. The polynomial h outputted by $\mathcal{B}1(F)$ lies in the kernel of ϕ, i.e., we have the equality $h(F(X)) = 0$ of polynomials in $\mathbb{Z}_q[X]$. In particular, we have $h(F(x)) = 0$ for each $x \in \mathbb{Z}_q^n$. Therefore, $\mathcal{A}1$ always outputs 0 if $b = 0$.
  If $b = 1$ in the security game in Definition 5, then the challenger $\mathcal{C}$ samples a uniformly random $y \leftarrow \mathbb{Z}_q^m$ and gives $y^* = y$ to $\mathcal{A}1$. Since h is non-zero and of degree $O(n^{1-\frac{e}{d-1}})$, the probability that h vanishes on y can be bounded by

$$\Pr_{y \leftarrow \mathbb{Z}_q^n}[h(y) = 0] \leq O(n^{1-\frac{e}{d-1}})/q \tag{83}$$

according to Lemma 1. Therefore, $\mathcal{A}1$ will output 1 in this case with probability at least $1 - O(n^{1-\frac{e}{d-1}})/q$.
  For the overall advantage of $\mathcal{A}1$, we get

$$\mathsf{adv}_F(\mathcal{A}1) = \Pr_{x \leftarrow \mathbb{Z}_q^n}[\mathcal{A}1(F, F_n(x)) = 0] + \Pr_{y \leftarrow \mathbb{Z}_q^m}[\mathcal{A}1(F, y) = 1] - 1 \tag{84}$$

$$\geq 1 + 1 - O(n^{1-\frac{e}{d-1}})/q - 1 = 1 - O(n^{1-\frac{e}{d-1}})/q. \tag{85}$$

Remark 4. Algorithm $\mathcal{A}1$ proceeds in two steps: in its first step, it uses $\mathcal{B}1$ to compute an algebraic relation h of F, and in its second step, it uses h to decide if the given image $y^* \in \mathbb{Z}_q^m$ is truly random.

However, since the PRG F is fixed and publicly known, the attack $\mathcal{A}1$ can be interpreted as an attack with preprocessing: In a first phase, the so-called *preprocessing* or *offline* phase, $\mathcal{A}1$ uses $\mathcal{B}1$ to compute an algebraic relation h of F of degree D (without seeing the value $y^* \in \mathbb{Z}_q^m$).

In a second phase, the so-called *online* phase, $\mathcal{A}1$ receives $y^* \in \mathbb{Z}_q^m$ and only needs to evaluate h on y^*.

If $m \geq n^{1+e}$, then the degree of h is bounded by $D \leq cn^{1-\frac{e}{d-1}}$ for some constant c. The evaluation of h requires $(D+1) \cdot \binom{m+D}{D}$ arithmetic operations over $\mathbb{Z}_q$ which will be much less than the time $\mathcal{B}1$ needs (since $\mathcal{B}1$ needs to reduce a matrix of shape $\binom{m+D}{D} \times \binom{n+d \cdot D}{d \cdot D}$).

Therefore, from a practical point of view, it makes more sense to interpret $\mathcal{A}1$ as an attack with preprocessing, where we invest a big one-time cost to find a relation h of F in the preprocessing phase, and then a smaller, but still subexponential, cost of $(D+1) \cdot \binom{m+D}{D}$ to decide challenges of F.

5   Attacks on Binary PRGs

We want to focus on the case $q = 2$ in this section. Note, that Theorem 2 does not give us a meaningful attack for small values of q like 2. In fact, if we were to use naively algorithm $\mathcal{B}1$ from Algorithm 1 on m polynomials over $\mathbb{Z}_2$, $\mathcal{B}1$ may return a field equation $Y_i^2 - Y_i$ for some $i \in [m]$. This field equation will not help us in distinguishing pseudo-random images from random images, since it will vanish on each $y \in \mathbb{Z}_2^m$.

To avoid trivial relations over $\mathbb{Z}_2$, we will present here a modified version of $\mathcal{B}1$ – that we will call $\mathcal{B}2$ – that will always find a non-trivial algebraic relation of polynomials over $\mathbb{Z}_2$. For this sake, we set by abuse of notation

$$R_2[X] := \mathbb{Z}_2[X_1, \ldots, X_n]/(X_1^2 - X_1, \ldots, X_n^2 - X_n), \tag{86}$$

$$R_2[Y] := \mathbb{Z}_2[Y_1, \ldots, Y_m]/(Y_1^2 - Y_1, \ldots, Y_m^2 - Y_m). \tag{87}$$

As explained in Remark 2, the rings $R_2[X]$ and $R_2[Y]$ are filtrated. For $\ell \in \mathbb{N}$, we have

$$R_2[X]^{\leq \ell} = \mathbb{Z}_2[X]^{\leq \ell}/\left(\mathbb{Z}_2[X]^{\leq \ell} \cap (X_1^2 - X_1, \ldots, X_n^2 - X_n)\right), \tag{88}$$

$$R_2[Y]^{\leq \ell} = \mathbb{Z}_2[Y]^{\leq \ell}/\left(\mathbb{Z}_2[Y]^{\leq \ell} \cap (Y_1^2 - Y_1, \ldots, Y_m^2 - Y_m)\right). \tag{89}$$

Now let F be a PRG of degree d over $\mathbb{Z}_2$ and let $f_1, \ldots, f_m \in \mathbb{Z}_2[X]$ be the polynomials that make up F. Without loss of generality, we can assume that $f_1, \ldots, f_m$ are reduced modulo the field equations $X_1^2 - X_1, \ldots, X_n^2 - X_n$. Therefore, by abuse of notation, we interpret $f_1, \ldots, f_m$ as elements of $R_2[X]$. Now, the dual map $\phi : \mathbb{Z}_2[Y] \to \mathbb{Z}_2[X]$ descends well-defined to a ring homomorphism

$$\phi_2 : R_2[Y] \longrightarrow R_2[X] \tag{90}$$

$$Y_i \longmapsto f_i(X). \tag{91}$$

For the kernel of ϕ_2, we have

$$\ker \phi_2 = (\ker \phi + (Y_1^2 - Y_1, \ldots, Y_m^2 - Y_m))/(Y_1^2 - Y_1, \ldots, Y_m^2 - Y_m). \quad (92)$$

I.e., $\ker \phi_2$ contains all algebraic relations of $\ker \phi$ modulo the trivial ones from the field equations of $\mathbb{Z}_2$. In particular, a non-zero element of $\ker \phi_2$ is now guaranteed to not vanish everywhere on $\mathbb{Z}_2^m$.

To find a non-zero element of $\ker \phi_2$, the algorithm $\mathcal{B}2$ will proceed similarly as $\mathcal{B}1$: For increasing $\ell = 1, \ldots, m$, the algorithm $\mathcal{B}2$ computes a basis of the $\mathbb{Z}_2$-vector space $\ker \phi_2 \cap R_2[Y]^{\leq \ell}$. If $\ker \phi_2 \cap R_2[Y]^{\leq \ell}$ is non-zero, $\mathcal{B}2$ returns a non-zero element of it and terminates. Otherwise, $\mathcal{B}2$ increments ℓ and repeats these computations. Formally, $\mathcal{B}2$ is given by:

Algorithm 3. The algorithm $\mathcal{B}2$ gets as input numbers $n, m, d \in \mathbb{N}$, and a description of a polynomial map $F : \mathbb{Z}_2^n \to \mathbb{Z}_2^m$. It has to output a non-zero element of $\ker \phi_2$.

For $\ell = 1, \ldots, m$, $\mathcal{B}2$ does the following:

1. $\mathcal{B}2$ computes $N := \dim_{\mathbb{Z}_2} \left(R_2[X]^{\leq d\ell} \right) = \sum_{i=0}^{\min(d\ell, n)} \binom{n}{i}$
   and $M := \dim_{\mathbb{Z}_2} \left(R_2[Y]^{\leq \ell} \right) = \sum_{i=0}^{\ell} \binom{m}{i}$.
2. $\mathcal{B}2$ computes a finite list $\left(Y_1^{a_1} \cdots Y_m^{a_m} \mid a_1, \ldots, a_m \in \{0,1\}, a_1 + \ldots + a_m \leq \ell \right) = (Y^{\alpha_1}, \ldots, Y^{\alpha_M})$ of all monomials in $R_2[Y]$ of degree $\leq \ell$.
3. $\mathcal{B}2$ applies ϕ_2 to each Y^{α_i} and computes a second list $(\phi_2(Y^{\alpha_1}), \ldots, \phi_2(Y^{\alpha_M}))$ of polynomials in $R_2[X]$ of degree $\leq d\ell$.
4. Let $X^{\beta_1}, \ldots, X^{\beta_N}$ be the set of all monomials in $R_2[X]$ of degree $\leq d\ell$ where each variable appears at most once. For each $\phi_2(Y^{\alpha_i})$ let $w_i = (w_{i,1}, \ldots, w_{i,N}) \in \mathbb{Z}_2^N$ be the unique column-vector s.t.

$$\phi_2(Y^{\alpha_i}) = \sum_{j=1}^{N} w_{i,j} \cdot X^{\beta_j}. \quad (93)$$

These vectors give us the matrix

$$W_\ell := \left(w_1 | \ldots | w_M \right) \in \mathbb{Z}_2^{N \times M}. \quad (94)$$

5. $\mathcal{B}2$ uses Gaussian elimination over $\mathbb{Z}_2$ to compute the kernel of W_ℓ

$$K_\ell := \left\{ r \in \mathbb{Z}_2^M \mid W_\ell \cdot r = 0 \right\}. \quad (95)$$

6. If K_ℓ is the trivial null-space, $\mathcal{B}2$ increases ℓ by one. If $\ell \leq m$, $\mathcal{B}2$ goes back to step 1. Otherwise, if $\ell = m + 1$, $\mathcal{B}2$ has exhausted the whole vector space $R_2[Y] = R_2[Y]^{\leq m}$. In this case, $\mathcal{B}2$ aborts, since now ϕ_2 must be injective.
7. If K_ℓ is not the null-space, $\mathcal{B}2$ chooses an arbitrary non-zero vector $r \in K_\ell$, computes the polynomial

$$h := r_1 \cdot Y^{\alpha_1} + \ldots + r_M \cdot Y^{\alpha_M} \in R_2[Y] \quad (96)$$

of total degree $\leq \ell$ and outputs it.

We have for $\mathcal{B}2$ similar time and space bounds as for $\mathcal{B}1$:

Lemma 8. *Assume that $\mathcal{B}2$ terminates after D iterations. Then, its space complexity can be bounded by $O(NM)$ and its time complexity can be bounded by $O(DN^2M)$ for $N = \sum_{i=0}^{\min(dD,n)} \binom{n}{i}$ and $M = \sum_{i=0}^{D} \binom{m}{i}$.*

Similarly, as in Sect. 3, one can show that $\mathcal{B}2$ will return an algebraic relation of minimal degree, if such a relation exists:

Lemma 9. *Let $n, m, d \in \mathbb{N}$. Let $f_1, \ldots, f_m \in R_2[X]$ be polynomials of degree $\leq d$. Assume that the corresponding morphism*

$$\phi_2 : R_2[Y] \longrightarrow R_2[X] \tag{97}$$
$$Y_i \longmapsto f_i \tag{98}$$

is not injective and set $D := \min\{\deg h \mid h \in \ker \phi_2, h \neq 0\}$. Then, $\mathcal{B}2$ terminates after D iterations and outputs a non-zero element of $\ker \phi_2$ of degree D.

Now, let $e > 0$ and $d \in \mathbb{N}$ be constants and assume $m \geq n^{1+e}$. The inequality in Lemma 7 has a pendant that states that for almost all n we have

$$\sum_{i=0}^{L} \binom{m}{i} > \sum_{i=0}^{dL} \binom{n}{i} \tag{99}$$

where $L = \lceil c \cdot n^{1-\frac{e}{d-1}} \rceil$. We give a formal proof of this inequality in the full version [45] of this text. However, its proof is very similar to the proof of Lemma 7. It follows that $\mathcal{B}2$'s complexity is subexponential for $m \geq n^{1+e}$ polynomials $f_1, \ldots, f_m$:

Theorem 3. *Let $d \in \mathbb{N}$, $e > 0$ be constants and $m \geq n^{1+e}$. Let $f_1, \ldots, f_m \in R_2[X]$ be polynomials of degree $\leq d$.*
Then, $\mathcal{B}2$ in Algorithm 3 outputs a non-trivial element of $\ker \phi_2$ of degree $O(n^{1-\frac{e}{d-1}})$. Its space and time complexities lie in $n^{O(n^{1-\frac{e}{d-1}})}$.

5.1   Binary PRGs of Constant Degree

$\mathcal{B}2$ gives rise to the following attacker $\mathcal{A}2$ on degree-d PRGs over $\mathbb{Z}_2$:

Algorithm 4. The algorithm $\mathcal{A}2$ receives as input a description of a PRG $F : \mathbb{Z}_2^n \to \mathbb{Z}_2^m$ of degree d, which includes the numbers $n, m, d \in \mathbb{N}$, and an element $y^* \in \mathbb{Z}_2^m$. The goal of $\mathcal{A}2$ is to output 0, if y^* lies in the image of F, and 1, otherwise.

$\mathcal{A}2$ proceeds in two simple steps:

1. $\mathcal{A}2$ executes $\mathcal{B}2$ from Algorithm 3 on the input n, m, d, F and receives a non-zero polynomial $h \in R_2[Y]$ as output.
2. $\mathcal{A}2$ outputs 0 if $h(y^*) = 0$. Otherwise, $\mathcal{A}2$ outputs 1.

It is clear that $\mathcal{A}2$'s space and time complexities are comparable to the space and time complexities of $\mathcal{B}2$. However, since the degree D of h will be much higher than the cardinality of $\mathbb{Z}_2$, we cannot apply the Schwartz-Zippel Lemma any more. Since h is not zero in $R_2[Y]$, we can only guarantee that h vanishes on at most $2^m - 2^{m-D}$ points of $\mathbb{Z}_2^m$ (we show this in the full version [45]). This gives us the following theorem:

Theorem 4. *Let $d \in \mathbb{N}, e > 0$ be constants. Let $F : \mathbb{Z}_2^n \to \mathbb{Z}_2^m$ be a PRG of degree d and stretch $m \geq n^{1+e}$.*

Then, there is an attack algorithm $\mathcal{A}2$ whose time and space complexities are bounded from above by $n^{O(n^{1-\frac{e}{d-1}})}$. Further, there exists a constant $c > 0$ s.t. $\mathcal{A}2$'s advantage in the security game in Definition 5 against F is lower bounded by

$$\mathsf{adv}_F(\mathcal{A}2) \geq 2^{-cn^{1-\frac{e}{d-1}}}. \tag{100}$$

Theorem 4 is unsatisfying, since $\mathcal{A}2$'s advantage can only be guaranteed to be at least subexponential. One solution for this problem is to look at a multi-challenge security game for the PRG F where the adversary receives Q challenges $y_1^*, \ldots, y_Q^* \in \mathbb{Z}_2^m$ and has to guess if all $y_1^*, \ldots, y_Q^*$ have been drawn uniformly and independently at random from $\mathbb{Z}_2^m$ or if all $y_1^*, \ldots, y_Q^*$ lie in the image of F.

If the number of challenges is $Q \in 2^{\Omega(n^{1-\frac{e}{d-1}})}$, then the advantage of $\mathcal{A}2$ can be amplified to a positive constant. We give here an informal theorem for this observation and flesh out the details in the full version [45] of this text:

Theorem 5 (Multi-challenge Attack (Informal)). *Let $d \in \mathbb{N}, e > 0$ be constants and let $F : \mathbb{Z}_2^n \to \mathbb{Z}_2^m$ be a PRG of degree d and poly-stretch $m \geq n^{1+e}$.*

Then, there is an attack algorithm whose time and space complexities are bounded from above by $n^{O(n^{1-\frac{e}{d-1}})}$ and whose advantage in breaking the pseudorandomness of F when given $Q \in 2^{\Omega(n^{1-\frac{e}{d-1}})}$ challenges is a constant greater than zero.

5.2 Binary PRGs of Constant Locality

Now, let $F : \mathbb{Z}_2^n \to \mathbb{Z}_2^m$ be a poly-stretch PRG of constant locality $d \in \mathbb{N}$, i.e., each output bit of F is determined by at most d input bits. In case of a PRG of constant locality we can perform a subexponential attack (for a single challenge value) where we can guarantee a much better advantage than for $\mathcal{A}2$ in Theorem 4.

Theorem 6. *Let $d \in \mathbb{N}$ and $e > 0$ be constants. Let $F : \mathbb{Z}_2^n \to \mathbb{Z}_2^m$ be a PRG of locality d with poly-stretch $m \geq n^{1+e}$.*

There is an attack $\mathcal{A}3$ on F and a constant $c > 0$ s.t. $\mathcal{A}3$'s space and time complexities are bounded by $2^{O(n^{1-\frac{e'}{d-1}})}$ for each constant $e' \in (0, e)$ and whose advantage in the security game of Definition 5 is at least

$$\mathsf{adv}_F(\mathcal{A}3) \geq 1 - cn^{-\frac{e'}{d-1}}. \tag{101}$$

The idea of $\mathcal{A}3$ is to convert F to a PRG $G : \mathbb{Z}_q^n \to \mathbb{Z}_q^{m'}$ of degree d over $\mathbb{Z}_q$ with stretch $m' = \lfloor m/(3\log(q)) \rfloor$ for a prime $q \geq n$.

Let $f_1, \ldots, f_m \in R_2[X]$ be the polynomials that make up F. Since each f_i is d-local, there are polynomials $f_1', \ldots, f_m' \in \mathbb{Z}_q[X]$ of degree $\leq d$ that coincide with $f_1, \ldots, f_m$ on $\{0,1\}^n$. In fact, for $i \in [m]$, let $j_1, \ldots, j_d \in [n]$ and $u_i : \{0,1\}^d \to \{0,1\}$ s.t. for all $x \in \{0,1\}^n$

$$f_i(x) = u_i(x_{j_1}, \ldots, x_{j_d}). \tag{102}$$

Then, the polynomial $f_i' \in \mathbb{Z}_q[X]$ is given by

$$f_i'(X) := \sum_{z \in \{0,1\}^d} u_i(z) \cdot (1 - z_1 - X_{j_1} + 2z_1 X_{j_1}) \cdots (1 - z_d - X_{j_d} + 2z_d X_{j_d}). \tag{103}$$

However, the image of the $f_1', \ldots, f_m'$ does not look random over $\mathbb{Z}_q$, since it is contained in $\{0,1\}^m$ (if the input is chosen from $\{0,1\}^n$). To compensate for that, we use the Leftover Hash Lemma. Let $F' = (f_1', \ldots, f_m') : \mathbb{Z}_q^n \to \mathbb{Z}_q^m$ be the collection of all f_i'. $\mathcal{A}3$ samples now a random matrix $A = (a_{i,j})_{i,j} \leftarrow \mathbb{Z}_q^{m' \times m}$ and defines a PRG $G : \mathbb{Z}_q^n \to \mathbb{Z}_q^{m'}$ by

$$G(X) := A \cdot F'(X). \tag{104}$$

I.e., if G consists of the polynomials $g_1, \ldots, g_{m'}$, each g_i is given by

$$g_i = \sum_{j=1}^{m} a_{i,j} \cdot f_j'. \tag{105}$$

Now, G is a degree-d PRG over $\mathbb{Z}_q$. According to Lemma 2, the image of G will *look random* (relative to $\mathbb{Z}_q^{m'}$) if the image of F looks random (relative to $\{0,1\}^m$). Finally, $\mathcal{A}3$ can use $\mathcal{A}1$ from Theorem 2 to break the pseudorandomness of G (and break therefore the pseudorandomness of F).

We will now formally define how $\mathcal{A}3$ proceeds:

Algorithm 5. Let $F : \mathbb{Z}_2^n \to \mathbb{Z}_2^m$ be a PRG of locality d consisting of polynomials $f_1, \ldots, f_m \in R_2[X]$. The algorithm $\mathcal{A}3$ receives as input a description of F, which includes the numbers $n, m, d \in \mathbb{N}$, and an element $y^* \in \mathbb{Z}_2^m$. The goal of $\mathcal{A}3$ is to output 0, if y^* lies in the image of F, and 1, otherwise.

$\mathcal{A}3$ proceeds in the following steps:

1. $\mathcal{A}3$ searches for a prime number $q \in \{n, n+1, \ldots, 2n\}$. Because of Bertrand's postulate we know that such a prime must exist.
2. $\mathcal{A}3$ sets $m' := \lfloor m/(3\log q) \rfloor$
3. $\mathcal{A}3$ computes polynomials $f_1', \ldots, f_m' \in \mathbb{Z}_q[X]$ that coincide with $f_1, \ldots, f_m$ on $\{0,1\}^n$.
4. $\mathcal{A}3$ draws a random matrix $A \leftarrow \mathbb{Z}_q^{m' \times m}$ and sets

$$G(X) := A \cdot F'(X). \tag{106}$$

Now, $G : \mathbb{Z}_q^n \to \mathbb{Z}_q^{m'}$ is a polynomial map of degree d.

5. $\mathcal{A}3$ interprets y^* as a binary vector in $\{0,1\}^m \subseteq \mathbb{Z}_q^m$ and computes

$$y'^* := A \cdot y^* \in \mathbb{Z}_q^m. \tag{107}$$

6. $\mathcal{A}3$ runs algorithm $\mathcal{A}1$ on (G, y'^*) and returns the output of $\mathcal{A}1$.

Now, let e', e'' be constants s.t. $0 < e' < e'' < e$ and assume that $\mathcal{A}3$ found the prime number q. Since $q \leq 2n$, we have $m' \geq \frac{m}{3 \log q} - 1 \geq \frac{n^{1+e}}{3 \log(n)+3} - 1$. The term on the right-hand side becomes greater than $n^{1+e''}$ for n big enough. Ergo, we have $m' \geq n^{1+e''}$ for almost all n. It is easy to see that the time and space complexities of $\mathcal{A}3$ are dominated by the complexities of $\mathcal{A}1$, which are upper-bounded by $n^{O(n^{1-\frac{e''}{d-1}})}$. For n large enough, $\mathcal{A}3$ will therefore have complexities upper-bounded by $2^{O(n^{1-\frac{e'}{d-1}})}$

To bound the advantage of $\mathcal{A}3$, we first distinguish two cases:

1. If $y^* = F(x)$ for some $x \in \mathbb{Z}_2^n$, then y'^* will be of the form

$$y'^* = Ay^* = AF'(x) = G(x). \tag{108}$$

   In those cases, $\mathcal{A}1$ will always output zero.
2. If y^* is a random element of $\{0,1\}^m$, then Lemma 2 states that the statistical distance of the distributions

$$(A, y'^*) \text{ and } (A, r) \tag{109}$$

for $r \leftarrow \mathbb{Z}_q^{m'}$ is less than $\frac{1}{2}\sqrt{2^{m' \log(q)-m}} \leq \frac{1}{2}q^{-m'}$. Therefore, the probability that $\mathcal{A}1$ outputs 1 in this case can be lower bounded by

$$1 - \frac{O(n^{1-\frac{e'}{d-1}})}{q} - \frac{1}{2}q^{-m'} \geq 1 - \frac{O(n^{1-\frac{e'}{d-1}})}{n} - \frac{1}{2}n^{-m'} \tag{110}$$

$$\geq 1 - O(n^{-\frac{e'}{d-1}}). \tag{111}$$

Now, we can bound the advantage of $\mathcal{A}3$ in the security-game of Definition 5 as follows:

$$\mathsf{adv}_F(\mathcal{A}3) \geq \Pr_{y \leftarrow \{0,1\}^m}[\mathcal{A}3(F, y) = 1] + \Pr_{x \leftarrow \{0,1\}^n}[\mathcal{A}3(F, F(x)) = 0] - 1 \tag{112}$$

$$\geq 1 - O(n^{-\frac{e'}{d-1}}) + 1 - 1 \geq 1 - O(n^{-\frac{e'}{d-1}}). \tag{113}$$

6   Avoiding Subexponential Attacks

Finally, we want to discuss three counter-measures in the design of PRGs that help to avoid the attacks presented in this paper:

Rational Functions. In case of a large modulus $q \geq n$, the algorithm $\mathcal{A}1$ in Theorem 2 gives a subexponential attack on constant-degree PRGs with non-negligible advantage.

To avoid $\mathcal{A}1$, one can consider PRGs $F : \mathbb{Z}_q^n \to \mathbb{Z}_q^m$ that incorporate rational functions of constant degree i.e. where each output value is computed by $f_i(X) := \frac{g_1(X)}{h_1(X)} + \ldots + \frac{g_\ell(X)}{h_\ell(X)}$ for polynomials $g_1, \ldots, g_\ell, h_1, \ldots, h_\ell \in \mathbb{Z}_q[X]$ of constant degree d. The functions $f_1, \ldots, f_m$ are still algebraically dependent, since $m > n$. However, we cannot bound the degree of the relation outputted by $\mathcal{B}1$, since the set $\left\{ \frac{f}{g} \mid f, g \in \mathbb{Z}_q[X]^{\leq d}, g \neq 0 \right\}$ is not contained in a finite-dimensional vector space any more.

We conjecture that if ℓ grows polynomially with n, then this kind of PRGs could even be resistant against Groebner basis-based attacks like F4/F5 and XL, since these algorithms need to multiply the equality $f_i(X) = y_i$ with $h_1 \cdots h_\ell$ to get a polynomial equality of non-constant degree $d \cdot \ell$.

As a concrete challenge, we propose a PRG – parametrized by n – where q is the smallest prime in $[2^n, 2^{n+1}]$, ℓ equals n, each g_i is one and each h_i is a random sum of two variables of $X_1, \ldots, X_n$. For $m \in \Omega(n^2)$, there is a trivial attack on this PRG. However, for smaller m, let's say $m = n^{1.9}$, we don't know a subexponential attack on this PRG with provably non-trivial advantage.

Non-constant Locality. In the case of binary poly-stretch PRGs of constant degree, we gave two attacks $\mathcal{A}2$ and $\mathcal{A}3$. For $\mathcal{A}2$, we can only guarantee a subexponentially small advantage. However, this is only a pessimistic lower-bound and does not exclude that $\mathcal{A}2$ may perform much better in praxis.

$\mathcal{A}3$ is guaranteed to have a high advantage, however it can only be applied on binary PRGs of constant locality. This means, that all PRG candidates in $\mathbf{NC}^0$ with poly-stretch are susceptible to subexponential attacks.

To avoid subexponential attacks for binary PRGs, the only option seems to be to design PRGs of non-constant locality.

Small Non-constant Modulus. The attack $\mathcal{A}1$ needs that the modulus, over which the PRG is evaluated, is large enough, while the attack $\mathcal{A}3$ needs that the modulus is constant (since otherwise the PRG constructed by $\mathcal{A}3$ will not have constant degree).

One can try to avoid both attacks by setting q to a number between both extremes (for example $q = \Theta(\sqrt{n})$ for $e < 0.5$). For such moduli q, neither $\mathcal{A}1$ nor $\mathcal{A}3$ can be applied and the attack $\mathcal{A}2$ must be used. If $\mathcal{B}2$ uses the appropriate field equations $Y_i^q - Y_i$, it will find a non-trivial algebraic relation of sublinear degree, however it is hard to show in such cases that this relation will not vanish on a non-negligible portion of $\mathbb{Z}_q^m$, since the Schwartz-Zippel Lemma cannot be applied.

References

1. Applebaum, B.: Pseudorandom generators with long stretch and low locality from random local one-way functions. In: Karloff, H.J., Pitassi, T. (eds.) 44th ACM STOC, pp. 805–816. ACM Press, May 2012. https://doi.org/10.1145/2213977. 2214050
2. Applebaum, B.: Cryptographic hardness of random local functions–survey. In: Sahai, A. (ed.) TCC 2013. LNCS, vol. 7785, pp. 599–599. Springer, Heidelberg (2013). https://doi.org/10.1007/978-3-642-36594-2_33
3. Applebaum, B.: The cryptographic hardness of random local functions - survey Cryptology ePrint Archive, Report 2015/165. https://eprint.iacr.org/2015/165 (2015)
4. Applebaum, B., Lovett, S.: Algebraic attacks against random local functions and their countermeasures. In: Wichs, D., Mansour, Y. (eds.) 48th ACM STOC, pp. 1087–1100. ACM Press, June 2016. https://doi.org/10.1145/2897518.2897554
5. Applebaum, B., Damgård, I., Ishai, Y., Nielsen, M., Zichron, L.: Secure arithmetic computation with constant computational overhead. In: Katz, J., Shacham, H. (eds.) CRYPTO 2017. LNCS, vol. 10401, pp. 223–254. Springer, Cham (2017). https://doi.org/10.1007/978-3-319-63688-7_8
6. Ars, G., Faugère, J.-C., Imai, H., Kawazoe, M., Sugita, M.: Comparison between XL and Gröbner basis algorithms. In: Lee, P.J. (ed.) ASIACRYPT 2004. LNCS, vol. 3329, pp. 338–353. Springer, Heidelberg (2004). https://doi.org/10.1007/978-3-540-30539-2_24
7. Barak, B., Brakerski, Z., Komargodski, I., Kothari, P.K.: Limits on low-degree pseudorandom generators (or: sum-of-squares meets program obfuscation). In: Nielsen, J.B., Rijmen, V. (eds.) EUROCRYPT 2018, Part II. LNCS, vol. 10821, pp. 649–679. Springer, Cham (2018). https://doi.org/10.1007/978-3-319-78375-8_21
8. Barak, B., Hopkins, S.B., Jain, A., Kothari, P., Sahai, A.: Sum-of-squares meets program obfuscation, revisited. In: Ishai, Y., Rijmen, V. (eds.) EUROCRYPT 2019, Part I. LNCS, vol. 11476, pp. 226–250. Springer, Cham (2019). https://doi.org/10.1007/978-3-030-17653-2_8
9. Bardet, M., Faugère, J.-C., Salvy, B.: Complexity of Gröbner basis computation for Semi-regular Overdetermined sequences over F_2 with solutions in F_2 Research Report RR-5049 (INRIA) (2003). https://hal.inria.fr/inria-00071534
10. Bardet, M., Faugère, J.-C., Salvy, B.: On the complexity of Gröbner basis computation of semi-regular overdetermined algebraic equations. https://doi.org/10.1016/j.jsc.2015.12.001
11. Bogdanov, A., Qiao, Y.: On the security of Goldreich's one-way function. In: Dinur, I., Jansen, K., Naor, J., Rolim, J. (eds.) APPROX/RANDOM -2009. LNCS, vol. 5687, pp. 392–405. Springer, Heidelberg (2009). https://doi.org/10.1007/978-3-642-03685-9_30
12. Buchmann, J.A., Ding, J., Mohamed, M.S.E., Mohamed, W.S.A.E.: MutantXL: solving multivariate polynomial equations for cryptanalysis. In: Handschuh, H., Lucks, S., Preneel, B., Rogaway, P. (eds.) Symmetric Cryptography 9031 (Schloss Dagstuhl - Leibniz-Zentrum für Informatik, Dagstuhl, Germany, 2009), pp. 1–7. https://drops.dagstuhl.de/opus/volltexte/2009/1945. https://doi.org/10.4230/DagSemProc.09031.10
13. Caminata, A., Gorla, E.: Solving multivariate polynomial systems and an invariant from commutative algebra. In: Bajard, J.C., Topuzoğlu, A. (eds.) WAIFI 2020. LNCS, vol. 12542, pp. 3–36. Springer, Cham (2021). https://doi.org/10.1007/978-3-030-68869-1_1. ISBN: 978-3-030-68869-1

14. Caminata, A., Gorla, E.: Solving degree, last fall degree, and related invariants. J. Symb. Comput. **114**, 322–335 (2023). ISSN: 0747-7171
15. Charikar, M., Wirth, A.: Maximizing quadratic programs: extending Grothendieck's inequality. In: 45th FOCS, pp. 54–60. IEEE Computer Society Press, October 2004. https://doi.org/10.1109/FOCS.2004.39
16. Cheng, C.-M., Chou, T., Niederhagen, R., Yang, B.-Y.: Solving quadratic equations with XL on parallel architectures. In: Prouff, E., Schaumont, P. (eds.) CHES 2012. LNCS, vol. 7428, pp. 356–373. Springer, Heidelberg (2012). https://doi.org/10.1007/978-3-642-33027-8_21
17. Courtois, N., Klimov, A., Patarin, J., Shamir, A.: Efficient algorithms for solving overdefined systems of multivariate polynomial equations. In: Preneel, B. (ed.) EUROCRYPT 2000. LNCS, vol. 1807, pp. 392–407. Springer, Heidelberg (2000). https://doi.org/10.1007/3-540-45539-6_27
18. Couteau, G., Dupin, A., Méaux, P., Rossi, M., Rotella, Y.: On the concrete security of Goldreich's pseudorandom generator. In: Peyrin, T., Galbraith, S. (eds.) ASIACRYPT 2018, Part II. LNCS, vol. 11273, pp. 96–124. Springer, Cham (2018). https://doi.org/10.1007/978-3-030-03329-3_4
19. Diem, C.: The XL-algorithm and a conjecture from commutative algebra. In: Lee, P.J. (ed.) ASIACRYPT 2004. LNCS, vol. 3329, pp. 323–337. Springer, Heidelberg (2004). https://doi.org/10.1007/978-3-540-30539-2_23
20. Ding, J., Schmidt, D.: Solving degree and degree of regularity for polynomial systems over a finite fields. In: Fischlin, M., Katzenbeisser, S. (eds.) Number Theory and Cryptography. LNCS, vol. 8260, pp. 34–49. Springer, Heidelberg (2013). https://doi.org/10.1007/978-3-642-42001-6_4
21. Dodis, Y., Reyzin, L., Smith, A.: Fuzzy extractors: how to generate strong keys from biometrics and other noisy data. In: Cachin, C., Camenisch, J.L. (eds.) EUROCRYPT 2004. LNCS, vol. 3027, pp. 523–540. Springer, Heidelberg (2004). https://doi.org/10.1007/978-3-540-24676-3_31
22. Dubois, V., Gama, N.: The degree of regularity of HFE systems. In: Abe, M. (ed.) ASIACRYPT 2010. LNCS, vol. 6477, pp. 557–576. Springer, Heidelberg (2010). https://doi.org/10.1007/978-3-642-17373-8_32
23. Faugère, J.C.: A new efficient algorithm for computing Gröbner bases without reduction to zero (F5). In: Proceedings of the 2002 International Symposium on Symbolic and Algebraic Computation, pp. 75–83. Association for Computing Machinery, Lille (2002). ISBN: 1581134843. https://doi.org/10.1145/780506.780516
24. Faugére, J.-C.: A new efficient algorithm for computing Gröbner bases (F4). J. Pure Appl. Algebra **139**, 61–88 (1999). ISSN: 0022-4049
25. Goemans, M.X., Williamson, D.P.: Improved approximation algorithms for maximum cut and satisfiability problems using semidefinite programming. J. ACM **42**, 1115–1145 (1995). ISSN: 0004-5411
26. Goldreich, O.: Candidate one-way functions based on expander graphs. In: Goldreich, O. (ed.) Studies in Complexity and Cryptography. Miscellanea on the Interplay between Randomness and Computation. LNCS, vol. 6650, pp. 76–87. Springer, Heidelberg (2011). https://doi.org/10.1007/978-3-642-22670-0_10. ISBN: 978-3-642-22670-0
27. Håstad, J., Impagliazzo, R., Levin, L.A., Luby, M.: A pseudorandom generator from any one-way function. SIAM J. Comput. **28**, 1364–1396 (1999)

28. Huang, M.-D.A., Kosters, M., Yeo, S.L.: Last fall degree, HFE, and Weil descent attacks on ECDLP. In: Gennaro, R., Robshaw, M. (eds.) CRYPTO 2015, Part I. LNCS, vol. 9215, pp. 581–600. Springer, Heidelberg (2015). https://doi.org/10.1007/978-3-662-47989-6_28

29. Impagliazzo, R., Wigderson, A.: P = BPP if E requires exponential circuits: derandomizing the XOR lemma. In: 29th ACM STOC, pp. 220–229. ACM Press, May 1997. https://doi.org/10.1145/258533.258590

30. Ishai, Y., Kushilevitz, E., Ostrovsky, R., Sahai, A.: Cryptography with constant computational overhead. In: Ladner, R.E., Dwork, C. (eds.) 40th ACM STOC, pp. 433–442. ACM Press, May 2008. https://doi.org/10.1145/1374376.1374438

31. Jain, A., Lin, H., Sahai, A.: Indistinguishability obfuscation from well- founded assumptions. In: Proceedings of the 53rd Annual ACM SIGACT Symposium on Theory of Computing, pp. 60–73. Association for Computing Machinery, Virtual (2021). ISBN: 9781450380539. https://doi.org/10.1145/3406325.3451093

32. Jain, A., Lin, H., Sahai, A.: Indistinguishability obfuscation from LPN over Fp, DLIN, and PRGs in NC0. In: Dunkelman, O., Dziembowski, S. (eds.) Advances in Cryptology - EUROCRYPT 2022, pp. 670–699. Springer, Cham (2022). ISBN: 978-3-031-06944-4. https://doi.org/10.1007/978-3-031-06944-4_23

33. Lang, S.: Algebra. Springer, New York (2002). ISBN: 9781461300410 146130041X. https://doi.org/10.1007/978-1-4613-0041-0

34. Lazard, D.: Gröbner bases, Gaussian elimination and resolution of systems of algebraic equations. In: van Hulzen, J.A. (ed.) EUROCAL 1983. LNCS, vol. 162, pp. 146–156. Springer, Heidelberg (1983). https://doi.org/10.1007/3-540-12868-9_99. ISBN: 978-3-540-38756-5

35. Macaulay, F.: The Algebraic Theory of Modular Systems. Cambridge Mathematical Library xxxi (1916). https://doi.org/10.3792/chmm/1263317740

36. Mohamed, M.S.E., Mohamed, W.S.A.E., Ding, J., Buchmann, J.: *MXL2*: solving polynomial equations over GF(2) using an improved mutant strategy. In: Buchmann, J., Ding, J. (eds.) PQCrypto 2008. LNCS, vol. 5299, pp. 203–215. Springer, Heidelberg (2008). https://doi.org/10.1007/978-3-540-88403-3_14

37. Mossel, E., Shpilka, A., Trevisan, L.: On e-biased generators in NC0. In: 44th FOCS, pp. 136–145. IEEE Computer Society Press, October 2003. https://doi.org/10.1109/SFCS.2003.1238188

38. Nisan, N., Wigderson, A.: Hardness vs. randomness (Extended Abstract). In: 29th FOCS, pp. 2–11. IEEE Computer Society Press, October 1988. https://doi.org/10.1109/SFCS.1988.21916

39. ODonnell, R., Witmer, D.: Goldreich's PRG: evidence for near-optimal polynomial stretch, pp. 1–12, June 2014. ISBN: 978-1-4799-3626-7. https://doi.org/10.1109/CCC.2014.9

40. Schwartz, J.T.: Fast probabilistic algorithms for verification of polynomial identities. J. ACM **27**, 701–717 (1980). ISSN: 0004-5411

41. Siegenthaler, T.: Correlation-immunity of nonlinear combining functions for cryptographic applications (Corresp.). IEEE Trans. Inform. Theory **30**, 776–780 (1984)

42. Sugita, M., Kawazoe, M., Imai, H.: Relation between the XL algorithm and Gröbner basis algorithms. IEICE Trans. Fundam. Electron. Commun. Comput. Sci. **E89-A**, 11–18 (2006). ISSN: 0916-8508

43. Viola, E.: The sum of d small-bias generators fools polynomials of degree d. In: 2008 23rd Annual IEEE Conference on Computational Complexity, pp. 124–127 (2008). https://doi.org/10.1109/CCC.2008.16

44. Yang, B.-Y., Chen, J.-M.: All in the XL family: theory and practice. In: Park, C., Chee, S. (eds.) ICISC 2004. LNCS, vol. 3506, pp. 67–86. Springer, Heidelberg (2005). https://doi.org/10.1007/11496618_7. ISBN: 978-3-540-32083-8
45. Ünal, A.: Worst-case subexponential attacks on prgs of constant degree or constant locality cryptology ePrint archive, Paper 2023/119 (2023). https://eprint.iacr.org/2023/119

Fine-Grained Non-interactive Key-Exchange: Constructions and Lower Bounds

Abtin Afshar[1], Geoffroy Couteau[2], Mohammad Mahmoody[1], and Elahe Sadeghi[3([⊠])]

[1] University of Virginia, Charlottesville, USA
{na6xg,abtin,mohammad}@virginia.edu
[2] CNRS, IRIF, Université Paris Cité, Paris, France
couteau@irif.fr
[3] University of Texas at Austin, Austin, USA
elahesadeghi@utexas.edu

Abstract. In this work, we initiate a study of K-NIKE protocols in the *fine-grained* setting, in which there is a *polynomial* gap between the running time of the honest parties and that of the adversary. Our goal is to show the possibility, or impossibility, of basing such protocols on weaker assumptions than those of K-NIKE for $K \geq 3$. Our contribution is threefold.

- We show that random oracles can be used to obtain fine-grained K-NIKE protocols for *every* constant K. In particular, we show how to generalize Merkle's two-party protocol to K parties in such a way that the honest parties ask n queries each, while the adversary needs $n^{K/(K-1)}$ queries to the random oracle to find the key.
- We then improve the security by further using algebraic structures, while avoiding pairings. In particular, we show that there is a 4-party NIKE in Shoup's generic group model with a *quadratic* gap between the number of queries by the honest parties vs. that of the adversary.
- Finally, we show a limitation of using purely algebraic methods for obtaining 3-NIKE. In particular, we show that any n-query 3-NIKE protocol in Maurer's generic group model can be broken by a $O(n^2)$-query attacker. Maurer's GGM is more limited compared with Shoup's both for the parties and the adversary, as there are no explicit labels for the group elements. Despite being more limited, this model still captures the Diffie Hellman protocol. Prior to our work, it was open to break 3-NIKE protocols in Maurer's model with *any* polynomial number of queries.

G. Couteau—Supported by the French Agence Nationale de la Recherche (ANR), under grant ANR-20-CE39-0001 (project SCENE), and by the France 2030 ANR Project ANR22-PECY-003 SecureCompute.
M. Mahmoody—Supported by NSF under grants CCF-1910681 and CNS19 36799.

C. Hazay and M. Stam (Eds.): EUROCRYPT 2023, LNCS 14004, pp. 55–85, 2023.
https://doi.org/10.1007/978-3-031-30545-0_3

1   Introduction

Non-interactive key exchange (NIKE), introduced in the seminal work of Diffie and Hellman [DH76], is a primitive of fundamental interest in cryptography. It allows a group of parties $P_1, \ldots, P_k$ to simultaneously publish a single message each, such that any party can recover (without further interaction) a common group key using their secret randomness and the common messages $(m_i)_{i \in [k]}$, in a way that the key remains hidden to any external observer who only gets to see $(m_i)_{i \in [k]}$. NIKE is an intriguing cryptographic object: although the first construction of a 2-party NIKE was given in one of the very first papers on public key cryptography, constructing NIKE for more parties is a notoriously hard problem. Even in the two party setting, NIKE is known only from a restricted set of assumptions, such as the Diffie-Hellman assumption [DH76], the LWE assumption with super-polynomial modulus-to-noise ratio [GKRS22], and from assumptions related to the hardness of factoring [FHKP13]. In the three-party setting, constructing NIKE was a major open problem until the breakthrough result of Joux [Jou00] from the bilinear Diffie-Hellman assumption over pairing groups, which introduced what remains to date the only known construction of 3-party NIKE under a standard assumption. Furthermore, all known constructions of K-party NIKE for $K > 3$ require much heavier cryptographic machinery, such as indistinguishability obfuscation [BZ14]. Hence, as of today, K-party NIKE with $K > 3$ belongs to the world of "obfustopia" primitives (alongside with primitives such as witness encryption or functional encryption), in spite of being seemingly a much simpler primitive than obfuscation.

Fine-Grained Cryptography. Traditional cryptography requires hardness of cryptographic primitives to hold against arbitrary polynomial-time adversaries. In contrast, *fine-grained* cryptography aims to study the feasibility of cryptographic primitives when the adversarial power is restricted, for example, to some fixed polynomial bound. While the study of fine-grained cryptography can be traced back to the seminal paper of Merkle [Mer74, Mer78] who constructed a 2-party NIKE from idealized hash functions with security against subquadratic-time adversaries, this primitive has recently spurred a renewed interest, leading to a collection of constructions [BGI08, BHK+11, DVV16, BRSV17, BRSV18, CG18, LLW19, EWT21, DH21, WP22] and lower bounds [BM09, BC22] for fine-grained cryptographic primitives.

A core motivation underlying the research on fine-grained cryptography is the hope that by relaxing the security to hold against less powerful adversaries, it might be possible to base the existence of fine-grained primitives on assumptions which are weaker than those known to imply their full-fledged counterpart. For some types of restrictions, this has been a fruitful endeavor so far; for example, when restricting the adversary to be of *constant depth* (in the complexity classes AC^0), this has led to the construction of many standard cryptographic primitives (one-way functions, pseudorandom generators, pseudorandom functions, public key encryption), with unconditional security [DVV16]. For adversaries of logarithmic depth (in the class NC^1), this resulted in the construction of most traditional cryptographic primitives under worst-case hardness assumptions [DVV16, CG18, EWT21, WP22].

Perhaps more interestingly, some results have been achieved when restricting only the *running time* of the adversary to be bounded by some fixed polynomial in the runtime of the honest parties (the degree of the polynomial is typically called the *security gap* of the scheme). The work of [BGI08], building upon [Mer78], showed that exponentially-secure one-way functions imply *key exchange and public key encryption* with near-quadratic security gap. More recently, the work of [BC22] showed that some strong forms of average-case hardness implies *one-way functions* with near-quadratic security gap. At the other end of the hardness spectrum, the work of [BJK+18] showed the existence of "quadratically efficient" witness encryption from the LWE assumption. In each of these examples, the fine-grained primitive is built from an assumption which seems to be of a weaker nature compared to the full-fledged version.

1.1   Our Contribution

In this work, we investigate multiparty non-interactive key-exchange in the setting of fine-grained security. We focus on the setting where the adversarial runtime is restricted to be bounded by a polynomial in the honest parties' runtime. Our main motivation is to understand the possibility of basing *fine-grained* multiparty NIKE on assumptions outside of the Obfustopia realm, and ideally on some of the traditional assumptions known to imply 2-party NIKE, such as the Diffie-Hellman assumption.

Below, we always denote by n the runtime of the honest participants, and write K-NIKE for K-party NIKE. Our main results are threefold:

1. In the random oracle model, we prove the existence of a fine-grained 3-NIKE protocol with security against $o(n^{1.5})$-time adversaries. Our result generalizes to K-NIKE with security against $o(n^{1+1/(K-1)})$-time adversaries. While this result is a relatively natural generalization of the seminal protocol of Merkle, to the best of our knowledge, it has never been found before.
2. We demonstrate that larger security gaps can be achieved by additionally relying on algebraic structure: in Shoup's generic group model [Sho97], we prove the existence of a 4-NIKE with security against $o(n^2)$-time adversaries. Our result generalizes to $2K$-NIKE with security against $o(n^2)$-time adversaries in the generic $(K-1)$-linear group model. In particular, this also yields a 6-NIKE with near-quadratic hardness in the generic bilinear group model.
3. We complement our positive result by proving a limitation on the fine-grained security of K-NIKE with $K > 2$ over generic groups. In particular, we prove that for $K > 2$ any K-NIKE protocol in Maurer's generic group model [Mau05] can be broken using $O(n^2)$ queries.[1] Our result extends to the setting of K-NIKE with imperfect correctness. An important point is that, even though our impossibility result only applies to the MGGM, the Diffie-Hellman protocol for 2-NIKE *can* be stated in the MGGM. Moreover, while it

---

[1] Our proof is for $K = 3$ which will directly imply the negative result for any $K \geq 3$.

is indeed true that negative results in the MGGM are generally weaker than those in the SGGM and should be interpreted cautiously [Zha22,DHH+21], our result is a natural first step towards proving a stronger negative result for a basic question of whether 3-NIKE can be based merely on simple algebraic assumptions without pairing.

Discussion. In our third contribution, we prove our lower bound in Maurer's generic group model, whereas our positive result holds in *Shoup*'s generic group model, which is more flexible: this leaves a gap between our positive and negative results. We refer to [Zha22] for an in-depth discussion on the differences between these two models. We view as an interesting question the goal of closing the gap between our positive and negative results, either by building a 4-NIKE protocol with quadratic security in Maurer's generic group model, or by extending our impossibility result to Shoup's generic group model.

1.2   Technical Overview: Building NIKE in the ROM and GGM

We start by covering our positive results. Our starting point is the classical 2-party NIKE of Merkle in the random oracle model, which works as follows: let $H : [n^2] \mapsto \{0,1\}^\lambda$ (for security parameter λ) be an injective random oracle. Alice and Bob sample $(a_1, \cdots, a_n) \xleftarrow{\$} [n^2]^n$ and $(b_1, \cdots, b_n) \xleftarrow{\$} [n^2]^n$ respectively, and exchange the hashes of these values: Alice sends $(H(a_1), \cdots, H(a_n))$, and Bob sends $(H(b_1), \cdots, H(b_n))$. By the birthday paradox, with some constant probability, there will be a collision $a_i = b_j$. Since H is injective, every hash collision corresponds to an input collision. Alice and Bob can identify (say) the first such collision, and set key $\leftarrow a_i = b_j$ to be their shared key. To find the shared key, any adversary must essentially query the random oracle on $\Omega(n^2)$ positions, hence the protocol has fine-grained security with near-quadratic gap. More generally, any $n^{2-\varepsilon}$-query adversary has probability $n^{-\varepsilon}$ of querying the shared key; this probability can be reduced to negligible by letting Alice and Bob send $n \cdot \log n$ hashes instead, and identifying $\ell(n) = \omega(\log n)$ collisions, defining the key as the XOR of the ℓ keys.

Fine-Grained Multiparty NIKE in the ROM. In this work, we show that the above protocol can be directly generalized to the K-party setting, if we set the domain size of the random oracle to $n^{1+1/(K-1)}$: this guarantees that K random $n \cdot \log n$-sized tuples will have $\ell(n)$ K-collision with some constant probability. The security analysis essentially unchanged, and shows that $n^{1+1/(K-1)-\varepsilon}$-query adversaries have negligible probability of finding the final key. Correctness is slightly more technical, as it requires proving that the number of K-collisions among K random $n \cdot \log n$-sized tuples is at least $\ell(n)$ with overwhelming probability. It follows from a sequence of concentration bounds: we identify some s_1 such that with overwhelming probability, the number of collisions among the hashes of the first two parties is at least s_1 (s_1 can be computed by a straightforward Chernoff bound). Then, we identify s_2 such that with overwhelming probability, for any fixed set of s_1 values, there will be at least s_2 collisions between this set and the third party's hashes. We proceed this way, using a sequence of K Chernoff bounds to identify $s_1 > s_2 > \cdots > s_{K-1} = \ell(n)$ such that the number of K-collisions is at least s_{K-1} with overwhelming probability. From here, correctness follows immediately from the injectivity of the oracle. Even though security against $n^{1+1/(K-1)-\varepsilon}$-query adversaries gets worse as K grows, for every constant K, it still shows a polynomial gap between the honest parties' running time and that of the adversary.

Fine-Grained 4-NIKE from Idealized 2-NIKE. The above protocol achieves K-NIKE, at the cost of strongly restricting the adversarial runtime: even for $K = 3$, the protocol only withstands $o(n^{1.5})$-time adversaries. However, since we only used a random oracle (*i.e.* an idealized hash function), one could reasonably hope that a better gap can be achieved if we start from stronger 'public key' primitives. As a starting point, we describe a construction of a 4-party NIKE starting from an idealized 2-NIKE oracle. While this construction does not directly yield a candidate classical instantiation (unlike ROM-based construction, which yield heuristic instantiation using a hash function), it captures the core intuition of our next construction, while abstracting out some of the technicalities. Concretely, we consider the following idealized 2-NIKE oracle with two procedures:

- $\mathsf{Msg} : [N] \mapsto \{0,1\}^*$ is an injective random oracle over the domain $[N]$.
- $\mathsf{Key} : [N] \times \{0,1\}^* \mapsto \{0,1\}^\lambda$, on input an element r of the domain $[N]$, and a bit-string s, it checks whether $s = \mathsf{Msg}(\mathsf{r}')$ for some r'. If there is such an r', it returns $h(\mathsf{r}_0, \mathsf{r}_1)$, where $(\mathsf{r}_0, \mathsf{r}_1)$ is a lexicographic ordering of $(\mathsf{r}, \mathsf{r}')$ and h is a random function from $[N] \times [N] \mapsto \{0,1\}^\lambda$.

Relative to $(\mathsf{Msg}, \mathsf{Key})$, it is straightforward to see that there exists an ideally-secure 2-NIKE scheme as follows: Alice and Bob broadcast $\mathsf{m_A} = \mathsf{Msg}(\mathsf{r_A})$ and $\mathsf{m_B} = \mathsf{Msg}(\mathsf{r_B})$ respectively, and obtain a shared key $\mathsf{key} = h(\mathsf{r_A}, \mathsf{r_B}) = \mathsf{Key}(\mathsf{r_A}, \mathsf{m_B}) = \mathsf{Key}(\mathsf{r_B}, \mathsf{m_A})$. Furthermore, interestingly there also exists a 4-NIKE relative to $(\mathsf{Msg}, \mathsf{Key})$ over domain $[N] = [n^2]$, with quadratic hardness gap (improving upon the collision-based approach of our construction of K-NIKE in the ROM) as follows. Fix four parties $(\mathsf{P}_1, \mathsf{P}_2, \mathsf{P}_3, \mathsf{P}_4)$. At a high level, the protocol proceeds by (1) letting $(\mathsf{P}_1, \mathsf{P}_2)$ agree on a common randomness r_{12} with associated message $\mathsf{m}_{12} = \mathsf{Msg}(\mathsf{r}_{12})$ by looking for a randomness collision, (2) letting $(\mathsf{P}_3, \mathsf{P}_4)$ agree on $(\mathsf{r}_{34}, \mathsf{m}_{34})$ via the same collision-finding procedure, and (3) letting $(\mathsf{P}_1, \mathsf{P}_2)$ and $(\mathsf{P}_3, \mathsf{P}_4)$ play the roles of Alice and Bob respectively and derive a shared key using the Key oracle. More precisely:

1. Each party P_i samples n random elements $(\mathsf{r}_1^{(i)}, \cdots, \mathsf{r}_n^{(i)}) \xleftarrow{\$} [n^2]$ and broadcasts $(\mathsf{m}_1^{(i)}, \cdots, \mathsf{m}_n^{(i)}) = (\mathsf{Msg}(\mathsf{r}_1^{(i)}), \cdots, \mathsf{Msg}(\mathsf{r}_n^{(i)}))$.
2. With some constant probability, there exists two positions j_0, j_1 such that $\mathsf{r}_{j_0}^{(1)} = \mathsf{r}_{j_1}^{(2)}$, leading to a hash collision. P_1 and P_2 identify this collision; let r_{12} denote the collision, and m_{12} denote the corresponding message.
3. Similarly, P_3 and P_4 identify a collision r_{34} with message m_{34} among their vectors of messages.

4. P_1 and P_2 output $\mathsf{Key}(r_{12}, m_{34})$, and P_3 and P_4 output $\mathsf{Key}(r_{34}, m_{12})$.

Correctness follows easily by inspection. For security, any adversary that manages to find the common key key with non-negligible advantage must have queried Key on either (r_{34}, m_{12}) or (r_{12}, m_{34}). Without loss of generality, we can assume that the adversary always queries message with its first input to Key: therefore, the adversary must have queried either r_{12} or r_{34} to Msg. By the same analysis as for Merkle puzzles, an $O(n^{2-\varepsilon})$-query adversary can find such a query with probability at most $n^{-\varepsilon}$. As before, one can reduce the adversary's advantage to negligible by generating $\ell(n) = \omega(\log n)$ collisions per pair of party instead, and defining the shared keys to be the XOR of the $\ell(n)$ outputs of Key.

Fine-Grained 4-NIKE in the SGGM. With the above template in mind, a natural idea is to replace the idealized oracle $(\mathsf{Msg}, \mathsf{Key})$ by a Diffie-Hellman key exchange, to get a 4-party NIKE over Diffie-Hellman groups with quadratic security gap. Unfortunately, this does not work! To see the issue, let us fix a cyclic group $\mathbb{G}$ of size n^2, with a generator g. Replacing $(\mathsf{Msg}, \mathsf{Key})$ by a Diffie-Hellman key exchange, we get the following (1st try) protocol:

1. Each party P_i samples n random elements $(r_1^{(i)}, \cdots, r_n^{(i)}) \xleftarrow{\$} [n^2]$ and broadcasts $(m_1^{(i)}, \cdots, m_n^{(i)}) = (g^{r_1^{(i)}}, \cdots, g^{r_n^{(i)}})$.
2. With some constant probability, there exists two positions j_0, j_1 such that $r_{j_0}^{(1)} = r_{j_1}^{(2)}$, leading to a collision between the group elements. P_0 and P_1 identify this collision; let r_{12} denote the collision, and m_{12} denote the corresponding message.
3. Similarly, P_3 and P_4 identify a collision r_{34} with message m_{34} among their vectors of messages.
4. P_1 and P_2 output $\mathsf{key} \leftarrow (m_{34})^{r_{12}}$, and P_3 and P_4 output $\mathsf{key} \leftarrow (m_{12})^{r_{34}}$.

The above protocol, however, turns out to be completely broken! The adversary can compute the discrete logarithm (in base g) of any group element in time $\sqrt{n^2} = n$, using a standard generic algorithm (e.g. Shank's baby-step giant-step algorithm [Sha71], or Pollard's rho algorithm [Pol75]). Hence, the adversary can recover $r_{12} = \mathsf{dlog}_g(m_{12})$ in time n and recompute the shared key.

Above, the issue is that our 4-NIKE from an idealized 2-NIKE crucially relied on its optimal security: it must be secure over a size-n^2 domain, when the honest parties can run in time n. However, over cryptographic groups, one can always get a quadratic speedup over naive brute-force. Fortunately, there is a way around. Our key idea is the following: we increase the group size to $|\mathbb{G}| = n^4$, so that generic discrete logarithm now takes $\Omega(n^2)$-time. Doing so, we strongly reduced the probability that the honest parties can find a collision among length-n vectors of group elements. To get around this issue, we make two important observations:

1. Although there will not be any full collision, we can guarantee that there will be a *prefix-collision* with some constant probability: a pair of group elements whose exponent share *the same first half*.

2. Assume that two parties identified a group element g^x such that (a) one of the parties knows x, and (b) the other party knows *the first half of the bits of x*. Then the second party can recover x entirely in time $O(n)$: there are only $\approx n^2$ possible exponents x consistent with the prefix known to the party. Furthermore, known generic discrete logarithm algorithms actually run in time *square root of the search space* when the exponent search space is an interval. Therefore, the party can recover x using, e.g., Pollard's rho algorithm in $O(n)$ time.

At a high level, our protocol combines (1) a Merkle-style 2-NIKE to identify a prefix-collision (hence using the ROM) and (2) a generic discrete logarithm computation running in time $\sqrt{T}$ for solving discrete logarithms with exponents in an interval of size T. Concretely, let $H : [n] \mapsto \{0,1\}^*$ be an injective random oracle, and let $\mathbb{G}$ be a cyclic group of prime order p with $p \approx n^4$ (we assume that the order is exactly n^4 below to simplify the description). Then, our actual protocol proceeds as follows.

1. P_1 samples n exponents $(\mathsf{r}_1, \cdots, \mathsf{r}_n) \xleftarrow{\$} [n^4]^n$. For each $i \leq n$, write $\mathsf{r}_i = a_i + n^2 \cdot b_i$ with $(a_i, b_i) \in [n^2] \times [n^2]$. P_0 broadcasts $(s_1, \cdots, s_n) \leftarrow (g^{\mathsf{r}_1}, \cdots, g^{\mathsf{r}_n})$ and $(H(a_1), \cdots, H(a_n))$.
2. P_2 samples n values $(a'_1, \cdots, a'_n) \xleftarrow{\$} [n^2]^n$ and broadcasts $(H(a'_1), \cdots, H(a'_n))$. This lets P_1 and P_2 identify a collision $a_i = a'_j$ with a constant probability.
3. P_2 computes $g^{n^2 \cdot b_i} = s_i / g^{a'_j}$. Note that $b_i \in [n^2]$. Hence, P_2 recovers b_i (and therefore $\mathsf{r}_i = a'_j + b_i \cdot n^2$) in time $O(n)$ by computing the discrete logarithm of $g^{n^2 \cdot b_i}$ in base g^{n^2} using e.g. Pollard's algorithm [Pol75][2]. At this stage, P_1 and P_2 agree on a common pair $(r, s) \leftarrow (\mathsf{r}_i, s_i)$ (and i, s_i are public).
4. P_3 and P_4 do similarly, and agree on (r', s') where s' is publicly known.
5. P_1 and P_2 output $(s')^r$, while P_3 and P_4 output $\mathsf{m}^{r'}$.

Correctness follows easily by inspection. In the body of the paper, we prove security in Shoup's generic group model (SGGM) together with the injective random oracle model. Using the random oracle, however, is merely for the ease of presentation, as the SGGM implies the existence of an injective random oracle, hence we get a 4-party NIKE with quadratic security gap in the SGGM.

Above, there is nothing specific to the 4-party setting: given a generic group $\mathbb{G}$ equipped with a $(K-1)$-linear map e, K parties can agree on a common key by each broadcasting a random group element $g_i = g^{\mathsf{r}_i}$, and outputting $\mathsf{key} = e((g_j)_{j \neq i})^{\mathsf{r}_i}$. Then, the above construction allows pairs of parties to agree on a common input (r_i, g_i) to this K-NIKE with a group of size $|\mathbb{G}| = n^4$ using $O(n)$ communication in a single round of interaction. Therefore, this yields a $2K$-NIKE with quadratic security gap in the generic $(K-1)$-linear group model. In particular, we can obtain a 6-NIKE with quadratic security in the generic bilinear group model.

---

[2] The seminal paper of Pollard describes two algorithms for solving discrete logarithms. The second, lesser known algorithm, usually called *Pollard's kangaroo algorithm*, solves discrete logarithms with exponents over intervals $[u, v]$ in time $\sqrt{v - u}$.

1.3 Technical Overview: Breaking 3-NIKE in Maurer's GGM

We also prove a limitation of how much algebraic structure, without pairing, can help building K-NIKE protocols for $K > 2$. In particular, we prove that in *Maurer's* generic group model (MGGM), where the access to the group is further limited through an oracle who does all the calculations, one cannot achieve more than quadratic gap between the honest parties and the adversary's query complexity. Recall that in MGGM, each party P has an array $\mathsf{Arr_P}$ that does the following operations: (1) $\mathsf{Arr_P}$ stores group elements from $\mathbb{G}$, starting with 1 written at the beginning, (2) it adds them (Add operation) when P asks $\mathsf{Arr_P}$ to do so, and stores the result at the end of the array, and (3) it can provide zero-tests (Zero operation) for all the stored group elements. We actually need to work with a generalization of this model in which parties can *exchange* group elements *directly* through their oracles (as group elements do not have an explicit representation). See Definition 14 for details. Finally, when it comes to key-agreement in MGGM, without loss of generality, we ask the parties to agree on a group element written in their oracle (see Remark 16.)

Here we highlight the key ideas in our attack on any 3-NIKE protocol Π in the MGGM. Our proof can be best explained in two steps: (1) Breaking Π, assuming that the honest parties do not ask any Zero queries. (2) Breaking Π, even if parties ask Zero queries by reducing this task to the case of protocols without Zero queries. Below, we explain both of these steps and their corresponding ideas.

Structure of the Key. For simplicity suppose $\mathsf{A}, \mathsf{B}, \mathsf{C}$, as part of Π, agree on a key key with probability 1. Let us focus on A and analyze the structure of the group element key_A that it produces as its key (see Definition 14). This key is a function of Alice's randomness r_A, the transcript tran and the group elements that Alice receives from Bob ($\overline{q}_B = (q_{B,1}, \cdots, q_{B,\gamma})$) and Charlie ($\overline{q}_C = (q_{C,1}, \cdots, q_{C,\gamma})$). Since Alice's algorithm is in the MGGM, the key key will, therefore, be a linear function of the components of $\overline{q}_B, \overline{q}_C$ with coefficients $\overline{a}_B, \overline{a}_C$ that can arbitrarily depend on Alice's randomness r_A and transcript tran (see Lemma 17). In particular, $\mathsf{key}_A = \overline{a}_B \cdot \overline{q}_B + \overline{a}_C \cdot \overline{q}_C$, where $\cdot$ is inner product.

Breaking 3-NIKEs without zero tests: randomness switching lemma. Suppose E starts by *re-sampling* Charlie's randomness into r'_C conditioned on the message m_C. This change will lead to a different set of group elements $\overline{q}'_C = (q'_{C,1}, \cdots, q'_{C,\gamma})$ broadcast by C, and hence Alice's key will change as well into $\mathsf{key}'_A = \overline{a}_B \cdot \overline{q}_B + \overline{a}_C \cdot \overline{q}'_C$. However, a crucial point is that the component $\overline{a}_B \cdot \overline{q}_B$ in this linear function *stays the same*. This important point is directly enabled by the fact that there are *three* parties involved, and we would not have this property in the 2-NIKE setting. Now, our attack will directly take advantage of this common part $\overline{a}_B \cdot \overline{q}_B$ in Alice's key when Charlie switches its randomness to r'_C. In particular, suppose $\mathsf{Key}_A(r'_A, r'_C)$ be Alice's key when Alice and Charlie use random seeds r'_A, r'_C (that are compatible with the text messages sent by Alice and Bob), and Bob's randomness is fixed to its true randomness r_B. Further using the same observation above about switching the randomness of a party, we show that when *both* Alice and Charlie resample their random seeds r'_A, r'_C, conditioned on the shared text messages (ignoring the group elements that are encoded), the common parts in Alice's key across these new "executions" of the protocol will cancel out each other and we obtain the following invariant,

$$\mathsf{Key}_A(r_A, r_C) = \mathsf{Key}_A(r_A, r'_C) + \mathsf{Key}_A(r'_A, r_C) - \mathsf{Key}_A(r'_A, r'_C),$$

which is formalized in Lemma 19 as the randomness switching lemma. Finally, the eavesdropper attacker can directly use the above equality to use re-sampled keys r'_A, r'_B (which she obtains using inverse sampling) to obtain all three fake keys on the right hand side, using which it can obtain the true key.

Breaking 3-NIKEs *with* zero tests: learning useful linear tests. We now describe the extra ideas needed to handle zero tests done by the parties. Firstly, we can assume without loss of generality that all zero tests by A, B, C are asked *after* they receive the text messages and the group elements (through their oracles). In particular, parties' randomness will directly determine their messages and the group elements they send. Eve, has direct access only to the text messages sent by the parties, because the group elements are encoded. However, Eve can also perform zero-test queries over the (vector of) group elements $\bar{q} = (\bar{q}_A, \bar{q}_B, \bar{q}_C)$. Eve's goal here is to learn any *useful* zero-test query over $\bar{q}$ such that the answer to the zero-test queries by A, B, C will follow. In particular, we say that a set of *linear constraints* LinCon (containing both linear equalities and inequalities) over $\bar{q}$ are $(1 - \varepsilon)$-*useful* if the following two properties hold.

1. *Pure restrictions.* We say that LinCon is pure if all of its constraints are over an *individual* party. Namely, for each constraint c in LinCon, there is a party $P \in \{A, B, C\}$ such that c is a constraint over $\bar{q}_P$.
2. *Covering heavy zero tests.* We say that (LinCon, tran) covers ε-*heavy* zero-tests, if for every zero test query f (over the variables $\bar{q} = (\bar{q}_A, \bar{q}_B, \bar{q}_C)$) whose answer is not implied by the equalities in LinCon (f is not trivially positive or negative using the equalities in LinCon), the probability of answering positively is at most ε over the randomness of the parties.

We first explain how we find useful sets of linear constraints. We then explain why finding them can be used for a successful attack by reduction to the setting of protocols with no zero tests.

Finding a useful set. Finding a useful set is rather straight forward. Eve will iteratively pick any *pure* zero test query (i.e., only dealing with one party's shared group elements) over $\bar{q}$ that is both ε-heavy to hold (positively) and that it is *not* in the span of the equalities already in LinCon. Since the dimension of the linear constraints over LinCon is limited by 3γ (i.e., the total number of group elements shared by the parties) this process will stop in about $3\gamma/\varepsilon$ steps. The proof is similar to the proof of efficiency of the heavy-learner of [BMG07,BM17].

Using a useful set. If a set LinCon is useful, then by the first (pure restrictions) property, it imposes a *product* distribution over the randomness of A, B, C. Therefore, one can define an imaginary protocol with respect to the fixed text messages tran and LinCon, in which A, B, C will pick their random seeds conditioned on (tran, LinCon) and run their key extraction algorithms to agree on a key. Furthermore, by the second (light tests) property, assuming ε is sufficiently small, with high probability *all* of the zero-test queries of A, B, C will be answered merely by LinCon, or that they will be answered negatively. Therefore, all such queries could be *removed* from the protocol, and we will be back to a protocol *without* any zero tests. This means that we are back to the simpler case of no zero tests, which was resolved already.

To see why the zero test queries can be compiled out of the protocol (conditioned on (tran, LinCon)), in the following for simplicity suppose Alice asks only one zero-test query. By the first (pure restrictions) property, one can fix this zero-test query without any further restriction on the distribution of the random seeds of Bob or Charlie. Therefore, all we need to show is that the answer to this (non-trivial) zero-test query will be negative with probability $1 - \varepsilon$. This would be the case if we had learned all the ε-heavy linear constraints that deal with the variables in *both* of $\overline{q}_B, \overline{q}_C$, while our set LinCon only contains heavy constraints that are pure. However, interestingly, one more application of the purity property shows that what we have learned in LinCon is already enough. In particular, we prove that, because of the independence of the distributions of r_B, r_C conditioned on (tran, LinCon), the existence of any unlearned ε-heavy zero-test (not spanned by the equalities in LinCon) over $\overline{q}_B, \overline{q}_C$ will automatically imply the existence of an unlearned pure ε-heavy linear restriction on *either* of $\overline{q}_B, \overline{q}_C$. But such heavy restrictions are already learned by Eve!

2   Preliminaries

Definition 1 (K-Party Non-interactive Key-Exchange (K-NIKE)).
For a security parameter λ, and a set of K parties $\{P_1, \cdots, P_K\}$, a K-party non-interactive key-exchange protocol for key space $\mathcal{KS}$ consists of a pair of algorithms (Msg, Key) defined as follows:

- Msg$(1^\lambda, i, r_i) \rightarrow m_i$: *The message generation algorithm takes as input the security parameter λ, an index $i \in [K]$ indicating the party P_i, and a randomness $r_i \in \{0,1\}^\lambda$, and outputs the corresponding message $m_i \in \{0,1\}^\lambda$. It is assumed that in the time of generating the messages, each party generates its message with the algorithm Msg and broadcasts it.*
- Key$(i, r_i, \mathsf{tran}) \rightarrow \mathsf{key}_i$: *The key generation algorithm takes as input the index $i \in [K]$ indicating the party P_i, P_i's randomness r_i and the transcript $\mathsf{tran} := (m_j)_{j \in [K]}$ consisting of all the broadcasted messages from the time of message generation, and outputs a (shared) key $\mathsf{key}_i \in \{0,1\}^m$.*

A K-NIKE protocol satisfies the following properties:

- **Correctness:** *We say the scheme has completeness error $\delta(\lambda)$, if for all security parameters $\lambda \in \mathbb{N}$, all indices $i, j \in [K]$, and all choices of randomnesses r_i and r_j,*

$$\Pr_{r_1, \ldots, r_K} [\mathsf{Key}(i, r_i, \mathsf{tran}) = \mathsf{Key}(j, r_j, \mathsf{tran})] \geq 1 - \delta(\lambda),$$

where tran $= (m_1, \ldots, m_K)$ *for* $m_i \leftarrow \mathsf{Msg}(1^\lambda, i, r_i)$. *We simply say the scheme is complete, if it has completeness error* $\delta(\lambda) \leq \mathsf{negl}(\lambda)$. *We say the scheme has perfect completeness if* $\delta(\lambda) = 0$.

– **Security:** *For all security parameters* $\lambda \in \mathbb{N}$, *and all efficient adversaries* $\mathcal{A}$, *we define the advantage of* $\mathcal{A}$ *as follows:*

$$\mathrm{Adv}_{\mathcal{A}}(\lambda) := \left| \Pr\left[\mathsf{key}_1 = \mathsf{key}_{\mathcal{A}}\right] - \frac{1}{|\mathcal{KS}|} \right|$$

where $\mathsf{key}_{\mathcal{A}} \leftarrow \mathcal{A}(1^\lambda, \mathsf{tran})$ *and* $\mathsf{key}_1 \leftarrow \mathsf{Key}(1, r_1, \mathsf{tran})$, *in which* tran $:= (m_i)_{i \in [K]}$ *for* $m_i \leftarrow \mathsf{Msg}(1^\lambda, i, r_i)$ *for all* $i \in [K]$. *A K-NIKE protocol is secure if* $\mathrm{Adv}_{\mathcal{A}}(\lambda) \leq \mathsf{negl}(n)$.

Note that randomnesses, messages, and keys can be viewed as vectors in the above definition. We can also define a fine-grained variant of K-NIKE as follows.

Definition 2 $((t, \varepsilon)$-**Secure K-NIKE**)**.** *For functions* $t = t(\cdot), \varepsilon = \varepsilon(\cdot)$ *a (fine-grained)* (t, ε)-*secure K-NIKE has the same syntax as the subroutines* Msg, Key *in Definition 1, with the following additional conditions on its correctness and security properties. There is a function* $n = n(\lambda)$, *such that:*

– **Correctness:** *All parties (i.e., both* Msg, Key *algorithms) run in time* $\tilde{O}(n)$.
– **Security:** *We only limit ourselves to adversaries who run in time* $t(n)$, *and for all such adversary their advantage shall be at most* $\varepsilon(n)$.

In other words, after changing the security parameter to n, *honest parties run in quasi-linear time, while the adversary needs time* t *to gain advantage* ε. *When the protocol is in an idealized model, we use the number of queries by the algorithms to the oracle as the measure of their running time.*

Definition 3 (Shoup's Generic Group Model (SGGM)). *Let* $p \in \mathbb{Z}$ *be a positive integer. For such fixed* p, *in Shoup's Generic Group Model (SGGM) all parties have access to an oracle with the following queries.*

– enc **query.** *Suppose* S *is a* label space *of size* $|S| \geq p$, *and let* enc *be a random injective function from* $\mathbb{Z}_p$ *to* S.
– Add **query.** *If* $z = c_1 \cdot x + c_2 \cdot y$, *then* $\mathsf{Add}(c_1, c_2, \mathsf{enc}(x), \mathsf{enc}(y)) = \mathsf{enc}(z)$.

In this paper, for simplicity of presentation, we denote $\mathsf{enc}(x)$ *by* g^x, *even when we are in the generic group model and* g^x *is not an actual exponentiation.*

Random Oracle Model. Recall that in the Random Oracle Model ROM, all parties have access to a function H randomly sampled from the set $\mathcal{H}$ of all functions $f : \mathcal{N} \rightarrow \mathcal{M}$, and the input/output spaces $\mathcal{N}, \mathcal{M}$ are chosen differently in different contexts. These variants can simulate each other, but when it comes to fine-grained efficiency and security properties, the choice of random oracle can be more important. In this model, we primarily count the number of oracle queries as the substitute for "running time."

Lemma 4 (Chernoff Bound). *Let $X = \Sigma_{i=1}^n X_i$, where $X_i = 1$ with probability p_i and $X_i = 0$ with probability $1 - p_i$, and all X_i are independent. Let $\mu = \mathbb{E}[X] = \Sigma_{i=1}^n p_i$. Then*

1. **Upper Tail:** $\Pr[\mathbf{X} \geq (1 + \delta)\mu] \leq e^{-\frac{\delta^2}{2+\delta}\mu}$ *for all $\delta > 0$;*
2. **Lower Tail:** $\Pr[\mathbf{X} \leq (1 - \delta)\mu] \leq e^{-\mu\frac{\delta^2}{2}}$ *for all $0 < \delta < 1$.*

3   3-NIKE in the Random Oracle Model

In this section, we construct a 3-party non-interactive key-exchange protocol in the random oracle model with non-trivial fine-grain security by generalizing Merkle Puzzles [Mer74]. To give a high-level idea of how the protocol works, we start with a similar idea of the classical 2-party NIKE of Merkle in random oracle model. Namely, for a security parameter λ and a given random oracle H, each of the three parties samples a set of secret values $\bar{r}_i$ of size $\lambda^2 \ell(\lambda)$, computes $H(\bar{r}_i)$, which is the output of the random oracle on each value of the set, and broadcasts it. It can be shown that with high probability, there will be a set of collisions of size at least $\ell(\lambda)$. Then, *without any further interaction*, the parties pick the first lexicographic $\ell(\lambda)$ collisions, or any other natural way of pre-agreeing on which subset to pick, and compute the shared key similar to the 2-party NIKE protocol of Merkle.

Construction 5 (3-NIKE ROM-Based Protocol). *For a security parameter λ, let $H : [\lambda^3] \to \{0,1\}^\lambda$ be a random oracle, and $\ell(\lambda) = \log^2(\lambda)$ a minimal intersection size parameter. The 3-NIKE protocol between parties $\{P_1, P_2, P_3\}$ would be as follows:*

- $\mathsf{Msg}(1^\lambda, i, \bar{r}_i) \to \bar{m}_i$: *For each party P_i, on input the security parameter λ and P_i's randomnesses $\bar{r}_i$, which is viewed as a set $\bar{r}_i \subset [\lambda^3]$ of size $\lambda^2 \cdot \log(\lambda)$, the message generation algorithm proceeds as follows:*
    1. *View $\bar{r}_i$ as $\{r_{ij}\}_{j \in \lambda^2 \cdot \log(\lambda)}$, and compute $H(\bar{r}_i) := \{H(r_{ij})\}_{j \in \lambda^2 \cdot \log(\lambda)}$.*
    2. *Output and broadcast the set of messages as $\bar{m}_i := H(\bar{r}_i)$.*
- $\mathsf{Key}(i, \bar{r}_i, \mathsf{tran}) \to \overline{\mathsf{key}}_i$: *On input an index $i \in [3]$, the party P_i's randomnesses $\bar{r}_i$, and the transcript $\mathsf{tran} := (\bar{m}_j)_{j \in [3]/\{i\}}$, the key generation algorithm proceeds as follow:*
    1. *Invoke the message generation algorithm to obtain $\bar{m}_i \leftarrow \mathsf{Msg}(1^\lambda, i, \bar{r}_i)$. If $|\cap_{j \in [3]} \bar{m}_j| < \ell(\lambda)$, the algorithm outputs 0 and aborts.*
    2. *Let $c_1, \cdots, c_{\ell(\lambda)}$ be the first $\ell(\lambda)$ lexicographic common outputs of $\cap_{j \in [3]} \bar{m}_j$.*
    3. *All parties P_1, P_2, P_3 are able to find the common inputs $s_1, \cdots, s_{\ell(\lambda)} \in \cap_{j \in [3]} \bar{r}_j$ such that $H(s_i) = c_i$.*
    4. *The shared (output) key will be $\overline{\mathsf{key}}_i := \bigoplus_{i=1}^{\ell(\lambda)} s_i$.*

In this section, we prove the following theorem.

Theorem 6. *Construction 5 is a (t, ε) 3-NIKE, where $t = n^{1.5}, \varepsilon = \mathsf{negl}(n)$.*

Proof. Let $n = \lambda^2$. The proofs of correctness and security are as follows.

Correctness. Due to $n = \lambda^2$, it holds that the algorithms running in $\tilde{O}(n)$.

We have three sets $\overline{m}_1$, $\overline{m}_2$, and $\overline{m}_3$ of size $\lambda^2 \log(\lambda)$ chosen randomly from the set $[\lambda^3]$. It is easy to see that since we are in the random oracle model, if the Key algorithm does not abort, all three parties will receive the same key with probability 1. Therefore, for $\ell(\lambda) = \log^2(\lambda)$, in order to show that the parties will successfully obtain one shared key with high probability after running the algorithms properly, it suffices to show that the probability of the Key algorithm aborts is negligible. More formally, we want to show

$$\Pr\left[| \cap_{j \in [3]} \overline{m}_j | \leq \ell(\lambda)\right] = \Pr[|\overline{m}_1 \cap \overline{m}_2 \cap \overline{m}_3| \leq \ell(\lambda)] \leq \mathsf{negl}(\lambda).$$

In order to prove this, we adopt the ideas used in [BGI08] in a similar context/goal (about amplifying security in a two-party key agreement) and use a chain of Chernoff bounds. We know

$$\Pr[|\overline{m}_1 \cap \overline{m}_2 \cap \overline{m}_3| \leq \ell(\lambda)] \leq 1 - \Pr[|\overline{m}_1 \cap \overline{m}_2 \cap \overline{m}_3| > \ell(\lambda)] \tag{1}$$

As a first step, it is easy to see that for every choice of $s \in [\lambda^2 \log(\lambda)]$, we have

$$\Pr[|\overline{m}_1 \cap \overline{m}_2 \cap \overline{m}_3| > \ell(\lambda)] \geq \Pr[|\overline{m}_1 \cap \overline{m}_2 \cap \overline{m}_3| > \ell(\lambda) \wedge |\overline{m}_1 \cap \overline{m}_2| \geq s]$$

$$= \Pr[|\overline{m}_1 \cap \overline{m}_2 \cap \overline{m}_3| > \ell(\lambda) \mid |\overline{m}_1 \cap \overline{m}_2| \geq s] \cdot \Pr[|\overline{m}_1 \cap \overline{m}_2| \geq s]. \tag{2}$$

Now we can analyze $\Pr[|\overline{m}_1 \cap \overline{m}_2| \geq s]$ for some $s \in [\lambda^2 \log(\lambda)]$, using a Chernoff bound similar to [BGI08]. Then viewing $\overline{m}_1 \cap \overline{m}_2$ as a set, we can use the same idea for analyzing $\Pr[|\overline{m}_1 \cap \overline{m}_2 \cap \overline{m}_3| > \ell(\lambda) \mid |\overline{m}_1 \cap \overline{m}_2| \geq s]$. Let

$$\overline{m}_1 = \{a_1, \cdots, a_{\lambda^2 \log(\lambda)}\}, \overline{m}_2 = \{b_1, \cdots, b_{\lambda^2 \log(\lambda)}\}, \overline{m}_3 = \{c_1, \cdots, c_{\lambda^2 \log(\lambda)}\}.$$

Now for analyzing the second probability in Eq. 2 (i.e. $\Pr[|\overline{m}_1 \cap \overline{m}_2| \geq s]$,) let X_i be the event that $b_i \in \overline{m}_1$ (i.e. $b_i \in \overline{m}_1 \cap \overline{m}_2$.) Therefore,

$$\mu := \mathbb{E}\left[\sum_{i=1}^{\lambda^2 \log(\lambda)} X_i\right] = \frac{\lambda^2 \log(\lambda)}{\lambda^3} \cdot \lambda^2 \log(\lambda) = \lambda \cdot \log^2(\lambda).$$

Based on the way the event X_i is defined, we can view $|\overline{m}_1 \cap \overline{m}_2|$ as $\sum_{i=1}^{\lambda^2 \log(\lambda)} X_i$,

$$\Pr[|\overline{m}_1 \cap \overline{m}_2| \geq s] = 1 - \Pr[\sum_{i=1}^{\lambda^2 \log(\lambda)} X_i < s].$$

By lower tail of Chernoff bound in Lemma 4,

$$\Pr\left[\sum_{i=1}^{\lambda^2 \log(\lambda)} X_i < (1 - \delta)\lambda \log^2(\lambda)\right] \leq e^{-\frac{\delta^2}{2}\lambda \log^2(\lambda)}.$$

This concludes that

$$\Pr\left[|\overline{m}_1 \cap \overline{m}_2| \geq s\right] \geq 1 - e^{-\frac{\delta^2}{2}\lambda \log^2(\lambda)}. \tag{3}$$

For analyzing the first probability in Eq. 2, we first simplify the probability as follows. Let $\overline{m} := \overline{m}_1 \cap \overline{m}_2$,

$$\Pr[|\overline{m}_1 \cap \overline{m}_2 \cap \overline{m}_3| > \ell(\lambda) \mid |\overline{m}_1 \cap \overline{m}_2| \geq s] = \Pr[|\overline{m} \cap \overline{m}_3| > \ell(\lambda) \mid |\overline{m}| \geq s]$$
$$\geq \Pr[|\overline{m} \cap \overline{m}_3| > \ell(\lambda) \mid |\overline{m}| = s]. \tag{4}$$

Now, using a similar approach as before, we can find a lower bound for the complement of the above probability which will give us an upper bound for the first part of Eq. 2. Namely,

$$1 - \Pr[|\overline{m}_1 \cap \overline{m}_2 \cap \overline{m}_3| > \ell(\lambda) \mid |\overline{m}_1 \cap \overline{m}_2| = s] = 1 - \Pr[|\overline{m} \cap \overline{m}_3| > \ell(\lambda) \mid |\overline{m}| = s]$$

Now, letting $\overline{m} = \{m_1, \ldots, m_s\}$ and Y_i be the event that $c_i \in \overline{m}$ (i.e. $c_i \in \overline{m} \cap \overline{m}_3$), we will have

$$\mu' := \mathbb{E}\left[\sum_{i=1}^{\lambda^2 \log(\lambda)} Y_i\right] = \frac{s}{\lambda^3}(\lambda^2 \log(\lambda)).$$

Using another Chernoff bound from Lemma 4,

$$\Pr\left[\sum_{i=1}^{\lambda^2 \log(\lambda)} Y_i \leq (1-\delta')\frac{s}{\lambda^3}(\lambda^2 \log(\lambda))\right] \leq e^{-\frac{\delta'^2}{2}\frac{s \log(\lambda)}{\lambda}},$$

which results in

$$1 - \Pr[|\overline{m} \cap \overline{m}_3| > \ell(\lambda) \mid |\overline{m}| = s] \leq e^{-\frac{\delta'^2}{2}\frac{s \log(\lambda)}{\lambda}}. \tag{5}$$

Using the above in Eq. 4 give us

$$\Pr[|\overline{m}_1 \cap \overline{m}_2 \cap \overline{m}_3| > \ell(\lambda) \mid |\overline{m}_1 \cap \overline{m}_2| \geq s] \geq 1 - e^{-\frac{\delta'^2}{2}\frac{s \log(\lambda)}{\lambda}}. \tag{6}$$

Set $\delta = \delta' = \frac{1}{2}$ and $s = \frac{\lambda}{2} \log^2(\lambda)$. Using Eqs. 3 and 6 in Eq. 2, we get

$$\Pr[|\overline{m}_1 \cap \overline{m}_2 \cap \overline{m}_3| > \ell(\lambda)] \geq (1 - e^{-\frac{\lambda}{8}\log^2(\lambda)})(1 - e^{-\frac{\log^3(\lambda)}{16}})$$
$$\geq 1 - 2e^{-\frac{\log^3(\lambda)}{16}} = 1 - \mathsf{negl}(\lambda).$$

which concludes the proof.

Security. We need to show that adversaries who ask $o(\lambda^3)$ queries have $\mathsf{negl}(\lambda)$ advantage of finding the shared key based on the transcript. In particular, we want to show that, any such adversary $\mathcal{A}$ will likely not query at least one of intersection points used by the key generation algorithm to compute the key.

Let $k = \lambda^3/3$ be the number of queries that the adversary $\mathcal{A}$ makes to the oracle, and assume w.l.o.g. that $\mathcal{A}$ does not repeat queries. Denote adversary's

i'th query by q_i and let X_{ij} be the event that $H(q_i) = c_j$ for some $j \in [\ell(\lambda)]$. For any $i \leq \lambda^3/3$ and any $q_i \notin \{q_1, \cdots, q_{i-1}\}$, $H(q_i)$ is distributed uniformly within the set $\{0,1\}^\lambda \setminus \{H(q_1), \cdots H(q_{i-1})\}$ from the view of $\mathcal{A}$ prior to q_i. Hence, for all i, j, $\Pr[X_{ij} = 1] \leq \frac{1}{2^\lambda - k}$, and letting $k' = 2^\lambda - k$ and $X_i = \sum_{j=1}^{\ell(\lambda)} X_{ij}$, for all $i \leq k$, $\Pr[\mathbf{X}_i = 1] \leq \frac{\ell(\lambda)}{k'}$ regardless of other X_i's. Let $p = \frac{\ell(\lambda)}{k'}$, and assume X_i's are independent and $\Pr[\mathbf{X}_i = 1] = p$. By using the upper tail of a Chernoff bound from Lemma 4 and letting $\mu := \mathbb{E}\left[\sum_{i=1}^k \mathbf{X}_i\right] = kp$, we have,

$$\Pr\left[\sum_{i=1}^k \mathbf{X}_i \geq \ell(\lambda)\right] = \Pr\left[\sum_{i=1}^k \mathbf{X}_i \geq \frac{k'}{k} \cdot (k \cdot \frac{\ell(\lambda)}{k'})\right] = \Pr\left[\sum_{i=1}^k \mathbf{X}_i \geq \frac{k'}{k} \cdot \mu\right]$$

where for large enough λ, the probability that $\mathcal{A}$ queries the oracle for all the common inputs (i.e. finding the shared key) will be bounded by:

$$\Pr\left[\sum_{i=1}^k \mathbf{X}_i \geq \ell(\lambda)\right] \leq e^{-\Omega(\ell(\lambda))} = \mathsf{negl}(\lambda)$$

where the last equality comes from $\ell(\lambda) = \log^2(\lambda)$. In the event that $\mathcal{A}$ did not query some s_i to the oracle, $\mathcal{A}$'s output is wrong with probability $\frac{1}{2}$ since from its point of view, the value of $\bigoplus_{i=1}^{\ell(\lambda)} s_i$ is 0 or 1 with equal probability. In other words, letting Y be the event that $\sum_{i=1}^k \mathbf{X}_i \geq \ell(\lambda)$,

$$\mathsf{Adv}_{\mathcal{A}}(\lambda) := \left| \Pr\left[\overline{\mathsf{key}_1} = \mathsf{key}_{\mathcal{A}}\right] - \frac{1}{2}\right|$$

$$= \left| \Pr\left[\overline{\mathsf{key}_1} = \mathsf{key}_{\mathcal{A}} \mid \mathbf{Y}\right] + \Pr\left[\overline{\mathsf{key}_1} = \mathsf{key}_{\mathcal{A}} \mid \neg\mathbf{Y}\right] - \frac{1}{2}\right|$$

$$\leq e^{-\Omega(\ell(\lambda))} + \frac{1}{2} - \frac{1}{2} = \mathsf{negl}(\lambda).$$

Therefore, for any $d < 3$, an $O(\lambda^d)$-bounded adversary cannot make more than $\frac{\lambda^3}{3}$ queries for large enough λ.

All in all, for any $d < 3$, any $O(\lambda^d)$-bounded adversary $\mathcal{A}$, when the probability is taken over the possibilities for the random function, $\mathcal{A}$ can guess the key only with negligible advantage.

Remark 7. Construction 5 can be generalized into a k-NIKE with $\Omega(\lambda^{k/(k-1)})$ security. The protocol will be similar to the above 3-NIKE protocol with a few changes. It will use a random oracle $H : [\lambda^k] \to \{0,1\}^\lambda$, and the randomness of each party should be from the set $[\lambda^k]$ and of size $\tilde{o}(\lambda^{k-1})$. The rest of the construction and the proofs will be similar with minor changes (e.g. there is a need for more applications of Chernoff bounds.)

Remark 8. We believe that with a similar approach to the one in [BGI08], one should be able to extend this result to getting a 3-NIKE similar to our Construction 5 from an "almost 1-1 OWF" instead of using a random oracle. We leave such studies for future work.

4   4-NIKE in Shoup's Generic Group Model

In this section, we construct a 4-NIKE protocol with quadratic security in Shoup's generic group model. As explained in the introduction, our construction can be interpreted as first constructing a 4-NIKE using an ideal 2-NIKE oracle, and then "substituting" the 2-NIKE ideal oracle with Shoup's GGM.

In this section, we introduce a candidate 4-NIKE protocol in the Shoup's Generic Group Model. To give a high-level intuition of the protocol, the idea of finding a shared key between four parties $\{P_1, P_2, P_3, P_4\}$ is as follows. All parties, similar to the previous section, will choose a secret set of random values and broadcast some message as its corresponding public values (the broadcast messages might differ for each party), such that after the interaction, P_1 and P_2 will be able to identify a single secret value where its corresponding public message has already been broadcast, and the same will hold for P_3 and P_4. From there, and *without any further interaction*, (P_1, P_2) will act as a single party, and so as (P_3, P_4). Therefore, one can simply run a 2-party NIKE between these two parties and without the need of an interaction.

Before going into details of the protocol, we should note that we use the fact that we can view $x \in [\lambda^4]$ as $(x_1, x_2) \in [\lambda^2] \times [\lambda^2]$ for two isomorphic groups of size $\theta(\lambda^4)$ and $\theta(\lambda^2) \times \theta(\lambda^2)$ throughout our construction and proofs.

Construction 9. *For a security parameter λ, let $H : [\lambda^2] \to \{0,1\}^\lambda$ be a random oracle, $\mathbb{G}$ be a generic group (in the sense of Shoup) of size $\theta(\lambda^4)$ whose encodings are denoted by the "generator" g. Let $\ell(\lambda) = \log^2(\lambda)$ be the minimal intersection size parameter. The NIKE protocol between parties $\{P_1, P_2, P_3, P_4\}$ is as follows:*

- $\mathsf{Msg}(1^\lambda, i, \bar{r}_i) \to \overline{m}_i$: *For each party P_i, on input the security parameter λ and P_i's randomnesses $\bar{r}_i$, which is a random set $\bar{r}_i \subset [\lambda^4]$ of size $\lambda \cdot \ell(\lambda)$, the message generation algorithm proceeds as follows:*
  1. *View $\bar{r}_i$ as $\{r_{ij}\}_{j \in [\lambda \cdot \ell(\lambda)]}$, and for $j \in [\lambda \cdot \ell(\lambda)]$, view each element as $r_{ij} := (r_{ij}^{(1)}, r_{ij}^{(2)}) \subset [\lambda^2] \times [\lambda^2]$, where $r_{ij}^{(1)}$ and $r_{ij}^{(2)}$ are the first and second half of the value r_{ij}, respectively.*
  2. *Compute $H(\bar{r}_i^{(1)}) := \left(H(r_{ij}^{(1)}) \right)_{j \in [\lambda \cdot \ell(\lambda)]}$, and $g^{\bar{r}_i} := (g^{r_{ij}})_{j \in [\lambda \cdot \ell(\lambda)]}$.*
  3. *Output and broadcast the messages as $\overline{m}_i = \left(H(\bar{r}_i^{(1)}), g^{\bar{r}_i} \right)$ for $i \in \{1, 3\}$, and $\overline{m}_i = H(\bar{r}_i^{(1)})$ for $i \in \{2, 4\}$.*
- $\mathsf{Key}(i, \bar{r}_i, \overline{tran}) \to key_i$: *On input an index $i \in [4]$, the party P_i's randomnesses $\bar{r}_i$, and the transcript $\overline{tran} := (\overline{m}_j)_{j \in [4]/\{i\}}$, the key generation algorithm proceeds as follows:*
  1. *Invoke the message generation and obtain $\overline{m}_i \leftarrow \mathsf{Msg}(1^\lambda, i, \bar{r}_i)$, and parse $\overline{m}_l = \left(H(\bar{r}_l^{(1)}), g^{\bar{r}_l} \right)$ or $\overline{m}_l = H(\bar{r}_l^{(1)})$ based on whether $l = 1, 3$ or $l = 2, 4$.*
  2. *If either $|H(\bar{r}_1^{(1)}) \cap H(\bar{r}_2^{(1)})| = 0$ or $|H(\bar{r}_3^{(1)}) \cap H(\bar{r}_4^{(1)})| = 0$, the algorithm outputs 0 and aborts.*
  3. *Let c be the first lexicographic common output of the $H(\bar{r}_1^{(1)}) \cap H(\bar{r}_2^{(1)})$, and c' be the first lexicographic common output of $H(\bar{r}_3^{(1)}) \cap H(\bar{r}_4^{(1)})$.*

4. *Parties* P_1 *and* P_2 *are able to find the common input* $s \in \bar{r}_1^{(1)} \cap \bar{r}_2^{(1)}$ *such that* $H(s) = c$. *And similarly,* P_3 *and* P_4 *are able to find the common input* $s' \in \bar{r}_3^{(1)} \cap \bar{r}_4^{(1)}$ *such that* $H(s') = c'$ *(there is no need of further interaction between the parties.)*

5. *Note that* s *is the first half of the corresponding element in* $\bar{r}_1 \cap \bar{r}_2$. *Having* $g^{\bar{r}_1}$ *from party* P_1 *'s message, party* P_2 *is able to find the other half of the corresponding element in the set* $\bar{r}_1$ *from* s *with a baby-step giant-step (BSGS) or Pollard's rho algorithm. Similarly, having* $g^{\bar{r}_3}$ *from party* P_3 *'s message, party* P_4 *is able to find the second half of the corresponding element in the set* $\bar{r}_3$ *from* s'.

6. *Now,* P_1 *and* P_2 *have a common randomness in the set* $\bar{r}_1$, *and* P_3 *and* P_4 *have a common randomness in* $\bar{r}_3$. *Let the common randomness of* P_1 *and* P_2 *be* $\hat{s} \subset \bar{r}_1$, *and the common randomness of* P_3 *and* P_4 *be* $\hat{s}' \subset \bar{r}_3$.

7. *View* P_1 *and* P_2 *as one party* $P_{12} = (P_1, P_2)$ *with the randomness* $r_{12} := \hat{s}$ *and their associated message* $m_{12} := g^{r_{12}} = g^{\hat{s}}$. *Similarly, view* P_3 *and* P_4 *as one party* $P_{34} = (P_3, P_4)$ *with the randomness* $r_{34} := \hat{s}'$ *and their associated message* $m_{34} := g^{r_{34}} = g^{\hat{s}'}$. P_{12} *and* P_{34} *can reach shared keys without any further interactions by a Diffie-Hellman Key-Exchange.*

8. *The shared (output) key will be* $\mathsf{key}_i = m_{34}^{r_{12}} = m_{12}^{r_{34}} := g^{\hat{s}\hat{s}'}$.

Theorem 10. *For any generic adversary* $\mathcal{A}$ *against the 4-party NIKE of Construction 9, which places* q *queries in total to either* H *or to the group operations (as in Shoup's GGM), the probability that* $\mathcal{A}$ *outputs the right key is*

$$O(q^2/\lambda^4 + q/\lambda^2 + \mathsf{polylog}(\lambda)/\lambda).$$

Before we proceed with the proof, we make two observations. First, we focus on bounding the probability that $\mathcal{A}$ *finds* the key, while K-NIKE requires that $\mathcal{A}$ cannot distinguish the key from random. However, given the shared key, all four parties can use the standard Goldreich-Levin theorem to extract a hardcore bit of the key, such that *guessing* this shared bit is as hard as *finding* the initial shared key. Hence, Theorem 10 actually implies the security of this modified 4-NIKE protocol. Second, both the construction and the adversary are allowed to query H and the generic group. However, Shoup's generic group model implies in particular the existence of an injective random oracle. Therefore, Theorem 10 further implies the existence of a quadratically secure 4-NIKE protocol in the 'bare' generic group model of Shoup.

4.1 Correctness

Let us first clarify why the protocol works correctly with a *single* round of interaction. Based on Theorem 10, after a single round of interaction (i.e. invoking the message generation algorithm once for every party,) all parties will have the following values:

- $\overline{m}_1 = \left(H\left(\overline{r}_1^{(1)} \right), g^{\overline{r}_1} \right)$ and $\overline{m}_2 = H\left(\overline{r}_2^{(1)} \right)$ for parties P_1 and P_2.
- $\overline{m}_3 = \left(H\left(\overline{r}_3^{(1)} \right), g^{\overline{r}_3} \right)$ and $\overline{m}_4 = H\left(\overline{r}_4^{(1)} \right)$ for parties P_3 and P_4.

Therefore, with the help of the baby-step giant-step or Pollard's rho algorithm, P_2 and P_4 can find $\hat{s} \subset \overline{r}_1$ and $\hat{s}' \subset \overline{r}_3$, having $g^{\overline{r}_1}$ and $g^{\overline{r}_3}$ respectively.

Since $H(s) \subset H\left(\overline{r}_1^{(1)} \right)$ and $H(s') \subset H\left(\overline{r}_3^{(1)} \right)$ were public from the interaction phase (where s and s' are the first half of $\hat{s}$ and $\hat{s}'$ resp.,) then all parties can find the corresponding values $g^{\hat{s}}$ and $g^{\hat{s}'}$ from $g^{\overline{r}_1}$ and $g^{\overline{r}_3}$ respectively. From there, it is easy to see that P_{12} and P_{34} (i.e. all parties,) can find the shared key $g^{\hat{s}\hat{s}'}$ from in steps 7 and 8 of the key generation algorithm.

Now to argue the correctness of the protocol, note that the Msg algorithm has $2 \cdot \lambda \ell(\lambda)$ computations, and the Key algorithm has constant number of computations along with running the Msg and BSGS algorithms. Therefore, the running time of both algorithms are of $\tilde{O}(\lambda)$. Moreover, the Key algorithm aborts and outputs 0 only if either $|H(\overline{r}_1^{(1)}) \cap H(\overline{r}_2^{(1)})| = 0$ or $|H(\overline{r}_3^{(1)}) \cap H(\overline{r}_4^{(1)})| = 0$, which by birthday paradox (and similar to [BGI08, Theorem 1]'s proof,) only happens with $\mathsf{negl}(\lambda)$ probability.

In order to prove the correctness of the scheme, we need to show that with overwhelming probability, all parties will find the same key. By correctness of the BSGS algorithm, it will follow from the construction that P_1 and P_2, as well as P_3 and P_4, will have the same and correct shared secret key. By correctness of the Diffie-Hellman key-exchange protocol, it follows that P_{12} and P_{34} (i.e. all the four parties) will agree on the same key. $\square$

4.2   Security Analysis

We prove that a generic adversary $\mathcal{A}$ making q queries (either to the injective random oracle or to the group) is able to output the shared key with probability at most $O(q^2/\lambda^4 + q/\lambda^2 + \mathsf{polylog}(\lambda)/\lambda)$. We start by analyzing the following simpler game G:

1. The adversary is given access to a generic group $\mathbb{G}$ of order $p \approx \lambda^4$, and to an injective random oracle H. It can ask q queries in total to either of them.
2. The game samples $(g, g^a, g^b) \xleftarrow{\$} \mathbb{G}^3$ and sends it to the adversary. Let us write $a = a_0 \| a_1$ and $b = b_0 \| b_1$, where the a_i, b_i are $2\log(\lambda)$-bit long. The game also computes $(h_a, h_b) \leftarrow (H(a_0), H(b_0))$ and sends it to $\mathcal{A}$.
3. The adversary outputs a group element g^c at the end of the game.

At the end of the game, we say that $\mathcal{A}$ wins if either of the two following conditions is fulfilled:

1. $c = a \cdot b$, or
2. the list L of all queries of $\mathcal{A}$ to H contains either a_0 or b_0.

Claim 11. $\Pr[\mathcal{A} \text{ wins in game } G] \leq q^2/\lambda^4 + 2q/\lambda^4 + 2q/\lambda^2$.

Proof. The proof follows closely to the blueprint of Shoup's proof [Sho97] that the advantage of any q-query adversary against the CDH problem is at most $(q^2+2q)/|\mathbb{G}|$. Recall that the generic oracle works as follows: an *encoding function* enc : $\mathbb{Z}_p \mapsto S$ is defined, where S is a set of bit-string. $\mathcal{A}$ sees group elements as encodings of integers: we identify g^a, g^b with enc(a), enc(b). Then, $\mathcal{A}$ can ask *addition queries*, which on input (enc(x), enc(y)) and a sign $+$ or $-$, outputs enc$(x \pm y)$. This more "limited" variant of SGGM is equivalent to Definition 3.

Consider the following variant of the game described above. We simulate all accesses to the generic group exactly as in Shoup's proof: we maintain a list of linear bivariate polynomials $(F_1, \cdots, F_k) \in \mathbb{Z}_p[X, Y]$ (initialized with $k = 3$, $F_1 = 1$, $F_2 = X$, and $F_3 = Y$), and a list of distinct values (enc$_1, \cdots$, enc$_k$) in S (initialized with three random distinct elements of S). For any addition query (i, j), we set $F_{k+1} \leftarrow F_i \pm F_j$. If F_{k+1} matches a polynomial F_t already in the list, let enc$_{k+1} \leftarrow$ enc$_t$, otherwise we set it to a uniformly random element in S.

Furthermore, we also simulate all queries to H as follows: we initially sample (h_a, h_b) uniformly at random from $\{0, 1\}^\lambda$. We maintain a list L of queries. Each time $\mathcal{A}$ queries i, we search if a tuple (i, h) exists in L; if it does not, we sample h uniformly at random from $\{0, 1\}^\lambda$, return h, and add (i, h) to L.

At the end of the game, we sample $(x, y) \overset{\$}{\leftarrow} \mathbb{Z}_p^2$ and check if (1) $F_i(x, y) = F_j(x, y)$ for some $i \neq y$, or (2) $F_i(x, y) = xy$ for some i, or (3) writing $x = x_0||x_1$ and $y = y_0||y_1$, the list L contains a pair (x_0, h) or a pair (y_0, h). By the Schwartz-Zippel lemma, the probability for a random (x, y) that (1) or (2) is satisfied is at most $q^2/\lambda^4 + 2q/\lambda^4 = O(q^2/\lambda^4)$. Furthermore, the probability to hit any entry of the L (whose size is at most q) with x_0 or y_0 (which are uniform over $[\lambda^2]$) is at most $2q/\lambda^2$. Overall, the probability that either (1), (2), or (3) holds is at most $q^2/\lambda^4 + 2q/\lambda^4 + 2q/\lambda^2$.

Furthermore, as in [Sho97], we observe that this simulated game differs from the real game exactly when (1), (2), or (3) happens, and that the adversary wins in the real game exactly when this happens: otherwise, the real and simulated game are perfectly indistinguishable. Therefore, the probability that $\mathcal{A}$ wins in the real game is at most $q^2/\lambda^4 + 2q/\lambda^4 + 2q/\lambda^2$; this concludes the proof.

The rest of the proof proceeds by reducing the existence of an adversary against Construction 9 to the existence of an adversary in the game G. Let $\mathcal{A}$ be a q-query adversary against Construction 9. The reduction proceeds as follow: it receives a challenge (enc(a), enc(b), h_a, h_b) from the game G. Then, it samples a random looking transcript of Construction 9, using $\tilde{O}(\lambda)$ queries to the group and to H to generate all group elements and hashes of prefixes, with the following difference: it replaces the lexicographically first collision in the message of P_1 by enc(a), and sets h_a to be the corresponding prefix hash. It also replaces the corresponding hash collision by h_a in the message of P_2. It does the same with (enc(b), h_b) with P_3 and P_4.

Observe that this simulated transcript is statistically indistinguishable from an honestly generated transcript of Construction 9: the simulation fails only when the transcript does not contain any hash collision between P_1 and P_2 or between P_3 and P_4. But the probability of not having a collision between $\lambda \cdot \ell(\lambda)$-sized tuples of random elements from $[\lambda^2]$ is negligible by a straightforward

Chernoff bound, similar to the proof of Claim 6. Furthermore, by construction, the corresponding shared key for the simulated transcript is exactly $\mathsf{enc}(ab)$.

Therefore, if there exists a q-query adversary against Construction 9 which finds the shared key with probability ε, then there exists a $(q + \tilde{O}(\lambda))$-query adversary against game G which wins the game with probability at least $\varepsilon -$ $\mathsf{negl}(\lambda)$. This concludes the proof. □

5   Impossibility Results

5.1   Defining 3-NIKE in Maurer's Generic Group Model

We first define the model and the problems. Then, we present our results.

Notation. We use bold font to represent random variables.

Definition 12 (Maurer's Generic Group Model (MGGM)). *Let $p \in \mathbb{Z}$ be a positive integer. Let $\mathsf{Arr_P}$ be an array for party P initialized to null at all indices except index 1 where it is initialized to be 1. Also, e is the last index of Arr that is not null (so, initially $e = 1$). Parties have access to group elements only through the following operations.*

- *Add query: The party P submits query $\mathsf{Add}(i_1, i_2, c_1, c_2)$ where $i_1, i_2 \in [e]$ and $c_1, c_2 \in \mathbb{Z}_p$. Then, the value $c_1.\mathsf{Arr_P}[i_1] + c_2.\mathsf{Arr_P}[i_2]$ will be written at $\mathsf{Arr_P}[e + 1]$ and e will be updated to $e + 1$.*
- *Equal query: The party P submits query $\mathsf{Equal}(i_1, i_2)$ where $i_1, i_2 \in [e]$. The party receives 1 if $\mathsf{Arr_P}[i_1] = \mathsf{Arr_P}[i_2]$ and 0 otherwise.*
  The following two queries are optional, as they can be obtained from the above (see Remark 13) but we define them as they sometimes help with a better presentation of algorithms in this model.
- *Write query: The party P submits query $\mathsf{Write}(x)$ for a group element $x \in \mathbb{Z}_q$ and then x is written to $\mathsf{Arr}[e + 1]$ followed by increasing e by one.*
- *Zero query: The party P submits query $\mathsf{Zero}(c_1, \ldots, c_e)$ where $c_1, \cdots, c_e \in \mathbb{Z}_p$. The party receives 1 if $\sum_{i \in [e]} c_i \mathsf{Arr_P}[i] = 0$ and 0 otherwise. When $\mathsf{Arr_P}[1] = 1$, this query can zero-test a general affine function over $\mathsf{Arr_P}[2], \ldots, \mathsf{Arr_P}[e]$.*

Remark 13 (Comparing queries and the default model). Note that the Equal queries can be simulated using a single call to an Zero query. Hence, Zero queries are as powerful. Conversely, an Zero query can be simulated using e queries to the Add followed by a single query to Equal that compares the result with a prepared encoding of zero. By default, we only allow $\mathsf{Add}, \mathsf{Zero}$ queries, but sometimes we state the availability of Write queries for a clearer presentation.

Definition 14 (3-NIKE in MGGM). *In this model, there are three parties Alice A, Bob B, and Charlie C. All parties receive a security parameter λ, and prime number p and a private randomness as inputs. Let their internal randomness be $\mathsf{r_A}, \mathsf{r_B}$, and $\mathsf{r_C}$ respectively. Each of the parties has access to a private MGGM oracle, but all parties' groups are defined over the same $\mathbb{Z}_p$. After making queries to the oracle, party P for all $\mathsf{P} \in \{\mathsf{A}, \mathsf{B}, \mathsf{C}\}$ will simultaneously perform the following actions:*

- P *sends a string* $\mathsf{m_P}$ *to the other parties. Define transcript* tran *as* tran $=$ $(\mathsf{m_A}, \mathsf{m_B}, \mathsf{m_C})$. *No-message protocols are a special case where* $\forall \mathsf{P}, \mathsf{m_P} = \emptyset$.
- P *submits query* $\mathsf{copy}(\gamma)$. *Upon such a query, the last* γ *indices of* P*'s array will be copied to the end of the other parties' arrays, for some publicly known value* $\gamma \leq \mathsf{poly}(\lambda)$ *that is fixed in the protocol and is the same for all three parties. Parties submit this operation at the same time, however, it will be processed first for* A, *second for* B *and last for* C. *Let the vector of group elements that* P *sends to others be* $\overline{q}_\mathsf{P} = (q_{\mathsf{P},1}, \cdots, q_{\mathsf{P},\gamma})$. *Additionally, let* $\overline{q}_{r_\mathsf{A}, r_\mathsf{B}, r_\mathsf{C}} = (\overline{q}_\mathsf{A}, \overline{q}_\mathsf{B}, \overline{q}_\mathsf{C})$ *in which if we run party* P *with internal randomness* r_P, *they will copy* $\overline{q}_\mathsf{P}$.

Without loss of generality (by Lemma 17), the parties in the steps above only use Write *queries to their oracle, as they will know the content of their arrays fully.*

In the second step, based on their private randomness r_P, *transcript* tran, *and their updated private oracles continue to interact with their MGGM oracles and will write a group element* $\mathsf{key_P}$ *to their local MGGM oracle.[3] Moreover, we ask that all the parties are efficient (so, they submit at most* $\mathsf{poly}(\lambda)$ *queries to the oracle). We enforce this by asking all parties to make a* copy *query with a fixed publicly known parameter* $\gamma \leq \mathsf{poly}(\lambda)$ *in their first step, and then (after receiving the exchanged messages) ask exactly* α Add *queries,* β Zero *queries for publicly known and fixed values of* $\alpha, \beta, \leq \mathsf{poly}(\lambda)$.

Completeness: *We say that parties agree on a key with probability* $1 - \delta$ *(where* δ *is called completeness error) if* $\Pr[\mathsf{key_A} = \mathsf{key_B} = \mathsf{key_C}] \geq 1 - \delta$, *where the probability is over the randomness of the parties. We say that the protocol has perfect completeness if* $\delta = 0$.

Soundness: *We say that Eve* E *breaks the protocol with advantage* ρ, *if she finds the key with probability at least than* $1/p + \rho$ *in the following game.* E *will get the transcript* tran *and has access to a private oracle* $\mathsf{Arr_E}$ *that gets as input the result of the copy operations of the all three parties. Namely,* E*'s MGGM oracle will contain 1 followed by* 3γ *group elements that are communicated by the parties in a canonical order. The scheme is secure if the advantage of any* $\mathsf{poly}(\lambda)$*-time* E *is at most* $\mathsf{negl}(\lambda)$.

Remark 15. The Diffie-Hellman protocol is a 2-party protocol that can be stated in the MGGM with perfect completeness, no (text) messages (in addition to the exchanged group elements), no zero-test queries are asked $(\beta = 0)$ *and only one group element is sent by each party* $(\gamma = 1)$.

Remark 16 (Why agreeing on group element in the oracle?). Here we further justify why the key in 3-NIKE protocols in MGGM are written in the $\mathsf{Arr_P}$ *oracle,*

---

[3] This writing could be due to a direct write operation or deriving the group element from other array elements (in which case the parties do not actually have direct access to the group element itself). However, note that if the group elements are eventually encoded, a la Shoup's model, the encoding of the group element will be accessible to the parties.

while the oracle's content is not directly accessible to the parties. Firstly, note that MGGM is an idealized model with an oracle Arr which will be eventually substituted with actual encodings (like Shoup's model). Therefore, if an MGGM protocol leads party to an agreement on the same group element x written in their oracles, this will imply an actual agreement when the oracle is substituted with actual encodings. Furthermore, if we ask the parties to agree on a *string* (as the key) in the MGGM, then (1) without loss of generality we can convert the protocol to agreeing on a key key $\in \mathbb{Z}_p$, one can always bootstrap even a binary key from $\{0, 1\}$ to a key from $\{0, 1\}^\lambda$, and then round it to a secure key in $\mathbb{Z}_p$, and then (2) the parties can write the secure key key $\in \mathbb{Z}_p$ in their corresponding oracle without losing any security, in which case they end up agreeing on a secure key as defined in Definition 14.

5.2 Breaking 3-NIKE in the MGGM Without Zero-Test Queries

Lemma 17 (Group Elements' Structure in MGGM). *Consider a party* P *who interacts with an MGGM oracle. Suppose* P *receives an input* input *and when it starts to interact with its oracle, there are already γ values written in* Arr$_P$ *(i.e., $e = \gamma$ at the beginning).*[4] *For a fixed $k > \gamma$, suppose the algorithm* P *has just written (directly or through an* Add *query) in* Arr$_P[k]$ *(i.e., e has become k), while we have the answer to all of its previous* Aff *queries encoded in a vector* vec. *Then, for any such fixed choices of* input, k, vec, *there are constants* $f_1, \ldots, f_\gamma \in \mathbb{Z}_p$, *such that*

$$\mathsf{Arr}_P[k] = \sum_{i \in [\gamma]} f_i \cdot \mathsf{Arr}_P[i].$$

In particular, if no Aff *queries are asked, then for any fixed* input, k, *the value of* Arr$_P[k]$ *is a linear function of the γ group elements that are written in its oracle at the beginning.*

Proof. This observation is used in previous papers (e.g., [FKL17]). In particular, the proof follows by a straightforward induction over k.

Definition 18 (Compatibility in MGGM). *For any $\mathcal{S} = \{s_1, \cdots, s_n\} \subseteq \{r_P, m_P, \overline{q}_P\}_{P \in \{A,B,C\}}$ in a 3-NIKE problem, we say they are compatible if there are internal randomness r_A, r_B, and r_C, using which if we run the protocol, then all $s_i \in S$ appears in the protocol. For example we say $\overline{q}_A$, m_A, and m_B are compatible if there exists r_A, r_B, and r_C using which if we run the protocol we have $\overline{q}_A = \overline{q}_A$, $m_A = m_A$, and $m_B = m_B$.*

Lemma 19 (Randomness Switching). *Consider a 3-NIKE protocol with no equality queries. Then for any* tran $\leftarrow$ trans, $r_A, r_A' \leftarrow r_A|$tran, $r_B \leftarrow r_B|$tran, *and* $r_C, r_C' \leftarrow r_C|$tran *following holds:*

$$\begin{aligned}
\mathsf{Key}_B&(r_B, \mathsf{tran}, \overline{q}_{r_A, r_B, r_C}) + \mathsf{Key}_B(r_B, \mathsf{tran}, \overline{q}_{r_A', r_B, r_C'}) \\
&= \mathsf{Key}_B(r_B, \mathsf{tran}, \overline{q}_{r_A, r_B, r_C'}) + \mathsf{Key}_B(r_B, \mathsf{tran}, \overline{q}_{r_A', r_B, r_C})
\end{aligned} \tag{7}$$

---

[4] One special case is that Arr$_P[1] = 1$, but this is not necessary in this Lemma 17.

Additionally, with probability $1 - 4\delta$ *over the randomness of* tran $\leftarrow$ **trans**, $r_A, r'_A \leftarrow r_A|$tran, $r_B \leftarrow r_B|$tran, *and* $r_C, r'_C \leftarrow r_C|$tran, *following holds:*

$$\mathsf{Key}_A(r_A, \mathsf{tran}, \overline{q}_{r_A, r_B, r_C}) + \mathsf{Key}_A(r'_A, \mathsf{tran}, \overline{q}_{r'_A, r_B, r'_C})$$
$$= \mathsf{Key}_C(r'_C, \mathsf{tran}, \overline{q}_{r_A, r_B, r'_C}) + \mathsf{Key}_A(r'_A, \mathsf{tran}, \overline{q}_{r'_A, r_B, r_C}) \tag{8}$$

Proof. By Lemma 17, the final key of Bob is of the following form:

$$\mathsf{key}_B = \mathsf{Key}_B(r_B, \mathsf{tran}, \overline{q}_{r_A, r_B, r_C})$$
$$= f_{B,B}(r_B, \mathsf{tran}) + \sum_{i=1}^{d} f_{B,A,i}(r_B, \mathsf{tran})q_{A,i} + \sum_{i=1}^{d} f_{B,C,i}(r_B, \mathsf{tran})q_{C,i}$$

Therefore we have:

$$\mathsf{Key}_B(r_B, \mathsf{tran}, \overline{q}_{r_A, r_B, r_C}) + \mathsf{Key}_B(r_B, \mathsf{tran}, \overline{q}_{r'_A, r_B, r'_C})$$
$$= \left(f_{B,B}(r_B, \mathsf{tran}) + \sum_{i=1}^{d} f_{B,A,i}(r_B, \mathsf{tran})q_{A,i} + \sum_{i=1}^{d} f_{B,C,i}(r_B, \mathsf{tran})q_{C,i} \right)$$
$$+ \left(f_{B,B}(r_B, \mathsf{tran}) + \sum_{i=1}^{d} f_{B,A,i}(r_B, \mathsf{tran})q'_{A,i} + \sum_{i=1}^{d} f_{B,C,i}(r_B, \mathsf{tran})q'_{C,i} \right)$$
$$+ \left(f_{B,B}(r_B, \mathsf{tran}) + \sum_{i=1}^{d} f_{B,A,i}(r_B, \mathsf{tran})q'_{A,i} + \sum_{i=1}^{d} f_{B,C,i}(r_B, \mathsf{tran})q_{C,i} \right)$$
$$+ \left(f_{B,B}(r_B, \mathsf{tran}) + \sum_{i=1}^{d} f_{B,A,i}(r_B, \mathsf{tran})q_{A,i} + \sum_{i=1}^{d} f_{B,C,i}(r_B, \mathsf{tran})q'_{C,i} \right)$$
$$= \mathsf{Key}_B(r_B, \mathsf{tran}, \overline{q}_{r'_A, r_B, r_C}) + \mathsf{Key}_B(r_B, \mathsf{tran}, \overline{q}_{r_A, r_B, r'_C})$$

This proves Eq. 7.

We say event E_{r_A, r_B, r_C} holds if Alice, Bob and Charlie when executed using randomness r_A, r_B, and r_C, agree on a key. namely:

$$\mathsf{Key}_A(r_A, \mathsf{tran}, \overline{q}_{r_A, r_B, r_C}) = \mathsf{Key}_B(r_B, \mathsf{tran}, \overline{q}_{r_A, r_B, r_C}) = \mathsf{Key}_C(r_C, \mathsf{tran}, \overline{q}_{r_A, r_B, r_C})$$

Note that by reverse sampling, the marginal distribution of $(r_A, r_B, r_C, \mathsf{tran})$ is the same as the marginal distribution of $(r'_A, r'_B, r'_C, \mathsf{tran}')$, where $(r_A, r_B, r_C) \leftarrow (r_A, r_B, r_C)$, tran is the transcript when we run the protocol with r_A, r_B, r_C, tran$' \leftarrow$ **trans**, and $(r'_A, r'_B, r'_C) \leftarrow (r_A|\mathsf{tran}', r_B|\mathsf{tran}', r_C|\mathsf{tran}')$. Thus any r_A, r_B, and r_C where tran $\leftarrow$ **trans**, $r_A \leftarrow r_A|$tran, $r_B \leftarrow r_B|$tran, and $r_C \leftarrow r_C|$tran, agree on a key with probability $1 - \delta$. Let $E^* = E_{r_A, r_B, r_C} \wedge E_{r'_A, r_B, r_C} \wedge E_{r_A, r_B, r'_C} \wedge E_{r'_A, r_B, r'_C}$, then by a union bound over the complements of the events on the right hand side of the equation, we have:

$$\Pr_{\mathsf{tran} \leftarrow \mathbf{trans}, r_A, r'_A \leftarrow r_A|\mathsf{tran}, r_B \leftarrow r_B|\mathsf{tran}, r_C, r'_C \leftarrow r_C|\mathsf{tran}} [E^*] \geq 1 - 4\delta \tag{9}$$

We finally use Eq. 9 to conclude the proof of Eq. 8 by switching the corresponding keys in Eq. 7.

Theorem 20 (Breaking 3-NIKE protocols without zero-test queries).
Suppose Π is a 3-NIKE protocol in the MGGM with no Equal *or* Zero *queries (i.e., $\beta = 0$) and completeness error δ. Then, there is an adversary Eve who, given the transcript* tran *and oracle access to the 3γ broadcast group elements finds Alice's key with probability $1 - 4\delta$ by asking $O(\alpha)$ queries to its* Add *oracle.*

Proof. Note that in a 3-NIKE in MGGM, by sampling r_P, $\{\overline{q}_P, m_P\}$ will also be sampled, and m_P only depends on r_P; namely, we can sample a randomness r_P such that (r_P, m_P) is compatible without any query to the MGGM operators. Thus in Lemma 19, given a transcript tran, we can sample any r_P with out any additional queries to the oracle.

Now to break the original protocol where Alice, Bob, and Charlie's respective internal randomness are r_A, r_B, and r_C, and their respective set of copied group elements and messages are $(\overline{q}_A, m_A)$, $(\overline{q}_B, m_B)$, and $(\overline{q}_C, m_C)$, consider the following attack:

Eve samples a new Alice $r'_A \leftarrow (r_A | \text{tran})$ and a new Charlie $r'_C \leftarrow (r_C | \text{tran})$, and computes their respective vector of copied group elements $\overline{q}'_A$, and $\overline{q}'_C$ by running their algorithms. Then Eve finds key_A as follows:

$$\text{key}_E = \text{Key}_E(r'_A, r'_C, \overline{q}_A, \overline{q}_B, \overline{q}_C, \overline{q}'_A, \overline{q}'_C, \text{tran})$$

$$= \text{Key}_C(r'_C, \text{tran}, \overline{q}_{r_A, r_B, r'_C}) + \text{Key}_A(r'_A, \text{tran}, \overline{q}_{r'_A, r_B, r_C}) - \text{Key}_A(r'_A, \text{tran}, \overline{q}_{r'_A, r_B, r'_C})$$

First note that Eve needs only $O(\alpha)$ queries to calculate the above formula. To prove that this is the actual key, first note that by reverse sampling the distribution of $(r_A, r_B, r_C) \leftarrow (r_A, r_B, r_C)$ is the same as the distribution of $(r_A, r_B, r_C) \leftarrow (r_A | \text{tran}, r_B | \text{tran}, r_C | \text{tran})$ where tran $\leftarrow \mathbf{trans}$. Thus we can w.l.o.g. assume that first the transcript was sampled and then Alice, Bob, and Charlie were sampled conditioned on the transcript. Now by Lemma 19, the following holds with probability at least $1 - 4\delta$:

$$\text{key}_E = \text{Key}_A(r_A, \text{tran}, \overline{q}_{r_A, r_B, r_C})$$

So Eve finds the key with probability $1 - 4\delta$ with $O(\alpha)$ queries.

5.3   Breaking 3-NIKE in the MGGM with Zero-Test Queries

Theorem 21 (Breaking 3-NIKE protocols with equality queries). *Suppose Π is a 3-NIKE protocol in the MGGM with parameters $\alpha, \beta, \gamma \leq \mathsf{poly}(\lambda)$ and completeness error δ (see Definition 14). Then, there is an adversary who, given the transcript* tran *and oracle access to the 3γ broadcast group elements finds Alice's key with probability $1 - 4\delta - \delta'$ by asking $\mathsf{poly}(\lambda)$ queries to its MGGM oracle. In particular, E will ask an expected number of $O(\gamma\beta/\delta')$* Zero *queries and $O(\alpha)$* Add *queries.*

Corollary: quadratic attack in MGGM. If honest parities ask n parties to their oracle and agree on a key with probability ≥ 0.99, then we have $\alpha, \beta, \gamma \leq n$.

In this case, E can choose $\delta' = 0.01$, and so it can find Alice's key with probability at least 0.95 by asking $O(n^2)$ queries in total.

In the rest of this subsection, we prove Theorem 21.

Before presenting the attack, we go over some relevant definitions.

Definition 22 (Notation and notions for the attack). *In the following, let fix γ to be known, and let $\mathsf{Aff}_\gamma = \mathbb{Z}_p^{\gamma+1}$. We interpret each $f = (a_0, \ldots, a_\gamma) \in \mathsf{Aff}_\gamma$ as an affine function from $\mathbb{Z}^\gamma$ to $\mathbb{Z}$ that maps $x = (x_1, \ldots, x_\gamma) \in \mathbb{Z}_p^\gamma$ to $f(x) = a_0 + \sum_{i \in [\gamma]} a_i \, x_i$. Using any such f, we can obtain two linear constraints: an equality $f(x) = 0$ and an inequality $f(x) \neq 0$. We represent the former constraint using (f, eql) and the latter as (f, nql). We call LinCon a set of linear constraints if LinCon contains elements that are of the form (f, c) where $f \in \mathsf{Aff}_\gamma, c \in \{\mathsf{eql}, \mathsf{nql}\}$. We say x satisfies the linear constraint (f, c), if $f(x) = 0$ for $c = \mathsf{eql}$ and $f(x) \neq 0$ for $c = \mathsf{nql}$. We say that x satisfies a set LinCon of linear constraints, if x satisfies all of the linear constraints in LinCon. For any party, let $\mathsf{LinEq}_\mathsf{P} = \{f \mid (f, \mathsf{eql}) \in \mathsf{LinCon}_\mathsf{P}\}$ be the set of linear equality constraints for party P. For two sets $\mathsf{LinEq}_\mathsf{B}, \mathsf{LinEq}_\mathsf{C} \subseteq \mathsf{Aff}_\gamma$ interpreted as affine constraints over two different set of variables, we define their combination $\mathsf{LinEq}_{\mathsf{B,C}} \subset \mathbb{Z}_{2\gamma+1}$ as the set of all vectors $(a_0, a_{\mathsf{B},1}, \ldots, a_{\mathsf{B},\gamma}, a_{\mathsf{C},1}, \ldots, a_{\mathsf{C},\gamma})$, such that either*

$$(a_0, a_{\mathsf{B},1}, \ldots, a_{\mathsf{B},\gamma}) \mathsf{LinEq}_\mathsf{B} \wedge (a_{\mathsf{C},1}, \ldots, a_{\mathsf{C},\gamma}) = (0, \ldots, 0)$$

or

$$(a_0, a_{\mathsf{C},1}, \ldots, a_{\mathsf{C},\gamma}) \in \mathsf{LinEq}_\mathsf{C} \wedge (a_{\mathsf{B},1}, \ldots, a_{\mathsf{B},\gamma}) = (0, \ldots, 0).$$

For a party P, a message m_P (sent by that party), and set of linear constraints LinCon, we define $\mathcal{R}_\mathsf{P} = \mathcal{R}_\mathsf{P}(\mathsf{LinCon}, \mathsf{m}_\mathsf{P})$ to be the set of random seeds for party P that are compatible with LinCon and m_P; namely, $r \in \mathcal{R}_\mathsf{P}$ if by using r, P outputs the message m_P and group elements $x = (x_1, \ldots, x_\gamma)$ (to be sent to other parties) such that x satisfies LinCon. For any distribution D over $\mathbb{Z}_p^\gamma$, we call $f \in \mathsf{Aff}_\gamma$ (interpreted as an equality constraint) ε-heavy for D, if $\Pr_{x \leftarrow D}[f(x) = 0] \geq \varepsilon$. We say that f is ε-heavy for party P conditioned on $(\mathsf{LinCon}, \mathsf{m}_\mathsf{P})$, if f is ε-heavy for the uniform D that is obtained by sampling $\mathsf{r} \leftarrow \mathcal{R}_\mathsf{P}(\mathsf{LinCon}, \mathsf{m}_\mathsf{P})$, and obtaining the γ shared group elements generated by party P from r; namely, if we sample a random seed for the party P conditioned on its message m_P and the linear constraints in LinCon over its produced group elements $x = (x_1, \ldots, x_\gamma)$ (to be sent to other parties), then x will satisfy f (as an equality) with probability at least ε. For any set of vectors V of the same dimension, $\mathsf{Span}(V)$ refers to their span using coefficients in $\mathbb{Z}_p$.

Construction 23 (Attack on protocols with zero tests). *The adversary E attacks 3-NIKE protocols with zero test queries as follows.*

- **Inputs to E:** *The adversary has access to $\mathsf{tran} = (\mathsf{m}_\mathsf{A}, \mathsf{m}_\mathsf{B}, \mathsf{m}_\mathsf{C})$ and has oracle access to an array that contains $1 + 3\gamma$ group elements: the first one being 1 followed by the 3γ group elements that are broadcast by $\mathsf{A}, \mathsf{B}, \mathsf{C}$. The adversary is also given an input parameter $\varepsilon \in (0, 1)$.*

    The attack has two phases, a learning phase followed by a sample phase.

- **Learning phase:** *Originally let three sets of linear constraints* LinCon$_P$, $P \in \{A, B, C\}$ *to be empty sets, and define* $\mathcal{R}_P$ *be the corresponding set of random seeds for the party* P *that is compatible with* m$_P$ *and the linear constraints* LinCon$_P$ *(see Definition 22).*

  Recall LinEq$_P = \{f \mid (f, \mathsf{eql}) \in \mathsf{LinCon}_P\}$. *Then, as long as there is any party* $P \in \{A, B, C\}$ *and any* $f \in \mathcal{A}\mathrm{ff}_\gamma$ *such that (1)* $f \notin \mathsf{Span}(\mathsf{LinEq}_P)$, *and (2)* f *(as a linear equality) is* ε-*heavy for party* P *conditioned on* $(\mathsf{m}_P, \mathsf{LinCon}_P)$, *then pick (the first lexicographic such)* f *and ask the corresponding* Zero *query from* Arr$_E$ *over the group elements shared by* P *to find out whether* $f(\overline{\mathsf{q}}_P) = 0$ *or not. If* $f(\overline{\mathsf{q}}_P) = 0$, *then add* (f, eql) *to* LinCon$_P$, *and add* (f, nql) *to* LinCon$_P$ *otherwise. Proceed to the next phase when no* ε-*heavy remains.*

- **Sampling phase:** *For the 3-NIKE protocol* (A', B', C') *defined below (in which no affine queries are asked) use the attack of Theorem 20 to find a key* key$_{A'}$ *for* A' *and output that key. For the fixed values of* $(\mathsf{LinCon}_P, \mathsf{m}_P), P \in \{A, B, C\}$, A', B', C', *work as follows.*

  1. *Party* $P \in \{A', B', C'\}$ *uniformly will pick* r$_P \in \mathcal{R}(\mathsf{m}_P, \mathsf{LinCon}_P)$. *Then,* P *will send the corresponding message* m$_P$ *and group elements* $\overline{\mathsf{q}}_P = (\mathsf{q}_{P,1}, \cdots, \mathsf{q}_{P,\gamma})$ *that are uniquely produced using* r$_P$. *Note that the messages of the parties will remain the same as the one fixed in the previous phase (e.g.,* m$_{A'}$ = m$_A$), *but their broadcast group elements might change. We explain the next step only for* A'; *algorithms for* B', C' *are similar.*

  2. *Party* A' *will run the same algorithm as* A *using* r$_{A'}$, *but when it comes to any* Zero *query* t, P' *will not ask it from its oracle and instead will do the following. By Lemma 17, any* Zero *query* t *by* A' *is equivalent to asking a query* $t' = (t_0, t_{B',1}, \ldots, t_{B',\gamma}, t_{C',1}, \ldots, t_{C',\gamma}) \in \mathbb{Z}_{2\gamma+1}$ *over the* 2γ *group elements* $\overline{\mathsf{q}}_{B'}, \overline{\mathsf{q}}_{C'}$ *that are copied to the array of* A' *by parties* B', C'. *Informally speaking,* t' *will be answered 1 if and only if this can be concluded from the equality constraints for* B, C. *More formally, let* LinEq$_{B,C} \subset \mathbb{Z}_{2\gamma+1}$ *be the combination of* LinEq$_B$, LinEq$_C$ *as in Definition 22, and answer the* Zero *query* t' *by 1 if and only if* $t' \in \mathsf{Span}(\mathsf{LinEq}_{B,C})$. *If* $t' \in \mathsf{Span}(\mathsf{LinEq}_{B,C})$, *we call* t' *a trivial query. After emulating* A, A' *will output the key* key$_{A'}$ *that* A *would output.*

Lemma 24 (Efficiency). *The expected number of zero-test queries asked by* E *in Construction 23 is* $\leq 3\gamma/\varepsilon$.

Proof. We prove that the expected number of the queries that E asks for each party $P \in \{A, B, C\}$ is at most γ/ε. Then, the lemma follows from the linearity of expectation. Now for a party P let $f_1, f_2, \cdots$ be the sequence of the queries that E asks, and if a query is not asked we let it be $\bot$. Let $p_i = \Pr[f_i \neq \bot]$. Let t be a random variable of the number of the zero-test queries that E ask over $\overline{\mathsf{q}}_P$, then $\mathbb{E}[t] = \sum p_i$. Additionally define ZT to be the set of *all* zero-tests that pass over $\overline{\mathsf{q}}_P$. Note that ZT is a random variable determined by the randomness of Alice. Moreover, define random variables $S_i = \mathsf{Span}(f_j \mid f_j \in \mathsf{ZT}$ for $j \leq i)$ $d_i = \dim(S_i)$. Note that as $\dim(\mathsf{ZT}) \leq \gamma$, $d_i \leq \gamma$ for all i. Now we claim that

$$\mathbb{E}[d_i] - \mathbb{E}[d_{i-1}] \geq p_i \cdot \varepsilon. \tag{10}$$

Since d_i is either d_{i-1} or $d_{i-1} + 1$, we have $\mathbb{E}[d_i] - \mathbb{E}[d_{i-1}] = \mathbb{E}[d_i - d_{i-1}] = \Pr[d_i = d_{i-1} + 1]$. By the definition, if $f_i \neq \bot$, then $f_i \notin S_{i-1}$, thus we have:

$$\Pr[d_i = d_{i-1} + 1] = \mathbb{E}_{f_1, \dots, f_{i-1}} \Pr[f_i \neq \bot \wedge f_i \in \mathsf{ZT} \mid f_1, \dots, f_{i-1}]$$

$$= \Pr[f_i \neq \bot \mid f_1, \dots, f_{i-1}] \cdot \Pr[f_i \in \mathsf{ZT} \mid f_1, \dots, f_{i-1}, f_i \neq \bot].$$

By the definition it holds that $\Pr[f_i \in \mathsf{ZT} \mid f_1, \dots, f_{i-1}, f_i \neq \bot] \geq \varepsilon$, and so

$$\Pr[d_i = d_{i-1} + 1] \geq \varepsilon \cdot \mathbb{E}_{f_1, \dots, f_{i-1}} \Pr[f_i \neq \bot \mid f_1, \dots, f_{i-1}] = \varepsilon \cdot p_i.$$

So we have proved the claim of Eq. 10. Note that the total number of linear constraints over γ variables is $p^{\gamma+1}$. Thus using Eq. 10 we have:

$$\sum_{i=q}^{p^{\gamma+1}} \mathbb{E}[d_i] \geq \sum_{i=1}^{p^{\gamma+1}} \mathbb{E}[d_{i-1}] + \sum_{i=0}^{p^{\gamma+1}} p_i . \varepsilon.$$

$$\to \gamma \geq \mathbb{E}[d_{p^{\gamma+1}}] \geq \sum_{i=0}^{p^{\gamma+1}} p_i . \varepsilon.$$

$$\to \gamma/\varepsilon \geq \mathbb{E}[d_{p^{\gamma+1}}] \geq \sum_{i=0}^{p^{\gamma+1}} p_i = \mathbb{E}[t].$$

This concludes the proof.

We will prove the following technical lemma, which will be useful for proving the success probability of the adversary of Construction 23.

Lemma 25 (Heaviness of pure vs. impure constraints). *Suppose we have*

1. *D_1 and D_2 are two distributions over $\mathbb{Z}_p^\gamma$.*
2. *$D_{1,2}$ is the distribution over $\mathbb{Z}_p^{2\gamma}$ that is obtained by independently sampling $\overline{x} = (x_1, \cdots, x_\gamma) \leftarrow D_1, \overline{y} = (y_1, \cdots, y_\gamma) \leftarrow D_2$ and outputting the vector $(\overline{x}, \overline{y})$ of dimension 2γ.*
3. *$\mathsf{LinEq}_1, \mathsf{LinEq}_2$ are subsets of $\mathsf{Aff}_\gamma = \mathbb{Z}_p^{\gamma+1}$.*
4. *If $\mathsf{P} \in \{1, 2\}$ and $f \in \mathsf{Aff}_\gamma$ is ε-heavy for D_P, then $f \in \mathsf{Span}(\mathsf{LinEq}_\mathsf{P})$.*

Then, for every $f \in \mathsf{Aff}_{2\gamma}$ that is ε-heavy for $D_{1,2}$, it holds that $f \in \mathsf{Span}(\mathsf{LinEq}_{1,2})$, where $\mathsf{LinEq}_{1,2}$ is the combination of $\mathsf{LinEq}_1, \mathsf{LinEq}_2$ as in Definition 22.

Proof. Let $f = (a_0, a_{1,1}, \cdots, a_{1,\gamma}, a_{2,1}, \cdots, a_{2,\gamma})$ be ε-heavy for $D_{1,2}$. For $j \in [p]$ define $\varepsilon_{1,j}$, and $\varepsilon_{2,j}$ as follows:

$$\Pr_{x \leftarrow D_1} \left[\sum_{i=1}^\gamma a_{1,i} x_i + j = 0 \mod p \right] = \varepsilon_{1,j},$$

$$\Pr_{y \leftarrow D_2} \left[\sum_{i=1}^\gamma a_{2t,i} x_i + a_0 - j = 0 \mod p \right] = \varepsilon_{2,j}.$$

Therefore, we have

$$\sum_{j=1}^{p} \varepsilon_{1,j}.\varepsilon_{2,j} = \Pr[f(\overline{x},\overline{y}) = 0] \geq \varepsilon.$$

Because $\sum_j \varepsilon_{1,j} = \sum_j \varepsilon_{2,j} = 1$, there are $j_1, j_2 \in [p]$ such that $\varepsilon_{1,j_1}, \varepsilon_{2,j_2} \geq \varepsilon$, and so $f_1 = (j_1, a_{1,1}, \cdots, a_{1,\gamma})$ is ε-heavy for D_1 and $f_2 = (a_0 - j_2, a_{2,1}, \cdots, a_{2,\gamma})$ is ε-heavy for D_2. Therefore, by Item 4, $f_1 \in \mathsf{Span}(\mathsf{LinEq}_1)$ and $f_2 \in \mathsf{Span}(\mathsf{LinEq}_2)$, which means $\varepsilon_{1,j_1} = \varepsilon_{2,j_2} = 1$. Furthermore, $\sum_{j=1}^{p} \varepsilon_{1,j} \cdot \varepsilon_{2,j}$ is 1 if $j_1 = j_2$ and is 0 otherwise. Since $\sum_{j=1}^{p} \varepsilon_{1,j}.\varepsilon_{2,j} \geq \varepsilon$, then $j_1 = j_2$. This means that $f \in \mathsf{Span}(\mathsf{LinEq}_{1,2})$.

For the next two lemmas, let $\mathsf{LinCon} = (\mathsf{LinCon}_P)_{P \in \{A,B,C\}}$ be the set of linear constraints discovered by E at the end of the learning phase in Construction 23.

Lemma 26 (Independence of random seeds). *For every fixed* tran, LinCon *at the end of learning phase, the following two distributions are the same:*

- *The joint distribution over the randomness of* A, B, C *conditioned on being compatible with* tran, LinCon.
- *Independently sampling randomness of each party* P *conditioned on being compatible with* (m_P, LinCon_P) *(and putting them together).*

Proof. The proof is similar to the observation that parties' randomness in interactive protocols, conditioned on the transcript, is always a product distribution.

If (r_A, r_B, r_C) is compatible with tran, LinCon, then clearly r_P is compatible with m_P, LinCon_P for all $P \in \{A, B, C\}$ as well. The more interesting observation is the reverse: if r_P is compatible with m_P, LinCon_P for all $P \in \{A, B, C\}$, then (r_A, r_B, r_C) is compatible with tran, LinCon. That is because, these local compatibilities will guarantee that the protocol will proceed consistently as a whole.

Lemma 27 (Statistical closeness of two protocols). *For every* tran, LinCon *at the end of learning phase, sample* r_A, r_B, r_C, *while* $r_P, P \in \{A, B, C\}$ *is sampled (only) conditioned on being compatible with* m_P, LinCon_P. *Then, do as follows.*

1. *Run the protocol* Π *(with zero-test queries) using the random seeds* r_A, r_B, r_C *and output the keys that the parties generate* $(\mathsf{key}_A, \mathsf{key}_B, \mathsf{key}_C)$.
2. *Run the protocol* Π' *(without zero-test queries) using the random seeds* r_A, r_B, r_C *and output the keys that parties generate* $(\mathsf{key}_{A'}, \mathsf{key}_{B'}, \mathsf{key}_{C'})$.

Then, for every fixed tran, LinCon *at the end of learning phase, with probability at least* $1 - 3\beta \cdot \varepsilon$ *over the randomness of sampling the random seeds, it holds that* $\mathsf{key}_P = \mathsf{key}_{P'}$ *for all* $P \in \{A, B, C\}$ *(simultaneously).*

Proof. For the same set of tran, LinCon and random seeds r_A, r_B, r_C the two protocols Π, Π' produce the same keys for the same parties if all the non-trivial zero-test queries are answered negatively.

We now prove that this is indeed the case, by proving that the two games will proceed the same with probability $1 - 3\beta \cdot \varepsilon$.

We define $3\beta + 1$ games $\Pi = \Pi_0, \ldots, \Pi_{3\beta} = \Pi'$ as follows. Let us imagine running A first, then B, and then C. This means that we have a total order on the 3β queries asked by them. In Π_i, the first i zero-test queries are answered similarly to Π' (i.e., using canonical answers) and the rest of them are answered similarly to how Π does answer them.

Let E_i be the event, defined in both Π_i and Π_{i-1}, that the answer to the ith query is not trivially yes, but it is indeed answered to be yes if asked from the real oracle (as if we are in Π_{i-1}). Note that the probability of E_i is the same in both Π_i and Π_{i-1}, and E_i happening is the only way that these experiments differ. All we have to do is to show that the probability of E_i is at most ε.

Suppose $\Pr[E_i] > \varepsilon$, and for simplicity suppose ith query is asked by A. Then, due to the independence of the random r_A, r_B, r_C, there is a way to fix r_A to r_A^0, such that $\Pr[E_i \mid r_A^0] > 0$. Fixing r_A^0 will fix the coefficients of the ith zero test. This means that there will be an affine test over the group elements shared by B, C that is zero with probability $> \varepsilon$. By Lemma 25, it means that for either of $P \in \{B, C\}$, there is an affine test over the group elements shared by P that is ε heavy, while it is not learned by E, which is a contradiction.

Finally, we prove Theorem 21 using the lemmas above.

Proof (of Theorem 21). The efficiency of the attacker of Construction 23 follows directly from Lemma 24. So, in the rest of the proof we focus on the success probability of the adversary in guessing Alice's key.

Let r_A, r_B, r_C be the randomness of the parties, tran be the transcript, and $\mathsf{LinCon} = (\mathsf{LinCon}_P)_{P \in \{A,B,C\}}$ be the result of the learning phase. Define $\delta_{\mathsf{tran},\mathsf{LinCon}}$ to be the completeness error *only conditioned* on $(\mathsf{tran}, \mathsf{LinCon})$. Then, we have $\mathbb{E}_{\mathsf{tran},\mathsf{LinCon}}[\delta_{\mathsf{tran},\mathsf{LinCon}}] = \delta$. We claim that for every fixed $(\mathsf{tran}, \mathsf{LinCon})$, the adversary finds Alice's true key with probability at least $1 - 4(3\beta\varepsilon + \delta_{\mathsf{tran},\mathsf{LinCon}}) - 3\beta\varepsilon$. Below, we prove this. By Lemma 26, sampling r_A, r_B, r_C *jointly* conditioned on $(\mathsf{tran}, \mathsf{LinCon})$ (which itself is equivalent to sampling everything according to the real protocol Π) is equivalent to sampling r_P independently only conditioned on (m_P, LinCon_P) for all $P \in \{A, B, C\}$. By Lemma 27, if we use the randomness r_A, r_B, r_C to run protocols Π or Π', with probability at least $1 - 3\beta\varepsilon$, the same set of keys will be produced.

Therefore, conditioned on $(\mathsf{tran}, \mathsf{LinCon})$, the protocol Π' (which is defined based on $\mathsf{tran}, \mathsf{LinCon}$) has completeness error at most $3\beta\varepsilon + \delta_{\mathsf{tran},\mathsf{LinCon}}$. This means that the attacker of Construction 23 will find Alice's key in Π' with probability at least $1 - 4(3\beta\varepsilon + \delta_{\mathsf{tran},\mathsf{LinCon}})$. By another application of Lemma 27, this means that the *same* attacker is finding the true key of Alice (in Π) with probability at least $1 - 4(3\beta\varepsilon + \delta_{\mathsf{tran},\mathsf{LinCon}}) - 3\beta\varepsilon$.

Putting things together, E finds Alice's *true* key with probability at least

$$\mathbb{E}_{\mathsf{tran},\mathsf{LinCon}}[1 - 15\beta\varepsilon - 4\delta_{\mathsf{tran},\mathsf{LinCon}}] = 1 - 15\beta\varepsilon - 4\mathbb{E}_{\mathsf{tran},\mathsf{LinCon}}[\delta_{\mathsf{tran},\mathsf{LinCon}}] = 1 - 15\beta\varepsilon - 4\delta.$$

By choosing $15\beta\varepsilon = \delta'$, the probability of not finding Alice's key will be at most $4\delta + \delta'$, while the expected number of its queries during the learning phase will be $3\gamma/\varepsilon = 45\gamma \cdot \beta/\delta'$.

References

[BC22] Brzuska, C., Couteau, G.: On building fine-grained one-way functions from strong average-case hardness. In: Dunkelman, O., Dziembowski, S. (eds.) EUROCRYPT 2022, Part II. LNCS, vol. 13276, pp. 584–613. Springer, Heidelberg (2022). https://doi.org/10.1007/978-3-031-07085-3_20

[BGI08] Biham, E., Goren, Y.J., Ishai, Y.: Basing weak public-key cryptography on strong one-way functions. In: Canetti, R. (ed.) TCC 2008. LNCS, vol. 4948, pp. 55–72. Springer, Heidelberg (2008). https://doi.org/10.1007/978-3-540-78524-8_4

[BHK+11] Brassard, G., Høyer, P., Kalach, K., Kaplan, M., Laplante, S., Salvail, L.: Merkle puzzles in a quantum world. In: Rogaway, P. (ed.) CRYPTO 2011. LNCS, vol. 6841, pp. 391–410. Springer, Heidelberg (2011). https://doi.org/10.1007/978-3-642-22792-9_22

[BJK+18] Brakerski, Z., Jain, A., Komargodski, I., Passelègue, A., Wichs, D.: Nontrivial witness encryption and null-iO from standard assumptions. In: Catalano, D., De Prisco, R. (eds.) SCN 2018. LNCS, vol. 11035, pp. 425–441. Springer, Cham (2018). https://doi.org/10.1007/978-3-319-98113-0_23

[BM09] Barak, B., Mahmoody-Ghidary, M.: Merkle puzzles are optimal — an $O(n^2)$-query attack on any key exchange from a random oracle. In: Halevi, S. (ed.) CRYPTO 2009. LNCS, vol. 5677, pp. 374–390. Springer, Heidelberg (2009). https://doi.org/10.1007/978-3-642-03356-8_22

[BM17] Barak, B., Mahmoody-Ghidary, M.: Merkle's key agreement protocol is optimal: an $O(n^2)$ attack on any key agreement from random oracles. J. Cryptol. **30**(3), 699–734 (2017)

[BMG07] Barak, B., Mahmoody-Ghidary, M.: Lower bounds on signatures from symmetric primitives. In: 48th Annual IEEE Symposium on Foundations of Computer Science (FOCS 2007), pp. 680–688. IEEE (2007)

[BRSV17] Ball, M., Rosen, A., Sabin, M., Vasudevan, P.N.: Average-case fine-grained hardness. In: 49th ACM STOC, pp. 483–496. ACM Press, June 2017

[BRSV18] Ball, M., Rosen, A., Sabin, M., Vasudevan, P.N.: Proofs of work from worst-case assumptions. In: Shacham, H., Boldyreva, A. (eds.) CRYPTO 2018, Part I. LNCS, vol. 10991, pp. 789–819. Springer, Cham (2018). https://doi.org/10.1007/978-3-319-96884-1_26

[BZ14] Boneh, D., Zhandry, M.: Multiparty key exchange, efficient traitor tracing, and more from indistinguishability obfuscation. In: Garay, J.A., Gennaro, R. (eds.) CRYPTO 2014, Part I. LNCS, vol. 8616, pp. 480–499. Springer, Heidelberg (2014). https://doi.org/10.1007/978-3-662-44371-2_27

[CG18] Campanelli, M., Gennaro, R.: Fine-grained secure computation. In: Beimel, A., Dziembowski, S. (eds.) TCC 2018, Part II. LNCS, vol. 11240, pp. 66–97. Springer, Cham (2018). https://doi.org/10.1007/978-3-030-03810-6_3

[DH76] Diffie, W., Hellman, M.E.: New directions in cryptography. IEEE Trans. Inf. Theory **22**(6), 644–654 (1976)

[DH21] Dinur, I., Hasson, B.: Distributed Merkle's puzzles. In: Nissim, K., Waters, B. (eds.) TCC 2021, Part II. LNCS, vol. 13043, pp. 310–332. Springer, Cham (2021). https://doi.org/10.1007/978-3-030-90453-1_11

[DHH+21] Döttling, N., Hartmann, D., Hofheinz, D., Kiltz, E., Schäge, S., Ursu, B.: On the impossibility of purely algebraic signatures. In: Nissim, K., Waters, B. (eds.) TCC 2021, Part III. LNCS, vol. 13044, pp. 317–349. Springer, Cham (2021). https://doi.org/10.1007/978-3-030-90456-2_11

[DVV16]   Degwekar, Akshay, Vaikuntanathan, Vinod, Vasudevan, Prashant Nalini: Fine-Grained Cryptography. In: Robshaw, Matthew, Katz, Jonathan (eds.) CRYPTO 2016, Part III. LNCS, vol. 9816, pp. 533–562. Springer, Heidelberg (2016). https://doi.org/10.1007/978-3-662-53015-3_19

[EWT21]   Egashira, S., Wang, Y., Tanaka, K.: Fine-grained cryptography revisited. J. Cryptol. 34(3), 23 (2021)

[FHKP13] Freire, E.S.V., Hofheinz, D., Kiltz, E., Paterson, K.G.: Non-Interactive Key Exchange. In: Kurosawa, K., Hanaoka, G. (eds.) PKC 2013. LNCS, vol. 7778, pp. 254–271. Springer, Heidelberg (2013). https://doi.org/10.1007/978-3-642-36362-7_17

[FKL17]   G. Fuchsbauer, E. Kiltz, and J. Loss. The algebraic group model and its applications. Cryptology ePrint Archive, Paper 2017/620, 2017. https://eprint.iacr.org/2017/620

[GKRS22] Guo, S., Kamath, P., Rosen, A., Sotiraki, K.: Limits on the efficiency of (ring) LWE-based non-interactive key exchange. J. Cryptol. 35(1), 1 (2022)

[Jou00]   Joux, Antoine: A one round protocol for tripartite Diffie–Hellman. In: Bosma, Wieb (ed.) ANTS 2000. LNCS, vol. 1838, pp. 385–393. Springer, Heidelberg (2000). https://doi.org/10.1007/10722028_23

[LLW19]   LaVigne, Rio, Lincoln, Andrea, Vassilevska Williams, Virginia: Public-key cryptography in the fine-grained setting. In: Boldyreva, Alexandra, Micciancio, Daniele (eds.) CRYPTO 2019, Part III. LNCS, vol. 11694, pp. 605–635. Springer, Cham (2019). https://doi.org/10.1007/978-3-030-26954-8_20

[Mau05]   Maurer, Ueli: Abstract models of computation in cryptography. In: Smart, Nigel P.. (ed.) Cryptography and Coding 2005. LNCS, vol. 3796, pp. 1–12. Springer, Heidelberg (2005). https://doi.org/10.1007/11586821_1

[Mer74]   Merkle, R.: C.s. 244 project proposal. Facsimile (1974). http://www.merkle.com/1974

[Mer78]   Merkle, R.C.: Secure communications over insecure channels. Commun. ACM 21(4), 294–299 (1978)

[Pol75]   Pollard, J.M.: A monte Carlo method for factorization. BIT 15, 331–334 (1975). http://cr.yp.to/bib/entries.html#1975/pollard

[Sha71]   Shanks, D.: Class number, a theory of factorization, and genera. In: Proceedings of Symposium Mathematical Society, pp. 41–440 (1971)

[Sho97]   Shoup, V.: Lower bounds for discrete logarithms and related problems. In: Fumy, W. (ed.) EUROCRYPT 1997. LNCS, vol. 1233, pp. 256–266. Springer, Heidelberg (1997). https://doi.org/10.1007/3-540-69053-0_18

[WP22]   Wang, Y., Pan, J.: Non-interactive zero-knowledge proofs with fine-grained security. In: EUROCRYPT 2022, Part II. LNCS, vol. 13276, pp. 305–335. Springer, Heidelberg (2022). https://doi.org/10.1007/978-3-031-07085-3_11

[Zha22]   Zhandry, M.: To label, or not to label (in generic groups). In: Dodis, Y., Shrimpton, T. (eds.) CRYPTO 2022. LNCS, vol. 13509, pp. 66–96. Springer, Cham (2022). https://doi.org/10.1007/978-3-031-15982-4_3

Speak Much, Remember Little: Cryptography in the Bounded Storage Model, Revisited

Yevgeniy Dodis[1], Willy Quach[2(✉)], and Daniel Wichs[3]

[1] New York University, New York, NY 10012, USA
dodis@cs.nyu.edu
[2] Northeastern University, Boston, MA 02115, USA
quach.w@northeastern.edu
[3] NTT Research, Sunnyvale, CA 94085, USA
wichs@ccs.neu.edu

Abstract. The goal of the *bounded storage model (BSM)* is to construct unconditionally secure cryptographic protocols, by only restricting the storage capacity of the adversary, but otherwise giving it unbounded computational power. Here, we consider a *streaming* variant of the BSM, where honest parties can stream huge amounts of data to each other so as to overwhelm the adversary's storage, even while their own storage capacity is significantly smaller than that of the adversary. Prior works showed several impressive results in this model, including *key agreement* and *oblivious transfer*, but only as long as adversary's storage $m = O(n^2)$ is at most quadratically larger than the honest user storage n. Moreover, the work of Dziembowski and Maurer (DM) also gave a seemingly matching lower bound, showing that key agreement in the BSM is impossible when $m > n^2$.

In this work, we observe that the DM lower bound only applies to a significantly more restricted version of the BSM, and does not apply to the streaming variant. Surprisingly, we show that it is possible to construct key agreement and oblivious transfer protocols in the streaming BSM, where the adversary's storage can be significantly larger, and even exponential $m = 2^{O(n)}$. The only price of accommodating larger values of m is that the round and communication complexities of our protocols grow accordingly, and we provide lower bounds to show that an increase in rounds and communication is necessary.

As an added benefit of our work, we also show that our oblivious transfer (OT) protocol in the BSM satisfies a simulation-based notion of security. In contrast, even for the restricted case of $m = O(n^2)$, prior solutions

---

The full version of this paper is available online [13].

Y. Dodis—Supported by gifts from VMware Labs and Algorand, and NSF grants 2055578 and 1815546.

W. Quach—Part of this work was completed during an internship at NTT Research.

D. Wichs—Research supported by NSF grant CNS-1750795, CNS-2055510 and the Alfred P. Sloan Research Fellowship.

C. Hazay and M. Stam (Eds.): EUROCRYPT 2023, LNCS 14004, pp. 86–116, 2023.
https://doi.org/10.1007/978-3-031-30545-0_4

only satisfied a weaker indistinguishability based definition. As an application of our OT protocol, we get general multiparty computation (MPC) in the BSM that allows for up to exponentially large gaps between m and n, while also achieving simulation-based security.

1 Introduction

It is well known that Alice and Bob cannot agree on a shared secret by communicating over public (authentic) channel, when the eavesdropper Eve has unbounded computational resources. Thus, traditional cryptography assumes that Eve is "resource bounded", and most commonly, bounds her run time. Many key agreement schemes have been constructed in this setting, starting with the seminal work of Diffie and Hellman [8], under various computational hardness assumptions. Of course, the dream of cryptography is to construct unconditionally secure protocols, without relying on any unproven assumptions, but unfortunately, this is currently beyond our reach, as it easily implies $P \neq NP$.

In contrast, the *Bounded Storage Model* (BSM), introduced in the pioneering work of Maurer [29], *only* assumes that Eve has bounded space rather than time. A long series of works [1,4,5,9–11,15,17,19,21,26,28,35,36,39] showed that it is possible to construct many kinds of unconditionally secure cryptographic schemes in this model, including key agreement and oblivious transfer over a public channel, provided that Eve's storage is not too large.

It turns out that there are several related-but-different variants of the BSM. In this work, we focus on a natural variant, which we refer to as the "streaming BSM". We first discuss this model, which will be the default throughout the paper. We will compare the streaming BSM model to other variants from the literature further below.

"Streaming" BSM. In this model, parties can generate and send huge amounts of data to each other, but only have limited local memory. The model is parametrized by two parameters: the honest parties' space capacity n, and the attacker's space capacity m, where $m \gg n$. We assume parties operate in the streaming model: they generate/receive communication one bit at a time, while only maintaining a small local memory throughout. The total communication k can be huge, say $k \gg m \gg n$, and can occur over multiple back-and-forth rounds.

For example, Alice can stream a huge random string X of length k to Bob by sampling it one bit at a time; both Alice and Bob can store some small subset of n physical locations of X, or they can store the parity of X computed in a streaming manner, but neither of them can remember all of X. The attacker Eve is also streaming, just like Alice and Bob, but has much larger memory capacity $m \gg n$. We call the resulting model the (n, m)-BSM, and it will be the default throughout the paper; sometimes, we will explicitly refer to it as the "streaming BSM" to disambiguate from other variants.

Prior Results. As with computational cryptography, in the BSM we can consider a symmetric-key setting, where honest parties can share a short secret key that can be used to encrypt arbitrarily many messages over time, or a public-key setting, where no shared key is available. In both cases the parties can freely communicate over a public channel, and the goal is to achieve unconditional, information-theoretic (IT) security, without making any additional computational assumptions.

In the symmetric-key setting, a series of beautiful papers [1,11,15,17,26,28, 29,35,36,39] showed that it is possible to achieve arbitrarily large gaps between the space of the attacker and that of the honest parties, up to exponential: $m = 2^{O(n)}$. (Of course, the price of allowing large values of m is that the ciphertext size has to grow proportionally, to ensure that we eventually overwhelm the adversary's storage capacity to overcome the Shannon lower bound. Therefore, if we want to limit ourselves to schemes with polynomial ciphertext size, then m is limited to some arbitrarily large polynomial.)

Amazingly, it is even possible to construct unconditionally secure public-key schemes in the BSM, and prior works [4,5,9,10,19,21] constructed BSM schemes for key agreement (KA) and oblivious transfer (OT), which is then complete for all multi-party computation (MPC) [23,25]. However, all of the prior works in the public-key setting allowed at most a quadratic gap between the adversarial and the honest users storage: $m = O(n^2)$. In fact, the work of Dziembowski and Maurer [16] seemed to suggest that this limitation is inherent, by showing there is no KA protocol in the BSM when $m > n^2$. Since OT directly implies KA, the same lower bound also extends to OT. So it may have appeared that the question of designing public-key cryptographic primitives in the BSM had been settled.

Our Question and Main Result. However, as we observe in this work, and discuss in Sect. 1.1, the lower bound of [16] was only shown in a *restricted* version of the BSM model, and does not apply to the more general "streaming" BSM. Most significantly, the authors critically assumed that there is *at most one* "long" communication round in the key agreement protocol, where the length k of the streamed message overwhelms the storage capacity m of the attacker. While this restriction was satisfied by many prior work in the BSM (see Sect. 1.1), this opens the possibility that it might be possible to break the quadratic barrier of [16] when parties use the full streaming power of the BSM, including the ability to stream *several* "long" messages to each other. This is the main question of this work:

Main Question: *Do there exist unconditionally secure key agreement (KA) and oblivious transfer (OT) protocols in the streaming (n, m)-BSM, when m is allowed to be much larger than n^2?*

We answer this question in the *affirmative*, and show that we can allow arbitrarily large gaps between m and n, up to exponential $m = 2^{O(n)}$. Surprisingly, this shows that unlike time-bounded public-key cryptography,—where we must rely on *additional* computational assumptions,—space-bounded public-key cryptography can be proven *unconditionally*, while supporting *arbitrary gaps* between the powers of honest parties and the attacker. The price of allowing large values of m is that the round and communication complexities of the protocols grow correspondingly and we also provide a lower bound to show that this is inherent. In particular, this means that if we want limit ourselves to protocols with polynomial (round/communication) efficiency, then m is limited to be some arbitrarily large polynomial.

Before describing our results in detail, we start by describing the different variants of the BSM, to understand the gap that we crucially exploit between the model used in the lower bound of [16] and the model for our upper bounds.

1.1   Modeling Gap: Breaking the Quadratic Barrier

Many of the prior works in the BSM, including the original work of [29] and the lower bound of Dziembowski and Maurer [16], considered a more restricted model, that we refer to as the "traditional BSM" to disambiguate from the "streaming BSM". In particular, they consider a variant where a single long random string X is broadcast by a third party, and the honest users can store a small subset of n physical locations of X (chosen non-adaptively). The adversary can store arbitrary information about X, as long as the amount of information is bounded by m bits. After this occurs, the adversary's storage becomes unbounded, and the honest parties can run some additional protocol, whose overall space and communication complexity is bounded by n. Protocols in the traditional BSM readily translate into the streaming BSM, by having one of the users stream X as the first message of the protocol.[1]

Compared to the streaming BSM, the traditional BSM can be seen as imposing additional restrictions on the honest parties Alice and Bob, and giving more power to the space-bounded attacker Eve, as follows:

(a) *Restricting Number of "Long" Rounds.* We make a distinction between "long" rounds, in which one of the parties streams a long message consisting of more than m bits of data, versus "short" rounds, consisting of fewer than m bits of data. Note that Eve can store the entire message in a short round. The traditional BSM allows only a single "long" round—the very first round of the protocol.

(b) *Uniformly Random "Long Rounds".* The traditional BSM requires that a "long" round should simply stream a uniformly random string X. When true, such X is called a *randomizer string* [29], and can also come externally (e.g., from nature) rather than being sampled by the parties.

(c) *Local Computability for Alice/Bob.* In the streaming BSM, when a party Alice streams a long string X to an honest party Bob, then Bob is allowed to arbitrarily process all of X in a streaming manner, as long as not using more than n bits of space. The traditional BSM demands a stricter property of n-*Local Computability* (LC) [39]: The honest parties can only access at

---

[1] This holds generically in the case of KA. In the case of OT, where the participants can be malicious, it may not be generically safe to allow one of the parties to chose X instead of having it sampled by a trusted third party. However, it was safe to do so for all the protocols in the literature.

most n (a-prior non-adaptively chosen) *physical* locations of each string X sent during a "long" round. [2]

(d) *Unlimited Short-term Memory for Eve.* In the streaming BSM, the adversary Eve is streaming and only has m bits of memory throughout the execution of the protocol. In the traditional BSM, we only require that Eve stores at most m bits immediately after observing each "long" round, but we allow her to use unlimited short-term memory to process the round, and do not restrict her memory during "short" rounds.

Clearly, enforcing any of the restrictions (a)–(d) makes any upper bound stronger, and hence all protocols in the traditional BSM model also apply to the streaming BSM. Indeed, most previous constructions in the traditional BSM satisfied all of these additional properties. For example, the symmetric-key results of [1,15,28,39] satisfied all of (a)–(d), as did the public-key results for key agreement and oblivious transfer of [4,5,10]. However, there were exceptions, pointing to the fact that these restrictions were not all seen as crucial. For example, the work of [9] required two "long" rounds, and therefore did not satisfy (a). Moreover, if one wanted to use OT as a sub-protocol in general MPC, then this would require running many sequential copies, meaning that even if the OT protocol satisfied (a), the resulting MPC would not.

More recently, the ground-breaking work of Raz et al. [17,26,35,36] (presented in terms of time-space tradeoffs for learning parity), constructed elegant symmetric-key encryption schemes in the streaming BSM that crucially *do not* satisfy (b)–(d); see Sect. 1.4. The work of [19], then lifted the techniques of Raz et al. [17,26,35,36] to build key agreement, oblivious transfer and bit commitment protocols in the streaming BSM, without satisfying (b)–(d). Nevertheless, the protocols of [19] have some advantages over prior works in the traditional BSM, such as smaller number of communication rounds, and perfect correctness.

Overall, looking at the literature, it appears that many works implicitly viewed the streaming BSM as the real conceptual goal, but ended up satisfying additional properties (a)–(d) that they incorporated into their formal model. This view seems to be shared by the more recent works of [17,19,26,35,36] that did not satisfy the additional properties, but still continued to refer to their model as the BSM, without carefully distinguishing between the variants. We continue in this vein, and view the streaming BSM as the main notion to strive for, while achieving the additional restrictions (a)–(d) can be seen as a nice bonus, but is not essential.

Moving to the lower bound of Dziembowski and Maurer [16], it turns out it critically used restriction (a), namely that there is only a single long round having large communication. Hence, to overcome the quadratic barrier imposed by [16], our protocols must use multiple long rounds.

Interestingly, we will be able to do so while still satisfying the additional restrictions (b)–(d). In particular, our protocols contains many long rounds, each of which involves generating a long uniformly random string X, while the honest

---

[2] For example, if local computability is demanded, parties cannot compute the parity of all the bits of X.

parties store some small set of at most n physical locations of X. The adversary is only restricted to storing at most m bits of information about each X sent in a long round, but gets unlimited memory otherwise (i.e. during the short rounds and for computing the functions that compresses each X into m bits). However, we will mostly view these additional features as secondary, and focus most of our discussion on the fully unrestricted streaming BSM. If follow-up works manage to get further improvements by also dropping the restrictions (b)-(d), much like the works of [17,19,26,35,36], this would be "fair game" and satisfy the main goal from our point of view.

To sum up, even though many prior works already departed from the traditional BSM and considered the streaming BSM as the main model, when it comes to public-key schemes, all prior works in the BSM were stuck at the quadratic gap between honest and adversarial storage. On the other hand, the quadratic lower bound of [16] does not extend to the streaming BSM, which opens the door for our results.

1.2   Our Results

As our main positive results, we design protocols for key agreement (KA), oblivious transfer (OT) and general multiparty computation (MPC) in the (n, m)-BSM, supporting up to an exponential gap between the honest user and adversary storage: $m = 2^{O(n)}$. This *qualitatively matches the positive results in the space-bounded symmetric-key setting*, albeit in (substantially) more rounds. In fact, we also show that large number of long rounds (and also overall large communication complexity) is essential when $m \gg n^2$, by non-trivially extending the lower bound of [16] to general BSM protocols. Details follow.

Key Agreement in BSM. Recall, the goal of a KA protocol is for Alice and Bob agree on a ℓ-bit key while talking over an authenticated-but-public channel. In Sect. 5, we show the following result in the (n, m)-BSM:

Theorem 1 (informal). *For any m, λ, there exists some $n_{min} = O(\log m + \lambda)$ such that for all $n \geq n_{min}$ there is an unconditionally secure key agreement protocol in the (n, m)-BSM that outputs an $\Omega(n)$-bit key and achieves security $2^{-\Omega(\lambda)}$. Furthermore:*

- *The number of rounds is $\widetilde{O}(\lceil m/n^2 \rceil \cdot \lambda)$.*
- *The communication complexity is $\widetilde{O}(m\lceil m/n^2 \rceil \cdot \lambda)$.*

Note that, although the adversary's storage bound m can even be exponentially larger than n, this comes at the cost of increasing the number of rounds and bits of communication. If we want the overall protocol to be polynomially efficient, then we must restrict m to be some arbitrarily large polynomial.

Oblivious Transfer and Beyond. As our second main result, we build an OT-protocol in (n, m)-BSM, achieving nearly the same parameters as our KA protocol from Theorem 1. Recall, in an OT protocol, sender Alice has two ℓ-bit messages $(\mathsf{msg}_0, \mathsf{msg}_1)$, and receiver Bob has a single choice bit $c \in \{0, 1\}$. At the end of the protocol, Alice should learn nothing, while Bob should learn msg_c, and get no information about msg_{1-c}. When ported to (n, m)-BSM, (1) honest Alice and Bob should use space at most n, (2) the privacy of choice bit c should hold even against malicious Alice with storage m, and (3) the privacy of m_{1-c} should hold even against malicious Bob with storage m.

In our work we will achieve receiver privacy guarantee (2) even against *unbounded* space sender, so we only rely on the BSM for sender privacy (3). Moreover, our protocol satisfies *simulation-based* security, with an efficient simulator. This means that our simulator only uses the attacker as a black-box and is efficient relative to the corresponding attacker. In contrast, prior OT works in the BSM [4,9,10,19] all satisfied a weaker indistinguishability-based variant of sender-privacy, which roughly corresponds to inefficient simulation. The problem of having an efficient simulator was explicitly stated as an interesting and challenging open problem in [10]. Our result, formally proven in Sect. 6, is summarized below:

Theorem 2 (informal). *For any m, λ, there exists some $n_{min} = O(\log m + \lambda)$ such that for all $n \geq n_{min}$ there is an unconditionally secure OT protocol with efficient simulator in the (n, m)-BSM with message size $\Omega(n)$ and security (and correctness) errors $2^{-\Omega(\lambda)}$. Furthermore:*

- *The number of rounds is $\widetilde{O}(\lceil m/n^2 \rceil \cdot \mathrm{poly}(\lambda))$.*
- *The communication complexity is $\widetilde{O}(m \cdot \lceil m/n^2 \rceil \cdot \mathrm{poly}(\lambda))$.*
- *Receiver security holds even against a malicious sender with unbounded space.*

To generalize our result to general MPC, recall that OT is information-theoretically complete for general MPC [23,25]. In Sect. 6.4, we observe that this result also extends to the (n, m)-BSM, provided we allow the honest parties' storage n, round complexity R, and communication complexity C to also polynomially-depend on the circuit size of the corresponding MPC functionality. Note that these parameters are completely independent of the adversary's storage bound m, which can still be arbitrarily (up to exponentially) larger than n. A similar observation that OT implies MPC in the BSM was already made in [10] and expanded on in [27], albeit in the setting where both the OT and the MPC only satisfy inefficient simulation.

We emphasize that the efficient simulation of our OT protocol is *critical* to achieve efficient simulation of the resulting MPC. If we apply our MPC to the special case of the zero-knowledge (ZK) functionality, we get the first ZK protocol in (n, m)-BSM with an *efficient simulator* and arbitrary gap between m and n. In contrast, if we only had indistinguishability-based OT, we would get ZK with an inefficient simulator (which is equivalent to witness indistinguishability), which is insufficient/uninteresting in many situations when the witness is unique. Indeed the prior works of [2,37] constructed (non-interactive) witness indistinguishable proofs in the BSM, and explicitly left zero-knowledge as an open problem, which we resolve here in the interactive setting.

Round and Communication Lower Bound. As we already mentioned, circumventing the lower bound [16] requires more than one long round. Also, any protocol in the (n, m)-BSM clearly requires more than m bits of communication. However, our protocols in Theorems 1 and 2 are noticeably less efficient: they use $\Omega(m/n^2)$ rounds and $\Omega(m^2/n^2)$ communication. This begs the question of whether large round and communication complexities of our protocols are inherent. In particular, when $m \gg n^2$, should the number of rounds R grow with m and should the communication C be super-linear in m?

Unfortunately, we show that the answer is affirmative (see Theorem 22). Specifically, we show that any KA and OT protocols must satisfy $R \geq \Omega((m/n^2)^{1/2})$ and $C \geq \Omega(m \cdot (m/n^2)^{1/2})$. While leaving a non-trivial gap with our upper bounds $R = \widetilde{O}(m/n^2)$ and $C = \widetilde{O}(m^2/n^2)$ when $m \gg n^2$, it still shows that the number of rounds grows with m, and the communication must be super-linear in m. It is an interesting open question to close this quantitative gap between our lower and upper bounds.

Our basic lower bound above only holds for BSM protocols where the attacker Eve is allowed unlimited short-term memory, and is only subject to keeping an m-bit state in between rounds (i.e., condition (d)). However, we also non-trivially extend our lower bound to show that it can even handle fully streaming adversaries that are restricted to m-bits of memory throughout the protocol execution, at the cost of a weaker quantitative bound: $R \geq \Omega((m/n^2)^{1/3})$, $C \geq \Omega(m \cdot (m/n^2)^{1/3})$. It is also an interesting open question to close the quantitative gap between this bound and the previous one.

1.3   Our Techniques

Bit-Entropy Lemma. As a crucial tool in our KA and OT constructions, we rely on a new technical lemma for min-entropy (Lemma 12). On a high level, the lemma says that if a long string $X \in \{0,1\}^k$ has high min-entropy (e.g., because it was chosen uniformly at random and the adversary could only remember $m \ll k$ bits of information about it, in which case X denotes the conditional distribution), then many individual bits $X[i]$ of X must have non-trivial min-entropy. Specifically, if $\mathbf{H}_\infty(X) \geq \delta \cdot k$, we show that $\sum_{i \in [k]} \mathbf{H}_\infty(X[i]) \geq \rho \cdot k$, where we (optimally) relate ρ to δ. For example, when $\delta = \Omega(1)$, then $\rho = \Omega(1)$. The technical lemma relates to conceptually similar lemmas in [3,33,39], showing that random subsets of bits in X have a high entropy rates. It also relates to quasi chain-rules for min-entropy [14,38]. However, to our knowledge, the single-bit version does not appear to follow easily from the prior results.

Key Agreement Protocol. The high-level idea for our KA protocol from Sect. 5.2 is surprisingly simple. For readers familiar with prior work on the bounded storage model, our protocol builds on a core template, introduced in [5] and further used in [4,9,10], which we adapt and extend to the interactive setting. The protocol consists of many rounds i, where Alice streams a ($k = 2m$)-bit random string X to Bob and remembers a single random location in the string $X[a]$. Similarly, as Bob receives the string X, he remembers a single random location $X[b]$. At the end of each round, Alice and Bob exchange their choice of locations a, b with each other; if $a = b$, they set $X[a] = X[b]$ as their shared key and terminate, else they erase all of their memory so far and go to the next round. Their storage only consists of a single index and is therefore $n = O(\log m)$. The probability of Alice and Bob agreeing in any round is $1/(2m)$ and therefore after $O(m)$ rounds they are likely to terminate. In the round i^* where they agree, the attacker can only remember m out of $2m$ bits of arbitrary information about the string X that was sent, and the choice of what information to remember is made before seeing Alice's and Bob's locations a, b. Therefore, the agreed upon location $X[a] = X[b]$ in that round has some constant amount of entropy from Eve's point of view.

The simple template above only outputs a 1-bit shared key, only guarantees that it has some low but non-trivial entropy from the point of view of the attacker (but does not guarantee that it is uniformly random), has a constant correctness error and and requires $O(m)$ rounds. However, it is easy to address these deficiencies. First, Alice/Bob can store $O(n/\log m)$ random locations (not just 1), which means they improve their odds of agreement in a given round from $1/m$ to roughly $O(n^2/m)$, to get round complexity $O(m/n^2)$ and communication complexity $O(m^2/n^2)$, respectively. Second, we can amplify security (and correctness) to ensure that the agreed upon key is $2^{-\lambda}$-statistically close to uniform, while simultaneously making the key longer (say, λ bits), by repeating the above $O(\lambda)$ times, and applying a randomness extractor to the $O(\lambda)$ agreed upon bit locations. Finally, once the symmetric-key is $O(\lambda)$ bits long, we amplify it to be $\Omega(n)$ bits, by adding an additional round, and using any of the optimal symmetric-key BSM protocols (e.g., [39]).

One crucial difference with the template of [5] and any single round in our interactive protocol is that, in our case, Alice and Bob agree on bits in a given round with very small probability $O(n^2/m) \ll 1$, as opposed to almost always agreeing in [5]. Our analysis is consequently significantly different, and builds on our bit-entropy lemma.

We also notice that, while our protocol takes many rounds (which we show to be inherent) and therefore does not satisfy restriction (a), it does satisfy the additional restrictions (b)–(d): each long string is truly random, Alice and Bob are "locally computable", and security holds even if Eve has an unrestricted amount of short-term local memory, as long as she can only remember at most m bits of information after seeing each string X.

Oblivious Transfer Protocol. In an OT protocol, sender Alice has two messages $(\mathsf{msg}_0, \mathsf{msg}_1)$, and receiver Bob has a single choice bit $c \in \{0, 1\}$. At the end of the protocol, Alice should learn nothing, while Bob learns msg_c, and gets no information about msg_{1-c}.

Our oblivious transfer crucially relies on a tool called *interactive hashing* [10,31]. This tool was also used to construct OT in the BSM by prior works [4,9,10] achieving a quadratic gap between the honest and adversarial storage. However, our protocol uses it in a substantially different way. In an interactive hashing protocol, a sender Bob has a random input $b \in [k]$, and at the end of the protocol, Alice can narrow down Bob's input to one of two possible choices b_0, b_1 such that $b \in \{b_0, b_1\}$, but Alice does not learn which of them it is; both options are equally likely. On the other hand, Bob cannot simultaneously control both of the values b_0, b_1 that Alice ends up with, and in particular he cannot cause both of them to land in some sparse subset $B \subseteq [k]$. Such interactive hashing protocols can be performed with 4 rounds of interactions and polylog(k) time/space. The security properties hold information-theoretically, even if the parties have unbounded computation and memory.

We now describe a simplified version of our OT protocol, which roughly corresponds to the case where honest users have $n = O(\log m)$ storage. We first rely on a component sub-protocol, which one can think of as an (imperfect) form of Rabin OT [34]: Alice outputs some bit r, and Bob either also outputs r or $\perp$, but Alice does not learn which of these occurred. We set the length of "long rounds" to $k = O(m \log(m))$:

- Alice and Bob choose random indices $a, b \leftarrow [k]$ respectively. Alice samples a random string $X \leftarrow \{0,1\}^k$ and sends it to Bob. Alice stores $X[a]$ and Bob stores $X[b]$.
- Alice and Bob run interactive hashing where Bob uses his index b. Alice learns that it is one of b_0, b_1.
- Alice checks if $a \in \{b_0, b_1\}$, and if not, then the parties go back to the beginning and try again. Else Alice sends a to Bob and outputs $r = X[a]$. Bob checks if $a = b$ and if so he outputs $r = X[b]$ else he outputs $\perp$.

The interactive hashing security ensures that even if Alice is malicious, she does not learn whether Bob outputs $\perp$ or r. On the other hand, even if Bob is malicious and has storage m, there is only a small $O(k/\log k)$ set of bad indices $B \subseteq [k]$ that he "knows" (have very small entropy given his state). The interactive hashing ensures that it's unlikely that both b_0, b_1 are in B, and Alice selects one of them at random (the one that matches her a). Therefore, in the execution where Alice accepts, with probability $\approx 1/2$, Alice's index satisfies $a \notin B$ and therefore Bob does not know $r = X[a]$.

To go from the above sub-protocol to full OT, we employ a variant of the trick of [7] to go from Rabin OT to the more standard 1-out-of-2 OT. The parties run the above sub-protocol for $t = 3\lambda$ iterations, where Alice outputs bits $(r_1, \ldots, r_t) \in \{0,1\}^t$ and Bob outputs $(r'_1, \ldots, r'_t) \in \{0, 1, \perp\}^t$ such that $r'_i \in \{r_i, \perp\}$ and roughly $1/2$ of them are $\perp$, but Alice does not know which. Bob selects two disjoint subsets $I_0, I_1 \subseteq [t]$ of size λ each at random, subject to I_c only containing values i for which $r'_i \neq \perp$. Alice applies an extractor on the values r_{I_0}, r_{I_1} and uses the outputs to one-time-pad her messages $\mathsf{msg}_0, \mathsf{msg}_1$. This allows Bob to recover msg_c. It's easy to see that the sets I_0, I_1 look identically distributed to Alice and so she does not learn Bob's choice bit c. On the other hand, since Bob only knows roughly $\frac{t}{2} = \frac{3\lambda}{2}$ of the values r_i, at least one of r_{I_0}, r_{I_1} must contain roughly $\frac{\lambda}{2}$ values that Bob does not know, and hence the corresponding extracted string will blind the message.

Note that in our scheme, security against an adversarial Bob (receiver) relies on him having bounded storage m, but security against an adversarial Alice (sender) does not impose any restrictions on her storage. The overall protocol requires $\widetilde{O}(m \cdot \lambda)$ rounds to terminate and $\widetilde{O}(m^2\lambda)$ communication. Our full protocol generalizes the above to settings where honest users have larger storage n to get $\widetilde{O}(\lceil m/n^2 \rceil \cdot \lambda)$ rounds and $\widetilde{O}(m \cdot \lceil m/n^2 \rceil \cdot \lambda)$ communication. This requires additional technical ideas to perform interactive hashing on sets of indices rather than just a single index; see Sect. 6.

One issue with the above idea, and indeed all prior constructions of OT in the BSM [4,9,10,19], is that it only satisfies a weak form of indistinguishability-based security, which is equivalent to security with an inefficient simulator. In particular, to simulate an adversarial Bob, we need to figure out his choice bit c, which requires figuring out which locations $X[a]$ he "knows" and which he does not. This can be done inefficiently (and non-black-box) by looking at Bob's state after processing X and figuring out the conditional entropy of each bit of X given the state; but there seems to be no hope to make this process efficient. We show how to overcome this via an efficient rewinding-based simulation strategy. The simulator forks off many copies of the interactive hashing protocol and figures out which indices show up as one of Alice's outputs with *high frequency*. We show that this serves as a good proxy for the indices that Bob knows – since he only knows $X[a]$ for very few locations a, he has to "play" such locations with high frequency if he wants to have a good chance of Alice selecting them. Therefore, by using the efficiently computable set of high-frequency indices as a proxy for the inefficiently computable set of indices that Bob knows, we can efficiently extract Bob's choice bit c.

Lower Bound. We prove a lower-bound for KA and, since OT directly gives KA, this also implies an identical lower bound for OT. Let us first recall the main intuition of the DM lower bound [16]. Let $m > n$ be the storage size of the adversary, and suppose the first message of the protocol is some large message M, potentially of size $|M| \gg m$ much larger than the adversary's storage. In the real protocol, the honest parties Alice and Bob respectively compute states s_A and s_B after processing M. DM shows that there exists some compact information s_E^* of size m, which (1) is publicly-computable given M, and (2) *decorrelates* the states s_A and s_B of Alice and Bob in the following sense: conditioned on s_E^*, the users' states s_A and s_B only share a low amount of mutual information, bounded by n^2/m. Therefore, if $m = O(n^2)$ is sufficiently large, the information shared between Alice and Bob conditioned on the adversary's view becomes too small (much less than 1 bit) for them to agree on a shared random key.

One obstacle towards extending DM to the interactive setting is that, even if the mutual information created in each round is very small $O(n^2/m)$, with sufficiently many rounds it can add up. Indeed, this is exactly what our upper bound exploits, and why one can allow large gaps between m and n with a large numbers of rounds! For our lower bound on rounds and communication, we want to show that this is essentially the best that one can do. There are two main obstacles. Firstly, the DM approach only works if Alice and Bob do not share any mutual information in the first place. This is true at the beginning of the protocol, which results in a candidate adversarial strategy for the first round of the protocol. But it is not clear whether it extends to any intermediate round within the protocol execution, where Alice and Bob managed to already get some, albeit small, amount of mutual information.[3] Moreover, a naive attempt would be to have Eve compute an appropriate s_E^* for every round, but then Eve would need to store all of these values throughout the duration of the protocol, thus blowing up her storage.

Instead, we approach the DM core idea from a different angle, by thinking of it as a *round reduction* step that allows us to convert an R round protocol into an $R - 1$ round protocol, with only a small loss in correctness and security. In particular, instead of having Alice send the long message M to Bob in the first round, we remove the first round entirely, and have Bob do the following: (1) sample M as Alice would, (2) (inefficiently) sample s_E^* given M as the adversary in DM, and (3) sample his state s_B conditioned on s_E^*; (4) use it to compute the next message M', and (5) send (s_E^*, M') as the new message to Alice. Alice then: (6) samples s_A conditioned on s_E^*; and (7) processes M' using s_A, as she would have done originally. Note that Alice and Bob are now inefficient, with unlimited short-term memory to process each round, but only keep short n-bit states between rounds, similar to feature (d) of Eve.[4]

We claim that the round reduction step preserves correctness and security up to some small loss. This holds because the original states s_A, s_B had small mutual information conditioned on s_E^*, which implies that they are statistically close to independent. Therefore, the new way of sampling s_A, s_B truly independently conditioned on s_E^* only introduces a small statistical error. On the other hand, any attack Eve can perform on the new protocol by observing both of the values (s_E^*, M') sent by Bob at the same time, she could have also performed originally by computing s_E^* from Alice's original message M, storing s_E^* locally in her m-bit state (here we crucially rely on it being small), and then performing the same computation on the values (s_E^*, M'), once Bob sends M'.

By performing the round-reduction steps iteratively, we eventually get a 0-round key agreement protocol, which leads to a contradiction. However, each time we perform the round-reduction step we incur some statistical error $\sqrt{n^2/m}$. The square-root comes from using Pinsker's inequality to convert from mutual information to statistical distance. Therefore, we only end up with a

---

[3] Indeed, it is not true in general that their mutual information can only increase by a small amount in each round; once Alice and Bob share even a small amount of mutual information (e.g., they share a short extractor seed, perhaps even only with small probability), they may be able to leverage it to derive much more mutual information in just one additional round (e.g., send a long message and extract).

[4] Note that allowing Alice and Bob to be stronger makes the resulting lower bound stronger as well.

secure protocol at the end, if the original protocol has $R = O(\sqrt{m/n^2})$ rounds, which gives our lower bound on rounds $R \geq \Omega(\sqrt{m/n^2})$. Note that this also gives a lower bound on communication C since $C \geq R$. However, we can get a stronger lower bound of $C \geq \Omega(m \cdot \sqrt{m/n^2})$ by showing how to remove "small" rounds (i.e., having communication smaller than m) for free, without any loss in correctness/security. We refer to Sect. 7.2 for more details.

As mentioned previously, this lower bound only rules out protocols secure against strong attackers Eve who have access to unbounded short-term memory to process each round, while storing m bits between rounds. We further adapt the techniques above to handle *fully streaming* adversaries, that are restricted to m bits of memory throughout the protocol. The main observation is that the only step in the round reduction procedure that requires Eve to have unbounded short-term memory is sampling s_E^* given M. We first observe that this step can be performed in a streaming manner using small local memory, as long as Alice and Bob are streaming algorithms with small local memory. However, even if the latter was the case in the initial protocol, once we start removing rounds, we required Alice and Bob to have large local memory to run Eve's attack. This turns into a recursive analysis, where the memory that Alice and Bob need to run the protocol after removing R rounds, depends on the memory Eve needs to attack on the protocol after removing $R - 1$ rounds, which depends on the memory Alice and Bob need to run the protocol after removing $R - 1$ rounds etc. By carefully analyzing this recursion, we show that Eve's short-term memory can be bounded to only be a factor of R larger than the previous bound we had on her long-term memory, which yields our new quantitatively weaker bounds of $R \geq \Omega((m/n^2)^{1/3})$ and $C \geq \Omega(m \cdot (m/n^2)^{1/3})$ for the fully streaming model. We refer to Sect. 7.4 for more details.

1.4   Related Work

We already extensively mentioned the prior work on the symmetric-key BSM [1,15,17,26,28,29,35,36,39] and the public-key BSM models [4,5,9,10,19,21]. In particular, the work of [17,26,35,36] constructed "reusable" n-bit-key symmetric-key encryption schemes, capable of encrypting exponentially many b-bit messages, where an individual ciphertext is "only" $O(mb/n)$ bits long.[5] When $b \ll n$, this is a huge saving compared to the prior symmetric-key schemes in the BSM, where each individual ciphertext had size greater than m, irrespective of message length. Interestingly, these works did not satisfy restrictions (b)-(d), critically using full features of the streaming BSM.

In the context of proof systems, [2,37] constructed non-interactive witness indistinguishable proofs secure against memory-bounded streaming verifiers, allowing arbitrary gap between the values n and m. In contrast, the proofs systems constructed in this work are full zero-knowledge, with efficient simulation,

---

[5] This is optimal, as otherwise Eve is capable of storing more than n/b ciphertexts in its memory, allowing the parties to encrypt more than $b \cdot n/b = n$ bits of information using an n-bit key, contradicting Shannon lower bound.

but use many rounds of interaction. In a related vein, a very recent work of [20] considered the notion of "disappearing cryptography" in the (streaming) BSM. Here, a component of the scheme (e.g., a ciphertext, signature, proof or program) is streamed bit by bit. The space-bounded receiver can get the functionality of the system once, after which the object "disappears" for subsequent use.

The work of [30] designed novel "timestamping" schemes in the (traditional) BSM. Here space-bounded sender and receiver have access to a long randomizer string X: the sender will timestamp a given document D at time t, and the receiver will prepare to verify D (which is yet unknown). The sender can then prove the timestamping of D to the receiver at a much later time, and the receiver is guaranteed that the sender is unable to timestamp a "very different" (i.e., high-entropy) document D'.

Finally, we mention the seminal works of [32,33] in the context of designing pseudorandom generators fooling space-bounded distinguishers. Unlike the BSM setting, the memory n of the generator must be necessarily higher than the memory m of the distinguisher, and the works of [32,33] come very close to this bound, unconditionally. In a similar vein, the work of [24] constructs deterministic randomness extractors for space-bounded sources of randomness.

2   Preliminaries

Notation. When X is a distribution, or a random variable following this distribution, we let $x \leftarrow X$ denote the process of sampling x according to the distribution X. If X is a set, we let $x \leftarrow X$ denote sampling x uniformly at random from X. We use the notation $[k] = \{1, \ldots, k\}$. If $x \in \{0,1\}^k$ and $i \in [k]$ then we let $x[i]$ denote the i'th bit of x. If $s \subseteq [k]$, we let $x[s]$ denote the list of values $x[i]$ for $i \in s$.

Statistical Distance. Let X, Y be random variables with supports S_X, S_Y, respectively. We define their *statistical difference* as

$$\mathbf{SD}(X,Y) = \frac{1}{2} \sum_{u \in S_X \cup S_Y} |\Pr[X = u] - \Pr[Y = u]|.$$

We write $X \approx_\varepsilon Y$ to denote $\mathbf{SD}(X,Y) \leq \varepsilon$.

Predictability and Entropy. The *predictability* of a random variable X is $\mathbf{Pred}(X) \overset{\text{def}}{=} \max_x \Pr[X = x]$. The *min-entropy* of a random variable X is $\mathbf{H}_\infty(X) = -\log(\mathbf{Pred}(X))$. Following Dodis et al. [12], we define the conditional predictability of X given Y as $\mathbf{Pred}(X|Y) \overset{\text{def}}{=} \mathbb{E}_{y \leftarrow Y}[\mathbf{Pred}(X|Y = y)]$ and the (average) conditional min-entropy of X given Y as: $\mathbf{H}_\infty(X|Y) = -\log(\mathbf{Pred}(X|Y))$. Note that $\mathbf{Pred}(X|Y)$ is the success probability of the optimal strategy for guessing X given Y.

Lemma 3 ([12]). *For any random variables X, Y, Z where Y is supported over a set of size T we have $\mathbf{H}_\infty(X|Y, Z) \leq \mathbf{H}_\infty(X|Z) - \log T$.*

Lemma 4 ([12]). *For any random variables X, Y, for every $\varepsilon > 0$ we have*

$$\Pr_{y \leftarrow Y}[\mathbf{H}_\infty(X|Y = y) \geq \mathbf{H}_\infty(X|Y) - \log(1/\varepsilon)] \geq 1 - \varepsilon.$$

Lemma 5. *If X and Y are independent conditioned on Z then $\mathbf{H}_\infty(X|Y) \geq \mathbf{H}_\infty(X|Y, Z) \geq \mathbf{H}_\infty(X|Z)$.*

Lemma 6. *If X and Y are independent conditioned on Z then $\mathbf{H}_\infty(X, Y|Z) \geq \mathbf{H}_\infty(X|Z) + \mathbf{H}_\infty(Y|Z)$.*

Shannon Entropy. The Shannon entropy of a random variable X is $\mathbf{H}(X) \overset{\text{def}}{=} \mathbf{E}_{x \leftarrow X}[-\log(\Pr[X = x])]$. The conditional Shannon entropy of X given Y is $\mathbf{H}(X|Y) \overset{\text{def}}{=} \mathbf{E}_{y \leftarrow Y} \mathbf{H}(X|Y = y) = \mathbf{E}_{(x,y) \leftarrow (X,Y)}[-\log(\Pr[X = x|Y = y])]$.

For $0 \leq p \leq 1$ we define the binary entropy function $\mathbf{h}(p) \overset{\text{def}}{=} \mathbf{H}(B_p)$, where B_p is a Bernoulli variable that outputs 1 with probability p and 0 with probability $1 - p$.

Lemma 7. *For any random variables X, Y, we have: $\mathbf{H}_\infty(X|Y) \leq \mathbf{H}(X|Y)$.*

Extractors. We review the notion of randomness extractors and known parameters.

Definition 8 ((Strong, Average-Case) Seeded Extractor [33]**).** *We say that an efficient function* $\mathsf{Ext} : \{0,1\}^n \times \{0,1\}^d \to \{0,1\}^\ell$ *is an (α, ε)-extractor if for all random variables (X, Z) such that X is supported over $\{0,1\}^n$ and $\mathbf{H}_\infty(X|Z) \geq \alpha$ we have $\mathbf{SD}((Z, S, \mathsf{Ext}(X; S)) , (Z, S, U_\ell)) \leq \varepsilon$ where S, U_ℓ are uniformly random and independent bit-strings of length d, ℓ respectively.*

Theorem 9 ([22]). *There exist an (α, ε)-extractor* $\mathsf{Ext} : \{0,1\}^n \times \{0,1\}^d \to \{0,1\}^\ell$ *as long as $\alpha \geq \ell + 2\log(1/\varepsilon)$. Furthermore, such an extractor can be computed in $O(n)$ time and space.*

Definition 10 (BSM Extractor [39]**).** *We say that an efficient function* $\mathsf{BSMExt} : \{0,1\}^k \times \{0,1\}^d \to \{0,1\}^\ell$ *is an (n, m, ε)-BSM extractor if:*

- *Given* seed $\in \{0,1\}^d$ *initially stored in memory, it is possible to compute* $\mathsf{BSMExt}(x; \text{seed})$ *given streaming access to $x \in \{0,1\}^k$ using at most n bits of total memory. Moreover, it can be done while only accessing at most n locations (chosen non-adaptively) in the string x.*
- BSMExt *is an (α, ε)-extractor (Definition 8) for $\alpha = k - m$.*

Note that a BSM Extractor gives a simple one-round protocol (n, m)-BSM protocol where Alice and Bob start with a uniformly random shared key key_0 of some small size d and derive a new shared key $\mathsf{key}_1 \in \{0,1\}^\ell$ of a larger size $\ell > d$. Alice just streams a random $x \in \{0,1\}^k$ to Bob and both parties compute $\mathsf{key}_1 = \mathsf{BSMExt}(x; \mathsf{key}_0)$. Security holds since the adversary can only store m-bits of information about x so it has $\alpha \geq k - m$ bits of entropy conditioned on the adversary's view, and key_0 acts as a random seed which is a-prior unknown to the adversary. Therefore $\mathsf{key}_1 = \mathsf{BSMExt}(x; \mathsf{key}_0)$ is ε-close to uniform given the adversary's view of the protocol.

Theorem 11 ([39]). *For any* $m \geq \ell, \lambda$, *there is a* (n, m, ε)-*BSM extractor* $\overrightarrow{\mathsf{BSMExt}}$: $\{0,1\}^k \times \{0,1\}^d \to \{0,1\}^\ell$ *with* $n = O(\ell + \lambda + \log m)$, $\varepsilon = 2^{-\Omega(\lambda)}$, $k = O(m + \lambda \log(\lambda))$, $d = O(\log m + \lambda)$.

3   Bit-Entropy Lemma

We prove a new lemma showing that if X has sufficiently high min-entropy, then many individual bits $X[i]$ have sufficiently high min-entropy as well.

For $q \in [0,1]$, we define $\mathbf{h}_+^{-1}(q)$ to be the unique value p such that $.5 \leq p \leq 1$ and $\mathbf{h}(p) = q$, where $\mathbf{h}$ is the binary entropy function defined above.

Lemma 12. *Assume* X, Y *are random variables, where* X *is distributed over* $\{0,1\}^k$. *Let* $X[i]$ *denote the* i'*th bit of* X. *If* $\mathbf{H}_\infty(X|Y) \geq \delta k$ *the following 3 statements hold:*

1. $\sum_i \mathbf{Pred}(X[i] \mid Y) \leq \mathbf{h}_+^{-1}(\delta)k.$
2. $\sum_i \mathbf{H}_\infty(X[i] \mid Y) \geq -\log(\mathbf{h}_+^{-1}(\delta))k.$
3. *If* I *is uniformly random over* $[k]$ *and independent of* X, Y *then* $\mathbf{H}_\infty(X[I] \mid Y, I) \geq -\log(\mathbf{h}_+^{-1}(\delta)).$

Proof. We have:

$$\delta k \leq \mathbf{H}_\infty(X|Y) \leq \mathbf{H}(X|Y) = \sum_{i \in [k]} \mathbf{H}(X[i] \mid X[1], ..., X[i-1], Y) \leq \sum_{i \in [k]} \mathbf{H}(X[i] \mid Y).$$

Therefore

$$\delta \leq \mathop{\mathbf{E}}_{i \leftarrow [k], Y \leftarrow y} \mathbf{H}(X[i] \mid Y = y).$$

Since $\mathbf{h}_+^{-1}$ is a decreasing and concave function, this means:

$$\mathbf{h}_+^{-1}(\delta) \geq \mathbf{h}_+^{-1}\left(\mathop{\mathbf{E}}_{i \leftarrow \{0,1\}^k, y \leftarrow Y} \mathbf{H}(X[i] \mid Y = y) \right)$$

$$\geq \mathop{\mathbf{E}}_{i \leftarrow [k], y \leftarrow Y} \mathbf{h}_+^{-1}(\mathbf{H}(X[i] \mid Y = y))$$

$$\geq \mathop{\mathbf{E}}_{i \leftarrow [k], y \leftarrow Y} (\max_{b \in \{0,1\}} \Pr[X[i] = b \mid Y = y])$$

$$\geq \mathop{\mathbf{E}}_{i \leftarrow [k]} \mathbf{Pred}(X[i]|Y).$$

This proves the first part of the theorem. Also the third part of the theorem follows since $\mathbf{H}_\infty(X[I] \mid Y, I) = -\log(\mathbf{E}_{i \leftarrow I} \mathbf{Pred}(X[I] \mid Y, I = i)) = -\log(\mathbf{E}_{i \leftarrow [k]} \mathbf{Pred}(X[i] \mid Y))$. The second part follows since $(-\log)$ is a decreasing and convex function so

$$-\log(\mathbf{h}_+^{-1}(\delta)) \leq -\log\left(\mathop{\mathbf{E}}_{i \leftarrow [k]} \mathbf{Pred}(X[i] \mid Y) \right)$$

$$\leq \mathop{\mathbf{E}}_{i \leftarrow [k]} -\log(\mathbf{Pred}(X[i] \mid Y))$$

$$\leq \mathop{\mathbf{E}}_{i \leftarrow [k]} \mathbf{H}_\infty(X[i] \mid Y) \qquad \square$$

Remark 13. To the best of our knowledge, the "bit-prediction" lemma above is new, as it talks about individual bit prediction; as opposed to "subkey-predcition" lemma studied in prior BSM literature [3,33,39], which talked about simultaneously predicting a large subset of bits. It also does not appear to follow directly from quasi chain-rules for min-entropy [14,38] that have a large loss in parameters that does not appear to give any non-trivial bounds in the bit setting. We also remark that our parameters are tight, as can be seen by taking X to be the uniform distribution over a hamming ball of radius pk, where $p = 1 - \mathbf{h}_+^{-1}(\delta) \leq 1/2$. The volume of this ball is roughly $2^{\mathbf{h}(p)k} = 2^{\delta k}$, so $\mathbf{H}_\infty(X) = \delta k$. Yet, each bit of X can be predicted with probability at least $1 - p = \mathbf{h}_+^{-1}(\delta)$.

Lemma 14. *For any* $0 < \varepsilon \leq 1$ *there is a* $\delta = \Omega(\varepsilon^2)$ *such that* $-\log(\mathbf{h}_+^{-1}(1 - \delta)) = (1 - \varepsilon)$.

Proof. Given ε we can solve:

$$-\log(\mathbf{h}_+^{-1}(1 - \delta)) = 1 - \varepsilon$$
$$\Rightarrow \qquad \mathbf{h}_+^{-1}(1 - \delta) = 2^\varepsilon/2$$
$$\Rightarrow \qquad 1 - \delta = \mathbf{h}(2^\varepsilon/2) = \mathbf{h}(1/2 + \Theta(\varepsilon)) = 1 - \Theta(\varepsilon^2).$$

where we rely on the bound $2^\varepsilon = (1 + \Theta(\varepsilon))$ and $\mathbf{h}(1/2 + \Theta(\varepsilon)) = 1 - \Theta(\varepsilon^2)$ (e.g. [6, Theorem 2.2]). □

4   Bounded Storage Model

A (n, m)-*bounded storage model (BSM)* protocol, is parametrized by a bound n on the memory of the honest parties, and a bound $m > n$ on the memory of the adversary. Communication between parties occurs in rounds where one party sends data to another party. Honest parties send and receive data in a *streaming* manner, by generating/reading the stream one bit at a time, while only using n bits of memory overall. The adversary is also a streaming algorithm with m bits of memory.

For all our constructions, we will satisfy additional properties, corresponding to properties (b)–(d) discussed in the introduction. The protocol consists of two types of rounds: "short rounds" are of size is $< n$, and can be fully generated, sent, and processed by the honest parties using only n bits of memory, without needing to be streamed one bit at a time, while "long rounds" are of size $> m$.[6] Our protocols satisfy the following additional properties:

---

[6] We will allow ourselves to split up the protocol into rounds arbitrarily, and may have two (or more) adjacent rounds where the same party A talks to party B.

– *Uniformly Random "Long Rounds".* Each long round consists of a uniformly random string x generated by some party A and sent to party B.
– *Local Computability for Honest Parties.* In each long round, the honest parties only read a small set of $< n$ locations of x and use these to update their state, while using only n bits of memory in total. Furthermore, the set of locations accessed is chosen non-adaptively at the beginning of the round, before seeing any bits of x.
– *Unlimited Short-term Memory for Adversary.* The adversary can generate and read the entire long round of communication at once, and can use unlimited amounts of short-term memory during this process, but can only store a compressed m-bit state immediately after the end of each long round. There are no restrictions on the adversary's memory during/after short rounds.

5   Key Agreement

5.1   Definition

A key agreement protocol in the (n, m)-BSM with security ε is a protocol between two honest users Alice and Bob with memory bound n. At the end of the protocol Alice and Bob outputs values $\mathsf{key}_A, \mathsf{key}_B \in \{0, 1\}^\ell$ respectively. For correctness, we require that when the protocol is executed honestly then $\Pr[\mathsf{key}_A = \mathsf{key}_B] = 1$. For security, we consider a passive BSM adversary Eve with memory bound m. Let view_{Eve} denote Eve's final state at the end of the protocol execution. We require that

$$(\mathsf{view}_{Eve}, \mathsf{key}_A) \approx_\varepsilon (\mathsf{view}_{Eve}, \mathsf{key}^*)$$

where $\mathsf{key}^* \leftarrow \{0, 1\}^\ell$ is chosen uniformly at random and independently of the protocol execution.

5.2   Construction

Theorem 15. *For any $m \geq \ell, \lambda$ there is some $n_{min} = O(\lambda + \ell + \log m)$ such that for all $n > n_{min}$ there is a key agreement protocol in the (n, m)-BSM that outputs an ℓ-bit key and has security $\varepsilon = 2^{-\Omega(\lambda)}$. The round complexity of the protocol is $O(\lceil (m/n^2) \rceil \cdot \lambda \cdot \mathrm{polylog}(m))$ and the communication complexity $O(m \cdot \lceil (m/n^2) \rceil \cdot \lambda \cdot \mathrm{polylog}(m + \lambda))$.*

Proof. We present the key agreement protocol between Alice and Bob. We refer to the full version [13] for a proof.

Construction. Given m, λ, ℓ we define additional parameters as follows.

– Let $k = 2m$.
– Let $d_1 = O(\lambda + \log m)$ and $n_1 = O(\lambda + \log m + \ell)$ and $k' = O(m + \lambda \log(\lambda))$ be some values such that there is a $(n_1, m, \varepsilon = 2^{-\Omega(\lambda)})$-BSM extractor $\mathsf{BSMExt} : \{0, 1\}^{k'} \times \{0, 1\}^{d_1} \to \{0, 1\}^\ell$ per Theorem 11.

- Let $t = O(\lambda + \log m)$ and $d_0 = O(t), n_0 = O(t)$ be some value such that there is a $(t/10, \varepsilon = 2^{-\Omega(\lambda)})$-extractor $\mathsf{Ext} : \{0,1\}^t \times \{0,1\}^{d_0} \to \{0,1\}^{d_1}$ that can be computed using n_0 space per Theorem 9.
- Define $n_{min} = \max(n_0, n_1, 2t + \lceil \log k \rceil + 1) = O(\lambda + \log m + \ell)$.
- For any $n \geq n_{min}$, define $\tilde{n} = \lfloor (n-t)/(\lceil \log k \rceil + 1) \rfloor = \Omega(n/\log m)$.

The protocol works as follows.

1. Set $i := 0$. Repeat the following until $i = t$:
   (a) Alice and Bob select uniformly random subsets $s_A, s_B \subseteq [k]$ of size $|s_A| = |s_B| = \tilde{n}$ respectively.
      Alice streams a uniformly random string $x \leftarrow \{0,1\}^k$ to Bob.
      Alice stores $x[s_A]$ while Bob stores $x[s_B]$.
   (b) Bob sends s_B to Alice.
   (c) If $s_A \cap s_B \neq \emptyset$ then Alice selects a random index $j \leftarrow s_A \cap s_B$ and sends j to Bob.
      Both Alice and Bob set $r_i = x[j]$ and increment $i := i+1$.
      Else if $s_A \cap s_B = \emptyset$ then Alice simply sends $j = \bot$ to Bob.
2. Alice and Bob set $r := (r_1, \ldots, r_t)$.
   Alice sends a random $\mathsf{seed}_0 \leftarrow \{0,1\}^{d_0}$ to Bob and both of them compute $\mathsf{seed}_1 = \mathsf{Ext}(r; \mathsf{seed}_0)$.
3. Alice streams a uniformly random string $x \leftarrow \{0,1\}^{k'}$ to Bob and both parties compute $\mathsf{key} = \mathsf{BSMExt}(x; \mathsf{seed}_1)$.

$\qquad\qquad\qquad\qquad\qquad\qquad\qquad\qquad\qquad\qquad\qquad\qquad\qquad\qquad\qquad\square$

6   Oblivious Transfer and Multiparty Computation

6.1   Definition of Oblivious Transfer

We define oblivious transfer (OT) in the BSM via a real/ideal framework. In the ideal model the sender (Alice) gives two messages $(\mathsf{msg}_0, \mathsf{msg}_1) \in (\{0,1\}^\ell)^2$ to an ideal functionality $\mathcal{F}_{OT}$ and the receiver (Bob) gives a bit $c \in \{0,1\}$. The ideal functionality $\mathcal{F}_{OT}$ gives msg_c to the receiver and gives nothing to the sender.

A protocol Π realizes $\mathcal{F}_{OT}$ in the (n, m)-BSM with security ε if:

- Π can be executed by honest parties with n-bit memory.
- There exists an efficient black-box simulator $\mathsf{Sim}^{\mathcal{A}}$ that runs in time $\mathsf{poly}(n, m, \lambda = \log(1/\varepsilon))$ with black-box (rewinding) access to the adversary $\mathcal{A}$, such that for any (inefficient) BSM-adversary $\mathcal{A}$ with m-bit state corrupting either the sender or the receiver and for any choice of inputs $\mathcal{Z} = (\mathsf{msg}_0, \mathsf{msg}_1, c)$ from the environment, we have

$$\mathsf{REAL}_{\mathcal{A}, \Pi, \mathcal{Z}} \approx_\varepsilon \mathsf{IDEAL}_{\mathsf{Sim}^{\mathcal{A}}, \mathcal{F}_{OT}, \mathcal{Z}}$$

where we define the distributions:

REAL$_{\mathcal{A},\Pi,\mathcal{Z}}$: denotes the real execution of Π with the adversary $\mathcal{A}$ taking on the role of either the sender or the receiver while the honest party uses the input specified by $\mathcal{Z}$; the output of the distribution consists of the output of $\mathcal{A}$ together with the inputs/outputs of the honest party.

IDEAL$_{\mathsf{Sim}^{\mathcal{A}},\mathcal{F}_{OT},\mathcal{Z}}$: denotes the ideal execution of $\mathcal{F}_{OT}$ with an ideal-adversary $\mathsf{Sim}^{\mathcal{A}}$ taking on the same role as $\mathcal{A}$, while the honest party uses the input specified by $\mathcal{Z}$; the output of the distribution consists of the output of $\mathsf{Sim}^{\mathcal{A}}$ together with the inputs/outputs of the honest party.

We further say that the protocol is secure against an *unbounded-memory* sender (resp. receiver) if we can drop the requirement on the storage of $\mathcal{A}$ when it corrupts the sender (resp. receiver).

We say that the protocol is only secure with *inefficient simulation*, if we drop the requirement on the efficiency of the simulator. Our default notion will be *efficient simulation*.

On Efficient Simulation. Note that we require efficient simulation even though the adversary may be computationally unbounded. This may seem strange at first, but is natural and is analogous to (e.g.,) requiring an efficient simulator for statistical Zero Knowledge proofs [18] or for information-theoretically secure MPC protocols. In particular, the definition is agnostic to whether or not the adversary is efficient, but ensures that the adversary cannot learn anything in the real world that it could not also learn with only polynomially *more* computational power in the ideal world. The need for an efficient simulator is crucial when leveraging OT to construct other more complex functionalities, as we will do in Sect. 6.4. For example, we can use our OT in the BSM to construct zero-knowledge (ZK) proofs in the BSM. If the OT simulator were inefficient, the resulting ZK proof would only be inefficiently simulatable (equivalently, would only be witness indistinguishable), which is completely meaningless in many scenarios where the witness is unique; the prover may as well just send the witness in the clear.

On the other hand, our simulator does not have bounded storage and can use more memory than the adversary. This naturally corresponds to the idea that having some a-priori (polynomial) bound on storage is only assumed to be a limitation in the real world, and is a useful limitation in helping us build secure protocols, but is not a fundamental restriction that we need to also preserve for the ideal-world adversary interacting with the ideal functionality.

6.2   Interactive Hashing

Basic Interactive Hashing. In an interactive hashing protocol a sender Bob has an input $u \in [k]$. The goal of the protocol is for Alice to narrow down Bob's input to one of two possible choices u_0, u_1 such that $u = u_b$ for one of $b = 0$ or $b = 1$, but Alice does not learn which. In particular, even if Alice acts maliciously, when Bob chooses his input $u \leftarrow [k]$ at random, then both choices of b appear equally likely from Alice's point of view. On the other hand, although Bob can choose an arbitrary input u and ensures $u = u_b$ for some $b \in \{0,1\}$, he cannot control the "other" value u_{1-b} too much. In particular, even if Bob is malicious during the protocol, for any sufficiently sparse subset $B \subseteq [k]$, it is highly unlikely that both of u_0, u_1 are contained in B.

Definition 16. *An interactive hashing protocol is a protocol between a public-coin randomized Alice (receiver) and a deterministic Bob (sender). Alice has no input and Bob has some input $u \in [k]$. At the end of the protocol, we denote the transcript (h, v), consisting of all the random messages h sent by Alice and all the responses v sent by Bob. We can think of h as defining a hash function that maps Bob's input u to his set of responses $v = h(u)$. The protocol has the following properties:*

- *2-to-1 Hash: Every possible choice of Alice's messages results in a hash function h which is 2-to-1, meaning that for every v in the image of h has exactly two pre-images: $|h^{-1}(v)| = 2$.*
- *(α, β)-Security: For any set $B \subseteq [k]$ of size $|B| \leq \beta \cdot k$, if Alice follows the protocol honestly and Bob acts arbitrarily resulting in some transcript (h, v) such that $\{u_0, u_1\} = h^{-1}(v)$ then $\Pr[\{u_0, u_1\} \subseteq B] \leq \alpha$.*

Note: the 2-to-1 hash property ensures that, if Bob chooses $u \leftarrow [k]$ uniformly at random and acts honestly during the protocol, then even if Alice acts maliciously resulting in some transcript (h, v) at the end of the protocol, if we define $\{u_0, u_1\} = h^{-1}(v)$ such that $u = u_b$, Alice cannot distinguish between b and $1 - b$.

We have constructions of interactive hashing (with security against arbitrary Alice and Bob, without any bound on their memory):

Theorem 17 ([10,31]). *There is an 4-round interactive hashing protocol with (α, β)-security for any $\beta < 1$ with $\alpha = O(\beta \log k)$. Furthermore, the execution of the protocol and the computation of h^{-1} can be done in $\mathrm{polylog} k$ time and space.*

Definition of Set Interactive Hashing. Here, we extend the notion of interactive hashing to the case where the sender Bob has an entire set of inputs $s_B \subseteq [k]$. Alice has her own set of inputs $s_A \subseteq [k]$. The goal of the protocol is to ensure that when there is a value in the intersection $s_A \cap s_B$ then there is a good chance that Alice will accept and output some value $u \in S_A$, in which case it then holds with probability $1/2$, that $u \in S_B$ and Bob accepts and outputs it, while with probability $1/2$ Bob rejects. Alice should not learn which of these two cases occur, even if she acts maliciously. On the other hand, even if Bob is malicious, he cannot have too much control over the value that Alice outputs: for any sufficiently sparse set $B \subseteq [k]$, he cannot ensure that the value u that Alice outputs (conditioned on her accepting) is in the set B with probability much higher than $1/2$.

Definition 18. *In a set interactive hashing protocol, Alice and Bob have sets $s_A, s_B \subseteq [k]$ of size $|s_A| = |s_B| = n$. At the end of the protocol, Alice either rejects* *by sending a special $\perp$ message to Bob, or she accepts and sends some $u \in S_A$ to Bob. If Alice sends $\perp$, then Bob always rejects and outputs $\perp$. Otherwise, Bob can either accept, in which case he outputs the same u as Alice and it must hold that $u \in S_B$, or he rejects. The protocol has (α, β)-security if it satisfies the following properties:*

- *Correctness: If Alice and Bob both execute the protocol honestly using random subsets $s_A, s_B \subseteq [k]$ of size $|s_A| = |s_B| = n$ then:*

$$\Pr[\text{Alice accepts}] \geq \Omega(\min(n^2/k, 1)) \quad , \quad \Pr[\text{Bob accepts} \mid \text{Alice accepts}] = \frac{1}{2}.$$

  Furthermore whenever Alice accepts with some value u, then it must be the case that $u \in S_A$ and if Bob also accepts then it must be the case that $u \in S_A \cap S_B$.
- *Security for Honest Bob: If Bob follows the protocol honestly using a random subset $s_B \subseteq [k]$ of size $|s_B| = n$ and Alice follows the protocol arbitrarily, then, even condition on any arbitrary protocol transcript in which Alice accepts (i.e., does not send $\perp$ to Bob as the last message) we have:*

$$\Pr[\text{Bob accepts}] = \frac{1}{2}.$$

- *(α, β)-Security for honest Alice: Let $B \subseteq [k]$ be a set of size $|B| \leq \beta \cdot k$. If Alice follows the protocol honestly using a random subset $s_A \subseteq [k]$ of size $|s_A| = n$ and Bob follows the protocol arbitrarily, then*

$$\Pr[\text{Alice outputs } u \in B \mid \text{Alice accepts}] \leq \frac{1}{2} + \alpha.$$

6.3 OT Construction

Theorem 19. *For any $m \geq \ell, \lambda$ there is some $n_{min} = \Omega(\log m + \ell + \lambda)$ such that for all $n \geq n_{min}$ there is an oblivious transfer protocol in the (n, m)-BSM with ℓ-bit messages and security $\varepsilon = 2^{-\Omega(\lambda)}$. The protocol is secure with efficient simulation, and it achieves security against an unbounded-memory sender. The round complexity is $O(\lceil m/n^2 \rceil \cdot \text{poly}(\lambda, \log m))$ and the communication complexity $O(m \cdot \lceil m/n^2 \rceil \cdot \text{poly}(\lambda, \log(m)))$.*

Proof. We describe the OT protocol between sender Alice and receiver Bob, and refer to the full version [13] for a proof.

Construction. Given m, λ, ℓ we define additional parameters as follows:

- Let $d_1 = O(\lambda + \log m)$ and $n_1 = O(\lambda + \log m + \ell)$ and $k' = O(m + \ell + \lambda \log(\lambda))$ be some values such that there is a $(n_1, m + \ell, \varepsilon = 2^{-\Omega(\lambda)})$-BSM extractor BSMExt : $\{0,1\}^{k'} \times \{0,1\}^{d_1} \to \{0,1\}^\ell$ per Theorem 11.
- Let $t = O(\lambda + \log m)$ and $d_0 = O(t), n_0 = O(t)$ be some value such that there is a $(t/40, \varepsilon = 2^{-\Omega(\lambda)})$-extractor Ext : $\{0,1\}^t \times \{0,1\}^{d_0} \to \{0,1\}^{d_1}$ that can be computed using n_0 space per Theorem 9.

– Set $k = (m + \lambda) \log^3(m + \lambda)$.
– Set $\alpha = \frac{1}{20}$ and let $\beta = 1/O(\log k)$ be such that (α, β)-security for interactive set hashing holds.
– Set $\delta = \Omega(\beta^2) = 1/O(\log^2 k))$ be such that $-\log(\mathbf{h}_+^{-1}(1 - \delta)) = (1 - \beta/2)$ by Lemma 14.
  This ensures that $\delta k \geq \Omega((m + \lambda) \log(m + \lambda))$.
– Let $g(k) = \text{poly} \log k$ be a parameter associated with set interactive hashing, such that an execution of the set interactive hashing protocol with parameters n, k can be done in $n \cdot g(k)$ time and space(see the full version [13] for more details). Assume $g(k) \geq \lceil \log k + 1 \rceil$.
– Define $n_{min} = \max(2n_0, 2n_1, 3t + g(k)) = O(\lambda + \log m + \ell)$.
– For any $n \geq n_{min}$, define $\tilde{n} = \lfloor (n - 2t)/g(k) \rfloor = \Omega(n/\text{polylog}(m + \lambda))$.
– Let $p = \Omega(\min(\tilde{n}^2/k, 1))$ be the correctness probability of Alice accepting during an honest execution of the set interactive hashing protocol with parameters $\tilde{n}, k$, per Definition 18.
  Set $R_{max} = 2t/p = O(t \cdot \lceil k/\tilde{n}^2 \rceil) = O(\lceil m/n^2 \rceil \cdot \text{poly}(\lambda, \log m))$.

The protocol works as follows.

Bob has a choice bit $c \in \{0, 1\}$ and Alice has two messages $\mathsf{msg}_0, \mathsf{msg}_1 \in \{0, 1\}^\ell$.

1. Alice and Bob initiate vectors $r_A \in \{0, 1\}^t, r_B \in \{0, 1, \perp\}^t$ respectively. They set $i := 0$.
   Repeat the following until $i = t$:
   (a) Alice and Bob select uniformly random subsets $s_A, s_B \subseteq [k]$ of size $|s_A| = |s_B| = \tilde{n}$ respectively.
       Alice streams a uniformly random string $x \leftarrow \{0, 1\}^k$ to Bob.
       Alice stores $x[s_A]$, and Bob stores $x[s_B]$.
   (b) Alice and Bob perform set interactive hashing, with Bob's input being s_B.
       – If Alice rejects, then both parties move to the next iteration.
       – Else, if Alice accepts with some value $u \in s_A$, then she sets $r_A[i] = x[u]$.
         • If Bob also accepts then it must be the case that $u \in s_B$ and he sets $r_B[i] = x[u]$.
         • Else, Bob sets $r_B[i] = \perp$.
       Both parties increment $i := i + 1$.
   If the number of iterations reaches R_{max} before $i = t$, the parties abort.
2. Bob sets $I := \{i \in [t] : r_B[i] \neq \perp\}$. If $|I| < \frac{2 \cdot t}{5}$ then Bob aborts. Else he chooses two sets I_0, I_1 of size $|I_0| = |I_1| = \frac{2 \cdot t}{5}$ by sub-selecting $I_c \subseteq I$ and $I_{1-c} \subseteq [t] \setminus I_c$ uniformly at random.
   Bob sends I_0, I_1 to Alice.
3. Alice checks that $|I_0| = |I_1| = \frac{2 \cdot t}{5}$ and $I_0 \cap I_1 = \emptyset$ and aborts otherwise.
   She chooses an extractor seed $\mathsf{seed} \leftarrow \{0, 1\}^{d_0}$ and sends seed to Bob.
   Alice computes $\mathsf{seed}_0 = \mathsf{Ext}(r_A[I_0]; \mathsf{seed})$, $\mathsf{seed}_1 = \mathsf{Ext}(r_A[I_1]; \mathsf{seed})$.
   Bob computes $\mathsf{seed}_c = \mathsf{Ext}(r_B[I_c]; \mathsf{seed})$.

4. Alice streams a uniformly random string $x \leftarrow \{0,1\}^{k'}$ to Bob.
   Alice computes $\mathsf{key}_0 = \mathsf{BSMExt}(x; \mathsf{seed}_0), \mathsf{key}_1 = \mathsf{BSMExt}(x; \mathsf{seed}_1)$.
   Bob computes $\mathsf{key}_c = \mathsf{BSMExt}(x; \mathsf{seed}_c)$.
5. Alice sends to Bob:

$$\mathsf{ct}_0 = \mathsf{key}_0 \oplus \mathsf{msg}_0, \quad \mathsf{ct}_1 = \mathsf{key}_1 \oplus \mathsf{msg}_1$$

and Bob outputs $\mathsf{msg} = \mathsf{ct}_c \oplus \mathsf{key}_c$.

$\square$

6.4   Multiparty Computation from OT

It is known that one can use the oblivious transfer (OT) ideal functionality as a black box to achieve general multi-party computation in the OT-hybrid model [23,25]. By plugging in our construction of OT in the BSM, one therefore gets general multiparty computation in the BSM with efficient simulation. A similar observation that OT implies MPC in the BSM was already made in [10] and expanded on in [27], albeit in the setting where both the OT and the MPC only satisfy inefficient simulation.

We provide some additional details. Assume we want to perform a multiparty computation of some circuit C with N parties and security parameter λ.

- Honest user storage: If we start with an OT protocol in the (n, m)-BSM and use it to construct MPC, the honest users need to keep in memory all of the intermediate state of the external MPC protocol in the OT-hybrid model. The size of this state is some $\mathrm{poly}(|C|, N, \lambda)$ completely independent of n, m. Therefore the resulting protocol will be in the (n', m)-BSM model with $n' = n + \mathrm{poly}(|C|, N, \lambda)$, which can still be arbitrarily smaller than the adversarial storage m.
- Adversary storage: We note that the MPC protocol only executes copies of the OT protocol sequentially. When the "outer" simulator of the overall MPC needs to simulate each OT execution, it can spawn of a fresh copy of an "inner" OT simulator. Although the outer simulator may need to store some additional state related to the outer MPC execution, this is completely unrelated to the inner OT. Therefore, the OT protocol only needs to achieve security against an OT adversary with the same storage bound m as the overall MPC adversary.

Summarizing we get the following theorem as a corollary of our OT protocol (Theorem 19) and the works of [23,25].

Theorem 20. *For any m, λ and any N-party ideal functionality $\mathcal{F}$ having circuit size $|\mathcal{F}|$, there is some $n_{min} = O(\log m) + \mathrm{poly}(|\mathcal{F}|, N, \lambda)$ such that for all $n \geq n_{min}$ there is a secure MPC protocol in the (n, m)-BSM with $\varepsilon = 2^{-\Omega(\lambda)}$ security against an adversary that can maliciously corrupt any number of parties. The round complexity is $O(\lceil m/n^2 \rceil \cdot \mathrm{poly}(|\mathcal{F}|, N, \lambda))$ and the communication complexity $O(m \cdot \lceil m/n^2 \rceil \cdot \mathrm{poly}(|\mathcal{F}|, N, \lambda))$.*

7   Lower Bounds on Rounds and Communication

In this section, we prove that achieving large memory gaps between adversaries and honest parties in the bounded storage model inherently requires large round complexity and communication. In Sect. 7.1, we introduce the specific BSM we use for our lower bound. In Sect. 7.2, we prove a lower bound on round complexity and communication in this model. Looking ahead, one drawback of this lower bound is that it only rules out protocols secure against somewhat strong, non-streaming adversaries. In Sect. 7.3, we introduce another variant of the BSM where adversaries are streaming, and prove an associated lower bound in Sect. 7.4.

7.1   Model for the Lower Bound: The Unbounded Processing Model

As mentioned in the introduction, our lower bound holds in a stronger model than the variant of streaming BSM we use for our positive results in Sect. 4. The main conceptual difference is that both the honest parties are only bound by their storage used between the rounds, but could compute its contents using unbounded temporary memory. We describe that model, and introduce notation in more details below. We develop in more details the relation with previously discussed notions of BSM in Remark 21.

A (n, m)-bounded storage model protocol Π in the *unbounded processing model*, is parametrized by a bound n on the storage of honest parties and a bound m on the storage of the adversary. In the case of two parties, Alice and Bob send (potentially large) messages to each other at every round. Every round i consists of one party, say Alice, sending a message to the other, say Bob, as follows: she computes

$$(s_A^{(i)}, M^{(i)}) \leftarrow \mathsf{send}_A^{(i)}(s_A^{(i-1)})$$

and Bob computes

$$s_B^{(i)} \leftarrow \mathsf{receive}_B^{(i)}(s_B^{(i-1)}, M^{(i)}),$$

and vice-versa if Bob sends the message in round i. $s_A^{(i)}$ and $s_B^{(i)}$ denote the local states kept by Alice and Bob respectively after round i, and $M^{(i)}$ denotes the message sent at round i. By convention their starting states are $s_A^{(0)} = s_B^{(0)} = \emptyset$. We require the states s_A and s_B to be of bounded size, namely $|s_A^{(i)}|, |s_B^{(i)}| \leq n$ for all i. There are however no restrictions on the complexity of the functions $\mathsf{send}_A^{(i)}, \mathsf{receive}_B^{(i)}$ in rounds i where Alice sends a message, or $\mathsf{send}_B^{(i)}, \mathsf{receive}_A^{(i)}$ in rounds i where Bob sends a message. We'll assume for convenience of notation that parties speak turn by turn, namely Alice sends messages in odd rounds and Bob sends messages in even rounds, or vice-versa.

Adversaries Adv in this model are similarly modeled as functions $\mathsf{Adv}^{(i)} : (s_E^{(i-1)}, M^{(i)})^{(i)} \mapsto s_E^{(i)}$, where there are no restrictions on the complexity of $\mathsf{Adv}^{(i)}$, up to the state $s_E^{(i)}$ having size at most m for all i.

We will respectively denote by C and R some upper bounds on the total communication and the number of rounds of Π, which hold over all possible executions of Π. In the case of key agreement, this is without loss of generality up to a constant loss in either security (having both parties abort and output 0) or correctness (having both parties abort and output a random value), using Markov's inequality.

We will furthermore suppose that the length of the message sent in any fixed round i is fixed by the protocol, and in particular does not depend on its internal randomness. We discuss how to relax this requirement in the full version [13]

We now define key agreement (with 1-bit output) in this model. A key agreement protocol Π in the (n, m)-BSM is a protocol with two parties, Alice and Bob, which results in a single-bit final state $s_A^{(R)}, s_B^{(R)} \in \{0, 1\}$. We require the following properties:

- δ-correctness: We have

$$\Pr[s_A^{(R)} = s_B^{(R)}] \geq 1/2 + \delta.$$

  for some constant $\delta \leq 1/2$.
- (m, ε)-Security: No adversary Adv with memory m (with the specifications above) can guess Alice's output $s_A^{(R)}$ at the end of the protocol:

$$\forall \mathsf{Adv}, \Pr[s_E^{(R)} = s_A^{(R)}] \leq 1/2 + \varepsilon,$$

  for constant $\varepsilon \leq 1/2$.
- We furthermore require $\delta - \varepsilon = \Theta(1)$.

The last requirement enforces that adversaries have strictly smaller probability of guessing the output of the honest parties than the other honest party.

Remark 21 (Comparison with previously discussed models). As mentioned before, this defines a more expressive model than the one in Sect. 4, as honest users for the definition above are stronger than in Sect. 4. The main differences are (1) there are no restrictions on the computational power of the *honest users* to compute their states kept between the rounds of the protocol, who can in particular use arbitrary large temporary memory, (2) they are neither bound to send uniformly random "long" messages, nor restricted to have local access to it. In the terminology we used in the introduction, the lower bound holds for honest users without restrictions (b), (c), but with the same capability (d) as Eve. All these capabilities make the resulting lower bound stronger.

However, we only consider strong adversaries with unlimited short-term memory (restriction (d) in the introduction). This does make our lower bound weaker than ideal, and leaves open the possibility of a tighter lower bound for more restricted classes of "streaming" adversaries. Looking ahead, in Sect. 7.3 and 7.4, we adapt this model and the subsequent lower bound to restrict adversaries to be streaming, albeit at the cost of slightly worse quantitative bounds.

To sum up, in this new model, the honest users have the same capabilities as the adversary, up to a smaller storage between rounds.

In terms of key agreement, we relax correctness and security to only be constants, as long as honest users have some non-trivial advantage in agreeing on the output bit compared to an adversary; this again makes our lower bound stronger.

7.2   Lower Bound in the Unbounded Processing Model

Theorem 22. *Let Π be a key agreement protocol in the unbounded processing model (Sect. 7.1), with honest storage n, satisfying δ-correctness and (m, ε) security, where $\delta - \varepsilon = \Omega(1)$. Suppose furthermore that for any execution of Π, the total communication between Alice and Bob is at most , and consists of at most R rounds. Then ,$\geq \Omega\left(\frac{m^{3/2}}{n}\right)$, and $R \geq \Omega\left(\frac{\sqrt{m}}{n}\right)$.*

Remark 23. (Lower Bound for OT). Because any OT protocol directly induces a key agreement protocol with identical round complexity and communication, the theorem directly extends to an identical lower bound for OT.

We refer to the full version [13] for a proof.

7.3   Model for a Lower Bound Against Streaming Adversaries

In the unbounded processing model for our lower bounds of Sects. 7.1 and 7.2, the only restriction, both for the honest parties and the adversary, is that their maintained state between rounds of communications has bounded size. In particular, they all can process messages from the protocol using potentially *unbounded* temporary memory, so long as they compress it to some limited amount of storage afterwards.

One natural setting left open, however, is the case where the adversary has bounded storage throughout the entire attack and only streaming access to messages sent. This makes the adversary *weaker* than in the model of Sect. 7.1, and it is not clear whether the subsequent lower bound extends. In this section, along with Sect. 7.3, we extend the lower bound of Sects. 7.1 and 7.2 to such adversaries, albeit at the cost of slightly worse parameters. Another difference is that while Sects. 7.1 and 7.2 also rule out protocols with unbounded processing *honest parties*, the model of this section and the subsequent lower bound in Sect. 7.3 only rule out *streaming* honest parties.

We first describe our model, that we call the *streaming model with CRS*. Honest parties send and receive messages in a *streaming manner*, using some bounded memory n, without any other restriction on the messages sent nor on the receiving algorithm. We will also consider adversaries which are similarly treating messages sent between the parties in a streaming manner using bounded memory $m > n$.

For comparison with Sect. 4, honest users are still more powerful, as having general streaming access to messages (as opposed to local access), and are not required to send uniformly random messages. In other words, honest parties neither have restriction (b) nor (c), but are still required now to be treating messages in a streaming manner. The adversary, however, is *weakened* to only have streaming access to the messages of the protocol, similar to honest users. Doing so makes the resulting lower bound stronger.

Compared with our previous lower bound (Sects. 7.1 and 7.2), both the honest parties and the adversary are weaker, as they are now both streaming, as opposed to having unbounded preprocessing. As a result, the resulting lower bounds are technically incomparable. Still, we believe that restricting ourselves to protocols where honest parties use bounded memory during the whole execution of the protocol is an extremely natural setting for protocols in the bounded storage model.

Optionally, we will consider a streaming model *in the common reference string model*, where a common reference string is available prior to protocol execution. The CRS is used to (independently) derive starting states for the parties of the protocol. We consider these processes (namely, the CRS generation and the user state generation) to be performed by a trusted party, which can potentially run in memory larger than n. Honest parties do not require knowledge of the CRS to execute the remainder protocol, but adversaries do have access to the CRS to mount attacks. For simplicity, we will only consider CRS that directly fit in the adversary's memory.

We define key agreement (with one-bit output) in a very similar way as in Sect. 7.1: we refer to that section for our notion of δ-correctness and (m, ε)-security. We further consider security against *non-uniform attacks* where adversaries obtain some non-uniform advice that can be generated using unbounded memory.

7.4   Lower Bound Against Streaming Adversaries

Theorem 24. *Let Π be a key agreement protocol in the streaming model (Sect. 7.3) with honest storage n, satisfying δ-correctness and (m, ε) security against non-uniform attacks, where $\delta - \varepsilon = \Omega(1)$. Suppose furthermore that for any execution of Π, the total communication between Alice and Bob is at most C and consists of at most R rounds. Then $C \geq \Omega\left(m \cdot \left(\frac{m}{n^2}\right)^{1/3}\right)$, and $R \geq \Omega\left(\left(\frac{m}{n^2}\right)^{1/3}\right)$.*

Remark 25 (Lower Bound for OT). Because any OT protocol directly induces a key agreement protocol with identical round complexity and communication, the theorem directly extends to an identical lower bound for OT.

References

1. Aumann, Y., Ding, Y.Z., Rabin, M.: Everlasting security in the bounded storage model. IEEE Trans. Inf. Theory **48**(6), 1668–1680 (2002). https://doi.org/10.1109/TIT.2002.1003845
2. Aumann, Y., Feige, U.: One message proof systems with known space verifiers. In: Stinson, D.R. (ed.) CRYPTO 1993. LNCS, vol. 773, pp. 85–99. Springer, Heidelberg (1994). https://doi.org/10.1007/3-540-48329-2_8

3. Bellare, M., Kane, D., Rogaway, P.: Big-key symmetric encryption: resisting key exfiltration. In: Robshaw, M., Katz, J. (eds.) CRYPTO 2016, Part I. LNCS, vol. 9814, pp. 373–402. Springer, Heidelberg (2016). https://doi.org/10.1007/978-3-662-53018-4_14

4. Cachin, C., Crépeau, C., Marcil, J.: Oblivious transfer with a memory-bounded receiver. In: 39th FOCS, pp. 493–502. IEEE Computer Society Press, Palo Alto, 8–11 November 1998. https://doi.org/10.1109/SFCS.1998.743500

5. Cachin, C., Maurer, U.: Unconditional security against memory-bounded adversaries. In: Kaliski, B.S. (ed.) CRYPTO 1997. LNCS, vol. 1294, pp. 292–306. Springer, Heidelberg (1997). https://doi.org/10.1007/BFb0052243

6. Calabro, C.: The exponential complexity of satisfiability problems. Ph.D. thesis, University of California, San Diego, USA (2009). http://www.escholarship.org/uc/item/0pk5w64k

7. Crépeau, C.: Equivalence between two flavours of oblivious transfers. In: Pomerance, C. (ed.) CRYPTO 1987. LNCS, vol. 293, pp. 350–354. Springer, Heidelberg (1988). https://doi.org/10.1007/3-540-48184-2_30

8. Diffie, W., Hellman, M.E.: New directions in cryptography. IEEE Trans. Inf. Theory $22(6)$, 644–654 (1976)

9. Ding, Y.Z.: Oblivious transfer in the bounded storage model. In: Kilian, J. (ed.) CRYPTO 2001. LNCS, vol. 2139, pp. 155–170. Springer, Heidelberg (2001). https://doi.org/10.1007/3-540-44647-8_9

10. Ding, Y.Z., Harnik, D., Rosen, A., Shaltiel, R.: Constant-round oblivious transfer in the bounded storage model. J. Cryptol. $20(2)$, 165–202 (2007). https://doi.org/10.1007/s00145-006-0438-1

11. Ding, Y.Z., Rabin, M.O.: Hyper-encryption and everlasting security. In: Alt, H., Ferreira, A. (eds.) STACS 2002. LNCS, vol. 2285, pp. 1–26. Springer, Heidelberg (2002). https://doi.org/10.1007/3-540-45841-7_1

12. Dodis, Y., Ostrovsky, R., Reyzin, L., Smith, A.D.: Fuzzy extractors: how to generate strong keys from biometrics and other noisy data. SIAM J. Comput. $38(1)$, 97–139 (2008). https://doi.org/10.1137/060651380

13. Dodis, Y., Quach, W., Wichs, D.: Speak much, remember little: cryptography in the bounded storage model, revisited. Cryptology ePrint Archive, Paper 2021/1270 (2021). https://eprint.iacr.org/2021/1270

14. Dziembowski, S., Kazana, T., Zdanowicz, M.: Quasi chain rule for min-entropy. Inf. Process. Lett. 134, 62–66 (2018). https://doi.org/10.1016/j.ipl.2018.02.007. https://www.sciencedirect.com/science/article/pii/S002001901830036X

15. Dziembowski, S., Maurer, U.M.: Tight security proofs for the bounded-storage model. In: 34th ACM STOC, pp. 341–350. ACM Press, Montréal, 19–21 May 2002. https://doi.org/10.1145/509907.509960

16. Dziembowski, S., Maurer, U.: On generating the initial key in the bounded-storage model. In: Cachin, C., Camenisch, J.L. (eds.) EUROCRYPT 2004. LNCS, vol. 3027, pp. 126–137. Springer, Heidelberg (2004). https://doi.org/10.1007/978-3-540-24676-3_8

17. Garg, S., Raz, R., Tal, A.: Extractor-based time-space lower bounds for learning. In: Diakonikolas, I., Kempe, D., Henzinger, M. (eds.) 50th ACM STOC, pp. 990–1002. ACM Press, Los Angeles, 25–29 June 2018. https://doi.org/10.1145/3188745.3188962

18. Goldwasser, S., Micali, S., Rackoff, C.: The knowledge complexity of interactive proof systems. SIAM J. Comput. $18(1)$, 186–208 (1989). https://doi.org/10.1137/0218012

19. Guan, J., Zhandary, M.: Simple schemes in the bounded storage model. In: Ishai, Y., Rijmen, V. (eds.) EUROCRYPT 2019, Part III. LNCS, vol. 11478, pp. 500–524. Springer, Cham (2019). https://doi.org/10.1007/978-3-030-17659-4_17

20. Guan, J., Zhandry, M.: Disappearing cryptography in the bounded storage model. In: Nissim, K., Waters, B. (eds.) TCC 2021. LNCS, vol. 13043, pp. 365–396. Springer, Cham (2021). https://doi.org/10.1007/978-3-030-90453-1_13

21. Hong, D., Chang, K.-Y., Ryu, H.: Efficient oblivious transfer in the bounded-storage model. In: Zheng, Y. (ed.) ASIACRYPT 2002. LNCS, vol. 2501, pp. 143–159. Springer, Heidelberg (2002). https://doi.org/10.1007/3-540-36178-2_9

22. Impagliazzo, R., Levin, L.A., Luby, M.: Pseudo-random generation from one-way functions. In: Proceedings of the Twenty-First Annual ACM Symposium on Theory of Computing, STOC 1989, pp. 12–24. Association for Computing Machinery, New York (1989). https://doi.org/10.1145/73007.73009

23. Ishai, Y., Prabhakaran, M., Sahai, A.: Founding cryptography on oblivious transfer – efficiently. In: Wagner, D. (ed.) CRYPTO 2008. LNCS, vol. 5157, pp. 572–591. Springer, Heidelberg (2008). https://doi.org/10.1007/978-3-540-85174-5_32

24. Kamp, J., Rao, A., Vadhan, S., Zuckerman, D.: Deterministic extractors for small-space sources. J. Comput. Syst. Sci. **77**(1), 191–220 (2011). https://doi.org/10.1016/j.jcss.2010.06.014. https://www.sciencedirect.com/science/article/pii/S002200001000098X. Celebrating Karp's Kyoto Prize

25. Kilian, J.: Founding cryptography on oblivious transfer. In: 20th ACM STOC, pp. 20–31. ACM Press, Chicago, 2–4 May 1988. https://doi.org/10.1145/62212.62215

26. Kol, G., Raz, R., Tal, A.: Time-space hardness of learning sparse parities. In: Hatami, H., McKenzie, P., King, V. (eds.) 49th ACM STOC, pp. 1067–1080. ACM Press, Montreal, 19–23 June 2017. https://doi.org/10.1145/3055399.3055430

27. Liu, J., Vusirikala, S.: Secure multiparty computation in the bounded storage model. In: Paterson, M.B. (ed.) IMACC 2021. LNCS, vol. 13129, pp. 289–325. Springer, Cham (2021). https://doi.org/10.1007/978-3-030-92641-0_14

28. Lu, C.-J.: Hyper-encryption against space-bounded adversaries from on-line strong extractors. In: Yung, M. (ed.) CRYPTO 2002. LNCS, vol. 2442, pp. 257–271. Springer, Heidelberg (2002). https://doi.org/10.1007/3-540-45708-9_17

29. Maurer, U.M.: Conditionally-perfect secrecy and a provably-secure randomized cipher. J. Cryptol. **5**(1), 53–66 (1992). https://doi.org/10.1007/BF00191321

30. Moran, T., Shaltiel, R., Ta-Shma, A.: Non-interactive timestamping in the bounded-storage model. J. Cryptol. **22**(2), 189–226 (2009). https://doi.org/10.1007/s00145-008-9035-9

31. Naor, M., Ostrovsky, R., Venkatesan, R., Yung, M.: Perfect zero-knowledge arguments for *NP* can be based on general complexity assumptions. In: Brickell, E.F. (ed.) CRYPTO 1992. LNCS, vol. 740, pp. 196–214. Springer, Heidelberg (1993). https://doi.org/10.1007/3-540-48071-4_14

32. Nisan, N.: Pseudorandom generators for space-bounded computations. In: Proceedings of the Twenty-Second Annual ACM Symposium on Theory of Computing, STOC 1990, pp. 204–212. Association for Computing Machinery, New York (1990). https://doi.org/10.1145/100216.100242

33. Nisan, N., Zuckerman, D.: Randomness is linear in space. J. Comput. Syst. Sci. **52**(1), 43–52 (1996). https://doi.org/10.1006/jcss.1996.0004

34. Rabin, M.O.: How to exchange secrets with oblivious transfer (1981). Harvard Aiken Computational Laboratory TR-81

35. Raz, R.: Fast learning requires good memory: a time-space lower bound for parity learning. In: Dinur, I. (ed.) 57th FOCS, pp. 266–275. IEEE Computer Society Press, New Brunswick, 9–11 October 2016. https://doi.org/10.1109/FOCS.2016.36

36. Raz, R.: A time-space lower bound for a large class of learning problems. In: Umans, C. (ed.) 58th FOCS, pp. 732–742. IEEE Computer Society Press, Berkeley, 15–17 October 2017. https://doi.org/10.1109/FOCS.2017.73

37. De Santis, A., Persiano, G., Yung, M.: One-message statistical zero-knowledge proofs and space-bounded verifier. In: Kuich, W. (ed.) ICALP 1992. LNCS, vol. 623, pp. 28–40. Springer, Heidelberg (1992). https://doi.org/10.1007/3-540-55719-9_61

38. Skorski, M.: Strong chain rules for min-entropy under few bits spoiled. In: 2019 IEEE International Symposium on Information Theory (ISIT), pp. 1122–1126 (2019). https://doi.org/10.1109/ISIT.2019.8849240

39. Vadhan, S.P.: Constructing locally computable extractors and cryptosystems in the bounded-storage model. J. Cryptol. **17**(1), 43–77 (2004). https://doi.org/10.1007/s00145-003-0237-x

Non-uniformity and Quantum Advice in the Quantum Random Oracle Model

Qipeng Liu[✉]

Simons Institute for the Theory of Computing, Berkeley, USA
qipengliu0@gmail.com

Abstract. QROM (quantum random oracle model), introduced by Boneh et al. (Asiacrypt 2011), captures all generic algorithms. However, it fails to describe non-uniform quantum algorithms with preprocessing power, which receives a piece of bounded classical or quantum advice.

As non-uniform algorithms are largely believed to be the right model for attackers, starting from the work by Nayebi, Aaronson, Belovs, and Trevisan (QIC 2015), a line of works investigates non-uniform security in the random oracle model. Chung, Guo, Liu, and Qian (FOCS 2020) provide a framework and establish non-uniform security for many cryptographic applications. Although they achieve nearly optimal bounds for many applications with classical advice, their bounds for quantum advice are far from tight.

In this work, we continue the study on quantum advice in the QROM. We provide a new idea that generalizes the previous multi-instance framework, which we believe is more quantum-friendly and should be the quantum analog of multi-instance games. To this end, we *match* the bounds with *quantum advice* to those with *classical advice* by Chung et al., showing quantum advice is almost as good/bad as classical advice for many natural security games in the QROM.

Finally, we show that for some contrived games in the QROM, quantum advice can be exponentially better than classical advice for some parameter regimes. To our best knowledge, it provides an evidence of a general separation between quantum and classical advice relative to an unstructured oracle.

1 Introduction

Many practical cryptographic constructions are analyzed in idealized models, for example, the random oracle model which treats an underlying hash function as a uniformly random oracle (ROM) [BR93]. On a high level, the random oracle model captures all algorithms that use the underlying hash function in a generic (black-box) way; often, the best attacks are generic. Whereas the random oracle methodology guides the actual security of practical constructions, it fails to describe non-uniform security: that is, an algorithm consists of two parts, the offline and the online part; the offline part can take forever, and at the end of the day, it produces a piece of bounded advice for its online part; the online part given the advice, tries to attack cryptographic constructions efficiently.

© International Association for Cryptologic Research 2023
C. Hazay and M. Stam (Eds.): EUROCRYPT 2023, LNCS 14004, pp. 117–143, 2023.
https://doi.org/10.1007/978-3-031-30545-0_5

Non-uniform algorithms are largely believed to be the right model for attackers and usually show advantages over uniform algorithms [Unr07, CDGS18, CDG18]. The famous non-uniform example is Hellman's algorithm [Hel80] for inverting permutations or functions. When a permutation of range and domain size N is given, Hellman's algorithm can invert any image (with certainty) with roughly advice size $\sqrt{N}$ and running time $\sqrt{N}$. In contrast, uniform algorithms require running time N to achieve constant success probability. Another more straightforward example is collision resistance. When non-uniform algorithms are presented, no single fixed hash function is collision-resistant as an algorithm can hardcode a pair of collisions in its advice.

Non-uniform security in idealized models has been studied extensively in the literature. Let us take the two most simple yet fundamental security games as examples: one search game and one decision game. The first one is one-way function inversion (or OWFs) as mentioned above. The goal is to invert a random image of the random oracle. The study was initialized by Yao [Yao90] and later improved by a line of works [DTT10, Unr07, DGK17, CDGS18]. They show that any T-query algorithm with arbitrary S-bit advice, can win this game with probability at most $\tilde{O}(ST/N)$, assuming the random oracle has equal domain and range size. The other example is pseudorandom generators (or PRG). The task is to distinguish between a random image $H(x)$ (x is uniformly at random and H is the hash function) or a random element y in its range. Since it is a decision game, some techniques for OWFs may not apply to PRGs, which we will see later. Its non-uniform security is $O(1/2 + T/N + \sqrt{ST/N})$ by Coretti et al. [CDGS18], and later improved by Garvin et al. [GGKL21].

The quantum setting is very similar to the classical one, except an algorithm can query the random oracle in superposition. Boneh et al. [BDF+11] justify the ability to make superposition queries since a quantum computer can always learn the description of a hash function and compute it coherently. Besides, advice can be either a sequence of **bits** or **qubits**. We should carefully distinguish between the two different models. Indeed, we believe non-uniform quantum algorithms with quantum advice are important to understand and should be considered the "right" attacker model when full-scale quantum computers are widely viable and quantum memory is affordable.

Nayebi, Aaronson, Belovs, and Trevisan [NABT14] initiated the study of quantum non-uniform security with classical advice of OWFs and PRGs. Hhan, Xagawa and Yamakawa [HXY19], Chung, Liao and Qian [CLQ19] extended the study to quantum advice. Most recently, Chung, Guo, Liu and Qian [CGLQ20] improved the bounds for both examples. For OWFs, their bounds are almost optimal in terms of query complexity for both classical and quantum advice. They show that to invert a random image with at least constant probability, advice size S and the number of queries T should satisfy $ST + T^2 \geq \tilde{\Omega}(N)$. However, a gap between classical and quantum advice appears when we choose security parameters for practical hash functions against non-uniform attacks. In practice, we ensure that an adversary with bounded resources (for example, $S = T = 2^{128}$) only has probability smaller than 2^{-128}. The bounds in [CGLQ20] suggest that for OWF, the security parameter needs to be $n = 384$ (and $N = 2^{384}$) for classical advice and $n = 640$ for quantum advice, leaving a big gap between two types of advice. Even worse, when it comes to PRGs, the security parameters are $n = 640$ for classical advice v.s. $n = 3200$ for quantum advice; not to mention a large gap between their query complexity, unlike OWFs.

As understanding quantum advice is beneficial to both practical cryptography efficiency and may inspire general computation theory (such as, QMA v.s. QCMA [AK07, Aar21] and BQP/poly v.s. BQP/qpoly [Aar05]), we raise the following natural question:

Can quantum advice outperform classical advice in the QROM?

In this work, we provide a new technique for analyzing quantum advice in the QROM and show that for many games, the non-uniform security with quantum advice matches the best-known security with classical advice, including OWFs and PRGs. It gives strong evidence that for many cryptographic games in the QROM, quantum advice provides no or little advantage over classical one.

So far, we have seen no advantage of quantum advice in the QROM for common cryptographic games. We then ask the second question:

Is there any (contrived) game in the QROM, in which quantum advice is "exponentially better" than classical advice?

We give an affirmative answer to this question, for some parameters of S, T. We show that when algorithms can not make online queries (i.e., $T = 0$), there is an exponential separation between quantum and classical advice for certain games. This result is inspired by the recent work by Yamakawa and Zhandry [YZ22] on verifiable quantum advantages in the QROM. We elaborate on both results now.

1.1 Our Results

Our first result is to give a quantum analog of "multi-instance games" via "alternating measurement games" (introduced in Sect. 5) and develop a new technique for analyzing non-uniform bounds with quantum advice. Our techniques do not need to rewind a non-uniform quantum algorithm and completely avoid the rewinding issues/difficulties in the prior work [CGLQ20].

To show the power of our technique, we incorporate it into three important applications: OWFs, PRGs, and salted cryptography. Note that our result below is a non-exhaustive list of applications. With little effort, we can show improved non-uniform security with quantum advice of Merkle-Damgård [GLLZ21], Yao's box [CGLQ20] and other games.

One-Way Functions. In this application, a random oracle is interpreted as a one-way function. A (non-uniform) algorithm needs to win the OWF security game with the random oracle as a OWF. Formally, let $H : [N] \to [M]$ be a random oracle.

1. A challenger samples a uniformly random input $x \in [N]$ and sends $y = H(x)$ to the algorithm.
2. The algorithm returns x' and it wins if and only if $H(x') = y$.

When both advice and queries are classical, the best lower bound is $\tilde{O}(ST/\alpha)$ by [CDGS18], where $\alpha = \min\{N, M\}$ and N, M are the domain and range size of the random oracle. In other words, no algorithm with S bits of advice and T classical queries can win with probability more than $\tilde{O}(ST/\alpha)$. There is a gap between this lower bound and the upper bound $\approx T/\alpha + (S^2T/\alpha^2)^{1/3}$ provided by Hellman's algorithm[1]. Later, Corrigan-Gibbs and Kogan [CGK19] study the possible improvement on the lower bound and conclude that any improvement will lead to improved results in circuit lower bounds. Thus, $\tilde{O}(ST/\alpha)$ is the best one can hope for in light of the barrier.

Chung et al. [CGLQ20] show that if S bits of classical advice and T quantum queries are given, the maximum winning probability is bounded by $\tilde{O}\left(\frac{ST+T^2}{\alpha}\right)$. They further argue that this bound is almost optimal. Intuitively, one can think of this as T^2/α comes from a brute-force Grover's algorithm [Gro96], without using any advice, and ST/α comes from classical advice and hits the classical barrier by [CGK19].

For quantum advice and quantum queries, they show the maximum success probability is $\tilde{O}\left(\frac{ST+T^2}{\alpha}\right)^{1/3}$. As mentioned early, although the bound is optimal regarding query complexity, the exponent seems non-tight. Thus, they ask the following question:

> ... Can this loss (of the exponent) be avoided, or is there any speed up in terms of S and T for sub-constant success probability?.

Our first result gives a positive answer to the above question and proves that the loss on exponent can be avoided.

Theorem 1. *Let H be a random oracle $[N] \to [M]$ and $\alpha = \min\{N, M\}$. One-way function games in the QROM have security $O\left(\frac{ST+T^2}{\alpha}\right)$ against non-uniform quantum algorithms with S-qubits of advice and T quantum queries.*

The theorem guides security parameter choices of hash functions to be secure against non-uniform attacks. The security parameter n should be 384 to have security 2^{-128} against non-uniform quantum attacks with $S = T = 2^{128}$. Another direct implication of our theorem is that, when quantum advice $S = O(\sqrt{\alpha})$, quantum advice is useless for speeding up function inversion. To put it in another way, Grover's algorithm can not be sped up and only has probability T^2/α to succeed even with quantum advice of size $O(\sqrt{\alpha})$, relative to a random oracle. We list a comparison of best-known bounds and our result below (Table 1).

---

[1] Hellman's algorithm on functions does not behave as well as on permutations. Upper and lower bounds meet at ST/α only when we consider permutations.

Table 1. Non-uniform security for OWFs with T queries and S bits (qubits) of advice, where $\alpha = \min\{N, M\}$ and N, M are the domain and range size of the random oracle. Our bound is a "big-O" instead of "big-$\tilde{O}$" as we also remove the dependence on $\log N$ and $\log M$.

Classical Advice in [CGLQ20]	Quantum Advice in [CGLQ20]	Quantum Advice in This Work
$\tilde{O}\left(\frac{ST+T^2}{\alpha}\right)$	$\tilde{O}\left(\frac{ST+T^2}{\alpha}\right)^{1/3}$	$O\left(\frac{ST+T^2}{\alpha}\right)$

Pseudorandom Generators. Another important application we will focus on is pseudorandom generators. One fundamental difference from one-way functions is its being a decision game. We will later see that publicly verifiable games such as one-way functions are easy to deal with in the previous work [CGLQ20]. For games that can not be publicly verified, such as decision games, [CGLQ20] often gives worse bounds.

In this game, an algorithm tries to distinguish between an image of a random input, and a uniformly random element in the range. Let $H : [N] \to [M]$ be a random oracle.

- A challenger samples a uniformly random bit b. If $b = 0$, it samples a uniformly random $x \in [N]$ and outputs $y = H(x)$; otherwise, it samples a uniform $y \in [M]$ and outputs y.
- The algorithm is given y and returns b'. It wins if and only if $b' = b$.

Our new technique demonstrates the following theorem about PRGs.

Theorem 2. *Let H be a random oracle $[N] \to [M]$. PRG games in the QROM have security $1/2 + O\left(\frac{T^2}{N}\right)^{1/2} + O\left(\frac{ST}{N}\right)^{1/3}$ against non-uniform quantum algorithms with S-qubits of advice and T quantum queries.*

"Salting Defeats Preprocessing". Finally, instead of proving more concrete non-uniform bounds like Merkle-Damgård [GLLZ21], we demonstrate that the generic mechanism "salting" helps prevent quantum preprocessing attacks even with quantum advice. Maybe the most illustrating example is collision-resistant hash functions. As mentioned before, no single fixed hash function can be collision resistant against non-uniform attacks. A typical solution is to add "salt" to the hash function. A salt is a piece of random data that will be fed into a hash function as an additional input. To attack a salted collision resistant hash function, an adversary gets a salt s and is required to come out with two input $m \neq m'$ such that the hash evaluation on (s, m) equals that of (s, m'). Intuitively, since salt s is chosen uniformly at random from a large space, advice is not long enough to include collisions for every possible salt. Thus, salting is a mechanism that compiles a game into another game, by adding a random extra input s and restricting the execution of the game always under oracle access to $H(s, \cdot)$ (Table 2).

Table 2. Non-uniform security of PRGs with T queries and S bits (qubits) of advice. Our bound also improves the previous result on classical advice by reducing the exponent on T^2/N from $1/3$ to $1/2$; we note that the improvement on the exponent only follows from a simple observation and can also be applied to the previous work as well.

Classical Advice in [CGLQ20]	Quantum Advice in [CGLQ20]	Quantum Advice in This Work
$\frac{1}{2} + \tilde{O}\left(\frac{ST+T^2}{N}\right)^{1/3}$	$\frac{1}{2} + \tilde{O}\left(\frac{S^5T+S^4T^2}{N}\right)^{1/19}$	$\frac{1}{2} + O\left(\frac{T^2}{N}\right)^{1/2} + O\left(\frac{ST}{N}\right)^{1/3}$

Chung et al. [CLMP13], and Coretti et al. [CDGS18] formally proved the non-uniform security of salted collision-resistant hash in the classical ROM. Chung et al. [CGLQ20] extended the statement in the quantum setting. For quantum advice, their result roughly says that if an underlying game G is publicly verifiable or a decision game, then the salted version of G is secure against non-uniform attacks.

Our third results improve the prior ones in two different aspects. First, our theorem works not only for publicly verifiable or decision games, but for any types of games (see our definition of games Definition 2). Second, our theorem is tighter and provides a more pictorial statement for "salting defeats preprocessing", elaborated below. Our bounds match those with classical advice in [CGLQ20].

Theorem 3 (Informal, Theorem 10). *For any game G in the QROM, let $\nu(T)$ be its uniform security in the QROM. Let G_S be the salted game with salt space $[K]$. Then G_S has security $\delta(S,T)$ against non-uniform quantum adversaries with T queries and S-qubits of advice,*

1. *$\delta(S,T) \leq 4\nu(T) + O(ST/K)$;*
2. *If G_S is a decision game, then $\delta(S,T) \leq \nu(T) + O(ST/K)^{1/3}$.*

That is to say, the non-uniform security of G_S and uniform security of G only differs by a term of $O(ST/K)$ or $O(ST/K)^{1/3}$ depending on the type of the game. When the game G is a search game, G_S has non-uniform security $4\nu(T) + O(ST/K)$. We can choose S to ensure $ST/K \leq \nu(T)$ so that the non-uniform security of G_S is in the same order of G's security $\nu(T)$. For decision games, we choose S such that $(ST/K)^{1/3}$ is extremely small.

In [CGLQ20], they show that for publicly verifiable games, $\delta := \delta(S,T)$ satisfies $\delta \leq \tilde{O}\left(\nu(T/\delta) + \frac{ST}{K\delta}\right)$ whereas ours works for any games and $\delta(S,T) \leq 4\nu(T) + O(ST/K)$. For decision games, ours also significantly improves prior results (see Table 3 and Theorem 7.6 in [CGLQ20] for a comparison). The dependence in their theorems on uniform security ν is much more complicated and yields loose bounds. Most notably, for decision games, when the salt size $K \to \infty$, the bound in [CGLQ20] does not rule out the speed up from having S-qubits of advice (corresponding to the term $\nu'(S^2T/\epsilon^8)$); whereas our bound gives $\nu(T)$ — exactly the security in the uniform case, completely ruling out the influence of quantum advice.

Table 3. Salting "defeats" preprocessing.

	Quantum Advice in [CGLQ20]	Quantum Advice in This Work
Any Games	$\delta \le \tilde{O}\left(\nu(T/\delta) + ST/(K\delta)\right)$	$\delta \le 4\nu(T) + O(ST/K)$
Decision Games	$\delta \le 1/2 + \epsilon$	$\delta \le \nu(T) + O(ST/K)^{1/3}$
	where $\epsilon \le \tilde{O}\left(\nu'(S^2T/\epsilon^8) + \sqrt{S^5T/(K\epsilon^{17})}\right)$	
	and $\nu'(T) := \nu(T) - 1/2$	

Separation of Quantum and Classical Advice in the QROM. So far, we have seen many examples that quantum advice is as good/bad as classical advice. Below, we show that it is not always the case in the QROM: there exists a game in the QROM such that quantum advice is exponentially better than classical advice.

Theorem 4 (Separation of Quantum and Classical Advice in the QROM). *Let H be a random oracle $[2^{\mathsf{poly}(n)}] \to \{0,1\}$. There exists a game G in the QROM such that,*

- *G has security $2^{-\Omega(n)}$ against non-uniform adversaries with S-bits of **classical** advice and making no queries, for $S = 2^{n^c}/n$ and some constant $0 < c < 1$;*
- *There is a non-uniform adversary with S-qubits of **quantum** advice and making no queries, that achieves winning probability $1 - \mathsf{negl}(n)$, for $S = \tilde{O}(n)$.*

Although the bound only works in the parameter regime $T = 0$, to our best knowledge, it is the first example of an exponential separation between quantum and classical advice in the QROM (or for inputs without structures).

Remark 1. For the parameter regime $T = 0$, the above separation can be alternatively viewed as an exponential separation of quantum/classical one-way communication complexity for some relation $\mathcal{R} \subseteq \mathcal{X} \times \mathcal{Y} \times Z$. In the context of one-way communication complexity, there are two players, Alice and Bob. Alice gets an input $x \in \mathcal{X}$ and Bob gets an input $y \in \mathcal{Y}$; Alice sends one (classical or quantum) message to Bob and Bob tries to output $z \in Z$ such that $(x, y, z) \in \mathcal{R}$. Our result in Theorem 4 is a separation of quantum/classical one-way communication complexity when $\mathcal{X} = \{0,1\}^{2^{\mathsf{poly}(n)}}$, $\mathcal{Y} = \{0,1\}^n$, $Z = \{0,1\}^{n \times \mathsf{poly}(n)}$; when the message is allow to be quantum, $\tilde{O}(n)$ qubits are sufficient; on the other hand, the classical communication complexity is $\Omega(2^{n^c}/n)$.

Exponential separation of quantum/classical one-way communication complexity is already known, starting from the work by [BYJK04] (later by [Gav08]) based on the so-called hidden matching problem. We believe the hidden matching problem can be also turned into a separation of quantum/classical advice in the parameter regime $T = 0$, in the QROM. However, [BYJK04] only proved *average-case* hardness against *deterministic* classical Bob. Therefore, we pick the recent result by Zhandry and Yamakawa for simplicity of presentation.

1.2   Organization

The rest of the paper is organized as follows. Section 2 and Sect. 3 recall the notations and backgrounds on quantum computing, random oracles models, non-uniform security and bit-fixing models. Section 4 introduces decomposition of advice with respect to a game, which helps the proof of our main theorem. Section 5 proves the main theorem whereas Sect. 6 applies the main theorem to various applications. Finally in Sect. 7, we give the separation of quantum and classical advice.

2   Preliminaries

We assume readers are familiar with the basics of quantum information and computation. All backgrounds on quantum information can be found in [NC10].

2.1   Quantum Random Oracle Model

In the quantum random oracle model, a hash function is modeled as a random classical function H. The function H is sampled at the beginning of any security game and then gets fixed. Oracle access to H is defined by a unitary U_H: $|x, y\rangle \rightarrow |x, y + H(x)\rangle$. A quantum oracle algorithm with oracle access to H is then denoted by a sequence of unitary $U_1, U_H, U_2, U_H, \cdots, U_T, U_H, U_{T+1}$ followed by a computational basis measurement, where U_i is a local unitary operating on the algorithm's internal register. The number of queries, in this case, is T—the number of U_H calls.

2.2   Other Useful Lemmas

We use the lemmas in this section to prove bounds in the alternating measurement games (Sect. 5). Readers can safely skip and return to this section for (Sect. 5).

We omit the proof for the following lemmas and refer readers to the appendix for more the proofs.

Lemma 1. *Let N be a positive integer and $p_1, \cdots, p_N \in \mathbb{R}^{\geq 0}$. Let $c_1, \cdots, c_N$ be a distribution over $[N]$. Assume $\sum_{i \in [N]} c_i p_i > 0$. Define S_k for every integer $k \geq 1$:*

$$S_k = \frac{\sum_{i \in [N]} c_i p_i^k}{\sum_{i \in [N]} c_i p_i^{k-1}}.$$

Then $\{S_k\}_{k \geq 1}$ is monotonically non-decreasing.

Lemma 2 (Jensen's inequality). *Let N, g be two positive integers and $p_1, \cdots, p_N \in \mathbb{R}^{\geq 0}$. Let $c_1, \cdots, c_N$ be a distribution over $[N]$. Assume $\sum_{i \in [N]} c_i p_i > 0$. If the following holds $\sum_{i \in [N]} c_i p_i^g \leq \delta^g$, then $\sum_{i \in [N]} c_i p_i \leq \delta$.*

3 (S, T) Quantum Algorithms and Games in the QROM

In this work, we consider non-uniform algorithms against games in the QROM. We start by defining (S, T) non-uniform quantum algorithms with either S classical bits of advice or S qubits of advice. The definitions below more or less follow definitions in [CGLQ20] but are adapted for our setting.

Definition 1 ((S, T) Non-uniform Quantum Algorithms in the QROM). *A (S, T) non-uniform quantum algorithm with* **classical** *advice in the QROM is modeled by a collection $\{s_H\}_{H:[N] \to [M]}$ and $\{U_{\mathsf{inp}}\}_{\mathsf{inp}}$: for every function H, s_H is a piece of S-bit advice and U_{inp}^H is a unitary that calls the oracle H at most T times.*

A (S, T) non-uniform quantum algorithm with **quantum** *advice in the QROM is modeled by a collection $\{|\sigma_H\rangle\}_H$ and $\{U_{\mathsf{inp}}\}_{\mathsf{inp}}$: for every function H, $|\sigma_H\rangle$ is a piece of S-qubit advice and U_{inp}^H is a unitary that calls the oracle H at most T times.*

Similarly, we denote a **uniform** *quantum algorithm by a collection of unitaries $\{U_{\mathsf{inp}}\}_{\mathsf{inp}}$: it is a non-uniform quantum algorithm satisfying $|\sigma_H\rangle = |0^S\rangle$ for all H.*

When the algorithm is working with oracle access to H, its initial state is $|s_H\rangle |0^L\rangle$ or $|\sigma_H\rangle |0^L\rangle$, respectively. On input inp, it applies U_{inp}^H on the initial state and measures its internal register in the computational basis.

Since we are working in the idealized model, we require neither L nor the size of the unitary U_{inp} to be polynomially bounded. In the rest of the work, we will focus on non-uniform algorithms with quantum advice as our new reduction works for both cases. Therefore, 'non-uniform algorithms' denotes 'non-uniform algorithms with quantum advice'.

Remark 2. We can assume quantum advice is a **pure** state. Due to convexity, the optimal non-uniform algorithm can always have advice as a pure state. If the advice is a mixed state and achieves a winning probability p, there always exists a pure state that achieves a winning probability at least p.

Next, we define games in the QROM.

Definition 2 (Games in the QROM). *A game G in the QROM is specified by two classical algorithms Samp^H and Verify^H:*

- *$\mathsf{Samp}^H(r)$: it is a deterministic algorithm that takes uniformly random coins $r \in \mathcal{R}$ as input, and outputs a challenge ch.*
- *$\mathsf{Verify}^H(r, \mathsf{ans})$: it is a deterministic algorithm that takes the same random coins for generating a challenge and an alleged answer ans, and outputs b indicating whether the game is won ($b = 0$ for winning).*

Let T_{Samp} be the number of queries made by Samp and T_{Verify} be the number of queries made by Verify.

For a fixed H and a quantum algorithm $\mathcal{A}$, the game $G_{\mathcal{A}}^H$ is executed as follows:

- A *challenger* $\mathcal{C}$ *samples* ch $\leftarrow$ Samp$^H(r)$ *using uniformly random coins* r.
- A *(uniform or non-uniform) quantum algorithm* $\mathcal{A}$ *has oracle access to* H, *takes* ch *as input and outputs* ans. *We call* $\mathcal{A}$ *an online adversary/algorithm.*
- $b \leftarrow$ Verify$^H(r, \text{ans})$ *is the game's outcome.*

Remark 3. In the above definition, a quantum algorithm makes at most T oracle queries to H. However, in some particular games, the algorithm can not get access to H. One famous example is Yao's box, in which an adversary is given a challenge input x and the goal is to output $H(x)$. The adversary can query H on any input except x (otherwise, the game is trivial). The definition Definition 2 does not capture this case. Nonetheless, we will stick with the current definition. For the special case when an algorithm has access to a different oracle H', the technique in this work extends as well. This extension requires a similar definition of games (Definition 3.3) in [CGLQ20].

Let us warm up by having a close look at the following examples.

Example 1. The first example is function inversion (or OWFs) G_{OWF}. $r = x \in [N]$ is a uniformly random pre-image and ch $:= H(x)$. The goal is to find a pre-image of ch. The verification procedure takes $r = x$ and ans $= x'$, it outputs 0 (winning) if and only if x' is a pre-image of $H(x)$.

The other example G_{PRG} is to distinguish images of PRG from a uniformly random element. In this example, r consists of (b, x, y) where b is a single bit, x is a uniformly random pre-image in $[N]$ and y is a uniformly random element in $[M]$. The challenge ch is $H(x)$ if $b = 0$, otherwise ch $= y$. The goal is to distinguish whether an image of a random input or a random element in the range is given. The verification procedure takes $r = (b, x, y)$ and ans $= b'$, it outputs 0 if and only if $b = b'$.

Definition 3. *We say a game G has $\delta(S, T) := \delta$ maximum winning probability (or has security δ, for cryptographic games) against all (S, T) non-uniform quantum adversaries with classical or quantum advice if*

$$\max_{\mathcal{A}} \Pr_H \left[G_{\mathcal{A}}^H = 1 \right] \leq \delta,$$

where max *is taken over all (S, T) non-uniform quantum adversaries $\mathcal{A}$ with classical or quantum advice, respectively.*

3.1   Quantum Bit-Fixing Model

Here we recall a different model called the quantum bit-fixing model. In the following sections, we will relate winning probability of a game G against (S, T) non-uniform quantum algorithms with that in the quantum bit-fixing model (BF-QROM). Since the previous quantum non-uniform bounds require analyzing the quantum bit-fixing model, winning probabilities in the bit-fixing model are already known for many games, and our improved bounds only need a new reduction. The following definitions are adapted from [GLLZ21].

Definition 4 (Games in the P-BF-QROM). *It is similar to games in the standard QROM, except now H has a different distribution.*

- *Before a game starts, a quantum algorithm f (having no input) with at most P queries to an oracle is picked and fixed by an adversary.*
- **Rejection Sampling Stage:** *A random oracle H is picked uniformly at random, then conditioned on f^H outputs 0. In other words, the distribution of H is defined by a rejection sampling:*
  1. *$H \leftarrow \{f : [N] \rightarrow [M]\}$.*
  2. *Run f^H and obtain a binary outcome b together with a quantum state τ^2.*
  3. *Restart from step 1 if $b \neq 0$.*
- **Online Stage:** *The game is then executed with oracle access to H, and an algorithm $\mathcal{B}$ gets τ.*

A (P, T) algorithm in the P-BF-QROM consists of f for sampling the distribution and $\mathcal{B}$ for playing the game, with f making at most P queries and $\mathcal{B}$ making at most T queries. We also call $\mathcal{B}$ an **online** algorithm/adversary.

We will also consider the following classical analog P-BF-ROM only when showing a separation between classical and quantum advice in Sect. 7.

Definition 5 (Games in the P-BF-ROM). *It is similar to the above Definition 4, except both f and $\mathcal{B}$ can only make classical queries.*

Definition 6. *We say a game G has $\nu(P, T) := \nu$ maximum winning probability (or is ν-secure, for cryptographic games) in the P-BF-QROM if*

$$\max_{f, \mathcal{B}} \Pr_H \left[f^H = 0 \wedge G_{\mathcal{B}}^H = 1 \right] \leq \nu,$$

where $\max$ is taken over all (P, T) quantum adversaries $(f, \mathcal{B})$ with f making at most P queries and $\mathcal{B}$ making at most T queries.

We know the following two lemmas from [CGLQ20, GLLZ21].

Lemma 3 (Function Inversion in the P-BF-QROM). *The OWF game has $\nu(P, T) = (P + T^2)/\min\{N, M\}$ in the P-BF-QROM.*

See the proof for Lemma 5.2 in [CGLQ20] and Lemma 10 in [GLLZ21].

Lemma 4 (PRGs in the P-BF-QROM). *The game PRG has $\nu(P, T) = 1/2 + \sqrt{(P + T^2)/N}$ in the P-BF-QROM.*

See the proof for Lemma 5.13 in [CGLQ20].

---

[2] In [GLLZ21], they do not need quantum or classical memory τ shared between f and $\mathcal{A}$. However, this is essential in our proof. Nonetheless, all security proofs in the P-BR-QROM work in the stronger setting (with τ shared between stages).

4   Games, POVMs and Decomposition of Advice

In this section, we will formalize an quantum algorithm's winning probability against a game in terms of POVMs and its corresponding eigenvectors.

For any game G and algorithm $\mathcal{A}$, let V_r^H be a projection that operates on the register of $\mathcal{A}$. V_r^H project a quantum state into a subspace spanned by basis states $|\text{ans}\rangle |z\rangle$ where $\text{Verify}^H(r, \text{ans}) = 1$ and z be any aux input (depending on the size of $\mathcal{A}$'s working register). As an example, for function inversion problem and $r = x$, V_r^H is defined as $\sum_{x':H(x')=H(x),z} |x', z\rangle \langle x', z|$.

Then for any non-uniform quantum algorithm $\mathcal{A} = (\{|\sigma_H\rangle\}_H, \{U_{\text{inp}}\}_{\text{inp}})$, by definition, its probability $\epsilon_{\mathcal{A}}$ for winning the game G with oracle access to H can be then written as:

$$\epsilon_{\mathcal{A},H} = \frac{1}{|\mathcal{R}|} \sum_{r \in \mathcal{R}} \left\| V_r^H U_{\text{Samp}^H(r)}^H |\sigma_H\rangle |0^L\rangle \right\|^2.$$

We define the following projections $P_r^H := \left(U_{\text{Samp}^H(r)}^H \right)^\dagger V_r^H U_{\text{Samp}^H(r)}^H$. Let P_H be a POVM: $P_H := \frac{1}{|\mathcal{R}|} \sum_{r \in \mathcal{R}} P_r^H$. We can equivalently write $\epsilon_{\mathcal{A},H}$ in terms of this POVM: $\epsilon_{\mathcal{A},H} = \langle \sigma_H, 0^L | P^H | \sigma_H, 0^L \rangle$. This is due to:

$$\epsilon_{\mathcal{A},H} = \frac{1}{|\mathcal{R}|} \sum_{r \in \mathcal{R}} \left\| V_r^H U_{\text{Samp}^H(r)}^H |\sigma_H\rangle |0^L\rangle \right\|^2$$

$$= \frac{1}{|\mathcal{R}|} \sum_{r \in \mathcal{R}} \langle \sigma_H | \langle 0^L | P_r^H |\sigma_H\rangle |0^L\rangle$$

$$= \langle \sigma_H, 0^L | P^H | \sigma_H, 0^L \rangle.$$

Since P_H is a Hermitian matrix and $0 \preceq P_H \preceq \mathbf{I}$, let $\{|\phi_{H,j}\rangle\}_j$ be the set of eigenbasis for P_H with eigenvalues $\{p_{H,j}\}_j$ between 0 and 1. We can decompose $|\sigma_H\rangle |0^L\rangle$ under the eigenbasis:

$$|\sigma_H\rangle |0^L\rangle = \sum_i \alpha_{H,i} |\phi_{H,i}\rangle.$$

Therefore, $\epsilon_{\mathcal{A},H}$ can be written in terms of $\alpha_{H,i}$ and $p_{H,i}$: $\epsilon_{\mathcal{A},H} = \sum_i |\alpha_{H,i}|^2 \cdot p_{H,i}$. This is because:

$$\epsilon_{\mathcal{A},H} = \langle \sigma_H, 0^L | P^H | \sigma_H, 0^L \rangle = \sum_i |\alpha_{H,i}|^2 \cdot p_{H,i}.$$

With all the above discussions, we conclude our lemma below.

Lemma 5. *Let G be a game and $\mathcal{A} = (\{|\sigma_H\rangle\}_H, \{U_{\text{inp}}\}_{\text{inp}})$ be any non-uniform quantum algorithm. Let P_H be the corresponding POVMs for function H. Let $\{|\phi_{H,j}\rangle\}_j$ be the set of eigenbasis for P_H with eigenvalues $\{p_{H,j}\}_j$.*

For each H, write $|\sigma_H\rangle |0^L\rangle$ as $\sum_i \alpha_{H,i} |\phi_{H,i}\rangle$. Let $\epsilon_{\mathcal{A}}$ be the winning probability of $\mathcal{A}$, when H is drawn uniformly at random. Then

$$\epsilon_{\mathcal{A}} = \mathbb{E}_H \left[\sum_i |\alpha_{H,i}|^2 \cdot p_{H,i} \right] = \frac{1}{N^M} \sum_H \sum_i |\alpha_{H,i}|^2 \cdot p_{H,i}.$$

5 Non-uniform Lower Bounds via Alternating Measurements

In this section, we prove the following theorem:

Theorem 5. *Let G be any game with $T_{\mathsf{Samp}}, T_{\mathsf{Verify}}$ being the number of queries made by Samp and Verify. For any S, T, let $P = S(T + T_{\mathsf{Verify}} + T_{\mathsf{Samp}})$.*

If G has security $\nu(P, T)$ in the P-BF-QROM, then it has security (maximum winning probability) $\delta(S, T) \leq 2 \cdot \nu(P, T)$ against (S, T) non-uniform quantum algorithms with quantum advice.

It also has security

$$\delta(S, T) \leq \min_{\gamma > 0} \left\{ \nu(P/\gamma, T) + \gamma \right\}$$

against (S, T) non-uniform quantum algorithms with quantum advice.

As a special case of the second result, when G is a decision game and is $\nu(P, T) = \frac{1}{2} + \nu'(P, T)$ secure in the P-BF-QROM, then it has security

$$1/2 + \min_{\gamma > 0} \left\{ \nu'(P/\gamma, T) + \gamma \right\}$$

against (S, T) non-uniform quantum algorithms with quantum advice.

The section is organized as follows: in the first subsection, we introduce a new multi-instance game, via the so-called alternating measurement games, the idea of alternating measurement was used in witness preserving amplification of QMA ([MW05]); in the next subsection, we elaborate on behaviors of any non-uniform quantum algorithm in the alternating measurement game; then we show that upper bounds (of success probabilities) in the bit-fixing model give rise to the probability of **uniform** quantum algorithms in the alternating measurement game; finally in the last subsection, we give the proof for our main theorem.

5.1 Multi-instance via Alternating Measurements

For a game G and a quantum non-uniform algorithm $\mathcal{A} = (\{|\sigma_H\rangle\}_H, \{U_{\mathsf{inp}}\}_{\mathsf{inp}})$, we start by recalling the following notations as in Sect. 4: $P_r^H, P_H, \{|\phi_{H,j}\rangle\}_j$ and $\{p_{H,i}\}_j$. Let **A** be the register that $\mathcal{A}$ operates on. The following controlled projection (as defined in [Zha20]) will be used heavily in this section.

Definition 7 (Controlled Projection). *The controlled projection for a game G and a quantum algorithm $\mathcal{A}$ is the following: for every H, the controlled projection is the measurement* $\mathsf{CP}^H = (\mathsf{CP}_0^H, \mathsf{CP}_1^H)$:

$$\mathsf{CP}_0^H = \sum_{r \in \mathcal{R}} |r\rangle\langle r|_{\mathbf{R}} \otimes P_r^H \quad \text{and} \quad \mathsf{CP}_1^H = \sum_{r \in \mathcal{R}} |r\rangle\langle r|_{\mathbf{R}} \otimes (\mathbf{I_A} - P_r^H).$$

Here CP^H operates on registers $\mathcal{R}\mathcal{A}$ where $\mathcal{R}$ are registers storing random coins and $\mathcal{A}$ are $\mathcal{A}$'s working registers.

Similarly, we define the following projection $\mathsf{IsUniform} = (|\mathbb{1}_{\mathcal{R}}\rangle\langle\mathbb{1}_{\mathcal{R}}| \otimes \mathbf{I_A}, (\mathbf{I_R} - |\mathbb{1}_{\mathcal{R}}\rangle\langle\mathbb{1}_{\mathcal{R}}|) \otimes \mathbf{I_A})$ over the same register as CP^H where $|\mathbb{1}_{\mathcal{R}}\rangle$ is a uniform superposition over $\mathcal{R}$: i.e., $|\mathbb{1}_{\mathcal{R}}\rangle = \frac{1}{|\mathcal{R}|}\sum_r |r\rangle$. We denote $|\mathbb{1}_{\mathcal{R}}\rangle\langle\mathbb{1}_{\mathcal{R}}| \otimes \mathbf{I_A}$ by $\mathsf{IsUniform}^0$ and $(\mathbf{I} - |\mathbb{1}_{\mathcal{R}}\rangle\langle\mathbb{1}_{\mathcal{R}}| \otimes \mathbf{I_A})$ by $\mathsf{IsUniform}^1$.

Now, We are ready to describe the new game via alternating measurements:

Definition 8 (Multi-instances via Alternating Measurments). *Fix a game G and an integer $k \geq 1$. A uniformly random H is sampled at the beginning. For a (potentially non-uniform) quantum algorithm $\mathcal{A}$, the multi-instance game $G^{\otimes k}$ is defined and executed as follows:*

- *A challenger $\mathcal{C}$ initializes a new register $|\mathbb{1}_{\mathcal{R}}\rangle_{\mathbf{R}}$ and controls $\mathcal{A}$'s register $\mathbf{A}$.*
- *It repeats the following procedures k times, for $i = 1, \cdots, k$:*
  - *If the current stage i is odd, $\mathcal{C}$ applies CP^H on $\mathbf{RA}$ and obtains a measurement outcome b_i.*
  - *If the current stage i is even, $\mathcal{C}$ applies $\mathsf{IsUniform}$ on $\mathbf{RA}$ and obtains a measurement outcome b_i.*
- *The game is won if and only if $b_1 = b_2 = \cdots = b_k = 0$.*

With this alternating measurement game, we describe the following theorem that relates the winning probability of a (non-uniform) $\mathcal{A}$ in the game G and that of $\mathcal{A}$ in the corresponding alternating measurement game $G^{\otimes k}$.

Theorem 6. *Let G be a game and $\mathcal{A} = (\{|\sigma_H\rangle\}_H, \{U_{\mathsf{inp}}\}_{\mathsf{inp}})$ be any non-uniform quantum algorithm for G. Let P_H be the corresponding POVMs for function H. Let $\{|\phi_{H,j}\rangle\}_j$ be the set of eigenbasis for P_H with eigenvalues $\{p_{H,j}\}_j$.*

For each H, write $|\sigma_H\rangle |0^L\rangle$ as $\sum_i \alpha_{H,i} |\phi_{H,i}\rangle$. Let $\epsilon_{\mathcal{A}}^{\otimes k}$ be the winning probability of $\mathcal{A}$ in the alternating measurement game $G^{\otimes k}$, when H is drawn uniformly at random. Then

$$\epsilon_{\mathcal{A}}^{\otimes k} = \frac{1}{N^M} \sum_H \sum_i |\alpha_{H,i}|^2 \cdot p_{H,i}^k.$$

We leave the explanation of the theorem to the appendix (the proof of Lemma 11) since it is similar to the analysis of QMA amplification [MW05] and quantum traitor tracing [Zha20]. We do not considered the proof as our main contribution. Nonetheless, we believe that the proof inspires our analysis for $\epsilon_{\mathcal{A}}^{\otimes k}$, which together with the new multi-instance reduction is considered the main contribution of this work.

By Lemma 2, we can easily conclude that any upper bound on $\mathcal{A}$'s success probability in $G^{\otimes k}$ yields an upper bound on its winning probability in G. The proof of the following lemma easily follows from Lemma 2.

Lemma 6. *Fix a game G and an integer $k \geq 1$. Let $\epsilon_{\mathcal{A}}$ be the success probability of (uniform or non-uniform) $\mathcal{A}$ in G and $\epsilon_{\mathcal{A}}^{\otimes k}$ be that of $\mathcal{A}$ in the alternating measurement game $G^{\otimes k}$. Then $\epsilon_{\mathcal{A}} \leq \left(\epsilon_{\mathcal{A}}^{\otimes k}\right)^{1/k}$.*

Thereby, to bound $\epsilon_{\mathcal{A}}$, it is enough to bound $\epsilon_{\mathcal{A}}^{\otimes k}$ for some appropriate positive integer k.

5.2 Advantages of Uniform Algorithms in Alternating Measurement Games

In this section, we relate success probabilities of **uniform** quantum algorithms in alternating measurements with probabilities in the corresponding bit-fixing model. We will show the following theorem:

Theorem 7. *Let G be a game in the QROM and $\mathcal{A}$ be any **uniform** quantum algorithm for G making T oracle queries. Let $\nu(P, T)$ be the security of G in the P-BF-QROM. For every $k > 0$, every $P \geq k\,(T + T_{\mathsf{Samp}} + T_{\mathsf{Verify}})$,*

$$\epsilon_{\mathcal{A}}^{\otimes k} \leq \nu(P, T)^k.$$

Recall that $T_{\mathsf{Samp}}, T_{\mathsf{Verify}}$ are the numbers of queries made by Samp and Verify, respectively.

To bound $\epsilon_{\mathcal{A}}^{\otimes k}$ for any uniform quantum algorithm, it is sufficient to bound the following conditional probability: $\epsilon_{\mathcal{A}}^{(t)}$ for $t = 1, \cdots, k$.

Definition 9 (Conditional Probability for the t-th Outcome). *$\epsilon_{\mathcal{A}}^{(t)}$ is the conditional probability $\Pr[b_t = 0 \,|\, \mathbf{b}_{<t} = \mathbf{0}]$, where $\mathbf{b}_{<t}$ and b_t are the first t outcomes produced by the game $G^{\otimes k}$ with $\mathcal{A}$, when H is picked uniformly at random.*

Next, we characterize the conditional probability in terms of eigenvalues $\{p_{H,j}\}_j$ and amplitudes under the corresponding eigenbasis $\{|\phi_{H,j}\rangle\}_j$.

Lemma 7. *Let G be a game and $\mathcal{A} = (\{U_{\mathsf{inp}}\}_{\mathsf{inp}})$ be any **uniform** quantum algorithm for G. Let P_H be the corresponding POVMs for function H. Let $\{|\phi_{H,j}\rangle\}_j$ be the set of eigenbasis for P_H with eigenvalues $\{p_{H,j}\}_j$.*

For each H, write the starting state $|0^S\rangle\,|0^L\rangle$ as $\sum_i \alpha_{H,i} |\phi_{H,i}\rangle$. Let $\epsilon_{\mathcal{A}}^{(t)}$ for $1 \leq t \leq k$ be the conditional probability defined in Definition 9. Then

$$\epsilon_{\mathcal{A}}^{(t)} = \frac{\sum_{H,i} |\alpha_{H,i}|^2 \cdot p_{H,i}^t}{\sum_{H,i} |\alpha_{H,i}|^2 \cdot p_{H,i}^{t-1}}.$$

Proof. By definition, $\epsilon_{\mathcal{A}}^{(t)} = \Pr[b_t = 0 \,|\, \mathbf{b}_{<t} = \mathbf{0}] = \Pr[\mathbf{b}_t = \mathbf{0}]/\Pr[\mathbf{b}_{t-1} = \mathbf{0}]$. Since $\Pr[\mathbf{b}_k = \mathbf{0}] = \sum_{H,i} |\alpha_{H,i}|^2 \cdot p_{H,i}^k$, we conclude the lemma. □

In order to bound $\epsilon_{\mathcal{A}}^{\otimes k}$, it is enough to bound $\epsilon_{\mathcal{A}}^{(t)}$ for every $1 \leq t \leq k$ and $\epsilon_{\mathcal{A}}^{\otimes k} = \prod_{1 \leq t \leq k} \epsilon_{\mathcal{A}}^{(t)}$. Indeed, with Lemma 1, we have the following straightforward corollary.

Corollary 1. *For every game G and* **uniform** *quantum algorithm $\mathcal{A}$, $\{\epsilon^{(t)}\}_{t \geq 1}$ is monotonically non-decreasing. Therefore, $\epsilon_{\mathcal{A}}^{\otimes k} \leq \left(\epsilon_{\mathcal{A}}^{(k^*)}\right)^k$ for any $k^* \geq k$. In particular, $\epsilon_{\mathcal{A}}^{\otimes k} \leq \left(\epsilon_{\mathcal{A}}^k\right)^k$.*

Proof. The proof is direct by setting $\{c_i\}$, $\{p_i\}$ in the statement of Lemma 1 as $\{|\alpha_{H,i}|^2 \cdot p_{H,i}^t / N^M\}$ and $\{p_{H,i}\}$. □

Finally, we show a connection between $\epsilon_{\mathcal{A}}^{(k)}$ and $\nu(P, T)$ of the game G in the P-BF-QROM for $P \geq k(T + T_{\mathsf{Samp}} + T_{\mathsf{Verify}})$.

Lemma 8. *For every game G and* **uniform** *quantum T-query algorithm $\mathcal{A}$, every* **odd** *$k > 0$, every $P \geq (k-1)(T + T_{\mathsf{Samp}} + T_{\mathsf{Verify}})$,*

$$\epsilon_{\mathcal{A}}^k \leq \nu(P, T).$$

As a direct corollary by the monotonicity of $\epsilon_{\mathcal{A}}^{(t)}$, for **even** *$k > 0$, every $P \geq k(T + T_{\mathsf{Samp}} + T_{\mathsf{Verify}})$,*

$$\epsilon_{\mathcal{A}}^k \leq \epsilon_{\mathcal{A}}^{(k+1)} \leq \nu(P, T).$$

Together with Corollary 1, we conclude the main theorem (Theorem 7) in this subsection.

Proof for Lemma 8. We only need to prove the lemma for odd k (or even $(k-1)$).

Recall in Definition 4, we need to specify a P-query quantum algorithm f and a T-query algorithm $\mathcal{B}$ to describe an algorithm in the P-BF-QROM. The game is executed if and only if f^H outputs 0. We define $f, \mathcal{B}$ as follows (Fig. 1).

P-query quantum algorithm f:
  - Initialize $|\mathbb{1}_{\mathcal{R}}\rangle_{\mathbf{R}} |0^S, 0^L\rangle_{\mathbf{A}}$.
  - Run the alternating measurement game for $(k-1)$-rounds (Definition 8). Let τ be the leftover state.
  - Let a boolean variable $b = 0$ if and only if all outcomes in $(k-1)$-rounds are 0s.
  - Output b and $\tau_{\mathbf{RA}}$.
T-query online algorithm $\mathcal{B}$:
  - Take $\tau_{\mathbf{RA}}$ as input.
  - On an online challenge ch $\leftarrow \mathsf{Samp}^H(r)$, it runs $\mathcal{A}$ on internal state $\tau[\mathbf{A}]$ and outputs the answer produced by $\mathcal{A}$.

Fig. 1. Turn $\mathcal{A}$ into an algorithm in the P-BF-QROM.

First, we show that $(f, \mathcal{B})$ is a (P, T) algorithm in the P-BR-QROM. It is easy to see that $\mathcal{B}$ makes at most T queries as $\mathcal{A}$ makes at most that many queries. The number of queries made by f is equal to that made in the alternating measurement game:

- In odd rounds, one needs to apply CP^H, which takes $2(T + T_{\mathsf{Samp}}) + T_{\mathsf{Verify}}$ queries; here $2(T + T_{\mathsf{Samp}})$ is for both $U^H_{\mathsf{Samp}^H(r)}$ and its inverse $\left(U^H_{\mathsf{Samp}^H(r)} \right)^\dagger$ and T_{Verify} is for applying the projection V^H_r (recall the definitions in Sect. 4).
- In even rounds, no queries are needed.

Thus, when $(k - 1)$ is even, the total number of queries is at most $(k - 1)(T + T_{\mathsf{Samp}} + T_{\mathsf{Verify}})$.

Next we prove that $(f, \mathcal{B})$ succeeds with probability $\epsilon^{(k)}_{\mathcal{A}}$. Thus by the definition of $\nu(P, T)$, $\epsilon^{(k)}_{\mathcal{A}}$ is at most $\nu(P, T)$, concluding the lemma.

For a fixed hash function H and even $(k - 1)$ (or equivalently, odd k), conditioned on f^H outputting 0, the leftover state $\tau_{\mathbf{RA}}$ is (by Lemma 11):

$$\tau_{\mathbf{RA}} \propto \sum_i \alpha_i p_i^{(k-1)/2} |v_i^0\rangle_{\mathbf{RA}} = |\mathbb{1}_{\mathcal{R}}\rangle_{\mathbf{R}} \otimes \sum_i \alpha_i p_i^{(k-1)/2} |\phi_i\rangle_{\mathbf{A}} .$$

Here we ignore H for subscripts or superscripts.

Therefore, $\tau[\mathbf{A}] = c \sum_i \alpha_i p_i^{(k-1)/2} |\phi_i\rangle_{\mathbf{A}}$ where c is a normalization factor such that $1/c^2 = \sum_i |\alpha_i|^2 p_i^{k-1}$. The winning probability of $\mathcal{B}$ for this fixed H is

$$\mathbb{E}_r \left[\left| V^H_r U^H_{\mathsf{Samp}^H(r)} \tau[\mathbf{A}] \right|^2 \right] = c^2 \sum_i |\alpha_i|^2 p_i^{(k-1)} \langle \phi_i | P_H | \phi_i \rangle$$
$$= c^2 \sum_i |\alpha_i|^2 p_i^k,$$

By taking the weighted sum of the winning probability for each H, the winning probability of $\mathcal{B}$ is

$$\frac{\sum_{H,i} |\alpha_{H,i}|^2 p_{H,i}^k}{\sum_{H,i} |\alpha_{H,i}|^2 p_{H,i}^{k-1}} = \epsilon^{(k)}_{\mathcal{A}} .$$

Finally, since G is $\nu(P, T)$ secure in the P-BF-QROM, $\epsilon^{(k)}_{\mathcal{A}} \leq \nu(P, T)$ for every T query quantum algorithm $\mathcal{A}$ and $P \geq (k - 1)(T + T_{\mathsf{Samp}} + T_{\mathsf{Verify}})$. $\qquad\square$

Lastly, we prove Theorem 7.

Proof for Theorem 7. It follows easily by combining Corollary 1 and Lemma 8. $\qquad\square$

5.3   Proof of Main Theorem

In this section, we prove our main theorem, Theorem 5.

We start by proving the first part of the theorem.

Proof for the First Part. Let G be any game. For any S, T, let $k = S$ and $P = k(T + T_{\mathsf{Samp}} + T_{\mathsf{Verify}}) = S(T + T_{\mathsf{Samp}} + T_{\mathsf{Verify}})$. G is $\nu(P, T)$ secure in the P-BF-QROM.

By Theorem 7, for any uniform T-query quantum algorithm and $k = S$, its winning probability in the alternating measurement game $G^{\otimes k}$ is at most $\nu(P, T)^k$.

Therefore, for any (S, T) non-uniform quantum algorithm $\mathcal{A}$, its success probability $\epsilon_{\mathcal{A}}^{\otimes k}$ is at most $2^S \nu(P, T)^k = (2\nu(P, T))^S$. This is because for any non-uniform algorithm of winning probability p with advice being an S-bit advice $|\sigma_H\rangle$, we can turn it into a uniform quantum algorithm with winning probability at least $2^{-S} p$ as follows ([Aar05]):

As the uniform algorithm does not know $|\sigma_H\rangle$, it samples an S-qubit maximally mixed state and runs the non-uniform algorithm on the maximally mixed state.

Since an S-qubit maximally mixed state can be written as $1/2^S |\sigma_H\rangle\langle\sigma_H| + (1 - 1/2^S)\sigma'$, the uniform algorithm has success probability at least $p/2^S$.

Finally, due to Lemma 6, any non-uniform algorithm $\mathcal{A}$ is at most $2\nu(P, T)$ secure in G for $P = S(T + T_{\mathsf{Samp}} + T_{\mathsf{Verify}})$.   □

The proof for the second part is similar but more laborious. Since we are dealing with decision games, we need to carefully deal with the factor 2^{-S} in the previous proof.

Proof for the Second Part. The theorem trivially holds when $\gamma \geq 1$. We prove it for $\gamma \in (0, 1]$.

Let G be a decision game. For any P, T, G is $\nu(P, T)$ secure in the P-BF-QROM.

Similarly by Theorem 7, for any uniform T-query quantum algorithm and k, its security in the alternating measurement game $G^{\otimes k}$ is at most $\nu(P, T)^k$ where $P = k(T + T_{\mathsf{Samp}} + T_{\mathsf{Verify}})$. Thus, for any (S, T) non-uniform quantum algorithm $\mathcal{A}$, $\epsilon_{\mathcal{A}}^{\otimes k}$ is at most $2^S \nu(P, T)^k$.

Since for any $\gamma \in (0, 1]$, $2 \leq (1 + \gamma)^{1/\gamma}$. By setting $k = S/\gamma$, we have:

$$\epsilon_{\mathcal{A}}^{\otimes k} \leq 2^S \nu(P, T)^k \leq ((1 + \gamma)\nu(P, T))^k \leq \left(\frac{1}{2} + \nu'(P, T) + \gamma\right)^k.$$

The last inequality follows the union bound and $\nu(P, T) = 1/2 + \nu'(P, T)$.

Since the above inequality holds for all $\gamma \in (0, 1]$, we conclude the second part of our theorem, following Lemma 6.   □

6   Applications

We show several applications of our main theorem (Theorem 5) in this section. We first apply our theorem to OWF and PRG games and achieve improved lower bounds for both games. The former ones are publicly verifiable, and the latter games are decision games and thus not publicly verifiable. The applications for both types of games show our main theorem is general and achieve pretty good bounds for almost all kinds of security games in the QROM against quantum/classical advice, as long as we can analyze their security in the P-BF-QROM.

Finally, we show that "salting defeats preprocessing" in the QROM, which extends the classical theorem by Coretti et al. [CDGS18] and improved the result by Guo et al. [CGLQ20].

OWF. Recall the definition of G_{OWF} in Example 1. It is shown that G_{OWF} has the following security in the in the P-BF-QROM, $\nu(P,T) = O\left((P+T^2)/\min\{N,M\}\right)$, where N and M are the sizes of the domain and range of the random oracle, by Lemma 1.5 in [CGLQ20].

By our main theorem Theorem 5, we have the following theorem.

Theorem 8. G_{OWF} *has security* $\delta(S,T) = O\left(\frac{ST+T^2}{\min\{N,M\}}\right)$ *against* (S,T) *non-uniform quantum adversaries, even with quantum advice.*

The above theorem improves the bound for quantum advice, which was shown to be $\tilde{O}\left(\frac{ST+T^2}{\min\{N,M\}}\right)^{1/3}$ in [CGLQ20].

PRG. Recall G_{PRG} is defined in Example 1. G_{PRG} has security $\nu(P,T) = 1/2 + O\left(\frac{P+T^2}{N}\right)^{1/2}$ where N is the size of the domain, by Lemma 1.6 in [CGLQ20]. Again by our main theorem Theorem 5, we have the following theorem.

Theorem 9. G_{PRG} *has security* $\delta(S,T) = 1/2 + O\left(\frac{T^2}{N}\right)^{1/2} + O\left(\frac{ST}{N}\right)^{1/3}$ *against* (S,T) *non-uniform quantum adversaries, even with quantum advice.*

This improves the previous result on G_{PRG} with quantum advice [CGLQ20], which was $1/2 + \tilde{O}\left(\frac{S^5T+S^4T^2}{N}\right)^{1/19}$.

6.1 Salting Defeats Quantum Advice

We start by defining the cryptographic mechanism called "salting".

Definition 10 (Salted Games in the QROM). *Let* G *be a game in the QROM as defined in Definition 2, with respect to a random oracle* $H : [N] \to [M]$. *It consists of two deterministic algorithms* Samp^H *and* Verify^H *and both algorithms make* T_{Samp} *(or* T_{Verify}*) queries, respectively.*

A salted game G_S *with salt space* $[K]$ *is defined as the following:* G_S *consists of two deterministic algorithms* Samp_S *and* Verify_S:

- Samp_S^H: *on input* s, r, *it returns* $(s, \mathsf{Samp}^{H_s}(r))$. *Here* H_s *denotes oracle access to the oracle* $H(s, \cdot)$.

- Verify_S^H : *on input* s, r, ans, *it returns* $\mathsf{Verify}^{H_s}(r, \mathsf{ans})$.

In other words, for a fixed $H : [K] \times [N] \to [M]$ and a quantum algorithm $\mathcal{A}$, the game $G_{S,\mathcal{A}}^H$ is executed as follows:

- *A challenger $\mathcal{C}$ samples a uniformly random salt $s \leftarrow [K]$ and $\mathsf{ch} \leftarrow \mathsf{Samp}^{H_s}(r)$ using uniformly random coins r.*
- *A (uniform or non-uniform) quantum algorithm $\mathcal{A}$ has oracle access to H, takes (s, ch) as input and outputs ans.*
- *$b \leftarrow \mathsf{Verify}^{H_s}(r, \mathsf{ans})$ is the outcome of the game.*

Lemma 9 (Salted Games in the P-BF-QROM, Lemma 7.2 in [CGLQ20]).
Let G be a game in the QROM, with security $\nu(T)$ against T-query quantum adversaries. Then for any P,

- *G has security $\nu(P, T) \leq 2\nu(T) + O(P/K)$ in the P-BF-QROM;*
- *G has security $\nu(P, T) \leq \nu(T) + O(\sqrt{P/K})$ in the P-BF-QROM.*

The second bullet point is better than the first one, when G is a decision game.

Proof. The proof is subsumed by the proof for Lemma 7.2 [CGLQ20]. Although Lemma 7.2 shows the multi-instance security of G_S, its P-BF-QROM security is an intermediate step. □

Combining with Theorem 5, we have the following results about salting in the QROM.

Theorem 10. *For any game G (as defined in Definition 2) in the QROM, let $\nu(T)$ be its security in the QROM. Let G_S be the salted game with salt space $[K]$. Then G_S has security $\delta(S, T)$ against (S, T) non-uniform quantum adversaries with quantum advice,*

- *$\delta(S, T) \leq 4\nu(T) + O(S(T + T_{\mathsf{Samp}} + T_{\mathsf{Verify}})/K)$;*
- *If G_S is a decision game, then $\delta(S, T) \leq \nu(T) + O(S(T + T_{\mathsf{Samp}} + T_{\mathsf{Verify}})/K)^{1/3}$.*

Proof. We only show the second bullet point. The first one is similar and more straightforward.

By Theorem 5, $\delta(S, T) \leq \min_{\gamma > 0} \{\gamma + \nu(P/\gamma, T)\}$ where $P = S(T + T_{\mathsf{Verify}} + T_{\mathsf{Samp}})$. Since $\nu(P/\gamma, T) \leq \nu(T) + O(\sqrt{P/(K\gamma)})$ by Lemma 9, $\delta(S, T)$ takes its minimum when $\gamma = O(P/K)^{1/3}$. Our second result follows. □

7   Advantages of Quantum Advice in the QROM

This section demonstrates a game in which non-uniform quantum algorithms with quantum advice have an exponential advantage over those with classical advice for some parameter regime S, T. Although the advantage only applies to some S, T ranges[3], we believe it is the first step toward understanding a game in which quantum advice has an exponential advantage over classical advice for a wider range of S, T.

The game is based on the recent work by Yamakawa and Zhandry [YZ22]. We start by explaining and recalling the basic ideas in their work.

Definition 11 ([YZ22], YZ Functions). *Let n be a positive integer, Σ be an exponentially (in n) sized alphabet and $C \subseteq \Sigma^n$ be an error correcting code over Σ. Let $H : [n] \times \Sigma \to \{0, 1\}$ be a random oracle. The following function is called a YZ function with respect to C and Σ:*

$$f_C^H : C \to \{0, 1\}^n$$
$$f_C^H(c_1, c_2, \cdots, c_n) = H(1, c_1) \| H(2, c_2) \| \cdots \| H(n, c_n)$$

We will consider the following game, which we call G_{YZ}. The game is to invert a uniformly random image with respect to the YZ function. More formally,

Definition 12 (Inverting YZ Functions). *The game G_{YZ} is specified by two classical algorithms:*

- $\mathsf{Samp}^H(r)$: *it samples a uniformly random image $y = r \in \{0, 1\}^n$;*
- $\mathsf{Verify}^H(r, \mathsf{ans})$: *it checks whether ans is a code in C and $f_C^H(\mathsf{ans}) = r$.*

The queries made by each algorithm satisfy $T_{\mathsf{Samp}} = 0$ and $T_{\mathsf{Verify}} = n$.

Their idea is that, if we want to find a pre-image in Σ^n of any $y \in \{0, 1\}^n$, it is easy: simply inverting each $H(i, y_i)$. Nevertheless, to find a pre-image in C, this entry-by-entry brute-force no longer works. In their work, Yamakawa and Zhandry show that for some appropriate C, the above function is classically one-way and quantumly easy to invert.

Theorem 11 (Theorem 6.1, Lemma 6.3 and 6.9 in [YZ22]). *There exists some appropriate C, such that*

- *The game G_{YZ} has security $2^{-\Omega(n)}$ against 2^{n^c}-query classical adversaries for some constant $0 < c < 1$;*
- *There is a $\tilde{O}(n)$-query quantum algorithm that wins the game G_{YZ} with probability $1 - \mathsf{negl}(n)$. Here $\tilde{O}$ hides a polylog factor.*

Moreover, we observe that the quantum algorithm makes non-adaptive queries and the queries are independent of the challenge. Upon a challenge y is received, the quantum algorithm does post-processing on the quantum queries without making further queries[4].

We show our separation result below.

Theorem 12 (Separation of classical and quantum advice in the QROM. *There exists some appropriate C (the same in [YZ22]) such that,*

---

[3] Specifically, we require $T = 0$, i.e., no online query.

[4] For more details, please refer to Fig 1. in [YZ22].

- G_{YZ} has security $2^{-\Omega(n)}$ against $(S, T = 0)$ non-uniform adversaries with **classical** advice, for $S = 2^{n^c}/n$ and some constant $0 < c < 1$;
- There is an $(S, T = 0)$ non-uniform adversary with **quantum** advice that achieves success probability $1 - \mathsf{negl}(n)$, for $S = \tilde{O}(n)$.

We refer readers to a detailed proof in the appendix.

Acknowledgements. We would like to thank Kai-Min Chung for his discussion on an early write-up and providing an intuitive explanation of the decomposition of quantum advice in our work; Jiahui Liu and Luowen Qian for their comments on an early draft of this paper; Luowen Qian and Makrand Sinha for mentioning the connections between our impossibility result and quantum one-way communication complexity.

Qipeng Liu is supported in part by the Simons Institute for the Theory of Computing, through a Quantum Postdoctoral Fellowship, by DARPA under Agreement No. HR00112020023 and by the NSF QLCI program through grant number OMA-2016245. Any opinions, findings and conclusions or recommendations expressed in this material are those of the author(s) and do not necessarily reflect the views of the United States Government or DARPA.

A   Proofs for the Useful Lemmas

Lemma 10. *Let N be a positive integer and $p_1, \cdots, p_N \in \mathbb{R}^{\geq 0}$. Let $\alpha_1, \cdots, \alpha_N$ be a distribution over $[N]$: i.e., $\alpha_i \in [0, 1]$ and $\sum_{i \in [N]} \alpha_i = 1$.*

Assume $\mu := \sum_{i \in [N]} \alpha_i p_i > 0$. Let $\beta_1, \cdots, \beta_N$ be another distribution over $[N]$: $\beta_i := \alpha_i p_i / \mu$. The following holds:

$$\sum_{i \in [N]} \beta_i p_i \geq \sum_{i \in [N]} \alpha_i p_i.$$

Proof. Let $\mathbf{X}$ be a random variable that takes value p_i w.p. α_i. It is easy to see that $\mathbb{E}[\mathbf{X}] = \sum_i \alpha_i p_i$ and $\mathbb{E}[\mathbf{X}^2] = \sum_i \alpha_i p_i^2$.

Since we assume $\mu = \mathbb{E}[\mathbf{X}] > 0$, we rewrite the inequality as follows:

$$\sum_i \alpha_i p_i^2 \geq \left(\sum_i \alpha_i p_i \right)^2.$$

The lemma holds by observing that L.H.S. is $\mathbb{E}[\mathbf{X}^2]$, R.H.S. is $\mathbb{E}[\mathbf{X}]^2$ and the fact that $\mathbf{Var}[\mathbf{X}] := \mathbb{E}[\mathbf{X}^2] - \mathbb{E}[\mathbf{X}]^2 \geq 0$.   □

Proof for Lemma 1. We fix any integer $k \geq 1$. Let $\alpha_i = c_i p_i^{k-1} / (\sum_i c_i p_i^{k-1})$. It it easy to see that $S_k = \sum_i \alpha_i p_i$.

Let $\beta_i = \alpha_i p_i / \mu$ where $\mu = \sum_i \alpha_i p_i$. We have

$$\beta_i = \alpha_i p_i / \mu$$
$$= \frac{c_i p_i^k}{\sum_i c_i p_i^{k-1} \cdot \mu}$$
$$= \frac{c_i p_i^k}{\sum_i c_i p_i^{k-1} \cdot \left(\sum_i c_i p_i^k / \left(\sum_i c_i p_i^{k-1}\right)\right)}$$
$$= \frac{c_i p_i^k}{\sum_i c_i p_i^k}.$$

Therefore, $S_{k+1} = \sum_i \beta_i p_i$. By Lemma 10, $S_{k+1} = \sum_i \beta_i p_i \geq \sum_i \alpha_i p_i = S_k$. $\square$

B   Characterization of Alternating Measurements and Proof of Theorem 6

Fixing a function H, the intial internal register $\mathbf{A}$ of $\mathcal{A}$ is $|\sigma_H\rangle |0^L\rangle = \sum_i \alpha_{H,i} |\phi_{H,i}\rangle$. Let us define the following states $|v_{H,i}^0\rangle, |v_{H,i}^1\rangle, |w_{H,i}^0\rangle, |w_{H,i}^1\rangle$ (for convenience, we ignore H in the subscripts in the analysis below). We will also ignore H for other notations like $P_r^H, |\phi_{H,i}\rangle, p_{H,i}$ as our analysis does not depend on H and the final conclusion follows by taking expectation over uniformly random functions H. Instead, we are using $P_r := P_r^H, |\phi_i\rangle := |\phi_{H,i}\rangle, p_i := p_{H,i}$ in the analysis.

1. $|w_i^0\rangle = \frac{1}{\sqrt{p_i |\mathcal{R}|}} \sum_r |r\rangle P_r |\phi_i\rangle$.

   It is easy to verify that it has norm 1:

   $$\langle w_i^0 | w_i^0 \rangle = \frac{1}{p_i |\mathcal{R}|} \sum_r \langle \phi_i | P_r | \phi_i \rangle = \frac{1}{p_i |\mathcal{R}|} \langle \phi_i | (\sum_r P_r) | \phi_i \rangle = \frac{p_i |\mathcal{R}|}{p_i |\mathcal{R}|} = 1.$$

   $\mathsf{CP}_0^H |w_i^0\rangle = |w_i^0\rangle$ and $\mathsf{CP}_1^H |w_i^0\rangle = 0$.

   After seeing the definition of $|v_i^0\rangle$ and $|v_i^1\rangle$ below, we also observe that $|w_i^0\rangle = \sqrt{p_i} |v_i^0\rangle + \sqrt{1 - p_i} |v_i^1\rangle$.
2. $|w_i^1\rangle = \frac{1}{\sqrt{(1-p_i)|\mathcal{R}|}} \sum_r |r\rangle (\mathbf{I_A} - P_r) |\phi_i\rangle$.

   Similarly, it has norm 1, $\mathsf{CP}_1^H |w_i^1\rangle = |w_i^1\rangle$ and $\mathsf{CP}_0^H |w_i^1\rangle = 0$.
3. $|v_i^0\rangle = |\mathbb{1}\rangle_{\mathcal{R}} |\phi_i\rangle = \sqrt{p_i} |w_i^0\rangle + \sqrt{1 - p_i} |w_i^1\rangle$.

   By the description of the game $G^{\otimes k}$ (Definition 8), the overall register $\mathbf{RA}$ at the beginning of the game can be written as $\sum_i \alpha_i |v_i^0\rangle$ (which we will prove below).

   The state has norm 1, $\mathsf{IsUniform}^0 |v_i^0\rangle = |v_i^0\rangle$ and $\mathsf{IsUniform}^1 |v_i^0\rangle = 0$.
4. $|v_i^1\rangle = \sqrt{1 - p_i} |w_i^0\rangle - \sqrt{p_i} |w_i^1\rangle$.

   We will not use the property of $|v_i^1\rangle$ in the proof and we thus omit all the details here.

Lemma 11. *For any fixed H, for any non-negative integer k, the leftover state over* **RA** *conditioned on all outcomes in the first k rounds being 0s is in proportion to:*

$$\sum_i \alpha_i p_i^{k/2} \begin{cases} |v_i^0\rangle & \text{if } k \text{ is even,} \\ |w_i^0\rangle & \text{if } k \text{ is odd.} \end{cases}$$

The probability of all outcomes being 0s is $\sum_i |\alpha_i|^2 p_i^k$.

The proof follows the proof of Claim 6.3 in [Zha20]. We reprove this claim for completeness.

Proof. This lemma holds for $k = 0$, when no measurement is applied. This is the state is

$$\sum_i \alpha_i |v_i^0\rangle = \sum_i \alpha_i |\mathbb{1}_\mathcal{R}\rangle_\mathbf{R} |\phi_i\rangle_\mathbf{A} = |\mathbb{1}_\mathcal{R}\rangle_\mathbf{R} |\sigma_H, 0^L\rangle_\mathbf{A} \,.$$

We now prove by induction. Assume the lemma holds up to some even k. We prove it holds for odd $k + 1$.

The leftover state after the first k rounds is $c \sum_i \alpha_i p_i^{k/2} |v_i^0\rangle$ for some normalization c. Note that $|v_i^0\rangle = \sqrt{p_i} |w_i^0\rangle + \sqrt{1 - p_i} |w_i^1\rangle$. The state can be rewritten as

$$c \sum_i \alpha_i p_i^{k/2} \left(\sqrt{p_i} |w_i^0\rangle + \sqrt{1 - p_i} |w_i^1\rangle \right) \,.$$

In the $(k + 1)$-th round, the challenger measures the state under CP^H. Note that $\mathsf{CP}_0^H |w_i^0\rangle = |w_i^0\rangle$ and $\mathsf{CP}_0^H |w_i^1\rangle = 0$. Thus, conditioned on the $(k + 1)$-th outcome being 0, the state is in proportion to $\sum_i \alpha_i p_i^{(k+1)/2} |w_i^0\rangle$. We complete the induction for k being even.

For odd k, the analysis is almost identical, by observing $|w_i^0\rangle = \sqrt{p_i} |v_i^0\rangle + \sqrt{1 - p_i} |v_i^1\rangle$ and also following from the fact that $\mathsf{IsUniform}^0 |v_i^0\rangle = |v_i^0\rangle$ and $\mathsf{IsUniform}^1 |v_i^0\rangle = 0$.

Finally, the probability can be bounded by looking at the un-normalized states above. □

Theorem 6 follows from summing over all functions H and Lemma 11.

C   Classical Version of Our Main Theorem

The following theorem is a classical version of our main theorem (Theorem 5), improved from Theorem 1 in [GLLZ21].

Theorem 13. *Let G be any game with $T_{\mathsf{Samp}}, T_{\mathsf{Verify}}$ being the number of queries made by Samp and Verify. For any S, T, let $P = S(T + T_{\mathsf{Verify}} + T_{\mathsf{Samp}})$.*

If G has security $\nu(P, T)$ in the P-BF-ROM, then it has security $\delta(S, T) \leq 2 \cdot \nu(P, T)$ against (S, T) non-uniform classical algorithms with classical advice.

In Theorem 1 in [GLLZ21], $P = (S + \log \gamma^{-1})(T + T_{\mathsf{Verify}} + T_{\mathsf{Samp}})$ and there is an extra additive term γ for $\delta(S, T)$.

Theorem 14 (Theorem 1 in [GLLZ21]). *Let G be any game with $T_{\mathsf{Samp}}, T_{\mathsf{Verify}}$ being the number of queries made by Samp and Verify. For any $S, T, \gamma > 0$, let $P = (S + \log \gamma^{-1})(T + T_{\mathsf{Verify}} + T_{\mathsf{Samp}})$.*

If G has security $\nu(P, T)$ in the P-BF-ROM, then it has security $\delta(S, T) \leq 2 \cdot \nu(P, T) + \gamma$ against (S, T) non-uniform classical algorithms with classical advice.

D Proof for the Separation Result

Proof. We first show the second bullet point. Let the quantum algorithm in Theorem 11 be $\mathcal{B}$. In the non-uniform quantum adversary, quantum advice is the non-adaptive queries made by $\mathcal{B}$ and the online stage is the post-processing by $\mathcal{B}$. It is straightforward that the non-uniform algorithm achieves the same probability as $\mathcal{B}$, which is $1 - \mathsf{negl}(n)$. Since each query has $O(\log n)$ qubits and $\mathcal{B}$ makes $\tilde{O}(n)$ queries, the total size of the quantum advice is still $\tilde{O}(n)$.

Next, we show the first bullet point. In the first bullet point of this theorem, we do not distinguish between non-uniform quantum adversaries with classical advice and non-uniform classical adversaries. The reason is that the online algorithm does not make any query, i.e., $T = 0$. These two types of algorithms are equivalent when $T = 0$.

Thus, we consider success probabilities of non-uniform classical adversaries. By a classical analog of our main theorem Theorem 5 (Theorem 13), we only need to show its success probability in the P-BF-ROM (Definition 5) where $P = S(T + T_{\mathsf{Samp}} + T_{\mathsf{Verify}}) = ST_{\mathsf{Verify}} = 2^{n^c}$.

Assume a random oracle is lazily sampled. In other words, an outcome of the random oracle on x is sampled only if the outcome is queried by an algorithm; otherwise, the outcome is marked as "not sampled". Conditioned on any P-query f outputs 0, the random oracle is only fixed on P positions and the rest of its outputs are still not sampled. The error correcting code C used in [YZ22] satisfies a property called (ζ, ℓ, L) list recoverability:

- For any subset $S_i \subseteq \Sigma$ such that $|S_i| \leq \ell$ for every $i \in [n]$, we have

$$|\mathsf{Good}| = |\{(x_1, \cdots, x_n) \in C : |\{i \in [n] : x_i \in S_i\}| \geq (1 - \zeta)n\}| \leq L.$$

In other words, the total number of codewords in C with hamming distance to $S_1 \times S_2 \times \cdots \times S_n$ smaller than ζn is bounded by L. Here hamming distance to $S_1 \times S_2 \times \cdots \times S_n$ is defined as the number of coordinates i whose x_i is not in the corresponding S_i.
We call this set of codewords Good.
- $P = 2^{n^c} < \ell$, $\zeta = \Omega(1)$ and $L = 2^{n^{c'}}$ for some $0 < c' < 1$.

In G_{YZ}, when a challenge y is sampled uniformly at random from $\{0,1\}^n$, there are two cases:

- **Case 1**: there exists a codeword c in Good, such that $y = f_C^H(c)$. This case happens with probability at most $|\text{Good}|/2^n \leq L/2^n$.
- **Case 2**: complement of Case 1. In this case, an adversary wins only if it outputs a codeword that is not in Good.

  For every codeword $c = (x_1, x_2, \cdots, x_n) \notin \text{Good}$, there are at least ζn coordinates whose random oracle outputs (i.e., $H(i, x_i)$) have not been sampled yet in the lazily sampled random oracle. For any $c \notin \text{Good}$, $\Pr[f_C^H(c) = y] \leq 2^{-\zeta n}$. Therefore, regardless of the algorithm's output, the success probability is at most $2^{-\zeta n}$.

The overall winning probability is bounded by $L/2^n + 2^{-\zeta n} = 2^{-\Omega(n)}$. We conclude the first bullet point of the theorem.

$\square$

References

[Aar05] Aaronson, S.: Limitations of quantum advice and one-way communication. Theory Comput. **1**(1), 1–28 (2005)

[Aar21] Aaronson, S.: Open problems related to quantum query complexity. ACM Trans. Quant. Comput. **2**(4), 1–9 (2021)

[AK07] Aaronson, S., Kuperberg, G.: Quantum versus classical proofs and advice. In: Twenty-Second Annual IEEE Conference on Computational Complexity (CCC 07), pp. 115–128. IEEE (2007)

[BDF+11] Boneh, D., Dagdelen, Ö., Fischlin, M., Lehmann, A., Schaffner, C., Zhandry, M.: Random oracles in a quantum world. In: Lee, D.H., Wang, X. (eds.) ASIACRYPT 2011. LNCS, vol. 7073, pp. 41–69. Springer, Heidelberg (2011). https://doi.org/10.1007/978-3-642-25385-0_3

[BR93] Bellare, M., Rogaway, P.: Random oracles are practical: a paradigm for designing efficient protocols. In: Proceedings of the 1st ACM Conference on Computer and Communications Security, pp. 62–73 (1993)

[BYJK04] Bar-Yossef, Z., Jayram, T.S., Kerenidis, I.: Exponential separation of quantum and classical one-way communication complexity. In: Proceedings of the Thirty-Sixth Annual ACM Symposium on Theory of Computing, pp. 128–137 (2004)

[CDG18] Coretti, S., Dodis, Y., Guo, S.: Non-uniform bounds in the random-permutation, ideal-cipher, and generic-group models. In: Shacham, H., Boldyreva, A. (eds.) CRYPTO 2018. LNCS, vol. 10991, pp. 693–721. Springer, Cham (2018). https://doi.org/10.1007/978-3-319-96884-1_23

[CDGS18] Coretti, S., Dodis, Y., Guo, S., Steinberger, J.: Random oracles and non-uniformity. In: Nielsen, J.B., Rijmen, V. (eds.) EUROCRYPT 2018. LNCS, vol. 10820, pp. 227–258. Springer, Cham (2018). https://doi.org/10.1007/978-3-319-78381-9_9

[CGK19] Corrigan-Gibbs, H., Kogan, D.: The function-inversion problem: barriers and opportunities. In: Hofheinz, D., Rosen, A. (eds.) TCC 2019. LNCS, vol. 11891, pp. 393–421. Springer, Cham (2019). https://doi.org/10.1007/978-3-030-36030-6_16

[CGLQ20] Chung, K.M., Guo, S., Liu, Q., Qian, L.: Tight quantum time-space trade-offs for function inversion. In: 2020 IEEE 61st Annual Symposium on Foundations of Computer Science (FOCS), pp. 673–684. IEEE (2020)

[CLMP13] Chung, K.M., Lin, H., Mahmoody, M., Pass, R.: On the power of nonuniformity in proofs of security. In: Proceedings of the 4th Conference on Innovations in Theoretical Computer Science, pp. 389–400 (2013)

[CLQ19] Chung, K.M., Liao, T.N., Qian, L.: Lower bounds for function inversion with quantum advice. arXiv preprint arXiv:1911.09176 (2019)

[DGK17] Dodis, Y., Guo, S., Katz, J.: Fixing cracks in the concrete: random oracles with auxiliary input, revisited. In: Coron, J.-S., Nielsen, J.B. (eds.) EUROCRYPT 2017. LNCS, vol. 10211, pp. 473–495. Springer, Cham (2017). https://doi.org/10.1007/978-3-319-56614-6_16

[DTT10] De, A., Trevisan, L., Tulsiani, M.: Time space tradeoffs for attacks against one-way functions and PRGs. In: Rabin, T. (ed.) CRYPTO 2010. LNCS, vol. 6223, pp. 649–665. Springer, Heidelberg (2010). https://doi.org/10.1007/978-3-642-14623-7_35

[Gav08] Gavinsky, D.: Classical interaction cannot replace a quantum message. In: Proceedings of the Fortieth Annual ACM Symposium on Theory of Computing, pp. 95–102 (2008)

[GGKL21] Gravin, N., Guo, S., Kwok, T.C., Lu, P.: Concentration bounds for almost k-wise independence with applications to non-uniform security. In: Proceedings of the 2021 ACM-SIAM Symposium on Discrete Algorithms (SODA), pp. 2404–2423. SIAM (2021)

[GLLZ21] Guo, S., Li, Q., Liu, Q., Zhang, J.: Unifying presampling via concentration bounds. In: Nissim, K., Waters, B. (eds.) TCC 2021. LNCS, vol. 13042, pp. 177–208. Springer, Cham (2021). https://doi.org/10.1007/978-3-030-90459-3_7

[Gro96] Grover, L.K.: A fast quantum mechanical algorithm for database search. In: Proceedings of the Twenty-Eighth Annual ACM Symposium on Theory of Computing, pp. 212–219 (1996)

[Hel80] Hellman, M.: A cryptanalytic time-memory trade-off. IEEE Trans. Inf. Theory **26**(4), 401–406 (1980)

[HXY19] Hhan, M., Xagawa, K., Yamakawa, T.: Quantum random oracle model with auxiliary input. In: Galbraith, S.D., Moriai, S. (eds.) ASIACRYPT 2019. LNCS, vol. 11921, pp. 584–614. Springer, Cham (2019). https://doi.org/10.1007/978-3-030-34578-5_21

[MW05] Marriott, C., Watrous, J.: Quantum arthur-merlin games. Comput. Complex. **14**(2), 122–152 (2005)

[NABT14] Nayebi, A., Aaronson, S., Belovs, A., Trevisan, L.: Quantum lower bound for inverting a permutation with advice. CoRR, abs/1408.3193 (2014)

[NC10] Nielsen, M.A., Chuang, I.L.: Quantum Computation and Quantum Information, 10th edn. Cambridge University Press, Cambridge (2010)

[Unr07] Unruh, D.: Random oracles and auxiliary input. In: Menezes, A. (ed.) CRYPTO 2007. LNCS, vol. 4622, pp. 205–223. Springer, Heidelberg (2007). https://doi.org/10.1007/978-3-540-74143-5_12

[Yao90] Yao, A.C.: Coherent functions and program checkers. In: Proceedings of the Twenty-Second Annual ACM Symposium on Theory of Computing, pp. 84–94 (1990)

[YZ22] Yamakawa, T., Zhandry, M.: Verifiable quantum advantage without structure. arXiv preprint arXiv:2204.02063 (2022)

[Zha20] Zhandry, M.: Schrödinger's Pirate: how to trace a quantum decoder. In: Pass, R., Pietrzak, K. (eds.) TCC 2020. LNCS, vol. 12552, pp. 61–91. Springer, Cham (2020). https://doi.org/10.1007/978-3-030-64381-2_3

Black-Box Separations for Non-interactive Classical Commitments in a Quantum World

Kai-Min Chung[1], Yao-Ting Lin[2(✉)], and Mohammad Mahmoody[3]

[1] Academia Sinica, New Taipei, Taiwan
kmchung@iis.sinica.edu.tw
[2] UCSB, Santa Barbara, USA
yao-ting_lin@ucsb.edu
[3] University of Virginia, Charlottesville, USA
mohammad@virginia.edu

Abstract. Commitments are fundamental in cryptography. In the classical world, commitments are equivalent to the existence of one-way functions. It is also known that the most desired form of commitments in terms of their round complexity, i.e., *non-interactive* commitments, *cannot* be built from one-way functions in a black-box way [Mahmoody-Pass, Crypto'12]. However, if one allows the parties to use quantum computation *and* communication, it is known that non-interactive commitments (to classical bits) are in fact possible [Koshiba-Odaira, Arxiv'11 and Bitansky-Brakerski, TCC'21].

We revisit the assumptions behind non-interactive commitments in a quantum world and study whether they can be achieved using quantum computation and *classical* communication based on a black-box use of one-way functions. We prove that doing so is impossible unless the Polynomial Compatibility Conjecture [Austrin et al. Crypto'22] is false. We further extend our impossibility to protocols with quantum decommitments. This complements the positive result of Bitansky and Brakerski [TCC'21], as they only required a classical decommitment message. Because non-interactive commitments can be based on injective one-way functions, assuming the Polynomial Compatibility Conjecture, we also obtain a black-box separation between one-way functions and injective one-way functions (e.g., one-way permutations) even when the construction and the security reductions are allowed to be quantum. This improves the separation of Cao and Xue [Theoretical Computer Science'21] in which they only allowed the *security reduction* to be quantum.

At a technical level, we prove that sampling oracles at random from "sufficiently large" sets (of oracles) will make them one-way against polynomial quantum-query adversaries who also get arbitrary polynomial-size quantum advice about the oracle. This gives a natural generalization of the recent results of Hhan et al. [Asiacrypt'19] and Chung et al. [FOCS'20].

K.-M. Chung—Supported in part by the NSTC QC project, under Grant no. NSTC 111-2119-M-001-004- and the Air Force Office of Scientific Research under award number FA2386-20-1-4066.

Y.-T. Lin—Part of the work was done when working at Academia Sinica.

M. Mahmoody—Supported by NSF grants CCF-1910681 and CNS1936799.

C. Hazay and M. Stam (Eds.): EUROCRYPT 2023, LNCS 14004, pp. 144–172, 2023.
https://doi.org/10.1007/978-3-031-30545-0_6

1   Introduction

Commitment schemes are one of the most basic building blocks in the foundations of cryptography with a variety of applications. In a non-interactive commitment scheme, a sender Sen who holds a (say single bit) message b sends a *commitment* message com to a receiver Rec in such a way that the com acts as a secure vault hiding b; this is formalized as follows. (1) The *hiding* property requires that com does not reveal anything about b to a computationally bounded receiver. (2) The *binding* property requires that after sending com, the sender is essentially bound to at most one $b \in \{0, 1\}$ and cannot change its mind afterwards. (3) The *completeness* of the scheme requires that the sender shall be able to convincingly reveal b using a *decommitment* message dec that functions like a password to the vault holding b.

In the classical setting, *interactive* commitments can be based on the *minimal* assumption that one-way functions exist [IL89, Nao90, HILL99]. However, when one wants to obtain the more desirable non-interactive variant, cryptographic primitives such as injective one-way functions [Yao82, GL89] and most public-key assumptions [LS19] have been shown to be sufficient. These constructions are black-box [IR89, RTV04, BBF13], in the sense that (1) they use the assumed primitive (e.g., in this case, one-way functions) as an oracle in their implementation, and (2) their security is proved by a reduction that treats the imagined adversary (breaking the construction) as an oracle as well. Moreover, it is known that OWFs cannot be used in a black-box way to obtain any of the primitives that are known to imply non-interactive commitments [MM11, IR89] or the non-interactive commitment itself [MP12].

Commitments in the Quantum Setting. With the rise of quantum computation in computer science and cryptography, questions that were previously considered to be well-understood in the classical setting are being revisited. In the quantum setting, we allow Sen, Rec to both run in *quantum* polynomial time, while the committed bit b is still classical. By default, the commitment and decommitment messages would also be quantum messages (but we would prefer them to be classical too, if possible). It has been shown [May97, LC97] that similarly to the classical setting, *some* form of computational intractability is necessary for commitments in the quantum setting, and (even interactive) commitments with statistical (hiding and binding) security cannot be achieved if adversaries are allowed to be quantum. When it comes to the *assumptions* behind commitments in the quantum setting, a sequence of works [DMS00, CLS01, KO09, LQWY14, Yan20] led to the perhaps surprising result that black-box constructions of non-interactive commitments (for classical messages) with various forms of binding properties that are meaningful in the quantum setting could in fact be constructed from (post-quantum) one-way functions [KO11, BB21] in the quantum setting.

The QCCC Model: Quantum Computation and Classical Communication. The full advantage of quantum cryptography will rely on using both quantum computation as well as quantum communication. However, the internet is currently a classical communication medium, so it is much more desirable to design protocols that stick to classical communication as much as possible, even if they rely on local quantum computation (and hardness assumptions). In fact, the recent active line of work on classically verifying quantum power [Mah18,CCY20,ACGH20,BKVV20,Zha21,Bar21] also falls into this quantum-computation and classical-communication (QCCC) model. Thus, we revisit constructing non-interactive commitments from OWFs in the quantum setting as well and ask the following question.

Can we construct non-interactive commitments from (post-quantum) one-way functions using quantum computation and (only) classical communication?

In fact, one can study a relaxed version of the question above by limiting only *one* of the commitment or decommitment messages to be quantum. The OWF-based constructions of [KO11,BB21] and the candidate OWF-based construction of [YWLQ15] all used *quantum* messages. Among them, the work of [BB21] managed to make the decommitment message classical (while using a quantum commitment). Hence, their work suggests that perhaps using quantum commitment messages is the key to getting non-interactive commitments from OWFs. Therefore, a natural related question is whether one can obtain non-interactive commitments from OWFs in the quantum setting while limiting the *commitment* message to be classical and allowing the decommitment to be quantum. Note that commitment messages are *stored* for a longer time between the two phases of the commitment scheme, decommitment messages are revealed at the *very end*. Therefore, if only one of these messages is going to be quantum, it is perhaps preferred that the decommitment message is the quantum one.

Quantum Binding vs. Classical Binding. We note that while hiding remains reasonably straightforward to define against quantum polynomial-time adversaries, binding is a subtle property and could be defined in different ways. In fact, for statistically hiding commitments, it is *impossible* to achieve the same strong notions of binding, similar to the classical variant, in which the commitment message essentially binds the committed bit to be at most one value [May97,LC97,BB21]. As a result, in the statistically-hiding setting, we usually settle down for the weaker notion of "sum binding", in which the probability p_b of opening successfully to b satisfies $p_0 + p_1 \leq 1 + \text{negl}(\kappa)$, where κ is the security parameter. For this setting, [Unr16a] proposed the alternative notion of "collapse-binding". By only requiring computational hiding, [BB21] showed that a very close notion to the classical form of binding is in fact possible if one allows the receiver to only make a (partial) measurement right after the commitment message is sent. Our main question above is meaningful with respect to all these variants of binding. Therefore, as we will clarify, it is *not* crucial for the reader to follow these subtle differences, as our (negative) results can be stated with a *weaker* notion of binding in which the adversary has to successfully decommit into both values of $0, 1$.

1.1   Our Results

At a high level, we answer our main question above negatively with respect to quantum black-box constructions [HY20], unless a recent conjecture about low-degree and low-influence polynomials is false [ACC+22]. The work of [ACC+22] showed that assuming this conjecture, one can break perfectly complete QCCC key-agreement protocols (with classical communication) in the Quantum Random Oracle Model [BDF+11] by asking only a polynomial number of queries to the oracle. As a result, they obtained black-box separations for perfectly complete key agreements in the QCCC model from OWFs. We first explain this conjecture and then will state our results based on it.

The Polynomial Compatibility Conjecture (PCC). Suppose $f = \sum_{S \subseteq [N]} \alpha_S \prod_{i \in S} x_i$ is a polynomial over Boolean variables $x_i \in \{\pm 1\}, i \in [N]$ and real coefficients $\alpha_S \in \mathbb{R}, S \subseteq [N]$. The degree of f is $\max_{\alpha_S \neq 0} |S|$ and $\|f\|_2 = \mathbb{E}_{\mathbf{x} \leftarrow \{\pm 1\}^N}[f(\mathbf{x})^2]$. The influence of x_i on f is $\mathrm{Inf}_i(f) = \sum_{i \in S} \alpha_S^2$, and for a distribution $\mathbf{F}$ over such polynomials, we let $\mathrm{Inf}_i(\mathbf{F}) = \mathbb{E}_{f \leftarrow \mathbf{F}}[\mathrm{Inf}_i(f)]$ be the *expected* influence. The PCC (for the group $\mathbb{Z}_2$) states that for sufficiently small $\delta(d) = 1/\mathrm{poly}(d)$, if $\mathbf{F}, \mathbf{G}$ are distributions over polynomials of degree d over variables $x_1, \ldots, x_N \in \{\pm 1\}$, $\|\cdot\|_2$-norm equal to 1, and expected influences $\mathrm{Inf}_i(\mathbf{F}), \mathrm{Inf}_i(\mathbf{G}) \leq \delta(d)$ for all $i \in [N]$, there exist $f \in \mathrm{supp}(\mathbf{F})$, $g \in \mathrm{supp}(\mathbf{G})$ and $\mathbf{x} \in \{\pm 1\}^N$ such that $f(\mathbf{x}) \cdot g(\mathbf{x}) \neq 0$. The work of [ACC+22] gave some evidence for the validity of the PCC by proving a weaker statement than the PCC in which the influences are exponentially $\exp(-d)$ small.[1]

We prove the following conditional black-box separation for non-interactive commitments in the quantum setting. Our result holds even for a "weak" variant of binding that is necessary for all the proposed forms of binding in the quantum setting. In particular, we say that a malicious sender breaks the weak binding if it can come up with a commitment message com and a pair of decommitment messages $(\mathrm{dec}_0, \mathrm{dec}_1)$ such that using dec_b allows the sender to successfully decommit com to b.

Theorem 1.1 (Black-box separation of QCCC commitments from OWFs). *Assuming the Polynomial Compatibility Conjecture, there is no black-box construction of non-interactive commitments from (post-quantum) one-way functions in the QCCC model. Moreover, this holds even if the decommitment message is allowed to be quantum.*

Theorem 1.1 complements the *positive* result of [BB21], in which they show that there is a commitment scheme with a quantum commitment and a classical decommitment based on post-quantum OWFs. In other words, our work (conditionally) shows that one cannot trade a quantum commitment message with a quantum decommitment message and still use post-quantum OWFs when constructing non-interactive commitments from OWFs in a black-box way.

Corollary: Separating Injective OWFs from OWFs in the Quantum Setting. Injective one-way functions (e.g., one-way permutations) with classical input/outputs imply non-interactive commitments in a black-box way [GL89]. Therefore, Theorem 1.1 also implies the corollary that assuming the PCC, black-box construction of injective one-way functions from general one-way functions does not exist, even if the construction is allowed to use quantum computation. The work of [CX21] proved such a separation only when the *security reduction* is quantum, but our result extends to fully quantum constructions (assuming the PCC).

---

[1] The PCC bears some similarities to a conjecture by Aaronson and Ambianis [AA09] that also deals with polynomials with a low degree and low influence and which is also proved for exponentially small influences. See [ACC+22] for more discussions and comparisons.

Corollary: Separating NICs from Pseudorandom States. The recent works of [AQY22, MY22] suggest that as opposed to the classical setting, OWFs might *not* be neces- sary for non-interactive commitments in the quantum setting: they could be constructed from "pseudorandom states" [BS20], which are weaker than OWFs [Kre21]. The work of [JLS18] showed that "pseudorandom states" (PRSs) can be based on OWFs in a black-box way. Therefore, as a corollary of our result, we obtain the separation between NICs and PRSs in the CCQD model (i.e., the model in which the commitment message is classical, but the decommitment is allowed to be quantum). We point out that the construction in [MY22] requires quantum commitment messages (but classical decom- mitment messages), and the construction in [AQY22] is interactive.

We will explain the key ideas behind the proof of Theorem 1.1 in Sect. 1.2. Before doing so we highlight one key technical tool that we develop along with the proof of Theorem 1.2 and believe to be of independent interest.

When are Randomized Oracles Quantum One-Way? It is known that if $\mathcal{H}_n$ denotes the set of all functions from $\{0,1\}^n$ to $\{0,1\}^n$, then a random oracles $f \leftarrow \mathcal{H}_n$ is one way against polynomial-time adversaries who even get arbitrary polynomial-size advice about the random oracle [IR89, GT00]. This classical result holds even if the adversary can ask quantum superposition queries to the (random *permutation*) oracle [NABT15], and even if the auxiliary information about the random oracle is quantum [HXY19, CGLQ20]. We revisit this phenomenon in a more general setting and ask the following question. What happens if the oracle $f : \{0,1\}^n \mapsto \{0,1\}^n$ is *not* completely random, yet it is sampled at random from a "large" set of oracles $\mathcal{F} \subseteq \mathcal{H}_n$. We give a concrete bound on how large $\mathcal{F}$ needs to be to make a random $f \leftarrow \mathcal{F}$ one-way against efficient non-uniform quantum adversaries that also receive quantum auxiliary advice about f.

Theorem 1.2 (One-wayness of oracles under quantum auxiliary input). *Suppose* $\mathcal{H}_n$ *denotes the set of all functions from* $\{0,1\}^n$ *to* $\{0,1\}^n$, *and that*

$$|\mathcal{F}| \geq 2^{-\frac{2^n}{n^{\omega(1)}}} \cdot |\mathcal{H}_n|$$

for a set of functions $\mathcal{F}$. *Then a randomly selected* $f \leftarrow \mathcal{F}$ *will be one-way against quantum adversaries who ask* $\mathrm{poly}(n)$ *quantum queries to* f *and receive at most* $\mathrm{poly}(n)$ *bits of quantum advice about* f.

See Sect. 3 for a more quantitative and general statement.

At a very high level, we use Theorem 1.2 to prove Theorem 1.1 by picking $\mathcal{F}$ to model a *large* set of oracles that can be used by a *cheating receiver*, while the advice about each oracle is a pair of decommitments to $b = 0, 1$. The security reduction of the supposedly black-box construction of non-interactive commitments from one-way functions would then lead to an adversary who inverts $f \leftarrow \mathcal{F}$ using $\mathrm{poly}(n)$ number of queries and $\mathrm{poly}(n)$ bits of advice, which is a contradiction due to Theorem 1.2.

1.2 Technical Overview

In this section, we explain some of the key ideas behind the proofs of Theorems 1.1 and 1.2 and the links between these two results. Our starting point for proving

Theorem 1.1 is the black-box separation of non-interactive commitments from one-way functions in the classical setting [MP12]. We first sketch the argument for the classical case and then explain the challenges that arise in the quantum setting.

Recap of the Proof for the Classical Setting. An approach for proving a black-box separation between primitives $\mathcal{Q}$ and OWFs is as follows. We show that the primitive $\mathcal{Q}$ can be broken relative to a *random oracle* h by asking only a polynomial number of queries.[2] However, when we want to separate commitments from OWFs (even in the classical setting), we cannot simply use random oracles as mentioned above. The reason is that the random oracle can indeed be used to obtain *injective* one-way functions (with high probability), which in turn do imply non-interactive commitments. That is why, in [MP12], the oracle h used for the separation is chosen from a more subtle distribution: h is chosen *either* at random, *or* from a "partially fixed" random oracle. The key idea is to show that *at least* one of these two oracle distributions leads to breaking the commitment scheme while one-way functions exist relative to both oracle distributions. In particular, each randomized oracle corresponds to one of the parties of the commitment scheme to be the cheater.

- *Cheating receiver* Rec^* *relative to a random oracle.* Let h be a (fully) random oracle $h\colon \{0,1\}^n \mapsto \{0,1\}^n$, where $n = \kappa$ is the security parameter. Suppose Sen is committing to a *random* $b \in \{0,1\}$ and sends message com to the receiver. Then, let $\mathsf{Rec}^*(\mathsf{com})$ be a cheating receiver who tries to learn the oracle answer to any query $x \in \{0,1\}^n$ such that x has been asked by Sen with probability at least ε, for a parameter $\varepsilon = 1/\operatorname{poly}(\kappa)$. Such queries were called "ε-heavy" in [BM09], and it was shown that regardless of com, there are (on average) at most d/ε of them if d is the number of oracle queries by Sen. Suppose the partial oracle $\mathcal{L}$ contains all the query-answer pairs learned by Rec^*. If Rec^* could now guess the random committed bit b (information-theoretically) with probability $1/2 + 1/\operatorname{poly}(\kappa)$, it means Rec^* has succeeded in its attack *in the random oracle* model. In this case, we would be done with the separation; the reason is that the security reduction S of the black-box construction shall now be able to use Rec^* and invert the random oracle h with non-negligible probability, which is in fact impossible because the combined algorithm S^{Rec^*} is still asking polynomially many queries to h
- *Cheating sender* Sen^* *relative to a non-random oracle.* Now, suppose the above attack by Rec^* does *not* succeed. In this case, we show that one can construct a cheating sender strategy Sen^* along with a fixed triple $(\mathsf{com}, \mathsf{dec}_0, \mathsf{dec}_1)$ and a distribution $\mathbf{h}$ over the oracles with the following.
  - com is a commitment message and dec_b is a decommitment message for b.
  - $\mathbf{h}$ is a distribution over oracles that are random everywhere except on a $\operatorname{poly}(n)$-size subset of the input domain $\{0,1\}^n$.
  - The honest receiver accepts both $(\mathsf{com}, \mathsf{dec}_b), b \in \{0,1\}$ relative to all $h \leftarrow \mathbf{h}$.
  If one can demonstrate the existence of the above triple $(\mathsf{com}, \mathsf{dec}_0, \mathsf{dec}_1, \mathbf{h})$, it again implies that black-box construction of Sen, Rec from one-way functions are impossible: the security reduction S shall again be able to use Sen^* and invert the partially fixed random oracle $h \leftarrow \mathbf{h}$, but that is again impossible because the oracle $\mathbf{h}$ is only partially fixed, and partially fixed random oracles are also one-way.

---

[2] E.g., one can re-interpret the proofs of [IR89, BM09] to fall into this framework.

The reason that such (com, dec_0, dec_1, **h**) exists is as follows. Since we assumed that Rec* had failed in its own attack above, conditioned on (com, $\mathcal{L}$), both bits $b = 0, 1$ are equally likely to be the truly committed bit. Therefore, if we further condition on $b = 0$ or $b = 1$, no 3ε-heavy queries would exist outside $\mathcal{L}$ (because both of the events $b = 0, 1$ have probability about $1/2$). Now, if we sample the view of the Sen twice, one conditioned on $b = 0$ and one conditioned on $b = 1$, two things happen: (1) we obtain decommitments two dec_0, dec_1 for $b = 0, 1$, and (2) we obtain *partial functions* h_0, h_1 that denote (only) the queries asked by Sen while committing to $0, 1$ to generate com and dec_0, dec_1. Due to the lack of heavy queries in both of these sampling processes, the partial oracles h_0, h_1 will be *disjoint* with (high) probability $1 - O(d\varepsilon)$, and so they can be combined into a *single* partial oracle $h_{0,1} = h_0 \cup h_1$. Together with the partial oracle $\mathcal{L}$, $h_{\mathsf{fixed}} = h_{0,1} \cup \mathcal{L}$ will shape the fixed part of the random oracles **h** that is useful for the cheating sender.

New Challenges in the Quantum Setting. When we move to the setting in which the honest parties are quantum, several steps of the argument above will break down. We go over these issues one by one and explain the ideas for resolving them.

1. *Quantum analogue of learning heavy queries.* Since Sen* can ask *quantum* queries to its oracle h (that is supposedly a random oracle), it no longer makes sense to use the classical ε-heavy query learners. However, the recent work of [ACC+22] showed how to extend this technique (by relying on ideas inspired by Zhandry's compressed oracle technique [Zha19]) to the quantum setting as follows. The receiver shall consider the sender's computation and the oracle all in a purified[3] way, while the oracle's answers are represented in the Fourier basis. This way, any query x that has at least ε chance of having a *nonzero* answer in the Fourier conditioned on the commitment message com, will be considered *quantum ε-heavy*. The intuition is that being zero in the Fourier basis is (almost) the same as not being read by anyone, and hence remaining uniform. Note that the heavy queries are classical. It can also be shown, just like in the classical setting, that the total number of quantum heavy queries is $O(d/\varepsilon)$ where d is the number of quantum queries by the sender.

2. *Quantum analogue of partially fixed oracles.* In the classical setting, we could fix the partial oracle $h_{\mathsf{fixed}} = h_{0,1} \cup \mathcal{L}$ that is consistent with two fixed openings dec_0, dec_1 as well as the learned and pick the rest of the oracle at random. However, in the quantum setting, it is no longer well-defined to refer to the "oracle queries asked by the sender" (i.e., $h_{0,1}$) as a partial oracle. That is because we cannot "record" the sender's queries, due to the quantum nature of its algorithm.

Below we explain how to resolve this challenge. It turns out that resolving this challenge is even harder to resolve for protocols with quantum decommitments, so we will first go over the easier case of protocols in the QCCC model, before discussing the classical commitment quantum decommitment (CCQD) case.

---

[3] In the context of quantum information theory, purifying a quantum process means delaying all intermediate measurements to the end at the cost of introducing additional qubits. So that the whole computation remains a pure state until the final measurement.

Finding Compatible Oracles. Suppose after the sender runs out of learning quantum ε-heavy queries, $|\phi_0\rangle, |\phi_1\rangle$ are the marginal quantum states of the sender and the oracle for the two cases of $b = 0, 1$, the same commitment string com, and the set of fixed oracle answers in $\mathcal{L}$. First, we show that if the Polynomial Compatibility Conjecture (PCC) of [ACC+22] holds, then there is *at least one* oracle h (in the computational basis) that is consistent with both quantum states $|\phi_0\rangle, |\phi_1\rangle$. To do this, first, assume that the decommitment messages are classical. This means one can find two ensembles $\mathbf{H}_0, \mathbf{H}_1$ of quantum states for the oracle registers such that (1) $\mathbf{H}_b$ denotes quantum states for the oracle compatible with committing to b, and (2) $\mathbf{H}_0, \mathbf{H}_1$ can be uniquely modeled using distributions $\mathbf{F}_0, \mathbf{F}_1$ over degree-d polynomials (where d is the number of oracle queries of the sender) of influence at most 3ε, and (3) the oracles compatible with decommitting to b are the non-zero points of the polynomials sampled from $\mathbf{F}_b$. Therefore, by the PCC, there are indeed samples $f_0 \leftarrow \mathbf{F}_0, f_1 \leftarrow \mathbf{F}_1$, and an oracle h such that $f_b(h) \neq 0$ for both $b \in \{0,1\}$. This means that the oracle h is compatible with two decommitments $\mathrm{dec}_0, \mathrm{dec}_1$ into both $b = 0, 1$ with respect to the same commitment com.

Boosting to Many Compatible Oracles. Having only one compatible oracle h that allows opening com successfully into both $b \in \{0,1\}$ using $\mathrm{dec}_0, \mathrm{dec}_1$ is not enough for proving the black-box separation, as h might be easy to invert. In particular, we need to show that such compatible oracle h can be found while it is also one-way. Our first idea for achieving this goal is that since the two polynomials f_0, f_1 have degree d, their (non-zero) product also has a degree at most $2d$. Therefore, we can use a variant of the Schwartz-Zippel lemma to conclude that at least 2^{-2d} fraction of all oracles h will satisfy $f_0(h) f_1(h) \neq 0$. When the group defining the oracle is not $\mathbf{Z}_2^n$, we can no longer apply the Schwartz-Zippel lemma, as the two functions $f_0(h) f_1(h)$ will not be low-degree polynomials, yet we derive a similar result using a generalization of the Schwartz-Zippel lemma known as the *Donoho-Stark support-size uncertainty principle* [DS89].

So far, we have shown that in the case of classical communication (including classical decommitments), the PCC implies that there is a *large* set of oracles $\mathcal{F}$ such that every $h \leftarrow \mathcal{F}$ is compatible with the commitment com followed by *both* decommitments $\mathrm{dec}_0, \mathrm{dec}_1$ into $0, 1$. It remains to show that a random sample $h \leftarrow \mathcal{F}$ is hard to invert by $\mathrm{poly}(n)$-query *quantum* adversaries. This idea is implicit in [HXY19] (about the one-wayness of random oracles under quantum queries and classical auxiliary information) and generalizes to the case of sampling an oracle from a large set of oracles as well. However, this approach does not work when we want to attack protocols with *quantum* decommitment messages, as that requires working with *quantum* auxiliary information.

For classical decommitments, we rely on the fact that we can sample decommitments to $0, 1$ and create an oracle (distribution) that is consistent with both. When decommitment messages are quantum, we can no longer measure the sender's registers to create cheating strategies, because the decommitment messages are *quantum* and need to be kept as such. Therefore, we need to modify the approach above. Let $\mathcal{F}_b$ be the set of oracles (in the computational basis) that are compatible with an opening into b. Since measuring (or not measuring) the sender's own registers (that will be used to produce the decommitment message) will *not* change the set $\mathcal{F}_b$, we first *pretend* that such measurement is happening to define two ensembles of oracles and use the PCC again to argue that the set $\mathcal{F} = \mathcal{F}_0 \cap \mathcal{F}_1$ contains at least an $\approx 1/d^{\Theta(n \cdot d)}$ fraction of the oracles that map $\{0,1\}^n$ to $\{0,1\}^n$.

To finish the proof, we need to prove two things: (1) for each $h \in \mathcal{F}$, there exist a pair of *quantum* decommitments $(\mathsf{dec}_0, \mathsf{dec}_1)$ that successfully decommit into $0, 1$ with respect to commitment message com, and (2) picking a random oracle $h \leftarrow \mathcal{F}$ will lead to h that is hard to invert by polynomial-query adversaries. Item (1) is rather straightforward, due to the fact that $f \in \mathcal{F}_0$ (resp. $f \in \mathcal{F}_1$) are already defined to be the set of oracles that are compatible with at least one decommitments to 0 (resp. 1) with respect to com. However, Item (2) is now more challenging to prove when the decommitments are quantum messages. That is because, the security reduction S, now has access to $f \in \mathcal{F}$ as well as a pair of "advice" $(\mathsf{dec}_0, \mathsf{dec}_1)$ which can be seen as a piece of *quantum auxiliary information* about f, and so we would need to prove the one-wayness of the oracle $f \leftarrow \mathcal{F}$ against adversaries with quantum auxiliary information about f. Below, we focus on explaining the ideas for proving this specific one-wayness as an independent problem of its own.

Functions Sampled from Large Sets are One-Way for Adversaries with Quantum Advice. As explained above, Theorem 1.1 reduces to Theorem 1.2, which states that any sufficiently large subset $\mathcal{F}$ of all oracles $\mathcal{H}_n = \{h \mid h \colon \{0,1\}^n \mapsto \{0,1\}^n\}$, a randomly selected function $h \leftarrow \mathcal{H}_n$ is "one-way" against any adversary who asks $\mathrm{poly}(n)$ quantum queries and gets $\mathrm{poly}(n)$ bits of quantum advice about f. At a high level, we prove this result through a reduction to carefully chosen results from [CGLQ20].

Below we first recall the results in [CGLQ20], which can be used to prove the hardness of *completely random* oracles against quantum adversaries with quantum advice, and then show how their approach can be adapted to our case, in which a function is sampled from a large set (rather than all) of functions.

– *Non-uniform one-wayness of fully random functions* [CGLQ20]. Here we describe the approach of [CGLQ20] for proving non-uniform hardness of fully random functions. We then describe how the components of the proof of [CGLQ20] can be adapted for our setting. Let $h \colon \{0,1\}^n \mapsto \{0,1\}^n$ be a function. Consider a classical adversary A who receives S bit classical advice $\alpha = \alpha(h)$ about h and can ask T queries to h and manages to invert h with probability $\geq \varepsilon$, i.e.,

$$\Pr_{A,h,x} [A^h(\alpha, h(x)) \in h^{-1}(h(x))] \geq \varepsilon,$$

where the probability is over the randomness of A and the random choices of the *completely random* h and x. Now, consider a different attacking algorithm B that can ask $k \cdot T$ queries to h, but it does not receive any advice. However, the job of B is harder, as it needs to solve a *multi-instance version* of the inversion problem as follows: B is asked to invert k challenges $h(x_1), \ldots, h(x_k)$. For each of these k challenges, the chance of inverting them is $O\left(\frac{kT}{2^n}\right)$ by a lazy-evaluation argument. Interestingly, as it is shown in [CGLQ20], and one can show that for the k-instance version, the success probability of any such algorithm B will decrease exponentially in k,

$$\Pr_{B,h,x_1,\ldots,x_k}[B^h(h(x_1),\ldots,h(x_k)) \text{ inverts } h(x_1),\ldots,h(x_k)] \leq O\left(\frac{kT}{2^n}\right)^k. \quad (1)$$

Now, we relate the success probability of A to that of B for bounding ε. First, using A we construct a new algorithm B' with S-bit classical advice and kT queries to h. B' simply uses the single copy of advice given to A and runs A to invert each $h(x_i)$ independently for all $i \in [k]$. To analyze the success probability of B', we use the following argument. By an averaging argument, with probability at least $\varepsilon/2$ over the choice of h, A can invert them successfully with probability $\varepsilon/2$. Denote the set of such "good" functions by $\mathcal{G}$. Then, we have

$$\Pr_{B',x_1,\ldots,x_k}[B'^h(\alpha,h(x_1),\ldots,h(x_k)) \text{ inverts } h(x_1),\ldots,h(x_k) \mid h \in \mathcal{G}] \geq \left(\frac{\varepsilon}{2}\right)^k.$$

Now, let B use B' and simply guess the advice α and use B'; we have,

$$O\left(\frac{kT}{2^n}\right)^k \geq \Pr[B \text{ guesses } \alpha \text{ correctly}] \cdot \Pr_h[h \in \mathcal{G}] \quad (2)$$

$$\cdot \Pr_{B,x_1,\ldots,x_k}[B^h(h(x_1),\ldots,h(x_k)) \text{ inverts } h(x_1),\ldots,h(x_k) \mid h \in \mathcal{G}] \quad (3)$$

$$\geq 2^{-S} \cdot \left(\frac{\varepsilon}{2}\right)^{k+1} \geq 2^{-S} \cdot \left(\frac{\varepsilon}{2}\right)^k. \quad (4)$$

By choosing k large enough $k = \widetilde{O}(S)$ we obtain the desired bound of $\varepsilon = \widetilde{O}(ST/2^n)$ between the adversary's number of queries, advice length, and its (small) chance of success. The main magic in the above argument is to leverage the exponential drop in success probability of the multi-instance game as shown in Eq. (1) and to absorb the loss caused by guessing the advice.

Even though the above sketch was for the case of classical advice, in which guessing the advice is rather easy to analyze, as it was shown in [CGLQ20], a similar argument can be used for "guessing" quantum advice as well and use the above blueprint for proving one-wayness of a truly random function against adversaries with quantum queries and quantum advice.

– *Non-uniform one-wayness of functions sampled from large sets.* We now explain how the outline above can be adapted to the setting where we work with an oracle h that is sampled from a large enough sets of oracles $\mathcal{F}$, instead of picking h completely at random. To achieve our results, we have a simple but extremely useful observation as follows. Let's start by assuming an algorithm A can invert $f(x)$ with probability ε, when $f \leftarrow \mathcal{F}$ and $x \in \{0,1\}^n$ are chosen uniformly at random. Using a similar averaging argument as the one above, we can still obtain a set of functions $\mathcal{G} \subseteq \mathcal{F}$ such that $|\mathcal{G}| \geq \varepsilon/2 \cdot |\mathcal{F}|$ such that A has success probability $\varepsilon/2$ conditioned on $h \in \mathcal{G}$. Going forward, the calculations in Eq. (2) break down. In particular, we previously had $\Pr[h \in \mathcal{G}] \geq \varepsilon/2$, while we know have $\Pr[h \in \mathcal{G}] \geq \rho \cdot \varepsilon/2$, where ρ is the fraction of $|\mathcal{F}|$ in the set of all functions.

Our key observation is that, although ρ is very small, we prove that it is not *too* small. Therefore, the loss in the calculation of Eq. (2) can be compensated by picking k

even larger than before. In particular, recall that increasing k can bound the success probability of adversary to be *exponentially* small in k. Therefore, by picking k large enough in a careful way, we can recover an argument similar to the case of "all oracles" as outlined above.

1.3 Further Related Work

Here we discuss further related works that were not mentioned above already.

Quantum Black-Box Separations. Hosoyamada and Yamakawa [HY20] initiated *quantum* black-box separations by formalizing quantum black-box constructions (for primitives with non-interactive security games) and ruling out the possibility of basing collision-resistant hash functions on one-way functions. Subsequently, [CX21] ruled out classical black-box constructions of post-quantum one-way permutations from post-quantum OWFs. The work of [ACC+22] ruled out quantum black-box constructions of perfectly complete key agreements from OWFs in the QCCC model. The work of [DLS22] ruled out quantum black-box reductions for proving the Fiat-Shamir heuristic, even in the presence of quantum shared entanglements.

Other Assumptions than OWFs. The recent work of [BCQ22] showed that sampling *statistically-far computationally-indistinguishable* pairs of (mixed) quantum states, as a primitive, is a minimal assumption for many quantum primitives such as commitments, oblivious transfer, and secure multiparty computation.

In the classical setting, [BOV03] showed how to derandomize Naor's 2-message commitment scheme that is based on OWFs and obtain a scheme that is non-interactive at the cost of introducing extra (derandomization-related) assumptions [NW94].

Post-quantum Security. Our focus here is on commitments in which parties are quantum. Another line of work studies the post-quantum security of classical constructions [Unr12, Unr16a, Unr16b]. Another exciting recent line of work studies constructing stronger cryptographic primitives (such as oblivious transfer) from the minimal assumption that post-quantum OWFs exist [CDMS04, BCKM21, GLSV21].

2   Preliminaries

Notation. By κ we denote the security parameter. We use bold letters (e.g., $\mathbf{f}$) to denote random variables and distributions. We use calligraphic letters (e.g., $\mathcal{X}$) to denote sets. We use $\mathcal{Y}^{\mathcal{X}}$ to denote the set of all functions from $\mathcal{X}$ to $\mathcal{Y}$.

Throughout this work, we use the standard bra-ket notation (e.g., $|\psi\rangle$) for quantum objects. For the basics of quantum computation, we refer readers to [NC10].

2.1 Quantum Computation

An *oracle-aided quantum algorithm* $\mathsf{A}^{(\cdot)}$ is a quantum algorithm with superposition query access to oracles. For any $d \geq 0$, an oracle quantum algorithm that makes d

queries to oracles can be specified by a sequence of unitaries $U_0, \ldots, U_d$, where the queries are executed between each unitary. Throughout this work, for any oracle $h :$ $\mathcal{X} \to \mathcal{Y}$, we additionally define the range of the oracle $\mathcal{Y}$ to be an additive abelian group. In particular, by O_h we denote the query operator that maps the state $|x, y\rangle$ to $|x, y + h(x)\rangle$, where the addition is associated with the corresponding abelian group. The algorithm also has access to the inverse of the query operator $O_h^\dagger$.

In the *quantum random oracle model* (QROM for short) [BDF+11], a random function $h \colon \{0,1\}^* \mapsto \{0,1\}^\kappa$ is sampled in the beginning. Every party in the protocol (including honest parties and adversaries) has quantum access to h. If an algorithm in the QROM asks at most d queries to the oracle, we call it a *d-query* algorithm.

Zhandry [Zha19] showed that the purified random oracle is perfectly indistinguishable from the (standard) quantum random oracle. Since the sampling of the oracle commutes with the operators of the algorithm accessing the oracle, it can be deferred to the end. Here, we consider a more general setting. Consider an algorithm A with classical input that accesses quantum random oracle and outputs classical transcripts (classical leakage) during its computation (e.g., during an interactive protocol). Inspired by Zhandry's work, we consider the *purified view* of such algorithms in the QROM. By the deferred measurement principle [NC10], all measurements of A can be replaced by unitaries if we introduce additional qubits for recording those measurement outcomes. After this modification, roughly speaking, by the purified view of A we mean the quantum state obtained by executing A from scratch in a coherent way, in which the sampling of the oracle and intermediate measurements are deferred. The formal definition follows.

Definition 2.1 (Purified view of algorithms with classical leakage in the QROM).
Let A be an algorithm with quantum access to a random oracle $h : \mathcal{X} \to \mathcal{Y}$ that takes as classical input b chosen randomly from some set $\mathcal{B}$ with probability p_b, and (possibly) outputs classical transcripts c (perhaps produced in several steps) during its computation. Suppose A consists of a sequence of unitaries and query operators (but no measurements). For ease of notation, we represent A as a sequence $V_1, \ldots, V_n$, where n is the size of A and each V_i is either a unitary operator or a query operator[4]. Let $\mathcal{B}$ be the input register, W be the workspace register, C be the transcript register, and H be the oracle register consisting of H_x for all $x \in \mathcal{X}$ while the content of each H_x stores $h(x)$. The purified view *of A, denoted by $|\psi_n\rangle$, is defined as*

$$|\psi_n\rangle := V_n V_{n-1} \ldots V_1 |\psi_0\rangle,$$

where

$$|\psi_0\rangle := \frac{1}{\sqrt{|\mathcal{Y}|^{|\mathcal{X}|}}} \sum_{b \in \mathcal{B}, h \in \mathcal{Y}^\mathcal{X}} \sqrt{p_b} |b\rangle_B |0\rangle_W |h\rangle_H |0\rangle_C.$$

Purified View of the Sender in Commitments. We now apply Definition 2.1 to senders in commitments as follows. Let A be the sender's algorithm; the register B stores the input bit $b \in \{0, 1\}$, the register C stores the classical commitment message com, and

---

[4] Since A takes b as input, each V_i is defined to be a controlled-unitary with the control bit b.

part of the register W stores the classical (resp. quantum) decommitment message in the QCCC (resp. CCQD) model.

In a seminal work [Zha19], Zhandry observes that any d-query algorithm in the QROM has a *sparse* Fourier representation. In this work, we closely follow the rephrased version based on [ACC+22] for our use.

Definition 2.2 (Non-zero queries in Fourier basis). *Let $\mathcal{Y}$ be a finite abelian group and $\hat{\mathcal{Y}}$ be the dual group. For any $\hat{h} \in \hat{\mathcal{Y}}^{\mathcal{X}}$, we define the size of $\hat{h}$ to be*

$$|\hat{h}| := |\{x : x \in \mathcal{X}, \hat{h}(x) \neq \hat{0}\}|.$$

Definition 2.3 (The computational and the Fourier basis). *Let $\mathcal{Y}$ be a finite abelian group with cardinality M. Let $\{|y\rangle\}_{y \in \mathcal{Y}}$ be an orthonormal basis of $\mathbb{C}^M$. We refer to this basis as the* computational basis. *Let $\hat{\mathcal{Y}}$ be the dual group which is known to be isomorphic to $\mathcal{Y}$. Recall that a member $\hat{y} \in \hat{\mathcal{Y}}$ is a character function (i.e., a function from $\mathcal{Y}$ to the multiplicative group of non-zero complex numbers). The* Fourier basis $\{|\hat{y}\rangle\}_{\hat{y} \in \hat{y}}$ *of $xcvmk^M$ is defined as*

$$|\hat{y}\rangle = \frac{1}{\sqrt{M}} \sum_y \hat{y}(y)^* |y\rangle \quad and \quad |y\rangle = \frac{1}{\sqrt{M}} \sum_y \hat{y}(y)|\hat{y}\rangle.$$

Lemma 2.4 (Sparse representation [Zha19], rephrased). *For any d-query algorithm A with classical leakage in the QROM with the oracle $h : \mathcal{X} \to \mathcal{Y}$, the purified view of A can be written as a (normalized) quantum state in the form of*

$$|\psi\rangle = \sum_{w,c,\hat{h}:|\hat{h}| \leq d} \alpha_{w,c,\hat{h}} |w\rangle_W |\hat{h}\rangle_H |c\rangle_C,$$

where W, H, and C, in order, denote the workspace of A, the oracle register, and the register recording the classical leakage.

When $\mathcal{Y}$ is a product of groups, i.e., $\mathcal{Y} = \mathcal{Y}_\circ^k$ for some integer $k \geq 1$ and abelian group $\mathcal{Y}_\circ$, then we immediately have the following corollary.

Corollary 2.5. *For any d-query algorithm A with classical leakage in the QROM with the oracle $h : \mathcal{X} \to \mathcal{Y}_\circ^k$, the purified view of A can be written as a normalized quantum state in the form of*

$$|\psi\rangle = \sum_{w,c,\hat{h}_\circ:|\hat{h}_\circ| \leq dk} \alpha_{w,c,\hat{h}_\circ} |w\rangle_W |\hat{h}_\circ\rangle_H |c\rangle_C,$$

where $\hat{h}_\circ \in \hat{\mathcal{Y}}_\circ^{\mathcal{X}}$ and W, H and C, in order, denotes the workspace of A, the oracle register, and the register recording the classical leakage.

Definition 2.6 (Oracle support). *For any quantum state $|\phi\rangle = \sum_{w,\hat{h}} \alpha_{w,\hat{h}} |w\rangle_W |\hat{h}\rangle_H$ defined on an arbitrary register W and the oracle register H, define the* oracle support *in the Fourier basis of $|\phi\rangle$ as*

$$\widehat{\text{supp}}^H(|\phi\rangle) := \{\hat{h} \mid \exists w : \alpha_{w,\hat{h}} \neq 0\}.$$

Let $\hat{h}_{\max}^H(|\psi\rangle)$ denote the function $\hat{h} \in \widehat{\mathrm{supp}}(|\phi\rangle)$ that has the largest size $|\hat{h}|$ (if such function is not unique, by default we pick the lexicographically first one). The definition extends naturally when the register W does not exist.

Definition 2.7 (Quantum ε-heavy queries [ACC+22]**).** *For any* $x \in \mathcal{X}$, *define the projector*

$$\Pi_x := \sum_{\hat{y} \in \hat{\mathcal{Y}} \setminus \{\hat{0}\}} |\hat{y}\rangle\langle\hat{y}|_{H_x}.$$

Given a quantum state $|\phi\rangle$ *over registers* W *and* H, *the quantum heaviness of any* $x \in \mathcal{X}$ *is defined as*

$$w(x) := \|\Pi_x|\phi\rangle\|^2,$$

i.e., the quantum heaviness of x *is the probability of obtaining a non-$\hat{0}$ outcome while measuring* H_x *in the Fourier basis. We call* x *a quantum ε-heavy query if* $w(x) \geq \varepsilon$.

2.2 Polynomial Compatibility Conjecture

In this section, we formally describe the Polynomial Compatibility Conjecture (PCC) of [ACC+22]. There are two equivalent formulations of this conjecture; one is based on low-degree polynomials, and the other is based on quantum states.

To keep the notation clean in this subsection, we identify $\mathcal{X}$ with $[N]$.

The Polynomial Formulation. Recall that for any $f : \mathcal{Y}^N \to \mathbb{C}$, it can be written in terms of its Fourier transform

$$f(\mathbf{x}) = \sum_{\chi \in \hat{\mathcal{Y}}^N} \hat{f}(\chi) \prod_{i=1}^N \chi_i(x_i),$$

where $\mathbf{x} = x_1 \| \dots \| x_N$. The *degree* of a character $\chi \in \hat{\mathcal{Y}}^N$ is $\deg(\chi) = |\{i \in [N] \mid \chi_i \neq \hat{0}\}|$, and the degree of f is $\deg(f) = \max\{\deg(\chi) \mid \hat{f}(\chi) \neq 0\}$. The ℓ_2-*norm* of a function f is defined as $\|f\|_2 := \sqrt{\mathbb{E}_{\mathbf{x} \leftarrow \mathcal{Y}^N} |f(\mathbf{x})|^2}$. We say that f is *normalized* if $\|f\|_2 = 1$. The *influence* of variable i on f is $\mathrm{Inf}_i(f) = \sum_{\substack{\chi \in \hat{\mathcal{Y}}^N \\ \chi_i \neq \hat{0}}} |\hat{f}(\chi)|^2$.

Conjecture 2.8. (Polynomial Compatibility). There exists a finite abelian group $\mathcal{Y}$ and a function $\delta(d) = 1/\mathrm{poly}(d)$ such that the following holds for all d, N. Let $\mathbf{F}$ and $\mathbf{G}$ be two distributions of functions from $\mathcal{Y}^N$ to $\mathbb{C}^5$ such that the following holds for all $f \in \mathrm{supp}(\mathbf{F})$ and $g \in \mathrm{supp}(\mathbf{G})$.

- **Unit ℓ_2 norm:** f and g have ℓ_2-norm 1.
- d-**degrees:** $\deg(f) \leq d$ and $\deg(g) \leq d$.
- δ-**influences on average:** For all $i \in [N]$, we have $\mathbb{E}_{f \leftarrow \mathbf{F}}[\mathrm{Inf}_i(f)] \leq \delta$ and $\mathbb{E}_{g \leftarrow \mathbf{G}}[\mathrm{Inf}_i(g)] \leq \delta$, where $\delta = \delta(d)$.

Then, there is an $f \in \mathrm{supp}(\mathbf{F})$, $g \in \mathrm{supp}(\mathbf{G})$, and $\mathbf{x} \in \mathcal{Y}^N$ such that $f(\mathbf{x}) \cdot g(\mathbf{x}) \neq 0$.

---

[5] As shown in [ACC+22], regardless of the image being $\mathbb{R}$ or $\mathbb{C}$, the conjectures are equivalent up to a constant factor in δ. For convenience, we use the version with $\mathbb{C}$.

Here we describe an equivalence between quantum states and polynomials. In Sect. 4, we first use the formulation of quantum states. After proving that the states possess certain properties, we will convert the states into polynomials by Lemma 2.12, which enables us to apply Conjecture 2.8. For completeness, we provide relevant definitions below; we refer readers to Sects. 4 and 5 in [ACC+22] for more details.

Definition 2.9 $((\mathcal{Y}, \delta, d, N)$-**state).** *Let H be a register over the Hilbert space $\mathbb{C}^{\mathcal{Y}^{\mathcal{X}}}$, where $|\mathcal{X}| = N$. A quantum state $|\psi\rangle$ over registers W and H is a $(\mathcal{Y}, \delta, d, N)$-state if it satisfies the following two conditions:*

- *d-**sparsity:** $|\hat{h}_{\max}^H(|\psi\rangle)| \leq d$. In other words, for any measurement of the registers H in the Fourier basis, the oracle support in the Fourier basis (as defined in Definition 2.6) is at most d (note that this is regardless of the basis in which we measure the register W).*
- *δ-**lightness:** For every $x \in \mathcal{X}$, it holds that $w(x) \leq \delta$.*

Definition 2.10 (State polynomial). *For a (normalized) quantum state $|\psi\rangle$ over the register H, the state polynomial of $|\psi\rangle$ is the function $f_\psi : \mathcal{Y}^N \to \mathbb{C}$ defined by*

$$f_\psi(h) = |\mathcal{Y}|^{N/2} \cdot \langle \psi | h \rangle = \sum_{\chi \in \hat{\mathcal{Y}}^N} \langle \psi | \chi \rangle \prod_{i=1}^N \chi_i(h_i). \tag{5}$$

Note that $\|f_\psi\|_2 = 1$.

Definition 2.11 (State polynomial distribution). *For a (normalized) quantum state $|\psi\rangle$ over registers W, H, the state polynomial distribution of $|\psi\rangle$ is the distribution $\mathbf{F}_\psi$ over (normalized) functions f which is sampled by measuring W in the computational basis and then taking the (normalized) state polynomial corresponding to the residual collapsed state over the register H. Explicitly, if $|\psi\rangle_{WH} = \sum_{w,\hat{h}} \alpha_{w\hat{h}} |w\rangle_W |\hat{h}\rangle_H$, then the support set of $\mathbf{F}_\psi$ consists of the state polynomial f_{Ψ_w} of the normalized state $|\psi_w\rangle := \sum_{\hat{h}} \alpha_{w\hat{h}} |\hat{h}\rangle_H / \left\| \sum_{\hat{h}} \alpha_{w\hat{h}} |\hat{h}\rangle_H \right\|$ for each w. The probability of each f_{Ψ_w} is defined to be $\left\| \sum_{\hat{h}} \alpha_{w\hat{h}} |\hat{h}\rangle_H \right\|^2$.*

Lemma 2.12. *Let $\mathbf{F}_\psi$ be the state polynomial distribution of an arbitrary $(\mathcal{Y}, \delta, d, N)$-state $|\psi\rangle$. Then the following folds.*

1. **Unit ℓ_2 norm:** *f has ℓ_2-norm 1 for every $f : \mathcal{Y}^N \to \mathbb{C}$ in the support set of $\mathbf{F}_\psi$.*
2. *d-**degrees:** $\deg(f) \leq d$ for every $f : \mathcal{Y}^N \to \mathbb{C}$ in the support set of $\mathbf{F}_\psi$.*
3. *δ-**influences on average:** For all $i \in [N]$, we have $\mathbb{E}_{f \leftarrow \mathbf{F}_\psi}[\mathrm{Inf}_i(f)] \leq \delta$.*

2.3   The Donoho-Stark Uncertainty Principle

We now explain the Donoho-Stark support-size uncertainty principle [DS89]. For our purpose, we use the following rephrased version from [WW21]. Informally, the uncertainty principle states that one cannot *simultaneously* obtain high-precision information of a state in the computational and Fourier basis. Consider the purified oracle as a motivating example. The oracle register in the Fourier basis starts with the all-zero state, while it is uniformly random in the computational basis. This phenomenon can be interpreted as the following: the algorithm knows the oracle with perfect precision in the Fourier basis while having absolutely no precision in the computational basis. Lemma 2.13 below provides a trade-off between the achievable precision in the computational and Fourier bases in terms of the size of supports.

Lemma 2.13 (Theorem 3.1 in [WW21]). *Let $\mathcal{Y}$ be a finite abelian group. If $f : \mathcal{Y} \to \mathbb{C}$ is a non-zero function and $\hat{f} : \hat{\mathcal{Y}} \to \mathbb{C}$ denotes its Fourier transform, then*

$$|\operatorname{supp}(f)| \cdot |\operatorname{supp}(\hat{f})| \geq |\mathcal{Y}|.$$

Corollary 2.14. *Given $f_0, f_1 : \mathcal{Y}^{\mathcal{X}} \to \mathbb{C}$ such that $\deg(f_0), \deg(f_1) \leq d$, we have*

$$|\operatorname{supp}(f_0) \cap \operatorname{supp}(f_1)| \geq \frac{|\mathcal{Y}|^{|\mathcal{X}|}}{O\left(d|\mathcal{X}|^{2d}|\mathcal{Y}|^{2d}\right)}.$$

Proof. Let $f := f_0 \cdot f_1$. It's easy to see that $\mathbf{x} \in \operatorname{supp}(f)$ if and only if $\mathbf{x} \in \operatorname{supp}(f_0) \cap \operatorname{supp}(f_1)$. Since the degree of each f_0 and f_1 is at most d, their Fourier expansion can be written as

$$f_b(\mathbf{x}) = \sum_{\chi \in \hat{\mathcal{Y}}^N : \deg(\chi) \leq d} \hat{f_b}(\chi) \prod_{i=1}^{N} \chi_i(x_i)$$

where $b \in \{0, 1\}$.

Therefore, in the Fourier expansion of f, the characters with non-zero coefficients are of degree at most $2d$. Then the size of $\operatorname{supp}(\hat{f})$ is at most the number of characters of degree at most $2d$. Namely,

$$|\operatorname{supp}(\hat{f})| \leq \sum_{i=0}^{2d} \binom{|\mathcal{X}|}{i} (|\mathcal{Y}| - 1)^i \leq (2d + 1) \cdot (|\mathcal{X}||\mathcal{Y}|)^{2d}.$$

Together with Lemma 2.13, this finishes the proof. □

2.4 Non-interactive Commitments

Below we define non-interactive commitments.

Models. By QCCC we refer to the *quantum-computation classical-communication* model in which all the communications (including the commitment and decommitment messages) are classical. By CCQD we refer to the *classical-commitment quantum-decommitment* model, which is only defined for commitment schemes.

We now define non-interactive commitments with an extremely weak notion of binding. To break the weak binding, the adversary needs to prepare two decommitments for both $b = 0, 1$ such that both will be accepted if used during the decommitment. Using this notion makes our negative result stronger.

Definition 2.15 (Non-interactive weakly-binding commitments in CCQD model).
A non-interactive commitment in the CCQD model consists of two quantum algorithms
Sen, Rec. *On input* $b \in \{0, 1\}$, *the sender* $\mathsf{Sen}(b, 1^\kappa)$ *starts with* $\mathrm{poly}(\kappa)$ *zero registers,*
$\mathrm{poly}(\kappa)$ *qubits of advice, and produces* classical commitment *message* com *and quantum decommitment message* dec. *The receiver (who also has* $\mathrm{poly}(\kappa)$ *zero registers)*
receives (com, b, dec) *and either accepts or rejects.*

- **Completeness.** $\Pr[\mathsf{Rec}(\mathsf{com}, b, \mathsf{dec}) = 1 \mid b \leftarrow \{0, 1\}, (\mathsf{com}, \mathsf{dec}) \leftarrow \mathsf{Sen}(b)] = 1.$
- **Hiding.** *We say* Rec^* *breaks hiding with advantage* ε, *if by picking* $b \leftarrow \{0, 1\}$ *at random,* $\mathsf{Rec}^*(\mathsf{com})$ *can correctly guess* b *with probability* $(1 + \varepsilon)/2$. *We call* Sen *hiding, if for every* $\mathrm{poly}(\kappa)$-*size quantum circuit* Rec^* *the advantage of* Rec^* *is at most* $\mathrm{negl}(\kappa)$.
- **Weak binding.** *We say* (com, dec_0, dec_1) *breaks the weak binding, if*

$$\Pr[\mathsf{Rec}(\mathsf{com}, b, \mathsf{dec}_b) = 1] = 1 \text{ for both } b \in \{0, 1\}.$$

We say that Rec *has weak binding, if for all sequence* $\{(\mathsf{com}_\kappa, \mathsf{dec}_{0,\kappa}, \mathsf{dec}_{1,\kappa})_\kappa\}$
where com_κ, $\mathsf{dec}_{0,\kappa}$, $\mathsf{dec}_{1,\kappa}$ *are of lengths at most* $\mathrm{poly}(\kappa)$, *for all but finitely many*
κ, $(\mathsf{com}_\kappa, \mathsf{dec}_{0,\kappa}, \mathsf{dec}_{1,\kappa})$ *does not break the weak binding of* Rec.

When the decommitment messages in a CCQD scheme are also classical, we say
the resulting scheme is in the QCCC (quantum-computation classical-communication)
model.

Note that in the definition above, we are implicitly working with poly-*size* (non-uniform) adversaries in our notion of weak binding. That is because a non-uniform adversary might simply know the best way to open into both cases of $0, 1$ without computational limitations. Having said that, even if we further weaken the security and ask for a *uniform* polynomial-time adversaries, it will not make a difference for a black-box separation (of an assumption behind non-interactive commitments). The reason is that the definition of black-box constructions (see below) requires the security reduction to work whenever it is given any *oracle* adversary regardless of its complexity.

Definition 2.16. *A quantum black-box construction of weakly-binding non-interactive*
commitments from (length preserving) one-way functions is a pair of uniform QPT
oracle-aided quantum algorithms (G, S) *as follows.*

- *For every abelian group* $\mathcal{Y}$ *and every* $f \colon \mathcal{Y}^\kappa \mapsto \mathcal{Y}^\kappa$, *the oracle-aided quantum algorithm* $G^f = (G_S^f, G_R^f)$ *implements a quantum commitment scheme (both for the sender and receiver).*
- *For every abelian group* $\mathcal{Y}$, *for every* $f \colon \mathcal{Y}^\kappa \mapsto \mathcal{Y}^\kappa$, *and any oracle adversary* $\mathsf{A} = (\mathsf{A}_h, \mathsf{A}_b)$ *who breaks the hiding or the weak binding of* G^f, *the algorithm* $S^{f, \mathsf{A}}$ *inverts* f *with a non-negligible probability. In particular,* S *consists of two algorithms* $S = (S_h, S_b)$, *and there is a function* $\delta = \mathrm{poly}(\varepsilon/\kappa)$ *such that: (1) if* A_h ε-*breaks the hiding of* G_S^f, *then* S_h^{f, A_h} *inverts* f *with probability* $\delta = \mathrm{poly}(\varepsilon/\kappa)$, *and (2) if* $\mathsf{A}_b = (\mathsf{com}_\kappa, \mathsf{dec}_{0,\kappa}, \mathsf{dec}_{1,\kappa})$ *breaks the weak binding of* G_R^f, *then* S_b^{f, A_b} *inverts* f *with probability* $\delta = \mathrm{poly}(1/\kappa)$.

Remark 2.17. First, restricting the OWFs to have the same input and output spaces is without loss of generality. Because according to the definition of black-box reduction, the construction of the commitment scheme should work for *any* OWF. Hence, toward a contradiction, it's sufficient to show that the commitment scheme is impossible to be constructed from some *specific* OWF in a black-box way.

Next, we note that in the quantum setting, the quantum oracle access to a classical function depends on the underlying abelian group. By default, we assume $\mathcal{Y} = \mathbb{Z}_2$ and $f : \{0,1\}^\kappa \mapsto \{0,1\}^\kappa$ simply uses $\mathbb{Z}_2^\kappa$ as the group used for writing the answers in the registers (by adding them in $\mathbb{Z}_2^\kappa$). However, when we say a black-box construction from OWFs exists, it means that there is a version of the construction for *any* abelian group G (of constant size) instead of $\mathbb{Z}_2$, in which case the one-way function would look like $f : G^\kappa \mapsto G^\kappa$. Moreover, there are finite groups of any order, so assuming the input and output spaces of the OWFs have group structure is also without loss of generality.

3 Non-uniform Hardness of Inverting Large Sets of Oracles

In this section, we analyze a variant of the standard random functions inversion game in which the function is uniformly chosen from a specific set of functions instead of the set of all functions. In particular, we formalize and prove Theorem 1.2 in this section.

We consider the adversaries which are given classical or quantum advice and have quantum query access to the oracle. Arguments implicit in [HXY19] can be used for obtaining similar results but only for classical advice. Our proof, however, uses definitions and technical tools from [CGLQ20], and even in the case of classical advice we can obtain sharper bounds (than those obtained by arguments implicit in [HXY19]).

3.1 Oracle Puzzles with Advice

Definition 3.1 (Oracle algorithm with advice). *An (S, T)-oracle-algorithm $\mathsf{A} = (\mathsf{A}_1, \mathsf{A}_2)$ with (oracle-dependent) advice consists of two procedures:*

- *$|\alpha\rangle \leftarrow \mathsf{A}_1(f)$, which is an arbitrary function of the oracle f, and outputs an S-qubit quantum state $|\alpha\rangle$;*
- *$|\mathsf{ans}\rangle \leftarrow \mathsf{A}_2^f(|\alpha\rangle, \mathsf{ch})$, which is a computationally unbounded algorithm that takes advice $|\alpha\rangle$, a challenge ch, makes at most T quantum queries to f, and outputs an answer $|\mathsf{ans}\rangle$, which we measure in the computational basis to obtain a classical answer ans if needed.*

Furthermore, we distinguish the following cases:

- *If the output of A_1 is classical, we call it a quantum algorithm with classical advice or an (S, T)-algorithm in the AI-QOM (auxiliary input quantum oracle model);*
- *If the output of A_1 is quantum, we call it a quantum algorithm with quantum advice or an (S, T)-algorithm in the QAI-QOM (quantum auxiliary input quantum oracle model);*
- *If $S = 0$, we call it a quantum algorithm without advice, or an algorithm in the QOM (quantum oracle model).*

In the following interactive setting, the two terms "algorithm" and "adversary" will be used interchangeably.

Definition 3.2 (Oracle puzzle). *An oracle puzzle $G = (\mathsf{Chal}, \mathbf{f})$ is specified by a challenger $\mathsf{Chal} = (\mathsf{Samp}, \mathsf{Ver})$ and a distribution $\mathbf{f}$ over oracles. In the beginning, an oracle is sampled $f \leftarrow \mathbf{f}$ and*

- *$\mathsf{ch} \leftarrow \mathsf{Samp}^f(r)$ is a deterministic classical algorithm that takes randomness r as input and outputs a classical challenge ch.*
- *$\mathsf{Ver}^f(r, \mathsf{ans})$ is a deterministic classical algorithm that takes as the input ans and outputs a decision b indicating whether the puzzle is won by the adversary.*

For every algorithm with advice, i.e., $\mathsf{A} = (\mathsf{A}_1, \mathsf{A}_2)$, we define

$$\mathsf{A}_{win}^f := \mathsf{Ver}^f\left(r, \mathsf{A}_2^f(\mathsf{A}_1(f), \mathsf{Samp}^f(r))\right)$$

to be the binary variable indicating whether A wins the oracle puzzle.

We define the security loss *in the AI-QOM, QAI-QOM of an oracle puzzle $G = (\mathsf{Chal}, \mathbf{f})$ to be*

$$\delta = \delta(S, T) := \sup_{\mathsf{A}} \Pr_{f \leftarrow \mathbf{f}, r, \mathsf{A}}[\mathsf{A}_{win}^f = 1],$$

where A in the probability denotes the randomness of the (quantum) algorithm, and supremum is taken over all (S, T)-adversaries A in the AI-QOM/QAI-QOM respectively. We say an oracle puzzle G is $(1 - \delta)$-secure if its security loss is at most δ.

In particular, we focus on a class of oracle puzzles in which the adversary can verify the answer by itself.

Definition 3.3 (Publicly-verifiable security game). *We call an oracle puzzle to be* publicly-verifiable *with verification time T_{Ver}, if $\mathsf{Ver}^f(r.\cdot) = \widetilde{\mathsf{Ver}}^f(\mathsf{ch}, \cdot)$ for some deterministic classical algorithm $\widetilde{\mathsf{Ver}}^f$ where ch is determined by r and T_{Ver} is the upper bound on the number of f queries for computing $\widetilde{\mathsf{Ver}}^f(\mathsf{ch}, \cdot)$.*

3.2   Multi-instance Oracle Puzzles

Definition 3.4 (Multi-instance oracle puzzle). *For any oracle puzzle $G = (\mathsf{Chal}, \mathbf{f})$ and any positive integer $k \geq 1$, we define the multi-instance oracle puzzle $G^{\otimes k} = (\mathsf{Chal}^{\otimes k}, \mathbf{f})$, where $\mathsf{Chal}^{\otimes k}$ is given as follows*

- *For $i \in [k]$, do:*
    1. *Sample fresh randomness r_i;*
    2. *Compute $\mathsf{ch}_i \leftarrow \mathsf{Chal}.\mathsf{Samp}^f(r_i)$ and send it to the adversary;*
    3. *Give the adversary oracle access to f until the adversary submits a quantum state $|\mathsf{ans}_i\rangle$;*
    4. *Let $\{P_0, P_1\}$ be a projective measurement where P_1 defines all ans's such that $\mathsf{Ver}(r, \mathsf{ans}) = 1$ and $P_0 = I - P_1$. Measure $|\mathsf{ans}_i\rangle$ in $\{P_0, P_1\}$ to get the quantum state $|\mathsf{ans}_i'\rangle$ and store the result in $b_i \in \{0, 1\}$;*

5. *Send* $|\text{ans}'_i\rangle$ *back to the adversary;*
- *Output* $b_1 \wedge b_2 \wedge \cdots \wedge b_k$;

Definition 3.5 (Multi-instance adversary). *A* (k, S, T)-*adversary with advice for a multi-instance oracle puzzle* $G^{\otimes k} = (\text{Chal}^{\otimes k}, \mathbf{f})$ *consists of* $\mathsf{A} = (\mathsf{A}_1, \mathsf{A}_2)$, *where the interaction between* $\mathsf{A}_2(|\alpha\rangle)$ *and* $\text{Chal}^{\otimes k}$ *is defined as follows:*

- $|\alpha\rangle \leftarrow \mathsf{A}_1(\mathbf{f})$, *which is an arbitrary (unbounded) function of* $\mathbf{f}$ *and outputs an S-qubit quantum state* $|\alpha\rangle$ *for* A_2;
- *For each* $i \in [k]$,
  1. A_2 *is given a challenge* ch_i *and the oracle access to* $\mathbf{f}$ *from* $\text{Chal}^{\otimes k}$;
  2. A_2 *makes at most T queries to* $\mathbf{f}$ *and prepares* $|\text{ans}_i\rangle$;
  3. A_2 *sends* $|\text{ans}_i\rangle$ *to* $\text{Chal}^{\otimes k}$ *and gets* $|\text{ans}'_i\rangle$ *back;*
- *Finally,* $\text{Chal}^{\otimes k}$ *outputs a bit b.*

In particular, if $S = 0$, we also call it a (k, T)-adversary (without advice), or a (k, T)-algorithm in the QOM. In the rest of the section, we sometimes use such notation when it is clear from the context.

For any A *which is a* (k, S, T)-*adversary with advice, we define* $\mathsf{A}_{win}^{\otimes k, f}$ *to be the binary variable indicating whether* A *wins the multi-instance oracle puzzle.*

We say a multi-instance oracle puzzle $G^{\otimes k}$ *is* $(1 - \delta)$-*secure[6] in the QOM if for any* (k, T)-*adversary* A *(without advice),*

$$\Pr_{f, \mathsf{A}, \text{Chal}^{\otimes k}}[\mathsf{A}_{win}^{\otimes k, f} = 1] \leq \delta^k = \delta(k, T)^k,$$

where A *in the probability denotes the randomness of the algorithm,* $\text{Chal}^{\otimes k}$ *in the probability denotes the randomness of the challenger.*

3.3   Function-Inversion Oracle Puzzles

Definition 3.6 (Function inversion oracle puzzle). *The oracle puzzle* $G_{\text{InvSet}, N, M, R} = (\text{Chal}, \mathbf{f})$ *parameterized by integers* $R, N, M \geq 0$ *is defined as follows:*

- $\mathbf{f}$ *is a uniform distribution over* $\mathcal{F} \subseteq [M]^{[N]}$ *such that* $|\mathcal{F}|$ *is at least* M^{N-R}.
- Samp^f *chooses x from $[N]$ uniformly at random, and outputs* $\text{ch} = f(x)$.
- $\text{Ver}^f(x, x')$ *outputs 1 if* $f(x) = f(x')$.

Notice that $G_{\text{InvSet}, N, M, R}$ *is publicly-verifiable with* $T_{\text{Ver}} = 1$. *When $R = 0$, as a special case, the oracle puzzle corresponds to the standard random functions inversion game denoted by* $G_{\text{InvAll}, N, M}$.

In particular, [CGLQ20] prove the security of multi-instance oracle puzzle $G_{\text{InvAll}, N, M}^{\otimes k}$ against (k, T)-adversaries in the quantum random oracle model (QROM). The formal statements are presented as follows.

---

[6] Actually, the security loss here is at most δ^k instead of δ. We follow this convention for ease of the presentation.

Lemma 3.7 (Lemma 5.2 in [CGLQ20]). $G^{\otimes k}_{\mathsf{InvAll}, N, M}$ is $(1 - \delta(k, T))$-secure[7] in the QROM, where

$$\delta(k, T) = O\left(\frac{kT + T^2}{\min\{N, M\}}\right).$$

3.4   Proof of One-Wayness Under Quantum Advice

The following lemma reduces the multi-instance oracle puzzle $G^{\otimes k}$ against a (k, T)-adversary (without advice) to the (single-instance) oracle puzzle G against an (S, T)-adversary (with *quantum* advice).

Lemma 3.8 (Corollary 4.14 in [CGLQ20]). *There exists a universal constant $c > 0$ such that the following holds. Given a publicly-verifiable oracle puzzle G with verification time T_{Ver}. Given an (S, T)-adversary A (with quantum advice) for G with winning probability δ, there exists a (k, T')-adversary A' (without advice) for the multi-instance oracle puzzle $G^{\otimes k}$ with winning probability at least $\delta' \geq 2^{-\ell S} \cdot (\delta/4)^{k+1}$ for any positive integer $k \geq 1$, where $T' = 2\ell(T + T_{\mathsf{Ver}})$ and $\ell = c \cdot \log(k + 1)/\delta$.*

Fact 3.9 (Fact 4.15 in [CGLQ20]). *Given any real $C \geq 0, D \geq 2$. If $k_0 = C + D + 14$ and $k = 2k_0 \log k_0$, then we have $k \geq C \log(k + 1) + D$.*

Now, we are ready to prove the function inversion oracle puzzle $G_{\mathsf{InvSet}, N, M, R}$ is secure against an (S, T)-adversary in the QAI-QOM.

Theorem 3.10. *For any integer $R \geq 0$, the oracle puzzle $G_{\mathsf{InvSet}, N, M, R}$ is $(1 - \delta(S, T))$-secure in the QAI-QOM, where*

$$\delta(S, T) = \tilde{O}\left(\sqrt[3]{\frac{(S + R \log M) \cdot T + T^2}{\min\{N, M\}}}\right).$$

In particulate, if $S(\kappa) = \mathrm{poly}(\kappa)$, $T(\kappa) = \mathrm{poly}(\kappa)$, $R(\kappa) = \mathrm{poly}(\kappa)$, $N = 2^{\Theta(\kappa)}$, and $M = 2^{\Theta(\kappa)}$, the security loss $\delta(\kappa)$ will be negligible in κ.

Proof. Suppose there exists an (S, T)-adversary A for $G_{\mathsf{InvSet}, N, M, R} = (\mathsf{Chal}, \mathbf{f})$ with winning probability $\delta = \delta(S, T)$. Then, by Lemma 3.8, there exists a (k, T')-adversary A' for $G^{\otimes k}_{\mathsf{InvSet}, N, M, R}$ with winning probability at least $\delta' \geq 2^{-\ell S} \cdot (\delta/4)^{k+1}$ for any $k \geq 1$, where $T' = 2\ell(T + T_{\mathsf{Ver}})$ and $\ell = c \cdot \log(k + 1)/\delta$.

Here, we construct an adversary A'' for $G^{\otimes k}_{\mathsf{InvAll}, N, M}$ by using A' as a black box. When A'' receives the challenge $f(x)$, it simply runs $\mathsf{A}'^f(f(x))$ and outputs whatever $\mathsf{A}'^f(f(x))$ outputs. The winning probability of A'', denoted by δ'', is at least

$$\delta'' \geq \Pr[f \in \mathrm{supp}(\mathbf{f})] \cdot \Pr[\mathsf{A}'^f(f(x)) \text{ wins} \mid f \in \mathrm{supp}(\mathbf{f})]$$
$$\geq M^{-R} \cdot \delta' \geq 2^{-\ell S - R \log M} \cdot (\delta/4)^{k+1},$$

where $\mathrm{supp}(\mathbf{f})$ denotes the support of $\mathbf{f}$.

---

[7] Recall that by our convention, the security loss is at most $\delta(k, T)^k$.

By the definition of multi-instance security of $G_{\mathsf{InvAll},N,M}^{\otimes k}$, for all $k \geq 1$ we have

$$\delta(k,T')^k \geq \delta'' \geq 2^{-\ell S - R \log M} \cdot (\delta/4)^{k+1} \geq 2^{-\ell S - R \log M} \cdot (\delta_0/4) \cdot (\delta/4)^k,$$

where $1/N \leq \delta_0 \leq \delta$ is the winning probability of an adversary that outputs a random answer without advice or making any query.

Pick $k_0 = \frac{c}{\delta} S + R \log M + \log(1/\delta_0) + 16$ and $k = 2k_0 \log k_0$. By Fact 3.9, let $C = \frac{c}{\delta} S$ and $D = \log(1/\delta_0) + 2 + R \log M$, we have $k \geq C \log(k+1) + D = c \log(k+1)S/\delta + \log(1/\delta_0) + 2 + R \log M$.

Therefore, we have

$$\begin{aligned}
\delta(k,T')^k &\geq 2^{-\ell S - R \log M} \cdot (\delta_0/4) \cdot (\delta/4)^k \\
&= 2^{-c \cdot \log(k+1)S/\delta} \cdot 2^{-\log(1/\delta_0) - 2 - R \log M} \cdot (\delta/4)^k \\
&\geq (\delta/8)^k
\end{aligned}$$

or equivalently

$$\delta \leq 8\delta(k,T'),$$

where $k = \widetilde{O}(S/\delta + R \log M)$ and $T' = \widetilde{O}(T + T_{\mathsf{Ver}})/\delta$.

By Lemma 3.7, it holds that

$$\delta \leq 8\delta(k,T') = \widetilde{O}\left(\frac{(\frac{S}{\delta} + R \log M) \cdot \frac{T}{\delta} + \frac{T^2}{\delta^2}}{\min\{N,M\}}\right)$$

which leads to

$$\delta = \widetilde{O}\left(\sqrt[3]{\frac{(S + R \log M) \cdot T + T^2}{\min\{N,M\}}}\right).$$

$\square$

4   Quantum Black-Box Separation from One-Way Functions

In this section, assuming Conjecture 2.8 is true, we show that there is no black-box construction of non-interactive commitments (with perfect completeness) from OWFs in the CCQD model. We emphasize that *all* known constructions of NICs that we are aware of have perfect completeness. The following theorem formalizes, and in fact generalizes, Theorem 1.1. In particular, Theorem 1.1 stated the result for the QCCC model (in which both messages are classical), while Theorem 4.1 allows the model to be CCQD, which lets the decommitment message to be quantum.

Theorem 4.1 (Black-box separation of CCQD commitments from OWFs). *Assuming Conjecture 2.8, there is no quantum black-box construction of non-interactive commitments in the CCQD model from one-way functions.*

We need the following notion characterizing the cardinality of sets of functions.

Definition 4.2 (α-flat distributions). *For $\alpha \in [0,1]$, a distribution $\mathbf{f}$ over functions from $\mathcal{X}$ to $\mathcal{Y}$ is called an α-flat distribution if the size of the support is at least an α fraction of $\mathcal{Y}^{\mathcal{X}}$, i.e., $|\mathrm{supp}(\mathbf{f})|/|\mathcal{Y}^{\mathcal{X}}| \geq \alpha$, and $\mathbf{f}$ is uniform over its support set.*

Next, we introduce a useful lemma from [ACC+22] that will help us argue about the efficiency of our attacks.

Lemma 4.3 (Efficiently learning quantum-heavy queries [ACC+22]).) *Let A be an algorithm that asks at most d quantum queries to the random oracle $h : \mathcal{X} \to \mathcal{Y}$ and outputs a classical message* com. *For any $0 < \varepsilon < 1$, there exists a deterministic learning algorithm that learns a list $\mathcal{L}$ of (classical) query-answer pairs from the random oracle (i.e., a partial function), such that the following two conditions hold.*

1. *Efficiency of the learner: $\mathbb{E}[|\mathcal{L}|] \leq d/\varepsilon$, where the expectation is over the randomness of the oracle and the algorithm A.*
2. *Learning quantum heavy queries: When the learner stops and learns a list $\mathcal{L}$, there is no $x \notin \mathcal{Q}_{\mathcal{L}}$ that is quantum ε-heavy in the purified view of A conditioned on knowing $\mathcal{L}$ and* com, *where $\mathcal{Q}_{\mathcal{L}}$ denotes the domain of $\mathcal{L}$.*

The rest of the section is dedicated to proving Theorem 4.1. For readability and simplicity of the presentation, we first assume the abelian group associated with the random oracle to be $\mathbb{Z}_2^{\kappa}$ and Conjecture 2.8 holds for $\mathbb{Z}_2$. For the general case in which Conjecture 2.8 holds for some abelian group $\mathcal{Y}_{\mathrm{o}}$, we instead pick the OWFs in Definition 2.16 as $f : \mathcal{Y}_{\mathrm{o}}^{\kappa} \mapsto \mathcal{Y}_{\mathrm{o}}^{\kappa}$. The following analysis still holds by replacing $\mathbb{Z}_2$ with $\mathcal{Y}_{\mathrm{o}}$.

We will use the following lemma as the key to our proof of Theorem 4.1.

Lemma 4.4. *If Conjecture 2.8 is true, then for any quantum-black-box implementation of non-interactive commitments from oracle $f : \{0,1\}^{\kappa} \mapsto \{0,1\}^{\kappa}$ in which the sender asks d quantum oracle queries, there are cheating strategies* Sen*, Rec* *such that at least one of the following holds.*

1. Rec* *asks d oracle queries such that: if the f is a random oracle, then* Rec* *has a non-negligible distinguishing advantage in breaking the hiding property of the commitment scheme.*
2. *There is a $2^{-\mathrm{poly}(\kappa)}$-flat distribution $\mathbf{f}$ over the oracles such for all $f \leftarrow \mathbf{f}$, there exists (an auxiliary information) (com, $\mathrm{dec}_0, \mathrm{dec}_1$) such that* com *is classical and $\mathrm{dec}_0, \mathrm{dec}_1$ are quantum messages and (com, $\mathrm{dec}_0, \mathrm{dec}_1$) breaks the weak binding of the scheme relative to f.[8]*

Proof. Suppose (Sen, Rec) is a quantum-black-box implementation of non-interactive commitment from one-way functions in the CCQD model.

Construction 4.5 (The cheating receiver Rec* with parameter ε). *Let d be the number of oracle queries asked by the sender. Given the commitment* com *which commits to a random bit $b \in \{0,1\}$, the description of the cheating receiver* Rec* *is as follows:*

---

[8] One can think of (com, $\mathrm{dec}_0, \mathrm{dec}_1$) as a cheating sender Sen*.

1. *Let* A *in Lemma 4.3 be* Sen *in which the sender commits to a random bit b. The output of* A *will be the commitment* com. *The cheating receiver* Rec* *runs the learning algorithm in Lemma 4.3 over* A *with the parameter* $\varepsilon = \frac{1}{10\delta(d\kappa)}$, *where* $\delta(\cdot)$ *is the function defined in Conjecture 2.8 for* $\mathcal{Y} = \mathbb{Z}_2$.

2. *The cheating receiver* Rec* *outputs the more likely input bit* $b \in \{0, 1\}$ *according to the purified view (i.e., conditioned on* com *and the learned classical queries* $\mathcal{L}$ *of the oracle) as its own output bit.*

If the conditional distribution of input bit b has already been noticeably biased after the learning algorithm, then Rec* would have a decent chance of breaking the hiding. Let $\mathcal{E}$ be the event that the distinguishing advantage

$$\frac{1}{2} \left| \Pr\left[b = 0 \mid \mathsf{com}, \mathcal{L} \right] - \Pr\left[b = 1 \mid \mathsf{com}, \mathcal{L} \right] \right|$$

is non-negligible holds. Then we either have $\Pr[\mathcal{E}] > 1/\kappa$ or $\Pr[\bar{\mathcal{E}}] \geq 1 - 1/\kappa$. If the former holds, it implies that Rec* has a non-negligible distinguishing advantage and thus the proof is done. Therefore, we assume that we are in the latter case. By Lemma 4.3 and an averaging argument, the number of queries asked by Rec* satisfies

$$\mathbb{E}[|\mathcal{L}| \mid \bar{\mathcal{E}}] \leq \frac{\mathbb{E}[|\mathcal{L}|]}{\Pr[\bar{\mathcal{E}}]} \leq \frac{1.01d}{\varepsilon}$$

for sufficiently large κ. Then by Markov's inequality, we have

$$\Pr\left[|\mathcal{L}| \geq \kappa^2 \cdot \frac{1.01d}{\varepsilon} \mid \bar{\mathcal{E}} \right] \leq \frac{1}{\kappa^2}.$$

Putting things together, we conclude that with probability at least $1 - O\left(1/\kappa^2\right)$, all of the following events hold:

- Rec* is efficient: Rec* asks at most $1.01\kappa^2 d/\varepsilon = \mathsf{poly}(d, \kappa)$ queries.
- No quantum ε-heavy query left: for all $x \notin \mathcal{Q}_\mathcal{L}$, $w(x) < \varepsilon$ where $w(\cdot)$ is defined in Definition 2.7.
- $b = 0, 1$ are almost as likely: $|\Pr[b = 0 \mid \mathsf{com}, \mathcal{L}] - \Pr[b = 1 \mid \mathsf{com}, \mathcal{L}]| = \mathsf{negl}(\kappa)$.

Let $\mathcal{G}$ denote the event that all the above three events hold.

Next, assuming that Rec* fails, we describe the cheating sender Sen* as follows.

Construction 4.6 (The cheating sender and the flat distribution). *Now, we describe the cheating sender's strategy* Sen* *and a corresponding α-flat distribution* f.

1. *The cheating sender* Sen* *samples* (com, $\mathcal{L}$) *according to the first step of the cheating receiver* Rec* *in Construction 4.5.*
   Before proceeding to the next step, we introduce some notations. Consider the purified view $|\Phi_{\mathsf{com},\mathcal{L}}\rangle$ *of the honest sender of the commitment conditioned on the (classical) commitment message* com *and the list* $\mathcal{L}$. *Let* $|\Phi_{0,\mathsf{com},\mathcal{L}}\rangle$ *and* $|\Phi_{1,\mathsf{com},\mathcal{L}}\rangle$ *be the purified views further conditioned on b being 0 and 1. That is,*

$$|\Phi_{\mathsf{com},\mathcal{L}}\rangle = \sqrt{\Pr[b = 0 \mid \mathsf{com}, \mathcal{L}]}|\Phi_{0,\mathsf{com},\mathcal{L}}\rangle + \sqrt{\Pr[b = 1 \mid \mathsf{com}, \mathcal{L}]}|\Phi_{1,\mathsf{com},\mathcal{L}}\rangle.$$

Let $\mathcal{X}' := \mathcal{X} \setminus \mathcal{Q}_{\mathcal{L}}$ and $N' := |\mathcal{X}'| = |\mathcal{X}| - |\mathcal{L}|$. Let H' be the oracle register corresponding to $\mathcal{X}'$. Note that conditioning on the list $\mathcal{L}$, the content of the oracle registers corresponding to $\mathcal{Q}_{\mathcal{L}}$ is fixed. So they are not entangled with H'. By abusing notation, for $b \in \{0, 1\}$, we also denote by $|\Phi_{b,\mathrm{com},\mathcal{L}}\rangle$ the state obtained by discarding the registers corresponding to $\mathcal{Q}_{\mathcal{L}}$. Let $\mathbf{F}_0$ be the state polynomial distribution of $|\Phi_{0,\mathrm{com},\mathcal{L}}\rangle$. Define $\mathbf{F}_1$ similarly.

2. Find $f_0 \in \mathrm{supp}(\mathbf{F}_0), f_1 \in \mathrm{supp}(\mathbf{F}_1)$ such that $f_0 \cdot f_1$ is not constant zero. If no such functions exist, then abort.
   Let $\mathcal{F}'$ be the set of all $h' \in \mathcal{Y}^{\mathcal{X}'}$ such that $(f_0 \cdot f_1)(h) \neq 0$, i.e.,

$$\mathcal{F}' := \{h' \in \mathcal{Y}^{\mathcal{X}'} \mid (f_0 \cdot f_1)(h) \neq 0\}.$$

The α-flat distribution $\mathbf{f}$ will be uniform over the set $\mathcal{F} \subseteq \mathcal{Y}^{\mathcal{X}}$ which contains all functions in $\mathcal{F}'$ combined with $\mathcal{L}$, i.e.,

$$\mathcal{F} := \{h \in \mathcal{Y}^{\mathcal{X}} \mid \exists h' \in \mathcal{F}': h = h' \cup \mathcal{L}\}.$$

3. The cheating sender Sen^* sends com as the commitment and uses the oracle-dependent quantum advice dec_b to decommit com into $b \in \{0, 1\}$.

Suppose $\mathcal{G}$ occurs in the rest of the proof. Before using Lemma 2.12 to relate quantum states with polynomials, we first show that the purified views satisfy certain properties. First, by Corollary 2.5, the purified views satisfy

$$|\hat{h}_{\max}^{H'}(|\Phi_{b,\mathrm{com},\mathcal{L}}\rangle)| \leq d \cdot \kappa$$

for $b \in \{0, 1\}$, where the degree is defined over $\mathbb{Z}_2$. Next, notice that after the first step, none of the conditional probability of each input is greater than $2/3$ for sufficiently large κ. That is, both probabilities $\Pr[b = 0 \mid \mathrm{com}, \mathcal{L}]$ and $\Pr[b = 1 \mid \mathrm{com}, \mathcal{L}]$ are between $1/3$ and $2/3$. Therefore, given that the purified view $|\Phi_{\mathrm{com},\mathcal{L}}\rangle$ has no quantum ε-heavy query in $\mathcal{X}'$, we can conclude that both $|\Phi_{0,,,\mathcal{L}}\rangle$ and $|\Phi_{1,,,\mathcal{L}}\rangle$ have no quantum 3ε-heavy query in $\mathcal{X}'$. By our choice of ε, we have $3\varepsilon \leq \delta(d\kappa)$. Consequently, we have both $|\Phi_{0,,,\mathcal{L}}\rangle$ and $|\Phi_{1,,,\mathcal{L}}\rangle$ are $(\mathbb{Z}_2, \delta(d\kappa), d\kappa, N')$-states. By Lemma 2.12, every $f: \mathbb{Z}_2^{N'} \to \mathbb{C}$ in the support set of $\mathbf{F}_0$ satisfies the following properties.

1. **Unit ℓ_2 norm:** f has ℓ_2-norm 1.
2. **$d\kappa$-degrees:** $\deg(f) \leq d\kappa$.
3. **δ-influences on average:** For all $i \in [N']$, we have $\mathbb{E}_{f \leftarrow \mathbf{F}_0}[\mathrm{Inf}_i(f)] \leq \delta(d\kappa)$.

The same conditions hold for $\mathbf{F}_1$ as well. Assuming Conjecture 2.8 holds for $\mathcal{Y} = \mathbb{Z}_2$, there must exist $f_0 \in \mathrm{supp}(\mathbf{F}_0)$ and $f_1 \in \mathrm{supp}(\mathbf{F}_1)$ such that $f_0 \cdot f_1 \neq 0$.

Finally, we show that the cardinality of $\mathcal{F}$ is large. By Corollary 2.14, it holds that the size of $\mathcal{F}'$ satisfies

$$\frac{|\mathcal{F}'|}{|\mathcal{Y}^{\mathcal{X}'}|} \geq \frac{1}{O\left(d\kappa|\mathcal{X}'|^{2d\kappa}|\mathcal{Y}|^{2d\kappa}\right)}.$$

Furthermore, note that the size of the sub-domain $\mathcal{Q}_{\mathcal{L}}$ fixed by $\mathcal{L}$ satisfies $|\mathcal{L}| \leq 100d/\varepsilon = \mathrm{poly}(\kappa, d)$. Therefore, it holds that

$$\frac{|\mathcal{F}|}{|\mathcal{Y}^{\mathcal{X}}|} = \frac{|\mathcal{F}'|}{|\mathcal{Y}^{\mathcal{X}}|} \geq |\mathcal{Y}|^{-|\mathcal{L}|} \cdot \frac{1}{O\left(d\kappa|\mathcal{X}'|^{2d\kappa}|\mathcal{Y}|^{2d\kappa}\right)} = 2^{-\mathrm{poly}(\kappa, d)} = 2^{-\mathrm{poly}(\kappa)},$$

which means the uniform distribution over $\mathcal{F}$ is a $2^{-\mathrm{poly}(\kappa)}$-flat distribution. $\square$

Finally, we use Lemma 4.4 to prove Theorem 4.1.

Proof of Theorem 4.1. Suppose there exists a black-box construction (G, S) of non-interactive commitments from OWF $f: \{0,1\}^\kappa \mapsto \{0,1\}^\kappa$ (as in Definition 2.16). By Lemma 4.4, at least one of the following holds.

1. Let f be a random oracle. There exist Rec^* and S_h^{f,Rec^*} such that S_h^{f,Rec^*} breaks the one-wayness of f by asking $\mathrm{poly}(\kappa)$ queries to f. However, then one can combine the algorithms S and Rec^* as a single algorithm that inverts a random oracle f with non-negligible probability by asking $\mathrm{poly}(\kappa)$ queries to it. This contradicts the known optimality of Grover search [BBBV97].

2. There exist Sen^* and S_b^{f,Sen^*} such that S_b^{f,Sen^*} breaks the one-wayness of f, where f has a $2^{-R(\kappa)}$-flat distribution with respect to Sen^*, where $R(\kappa) = \mathrm{poly}(\kappa)$. In detail, for each query asked to Sen^*, it outputs polynomially many classical bits as the commitment and polynomially many qubits as for the two decommitment. By assumption, S_b^{f,Sen^*} asks only a polynomial number of queries to both f and Sen^*, but the answer by Sen^* is already fixed and so not worth asking them more than once. The answers that Sen^* provides could be interpreted as polynomial-size quantum advice about the oracle f that is passed down to the security reduction S. Putting things together, we conclude that S_b^{f,Sen^*} is an algorithm that inverts f with non-negligible probability by asking $S(\kappa) = \mathrm{poly}(\kappa)$ number of queries and having $T(\kappa) = \mathrm{poly}(\kappa)$ many bits of quantum advice about f. However, this contradicts the one-wayness of f as proven in Theorem 3.10.

□

References

AA09. Aaronson, S., Ambainis, A.: The need for structure in quantum speedups. arXiv preprint arXiv:0911.0996 (2009)

ACC+22. Austrin, P., Chung, H., Chung, K.M., Fu, S., Lin, Y.T., Mahmoody, M.: On the impossibility of key agreements from quantum random oracles. In: Dodis, Y., Shrimpton, T. (eds.) CRYPTO 2022. LNCS, vol. 13508, pp. 165–194. Springer, Cham (2022). https://doi.org/10.1007/978-3-031-15979-4_6

ACGH20. Alagic, G., Childs, A.M., Grilo, A.B., Hung, S.-H.: Non-interactive classical verification of quantum computation. In: Pass, R., Pietrzak, K. (eds.) TCC 2020. LNCS, vol. 12552, pp. 153–180. Springer, Cham (2020). https://doi.org/10.1007/978-3-030-64381-2_6

AQY22. Ananth, P., Qian, L., Yuen, H.: Cryptography from pseudorandom quantum states. In: Dodis, Y., Shrimpton, T. (eds.) CRYPTO 2022. LNCS, vol. 13507, pp. 208–236. Springer, Cham (2022). https://doi.org/10.1007/978-3-031-15802-5_8

Bar21. Bartusek, J.: Secure quantum computation with classical communication. Cryptology ePrint Archive, Report 2021/964 (2021). https://ia.cr/2021/964

BB21. Bitansky, N., Brakerski, Z.: Classical binding for quantum commitments. In: Nissim, K., Waters, B. (eds.) TCC 2021. LNCS, vol. 13042, pp. 273–298. Springer, Cham (2021). https://doi.org/10.1007/978-3-030-90459-3_10

BBBV97. Bennett, C.H., Bernstein, E., Brassard, G., Vazirani, U.: Strengths and weaknesses of quantum computing. SIAM J. Comput. 26(5), 1510–1523 (1997)

BBF13.   Baecher, P., Brzuska, C., Fischlin, M.: Notions of black-box reductions, revisited. In: Sako, K., Sarkar, P. (eds.) ASIACRYPT 2013. LNCS, vol. 8269, pp. 296–315. Springer, Heidelberg (2013). https://doi.org/10.1007/978-3-642-42033-7_16

BCKM21. Bartusek, J., Coladangelo, A., Khurana, D., Ma, F.: One-way functions imply secure computation in a quantum world. In: Malkin, T., Peikert, C. (eds.) CRYPTO 2021. LNCS, vol. 12825, pp. 467–496. Springer, Cham (2021). https://doi.org/10.1007/978-3-030-84242-0_17

BCQ22.   Brakerski, Z., Canetti, R., Qian, L.: On the computational hardness needed for quantum cryptography. Cryptology ePrint Archive, Paper 2022/1181 (2022). https://eprint.iacr.org/2022/1181

BDF+11. Boneh, D., Dagdelen, Ö., Fischlin, M., Lehmann, A., Schaffner, C., Zhandry, M.: Random oracles in a quantum world. In: Lee, D.H., Wang, X. (eds.) ASIACRYPT 2011. LNCS, vol. 7073, pp. 41–69. Springer, Heidelberg (2011). https://doi.org/10.1007/978-3-642-25385-0_3

BKVV20. Brakerski, Z., Koppula, V., Vazirani, U., Vidick, T.: Simpler proofs of quantumness. arXiv preprint arXiv:2005.04826 (2020)

BM09.   Barak, B., Mahmoody-Ghidary, M.: Merkle puzzles are optimal — An $O(n^2)$-query attack on any key exchange from a random oracle. In: Halevi, S. (ed.) CRYPTO 2009. LNCS, vol. 5677, pp. 374–390. Springer, Heidelberg (2009). https://doi.org/10.1007/978-3-642-03356-8_22

BOV03.   Barak, B., Ong, S.J., Vadhan, S.: Derandomization in cryptography. In: Boneh, D. (ed.) CRYPTO 2003. LNCS, vol. 2729, pp. 299–315. Springer, Heidelberg (2003). https://doi.org/10.1007/978-3-540-45146-4_18

BS20.   Brakerski, Z., Shmueli, O.: Scalable pseudorandom quantum states. In: Micciancio, D., Ristenpart, T. (eds.) CRYPTO 2020. LNCS, vol. 12171, pp. 417–440. Springer, Cham (2020). https://doi.org/10.1007/978-3-030-56880-1_15

CCY20.   Chia, N.-H., Chung, K.-M., Yamakawa, T.: Classical verification of quantum computations with efficient verifier. In: Pass, R., Pietrzak, K. (eds.) TCC 2020. LNCS, vol. 12552, pp. 181–206. Springer, Cham (2020). https://doi.org/10.1007/978-3-030-64381-2_7

CDMS04. Crépeau, C., Dumais, P., Mayers, D., Salvail, L.: Computational collapse of quantum state with application to oblivious transfer. In: Naor, M. (ed.) TCC 2004. LNCS, vol. 2951, pp. 374–393. Springer, Heidelberg (2004). https://doi.org/10.1007/978-3-540-24638-1_21

CGLQ20. Chung, K.M., Guo, S., Liu, Q., Qian, L.: Tight quantum time-space tradeoffs for function inversion. In: 61st Annual Symposium on Foundations of Computer Science, Durham, NC, USA, 16–19 November 2020, pp. 673–684. IEEE Computer Society Press (2020)

CLS01.   Crépeau, C., Légaré, F., Salvail, L.: How to convert the flavor of a quantum bit commitment. In: Pfitzmann, B. (ed.) EUROCRYPT 2001. LNCS, vol. 2045, pp. 60–77. Springer, Heidelberg (2001). https://doi.org/10.1007/3-540-44987-6_5

CX21.   Cao, S., Xue, R.: Being a permutation is also orthogonal to one-wayness in quantum world: impossibilities of quantum one-way permutations from one-wayness primitives. Theor. Comput. Sci. **855**, 16–42 (2021)

DLS22.   Dupuis, F., Lamontagne, P., Salvail, L.: Fiat-shamir for proofs lacks a proof even in the presence of shared entanglement. Cryptology ePrint Archive, Report 2022/435 (2022). https://eprint.iacr.org/2022/435

DMS00.   Dumais, P., Mayers, D., Salvail, L.: Perfectly concealing quantum bit commitment from any quantum one-way permutation. In: Preneel, B. (ed.) EUROCRYPT 2000. LNCS, vol. 1807, pp. 300–315. Springer, Heidelberg (2000). https://doi.org/10.1007/3-540-45539-6_21

DS89. Donoho, D.L., Stark, P.B.: Uncertainty principles and signal recovery. SIAM J. Appl. Math. **49**(3), 906–931 (1989)

GL89. Goldreich, O., Levin, L.A.: A hard-core predicate for all one-way functions. In: 21st Annual ACM Symposium on Theory of Computing, Seattle, WA, USA, 15–17 May 1989, pp. 25–32. ACM Press (1989)

GLSV21. Grilo, A.B., Lin, H., Song, F., Vaikuntanathan, V.: Oblivious transfer is in MiniQCrypt. In: Canteaut, A., Standaert, F.-X. (eds.) EUROCRYPT 2021. LNCS, vol. 12697, pp. 531–561. Springer, Cham (2021). https://doi.org/10.1007/978-3-030-77886-6_18

GT00. Gennaro, R., Trevisan, L.: Lower bounds on the efficiency of generic cryptographic constructions. In: 41st Annual Symposium on Foundations of Computer Science, Redondo Beach, CA, USA, 12–14 November 2000, pp. 305–313. IEEE Computer Society Press (2000)

HILL99. Håstad, J., Impagliazzo, R., Levin, L.A., Luby, M.: A pseudorandom generator from any one-way function. SIAM J. Comput. **28**(4), 1364–1396 (1999)

HXY19. Hhan, M., Xagawa, K., Yamakawa, T.: Quantum random oracle model with auxiliary input. In: Galbraith, S.D., Moriai, S. (eds.) ASIACRYPT 2019. LNCS, vol. 11921, pp. 584–614. Springer, Cham (2019). https://doi.org/10.1007/978-3-030-34578-5_21

HY20. Hosoyamada, A., Yamakawa, T.: Finding collisions in a quantum world: quantum black-box separation of collision-resistance and one-wayness. In: Moriai, S., Wang, H. (eds.) ASIACRYPT 2020. LNCS, vol. 12491, pp. 3–32. Springer, Cham (2020). https://doi.org/10.1007/978-3-030-64837-4_1

IL89. Impagliazzo, R., Luby, M.: One-way functions are essential for complexity based cryptography (extended abstract). In: 30th Annual Symposium on Foundations of Computer Science, Research Triangle Park, NC, USA, 30 October–1 November 1989, pp. 230–235. IEEE Computer Society Press (1989)

IR89. Impagliazzo, R., Rudich, S.: Limits on the provable consequences of one-way permutations. In: 21st Annual ACM Symposium on Theory of Computing, Seattle, WA, USA, 15–17 May 1989, pp. 44–61. ACM Press (1989)

JLS18. Ji, Z., Liu, Y.-K., Song, F.: Pseudorandom quantum states. In: Shacham, H., Boldyreva, A. (eds.) CRYPTO 2018. LNCS, vol. 10993, pp. 126–152. Springer, Cham (2018). https://doi.org/10.1007/978-3-319-96878-0_5

KO09. Koshiba, T., Odaira, T.: Statistically-hiding quantum bit commitment from approximable-preimage-size quantum one-way function. In: Childs, A., Mosca, M. (eds.) TQC 2009. LNCS, vol. 5906, pp. 33–46. Springer, Heidelberg (2009). https://doi.org/10.1007/978-3-642-10698-9_4

KO11. Koshiba,T., Odaira, T.: Non-interactive statistically-hiding quantum bit commitment from any quantum one-way function. arXiv preprint arXiv:1102.3441 (2011)

Kre21. Kretschmer, W.: Quantum pseudorandomness and classical complexity. arXiv preprint arXiv:2103.09320 (2021)

LC97. Hoi-Kwong Lo and Hoi Fung Chau: Is quantum bit commitment really possible? Phys. Rev. Lett. **78**(17), 3410 (1997)

LQWY14. Lin, D., Quan, Y., Weng, J., Yan, J.: Quantum bit commitment with application in quantum zero-knowledge proof. Cryptology ePrint Archive, Report 2014/791 (2014). https://eprint.iacr.org/2014/791

LS19. Lombardi, A., Schaeffer, L.: A note on key agreement and non-interactive commitments. Cryptology ePrint Archive, Report 2019/279 (2019). https://eprint.iacr.org/2019/279

Mah18. Mahadev, U.: Classical verification of quantum computations. In: 2018 IEEE 59th Annual Symposium on Foundations of Computer Science (FOCS), pp. 259–267. IEEE (2018)

May97. Mayers, D.: Unconditionally secure quantum bit commitment is impossible. Phys. Rev. Lett. **78**(17), 3414 (1997)

MM11. Matsuda, T., Matsuura, K.: On black-box separations among injective one-way functions. In: Ishai, Y. (ed.) TCC 2011. LNCS, vol. 6597, pp. 597–614. Springer, Heidelberg (2011). https://doi.org/10.1007/978-3-642-19571-6_36

MP12. Mahmoody, M., Pass, R.: The curious case of non-interactive commitments – on the power of black-box vs. non-black-box use of primitives. In: Safavi-Naini, R., Canetti, R. (eds.) CRYPTO 2012. LNCS, vol. 7417, pp. 701–718. Springer, Heidelberg (2012). https://doi.org/10.1007/978-3-642-32009-5_41

MY22. Morimae, T., Yamakawa, T.: Quantum commitments without one-way functions. In: International Cryptology Conference CRYPTO (2022)

NABT15. Nayebi, A., Aaronson, S., Belovs, A., Trevisan, L.: Quantum lower bound for inverting a permutation with advice. Quant. Inf. Comput. **15**(11–12), 901–913 (2015)

Nao90. Naor, M.: Bit commitment using pseudo-randomness. In: Brassard, G. (ed.) CRYPTO 1989. LNCS, vol. 435, pp. 128–136. Springer, New York (1990). https://doi.org/10.1007/0-387-34805-0_13

NC10. Nielsen, M.A., Chuang, I.L.: Quantum Computation and Quantum Information. Cambridge University Press, Cambridge (2010)

NW94. Nisan, N., Wigderson, A.: Hardness vs randomness. J. Comput. Syst. Sci. **49**(2), 149–167 (1994)

RTV04. Reingold, O., Trevisan, L., Vadhan, S.: Notions of reducibility between cryptographic primitives. In: Naor, M. (ed.) TCC 2004. LNCS, vol. 2951, pp. 1–20. Springer, Heidelberg (2004). https://doi.org/10.1007/978-3-540-24638-1_1

Unr12. Unruh, D.: Quantum proofs of knowledge. In: Pointcheval, D., Johansson, T. (eds.) EUROCRYPT 2012. LNCS, vol. 7237, pp. 135–152. Springer, Heidelberg (2012). https://doi.org/10.1007/978-3-642-29011-4_10

Unr16a. Unruh, D.: Collapse-binding quantum commitments without random oracles. In: Cheon, J.H., Takagi, T. (eds.) ASIACRYPT 2016. LNCS, vol. 10032, pp. 166–195. Springer, Heidelberg (2016). https://doi.org/10.1007/978-3-662-53890-6_6

Unr16b. Unruh, D.: Computationally binding quantum commitments. In: Fischlin, M., Coron, J.-S. (eds.) EUROCRYPT 2016. LNCS, vol. 9666, pp. 497–527. Springer, Heidelberg (2016). https://doi.org/10.1007/978-3-662-49896-5_18

WW21. Wigderson, A., Wigderson, Y.: The uncertainty principle: variations on a theme. Bull. Am. Math. Soc. **58**(2), 225–261 (2021)

Yan20. Yan, J.: General properties of quantum bit commitments. Cryptology ePrint Archive, Paper 2020/1488 (2020). https://eprint.iacr.org/2020/1488

Yao82. Yao, A.C.C.: Theory and applications of trapdoor functions (extended abstract). In: 23rd Annual Symposium on Foundations of Computer Science, pages 80–91, Chicago, Illinois, 3–5 November 1982. IEEE Computer Society Press (1982)

YWLQ15. Yan, J., Weng, J., Lin, D., Quan, Y.: Quantum bit commitment with application in quantum zero-knowledge proof (extended abstract). In: Elbassioni, K., Makino, K. (eds.) ISAAC 2015. LNCS, vol. 9472, pp. 555–565. Springer, Heidelberg (2015). https://doi.org/10.1007/978-3-662-48971-0_47

Zha19. Zhandry, M.: How to record quantum queries, and applications to quantum indifferentiability. In: Boldyreva, A., Micciancio, D. (eds.) CRYPTO 2019. LNCS, vol. 11693, pp. 239–268. Springer, Cham (2019). https://doi.org/10.1007/978-3-030-26951-7_9

Zha21. Zhang, J.: Succinct blind quantum computation using a random oracle. In STOC 2021: 53rd Annual ACM SIGACT Symposium on Theory of Computing, Virtual Event, Italy, 21–25 June 2021, pp. 1370–1383 (2021)

On Non-uniform Security for Black-Box Non-interactive CCA Commitments

Rachit Garg[1]($\boxtimes$), Dakshita Khurana[2], George Lu[1], and Brent Waters[1,3]

[1] University of Texas at Austin, Austin, TX, USA
rachg96@cs.utexas.edu
[2] University of Illinois Urbana-Champaign, Champaign, IL, USA
[3] NTT Research, Sunnyvale, CA, USA

Abstract. We obtain a black-box construction of non-interactive CCA commitments against non-uniform adversaries. This makes black-box use of an appropriate base commitment scheme for small tag spaces, variants of sub-exponential hinting PRG (Koppula and Waters, Crypto 2019) and variants of keyless sub-exponentially collision-resistant hash function with security against non-uniform adversaries (Bitansky, Kalai and Paneth, STOC 2018 and Bitansky and Lin, TCC 2018).

All prior works on non-interactive non-malleable or CCA commitments without setup first construct a "base" scheme for a relatively small identity/tag space, and then build a tag amplification compiler to obtain commitments for an exponential-sized space of identities. Prior black-box constructions either add multiple rounds of interaction (Goyal, Lee, Ostrovsky and Visconti, FOCS 2012) or only achieve security against uniform adversaries (Garg, Khurana, Lu and Waters, Eurocrypt 2021).

Our key technical contribution is a novel tag amplification compiler for CCA commitments that replaces the non-interactive proof of consistency required in prior work. Our construction satisfies the strongest known definition of non-malleability, i.e., CCA2 (chosen commitment attack) security. In addition to only making black-box use of the base scheme, our construction replaces sub-exponential NIWIs with sub-exponential hinting PRGs, which can be obtained based on assumptions such as (sub-exponential) CDH or LWE.

1 Introduction

Non-malleable commitments [18] and their stronger counterparts CCA commitments [12] are core cryptographic primitives that provide security in the presence of "man in the middle" attacks. They ensure that a man-in-the-middle adversary, that simultaneously participates in two or more protocol sessions, cannot use information obtained in one session to breach security in another. They also enable secure multi-party computation, coin flipping and auctions.

This work builds non-interactive CCA commitments, which involve just a single commit message from the committer. We focus on the (standard) notion of security against non-uniform adversaries, which necessitates that these commitments be perfectly binding and computationally hiding. For these commitments,

© International Association for Cryptologic Research 2023
C. Hazay and M. Stam (Eds.): EUROCRYPT 2023, LNCS 14004, pp. 173–204, 2023.
https://doi.org/10.1007/978-3-031-30545-0_7

the perfect binding requirement is that for any commitment string c generated maliciously with potentially an arbitrary amount of preprocessing, there do not exist two openings to messages m and m' such that $m \neq m'$. The (computational) hiding property requires that for every pair of equal-length messages m and m', the distributions of commitments $\mathsf{com}(m)$ and $\mathsf{com}(m')$ are computationally indistinguishable.

The notion of CCA security for commitments is defined analogously to encryption schemes, except that the adversary is given access to a decommitment oracle. However, unlike the case of encryption, non-interactive commitments without setup do not allow for efficient decommitment given a trapdoor/secret key. In more detail, the hiding game is strengthened significantly to give the adversary oracle access to an *inefficient* decommitment/value function $\mathsf{CCA.Val}$ where on input a string c, $\mathsf{CCA.Val}(\mathsf{tag}, c)$ will return m if $\mathsf{CCA.Com}(\mathsf{tag}, m; r) \rightarrow c$ for some r. The adversary must first specify a challenge tag tag^*, along with messages m_0^*, m_1^*. It is then allowed oracle access to $\mathsf{CCA.Val}(\mathsf{tag}, \cdot)$ for every $\mathsf{tag} \neq \mathsf{tag}^*$, and can make an arbitrary (polynomial) number of queries before and after obtaining the challenge commitment.[1]

This CCA-based definition is the strongest known definition of non-malleability. In the non-interactive setting, the often-used definition of (concurrent) non-malleability with respect to commitment is a special case of this definition where the adversay is only allowed to make parallel oracle queries once it obtains the challenge commitment.

Prior Work on Non-malleable Commitments. There have been several results [4, 14, 15, 18, 21–25, 30, 32, 34–38, 40–42, 44] that gradually reduced the round complexity and the cryptographic assumptions required to achieve non-malleable commitments. In the non-interactive setting, Pandey, Pass and Vaikuntanathan [38] first obtained non-malleable commitments from a strong non-falsifiable assumption. A lower bound due to Pass [39] demonstrated the difficulty of obtaining a non-interactive construction from standard assumptions.

Nevertheless, recent works of Lin, Pass and Soni [36], Bitansky and Lin [8], Kalai and Khurana [29], Garg et al. [19] and Khurana [31] made progress towards improving these assumptions. These works proceed in two steps: the first step builds a "base" scheme supporting a small (typically, constant-sized) tag space and the second step converts commitments supporting a small tag space to commitments that support a much larger tag space.

Base Constructions. Three recent works [8, 29, 36] build non-interactive base schemes: non-malleable commitments for a tag space of size $c \log \log \kappa$ for a specific constant $c > 0$, based on various hardness assumptions. Specifically, Lin, Pass and Soni [36] assume a sub-exponential variant of the hardness of time-lock puzzles, and Bitansky and Lin [8] rely on sub-exponentially hard injective

---

[1] The assumption that the commitment takes input a tag is without loss of generality when the tag space is exponential. As is standard with non-malleable commitments, tags can be generically removed by setting the tag as the verification key of a signature scheme, and signing the commitment string using the signing key.

one-way functions that admit hardness amplification beyond negligible. Finally, Kalai and Khurana [29] assume classically sub-exponentially hard but quantum easy non-interactive commitments (which can be based, e.g., on sub-exponential hardness of DDH), and sub-exponentially quantum hard non-interactive commitments (which can be based, e.g., on sub-exponential hardness of LWE).

Tag Amplification. The second step, as discussed above, builds a tag amplification compiler that increases the tag space exponentially. Starting with non-malleable commitments for a tag space of size $c \log \log \kappa$ for a specific constant $c > 0$ (or sometimes even smaller), multiple applications of this compiler yield commitments for a tag space of size 2^κ.

This step, which is also the focus of the current work, typically involves encoding a single tag from a larger space into many tags from a smaller space, and then committing to a given message several times, once w.r.t. each small tag. In addition, an implicit/explicit *proof of consistency* of these commitments is provided, and this proof is required to hide the committed message. Such a proof becomes challenging to implement in the non-interactive setting without setup.

Nevertheless, tag amplification was obtained in [36] against *uniform* man-in-the-middle adversaries based on sub-exponential non-interactive witness indistinguishable (NIWI) proofs and keyless collision resistant hash functions against uniform adversaries. It was also obtained in [8] against *non-uniform* man-in-the-middle adversaries based on sub-exponential non-interactive witness indistinguishable (NIWI) proofs and keyless collision resistant hash functions with a form of collision resistance even against *non-uniform* adversaries. Somewhat orthogonally, [31] obtained tag amplification from sub-exponential indistinguishability obfuscation and sub-exponential one-way functions, while avoiding the need for keyless collision resistant hashing.

Black-Box Tag Amplification. Recently, [19] developed the first tag amplification technique that only made *black-box use of the base commitment.* That work additionally assumed (black-box access to) hinting PRGs and keyless collision resistant hash functions against uniform adversaries. Hinting PRGs themselves admit constructions from the CDH and LWE assumptions. Besides being black-box , this was the first solution that *did not* rely on non-interactive witness indistinguishable (NIWI) proofs, which so far are only known based on the hardness of the decisional linear problem over bilinear maps [26], or derandomization assumptions and trapdoor permutations [5], or indistinguishability obfuscation and one-way functions [9]. However, GKLW only obtain security against uniform adversaries.

But non-uniform security is often necessary when using non-malleable commitments within a bigger protocol. For instance, round efficient secure multiparty computation protocols in the plain model [1,2,6,10,13,27] against malicious adversaries usually include a step where participants commit to their inputs via a non-malleable/CCA commitment, in addition to providing a proof that the CCA commitment is consistent with other messages sent in the protocol.

In low-interaction settings such as those of super-polynomial secure MPC in two or three [3] messages, these proofs of consistency are often simulated non-uniformly, which ends up necessitating the use of non-malleable commitments with security against non-uniform adversaries.

Our work addresses the following natural gap in our understanding of non-interactive non-malleable/CCA commitments.

Is it possible to obtain black-box non-interactive CCA commitments against non-uniform adversaries?

Our Results. This work provides a *black-box approach* to achieving non-interactive CCA commitments with security against *non-uniform adversaries*, by relying on keyless hash functions that satisfy collision-resistance against non-uniform adversaries, and by overcoming seemingly fundamental limitations from the prior work of [19]. In addition, our tag amplification technique achieves provable security without the need for NIWIs as in prior work [8], and by instead relying on a sub-exponentially secure variant of hinting PRGs, which can themselves be obtained from (sub-exponential) CDH or LWE just like their counterparts in [33].

2   Overview of Techniques

We now give an overview of our amplification technique, where the goal is to amplify a scheme for $O(N)$ tags to a scheme for 2^N tags, with computational cost that grows polynomially with N and the security parameter κ. This process can be applied iteratively $c + 1$ times to a base NM commitment scheme that handles tags of size $\underbrace{\lg \lg \cdots \lg(\kappa)}_{c \text{ times}}$ for some constant c and results in a scheme that handles tags of size 2^κ.

Templates for Tag Amplification. To perform tag amplification, we will build on a tag encoding scheme that was first suggested by [18]. They suggest a method of breaking a large tag T^j (say, in $[2^N]$) into N small tags $t_1^j, t_2^j, \ldots t_N^j$, each in $2N$, such that for two different large tags $T^1 \neq T^2$, there exists at least one index i such that $t_i^2 \notin \{t_1^1, t_2^1, \ldots t_N^1\}$. This is achieved by setting $t_i^j = i || T^j[i]$, where $T^j[i]$ denotes the ith bit of T^j.

Given this tag amplification technique, we start by describing a template for non-interactive tag amplification suggested in [32,36]. A CCA commitment scheme for tags in 2^N will generate a commitment to a message m as CCA.Com$(1^\kappa, \text{tag}, m; r) \to \text{com}$. The string com is generated by first applying the DDN encoding to tag to obtain N tags $t_1, \ldots t_N$. Next, these (smaller) tags are used to generate commitments to m in the smaller tag scheme as $c_i = \text{Small.Com}(1^\kappa, (t_i), \text{msg} = m; r_i)$ for $i \in [N]$. The intuition for security is as follows: recall that the DDN encoding ensures that for two different large tags $T^1 \neq T^2$, there exists at least one index i such that $t_i^2 \notin \{t_1^1, t_2^1, \ldots t_N^1\}$. This (roughly) implies that the commitment generated by an adversary w.r.t. tag t_i^2

is *independent* of the challenge commitment string, as we desire. However, the commitments w.r.t. other tags t_j^2 could potentially depend on the challenge commitment, which is undesirable. To get around this issue, the templates in [32, 36][2] suggest that the committer attach a type of zero knowledge (ZK) proof that all commitments are to the same message m using the random coins as a witness. In the setting of non-interactive amplification, the ZK proof will need to be non-interactive. For technical reasons, it is in fact required to be ZK against adversaries running in time T, where T is the time required to brute-force break the underlying CCA scheme for small tags.

Since non-interactive ZK proofs do not exist without trusted setup, the techniques in [8, 29, 32, 36] rely on weaker variants of ZK such as NIWIs, and [8, 32, 36] combine NIWIs with a trapdoor statement that an (inefficient) ZK simulator uses to simulate the ZK proof. At the same time, for soundness, we require that an adversary cannot use the trapdoor statement to cheat. This is challenging when the trapdoor statement is fixed independently of the statement being proven, because a *non-uniform* adversary can always hardwire the trapdoor and use this to provide convincing proofs of false statements.

Given this barrier, [36] restricted themselves to achieving tag amplification against *uniform adversaries*, based on (sub-exponential) NIWIs and keyless collision-resistant hash functions against uniform adversaries. Subsequently [8] developed a technique to obtain tag amplification against *non-uniform adversaries*, based on NIWIs and assuming the existence of keyless collision-resistant hash functions that satisfy some form of security against non-uniform adversaries. Very roughly, they assume that no adversary with non-uniform advice of size S can find more than $\mathsf{poly}(S)$ collisions[3].

More recently, [19] developed a method for performing non-interactive tag amplification without NIWIs, and while only making *black-box use* of the underlying base commitment. However, the resulting scheme is secure only against *uniform adversaries*. On the other hand, the goal of this work is to achieve a *black-box construction* that avoids NIWIs and achieves security against *non-uniform adversaries*, under a similar keyless assumption as [8]. To highlight the bottlenecks in the non-uniform setting, we give a brief overview of the technique of [19].

Black-Box Tag Amplification. To begin, we note that the tag amplification technique sketched above is not black-box in the base commitment due to the use of variants of ZK. Recall that ZK is used to ensure consistency of adversarial commitments generated w.r.t. different small tags. In the CCA setting, this allows using a CCA decommitment oracle that opens a commitment under any

---

[2] These are the non-interactive versions of templates previously suggested in [18, 34, 44].

[3] Technically, they rely on a more general notion of incompressible problems, which is a collection of efficiently recognizable and sufficiently dense sets, one for each security parameter, for which no adversary with non-uniform description of polynomial size in S can find more than $K(S)$ elements in the set.

one of the adversary's small tags, without the adversary noticing which one was opened. In other words, ZK is used to establish a system where the adversary cannot submit a commitment such that its opening will be different under oracle functions that open different commitments, which turns out to be crucial to achieving CCA security.

In [19], this system is established by means of a *hinting PRG* [33]. At a high level, the construction in [19] sets things up so that the CCA oracle that opens a commitment under one of the adversary's small tags will recover a candidate PRG seed s. This seed deterministically generates (a significant part of) the randomness used to create commitments with respect to *all* the adversary's small tags. The oracle uses this property to check for consistency by re-evaluating the underlying small-tag commitments, and checking them against the original. These checks intuitively serve as a substitute for ZK proofs, however they differ from ZK in that the checking algorithm sometimes allows partially malformed commitments to be opened to valid values. While creating such partially malformed commitments is actually easy for the adversary, the adversary is still unable to distinguish between oracles that open different small tag commitments.

The work [19] converts CCA commitments with $4N$ tags to CCA commitments with 2^N tags, assuming hinting PRGs and statistically equivocal commitments without setup, that satisfy binding against uniform adversaries. A hinting PRG satisfies the following property: for a uniformly random short seed s, expand $PRG(s) = z_0 z_1 z_2 \ldots z_n$. Then compute matrix x by sampling uniformly random $v_1 v_2 \ldots v_n$, and setting for all $i \in [n]$, $M_{s_i, i} = z_i$ and $M_{1-s_i, i} = v_i$. The requirement is that z_0, M generated using a uniformly random seed must be indistinguishable from a uniform random string.

Here, we actually note that prior works [19,33] can be made to work based on a hinting PRG that actually satisfies a weaker property: namely, that z_0, M obtained as described above should be indistinguishable from u, M where u is generated uniformly at random and M is generated as described above. Looking ahead, we will define a variant of a hinting PRG and will rely on the fact that this weaker property can be used instead.

Hinting PRGs were built based on CDH, LWE [33], as well as more efficient versions based on the ϕ-hiding and DBDHI assumptions [20]. The required equivocal commitments can be obtained from keyless collision resistant hash functions against uniform adversaries, based on the blueprint of [17] and [28], and more recently [7], in the keyless hash setting.

The [19] *Technique.* We now provide a brief overview of the [19] technique, since their construction will serve as a starting point for our work.

Let (Small.Com, Small.Val, Small.Recover) be a CCA commitment for $4N$ tags. Then [19] assume tags take identities of the form $(i, \beta, \gamma) \in [N] \times \{0, 1\} \times \{0, 1\}$ and that the Small.Com algorithm requires randomness of length $\ell(\kappa)$. Their transformation produces three algorithms, (CCA.Com, CCA.Val, CCA.Recover). The CCA.Com algorithm on input a tag tag from the large tag space, an input message, and uniform randomness, first samples a seed s of size n for a hinting PRG. It uses the first co-ordinate z_0 (of the output of the hinting PRG on input s), as a one-time pad to mask the message m, resulting in string c. Next, it generates n equivocal commitments $\{\sigma_i\}_{i \in [n]}$, one to each bit of s. We will let y_i denote the opening of the ith equivocal commitment (this includes the ith bit s_i of s). Finally, it 'signals' each of the bits of s by generating commitments $\{c_{x,i,b}\}_{x \in [N], i \in [n], b \in \{0,1\}}$ using the small tag scheme. For every $i \in [n]$, the commitments $\{c_{x,i,0}\}_{x \in [N]}$ and $\{c_{x,i,1}\}_{x \in [N]}$ are generated as follows:

1. If $s_i = 0$
   (a) $c_{x,i,0} = \mathsf{Small.Com}(1^\kappa, (x, \mathsf{tag}_x, 0), \mathsf{msg} = y_i; r_{x,i})$
   (b) $c_{x,i,1} = \mathsf{Small.Com}(1^\kappa, (x, \mathsf{tag}_x, 1), \mathsf{msg} = y_i; \tilde{r}_{x,i})$
2. If $s_i = 1$
   (a) $c_{x,i,0} = \mathsf{Small.Com}(1^\kappa, (x, \mathsf{tag}_x, 0), \mathsf{msg} = y_i; \tilde{r}_{x,i})$
   (b) $c_{x,i,1} = \mathsf{Small.Com}(1^\kappa, (x, \mathsf{tag}_x, 1), \mathsf{msg} = y_i; r_{x,i})$

where all the $\tilde{r}_{x,i}$ values are uniformly random, whereas $r_{x,i}$ values correspond to the output of the hinting PRG on seed s. The output of CCA.Com is $\mathsf{tag}, c, \{\sigma_i\}_{i \in [n]}, \{c_{x,i,b}\}_{x \in [N], i \in [n], b \in \{0,1\}}$.

On an oracle query of the form $\mathsf{CCA.Val}(\mathsf{tag}, \mathsf{com})$, we must return the message committed in the string com, if one exists. To do this, we parse $\mathsf{com} = \mathsf{tag}, c, \{\sigma_i\}_{i \in [n]}, \{c_{x,i,b}\}_{x \in [N], i \in [n], b \in \{0,1\}}$, and then recover the values committed under small tags $(1, \mathsf{tag}_1, 0)$ and $(1, \mathsf{tag}_1, 1)$, which also helps recover the seed s of the hinting PRG. Next, we check that for every $i \in [n]$, the recovered values correspond to openings of the respective σ_i. We also compute hinting $\mathsf{PRG}(s)$, and use the resulting randomness to check that for all $x \in [N]$, the commitments that were supposed to use the outcome of the PRG were correctly constructed. If any of these checks fail, we know that the commitment string com cannot be a well-formed commitment to any message. Therefore, if any of the checks fail, the oracle outputs $\perp$. These checks are inspired by [33], and intuitively, ensure that it is computationally infeasible for an adversary to query the oracle on commitment strings that lead to different outcomes depending on which small tag was used. If all these checks pass, the CCA.Val algorithm uses c to recover and output m.

To prove that the resulting scheme is CCA secure against uniform adversaries, note that the set $\{(x, \mathsf{tag}_x)\}_{x \in [N]}$ is nothing but the DDN encoding of the tag tag. This means that for our particular method of generating the commitments $c_{x,i,b}$ described above, for each of the adversary's oracle queries, there will be an index $x' \in [N]$ such that the tags $(x', \mathsf{tag}_{x'}, 0)$ and $(x', \mathsf{tag}_{x'}, 1)$ used to generate $\{c_{x',i,b}\}_{i \in [n], b \in \{0,1\}}$ in that query will differ from *all small tags used to generate the challenge commitment*.

The first step towards proving security of the resulting commitment will be to define an alternative CCA.ValAlt algorithm, that instead of recovering the values committed under tags $(1, \mathsf{tag}_1, 0)$ and $(1, \mathsf{tag}_1, 1)$, recovers values committed under $(x', \mathsf{tag}_{x'}, 0)$ and $(x', \mathsf{tag}_{x'}, 1)$. The goal is to ensure that it is computationally infeasible for an adversary to query the oracle on commitment strings for which CCA.Val and CCA.ValAlt lead to different outcomes. In more detail, because of the checks performed by the valuation algorithms, it is possible to argue that any adversary that distinguishes CCA.Val from CCA.ValAlt must query the oracle with a commitment string that has following property: For some $i \in [n], x \in [N]$, $c_{x,i,0}$ and $c_{x,i,1}$ are small tag commitments to openings of the equivocal commitment to some bit b and $1 - b$ respectively. One can then brute-force extract these openings from $c_{x,i,0}$ and $c_{x,i,1}$ to contradict the binding property of the commitment against *uniform* sub-exponential adversaries.

This first step already becomes a bottleneck in the non-uniform setting: in general, an adversary with bounded polynomial advice can always sample an equivocal (non-interactive) commitment string together with an opening to 0 and another opening to 1.

The Problem in the Non-uniform Case. As discussed above, the proof/ construction in [19] falls apart in the very first step when considering a non-uniform adversary. In fact, such an adversary can attack the [19] scheme by non-uniformly sampling equivocal commitments $\{\widetilde{\sigma}_i\}_{i \in [n]}$ together with randomness $\{\widetilde{y}_{0,i}\}_{i \in [n]}$ and $\{\widetilde{y}_{1,i}\}_{i \in [n]}$ that can be used to open these commitments to both 0 and 1 respectively. Next, it can set the components $\{\widetilde{c}_{x,i,b}\}_{x \in [N], i \in [n], b \in \{0,1\}}$ as small-tag commitments to both types of openings. This allows the attacker to explicitly break CCA2 security, as we describe next.

Let $x' \in [N]$ be an index such that the tags $(x', \mathsf{tag}_{x'}, 0)$ and $(x', \mathsf{tag}_{x'}, 1)$ used to generate $\{c_{x',i,b}\}_{i \in [n], b \in \{0,1\}}$ in that query differ from *all small tags used to generate the challenge commitment.* On one hand, CCA2 security of the small-tag scheme will ensure that seed recovered from small-tag commitments $(x', \widetilde{\mathsf{tag}}_{x'}, 0)$ and $(x', \widetilde{\mathsf{tag}}_{x'}, 1)$ are independent of the seed in the challenge commitment. On the other hand, the actual committed value, which is defined via the seed recovered from $(1, \widetilde{\mathsf{tag}}_1, 0), (1, \widetilde{\mathsf{tag}}_1, 1)$ will exactly match the value in the challenge commitment, allowing this adversary to break CCA2 security. The equivocation described above would allow the adversary to ensure that all the hinting PRG checks pass, despite the use of different types of seeds in small tags $(1, \widetilde{\mathsf{tag}}_1, 0), (1, \widetilde{\mathsf{tag}}_1, 1)$ versus $(x', \widetilde{\mathsf{tag}}_{x'}, 0), (x', \widetilde{\mathsf{tag}}_{x'}, 1)$.

Towards a Solution. Now, one could hope to rely on some form of *non-uniform* security of keyless hash functions [7,8]. Prior works [7,8] have formulated and used the assumption that there exist keyless hash functions where any adversary with non-uniform advice of size S can only find $\mathsf{poly}(S)$ collisions. Inspired by a technique in [8], we could hope to define a "bad" CCA2 query as one that contains openings to both a zero and a one for the equivocal commitment. Next, we could hope to limit the number of "bad" CCA2 queries that a non-uniform adversary will make to its decommitment oracle. As long as this set of "bad" queries is bounded and is just a function of the adversary's non-uniform advice, our challenger could also hope to non-uniformly obtain answers to such queries and use these instead of running the CCA.Val or CCA.ValAlt function.

Unfortunately, in the [19] protocol, even given just bounded (polynomial) non-uniform advice, an adversary will be able to equivocate *all of its* commitments and generate an *unbounded* number of bad queries. Moreover, because the hinting PRG is not injective, each bad query could have multiple possible openings to different seeds. This indicates that the [19] protocol needs to be fundamentally modified to enable security against non-uniform attacks.

Our Approach. We begin by understanding how the [19] protocol can possibly be modified to disallow the attack described above.

- As described above, we want to force the adversary to "use up" bits of non-uniform advice for each new bad query that it makes. This will hopefully help limit the number of unique bad queries, and our reduction could then non-uniformly obtain answers to each of these queries.
- To allow the reduction to non-uniformly answer bad queries, we will aim to pair every possible bad query with a *unique* seed value that can be used to answer this bad query in place of running the CCA.Val or CCA.ValAlt function.

Limiting Bad Seeds Instead of Bad Queries. The first bullet aims to *limit the number of bad queries*. While we will not be able to achieve this, we will achieve a slightly weaker property that will nevertheless suffice for our proof idea to go through. In more detail, we will tie every CCA2 query, and in particular the *equivocal commitment part of every CCA2 query* to an auxiliary input parameter. That is, in addition to message and randomness, each equivocal commitment will obtain as input an auxiliary parameter. There will be no hiding requirement on the auxiliary parameter; it will only serve to strengthen the binding property of the equivocal commitment. We will require that there exists a fixed polynomial $K(\cdot)$ such that any adversary with non-uniform advice of size S is unable to output $K(S)$ different pairs of auxiliary parameters and commitment strings, with valid openings for each pair to both a zero and a one. We will rely on keyless collision-resistant hash functions against non-uniform adversaries to build modified equivocal commitments with this guarantee. While this does not limit the number of bad queries that an adversary can make, it does limit the number of unique auxiliary input parameters that an adversary can use to generate CCA2 queries where it is able to open the equivocal commitments to both a zero and a one.

The goal of the second bullet is to allow a reduction to answer all bad queries by pairing every such query with a *unique seed* that can be used to non-uniformly answer this query in place of running the CCA.Val or CCA.ValAlt function. To get this idea to work, we must assign a "right" candidate seed to each bad query. As discussed above, in the [19] protocol, any adversary that can find two openings for the equivocal commitments could submit a bad query where multiple possible seed values match the output of the HPRG. To prevent this, we will explicitly force the HPRG to be injective. In more detail, we add what we call an "injective extension" to the HPRG. This is an additional algorithm $\mathsf{ExtEval}(s) \to r_{ext}$ that is an injective function on the HPRG seed s. The HPRG security requirement is also slightly modified to ensure that an adversary will not be able to distinguish the PRG output z from uniform given the hint matrix M (described above) and *additionally given* r_{ext}.

Now the CCA2 commitment will additionally consist of the value $r_{ext} = \mathsf{ExtEval}(s)$, and CCA.Val/CCA.ValAlt will reject if for a recovered candidate seed

s', $\mathsf{ExtEval}(s') \neq r_{\mathsf{ext}}$. As a result, there will be at most a single seed s that will be "compatible" with any commitment string.

Going back to the construction of our CCA2 commitment, we will compute the modified equivocal commitments with auxiliary parameter set to r_{ext}, where recall that $r_{\mathsf{ext}} = \mathsf{ExtEval}(s)$. At this point, we will be able to assign (at most) one unique 's' to each auxiliary parameter. Moreover, by the (strengthened) binding property of equivocal commitments, any non-uniform attacker will be able to equivocate on at most a small number of auxiliary parameter values.

Analyzing Security. To prove CCA2 security of the resulting construction, we will proceed as follows. In the first hybrid (Game 1), we will switch to a challenger that depending on the adversary's non-uniform advice, stores a "cheat-sheet" consisting of all 'bad' r_{ext} that the adversary can query on (with more than a certain inverse-polynomial probability), together with their inverses s under the injective algorithm $\mathsf{ExtEval}(\cdot)$. Our challenger will (1) rely on the cheat-sheet to answer any adversarial queries for which r_{ext} lies on the cheat-sheet, and (2) use $\mathsf{CCA.Val}$ to decrypt only those queries for which r_{ext} lies outside the cheat-sheet.

In the second hybrid (Game 2), the challenger will behave similarly as the previous hybrid, except using $\mathsf{CCA.ValAlt}$ to decrypt queries for which r_{ext} lies outside the cheat-sheet. By the strong binding property of the equivocal commitment, the adversary is guaranteed to not equivocate on these queries (except with low probability). Therefore by the argument outlined in the proof of the [19] technique, the outputs of $\mathsf{CCA.Val}$ and $\mathsf{CCA.ValAlt}$ will be indistinguishable on these queries. The rest of the proof will follow similarly to [19]. There is one major hurdle in realizing this outline, as we discuss next.

Modifying the $\mathsf{CCA.Val}$ *Algorithm.* The first hybrid (Game 1) described above will actually *not* be indistinguishable from the output of the actual CCA2 game. This is because a non-uniform adversary may generate equivocation queries for which r_{ext} lies on the cheat-sheet and has an inverse (a hinting PRG seed), but the $\mathsf{CCA.Val}$ algorithm run by the CCA2 challenger may *not* be able to find this seed. To deal with this issue, we will change the $\mathsf{CCA.Val}$ algorithm so that it performs a brute-force search through all possible seeds to find the one (if any) that matches r_{ext}.

At first it appears that the rest of the proof should be easy once this is done. It should be possible to rely on security of the (1) auxiliary-input equivocal commitments and (2) hinting PRGs with injective extension, to show that the (updated) CCA2 game is indistinguishable from the first hybrid. However, while this is true, proving it turns out to be fairly tricky. To prove indistinguishability, we must design an efficient reduction B that has oracle access to an adversary A which distinguishes between the CCA2 game and the first hybrid. This reduction B should be able to use such an adversary to break security of equivocal commitments, by generating many more equivocal openings than its (non-uniform) advice would allow it to. The adversary A is a CCA2 adversary, which means it makes multiple (a-priori unbounded) calls to a $\mathsf{CCA.Val}$ oracle, and B must find a way to answer these queries. But recall that the oracle needs to perform a brute-force search through all possible seeds to find the one (if any) that matches r_{ext} – simulating this process will make B inefficient. As such, B will need to maintain its own cheat-sheet to answer CCA.Val queries. Even with such a cheat-sheet, the proof is not straightforward: the set of most common equivocal queries in the CCA2 game may in general be different from the set of most common queries when B answers from its cheat-sheet.

Intermediate Cheat-Sheets. To make the proof go through, we will rely on a sequence of carefully defined intermediate cheat-sheets (that we will call lists from this point on). These will be defined inductively, and in the base case $\mathcal{L}^{(0)}$ will be empty. Let $Q = Q(\kappa)$ denote the total number of oracle calls that the attacker makes. For $j \in [1, Q]$, the jth intermediate list, denoted by $\mathcal{L}^{(j)}$ will contain the r_{ext} values and corresponding seeds for A's most common equivocal queries in its first j oracle calls. Note that this does not suffice to fully define $\mathcal{L}^{(j)}$, since we also need to determine how the first $j - 1$ oracle calls of A will be answered: in the definition of $\mathcal{L}^{(j)}$, the first j oracle calls will be answered using the CCA.ValAlt algorithm with access to the list $\mathcal{L}^{(j-1)}$. The final list $\mathcal{L}$ used by CCA.ValAlt in Game 1 will correspond exactly to $\mathcal{L} = \mathcal{L}^{(Q)}$. We show the following inductively for every j: when the first $j - 1$ CCA.Val queries are answered using list $\mathcal{L}^{(j-1)}$, then it is possible to add new common equivocal queries and update the list to $\mathcal{L}^{(j)}$. This will eventually allow us to switch to the first hybrid described above, which uses CCA.ValAlt (plus the final list $\mathcal{L}^{(Q)}$).

We point the reader to our full version for a more detailed overview of this part of the proof. There we also discuss why for technical reasons, we require as building blocks for our equivocal commitment, keyless hash functions with specific parameters. In more detail, we require that an adversary with $S(\kappa)$ bits of advice cannot produce more than $S(\kappa) \cdot p(\kappa)$ pairs of "distinct collisions" for some a-priori fixed polynomial $p(\cdot)$, where "distinct collisions" means that no entry in any pair of collisions matches an entry in another pair. The assumption is described formally and analyzed in Sect. 4.1.

Completing the Analysis. After switching to CCA.ValAlt (plus the cheat-sheet), the next hybrid will sample equivocal commitments $\{\sigma_i\}_{i\in[n]}$, for the challenge commitment, together with randomness $\{y_{0,i}\}_{i\in[n]}$ and $\{y_{1,i}\}_{i\in[n]}$ that can be used to equivocally open these commitments to 0 and 1 respectively. Next, inspired by [33] the components $\{c^*_{x,i,b}\}_{x\in[N],i\in[n],b\in\{0,1\}}$ are modified in the challenge commitment to "drown" out information about s via noise, while relying on CCA2 security of the underlying small tag scheme to run the CCA.ValAlt function and recover values committed under $(x', \mathsf{tag}_{x'}, 0)$ and $(x', \mathsf{tag}_{x'}, 1)$. This step crucially makes use of the fact that the tags $(x', \mathsf{tag}_{x'}, 0)$ and $(x', \mathsf{tag}_{x'}, 1)$ differ from *all small tags used to generate the challenge commitment*. Finally, we rely on the security of the hinting PRG to switch to using uniform randomness everywhere.

Hinting PRGs with Injective Extension. We now describe how to achieve hinting PRGs with injective extension by modifying the constructions in [33]. Recall that we require hinting PRGs with injective extensions that satisfy a different security property than prior work: namely, for a uniformly random short seed s, expand $PRG(s) = z_0 z_1 z_2 \ldots z_n$ and compute the injective output r_{ext}. Then compute matrix M by sampling uniformly random $v_1 v_2 \ldots v_n$, and setting for all $i \in [n]$, $M_{s_i, i} = z_i$ and $M_{1-s_i, i} = v_i$. The requirement is that z_0 generated using a uniformly random seed must be indistinguishable from uniform, *even given M and given the output r_{ext} of the injective extension.*

We build hinting PRGs with an injective extension by modularly combining the constructions in [33] with any leakage-resilient injective one-way function (LRIOWF). To enable this, we note that hinting PRG constructions in [33] from CDH and LWE have a "lossy" property, where PRG parameters can be generated in lossy mode in such a way that the output of the hinting PRG is simulatable given just a small amount of advice. We call the resulting abstraction a lossy hinting function. To achieve injectivity, we rely on a leakage resilient injective one-way function (LRIOWF) applied to the seed s of the lossy hinting function[4]. Finally, we generate the 'mask' z_0 of the hinting PRG as the Goldreich-Levin hardcore bits of the LRIOWF. To prove that z_0 is pseudorandom even in the presence of r_{ext} and M, we will switch the lossy hinting function to lossy mode. In this mode the hinting function will only leak a few bits about the inverse s of the LRIOWF. We will then invoke the Goldreich-Levin theorem to argue that distinguishing the mask from uniform will require inverting the LRIOWF given just a few bits of leakage on s, which is impossible by assumption on the LRIOWF. This completes an overview of our techniques.

Comparison with Prior Work. We conclude with a comparison of our techniques against prior work that relies on keyless collision-resistant hash functions against non-uniform adversaries. While [7] relies on this assumption to obtain 3-message zero-knowledge via substantially different techniques, [8] applies this to a setting that is much closer to our work, that is, to achieving non-interactive non-malleable commitments. In more detail, [8] use keyless hash functions against non-uniform adversaries to build a special type of 1-message zero-knowledge for NP with a *weak* soundness guarantee against non-uniform provers. They achieve this by building on the usual template for 1-message ZK, where a prover proves (via a NIWI) that either $x \in L$ or that the prover knows a trapdoor. The trapdoor, roughly, corresponds to a collision in a keyless hash function; and is derived as a function of the statement x. This ensures that a prover that can (non-uniformly) find a fixed set of non-uniform collisions will only be able to provide convincing proofs for a fixed set of statements. In their construction of non-malleable commitments, the use of NIWIs to prove a statement of the form "$x \in L$ or the prover knows a trapdoor" results in non-black-box use of the underlying base scheme.

Unlike [8], we do not construct any variant of non-interactive ZK (or rely on assumptions like NIWI that imply non-interactive ZK). We develop a new

---

[4] For example, any sub-exponentially secure injective one-way function will suffice for our purposes.

template to directly achieve tag amplification for non-malleable commitments against non-uniform adversaries, without reliance on NIWIs. Our methodology to "tie" together the set of collisions an adversary can find with the number of commitments that an adversary can cheat on is entirely different from that of [8].

3 Background

3.1 Non-uniform Security

We say that a cryptographic game is $T(\cdot)$-non-uniform secure if for any Turing Machine in $\mathsf{poly}(T(\kappa))$ time with $\mathsf{poly}(\kappa)$ non-uniform advice only has only negligible advantage in said game. We will refer to $\mathsf{poly}(\cdot)$-non-uniform secure schemes as achieving 'plain' non-uniform security.

In addition, we will say a cryptographic scheme is subexponentially secure against non-uniform adversaries if there exists some constant $c > 0$ such that the scheme is 2^{n^c}-non-uniform secure. When the constant c is explicitly required, we will say c-subexponentially secure.

3.2 CCA Commitments

We present our definition of CCA secure commitments [12], which is derived from [19] with modifications made for defining security against non-uniform attackers. Intuitively, these are tagged commitments where a commitment to message m under tag tag and randomness r is created as $\mathsf{CCA.Com}(\mathsf{tag}, m; r) \to \mathsf{com}$. The scheme will be statistically binding, i.e., for all $\mathsf{tag}_0, \mathsf{tag}_1$, r_0, r_1 and $m_0 \neq m_1$ we have that $\mathsf{CCA.Com}(\mathsf{tag}_0, m_0; r_0) \neq \mathsf{CCA.Com}(\mathsf{tag}_1, m_1; r_1)$.

The hiding property is a strengthened CCA2-style definition where an attacker outputs a challenge tag tag^* along with messages m_0, m_1 and receives a challenge commitment com^* to either m_0 or m_1. The attacker's job is to guess the message that was committed to with oracle access to an (inefficient) value function $\mathsf{CCA.Val}$ where $\mathsf{CCA.Val}(\mathsf{com})$ will return m if $\mathsf{CCA.Com}(\mathsf{tag}, m; r) \to \mathsf{com}$ for some r. The attacker is allowed oracle access to $\mathsf{CCA.Val}(\cdot)$ for any $\mathsf{tag} \neq \mathsf{tag}^*$. In the non-interactive setting, the traditional notion of non-malleability (as seen in [8,29], etc.) is simply a restriction of the CCA game where the adversary is only allowed to simultaneously submit a single set of decommitment queries. The proof of this is immediate and can be found in [11].

We mention two distinct features of our definition. First, we explicitly denote the running time of the $\mathsf{CCA.Val}$ algorithm despite the fact that it is not polynomial time. Explicitly specifying the runtime of the $\mathsf{CCA.Val}$ oracle will help us in complexity leveraging when performing tag amplification. We will call the commitment scheme to be 2^{κ^v}-efficient, i.e. can run in time (polynomially in) 2^{κ^v} where $v \geq 1$ and the security of the scheme is considered for subexponential adversaries. This additional specification was not required in [19].

Second, (as in [19]) we require a recover from randomness property, which allows one to open the commitment given all the randomness used to generate said commitment. This can be achieved generically with no additional assumptions.

Remark 3.1. We note that by considering non-uniform attackers our definition actually becomes simpler than that of [19] where they considered security against a stronger than uniform adversary, which they labeled as *e*-computationally enabled security. Such an adversary can run any Turing Program that runs in time $\mathsf{poly}(2^{\kappa^e})$ and obtain it's output as a non-uniform advice. This notion helped them perform complexity leveraging and obtain a uniformly secure non-malleable commitment scheme. Since we consider security against non-uniform adversaries, which are allowed to obtain non-uniform advice that may take an arbitrary amount of time to compute, our presentation is simpler.

Definition. A CCA secure commitment is parameterized by a tag space of size $N = N(\kappa)$ where tags are in $[1, N]$ for message space $\mathcal{M} = \{0,1\}^{w(\kappa)}$ where $w(\cdot)$ is a polynomial function (for simplicity in notation we often skip the dependence on κ). It consists of three algorithms:

$\mathsf{CCA.Com}(1^\kappa, \mathsf{tag}, m; r) \rightarrow \mathsf{com}$ is a randomized PPT algorithm that takes as input the security parameter κ, a tag $\mathsf{tag} \in [N]$, a message $m \in \{0,1\}^w$ and outputs a commitment com, including the tag $\mathsf{com.tag}$. We denote the random coins explicitly as r.

$\mathsf{CCA.Val}(\mathsf{com}) \rightarrow m \cup \perp$ is a deterministic inefficient algorithm that takes in a commitment com and outputs either a message $m \in \{0,1\}^w$ or a reject symbol $\perp$.

$\mathsf{CCA.Recover}(\mathsf{com}, r) \rightarrow m$ is a deterministic algorithm which takes a commitment com and the randomness r used to generate com and outputs the underlying message m.

We now define the correctness, efficiency properties, as well as the security properties of perfect binding and message hiding.

Correctness

Definition 3.2. *We say that our CCA secure commitment scheme is perfectly correct if the following holds.* $\forall m \in \{0,1\}^w$, $\mathsf{tag} \in [N]$ *and* r *we have that*

$$\mathsf{CCA.Val}(\mathsf{CCA.Com}(1^\kappa, \mathsf{tag}, m; r)) = m.$$

Efficiency

Definition 3.3. *We say that our CCA secure commitment scheme is* $\mathsf{T}(\cdot)$-*efficient, if* $\mathsf{CCA.Com}, \mathsf{CCA.Recover}$ *run in time* $\mathsf{poly}(|m|, \kappa)$, *while* $\mathsf{CCA.Val}$ *runs in time* $\mathsf{poly}(|m|, \mathsf{T}(\kappa))$.[5]

---

[5] In order for the scheme to be secure, the runtime of the CCA.Val oracle should be bigger than the runtime of the subexponential adversary. We will imagine runtime of the CCA.Val oracle to be 2^{κ^v} where $v > 1$.

Security

Binding

Definition 3.4. *We say that our CCA secure commitment is perfectly binding if $\forall c, \forall m_0, m_1 \in \{0,1\}^w$ s.t. $m_0 \neq m_1$ and $\mathsf{CCA.Val}(c) \in \{m_1, \perp\}$, there does not exist r such that*

$$\mathsf{CCA.Recover}(c, r) = m_0$$

Moreover, for any c such that $\mathsf{CCA.Val}(c) = m_1 \neq \perp$, then there exists r such that $\mathsf{CCA.Recover}(c, r) = m_1$.

Weak Binding

Definition 3.5. *We say that our CCA secure commitment is perfectly binding if $\forall c, \forall m_0, m_1 \in \{0,1\}^w$ s.t. $m_0 \neq m_1$ and $\mathsf{CCA.Val}(c) \in \{m_1, \perp\}$, there does not exist r such that*

$$\mathsf{CCA.Recover}(c, r) = m_0$$

CCA Hiding. We also define a CCA message hiding game between a challenger and an attacker. The game is parameterized by a security parameter κ.

1. The attacker sends a "challenge tag" $\mathsf{tag}^* \in [N]$.
2. The attacker makes a polynomial number of repeated commitment queries com. If $\mathsf{com.tag} = \mathsf{tag}^*$ the challenger responds with $\perp$. Otherwise it responds as
$$\mathsf{CCA.Val(com)}.$$
3. The attacker sends two messages $m_0, m_1 \in \{0,1\}^w$.
4. The challenger flips a coin $b \in \{0,1\}$ and sends $\mathsf{com}^* = \mathsf{CCA.Com}(\mathsf{tag}^*, m_b; r)$ for randomly chosen r.
5. The attacker again makes a polynomial number of repeated queries of commitment com. If $\mathsf{com.tag} = \mathsf{tag}^*$ the challenger responds with $\perp$. Otherwise it responds as
$$\mathsf{CCA.Val(com)}.$$
6. The attacker finally outputs a guess b'.

We define the attacker's advantage in the game to be $\Pr[b' = b] - \frac{1}{2}$ where the probability is over all the attacker and challenger's coins.

Definition 3.6. *A CCA secure commitment scheme scheme given by algorithms* (CCA.Com, CCA.Val, CCA.Recover) *is said to be* $T(\cdot)$-CCA *secure if for any* $T(\cdot)$-*non-uniform adversary $\mathcal{A}$ there exists a negligible function $\mathsf{negl}(\cdot)$ such that the attacker's advantage in the game is $\mathsf{negl}(\kappa)$.*

We also define another notion of security which we call "same tag" computation enabled secure for a weaker class of adversaries who only submit challenge queries that all have the same tag.

Definition 3.7. *A CCA secure commitment scheme scheme given by algorithms* (CCA.Com, CCA.Val, CCA.Recover) *is said to be "same tag"* $\mathsf{T}(\cdot)$-*CCA secure if for any* $\mathsf{T}(\cdot)$-*non-uniform adversary* $\mathcal{A}$ *which generates queries such that all commitment queries submitted by* $\mathcal{A}$ *are on the same tag, there exists a negligible function* negl$(\cdot)$ *such that the attacker's advantage in the game is* negl(κ).

Recovery from Randomness

Definition 3.8. *We say that our CCA secure commitment scheme can be recovered from randomness if the following holds. For all* $m \in \{0,1\}^w$, tag $\in [N]$, *and* r *we have that*

$$\mathsf{CCA.Recover}(\mathsf{CCA.Com}(1^\kappa, \mathsf{tag}, m; r), r) = m.$$

4   Setupless Equivocal Commitments Against Non-uniform Adversaries

Equivocal commitments are commitments introduced by DiCrescenzo et al. [16] that have two computationally indistinguishable modes of setup. In the normal mode the setup outputs public parameters such that the commitment is statistically binding. In the alternate mode, the setup outputs public parameters and a trapdoor which can output commitments that open to both 0 and 1.

A setupless equivocal commitment sceme doesn't have a trusted setup algorithm. Instead we have an inefficient equivocation algorithm that can output commitments to both 0 and 1. The security of the scheme is guaranteed for adversaries that run in less than the equivocation time. A setupless equivocal commitment scheme, secure against uniform adversaries can be constructed from any setupless statistical hiding, computationally binding commitment scheme [19]. These can be built using a strong extractor and a keyless collision resistant hash function ([7,17,28]). But for non-uniform adversaries, it is easy to hardwire collisions for the setupless collision resistant hash function and hence break binding security of the scheme.

In order to achieve non-uniform security, Bitansky et al. [7], suggested a multi-collision resistance assumption that essentially claims that hardwiring collisions is the best that an adversary can do. Informally, the K strong multi-collision resistant property states that any non-uniform adversary with advice advice can not output more than K(|advice|) many collisions (assume that K blows up the length). This assumption was used by Bitansky et al. [7] to create statistically hiding commitments with a special binding against non-uniform adversaries.

We introduce a modified notion called "Setupless Equivocal Commitment with Auxiliary Input" that builds on these prior work, assumptions and takes in an auxiliary input aux $\in \{0,1\}^*$ additionally and commits to a bit b and aux. The inefficient equivocation algorithm can take in any aux and output a commitment that can be open to both 0 and 1. We hide b (aux can not be hidden) while guaranteeing computational binding against non-uniform adversaries. We show that a similar construction showed by [7] using multi-collision resistant hash functions and a strong extractor also gives this notion.

4.1 Distinct Strong Keyless Multi-collision Resistance

The definition from [7,8] states that a non-uniform attacker with advice string advice cannot output more than $\mathsf{K}(\kappa, |\mathsf{advice}|)$ collisions (one can think of K as a polynomial that grows the advice length, [8] say this could, for instance, be a quadratic polynomial). We further weaken the definition so that the adversary is required to output all distinct elements in its pairs of collisions, i.e. letting $\mathbf{X} = \left(X_1^{(0)}, X_1^{(1)}, \ldots, X_K^{(0)}, X_K^{(1)} \right)$, we require that there do not exist any $i, j \in [K]^2$, $b, c \in \{0,1\}^2$ such that $X_i^{(b)} = X_j^{(c)}$. We call this modified notion distinct strong multi-collision resistance. Formally,

Definition 4.1 ((T, K)-Distinct Strong Multi-collision Resistance). *Let $\mathsf{T} = \mathsf{T}(\cdot)$ and $\mathsf{K} = \mathsf{K}(\cdot, \cdot)$ be functions of the security parameter κ. A keyless hash function $\mathsf{H} : \{0,1\}^* \to \{0,1\}^\kappa$ is (T, K) distinct strong multi-collision resistant if there is a negligible function negl such that for every polynomial size non-uniform adversary $\mathcal{A}$ that runs in time $\mathsf{poly}(\mathsf{T})$ and is given advice advice of length $\mathsf{poly}(\kappa)$, for every security parameter κ, for $\mathsf{T} = \mathsf{T}(\kappa)$ and $K = \mathsf{K}(\kappa, |\mathsf{advice}|)$,*

$$\Pr \left[\begin{array}{c} \left(X_1^{(0)}, X_1^{(1)}, \ldots, X_K^{(0)}, X_K^{(1)} \right) \\ \leftarrow \mathcal{A}(1^\kappa) \end{array} : \begin{array}{c} \forall (i, b) \neq (j, c) \in [K] \times \{0, 1\}, \\ X_i^{(b)} \neq X_j^{(c)}, \\ \forall i \in [K], \mathsf{H}.\mathsf{Hash}(1^\kappa, X_0^{(i)}) = \\ \mathsf{H}.\mathsf{Hash}(1^\kappa, X_1^{(i)}) \end{array} \right] \leq \mathsf{negl}(\kappa).$$

While this is not part of our definition, for applications we will require that the number of collisions remain linear in the size of advice, i.e., there is a fixed polynomial $p(\cdot)$ such that $\mathsf{K}(\kappa, |\mathsf{advice}|) \leq p(\kappa) \cdot |\mathsf{advice}|$. In our full version, we show that our assumption, namely (T, K)-distinct strong multi-collision resistance holds in the auxiliary-input random oracle model [43] with $p(\kappa)$ as small as 1, i.e. $\mathsf{K}(\kappa, |\mathsf{advice}|) \leq |\mathsf{advice}|$.

4.2 Setupless Equivocal Commitment with Auxillary Input

An auxiliary input equivocal commitment scheme AuxEquiv without setup consists of the algorithms:

AuxEquiv.Com(1^κ, aux, b) $\to (c, d)$ is a randomized PPT algorithm that takes in a bit $b \in \{0, 1\}$, some auxiliary information aux $\in \{0, 1\}^*$ and security parameter $\kappa \in \mathbb{N}$ and outputs a commitment c, decommitment string d.
AuxEquiv.Decom(aux, c, d) $\to \{0, 1, \bot\}$ is a deterministic polytime algorithm that takes in the commitment c along with the auxiliary information aux and it's opening d and reveals the bit that it was committed to or $\bot$ to indicate failure.

AuxEquiv.Equivocate$(1^\kappa, \mathsf{aux}) \rightarrow (c, d_0, d_1)$ is an (inefficient) randomized algorithm that takes in the security parameter and some auxiliary information aux and outputs a commitment string c and decommitment strings to both 0 and 1.

Definition 4.2. *Correctness - We say an equivocal commitment scheme is perfectly correct if for all $b \in \{0, 1\}, \mathsf{aux} \in \{0, 1\}^*,$*

$$\Pr \begin{bmatrix} (c, d) \leftarrow \mathsf{AuxEquiv.Com}(1^\kappa, \mathsf{aux}, b) \\ b' \leftarrow \mathsf{AuxEquiv.Decom}(\mathsf{aux}, c, d) \\ b' = b \end{bmatrix} = 1$$

Definition 4.3. *Efficiency - We say an equivocal commitment scheme is efficient if* AuxEquiv.Com *and* AuxEquiv.Decom *run in* poly$(\kappa, |\mathsf{aux}|)$ *time, and* AuxEquiv.Equivocate *runs in time* poly$(2^\kappa, |\mathsf{aux}|)$.

We now define the binding and equivocal properties.

Definition 4.4. *An equivocal commitment without setup scheme is said to be* $(\mathsf{T}(\cdot), \mathsf{K}(\cdot))$ *binding secure if for any* non-uniform *adversary* $\mathcal{A}$ *running in time* poly$(\mathsf{T}(\kappa))$ *for some polynomial and given an advice* advice(κ) *(for simplicity, denoted as* advice*) of length* poly(κ) *and a setting of* $K = \mathsf{K}(|\mathsf{advice}|, \kappa)$, *there exists a negligible function* negl$(\cdot)$ *such that,*

$$\Pr \begin{bmatrix} & \forall i \in [K], \\ \left((\mathsf{aux}^{(1)}, c^{(1)}, d_0^{(1)}, d_1^{(1)}), \dots, & \mathsf{Decom}(\mathsf{aux}^{(i)}, c^{(i)}, d_0^{(i)}) = 0, \\ (\mathsf{aux}^{(K)}, c^{(K)}, d_0^{(K)}, d_1^{(K)})\right) \leftarrow \mathcal{A}(1^\kappa) & : \mathsf{Decom}(\mathsf{aux}^{(i)}, c^{(i)}, d_1^{(i)}) = 1 \\ & \forall i \neq j \in [K], \mathsf{aux}^{(i)} \neq \mathsf{aux}^{(j)} \end{bmatrix} \leq \mathsf{negl}(\kappa).$$

Definition 4.5. *We say that a scheme is equivocal if for all $b \in \{0, 1\}, \mathsf{aux} \in \{0, 1\}^*$ the statistical difference between the following two distributions is negligible in κ.*

- $\mathcal{D}_0 = (\mathsf{aux}, c, d)$ *where* AuxEquiv.Com$(1^\kappa, \mathsf{aux}, b) \rightarrow (c, d)$.
- $\mathcal{D}_1 = (\mathsf{aux}, c, d_b)$ *where* AuxEquiv.Equivocate$(1^\kappa, \mathsf{aux}) \rightarrow (c, d_0, d_1)$.

4.3   Construction

We construct auxiliary-input equivocal commitments assuming a keyless hash function that is distinct strong multi-collision resistant and a strong extractor. This is based on constructions introduced and presented in [7,17,28]. Let the keyless hash function be $\mathsf{H} : \{0, 1\}^* \rightarrow \{0, 1\}^\kappa$. A $(\kappa, \mathsf{negl}(\kappa))$ strong extractor SExt (see full version for detailed preliminaries) that takes a seed of κ bits and an input of 3κ bits and outputs a single bit, SExt : $\{0, 1\}^\kappa \times \{0, 1\}^{3\kappa} \rightarrow \{0, 1\}$.

AuxEquiv.Com$(1^\kappa, \text{aux}, b) \rightarrow (c, d)$.

  Sample a seed $g \leftarrow \{0,1\}^\kappa$. Choose $v \leftarrow \{0,1\}^{3\kappa}$. Compute $w = b \oplus \text{SExt}(g, v)$. Compute $h = \text{H.Hash}(1^\kappa, (\text{aux}, v))$. Compute $c = (g, w, h)$ and $d = v$.

AuxEquiv.Decom$(\text{aux}, c, d) \rightarrow \{0, 1, \bot\}$

  Parse c as (g, w, h). Check if $h = \text{H.Hash}(1^\kappa, (\text{aux}, d))$, output $\bot$ if fails. Output $w \oplus \text{SExt}(g, d)$.

AuxEquiv.Equivocate$(1^\kappa, \text{aux}) \rightarrow (c, d_0, d_1)$

  Sample a seed $g \leftarrow \{0,1\}^\kappa$ for a SExt. Sample $w \leftarrow \{0,1\}$. Sample $t \xleftarrow{R} \{0,1\}^{3\kappa}$.

  Define $\mathcal{V}_t = \{v : \text{H.Hash}(1^\kappa, (\text{aux}, v)) = \text{H.Hash}(1^\kappa, (\text{aux}, t))\}$. Partition $\mathcal{V}_t = \mathcal{V}_t^0 \cup \mathcal{V}_t^1$ where $\mathcal{V}_t^i = \{v : v \in \mathcal{V}_t \wedge \text{SExt}(g, v) = i\}$, output $\bot$ if either $\mathcal{V}_t^0$ or $\mathcal{V}_t^1$ are $\emptyset$.

  Sample $v_0 \xleftarrow{R} \mathcal{V}_t^w, v_1 \xleftarrow{R} \mathcal{V}_t^{w \oplus 1}$. Output $\bot$ if no such v_0 or v_1 exist. $h \leftarrow \text{H.Hash}(1^\kappa, (\text{aux}, t))$. Output $((g, w, h), v_0, v_1)$.

We defer the analysis of this construction and a proof of the following lemma to the full version.

Lemma 4.6. *If* $\text{H}(\cdot)$ *is a* $(\text{T}(\cdot), \text{K}(\cdot, \cdot))$ *distinct strong multi-collision resistant keyless hash function against non-uniform adversaries and* SExt *is a* $(k, \epsilon) = (\kappa, \text{negl}(\kappa))$ *Strong Seeded extractor, then the construction above is a correct and efficient equivocal commitment scheme (Definition 4.3), and is* $(\text{T}(\cdot), \text{K}(\cdot, \cdot))$-*binding secure (Definition 4.4).*

4.4   Amplification

Lemma 4.7. *If there exists a* $(\text{T}(\cdot), \text{K}(\cdot, \cdot))$-*binding equivocal commitment scheme, then for any polynomial* $p(\cdot)$, *there exists a* $(\text{T}(\cdot), \text{K}(\cdot, \cdot))/p(\kappa))$-*binding equivocal commitment scheme.*

Proof. Let Small.AuxEquiv.Com, Small.AuxEquiv.Decom, Small.AuxEquiv.Equivo$-$cate be a $(\text{T}(\cdot), \text{K}(\cdot))$-binding equivocal commitment scheme. Consider a $p(\cdot)$-parallel repetition of Small.AuxEquiv

AuxEquiv.Com$(1^\kappa, \text{aux}, b) \rightarrow (c, d)$.

  For $i \in [p(\kappa)]$, run $(c_i, d_i) \leftarrow \text{Small.AuxEquiv.Com}(1^\kappa, (\text{aux}, i), b)$. Output $(c = \{c_i\}, d = \{d_i\})$

AuxEquiv.Decom$(\text{aux}, c, d) \rightarrow \{0, 1, \bot\}$

  If $\exists b \in \{0,1\} : \forall i \in [p(\kappa)]$, AuxEquiv.Decom$((\text{aux}, i), c_i, d_i) = b$, output b. Otherwise output $\bot$.

AuxEquiv.Equivocate$(1^\kappa, \text{aux}) \rightarrow (c, d_0, d_1)$

  For $i \in [p(\kappa)]$, run $(c_i, d_{0,i}, d_{1,i}) \leftarrow \text{Small.AuxEquiv.Equivocate}(1^\kappa, (\text{aux}, i))$. Output $(c = \{c_i\}, d_0 = \{d_{0,i}\}, d_1 = \{d_{1,i}\})$

We defer the analysis of this construction to the full version.   □

Corollary 4.8. *Suppose there exists a* $(\mathsf{T}(\cdot), \mathsf{K}(\cdot, \cdot))$ *distinct strong collision resistant hash function satisfying Definition 4.1, for some* $\mathsf{K}(\kappa, |\mathsf{advice}|) = |\mathsf{advice}| \cdot p(\kappa)$ *for some* $p \in \mathsf{poly}(\kappa)$. *Then for every polynomial* $\mathsf{poly}(\cdot)$, *there exists a* $(\mathsf{T}(\cdot), \frac{|\mathsf{advice}|}{\mathsf{poly}(\kappa)})$-*binding equivocal commitment scheme.*

Proof. Fix the polynomial $p(\cdot)$ and the distinct strong collision resistant hash function that is guaranteed by the assumption. By lemma 4.6, there exists a correct and efficienct equivocal commitment that is $(\mathsf{T}(\cdot), p(\kappa) \cdot |\mathsf{advice}|)$-binding. Fix any polynomial $\mathsf{poly}(\kappa)$. Then by invoking lemma 4.7 on the polynomial $\mathsf{poly}(\kappa) \cdot p(\kappa)$, we have that there exists a $(\mathsf{T}(\cdot), \frac{|\mathsf{advice}|}{\mathsf{poly}(\kappa)})$-binding equivocal commitment scheme. □

5   Hinting PRGs with Injective Extension

A hinting pseudorandom generator as introduced by Koppula and Waters [33] is a pseudorandom generator with an enhanced security property. In this security game blocks that are output from the PRG are interspersed with random blocks where the placement is according to the seed of the PRG.

In this section we introduce a variant of Hinting PRGS that we call Hinting PRGs with injective extension. Our variant follows along the lines of the original, but with two critical modifications. The first is that we slightly relax the security game. On a seed s of length n bits, the hinting PRG outputs length $n+1$ blocks each consisting of ℓ bits. Informally, our security guarantee is that the adversary cannot distinguish between the following two distributions, each consisting of $(2n + 1)$ blocks. In both distributions, all blocks but the first are generated identically: these output as a $2 \times n$ matrix where for all $i \in [n]$ the $(s_i, i)^{th}$ entry is set according to the $(i+1)^{th}$ block of the PRG evaluation, while the $(1 - s_i, i)^{th}$ entry is a uniformly random string. In the first distribution, the first ℓ-bit block is set as the first block of the PRG evaluation, and in the second distribution, the first ℓ-bit block is set uniformly at random.

This relaxed security definition differs from the original security definition in which the second distribution consists of all random blocks. It is fairly easy to observe that our relaxed notion also suffices for performing the CCA transformation of [33] and will also suffice for our purposes. The primary reason for relaxing the security definition, is that it makes it easier to realize our second modification.

We additionally define an injective extension for the hinting PRG, where we require that the Hinting PRG evaluation algorithm additionally outputs a separate block that is injective with respect to the seed. To ensure injectivity we will define an algorithm that checks the Hinting PRG public parameters and outputs 0 if the public parameters were sampled so that the extended block might not be an injective function of the seed. That is there could be two seeds that output the same extended block. If the check function outputs 1, the extended block will be an injective function of the seed. The hinting PRG scheme consists of the following algorithms,

$\mathsf{Setup}(1^\kappa, 1^\ell)$: The setup algorithm takes as input the security parameter κ, and length parameter ℓ, and outputs public parameters pp and input length $n = n(\kappa, \ell)$

$\mathsf{Eval}(\mathsf{pp}, s \in \{0,1\}^n, i \in [n] \cup \{0\})$: The evaluation algorithm takes as input the public parameters pp, an n bit string s, an index $i \in [n] \cup \{0\}$ and outputs an ℓ bit string y.

$\mathsf{ExtEval}(\mathsf{pp}, s \in \{0,1\}^n)$: The extended evaluation algorithm takes as input the public parameters pp, an n bit string s and outputs a string of length $m = m(\kappa, \ell)$.

$\mathsf{CheckParams}(\mathsf{pp}, n)$: The algorithm takes as input the public parameters pp, the seed input length n and checks them to see if the function sampled is injective or not. It outputs $\{0, 1\}$ accordingly.

Definition 5.1. *A hinting PRG scheme is said to be non-uniform $T(\cdot)$-secure if for any polynomial $\ell(\cdot)$ and any adversary $\mathcal{A}$ running in time $\mathsf{poly}(T(\kappa))$ and $\mathsf{poly}(\kappa)$ advice, there exists a negligible function $\mathsf{negl}(\cdot)$ such that the following holds:*

$$\left| \Pr\left[\begin{array}{c} \beta \leftarrow \mathcal{A}\left(\mathsf{pp}, \left(r_0^\beta, r_{\mathsf{ext}},\right.\right. \\ \left.\left.\{r_{i,b}\}_{i \in [n], b \in \{0,1\}}\right)\right) \end{array} : \begin{array}{c} (\mathsf{pp}, n) \leftarrow \mathsf{Setup}(1^\kappa, 1^{\ell(\kappa)}), s \leftarrow \{0,1\}^n, \\ r_0^0 = \mathsf{Eval}(\mathsf{pp}, s, 0), r_0^1 \leftarrow \{0,1\}^\ell, \\ r_{\mathsf{ext}} = \mathsf{ExtEval}(\mathsf{pp}, s), \beta \leftarrow \{0,1\}, \\ r_{i,s_i} = \mathsf{Eval}(\mathsf{pp}, s, i), r_{i,\overline{s_i}} \leftarrow \{0,1\}^\ell \; \forall \, i \in [n] \end{array} \right] - \frac{1}{2} \right| \leq \mathsf{negl}(\kappa).$$

Definition 5.2. *A hinting PRG scheme is said to be extended injectively if for any security parameter $\kappa \in \mathbb{N}$, any polynomial $\ell(\cdot)$ and any $\mathsf{pp} \in \{0,1\}^*$ the following holds,*

$$\Pr\left[\begin{array}{c} \exists s_1 \neq s_2 \in \{0,1\}^n, \\ \mathsf{ExtEval}(\mathsf{pp}, s_1) = \mathsf{ExtEval}(\mathsf{pp}, s_2) \end{array} : \begin{array}{c} n \in \mathbb{N} \\ \mathsf{CheckParams}(\mathsf{pp}, n) = 1 \end{array} \right] = 0.$$

Definition 5.3. *A hinting PRG scheme is setup such that it outputs injective parameters if for any security parameter $\kappa \in \mathbb{N}$, any polynomial $\ell(\cdot)$ the following holds,*

$$\Pr\left[\mathsf{CheckParams}(\mathsf{pp}, n) = 0 : (\mathsf{pp}, n) \leftarrow \mathsf{Setup}(1^\kappa, 1^{\ell(\kappa)}) \right] = 0.$$

Definition 5.4. *A hinting PRG scheme is succinct if the length of the seed n, public parameters and injective extension are independent of the block length parameter ℓ.*

Theorem 5.5. *If there exists an injective sub-exponentially secure one way function, either of the three assumptions - DDH, CDH or LWE - are sub-exponentially secure, and there exists a sub-exponentially secure pseudorandom generator, then there exists a hinting PRG scheme that can be extended injectively, outputs injective parameters, is succinct and for some constant $\delta \in (0,1)$, satisfies non-uniform 2^{κ^δ}-security.*

We defer the construction and its analysis to the full version.

6   Tag Amplification

We discuss how to amplify a non-uniform subexponentially secure CCA scheme for $N' = 4N$ tags to a scheme with 2^N tags. We will perform the amplification using non uniform subexponentially secure primitives AuxEquiv (Sect. 4), extended hinting PRG (Sect. 5). The amplification algorithm runs in time polynomial in N and the runtime of the primitives involved, thus N should always stay polynomial in the security parameter for the amplification to be an efficient algorithm.

Let the hinting PRG scheme (Setup, Eval, ExtEval, CheckParams) be a succinct $T = 2^{\kappa^\gamma}$ secure for some constant $\gamma \in (0,1)$. Let AuxEquiv be $T = 2^{\kappa^\delta}$-binding secure and statistically hiding where $\delta \in (0,1)$. Let (Small.Com, Small.Val, Small.Recover) be a 2^{κ^c}-subexponentially secure, weak binding, 2^{κ^v}-efficient CCA commitment scheme for $N'(\kappa) = N' = 4N$ tags where $c < 1$ and $v \geq 1$ for message length $u(\kappa)^6$. We will assume tags take identities of the form $(i, \beta, \Gamma) \in [N] \times \{0,1\} \times \{0,1\}$ and that the Small.Com algorithm take in random coins of length $\ell(\kappa)$.

Let m be the message input to the commitment algorithm and length be denoted by $|m|$. Let $n' = n'(\kappa)$ be the length of the seed plus public parameters plus injective extension of the hinting PRG scheme when invoked on security parameter $\kappa'' = \kappa^{\frac{v}{\delta \gamma}}$. Since the scheme is succinct, n' is a function of only κ'' (and hence κ) and not the block length, which we will specify later. By Lemma 4.7, we will use a $(2^{\kappa^\delta}, \frac{|\text{advice}|}{2 \cdot n'})$-binding secure commitment scheme AuxEquiv, and let $|y|$ refer to the length of the decommitment strings of said scheme. Finally, we run Small.Com on messages of size $|y|$, and let ℓ be the size of randomness used by Small.Com on said input size. We set the block size of our hinting PRG scheme to be the maximum of $|m|, N \cdot \ell$. For ease of notation we assume that HPRG.Eval(pp, s, 0) $\in \{0,1\}^{|m|}$ and $\forall i \in [n]$, HPRG.Eval(pp, s, i) $\in \{0,1\}^{\ell \cdot N}$, i.e. we ignore any extra bits output by the HPRG.Eval algorithm. Let $\Theta(\kappa^{\tilde{v}})$ denote the length of the seed n in relation to the security parameter.

Our transformation will produce three algorithms, (CCA.Com, CCA.Val, CCA.Recover) which we prove non-uniform 2^{κ^c}-subexponentially secure and $2^{\kappa^{v'}}$-efficient where $v' = \frac{v \cdot \tilde{v}}{\delta \cdot \gamma}$. The construction will call AuxEquiv on security param-

---

[6] Recall from Definition 3.3 that a 2^{κ^v}-efficient scheme with $v \geq 1$ implies that the runtime of Small.Val is polynomial in 2^{κ^v}.

eter $\kappa' = \kappa^{\frac{v}{\delta}}$, HPRG on security parameter $\kappa'' = \kappa^{\frac{v}{\delta \cdot \gamma}}$ and Small on security parameter κ.

The different parameters will help us perform complexity leveraging. For simplicity, we assume that the message space of Small, $u(\kappa)$ is equal to the length of the decommitment string of the equivocal commitment called on κ'. We will ensure this property is satisfied in Sect. 7 when we recursively amplify the tags. The CCA.Val procedure in our transformation will be an inefficient algorithm that brute forces through each hinting PRG seed and run in time 2^n where $n = \Theta(\kappa''^{\tilde{v}})$. Thus our transformation will increase the runtime of CCA.Val from Small.Val that runs in time 2^{κ^v} to $2^{\kappa^{v'}}$.

Additionally, we will also present a fourth non-uniform algorithm CCA.ValAlt, which is only used in the proof and depends on the non-uniform advice it gets. In our proof we will first change how we answer an adversary's decommitment queries by using CCA.ValAlt to answer instead of CCA.Val. Since the queries made to the CCA.Val oracles differ in at least one position from tag*, CCA.ValAlt will crucially rely on the security of Small.Com at this position by making calls to Small.Val to help in decommitment.

CCA.ValAlt(tag*, com, $\mathcal{L}$) $\to m \cup \bot$ is a deterministic inefficient algorithm that takes in tag*, a commitment com and a non-uniform advice list $\mathcal{L}$ and outputs either a message $m \in \{0,1\}^w$ or a reject symbol $\bot$. It will be used solely as an instrument in proving the scheme secure and not exported as part of the interface. Figures 1, 2 and 3 describe algorithms that are exposed and repeated in the construction and proof.

CCA.FindSeed(aux)

Inputs: String aux = (HPRG.pp, aux$'$)   **Output:** $\tilde{s} \in \{0,1\}^n \cup \bot$

- Parse aux as (HPRG.pp, aux$'$)
- Iterate through all $\tilde{s} \in \{0,1\}^n$
  - If aux$'$ = HPRG.ExtEval(HPRG.pp, $\tilde{s}$), return s.
- Return $\bot$

Fig. 1. Routine CCA.FindSeed

We now describe our transformation.

Transformation   Amplify(Small   =   (Small.Com, Small.Val, Small.Recover), HPRG, AuxEquiv, $w(\kappa), v'$) $\to$ NM = (CCA.Com, CCA.Val, CCA.Recover) :

CCA.Com(1^κ, tag, $m \in \{0,1\}^{w(\kappa)}; r$) $\to$ com
   1. Compute $\kappa' = \kappa^{\frac{v}{\delta}}$. Compute $\kappa'' = \kappa'^{\frac{1}{\gamma}}$.[7]

---

[7] The variables δ and γ are known from the security guarantees of AuxEquiv, HPRG respectively.

CCA.Check($\tilde{s}$, ,)

Inputs: Seed candidate $\tilde{s} = \tilde{s}_1, \tilde{s}_2, \ldots, \tilde{s}_n$

Commitment $, = \left(\text{tag}, \text{aux}, c, (\sigma_i, (c_{x,i,0}, c_{x,i,1})_{x \in [N]})_{i \in [n]}\right)$

Output: $\{0, 1\}$

- For $i \in [n]$
  1. Compute $(r_{1,i}, r_{2,i}, \ldots, r_{N,i}) = \text{HPRG.Eval}(\text{HPRG.pp}, \tilde{s}, i)$
  2. For $x \in [N]$
     (a) Let $\tilde{y}_i = \text{Small.Recover}(c_{x,i,\tilde{s}_i}, r_{x,i})$. If $\tilde{y}_i = \bot$, output 0.
     (b) If $c_{x,i,\tilde{s}_i} \neq \text{Small.Com}(1^\kappa, (x, \text{tag}_x, \tilde{s}_i), \tilde{y}_i; r_{x,i})$, output 0.
     (c) If $\tilde{s}_i \neq \text{AuxEquiv.Decom}(\text{aux}, \sigma_i, \tilde{y}_i)$, output 0.
- Parse aux as $(\text{HPRG.pp}, \text{aux}')$.
- If $\text{HPRG.CheckParams}(\text{HPRG.pp}, n) = 0$, output 0.
- If $\text{aux}' \neq \text{HPRG.ExtEval}(\text{HPRG.pp}, s)$ output 0.
- If all the above checks have passed, output 1.

Fig. 2. Routine CCA.Check

CCA.FindAlt(x', , , $\mathcal{L}$)

Inputs: Index $x' \in [N]$

Commitment $, = \left(\text{tag}, \text{aux}, c, (\sigma_i, (c_{x,i,0}, c_{x,i,1})_{x \in [N]})_{i \in [n]}\right)$

Polynomial Size Non-Uniform Advice List $\mathcal{L}$

Output: $\tilde{s} \in \{0, 1\}^n$

- If for some $\tilde{s} \in \{0, 1\}^n$, $(, .\text{aux}, \tilde{s}) \in \mathcal{L}$, where $\tilde{s}$ is the seed recorded from the advice. Output $\tilde{s}$.
- Else if $, .\text{aux}$ is not recorded in $\mathcal{L}$,
  - For each $i \in [n]$
    1. Let $\tilde{y}_i = \text{Small.Val}(c_{x',i,0})$
    2. Set $\tilde{z}_i = \text{AuxEquiv.Decom}(\text{aux}, \sigma_i, \tilde{y}_i)$. If $\tilde{z}_i = \bot$, set $\tilde{s}_i = 1$. Else, set $\tilde{s}_i = \tilde{z}_i$.
  - Output $\tilde{s} = \tilde{s}_1, \tilde{s}_2, \ldots, \tilde{s}_n$.

Fig. 3. Routine CCA.FindAlt

---

2. Sample $(\text{HPRG.pp}, n) \leftarrow \text{HPRG.Setup}(1^{\kappa''}, 1^{\max(|m|, N \cdot \ell)})$.
3. Sample $s = s_1 \ldots s_n \xleftarrow{R} \{0, 1\}^n$ as the seed of the extended hinting PRG.
4. Set $\text{aux} = (\text{HPRG.pp}, \text{HPRG.ExtEval}(\text{HPRG.pp}, s))$.
5. For all $i \in [n]$ run $\text{AuxEquiv.Com}(1^\kappa, \text{aux}, s_i) \rightarrow (\sigma_i, y_i)$.
6. Let for $x \in [N], i \in [n], r_{x,i}, \tilde{r}_{x,i} \in \{0, 1\}^\ell$ be defined as follows:
7. For $i \in [n]$
   (a) Compute $(r_{1,i}, r_{2,i}, \ldots, r_{N,i}) = \text{HPRG.Eval}(\text{HPRG.pp}, s, i)$

(b) Sample $(\tilde{r}_{1,i}, \tilde{r}_{2,i}, \ldots, \tilde{r}_{N,i}) \xleftarrow{R} \{0,1\}^{N \cdot \ell}$

8. Compute $c = m \oplus \mathsf{HPRG.Eval}(\mathsf{HPRG.pp}, s, 0)$

9. For $i \in [n]$, $x \in [N]$
   (a) If $s_i = 0$
      i. $c_{x,i,0} = \mathsf{Small.Com}(1^\kappa, (x, \mathsf{tag}_x, 0), \mathsf{msg} = y_i; r_{x,i})$
      ii. $c_{x,i,1} = \mathsf{Small.Com}(1^\kappa, (x, \mathsf{tag}_x, 1), \mathsf{msg} = y_i; \tilde{r}_{x,i})$
   (b) If $s_i = 1$
      i. $c_{x,i,0} = \mathsf{Small.Com}(1^\kappa, (x, \mathsf{tag}_x, 0), \mathsf{msg} = y_i; \tilde{r}_{x,i})$
      ii. $c_{x,i,1} = \mathsf{Small.Com}(1^\kappa, (x, \mathsf{tag}_x, 1), \mathsf{msg} = y_i; r_{x,i})$

10. Output $\mathsf{com} = \left(\mathsf{tag}, \mathsf{aux}, c, (\sigma_i, (c_{x,i,0}, c_{x,i,1})_{x \in [N]})_{i \in [n]}) \right)$ as the commitment. All of the randomness is used as the decommitment string.

$\mathsf{CCA.Val}(\mathsf{com}) \to m \cup \perp$
   1. Set $\tilde{s} = \mathsf{CCA.FindSeed}(\mathsf{com.aux})$.
   2. If $\mathsf{CCA.Check}(\tilde{s}, \mathsf{com}) = 0$ output $\perp$.
   3. Output $c \oplus \mathsf{HPRG.Eval}(\mathsf{HPRG.pp}, \tilde{s}, 0)$.

$\mathsf{CCA.ValAlt}(\mathsf{tag}^*, \mathsf{com}, \mathcal{L}) \to m \cup \perp$
   1. If $\mathsf{com.tag} = \mathsf{tag}^*$, output $\perp$.
   2. Let x^* be the smallest index where the bits of $\mathsf{tag}^*, \mathsf{com.tag}$ differ.
   3. Set $\tilde{s} = \mathsf{CCA.FindAlt}(x^*, \mathsf{com}, \mathcal{L})$.
   4. If $\mathsf{CCA.Check}(\tilde{s}, \mathsf{com}) = 0$ output $\perp$.
   5. Output $c \oplus \mathsf{HPRG.Eval}(\mathsf{HPRG.pp}, \tilde{s}, 0)$.

$\mathsf{CCA.Recover}(\mathsf{com}, r) \to m \cup \perp$
   1. From r, parse the seed s of the Hinting PRG.
   2. If $\mathsf{CCA.Check}(s, \mathsf{com}) = 0$, output $\perp$.
   3. From com, parse the commitment component c and the public parameter $\mathsf{HPRG.pp}$.
   4. Output $c \oplus \mathsf{HPRG.Eval}(\mathsf{HPRG.pp}, s, 0)$.

7 Compilation of Transformations

We show how to combine our transformations Amplify and OneToMany to prove that if we start with a base scheme that is secure against non-uniform "same tag" adversaries (see Definition 3.7) for $32 \cdot \mathsf{ilog}(q, \kappa)$ tags where the notation $\mathsf{ilog}(q, \kappa)$ denotes $\underbrace{\lg \lg \cdots \lg(\kappa)^8}_{q \text{ times}}$ and q is some constant, then using our described transformations, we can construct a scheme that is secure against non-uniform adversaries (see Definition 3.6) for $16 \cdot 2^\kappa$ tags.

Our sequence of transformations is very similar to [19], where we start with a base scheme BaseCCA that satisfies property Definition 3.8. We then remove the same tag restriction on the adversary by using the transformation OneToMany (described in the full version) and then amplify the tag space by using the transformation Amplify in Sect. 6 $q + 1$ times. The two main deviations from the formal treatment of [19] is due to our proof technique, i.e. we need to keep track

---

[8] The notation $\mathsf{ilog}(0, \kappa)$ is defined as κ.

of the message and efficiency of the val oracle when we perform the sequence of transformations.

We remind the reader that the order of the sequence of transformations is important as to perform Amplify and OneToMany we need the commitment scheme to be recoverable from randomness. Additionally, OneToMany does computation that is polynomial in the number of tags for the input scheme. Thus, we must remove the "same tag" restriction from our adversary before amplifying our tags with Amplify. Based on the sequence of transformations we have discussed, our tag space will amplify as follows. At the end of OneToMany, we will end up with $16 \cdot \mathsf{ilog}(q, \kappa)$ sized tag space. And after $q + 1$ applications of Amplify, we will end up with $16 \cdot 2^\kappa$ sized tag space. One application of Amplify converts a $4N$ tag space scheme to a 2^N tag space scheme. Thus on input a $4 \cdot 4 \cdot \mathsf{ilog}(q, \kappa)$ tag space, one gets a $2^{4 \cdot \mathsf{ilog}(q,\kappa)} = 16 \cdot \mathsf{ilog}(q - 1, \kappa)$ tag space.

Additionally, when using the schemes in a sequence of transformations we need to keep track of the message spaces we chose in our output scheme. For instance, to perform the transformation Amplify and OneToMany, the constructions output committment σ to each seed bit of the hinting PRG. The base scheme here takes in the decommitment string of σ as input. Thus the length of the base scheme being transformed should be able to support messages of this length for the transformation to be correct. Let the length of the decommitment string be denoted by a polynomial function $\mathsf{DecomLen}(\cdot)$ that takes as input the security parameter κ[9]. Thus for the transformations Amplify and OneToMany, u (input message length of the base scheme) should be equal to $\mathsf{DecomLen}(\kappa')$ where κ' is the security parameter input to the equivocal commitment. In our transformations κ' is set as $\kappa^{\frac{v}{\delta}}$ where there exists a constant δ such that the setupless equivocal commitment scheme is 2^{κ^δ}-hiding secure and the base scheme is 2^{κ^v}-efficient[10].

Our formal transformation is below. We start with a base commitment scheme BaseCCA and output the scheme $(\mathsf{AmplifiedCCA}^{q+1}.\mathsf{Com}, \mathsf{AmplifiedCCA}^{q+1}.\mathsf{Val})$. We list a few assumptions on our transformation -

- Let there exist variables $\delta, \gamma, \tilde{v}$ such that $\delta \in (0, 1)$ and the setupless equivocal commitment scheme is 2^{κ^δ}-hiding secure, $\gamma \in (0, 1)$ and the hinting PRG with injective extension is 2^{κ^γ}-secure and the dependence of seed on the security parameter be such that seed length $n = \Theta(\kappa^{\tilde{v}})$.
- We start with a base scheme that is 2^κ-efficient and secure against non-uniform "same tag" 2^{κ^c}-subexponentially secure adversaries for tag space $32\mathsf{ilog}(q, \kappa)$ tags for any constant q.
  If the base scheme runs in time some constant $\mathsf{poly}(2^{\kappa^a})$ where $a \in (0, 1)$ then the scheme is 2^κ-efficient. Otherwise, on input security parameter κ, we can

---

[9] The length of the decommitment string can depend on aux, but since aux is also called with a polynomial function in κ based on the hinting PRG construction, we simplify the notation. In our specific construction for AuxEquiv in Sect. 4, the decommitment string length doesn't depend on aux.

[10] Recall from Definition 3.3 that a 2^{κ^v}-efficient scheme with $v \geq 1$ implies that the runtime of Small.Val is polynomial in 2^{κ^v}.

run the scheme with parameters $\kappa^{\frac{1}{a}}$ to get a 2^{κ}-efficent scheme that is still 2^{κ^c} sub-exponentially secure with $c \in (0,1)$ for some constant c. Thus we can wlog claim that we start with a 2^{κ}-efficient scheme. This will help simplify notation.

– Let the base scheme support messages of length $u = \mathsf{AuxEquiv.DecomLen}(\kappa^{\frac{1}{\delta}})$ and the final scheme support messages of length w.

Recall that the transformations OneToMany (see full version) and Amplify (Sect. 6) take in the following parameters - a scheme to be transformed, hinting PRG with injective extension HPRG, setupless equivocal commitment scheme AuxEquiv, the length of the messages supported by the output scheme and an efficiency parameter v such that the output scheme is 2^{κ^v}-efficient.

$\mathsf{CompiledAmplify(BaseCCA}$ =
$\quad$ (BaseCCA.Com, BaseCCA.Val, u), HPRG, AuxEquiv, w)
$\quad$ 1. $\mathsf{AmplifiedCCA}^0 \leftarrow$
$\qquad$ OneToMany(BaseCCA, HPRG, AuxEquiv, $\mathsf{AuxEquiv.DecomLen}(\kappa^{\frac{v_0}{\delta}}), v_0$)
$\qquad$ where $v_0 = \frac{\tilde{v}}{\delta \cdot \gamma}$.
$\quad$ 2. For $i \in [q]$,
$\qquad$ (a) $\mathsf{AmplifiedCCA}^i \leftarrow \mathsf{Amplify}(\mathsf{AmplifiedCCA}^{i-1}, \mathsf{HPRG},$
$\qquad\qquad$ AuxEquiv, $\mathsf{AuxEquiv.DecomLen}(\kappa^{\frac{v_i}{\delta}}), v_i$) where $v_i = \left(\frac{\tilde{v}}{\delta \cdot \gamma}\right)^{i+1}$.
$\quad$ 3. $\mathsf{AmplifiedCCA}^{q+1} \leftarrow \mathsf{Amplify}(\mathsf{AmplifiedCCA}^q, \mathsf{HPRG}, \mathsf{AuxEquiv}, w, v_{q+1})$
$\qquad$ where $v_{q+1} = \left(\frac{\tilde{v}}{\delta \cdot \gamma}\right)^{q+2}$.
$\quad$ 4. Output $(\mathsf{AmplifiedCCA}^{q+1}.\mathsf{Com}, \mathsf{AmplifiedCCA}^{q+1}.\mathsf{Val})$

Below we analyze CompiledAmplify by stating theorems on correctness, efficiency and security.

Theorem 7.1. *For every* $\kappa \in \mathbb{N}$, *any constant* q, *any polynomial* w, *let* BaseCCA = (BaseCCA.Com, BaseCCA.Val, u) *be a perfectly correct CCA commitment scheme for message space* $\{0,1\}^u$ *by Definition 3.2 with tag space* $32 \cdot \mathsf{ilog}(q, \kappa)$. *Let* AuxEquiv = (AuxEquiv.Com, AuxEquiv.Decom, AuxEquiv.Equivocate) *be a perfectly correct equivocal commitment scheme by Definition 4.2. Let there exist a constant* δ *such that* $u = \mathsf{AuxEquiv.DecomLen}(\kappa^{\frac{1}{\delta}})$.
$\quad$ *Then, we have that the scheme* CompiledAmplify(BaseCCA, HPRG, AuxEquiv, w) *is a perfectly correct CCA commitment scheme for* $16 \cdot 2^{\kappa}$ *tags.*

Theorem 7.2. *For every* $\kappa \in \mathbb{N}$, *any constant* q, *any polynomial* w, *let* BaseCCA = (BaseCCA.Com, BaseCCA.Val, u) *be an* 2^{κ}-*efficient CCA commitment scheme by Definition 3.3 with tag space* $32 \cdot \mathsf{ilog}(q, \kappa)$. *Let* AuxEquiv = (Equiv.Com, Equiv.Decom, Equiv.Equivocate) *be an efficient equivocal commitment scheme by Definition 4.3. Let there exist constants* $\delta, \gamma, \tilde{v}$ *such that setupless equivocal commitment scheme is* $2^{\kappa^{\delta}}$-*hiding secure and* $u = \mathsf{AuxEquiv.DecomLen}(\kappa^{\frac{1}{\delta}}); \gamma \in (0,1)$ *and the hinting PRG with injective extension is* $2^{\kappa^{\gamma}}$-*secure; the dependence of seed on the security parameter be such that* $n = \Theta(\kappa^{\tilde{v}})$.

Then, CompiledAmplify(BaseCCA, HPRG, AuxEquiv, w) *is an* $2^{\kappa^v_{q+1}}$*-efficient CCA commitment scheme for* $16 \cdot 2^\kappa$ *tags where* $v_{q+1} = \left(\frac{\tilde{v}}{\delta \cdot \gamma}\right)^{q+2}$.

Theorem 7.3. *For every* $\kappa \in \mathbb{N}$*, any constant* q*, any polynomial* w*, let* BaseCCA = (BaseCCA.Com, BaseCCA.Val, u) *be a CCA commitment scheme that is hiding against non-uniform "same tag"* 2^{κ^c}*-subexponential adversaries according to Definition 3.7 for tag space* $32 \cdot \text{ilog}(q, \kappa)$*. HPRG =* (HPRG.Setup, HPRG.Eval) *be a hinting PRG scheme with injective extension that is* $T = 2^{\kappa^\gamma}$ *secure by Definition 5.1 for* $\gamma \in (0, 1)$*. AuxEquiv =* (AuxEquiv.Com, AuxEquiv.Decom, AuxEquiv.Equivocate) *be an equivocal commitment without setup scheme that is* $T = 2^{\kappa^\delta}$ *binding secure Definition 4.4 and statistically hiding for some constant* $\delta \in (0, 1)$*. Let* u *be equal to* AuxEquiv.DecomLen($\kappa^{\frac{1}{\delta}}$)*.*

Then, CompiledAmplify(BaseCCA, HPRG, AuxEquiv, w) *is a CCA commitment scheme that is hiding against non-uniform* 2^{κ^c}*-subexponential adversaries according to Definition 3.6 for tag space* $16 \cdot 2^\kappa$*.*

We import the following theorems about instantiating base schemes, from prior work.

Theorem 7.4. [29]. *For every constant* $c > 0$*, there exist correct, polynomially efficient, binding (3.4), same-tag CCA secure commitments with randomness recovery satisfying Definition 3.7 against non-uniform adversaries, with tag space* ($c \lg \lg \lg \kappa$)*, message space* $u = \text{poly}(\kappa)$ *that make black-box use of subexponential quantum hard non-interactive commitments and subexponential classically hard non-interactive commitments in* BQP*, both with randomness recovery.*

Theorem 7.5. [36]. *For every constant* $c > 0$*, there exist correct, polynomially efficient, weak binding (3.5), same-tag CCA secure commitments with randomness recovery satisfying same-tag CCA security according to Definition 3.7 against non-uniform adversaries, with tag space* ($c \lg \lg \lg \kappa$)*, that make black-box use of subexponential time-lock puzzles [36].*

We remark that while [29,36] prove that their constructions satisfy non-malleability with respect to commitment, their proof techniques also extend to exhibit same-tag CCA security against non-uniform adversaries. In a nutshell, both these works rely on two simultaneous axes of hardness to build their base schemes. As a consequence of this in the same-tag setting, for any pair of tags (tag, $\widetilde{\text{tag}}$) corresponding to the challenge query and CCA oracle queries of the adversary respectively, there is an oracle that inverts all commitments generated under $\widetilde{\text{tag}}$ but where commitments under tag remain secure in the presence of this oracle. In both these works [29,36], we note that while the specific oracle is only used to invert parallel queries of the adversary (thereby obtaining many-many non-malleability), the oracle is actually capable of inverting (unbounded) polynomially many *adaptive* queries, thereby also achieving same-tag CCA security. In [36], this oracle over-extracts, therefore achieving the weaker property of same-tag CCA security with weak binding. The [29] scheme does not suffer from over-extraction and achieves the stronger notion of (standard) binding. The [29] scheme can be observed to satisfy randomness recovery by relying on the recovery algorithm of the underlying commitments. The [36] scheme outputs a commitment to a bit b as

$$f(s;r), r', \langle s, r' \rangle \oplus b$$

which satisfies randomness recovery given all the randomness used to commit.

Combining this theorem with Theorem 7.3, we obtain the following corollaries.

Corollary 7.6. *There exists a perfectly correct, polynomially efficient, binding (Definition 3.4) and CCA secure commitment satisfying Definition 3.6 against non-uniform adversaries, with tag space 2^κ for security parameter κ, that makes black-box use of subexponential quantum hard one-way functions, subexponential classically hard one-way functions in* BQP, *subexponential hinting PRGs and subexponential keyless collision-resistant hash functions.*

Corollary 7.7. *There exists a perfectly correct, polynomially efficient, binding (Definition 3.4) and CCA secure commitment satisfying Definition 3.6 against non-uniform adversaries, with tag space 2^κ for security parameter κ, that makes black-box use of subexponential time-lock puzzles as used in [36], subexponential hinting PRGs and subexponential keyless collision-resistant hash functions.*

Finally, we point out that while all our formal theorems discuss CCA security, our transformations also apply as is to the case of amplifying parallel CCA security (equivalently, concurrent non-malleability w.r.t. commitment). That is, given a base scheme that is only same-tag parallel CCA secure (or non-malleable w.r.t. commitment) for small tags, our transformations yield a scheme for all tags that is parallel CCA secure (or concurrent non-malleable w.r.t. commitment) for tags in 2^κ, without the same tag restriction.

Acknowledgments. We thank Daniel Wichs for a useful discussion about the construction of our new Hinting PRGs, anonymous reviewers for helpful feedback on a preliminary version of this work, and Nir Bitansky and Rachel Lin for answering our questions about keyless collision-resistant hash functions.

D. Khurana was supported in part by NSF CNS - 2238718, DARPA SIEVE and a gift from Visa Research. This material is based upon work supported by the Defense Advanced Research Projects Agency through Award HR00112020024. Brent Waters was supported by NSF CNS-1908611, Simons Investigator award and Packard Foundation Fellowship.

References

1. Ananth, P., Choudhuri, A.R., Jain, A.: A new approach to round-optimal secure multiparty computation. In: Katz, J., Shacham, H. (eds.) CRYPTO 2017. LNCS, vol. 10401, pp. 468–499. Springer, Cham (2017). https://doi.org/10.1007/978-3-319-63688-7_16

2. Badrinarayanan, S., Goyal, V., Jain, A., Kalai, Y.T., Khurana, D., Sahai, A.: Promise zero knowledge and its applications to round optimal MPC. In: Shacham, H., Boldyreva, A. (eds.) CRYPTO 2018. LNCS, vol. 10992, pp. 459–487. Springer, Cham (2018). https://doi.org/10.1007/978-3-319-96881-0_16

3. Badrinarayanan, S., Goyal, V., Jain, A., Khurana, D., Sahai, A.: Round optimal concurrent MPC via strong simulation. In: Kalai, Y., Reyzin, L. (eds.) TCC 2017. LNCS, vol. 10677, pp. 743–775. Springer, Cham (2017). https://doi.org/10.1007/978-3-319-70500-2_25

4. Barak, B.: Constant-round coin-tossing with a man in the middle or realizing the shared random string model. In: FOCS (2002)

5. Barak, B., Ong, S.J., Vadhan, S.P.: Derandomization in cryptography. SIAM J. Comput. **37**, 380–400 (2007)

6. Benhamouda, F., Lin, H.: k-round multiparty computation from k-round oblivious transfer via garbled interactive circuits. In: Nielsen, J.B., Rijmen, V. (eds.) EUROCRYPT 2018. LNCS, vol. 10821, pp. 500–532. Springer, Cham (2018). https://doi.org/10.1007/978-3-319-78375-8_17

7. Bitansky, N., Kalai, Y.T., Paneth, O.: Multi-collision resistance: a paradigm for keyless hash functions. In: STOC (2018)

8. Bitansky, N., Lin, H.: One-message zero knowledge and non-malleable commitments. In: Beimel, A., Dziembowski, S. (eds.) TCC 2018. LNCS, vol. 11239, pp. 209–234. Springer, Cham (2018). https://doi.org/10.1007/978-3-030-03807-6_8

9. Bitansky, N., Paneth, O.: ZAPs and non-interactive witness indistinguishability from indistinguishability obfuscation. In: Dodis, Y., Nielsen, J.B. (eds.) TCC 2015. LNCS, vol. 9015, pp. 401–427. Springer, Heidelberg (2015). https://doi.org/10.1007/978-3-662-46497-7_16

10. Brakerski, Z., Halevi, S., Polychroniadou, A.: Four round secure computation without setup. In: Kalai, Y., Reyzin, L. (eds.) TCC 2017. LNCS, vol. 10677, pp. 645–677. Springer, Cham (2017). https://doi.org/10.1007/978-3-319-70500-2_22

11. Broadnax, B., Fetzer, V., Müller-Quade, J., Rupp, A.: Non-malleability vs. cca-security: the case of commitments. In: IACR International Workshop on Public Key Cryptography (2018)

12. Canetti, R., Lin, H., Pass, R.: Adaptive hardness and composable security in the plain model from standard assumptions. In: FOCS (2010)

13. Choudhuri, A.R., Ciampi, M., Goyal, V., Jain, A., Ostrovsky, R.: Round optimal secure multiparty computation from minimal assumptions. Cryptology ePrint Archive, Report 2019/216 (2019)

14. Ciampi, M., Ostrovsky, R., Siniscalchi, L., Visconti, I.: Concurrent non-malleable commitments (and more) in 3 rounds. In: Robshaw, M., Katz, J. (eds.) CRYPTO 2016. LNCS, vol. 9816, pp. 270–299. Springer, Heidelberg (2016). https://doi.org/10.1007/978-3-662-53015-3_10

15. Ciampi, M., Ostrovsky, R., Siniscalchi, L., Visconti, I.: Four-round concurrent non-malleable commitments from one-way functions. In: Katz, J., Shacham, H. (eds.) CRYPTO 2017. LNCS, vol. 10402, pp. 127–157. Springer, Cham (2017). https://doi.org/10.1007/978-3-319-63715-0_5

16. Crescenzo, G.D., Ishai, Y., Ostrovsky, R.: Non-interactive and non-malleable commitment. In: Vitter, J.S. (ed.) STOC (1998)

17. Damgård, I.B., Pedersen, T.P., Pfitzmann, B.: On the existence of statistically hiding bit commitment schemes and fail-stop signatures. In: Stinson, D.R. (ed.) CRYPTO 1993. LNCS, vol. 773, pp. 250–265. Springer, Heidelberg (1994). https://doi.org/10.1007/3-540-48329-2_22

18. Dolev, D., Dwork, C., Naor, M.: Non-malleable cryptography (extended abstract). In: STOC (1991)
19. Garg, R., Khurana, D., Lu, G., Waters, B.: Black-box non-interactive non-malleable commitments. In: Canteaut, A., Standaert, F.-X. (eds.) EUROCRYPT 2021. LNCS, vol. 12698, pp. 159–185. Springer, Cham (2021). https://doi.org/10.1007/978-3-030-77883-5_6
20. Goyal, R., Vusirikala, S., Waters, B.: New constructions of hinting prgs, owfs with encryption, and more. IACR Cryptology ePrint Archive (2019)
21. Goyal, V.: Constant round non-malleable protocols using one-way functions. In: STOC (2011)
22. Goyal, V., Lee, C.K., Ostrovsky, R., Visconti, I.: Constructing non-malleable commitments: a black-box approach. In: FOCS (2012)
23. Goyal, V., Pandey, O., Richelson, S.: Textbook non-malleable commitments. In: STOC (2016)
24. Goyal, V., Richelson, S.: Non-malleable commitments using goldreich-levin list decoding. In: FOCS (2019)
25. Goyal, V., Richelson, S., Rosen, A., Vald, M.: An algebraic approach to non-malleability. In: FOCS (2014)
26. Groth, J., Ostrovsky, R., Sahai, A.: New techniques for noninteractive zero-knowledge. J. ACM **59**, 1–35 (2012)
27. Halevi, S., Hazay, C., Polychroniadou, A., Venkitasubramaniam, M.: Round-optimal secure multi-party computation. J. Cryptol. **34**(3), 1–63 (2021). https://doi.org/10.1007/s00145-021-09382-3
28. Halevi, S., Micali, S.: Practical and provably-secure commitment schemes from collision-free hashing. In: Koblitz, N. (ed.) CRYPTO 1996. LNCS, vol. 1109, pp. 201–215. Springer, Heidelberg (1996). https://doi.org/10.1007/3-540-68697-5_16
29. Kalai, Y.T., Khurana, D.: Non-interactive non-malleability from quantum supremacy. In: Boldyreva, A., Micciancio, D. (eds.) CRYPTO 2019. LNCS, vol. 11694, pp. 552–582. Springer, Cham (2019). https://doi.org/10.1007/978-3-030-26954-8_18
30. Khurana, D.: Round optimal concurrent non-malleability from polynomial hardness. In: Kalai, Y., Reyzin, L. (eds.) TCC 2017. LNCS, vol. 10678, pp. 139–171. Springer, Cham (2017). https://doi.org/10.1007/978-3-319-70503-3_5
31. Khurana, D.: Non-interactive distributional indistinguishability (NIDI) and non-malleable commitments. In: Canteaut, A., Standaert, F.-X. (eds.) EUROCRYPT 2021. LNCS, vol. 12698, pp. 186–215. Springer, Cham (2021). https://doi.org/10.1007/978-3-030-77883-5_7
32. Khurana, D., Sahai, A.: How to achieve non-malleability in one or two rounds. In: FOCS (2017)
33. Koppula, V., Waters, B.: Realizing chosen ciphertext security generically in attribute-based encryption and predicate encryption. In: Boldyreva, A., Micciancio, D. (eds.) CRYPTO 2019. LNCS, vol. 11693, pp. 671–700. Springer, Cham (2019). https://doi.org/10.1007/978-3-030-26951-7_23
34. Lin, H., Pass, R.: Non-malleability Amplification. In: STOC (2009)
35. Lin, H., Pass, R.: Constant-round Non-malleable Commitments from Any One-way Function. In: STOC (2011)
36. Lin, H., Pass, R., Soni, P.: Two-round and non-interactive concurrent non-malleable commitments from time-lock puzzles. In: FOCS (2017)

37. Lin, H., Pass, R., Venkitasubramaniam, M.: Concurrent non-malleable commitments from any one-way function. In: Canetti, R. (ed.) TCC 2008. LNCS, vol. 4948, pp. 571–588. Springer, Heidelberg (2008). https://doi.org/10.1007/978-3-540-78524-8_31

38. Pandey, O., Pass, R., Vaikuntanathan, V.: Adaptive one-way functions and applications. In: Wagner, D. (ed.) CRYPTO 2008. LNCS, vol. 5157, pp. 57–74. Springer, Heidelberg (2008). https://doi.org/10.1007/978-3-540-85174-5_4

39. Pass, R.: Unprovable security of perfect NIZK and non-interactive non-malleable commitments. Comput. Complex. **25**(3), 607–666 (2016). https://doi.org/10.1007/s00037-016-0122-2

40. Pass, R., Rosen, A.: Concurrent non-malleable commitments. In: FOCS (2005)

41. Pass, R., Rosen, A.: New and improved constructions of nonmalleable cryptographic protocols. SIAM J. Comput. (2008)

42. Pass, R., Wee, H.: Constant-round non-malleable commitments from subexponential one-way functions. In: Gilbert, H. (ed.) EUROCRYPT 2010. LNCS, vol. 6110, pp. 638–655. Springer, Heidelberg (2010). https://doi.org/10.1007/978-3-642-13190-5_32

43. Unruh, D.: Random oracles and auxiliary input. In: Menezes, A. (ed.) CRYPTO 2007. LNCS, vol. 4622, pp. 205–223. Springer, Heidelberg (2007). https://doi.org/10.1007/978-3-540-74143-5_12

44. Wee, H.: Black-box, round-efficient secure computation via non-malleability amplification. In: FOCS (2010)

Polynomial-Time Cryptanalysis of the Subspace Flooding Assumption for Post-quantum $i\mathcal{O}$

Aayush Jain[1], Huijia Lin[2], Paul Lou[3(✉)], and Amit Sahai[3]

[1] Carnegie Mellon University, Pittsburgh, USA
aayushja@andrew.cmu.edu
[2] University of Washington, Seattle, USA
rachel@cs.washington.edu
[3] UCLA, Los Angeles, USA
{pslou,sahai}@cs.ucla.edu

Abstract. Indistinguishability Obfuscation ($i\mathcal{O}$) is a highly versatile primitive implying a myriad advanced cryptographic applications. Up until recently, the state of feasibility of $i\mathcal{O}$ was unclear, which changed with works (Jain-Lin-Sahai STOC 2021, Jain-Lin-Sahai Eurocrypt 2022) showing that $i\mathcal{O}$ can be finally based upon well-studied hardness assumptions. Unfortunately, one of these assumptions is broken in quantum polynomial time. Luckily, the line work of Brakerski et al. Eurocrypt 2020, Gay-Pass STOC 2021, Wichs-Wee Eurocrypt 2021, Brakerski et al. ePrint 2021, Devadas et al. TCC 2021 simultaneously created new pathways to construct $i\mathcal{O}$ with plausible post-quantum security from new assumptions, namely a new form of circular security of LWE in the presence of leakages. At the same time, effective cryptanalysis of this line of work has also begun to emerge (Hopkins et al. Crypto 2021).

It is important to identify the simplest possible conjectures that yield post-quantum $i\mathcal{O}$ and can be understood through known cryptanalytic tools. In that spirit, and in light of the cryptanalysis of Hopkins et al., recently Devadas et al. gave an elegant construction of $i\mathcal{O}$ from a fully-specified and simple-to-state assumption along with a thorough initial cryptanalysis.

Our work gives a polynomial-time distinguisher on their "final assumption" for their scheme. Our algorithm is extremely simple to describe: Solve a carefully designed linear system arising out of the assumption. The argument of correctness of our algorithm, however, is nontrivial.

We also analyze the "T-sum" version of the same assumption described by Devadas et al. and under a reasonable conjecture rule out the assumption for any value of T that implies $i\mathcal{O}$.

The full version of this paper can be found at https://eprint.iacr.org/2022/1637.

Supplementary Information The online version contains supplementary material available at https://doi.org/10.1007/978-3-031-30545-0_8.

© International Association for Cryptologic Research 2023
C. Hazay and M. Stam (Eds.): EUROCRYPT 2023, LNCS 14004, pp. 205–235, 2023.
https://doi.org/10.1007/978-3-031-30545-0_8

1   Introduction

Indistinguishability obfuscation ($i\mathcal{O}$) for programs computable in polynomial-time [11] makes a program as unintelligble as possible while preserving the functionality. Mathematically, $i\mathcal{O}(P)$ is indistinguishable to $i\mathcal{O}(P')$ for any functionally equivalent programs P, P' of the same size. $i\mathcal{O}$'s importance is evident in its central position as a powerful and versatile primitive for building a wide variety of modern cryptographic tools (see e.g., [6,15,21,22,25,38,46,55]). Up until recently, the feasibility of $i\mathcal{O}$ from well-established assumptions was not known. In recent works, Jain, Lin, and Sahai [44,45] constructed $i\mathcal{O}$ from three well-studied assumption: Decisional Linear assumption (DLIN) over bilinear maps [8], Learning Parity with Noise over general fields [42], and Pseudorandom Generators in NC_0 [37]. DLIN over bilinear maps, however, is an assumption broken in quantum polynomial time.

In an effort to construct $i\mathcal{O}$ from conjectured post-quantum secure assumptions, specifically lattice-based ones, an exciting line of works [18,33,56] construct $i\mathcal{O}$ based on new circular security type assumptions of LWE in the presence of structured leakages of their errors. Typically there is a lot of room in how you can instantiate leakages that imply $i\mathcal{O}$, and at the moment we do not have a stable understanding of what constitutes an acceptable leakage. In fact, very recently [40] showed that instantiations of several assumptions of Gay-Pass and Wee-Wichs can be broken in classical polynomial time.

Ideally we would like to construct post-quantum $i\mathcal{O}$ based solely on well-studied post-quantum assumptions such as LWE/LPN. Unfortunately, however, our understanding of conjectures implying post-quantum $i\mathcal{O}$ is severely limited, and our confidence in them is much lower than those in classical constructions (LPN, DLIN and PRGs). Therefore, it is important that we strive to identify assumptions that are:

- Simple-to-state, and yet imply $i\mathcal{O}$,
- Can be reasoned about with cryptanalytic study.

We believe that this symbiotic relationship between constructions and constructive cryptanalysis could further understanding of how to securely instantiate assumptions. To be clear, we do not endorse an unchecked break and repair cycle, but a cycle that identifies new conceptual pathways. In this spirit, following the cryptanalysis of [40], the work of Devadas et al. [29] recently gave an elegant construction from a *fully-specified* and simple-to-state assumption implying $i\mathcal{O}$. We emphasize that their construction has all parameters *fully-specified*. This is unlike the previous assumption of [56] which was very general, and required that for some implementation choices such as PRF scheme involved, the resulting assumption is secure. The same is true with the assumption of [33], where the circuit implementations of functions involved were not fully specified.

Moreover, Devadas et al. back their instantiation with a thorough (initial) cryptanalysis.

Lessons from Our Work. A major open area is constructing post-quantum $i\mathcal{O}$. The most promising approach currently being explored is formulating simple variations of LWE with certain leakage that are sufficient. The recent work of [40] shows the importance of fully specifying the assumption and cryptanalysis (indeed, the attack of [40] exploits freedom in specification). Incorporating these insights, the [29] assumption is fully specified, relatively simple, avoids [40] attacks, Furthermore, the authors of [29] performed cryptanalysis using existing techniques. The purpose of our work is to identify and understand weaknesses in the approach of [29] so that these may be overcome in future work.

On a very high level, the intuition of [29] was that tensored polynomial systems derived from LWE not only bypasses the previous two attacks (as far as we know, the parameters are set so that sum-of-squares attacks of [12] do not apply, and at the same time, the specifications are set so that the attacks of [40] do not apply). Our main result shows a new way to get around the apparent difficulties introduced by tensoring. Therefore, we view our result contributing a new insight that will be useful in designing better assumptions.

A key aspect in which our attacks differs from previous attacks [12, 40] on the new "LWE+Leakage" assumptions [3, 18, 33, 43, 56] is that all previous attacks apply to part of the leakage that is obtained over integer/small-valued domains such as the error or the polynomial evaluations. On the other hand, our attack applies to the leakage that is given out over the prime fields (the leakage on the secret in the LWE sample). This points to a new vulnerability in designing such assumptions towards the grand goal of achieving $i\mathcal{O}$.

Our Technical Contribution. In this work, we give a polynomial-time distinguisher and recovery algorithm on the "final assumption" of [29] (stated on page 7; also formulated as Conjecture 2 on page 25) with parameters as suggested (page 23, Sect. 4.3). Our attack is algorithmically simple to describe: solve a carefully designed linear system of equations. Our analysis, on the other hand, requires a significant amount of care. In particular, the techniques we present and introduce in our analysis are of general interest to the studying the usage of tensor products in cryptographic constructions. We contribute the following general ideas.

1. We first show that Kilian randomization on highly tensored matrices does not kill the tensor structure. Consider positive integers $m \gg w$ and consider the equation

$$\left[\mathbf{U}_1 \otimes \mathbf{I} \| \mathbf{I} \otimes \mathbf{U}_2\right] = \mathbf{Y}$$

where $\mathbf{I}$ denotes a $m \times m$ square identity matrix, the matrices $\mathbf{U}_1, \mathbf{U}_2$ are unknown and of shape $m \times w$, and $\mathbf{Y}$, of shape $m^2 \times 2mw$, is given as input to the algorithm. Suppose $\mathbf{Y} \leftarrow \left[\mathbf{A}_1 \otimes \mathbf{I} \| \mathbf{I} \otimes \mathbf{A}_2\right] \cdot \mathbf{R}$ for some tall random matrices $\mathbf{A}_1, \mathbf{A}_2 \in \mathbb{Z}_q^{m \times w}$ and some Kilian matrix $\mathbf{R} \in \mathbb{Z}_q^{2mw \times 2mw}$, all of which are unknown to the algorithm. Right-multiplication by the matrix $\mathbf{R}$ seemingly mixes up the columns of matrices $\mathbf{A}_1 \otimes \mathbf{I}$ and $\mathbf{I} \otimes \mathbf{A}_2$, preventing the recovery of $\mathbf{A}_1$ and $\mathbf{A}_2$. By considering column spans, however, we observe that $\mathrm{Colspan}(\mathbf{A}_1 \otimes \mathbf{I})$ and $\mathrm{Colspan}(\mathbf{I} \otimes \mathbf{A}_2)$ have significant non-overlap (linearly independent columns) and right multiplication by an invertible matrix preserves this non-overlap. We will show that this non-overlap enables a linear independence argument, involving a small number of carefully chosen linearly independent vectors, that shows that we can recover $\mathbf{A}_1$ and $\mathbf{A}_2$ up to a unique representation. More precisely, we show how to recover a normal form of $\mathbf{A}_i$, given by $\mathbf{U}_i = \mathbf{A}_i \cdot \mathbf{A}_{i,T}^{-1}$, where $\mathbf{A}_{i,T} \in \mathbb{Z}_q^{w \times w}$ denotes the top $w \times w$ block of $\mathbf{A}_i$ for $i \in \{1, 2\}$ (these inverses exist with high probability).

2. Consider a random matrix $\mathbf{P}$ with M rows and N columns. We conjecture that, with overwhelming probability over the choice of a random matrix $\mathbf{P}$, for any set of vectors $\{\mathbf{v}_1, \ldots, \mathbf{v}_T\}$ of linearly independent vectors, where $T \ll M$ and $T \leq N$, the set of vectors $\{\mathbf{P} \cdot \mathbf{v}_1, \ldots, \mathbf{P} \cdot \mathbf{v}_T\}$ is linearly independent. We demonstrate how to use the conjecture to prove the uniqueness of solutions and compute the rank of relevant matrices as we shortly explain.

   The parameter settings relevant to the DQVWW construction consider matrices $\mathbf{P}$ that are only slightly dimension shrinking and for which the conjecture is applicable (M is still sufficiently large with respect to the sets of vectors we consider). In this setting, we cannot use matrices $\mathbf{P}$ with a very small number of rows M because we require certain expansion properties for $i\mathcal{O}$.

3. Using the conjecture, we can show that left-multiplication by a random matrix $\mathbf{P}$ fails to destroy the tensor structure present if it is insufficiently dimension shrinking. For example, we show that we can still recover the matrices $\mathbf{A}_1, \mathbf{A}_2$ above up to a unique representation from the equation,

$$\mathbf{P} \cdot \big[\mathbf{U}_1 \otimes \mathbf{I} \| \mathbf{I} \otimes \mathbf{U}_2\big] = \mathbf{Y}$$

where $\mathbf{P} \in \mathbb{Z}_q^{m^{3/2} \times m^2}$ is a known matrix, and where the matrix $\mathbf{Y}$ is generated as $\mathbf{Y} \leftarrow \mathbf{P} \cdot \big[\mathbf{A}_1 \otimes \mathbf{I} \| \mathbf{I} \otimes \mathbf{A}_2\big] \cdot \mathbf{R}$, differing from the above generation process only by the left-multiplication by $\mathbf{P}$. Our main observation here is that the linear independence of the same small set of linearly independent vectors identified above will be preserved by $\mathbf{P}$, enabling the same argument to show the recovery of a unique representation for $\mathbf{A}_1$ and $\mathbf{A}_2$.

   While many previous linear-algebraic cryptanalytic works present attacks from a matrix point of view, we show that considering column spans instead allows us to better analyze the tensor structure especially in the presence of the structure destroying matrix $\mathbf{P}$ and the randomizing matrix $\mathbf{R}$.

4. Finally, we give a technique for proving the uniqueness of solutions to $\mathbf{X}$ (when such uniqueness exists) in the equation

$$\mathbf{A}\mathbf{X} + \mathbf{B}\mathbf{Y} = \mathbf{C}$$

where $\mathbf{A}, \mathbf{B}, \mathbf{C}$ are known coefficient matrices such that the column span of $\mathbf{A}$ has a sufficient amount of non-overlap with the column span of $\mathbf{B}$, and $\mathbf{X}$ and $\mathbf{Y}$ are unknown matrices. By considering the homogeneous version of the above equation, in which $\mathbf{C} = \mathbf{0}$ and which corresponds to taking the difference of two solutions for the inhomogeneous version, and by identifying how many columns in $\mathbf{A}$ do not overlap with Colspan$(\mathbf{B})$, we can isolate an equation of the form $\mathbf{A}'\mathbf{X} = \mathbf{0}$ for some matrix $\mathbf{A}'$. This allows us to use standard rank arguments that depend on the shape of $\mathbf{A}'$ to show that the only solution to $\mathbf{X}$ in the homogeneous equation is $\mathbf{0}$, which implies that there is a unique solution to $\mathbf{X}$ in the inhomogeneous equation. Here, the conjecture above also extends our technique to the setting of proving the uniqueness of solutions to $\mathbf{X}$ (when such uniqueness exists) in equations of the form

$$\mathbf{PAX} + \mathbf{PBY} = \mathbf{C}.$$

In particular, if we can compute the size of the overlap of $\mathrm{Colspan}(\mathbf{A})$ and $\mathrm{Colspan}(\mathbf{B})$, then the conjecture allows us to compute the size of the overlap of $\mathrm{Colspan}(\mathbf{PA})$ and $\mathrm{Colspan}(\mathbf{PB})$.

Related Works. There is a huge body of other works $[1,2,5,7,10,13,19,20,23,24,$ $26\text{--}28,30,32,35,39,41,43,47,48,50,53]$ that construct $i\mathcal{O}$ candidates from plausible post-quantum assumptions (some of which are subject to prior cryptanalysis). This list includes constructions based on candidate multi-linear maps $[31,32,34]$, from noisy linear functional encryption $[1,2]$ and affine determinant programs $[13]$. Similarly, cryptanalysis was performed to better understand these assumptions $[9,12,17,19,23,24,26,39\text{--}41,51,53,54]$. Our work does not consider these lines of constructions.

Organization of the Paper. The technical overview is nearly complete in of itself. Due to space constraints we place the proof of uniqueness for recovering $\mathbf{V}_1$ in the Supplementary Materials in Sect. 4.1. We also place the extension to the T-sum case in the Supplementary Materials in Sect. 4.2. Basic linear algebraic facts and proofs about the tensor structure are found in the Supplementary Materials in Sect. 4.4 and Sect. 4.5 (resp.). A full version can be found as a separate supplementary file.

2   Technical Overview

We start by reviewing the construction idea of $[29]$. The work is built upon $[56]$, which was a follow up of $[18]$. The works $[29,56]$ construct $i\mathcal{O}$ by constructing a non-trivial obfuscation $xi\mathcal{O}$. The works of $[4,14,16,49]$ showed that, under a subexponential security loss, an $xi\mathcal{O}$ scheme can be generically lifted to a construction of an indistinguishability obfuscation scheme further assuming LWE. Recall that in an $xi\mathcal{O}$ scheme, the goal is to obfuscate circuits $C : \{0,1\}^n \to \{0,1\}^m$, where the size of the obfuscation must be marginally better than the size of the truth-table for C i.e. bounded by $2^{\epsilon \cdot n} \, \mathsf{poly}(\lambda, |C|)$ for some constant $\epsilon < 1$, whereas the running time could be as large as $2^n \, \mathsf{poly}(\lambda, |C|)$.

The Overall Approach of $[29,56]$. The main starting observation of the works $[29,56]$ is the following. Consider a function $f : \{0,1\}^\ell \to \{0,1\}^{M \times K}$ where $M \cdot K = 2^n \cdot m$ (the size of the truth table for C). We intend the function f to take as input the bit description of a circuit C, and output its truth table. Now consider ciphertexts encrypting bits of the circuit C, encrypted using the dual GSW variant of homomorphic encryption scheme $[36]$ $\{\mathsf{CT}_i = \mathbf{A}\mathbf{S}_i + \mathbf{E}_i + C_i\mathbf{G}\}_{i \in [\ell]}$ where $\mathbf{A} \in \mathbb{Z}_q^{M \times w}$ and $\mathbf{S}_i \in \mathbb{Z}_q^{w \times M \log q}$ and $\mathbf{G}$ is the gadget matrix defined by $[52]$ and $w \ll M, K$. Then the idea is that, one can homomorphically evaluate on these ciphertexts to compute an encoding:

$$\mathsf{CT}_f = \mathbf{A}\mathbf{S}_f + \mathbf{E}_f + \mathbf{M}_f \left\lceil \frac{q}{2} \right\rceil$$

where $\mathbf{S}_f \in \mathbb{Z}_q^{w \times K}$ and $\mathbf{M}_f$ is a matrix of dimension $M \times K$, that arranges outputs of $f(C)$ in a matrix form, and $\mathbf{E}_f$ is a matrix with ℓ_2 norm much smaller than q. This is a ciphertext that has an opening that is much shorter in size than $M \cdot K$. The opening is simply $\mathbf{S}_f$ which is of the size $w \cdot K \log q \ll M \cdot K$.

Thus, a first candidate could be one in which the obfuscator gives out $\{\mathsf{CT}_i\}_{i \in [\ell]}$ along with $\mathbf{S}_f$. Unfortunately, this is easily attackable, because this let's one learn $\mathbf{E}_f$, which lies in a linear subspace which is some function of the circuit C. Thus given $\mathbf{E}_f$ one can test if the ciphertexts encrypt C_0 or C_1.

Relying on Fresh LWE Samples with Large Error. To address this issue, [18,56] observed that access to fresh LWE samples $\mathbf{D} = \mathbf{AR} + \mathbf{F}$ where $\mathbf{R} \in \mathbb{Z}_q^{w \times K}$ and $\mathbf{F} \in \chi_{\mathsf{flood}}^{M \times K}$ from some distribution χ_{flood} can drown out $\mathbf{E}_f$. Then, one can give out $\mathbf{S}_f + \mathbf{R}$ (in addition to $\mathbf{D}, \{\mathsf{CT}_i\}$) which lets one learn $\mathbf{E}_f + \mathbf{F} + \mathbf{M}_f \lceil \frac{q}{2} \rceil$. In fact, this system can be proven secure under LWE. Unfortunately, now the problem is that $\mathbf{D}$ is too big! We don't obtain any compression if we give such a matrix out. To address this issue, [56] suggested pseudorandomly generating LWE samples, motivating a source of new hardness assumptions in [56] as well as the paper under consideration in our work [29].

Pseudorandomly Sampling LWE. To obtain compression, [56] suggested that we come up with a way where one uses a small set of encryptions (encrypting say a PRF key) $\{\mathsf{CT}'_i = \mathbf{AS}'_i + \mathbf{E}'_i + k_i \mathbf{G}\}_{i \in [\ell']}$ and then using this compute a larger number of LWE samples of the same kind as $\mathbf{D}$. The work showed that by homomorphically evaluating PRF and relying on packing techniques, one could generate a larger sample of the required form $\mathbf{D} = \mathbf{AR}' + \mathbf{F}'$. Now one could give out $\mathbf{S}_f + \mathbf{R}'$ and this could effectively replace the role of a fresh LWE sample $\mathbf{D}$. Unfortunately, this assumption is heuristic in nature, and is contingent on the exact specification of the circuit implementation of the PRF used. The work of [40] pointed out that for every PRF, if the circuit implementation is not chosen carefully, the assumption could be attacked.

Simplifying Assumption. The main contribution of [29] is a significantly simpler scheme that involves computation of a fully specified structured constant-degree polynomials rather than a PRF. The purpose is to identify the simplest possible assumption that suffices to build $i\mathcal{O}$, and can be reasoned with respect to broad classes of cryptanalysis algorithms. In order to generate "LWE" type samples, the work of [29] gives out d LWE matrices for some constant $d \in \mathbb{N}$:

$$\mathbf{B}_i = \mathbf{A}_i \mathbf{S}_i + \mathbf{E}_i \mod q,$$

for $i \in [d]$ where $\mathbf{A}_i \leftarrow \mathbb{Z}_q^{m \times w}$ and $\mathbf{S}_i \leftarrow \mathbb{Z}_q^{w \times k}$ and $\mathbf{E}_i \leftarrow \chi^{m \times k}$. Here $w \ll m \ll k$

The point of this is that now one can compute $\mathbf{B}' = \mathbf{B}_1 \otimes \ldots \otimes \mathbf{B}_d$ given these matrices resulting in a matrix of much larger dimension. This matrix can be expressed as:

$$\mathbf{B}_1 \otimes \ldots \otimes \mathbf{B}_d = \mathbf{A}' \cdot \mathbf{S}' + \mathbf{E}',$$

where,

$$\mathbf{A}' = (\mathbf{A}_1 \otimes \mathbf{I}_m \otimes \ldots \mathbf{I}_m \| \mathbf{I}_m \otimes \mathbf{A}_2 \otimes \ldots \mathbf{I}_m \| \ldots \| \mathbf{I}_m \otimes \mathbf{I}_m \otimes \ldots \mathbf{A}_d),$$

$$\mathbf{S}' = \begin{pmatrix} \mathbf{S}_1 \otimes \mathbf{B}_2 \otimes \mathbf{B}_3 \otimes \ldots \mathbf{B}_{d-1} \otimes \mathbf{B}_d \\ \mathbf{E}_1 \otimes \mathbf{S}_2 \otimes \mathbf{B}_3 \otimes \ldots \mathbf{B}_{d-1} \otimes \mathbf{B}_d \\ \vdots \\ \mathbf{E}_1 \otimes \mathbf{E}_2 \otimes \mathbf{E}_3 \otimes \ldots \mathbf{E}_{d-1} \otimes \mathbf{S}_d \end{pmatrix},$$

$$\mathbf{E}' = \mathbf{E}_1 \otimes \ldots \otimes \mathbf{E}_d.$$

At this point it is tempting to use $\mathbf{B}'$ to instantiate the template above. Indeed the dimension of $\mathbf{S}'$ is much smaller than the dimension of $\mathbf{B}'$. Unfortunately, this can be attacked using the sum-of-squares algorithm. The sample $\mathbf{E}' + \mathbf{M}_f \lceil \frac{q}{2} \rceil + \mathbf{E}_f$ does not hide $\mathbf{E}_f$. $\mathbf{E}'$ consists of all degree d monomials of $\mathbf{E}_1, \ldots, \mathbf{E}_d$, and if $\|\mathbf{E}_f\|_2 \ll \|\mathbf{E}'\|_2$, using ideas similar to [12] we can recover $\{\mathbf{E}_i\}$ uniquely with high probability in polynomial time. For ruling out such attacks, we require that for any system of polynomials of degree d over n variables, the number of equations be less than $n^{d/2}$, whereas in this case we are giving out n^d equations.

Thus, [29] suggested multiplying $\mathbf{B}'$ by matrices $\mathbf{P}$ and $\mathbf{P}'$ (which are both a part of some crs) with integer Gaussian entries to compute $\mathbf{B}^* = \mathbf{P}\mathbf{B}'\mathbf{P}'$ where $\mathbf{P} \in \mathbb{Z}^{M \times m^d}$ and $\mathbf{P}' \in \mathbb{Z}^{k^d \times K}$. This yields $\mathbf{B}^* = \mathbf{A}^* \cdot \mathbf{S}^* + \mathbf{E}^*$ where $\mathbf{S}^* = \mathbf{S}' \cdot \mathbf{P}'$ and $\mathbf{E}^* = \mathbf{P}(\mathbf{E}_1 \otimes \ldots \otimes \mathbf{E}_d)\mathbf{P}'$. We can now use $\mathbf{E}^*$ as the smudging polynomial. The dimension M and K are set so that $M \cdot K \ll (m \cdot k)^{d/2}$ to resist sum-of-squares attacks and at the same time also give the compression needed to give rise to $i\mathcal{O}$.

While this is the main idea, there are several additional ideas that are needed to turn the intuition above into a scheme. Observe that in $\mathbf{B}^* = \mathbf{P}\mathbf{A}'\mathbf{S}'\mathbf{P}' + \mathbf{E}^*$, $\mathbf{A}'$ and $\mathbf{S}'$ are highly structured. Instead of releasing matrices $\overline{\mathbf{A}}^* = \mathbf{P}\mathbf{A}'$ in the clear, one gives out Kilian randomized version of $\overline{\mathbf{A}}^*$, which we denote by $\mathbf{A}^*$ with the same column span as that of $\mathbf{P}\mathbf{A}'$. Still, several issues remain: For example, the construction is in the CRS model, and the assumption is associated with a CRS. We now describe the assumption below and then give a sketch of our attack.

Succinct LWE Sampling Assumption. The assumption on a broad level roughly says that for some constant $d \in \mathbb{N}$:

$$(\{\mathbf{A}_i\mathbf{S}_i + \mathbf{E}_i\}_{i \in [d]}, \mathbf{A}^*, \bar{Q}, \bar{Q}(\mathbf{E}_1, \ldots, \mathbf{E}_d) + \mathsf{Z}_0, \mathsf{aux}_0) \approx_c$$
$$(\{\mathbf{A}_i\mathbf{S}_i + \mathbf{E}_i\}_{i \in [d]}, \mathbf{A}^*, \bar{Q}, \bar{Q}(\mathbf{E}_1, \ldots, \mathbf{E}_d) + \mathsf{Z}_1, \mathsf{aux}_1)$$

where $\bar{Q}$ is a fully specified degree-d polynomial map over the integers chosen at random from some distribution which we will specify below. For $b \in \{0, 1\}$, Z_b is a distribution that needs to be smudged and aux_b is auxiliary information about the distribution. On a very high level, the assumption has a structure that is reminiscent of the assumptions made by [3,43]. However, there are differences in what set of polynomials that $\bar{Q}$ can be supported and the auxiliary information. As described above, the polynomial map that [29] considers is of the form: $\bar{Q}(\mathbf{E}_1,\ldots,\mathbf{E}_d) = \mathbf{P}(\mathbf{E}_1 \otimes \ldots \mathbf{E}_d)\mathbf{P}'$ where the polynomial first computes multilinear degree d monomials by computing $\mathbf{E}_1 \otimes \ldots \otimes \mathbf{E}_d$ and then multiplies it on both sides by matrices $\mathbf{P}, \mathbf{P}'$ of appropriately chosen dimensions where the entries are chosen from a discrete Gaussian distribution. Our attacks do not apply to the assumptions made in [3,43], which are structurally similar on a very high level. The reason for this is that our attack uses the structure of the polynomial $\bar{Q}$ in a crucial way. Our results, in fact, suggest that there are distributions of polynomials $\bar{Q}$, such that $\bar{Q}(\mathbf{E}_1,\ldots,\mathbf{E}_d)$ may be secure to release (from the point of view of SoS, linearizations and other attacks) but together with the LWE samples, might end up being invertible. This conclusion suggests that these types of assumptions of LWE sampling with polynomial leakage on the errors need to be thoroughly investigated.

We now describe the assumption in full specification below.

2.1   The DQVWW Assumption Implying $i\mathcal{O}$

We now describe the assumption of [29] implying $i\mathcal{O}$. The assumption appears as the "final assumption" on page 7 as well as Conjecture 2 in [29]. We emphasize unlike previous works in this line, the assumption of [29] is *fully-specified*, meaning all parameters/implementations are fully specified.

We first set some parameters that will be used to define the conjecture.

- $d \geq 3$ is a constant integer.
- w is a security/dimension parameter,
- m, n, k, M, N, W are other dimension parameters which are polynomials in w.
- In their candidate, $M = m^{d-1/2}$ and $K = m^{d+1/2}$, $m \geq w^3$ and $m^3 \leq k \leq m^{2d-7/6}$ and $W = O(dwm^{d-1})$.
- q is a prime, $\chi, \bar{\chi}, \chi_{\mathsf{flood}}$ are LWE error distributions with different parameters. We note that there is a bound of $q \leq 2^{O(m)}$ for LWE security to hold, a point which we expound on in Remark 1.

The assumption is regarding indistinguishability of two distributions $\mathcal{D}_b$ for $b \in \{0,1\}$. We describe both the distributions below.

Distribution $\mathcal{D}_b$.

- For $i \in [d]$, sample $\mathbf{A}_i \leftarrow \mathbb{Z}_q^{m \times w}$, $\mathbf{S}_i \leftarrow \mathbb{Z}_q^{w \times k}$, $\mathbf{E}_i \leftarrow \chi^{m \times k}$. Set $\mathbf{B}_i = \mathbf{A}_i \cdot \mathbf{S}_i + \mathbf{E}_i$. Visually, the $\mathbf{A}_i$'s are tall, the $\mathbf{S}_i$'s are wide, and the $\mathbf{B}_i$'s and the $\mathbf{E}_i$'s are wide.
- Sample $\mathbf{P} \leftarrow \chi^{M \times m^d}$ and $\mathbf{P}' \leftarrow \chi^{k^d \times K}$. Visually, $\mathbf{P}$ is a wide matrix and $\mathbf{P}'$ is a tall matrix.
- Set $\bar{\mathbf{A}}^* = \mathbf{P} \cdot \left(\mathbf{A}_1 \otimes \mathbf{I}_m^{\otimes(d-1)} \| \mathbf{I}_m \otimes \mathbf{A}_2 \otimes \mathbf{I}_m^{\otimes(d-2)} \| \ldots \| \mathbf{I}_m^{\otimes(d-1)} \otimes \mathbf{A}_d\right) \in \mathbb{Z}_q^{M \times dwm^{d-1}}$. Visually, $\bar{\mathbf{A}}^*$ is a tall matrix.

– Set $\bar{\mathbf{S}}^* = \begin{pmatrix} \mathbf{S}_1 \otimes \mathbf{B}_2 \otimes \mathbf{B}_3 \otimes \ldots \otimes \mathbf{B}_{d-1} \otimes \mathbf{B}_d \\ \mathbf{E}_1 \otimes \mathbf{S}_2 \otimes \mathbf{B}_3 \otimes \ldots \otimes \mathbf{B}_{d-1} \otimes \mathbf{B}_d \\ \vdots \\ \mathbf{E}_1 \otimes \mathbf{E}_2 \otimes \mathbf{E}_3 \otimes \ldots \otimes \mathbf{E}_{d-1} \otimes \mathbf{S}_d \end{pmatrix} \cdot \mathbf{P}' \in \mathbb{Z}_q^{dwm^{d-1} \times K}$ Visually,

$\bar{\mathbf{S}}^*$ is a wide matrix.

– (Killian Randomization) Find random full rank matrices $\mathbf{A}^* \in \mathbb{Z}_q^{M \times W}, \mathbf{S}^* \in \mathbb{Z}_q^{W \times K}$ such that $\mathbf{A}^* \cdot \mathbf{S}^* = \bar{\mathbf{A}}^* \cdot \bar{\mathbf{S}}^*$. Visually, $\mathbf{A}^*$ is a tall matrix and $\mathbf{S}^*$ is a wide matrix.

– Observe that if one sets $\mathbf{B}^* = \mathbf{P} \cdot (\mathbf{B}_1 \otimes \ldots \otimes \mathbf{B}_d) \cdot \mathbf{P}'$ and $\mathbf{E}^* = \mathbf{P} \cdot (\mathbf{E}_1 \otimes \ldots \otimes \mathbf{E}_d) \cdot \mathbf{P}'$, then it holds that $\mathbf{B}^* - \mathbf{A}^*\mathbf{S}^* = \mathbf{E}^*$. Set seed $= \{\mathbf{B}_i\}_{i \in [d]}, \mathbf{A}^*, \mathbf{S}^*$.

– Set $\hat{\mathbf{B}} = \mathbf{A}^*\mathbf{S}_0 + \mathbf{F}$, where $\mathbf{S}_0 \leftarrow \mathbb{Z}_q^{W \times K}$ and $\mathbf{F} \leftarrow \chi_{\text{flood}}^{M \times K}$.

– Set $\mathbf{C} = \mathbf{A}^*\mathbf{R} + \mathbf{E} - b\mathbf{G}$, where $\mathbf{R} \leftarrow \mathbb{Z}_q^{W \times M \log q}$ and $\mathbf{E} \leftarrow \bar{\chi}^{M \times M \log q}$.

Output of $\mathcal{D}_b$ consists of the following tuple:

$$\Delta_b = (\mathbf{P}, \mathbf{P}', \mathbf{A}^*, \{\mathbf{B}_i\}_{i \in [d]}, \hat{\mathbf{B}}, \mathbf{C}, \mathbf{E}^* + \mathbf{E}\mathbf{G}^{-1}(\hat{\mathbf{B}}) - b\mathbf{F})$$

We note that $\mathbf{E}^* + \mathbf{E}\mathbf{G}^{-1}(\hat{\mathbf{B}}) - b\mathbf{F}$ let's one derive $\mathbf{A}^* \cdot (\mathbf{S}^* + \mathbf{R}\mathbf{G}^{-1}(\hat{\mathbf{B}}) - b\mathbf{S}_0)$. This is because $\mathbf{B}^* + \mathbf{C}\mathbf{G}^{-1}(\hat{\mathbf{B}}) = \mathbf{A}^*(\mathbf{S}^* + \mathbf{R}\mathbf{G}^{-1}(\hat{\mathbf{B}}) - b\mathbf{S}_0) + \mathbf{E}^* + \mathbf{E}\mathbf{G}^{-1}(\hat{\mathbf{B}}) - b\mathbf{F}$.

The Assumption of [29]**.** For the distribution $\mathcal{D}_0, \mathcal{D}_1$ defined above, $\mathcal{D}_0$ is computationally indistinguishable to $\mathcal{D}_1$.

Remark 1. For simplicity, consider the LWE error distribution χ to be uniform over $[0, B - 1]$. In general, the security of LWE itself requires that $B/q \geq 2^{-w}$ where w is the security parameter (It's also the length of the secret, observe that each matrix $\mathbf{S}_i$ is of dimension $w \times k$ and every column, say $\mathbf{s}_{i,j} \in \mathbb{Z}_q^w$ of $\mathbf{S}_i$ defines a fresh LWE sample given by $\mathbf{A}_i\mathbf{s}_{i,j} + \mathbf{e}_{i,j}$, where $\mathbf{e}_{i,j} \in \mathbb{Z}_q^k$ is the jth column of $\mathbf{E}_i$). Moreover, we know that the total entropy in a LWE matrix is upper bounded by $wk \log q + mk \log B$ and this total entropy must be upper bounded by the entropy in a truly random matrix of dimension $m \times k$, so we have $mk \log q \geq wk \log q + mk \log B$. Substituting the constraint on the noise-to-modulus ratio into the entropy bound gives us that $m \geq \log q$, so $q \leq 2^{O(m)}$ so that LWE security holds. An analogous constraint holds on Gaussian distributions with respect to the width.

2.2 Overview of the Attack

We begin by describing a recovery algorithm for the error term $\mathbf{E}_1$ in the case that $b = 0$. To break the assumption, the algorithm is given a tuple

$$(\mathbf{P}, \mathbf{P}', \mathbf{A}^*, \{\mathbf{B}_i\}_{i \in [d]}, \hat{\mathbf{B}}, \mathbf{C}, \mathbf{E}^* + \mathbf{E}\mathbf{G}^{-1}(\hat{\mathbf{B}}) - b\mathbf{F})$$

for some $b \in \{0, 1\}$, and the algorithm needs to identify the value of $b \in \{0, 1\}$. We show that in the case of $b = 0$, we can construct an algorithm $\mathcal{A}$ that recovers the matrices $\mathbf{A}_1, \ldots, \mathbf{A}_d$ up to a unique representation, and then recovers the secret $\mathbf{S}_1$ up to a unique representation. If we recover $\mathbf{A}_1$ and $\mathbf{S}_1$ up to a unique representation, then we can recover $\mathbf{E}_1$ from $\mathbf{B}_1$. The same attack can then iteratively recover $\mathbf{E}_i$ for all $i \in [d]$. This recovery algorithm for the case that $b = 0$ heuristically gives rise to a distinguisher which we explain in Sect. 3.1.

A Unique Representation. Observe that if one was to naively solve for $\mathbf{A}_i, \mathbf{S}_i$, there could be many solutions simultaneously satisfying all the constraints. In particular, there are many possible values of $\mathbf{U}_i, \mathbf{V}_i$ that satisfy $\mathbf{B}_i = \mathbf{U}_i \cdot \mathbf{V}_i + \mathbf{E}_i$ where $\mathbf{U}_i \in \mathbb{Z}_q^{m \times w}$, $\mathbf{V}_i \in \mathbb{Z}_q^{w \times k}$ and $\mathbf{A}^* = \mathbf{P}\left[\mathbf{U}_1 \otimes \mathbf{I}^{\otimes(d-1)} \| \cdots \| \mathbf{I}^{\otimes(d-1)} \otimes \mathbf{U}_d\right]\mathbf{T}$ for a matrix $\mathbf{T} \in \mathbb{Z}_q^{dwm^{d-1} \times W}$. This large solution space, for example, contains all solutions of the form $\mathbf{U}_i = \mathbf{A}_i\mathbf{R}$ and $\mathbf{V}_i = \mathbf{R}^{-1}\mathbf{S}_i$ for any invertible matrix $\mathbf{R} \in \mathbb{Z}_q^{w \times w}$. Any such choice of $\mathbf{U}_i$ and $\mathbf{V}_i$ also gives rise to a solution of $\mathbf{A}^*\mathbf{S}^* = \bar{\mathbf{U}}^*\bar{\mathbf{V}}^*$ where

$$\bar{\mathbf{U}}^* = \mathbf{P}\left[\mathbf{U}_1 \otimes \mathbf{I}^{\otimes(d-1)} \| \cdots \| \mathbf{I}^{\otimes(d-1)} \otimes \mathbf{U}_d\right]$$

$$\bar{\mathbf{V}}^* = \begin{bmatrix} \mathbf{V}_1 \otimes \mathbf{B}_2 \otimes \mathbf{B}_3 \otimes \ldots \otimes \mathbf{B}_{d-1} \otimes \mathbf{B}_d \\ \mathbf{E}_1 \otimes \mathbf{V}_2 \otimes \mathbf{B}_3 \otimes \ldots \otimes \mathbf{B}_{d-1} \otimes \mathbf{B}_d \\ \vdots \\ \mathbf{E}_1 \otimes \mathbf{E}_2 \otimes \mathbf{E}_3 \otimes \ldots \otimes \mathbf{E}_{d-1} \otimes \mathbf{V}_d \end{bmatrix} \cdot \mathbf{P}'.$$

In order to make a *unique* search possible, we observe that for any LWE sample,

$$\mathbf{B}_i = \mathbf{A}_i \cdot \mathbf{S}_i + \mathbf{E}_i$$

for a planted $\mathbf{A}_i \in \mathbb{Z}_q^{m \times w}$, $\mathbf{S}_i \in \mathbb{Z}_q^{w \times k}$ and $\mathbf{E}_i \leftarrow \chi^{m \times k}$, with high probability, can be uniquely written as:

$$\mathbf{B}_i = \mathbf{U}_i \cdot \mathbf{V}_i + \mathbf{E}_i$$

where we insist that $\mathbf{U}_i$ is uniquely structured, namely in its Hermite normal form (reduced echelon form). That is, we set $\mathbf{U}_i = \begin{bmatrix} \mathbf{I}_w \\ \tilde{\mathbf{A}}_i \end{bmatrix}$, by setting the top $w \times w$ submatrix of $\mathbf{U}_i$ to be identity. The purported solution value of $\mathbf{U}_i$ is supposed to be $\mathbf{A}_i \cdot \mathbf{A}_{i,T}^{-1}$ where $\mathbf{A}_{i,T}^{-1}$ is the top $w \times w$ submatrix of $\mathbf{A}_i$. Similarly, the intended solution for $\mathbf{V}_i$ is supposed to be $\mathbf{A}_{i,T} \cdot \mathbf{S}_i$. Note that if this happens, then we still have the desired relation:

$$\mathbf{A}_i \cdot \mathbf{S}_i = \mathbf{U}_i \cdot \mathbf{V}_i$$

Our Algorithm. We now state our recovery algorithm that recovers $\mathbf{E}_1$ in two simple steps:

─────────────── **Main Recovery Algorithm** $\mathcal{A}$ ───────────────

Input: $(\mathbf{P}, \mathbf{P}', \mathbf{A}^*, \{\mathbf{B}_i\}_{i \in [d]}, \hat{\mathbf{B}}, \mathbf{C}, \mathbf{E}^* + \mathbf{EG}^{-1}(\hat{\mathbf{B}}))$.
Output: $\mathbf{V}_1, \mathbf{E}_1$.

1. **Recover $\mathbf{U}_1, \ldots, \mathbf{U}_d$**: Solve the affine system of equations defined by

$$\mathbf{P} \cdot \left[\mathbf{U}_1 \otimes \mathbf{I}_m^{\otimes(d-1)} \| \mathbf{I}_m \otimes \mathbf{U}_2 \otimes \mathbf{I}_m^{\otimes(d-2)} \| \cdots \| \mathbf{I}_m^{\otimes(d-1)} \otimes \mathbf{U}_d \right] = \mathbf{A}^* \cdot \mathbf{M} \tag{1}$$

where $\mathbf{U}_i = \begin{bmatrix} \mathbf{I}_w \\ \tilde{\mathbf{A}}_i \end{bmatrix}$, for $i \in [d]$, and the variables are given by the entries of $\tilde{\mathbf{A}}_1, \ldots, \tilde{\mathbf{A}}_d \in \mathbb{Z}_q^{(m-w)\times w}$ and the entries of $\mathbf{M} \in \mathbb{Z}_q^{W \times dwm^{d-1}}$. Even more precisely, every entry of the matrix

$$\mathbf{P} \cdot \left[\mathbf{U}_1 \otimes \mathbf{I}_m^{\otimes(d-1)} \| \mathbf{I}_m \otimes \mathbf{U}_2 \otimes \mathbf{I}_m^{\otimes(d-2)} \| \cdots \| \mathbf{I}_m^{\otimes(d-1)} \otimes \mathbf{U}_d \right] - \mathbf{A}^* \cdot \mathbf{M}$$

defines an equation in the above described variables, where the coefficients are given by the entries of $\mathbf{A}^*$ and $\mathbf{P}$. We will show there is a unique solution for $\{\tilde{\mathbf{A}}_i\}_{i\in[d]}$, namely the fact that there is only one possible solution for all the entries of $\{\tilde{\mathbf{A}}_i\}_{i\in[d]}$ regardless of the solution found for the entries of $\mathbf{M}$.

2. **Recover $\mathbf{V}_1$**: Having recovered the unique matrices $\{\tilde{\mathbf{A}}_i\}_{i\in[d]}$, our algorithm now aims to recover $\mathbf{V}_1$ such that $\mathbf{U}_1 \cdot \mathbf{V}_1 = \mathbf{A}_1 \cdot \mathbf{S}_1$. To do this, our algorithm computes

$$\mathbf{Y} = \mathbf{A}^* \cdot (\mathbf{S}^* + \mathbf{R} \cdot \mathbf{G}^{-1}(\hat{\mathbf{B}}))$$

by subtracting off the error $\mathbf{E}^* + \mathbf{E} \cdot \mathbf{G}^{-1}(\hat{\mathbf{B}})$ from $\mathbf{B}^* + \mathbf{C} \cdot \mathbf{G}^{-1}(\mathbf{B})$. Then it computes, via standard linear algebra, a full rank annihilator matrix $\mathbf{Q} \in \mathbb{Z}_q^{K \times (K - M \log q)}$ such that $\mathbf{G}^{-1}(\hat{\mathbf{B}}) \cdot \mathbf{Q} = \mathbf{0}$, obtaining the equation,

$$\mathbf{A}^* \cdot \mathbf{S}^* \cdot \mathbf{Q} = \mathbf{Y} \cdot \mathbf{Q}.$$

Finally, it solves the linear system of equations defined by

$$\mathbf{P} \left[\mathbf{U}_1 \otimes \mathbf{I}_m^{\otimes(d-1)} \| \cdots \| \mathbf{I}_m^{\otimes(d-1)} \otimes \mathbf{U}_d \right] \begin{bmatrix} \mathbf{V}_1 \otimes \mathbf{B}_2' \\ \mathbf{Z} \end{bmatrix} \mathbf{P}' \cdot \mathbf{Q} = \mathbf{Y} \cdot \mathbf{Q} \tag{2}$$

where $\mathbf{B}_2' = \mathbf{B}_2 \otimes \ldots \otimes \mathbf{B}_d$ and where the variables are the entries of $\mathbf{V}_1$ and $\mathbf{Z}$ and the coefficients are given by the entries of $\mathbf{P}, \mathbf{P}', \mathbf{Q}, \mathbf{Y}, \mathbf{U}_i$, for $i \in [d]$, and $\mathbf{B}_2'$. We will show that $\mathbf{V}_1$ has a unique solution, namely the fact that there is only one possible solution for the entries of $\mathbf{V}_1$ regardless of the solution found for the entries of $\mathbf{Z}$. Finally, $\mathbf{E}_1$ is now recovered by computing $\mathbf{B}_1 - \mathbf{U}_1 \cdot \mathbf{V}_1$.

Observe that in each of the two steps above, our algorithm sets up a simple, explicit affine (linear in Step 2) system of equations. Correctness of the algorithm is entirely determined by showing, for Step 1, the uniqueness of the solution to $\{\tilde{\mathbf{A}}_i\}_{i\in[d]}$, and showing, for Step 2, the uniqueness of the solution to $\mathbf{V}_1$.

This analysis is intricate and benefits from being viewed in a specific lens as we shortly explain.

> *Remark 2.* We will place basic linear algebra facts and linear algebraic statements about the tensor structure used in the DQVWW construction in a shaded box. This is done to minimize the number of distractions the reader encounters. A reference to the corresponding statement in the Appendix will be included. A compendium of these facts and their proofs is found in Appendix 4.4 and Appendix 4.5.

2.3   The Importance of Column Spans

To show uniqueness in Step 1, we will analyze column spans instead of analyzing matrix equations. There are two reasons for analyzing the column spans: First, reasoning about column spans allows us to disregard the matrix $\mathbf{M}$ in Eq. 1 by taking advantage of the fact that the column span of $\mathbf{A}^* \cdot \mathbf{M}$ is contained in the column span of $\mathbf{A}^*$, a fact which we will recall shortly.

Our second, and principal, reason for analyzing column spans is that it allows us to continue to see the tensor structure even after left-multiplication by the matrix $\mathbf{P}$. If $\mathbf{P}$ were not present, then we observe that a straightforward linear independence argument, which uses the tensor structure of the matrix in the LHS of the below equation, shows that there is a unique choice of $\{\tilde{\mathbf{A}}_i\}_{i \in [d]}$ that satisfies the equation

$$\left[\mathbf{U}_1 \otimes \mathbf{I}_m^{\otimes(d-1)} \| \mathbf{I}_m \otimes \mathbf{U}_2 \otimes \mathbf{I}_m^{\otimes(d-2)} \| \cdots \| \mathbf{I}_m^{\otimes(d-1)} \otimes \mathbf{U}_d\right] = \mathbf{A}^* \cdot \mathbf{M}.$$

We will explicitly analyze this case without $\mathbf{P}$ later in this overview as a simple example to build intuition. Under a reasonable conjecture about random matrices being injective on subspaces of small dimension, we can directly extend this linear independence argument for the simple example to the general case when we have left-multiplication by $\mathbf{P}$. This extension reveals that left-multiplication by $\mathbf{P}$ does not sufficiently destroy, nor scramble, the tensor structure of the LHS above. Yet, this observation is completely hidden from view when considering the matrix view

$$\mathbf{P} \cdot \left[\mathbf{U}_1 \otimes \mathbf{I}_m^{\otimes(d-1)} \| \mathbf{I}_m \otimes \mathbf{U}_2 \otimes \mathbf{I}_m^{\otimes(d-2)} \| \cdots \| \mathbf{I}_m^{\otimes(d-1)} \otimes \mathbf{U}_d\right]$$

Since $\mathbf{P}$, in general, is not decomposable into a tensor product, directly analyzing the matrix product makes the tensor structure appear to be completely lost!

From a column span view, however, this tensor structure is still very much accessible. Extending the above mentioned linear independence argument to the general case, in which $\mathbf{P}$ is present, turns out to exactly require analyzing the column span $\text{Colspan}\left(\mathbf{P}\left[\mathbf{U}_1 \otimes \mathbf{I}_m^{\otimes(d-1)} \| \cdots \| \mathbf{I}_m^{\otimes(d-1)} \otimes \mathbf{U}_d\right]\right)$. A more detailed overview is given below.

Framework for Column Spans. To analyze the column span of the following matrix

$$\left[\mathbf{U}_1 \otimes \mathbf{I}_m^{\otimes(d-1)} \| \mathbf{I}_m \otimes \mathbf{U}_2 \otimes \mathbf{I}_m^{\otimes(d-2)} \| \cdots \| \mathbf{I}_m^{\otimes(d-1)} \otimes \mathbf{U}_d\right].$$

where the matrices $\mathbf{U}_i \in \mathbb{Z}_q^{m \times w}$ are of the stipulated form (with a top $w \times w$ identity block, so of full column rank w), it is useful to make the following extension of each $\mathbf{U}_i$ to a full basis for $\mathbb{Z}_q^m$. The column span of this matrix is some subspace of the vector space over $\underbrace{\mathbb{Z}_q^m \otimes \cdots \otimes \mathbb{Z}_q^m}_{d \text{ times}}$. Considering $\mathbb{Z}_q^m$ as a

vector space, we consider the following bases for $\mathbb{Z}_q^m$. For $i \in [d]$, let $\mathcal{B}_i$ be a basis for $\mathbb{Z}_q^m$ obtained by extending the set of column vectors in $\mathbf{U}_i = \begin{bmatrix} \mathbf{I}_w \\ \tilde{\mathbf{A}}_i \end{bmatrix}$ to the following full rank, lower-triangular matrix

$$\mathcal{B}_i \triangleq \begin{bmatrix} \mathbf{I}_w & \mathbf{0}_{w \times (m-w)} \\ \tilde{\mathbf{A}}_i & \mathbf{I}_{m-w} \end{bmatrix} \in \mathbb{Z}_q^{m \times m},$$

and let $(\mathbf{e}_1^{(i)}, \ldots, \mathbf{e}_m^{(i)})$ denote the columns of $\mathcal{B}_i$ (the basis vectors).

2.4 Correctness of Step 1

We aim to build simple intuition about the correctness of our algorithm in this overview and leave the full details to the main technical content. Our overview first shows the existence of one solution to $\{\mathbf{U}_i\}_{i \in [d]}$ in Eq. 1, namely a solution to $\mathbf{U}_i$ is the Hermite normal form of $\mathbf{A}_i \in \mathbb{Z}_q^{m \times w}$, which has full column rank with overwhelming probability by property of random matrices. Then we explain why this is the only solution with overwhelming probability.

(Step 1) Existence of a Structured Solution : First, there exists at least one solution to $\{\mathbf{U}_i\}_{i \in [d]}$ and $\mathbf{M}$ in Eq. 1 in which for all $i \in [d]$, we have $\mathbf{U}_i \leftarrow \mathbf{A}_i \cdot \mathbf{A}_{i,T}^{-1}$, where we recall that $\mathbf{A}_{i,T} \in \mathbb{Z}_q^{w \times w}$ is defined to be the top $w \times w$ block of $\mathbf{A}_i$. Put equivalently, a solution to $\mathbf{U}_i$ is the Hermite normal form of $\mathbf{A}_i$. To see why, for $i \in [d]$, define the invertible matrix $\mathbf{N}_i = \mathbf{I}_m^{\otimes(i-1)} \otimes \mathbf{A}_{i,T}^{-1} \otimes \mathbf{I}_m^{\otimes(d-i)}$ and use the following two linear algebraic facts.

Lemma 1. *For any matrices $\mathbf{M}_1, \mathbf{M}_2$, there exists a matrix $\mathbf{N}$ such that $\mathbf{M}_1 \cdot \mathbf{N} = \mathbf{M}_2$ if and only if $\mathrm{Colspan}(\mathbf{M}_2) \subseteq \mathrm{Colspan}(\mathbf{M}_1)$.*

Corollary 1. *For any matrices $\mathbf{M}_1, \mathbf{M}_2$ and for any invertible matrices $\mathbf{N}_1, \mathbf{N}_2$ of the appropriate dimensions, we have that*

$$\mathrm{Colspan}\left([\mathbf{M}_1 \| \mathbf{M}_2]\right) = \mathrm{Colspan}\left([\mathbf{M}_1 \mathbf{N}_1 \| \mathbf{M}_2 \mathbf{N}_2]\right).$$

These statements and their proofs can be found in Appendix 4.4, under Lemma 12 and Corollary 6.

By Corollary 1 we have,

$$\text{Colspan}\left(\mathbf{P} \cdot \left[\mathbf{A}_1 \otimes \mathbf{I}_m^{\otimes(d-1)} \| \cdots \| \mathbf{I}_m^{\otimes(d-1)} \otimes \mathbf{A}_d\right]\right)$$

$$= \text{Colspan}\left(\mathbf{P} \cdot \left[\left(\mathbf{A}_1 \otimes \mathbf{I}_m^{\otimes(d-1)}\right) \cdot \mathbf{N}_1 \| \cdots \| \left(\mathbf{I}_m^{\otimes(d-1)} \otimes \mathbf{A}_d\right) \cdot \mathbf{N}_d\right]\right)$$

$$= \text{Colspan}\left(\mathbf{P} \cdot \left[\mathbf{A}_1 \cdot \mathbf{A}_{1,T}^{-1} \otimes \mathbf{I}_m^{\otimes(d-1)} \| \cdots \| \mathbf{I}_m^{\otimes(d-1)} \otimes \mathbf{A}_d \cdot \mathbf{A}_{d,T}^{-1}\right]\right).$$

By definition of the scheme,

$$\mathbf{A}^* = \mathbf{P} \cdot \left[\mathbf{A}_1 \otimes \mathbf{I}_m^{\otimes(d-1)} \| \cdots \| \mathbf{I}_m^{\otimes(d-1)} \otimes \mathbf{A}_d\right] \cdot \mathbf{K}$$

for some matrix $\mathbf{K} \in \mathbb{Z}_q^{dwm^{d-1} \times W}$ that preserves the column span of

$$\mathbf{P} \cdot \left[\mathbf{A}_1 \otimes \mathbf{I}_m^{\otimes(d-1)} \| \cdots \| \mathbf{I}_m^{\otimes(d-1)} \otimes \mathbf{A}_d\right].$$

Since the column span is preserved by $\mathbf{K}$,

$$\text{Colspan}(\mathbf{A}^*) = \text{Colspan}\left(\mathbf{P} \cdot \left[\mathbf{A}_1 \cdot \mathbf{A}_{1,T}^{-1} \otimes \mathbf{I}_m^{\otimes(d-1)} \| \cdots \| \mathbf{I}_m^{\otimes(d-1)} \otimes \mathbf{A}_d \cdot \mathbf{A}_{d,T}^{-1}\right]\right)$$

which implies, by Lemma 1, that there exists some matrix $\mathbf{M}$ that satisfies Eq. 1 when we consider $\mathbf{U}_i \leftarrow \mathbf{A}_i \cdot \mathbf{A}_{i,T}^{-1}$ for all $i \in [d]$.

(Step 1) Uniqueness When P is Absent: To build intuition for the full uniqueness argument, we present it in the simpler setting in which $\mathbf{P}$ is entirely absent from the scheme in the DQVWW assumption. Let us also consider the simple case when $d = 2$. In this toy case, there is no matrix $\mathbf{P}$ used to generate $\mathbf{A}^*$, so for this simple case we instead consider when the algorithm is given a matrix of the form $\mathbf{T}^* = \left[\mathbf{A}_1 \otimes \mathbf{I}_m \| \mathbf{I}_m \otimes \mathbf{A}_2\right] \mathbf{K}$ for some column span preserving Kilian matrix $\mathbf{K}$. We show the following claim.

Lemma 2 (Simple case without P). *For matrices* $\mathbf{U}_1 = \begin{bmatrix} \mathbf{I}_w \\ \tilde{\mathbf{A}}_1 \end{bmatrix}, \mathbf{U}_2 = \begin{bmatrix} \mathbf{I}_w \\ \tilde{\mathbf{A}}_2 \end{bmatrix}, \mathbf{U}_1' = \begin{bmatrix} \mathbf{I}_w \\ \tilde{\mathbf{A}}_1' \end{bmatrix}, \mathbf{U}_2' = \begin{bmatrix} \mathbf{I}_w \\ \tilde{\mathbf{A}}_2' \end{bmatrix} \in \mathbb{Z}_q^{m \times w},$ *if*

$$\text{Colspan}\left(\left[\mathbf{U}_1 \otimes \mathbf{I}_m \| \mathbf{I}_m \otimes \mathbf{U}_2\right]\right) = \text{Colspan}\left(\left[\mathbf{U}_1' \otimes \mathbf{I}_m \| \mathbf{I}_m \otimes \mathbf{U}_2'\right]\right). \quad (3)$$

then $\tilde{\mathbf{A}}_i = \tilde{\mathbf{A}}_i'$ *for* $i \in [2]$ *so that* $\mathbf{U}_1 = \mathbf{U}_1'$ *and* $\mathbf{U}_2 = \mathbf{U}_2'$.

Before we show how to prove Lemma 2, let us show that Lemma 2 implies uniqueness. In particular, we now explain why it is reasonable to require in the statement of Lemma 2 that the column spans are *equal*.

Recall that the algorithm finds a solution to $\{\tilde{\mathbf{A}}_i\}_{i \in [2]}$ and $\mathbf{M}$ in Eq. 1 which is of the following form in the simplified setting:

$$\left[\mathbf{U}_1 \otimes \mathbf{I}_m \| \mathbf{I}_m \otimes \mathbf{U}_2\right] = \mathbf{T}^* \cdot \mathbf{M}.$$

Then, by Lemma 1, any solution to $\{\tilde{\mathbf{A}}_i\}_{i \in [2]}$ satisfies the set *containment* $\text{Colspan}\left(\left[\mathbf{U}_1 \otimes \mathbf{I}_m \| \mathbf{I}_m \otimes \mathbf{U}_2\right]\right) \subseteq \text{Colspan}(\left[\mathbf{A}_1 \otimes \mathbf{I}_m \| \mathbf{I}_m \otimes \mathbf{A}_2\right]).$

Corollary 2 *With overwhelming probability over the choice of random* $\mathbf{A}_i \in \mathbb{Z}_q^{m \times w}$, *for* $i \in [d]$, *if*

$$\mathrm{Colspan}\left(\left[\mathbf{U}_1 \otimes \mathbf{I}_m^{\otimes(d-1)} \| \cdots \| \mathbf{I}_m^{\otimes(d-1)} \otimes \mathbf{U}_d\right]\right)$$

$$\subseteq \mathrm{Colspan}\left(\left[\mathbf{A}_1 \otimes \mathbf{I}_m^{\otimes(d-1)} \| \cdots \| \mathbf{I}_m^{\otimes(d-1)} \otimes \mathbf{A}_d\right]\right)$$

then

$$\mathrm{Colspan}\left(\left[\mathbf{U}_1 \otimes \mathbf{I}_m^{\otimes(d-1)} \| \cdots \| \mathbf{I}_m^{\otimes(d-1)} \otimes \mathbf{U}_d\right]\right)$$

$$= \mathrm{Colspan}\left(\left[\mathbf{A}_1 \otimes \mathbf{I}_m^{\otimes(d-1)} \| \cdots \| \mathbf{I}_m^{\otimes(d-1)} \otimes \mathbf{A}_d\right]\right)$$

The proof sketch can be found in Supp. Materials Sect. 4.5 under Corollary 11.

By Corollary 2, with overwhelming probability over the choice $\mathbf{A}_1, \mathbf{A}_2$, set containment in this setting actually implies set *equality*:

$$\mathrm{Colspan}\left(\left[\mathbf{U}_1 \otimes \mathbf{I}_m \| \mathbf{I}_m \otimes \mathbf{U}_2\right]\right) = \mathrm{Colspan}(\left[\mathbf{A}_1 \otimes \mathbf{I}_m \| \mathbf{I}_m \otimes \mathbf{A}_2\right]).$$

Therefore, any solution found for the simplified version of Eq. 1 satisfies the above set equality, and our new Lemma 2 implies that there is only one such choice of $\{\tilde{\mathbf{A}}_i\}_{i \in [2]}$ that satisfies this equality.

Proof (Proof of Lemma 2). Proving this fact is done by a linear independence argument enabled by the structure of matrices $\mathbf{U}_i$ and by the tensor construction.

We now give a direct argument for uniqueness by showing that $\mathbf{U}_1 = \mathbf{U}_1'$ column-by-column. To show, for example, that the first column $\mathbf{v} = \mathbf{e}_1^{(1)}$ of $\mathbf{U}_1 = \begin{bmatrix} \mathbf{I}_w \\ \tilde{\mathbf{A}}_1 \end{bmatrix}$ is equal to the first column of $\mathbf{v}'$ of $\begin{bmatrix} \mathbf{I}_w \\ \tilde{\mathbf{A}}_1' \end{bmatrix}$, we perform the following steps.

- We observe that $\mathbf{v}'$ can expressed in the basis $\mathcal{B}_1$ in a special linear combination: $\mathbf{v}' = \mathbf{e}_1^{(1)} + \sum_{j \in \{w+1,\dots,m\}} \alpha_j' \mathbf{e}_j^{(1)}$ for some coefficients α_j'.
- We consider the vector $\mathbf{v}' \otimes \mathbf{e}_m^{(2)}$ which is in both the LHS and RHS of Eq. 3. Because it is in both column spans, this vector can be written as

$$\mathbf{v}' \otimes \mathbf{e}_m^{(2)} = \sum_{i \leq w \text{ or } j \leq w} \lambda_{i,j} \cdot \mathbf{e}_i^{(1)} \otimes \mathbf{e}_j^{(2)}.$$

On the other hand, substituting for $\mathbf{v}'$ and rearranging gives

$$0 = (\lambda_{1,m} - 1) \cdot \mathbf{e}_1^{(1)} \otimes \mathbf{e}_m^{(2)} - \sum_{j \in \{w+1,\dots,m\}} \alpha_j' \cdot \mathbf{e}_j^{(1)} \otimes \mathbf{e}_m^{(2)}$$

$$+ \sum_{i \leq w \text{ or } j \leq w} \lambda_{i,j} \cdot \mathbf{e}_i^{(1)} \otimes \mathbf{e}_j^{(2)}. \tag{4}$$

– $\mathcal{B}_1 \otimes \mathcal{B}_2 = \{\mathbf{e}_i^{(1)} \otimes \mathbf{e}_j^{(2)}\}_{i,j \in [m]}$ is a basis for $\mathbb{Z}_q^m \otimes \mathbb{Z}_q^m$. Therefore, the vectors in each of the terms above are linearly independent. This implies that for $j \in \{w+1, \ldots, m\}$, $\alpha'_j = 0$, and $\lambda_{1,m} = 1$, and for all other values of i, j we have $\lambda_{i,j} = 0$.

The same outline of steps can be repeated column-by-column.

While this argument suffices to handle the case when $\mathbf{P}$ is absent, when $\mathbf{P}$ is present we exploit the following observation. In the argument above for the case of $d = 2$, we needed the linear independence of $m^2 - (m-w)^2 + (m-w) + 1$ many vectors (given by each of the terms in Eq. 4, although note that the first term will vary depending on which of the w columns we are considering) which is a much smaller set of vectors than the total size of the basis for $\mathbb{Z}_q^m \otimes \mathbb{Z}_q^m$, which is m^2. For the argument to continue to hold when $\mathbf{P}$ is present, $\mathbf{P}$ only needs to preserve the linear independence of this small set of vectors. A formal statement and proof of this uniqueness is found in Theorem 2.

(Step 1) Uniqueness in the General Case : Having seen the uniqueness argument in the simple case above without $\mathbf{P}$, we now address the general case where $\mathbf{P}$ is present.

In the general case, we introduce a single, reasonable conjecture about $\mathbf{P}$ being rank preserving on low-dimensional subspaces. Namely, we conjecture that with overwhelming probability over the choice of $\mathbf{P}$ whose entries are sampled from χ where $\mathbf{P}$ has M rows, for $T \ll M$, and for any set of T linearly independent vectors $\{\mathbf{v}_i\}_{i \in [T]}$, the set $\{\mathbf{P} \cdot \mathbf{v}_i\}_{i \in [T]}$ remains linearly independent. This conjecture enables us to firstly show that all solutions satisfy a column span set equality and secondly enable the same linear independence argument that shows that this set equality implies unique solutions.

We first note that the application of Lemma 1 on Eq. 1, which we now restate,

$$\mathbf{P} \cdot \left[\mathbf{U}_1 \otimes \mathbf{I}_m^{\otimes(d-1)} \| \mathbf{I}_m \otimes \mathbf{U}_2 \otimes \mathbf{I}_m^{\otimes(d-2)} \| \cdots \| \mathbf{I}_m^{\otimes(d-1)} \otimes \mathbf{U}_d\right] = \mathbf{A}^* \cdot \mathbf{M}$$

shows that any solution to $\{\mathbf{U}_i\}_{i \in [d]}$ in Eq. 1, satisfies the set *containment*

$$\mathrm{Colspan}\left(\mathbf{P}\left[\mathbf{U}_1 \otimes \mathbf{I}_m^{\otimes(d-1)} \| \cdots \| \mathbf{I}_m^{\otimes(d-1)} \otimes \mathbf{U}_d\right]\right) \subseteq \mathrm{Colspan}\left(\mathbf{A}^*\right). \qquad (5)$$

To extend the uniqueness argument from above, we desire to show that any solution to $\{\mathbf{U}_i\}_{i \in [d]}$ in Eq. 1 in fact satisfies the set *equality*:

$$\mathrm{Colspan}\left(\mathbf{P}\left[\mathbf{U}_1 \otimes \mathbf{I}_m^{\otimes(d-1)} \| \cdots \| \mathbf{I}_m^{\otimes(d-1)} \otimes \mathbf{U}_d\right]\right) = \mathrm{Colspan}(\mathbf{A}^*). \qquad (6)$$

To see that the set containment implies set equality, we first observe that Corollary 2 gives us

$$\text{rk}\left(\left[\mathbf{A}_1 \otimes \mathbf{I}_m^{\otimes(d-1)} \|\cdots\| \mathbf{I}_m^{\otimes(d-1)} \otimes \mathbf{A}_d\right]\right)$$
$$= \text{rk}\left(\left[\mathbf{U}_1 \otimes \mathbf{I}_m^{\otimes(d-1)} \|\cdots\| \mathbf{I}_m^{\otimes(d-1)} \otimes \mathbf{U}_d\right]\right).$$

Then we use the assumption that $\mathbf{P}$ preserves the rank of low-dimensional subspaces. This assumption implies firstly that

$$\text{rk}\left(\mathbf{P}\left[\mathbf{U}_1 \otimes \mathbf{I}_m^{\otimes(d-1)} \|\cdots\| \mathbf{I}_m^{\otimes(d-1)} \otimes \mathbf{U}_d\right]\right)$$
$$= \text{rk}\left(\left[\mathbf{U}_1 \otimes \mathbf{I}_m^{\otimes(d-1)} \|\cdots\| \mathbf{I}_m^{\otimes(d-1)} \otimes \mathbf{U}_d\right]\right)$$

and, recalling that $\mathbf{A}^* = \mathbf{P} \cdot \left[\mathbf{A}_1 \otimes \mathbf{I}_m^{\otimes(d-1)} \|\cdots\| \mathbf{I}_m^{\otimes(d-1)} \otimes \mathbf{A}_d\right] \cdot \mathbf{K}$ for some column span preserving matrix $\mathbf{K}$, the assumption implies secondly that

$$\text{rk}\left(\mathbf{A}^*\right) = \text{rk}\left(\left[\mathbf{A}_1 \otimes \mathbf{I}_m^{\otimes(d-1)} \|\cdots\| \mathbf{I}_m^{\otimes(d-1)} \otimes \mathbf{A}_d\right]\right)$$

Then we apply the following linear algebraic fact,

Lemma 3. *For any matrices* $\mathbf{M}, \mathbf{N}$ *with finitely many rows and columns such that* $\text{Colspan}(\mathbf{M}) \subseteq \text{Colspan}(\mathbf{N})$, *if* $\text{rk}(\mathbf{M}) = \text{rk}(\mathbf{N})$, *then* $\text{Colspan}(\mathbf{M}) = \text{Colspan}(\mathbf{N})$.

The proof can be found in Appendix 4.4 under Lemma 13.

To see that any solution $\{\mathbf{U}_i\}_{i\in[d]}$ that satisfies the set containment in Eq. 5, also satisfies the set equality found in Eq. 6. A formal statement of the conjecture on $\mathbf{P}$ and is given in Sect. 3.2.

Now that we've established this set equality, we return to our previous linear independence argument.

Lemma 4 (Simple case with P). *For matrices* $\mathbf{U}_1 = \begin{bmatrix} \mathbf{I}_w \\ \tilde{\mathbf{A}}_1 \end{bmatrix}, \mathbf{U}_2 = \begin{bmatrix} \mathbf{I}_w \\ \tilde{\mathbf{A}}_2 \end{bmatrix}$, $\mathbf{U}'_1 = \begin{bmatrix} \mathbf{I}_w \\ \tilde{\mathbf{A}}'_1 \end{bmatrix}, \mathbf{U}'_2 = \begin{bmatrix} \mathbf{I}_w \\ \tilde{\mathbf{A}}'_2 \end{bmatrix} \in \mathbb{Z}_q^{m\times w}$, *if*

$$\text{Colspan}\left(\mathbf{P} \cdot \left[\mathbf{U}_1 \otimes \mathbf{I}_m \| \mathbf{I}_m \otimes \mathbf{U}_2\right]\right) = \text{Colspan}\left(\mathbf{P} \cdot \left[\mathbf{U}'_1 \otimes \mathbf{I}_m \| \mathbf{I}_m \otimes \mathbf{U}'_2\right]\right). \quad (7)$$

then $\tilde{\mathbf{A}}_i = \tilde{\mathbf{A}}'_i$ *for* $i \in [2]$ *so that* $\mathbf{U}_1 = \mathbf{U}'_1$ *and* $\mathbf{U}_2 = \mathbf{U}'_2$.

We leave the formal proof to the technical section and instead take the opportunity to demonstrate how the conjecture naturally extends the proof above (proof of Lemma 2) to this setting in which $\mathbf{P}$ is present. To show, for example, that the first column $\mathbf{v} = \mathbf{e}_1^{(1)}$ of $\mathbf{U}_1 = \begin{bmatrix} \mathbf{I}_w \\ \tilde{\mathbf{A}}_1 \end{bmatrix}$ is equal to the first column of $\mathbf{v}'$ of $\begin{bmatrix} \mathbf{I}_w \\ \tilde{\mathbf{A}}_1' \end{bmatrix}$, we perform the almost identical steps as done before. We observe that $\mathbf{v}'$ can expressed in the basis $\mathcal{B}_1$ in a special linear combination: $\mathbf{v}' = \mathbf{e}_1^{(1)} + \sum_{j \in \{w+1,\dots,m\}} \alpha'_j \mathbf{e}_j^{(1)}$ for some coefficients α'_j. Then, using the set equality we showed above, we see that the vector $\mathbb{P} \cdot (\mathbf{v}' \otimes \mathbf{e}_m^{(2)})$, is in both $\mathrm{Colspan}\left(\mathbb{P} \cdot \left[\mathbf{U}_1 \otimes \mathbf{I}_m^{\otimes(d-1)} \| \cdots \| \mathbf{I}_m^{\otimes(d-1)} \otimes \mathbf{U}_d \right] \right)$ and in $\mathrm{Colspan}(\mathbf{A}^*)$ where $\mathbf{A}^*$ was generated in a process that left-multiplied by $\mathbb{P}$. Therefore, it can also be expressed as

$$\mathbb{P} \cdot \mathbf{v}' \otimes \mathbf{e}_m^{(2)} = \mathbb{P} \cdot \left(\mathbf{e}_1^{(1)} \otimes \mathbf{e}_m^{(2)} \right) + \sum_{j \in \{w+1,\dots,m\}} \alpha'_j \cdot \mathbb{P} \cdot \left(\mathbf{e}_j^{(1)} \otimes \mathbf{e}_m^{(2)} \right)$$

or as

$$\mathbb{P} \cdot \left(\mathbf{v}' \otimes \mathbf{e}_m^{(2)} \right) = \sum_{i \leq w \text{ or } j \leq w} \lambda_{i,j} \cdot \mathbb{P} \cdot \left(\mathbf{e}_i^{(1)} \otimes \mathbf{e}_j^{(2)} \right).$$

Taking the difference gives us the equation,

$$0 = (\lambda_{1,m} - 1) \cdot \mathbb{P} \cdot \left(\mathbf{e}_1^{(1)} \otimes \mathbf{e}_m^{(2)} \right) - \sum_{j \in \{w+1,\dots,m\}} \alpha'_j \cdot \mathbb{P} \cdot \left(\mathbf{e}_j^{(1)} \otimes \mathbf{e}_m^{(2)} \right)$$
$$+ \sum_{i \leq w \text{ or } j \leq w} \lambda_{i,j} \cdot \mathbb{P} \cdot \left(\mathbf{e}_i^{(1)} \otimes \mathbf{e}_j^{(2)} \right).$$

For us to finish arguing that all the coefficients $\alpha'_j = 0$, for $j \in \{w+1,\dots,m\}$, we need the linearly independence of the following set of vectors

$$\left\{ \mathbb{P} \cdot \left(\mathbf{e}_1^{(1)} \otimes \mathbf{e}_m^{(2)} \right) \right\} \cup \left\{ \mathbb{P} \cdot \left(\mathbf{e}_j^{(1)} \otimes \mathbf{e}_m^{(2)} \right) \right\}_{j \in \{w+1,\dots,m\}} \cup \left\{ \mathbb{P} \cdot \left(\mathbf{e}_i^{(1)} \otimes \mathbf{e}_j^{(2)} \right) \right\}_{i \leq w \text{ or } j \leq w}.$$

The proposed conjecture above that $\mathbf{P}$ preserves the linear independence of this small number of vectors directly addresses this.

2.5   Correctness of Step 2

In Step 2, we assume that the algorithm has already recovered the unique solution for $\{\tilde{\mathbf{A}}_i\}_{i \in [d]}$ (therefore, it has also recovered a unique solution for $\{\mathbf{U}_i\}_{i \in [d]}$) in Step 1. We claim that in Step 2 of the algorithm above, there exists a unique solution for $\mathbf{V}_1$ in Eq. 2, which is restated below:

$$\mathbf{P} \left[\mathbf{U}_1 \otimes \mathbf{I}_m^{\otimes(d-1)} \| \cdots \| \mathbf{I}_m^{\otimes(d-1)} \otimes \mathbf{U}_d \right] \begin{bmatrix} \mathbf{V}_1 \otimes \mathbf{B}_2' \\ \mathbf{Z} \end{bmatrix} \mathbf{P}' \cdot \mathbf{Q} = \mathbf{Y} \cdot \mathbf{Q}.$$

To show uniqueness in Step 2, we consider the homogeneous version (when the RHS is $\mathbf{0}$) of Eq. 2:

$$\mathbf{P} \left[\mathbf{U}_1 \otimes \mathbf{I}_m^{\otimes(d-1)} \| \cdots \| \mathbf{I}_m^{\otimes(d-1)} \otimes \mathbf{U}_d \right] \begin{bmatrix} \mathbf{V}_1 \otimes \mathbf{B}_2' \\ \mathbf{Z} \end{bmatrix} \mathbf{P}' \cdot \mathbf{Q} = \mathbf{0}.$$

Any solution for $\mathbf{V}_1$ and $\mathbf{Z}$ in the homogeneous version is exactly the difference of two solutions for $\mathbf{V}_1$ and $\mathbf{Z}$ in the inhomogeneous version. Therefore, by showing that the only solution for $\mathbf{V}_1$ in the homogeneous system is the zero matrix, we show that there is a unique solution for inhomogeneous version.

Intuitively, one sees that uniqueness is possible by observing that in the block $\mathbf{V}_1 \otimes \mathbf{B}_2'$ is linear in the entries of $\mathbf{V}_1$ and there are only wk unknowns but many equations (as many as the number of entries in $\mathbf{V}_1 \otimes \mathbf{B}_2'$). On the other hand, in terms of uniqueness, one should be concerned about the unknown matrix $\mathbf{Z}$ in Eq. 2. However, we show how to isolate a linear equation in only $\mathbf{V}_1$ (removing $\mathbf{Z}$) thereby revealing that $\mathbf{V}_1$ must have a unique solution with high probability. The proof of uniqueness then proceeds by a rank argument. We present an overview of this proof in three steps: firstly, we show that there always exists a solution, secondly we give a simple observation for when $\mathbf{P}$ is not present, and finally we give the high level argument for when $\mathbf{P}$ is present.

(Step 2) Existence of a Solution : By definition of the scheme, $\mathbf{A}^* \cdot \mathbf{S}^* = \bar{\mathbf{A}}^* \cdot \bar{\mathbf{S}}^*$ where,

$$\bar{\mathbf{A}}^* = \mathbf{P}(\mathbf{A}_1 \otimes \mathbf{I} \otimes \ldots \otimes \mathbf{I} | \ldots | \mathbf{I} \otimes \mathbf{I} \otimes \ldots \otimes \mathbf{A}_d),$$

$$\bar{\mathbf{S}}^* = \begin{pmatrix} \mathbf{S}_1 \otimes \mathbf{B}_2 \otimes \mathbf{B}_3 \otimes \ldots \mathbf{B}_{d-1} \otimes \mathbf{B}_d \\ \mathbf{E}_1 \otimes \mathbf{S}_2 \otimes \mathbf{B}_3 \otimes \ldots \mathbf{B}_{d-1} \otimes \mathbf{B}_d \\ \vdots \\ \mathbf{E}_1 \otimes \mathbf{E}_2 \otimes \mathbf{E}_3 \otimes \ldots \mathbf{E}_{d-1} \otimes \mathbf{S}_d \end{pmatrix} \cdot \mathbf{P}'$$

Thus, due to the properties of tensor products $\mathbf{A}^* \cdot \mathbf{S}^* = \mathbf{L}_1 \cdot \mathbf{L}_2$, where,

$$\mathbf{L}_1 = \mathbf{P}(\mathbf{A}_1 \cdot \mathbf{A}_{1,T}^{-1} \otimes \mathbf{I} \otimes \ldots \otimes \mathbf{I} | \ldots | \mathbf{I} \otimes \mathbf{I} \otimes \ldots \otimes \mathbf{A}_d \cdot \mathbf{A}_{d,T}^{-1}),$$

$$\mathbf{L}_2 = \begin{pmatrix} \mathbf{A}_{1,T} \cdot \mathbf{S}_1 \otimes \mathbf{B}_2 \otimes \mathbf{B}_3 \otimes \ldots \mathbf{B}_{d-1} \otimes \mathbf{B}_d \\ \mathbf{E}_1 \otimes \mathbf{A}_{2,T}\mathbf{S}_2 \otimes \mathbf{B}_3 \otimes \ldots \mathbf{B}_{d-1} \otimes \mathbf{B}_d \\ \vdots \\ \mathbf{E}_1 \otimes \mathbf{E}_2 \otimes \mathbf{E}_3 \otimes \ldots \mathbf{E}_{d-1} \otimes \mathbf{A}_{d,T}\mathbf{S}_d \end{pmatrix} \cdot \mathbf{P}'$$

Therefore, there is a solution to Eq. 2 where $\mathbf{V}_1 = \mathbf{A}_{1,T} \cdot \mathbf{S}_1$.

(Step 2) Uniqueness When P is Absent: Uniqueness is argued by considering the homogeneous version of Eq. 2 (obtained by taking the difference of two candidate solutions) and arguing that the only solution is the zero solution (the difference is zero, so the two solutions are equal). Consider the homogeneous equation when $\mathbf{P}$ is absent:

$$\left[\mathbf{U}_1 \otimes \mathbf{I}_m^{\otimes(d-1)} \| \cdots \| \mathbf{I}_m^{\otimes(d-1)} \otimes \mathbf{U}_d \right] \begin{bmatrix} \mathbf{V}_1' \otimes \mathbf{B}_2' \\ \mathbf{Z}' \end{bmatrix} \mathbf{P}' \cdot \mathbf{Q} = \mathbf{0} \tag{8}$$

where the entries of $\mathbf{V}_1', \mathbf{Z}'$ are the unknowns. In this case, it easy to see that $\mathbf{V}_1' = \mathbf{0}$ since we can remove $\mathbf{Z}'$ by left multiplying both sides of Eq. 8 by the matrix

$$\mathbf{U}^{\perp} \triangleq \left[\mathbf{I}_m \otimes \mathbf{U}_2^{\perp} \otimes \cdots \mathbf{U}_d^{\perp} \right]$$

where $\mathbf{U}_i^{\perp} \in \mathbb{Z}_q^{(m-w) \times m}$ are full rank annihilators of $\mathbf{U}_i$, that is $\mathbf{U}_i^{\perp} \mathbf{U}_i = \mathbf{0}$. Moreover, observe that if $\mathbf{U}_i$ are the Hermite normal forms of $\mathbf{A}_i$, then $\mathbf{U}_i^{\perp}$ also annihilates $\mathbf{A}_i$. Left multiplying both sides of Eq. 8 by $\mathbf{U}^{\perp}$ and expanding $\mathbf{B}_2' = \mathbf{B}_2 \otimes \cdots \otimes \mathbf{B}_d$ where $\mathbf{B}_i = \mathbf{A}_i \mathbf{S}_i + \mathbf{E}_i$ gives:

$$\left(\mathbf{U}_1 \cdot \mathbf{V}_1' \otimes \mathbf{U}_2^{\perp} \cdot \mathbf{E}_2 \otimes \cdots \otimes \mathbf{U}_d^{\perp} \cdot \mathbf{E}_d \right) \cdot \mathbf{P}' \cdot \mathbf{Q} = \mathbf{0}. \tag{9}$$

This equation implies that $\mathbf{V}_1' = \mathbf{0}$ with high probability. Observe that the error terms $\mathbf{E}_i$, the matrix $\mathbf{P}'$, and the matrix $\mathbf{Q}$ are independently produced. Moreover, with high probability over the choice of error terms $\mathbf{E}_i$, we have $\mathbf{U}_i^{\perp} \cdot \mathbf{E}_i \neq \mathbf{0}$. If $\mathbf{V}_1'$ is non-zero then $\mathbf{U}_1 \cdot \mathbf{V}_1' \neq \mathbf{0}$, since $\mathbf{U}_1$ has full column rank, which would imply that the LHS of Eq. 9 is non-zero, a contradiction. Therefore, $\mathbf{V}_1' = \mathbf{0}$ with high probability and we have uniqueness for a solution to $\mathbf{V}_1$ when $\mathbf{P}$ is absent.

(Step 2) Uniqueness When P is Present: Now we consider the homogeneous equation with $\mathbf{P}$:

$$\mathbf{P} \cdot \left[\mathbf{U}_1 \otimes \mathbf{I}_m^{\otimes(d-1)} \| \cdots \| \mathbf{I}_m^{\otimes(d-1)} \otimes \mathbf{U}_d \right] \begin{bmatrix} \mathbf{V}_1' \otimes \mathbf{B}_2' \\ \mathbf{Z}' \end{bmatrix} \mathbf{P}' \cdot \mathbf{Q} = \mathbf{0} \tag{10}$$

where $\mathbf{V}_1'$ and $\mathbf{Z}'$ are the unknowns. Here, from the matrix point of view the tensor structure is destroyed by the action of $\mathbf{P}$, for example consider $\mathbf{P} \cdot (\mathbf{U}_1 \otimes \mathbf{I}_m^{\otimes(d-1)})$, obstructing us from using the simple argument for uniqueness above. An argument using column spans is also inhibited because the matrix of interest $\begin{bmatrix} \mathbf{V}_1' \otimes \mathbf{B}_2' \\ \mathbf{Z}' \end{bmatrix}$ is left-multiplied by the matrix

$$\mathbf{P} \left[\mathbf{U}_1 \otimes \mathbf{I}_m^{\otimes(d-1)} \| \cdots \| \mathbf{I}_m^{\otimes(d-1)} \otimes \mathbf{U}_d \right] .$$

The key insight from the simple argument above is that it allowed us to isolate $\mathbf{V}_1'$ in a simple homogeneous equation where $\mathbf{Z}'$ is absent. Therefore, we aim to again isolate $\mathbf{V}_1'$ in a simple homogeneous equation to prove uniqueness in this general setting, we first expand Eq. 10:

$$\mathbf{P} \cdot \left[\mathbf{U}_1 \otimes \mathbf{I}_m^{\otimes(d-1)} \right] (\mathbf{V}_1' \otimes \mathbf{B}_2') \cdot \mathbf{P}' \cdot \mathbf{Q}$$
$$+ \mathbf{P} \cdot \left[\mathbf{I}_m \otimes \mathbf{U}_2 \otimes \mathbf{I}_m^{\otimes(d-2)} \| \cdots \| \mathbf{I}_m^{\otimes(d-1)} \otimes \mathbf{U}_d \right] \mathbf{Z}' \cdot \mathbf{P}' \cdot \mathbf{Q} = \mathbf{0}$$

Applying the principle of wishful thinking, if the columns of $\mathbf{P} \cdot \left[\mathbf{U}_1 \otimes \mathbf{I}_m^{\otimes(d-1)} \right]$ were linearly independent from those of $\mathbf{P} \cdot \left[\mathbf{I}_m \otimes \mathbf{U}_2 \otimes \mathbf{I}_m^{\otimes(d-2)} \| \cdots \| \mathbf{I}_m^{\otimes(d-1)} \otimes \mathbf{U}_d \right]$ then the first term alone must satisfy $\mathbf{P} \cdot \left[\mathbf{U}_1 \otimes \mathbf{I}_m^{\otimes(d-1)} \right] (\mathbf{V}_1' \otimes \mathbf{B}_2') \cdot \mathbf{P}' \cdot \mathbf{Q} = \mathbf{0}$, thereby isolating $\mathbf{V}_1'$ in a new homogeneous equation without the presence of $\mathbf{Z}'$. This independence, however, is false. The two column spans certainly overlap.

To make this approach work, a simple modification suffices: we can take a submatrix of $\mathbf{P} \cdot \left[\mathbf{U}_1 \otimes \mathbf{I}_m^{\otimes(d-1)}\right]$ and remove from consideration all the columns of $\mathbf{P} \cdot \left[\mathbf{U}_1 \otimes \mathbf{I}_m^{\otimes(d-1)}\right]$ contained in

$$\mathrm{Colspan}\left(\mathbf{P} \cdot \left[\mathbf{I}_m \otimes \mathbf{U}_2 \otimes \mathbf{I}_m^{\otimes(d-2)} \| \cdots \| \mathbf{I}_m^{\otimes(d-1)} \otimes \mathbf{U}_d\right]\right).$$

Moreover, we can compute the exact rank of this submatrix combinatorially as $w(m - w)^{d-1}$. Leaving the exact details to the main technical body, this observation leads us to an equation of the form

$$\mathbf{X}_1 \cdot (\mathbf{V}_1' \otimes \mathbf{B}_2') \cdot \mathbf{P}' \cdot \mathbf{Q} = 0.$$

for some matrix $\mathbf{X}_1$ that has a nullspace of dimension $O(w^2 m^{d-2})$. On the other hand, we will observe that when $\mathbf{V}_1' \neq 0$, $\mathbf{V}_1' \otimes \mathbf{B}_2'$ has rank at least $O(m^{d-1})$. Therefore, it must be the case that $\mathbf{V}_1' = 0$ if $m = \omega(w^2)$ and we observe that the initial work of [29] sets $m \geq w^3$. In a nutshell, the significant amount of non-overlap of the column span of $\mathbf{P} \cdot \left[\mathbf{U}_1 \otimes \mathbf{I}_m^{\otimes(d-1)}\right]$ with the column span $\mathrm{Colspan}\left(\mathbf{P} \cdot \left[\mathbf{I}_m \otimes \mathbf{U}_2 \otimes \mathbf{I}_m^{\otimes(d-2)} \| \cdots \| \mathbf{I}_m^{\otimes(d-1)} \otimes \mathbf{U}_d\right]\right)$ is still enough to argue uniqueness of $\mathbf{V}_1$. The full details of this uniqueness claim can be found in Sect. 4.1.

3   Our Attack

Theorem 1. *Under Conjecture 1, there exists a polynomial time probabilistic algorithm that recovers $\{\mathbf{E}_i\}_{i\in[d]}$ for $i \in [d]$ when given an input from $\mathcal{D}_0$.*

Proof. We construct an algorithm $\mathcal{A}$ that takes an input

$$\Delta_0 = (\mathbf{P}, \mathbf{P}', \mathbf{A}^*, \{\mathbf{B}_i\}_{i\in[d]}, \hat{\mathbf{B}}, \mathbf{C}, \mathbf{E}^* + \mathbf{E} \cdot G^{-1}(\hat{\mathbf{B}})),$$

and outputs $\{\mathbf{E}_i\}_{i\in[d]}$. In a nutshell, the algorithm will be able to compute matrices $\mathbf{V}_1 \in \mathbb{Z}_q^{m\times w}$ and $\mathbf{U}_1 \in \mathbb{Z}_q^{w\times k}$ such that $\mathbf{B}_1 \in \mathbb{Z}_q^{m\times k}$ such that $\mathbf{B}_1 = \mathbf{U}_1 \cdot \mathbf{V}_1 + \mathbf{E}_1 \in \mathbb{Z}_q^{m\times k}$ such that $\mathbf{E}_1 \in \mathbb{Z}_q^{m\times k}$ has a small norm. Our attack recovers all the errors $\mathbf{E}_i$ for $i \in [d]$, giving a full recovery algorithm.

As described in the overview, there are only two steps where each step only uses Gaussian Elimination on polynomial sized systems of equations.

──────────── **Algorithm for Recovery of $\mathbf{E}_1$** ────────────

Input: $(\mathbf{P}, \mathbf{P}', \mathbf{A}^*, \{\mathbf{B}_i\}_{i\in[d]}, \hat{\mathbf{B}}, \mathbf{C}, \mathbf{E}^* + \mathbf{E}G^{-1}(\hat{\mathbf{B}}))$.
Output: $\{\tilde{\mathbf{A}}_i\}_{i\in[d]}, \mathbf{V}_1, \mathbf{E}_1$.

1. **Recover** $\mathbf{U}_1, \ldots, \mathbf{U}_d$: Solve the affine system of equations defined by

$$\mathbf{P} \cdot \left[\mathbf{U}_1 \otimes \mathbf{I}_m^{\otimes(d-1)} \| \mathbf{I}_m \otimes \mathbf{U}_2 \otimes \mathbf{I}_m^{\otimes(d-2)} \| \cdots \| \mathbf{I}_m^{\otimes(d-1)} \otimes \mathbf{U}_d\right] = \mathbf{A}^* \cdot \mathbf{M}$$

where $\mathbf{U}_i = \begin{bmatrix} \mathbf{I}_w \\ \tilde{\mathbf{A}}_i \end{bmatrix}$, for $i \in [d]$, and the variables are given by the entries of $\tilde{\mathbf{A}}_1, \ldots, \tilde{\mathbf{A}}_d \in \mathbb{Z}_q^{(m-w) \times w}$ and the entries of $\mathbf{M} \in \mathbb{Z}_q^{W \times dwm^{d-1}}$ and the coefficients are given by the entries of $\mathbf{A}^*$ and $\mathbf{P}$. We discuss this step in detail in Sect. 3.2.

2. **Recover** $\mathbf{V}_1$: Having recovered the unique matrices $\{\tilde{\mathbf{A}}_i\}_{i \in [d]}$, our algorithm now aims to recover $\mathbf{V}_1$ such that $\mathbf{U}_1 \cdot \mathbf{V}_1 = \mathbf{A}_1 \cdot \mathbf{S}_1$. To do this, our algorithm computes

$$\mathbf{Y} = \mathbf{A}^* \cdot (\mathbf{S}^* + \mathbf{R} \cdot \mathbf{G}^{-1}(\hat{\mathbf{B}}))$$

by subtracting off the error $\mathbf{E}^* + \mathbf{E} \cdot \mathbf{G}^{-1}(\hat{\mathbf{B}})$ from $\mathbf{B}^* + \mathbf{C} \cdot \mathbf{G}^{-1}(\mathbf{B})$. Then it computes, via standard linear algebra, a full rank annihilator matrix $\mathbf{Q} \in \mathbb{Z}_q^{K \times (K - M \log q)}$ such that $\mathbf{G}^{-1}(\hat{\mathbf{B}}) \cdot \mathbf{Q} = \mathbf{0}$, obtaining the equation,

$$\mathbf{A}^* \cdot \mathbf{S}^* \cdot \mathbf{Q} = \mathbf{Y} \cdot \mathbf{Q}.$$

Finally, it solves the linear system of equations defined by

$$\mathbf{P} \left[\mathbf{U}_1 \otimes \mathbf{I}_m^{\otimes(d-1)} \| \cdots \| \mathbf{I}_m^{\otimes(d-1)} \otimes \mathbf{U}_d\right] \begin{bmatrix} \mathbf{V}_1 \otimes \mathbf{B}_2' \\ \mathbf{Z} \end{bmatrix} \mathbf{P}' \cdot \mathbf{Q} = \mathbf{Y} \cdot \mathbf{Q}$$

where $\mathbf{B}_2' = \mathbf{B}_2 \otimes \ldots \otimes \mathbf{B}_d$ and where the variables are the entries of $\mathbf{V}_1$ and $\mathbf{Z}$ and the coefficients are given by the entries of $\mathbf{P}, \mathbf{P}', \mathbf{Q}, \mathbf{Y}, \mathbf{U}_i$, for $i \in [d]$, and $\mathbf{B}_2'$. Finally, $\mathbf{E}_1$ is now recovered by computing $\mathbf{B}_1 - \mathbf{U}_1 \cdot \mathbf{V}_1$. We discuss this step in Sect. 4.1.

The above two steps details the main step of the algorithm. Having recovered $\mathbf{U}_1, \mathbf{V}_1$, we can now recover $\mathbf{E}_1$ from $\mathbf{B}_1$. We now describe how to extend the same recovery algorithm to $\mathbf{E}_2, \ldots, \mathbf{E}_d$. First consider the case of recovering $\mathbf{E}_2$.

Extension to $\mathbf{E}_2$: The algorithm described above allows us to learn recover $\mathbf{V}_1$ and $\mathbf{E}_1$ where $\mathbf{B}_1 - \mathbf{U}_1 \mathbf{V}_1 = \mathbf{E}_1$. The idea is that we can repeat this process to learn $\mathbf{E}_2, \ldots, \mathbf{E}_d$. Note that in the equation

$$\mathbf{P}(\mathbf{U}_1 \otimes \mathbf{I}_m^{\otimes(d-1)} \| \cdots \| \mathbf{I}_m^{\otimes(d-1)} \otimes \mathbf{U}_d) \cdot \begin{bmatrix} \mathbf{V}_1 \otimes \mathbf{B}^{(2,\ldots,d)} \\ \mathbf{Z} \end{bmatrix} \mathbf{P}' \mathbf{Q} = \mathbf{Y} \mathbf{Q},$$

once $\mathbf{V}_1$ is known, we can begin exploiting the structure of a candidate solution to $\mathbf{Z}$. In particular, there exists a solution for $\mathbf{Z}$ which is of the form:

$$\bar{\mathbf{Z}} = \begin{pmatrix} \mathbf{E}_1 \otimes \mathbf{A}_{2,T} \cdot \mathbf{S}_2 \otimes \mathbf{B}_3 \otimes \ldots \otimes \mathbf{B}_{d-1} \otimes \mathbf{B}_d \\ \vdots \\ \mathbf{E}_1 \otimes \mathbf{E}_2 \otimes \mathbf{E}_3 \otimes \ldots \otimes \mathbf{E}_{d-1} \otimes \mathbf{A}_{d,T}\mathbf{S}_d \end{pmatrix} \cdot \mathbf{P}'.$$

This form allows us to solve for $\mathbf{V}_2, \mathbf{Z}_2$, once we have $\mathbf{V}_1, \mathbf{E}_1$, by setting up the system of affine equations given by:

$$\mathbf{P}(\mathbf{U}_1 \otimes \mathbf{I}_m^{\otimes(d-1)} \| \cdots \| \mathbf{I}_m^{\otimes(d-1)} \otimes \mathbf{U}_d) \cdot \begin{bmatrix} \mathbf{V}_1 \otimes \mathbf{B}^{(2,\ldots,d)} \\ \mathbf{E}_1 \otimes \mathbf{V}_2 \otimes \mathbf{B}_3 \otimes \ldots \otimes \mathbf{B}_{d-1} \otimes \mathbf{B}_d \\ \mathbf{Z}_2 \end{bmatrix} \mathbf{P}'\mathbf{Q}$$

$$= \mathbf{YQ}$$

for which we know a candidate solution for $\mathbf{V}_2$ is $\mathbf{A}_{2,T}\mathbf{S}_2$. Here the unknowns are the entries of $\mathbf{V}_2, \mathbf{Z}_2$ and the coefficients are given by all the other matrices' entries. We solve for $\mathbf{V}_2$ as the equation is now linear in $\mathbf{V}_2$. Proving that this solution is unique will use the exact same ideas as above, except on a smaller system of equations which are affine instead of linear. We will continue this way for all remaining indices $i \in [d]$. We prove this uniqueness formally for the case of $i = 1$ in Sect. 4.1 and remark here that uniqueness in the other cases follow similarly.

Remark 3. Theorem 1 shows a full recovery attack for the case that the input is from $\mathcal{D}_0$ and can be extended via a heuristic argument to a distinguisher between $\mathcal{D}_0$ and $\mathcal{D}_1$ which we discuss in Sect. 3.1.

3.1 Distinguishing $\mathcal{D}_0$ from $\mathcal{D}_1$

To come up with a distinguisher which takes an instance from $\mathcal{D}_b$ for some $b \in \{0, 1\}$, we follow the following approach:

- We use the algorithm described in Theorem 1 to learn $\mathbf{E}_1, \ldots, \mathbf{E}_d$. As a remark, we note that equations solved for in the algorithm can be set up regardless of whether $b = 0$ or $b = 1$. What we show is that the recovery will succeed with high probability when $b = 0$.
- Once we have $\mathbf{E}_1, \ldots, \mathbf{E}_d$ we can compute $\mathbf{E}^* = \mathbf{P} \cdot (\mathbf{E}_1 \otimes \cdots \otimes \mathbf{E}_d) \cdot \mathbf{P}'$. Then, we can use the error leakage from the assumption $\mathbf{E}^* + \mathbf{E} \cdot G^{-1}(\hat{\mathbf{B}})$ to learn $\mathbf{E} \cdot G^{-1}(\hat{\mathbf{B}})$. We simply check that this is annihilated by multiplying by $\mathbf{Q}$. This will succeed in the case that $b = 0$.
- In the case when $b = 1$, the check will not pass because of the presence of a random error matrix $\mathbf{F}$, namely the leakage term is given by $\mathbf{E}^* + \mathbf{E} \cdot G^{-1}(\hat{\mathbf{B}}) - \mathbf{F}$ and even if we solve for $\mathbf{E}^*$ and attempt to annihilate the remaining terms, the term $\mathbf{E} \cdot G^{-1}(\hat{\mathbf{B}}) - \mathbf{F}$ cannot be annihilated because heuristically a random matrix $\mathbf{F}$ is unlikely to lie in the row span of $G^{-1}(\hat{\mathbf{B}})$ (note that $G^{-1}(\hat{\mathbf{B}})$ is a wide matrix with a large right nullspace) .

3.2   Recovery of Unique $\tilde{\mathbf{A}}_i$'s

Our first objective is to recover the matrices $\mathbf{A}_1, \ldots, \mathbf{A}_d$ up to a unique representation $\mathbf{U}_1 = \begin{bmatrix} \mathbf{I}_w \\ \tilde{\mathbf{A}}_1 \end{bmatrix}, \ldots, \mathbf{U}_d = \begin{bmatrix} \mathbf{I}_w \\ \tilde{\mathbf{A}}_d \end{bmatrix}$. The intuition for the below section is provided in detail in Sect. 2.4.

Useful Claims and Conjectures

Conjecture 1 (Linear independence preservation under $\mathbf{P}$). Let $m, w, d, k, K,$ M, q, χ be parameters defined previously. If $\mathbf{v}_1, \ldots, \mathbf{v}_T$ are arbitrary linearly independent vectors in $\mathbb{Z}_q^{\otimes d}$, where $T = m^d - (m-w)^d + d \cdot m$ then with probability $1 - q^{-\Omega(w^2 m)}$ over the choice of $\mathbf{P} \leftarrow \chi^{M \times m^d}$, we have that $\mathbf{P} \cdot \mathbf{v}_1, \ldots, \mathbf{P} \cdot \mathbf{v}_T$ are linearly independent.

Remark 4 (Limit on Modulus Size). Naively using exponential modulus-to-noise ratios does not break the conjecture because the hardness of LWE puts a limit on this ratio. As a concrete attempt to break the conjecture, let us focus on the probability of sampling the zero-matrix, $\mathbf{P} \leftarrow \mathbf{0}$, given by $B^{-m^d \cdot M} = B^{-m^{2d-(1/2)}}$. The zero-matrix is not injective on any non-trivial subspace so to attempt to break the conjecture, we can set the modulus q such that the probability of sampling the zero-matrix is larger than $q^{-\Omega(w^2 m)}$. For this attempt to be succeed, we require the relation $B^{-m^{2d-(1/2)}} \geq q^{-\Omega(w^2 m)}$ which implies that setting $q \geq B^{\Omega(m^{2d-3/2}/w^2)} \geq 2^{\Omega(m^{2d-3/2}/w^2)}$ (since $B \geq 2$) is enough to refute the conjecture. Since $d \geq 3$ and $m \geq w^3$, this setting of modulus q is much too large for LWE security to hold as security requires $q \leq 2^{O(m)}$. In other words, in this setting, the distribution χ is *not* an LWE-friendly error distribution and is not an admissible choice of χ allowed in the original assumptions (see Sect. 2.1 and Remark 1).

Remark 5. If $\mathbf{P}$ is a uniformly random matrix over $\mathbb{Z}_q^{M \times m^d}$, a straightforward counting argument suffices to prove the above conjecture. If $\mathbf{P}$ is random, then $\mathbf{P}\mathbf{v}_1, \ldots, \mathbf{P}\mathbf{v}_T$ are jointly distributed as random vectors over $\mathbb{Z}_q^M$ provided $T \ll M$. For random vectors, the probability that they are linearly independent is at least $1 - O(T \cdot \frac{q^{T-1}}{q^M}) = 1 - O(q^{-M/2})$ when $T \ll M$.

Now we use the conjecture and express it in a notation useful to our proofs.

Corollary 3 (Linear independence preservation under P, Useful Notation). *Let $m, w, d, k, K, M, q, \chi$ be parameters defined previously. Let $\mathbf{e}_j^{(i)}$ denote the jth column of the matrix $\mathcal{B}_i$, which was defined in Sect. 2.3 so that for $i \in [d]$, the set $\{\mathbf{e}_1^{(i)}, \mathbf{e}_2^{(i)}, \ldots, \mathbf{e}_m^{(i)}\}$ is a basis for $\mathbb{Z}_q^m$. Then define*

$$\mathcal{B} \triangleq \left\{ \mathbf{e}_{i_1}^{(1)} \otimes \cdots \otimes \mathbf{e}_{i_d}^{(d)} : i_1, \ldots, i_d \in [m] \wedge \exists j \in [d], i_j \leq w, \right\}$$

$$\cup \bigcup_{k=1}^{d} \left\{ \mathbf{e}_m^{(1)} \otimes \cdots \otimes \mathbf{e}_m^{(k-1)} \otimes \mathbf{e}_\ell^{(k)} \otimes \mathbf{e}_m^{(k+1)} \otimes \cdots \otimes \mathbf{e}_m^{(d)} : \ell \in [m] \right\}.$$

Assuming Conjecture 1 and $\mathbf{P}$ *is sampled from* $\chi^{M \times m^d}$, *with probability* $1 - q^{-\Omega(w^2 m)}$, *the vectors in the set* $\mathcal{B}^{\mathbf{P}} \triangleq \{\mathbf{P} \cdot \mathbf{v} : \mathbf{v} \in \mathcal{B}\}$ *are linearly independent.*

Proof. Set $\mathbf{v}_1, \ldots, \mathbf{v}_T$ to the vectors in $\mathcal{B}$.

We now show that under Conjecture 1, for a random choice of $\mathbf{P}$ from χ, with overwhelming probability there is no choice of matrices $\{\tilde{\mathbf{A}}_i\}_{i \in [d]}$ for which $\mathbf{P}$ does not preserve the linear independence of the set $\mathcal{B}$.

Lemma 5. *Let* $\mathbf{P} \leftarrow \chi^{M \times m^d}$ *and for* $i \in [d]$, *let* $\tilde{\mathbf{A}}_i \in \mathbb{Z}_q^{(m-w) \times w}$. *Assuming Conjecture 1,*

$$\Pr_{\mathbf{P}}\left[\exists \{\tilde{\mathbf{A}}_i\}_{i \in [d]} \text{ s.t. } \mathcal{B}^{\mathbf{P}} \text{ not linearly independent}\right] = q^{-\Omega(w^2 m)} = \mathsf{negl}(w)$$

Proof. By Corollary 3, the probability over choice of $\mathbf{P}$ that $\mathbf{P}$ preserves the linear independence of $\mathcal{B}$ defined with respect to a fixed set of $\{\tilde{\mathbf{A}}_i\}_{i \in [d]}$ is $1 - q^{-\Omega(w^2 m)}$. Taking a union bound over all possible values of $\{\tilde{\mathbf{A}}_i\}_{i \in [d]}$, for which there are $q^{dw(m-w)}$ many, we have

$$\Pr_{\mathbf{P}}[\exists \{\tilde{\mathbf{A}}_i\}_{i \in [d]} \text{ s.t. } \mathcal{B}^{\mathbf{P}} \text{ not linearly independent}] = q^{-\Omega(w^2 m) + dw(m-w)} = q^{-\Omega(w^2 m)}.$$

Lemma 6. *For* $i \in [d]$, *let* $\mathbf{L}_i \triangleq \mathbf{I}_m^{\otimes(i-1)} \otimes \begin{bmatrix} \mathbf{I}_w \\ \tilde{\mathbf{A}}_i \end{bmatrix} \otimes \mathbf{I}_m^{\otimes(d-i)}$ *and let* $\tilde{\mathbf{A}} \triangleq [\mathbf{L}_1 \| \mathbf{L}_2 \| \cdots \| \mathbf{L}_d]$. *Under Conjecture 1, with overwhelming probability over the choice of* $\mathbf{P} \leftarrow \chi^{M \times m^d}$, *we have that the following holds for any set of matrices* $\{\tilde{\mathbf{A}}_i\}_{i \in [d]}$.

$$\forall i \in [d], \dim(\mathbf{P} \cdot \mathbf{L}_i) = wm^{d-1}$$

$$\dim\left(\mathrm{Colspan}\left([\mathbf{P} \cdot \mathbf{L}_1 \| \mathbf{P} \cdot \mathbf{L}_2 \| \ldots \| \mathbf{P} \cdot \mathbf{L}_d]\right)\right) = m^d - (m-w)^d = dwm^{d-1} - O\left(w^2 m^{d-2}\right)$$

$$\dim\left(\mathrm{Colspan}(\mathbf{P} \cdot \mathbf{L}_1) \cap \mathrm{Colspan}\left([\mathbf{P} \cdot \mathbf{L}_2 \| \ldots \| \mathbf{P} \cdot \mathbf{L}_d]\right)\right) = wm^{d-1} - w(m-w)^{d-1}$$

Proof. The proof can be found in the Supplementary Materials (under Lemma 18).

Main Theorem for the Recovery of $\tilde{\mathbf{A}}_i$'s. The following theorem immediately gives rise to our recovery algorithm.

Theorem 2 (Unique solutions for $\tilde{\mathbf{A}}_i$). *Let* M, m, w, k, d, q, χ *be parameters as defined previously. Sample* $\mathbf{P} \leftarrow \chi^{M \times m^d}$. *Then with probability* $1 - \mathsf{negl}(m)$, *over the choice of* $\mathbf{P}$ *we have that for any choice of* $\tilde{\mathbf{A}}_i \in \mathbb{Z}_q^{(m-w) \times w}$ *for* $i \in [d]$ *and* $\tilde{\mathbf{A}}_i'$, *we have the following where we define*

$$\tilde{\mathbf{A}} \triangleq \left[\begin{bmatrix} \mathbf{I}_w \\ \tilde{\mathbf{A}}_1 \end{bmatrix} \otimes \mathbf{I}_m^{\otimes(d-1)} \| \mathbf{I}_m \otimes \begin{bmatrix} \mathbf{I}_w \\ \tilde{\mathbf{A}}_2 \end{bmatrix} \otimes \mathbf{I}_m^{\otimes(d-2)} \| \cdots \| \mathbf{I}_m^{\otimes(d-1)} \otimes \begin{bmatrix} \mathbf{I}_w \\ \tilde{\mathbf{A}}_d \end{bmatrix} \right]$$

$$\tilde{\mathbf{A}}' \triangleq \left[\begin{bmatrix} \mathbf{I}_w \\ \tilde{\mathbf{A}}_1' \end{bmatrix} \otimes \mathbf{I}_m^{\otimes(d-1)} \| \mathbf{I}_m \otimes \begin{bmatrix} \mathbf{I}_w \\ \tilde{\mathbf{A}}_2' \end{bmatrix} \otimes \mathbf{I}_m^{\otimes(d-2)} \| \cdots \| \mathbf{I}_m^{\otimes(d-1)} \otimes \begin{bmatrix} \mathbf{I}_w \\ \tilde{\mathbf{A}}_d' \end{bmatrix} \right].$$

1. *If,* Colspan $\left(\mathbf{P}\tilde{\mathbf{A}}'\right) \subseteq$ Colspan $\left(\mathbf{P}\tilde{\mathbf{A}}\right)$, *then* Colspan $\left(\mathbf{P}\tilde{\mathbf{A}}'\right) =$ Colspan $\left(\mathbf{P}\tilde{\mathbf{A}}\right)$.

2. *Furthermore, if* Colspan $\left(\mathbf{P}\tilde{\mathbf{A}}'\right) =$ Colspan $\left(\mathbf{P}\tilde{\mathbf{A}}\right)$ *for all* $i \in [d]$, *then* $\tilde{\mathbf{A}}_i = \tilde{\mathbf{A}}'_i$.

Proof. The proof of the first claim was fully addressed in Sect. 2.4 in *(Step 1) Uniqueness in the general case.*

We now address the second claim. The proof proceeds column-by-column of $\begin{bmatrix} \mathbf{I}_w \\ \tilde{\mathbf{A}}'_i \end{bmatrix}$ for $i \in [d]$ and shows that each column of $\begin{bmatrix} \mathbf{I}_w \\ \tilde{\mathbf{A}}_i \end{bmatrix}$ is equal to its corresponding column in $\begin{bmatrix} \mathbf{I}_w \\ \tilde{\mathbf{A}}_i \end{bmatrix}$. We'll show that the first column of $\begin{bmatrix} \mathbf{I}_w \\ \tilde{\mathbf{A}}'_1 \end{bmatrix}$, say $\mathbf{d}_1^{(1)}$, is equal to the first column of $\begin{bmatrix} \mathbf{I}_w \\ \tilde{\mathbf{A}}_1 \end{bmatrix}$.

First, for every $i \in [d]$ extend the columns of $\begin{bmatrix} \mathbf{I}_w \\ \tilde{\mathbf{A}}_i \end{bmatrix}$ to a basis for $\mathbb{Z}_q^m$ given by the columns of the matrix $\mathcal{B}_i$ below:

$$\mathcal{B}_i \triangleq \begin{bmatrix} \mathbf{I}_w & \mathbf{0}_{w \times (m-w)} \\ \tilde{\mathbf{A}}_i & \mathbf{I}_{m-w} \end{bmatrix} \in \mathbb{Z}_q^{m \times m}.$$

Let $\mathbf{e}_j^{(i)}$ denote the jth column in $\mathcal{B}_i$ and observe that for all the jth columns of $\mathcal{B}_i$ for $j \in [w+1, m]$ are all elementary vectors. That is, for $i \in [d]$ and for $j \in \{w+1, \dots, d\}$, $\mathbf{e}_j^{(i)} = \mathbf{e}_j$ where $\mathbf{e}_j$ is the jth elementary vector. Now we aim to show that $\mathbf{d}_1^{(1)} = \mathbf{e}_1^{(1)}$.

Take a carefully chosen column of $\mathbf{P}\tilde{\mathbf{A}}'$, namely $\mathbf{P} \cdot \left(\mathbf{d}_1^{(1)} \otimes \mathbf{e}_m^{(2)} \otimes \cdots \otimes \mathbf{e}_m^{(d)}\right) \in$ Colspan $\left(\mathbf{P}\tilde{\mathbf{A}}'\right) =$ Colspan $\left(\mathbf{P}\tilde{\mathbf{A}}\right)$. Therefore, we can write an equation:

$$\mathbf{P} \cdot \left(\mathbf{d}_1^{(1)} \otimes \mathbf{e}_m^{(2)} \otimes \cdots \otimes \mathbf{e}_m^{(d)}\right) \tag{*}$$

$$= \sum_{i_1, i_2, \dots, i_d \in [m] \exists j \in [d] \text{ s.t. } i_j \in [w]} \lambda_{i_1, \dots, i_d} \cdot \mathbf{P} \cdot (\mathbf{e}_{i_1}^{(1)} \otimes \cdots \otimes \mathbf{e}_{i_d}^{(d)})$$

Now observe that, $\mathbf{d}_1^{(1)}$ has a special form. Namely, the first column $\mathbf{d}_1^{(1)}$ must be of the form $\mathbf{d}_1^{(1)} = \mathbf{e}_1^{(1)} + \sum_{w < j \le m} \alpha_j^{(1)} \mathbf{e}_j^{(1)}$ for some coefficients $\alpha_j^{(1)} \in \mathbb{Z}_q$, $j \in \{w+1, \dots, m\}$. If we show that $\alpha_j^{(1)} = 0$ for all $j \in \{w+1, \dots, m\}$, then $\mathbf{d}_1^{(1)} = \mathbf{e}_1^{(1)}$ and $\mathbf{e}_1^{(1)}$ is the first column of $\begin{bmatrix} \mathbf{I}_w \\ \tilde{\mathbf{A}}_1 \end{bmatrix}$.

Substituting for $\mathbf{d}_1^{(1)}$, we have

$$\mathbf{P} \cdot \left(\mathbf{d}_1^{(1)} \otimes \mathbf{e}_m^{(2)} \otimes \cdots \otimes \mathbf{e}_m^{(d)} \right) \tag{$**$}$$

$$= \mathbf{P} \cdot \left(\left(\mathbf{e}_1^{(1)} + \sum_{j>w} \alpha_j^{(1)} \mathbf{e}_j^{(1)} \right) \otimes \mathbf{e}_m^{(2)} \otimes \cdots \mathbf{e}_m^{(d)} \right)$$

$$= \mathbf{P} \cdot \left(\mathbf{e}_1^{(1)} \otimes \mathbf{e}_m^{(2)} \otimes \cdots \mathbf{e}_m^{(d)} \right) + \sum_{j>w} \alpha_j^{(1)} \mathbf{P} \cdot \left(\mathbf{e}_j^{(1)} \otimes \mathbf{e}_m^{(2)} \otimes \cdots \mathbf{e}_m^{(d)} \right)$$

Taking the difference of equation (*) and (**), we see that we have

$$0 = (\lambda_{1,m,m,\dots,m} - 1) \cdot \mathbf{P} \cdot (\mathbf{e}_1^{(1)} \otimes \mathbf{e}_m^{(2)} \otimes \cdots \mathbf{e}_m^{(d)})$$

$$+ \sum_{i_1 \in \{w+1,\dots,m\}} \alpha_j^{(1)} \cdot \mathbf{P} \cdot (\mathbf{e}_{i_1}^{(1)} \otimes \mathbf{e}_m^{(2)} \otimes \cdots \otimes \mathbf{e}_m^{(d)})$$

$$+ \sum_{i_1,i_2,\dots,i_d \in [m] \exists j \in [d]\ \mathrm{s.t.}\ i_j \in [w]} \lambda_{i_1,\dots,i_d} \cdot \mathbf{P} \cdot (\mathbf{e}_{i_1}^{(1)} \otimes \cdots \otimes \mathbf{e}_{i_d}^{(d)})$$

Now observe that every vector in this linear combination is linearly independent by Lemma 5 which states that

$$\mathcal{B}^{\mathbf{P}} = \left\{ \mathbf{P} \cdot \left(\mathbf{e}_{i_1}^{(1)} \otimes \cdots \otimes \mathbf{e}_{i_d}^{(d)} \right) : i_1,\dots,i_d \in [m] \wedge \exists j \in [d], i_j \leq w, \right\}$$

$$\cup \bigcup_{k=1}^{d} \left\{ \mathbf{P} \cdot \left(\mathbf{e}_m^{(1)} \otimes \cdots \mathbf{e}_m^{(k-1)} \otimes \mathbf{e}_\ell^{(k)} \otimes \mathbf{e}_m^{(k+1)} \otimes \cdots \otimes \mathbf{e}_m^{(d)} \right) : \ell \in \{w+1,\dots,m\} \right\}$$

is a linearly independent set of vectors. Therefore, $\lambda_{1,m,m,\dots,m} = 1$ and $\alpha_j^{(1)} = 0$ for all $j \in \{w+1,\dots,d\}$. Therefore, $\mathbf{d}_1^{(1)} = \mathbf{e}_1^{(1)}$. To show that the ℓth column of $\begin{bmatrix} \mathbf{I}_w \\ \tilde{\mathbf{A}}_i' \end{bmatrix}$, denoted $\mathbf{d}_\ell^{(i)}$, is the ℓth column of $\begin{bmatrix} \mathbf{I}_w \\ \tilde{\mathbf{A}}_i \end{bmatrix}$, denoted $\mathbf{e}_\ell^{(i)}$, apply the same argument on the vector $\mathbf{P} \cdot \left(\mathbf{e}_m^{\otimes (i-1)} \otimes \mathbf{d}_\ell^{(i)} \otimes \mathbf{e}_m^{\otimes (d-i)} \right)$.

Acknowledgement. Aayush Jain is supported by the Computer Science Department, CMU and a seed grant from the CYLAB security and the privacy institute, CMU. Amit Sahai was supported in part from a Simons Investigator Award, DARPA SIEVE award, NTT Research, NSF Frontier Award 1413955, BSF grant 2012378, a Xerox Faculty Research Award, a Google Faculty Research Award, and an Okawa Foundation Research Grant. This material is based upon work supported by the Defense Advanced Research Projects Agency through Award HR00112020024. Huijia Lin was supported by NSF grants CNS-1936825 (CAREER), CNS-2026774, a JP Morgan AI research Award, a Cisco research award, and a Simons Collaboration on the Theory of Algorithmic Fairness. This work was done (in part) while Paul Lou was visiting the Simons Institute for the Theory of Computing.

We gratefully thank Hoeteck Wee for several extended technical discussions which greatly developed the presentation of our attack. We are also grateful to the anonymous TCC reviewers for graciously providing a thorough review process and giving us very useful feedback about our presentation.

References

1. Agrawal, S.: Indistinguishability obfuscation without multilinear maps: new methods for bootstrapping and instantiation. In: Ishai, Y., Rijmen, V. (eds.) EUROCRYPT 2019, Part I. LNCS, vol. 11476, pp. 191–225. Springer, Heidelberg (2019). https://doi.org/10.1007/978-3-030-17653-2_7

2. Agrawal, S., Pellet-Mary, A.: Indistinguishability obfuscation without maps: attacks and fixes for noisy linear FE. In: Canteaut, A., Ishai, Y. (eds.) EUROCRYPT 2020, Part I. LNCS, vol. 12105, pp. 110–140. Springer, Heidelberg (2020). https://doi.org/10.1007/978-3-030-45721-1_5

3. Ananth, P., Jain, A., Lin, H., Matt, C., Sahai, A.: Indistinguishability obfuscation without multilinear maps: new paradigms via low degree weak pseudorandomness and security amplification. In: Boldyreva, A., Micciancio, D. (eds.) CRYPTO 2019, Part III. LNCS, vol. 11694, pp. 284–332. Springer, Heidelberg (2019). https://doi.org/10.1007/978-3-030-26954-8_10

4. Ananth, P., Jain, A.: Indistinguishability obfuscation from compact functional encryption. In: Gennaro, R., Robshaw, M.J.B. (eds.) CRYPTO 2015, Part I. LNCS, vol. 9215, pp. 308–326. Springer, Heidelberg (2015). https://doi.org/10.1007/978-3-662-47989-6_15

5. Ananth, P., Sahai, A.: Projective arithmetic functional encryption and indistinguishability obfuscation from degree-5 multilinear maps. In: Coron, J.S., Nielsen, J.B. (eds.) EUROCRYPT 2017, Part I. LNCS, vol. 10210, pp. 152–181. Springer, Heidelberg (2017). https://doi.org/10.1007/978-3-319-56620-7_6

6. Badrinarayanan, S., Goyal, V., Jain, A., Sahai, A.: Verifiable functional encryption. In: Cheon, J.H., Takagi, T. (eds.) ASIACRYPT 2016, Part II. LNCS, vol. 10032, pp. 557–587. Springer, Heidelberg (2016). https://doi.org/10.1007/978-3-662-53890-6_19

7. Badrinarayanan, S., Miles, E., Sahai, A., Zhandry, M.: Post-zeroizing obfuscation: new mathematical tools, and the case of evasive circuits. In: Fischlin, M., Coron, J.S. (eds.) EUROCRYPT 2016, Part II. LNCS, vol. 9666, pp. 764–791. Springer, Heidelberg (2016). https://doi.org/10.1007/978-3-662-49896-5_27

8. Ballard, L., Green, M., de Medeiros, B., Monrose, F.: Correlation-resistant storage via keyword-searchable encryption. Cryptology ePrint Archive, Report 2005/417 (2005). https://eprint.iacr.org/2005/417

9. Barak, B., Brakerski, Z., Komargodski, I., Kothari, P.K.: Limits on low-degree pseudorandom generators (or: sum-of-squares meets program obfuscation). Electron. Colloquium Comput. Complexity (ECCC) **24**, 60 (2017)

10. Barak, B., Garg, S., Kalai, Y.T., Paneth, O., Sahai, A.: Protecting obfuscation against algebraic attacks. In: Nguyen, P.Q., Oswald, E. (eds.) EUROCRYPT 2014. LNCS, vol. 8441, pp. 221–238. Springer, Heidelberg (2014). https://doi.org/10.1007/978-3-642-55220-5_13

11. Barak, B., et al.: On the (im)possibility of obfuscating programs. In: Kilian, J. (ed.) CRYPTO 2001. LNCS, vol. 2139, pp. 1–18. Springer, Heidelberg (2001). https://doi.org/10.1007/3-540-44647-8_1

12. Barak, B., Hopkins, S.B., Jain, A., Kothari, P., Sahai, A.: Sum-of-squares meets program obfuscation, revisited. In: Ishai, Y., Rijmen, V. (eds.) EUROCRYPT 2019, Part I. LNCS, vol. 11476, pp. 226–250. Springer, Heidelberg (2019). https://doi.org/10.1007/978-3-030-17653-2_8

13. Bartusek, J., Ishai, Y., Jain, A., Ma, F., Sahai, A., Zhandry, M.: Affine determinant programs: a framework for obfuscation and witness encryption. In: Vidick, T. (ed.) ITCS 2020, vol. 151, pp. 82:1–82:39. LIPIcs, January 2020. https://doi.org/10.4230/LIPIcs.ITCS.2020.82

14. Bitansky, N., Nishimaki, R., Passelègue, A., Wichs, D.: From Cryptomania to Obfustopia through secret-key functional encryption. In: Hirt, M., Smith, A.D. (eds.) TCC 2016-B, Part II. LNCS, vol. 9986, pp. 391–418. Springer, Heidelberg (2016). https://doi.org/10.1007/978-3-662-53644-5_15

15. Bitansky, N., Paneth, O., Rosen, A.: On the cryptographic hardness of finding a Nash equilibrium. In: Guruswami, V. (ed.) 56th FOCS, pp. 1480–1498. IEEE Computer Society Press, October 2015. https://doi.org/10.1109/FOCS.2015.94

16. Bitansky, N., Vaikuntanathan, V.: Indistinguishability obfuscation from functional encryption. In: Guruswami, V. (ed.) 56th FOCS, pp. 171–190. IEEE Computer Society Press, October 2015. https://doi.org/10.1109/FOCS.2015.20

17. Boneh, D., Wu, D.J., Zimmerman, J.: Immunizing multilinear maps against zeroizing attacks. Cryptology ePrint Archive, Report 2014/930 (2014)

18. Brakerski, Z., Döttling, N., Garg, S., Malavolta, G.: Candidate iO from homomorphic encryption schemes. In: Canteaut, A., Ishai, Y. (eds.) EUROCRYPT 2020, Part I. LNCS, vol. 12105, pp. 79–109. Springer, Heidelberg (2020). https://doi.org/10.1007/978-3-030-45721-1_4

19. Brakerski, Z., Gentry, C., Halevi, S., Lepoint, T., Sahai, A., Tibouchi, M.: Cryptanalysis of the quadratic zero-testing of GGH. Cryptology ePrint Archive, Report 2015/845 (2015). http://eprint.iacr.org/

20. Brakerski, Z., Rothblum, G.N.: Virtual black-box obfuscation for all circuits via generic graded encoding. In: Lindell, Y. (ed.) TCC 2014. LNCS, vol. 8349, pp. 1–25. Springer, Heidelberg (2014). https://doi.org/10.1007/978-3-642-54242-8_1

21. Brzuska, C., Farshim, P., Mittelbach, A.: Indistinguishability obfuscation and UCEs: the case of computationally unpredictable sources. In: Garay, J.A., Gennaro, R. (eds.) CRYPTO 2014, Part I. LNCS, vol. 8616, pp. 188–205. Springer, Heidelberg (2014). https://doi.org/10.1007/978-3-662-44371-2_11

22. Canetti, R., Lin, H., Tessaro, S., Vaikuntanathan, V.: Obfuscation of probabilistic circuits and applications. In: Dodis, Y., Nielsen, J.B. (eds.) TCC 2015, Part II. LNCS, vol. 9015, pp. 468–497. Springer, Heidelberg (2015). https://doi.org/10.1007/978-3-662-46497-7_19

23. Cheon, J.H., Han, K., Lee, C., Ryu, H., Stehlé, D.: Cryptanalysis of the multilinear map over the integers. In: Oswald, E., Fischlin, M. (eds.) EUROCRYPT 2015. LNCS, vol. 9056, pp. 3–12. Springer, Heidelberg (2015). https://doi.org/10.1007/978-3-662-46800-5_1

24. Cheon, J.H., Lee, C., Ryu, H.: Cryptanalysis of the new CLT multilinear maps. Cryptology ePrint Archive, Report 2015/934 (2015). http://eprint.iacr.org/

25. Chung, K.M., Lin, H., Pass, R.: Constant-round concurrent zero-knowledge from indistinguishability obfuscation. In: Gennaro, R., Robshaw, M.J.B. (eds.) CRYPTO 2015, Part I. LNCS, vol. 9215, pp. 287–307. Springer, Heidelberg (2015). https://doi.org/10.1007/978-3-662-47989-6_14

26. Coron, J.-S., et al.: Zeroizing without low-level zeroes: new MMAP attacks and their limitations. In: Gennaro, R., Robshaw, M. (eds.) CRYPTO 2015. LNCS, vol. 9215, pp. 247–266. Springer, Heidelberg (2015). https://doi.org/10.1007/978-3-662-47989-6_12

27. Coron, J.S., Lepoint, T., Tibouchi, M.: Practical multilinear maps over the integers. In: Canetti, R., Garay, J.A. (eds.) CRYPTO 2013, Part I. LNCS, vol. 8042, pp. 476–493. Springer, Heidelberg (2013). https://doi.org/10.1007/978-3-642-40041-4_26

28. Coron, J.S., Lepoint, T., Tibouchi, M.: New multilinear maps over the integers. In: Gennaro, R., Robshaw, M.J.B. (eds.) CRYPTO 2015, Part I. LNCS, vol. 9215, pp.

267–286. Springer, Heidelberg (2015). https://doi.org/10.1007/978-3-662-47989-6_13

29. Devadas, L., Quach, W., Vaikuntanathan, V., Wee, H., Wichs, D.: Succinct LWE sampling, random polynomials, and obfuscation. In: Nissim, K., Waters, B. (eds.) TCC 2021. LNCS, vol. 13043, pp. 256–287. Springer, Cham (2021). https://doi.org/10.1007/978-3-030-90453-1_9

30. Döttling, N., Garg, S., Gupta, D., Miao, P., Mukherjee, P.: Obfuscation from low noise multilinear maps. IACR Cryptology ePrint Archive 2016, 599 (2016)

31. Garg, S., Gentry, C., Halevi, S.: Candidate multilinear maps from ideal lattices. In: Johansson, T., Nguyen, P.Q. (eds.) EUROCRYPT 2013. LNCS, vol. 7881, pp. 1–17. Springer, Heidelberg (2013). https://doi.org/10.1007/978-3-642-38348-9_1

32. Garg, S., Gentry, C., Halevi, S., Raykova, M., Sahai, A., Waters, B.: Candidate indistinguishability obfuscation and functional encryption for all circuits. In: 54th FOCS, pp. 40–49. IEEE Computer Society Press, October 2013. https://doi.org/10.1109/FOCS.2013.13

33. Gay, R., Pass, R.: Indistinguishability obfuscation from circular security, pp. 736–749. ACM Press (2021). https://doi.org/10.1145/3406325.3451070

34. Gentry, C., Gorbunov, S., Halevi, S.: Graph-induced multilinear maps from lattices. In: Dodis, Y., Nielsen, J.B. (eds.) TCC 2015, Part II. LNCS, vol. 9015, pp. 498–527. Springer, Heidelberg (2015). https://doi.org/10.1007/978-3-662-46497-7_20

35. Gentry, C., Jutla, C.S., Kane, D.: Obfuscation using tensor products. Electron. Colloquium Comput. Complexity (ECCC) 25, 149 (2018)

36. Gentry, C., Sahai, A., Waters, B.: Homomorphic encryption from learning with errors: conceptually-simpler, asymptotically-faster, attribute-based. In: Canetti, R., Garay, J.A. (eds.) CRYPTO 2013, Part I. LNCS, vol. 8042, pp. 75–92. Springer, Heidelberg (2013). https://doi.org/10.1007/978-3-642-40041-4_5

37. Goldreich, O.: Candidate one-way functions based on expander graphs. IACR Cryptol. ePrint Arch. 2000, 63 (2000)

38. Goldwasser, S., et al.: Multi-input functional encryption. In: Nguyen, P.Q., Oswald, E. (eds.) EUROCRYPT 2014. LNCS, vol. 8441, pp. 578–602. Springer, Heidelberg (2014). https://doi.org/10.1007/978-3-642-55220-5_32

39. Halevi, S.: Graded encoding, variations on a scheme. IACR Cryptol. ePrint Arch. 2015, 866 (2015)

40. Hopkins, S.B., Jain, A., Lin, H.: Counterexamples to new circular security assumptions underlying iO. In: Malkin, T., Peikert, C. (eds.) CRYPTO 2021, Part II. LNCS, vol. 12826, pp. 673–700, Virtual Event. Springer, Heidelberg (2021). https://doi.org/10.1007/978-3-030-84245-1_23

41. Hu, Y., Jia, H.: Cryptanalysis of GGH map. IACR Cryptol. ePrint Arch. 2015, 301 (2015)

42. Ishai, Y., Prabhakaran, M., Sahai, A.: Secure arithmetic computation with no honest majority. In: Reingold, O. (ed.) TCC 2009. LNCS, vol. 5444, pp. 294–314. Springer, Heidelberg (2009). https://doi.org/10.1007/978-3-642-00457-5_18

43. Jain, A., Lin, H., Matt, C., Sahai, A.: How to leverage hardness of constant-degree expanding polynomials over $\mathbb{R}$ to build $i\mathcal{O}$. In: Ishai, Y., Rijmen, V. (eds.) EUROCRYPT 2019, Part I. LNCS, vol. 11476, pp. 251–281. Springer, Heidelberg (2019). https://doi.org/10.1007/978-3-030-17653-2_9

44. Jain, A., Lin, H., Sahai, A.: Indistinguishability obfuscation from well-founded assumptions, pp. 60–73. ACM Press (2021). https://doi.org/10.1145/3406325.3451093

45. Jain, A., Lin, H., Sahai, A.: Indistinguishability obfuscation from LPN over $\mathbb{F}_p$, DLIN, and PRGs in NC^0. In: Dunkelman, O., Dziembowski, S. (eds.) Advances in Cryptology - EUROCRYPT 2022–41st Annual International Conference on the Theory and Applications of Cryptographic Techniques, Trondheim, Norway, 30 May–3 June 2022, Proceedings, Part I. LNCS, vol. 13275, pp. 670–699. Springer, Cham (2022). https://doi.org/10.1007/978-3-031-06944-4_23

46. Khurana, D., Rao, V., Sahai, A.: Multi-party key exchange for unbounded parties from indistinguishability obfuscation. In: Iwata, T., Cheon, J.H. (eds.) ASIACRYPT 2015, Part I. LNCS, vol. 9452, pp. 52–75. Springer, Heidelberg (2015). https://doi.org/10.1007/978-3-662-48797-6_3

47. Lin, H.: Indistinguishability obfuscation from constant-degree graded encoding schemes. In: Fischlin, M., Coron, J.S. (eds.) EUROCRYPT 2016, Part I. LNCS, vol. 9665, pp. 28–57. Springer, Heidelberg (2016). https://doi.org/10.1007/978-3-662-49890-3_2

48. Lin, H.: Indistinguishability obfuscation from SXDH on 5-linear maps and locality-5 PRGs. In: Katz, J., Shacham, H. (eds.) CRYPTO 2017, Part I. LNCS, vol. 10401, pp. 599–629. Springer, Heidelberg (2017). https://doi.org/10.1007/978-3-319-63688-7_20

49. Lin, H., Pass, R., Seth, K., Telang, S.: Indistinguishability obfuscation with non-trivial efficiency. In: Cheng, C.M., Chung, K.M., Persiano, G., Yang, B.Y. (eds.) PKC 2016, Part II. LNCS, vol. 9615, pp. 447–462. Springer, Heidelberg (2016). https://doi.org/10.1007/978-3-662-49387-8_17

50. Lin, H., Tessaro, S.: Indistinguishability obfuscation from trilinear maps and block-wise local PRGs. In: Katz, J., Shacham, H. (eds.) CRYPTO 2017, Part I. LNCS, vol. 10401, pp. 630–660. Springer, Heidelberg (2017). https://doi.org/10.1007/978-3-319-63688-7_21

51. Lombardi, A., Vaikuntanathan, V.: Limits on the locality of pseudorandom generators and applications to indistinguishability obfuscation. In: Kalai, Y., Reyzin, L. (eds.) TCC 2017, Part I. LNCS, vol. 10677, pp. 119–137. Springer, Heidelberg (2017). https://doi.org/10.1007/978-3-319-70500-2_5

52. Micciancio, D., Peikert, C.: Hardness of SIS and LWE with small parameters. In: Canetti, R., Garay, J.A. (eds.) CRYPTO 2013, Part I. LNCS, vol. 8042, pp. 21–39. Springer, Heidelberg (2013). https://doi.org/10.1007/978-3-642-40041-4_2

53. Miles, E., Sahai, A., Zhandry, M.: Annihilation attacks for multilinear maps: cryptanalysis of indistinguishability obfuscation over GGH13. In: Advances in Cryptology - CRYPTO (2016)

54. Minaud, B., Fouque, P.A.: Cryptanalysis of the new multilinear map over the integers. Cryptology ePrint Archive, Report 2015/941 (2015). http://eprint.iacr.org/

55. Sahai, A., Waters, B.: How to use indistinguishability obfuscation: deniable encryption, and more. In: Shmoys, D.B. (ed.) 46th ACM STOC, pp. 475–484. ACM Press, May/June 2014. https://doi.org/10.1145/2591796.2591825

56. Wee, H., Wichs, D.: Candidate obfuscation via oblivious LWE sampling. In: Canteaut, A., Standaert, F.X. (eds.) EUROCRYPT 2021, Part III. LNCS, vol. 12698, pp. 127–156. Springer, Heidelberg (2021). https://doi.org/10.1007/978-3-030-77883-5_5

Oblivious Transfer and Data Access

Reverse Firewalls for Oblivious Transfer Extension and Applications to Zero-Knowledge

Suvradip Chakraborty[1], Chaya Ganesh[2], and Pratik Sarkar[3]([✉])

[1] Visa Research, Palo Alto, USA
[2] Indian Institute of Science, Bengaluru, India
[3] Department of Computer Science, Boston University, Boston, USA
pratik93@bu.edu

Abstract. In the setting of subversion, an adversary tampers with the machines of the honest parties thus leaking the honest parties' secrets through the protocol transcript. The work of Mironov and Stephens-Davidowitz (*EUROCRYPT'15*) introduced the idea of reverse firewalls (RF) to protect against tampering of honest parties' machines. All known constructions in the RF framework rely on the malleability of the underlying operations in order for the RF to rerandomize/sanitize the transcript. RFs are thus limited to protocols that offer some structure, and hence based on public-key operations. In this work, we initiate the study of *efficient* Multiparty Computation (MPC) protocols in the presence of tampering. In this regard,

- We construct the *first* Oblivious Transfer (OT) extension protocol in the RF setting. We obtain $\mathsf{poly}(\kappa)$ maliciously-secure OTs using $\mathcal{O}(\kappa)$ public key operations and $\mathcal{O}(1)$ inexpensive symmetric key operations, where κ is the security parameter.
- We construct the *first* Zero-knowledge protocol in the RF setting where each multiplication gate can be proven using $\mathcal{O}(1)$ symmetric key operations. We achieve this using our OT extension protocol and by extending the ZK protocol of Quicksilver (Yang, Sarkar, Weng and Wang, *CCS'21*) to the RF setting.
- Along the way, we introduce new ideas for malleable interactive proofs that could be of independent interest. We define a notion of *full malleability* for Sigma protocols that unlike prior notions allow modifying the instance as well, in addition to the transcript. We construct new protocols that satisfy this notion, construct RFs for such protocols and use them in constructing our OT extension.

The key idea of our work is to demonstrate that correlated randomness may be obtained in an RF-friendly way *without* having to rerandomize the entire transcript. This enables us to avoid expensive public-key operations that grow with the circuit-size.

S. Chakraborty—The work was done while the author was at ETH Zurich. The author is supported in part by ERC grant 724307.

C. Ganesh—The author is supported by a Google India Faculty Research Award, and Infosys Young Investigator Award, Infosys Foundation.

P. Sarkar—The author is supported by NSF Awards 1931714, 1414119, and the DARPA SIEVE program.

C. Hazay and M. Stam (Eds.): EUROCRYPT 2023, LNCS 14004, pp. 239–270, 2023.
https://doi.org/10.1007/978-3-031-30545-0_9

1 Introduction

Protocols in cryptography are proven secure under standard definitions where the assumption is that the honest parties trust their machines to implement their computation. This assumption breaks down in the real world, where even honest parties' computations are performed on untrusted machines. The security guarantees of these protocols fall short of protecting against attacks that take advantage of the *implementation* details instead of merely treating the algorithm as a black-box. Such attacks are indeed realistic, both because users are compelled to use third-party hardware due to lack of expertise, software mandated due to standardization, or even because of intentional *tampering* due to subversion. The threat of a powerful adversary modifying the implementation so that the subverted algorithm remains indistinguishable from the specification in black-box interface, while leaking secrets is not overkill. Snowden revelations [2] show that one of the potential mechanisms for large scale mass surveillance is subversion of cryptographic standards and tampering of hardware.

Reverse Firewalls. The framework of cryptographic reverse firewalls was introduced by Mironov and Stephens-Davidowitz [32] for designing protocols secure against adversaries that can corrupt the machines of honest parties in order to compromise their security. In such a setting, all parties are equipped with their own reverse firewall (RF), which sits between the party and the external world and sanitizes the parties' incoming and outgoing messages. The parties do not trust the RF, the RF cannot create security and the hope is for the RF to preserve security in the face of subversion. Roughly, the security properties desired from an RF are: (i) *exfiltration-resistance*: the firewall prevents the machine from leaking any information to the outside world regardless of how the user's machine behaves. (ii) *security preservation*: the protocol with the firewall is secure even when honest parties' machines are tampered.

The work of [32] provides a construction of a two-party passively secure computation protocol with a reverse firewall in addition to introducing the RF framework. Feasibility of RF for multi-party computation (MPC) was shown in [10] who constructed RFs for MPC protocols in the malicious setting. The recent work of [11] constructs MPC protocols with RF in the presence of adaptive corruptions. We discuss other works in the RF framework and related models for subversion resistance in Sect. 1.3.

Motivation. We begin by observing that both existing works that construct RFs for maliciously-secure MPC protocols [10,11] follow roughly the same template – that of the GMW compiler [26]. Both constructions are essentially compilers: they take a semi-honest secure MPC protocol and run GMW-like steps in the reverse firewall setting to yield a secure MPC protocol with reverse firewalls. In the process, they design secure protocols for the underlying primitives (like augmented coin-tossing and zero knowledge) in the GMW compiler, construct reverse firewalls for each of the primitives, and finally, show that the compiled

MPC protocol is secure in the presence of tampering of honest parties. This renders the resulting protocols inefficient for practical purposes.

The current techniques for constructing the RFs crucially make use of malleability. This is because, the constructions rely on the ability of the RF to randomize/maul messages to prevent exfiltration. In order to not break correctness, such mauling has to be on messages that are malleable and therefore requires the underlying primitives to be homomorphic. Indeed, the RFs for Sigma protocols of [24] rely on malleability of Sigma protocol, and message and key homomorphism of Pedersen commitment. The RF of [10] relies on controlled malleable non-interactive zero-knowledge proofs (NIZK) [14], and the constructions of [11] need primitives like homomorphic commitment scheme, homomorphic public-key encryption and homomorphic Sigma protocols for NP (which are secure against adaptive corruption) [9]. These randomization techniques for constructing the RF necessitates the MPC protocol to use homomorphic primitives based on expensive public-key operations. In particular, the GMW approach of [10, 11] require number of public-key operations that is proportional to the size of the circuit being computed by the protocol. However, progress in MPC has resulted in several efficient protocols [22, 28, 37] based on Oblivious Transfer (OT) extension [7, 16, 27, 29, 34, 40] that only rely on cheap symmetric key operations and few public key operations. A recent line of works [3, 38] presented interactive ZK protocols for circuits in the vector OLE (Oblivious Linear Evaluation) model [5, 16, 40]. Now that we know feasibility of RF for MPC via generic compilers, can we construct RFs for efficient MPC protocols like those based on OT extension? All known techniques to construct RFs rely on some form of malleability/homomorphism of the underlying protocol so that the RF can randomize the messages. It is unclear how such randomization would work when the protocol messages are unstructured. Modifying the protocol to be homomorphic so as to be RF friendly defeats the purpose of protocols like OT extension where the goal is to minimize the number of public key operations. This motivates us to ask the following question:

Can we construct an MPC protocol in the reverse firewall setting where the number of public key operations is independent of the size of the circuit being computed?

We answer the above question in the affirmative by constructing such protocols for specific functions like OT extension and Zero-Knowledge (ZK). Constructing reverse firewalls for such protocols requires new techniques since the transcript resulting from symmetric key operations are unstructured and do not render themselves well to randomization.

1.1 Our Contributions

We initiate the study of efficient MPC protocols in the RF setting. Towards this end, we make the following contributions.

– We construct a variant of the KOS OT extension protocol [29] together with an RF in the random oracle $\mathcal{F}_{\mathsf{RO}}$ model. Our protocol constructs $m = \mathsf{poly}(\kappa)$ correlated OT (cOT)[1] using only $\mathcal{O}(\kappa)$ public key operations. All prior constructions of maliciously secure OT [10,11] require $\mathsf{poly}(\kappa)$ public key operations *per OT* due to their reliance on the GMW compiler and expensive ZK proofs. See Sects. 2.1 and 2.2 for an overview of our cOT functionality $\mathcal{F}_{\mathsf{cOT}}$ (in Fig. 1) and cOT extension protocol respectively.
– We construct a new base (random) OT protocol, which we use for our OT extension. In constructing the base OT protocol and RF (an overview of these ideas in Sect. 2.3), we employ new ideas for malleable interactive proofs.
– We define a notion of *full malleability* for Sigma protocols that unlike prior notions allow randomizing the instance as well. We construct RFs for Sigma protocols and for OR composition that sanitize both the instance and the transcript. We show that ZK protocol resulting from the standard compilation of a Sigma protocol is fully malleable and construct an RF for it. These results could be of independent interest. We provide an overview of these ideas in Sect. 2.4.

Each base OT protocol require 35 exponentiations. For $\ell \leq \kappa$ base OTs in the OT extension, the cost of computing 35ℓ exponentiations gets amortized by generating $\mathsf{poly}(\kappa)$ extended cOTs. As a result each extended cOT communicates κ bits and computes roughly 4 symmetric key operations. Our correlated OT extension protocol in the firewall setting is captured in Theorem 1.

Theorem 1. *(Informal) Assume there exists an additively homomorphic commitment scheme* Com, *a collision resistant hash function* H, *a pseudorandom generator* PRG, *and that the Discrete Log assumption holds. We obtain a correlated OT extension protocol* π_{cOT} *with reverse firewalls that implements* $\mathcal{F}_{\mathsf{cOT}}$ *in* $\mathcal{F}_{\mathsf{RO}}$-*model when the honest parties' machines can be tampered and the adversary can maliciously corrupt either the sender or the receiver.*

We then show application of our cOT extension protocol in constructing efficient Zero-knowledge protocols. We build upon the recent interactive ZK protocol of Quicksilver [38] to obtain the first efficient ZK protocol for all of NP in the RF setting. We capture our contribution by the following theorem.

Theorem 2. *(Informal) Assuming* H *is a collision resistant hash function and* Com *is an additively homomorphic commitment scheme,* π_{QS} *implements the Zero-knowledge* $\mathcal{F}_{\mathsf{ZK}}$ *functionality in the* $\mathcal{F}_{\mathsf{cOT}}$ *model for NP in the presence of reverse firewalls where the honest parties' machines can be tampered and the adversary can maliciously corrupt either the prover or the verifier. Our construction requires* $(n + t)$ *invocations to* $\mathcal{F}_{\mathsf{cOT}}$, *where* n *is the number of input wires and* t *is the number of multiplication gates in the NP verification circuit for the statement.*

---

[1] Our cOT protocol allows the receiver to learn c bits of sender's secret with probability 2^{-c}. We capture this leakage in the ideal functionality $\mathcal{F}_{\mathsf{cOT}}$, and show that this weakened functionality suffices for constructing OT-based RF friendly ZK protocol.

In π_{QS}, proving each multiplication gate requires one cOT, as in the original Quicksilver protocol. Instantiating $\mathcal{F}_{cOT}$ with our π_{cOT} results in a proof size of $(n+t)\kappa$ bits. In comparison, the original Quicksilver implements $\mathcal{F}_{cOT}$ using Silent-OT extension protocol [40] yielding a proof size of $(n+t)$ bits. We provide an overview of our Quicksilver variant and its RF in Sect. 2.5.

Key Idea. The central idea of our work is to generate correlated data (cOTs in our case) between two parties to compute a circuit. We show how these correlated data can be generated from symmetric key operations and in an RF-friendly way. Previously, all RF-friendly techniques were for protocols relying on public-key primitives and the RF exploits the natural "structure". Our work shows that there is no inherent barrier for constructing RFs for protocols that rely on symmetric-key primitives. Concretely, we only need cheap symmetric key operations, and the number of public key operations (e.g. the base OTs) are independent of the size of the circuit to be computed. Looking ahead, this correlation allows the parties to verify a protocol transcript (e.g. the RF-compatible Quicksilver) efficiently. This verification can be performed using an inexpensive (solely based on symmetric key operations) consistency check. In contrast, if we were to use ZK proofs (GMW paradigm) for verification, RF-compatibility requires ZK to be controlled-malleable which are algebraic and inherently require public key operations. We believe our ideas to deal with unstructured data opens up a new paradigm for constructing more efficient RF-compatible protocols, especially as a stepping stone towards MPC protocols based on silent OT extension.

1.2 Future Work

Our RF-friendly OT extension protocol can be used in a straightforward way to achieve an efficient semi-honest secure MPC using the GMW protocol. This protocol requires the parties to sample randomness for input sharing and evaluation phases. Rest of the GMW protocol is deterministic and hence would be exfiltration resistant when the parties are tampered or are semi-honest. Our RF compatible extended OTs can be used in the evaluation of multiplication gates. However, constructing a maliciously-secure MPC protocol in the GMW paradigm will require much more work. One of the reasons being the requirement of a controlled-malleable ZK protocol to ensure security against malicious adversaries in the RF setting. However, we do not know of an efficient RF-friendly instantiation, where the number of public-key operations are sub-linear in the size of the verification circuit. For other OT-based MPC protocols that rely on garbled circuits (GC), lifting our OT extension protocol to give a full-fledged RF-friendly and efficient MPC protocol seems to be more challenging. Even with our efficient OT extension protocol, one of the main bottlenecks is that we will need a *re-randomizable* GC, for which currently no efficient (in terms of public-key operations) constructions are known.

A natural extension of our work is to construct Silent OT extension family of protocols [5,16,40] in the RF setting. Current techniques in Silent OT extension paradigm require the receiver to compute LPN samples and use them in the underlying bootstrapping protocol. In the RF setting, this is a non-trivial task since the LPN samples might be leaky due to bad randomness. It is not obvious how to sanitize them without relying on expensive public key operations or generic zero-knowledge. Our work shows that our correlated OTs suffice for designated-verifier ZK protocols. We believe that similar ideas could be useful in other designated-verifier settings, like silent-OT and authenticated garbling [39].

1.3   Related Work

Reverse Firewalls. The work of [32] constructs RFs for a variant of the Naor-Pinkas OT protocol [33]. Their construction only provides passive security, whereas we are in the malicious setting. The work of [15] constructs an OT protocol from graded rings, incurring $\mathsf{poly}(\kappa)$ public key operations for each OT. While these works show feasibility, we focus on constructing OT extension protocols in the RF setting with malicious security, while retaining the advantage of OT extension – create $\mathsf{poly}(\kappa)$ OTs with *symmetric key operations* starting from κ base OTs. The other approaches via generic MPC compilers [10,11] incur $\mathsf{poly}(\kappa)$ public key operations for each OT instance. In their original paper, Mironov and Stephens-Davidowitz [32] show how to construct reverse firewalls for oblivious transfer (OT) and two-party computation with semi-honest security. Follow-up research showed how to construct reverse firewalls for a plethora of cryptographic primitives and protocols including: secure message transmission and key agreement [15,21], signature schemes [1], interactive proof systems [24], and maliciously secure MPC for both the case of static [10] and adaptive [11] corruptions. The recent work of [13] also introduced the notion of Universally Composable Subversion-Resilient security. Extending our results in their model is an interesting direction for future work.

As already mentioned in the introduction, all the above constructions use the ability of the RF to maul (in a controlled way) the transcript of the protocols to prevent exfiltration, which in turn required the underlying building blocks to be (controlled) homomorphic. Hence, the number of public key operations depends on the size of the circuit (representing the function) to be computed securely. This is in sharp contrast to our OT and (interactive) ZK protocols where the resulting protocols after RF sanitization performs a number of public key operations that are independent of the size of the circuit being computed.

Remark. Since our focus is on efficient MPC protocols and RFs, the RF-friendly protocols we construct are based on symmetric-key primitives like hash functions and Pseudorandom generators (PRGs). While backdooring of such primitives is also of concern in the subversion setting, we argue that it is an issue orthogonal to the issue of *tampering of implementations* that we consider in this work. We also note that both prior works that construct RFs for MPC protocols [10,11] are generic compilers and therefore also implicitly assume that all the primitives used by the underlying MPC protocol are backdoorless. We provide a more detailed discussion comparing tampering of implementations and backdooring of primitives in the full version [12]. We prove security of our protocols in the

Random Oracle (RO) model, and it is known how to immunize backdoored primitives like PRGs in the RO model [20]. Once the RO is instantiated with a hash function like SHA-256, the assumption presumes that SHA-256 is itself not backdoored. The works of [19, 23] show how to immunize backdoored ROs and backdoored hash functions. Combining these immunization techniques with RFs to construct end-to-end solutions that address subversion is an interesting direction for future work. Countering both tampering of implementation and subversion of primitives simultaneously is important but not in the scope of the current work. We also refer to the full version [12] for more related works on other forms of subversion resilience based on watch-dog, self-guarding and tackling backdooring of primitives.

2   Technical Overview

In this section, we discuss state-of-the-art protocols, some hurdles in adapting them to the RF setting and outline our techniques to overcome them. Our protocols are shown secure in the RF setting by relying on the recent result of [11], which showed that 1) if an MPC protocol satisfies simulation-based security, and 2) the firewall is functionality maintaining and provides exfiltration resistance, then the firewall preserves security of the protocol in the presence of functionality maintaining tampering. Theorem 3 in Sect. 3.1 formally summarizes the result. For every protocol we prove that it satisfies simulation-based security and their respective firewall provides exfiltration resistance. Combining Theorem 3 with simulation security and exfiltration resistance provides us the desired security guarantee.

2.1   Correlated OT with Leakage Functionality

We initiate our overview discussion with the correlated OT functionality $\mathcal{F}_{\mathsf{cOT}}$ in Fig. 1 (taken from [29]). It allows some leakage to a corrupt receiver. The receiver has a choice bit vector $\mathbf{b} \in \{0,1\}^{\ell}$. The functionality samples $\mathbf{s} \leftarrow_R \{0,1\}^{\kappa}$, $\mathbf{M} \leftarrow_R \{0,1\}^{\ell \times \kappa}$ and sets $\mathbf{Q}_j = \mathbf{M}_j \oplus (\mathbf{s} \odot b_j)$ for $j \in [\ell]$. The functionality sets $\mathbf{Q} = \{\mathbf{Q}_j\}_{j \in [j \in [\ell]]}$ and returns $\mathbf{M}$ to the receiver and the $(\mathbf{s}, \mathbf{Q})$ to the sender. The functionality allows the receiver to guess c bits of $\mathbf{s}$ and the receiver gets caught with $1 - 2^{-c}$ probability. We show that this weaker functionality suffices for the ZK protocol of Quicksilver [38].

2.2   Correlated Oblivious Transfer Extension in the RF Setting

We use the KOS [29] OT extension to implement the $\mathcal{F}_{\mathsf{cOT}}$ functionality. We recall the KOS protocol as follows:

Recalling KOS OT Extension: In the KOS OT extension, the sender $\mathsf{S}_{\mathsf{Ext}}$ and receiver $\mathsf{R}_{\mathsf{Ext}}$ generate m ($= \mathsf{poly}(\kappa)$) OTs using κ invocations to the random OT functionality, i.e. $\mathcal{F}_{\mathsf{rOT}}{}^2$ (Fig. 5), (implemented by base OTs) and symmetric key

---

2   Each invocation of $\mathcal{F}_{\mathsf{rOT}}$ returns (a_0, a_1) to the sender and (b, a_b) to the receiver where $a_0, a_1 \leftarrow_R \{0,1\}^{\kappa}$ and $b \leftarrow_R \{0,1\}$ are randomly sampled by the functionality.

Functionality $\mathcal{F}_{\mathsf{cOT}}$

Upon receiving $(\textsc{Initiate}, \mathsf{sid}, \ell)$ from sender S and receiving $(\textsc{Initiate}, \mathsf{sid}, \ell)$ from receiver R, the functionality $\mathcal{F}_{\mathsf{cOT}}$ interacts as follows:

- Sample $\mathbf{b} = (b_1, \ldots, b_\ell)$ where $b_j \in \{0, 1\}$ for $j \in [\ell]$.

- If S is corrupted receive $\mathbf{s} \in \{0, 1\}^\kappa$ from the sender. Sample $\mathbf{Q} \leftarrow_R \{0, 1\}^{\ell \times \kappa}$. Set $\mathbf{M}_j = \mathbf{Q}_j \oplus (\mathbf{s} \odot b_j)$ for $j \in [\ell]$.

- If R is corrupted then receive $\mathbf{M} \in \{0, 1\}^{\ell \times \kappa}$ from the receiver, sample $\mathbf{s} \leftarrow_R \{0, 1\}^\kappa$ and set $\mathbf{Q}_j = \mathbf{M}_j \oplus (\mathbf{s} \odot b_j)$ for $j \in [\ell]$.

- When a corrupt R guesses c bits of $\mathbf{s}$ by invoking $(\textsc{Guess}, \mathsf{sid}, \{i\}_{I \in [c]}, \{s'_i\}_{i \in [c]})$: $\mathcal{F}_{\mathsf{rOT}}$ aborts if $s'_i \neq s_i$ for any $i \in [c]$; otherwise all the guesses are correct and $\mathcal{F}_{\mathsf{rOT}}$ sends $(\textsc{Undetected}, \mathsf{sid})$ to $\mathcal{A}$.

- If both parties are honest, then sample $\mathbf{s} \leftarrow_R \{0, 1\}^\kappa$, $\mathbf{M} \leftarrow_R \{0, 1\}^{\ell \times \kappa}$ and set $\mathbf{Q}_j = \mathbf{M}_j \oplus (\mathbf{s} \odot b_j)$ for $j \in [\ell]$.

Denote $\mathbf{Q} = \{\mathbf{Q}_j\}_{j \in [\ell]}$ and $\mathbf{M} = \{\mathbf{M}_j\}_{j \in [\ell]}$. Send $(\mathsf{sent}, \mathsf{sid}, \mathbf{M}, \mathbf{b})$ to R and $(\mathsf{sent}, \mathsf{sid}, (\mathbf{s}, \mathbf{Q}))$ to S and store $(\mathsf{sen}, \mathsf{sid}, \ell, (\mathbf{b}, \mathbf{M}, \mathbf{Q}))$ in memory. Ignore future messages with the same sid.
If a corrupt sender (resp. receiver) sends $\bot$ to the $\mathcal{F}_{\mathsf{cOT}}$ then $\mathcal{F}_{\mathsf{cOT}}$ delivers the output of the corrupt sender (resp. receiver) to the corrupt sender (resp. receiver) and aborts.

Fig. 1. Ideal functionality $\mathcal{F}_{\mathsf{cOT}}$ for Correlated Oblivious Transfer with leakage

operations. In the base OTs, the sender $\mathsf{S}_{\mathsf{Ext}}$ plays the role of a receiver, and the receiver $\mathsf{R}_{\mathsf{Ext}}$ plays the role of a sender. The ith invocation of $\mathcal{F}_{\mathsf{rOT}}$ functionality returns random strings $(k_{i,0}, k_{i,1}) \leftarrow_R \{0, 1\}^\kappa$ to the sender and (s_i, k_{i,s_i}) to the receiver where $s_i \leftarrow_R \{0, 1\}$. The input of $\mathsf{R}_{\mathsf{Ext}}$ is bit string $\mathbf{r} \in \{0, 1\}^m$ for m correlated extended-OTs. The receiver also samples κ random bits $\tau \leftarrow_R \{0, 1\}^\kappa$ and sets $\mathbf{r}' = (\mathbf{r} \| \tau) \in \{0, 1\}^{m+\kappa}$. This is done to prevent leakage of input choice bits during the consistency checks. The receiver computes the choice bit matrix $\mathbf{R} \in \{0, 1\}^{(m+\kappa) \times \kappa}$ where the jth row of $\mathbf{R}$ denoted as $\mathbf{R}_j$ is computed as follows:

$$\mathbf{R}_j = (r'_j, \ldots, r'_j) \text{ for } j \in [m + \kappa].$$

$\mathsf{R}_{\mathsf{Ext}}$ computes a matrix $\mathbf{M} \in \{0, 1\}^{(m+\kappa) \times \kappa}$ such that the ith column of $\mathbf{M}$ denoted as $\mathbf{M}^i$ is computed as follows:

$$\mathbf{M}^i = \mathsf{PRG}(k_{i,0}) \text{ for } i \in [\kappa],$$

where $\mathsf{PRG} : \{0, 1\}^\kappa \to \{0, 1\}^{m+\kappa}$. $\mathsf{R}_{\mathsf{Ext}}$ sends a mapping $\mathbf{D}$ from his choice bits $\mathbf{r}' \in \{0, 1\}^m$ to the $(\mathbf{k}_{i,0}, \mathbf{k}_{i,1})$ values. The ith column of $\mathbf{D}$ is denoted as $\mathbf{D}^i$ and is computed as follows:

$$\mathbf{D}^i = \mathsf{PRG}(k_{i,0}) \oplus \mathsf{PRG}(k_{i,1}) \oplus \mathbf{R}^i \text{ for } i \in [\kappa].$$

Upon obtaining this mapping $\mathbf{D}$ and the base-OT output, the sender computes his mapping as $\mathbf{Q}$ where the ith column of $\mathbf{Q}$ is denoted as follows:

$$\mathbf{Q}^i = \left(s_i \odot \mathbf{D}^i\right) \oplus \mathsf{PRG}(k_{i,s_i}) \text{ for } i \in [\kappa],$$

The jth row of $\mathbf{Q}$ denoted as $\mathbf{Q}_j$ satisfies the following relation:

$$\mathbf{Q}_j = \mathbf{M}_j \oplus (\mathbf{s} \odot \mathbf{R}_j) = \mathbf{M}_j \oplus (\mathbf{s} \odot r_j) \text{ for } j \in [m].$$

In addition to the above, the sender performs consistency checks [18]. A corrupt receiver can leak bits of $\mathbf{s}$ if the rows of $\mathbf{R}$ are not monochrome, i.e. $\exists j \in [m]$ s.t. $\mathbf{R}_j$ is neither 0^κ nor 1^κ. Such an attack can be launched by the corrupt receiver if $\mathbf{D}$ is malformed. To detect such malicious behaviour, the sender performs a consistency check on matrix $\mathbf{D}$. In the original KOS paper, the protocol consists of an interactive check phase. The receiver and sender perform a coin-tossing protocol to generate $m + \kappa$ fields elements $\chi \leftarrow_R \mathbb{F}^{m+\kappa}$ using a random oracle $\mathcal{F}_{\mathsf{RO}}$, where $\mathbb{F} = \mathcal{O}(2^\mu)$ and μ is the statistical security parameter. The receiver computes $\mathbf{u}$ and $\mathbf{v}$ as part of the consistency check on $\mathbf{D}$:

$$\mathbf{u} = \bigoplus_{j \in (m+\kappa)} (\chi_j \cdot \mathbf{M}_j), \mathbf{v} = \bigoplus_{j \in (m+\kappa)} (\chi_j \cdot \mathbf{R}_j)$$

The receiver sends $(\mathbf{u}, \mathbf{v})$ to the sender as the response of the consistency checks. The sender computes $\mathbf{w}$ as follows:

$$\mathbf{w} = \bigoplus_{j \in (m+\kappa)} (\chi_j \cdot \mathbf{Q}_j).$$

The sender aborts if $\mathbf{w} \neq \mathbf{u} \oplus \mathbf{s} \cdot \mathbf{v}$. The consistency checks ensure that the receiver learns only c bits of $\mathbf{s}$ with probability 2^{-c} probability. We follow the same approach. Once the consistency checks pass, the receiver sets $\{r_j, \mathbf{M}_j\}$ as the output of the jth cOT for $j \in [m]$. The sender sets $(\mathbf{s}, \mathbf{Q}_j)$ as the output of the jth cOT.

Obstacles in RF Setting and Key Insights. The above protocol fails to provide exfiltration resistance in the RF setting. We highlight the problems and outline solution ideas.

- **Implementing $\mathcal{F}_{\mathsf{cOT}}$:** There is no protocol π_{rOT} in MPC literature that implements $\mathcal{F}_{\mathsf{rOT}}$ functionality while providing ER for tampered honest parties. In order to provide ER, the firewall needs to rerandomize the OT protocol transcript such that the receiver's choice bit gets randomized and the sender's messages are rerandomized. The state-of-the-art OT protocols of [8,35] are in the setup string model where the setup string can be tampered. Moreover, a firewall cannot rerandomize the first message of the receiver to rerandomize the receiver's choice bit since the tampered receiver would then be unable to decrypt the sanitized OT transcript. Meanwhile, the protocols of [6,7,30] are in the random oracle model where the messages in the OT transcript consists of random oracle outputs. It is unclear how a firewall could rerandomize such transcripts since it would require computing the preimage of the random oracle output. To address this issue, we build a new base OT protocol π_{rOT} which implements $\mathcal{F}_{rOT}$ functionality and provides exfiltration resistance for tampered parties. Overview of the base OT protocol is discussed in Sect. 2.3.

- **Rerandomizing D Matrix:** A malicious receiver could send a "signal" such that a tampered sender behaves differently thereby leaking one bit of the honest (tampered) sender's input. For instance, a malicious receiver can choose its choice bits $\mathbf{r}$ in a way such that $\mathbf{D}$ lies in a particular distribution (e.g. the first column of $\mathbf{D}$ is all 0s). A tampered sender aborts upon receiving this malformed $\mathbf{D}$ matrix while an honest sender does not. This leaks one bit of the sender's input violating exfiltration resistance. We address this issue by using a technique such that the $\mathbf{r}$ vector is randomly chosen as part of the protocol. The receiver and the sender perform an augmented coin-tossing protocol where the receiver obtains random coins coin and the sender obtains a commitment to the coin as c_{coin}. The receiver generates the first column of $\mathbf{D}$, denoted as $\mathbf{D}^1$, by invoking the random oracle $\mathcal{F}_{RO}$ on coin. The receiver is required to compute the choice bit vector(and the padding bits) $\mathbf{r}' = \mathbf{r}||\tau$ from $\mathbf{D}^1$ and the outputs of the base OTs as follows:

$$\mathbf{r}' = \mathbf{D}^1 \oplus \mathsf{PRG}(k_{1,0}) \oplus \mathsf{PRG}(k_{1,1})$$

This rerandomizes the $\mathbf{r}'$ vector, and as a result the $\mathbf{D}$ matrix cannot be used to exfiltrate by choosing a tampered choice bit vector $\mathbf{r}$ (or τ). The receiver is required to decommit to c_{coin} when it sends $\mathbf{D}$ to the sender. The sender verifies the opening and also verifies that the first column of $\mathbf{D}$ is generated by invoking the random oracle $\mathcal{F}_{RO}$ on coin as $\mathcal{F}_{RO}(0, \text{coin})$[3].

- **Consistency Checks:** A malicious receiver can still send a badly constructed $\mathbf{D}$ (rows of the computed $\mathbf{R}$ are not monochrome) which might trigger a tampered sender. Upon obtaining $\mathbf{D}$ the tampered sender can abort thus leaking one bit of its input. In contrast, an honest sender does not abort until the end of the consistency checks. This behaviour could exfiltrate secrets of a tampered sender to a malicious receiver. We observe that if a malicious receiver sends a malformed $\mathbf{D}$ and the consistency check is performed correctly then a tampered sender aborts, similar to an honest sender, since the tampering is functionality maintaining. However, the sender should obtain $\mathbf{D}$ and the receiver's response for the consistency check in the same round. In such a case, an honest sender also aborts if $\mathbf{D}$ is malformed as this is detected in the consistency check. A tampered sender also aborts and now this prevents exfiltration even if $\mathbf{D}$ contains hidden triggers since the abort is due to the checks failing. The behaviour of the tampered sender is statistically indistinguishable from an honest sender: they only differ when the checks fail to detect inconsistency which occurs with probability $\frac{1}{|\mathbb{F}|}$. This observation leads

---

[3] The $\mathcal{F}_{RO}$ functionality is parametrized by 0 so that we can reuse the same functionality later for a different input/output pair by changing the parameter to 1.

us to a modified protocol such that it provides ER for a tampered sender.

After computing the base OTs, the corrupt receiver commits to the hash of $\mathbf{D}$ using an additively homomorphic commitment scheme as $c_{\mathbf{D}}$. Additive homomorphism allows rerandomization of the commitment by the firewall. The parties then generate the coins seed for the consistency check using an RF-compatible augmented coin-tossing protocol. The randomness for the consistency checks are derived from $\mathcal{F}_{\mathsf{RO}}(1, \mathsf{seed})$, where $\mathcal{F}_{\mathsf{RO}}$ is the random oracle. Finally, the receiver sends $\mathbf{D}$, the decommitment of $c_{\mathbf{D}}$ to $H(\mathbf{D})$ and the response to the consistency checks. The sender verifies the decommitment and the response to the consistency check.

The hash function and $c_{\mathbf{D}}$ forces a corrupt receiver to succinctly commit to $\mathbf{D}$ and allows it to decommit to $\mathbf{D}$ along with the response to the consistency check. The consistency check forces a tampered sender to abort if $\mathbf{D}$ is malformed in a way oblivious to any hidden triggers. This provides exfiltration resistance for the sender. The commitment $c_{\mathbf{D}}$ is rerandomized by the firewall. seed is rerandomized by the firewall to $\widetilde{\mathsf{seed}} = \mathsf{seed} + \widetilde{\mathsf{seed}}$. To incorporate $\widetilde{\mathsf{seed}}$ into c_{seed} the firewall computes $\widehat{c_{\mathsf{seed}}} = c_{\mathsf{seed}} \cdot \mathsf{Com}(\widetilde{\mathsf{seed}}; \widetilde{\delta_{\mathsf{seed}}})$ and sends $\widehat{c_{\mathsf{seed}}}$ to receiver on behalf of sender. The firewall also sends $\widehat{c_{\mathsf{R}}} = \mathsf{seed}_{\mathsf{R}} + \widetilde{\mathsf{seed}}$ to the sender on behalf of the receiver. When sender opens c_{seed} to $(\mathsf{seed}_{\mathsf{S}}; \delta_{\mathsf{seed}})$ the firewall sends $(\mathsf{seed}_{\mathsf{S}} + \widetilde{\mathsf{seed}}, \delta_{\mathsf{seed}} + \widetilde{\delta_{\mathsf{seed}}})$ to the receiver. This ensures that both parties obtain the coins as $\widetilde{\mathsf{seed}}$. We also assume that the commitments are additively homomorphic so that they can be rerandomized by the firewall. The only way to tamper $\mathbf{D}$ matrix and not get caught is when the receiver guesses κ bits of $\mathbf{s}$ to pass the consistency checks. However, the checks ensure that such an event occurs with $2^{-\kappa}$ probability.

The protocol with the three changes gives us a correlated OT (with leakage) extension protocol π_{cOT}. The protocol is presented in Fig. 3 and the firewall in Fig. 4. Our correlated OT with leakage is weaker than correlated OT of [38] since it allows a corrupt receiver to compute c bits of sender's secret key $\mathbf{s}$ with probability 2^{-c}. However, as we show in Sect. 2.5, this suffices for Quicksilver [38]. Next, we build our base OT protocol π_{rOT} which implements $\mathcal{F}_{\mathsf{rOT}}$.

2.3   Base Oblivious Transfer Protocols in the RF Setting

As discussed above, the state-of-the-art OT protocols [7,8,30,35] fail to give π_{rOT} in the presence of functionality maintaining tampering. The OT protocol of [32] provides only passive security in the RF setting and no guarantees against active corruption of the receiver. We construct π_{rOT} by building upon the classical OT protocol of [4] in the plain model. For the sake of completeness, we first recall the protocol.

Protocol of [4]. The sender samples a field element q and computes group element $Q = g^q$ and sends Q to the receiver. The receiver has a choice bit b and it samples two public keys $(\mathsf{pk}_0, \mathsf{pk}_1)$ such that $\mathsf{pk}_b = g^{\mathsf{sk}}$ for secret key sk and $Q = \mathsf{pk}_0 \cdot \mathsf{pk}_1$.

The receiver sends pk_0 to the sender. The sender samples $r_0, r_1 \leftarrow_R \mathbb{Z}_q$, and computes $R_0 = g^{r_0}$ and $R_1 = g^{r_1}$. The sender sets the output as $k_0 = H(\mathsf{pk}_0^{r_0})$ and $k_1 = H(\mathsf{pk}_1^{r_1})$ where H is the Goldreich-Levin hash function or a random oracle. The sender sends (R_0, R_1) to the receiver. The receiver outputs $k_b = H(R_b^{\mathsf{sk}})$.

Modifications for Simulation-Based Security. The protocol of [4] only provides semantic security. The receiver's choice bit is perfectly hidden in the first message pk_0 and the sender's messages are (k_0, k_1) not extractable. We make the following changes in order to allow for simulation based security:

- **Sender Input Extraction:** To extract the sender's input, we modify the protocol so that the sender proves knowledge of q such that $Q = g^q$ through an interactive protocol zero knowledge proof of knowledge (ZKPOK) with the receiver as the verifier. The simulator extracts q from the ZKPOK and sets the secret keys as $\mathsf{sk}_0 \leftarrow_R \mathbb{Z}_q$ and $\mathsf{sk}_1 = q - \mathsf{sk}_0$. The knowledge of the two secret keys enables the simulator to extract the corrupt sender's outputs (k_0, k_1). The ZK property of the proof ensures that q is hidden from a corrupt receiver.

- **Receiver Input Extraction:** To extract the receiver's input, we modify the protocol so that the receiver proves knowledge of sk for the statement $((\mathsf{pk}_0, \mathsf{pk}_1, \mathbb{G}, \mathbb{Z}_q) : \exists \mathsf{sk} \in \mathbb{Z}_q, b \in \{0, 1\} \text{ s.t. } (\mathsf{pk}_0 = g^{\mathsf{sk}} \vee \mathsf{pk}_1 = g^{\mathsf{sk}}))$ using a Witness indistinguishability proof of knowledge (WIPOK). The simulator extracts (sk, b) from the WI proof. Meanwhile, the simulator against a corrupt sender is able to simulate the proof by setting $\mathsf{pk}_0 = g^{\mathsf{sk}}$ and $b = 0$ by relying on the WI property. We also set $k_0 = \mathsf{pk}_0^{r_0}$ and $k_1 = \mathsf{pk}_1^{r_1}$ for efficiency purposes and remove the Goldreich-Levin hash function. The WI proof ensures that if the proof accepts then the receiver has full knowledge of (sk, b). Using the knowledge of sk, we reduce a corrupt receiver breaking semantic security of the OT scheme to an adversary breaking DDH.

Modifications in RF Setting. The above protocol fails to provide exfiltration resistance. We highlight some problems and suggest solutions.

- **Rerandomizing OT parameter Q:** A malicious sender can malform Q and use it as a trigger for a tampered receiver. To address this issue, we generate Q using coin tossing where the receiver sends $T = \mathsf{Com}(Q_R)$ and the sender sends a share Q_S. The receiver later decommits to Q_R and both parties set $Q = Q_R \cdot Q_S$ as the parameter. A firewall can sanitize this: sample $\widetilde{q} \leftarrow_R \mathbb{Z}_q, \widetilde{t} \leftarrow_R \{0, 1\}^*$ and sanitize the commitment as $\widehat{T} = T \cdot \mathsf{Com}(g^{\widetilde{q}}; \widetilde{t})$ and sanitize Q_S as $\widehat{Q_S} = Q_S \cdot g^{\widetilde{q}}$ such that the new parameter is $\widehat{Q} = Q \cdot g^{\widetilde{q}}$ where $\widetilde{q} \leftarrow_R \mathbb{Z}_q$. The firewall also invokes the firewall of the ZK protocol with instance rerandomizer $\widetilde{q}$ since the receiver produces a ZK proof for $(Q_S, \mathbb{G}, \mathbb{Z}_q)$ and the firewall sanitizes it to a proof of $(Q_S \cdot g^{\widetilde{q}}, \mathbb{G}, \mathbb{Z}_q)$. More discussion about the ZK firewall can be found in Sect. 2.4. This transformation provides ER to both parties corresponding to the OT parameters and the ZK proof.

– **Rerandomizing Receiver's choice bit and public keys:** The firewall needs to rerandomize the receiver's choice bit and the public keys to implement $\mathcal{F}_{rOT}$ functionality and prevent exfiltration through the public keys. To enable this, we have the sender commit to a pad $p \leftarrow_R \mathbb{Z}_q$ using an additively homomorphic commitment as $c^S = \mathsf{Com}(p; d^S)$. When the sender receives $(\mathsf{pk}_0, \mathsf{pk}_1)$ the sender decommits to p and the receiver sets the new public keys as $\mathsf{pk}_0' = \mathsf{pk}_0 \cdot g^p$ and $\mathsf{pk}_1' = \mathsf{pk}_1 \cdot g^{-p}$. These new public keys maintain the invariant that $\mathsf{pk}_0' \cdot \mathsf{pk}_1' = Q$. The firewall sanitizes the public keys by changing p to $\widehat{p} = p + \widetilde{p}$. The commitment is modified to $\widehat{c^S} = c^S \cdot \mathsf{Com}(\widetilde{p}; \widetilde{d^S})$. Upon receiving the decommitment (p, d^S) the firewall modifies it to $(\widehat{p}, d^S + \widetilde{d^S})$. Upon receiving the public keys $(\mathsf{pk}_0, \mathsf{pk}_1)$ the firewall changes it to $(\widehat{\mathsf{pk}_0 \cdot g^{\widetilde{p}}}, \mathsf{pk}_1 \cdot g^{-\widetilde{p}})$. This allows both parties to get sanitized public keys $(\widehat{\mathsf{pk}_0}, \widehat{\mathsf{pk}_1}) = (\mathsf{pk}_0 \cdot g^{p+\widetilde{p}}, \mathsf{pk}_1 \cdot g^{-p-\widetilde{p}})$. It is ensured that $\widehat{\mathsf{pk}_0} \cdot \widehat{\mathsf{pk}_1} = \widehat{Q}$ thus preventing any exfiltration through the public keys. Next, we rerandomize the choice bit of the receiver where the sender sends a random bit ρ in the last message of the OT protocol. The receiver's new choice bit is set to $s = b \oplus \rho$ where b was initially chosen by the receiver by sampling $\mathsf{sk} \leftarrow_R \mathbb{Z}_q$ and setting $\mathsf{pk}_b = g^{\mathsf{sk}}$. The firewall sanitises ρ to $\widehat{\rho} = \rho \oplus \widetilde{\rho}$ and it permutes the order of pk_0 and pk_1 if $\widetilde{\rho} = 1$. The firewall also modifies the commitment c^{seed} accordingly so that the order of the sanitised public keys are consistent for both parties. Finally, these changes are also reflected in the WIPOK proof performed by the receiver as the prover. Recall that the receiver proves knowledge of witness for the statement $((\mathsf{pk}_0, \mathsf{pk}_1, \mathbb{G}, \mathbb{Z}_q) : \exists w \in \mathbb{Z}_q, b \in \{0,1\}$ s.t. $(\mathsf{pk}_0 = g^w \vee \mathsf{pk}_1 = g^w))$ using a WIPOK. The firewall sanitizes the proof such that it is consistent with the sanitized public keys and the order of the keys. In particular, if $\widetilde{\rho} = 0$ the new statement is $((\mathsf{pk}_0 \cdot g^{\widetilde{p}}, \mathsf{pk}_1 \cdot g^{-\widetilde{p}}, \mathbb{G}, \mathbb{Z}_q) : \exists w \in \mathbb{Z}_q, b \in \{0,1\}$ s.t. $(\mathsf{pk}_0 \cdot g^{\widetilde{p}} = g^w \vee \mathsf{pk}_1 \cdot g^{-\widetilde{p}} = g^w))$. If $\widetilde{\rho} = 1$ the new statement is $((\mathsf{pk}_0 \cdot g^{\widetilde{p}}, \mathsf{pk}_1 \cdot g^{-\widetilde{p}}, \mathbb{G}, \mathbb{Z}_q) : \exists w \in \mathbb{Z}_q, b \in \{0,1\}$ s.t. $(\mathsf{pk}_0 \cdot g^{\widetilde{p}} = g^w \vee \mathsf{pk}_1 \cdot g^{-\widetilde{p}} = g^w))$. This is performed by constructing malleable Interactive WIPOKs in the RF setting where the *instance* is also sanitized. The firewall for the OT protocol invokes the WI RF with input $((\widetilde{p}, -\widetilde{p}), \widetilde{\rho})$. Detailed discussion about WI is in Sect. 2.4.

– **Rerandomizing sender's messages:** Finally the sender's pads (R_0, R_1) for the OT protocol needs to be rerandomized to implement $\mathcal{F}_{rOT}$ functionality. The receiver commits to $(v_0, v_1) \leftarrow_R \mathbb{Z}_q$ and sends the commitments along-with the public keys. Upon receiving (R_0, R_1), the receiver opens to (v_0, v_1) and considers the sender's random pads as $(R_0 \cdot g^{v_0}, R_1 \cdot g^{v_1})$. The sender sets the new randomness as $(r_0 + v_0, r_1 + v_1)$. The firewall sanitizes the commitment and the interaction such that the random pads are $(R_0 \cdot g^{v_0} \cdot g^{\widetilde{v_0}}, R_1 \cdot g^{v_1} \cdot g^{\widetilde{v_1}})$ and the sender's randomness are $(r_0 + v_0 + \widetilde{v_0}, r_1 + v_1 + \widetilde{v_1})$. This ensures that the tampered sender's pads are indistinguishable from an honestly generated sender random pads.

We obtain our base OT protocol implementing $\mathcal{F}_{\mathsf{rOT}}$ in Figs. 6 and 7 by carefully putting together the above ideas. While this overview is for $\ell = 1$ for simplicity, the final protocol implements $\mathcal{F}_{\mathsf{rOT}}$ for general ℓ. The protocol and the firewall are presented in Sect. 5. Each OT instance communicates 13 group elements + 15 field elements + 1 bit, and performs 35 exponentiations. In comparison, previous maliciously secure OT protocols [10,11] rely on the GMW compiler, and compute $\mathsf{poly}(\kappa)$ exponentiations and communicate $\mathsf{poly}(\kappa)$ bits.

2.4   Malleable Interactive Protocols in the RF Setting

We consider a class of interactive protocols based on Sigma protocols. For the sake of concreteness, consider the classical Sigma protocol for proving knowledge of a discrete logarithm [36]. The statement consists of the description of a cyclic group $\mathbb{G}$ of prime order q, a generator g and an instance $x = g^w$, for $w \in \mathbb{Z}_q$. The prover's first message is a random group element $a = g^\alpha$. For a verifier's challenge $c \in \mathbb{Z}_q$, the prover's response is $z = a + wc$. The transcript $\tau = (a, c, z)$ is accepting if $g^z = ax^c$. We need to rerandomize the transcript without breaking the completeness condition, and without knowing the witness. In addition, since we use these interactive protocols in constructing our OT protocol, the instance x could also potentially be subliminal and therefore, we need to randomize the instance as well, to generate a randomized transcript $(\hat{x}, \hat{\tau})$. In order to build RFs for the ZK protocol obtained by compiling a Sigma protocol, we need to sanitize additional messages. Here, we rely on the key and message homomorphism of the Pedersen commitment scheme to randomize the commitment key, the commitment, and the message inside the commitment. Finally, we construct an RF for the OR composition that not only randomizes each instance in the compound statement, but the *entire* statement (by permuting the clauses). This is necessary since we use the OR protocol as a building block in a larger protocol where the statement itself could be tampered and needs to be sanitized.

We emphasize that our RFs randomize not just the transcript (a, c, z), but also the instance x, as opposed to the RF constructions in [24] where the sanitized transcript still verifies for the same instance x. In our setting, crucially, the instance could also potentially be subliminal and therefore, needs to be randomized to prevent exfiltration. Our notion of fully malleable Sigma protocol is stronger than the malleability considered in [24].

2.5   Efficient Zero-Knowledge in the RF Setting

The recent works of [3,38] present interactive ZK protocols for circuits in the vector OLE model [5,40]. We focus on the work of Quicksilver [38] for binary circuits. In this setting, the vector OLE over binary field is modeled by the $\mathcal{F}_{\mathsf{cOT}}$ functionality. In Quicksilver, the parties run an interactive preprocessing phase which depends only on the security parameter. The parties obtain correlated randomness through this phase. In the online phase the prover obtains the NP verification circuit C and the witness wire assignment $\mathbf{w}$. The verifier obtains the circuit C. The parties locally expand their correlated randomness. The prover obtains $\mathbf{M} \in \{0,1\}^{\ell \times \kappa}$ and a random $\mathbf{b} \in \{0,1\}^{\ell}$, the verifier obtains $\mathbf{K} \in \{0,1\}^{\ell \times \kappa}$ and a random $\Delta \in \{0,1\}^{\kappa}$ such that the following holds for $i \in [\ell]$, where $\mathbf{K} = \{K_i\}_{i \in [\ell]}$, $\mathbf{M} = \{M_i\}_{i \in [\ell]}$, $\mathbf{b} = \{b_i\}_{i \in [\ell]}$:

$$K_i = M_i \oplus b_i \odot \Delta$$

Assume that the number of input wires to the circuit is n, the number of multiplication gates is t and $\ell = n + t$. The prover commits to the $n + t$ wire assignments for the input wires and multiplication gates by sending the mapping $d_i = w_i \oplus b_i$ to the verifier. Addition gates are free due to additive homomorphism and can be verified locally. The verifier updates K_i as follows for $i \in [n + t]$:

$$K_i = K_i \oplus d_i \odot \Delta = (M_i \oplus b_i \odot \Delta) \oplus (w_i \oplus b_i) \odot \Delta = M_i \oplus w_i \odot \Delta.$$

The prover P proves that the committed values w_i corresponding to the multiplication gates are correct by executing a batched verification phase with the verifier V. For each multiplication gate (α, β, γ) with input wires α and β and output wire γ, the prover P has $(w_\alpha, M_\alpha), (w_\beta, M_\beta), (w_\gamma, M_\gamma)$ and the verifier V holds $K_\alpha, K_\beta, K_\gamma, \Delta$ such that the following four equations should hold:

$$w_\gamma = w_\alpha \cdot w_\beta \quad \text{and} \quad M_i = K_i \oplus w_i \odot \Delta \text{ for } i \in \{\alpha, \beta, \gamma\}.$$

This can be verified by the verifier by performing the following check where prover sends $A_{i,0}$ and $A_{i,1}$:

$$\overbrace{B_i = K_\alpha \cdot K_\beta \oplus K_\gamma \cdot \Delta}^{\text{known to V}} \overset{?}{=} \overbrace{M_\alpha \cdot M_\beta + (w_\beta \cdot M_\alpha \oplus w_\alpha \cdot M_\beta \oplus M_\gamma)}^{\text{known to P}} \cdot \overbrace{\Delta}^{\text{known to V}}$$
$$= A_{i,0} \oplus A_{i,1} \cdot \Delta$$

A corrupt prover passes the check even if $w_\gamma \neq w_\alpha \cdot w_\beta$ if it correctly guesses Δ, which occurs with $2^{-\kappa}$ probability. This covers the case for one gate. To check t multiplication gates in a batch the verifier sends a challenge χ. The prover and verifier also generates a random linear relationship $B^* = A_0^* \oplus A_1^* \cdot \Delta$ to mask the prover's inputs. This is performed using additional κ cOTs. The prover computes (U, V) as described below. The prover sends (U, V) and the verifier locally computes W.

$$U = \bigoplus_{i \in [n+t]} A_{i,0} \oplus A_0^* \quad , \quad V = \bigoplus_{i \in [n+t]} A_{i,1} \oplus A_1^* \quad , \quad W = \bigoplus_{i \in [n+t]} B_i \oplus B^*$$

The verifier outputs accept if $(W == U \oplus V \cdot \Delta)$ and rejects the proof if the equation fails to satisfy. A corrupt prover successfully cheats in the batch verification with probability $2^{-\kappa}$ by guessing Δ. Meanwhile, the ZK simulator simulates the proof by passing the check, given the knowledge of $(\mathbf{K}, \Delta)$ from $\mathcal{F}_{\mathsf{cOT}}$. The simulator computes W, samples $V \leftarrow_R \{0,1\}^{\kappa}$ and sets $U = W \oplus V \cdot \Delta$.

Modifications in RF Setting. In order to achieve ER in the firewall setting, we make the following changes to the above protocol.

- **Preprocessing Phase:** The above protocol provides ER for the preprocessing phase if we implement $\mathcal{F}_{cOT}$ with π_{cOT} with parameter $\ell = n + t + \kappa$. However, the parties need to know the number of extended correlated OTs (i.e. $n + t + \kappa$) in π_{cOT} during the preprocessing phase and perform communication proportional to it.

- **Batch Verification:** The mappings **d** maybe malformed and can be used to leak **w**. Similarly, the challenge χ maybe malformed and can be used by a malicious verifier to trigger a tampered prover. We address these issues by following an approach similar to the consistency check in π_{cOT}. The prover commits to hash of **d** as $c_{\mathbf{d}}$. Upon receiving the commitment, the parties participate in an interactive coin tossing protocol to generate the challenge χ. Upon receiving the challenge, the prover decommits **d** and computes the response to the batch verification (following the original Quicksilver protocol). The verifier checks the decommitment to **d** and performs the verifier algorithm of the original quicksilver protocol. The soundness argument of the check is preserved if the hash is collision resistant, $c_{\mathbf{d}}$ is instantiated using a binding commitment scheme and the coin-tossing returns a random χ in the presence of functionality maintaining tamperings. The coin-tossing subprotocol is same as the coin tossing protocol in π_{cOT}. The firewall construction is also the same and this ensures ER for the coin-tossing. We refer to the *Consistency Checks* Sect. 2.2 for the discussion on the coin-tossing. Given that Δ is random and the challenge is sanitized by the firewall, a corrupt prover gets caught if **d** vector is malformed such that the underlying $\mathbf{w} = \mathbf{b} \oplus \mathbf{d}$ is invalid, i.e. $C(\mathbf{w}) = 0$. The complete protocol π_{QS} cna be found in Sect. 7.

The original quicksilver paper achieves communication complexity of 1 bit per multiplication gate. We incur a cost of $\kappa(1 + o(1)) < 2\kappa$ bits per multiplication gate. The number of public key operations is $\mathcal{O}(\kappa)$. The prover and verifier can run our protocol to verify a batch of m different circuits $(C_1, C_2, \ldots, C_m)$ with parameters $(\ell_1, \ell_2, \ldots, \ell_m)$ where ℓ_i denotes the number of input wires and multiplication gates in C_i. In such a case the parties invoke $\mathcal{F}_{cOT}$ with parameter $L = \Sigma_{i \in [m]} \ell_i$. The number of public key operations for the base OTs gets amortized over m runs of the ZK protocol.

3   Preliminaries

Notations: We denote by $a \leftarrow D$ a uniform sampling of an element a from a distribution D. The set of elements $\{1, \ldots, n\}$ is represented by $[n]$. We denote the computational security parameter by κ and statistical security parameter by μ respectively. Let $\mathbb{Z}_q$ denote the field of order q, where $q = \frac{p-1}{2}$ and p are primes. Let $\mathbb{G}$ be the multiplicative group corresponding to $\mathbb{Z}_p^*$ with generator g, where CDH assumption holds. We denote a field of size $\mathcal{O}(2^\mu)$ as $\mathbb{F}$. For a bit

$b \in \{0,1\}$, we denote $1 - b$ by $\bar{b}$. We denote a matrix by $\mathbf{M}$ and let $\mathbf{M}^i$ refer to the ith column and $\mathbf{M}_j$ to the jth row of $\mathbf{M}$ respectively. Given a field element $x \in \mathbb{F}$ and a bit vector $\mathbf{a} = (a_1, a_2, \ldots, a_\kappa)$ we write component-wise multiplication as $x \cdot \mathbf{a} = (a_1 \cdot x, a_2 \cdot x, \ldots, a_\kappa \cdot x)$. Given two vectors $\mathbf{a}, \mathbf{b} \in \{0,1\}^n$, we denote component-wise multiplication by $\mathbf{a} \odot \mathbf{b} = (a_1 \cdot b_1, \ldots, a_n \cdot b_n)$.

Commitment Schemes: We define a non-interactive commitment scheme Com as a tuple of two algorithms (Gen, Com) such that it satisfies the properties of computational binding, computational hiding. Additionally, we require Com to be additively homomorphic over the message space $\mathcal{M}$ and randomness space $\mathcal{R}$, which are written additively, such that for all $m, m' \in \mathcal{M}$, $r, r' \in \mathcal{R}$ we have: $\mathsf{Com}(\mathsf{pp}, m; r) \cdot \mathsf{Com}(\mathsf{pp}, m'; r') = \mathsf{Com}(\mathsf{pp}, m + m'; r + r')$, where pp are the public parameters generated by Gen. For our protocols we require additively homomorphic commitments over $\mathbb{Z}_q$ and $\mathbb{G}$ message spaces. We use Pedersen and Elgamal commitments respectively for this purpose. More details can be found in the full version [12].

3.1 Cryptographic Reverse Firewalls

In this section we recall the basic definitions of reverse firewalls following [10,11, 32]. We focus on the setting of two parties.

Notation. Let Π denote a ℓ-round two-party protocol, for some arbitrary polynomial $\ell(\cdot)$ in the security parameter κ. For a party P and reverse firewall RF we define $\mathsf{RF} \circ P$ as the "composed" party in which the incoming and outgoing messages of A are "sanitized" by RF. The firewall RF is a *stateful* algorithm that is only allowed to see the public parameters of the system, and does not get to see the inputs and outputs of the party P. We denote the tampered implementation of a party P by $\overline{P}$. We write $\Pi_{\mathsf{RF} \circ P}$ (resp. $\Pi_{\overline{P}}$) to represent the protocol Π in which the role of a party P is replaced by the composed party $\mathsf{RF} \circ P$ (resp. the tampered implementation $\overline{P}$). We now define the properties that a reverse firewall must satisfy.

Definition 1 (Functionality maintaining). *For any reverse firewall* RF *and a party* P, *let* $\mathsf{RF}^1 \circ P = \mathsf{RF} \circ P$, *and* $\mathsf{RF}^k \circ P = \underbrace{\mathsf{RF} \circ \cdots \circ \mathsf{RF}}_{k \ times} \circ P$. *For a protocol* Π *that satisfies some functionality requirements* $\mathcal{F}$, *we say that a reverse firewall* RF *maintains functionality* $\mathcal{F}$ *for a party* P *in protocol* Π *if* $\Pi_{\mathsf{RF}^k \circ P}$ *also satisfies* $\mathcal{F}$, *for any polynomially bounded* $k \geq 1$.

Definition 2 (Security preservation). *A reverse firewall weakly preserves security* $\mathcal{S}$ *for party* P *in protocol* Π *if protocol* Π *satisfies* $\mathcal{S}$, *and for any polynomial-time algorithm* $\overline{P}$ *such that* $\Pi_{\overline{P}}$ *satisfies* $\mathcal{F}$, *the protocol* $\Pi_{\mathsf{RF} \circ \overline{P}}$ *satisfies* $\mathcal{S}$. *(i.e., the firewall can guarantee security even when an adversary has tampered with* P, *provided that the tampered implementation does not break the functionality of the protocol).*

A *reverse firewall* strongly preserves security $\mathcal{S}$ for party P in protocol Π *if protocol Π satisfies $\mathcal{S}$, and for any polynomial-time algorithm $\overline{P}$, the protocol $\Pi_{\mathsf{RF} \circ \overline{P}}$ satisfies $\mathcal{S}$. (i.e., the firewall can guarantee security even when an adversary has tampered with party P.)*

We now define exfiltration resistance, which intuitively asks the adversary to distinguish between a tampered implementation $\overline{P}$ of party P from an honest implementation (via the reverse firewall). This prevents, for e.g., for a tampered implementation $\overline{P}$ to leak the secrets of P.

Definition 3 (Exfiltration resistance). *A reverse firewall is* weak exfiltration resistant for party P_1 against party P_2 in protocol Π *satisfying functionality $\mathcal{F}$ if no PPT adversary $\mathcal{A}_{\mathsf{ER}}$ with output circuits $\overline{P_1}$ and $\overline{P_2}$ such that $\Pi_{\overline{P_1}}$ and $\Pi_{\overline{P_2}}$ satisfies $\mathcal{F}$ has non-negligible advantage in the game* $\mathsf{LEAK}(\Pi, P_1, P_2, \mathsf{RF}, \kappa)$ *(see Fig. 2). If P_2 is empty, then we simply say that the firewall is* weak exfiltration resistant.

A reverse firewall is strongly exfiltration resistant for party P_1 against party P_2 in protocol Π *if no PPT adversary $\mathcal{A}_{\mathsf{ER}}$ has non-negligible advantage in the game* $\mathsf{LEAK}(\Pi, P_1, P_2, \mathsf{RF}, \kappa)$. *If P_2 is empty, then we simply say that the firewall is* strongly exfiltration resistant.

$$\frac{\mathsf{LEAK}(\Pi, P_1, P_2, \mathsf{RF}, \kappa)}{(\overline{P_1}, \overline{P_2}, I) \leftarrow \mathcal{A}_{\mathsf{ER}}(1^\kappa)}$$

$$b \xleftarrow{\$} \{0, 1\};$$
$$\text{If } b = 1, P_1^* \leftarrow \mathsf{RF}_1 \circ \overline{P_1}$$
$$\text{Else, } P_1^* \leftarrow \mathsf{RF}_1 \circ P_1.$$
$$\tau^* \leftarrow \Pi_{P_1^*, \{P_2 \rightarrow \overline{P_2}\}}(I).$$
$$b^* \leftarrow \mathcal{A}_{\mathsf{ER}}(\tau^*, \{\mathsf{st}_{\overline{P_2}}\}).$$
$$\text{Output } (b = b^*).$$

Fig. 2. $\mathsf{LEAK}(\Pi, P_1, P_2, \mathsf{RF}, \kappa)$ is the exfiltration-resistance security game for a reverse firewall RF_1 for party P_1 in the protocol Π against party P_2 with input I. Here, $\mathcal{A}_{\mathsf{ER}}$ is the adversary, $\mathsf{st}_{\overline{P_2}}$ denote the state of party P_2 after the run of the protocol, and τ^* denote the transcript of the protocol $\Pi_{P_1^*, \{P_2 \rightarrow \overline{P_2}\}}$ with input I.

We recall the *transparency* property [11] that intuitively, requires that the behavior of $\mathsf{RF} \circ P$ is identical to the behavior of P if P is the honest implementation.

Throughout the paper we refer to weak exfiltration resistance as exfiltration resistance. We will also use the following result established in [11]. It basically states that exfiltration resistance implies security preservation for protocols satisfying simulation-based definition of security.

Theorem 3 ([11] Exfiltration resistance implies Security preservation). *Let Π denote a two-party protocol running between P_1 and P_2 that securely* *computes some function f with abort in presence of malicious adversaries in the simulation-based setting. Assume w.l.o.g, that P_1 is honest (i.e., not maliciously corrupted). Then if the reverse firewall RF_1 is functionality-maintaining, (strongly/weakly) exfiltration resistant for P_1 against P_2, and transparent, then for all PPT adversaries $\mathcal{A}$ and all PPT tempering $\overline{P_1}$ provided by $\mathcal{A}$, the firewall RF_1 (strongly/weakly) preserve security of the party P_1 in the protocol Π according to Definition 2.*

4   Correlated OT Extension in the Firewall Setting

We describe our revised cOT extension protocol in Fig. 3 and the corresponding firewall can be found in Fig. 4. High level overview can be found in Sect. 2.2. We show security of our protocol by proving Theorem 4 in the full version [12].

Theorem 4. *Assuming π_{rOT} implements $\mathcal{F}_{\mathsf{rOT}}$ functionality, Com is a binding and hiding commitment scheme, PRG is a pseudorandom generator and H is a collision resistant hash function, then π_{cOT} implements $\mathcal{F}_{\mathsf{cOT}}$ functionality against active corruption of parties in the $\mathcal{F}_{\mathsf{RO}}$ model.*

We show that our protocol provides weak exfiltration resistance against tampering of honest parties by proving Theorem 5 as follows.

Theorem 5. *Assuming Com is an additively homomorphic, binding and hiding commitment scheme, and $\mathsf{RF}_{\mathsf{rOT\text{-}R}}$ provides weak exfiltration resistance for the receiver (of base OT) in π_{rOT} then $\mathsf{RF}_{\mathsf{cOT\text{-}S}}$ (Fig. 4) provides weak exfiltration resistance for a tampered sender of π_{cOT}. Similarly if $\mathsf{RF}_{\mathsf{rOT\text{-}S}}$ provides weak exfiltration resistance for the sender (of base OT) in π_{rOT} then $\mathsf{RF}_{\mathsf{cOT\text{-}R}}$ (Fig. 4) provides weak exfiltration resistance for a tampered receiver in π_{cOT}.*

Proof. We argue weak exfiltration resistance for each phase as follows:

- The $\mathsf{RF}_{\mathsf{rOT}}$ transcript provides ER to the sender and receiver due to ER of $\mathsf{RF}_{\mathsf{cOT\text{-}R}}$ and $\mathsf{RF}_{\mathsf{cOT\text{-}S}}$ respectively.
- In the OT extension phase, the $\widehat{c_{\mathsf{coin}}}$ and $\widehat{c_{\mathsf{D}}}$ provides ER due to homomorphism and hiding property of the commitment scheme.
- In the consistency check phase if a receiver passes the consistency check the random oracle $\mathcal{F}_{\mathsf{RO}}(\mathsf{sid}, 0, \mathsf{coin})$, $\mathsf{PRG}(k_{1,0})$ and $\mathsf{PRG}(k_{1,1})$ ensures that the first column of $\mathbf{D}$ is randomly distributed and as a result $\mathbf{r}'$ is random. Both parties generate the sanitized $\mathbf{r}'$ as follows:

$$\mathbf{r}' = \mathcal{F}_{\mathsf{RO}}(\mathsf{sid}, 0, \mathsf{coin}_{\mathsf{R}} + \mathsf{coin}_{\mathsf{S}} + \widetilde{\mathsf{coin}}) \oplus \mathsf{PRG}(k_{1,0}) \oplus \mathsf{PRG}(k_{1,1}),$$

where $k_{1,0}$ and $k_{1,1}$ are outputs from the sanitized base OT protocols. $\widehat{c_{\mathsf{seed}}}$ provides ER due to homomorphism and hiding property of the commitment scheme. The consistency check ensures that a malformed $\mathbf{D}$ is detected. For example if the ith column of $\mathbf{D}$ is malformed such that $\mathbf{R}^i \neq \mathbf{r}$ then the check detects and the honest and tampered party aborts when $s_i == 1$.

- **Private Inputs:** R and S do not possess any private inputs.
- **Primitives:** Pseudorandom Generators PRG $: \{0,1\}^{\kappa} \rightarrow \{0,1\}^{m+\kappa}$, $H :$ $\{0,1\}^{(m+\kappa)\times\kappa} \rightarrow \{0,1\}^{\kappa}$ is a Collision Resistant Hash function and Com $:$ $\{0,1\}^{\kappa} \rightarrow \{0,1\}^{\kappa}$ is a string commitment scheme. $\mathcal{F}_{\mathsf{RO}}$ is a random oracle functionality such that $\mathcal{F}_{\mathsf{RO}} : \{0,1\}^{\kappa} \times \{0\} \rightarrow \{0,1\}^{m+\kappa}$ and $\mathcal{F}_{\mathsf{RO}} : \{0,1\}^{\kappa} \times \{1\} \rightarrow \mathbb{F}^{m+\kappa}$.

- **Subprotocols:** Subprotocol π_{rOT} computes ℓ instance of random OT.

Seed OT Phase:

1. S and R participate in π_{rOT} protocol (implementing the $\mathcal{F}_{\mathsf{rOT}}$ functionality) as receiver and sender respectively.
2. R receives $(\mathbf{k}_0, \mathbf{k}_1)$ as output where $\mathbf{k}_{\alpha} = \{k_{i,\alpha}\}_{i\in[\kappa]}$ and $k_{i,\alpha} \in \{0,1\}^{\kappa}$ for $\alpha \in \{0,1\}, i \in [\kappa]$.
3. S receives $\mathbf{s} \in \{0,1\}^{\kappa}$ and $\mathbf{k}'$ where $\mathbf{k}' = \{k'_i\}_{i\in[\kappa]}$ and $k'_i = k_{i,s_i}$ for $i \in [\kappa]$.

OT Extension Phase:

1. R and S perform a coin tossing protocol as follows:
   - R samples $\mathsf{coin}_{\mathsf{R}} \leftarrow_R \{0,1\}^{\kappa}$ and sends $c_{\mathsf{coin}} = \mathsf{Com}(\mathsf{coin}_{\mathsf{R}}; \delta_{\mathsf{coin}})$ to S.
   - S obtains c_{coin} and samples $\mathsf{coin}_{\mathsf{S}} \leftarrow_R \{0,1\}^{\kappa}$ and sends $\mathsf{coin}_{\mathsf{S}}$ to R.
   - R computes $\mathsf{coin} = \mathsf{coin}_{\mathsf{R}} \oplus \mathsf{coin}_{\mathsf{S}}$.
2. R forms three $(m+\kappa) \times \kappa$ matrices $\mathbf{M}$, $\mathbf{R}$ and $\mathbf{D}$ in the following way:
   - Sets $\mathbf{M}^i = \mathsf{PRG}(k_{i,0})$ for $i \in [\kappa]$.
   - Sets $\mathbf{D}^1 = \mathcal{F}_{\mathsf{RO}}(\mathsf{sid}, 0, \mathsf{coin})$. Computes $\mathbf{r}' = \mathbf{D}^1 \oplus \mathbf{M}^1 \oplus \mathsf{PRG}(k_{1,1})$.
   - Parses $\mathbf{r}' = \mathbf{r}\|\tau$ where $\mathbf{r} \in \{0,1\}^m$ and $\tau \in \{0,1\}^{\kappa}$.
   - Sets $\mathbf{R}_j = (r'_j, \ldots, r'_j)$ for $j \in [m+\kappa]$. Clearly, $\mathbf{R}^i = \mathbf{r}'$ for $i \in [\kappa]$.
   - Set $\mathbf{D}^i = \mathbf{M}^i \oplus \mathsf{PRG}(k_{i,1}) \oplus \mathbf{R}^i$ for $i \in [\kappa]$.
   R sets $\mathbf{D} = \{\mathbf{D}^i\}_{i\in[\kappa]}$. R commits to $\mathbf{D}$ as $c_{\mathbf{D}} = \mathsf{Com}(H(\mathbf{D}); \delta_{\mathbf{D}})$ using randomness d and sends $c_{\mathbf{D}}$ to S.

Consistency Check Phase:

1. S and R performs a coin tossing protocol as follows:
   - S samples $\mathsf{seed}_{\mathsf{S}} \leftarrow_R \{0,1\}^{\kappa}$ and sends $c_{\mathsf{seed}} = \mathsf{Com}(\mathsf{seed}_{\mathsf{S}}; \delta_{\mathsf{seed}})$ to R.
   - R obtains c_{seed} and samples $\mathsf{seed}_{\mathsf{R}} \leftarrow_R \{0,1\}^{\kappa}$ and sends $\mathsf{seed}_{\mathsf{R}}$ to S.
   - S opens c_{seed} by sending $(\mathsf{seed}_{\mathsf{S}}, \delta_{\mathsf{seed}})$ to R and sets $\mathsf{seed} = \mathsf{seed}_{\mathsf{S}} + \mathsf{seed}_{\mathsf{R}}$.
2. R aborts if $c_{\mathsf{seed}} \neq \mathsf{Com}(\mathsf{seed}_{\mathsf{S}}; \delta_{\mathsf{seed}})$. Else R computes challenge from the output of the coin tossing protocol, as $\chi = \{\chi_1, \ldots, \chi_{m+\kappa}\} = \mathcal{F}_{\mathsf{RO}}(\mathsf{sid}, 1, \mathsf{seed}_{\mathsf{S}} + \mathsf{seed}_{\mathsf{R}})$.
3. R computes $\mathbf{u} = \bigoplus_{j\in(m+\kappa)}(\chi_j \cdot \mathbf{M}_j)$ and $\mathbf{v} = \bigoplus_{j\in(m+\kappa)}(\chi_j \cdot \mathbf{R}_j)$. R sends $(\mathbf{D}, \delta_{\mathbf{D}}, \mathbf{u}, \mathbf{v})$ to S as the response. R also decommits c_{coin} to $\mathsf{coin}_{\mathsf{R}}$ by sending $(\mathsf{coin}_{\mathsf{R}}, \delta_{\mathsf{coin}})$.
4. On receiving $\mathbf{D}$, S aborts if $c_{\mathbf{D}} \neq \mathsf{Com}(H(\mathbf{D}); \delta_{\mathbf{D}})$ or $c_{\mathsf{coin}} \neq \mathsf{Com}(\mathsf{coin}_{\mathsf{R}}; \delta_{\mathsf{coin}})$ or $\mathbf{D}^1 \neq \mathcal{F}_{\mathsf{RO}}(\mathsf{sid}, 0, \mathsf{coin}_{\mathsf{R}} \oplus \mathsf{coin}_{\mathsf{S}})$. S forms $(m+\kappa) \times \kappa$ bit-matrix $\mathbf{Q}$ with the ith column of $\mathbf{Q}$ set as $\mathbf{Q}^i = (s_i \odot \mathbf{D}^i) \oplus \mathsf{PRG}(k'_i)$. Clearly, (i) $\mathbf{Q}^i = (\mathbf{M}^i \oplus (s_i \odot \mathbf{R}^i))$ and (ii) $\mathbf{Q}_j = (\mathbf{M}_j \oplus (\mathbf{s} \odot \mathbf{R}_j)) = (\mathbf{M}_j \oplus (\mathbf{s} \odot r_j))$.
5. S constructs $\chi = \mathcal{F}_{\mathsf{RO}}(\mathsf{sid}, 1, \mathsf{seed})$ and computes $\mathbf{w} = \bigoplus_{j\in(m+\kappa)}(\chi_j \cdot \mathbf{Q}_j)$. S aborts if $\mathbf{w} \neq \mathbf{u} \oplus \mathbf{s} \cdot \mathbf{v}$.

Output Phase:
S sets $(\mathbf{s}, \{\mathbf{Q}_j\}_{j\in[m]})$ as the output. R sets $(\mathbf{r}, \{\mathbf{M}_j\}_{j\in[m]})$ as the output.

Fig. 3. Correlated OT Extension π_{cOT} in the RF setting

Com is an additively homomorphic commitment where $\mathsf{Com}(m_1; r_1) \cdot \mathsf{Com}(m_2; r_2) = \mathsf{Com}(m_1 + m_2; r_1 + r_2)$.

Seed OT Phase:

$\mathsf{RF}_{\mathsf{cOT\text{-}S}}$ (resp. $\mathsf{RF}_{\mathsf{cOT\text{-}R}}$) invokes the firewall $\mathsf{RF}_{\mathsf{rOT\text{-}R}}$ (resp. $\mathsf{RF}_{\mathsf{rOT\text{-}S}}$) of base-OT receiver (resp. sender) for sanitising the cOT-extension sender's (resp. receiver's) π_{rOT} messages.

OT Extension Phase:

1. The firewall sanitizes the coin-tossing protocol as follows:
   - Upon receiving c_{coin} from R the firewall samples $\widehat{c_{\mathsf{coin}}} = c_{\mathsf{coin}} \cdot \mathsf{Com}(\widetilde{\mathsf{coin}}; \widetilde{\delta_{\mathsf{coin}}})$ where $\widetilde{\mathsf{coin}} \leftarrow_R \{0,1\}^*$ and $\widetilde{\delta_{\mathsf{coin}}} \leftarrow_R \{0,1\}^*$. The firewall sends $\widehat{c_{\mathsf{coin}}}$ to the sender.
   - Upon receiving $\mathsf{coin}_{\mathsf{S}}$ from the sender, the firewall sends $\widehat{\mathsf{coin}_{\mathsf{S}}} = \mathsf{coin}_{\mathsf{S}} + \widetilde{\mathsf{coin}}$ to the receiver.
2. Upon receiving $c_{\mathbf{D}}$ from receiver, the firewall computes $\widehat{c_{\mathbf{D}}} = c_{\mathbf{D}} \cdot \mathsf{Com}(0; \widetilde{\delta_{\mathbf{D}}})$ where $\widetilde{\delta_{\mathbf{D}}} \leftarrow_R \{0,1\}^*$. The firewall sends $\widehat{c_{\mathbf{D}}}$ to the receiver.

Consistency Check Phase:

1. The firewall sanitizes the coin tossing protocol messages as follows:
   - When S sends c_{seed}, the firewall samples $\widetilde{\mathsf{seed}}$ and computes the sanitized commitment as $\widehat{c_{\mathsf{seed}}} = c_{\mathsf{seed}} \cdot \mathsf{Com}(\widetilde{\mathsf{seed}}; \widetilde{\delta_{\mathsf{seed}}})$ where $\widetilde{\delta_{\mathsf{seed}}} \leftarrow_R \{0,1\}^*$. the firewall sends $\widehat{c_{\mathsf{seed}}}$ to the receiver R.
   - When R sends $\mathsf{seed}_{\mathsf{R}}$, the firewall sends $\widehat{\mathsf{seed}_{\mathsf{R}}} = \mathsf{seed}_{\mathsf{R}} + \widetilde{\mathsf{seed}}$ to the sender S.
   - When S sends $(\mathsf{seed}_{\mathsf{S}}, \delta_{\mathsf{seed}})$, the firewall sends $(\widehat{\mathsf{seed}_{\mathsf{S}}}, \widehat{\delta_{\mathsf{seed}}}) = (\mathsf{seed}_{\mathsf{S}} + \widetilde{\mathsf{seed}}, \delta_{\mathsf{seed}} + \widetilde{\delta_{\mathsf{seed}}})$ to the receiver R.
2. When R sends $(\mathbf{D}, \delta_{\mathbf{D}}, \mathbf{u}, \mathbf{v})$, the firewall computes $\widehat{\delta_{\mathbf{D}}} = \delta_{\mathbf{D}} + \widetilde{\delta_{\mathbf{D}}}$ and sends $(\mathbf{D}, \widehat{\delta_{\mathbf{D}}}, \mathbf{u}, \mathbf{v})$ to S. When R sends $(\mathsf{coin}_{\mathsf{R}}, \delta_{\mathsf{coin}})$, the firewall sends $(\mathsf{coin}_{\mathsf{R}} + \widetilde{\mathsf{coin}}, \delta_{\mathsf{coin}} + \widetilde{\delta_{\mathsf{coin}}})$ to the sender.

Fig. 4. Sender's (resp. Receiver's) Firewall $\mathsf{RF}_{\mathsf{cOT\text{-}S}}$ (resp. $\mathsf{RF}_{\mathsf{cOT\text{-}R}}$) in π_{cOT}

When $s_i == 0$ the check fails to detect it and the adversary is able to leak the ith bit of $\mathbf{s}$. The honest sender does not abort following the protocol and the tampered sender also doesn't abort since it is functionality maintaining w.r.t $\mathcal{F}_{\mathsf{cOT}}$ which enables adversary to guess c bits of $\mathbf{s}$. □

By composing Theorems 3, 5 and 4 we show that the firewalls $\mathsf{RF}_{\mathsf{cOT\text{-}R}}$ and $\mathsf{RF}_{\mathsf{cOT\text{-}S}}$ (Fig. 4) preserves the security of the underlying protocol π_{cOT} and that proves Theorem 1.

5   Implementing $\mathcal{F}_{\mathsf{rOT}}$ in the Firewall Setting

In this section we implement $\mathcal{F}_{\mathsf{rOT}}$ (Fig. 5) for base OT protocol. Our protocol π_{rOT} can be found in the full version [12]. Detailed overview can be found in Sec. 2.3. We show simulation based security of π_{rOT} by proving Theorem 6 in the full version [12]. We implement the ZK protocol in Fig. 9 and WI protocol in Fig. 10 in Sect. 6.

Functionality $\mathcal{F}_{\mathsf{rOT}}$

Upon receiving (INITIATE, sid, ℓ) from sender S and a receiver R, the functionality $\mathcal{F}_{\mathsf{rOT}}$ interacts as follows:

- If S is corrupted receive $(\mathbf{a}_0, \mathbf{a}_1) \in \{0,1\}^{\ell \times \kappa}$ from the sender. Else, sample $a_{i,0}, a_{i,1} \leftarrow_R \{0,1\}^\kappa$ for $i \in [\ell]$ and set $(\mathbf{a}_0, \mathbf{a}_1) = \{a_{i,0}, a_{i,1}\}_{i \in [\ell]}$.
- If R is corrupted then receive $\mathbf{b} \in \{0,1\}^\ell$ and $\mathbf{a}' \in \{0,1\}^{\ell \times \kappa}$ from the receiver, and set $a_{i,b_i} = a'_i$ for $i \in [\ell]$. Else, sample $\mathbf{b} \leftarrow_R \{0,1\}^\ell$.
- Denote $\mathbf{b} = \{b_i\}_{i \in [\ell]}$. Set $\mathbf{a}' = \{a'_i\}_{i \in [\ell]}$ where $a'_i = a_{i,b_i}$ for $i \in [\ell]$.

Send (sent, sid, $(\mathbf{b}, \mathbf{a}')$) to R and (sent, sid, $(\mathbf{a}_0, \mathbf{a}_1)$) to S and store (sen, sid, ℓ, $(\mathbf{b}, \mathbf{a}_0, \mathbf{a}_1)$) in memory. Ignore future messages with the same sid.

Fig. 5. The ideal functionality $\mathcal{F}_{\mathsf{rOT}}$ for Oblivious Transfer with random inputs

Theorem 6. *Assuming $\mathsf{Com}_{\mathbb{G}}$ and Com_q be computationally binding and hiding commitment schemes where they are rerandomizable and additively homomorphic for message spaces over $\mathbb{G}$ and $\mathbb{Z}_q$ elements respectively, $\pi_{\mathsf{ZK}}^{\mathsf{DL}}$ implement $\mathcal{F}_{\mathsf{ZK}}$ functionality for the Discrete Log relation $\mathcal{R}_{\mathsf{DL}}$, $\pi_{\mathsf{WI}}^{\mathsf{OR}}$ be a protocol for Witness Indistinguishability with proof of knowledge for the relation $\mathcal{R}_{\mathsf{OR}}$ and DDH assumption holds in group $\mathbb{G}$, then π_{rOT} implements $\mathcal{F}_{\mathsf{rOT}}$ against active corruption of parties.*

We provide the reverse firewall $\mathsf{RF}_{\mathsf{rOT}}$ for protocol π_{rOT} in the full version [12]. We show that the firewall maintains functionality and provides ER for a tampered sender against a receiver and also provides ER for a tampered receiver against a sender by proving Theorem 7.

Theorem 7. *Assuming $\mathsf{Com}_{\mathbb{G}}$ and Com_q be computationally binding and hiding commitment schemes where they are rerandomizable and additively homomorphic for message spaces over $\mathbb{G}$ and $\mathbb{Z}_q$ elements respectively, $\mathsf{RF}_{\mathsf{ZK}}$ and $\mathsf{RF}_{\mathsf{WI}}$ provides weak exfiltration resistance for the tampered parties in $\pi_{\mathsf{ZK}}^{\mathsf{DL}}$ and $\pi_{\mathsf{WI}}^{\mathsf{OR}}$ respectively, then the above firewall $\mathsf{RF}_{\mathsf{rOT}}$ provides weak exfiltration resistance for a tampered sender against a receiver, and for a tampered receiver against a sender.*

Cost. The protocol π_{rOT} implements $\mathcal{F}_{\mathsf{rOT}}$ by producing ℓ random OT instances. Each random OT instance communicates 13 group elements + 15 field elements + 1 bit, and performs 35 exponentiations.

6 Fully Malleable Sigma Protocols

We denote a Sigma protocol by $\Sigma = (\mathsf{P}, \mathsf{V})$, where P_1 and P_2 are algorithms that compute, respectively, the prover's first message a, and the prover's last

$\mathsf{Com}_{\mathbb{G}}$ and Com_q are commitments for group elements and field elements respectively. $\pi_{\mathsf{ZK}}^{\mathsf{DL}}$ is a ZK proof for the statement $(x, \mathbb{G}, \mathbb{Z}_q)$ corresponding to relation $\mathcal{R}_{\mathsf{DL}} = (\exists w \in \mathbb{Z}_q : x = g^w)$. $\pi_{\mathsf{WI}}^{\mathsf{OR}}$ is a WI proof for the statement $(x_0, x_1, \mathbb{G}, \mathbb{Z}_q)$ corresponding to relation $\mathcal{R}_{\mathsf{OR}} = (\exists w \in \mathbb{Z}_q, b \in \{0,1\} : x_0 = g^w \vee x_1 = g^w)$.

---

1. **Receiver's Coin-tossing for Parameters:** The receiver samples $Q_{\mathsf{R}} \leftarrow_R \mathbb{G}$ and sends $T = \mathsf{Com}_{\mathbb{G}}(Q_{\mathsf{R}}; t)$ to the sender.
2. **Sender's Coin-tossing for Parameters and Receiver's Public Key:** The sender samples $q \leftarrow_R \mathbb{Z}_q$ and computes $Q_{\mathsf{S}} = g^q$. For $i \in [\ell]$ the sender performs the following:
   - The sender samples $p_i \leftarrow_R \mathbb{Z}_q$ to rerandomize the receiver public key.
   - The sender computes $c_i^{\mathsf{S}} = \mathsf{Com}_q(p_i; d_i^{\mathsf{S}})$.

   The sender sends $(Q_{\mathsf{S}}, \mathbf{C}^{\mathsf{S}})$ to the receiver, where $\mathbf{C}^{\mathsf{S}} = \{c_i^{\mathsf{S}}\}_{i \in [\ell]}$.
3. **Sender's Zero-Knowledge Proof for Parameters:** The sender and the receiver run $\pi_{\mathsf{ZK}}^{\mathsf{DL}}$ protocol where sender is the prover for the statement $(Q_{\mathsf{S}}, \mathbb{G}, \mathbb{Z}_q)$ corresponding to witness q.
4. **Receiver's generates Public Keys and Performs Coin-tossing for Sender's OT message:** The receiver computes $Q = Q_{\mathsf{R}} \cdot Q_{\mathsf{S}}$. The receiver samples random choice bits $\mathbf{b} \leftarrow_R \{0,1\}^{\ell}$. For $i \in [\ell]$ the receiver performs the following:
   - The receiver samples $\mathsf{sk}_i \leftarrow_R \mathbb{Z}_q$ and computes $\mathsf{pk}_{i,b} = g^{\mathsf{sk}_i}$.
   - The receiver computes $\mathsf{pk}_{i,\bar{b}} = \frac{Q}{\mathsf{pk}_{i,b}}$.
   - The receiver samples shares for sender's OT randomness $v_{i,0}, v_{i,1} \leftarrow_R \mathbb{Z}_q$.
   - The receiver commits to the shares as $c_{i,0}^{\mathsf{R}} = \mathsf{Com}_q(v_{i,0}; d_{i,0}^{\mathsf{R}})$ and $c_{i,1}^{\mathsf{R}} = \mathsf{Com}_q(v_{i,1}; d_{i,1}^{\mathsf{R}})$.

   The receiver decommits to T by sending (Q_{R}, t). The receiver also sends the commitments - $(\mathbf{C}_0^{\mathsf{R}}, \mathbf{C}_1^{\mathsf{R}})$ where $\mathbf{C}_0^{\mathsf{R}} = \{c_{i,0}^{\mathsf{R}}\}_{i \in [\ell]}$ and $\mathbf{C}_1^{\mathsf{R}} = \{c_{i,1}^{\mathsf{R}}\}_{i \in [\ell]}$ and the public keys $\{\mathsf{pk}_{i,0}\}_{i \in [\ell]}$.
5. **Receiver's WI Proof for Secret Keys:** For $i \in [\ell]$, the receiver and the sender parallely run $\pi_{\mathsf{WI}}^{\mathsf{OR}}$ protocol where receiver is the prover for the statement $\{\mathsf{pk}_{i,0}, \mathsf{pk}_{i,1}, \mathbb{G}, \mathbb{Z}_q\}_{i \in [\ell]}$ corresponding to witness $\{\mathsf{sk}_i, b_i\}_{i \in [\ell]}$.
6. **Sender generates OT message, Rerandomizes and Permutes Receiver's Public Keys:** The sender aborts if $T \neq \mathsf{Com}_{\mathbb{G}}(Q_{\mathsf{R}}; t)$ else it sets $Q = Q_{\mathsf{S}} \cdot Q_{\mathsf{R}}$. The sender samples random choice bit permutation $\boldsymbol{\rho} \leftarrow_R \{0,1\}^{\ell}$. For $i \in [\ell]$ the sender performs the following:
   - The sender computes $\mathsf{pk}_{i,1} = \frac{Q}{\mathsf{pk}_{i,0}}$.
   - The sender samples $r_{i,0}, r_{i,1} \leftarrow_R \mathbb{Z}_q$.
   - The sender computes $R_{i,0} = g^{r_{i,0}}$ and $R_{i,1} = g^{r_{i,1}}$.

   The sender sends $(\boldsymbol{\rho}, \{R_{i,0}, R_{i,1}, p_i, d_i^{\mathsf{S}}\}_{i \in [\ell]})$ to the receiver.
7. **Receiver Rerandomizes Sender's OT message and Computes Output:** The receiver sets the random choice bit string as $\mathbf{s} = \mathbf{b} \oplus \boldsymbol{\rho}$. For $i \in [\ell]$, the receiver performs the following:
   - The receiver aborts if $c_i^{\mathsf{S}} \neq \mathsf{Com}_q(p_i; d_i^{\mathsf{S}})$.
   - The receiver sets $p_{i,0} = p_i$ and $p_{i,1} = -p_i$.
   - The receiver updates $\mathsf{sk}_i = \mathsf{sk}_i + p_{i,b_i}$ and computes $k_i' = (R_{i,s_i} \cdot g^{v_{i,s_i}})^{\mathsf{sk}_i}$.

   The receiver outputs $(\mathbf{s}, \mathbf{k}')$ where $\mathbf{k}' = \{k_i'\}_{i \in [\ell]}$. The receiver decommits $(\mathbf{C}_0^{\mathsf{R}}, \mathbf{C}_1^{\mathsf{R}})$ by sending $\{v_{i,0}, d_{i,0}^{\mathsf{R}}, v_{i,1}, d_{i,1}^{\mathsf{R}}\}_{i \in [\ell]}$ to sender.

Fig. 6. Protocol π_{rOT} implementing $\mathcal{F}_{\mathsf{rOT}}$

8. **Sender Computes Rerandomized Output:** For $i \in [\ell]$ the sender computes the following:
   - For $\beta \in \{0,1\}$: The sender aborts if $c_{i,\beta}^R \neq \mathsf{Com}_q(v_{i,\beta}; d_{i,\beta}^R)$.
   - Sets $p_{i,0} = p_i$ and $p_{i,1} = -p_i$.
   - The sender computes $k_{i,0}$ and $k_{i,1}$ based on ρ_i by considering the following two cases:
     - If ($\rho_i == 0$): the sender computes the output messages $k_{i,0} = (\mathsf{pk}_{i,0} \cdot g^{p_{i,0}})^{r_{i,0}+v_{i,0}}$ and $k_{i,1} = (\mathsf{pk}_{i,1} \cdot g^{p_{i,1}})^{r_{i,1}+v_{i,1}}$.
     - If ($\rho_i == 1$): the sender computes the output messages $k_{i,0} = (\mathsf{pk}_{i,1} \cdot g^{p_{i,1}})^{r_{i,0}+v_{i,0}}$ and $k_{i,1} = (\mathsf{pk}_{i,0} \cdot g^{p_{i,0}})^{r_{i,1}+v_{i,1}}$.

     More generally, the sender computes $k_{i,0} = (\mathsf{pk}_{i,\rho_i} \cdot g^{p_{i,\rho_i}})^{r_{i,0}+v_{i,0}}$ and $k_{i,1} = (\mathsf{pk}_{i,\overline{\rho_i}} \cdot g^{p_{i,\overline{\rho_i}}})^{r_{i,1}+v_{i,1}}$.

   The sender sets $(\mathbf{k}_0, \mathbf{k}_1) = \{k_{i,0}, k_{i,1}\}_{i \in [\ell]}$ as the output.

Fig. 7. Protocol π_{rOT} implementing $\mathcal{F}_{\mathsf{rOT}}$

message (response) z. Moreover we require the Sigma protocol to be "unique response", i.e., it is infeasible to find two distinct valid responses for a given first message and fixed challenge. Let $\mathcal{A}$ be the space of all possible prover's first messages; membership in $\mathcal{A}$ can be tested efficiently, so the V always outputs $\bot$ when $a \notin \mathcal{A}$. Also, let $\mathcal{C}$ denote the challenge space of the verifier.

6.1 Malleability

The work of [24] defines the notion of malleability. A Sigma protocol is malleable if the prover's first message a can be randomized into $\hat{a}$ that is distributed identically to the first message of an honest prover. In addition, for any challenge c, given the coins used to randomize a and any response z yielding an accepting transcript $\tau = (a, c, z)$, a balanced response $\hat{z}$ can be computed such that $(\hat{a}, c, \hat{z})$ is also an accepting transcript. In our constructions, we need a stronger notion of malleability: we will need to randomize the *instance* in addition to the transcript. We demonstrate that the sigma protocol for discrete log is malleable in Fig. 8.

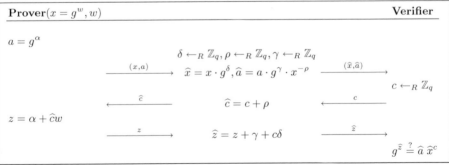

Fig. 8. Fully Malleable Sigma protocol for discrete log

We now formally define our notion of fully malleable Sigma protocols.

Definition 4 (Fully Malleable Sigma protocol). *Let $\Sigma = (P_1, P_2, V)$ be a Sigma protocol for a relation $\mathcal{R}$. Σ is said to be* fully malleable *if there exists a tuple of polynomial-time algorithms* (Maul, MaulCh, Bal) *specified as follows:*

(i) Maul *is a probabilistic algorithm that takes as input an instance x, $a \in \mathcal{A}$ (recall that $\mathcal{A}$ is set of all possible prover's first messages), instance randomizer δ and outputs an instance $\widehat{x}$, and $\widehat{a} \in \mathcal{A}$ and state $\sigma \in \{0, 1\}^*$;*

(ii) MaulCh *is a probabilistic algorithm that takes as input a challenge c and a randomizer ρ and returns a modified challenge $\widehat{c}$.*

(iii) Bal *is a deterministic algorithm that takes as input x, z, the state σ output by* Maul, *a challenge c and returns a balanced response $\widehat{z}$.*

The following properties need to be satisfied.

- **Uniformity.** *For all $(x, w) \in \mathcal{R}$, and for all $a \in \mathcal{A}$, $\widehat{x}$ is a uniformly distributed instance in $\mathcal{L}$, and the distribution of $\widehat{a}$ is identical to that of $P_1(\widehat{x}, \widehat{w})$, where $(\widehat{x}, \widehat{a}, \sigma) \leftarrow_R$ Maul(x, a, δ) such that $(\widehat{x}, \widehat{w}) \in \mathcal{R}$. Moreover, for all $c \in \mathcal{C}$ (recall that $\mathcal{C}$ denotes the challenge space) and uniformly random $\rho \leftarrow_R \mathbb{Z}_q$, $\widehat{c}$ is uniformly distributed in $\mathcal{C}$, where $\widehat{c} \leftarrow_R$ MaulCh$(c; \rho)$*
- **Malleability.** *For all $x \in \mathcal{L}$, for all $\rho \leftarrow_R \mathbb{Z}_q$ and for all $\tau = (a, \widehat{c}, z)$ such that $V(x, (a, \widehat{c}, z)) = 1$, where $\widehat{c} \leftarrow_R$ MaulCh$(c; \rho)$, the following holds:*

$$\Pr[V(\widehat{x}, (\widehat{a}, c, \widehat{z})) = 1 : (\widehat{x}, \widehat{a}, \sigma) \leftarrow \mathsf{Maul}(x, a, \delta); \widehat{z} = \mathsf{Bal}(x, z, \sigma, c)] = 1,$$

where the probability is over the randomness of Maul *and* MaulCh.

Lemma 1. *The Sigma protocol for Discrete Log is fully malleable as per Definition 4. The construction is shown in Fig. 8.*

Proof. We instantiate Maul, MaulCh and Bal algorithms for knowledge of discrete logarithm, where $\gamma \leftarrow_R \mathbb{Z}_q$:

$$\mathsf{Maul}(x, a, \rho, \delta) = (x \cdot g^\delta, a \cdot g^\gamma \cdot x^{-\rho}, (\gamma, \delta)) \quad \mathsf{MaulCh}(c, \rho) = c + \rho$$
$$\mathsf{Bal}(x, z, (\gamma, \delta), c) = z + \gamma + c\delta$$

- *Uniformity:* For all $(x, w), x = g^w$, for all $\alpha \in \mathbb{Z}_q$, the distribution of $\widehat{a} = a \cdot g^\gamma \cdot x^{-\rho} = g^\alpha \cdot g^\gamma \cdot g^{-\rho w}$ over the choice of $\gamma \leftarrow_R \mathbb{Z}_q$ is identical to the distribution of $a = g^\alpha$ over the choice of $\alpha \in \mathbb{Z}_q$. Moreover, for all uniformly random $\rho \leftarrow_R \mathbb{Z}_q$, the value $\widehat{c} = c + \rho$ is uniformly distributed in the challenge space.
- *Malleability:* For all $x \in \mathcal{L}$, for all $\rho \in \mathbb{Z}_q$, and for all $\tau = (a, \widehat{c}, z)$ such that $g^z = ax^{-\widehat{c}}$, where $\widehat{c} = c + \rho$, the following holds:

$$\widehat{a}\widehat{x}^{-c} = ag^\gamma x^{-\rho}\widehat{x}^{-c} = ag^\gamma x^{-c-\rho}g^{-\delta c} = ag^\gamma x^{-\widehat{c}}g^{-\delta c} = g^z g^\gamma g^{-\delta c} = g^{\widehat{z}}$$

$\square$

We note that Maul and Bal easily generalize to the unifying Sigma protocol for proving knowledge of preimage of a homomorphism [31]. This generalization gives an RF for the unifying Sigma protocol, even though we only need the protocol for knowledge of discrete logarithm in our applications.

In general, Sigma protocols are not full-fledged zero knowledge or zero-knowledge proof of knowledge (ZKPoK) protocols. However, standard techniques [25] allow to compile a Sigma protocol into a zero knowledge protocol. We recall the ZKPoK protocol $\pi_{\mathsf{ZK}}^{\mathsf{DL}}$ for the discrete logarithm problem in the full version [12] and we provide an RF for it in Fig. 9 and prove Theorem 8.

Theorem 8. *Let Σ be a fully malleable unique-response Sigma protocol for $\mathcal{R}$ as in Definition 4. The RF $\mathsf{RF}_{\mathsf{ZK}}$ in Fig. 9 is functionality-maintaining, weakly ZK preserving and weak exfiltration resistant for the ZK protocol $\pi_{\mathsf{ZK}}^{\mathsf{DL}}$ of discrete log.*

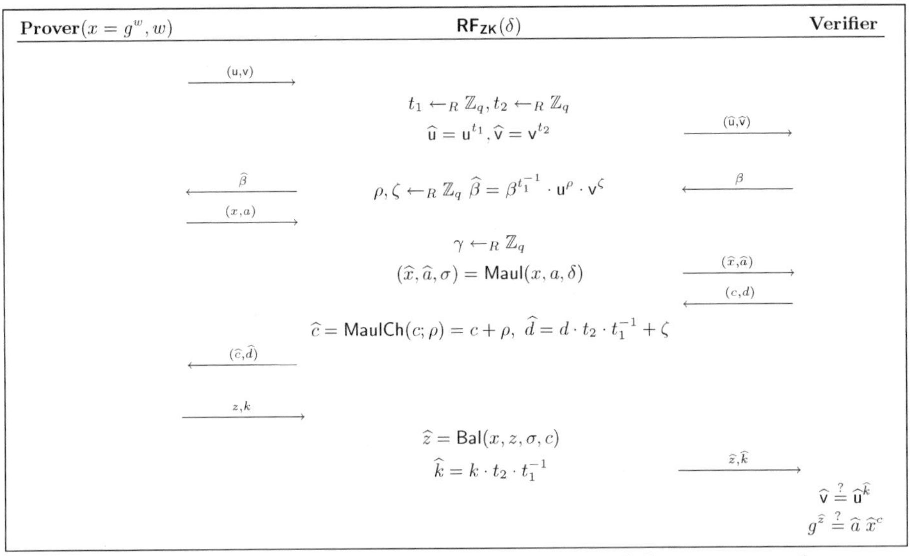

Fig. 9. Reverse Firewall $\mathsf{RF}_{\mathsf{ZK}}$ for ZK compiled Sigma protocol

6.2 RF for OR Transform Sigma Protocol

OR Transform. Given x_0, x_1, a prover wishes to prove to a verifier that either $x_0 \in \mathcal{L}_0$ or $x_1 \in \mathcal{L}_1$ without revealing which one is true. The OR relation is given by: $\mathcal{R}_{\mathsf{OR}} = \{((x_0, x_1), w) : (x_0, w) \in \mathcal{R}_0 \vee (x_1, w) \in \mathcal{R}_1\}$.

Let $\Sigma_0 = ((\mathsf{P}_1^0, \mathsf{P}_2^0), \mathsf{V}^0)$ (resp. $\Sigma_1 = ((\mathsf{P}_1^1, \mathsf{P}_2^1), \mathsf{V}^1)$) be a Sigma protocol for language $\mathcal{L}_0$ (resp. $\mathcal{L}_1$). Let Sim^0 (resp. Sim^1) be the HVZK simulator for Σ_0 (resp. Σ_1). A Sigma protocol $\pi_{\mathsf{WI}}^{\mathsf{OR}}$ for the relation $\mathcal{R}_{\mathsf{OR}}$ was constructed in [17]. We describe the protocol $\pi_{\mathsf{WI}}^{\mathsf{OR}}$ in Fig. 10. $\pi_{\mathsf{WI}}^{\mathsf{OR}}$ satisfies perfect special HVZK and perfect WI.

RF for OR Protocol. In order to construct an RF for the OR transform, we need to maul the prover's first message in such a way that the verifier's challenge can be balanced in addition to the prover's last message. We note that [24] considers an RF for the OR composition, however that definition and construction does not suffice for our application since we need to randomize the instance as well. We present the WI protocol for OR composition the full version [12]. We show the RF for the OR composition in Fig. 10 and demonstrate that it provides ER by proving Theorem 9.

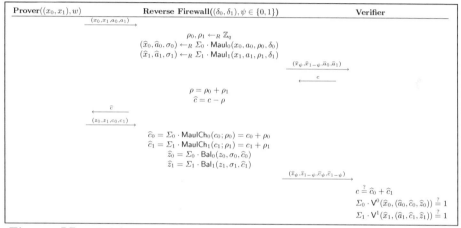

Fig. 10. $\mathsf{RF_{WI}}$: RF for the OR composition of Sigma protocols, where $(x_b, w) \in \mathcal{R}_b$ for $b \in \{0, 1\}$. The bit ψ is an additional input to $\mathsf{RF_{WI}}$ provided by a RF of an higher-level protocol (in our case the RF of our base OT protocol)

Theorem 9. *Let Σ_0 and Σ_1 be fully malleable unique-response Sigma protocols for $\mathcal{R}_0$ and $\mathcal{R}_1$ respectively. The RF $\mathsf{RF_{WI}}$ in Fig. 10 preserves completeness, is weakly HVZK/WI preserving and weak exfiltration resistant for π_{WI}^{OR}.*

7   Quicksilver with Reverse Firewall

We present a variant of Quicksilver [38] in the firewall setting, π_{QS}, in the full version [12]. It is in the $\mathcal{F}_{cOT}$ model and provides efficient interactive ZK for binary circuits. For a circuit with number of input wires n and the number of multiplication gate t, the proof size is $(n+t)$ bits in the $\mathcal{F}_{cOT}$ model. Instantiating $\mathcal{F}_{cOT}$ with π_{cOT} the concrete proof size of π_{QS} is $(n+t)\kappa + \mathcal{O}(\kappa^2)$ bits. The number of public key operations is $\mathcal{O}(\kappa)$ and is independent of t. Detailed overview can be found in Sect. 2.5. Security of π_{QS} is summarized in Theorem 10. More details can be found in the full version [12].

Theorem 10. *Assuming H is a collision resistant hash function and Com is a computationally hiding and binding commitment scheme then π_{QS} implements $\mathcal{F}_{ZK}$ functionality in the $\mathcal{F}_{cOT}$ model.*

Proof Sketch. A corrupt prover breaks soundness of the protocol if it 1) breaks binding of $c_{\mathbf{d}}$, or 2) finds a collision in H, or 3) breaks hiding of c_{seed}, or it passes the batch verification phase for a circuit C such that $\forall \mathbf{w}, C(\mathbf{w}) = 0$. Breaking binding of $c_{\mathbf{d}}$ or finding a collision in H allows the prover to open the commitment to a different $\mathbf{d}'$ after obtaining the challenge χ and hence passing the batch verification. Breaking hiding of c_{seed} allows the prover to fix the challenge to a particular value for which it passes the challenge. Finally, assuming the above attacks fail the prover can still pass the batch verification checks if it correctly guesses the entire Δ^{κ} of the V. The functionality $\mathcal{F}_{cOT}$ allows the prover to leak c bits of 2^{-c} bits. However, it successfully guesses the entire $\Delta \in \{0,1\}^{\kappa}$ with $2^{-\kappa}$ probability. Zero knowledge of the protocol follows from the security for a receiver in π_{cOT}. The pads (A_0^*, A_1^*) perfectly hides the inputs of the prover and the ZK simulator simulates the proof given corrupt verifier's input Δ to $\mathcal{F}_{cOT}$.

Com is an additively homomorphic commitment scheme. $\mathsf{RF}_{cOT\text{-}R}$ and $\mathsf{RF}_{cOT\text{-}S}$ provides exfiltration resistance for a tampered receiver and a tampered sender in π_{cOT}.

Preprocessing phase:
The firewall for the prover invokes the firewall $\mathsf{RF}_{cOT\text{-}R}$ (resp. $\mathsf{RF}_{cOT\text{-}S}$) to sanitize the transcript of π_{cOT} for the prover (resp. verifier).

Online phase:
Now the circuit and witness are known by the parties.

4. *Input Wire Mapping:* This step only includes local computation.
5. *Gate Computation:* Upon receiving $c_{\mathbf{d}}$ from the prover the firewall computes $\widehat{c}_{\mathbf{d}} = c_{\mathbf{d}} \cdot \mathsf{Com}(0; \widetilde{\delta}_{\mathbf{d}})$ by sampling $\widetilde{\delta}_{\mathbf{d}} \leftarrow_R \{0,1\}^{\kappa}$. The firewall sends $\widehat{c}_{\mathbf{d}}$ to the verifier.
6. *Batch Verification Challenge:* The steps of the coin tossing protocol are sanitised as follows:
   - Upon receiving c_{seed} from verifier the firewall computes $\widehat{c}_{\mathsf{seed}} = c_{\mathsf{seed}} \cdot \mathsf{Com}(\widetilde{\mathsf{seed}}; \widetilde{\delta}_{\mathsf{seed}})$ by sampling $\widetilde{\mathsf{seed}} \leftarrow_R \{0,1\}^{\kappa}$ and $\widetilde{\delta}_{\mathsf{seed}} \leftarrow_R \{0,1\}^*$. The firewall sends $\widehat{c}_{\mathsf{seed}}$ to the P.
   - Upon receiving seed_P from the prover the firewall sends $\widetilde{\mathsf{seed}}_P = \mathsf{seed}_P \oplus \widetilde{\mathsf{seed}}$ to the V.
   - Upon receiving $(\mathsf{seed}_V, \delta_{\mathsf{seed}})$ from the verifier, the firewall sends $(\mathsf{seed}_V \oplus \widetilde{\mathsf{seed}}, \delta_{\mathsf{seed}} \oplus \widetilde{\delta}_{\mathsf{seed}})$ to the prover.
7. *Batch Verification Response:* Upon receiving $(\mathbf{d}, \delta_{\mathbf{d}}, U, V)$ from the prover, the firewall sends $(\mathbf{d}, \delta_{\mathbf{d}} \oplus \widetilde{\delta}_{\mathbf{d}}, U, V)$ to the verifier as the response.
8. *Batch Verification:* This step only includes local computation.

Fig. 11. Reverse Firewalls $\mathsf{RF}_{QS\text{-}P}$ (resp. $\mathsf{RF}_{QS\text{-}V}$) providing exfiltration resistance for a tampered prover (resp. verifier) in π_{QS}

The Firewall Construction. We provide the firewalls in Fig. 11. Assuming $\mathcal{F}_{cOT}$ is implemented by π_{cOT} in π_{QS}, the firewall $\mathsf{RF}_{cOT\text{-}S}$ for the sender in π_{cOT} provides ER to the prover in the preprocessing phase of π_{QS}. Similarly, the firewall $\mathsf{RF}_{cOT\text{-}R}$ for the receiver in π_{cOT} provides ER to the verifier in the preprocessing phase. The coin χ is rerandomized by the firewall to prevent any exfiltration through the coin-tossing. Similarly, the commitments are also rerandomized to prevent exfiltration. Theorem 11 summarizes the RF security.

Theorem 11. *Let π_{cOT} implement $\mathcal{F}_{cOT}$ in π_{QS}. Assuming* Com *is an additively homomorphic, binding and hiding commitment scheme,* $\mathsf{RF}_{cOT\text{-}R}$ *provides weak exfiltration resistance for a tampered receiver in π_{rOT} and* $\mathsf{RF}_{cOT\text{-}S}$ *provides weak exfiltration resistance for a tampered sender of π_{cOT} then* $\mathsf{RF}_{QS\text{-}P}$ *provides weak exfiltration resistance for the prover in π_{QS} and* $\mathsf{RF}_{QS\text{-}V}$ *provides weak exfiltration resistance for the verifier in π_{QS} respectively.*

By composing Theorems 3, 10 and 11 we show that the firewalls $\mathsf{RF}_{QS\text{-}V}$ and $\mathsf{RF}_{QS\text{-}P}$ (Fig. 11) preserves the security of the underlying protocol π_{QS} thus proving Theorem 2.

Optimizations. Our protocol admits batching: the prover and verifier can run our protocol to verify m different circuits $(C_1, C_2, \ldots, C_m)$ with parameters $(\ell_1, \ell_2, \ldots, \ell_m)$ where ℓ_i denotes the number of input wires and multiplication gates in C_i. The parties invoke $\mathcal{F}_{cOT}$ with parameter $\ell = \Sigma_{i \in [m]} \ell_i$, the combined witness $\mathbf{w}$ consists of the individual witnesses $(\mathbf{w}_1, \mathbf{w}_2, \ldots, \mathbf{w}_m)$ and circuit $C(\mathbf{w}) = 1$ when $\forall i \in [m], C_i(\mathbf{w}_i) = 1$. In this batched setting, the number of public key operations for the base OTs gets amortized over m runs of the ZK protocol.

References

1. Ateniese, G., Magri, B., Venturi, D.: Subversion-resilient signature schemes. In: Ray, I., Li, N., Kruegel, C. (eds.) ACM CCS 2015, pp. 364–375. ACM Press, October 2015. https://doi.org/10.1145/2810103.2813635

2. Ball, J., Borger, J., Greenwald, G., et al.: Revealed: how US and UK spy agencies defeat internet privacy and security. Know Your Neighborhood (2013)

3. Baum, C., Malozemoff, A.J., Rosen, M.B., Scholl, P.: Mac'n'cheese: zero-knowledge proofs for boolean and arithmetic circuits with nested disjunctions. In: Malkin, T., Peikert, C. (eds.) CRYPTO 2021, Part IV. LNCS, vol. 12828, pp. 92–122, Virtual Event. Springer, Cham (2021). https://doi.org/10.1007/978-3-030-84259-8_4

4. Bellare, M., Micali, S.: Non-interactive oblivious transfer and applications. In: Brassard, G. (ed.) CRYPTO 1989. LNCS, vol. 435, pp. 547–557. Springer, Cham (1990). https://doi.org/10.1007/0-387-34805-0_48

5. Boyle, E., et al.: Efficient two-round OT extension and silent non-interactive secure computation. In: Cavallaro, L., Kinder, J., Wang, X., Katz, J. (eds.) ACM CCS 2019, pp. 291–308. ACM Press, November 2019. https://doi.org/10.1145/3319535.3354255

6. Byali, M., Patra, A., Ravi, D., Sarkar, P.: Fast and universally-composable oblivious transfer and commitment scheme with adaptive security. Cryptology ePrint Archive, Report 2017/1165 (2017). https://eprint.iacr.org/2017/1165

7. Canetti, R., Sarkar, P., Wang, X.: Blazing fast OT for three-round UC OT extension. In: Kiayias, A., Kohlweiss, M., Wallden, P., Zikas, V. (eds.) PKC 2020, Part II. LNCS, vol. 12111, pp. 299–327. Springer, Cham (2020). https://doi.org/10.1007/978-3-030-45388-6_11

8. Canetti, R., Sarkar, P., Wang, X.: Efficient and round-optimal oblivious transfer and commitment with adaptive security. In: Moriai, S., Wang, H. (eds.) ASIACRYPT 2020, Part III. LNCS, vol. 12493, pp. 277–308. Springer, Cham (2020). https://doi.org/10.1007/978-3-030-64840-4_10

9. Canetti, R., Sarkar, P., Wang, X.: Triply adaptive UC NIZK. In: Agrawal, S., Lin, D. (eds.) Advances in Cryptology - ASIACRYPT 2022–28th International Conference on the Theory and Application of Cryptology and Information Security, Taipei, Taiwan, 5–9 December 2022, Proceedings, Part II. LNCS, vol. 13792, pp. 466–495. Springer, Cham (2022). https://doi.org/10.1007/978-3-031-22966-4_16

10. Chakraborty, S., Dziembowski, S., Nielsen, J.B.: Reverse firewalls for actively secure MPCs. In: Micciancio, D., Ristenpart, T. (eds.) CRYPTO 2020, Part II. LNCS, vol. 12171, pp. 732–762. Springer, Cham (2020). https://doi.org/10.1007/978-3-030-56880-1_26

11. Chakraborty, S., Ganesh, C., Pancholi, M., Sarkar, P.: Reverse firewalls for adaptively secure MPC without setup. In: Tibouchi, M., Wang, H. (eds.) ASIACRYPT 2021. LNCS, vol. 13091, pp. 335–364. Springer, Cham (2021). https://doi.org/10.1007/978-3-030-92075-3_12

12. Chakraborty, S., Ganesh, C., Sarkar, P.: Reverse firewalls for oblivious transfer extension and applications to zero-knowledge. IACR Cryptol. ePrint Arch., p. 1535 (2022). https://eprint.iacr.org/2022/1535, https://eprint.iacr.org/2022/1535

13. Chakraborty, S., Magri, B., Nielsen, J.B., Venturi, D.: Universally composable subversion-resilient cryptography. In: Dunkelman, O., Dziembowski, S. (eds.) Advances in Cryptology - EUROCRYPT 2022–41st Annual International Conference on the Theory and Applications of Cryptographic Techniques, Trondheim, Norway, 30 May–3 June 2022, Proceedings, Part I. LNCS, vol. 13275, pp. 272–302. Springer, Cham (2022). https://doi.org/10.1007/978-3-031-06944-4_10

14. Chase, M., Kohlweiss, M., Lysyanskaya, A., Meiklejohn, S.: Malleable proof systems and applications. In: Pointcheval, D., Johansson, T. (eds.) EUROCRYPT 2012. LNCS, vol. 7237, pp. 281–300. Springer, Cham (2012). https://doi.org/10.1007/978-3-642-29011-4_18

15. Chen, R., Mu, Y., Yang, G., Susilo, W., Guo, F., Zhang, M.: Cryptographic reverse firewall via malleable smooth projective hash functions. In: Cheon, J.H., Takagi, T. (eds.) ASIACRYPT 2016, Part I. LNCS, vol. 10031, pp. 844–876. Springer, Cham (2016). https://doi.org/10.1007/978-3-662-53887-6_31

16. Couteau, G., Rindal, P., Raghuraman, S.: Silver: silent VOLE and oblivious transfer from hardness of decoding structured LDPC codes. In: Malkin, T., Peikert, C. (eds.) CRYPTO 2021, Part III. LNCS, vol. 12827, pp. 502–534, Virtual Event. Springer, Cham (2021). https://doi.org/10.1007/978-3-030-84252-9_17

17. Cramer, R., Damgård, I., Schoenmakers, B.: Proofs of partial knowledge and simplified design of witness hiding protocols. In: Desmedt, Y. (ed.) CRYPTO 1994. LNCS, vol. 839, pp. 174–187. Springer, Cham (1994). https://doi.org/10.1007/3-540-48658-5_19

18. Diamond, B.E.: On the security of KOS. Cryptology ePrint Archive, Paper 2022/1371 (2022). https://eprint.iacr.org/2022/1371, https://eprint.iacr.org/2022/1371

19. Dodis, Y., Farshim, P., Mazaheri, S., Tessaro, S.: Towards defeating backdoored random oracles: indifferentiability with bounded adaptivity. In: Pass, R., Pietrzak, K. (eds.) TCC 2020, Part III. LNCS, vol. 12552, pp. 241–273. Springer, Cham (2020). https://doi.org/10.1007/978-3-030-64381-2_9

20. Dodis, Y., Ganesh, C., Golovnev, A., Juels, A., Ristenpart, T.: A formal treatment of backdoored pseudorandom generators. In: Oswald, E., Fischlin, M. (eds.) EUROCRYPT 2015, Part I. LNCS, vol. 9056, pp. 101–126. Springer, Cham (2015). https://doi.org/10.1007/978-3-662-46800-5_5

21. Dodis, Y., Mironov, I., Stephens-Davidowitz, N.: Message transmission with reverse firewalls–secure communication on corrupted machines. In: Robshaw, M., Katz, J. (eds.) CRYPTO 2016, Part I. LNCS, vol. 9814, pp. 341–372. Springer, Cham (2016). https://doi.org/10.1007/978-3-662-53018-4_13

22. Doerner, J., Kondi, Y., Lee, E., Shelat, A.: Secure two-party threshold ECDSA from ECDSA assumptions. In: 2018 IEEE Symposium on Security and Privacy, pp. 980–997. IEEE Computer Society Press, May 2018. https://doi.org/10.1109/SP.2018.00036

23. Fischlin, M., Janson, C., Mazaheri, S.: Backdoored hash functions: Immunizing HMAC and HKDF. In: Chong, S., Delaune, S. (eds.) CSF 2018 Computer Security Foundations Symposium, pp. 105–118. IEEE Computer Society Press (2018). https://doi.org/10.1109/CSF.2018.00015

24. Ganesh, C., Magri, B., Venturi, D.: Cryptographic reverse firewalls for interactive proof systems. In: Czumaj, A., Dawar, A., Merelli, E. (eds.) ICALP 2020. LIPIcs, vol. 168, pp. 55:1–55:16. Schloss Dagstuhl, July 2020. https://doi.org/10.4230/LIPIcs.ICALP.2020.55

25. Goldreich, O., Kahan, A.: How to construct constant-round zero-knowledge proof systems for NP. J. Cryptol. 9(3), 167–190 (1996)

26. Goldreich, O., Micali, S., Wigderson, A.: How to play any mental game or a completeness theorem for protocols with honest majority. In: Aho, A. (ed.) 19th ACM STOC, pp. 218–229. ACM Press, May 1987. https://doi.org/10.1145/28395.28420

27. Ishai, Y., Kilian, J., Nissim, K., Petrank, E.: Extending oblivious transfers efficiently. In: Boneh, D. (ed.) CRYPTO 2003. LNCS, vol. 2729, pp. 145–161. Springer, Cham (2003). https://doi.org/10.1007/978-3-540-45146-4_9

28. Jawurek, M., Kerschbaum, F., Orlandi, C.: Zero-knowledge using garbled circuits: how to prove non-algebraic statements efficiently. In: Sadeghi, A.R., Gligor, V.D., Yung, M. (eds.) ACM CCS 2013, pp. 955–966. ACM Press, November 2013. https://doi.org/10.1145/2508859.2516662

29. Keller, M., Orsini, E., Scholl, P.: Actively secure OT extension with optimal overhead. In: Gennaro, R., Robshaw, M.J.B. (eds.) CRYPTO 2015, Part I. LNCS, vol. 9215, pp. 724–741. Springer, Heidelberg (2015). https://doi.org/10.1007/978-3-662-47989-6_35

30. Masny, D., Rindal, P.: Endemic oblivious transfer. In: Cavallaro, L., Kinder, J., Wang, X., Katz, J. (eds.) ACM CCS 2019, pp. 309–326. ACM Press, November 2019. https://doi.org/10.1145/3319535.3354210

31. Maurer, U.: Unifying zero-knowledge proofs of knowledge. In: Preneel, B. (ed.) AFRICACRYPT 2009. LNCS, vol. 5580, pp. 272–286. Springer, Heidelberg (2009). https://doi.org/10.1007/978-3-642-02384-2_17

32. Mironov, I., Stephens-Davidowitz, N.: Cryptographic reverse firewalls. In: Oswald, E., Fischlin, M. (eds.) EUROCRYPT 2015, Part II. LNCS, vol. 9057, pp. 657–686. Springer, Cham (2015). https://doi.org/10.1007/978-3-662-46803-6_22

33. Naor, M., Pinkas, B.: Efficient oblivious transfer protocols. In: Kosaraju, S.R. (ed.) 12th SODA, pp. 448–457. ACM-SIAM, January 2001

34. Patra, A., Sarkar, P., Suresh, A.: Fast actively secure OT extension for short secrets. In: 24th Annual Network and Distributed System Security Symposium, NDSS 2017, San Diego, California, USA, 26 February–1 March 2017. The Internet Society (2017)

35. Peikert, C., Vaikuntanathan, V., Waters, B.: A framework for efficient and composable oblivious transfer. In: Wagner, D. (ed.) CRYPTO 2008. LNCS, vol. 5157, pp. 554–571. Springer, Cham (2008). https://doi.org/10.1007/978-3-540-85174-5_31

36. Schnorr, C.P.: Efficient identification and signatures for smart cards. In: Brassard, G. (ed.) CRYPTO 1989. LNCS, vol. 435, pp. 239–252. Springer, Cham (1990). https://doi.org/10.1007/0-387-34805-0_22

37. Wang, X., Ranellucci, S., Katz, J.: Authenticated garbling and efficient maliciously secure two-party computation. In: Thuraisingham, B.M., Evans, D., Malkin, T., Xu, D. (eds.) ACM CCS 2017, pp. 21–37. ACM Press, October/November 2017. https://doi.org/10.1145/3133956.3134053

38. Yang, K., Sarkar, P., Weng, C., Wang, X.: QuickSilver: efficient and affordable zero-knowledge proofs for circuits and polynomials over any field. In: Kim, Y., Kim, J., Vigna, G., Shi, E. (eds.) CCS 2021: 2021 ACM SIGSAC Conference on Computer and Communications Security, Virtual Event, Republic of Korea, 15–19 November 2021, pp. 2986–3001. ACM (2021)

39. Yang, K., Wang, X., Zhang, J.: More efficient MPC from improved triple generation and authenticated garbling. In: Ligatti, J., Ou, X., Katz, J., Vigna, G. (eds.) ACM CCS 2020, pp. 1627–1646. ACM Press, November 2020. https://doi.org/10.1145/3372297.3417285

40. Yang, K., Weng, C., Lan, X., Zhang, J., Wang, X.: Ferret: fast extension for correlated OT with small communication. In: Ligatti, J., Ou, X., Katz, J., Vigna, G. (eds.) ACM CCS 2020, pp. 1607–1626. ACM Press, November 2020. https://doi.org/10.1145/3372297.3417276

Oblivious Transfer with Constant Computational Overhead

Elette Boyle[1], Geoffroy Couteau[2], Niv Gilboa[3], Yuval Ishai[4], Lisa Kohl[5],
Nicolas Resch[6(✉)], and Peter Scholl[7]

[1] IDC Herzliya and NTT Research, Sunnyvale, USA
[2] IRIF, Paris, France
geoffroy.couteau@irif.fr
[3] Ben-Gurion University, Beersheba, Israel
[4] Technion, Haifa, Israel
[5] Cryptology Group, CWI Amsterdam, Amsterdam, The Netherlands
[6] University of Amsterdam, Amsterdam, The Netherlands
n.a.resch@uva.nl
[7] Aarhus University, Aarhus, Denmark

Abstract. The *computational overhead* of a cryptographic task is the asymptotic ratio between the computational cost of securely realizing the task and that of realizing the task with no security at all.

Ishai, Kushilevitz, Ostrovsky, and Sahai (STOC 2008) showed that secure two-party computation of Boolean circuits can be realized with *constant* computational overhead, independent of the desired level of security, assuming the existence of an oblivious transfer (OT) protocol and a local pseudorandom generator (PRG). However, this only applies to the case of semi-honest parties. A central open question in the area is the possibility of a similar result for *malicious* parties. This question is open even for the simpler task of securely realizing many instances of a constant-size function, such as OT of bits.

We settle the question in the affirmative for the case of OT, assuming: (1) a standard OT protocol, (2) a slightly stronger "correlation-robust" variant of a local PRG, and (3) a standard sparse variant of the Learning Parity with Noise (LPN) assumption. An optimized version of our construction requires fewer than 100 bit operations per party per bit-OT. For 128-bit security, this improves over the best previous protocols by 1–2 orders of magnitude.

We achieve this by constructing a constant-overhead *pseudorandom correlation generator* (PCG) for the bit-OT correlation. Such a PCG generates N pseudorandom instances of bit-OT by locally expanding short, correlated seeds. As a result, we get an end-to-end protocol for generating N pseudorandom instances of bit-OT with $o(N)$ communication, $O(N)$ computation, and security that scales sub-exponentially with N.

Finally, we present applications of our main result to realizing other secure computation tasks with constant computational overhead. These include protocols for general circuits with a relaxed notion of security against malicious parties, protocols for realizing N instances of natural constant-size functions, and reducing the main open question to a potentially simpler question about fault-tolerant computation.

© International Association for Cryptologic Research 2023
C. Hazay and M. Stam (Eds.): EUROCRYPT 2023, LNCS 14004, pp. 271–302, 2023.
https://doi.org/10.1007/978-3-031-30545-0_10

1   Introduction

A dream goal in cryptography is obtaining security "for free," without any slow-down. How close can we get to this goal in the context of secure computation?

A theoretical study of this question was initiated in the work of Ishai, Kushile-vitz, Ostrovsky, and Sahai [52] (IKOS). For secure two-party computation of Boolean circuits, they showed that it is possible to achieve *constant computa-tional overhead* under plausible cryptographic assumptions. Concretely, there is a multiplicative constant c, independent of the desired security level, such that every sufficiently big Boolean circuit of size N can be securely evaluated by two parties which are implemented by Boolean circuits of size cN.[1] This means that the *amortized* slowdown factor can be independent of the security level.[2]

The IKOS protocol combines a technique of Beaver [19] with a *local PRG* [10,46,62], namely a pseudorandom generator $G : \{0,1\}^\kappa \to \{0,1\}^{n(\kappa)}$ that has polynomial stretch ($n = \Omega(\kappa^d)$ for some $d > 1$) and such that every output bit of G depends on a constant number of input bits. While the existence of such local PRGs was considered quite speculative at the time, it is now widely accepted as a standard cryptographic assumption.

A major limitation of the IKOS protocol is that its security is restricted to the case of semi-honest parties. The possibility of a similar result for *malicious* parties was the main question left open by [52]. In spite of significant progress on this and related problems, including constant-overhead protocols for *arith-metic* circuits over large fields [8,24], a solution to the above main question is still elusive; see [36,55] for a survey of related work. The question is open even for simpler tasks, such as computing N instances of a nontrivial constant-size function. To make things worse, strong cryptographic primitives such as indis-tinguishability obfuscation do not seem helpful. In fact, even entirely heuristic solutions are not currently known. Our work is motivated by the goal of solving useful special cases of this central open question.

The Overhead of Oblivious Transfer. A common framework toward secure computation, including the protocol of IKOS, follows a two-phase approach: first run an input-independent preprocessing protocol for secure distributed genera-tion of useful correlated secret randomness, and then consume these correlations within an online protocol that performs a secure computation on the inputs [18]. An important example is the random *oblivious transfer* (OT) correlation,[3] in

---

[1] Here the default security requirement is that any $\mathsf{poly}(N)$-time adversary can only obtain a $\mathsf{negl}(N)$ advantage. Alternatively, using a separate security parameter λ, the cN bound holds when N is sufficiently (but polynomially) larger than λ.

[2] See Sect. 2.1 for more details on our specific cost model. Briefly, functions and proto-cols are implemented as bounded fan-in Boolean circuits, and the computational cost is the number of gates. For *concrete* computational costs, we allow any bit operation over *two-bit* inputs.

[3] In this work, OT refers by default to bit-OT, namely oblivious transfer of pairs of *bits*. However, as discussed below (cf. Sect. 5), our results apply to most other natural flavors of OT.

which Alice and Bob receive (s_0, s_1) and (b, s_b) respectively, where s_0, s_1, b are random bits. Given $2N$ independent instances of this OT correlation, Alice and Bob can evaluate any Boolean circuit with N gates (excluding "free" XOR and NOT gates) on their inputs, with perfect semi-honest security, by each sending 2 bits and performing a small constant number of bit operations per gate [47,48]. Indeed, IKOS protocol obtains constant-overhead general secure two-party computation precisely by achieving this goal for generation of random bit-OTs.

Generating random bit-OTs with *malicious* security, however, is much more challenging. In particular, the IKOS protocol is not secure in this setting[4] The best known solutions incur polylogarithmic computational overhead [36,41]. A natural approach for improvement would be to follow the "GMW-paradigm" [48], applying zero-knowledge proofs to enforce honest behavior in the IKOS protocol. However, the existence of such proofs with constant computational overhead for the satisfiability of Boolean circuits is also wide open: even there, the best known solutions have polylogarithmic overhead [41]. A number of works developed special-purpose cut-and-choose techniques for protecting efficient OT extension protocols against malicious parties with a very low overhead [15,56,65]. However, these techniques are inherently tied to string-OTs whose length is proportional to a security parameter, and seem to require (at least) a polylogarithmic computational overhead when adapted to the case of bit-OT. Part of the challenge of protecting "traditional" OT generation protocols against malicious adversaries is that the underlying semi-honest protocols require $\Omega(N)$ communication for generating N OT correlation instances, which must somehow be checked or verified.

Pseudorandom Correlation Generators. A recent alternative approach to OT generation is via the tool of *pseudorandom correlation generators* (PCG), put forth in [25,28,30]. The PCG approach enables fast generation of short correlated seeds, of length $o(N)$, that can be locally expanded without interaction to N instances of OT (or other) correlations. Unlike the traditional protocols from above, the structure of PCG-based protocols directly gives rise to secure computation of N pseudorandom OT correlations with *sublinear $o(N)$* communication cost. This is an appealing feature, not only as a concrete efficiency benefit (indeed, communication costs often form the practical efficiency bottleneck), but also as a promising starting point for obtaining *malicious* security with low overhead. Indeed, since the local expansion from short PCG seed to long OT output is deterministic, it suffices to ensure that the short seeds be generated correctly, reducing the malicious-security problem to an instance of sublinear size.

However, existing PCG constructions do not yet suffice for our goal. While the communication cost of PCG-based protocols is sublinear in N, the required *computation* costs are quite high. In existing constructions [26–28,40,69], even just the *amortized* cost of generating each final bit-OT correlation (corresponding to simply 2 output bits per party) requires generating security-parameter many pseudorandom bits, and then hashing them down.

---

[4] See the full version for an explicit attack.

1.1   Our Results

We present new constructions of pseudorandom correlation generators for N instances of the bit-OT correlation, which not only have sublinear communication in N but also achieve *constant* computational overhead. As a direct consequence, we obtain the first constant-overhead protocol for realizing N instances of bit-OT with security against *malicious* parties. As we further discuss below, this result extends beyond OT to other natural secure computation tasks.

Theorem 1 (Constant-overhead PCG for OT, informal). *Suppose that the following assumptions hold:*

- *There is a local PRG with an additional "correlation robustness" property;*
- *There are sparse generating matrices of codes for which Learning Parity with Noise is hard.*

Then, there is a pseudorandom correlation generator for the bit-OT correlation, with polynomial stretch, where the local expansion function PCG.Expand *has constant computational overhead.*

In fact, we present two variants of this main result: one based on a *primal-LPN* assumption, which has better amortized cost but a small (sub-quadratic) stretch, and one based on *dual-LPN* that can achieve an arbitrary polynomial stretch at the cost of a slightly increased (constant) overhead.

By applying a general-purpose secure computation protocol to distribute the PCG seed generation, we obtain the following corollary.

Corollary 2 (Constant-overhead malicious OT, informal). *Assuming the existence of a standard OT protocol along with the assumptions of Theorem 1, there exists a two-party protocol for realizing N instances of bit-OT with security against malicious parties and a constant computational overhead.*

About the Assumptions. Our protocols require three types of assumptions: (1) the (necessary) existence of standard OT; (2) a slight strengthening of local PRGs that we refer to as *correlation robustness*; and (3) a "sparse" form of the Learning Parity with Noise (LPN) assumption.

As discussed above, local PRGs (more concretely, PRGs with constant locality and polynomial stretch) were already used in the IKOS protocol [52]. A well-known candidate is Goldreich's PRG [46], where significant study has gone toward proving resilience against classes of attacks for particular choices of output predicates P_i [4,5,7,12,20,30,38,39,61,63]. Correlation robustness of a PRG $G : \{0,1\}^\kappa \to \{0,1\}^N$ requires that for any choice of offsets $\Delta_1, \ldots, \Delta_N \in \{0,1\}^\kappa$, the output $(P_1(x \oplus \Delta_1), \ldots, P_N(x \oplus \Delta_N)) \in \{0,1\}^N$ appears pseudorandom for random x. For a local PRG, this corresponds to fixed xor-shifts of the corresponding output local predicates. In the full version we investigate the potential correlation robustness of the Goldreich local PRG construction, demonstrating that "good" properties of PRG output predicates P_i are *preserved* under fixed xor-shift. In turn, we conclude that the same classes of attacks can be ruled out for correlation robustness of the PRG as well as for standard pseudorandomness.

"Sparse" LPN, first put forth by Alekhnovich [2], corresponds to a form of LPN whose code generator matrix (i.e., coefficients of noisy linear equations) has constant row sparsity. The assumption states that the mapping $(\vec{s}, \vec{e}) \mapsto \mathbf{G} \cdot \vec{s} + \vec{e}$ is a PRG, where $\vec{s}$ is a short uniform seed of length n, $\mathbf{G} \in \{0,1\}^{N \times n}$ is a suitably chosen sparse matrix and $\vec{e}$ is a noise vector of weight $t \ll N$. In such a scenario we can have polynomial stretch (i.e., both n, t are at most $N^{1-\epsilon}$ for some $\epsilon > 0$) but the stretch is fairly limited.

We also consider the dual variant of LPN directly, where the seed is viewed as a length M error vector $\vec{e}$ and the mapping sends $\vec{e} \mapsto \mathbf{H} \cdot \vec{e}$ for a suitably chosen $\mathbf{H} \in \{0,1\}^{N \times M}$ with $M > N$. By choosing $\mathbf{H}$ to have a *repeat-accumulate* structure, we get desirable efficiency properties (analogous to the efficiency the sparsity of $\mathbf{G}$ earns us in the primal case) while allowing for arbitrary polynomial stretch.

To evaluate the plausibility of our LPN-assumptions we follow the *linear tests*-framework, which was implicit in [29,40] and made explicit in [26]. Briefly, this means that we need to verify that the distance of a code related to the matrix is not too small.

Concrete Amortized Cost. We estimate that, when producing a sufficiently large number N of OTs, our construction based on primal-LPN can have a concrete, amortized cost of 243 bit operations per party, per OT, while achieving sublinear communication complexity. This figure is based on using a PRG with locality 9, which asymptotically is believed to be secure with stretch as large as $\kappa^{2.49}$, and a primal-LPN matrix with row sparsity of $d = 18$. For the dual LPN variant, we can rely on a PRG with locality 5, achieving amortized costs of 91 bit operations per party.

In comparison, with 128 bits of security against malicious parties, the amortized cost of all previous protocols is bigger by 1–2 orders of magnitude, even when using a best-possible implementation of the underlying primitives (e.g., using a local PRG for generating pseudorandom bits). This applies both to protocols with linear communication [15,50,56,65] and to PCG-based protocols with sublinear communication [26–28,40,69].

Counting bit operations does not reflect true performance on standard architectures, and in particular does not take into account additional costs such as memory access. However, the extra costs can be amortized by performing many identical computations in parallel. We leave a more thorough investigation of concrete efficiency and further optimizations to future work.

Beyond Oblivious Transfer. While our main result only refers to the specific task of securely realizing N instances of OT, the ubiquity of OT in cryptography makes it relevant to many applications. Even in the strict context of secure computation with constant computational overhead, our results have broader implications to other useful secure computation tasks. We summarize them below.

- *General protocols with relaxed security.* Given our constant-overhead realization of (malicious-secure) OT, one can securely compute *every* Boolean circuit with constant computational overhead by settling for *security up to additive attacks* [43]. In this relaxed security model, the malicious party can (blindly) choose a subset of the circuit wires to toggle, independently of the honest party's input. While devastating in some applications, such as zero-knowledge proofs, additive attacks can be tolerable in others. This may be the case, for example, when computing functions with long inputs and short outputs, and when the main concern is about the *amount of information* that a malicious party can learn.
- *Leveraging perfect security.* Consider the case of realizing N instances of a "constant-size" functionality f. If f has *perfect* security against *malicious* parties in the *OT-hybrid* model, namely using ideal calls to a bit-OT oracle, then our main result implies a constant-overhead protocol in the plain model. While the question of characterizing such f is still open, positive examples include other flavors of OT [34,54], simple noisy channels such as a BSC channel and, more surprisingly, a broad class of functionalities that includes constant-size instances of the millionaire's problem and many others [3].
- *Reducing security to fault-tolerance.* Finally, given our constant-overhead realization of the OT-hybrid model, settling the general open question reduces to settling it in this model. This, in turn, reduces to a constant-overhead construction of Boolean *AMD circuits* — randomized circuits that are resilient to additive attacks [43]. The best known construction of such circuits has polylogarithmic overhead [44].

1.2 Technical Overview

At a high-level, our approach follows the construction of PCGs for random bit-OT via subfield vector oblivious linear evaluation (sVOLE) [25,28]. We first recall their approach, and then explain how to achieve constant overhead.

PCGs for sVOLE from LPN [25,28]. Recall that an sVOLE instance is of the form $(\vec{b}, \vec{z}_0), (x, \vec{z}_1)$, where $x \in \{0,1\}^\kappa, \vec{b} \in \{0,1\}^N, \vec{z}_0 \in (\{0,1\}^\kappa)^N, \vec{z}_1 \in (\{0,1\}^\kappa)^N$ such that $x \cdot \vec{b} = \vec{z}_0 \oplus \vec{z}_1$, where $x \cdot \vec{b} := (b_1 \cdot x, \ldots, b_N \cdot x) \in (\{0,1\}^\kappa)^N$. (Note that typically x is considered as element $x \in \mathbb{F}_{2^\kappa}$, which is where the name subfield VOLE comes from. Here, however, it will be more convenient to think of x as a bitstring $x \in \{0,1\}^\kappa$, since this will later be input to a local PRG.)

The first ingredient of the PCG construction is a pseudorandom generator from the learning parity with noise assumption. Let $n, N \in \mathbb{N}$ with $n < N$. The *primal learning parity with noise assumption* states that, relative to some code generator $\mathbf{C}$ returning matrices in $\{0,1\}^{N \times n}$ and noise distribution $\mathcal{D}$ over $\{0,1\}^N$, $(\mathbf{G}, \mathbf{G} \cdot \vec{s} \oplus \vec{e}) \overset{c}{\approx} (\mathbf{G}, \vec{b})$, where $\mathbf{G} \leftarrow \mathbf{C}, \vec{s} \overset{\$}{\leftarrow} \{0,1\}^n, \vec{e} \leftarrow \mathcal{D}$ and $\vec{b} \overset{\$}{\leftarrow} \{0,1\}^N$. Here, we consider noise distributions $\mathcal{D}$ that return t-sparse vectors, i.e., vectors containing at most t non-zero entries.

The second ingredient is a (known-index) function secret sharing (FSS) scheme to generate a succinct secret sharing of $x \cdot \vec{e}$, where $x \in \{0,1\}^\kappa$ as above, and $\vec{e}$ is a t-sparse noise vector. Roughly, a function secret sharing scheme consists of a tuple of algorithms (Setup, FullEval), such that Setup($1^\lambda, \hat{v}$) (where $\hat{v}$ is the succinct representation of the vector $\vec{v} = x \cdot \vec{e}$) returns a tuple of succinct (i.e., polynonomial in the size of $\hat{v}$) keys (K_0, K_1) and FullEval(σ, K_σ) returns a vector $\vec{y}_\sigma \in (\{0,1\}^\kappa)^N$ such that $\vec{y}_0 \oplus \vec{y}_1 = \vec{v}$. The security requirement states, essentially, that even given $\vec{y}_b$ for either $b = 0$ or $b = 1$, one cannot derive any information about $\vec{v}$.

Function secret sharing schemes for so-called t-sparse point functions are known to exist from one-way functions [31,45]. Further, as observed in [27,66] for the purpose of constructing PCGs for sVOLE a so-called *known-index* FSS scheme is sufficient, where one party learns the positions of the non-zero entries. Known-index FSS for point functions are implied by simpler constructions of puncturable pseudorandom functions [23,33,58].

Now, given these two ingredients, the PCG construction for sVOLE can be obtained as follows:

- Sample $x \xleftarrow{\$} \{0,1\}^\kappa$ as input for P_1.
- Sample $\vec{s} \xleftarrow{\$} \{0,1\}^n$, $\vec{e} \xleftarrow{\$} \mathcal{D}$ and give $\vec{s}$, as well as a succinct description of $\vec{e}$ to P_0, who can then compute $\vec{b} := \mathbf{G} \cdot \vec{s} \oplus \vec{e}$.
- Generate a succinct secret sharing of $x \cdot \vec{b}$ as follows:
  1. Generate additive secret shares $\vec{r}_0, \vec{r}_1$ such that $\vec{r}_0 \oplus \vec{r}_1 = x \cdot \vec{s} \in (\{0,1\}^\kappa)^n$.
  2. Generate function secret shares $(K_0, K_1) \leftarrow$ Setup($1^\lambda, \hat{v}$), where $\vec{v} := x \cdot \vec{e}$.

By the correctness of the FSS and linearity of the code, it now holds

$$x \cdot \vec{b} = x \cdot (\mathbf{G} \cdot \vec{s} \oplus \vec{e}) = \mathbf{G} \cdot (\vec{r}_0 \oplus \vec{r}_1) \oplus \text{Eval}(0, K_0) \oplus \text{Eval}(1, K_1) = \vec{z}_0 \oplus \vec{z}_1,$$

where $\vec{z}_\sigma := \mathbf{G} \cdot \vec{r}_\sigma + \text{FullEval}(\sigma, K_\sigma)$ for $\sigma \in \{0,1\}$.

From sVOLE to bit-OT. The transformation from sVOLE to bit-OT follows the strategy of [50]. Namely, an instance of N-dimensional sVOLE can be considered as N instances of correlated string-OT with offset x as follows. The vector $\vec{b}$ corresponds to the choice vector of the "receiver" P_0. Further, for each entry b_i, the receiver obtains $z_{0,i} = z_{1,i} \oplus b_i \cdot x$, i.e., either the bit-string $z_{1,i} \in \{0,1\}^\kappa$ or the bit-string $z_{1,i} \oplus x \in \{0,1\}^\kappa$ held by the "sender" P_1. These correlations can be removed by applying a correlation-robust hash function $H \colon \{0,1\}^\kappa \to \{0,1\}$. Roughly, a correlation-robust hash function has the property that applied to values related by an (adversarially chosen) Δ, the outputs are indistinguishable from the output on uncorrelated values. With this, the j-th bit OT can be obtained as

$$\big(b_j, H(z_{0,j})\big), \big(H(z_{0,j}), H(z_{0,j} \oplus x)\big).$$

Choosing κ, n, t such that $\kappa \cdot n + t \cdot \log N \in N^{1-\epsilon}$ for some $\epsilon > 0$, the above PCG construction allows to obtain N bit-OTs with communication $o(N)$. On the negative side, it does not achieve constant computational-overhead. The most crucial reason for this is that the sVOLE instance itself introduces an overly large overhead: for each bit-OT, the above transformation requires one to hash κ-bits, introducing a factor κ-overhead (even if all other building blocks are assumed to be constant time). Note that in the above construction it is essential that κ is large, since otherwise a corrupt receiver could guess x and thereby violate the security of the OT.

Towards PCGs for bit-OT with Constant Overhead. The central idea of this work is to replace the correlation-robust hash function H by a *local pseudorandom generator* G. More precisely, recall that a local PRG is of the form

$$G(x) = P_1(\pi_1(x)) \| \ldots \| P_N(\pi_N(x)),$$

where each π_i projects x to an ℓ-sized subset of its coordinates, and $P_i \colon \{0,1\}^\ell \to \{0,1\}$ is a predicate.

Given a local PRG with constant locality ℓ, we can obtain N bit-OTs from an sVOLE instance $x \cdot \vec{b} = \vec{z}_0 \oplus \vec{z}_1$ as

$$\left(b_j, P_j(\pi_j(z_{0,j}))\right), \left(P_j(\pi_j(z_{1,j})), P_j(\pi_j(z_{1,j} \oplus x))\right).$$

In other words, in the j-th bit-OT instance, we replace H by $P_j \circ \pi_j$. Now, it can be shown that if the PRG G additionally satisfies a form of correlation robustness[5], then replacing the correlation-robust hash function by a local PRG preserves correctness and security of the PCG for bit-OT.

This observation does not yet suffice to achieve constant overhead, since the starting point is still an instance of sVOLE with vectors in $(\{0,1\}^\kappa)^N$. Observe though that the parties actually do not need to generate $\vec{z}_0, \vec{z}_1 \in (\{0,1\}^\kappa)^N$, such that $\vec{z}_0 \oplus \vec{z}_1 = x \cdot \vec{b}$. Instead, it suffices to generate $\vec{v}_0, \vec{v}_1 \in (\{0,1\}^\ell)^N$, such that

$$\pi_j(x) \cdot b_j = v_{0,j} \oplus v_{1,j}$$

for all $j \in [N]$, where $\ell \in \mathbb{N}$ is constant. The above generation of bit-OTs can then be simplified as

$$\left(b_j, P_j(v_{0,j})\right), \left(P_j(v_{j,1}), P_j(v_{j,1} \oplus \pi_j(x))\right),$$

where equality holds since the projection functions are linear. We will refer to this correlation as *projected-payload sVOLE* in the following. It remains to discuss how to generate a projected payload sVOLE PCG with constant overhead.

Projected Payload sVOLE via Primal LPN. Recall that we need to generate compressed secret sharings of $x \cdot \vec{b} = \mathbf{G} \cdot (x \cdot \vec{s}) + x \cdot \vec{e}$. Towards constant overhead, we first replace $\mathbf{G}$ by a sparse matrix, for which each row only contains a constant number d of non-zero entries. By an Alekhnovich variant of the LPN assumption [2], the resulting $\vec{b}$ is still computationally hard to distinguish from random (given a suitable choice of parameters). This allows P_0 to compute $\vec{b} = \mathbf{G} \cdot \vec{s} + \vec{e}$ with constant overhead $O(d \cdot N + t \cdot \log N)$.

---

[5] Namely, we require $\{P_j(\Delta_j \oplus \pi_j(x))\}_{j \in N}$ is indistinguishable from random, where $\Delta_1, \ldots, \Delta_N$ are pseudorandom with seed known to the adversary.

Again, we generate secret shares $\vec{r}_0, \vec{r}_1$ such that $\vec{r}_0 \oplus \vec{r}_1 = x \cdot s \in (\{0,1\}^\kappa)^n$. If $\kappa \cdot n < N$, these shares have size $< N$ as required. For expansion, note that for each $j \in [N]$ it is sufficient to compute

$$\pi_j(x) \cdot \mathbf{G}_j \cdot \vec{s} = \mathbf{G}_j \cdot (\pi_j(x) \cdot \vec{s}) = \mathbf{G} \cdot (\Pi_j(\vec{r}_0) \oplus \Pi_j(\vec{r}_1)),$$

where $\mathbf{G}_j$ is the j-th row of $\mathbf{G}$, and $\Pi_j \colon (\{0,1\}^\kappa)^N \to (\{0,1\}^\ell)^N$ is obtained by applying π_j componentwise. Overall, expansion requires $d \cdot N$ operations.

Finally, recall that by above considerations it is left to generate secret shares $\vec{v}_0, \vec{v}_1 \in (\{0,1\}^\ell)^N$ such that $v_{0,j} \oplus v_{1,j} = \pi_j(x) \cdot e_j$.

We can do this with constant overhead by relying on LPN with regular noise, i.e., where $\vec{e}$ is split into N/t intervals, each containing exactly one non-zero noise coordinate. For the corresponding class $\{\pi_j(x) \cdot e_j\}_{j \in [N]}$, one can achieve a known-index FSS with constant overhead by using the puncturable PRF construction of [23,33,58] together with an observation in [25], which allows to remove a factor-λ overhead. This only requires a length-doubling PRG, which can be instantiated with constant overhead using the same PRG with constant locality as before.

Projected-Payload sVOLE via Dual LPN. The above construction suffices for constant-overhead OT, although the PCG is limited to subquadratic stretch. We can obtain arbitrary polynomial stretch by generating $\vec{b}$ via *dual LPN*, i.e., as $\vec{b} = \mathbf{H} \cdot \vec{e}$, where $\mathbf{H} \in \{0,1\}^{N \times M}$, $\vec{e} \in \{0,1\}^M$ (where $M = d \cdot N$). To achieve constant locality, we choose $\mathbf{H}$ such that $\mathbf{H} = \mathbf{B} \cdot \mathbf{A}$, where $\mathbf{A}$ is an accumulator matrix (i.e., an all-one lower-triangular matrix) and $\mathbf{B}$ has only a constant number d of non-zero entries in each column. The security is based on a "repeat-accumulate" variant of LPN, which is analogous to the expand-accumulate LPN assumption that appeared recently [26].

In this case, for $\vec{b} = \mathbf{H} \cdot \vec{e}$, the goal is now to generate compressed secret shares of $(b_1 \cdot \pi_1(x), b_2 \cdot \pi_2(x), \ldots, b_N \cdot \pi_N(x))$. Fortunately for us, we know how to share $\vec{a} := \mathbf{A} \cdot \vec{e}$ in a compressed manner: $\vec{a}$ is a multi-interval noise vector, and so we can share it using function secret-sharing for multi-interval functions. More precisely, by a t-multi-interval noise vector we mean a vector in which there are at most t coordinates $i \geq 2$ for which the i-th coordinate differs from the $(i-1)$-st. However, as $\vec{b} = \mathbf{B} \cdot \vec{a}$, we need to work a bit harder.

Fortunately, recall that each row of $\mathbf{B}$ only has d nonzero entries, and d is a *constant*. Let $S_j \subseteq [M]$ be such that $b_j = \bigoplus_{i \in S_j} a_i$. To get shares of $b_j \pi_j(x)$, it suffices to secret share $a_i \cdot \pi_j(x)$ for exactly these d choices of $i \in S_j$. We thereby get secret shares $\vec{v}^0, \vec{v}^1 \in (\{0,1\}^\ell)^M$. In particular, to obtain an *additive* secret-sharing of $b_j \cdot \pi_j(x)$ for $j \in [N]$, each party $\sigma \in \{0,1\}$ just needs to locally compute $\bigoplus_{i \in S_j} v_i^\sigma$. That is, $\bigoplus_{i \in S_j} v_i^0 \oplus \bigoplus_{i \in S_j} v_i^1 = b_j \cdot \pi_j(x)$.

To distribute the shares $\vec{v}_0, \vec{v}_1$, we introduce an FSS variant called *projected-payload distributed comparison function*, which optimizes for the fact that, at each index j, only the projection $\pi_j(x)$ is multiplied with the bits a_i of the interval vector for $i \in S_j$. This is contrasted with a standard distributed comparison function, where the whole of the κ-bit x is multiplied for every a_i.

We show how to build projected-payload DCF with constant overhead, by carefully combining a standard (known-index) DCF with a DPF. In a nutshell, we use a DPF and DCF which both correspond to a truncated binary tree, with N/κ leaves instead of N. The DCF is set to give out shares of the full payload x for indices i such that $\lceil i/\kappa \rceil < \alpha'$, where $\alpha' = \lceil \alpha/\kappa \rceil$, and shares of 0 otherwise. Note that this already allows the parties to obtain shares of the *projected* evaluations $a_i \cdot \pi_i(x)$, for all $i \in [N]$ except those whose prefix is α'. To correct for the indices with prefix α', we give out an $\ell\kappa$-bit correction word, which is masked using the missing expanded output of the DPF, and allows the party who knows α to correct its outputs to the right value.

2   Preliminaries

2.1   Computational Model and Cost Measure

Computational Cost. Similarly to prior works [9,13,22,36,37,42,52,55,64], we assume that functions and protocols are implemented using Boolean circuits with bounded fan-in gates. Computational cost is then measured by the circuit size, namely the number of gates. Note that this cost measure is robust to the exact fan-in or the type of gates used, which can only change the cost by a constant multiplicative factor. This should be contrasted with counting atomic operations in more liberal computational models, such as arithmetic circuits or RAM programs, which are more sensitive to model variations such as the underlying ring or the allowable word size. See [67] for discussion.

Concrete Cost. When we refer to *concrete* computational costs, we count the number of *bit operations* by considering the size of a circuit over the full binary basis, namely where a gate can compute any mapping from two bits to one bit. For instance, the concrete computational cost of the predicate $P_5 =: (x_1 \wedge x_2) \oplus x_3 \oplus x_4 \oplus x_5$ is 4. This is a standard concrete cost measure in complexity theory.

Setup. When considering the computational cost of cryptographic tasks, we allow a one-time PPT setup that given a security parameter 1^λ and a task description, outputs a circuit implementation for the task. For instance, for the task of generating N instances of random bit-OT, the task description is 1^N and the implementation includes circuits computing the next-message functions of the protocol. Since the setup cost is amortized away, we do not consider its complexity except for requiring it to run in polynomial time. The setup will typically need to generate constant-degree bipartite expander graphs in which one side is polynomially bigger than the other. A recent PPT construction of such graphs with negligible failure probability was given in [11]. Alternatively, the failure probability can be eliminated assuming the conjectured existence of explicit unbalanced expanders or similar combinatorial objects; see, e.g., [8,52] for discussion. Under this assumption, the setup required by our protocols can be implemented in deterministic polynomial time.

Computational Overhead. We will be interested in minimizing the amortized computational cost of a task of size N (e.g., N instances of random bit-OT), when N tends to infinity. Here we allow $N = N(\lambda)$ to be an arbitrarily big polynomial in the security parameter, effectively ignoring lower order additive terms that may depend polynomially on λ and sublinearly on N.[6] We say that the implementation has *computational overhead (at most)* $c = c(\lambda)$ if there is a polynomial $N = N(\lambda)$ such that ratio between the implementation cost and $N(\lambda)$ is at most $c(\lambda)$ for all sufficiently large λ. We say that the implementation has *constant computational overhead* if $c(\lambda) = O(1)$.

As discussed in [52], a cleaner alternative is to use N both as a size parameter and a security parameter, similarly to textbook definitions of basic cryptographic primitives. (Here security means that every poly(N)-size adversary only has a negl(N) advantage.) The separation between the two parameters serves to simplify the presentation and give a better sense of concrete efficiency.

Cost of Pseudorandomness. Sometimes, it will be convenient to refer to the amortized cost of outputting n pseudorandom bits from a PRG seed. We write this as $C_{\mathsf{prg}}(n)$.

Note that using local PRGs, we have $C_{\mathsf{prg}}(n) = O(n)$, where the best concrete candidate (using the P_5 predicate described above) has cost $C_{\mathsf{prg}}(n) = 4n$. To analyze efficiency on modern CPUs, it can be useful to measure this cost separately due to the prevalence of built-in hardware support for AES. However, note that for large values of n, a "bitsliced" implementation of a local PRG (evaluating many PRG copies in parallel using *bitwise* AND and XOR operations) may have better performance, at the expense of using a much bigger seed.

2.2 Correlation Robust Local PRGs

In this section we recall local pseudorandom generators and introduce the notion of *correlation-robustness* in the context of local PRGs.

Definition 3 (Pseudorandom Generator). *Let* $\kappa = \kappa(\lambda), N = N(\lambda) \in \mathbb{N}$. *We say a family of functions* $G = \{G_\lambda \colon \{0,1\}^{\kappa(\lambda)} \to \{0,1\}^{N(\lambda)}\}_{\lambda \in \mathbb{N}}$ *is a pseudorandom generator (PRG), if for all polynomial-time non-uniform adversaries* $\mathcal{A}$, *there exists a negligible function* $\mathsf{negl} \colon \mathbb{N} \to R_{\geq 0}$ *such that for all* $\lambda \in \mathbb{N}$:

$$\left| \Pr[\mathcal{A}(1^\lambda, G_\lambda(x)) = 1 \mid x \leftarrow \{0,1\}^\kappa] - \Pr[\mathcal{A}(1^\lambda, u) = 1 \mid u \leftarrow \{0,1\}^N] \right| \leq \mathsf{negl}(\lambda).$$

---

[6] This should be contrasted with a more fine-grained measure of overhead considered in [17,22,36], which requires *exponential* security in λ (rather than superpolynomial), measures the overhead with respect to $N+\lambda$, and requires the overhead to apply to all choices of N and λ (e.g., even when $N = \lambda$).

Definition 4 (Subset projection). *Let $\kappa, \ell \in \mathbb{N}$ with $\kappa > \ell$. We say a mapping $\pi \colon \{0,1\}^\kappa \to \{0,1\}^\ell$ is a subset projection (or simply projection), if there exists a size-ℓ set $S \subset \{1, \ldots, \kappa\}$ such that $\pi(x) = (x_i)_{i \in S}$ for all $x \in \{0,1\}^\kappa$.*

Definition 5 (Local family of functions). *Let $\kappa = \kappa(\lambda), N = N(\lambda), \ell = \ell(\lambda) \in \mathbb{N}$ with $\ell \ll \kappa$ (e.g., $\ell = O(\log \kappa)$ or $\ell = O(1)$). We say a family of functions $G = \{G_\lambda \colon \{0,1\}^{\kappa(\lambda)} \to \{0,1\}^{N(\lambda)}\}_{\lambda \in \mathbb{N}}$ is ℓ-local if there exists families of subset projections $\pi_1, \ldots, \pi_{N(\lambda)} \colon \{0,1\}^\kappa \to \{0,1\}^{\ell(\lambda)}$ and families of predicates $P_1, \ldots, P_{N(\lambda)} \colon \{0,1\}^{\ell(\lambda)} \to \{0,1\}$, such that for every $\lambda \in \mathbb{N}$,*

$$G(x) = P_1(\pi_1(x)) \| \ldots \| P_{N(\lambda)}(\pi_{N(\lambda)}(x))$$

for all $x \in \{0,1\}^{\kappa(\lambda)}$. We say G has constant locality if $\ell \in O(1)$.

Definition 6 (Δ-shift). *Let $\kappa, N, \ell \in \mathbb{N}$ with $\ell < \kappa$ and let $G \colon \{0,1\}^\kappa \to \{0,1\}^N$ be a ℓ-local function with subset projections $\pi_1, \ldots, \pi_N \colon \{0,1\}^\kappa \to \{0,1\}^\ell$ and predicates $P_1, \ldots, P_N \colon \{0,1\}^\ell \to \{0,1\}$. For $\Delta = (\Delta_1, \ldots, \Delta_N) \in \{0,1\}^N$, we define the Δ-shift of G as*

$$G^\Delta(x) = P_1(\pi_1(x) \oplus \Delta_1) \| \ldots \| P_N(\pi_N(x) \oplus \Delta_N)$$

for all $x \in \{0,1\}^\kappa$.

Definition 7 (Correlation-robust local PRG). *Let $\kappa = \kappa(\lambda), N = N(\lambda), \ell = \ell(\lambda) \in \mathbb{N}$. Let $G = \{G_\lambda \colon \{0,1\}^{\kappa(\lambda)} \to \{0,1\}^{N(\lambda)}\}_{\lambda \in \mathbb{N}}$ be a family of local functions with ℓ-locality.*

We say that G is a correlation-robust ℓ-local PRG, if for all polynomial-time non-uniform adversaries $\mathcal{A}$, there exists a negligible function $\mathsf{negl} \colon \mathbb{N} \to \mathbb{R}_{\geq 0}$ such that for all $\lambda \in \mathbb{N}$

$$\left| \Pr\left[\mathcal{A}_2(\mathsf{st}, y) = 1 \,\middle|\, \begin{matrix} (\Delta, \mathsf{st}) \leftarrow \mathcal{A}_1(1^\lambda) \\ x \xleftarrow{\$} \{0,1\}^{\kappa(\lambda)} \\ y = G_\lambda^\Delta(x) \end{matrix} \right] - \Pr\left[\mathcal{A}_2(\mathsf{st}, y) = 1 \,\middle|\, \begin{matrix} (\Delta, \mathsf{st}) \leftarrow \mathcal{A}_1(1^\lambda) \\ y \xleftarrow{\$} \{0,1\}^{N(\lambda)} \end{matrix} \right] \right|$$

$$\leq \mathsf{negl}(\lambda),$$

where $\Delta \in \{0,1\}^{N(\lambda)}$ and G_λ^Δ is the Δ-shift of G^λ, as defined in Def. 6.

Note that this definition implies the standard definition of pseudorandomness since the adversary can choose $\Delta = 0$. Further, note that for our constructions it is actually sufficient to rely on a *weaker* distributional version of correlation-robustness, where the adversary does not have control over Δ. For simplicity we will rely on the stronger version in the body of the paper. For a formal definition of distributional correlation-robustness, we refer to the full version.

2.3   Pseudorandom Correlation Generators

We recall the notion of pseudorandom correlation generator (PCG) from [28]. At a high level, a PCG for some target ideal correlation takes as input a pair of short, correlated seeds and outputs long correlated pseudorandom strings, where the expansion procedure is deterministic and can be applied locally.

Definition 8 (Correlation Generator). *A PPT algorithm $\mathcal{C}$ is called a correlation generator, if $\mathcal{C}$ on input 1^λ outputs a pair of strings in $\{0,1\}^{\ell_0 \cdot N} \times \{0,1\}^{\ell_1 \cdot N}$ for $\ell_0, \ell_1, N \in \mathsf{poly}(\lambda)$.*

The correlation we consider in this paper is the *bit-OT correlation*, where $\ell_0 = \ell_1 = 2$, and $\mathcal{C}$ outputs N uniformly random tuples of the form $((b, s_b), (s_0, s_1))$ (where $b, s_0, s_1 \in \{0,1\}$).

The security definition of PCGs requires the target correlation to satisfy a technical requirement, which roughly says that it is possible to efficiently sample from the conditional distribution of R_0 given $R_1 = r_1$ and vice versa. It is easy to see that this is true for the bit-OT correlation.

Definition 9 (Reverse-sampleable Correlation Generator). *Let $\mathcal{C}$ be a correlation generator. We say $\mathcal{C}$ is* reverse sampleable *if there exists a PPT algorithm RSample such that for $\sigma \in \{0,1\}$ the correlation obtained via:*

$$\{(R_0', R_1') \,|\, (R_0, R_1) \xleftarrow{\$} \mathcal{C}(1^\lambda), R_\sigma' := R_\sigma, R_{1-\sigma}' \xleftarrow{\$} \mathsf{RSample}(\sigma, R_\sigma)\}$$

is computationally indistinguishable from $\mathcal{C}(1^\lambda)$.

The following definition of pseudorandom correlation generators is taken almost verbatim from [28]; it generalizes an earlier definition of pseudorandom VOLE generator in [25].

Definition 10 (Pseudorandom Correlation Generator (PCG) [28]). *Let $\mathcal{C}$ be a reverse-sampleable correlation generator. A PCG for $\mathcal{C}$ is a pair of algorithms* (PCG.Gen, PCG.Expand) *with the following syntax:*

- PCG.Gen(1^λ) *is a PPT algorithm that given a security parameter λ, outputs a pair of seeds* $(\mathsf{k}_0, \mathsf{k}_1)$;
- PCG.Expand$(\sigma, \mathsf{k}_\sigma)$ *is a polynomial-time algorithm that given party index $\sigma \in \{0,1\}$ and a seed k_σ, outputs a bit string $R_\sigma \in \{0,1\}^{\ell_\sigma}$.*

The algorithms (PCG.Gen, PCG.Expand) *should satisfy the following:*

- **Correctness.** *The correlation obtained via:*

$$\{(R_0, R_1) \,|\, (\mathsf{k}_0, \mathsf{k}_1) \xleftarrow{\$} \mathsf{PCG.Gen}(1^\lambda), (R_\sigma \leftarrow \mathsf{PCG.Expand}(\sigma, \mathsf{k}_\sigma))_{\sigma=0,1}\}$$

  is computationally indistinguishable from $\mathcal{C}(1^\lambda)$.
- **Security.** *For any $\sigma \in \{0,1\}$, the following two distributions are computationally indistinguishable:*

$$\{(\mathsf{k}_{1-\sigma}, R_\sigma) \,|\, (\mathsf{k}_0, \mathsf{k}_1) \xleftarrow{\$} \mathsf{PCG.Gen}(1^\lambda), R_\sigma \leftarrow \mathsf{PCG.Expand}(\sigma, \mathsf{k}_\sigma)\} \text{ and}$$
$$\{(\mathsf{k}_{1-\sigma}, R_\sigma) \,|\, (\mathsf{k}_0, \mathsf{k}_1) \xleftarrow{\$} \mathsf{PCG.Gen}(1^\lambda), R_{1-\sigma} \leftarrow \mathsf{PCG.Expand}(\sigma, \mathsf{k}_{1-\sigma}),$$
$$R_\sigma \xleftarrow{\$} \mathsf{RSample}(\sigma, R_{1-\sigma})\}$$

  where RSample is the reverse sampling algorithm for correlation $\mathcal{C}$.

2.4   Learning Parity with Noise

We define the LPN assumption over a ring $\mathcal{R}$ with number of samples N w.r.t. a code generation algorithm $\mathbf{C}$ and a noise distribution $\mathcal{D}$. In the following we state a primal and a dual version of the LPN assumption. Note that we consider LPN and dual-LPN in the bounded sample regime, which is commonly referred to as the *syndrome decoding assumption* in the code-based cryptography literature.

Definition 11 (Primal LPN). *Let $\mathcal{D}(\mathcal{R}) = \{\mathcal{D}_{n,N}(\mathcal{R})\}_{n,N\in\mathbb{N}}$ denote a family of distributions over a ring $\mathcal{R}$, such that for any $n, N \in \mathbb{N}$, $\mathsf{Im}(\mathcal{D}_{n,N}(\mathcal{R})) \subseteq \mathcal{R}^N$. Let $\mathbf{C}$ be a probabilistic code generation algorithm such that $\mathbf{C}(N, n, \mathcal{R})$ outputs a matrix $\mathbf{G} \in \mathcal{R}^{N\times n}$. For dimension $n = n(\lambda)$, number of samples (or block length) $N = N(\lambda)$, and ring $\mathcal{R} = \mathcal{R}(\lambda)$, the (primal) $(\mathcal{D}, \mathbf{C}, \mathcal{R})$-LPN$(n, N)$ assumption states that*

$$\{(\mathbf{G}, \vec{b}) \mid \mathbf{G} \xleftarrow{\$} \mathbf{C}(N, n, \mathcal{R}), \vec{e} \xleftarrow{\$} \mathcal{D}_{n,N}(\mathcal{R}), \vec{s} \xleftarrow{\$} \mathcal{R}^n, \vec{b} \leftarrow \mathbf{G} \cdot \vec{s} + \vec{e}\}$$

$$\stackrel{c}{\approx} \{(\mathbf{G}, \vec{b}) \mid \mathbf{G} \xleftarrow{\$} \mathbf{C}(N, n, \mathcal{R}), \vec{b} \xleftarrow{\$} \mathcal{R}^N\}$$

Definition 12 (Dual LPN). *Let $\mathcal{D}(\mathcal{R}) = \{\mathcal{D}_{N,M}(\mathcal{R})\}_{n,N\in\mathbb{N}}$ denote a family of efficiently sampleable distributions over a ring $\mathcal{R}$, such that for any $N, M \in \mathbb{N}$, $\mathsf{Im}(\mathcal{D}_{N,M}(\mathcal{R})) \subseteq \mathcal{R}^M$. Let $\mathbf{C}$ be a probabilistic code generation algorithm such that $\mathbf{C}(N, M, \mathcal{R})$ outputs a matrix $\mathbf{H} \in \mathcal{R}^{N\times M}$. For dimension $M = M(\lambda)$, number of samples $N = N(\lambda)$, and ring $\mathcal{R} = \mathcal{R}(\lambda)$, the (dual) $(\mathcal{D}, \mathbf{C}, \mathcal{R})$-LPN$(N, M)$ assumption states that*

$$\{(\mathbf{H}, \vec{b}) \mid \mathbf{H} \xleftarrow{\$} \mathbf{C}(N, M, \mathcal{R}), \vec{e} \xleftarrow{\$} \mathcal{D}_{N,M}(\mathcal{R}), \vec{b} \leftarrow \mathbf{H} \cdot \vec{e}\}$$

$$\stackrel{c}{\approx} \{(\mathbf{H}, \vec{b}) \mid \mathbf{H} \xleftarrow{\$} \mathbf{C}(N, M, \mathcal{R}), \vec{b} \xleftarrow{\$} \mathcal{R}^N\}.$$

If $\mathbf{C}(N, n, \mathcal{R})$ always outputs the same matrix $\mathbf{G} \in \mathcal{R}^{N\times n}$ (in the primal case) or $\mathbf{H} \in \mathcal{R}^{N\times M}$ (in the dual case), we simplify the notation to $(\mathcal{D}, \mathbf{G}, \mathcal{R})$-LPN$(n, N)$ (in the primal case) or $(\mathcal{D}, \mathbf{H}, \mathcal{R})$-LPN$(N, M)$ (in the dual case).

Remark 13 (LPN with regular noise). In this work, for the noise distribution we will use $\mathsf{Reg}_t^N(\{0,1\})$ which outputs a concatenation of t random unit vectors from $\{0,1\}^{N/t}$. This variant of choosing regular noise was introduced in [16], has been further analysed in [25,49], and has found applications in the PCG line of work as it significantly improves efficiency [25,27,28]. While building on regular noise does not seem to affect security of dual LPN in the parameter regimes considered in the line of work on PCGs, it requires a more careful parameter instantiation for primal LPN. For more details we refer to the full version.

LPN-Friendliness. In order to develop more efficient protocols, we will consider code generation algorithms that output matrices with useful structure. To determine when the primal/dual-LPN assumption plausibly holds, we follow the recently proposed heuristic of *resilience to linear tests*. As discussed in detail in [26],[7] essentially all attacks on the LPN problem for our range of parameters involve choosing a nonzero attack vector $\vec{u} \in \{0,1\}^N \setminus \{\vec{0}\}$ and then computing the dot product $\vec{u}^\top \cdot \vec{b}$, where either $\vec{b} \xleftarrow{\$} \{0,1\}^N$, or $\vec{b} = \mathbf{G} \cdot \vec{s} + \vec{e}$ in the primal case or $\vec{b} = \mathbf{H} \cdot \vec{e}$ in the dual case. The hope is to detect a noticeable bias in the bit $\vec{u}^\top \cdot \vec{b}$, as in the case $\vec{b}$ is uniform the bit $\vec{u}^\top \cdot \vec{b}$ is perfectly unbiased. Concretely, for a vector $\vec{v} \in \{0,1\}^N$ and a distribution $\mathcal{D}$ with $\mathsf{Im}(\mathcal{D}) \subseteq \{0,1\}^N$ we define the *bias* of $\vec{v}$ with respect to $\mathcal{D}$ as

$$\mathsf{bias}_{\vec{v}}(\mathcal{D}) = \left| \mathbb{E}_{\vec{x} \sim \mathcal{D}}[\vec{v}^\top \cdot \vec{x}] - \frac{1}{2} \right| .$$

Concretely, for a vector $\vec{v} \in \{0,1\}^N$ of weight D we have $\mathsf{bias}_{\vec{v}}(\mathsf{Reg}_t^N) \leq (1 - 2(D/t)/(N/t))^t < e^{-2tD/N}$.

For the primal case, to rule out the existence of a good linear test it suffices to show that the code generated by $\mathbf{G}$ has good dual distance. More concretely, letting $\mathsf{HW}(\vec{u})$ denote the number of nonzero entries the vector (its *weight*) it should be that any nonzero vector $\vec{u}$ satisfying $\vec{u}^\top \cdot \mathbf{G} = \vec{0}^\top$ has $\mathsf{HW}(\vec{u}) \geq D$ (say). To see this, note that if $\vec{u}^\top \cdot \mathbf{G} \neq \vec{0}^\top$ then $\vec{u}^\top \cdot (\mathbf{G} \cdot \vec{s})$ will be perfectly unbiased (since $\vec{s} \xleftarrow{\$} \{0,1\}^n$), so $\vec{u}^\top \cdot \vec{b}$ will be perfectly unbiased. Otherwise $\vec{u}^\top \cdot \vec{b} = \vec{u}^\top \cdot \vec{e}$ whose bias will not be too large assuming both $\mathsf{HW}(\vec{u}) \geq D$ and $\mathsf{HW}(\vec{e}) \geq t$. In particular, once $Dt > \lambda N \ln(2)/2$ the bias will be at most $2^{-\lambda}$.

The dual case is similar: we would like that there is no light vector of the form $\vec{u}^\top \cdot \mathbf{H}$ for $\vec{u} \in \{0,1\}^N \setminus \{\vec{0}\}$, as if all such vectors $\vec{u}$ satisfy $\mathsf{HW}(\vec{u}^\top \cdot \mathbf{H}) \geq D$ then the bias of $\vec{u}^\top \cdot \mathbf{H} \cdot \vec{e}$ will be at most $e^{-2Dt/M}$, so we can take $Dt > \lambda M \ln(2)/2$ to guarantee bias at most $2^{-\lambda}$.

2.5   (Known Index) Function Secret Sharing

We use several types of function secret sharing for different function classes, including point functions and interval functions. We relax the standard definition [32] by allowing some additional leakage given to one of the parties. The leakage will be the point/interval positions to party P_0. As observed in [27,66], in the context of PCGs for OT and VOLE, allowing this leakage can give rise to more efficient instantiations without hurting security (since P_0 already knows the LPN noise values anyway).

FSS with per-party leakage. Following the syntax of [32], we consider a function family to be defined by a pair $\mathcal{F} = (P_{\mathcal{F}}, E_{\mathcal{F}})$, where $P_{\mathcal{F}}$ is an infinite collection of function descriptions $\hat{f}$ (containing the input domain D_f and output domain R_f), and $E_{\mathcal{F}} \colon P_{\mathcal{F}} \times \{0,1\}^* \to \{0,1\}^*$ is a polynomial-time algorithm defining the function described by $\hat{f}$. More concretely, each $\hat{f} \in P_{\mathcal{F}}$ describes a corresponding function $f \colon D_f \to R_f$ defined by $f(x) = E_{\mathcal{F}}(\hat{f}, x)$. In the following, we will typically have $D_f = [N]$ (where $[N] = \{1, \ldots, N\}$), and $R_f = \mathbb{G}$ for some group $\mathbb{G}$.

---

[7] We refer the interested reader to this work for more details.

Note that as a difference to the original definition, we include FullEval in the full definition for the following reason. While Eval implies the existence of FullEval (and vice versa), considering the two independently can give rise to more efficient implementations. If only considering FullEval for evaluation, we will sometimes write FSS = (Setup, FullEval).

Definition 14 (FSS Syntax). *A (2-party) function secret sharing scheme (FSS) is a pair of algorithms* (Setup, Eval, FullEval) *with the following syntax:*

- Setup$(1^\lambda, \hat{f})$ *is a PPT algorithm, which on input of the security parameter* 1^λ) *and the description of a function* $\hat{f} \in \{0,1\}^*$ *outputs a tuple of keys* (K_0, K_1).
- Eval(σ, K_σ, x) *is a polynomial-time algorithm, which on input of the party index* $\sigma \in \{0,1\}$, *key* K_σ, *and input* $x \in [N]$, *outputs a group element* $y_\sigma \in \mathbb{G}$.
- FullEval(σ, K_σ) *is a polynomial-time algorithm, which on input of the party index* $\sigma \in \{0,1\}$ *and key* K_σ, *outputs a vector* $(\vec{y}_\sigma) \in \mathbb{G}^N$.

Definition 15 (FSS Security). *Let* $\mathcal{F} = (P_\mathcal{F}, E_\mathcal{F})$ *be a function family and* Leak$_0$, Leak$_1 : \{0,1\}^* \to \{0,1\}^*$ *be the respective leakage functions. A secure FSS for* $\mathcal{F}$ *with leakage* Leak *is a pair* (Setup, Eval, FullEval) *as in Definition 14, satisfying the following:*

- **Correctness:** *For all* $\hat{f} \in P_\mathcal{F}$ *describing* $f : [N] \to \mathbb{G}$, *and every* $x \in [N]$, *if* $(K_0, K_1) \leftarrow$ Setup$(1^\lambda, \hat{f})$, *then*

$$\Pr[\mathsf{Eval}(0, K_0, x) + \mathsf{Eval}(1, K_1, x) = f(x)] = 1 \ and$$

$$\Pr[\mathsf{FullEval}(0, K_0) + \mathsf{FullEval}(1, K_1) = \{f(x)\}_{x \in [N]}] = 1$$

- **Secrecy:** *For each* $\sigma \in \{0,1\}$, *there exists a PPT algorithm* Sim *such that for every sequence* $\hat{f}_1, \hat{f}_2, \ldots$ *of polynomial-size function descriptions from* $P_\mathcal{F}$, *the outputs of the following experiments* Real *and* Ideal *are computationally indistinguishable:*
  - Real(1^λ) : *Sample* $(K_0, K_1) \leftarrow$ Setup$(1^\lambda, \hat{f}_\lambda)$ *and output* K_σ.
  - Ideal(1^λ) : *Output* Sim$(1^\lambda, \mathsf{Leak}_\sigma(\hat{f}_\lambda))$.

In the following, when referring to an FSS, we always assume the FSS to satisfy correctness and secrecy.

Remark 16 (Pseudorandomness of the output shares). In [31] it was shown that for any sufficiently rich function class (including point functions and interval functions considered below), secrecy implies pseudorandomness of the output shares.

Remark 17 (Succinctness). Note that the running time of the Setup algorithm (and therefore the key sizes) are only allowed to depend polynomially on the size of the description $\hat{f}$ of f. We will refer to the computational cost of Setup as $C_{\mathsf{FSS.Setup}}$.

In the following, we define the *computational overhead* of an FSS.

Definition 18 (FSS Cost). *For an* FSS $=$ (Setup, Eval, FullEval) *we define the cost functions* $C_{\mathsf{FSS}}^0, C_{\mathsf{FSS}}^1$ *as the circuit sizes (over the full binary basis) of* FullEval$(0, \cdot)$ *and* FullEval$(1, \cdot)$, *respectively. If* $C_{\mathsf{FSS}}^\sigma(\lambda) = c \cdot N + \mathsf{poly}(\lambda)$ *for some constant* $c \in O(1)$, *for* $\sigma \in \{0, 1\}$, *we say that* FSS *has* constant overhead.

Multi-point and multi-interval functions. In the following we give the definition of regular multi-point functions and projected-payload multi-interval function. For more definitions we refer to the full version.

Definition 19 (Regular multi-point function). *Let* $t \in \mathbb{N}, N \in \mathbb{N}$, $\alpha_1, \ldots, \alpha_t \in [N/t]$, $\mathbb{G}$ *be an additive group and* $\beta_1, \ldots, \beta_t \in \mathbb{G}$. *The* regular multi-point *function defined by* $\vec{\alpha} = (\alpha_1, \ldots, \alpha_t)$ *and* $\vec{\beta} = (\beta_1, \ldots, \beta_t)$ *is then*

$$f_{\vec{\alpha}}^{\vec{\beta}} \colon [N] \to \mathbb{G}, \ f_{\vec{\alpha}}^{\vec{\beta}}(x) := \begin{cases} \beta_i & \text{if } x = \alpha_i + \frac{N}{t} \cdot (i-1) \\ 0 & \text{else} \end{cases}.$$

Definition 20 (Projected-payload multi-interval function). *Let* $N \in \mathbb{N}$ *be the domain size,* $\kappa, \ell \in \mathbb{N}$, $\mathbb{G} = \{0,1\}^\kappa$ *be the group of* κ-*length bit-strings and* $\pi_i \colon \{0,1\}^\kappa \to \{0,1\}^\ell$ *for* $i \in [N]$ *projection functions. Let further* $\alpha_1, \ldots, \alpha_t \in [N]$ *be pairwise different and* $\beta \in \{0,1\}^\kappa$. *Then, we define the projected-payload interval function specified by* $\vec{\alpha} = (\alpha_1, \ldots, \alpha_t)$, β *and* $\vec{\pi} := (\pi_1, \ldots, \pi_N)$ *as*

$$f_{<\vec{\alpha}}^{\beta, \vec{\pi}}(x) = \begin{cases} \pi_x(\beta) & \text{if } |\{i \in [t] : \alpha_i < x\}| \equiv 1 \pmod 2 \\ 0^\ell & \text{else} \end{cases}.$$

Known-Index FSS. In known-index FSS for point functions, introduced in [66], the index α is allowed to be leaked to party P_0. As observed in [27,66], a puncturable PRF suffices to instantiate known-index FSS for point-functions. Similarly, a t-puncturable PRF suffices to instantiate known-index FSS for t-point functions. In [26], it was further observed that allowing to leak the index can also give efficiency improvements for interval FSS, through known-index interval FSS (in their work, this is referred to as *relaxed distributed comparison function*).

In the full version we give the formal definitions of these flavors of FSS, present constructions and analyze their circuit complexity. For known-index DPF and known-index interval FSS, the constructions are based on prior works, while for projected-payload FSS, we devise a new construction.

3   Constant-Overhead PCG for OT from Primal LPN

In this section give a PCG for OT with constant overhead in Fig. 1. An inherent limitation to this approach is that primal LPN is limited to subquadratic stretch.

First, following Alekhnovich [2], we will consider a primal code generation procedure that outputs matrices $\mathbf{G}$ that are *very sparse*. In particular, $\mathbf{G}$ will be sampled uniformly at random subject to the constraint that every row has exactly d 1's. Alekhnovich already conjectured this is hard when $d = 3$ if $N, t = O(n)$, where the noise is sampled to have weight t. Polynomial-time attacks exist with $N = \Omega(n^{d/2})$ [6,21]: one hopes for there to be two rows of $\mathbf{G}$ which agree (which occurs with probability $\frac{\binom{N}{2}}{\binom{n}{d}}$). This is the same as saying the dual distance of $\mathbf{G}$ is 2.

However, as discussed in Sect. 2.4 when the dual distance D is larger we obtain security against linear tests: the security is at most $2^{-\lambda}$ when $Dt \geq (\ln 2)\lambda N/2$. In general, for any $\gamma > 0$ it is feasible to have a d-sparse matrix $\mathbf{G} \in \{0,1\}^{N \times n}$ with dual distance $D = \Omega_d(n^\gamma)$ and $N = n^{\frac{1-\gamma}{2}d+\gamma}$. In particular we can choose $\gamma = 9/10$ to get $D = \Theta_d(n^{9/10})$ and $N = n^{\frac{d+18}{20}}$, so if we wish to have $N\lambda = O(tD)$ to guarantee exponentially small in λ security against linear tests we may choose $t = \Theta_d(\lambda n^{\frac{d}{18+d}})$.

We must also be careful in light of the attack by Arora and Ge [14], which is effective when $N = \Omega(n^2)$. For this reason, we will ensure $N = o(n^2)$.

In what follows (and in the rest of the paper), we assume the existence of an *explicitly generated* matrix $\mathbf{G}$ with sparsity $d = O(1)$ for which the primal $(\mathsf{Reg}_t^N(\{0,1\}), \mathbf{G}, \{0,1\})$-LPN$(n, N)$ holds with $n, t \leq N^{1-\gamma}$ for some $\gamma > 0$. Alternatively, we conjecture that the randomized expander generation algorithm from [11] can be used to efficiently generate such $\mathbf{G}$ with negligible failure probability.

We show security of the PCG in the theorem below, and then analyze its overhead.

Theorem 21. *Let $N = N(\lambda), n = n(\lambda), t = t(\lambda), \kappa = \kappa(\lambda) \in \mathbb{N}$ and let $\ell, d \in \mathbb{N}$ be constant and $\mathbf{C}$ a primal code generation algorithm with constant sparsity d (i.e., generating code matrices, where each row has at most d non-zero entries). If the (primal) $(\mathsf{Reg}_t^N(\mathbb{F}_2), \mathbf{C}, \mathbb{F}_2)$-LPN$(n, N)$-assumption holds, if $G: \{0,1\}^\kappa \to \{0,1\}^N$ is a correlation-robust ℓ-local PRG, and if $\mathsf{FSS} = (\mathsf{Setup}, \mathsf{FullEval})$ is a known-index regular t-point FSS, then the PCG as defined in Fig. 1 is a PCG for generating N instances of the bit-OT correlation.*

The proof is provided in the full version.

Lemma 22. *The $\mathsf{PCG.Gen}$ algorithm in Fig. 1 has circuit size $O(\kappa \cdot n + C_{\mathsf{FSS.Setup}})$. Furthermore, if $C_{\mathsf{FSS}}^\sigma(\lambda)$ is the cost of $\mathsf{FSS.FullEval}(\sigma, \cdot)$ and C_P is an upper bound on the cost of evaluating one predicate in the local PRG G, then the $\mathsf{PCG.Expand}(\sigma, \cdot)$ phase has circuit size*

$$\ell dN + C_{\mathsf{FSS}}^\sigma(\lambda) + (1 - \sigma)dN + (1 + \sigma)(C_P + 1)N.$$

So, if FSS has constant overhead then $\mathsf{PCG.Expand}$ has constant overhead.

Proof. For key generation, generating the secret shares $\vec{r}_0, \vec{r}_1$ requires $O(n \cdot \kappa)$ operations. The remainder of the setup is dominated by $\mathsf{FSS.Setup}$, giving $O(\kappa \cdot n + C_{\mathsf{FSS.Setup}}(\lambda))$.

For expansion, the cost derivation is as follows.

Construction $\mathsf{PCG}_{\mathsf{OT}}^{\mathsf{primal}}$

PARAMETERS:

- Security parameter $\lambda \in \mathbb{N}$, matrix parameters $N = N(\lambda), n = n(\lambda) \in \mathbb{N}$ with $N > n$, constant matrix sparsity parameter $d \in \mathbb{N}$, noise weight $t = t(\lambda) \in \mathbb{N}$, local PRG input length $\kappa = \kappa(\lambda) \in \mathbb{N}$, constant locality $\ell \in \mathbb{N}$.
- A *primal* sparse code generation algorithm $\mathbf{C}$ returning matrices in $\{0,1\}^{N \times n}$ with d non-zero entries per row and a public matrix $\mathbf{G} \xleftarrow{\$} \mathbf{C}(N, n, \mathbb{F}_2)$ sampled according to $\mathbf{C}$.
- A constant-overhead known-index regular t-point FSS $\mathsf{FSS} = (\mathsf{Setup}, \mathsf{FullEval})$ over domain $[N]$ and range $\{0,1\}^\ell$.
- A correlation-robust ℓ-local PRG $G \colon \{0,1\}^\kappa \to \{0,1\}^N$ with $G(x) = P_1(\pi_1(x)) \| \ldots \| P_N(\pi_N(x))$ for all $x \in \{0,1\}^\kappa$.

CORRELATION: Outputs N tuples $((b, w), (w_0, w_1))$, where b, w_0, w_1 are random bits and $w = w_b$.

GEN:

- Pick a *local PRG seed* $x \xleftarrow{\$} \{0,1\}^\kappa$ at random.
- Pick an *LPN seed* $\vec{s} \xleftarrow{\$} \{0,1\}^n$ at random.
- Generate a random additive secret sharing of $\vec{r} := (s_1 \cdot x, s_2 \cdot x, \ldots, s_N \cdot x)$, i.e., choose $\vec{r}_1 \xleftarrow{\$} (\{0,1\}^\kappa)^n$ and set $\vec{r}_1 := \vec{r}_0 \oplus \vec{r}$.
- Choose *regular noise positions* $\vec{\alpha} \xleftarrow{\$} [N/t]^t$ at random.
- Set $\beta_i := \pi_{\alpha_i + \frac{N}{t} \cdot (i-1)}(x) \in \{0,1\}^\ell$ for each $i \in [t]$ and set $\vec{\beta} := (\beta_1, \ldots, \beta_t)$.
- Set $(K_0, K_1) \leftarrow \mathsf{FSS}.\mathsf{Setup}(1^\lambda, \vec{\alpha}, \vec{\beta})$.
- Set $\mathsf{k}_0 := (\vec{s}, \vec{r}_0, \vec{\alpha}, K_0)$ and $\mathsf{k}_1 := (x, \vec{r}_1, K_1)$ and output $(\mathsf{k}_0, \mathsf{k}_1)$.

EXPAND: On input $(\sigma, \mathsf{k}_\sigma)$:

1. If $\sigma = 0$, parse k_0 as $(\vec{s}, \vec{r}_0, \vec{\alpha}, K_0)$ and proceed as follows:
   - Let $\vec{\mu} \in \{0,1\}^N$ be the regular noise vector defined by $\vec{\alpha}$, i.e.,

   $$\mu_j = \begin{cases} 1 & \text{if } j = \alpha_i + \frac{N}{t} \cdot (i-1) \\ 0 & \text{else} \end{cases}.$$

   - Set $\vec{b} := \mathbf{G} \cdot \vec{s} \oplus \vec{\mu} \in \{0,1\}^N$.
   - Set $\vec{y}^0 := \mathbf{G} \cdot \vec{r}_0 \in (\{0,1\}^\kappa)^N$. //Note that we only need the ℓ entries $\pi_j(\vec{y}_j^0) \in \{0,1\}^\ell$ to continue. Towards constant overhead this step can therefore be computed in $N \cdot d \cdot \ell \in O(N)$ operations (by only computing relevant parts of the matrix-vector product).
   - Compute $\vec{v}^0 \leftarrow \mathsf{FSS}.\mathsf{FullEval}(0, K_0) \in (\{0,1\}^\ell)^N$.
   - For each $j \in [N]$, compute $w_j := P_j(\pi_j(y_j^0) \oplus v_j^0) \in \{0,1\}$.
   - Output $\{(b_j, w_j)\}_{j \in [N]}$.
2. If $\sigma = 1$, parse k_1 as $(\vec{x}, \vec{r}_1, K_1)$ and proceed as follows:
   - Set $\vec{y}^1 := \mathbf{G} \cdot \vec{r}_1 \in (\{0,1\}^\kappa)^N$.
   - Compute $\vec{v}_1 \leftarrow \mathsf{FSS}.\mathsf{FullEval}(1, K_1) \in (\{0,1\}^\ell)^N$.
   - For $j \in [N]$, $b \in \{0,1\}$, compute $w_{j,b} := P_j(\pi_j(y_j^1) \oplus \vec{v}_j^1 \oplus b \cdot \pi_j(\vec{x}))$.
   - Output $\{(w_{j,0}, w_{j,1})\}_{j \in [N]}$.

Fig. 1. Constant-overhead PCG for N instances of random bit-OT.

- Computing each entry of $\vec{b}$ (for $\sigma = 0$) can be done with d XORs, for a total of dN gates.
- Since one only has to compute the ℓ-bit projections π_j of $\vec{y}^0$, $\vec{y}^1$ (as explained in the protocol description), these cost at most ℓdN XOR gates.
- Computing $\vec{v}^\sigma$ costs $C_{\text{FSS}}^\sigma(\lambda) \cdot N$ gates.
- Each $w_j / w_{j,0}, w_{j,1}$ can be computed with $C_P + 1$ gates, resulting in either $(C_P + 1)N$ (for $\sigma = 0$) or $2(C_P + 1)N$ ($\sigma = 1$) for the last step.

We can instantiate the FSS construction with the naive "square-root" construction of known-index DPF from the full version. This gives $C_{\text{FSS}}^\sigma(\lambda) \leq C_{\text{prg}}(\ell) + (1 - \sigma)2\ell$. With regular noise, the setup cost of the FSS is $O(t\lambda\sqrt{N/t}) = O(\lambda\sqrt{Nt})$. For the PCG to be sublinear, we therefore get the constraint that $\kappa n + \lambda\sqrt{Nt} = o(N)$

Based on the above analysis, we now obtain our main result on maliciously secure bit-OT, by replacing PCG.Gen with a secure 2-PC protocol.

Corollary 23. *Suppose OT exists. Suppose the* $(\text{Reg}_t^N(\mathbb{F}_2), \mathbf{C}, \mathbb{F}_2)$*-LPN$(n, N)$-assumption holds for some n, t, N and matrix $\mathbf{G}$ with constant sparsity d, and suppose there exists a correlation-robust ℓ-local PRG for constant ℓ that stretches $N^{1-\varepsilon}$ to N bits for some $\varepsilon \in (0, 1)$, where $19\varepsilon/20 \geq \frac{20}{d+18}$ and $0.9 \cdot (19\varepsilon/20) + 9\varepsilon/10 > 1$. Then, there exists a protocol for securely computing N instances of random bit-OT with malicious security, $o(N)$ communication and an average, amortized per-party computation of $\ell(d + 1) + \frac{d}{2} + C_{\text{prg}}(\ell) + \frac{3}{2}(C_P + 1)$ Boolean gates per OT.*

Proof. Assuming OT and using standard 2-PC protocols like [54], there is a polynomial p such that for all λ and circuits C, there is a malicious 2-PC protocol that securely computes C with computation complexity $O(|C|) \cdot p(\lambda)$. Based on Lemma 22 and plugging in the square-root FSS construction, we obtain a protocol that securely computes the PCG.Gen algorithm from Fig. 1 with complexity $(\kappa n + \lambda\sqrt{Nt}) \cdot p(\lambda)$. Following [28, Theorem 19], by running the 2-PC protocol and then locally evaluating PCG.Expand, the resulting protocol securely realizes the functionality for N instances of random bit-OT.

We show how to choose parameters such that the complexity of the 2-PC phase is sublinear in N for sufficiently large N. This means the $p(\lambda)$ overhead of 2-PC amortizes and the total computational cost is dominated by the expand phase. With $\kappa = N^{1-\varepsilon}$, we set $n = N^{19\varepsilon/20}$ and $t = N^{9\varepsilon/10}$. Further, we obtain complexities of $\kappa n = N^{1-\varepsilon/20}$ and $\lambda\sqrt{Nt} = \lambda N^{\frac{1}{2}+\frac{9}{20}\varepsilon}$. These are both sublinear in N. Regarding security of primal-LPN, note that by assumption we have $n \geq N^{20/(d+18)}$, which is enough to give dual distance $D = \Theta(n^{9/10})$. We also have $tn^{9/10} = \Omega(N\lambda)$ for large enough N by assumption, giving exponential security in λ.

Finally, to compute the computational complexity of PCG.Expand, we plug in the cost of the square-root FSS construction to the formula from Lemma 22, and average the result over the two parties $\sigma = 0$ and $\sigma = 1$. This is possible as random bit-OT is symmetric, so the parties can run two instances of the protocol of size $N/2$, reversing the roles of sender and receiver.

Concrete Complexity. We now estimate the constant overhead of our construction, at least asymptotically as N grows large. We need to choose the LPN degree d and ℓ-local correlation robust PRG, which determines the predicate cost C_P and the PRG seed size $\kappa = N^{1-\varepsilon}$ bits. We also need to instantiate the PRG used in the FSS scheme, for which we use a 5-local PRG, giving $C_{\mathsf{prg}}(\ell) = C_{P_5}\ell = 4\ell$ (unlike the other PRG, this one only needs to have constant stretch, since it can be used iteratively). Using the $\mathsf{XOR}_4 \oplus \mathsf{MAJ}_5$ predicate in our PCG, we have $\ell = 9$, $C_P = 17$ and a plausible stretch of $\kappa^{2.49}$, giving $\varepsilon = 1 - 1/2.49$. This satisfies $19\varepsilon/20 > \frac{20}{d+18}$ for $d = 18$, and furthermore that $0.9 \cdot (19\varepsilon/20) + 9\varepsilon/10 > 1$. Note further that $19\varepsilon/20 > 0.5$, so $n = N^{19\varepsilon/20} = \omega(\sqrt{N})$, ruling out the Arora-Ge attack [14]. Furthermore $t = N^{9\varepsilon/10} = o(n)$, which is necessary for building on LPN with regular noise. Overall, we get a cost of 243 gates per party.

Remark 24. (Iterative constant overhead). If the FSS scheme supports single evaluation Eval with constant cost $c \in O(1)$, the above construction yields a PCG with iterative constant overhead, i.e., where a single bit-OT can be computed at constant cost. This property in fact already holds of the square-root FSS construction when instantiated with a local PRG.

Remark 25. (Building on LPN with standard noise). To build on LPN with the more standard Bernoulli noise, one has to replace the t-regular FSS by a more general multi-point FSS. Known-index multi-point FSS with constant overhead can be obtained generically from single-point FSS with constant overhead via batch codes. For details we refer to [25].

4 Constant-Overhead PCG for OT from Dual LPN

In this section we provide a PCG for OT with constant computational overhead based on a dual-LPN assumption. This will allow us to achieve an arbitrary polynomial stretch. All proofs in this section are provided in the full version.

Repeat-Accumulate (RA) Codes. We consider the following dual code generation procedure, which essentially outputs generator matrices for *repeat-accumulate (RA) codes*.

Definition 26. *Let $d, N \in \mathbb{N}$ with $d \geq 3$ and let $M = dN$. A* repeat-accumulate (RA) *matrix $\mathbf{H}$ is a matrix of the form $\mathbf{H} = \mathbf{BA}$, where $\mathbf{B} \in \{0,1\}^{N \times M}$ has exactly d nonzero entries per row and 1 nonzero entry per column and $\mathbf{A} \in \{0,1\}^{M \times M}$ is an accumulator matrix which has 1's on and below the main diagonal.*

The code $\{\vec{u}^\top \cdot \mathbf{BA} : \vec{u} \in \{0,1\}^N\}$ is well-studied in coding theory (it is called a repeat-accumulate (RA) code). In particular, for fixed $\gamma > 0$ it is known that they achieve minimum distance $D = M^{1-2/d-\gamma}$ with good probability over a random choice of $\mathbf{B}$. This means that if $\vec{e} \xleftarrow{\$} \mathsf{Reg}_t^M(\{0,1\})$, recalling that the bias of the dot-product between a vector of weight D and $\vec{e}$ is at most $e^{-2tD/M}$ we will require $t \geq \ln 2 \cdot \lambda \cdot M^{2/d+\gamma}$.

Unfortunately, the failure probability is not negligible (an inspection of the proof of [60, Theorem 1] shows that it is roughly of the order $M^{-\gamma d/2}$). Thus, as before we will assume access to a *explicitly generated* RA matrix $\mathbf{H} = \mathbf{BA}$ and assume that the dual $(\mathsf{Reg}_t^M(\{0,1\}), \mathbf{H}, \{0,1\}\text{-LPN}(N, dN)$ holds with respect to it.[8]

Theorem 27. *Let $N = N(\lambda), t = t(\lambda), \kappa = \kappa(\lambda) \in \mathbb{N}$, let $\ell, d \in \mathbb{N}$ be constants, let $M = dN$ and let $\mathbf{H} = \mathbf{BA}$ be an $N \times M$ repeat-accumulate matrix. If the dual $(\mathsf{Reg}_t^M(\{0,1\}), \mathbf{H}, \{0,1\})\text{-LPN}(N, M)$-assumption holds, if $G: \{0,1\}^\kappa \to \{0,1\}^N$ is a correlation-robust ℓ-local PRG, and if FSS is a known-index projected-payload t-interval FSS, then the PCG as defined in Fig. 2 is a constant-overhead PCG for generating N instances of the bit-OT correlation.*

Lemma 28. *The PCG.Gen algorithm in Fig. 2 has circuit size $O(t \log(N/t) + C_{\mathsf{FSS.Setup}}(\lambda))$. Furthermore, if $C_{\mathsf{FSS}}^\sigma(\lambda)$ is the cost of FSS.FullEval$(\sigma, \cdot)$ and C_P is an upper bound on the cost of evaluating one predicate in the local PRG G, then the PCG.Expand$(\sigma, \cdot)$ phase has circuit size*

$$C_{\mathsf{FSS}}^\sigma(\lambda) + (1 - \sigma)(2Nd - 1) + (d\ell + C_P)N + \sigma((d+1)\ell + C_P)N .$$

Corollary 29. *Suppose OT exists. Suppose the $(\mathsf{Reg}_t^M(\mathbb{F}_2), \mathbf{H}, \mathbb{F}_2)\text{-LPN}(N, M)$-assumption holds for some RA matrix $\mathbf{H}$ with $M = dN$ for constant integer d, and suppose there exists a correlation-robust ℓ-local PRG for constant ℓ that stretches $N^{1-\varepsilon}$ to N bits for some $\varepsilon > 0$. Then, there exists a protocol for securely computing N instances of random bit-OT with malicious security, $o(N)$ communication and an average, amortized per-party computation of*

$$\frac{3}{2}d\ell + d + \frac{5\ell}{2} + \frac{3}{2}C_P + C_{\mathsf{prg}}(2\ell) + \frac{1}{\kappa}C_{\mathsf{prg}}(2\lambda + \kappa) + 3$$

Boolean gates per OT. In particular, if $C_{\mathsf{prg}}(k) = O(k)$ for integer k, then the amortized per-party computation is constant.

Concrete Complexity. Choose $d = 3$. Now we choose the P_5 predicate for the local PRG so that $\ell = 5$ and $C_P = 4$. Further we use a constant stretch PRG for the FSS satisfying $C_{\mathsf{prg}}(\ell) = 4\ell$. Asymptotically we then compute 91 bit operations per output, beating the primal construction. Furthermore, note with this value of d we are stretching roughly $N^{2/3}$ bits to N bits (we can choose $t = M^{2/3+\varepsilon}$). For general d we can get stretch $(dN)^{2/d+\varepsilon}$ bits to N bits, yielding arbitrary polynomial stretch (although the complexity per OT output does increase commensurately).

5   Beyond Oblivious Transfer

In this section we discuss applications of our main result to constant-overhead implementations of other secure computation tasks. For simplicity, we refer here

---

[8] Instead of RA codes we could have used a code of Tillich and Zémor [68]; however the effect on the computational complexity is essentially nil.

Construction $\mathsf{PCG}_{\mathsf{OT}}^{\mathsf{dual}}$

PARAMETERS:

- Security parameter $\lambda \in \mathbb{N}$, matrix parameters $M = M(\lambda), N = N(\lambda) \in \mathbb{N}$ with $M = dN$ for constant matrix sparsity parameter $d \in \mathbb{N}$, noise weight $t = t(\lambda) \in \mathbb{N}$, local PRG input length $\kappa = \kappa(\lambda) \in \mathbb{N}$, constant locality $\ell \in \mathbb{N}$.
- An RA matrix $\mathbf{H} = \mathbf{BA} \in \{0,1\}^{N \times M}$ for which the dual $(\mathsf{Reg}_t^M(\{0,1\}), \mathbf{H}, \{0,1\})\text{-}\mathsf{LPN}(N, dN)$ holds. Let S_j for $j \in [N]$ denote the support of the j-th row of $\mathbf{B}$ (each of which has size d) and for $i \in [M]$ let $\tau(i) \in [N]$ denote the nonzero coordinate of the i-th column of $\mathbf{B}$. $//$Note that $S_j = \{i \in [M] : \tau(i) = j\} = \tau^{-1}(j)$.
- A constant overhead regular known-index projected-payload t-interval FSS $\mathsf{FSS} = (\mathsf{Setup}, \mathsf{Eval})$ over domain $[M]$ with output bit length κ and projected output length ℓ.
- A correlation-robust ℓ-local PRG $G \colon \{0,1\}^\kappa \to \{0,1\}^N$ with $G(x) = P_1(\pi_1(x)) \| \dots \| P_N(\pi_N(x))$ for all $x \in \{0,1\}^\kappa$.

CORRELATION: Outputs N tuples $((b,w),(w_0,w_1))$, where b, w_0, w_1 are random bits and $w = w_b$.

GEN:

- Pick a *local PRG seed* $x \xleftarrow{\$} \{0,1\}^\kappa$ at random.
- Choose *regular noise positions* $\vec{\alpha} \xleftarrow{\$} [M/t]^t$ at random.
- Set $\beta := x \in \{0,1\}^\kappa$.
- Denote $\vec{\psi} = (\pi_{\tau(1)}, \dots, \pi_{\tau(M)})$.
- Set $(K_0, K_1) \leftarrow \mathsf{FSS.Setup}(1^\lambda, (\vec{\alpha}, \beta, \vec{\psi}))$.
- Set $\mathsf{k}_0 := (\vec{\alpha}, K_0)$ and $\mathsf{k}_1 := (x, K_1)$ and output $(\mathsf{k}_0, \mathsf{k}_1)$.

EXPAND: On input $(\sigma, \mathsf{k}_\sigma)$:

1. If $\sigma = 0$, parse k_0 as $(\vec{\alpha}, K_0)$ and proceed as follows:
   - Let $\vec{a} \in \{0,1\}^M$ be the regular interval noise vector defined by $\vec{\alpha}$, i.e., a_i is equal to the parity of $|\{\iota \in [t] : \alpha_\iota + (M/t) \cdot (\iota - 1) \le i\}|$.
   - Compute $\vec{b} := \mathbf{B} \cdot \vec{a}$.
   - Compute $\vec{v}^0 \leftarrow \mathsf{FSS.FullEval}(0, K_0) \in (\{0,1\}^\ell)^M$.
   - For $j \in [N]$ compute $w_j := P_j\left(\bigoplus_{i \in S_j} v_i^0\right)$.
   - Output $\{(b_j, w_j)\}_{j \in [N]}$.
2. If $\sigma = 1$, parse k_1 as (x, K_1) and proceed as follows:
   - Compute $\vec{v}^1 \leftarrow \mathsf{FSS.FullEval}(1, K_1) \in (\{0,1\}^\ell)^M$.
   - For $j \in [N], b \in \{0,1\}$ compute $w_{j,b} := P_j\left(\left(\bigoplus_{i \in S_j} v_i^1\right) \oplus b \cdot \pi_j(x)\right)$.
   - Output $\{(w_{j,0}, w_{j,1})\}_{j \in [N]}$.

Fig. 2. Constant-overhead PCG for N instances of random bit-OT.

only to the two-party case, though most of the results in this section apply also to MPC with a constant number of parties with the same asymptotic cost. We will also refer to security against malicious parties by default.

One of the main open questions about the asymptotic complexity of cryptography is the possibility of securely computing Boolean circuits with constant computational overhead. While in the semi-honest model such a result can be based on local PRGs [52], extending this to the malicious model was posed as an open question.[9] The overhead of the best known protocols grows polylogarithmically with the security parameter and the circuit size [41].

Our main result allows us to make progress on this question, by obtaining partial positive results and reducing the general question to simpler questions.

5.1   General Protocols with Relaxed Security

Our main result gives the first constant-overhead implementation of (malicious bit-) OT. However, extending this to general functionalities is challenging. While it is well-known that OT is complete for secure computation [54,59], the best known protocols for Boolean circuits in the OT-hybrid model have polylogarithmic overhead [41,44]. In contrast, in the *semi-honest* OT-hybrid model, a simple "textbook" protocol [47,48], commonly referred to as the (semi-honest) *GMW protocol*, achieves perfect security with a small constant overhead.

A key observation from [43] is that this textbook protocol actually achieves a nontrivial notion of security even against malicious parties: it is secure up to *additive attacks*. For Boolean circuits, this means that the adversary's attack capability is limited to choosing a subset of the circuit wires that are toggled. This is formalized by modifying the ideal functionality to take from the adversary an additional input bit for each wire, specifying whether to insert a NOT gate into the middle of the wire. Combining this with a standard composition theorem [35,47], we get the following application of our main result.

Theorem 30 (Constant overhead with additive attacks). *Suppose there exists a constant-overhead OT protocol with security against malicious parties. Then there exists a constant-overhead protocol for Boolean circuits with security up to additive attacks.*

Additive attacks can render security meaningless for some applications. For instance, capturing a zero-knowledge proof as a secure computation of the verification predicate, a malicious prover can make the verifier accept a false statement by simply toggling the final decision bit.

In some other cases, however, security up to additive attacks is still meaningful. Consider a secure computation task that has long inputs and a short output, such as applying a complex search query to a big database or a

---

[9] In fact, the question is open even in the simpler special case of zero-knowledge functionalities. A solution for this special case would imply a solution for the general case by applying the GMW compiler [48] to a constant-overhead protocol with semi-honest security.

data-mining algorithm to the union of two databases. In such cases, it is often hard to reason about the security features of an ideal-model implementation, except for the syntactic guarantee that a malicious party can only learn a small amount of information about the honest party's input. The same kind of guarantee is given by a protocol with security up to additive attacks. In contrast, applying the constant-overhead semi-honest protocol from [52] to such a functionality may allow a malicious party to learn the entire input of the honest party.

5.2   Leveraging Perfect Security

Consider the case of evaluating N instances of a constant-size f on different sets of inputs. If f admits a *perfectly* secure protocol in the OT-hybrid model, then the protocol necessarily uses a fixed number of bit operations, independent of any security parameter. Combining N instances of such a protocol with the constant-overhead OT from this work, we get a constant-overhead protocol for evaluating N instances of f.

Theorem 31 (Constant overhead from perfect security). *Let f be a constant-size functionality that can be computed with perfect security in the OT-hybrid model. Then, a constant-overhead OT protocol with security against malicious parties implies a constant-overhead protocol for computing N instances of f.*

The existence of perfectly secure protocols in the OT-hybrid model is still quite far from understood. There are negative results for functionalities with big inputs (assuming that the protocol's running time must be polynomial in the input length), as well as for constant-size two-sided functionalities delivering outputs to both parties [51]. The general case of constant-size *one-sided* functionalities is still open, but positive results for natural functionalities appear in the literature.

Early examples include other flavors of OT, including 1-out-of-k bit-OT, its extension to string-OT (of any fixed length) [34], and instances of "Rabin-OT" that correspond to erasure channels with a rational erasure probability [54].

Perfectly secure protocols for a much broader class of one-sided functionalities were recently obtained in [3]. This class includes natural functionalities such as small instances of the millionaire's problem, as well as almost all Boolean one-sided functionalities where the party receiving the output has a smaller input domain than the other party.

Realizing a BSC. An even simpler corollary of Theorem 31 is a constant-overhead protocol for securely realizing N instances of a *binary symmetric channel* (BSC). The feasibility and complexity of securely realizing BSC and other channels was studied in several previous works [1,53,57].

Corollary 32 (Constant-overhead BSC). *Suppose there exists a constant-overhead OT protocol with security against malicious parties. Then there exists a constant-overhead protocol for realizing N instances of the $BSC_{0.25}$ functionality,* *which takes a bit b from the sender and delivers $b \oplus e$ to the receiver, where $e = 1$ with probability 0.25 and $e = 0$ otherwise.*

Proof. By Theorem 31, it suffices to show that $\mathsf{BSC}_{0.25}$ perfectly reduces to OT. Consider a deterministic functionality f that takes bits b, e_1^S, e_2^S from the sender and bits e_1^R, e_2^R from the receiver, and delivers $b \oplus ((e_1^S \oplus e_1^R) \wedge (e_2^S \oplus e_2^R))$ to the receiver. Let C_f be a Boolean circuit computing f in the natural way. By the above mentioned theorem of [43], there is a perfectly secure protocol for C_f in the OT-hybrid model with security up to additive attacks. We argue that applying this protocol with randomly chosen inputs $e_1^S, e_2^S, e_1^R, e_2^R$ yields a perfectly secure protocol for $\mathsf{BSC}_{0.25}$ in the OT-hybrid model. Indeed, letting $e = (e_1^S \oplus e_1^R) \wedge (e_2^S \oplus e_2^R)$, it is not hard to see that a single malicious party cannot bias nor learn any information about e by toggling wire values of C_f. Furthermore, toggling b or the output can be trivially simulated in the ideal model.

5.3   Reducing the Main Open Question to Simpler Questions

Finally, while we leave open the existence of constant-overhead protocols for general Boolean circuits, our result for OT allows us to reduce this question to a question about a special kind of fault-tolerant circuits.

An Algebraic Manipulation Detection (AMD) circuit [43] for f is a randomized circuit $\widehat{C}$ that computes f while resisting additive attacks in the following sense: the effect of every additive attack on the wires of $\widehat{C}$ can be simulated by an ideal additive attack on the inputs and outputs of f. As before, in the Boolean case an additive attack can toggle an arbitrary subset of the wires. More formally:

Definition 33 (Boolean AMD circuit).   *Let $C : \{0,1\}^n \to \{0,1\}^k$ be a (deterministic or randomized) Boolean circuit. We say that a randomized Boolean circuit $\widehat{C} : \{0,1\}^n \to \{0,1\}^k$ is an ϵ-secure AMD implementation of C if the following holds:*

- *Completeness. For all $x \in \{0,1\}^n$, $\widehat{C}(x) \equiv C(x)$.*
- *Security against additive attacks. For any additive attack A, toggling a subset of the wires of $\widehat{C}$, there exist distributions Δ_{in} over $\{0,1\}^n$ and Δ_{out} over $\{0,1\}^k$ such that for every $x \in \{0,1\}^n$ it holds that*

$$SD\left(\widetilde{C}(x), C(x \oplus \Delta_{\mathsf{in}}) \oplus \Delta_{\mathsf{out}}\right) \leq \epsilon,$$

where $\widetilde{C} \leftarrow A(\widehat{C})$ and SD denotes statistical distance.

Boolean AMD circuits are motivated by the goal of obtaining efficient secure computation protocols in the OT-hybrid model. Indeed, applying the semi-honest GMW protocol [47,48] to the AMD circuit $\widehat{C}$, with a suitable encoding to protect the input and output, yields a secure protocol for C [43,44]. Combined with a constant-overhead OT protocol, this reduces an affirmative answer to the main open question to the design of constant-overhead AMD circuits.

Theorem 34 (Cf. [44], Claim 18). *Suppose that every Boolean circuit C admits a $2^{-\lambda}$-secure AMD implementation $\widehat{C}$ of size $O(|C|) + \mathsf{poly}(\lambda) \cdot |C|^{0.9}$. Then, a constant-overhead OT protocol implies a constant-overhead protocol for general Boolean circuits.*

The main result of [44] is a construction of AMD circuits with polylogarithmic overhead (in $|C|, \lambda$). Whether this can be improved was left open, but the question was further reduced to the design of two kinds of simple protocols in the honest-majority setting: a protocol that only provides semi-honest security (with a constant fraction of corrupted parties) and a protocol that only guarantees the correctness of the output. This should be contrasted to the approach from [41,54], which reduces the question to the design of honest-majority protocols with security against *malicious* parties.

Acknowledgements. E. Boyle supported by AFOSR Award FA9550-21-1-0046, ERC Project HSS (852952), and a Google Research Award. G. Couteau supported by the ANR SCENE. N. Gilboa supported by ISF grant 2951/20, ERC grant 876110, and a grant by the BGU Cyber Center. Y. Ishai supported by ERC Project NTSC (742754), BSF grant 2018393, and ISF grant 2774/20. L. Kohl is funded by NWO Gravitation project QSC. N. Resch supported in part by ERC H2020 grant No.74079 (ALGSTRONGCRYPTO). P. Scholl is supported by the Danish Independent Research Council under project number 0165-00107B (C3PO) and an Aarhus University Research Foundation starting grant.

References

1. Agarwal, P., Narayanan, V., Pathak, S., Prabhakaran, M., Prabhakaran, V.M., Rehan, M.A.: Secure non-interactive reduction and spectral analysis of correlations. In: Dunkelman, O., Dziembowski, S. (eds.) Advances in Cryptology - EUROCRYPT 2022–41st Annual International Conference on the Theory and Applications of Cryptographic Techniques, Trondheim, Norway, May 30 - June 3, 2022, Proceedings, Part III. Lecture Notes in Computer Science, vol. 13277, pp. 797–827. Springer (2022). https://doi.org/10.1007/978-3-031-07082-2_28
2. Alekhnovich, M.: More on average case vs approximation complexity. In: 44th Symposium on Foundations of Computer Science (FOCS 2003), 11–14 October 2003, Cambridge, MA, USA, Proceedings, pp. 298–307. IEEE Computer Society (2003). https://doi.org/10.1109/SFCS.2003.1238204
3. Alon, B., Paskin-Cherniavsky, A.: On perfectly secure 2PC in the OT-hybrid model. Theor. Comput. Sci. **891**, 166–188 (2021). https://doi.org/10.1016/j.tcs.2021.08.035
4. Applebaum, B.: Pseudorandom generators with long stretch and low locality from random local one-way functions. In: 44th ACM STOC (May 2012)
5. Applebaum, B.: The cryptographic hardness of random local functions - survey. Cryptology ePrint Archive, Report 2015/165 (2015). https://eprint.iacr.org/2015/165
6. Applebaum, B.: Cryptographic hardness of random local functions. Comput. complex. **25**(3), 667–722 (2016)

7. Applebaum, B., Bogdanov, A., Rosen, A.: A dichotomy for local small-bias generators. Journal of Cryptology (3) (Jul 2016)
8. Applebaum, B., Damgård, I., Ishai, Y., Nielsen, M., Zichron, L.: Secure arithmetic computation with constant computational overhead. In: Katz, J., Shacham, H. (eds.) CRYPTO 2017. LNCS, vol. 10401, pp. 223–254. Springer, Cham (2017). https://doi.org/10.1007/978-3-319-63688-7_8
9. Applebaum, B., Haramaty, N., Ishai, Y., Kushilevitz, E., Vaikuntanathan, V.: Low-complexity cryptographic hash functions. In: ITCS 2017 (Jan 2017)
10. Applebaum, B., Ishai, Y., Kushilevitz, E.: Cryptography in NC^0. In: 45th FOCS (Oct 2004)
11. Applebaum, B., Kachlon, E.: Sampling graphs without forbidden subgraphs and unbalanced expanders with negligible error. In: Zuckerman, D. (ed.) 60th IEEE Annual Symposium on Foundations of Computer Science, FOCS 2019, Baltimore, Maryland, USA, November 9–12, 2019, pp. 171–179. IEEE Computer Society (2019). https://doi.org/10.1109/FOCS.2019.00020
12. Applebaum, B., Lovett, S.: Algebraic attacks against random local functions and their countermeasures. In: 48th ACM STOC (Jun 2016)
13. Applebaum, B., Moses, Y.: Locally computable uowhf with linear shrinkage. In: Johansson, T., Nguyen, P.Q. (eds.) EUROCRYPT 2013. LNCS, vol. 7881, pp. 486–502. Springer, Heidelberg (2013). https://doi.org/10.1007/978-3-642-38348-9_29
14. Arora, S., Ge, R.: New algorithms for learning in presence of errors. In: Aceto, L., Henzinger, M., Sgall, J. (eds.) ICALP 2011. LNCS, vol. 6755, pp. 403–415. Springer, Heidelberg (2011). https://doi.org/10.1007/978-3-642-22006-7_34
15. Asharov, G., Lindell, Y., Schneider, T., Zohner, M.: More efficient oblivious transfer extensions. J. Cryptol. 30(3), 805–858 (2016). https://doi.org/10.1007/s00145-016-9236-6
16. Augot, D., Finiasz, M., Sendrier, N.: A fast provably secure cryptographic hash function. Cryptology ePrint Archive, Report 2003/230 (2003). https://eprint.iacr.org/2003/230
17. Baron, J., Ishai, Y., Ostrovsky, R.: On linear-size pseudorandom generators and hardcore functions. Theor. Comput. Sci. 554, 50–63 (2014). https://doi.org/10.1016/j.tcs.2014.06.013
18. Beaver, D.: Foundations of secure interactive computing. In: Feigenbaum, J. (ed.) CRYPTO 1991. LNCS, vol. 576, pp. 377–391. Springer, Heidelberg (1992). https://doi.org/10.1007/3-540-46766-1_31
19. Beaver, D.: Correlated pseudorandomness and the complexity of private computations. In: Proceedings of the Twenty-Eighth Annual ACM Symposium on Theory of Computing, pp. 479–488 (1996)
20. Bogdanov, A., Qiao, Y.: On the security of Goldreich's one-way function. In: Dinur, I., Jansen, K., Naor, J., Rolim, J. (eds.) APPROX/RANDOM -2009. LNCS, vol. 5687, pp. 392–405. Springer, Heidelberg (2009). https://doi.org/10.1007/978-3-642-03685-9_30
21. Bogdanov, A., Sabin, M., Vasudevan, P.N.: Xor codes and sparse learning parity with noise. In: Proceedings of the Thirtieth Annual ACM-SIAM Symposium on Discrete Algorithms, pp. 986–1004. SIAM (2019)

22. Boneh, D., Ishai, Y., Sahai, A., Wu, D.J.: Quasi-optimal SNARGs via linear multi-prover interactive proofs. In: Nielsen, J.B., Rijmen, V. (eds.) EUROCRYPT 2018. LNCS, vol. 10822, pp. 222–255. Springer, Cham (2018). https://doi.org/10.1007/978-3-319-78372-7_8

23. Boneh, D., Waters, B.: Constrained Pseudorandom Functions and Their Applications. In: Sako, K., Sarkar, P. (eds.) ASIACRYPT 2013. LNCS, vol. 8270, pp. 280–300. Springer, Heidelberg (2013). https://doi.org/10.1007/978-3-642-42045-0_15

24. Bootle, J., Cerulli, A., Ghadafi, E., Groth, J., Hajiabadi, M., Jakobsen, S.K.: Linear-time zero-knowledge proofs for arithmetic circuit satisfiability. In: Takagi, T., Peyrin, T. (eds.) ASIACRYPT 2017. LNCS, vol. 10626, pp. 336–365. Springer, Cham (2017). https://doi.org/10.1007/978-3-319-70700-6_12

25. Boyle, E., Couteau, G., Gilboa, N., Ishai, Y.: Compressing vector OLE. In: ACM CCS 2018 (Oct 2018)

26. Boyle, E., Couteau, G., Gilboa, N., Ishai, Y., Kohl, L., Resch, N., Scholl, P.: Correlated pseudorandomness from expand-accumulate codes. In: Advances in Cryptology - CRYPTO 2022 (2022). https://eprint.iacr.org/2022/1014

27. Boyle, E., et al.: Efficient two-round OT extension and silent non-interactive secure computation. In: ACM CCS 2019 (Nov 2019)

28. Boyle, E., Couteau, G., Gilboa, N., Ishai, Y., Kohl, L., Scholl, P.: Efficient pseudorandom correlation generators: silent OT extension and more. In: Boldyreva, A., Micciancio, D. (eds.) CRYPTO 2019. LNCS, vol. 11694, pp. 489–518. Springer, Cham (2019). https://doi.org/10.1007/978-3-030-26954-8_16

29. Boyle, E., Couteau, G., Gilboa, N., Ishai, Y., Kohl, L., Scholl, P.: Correlated pseudorandom functions from variable-density LPN. In: 61st FOCS (Nov 2020)

30. Boyle, E., Couteau, G., Gilboa, N., Ishai, Y., Orrù, M.: Homomorphic secret sharing: Optimizations and applications. In: ACM CCS 2017 (Oct / Nov 2017)

31. Boyle, E., Gilboa, N., Ishai, Y.: Function secret sharing. In: Oswald, E., Fischlin, M. (eds.) EUROCRYPT 2015. LNCS, vol. 9057, pp. 337–367. Springer, Heidelberg (2015). https://doi.org/10.1007/978-3-662-46803-6_12

32. Boyle, E., Gilboa, N., Ishai, Y.: Function secret sharing: Improvements and extensions. In: ACM CCS 2016 (Oct 2016)

33. Boyle, E., Goldwasser, S., Ivan, I.: Functional signatures and pseudorandom functions. In: Krawczyk, H. (ed.) PKC 2014. LNCS, vol. 8383, pp. 501–519. Springer, Heidelberg (2014). https://doi.org/10.1007/978-3-642-54631-0_29

34. Brassard, G., Crépeau, C., Robert, J.: Information theoretic reductions among disclosure problems. In: 27th Annual Symposium on Foundations of Computer Science, Toronto, Canada, 27–29 October 1986, pp. 168–173. IEEE Computer Society (1986). https://doi.org/10.1109/SFCS.1986.26

35. Canetti, R.: Security and composition of multiparty cryptographic protocols. J. Cryptol. **13**(1), 143–202 (2000). https://doi.org/10.1007/s001459910006

36. de Castro, L., Hazay, C., Ishai, Y., Vaikuntanathan, V., Venkitasubramaniam, M.: Asymptotically quasi-optimal cryptography. In: Dunkelman, O., Dziembowski, S. (eds.) Advances in Cryptology - EUROCRYPT 2022–41st Annual International Conference on the Theory and Applications of Cryptographic Techniques, Trondheim, Norway, May 30 - June 3, 2022, Proceedings, Part I. Lecture Notes in Computer Science, vol. 13275, pp. 303–334. Springer (2022). https://doi.org/10.1007/978-3-031-06944-4_11

37. Chen, L., Li, J., Yang, T.: Extremely Efficient Constructions of Hash Functions, with Applications to Hardness Magnification and PRFs. In: Lovett, S. (ed.) 37th Computational Complexity Conference (CCC 2022). Leibniz International Proceedings in Informatics (LIPIcs), vol. 234, pp. 23:1–23:37. Schloss Dagstuhl - Leibniz-Zentrum für Informatik, Dagstuhl, Germany (2022). https://doi.org/10.4230/LIPIcs.CCC.2022.23, https://drops.dagstuhl.de/opus/volltexte/2022/16585

38. Cook, J., Etesami, O., Miller, R., Trevisan, L.: On the one-way function candidate proposed by goldreich. ACM Trans. Comput. Theor. (TOCT) 6(3), 14 (2014)

39. Couteau, G., Dupin, A., Méaux, P., Rossi, M., Rotella, Y.: On the concrete security of Goldreich's pseudorandom generator. In: ASIACRYPT 2018, Part II (Dec 2018)

40. Couteau, G., Rindal, P., Raghuraman, S.: Silver: silent VOLE and oblivious transfer from hardness of decoding structured LDPC codes. In: Malkin, T., Peikert, C. (eds.) CRYPTO 2021. LNCS, vol. 12827, pp. 502–534. Springer, Cham (2021). https://doi.org/10.1007/978-3-030-84252-9_17

41. Damgård, I., Ishai, Y., Krøigaard, M.: Perfectly secure multiparty computation and the computational overhead of cryptography. In: Gilbert, H. (ed.) EUROCRYPT 2010. LNCS, vol. 6110, pp. 445–465. Springer, Heidelberg (2010). https://doi.org/10.1007/978-3-642-13190-5_23

42. Fan, Z., Li, J., Yang, T.: The exact complexity of pseudorandom functions and the black-box natural proof barrier for bootstrapping results in computational complexity. In: Leonardi, S., Gupta, A. (eds.) STOC '22: 54th Annual ACM SIGACT Symposium on Theory of Computing, Rome, Italy, June 20–24, 2022, pp. 962–975. ACM (2022). https://doi.org/10.1145/3519935.3520010

43. Genkin, D., Ishai, Y., Prabhakaran, M., Sahai, A., Tromer, E.: Circuits resilient to additive attacks with applications to secure computation. In: 46th ACM STOC (May / Jun 2014)

44. Genkin, D., Ishai, Y., Weiss, M.: Binary AMD circuits from secure multiparty computation. In: Hirt, M., Smith, A. (eds.) TCC 2016. LNCS, vol. 9985, pp. 336–366. Springer, Heidelberg (2016). https://doi.org/10.1007/978-3-662-53641-4_14

45. Gilboa, N., Ishai, Y.: Distributed point functions and their applications. In: Nguyen, P.Q., Oswald, E. (eds.) EUROCRYPT 2014. LNCS, vol. 8441, pp. 640–658. Springer, Heidelberg (2014). https://doi.org/10.1007/978-3-642-55220-5_35

46. Goldreich, O.: Candidate one-way functions based on expander graphs. Cryptology ePrint Archive, Report 2000/063 (2000), https://eprint.iacr.org/2000/063

47. Goldreich, O.: Foundations of cryptography: volume 2, basic applications. Cambridge University Press (2009)

48. Goldreich, O., Micali, S., Wigderson, A.: How to play any mental game or A completeness theorem for protocols with honest majority. In: Aho, A.V. (ed.) Proceedings of the 19th Annual ACM Symposium on Theory of Computing, 1987, New York, New York, USA. pp. 218–229. ACM (1987). https://doi.org/10.1145/28395.28420

49. Hazay, C., Orsini, E., Scholl, P., Soria-Vazquez, E.: TinyKeys: a new approach to efficient multi-party computation. In: Shacham, H., Boldyreva, A. (eds.) CRYPTO 2018. LNCS, vol. 10993, pp. 3–33. Springer, Cham (2018). https://doi.org/10.1007/978-3-319-96878-0_1

50. Ishai, Y., Kilian, J., Nissim, K., Petrank, E.: Extending oblivious transfers efficiently. In: Boneh, D. (ed.) CRYPTO 2003. LNCS, vol. 2729, pp. 145–161. Springer, Heidelberg (2003). https://doi.org/10.1007/978-3-540-45146-4_9

51. Ishai, Y., Kushilevitz, E., Meldgaard, S., Orlandi, C., Paskin-Cherniavsky, A.: On the power of correlated randomness in secure computation. In: Sahai, A. (ed.) TCC

2013. LNCS, vol. 7785, pp. 600–620. Springer, Heidelberg (2013). https://doi.org/10.1007/978-3-642-36594-2_34

52. Ishai, Y., Kushilevitz, E., Ostrovsky, R., Sahai, A.: Cryptography with constant computational overhead. In: 40th ACM STOC (May 2008)

53. Ishai, Y., Kushilevitz, E., Ostrovsky, R., Sahai, A.: Extracting correlations. In: 50th Annual IEEE Symposium on Foundations of Computer Science, FOCS 2009, October 25–27, 2009, Atlanta, Georgia, USA. pp. 261–270. IEEE Computer Society (2009). https://doi.org/10.1109/FOCS.2009.56

54. Ishai, Y., Prabhakaran, M., Sahai, A.: Founding cryptography on oblivious transfer – efficiently. In: Wagner, D. (ed.) CRYPTO 2008. LNCS, vol. 5157, pp. 572–591. Springer, Heidelberg (2008). https://doi.org/10.1007/978-3-540-85174-5_32

55. Justin Holmgren, R.R.: Faster sounder succinct arguments and iops. In: Crypto 2022 (2022). https://doi.org/10.1007/978-3-031-15802-5_17

56. Keller, M., Orsini, E., Scholl, P.: Actively secure OT extension with optimal overhead. In: Gennaro, R., Robshaw, M. (eds.) CRYPTO 2015. LNCS, vol. 9215, pp. 724–741. Springer, Heidelberg (2015). https://doi.org/10.1007/978-3-662-47989-6_35

57. Khorasgani, H.A., Maji, H.K., Nguyen, H.H.: Secure non-interactive simulation: Feasibility and rate. In: Dunkelman, O., Dziembowski, S. (eds.) Advances in Cryptology - EUROCRYPT 2022–41st International Conference on the Theory and Applications of Cryptographic Techniques, Trondheim, Norway, May 30 - June 3, 2022, Proceedings, Part III. Lecture Notes in Computer Science, vol. 13277, pp. 767–796. Springer (2022). https://doi.org/10.1007/978-3-031-07082-2_27

58. Kiayias, A., Papadopoulos, S., Triandopoulos, N., Zacharias, T.: Delegatable pseudorandom functions and applications. In: ACM CCS 2013 (Nov 2013)

59. Kilian, J.: Founding cryptography on oblivious transfer. In: Simon, J. (ed.) Proceedings of the 20th Annual ACM Symposium on Theory of Computing, May 2–4, 1988, Chicago, Illinois, USA, pp. 20–31. ACM (1988). https://doi.org/10.1145/62212.62215

60. Kliewer, J., Zigangirov, K.S., Costello Jr, D.J.: New results on the minimum distance of repeat multiple accumulate codes. In: Proceedings 45th Annual Allerton Conf. Commun., Control, and Computing (2007)

61. Lombardi, A., Vaikuntanathan, V.: Limits on the locality of pseudorandom generators and applications to indistinguishability obfuscation. In: Kalai, Y., Reyzin, L. (eds.) TCC 2017. LNCS, vol. 10677, pp. 119–137. Springer, Cham (2017). https://doi.org/10.1007/978-3-319-70500-2_5

62. Mossel, E., Shpilka, A., Trevisan, L.: On e-biased generators in NC0. In: 44th FOCS (Oct 2003)

63. ODonnell, R., Witmer, D.: Goldreich's prg: evidence for near-optimal polynomial stretch. In: Computational Complexity (CCC), 2014 IEEE 29th Conference on, pp. 1–12. IEEE (2014)

64. Ron-Zewi, N., Rothblum, R.D.: Proving as fast as computing: succinct arguments with constant prover overhead. In: Leonardi, S., Gupta, A. (eds.) STOC '22: 54th Annual ACM SIGACT Symposium on Theory of Computing, Rome, Italy, June 20–24, 2022, pp. 1353–1363. ACM (2022). https://doi.org/10.1145/3519935.3519956

65. Roy, L.: Softspokenot: Communication-computation tradeoffs in OT extension. In: Crypto 2022 (2022)
66. Schoppmann, P., Gascón, A., Reichert, L., Raykova, M.: Distributed vector-OLE: Improved constructions and implementation. In: ACM CCS 2019 (Nov 2019)
67. Spielman, D.A.: Linear-time encodable and decodable error-correcting codes. In: Leighton, F.T., Borodin, A. (eds.) Proceedings of the Twenty-Seventh Annual ACM Symposium on Theory of Computing, 29 May-1 June 1995, Las Vegas, Nevada, USA. pp. 388–397. ACM (1995). https://doi.org/10.1145/225058.225165
68. Tillich, J.P., Zémor, G.: On the minimum distance of structured ldpc codes with two variable nodes of degree 2 per parity-check equation. In: 2006 IEEE International Symposium on Information Theory, pp. 1549–1553. IEEE (2006)
69. Yang, K., Weng, C., Lan, X., Zhang, J., Wang, X.: Ferret: Fast extension for correlated OT with small communication. In: ACM CCS 2020 (Nov 2020)

Endemic Oblivious Transfer via Random Oracles, Revisited

Zhelei Zhou[1,2], Bingsheng Zhang[1,2(✉)], Hong-Sheng Zhou[3(✉)], and Kui Ren[1,2]

[1] Zhejiang University, Hangzhou, China
{zl_zhou,bingsheng,kuiren}@zju.edu.cn
[2] ZJU-Hangzhou Global Scientific and Technological Innovation Center,
Hangzhou, China
[3] Virginia Commonwealth University, Richmond, USA
hszhou@vcu.edu

Abstract. The notion of Endemic Oblivious Transfer (EOT) was introduced by Masny and Rindal (CCS'19). EOT offers a weaker security guarantee than the conventional random OT; namely, the malicious parties can fix their outputs arbitrarily. The authors presented a 1-round UC-secure EOT protocol under a tailor-made and non-standard assumption, Choose-and-Open DDH, in the RO model.

In this work, we systematically study EOT in the UC/GUC framework. We present a new 1-round UC-secure EOT construction in the RO model under the DDH assumption. Under the GUC framework, we propose the first 1-round EOT construction under the CDH assumption in the Global Restricted Observable RO (GroRO) model proposed by Canetti *et al.* (CCS'14). We also provide an impossibility result, showing there exist *no* 1-round GUC-secure EOT protocols in the Global Restricted Programmable RO (GrpRO) model proposed by Camenisch *et al.* (Eurocrypt'18). Subsequently, we provide the first round-optimal (2-round) EOT protocol with adaptive security under the DDH assumption in the GrpRO model. Finally, we investigate the relations between EOT and other cryptographic primitives.

As side products, we present the first 2-round GUC-secure commitment in the GroRO model as well as a separation between the GroRO and the GrpRO models, which may be of independent interest.

1 Introduction

The security of a cryptographic protocol is typically analyzed under the simulation paradigm [27], where the "formal specification" of the security requirements is modeled as an ideal process, and a real-world protocol is said to securely realize

Z. Zhou and B. Zhang—Work supported by the National Key R&D Program of China (No. 2021YFB3101601), the National Natural Science Foundation of China (Grant No. 62072401), "Open Project Program of Key Laboratory of Blockchain and Cyberspace Governance of Zhejiang Province", and Input Output (iohk.io).
H.-S. Zhou—Work supported in part by NSF grant CNS-1801470, and a Google Faculty Research Award.

C. Hazay and M. Stam (Eds.): EUROCRYPT 2023, LNCS 14004, pp. 303–329, 2023.
https://doi.org/10.1007/978-3-031-30545-0_11

the specification if it "emulates" the ideal process. In the past decades, many variants were proposed: Initially, protocol security was considered in the *standalone* setting, in the sense that the challenged protocol is executed in isolation. Later, *Universal Composibility* (UC) [6] was introduced to analyze protocol security in arbitrary execution environments; in particular, multiple protocol sessions may be executed concurrently in an adversarially coordinated way. Note that protocols in the UC framework must be *subroutine respecting*, in the sense that all the underlying subroutines are only created for the challenged protocol instance and cannot be directly accessed by any other protocols or even the other instances of the same protocol. To address this drawback, Canetti *et al.* [7] proposed the Generalized Universal Composibility (GUC) framework.

Endemic Oblivious Transfer. The notion of *Endemic Oblivious Transfer* (EOT) was introduced by Masny and Rindal [34] as a weaker version of Random OT (ROT). In an EOT protocol, the sender has no input, and the receiver inputs a choice bit $b \in \{0, 1\}$; at the end of EOT, the sender outputs two random elements (m_0, m_1), and the receiver outputs m_b. Although EOT looks similar to the conventional ROT, EOT offers a weaker security guarantee—the malicious sender can fix its output (m_0, m_1) arbitrarily, and the malicious receiver can fix its output m_b arbitrarily. The first 1-round[1] (a.k.a. non-interactive) EOT/ROT protocol was proposed by Bellare and Micali [1]. It achieves standalone security against semi-honest adversaries under the DDH assumption in the Common Reference String (CRS) model. As shown in [25], this scheme can also be transformed to achieve malicious security using the Groth-Sahai proof [28]. Later, Garg *et al.* proposed several 1-round UC-secure EOT protocols under the well-understood assumptions, (e.g., Decisional Diffie-Hellman (DDH), Quadratic Residuosity (QR) and Learning With Errors (LWE)), in the CRS model [23]. Recently, Masny and Rindal [34] demonstrated a generic construction for 1-round EOT by using any non-interactive key exchange scheme in the Random Oracle (RO) model; however, their generic construction only achieves standalone security. Masny and Rindal [34,35] then provided a 1-round *UC-secure* EOT protocol but under a tailor-made computational assumption called "*Choose-and-Open DDH* (CODDH)", in the RO model. We remark that, different from the DDH, the CODDH is a new assumption, and its hardness is yet to be further studied.

(Global) Random Oracles. Random oracle (RO) model [2] is a popular idealized setup model that has been widely used to justify the security of efficient cryptographic protocols. In spite of its known inability to provide provable guarantees when RO is instantiated with a real-world hash function [8], RO is still a promising setup since it is generally accepted that security analysis in the RO model does provide strong evidences to the resilience of the protocol in

---

[1] In this work, we consider the simultaneous communication model with a rushing adversary, where both parties can send messages to each other within the same round. The rushing adversary can delay sending messages on behalf of corrupted parties in a given round until the messages sent by all the uncorrupted parties in that round have been received. Note that this is different from the simultaneous messaging requirement in [30], which deals with a non-rushing adversary.

question in the presence of practical attacks [9]. In fact, RO model draws increasing attention along with recent advancement of the blockchain technology.

Local RO Model vs. Global RO Models. The "local" RO model is often used in the UC framework where the simulator is allowed to simulate it in the ideal world, and it grants the simulator two advantages: (i) observability: the simulator can see what values the parties query the RO on; (ii) programability: the simulator can program RO query responses as long as they "look" indistinguishable from the real ones. In the GUC framework [7], a "global" RO is external to the simulator; to facilitate simulation, some "extra power" needs to be granted to the simulator. In the literature, two main strengthened variants of the global RO model were proposed: global RO with restricted observability (GroRO) model proposed by Canetti *et al.* [9] and global RO with restricted programmability (GrpRO) model proposed by Camenisch *et al.* [5]. Here, the restricted observability and programmability stand for the "extra power" that the simulator has but the adversary does not have.

1.1 Problem Statement

Constructing EOT in (Global) RO Models. As mentioned above, it is known that one can build a 1-round UC-secure EOT protocol under the well-known assumptions in the local CRS model [23]; however, in the local RO model, the recent construction by Masny and Rindal [34,35] was based on a *non-standard* assumption i.e., the CODDH assumption. A natural question to ask is: can we construct a 1-round UC-secure EOT protocol under well-understood assumptions (e.g., DDH assumption) in the local RO model?

Compared to local setups (e.g., local CRS and local RO), global setups are more practical in real life applications. However, very little research work has been done for constructing EOT protocols under a global setup. Our main goal here is to construct a 1-round EOT protocol using global setups. We emphasize that local setups are helpful for us to construct a provably secure 1-round EOT protocol. For example, in the local CRS model, both parties can utilize the shared string, i.e., the CRS, to generate the correlated information for the remaining protocol execution. In other words, *the CRS can be viewed as an extra round of communication messages* during the protocol execution. Intuitively, the security analysis can go through: the simulator is allowed to generate the CRS along with the trapdoor; then the trapdoor information will help the simulator to complete the simulation. In the local RO model, the situation is similar: in the protocol execution, the protocol players may query the RO at certain predefined points to obtain corresponding responses; in a very fuzzy way, it also can be viewed as an extra round of communication messages. In the security analysis, the simulator is allowed to program the RO on those predefined points; this gives the simulator advantages over the adversary which will help the simulator to complete the simulation.

The situation is very different when we use a **global** setup for constructing 1-round EOT protocols. First, we remark that, as already proven in [7], it is impossible to construct a non-trivial two-party computation protocols (including EOT) using a global CRS. To bypass this impossibility, Canetti *et al.* proposed the Augmented CRS (ACRS) model [7]; however, known technique of building non-trivial two-party computation protocols in the ACRS model requires coin-flipping [7,18], which increases round complexity. The good news is that it might be possible to construct a 1-round EOT protocol using a global RO model; note that, different global RO models (e.g., the GroRO [9] and the GrpRO [5]) have been introduced for constructing non-trivial two-party computation protocols. We must remark that, technical difficulty remains. Typically, a global RO is instantiated with a predefined hash function. It seems that the aforementioned design and analysis ideas using local ROs still work: both parties may still be able to utilize the shared hash function on some predefined points to generate the corresponding responses for the remaining protocol execution; unfortunately, it is not true. Below, we provide our elaboration: (1) in the GroRO model, the simulator is not allowed to program the global RO and thus cannot obtain the "trapdoor" of the corresponding responses; as a result, it is unclear how we will be able to complete the security analysis; (2) in the GrpRO model, the simulator is only allowed to program the unqueried points, and the simulator may not be able to program the global RO on those predefined points since the environment may have already queried them before the protocol execution. Given the technical difficulty, we ask the following major research question:

> *In the GUC framework, does there exist a 1-round EOT protocol under well-understood assumptions in the GroRO/GrpRO model?*

For completeness, we also construct new 1-round UC-secure EOT protocols in the local RO model.

Understanding the Complexity of EOT. In addition to the concrete protocol constructions, we are also interested in understanding the complexity, including the power and the limits, of the cryptographic task of EOT. More precisely, what are the relations between EOT and other well-known secure computation tasks? For example, is EOT fundamentally different from ROT or (1-out-of-2) OT? In [34], Masny and Rindal have already initialized the investigation of this interesting problem: They proposed a new OT notion called Uniform OT (UOT) which also looks similar to the conventional ROT, except that it offers a strong security guarantee that no adversary can bias the distribution of the ROT outputs. They showed that it is possible to build UOT based on an EOT and a coin-tossing protocol; however, it is unclear if the coin-tossing protocol can be built from an EOT protocol. We thus ask the following question:

> *What is the relation between the EOT and other cryptographic primitives (such as coin-tossing and UOT etc.)?*

Understanding the Complexity of Global RO Models. Finally, let us go back to the global setups we used in this work. Recall that, the GroRO and the GrpRO models provide different aspects of "extra power" to the simulator. Are these two different global RO models, essentially equivalent? Or one is strictly stronger than the other? It raises our last question:

What is the relation between the GroRO model and the GrpRO model?

Our goal is to provide a comprehensive and thorough investigation of constructing EOT via ROs. From a practical point of view, if the above questions could be answered, we would see highly efficient constructions for EOT. From a theoretical point of view, if (some of) the above questions could be answered, we would have a better understanding of the relation between EOT and many secure computation tasks; we could also have a better understanding of the power and limits of different global RO models.

1.2   Our Results

In this work, we investigate the above problems. Our results can be summarized as follows.

Constructing EOT via (Global) ROs. Table 1 depicts a selection of our new constructions.

Table 1. Comparison with state-of-the-art round-optimal EOT protocols under computational assumptions that related to the cyclic groups.

Protocol	#Round	Security	Computational Assumption	Setup Assumption
Garg *et al.* [23, 24][a]	1	UC+Static	DDH	CRS
Masny and Rindal [34, 35]	1	UC+Static	CODDH [b]	RO
Canetti *et al.* [11]	1	UC+Adaptive	DDH	GrpRO+CRS
$\Pi_{\text{EOT-RO}}$ (Sect. 3)	1	UC+Static	DDH	RO
$\Pi_{\text{EOT-GroRO}}$ (Sect. 5.1)[c]	1	GUC+Static	CDH	GroRO
$\Pi_{\text{EOT-GrpRO}}$ (Sect. 5.2)[d]	2	GUC+Adaptive	DDH	GrpRO

[a] Garg et al's constructions can be instantiated from different assumptions (e.g., DDH, LWE and QR); but in this table, we focus on constructions using (cyclic) group based assumptions.

[b] Here, CODDH refers to the "Choose-and-Open DDH" assumption which is not known to be reducible to the DDH assumption.

[c] Although protocol $\Pi_{\text{EOT-GroRO}}$ uses a weaker computational assumption and a less idealized setup than protocol $\Pi_{\text{EOT-RO}}$ does, the former is less efficient than the latter.

[d] This construction is round-optimal due to Theorem 5, below.

Next, we provide the technical overview for our EOT protocol constructions in the (global) RO models. We first show how to construct a 1-round UC-secure EOT protocol under DDH assumption in the RO model against static adversaries. After that, we turn to the global RO models and show how to construct a 1-round GUC-secure EOT protocol under CDH assumption in the GroRO model. Note that, the situation in the GrpRO model is complicated: We find that there exists no 1-round GUC-secure EOT protocols in the GrpRO model even with static security, and we give a round-optimal (2-round) EOT protocol under DDH assumption against adaptive adversaries.

New Technique: 1-round UC-secure EOT Protocol in the RO Model. We present a new technique that enables the first UC-secure 1-round EOT protocol in the RO model under the DDH assumption (cf. Sect. 3). The basic scheme achieves static security. Intuitively, our technique is as follows. We start with the two-round standalone ROT/EOT protocol in the RO model proposed in [13]. In the 1st round, the sender sends $h := g^s$ to the receiver; in the 2nd round, the receiver uses sender's message to compute $B := g^r h^b$ and sends B back, where $b \in \{0, 1\}$ is the choice bit; finally, the sender outputs $m_0 := \text{Hash}(B^s)$ and $m_1 := \text{Hash}((\frac{B}{h})^s)$, where Hash is a predefined hash function and it is modeled as a RO; the receiver outputs $m_b := \text{Hash}(h^r)$. Although this protocol is simple and efficient, it cannot achieve UC security [26, 33].

Our technique is presented as follows. The dependence of the sender's message in [13] can be eliminated such that the receiver's message can be produced simultaneously in the same round. The idea is to let the receiver produce the commitment key h instead of waiting it from the sender. How to generate a random group element and be oblivious to its discrete logarithm? This can be achieved by setting $h := \text{Hash}(\text{seed})$, where seed is some randomly sampled string. Similar technique can be found in [11]. Now the 1-round (non-interactive) version of [13] roughly works as follows. The sender sends $z := g^s$ to the receiver; meanwhile, the receiver picks $h := \text{Hash}(\text{seed})$ and computes $B := g^r h^b$, and then it sends (seed, B) to the sender; finally, the sender computes $h := \text{Hash}(\text{seed})$ and outputs $m_0 := \text{Hash}(B^s)$ and $m_1 := \text{Hash}((\frac{B}{h})^s)$; the receiver outputs $m_b := \text{Hash}(z^r)$.

Further, to make the protocol UC-secure, certain *extractability* is needed: (i) when the sender is malicious, the simulator should be able to extract the sender's private randomness s, so the simulator can compute both m_0 and m_1; (ii) when the receiver is malicious, the simulator should be able to extract the receiver's choice bit. In order to extract the sender's s, we let the sender additionally generate a RO-based straight-line extractable NIZK argument [22, 32, 38]. In order to extract the receiver's choice bit b, we let the receiver computes the ElGamal encryption of b instead of the Pedersen commitment. We then let the receiver additionally generate a NIZK argument to ensure the correctness of the ElGamal encryption. Note that, we do not need the straight-line extractability here, since the simulator can program the RO to obtain $\log_g h$ and thus be able to decrypt the ElGamal ciphertext to extract b.

1-round GUC-secure EOT Protocol in the GroRO Model. Turning to the GUC setting, we propose the first 1-round EOT construction under the CDH assumption in the GroRO model (cf. Sect. 5.1). Compared to our UC-secure construction, this one requires *weaker* a computational assumption.

Recall that, in our UC-secure EOT protocol, we let the sender send $z := g^s$ together with a straight-line extractable NIZK argument. The straight-line extractable NIZK argument gives the simulator the ability to extract s. However,

Pass showed that it is impossible to construct NIZK arguments in observable RO model [38], let alone NIZK arguments with straight-line extractability. The good news is that straight-line extractable NIWH argument is sufficient for our purpose, and it exists in the GroRO model [38]. Therefore, we let the sender generate a straight-line extractable NIWH argument of s such that $z = g^s$ instead. Next, to extract the receiver's choice bit, our UC-secure construction utilizes the programmability of RO; however, $\mathcal{G}_{roRO}$ does not offer programability, so a different approach shall be taken. In particular, we let the receiver compute a Pedersen commitment to the choice bit $B := g^r h^b$, and generate a straight-line extractable NIWH argument of (r, b) such that $B = g^r h^b$. Analogously to the sender side, the straight-line extractable NIWH argument gives the simulator extractability.

Understanding the Power/Limits of Different Global ROs. Here we discuss the feasibility result and impossible result in the GrpRO model. In addition to that, we also reveal a separation between the GroRO and the GrpRO model.

A Separation Between the GroRO Model and the GrpRO Model. To show this separation, we first give a new impossibility result, showing that there exists *no* 1-round GUC-secure EOT protocol in the GrpRO model even with static security (cf. Sect. 5.2). By combining this negative result in the GrpRO model and the aforementioned positive result in the GroRO model, we demonstrate a separation between the GroRO model and the GrpRO model. More precisely, let $\mathcal{G}_{roRO}, \mathcal{G}_{rpRO}$ be the functionalities of the GroRO and the GrpRO model, we present the relation of these global RO models in Fig. 1.

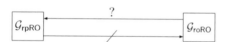

Fig. 1. The relation between the $\mathcal{G}_{roRO}$ model and the $\mathcal{G}_{rpRO}$ model. Here, "A $\nrightarrow$ B" denotes that A does not imply B. In addition, "A $\overset{?}{\rightarrow}$ B" denotes that whether A implies B remains unknown.

New Impossibility Results in the GrpRO Model. Here we will present more details about the aforementioned impossibility result in the GrpRO model. The impossibility is proven by contradiction (cf. Sect. 5.2). Suppose that there exists such a 1-round GUC-secure EOT protocol in the GrpRO model. Let us first consider the case where the receiver is corrupted, and the simulator needs to extract the choice bit of the receiver from its message. Recall that, the GrpRO only grants the simulator the restricted programmability: the simulator can program the unqueried points without being detected. More importantly, unlike local RO, the simulator cannot program a global RO on the fly, as it cannot see which point is queried at this moment. Thus, the simulator needs to find a way to enforce the corrupt receiver to query the simulator's programmed points. However, in a one simultaneous round protocol, the messages between parties have no dependency. Hence the simulator cannot enforce the corrupt receiver to produce its message on the programmed points, and has no advantages. If the simulator still succeeds to extract the corrupted receiver's choice bit, then we have the following attack. The adversary corrupts the sender, and instructs the sender to run the simulator algorithm above to extract the choice bit from the message sent by the receiver/simulator. However, the simulator has no idea about the real choice bit, thus with $1/2$ probability the simulation would fail.

New Feasibility: Round-Optimal GUC-secure EOT Protocol in the GrpRO Model.
To complete the picture, we also give a round-optimal (2-round) EOT protocol with adaptive security under the DDH assumption in the GrpRO model (cf. Sect. 5.2). Here, we do not consider simultaneous messaging in the same round. Our intuition comes from the UC-secure EOT protocol in the CRS+GrpRO model proposed by Canetti *et al.* [11]. In their protocol, the CRS consists of two group elements $g, h \in \mathbb{G}$, and the simulator knows $\log_g h$. The sender computes $z := g^r h^s$, while the receiver generates $(G, H) := \mathsf{Hash}(\mathsf{seed})$ and computes two Pedersen commitments to the choice bit using two sets of the parameter, i.e., (g, G) and (h, H), and the same randomness.

To eliminate the CRS, we let the sender generate the first set of the parameter $(g, h) := \mathsf{Hash}(\mathsf{seed}_1)$ where seed_1 is an uniformly sampled string. At the same time, the sender computes $z := g^r h^s$ using random $r, s \leftarrow \mathbb{Z}_q$ and sends seed, z to the receiver in the first round. In the second round, the receiver first checks if seed_1 is a programmed point. If not, the receiver generates the second set of the parameter $(G, H) := \mathsf{Hash}(\mathsf{seed}_2)$ where seed_2 is an uniformly sampled string. Then the receiver can compute two Pedersen commitments to the choice bit, i.e., $(B_1, B_2) := (g^x G^b, h^x H^b)$ using random $x \leftarrow \mathbb{Z}_q$. Finally, we let the receiver send $(\mathsf{seed}_2, B_1, B_2)$ to the sender. How to make the protocol simulatable in the GrpRO model? We show the simulation strategy as follows: when the receiver is malicious (and the sender is honest), the simulator can extract the receiver's choice bit b by programming the GrpRO (the simulator always succeeds to program the GrpRO since seed_1 is sampled by the honest sender itself) and knowing α such that $h = g^\alpha$; when the sender is malicious (and the receiver is honest), the simulator can compute both m_0 and m_1 by programming the GrpRO (the simulator always succeeds to program the GrpRO since seed_2 is sampled by the honest receiver itself) such that (g, h, G, H) is a DDH tuple.

Understanding the Relation Between EOT and Other Cryptographic Primitives.

Here we discuss the complexity of EOT. Our results can be summarized as follows.

EOT Implies UOT and Commitment. In [34], the authors showed that UOT implies EOT. But the work on the opposite direction is incomplete. Let $\mathcal{F}_{\mathsf{EOT}}$, $\mathcal{F}_{\mathsf{UOT}}$ and $\mathcal{F}_{\mathsf{Coin}}$ be the ideal functionalities of EOT, UOT and coin-tossing protocol, respectively. They showed that a UOT protocol can be constructed in the $\{\mathcal{F}_{\mathsf{EOT}}, \mathcal{F}_{\mathsf{Coin}}\}$-hybrid world with unconditional security, and they constructed $\mathcal{F}_{\mathsf{Coin}}$ via only $\mathcal{F}_{\mathsf{UOT}}$. However, it remains unclear whether $\mathcal{F}_{\mathsf{Coin}}$ can be constructed via only $\mathcal{F}_{\mathsf{EOT}}$; therefore, it is still an open question on whether EOT implies UOT? We present the relations that they claimed in Fig. 2(a).

Recall that, Brzuska *et al.* proved that bit commitment can be constructed via 1-out-of-2 OT with unconditional security [3]. What about EOT? Nevertheless, surprisingly, we show that bit commitment can be constructed via a weaker primitive, i.e., EOT with unconditional security (cf. Sect. 4.1).

Our key observation is that the receiver's message can be viewed as the commitment to the choice bit b, and the locally computed message m_b together with b can be viewed as the opening. Typically, a commitment protocol requires both hiding and binding properties. The hiding property holds since the malicious receiver in the EOT cannot learn m_{1-b}, even if it can influence the distribution of m_b. The binding property holds since the malicious sender in the EOT cannot know which message is received by the receiver, even if it can influence the distributions of both m_0 and m_1.

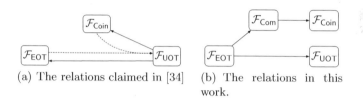

(a) The relations claimed in [34]   (b) The relations in this work.

Fig. 2. The relations between EOT and other primitives. "A → B" denotes that A implies B. "A --→ B" denotes that A can be transformed into B.

Since it is well-known how to construct $\mathcal{F}_{\mathsf{Coin}}$ via only $\mathcal{F}_{\mathsf{Com}}$, where $\mathcal{F}_{\mathsf{Com}}$ is the commitment functionality, we show that EOT implies UOT and completes the relation between EOT and UOT (cf. Sect. 4.2). We present the relations that explored in this work in Fig. 2(b).

Furthermore, as a side product, we present the first 2-round GUC-secure commitment in the GroRO model (cf. Sect. 5.1), which may be of independent interest. The previous state-of-the-art protocols need 3 rounds [36,42]. Note that this result does not contradict Zhou *et al.*'s impossibility result [42], as their work did not consider simultaneous communication model.

1.3 Related Work

In this work, we mainly focus on the EOT (and OT) protocols in the different variants of RO models, i.e. the local RO model, the GroRO model and the GrpRO model. The EOT (and OT) results in the CRS model can be found in the full version of this paper [41].

In terms of the local RO model, Chou and Orlandi proposed a 3-round OT protocol called "the simplest OT protocol" [13]. This protocol and the protocol in [29] have been found to suffer from a number of issues [4,26,33] and are not UC-secure. In the following, Masny and Rindal showed how to construct EOT protocols from the key exchange schemes in the local RO model [34]. In particular, they provided a 1-round UC-secure construction under a non-standard assumption, i.e., Choose-and-Open DDH (CODDH) assumption [34,35].

Regarding the GroRO model, Canetti *et al.* proposed a 2-round OT protocol under DDH assumption [9], but their protocol is only one-sided GUC-simulatable. Later, fully GUC-secure OT protocols in the GroRO model are proposed [16,19]. Their protocols only need CDH assumption but require no less than 5 rounds of communication. To achieve round-optimal, Canetti *et al.* proposed a 2-round GUC-secure OT protocol in the GroRO model [11], but their protocol requires a stronger assumption, i.e., DDH assumption.

As for the GrpRO model, Canetti *et al.* proposed an adaptive-secure 1-round EOT protocol in the GrpRO+CRS hybrid model [11], but their protocol is only UC-secure since their simulator must know the trapdoor of the CRS.

2   Preliminaries

2.1   Notations

We denote by $\lambda \in \mathbb{N}$ the security parameter. We say that a function $\mathsf{negl} : \mathbb{N} \to \mathbb{N}$ is negligible if for every positive polynomial $\mathsf{poly}(\cdot)$ and all sufficiently large λ, it holds that $\mathsf{negl}(\lambda) < \frac{1}{\mathsf{poly}(\lambda)}$. We use the abbreviation PPT to denote probabilistic polynomial-time. For an NP relation $\mathcal{R}$, we denote by $\mathcal{L}$ its associate language, i.e. $\mathcal{L} = \{x \mid \exists w \text{ s.t. } (x, w) \in \mathcal{R}\}$. We denote by $y := \mathsf{Alg}(x; r)$ the event where the algorithm Alg on input x and randomness r, outputs y. We denote by $y \leftarrow \mathsf{Alg}(x)$ the event where Alg selects a randomness r and sets $y := \mathsf{Alg}(x; r)$. We denote by $y \leftarrow S$ the process for sampling y uniformly at random from the set S. Let q be a λ-bit prime, and $p = 2q + 1$ also be a prime. Let $\mathbb{G}$ be a subgroup of order q of $\mathbb{Z}_p^*$ with the generator g.

2.2   Universal Composability

We formalize and analyze the security of our protocols in the Canetti's Universal Composability (UC) framework [6] and Canetti *et al*'s Generalized UC (GUC) framework [7]. The main difference between the UC and the GUC framework is that the environment $\mathcal{Z}$ cannot have direct access to the setups in the UC framework, whereas $\mathcal{Z}$ is "unconstrained" and can access the setups directly in the GUC framework. The local setups in the UC framework are often modeled as ideal functionalities, whereas the global setups in the GUC framework are often modeled as the *shared functionalities* which are completely analogous to ideal functionalities, except that they may interact with more than one protocol sessions. For that reason, the simulator in the UC framework can simulate the local setups and have the full control over it; whereas, the simulator in the GUC framework has no control over the global setups. We refer interesting readers to see more details in [6,7].

Adversarial Model. In this work, we consider both static corruption (where the adversary corrupts the parties at the beginning of the protocol) and adaptive corruption (where the adversary corrupts the parties at any time). We also consider *rushing* adversaries, who may delay sending messages on behalf of corrupted parties in a given round until the messages sent by all the uncorrupted parties in that round have been received [30].

Secure Communication Model. Many UC-secure protocols assume the parties are interconnected with secure or authenticated channels [7,10]. The secure channel and authenticated channel can be modeled as ideal functionalities $\mathcal{F}_{SC}$ and $\mathcal{F}_{Auth}$ respectively [6]. In this work, most of our protocols are designed in the simultaneous communication channel with rushing adversaries, which is different from that [30] deals with non-rushing adversaries. For this reason, we often assume the synchronous channel which can be modeled as $\mathcal{F}_{Syn}$ [6]. Note that, intuitively, $\mathcal{F}_{Syn}$ can be viewed an authenticated communication network with storage, which proceeds in a round-based fashion [6,31]. For readability, we will mention which secure communication channel is used in the context and omit it in the protocol description.

2.3 Ideal Functionalities

In this section, we provide ideal functionalities that will be used in UC/GUC security analysis.

OT, UOT and EOT. We start with the Oblivious Transfer (OT). In a OT protocol, there is a sender S holding two private input $m_0, m_1 \in \{0,1\}^\lambda$ and a receiver R holding a choice bit $b \in \{0,1\}$. At the end of the honest execution of the OT protocol, the receiver R will compute m_b. At the same time, the sender should learn nothing about b while the receiver should learn nothing about m_{1-b}. We present the OT functionality $\mathcal{F}_{OT}$ in Fig. 3.

Functionality $\mathcal{F}_{OT}$

It interacts with two parties S, R and an adversary $\mathcal{S}$.

Transfer. Upon receiving (SEND, sid, S, R, m_0, m_1) from the sender S, do:

- Record (sid, S, R, m_0, m_1), and send (SEND, sid, S, R) to R and the adversary $\mathcal{S}$.
- Ignore any subsequent SEND commands.

Choose. Upon receiving (RECEIVE, sid, S, R, b) from R where $b \in \{0,1\}$, do:

- Record (sid, S, R, b), and send (RECEIVE, sid, S, R) to the sender S and the adversary $\mathcal{S}$.
- Ignore any subsequent RECEIVE commands.

Process. When both (sid, S, R, m_0, m_1) and (sid, S, R, b) are recorded, do:

- Send (PROCEED?, sid, S, R) to the adversary $\mathcal{S}$.
- Upon receiving (PROCEED, sid, S) from the adversary $\mathcal{S}$, output (RECEIVED, sid, S, R) to the sender S; Upon receiving (NO, sid, S) from the adversary $\mathcal{S}$, output (ABORT, sid, S) to the sender S. Upon receiving (PROCEED, sid, R) from the adversary $\mathcal{S}$, output (RECEIVED, sid, S, R, m_b) to R; Upon receiving (NO, sid, R) from the adversary $\mathcal{S}$, output (ABORT, sid, R) to R.

Fig. 3. The Ideal Functionality $\mathcal{F}_{OT}$ for Oblivious Transfer

In [34], Masny and Rindal proposed two notions that called Uniform OT (UOT) and Endemic OT (EOT). Both of them are similar to OT, except that the senders have no inputs. The main difference between the UOT and the EOT is that they provide different levels of security guarantees. We describe the UOT first. The UOT functionality samples two uniformly random strings m_0, m_1, and outputs m_0, m_1 to the (potentially malicious) sender and m_b to the (potentially malicious) receiver. The UOT gives a strong security guarantee that any malicious party cannot influence the distribution of the OT messages. Formally, we put the UOT functionality $\mathcal{F}_{\mathsf{UOT}}$ in Fig. 4.

Functionality $\mathcal{F}_{\mathsf{UOT}}$

It interacts with two parties S, R and an adversary $\mathcal{S}$.

Transfer. Upon receiving (SEND, sid, S, R) from S, do:

- Sample $m_0, m_1 \leftarrow \{0,1\}^\lambda$, record (sid, S, R, m_0, m_1), and send (SEND, sid, S, R) to R and the adversary $\mathcal{S}$.
- Ignore any subsequent SEND commands.

Choose. Upon receiving (RECEIVE, sid, S, R, b) from R where $b \in \{0,1\}$, do:

- Record (sid, S, R, b), and send (RECEIVE, sid, S, R) to the sender S and the adversary $\mathcal{S}$.
- Ignore any subsequent RECEIVE commands.

Process. When both (sid, S, R, m_0, m_1) and (sid, S, R, b) are recorded, do:

- Send (PROCEED?, sid, S, R) to the adversary $\mathcal{S}$.
- Upon receiving (PROCEED, sid, S) from the adversary $\mathcal{S}$, output (RECEIVED, sid, S, R, m_0, m_1) to the sender S; Upon receiving (NO, sid, S) from the adversary $\mathcal{S}$, output (ABORT, sid, S) to the sender S. Upon receiving (PROCEED, sid, R) from the adversary $\mathcal{S}$, output (RECEIVED, sid, S, R, m_b) to R; Upon receiving (NO, sid, R) from the adversary $\mathcal{S}$, output (ABORT, sid, R) to R.

Fig. 4. The Ideal Functionality $\mathcal{F}_{\mathsf{UOT}}$ for Uniform Oblivious Transfer

Now let us turn to EOT. Compared to UOT, the EOT functionality gives a weak security guarantee: no matter whether the sender or the receiver is malicious, the malicious party can always determine the distribution of the OT messages. Roughly speaking, if both sender and receiver are honest, the EOT functionality acts as the UOT functionality. If the sender is malicious and the receiver is honest, the EOT functionality lets the adversary determine the message strings m_0, m_1, and it returns the adversarial chosen m_b to the honest receiver after receiving b. If the receiver is malicious and the sender is honest, the EOT functionality lets the adversary determine the message string m_b, and it returns the adversarial chosen m_b and an uniformly sampled m_{1-b} to the honest sender. If both sender and receiver are malicious, the EOT functionality simply aborts. Formally, we put the EOT functionality $\mathcal{F}_{\mathsf{EOT}}$ in Fig. 5.

Random Oracles. Here we introduce two well-known global RO models: Global Restricted Programmable Random Oracle (GrpRO) model proposed by Camenisch et al. [5] and Global Restricted Observable Random Oracle (GroRO) model proposed by Canetti et al. [9]. We omit the formal description of the well-known local RO functionality $\mathcal{F}_{\mathsf{RO}}$.

Functionality $\mathcal{F}_{\mathsf{EOT}}$

It interacts with two parties S, R and an adversary $\mathcal{S}$.

Transfer/Choose. Upon receiving (SEND, sid, S, R) from the sender S or (RECEIVE, sid, S, R, b) from the receiver R, do the same as $\mathcal{F}_{\mathsf{UOT}}$ that depicted in Figure 4.

Process. When both (sid, S, R, m_0, m_1) and (sid, S, R, b) are recorded, do:

- If both the sender S and the receiver R are honest, output (RECEIVED, sid, S, R, m_0, m_1) to the sender S, (RECEIVED, sid, S, R, m_b) to R and (RECEIVED, sid, S, R) to the adversary $\mathcal{S}$.
- Else if the sender S is corrupted and the receiver R is honest, send (PROCEED?, sid, R) to the adversary $\mathcal{S}$. Upon receiving (PROCEED, sid, R, m_0^*, m_1^*) from the adversary $\mathcal{S}$, set $m_0 := m_0^*$, $m_1 := m_1^*$, and output (RECEIVED, sid, S, R, m_0, m_1) to the sender S, (RECEIVED, sid, S, R, m_b) to R; Upon receiving (NO, sid, R) from the adversary $\mathcal{S}$, output (ABORT, sid, R) to R.
- Else if the sender S is honest and the receiver R is corrupted, send (PROCEED?, sid, S) to the adversary $\mathcal{S}$. Upon receiving (PROCEED, sid, S, m_b^*) from the adversary $\mathcal{S}$, set $m_b := m_b^*$, and output (RECEIVED, sid, S, R, m_0, m_1) to the sender S, (RECEIVED, sid, S, R, m_b) to R; Upon receiving (NO, sid, S) from the adversary $\mathcal{S}$, output (ABORT, sid, S) to the sender S.
- Else if both the sender S and the receiver R are corrupted, halt.

Fig. 5. The Ideal Functionality $\mathcal{F}_{\mathsf{EOT}}$ for Endemic Oblivious Transfer

The GrpRO Model. Compared to $\mathcal{F}_{\mathsf{RO}}$, the GrpRO is modeled as a shared functionality $\mathcal{G}_{\mathsf{rpRO}}$ which may interact with more than one protocol sessions. The $\mathcal{G}_{\mathsf{rpRO}}$ answers to the queries in the same way as $\mathcal{F}_{\mathsf{RO}}$: Upon receiving (QUERY, sid, x) from any party, $\mathcal{G}_{\mathsf{rpRO}}$ first checks whether the query (sid, x) has been queried before. If not, $\mathcal{G}_{\mathsf{rpRO}}$ selects a random value of pre-specified length $v \leftarrow \{0, 1\}^{\ell_{\mathsf{out}}(\lambda)}$, answers with the value v and records the tuple (sid, x, v); otherwise, the previously chosen value v is returned again, even if the earlier query was made by another party. The simulator is only granted the restricted programmability: both the adversary and the simulator are allowed to program the unqueried points of the random oracle, but only the simulator can program it without being detected. More precisely, as depicted in Fig. 6, upon receiving (PROGRAM, sid, x, v) from the simulator/adversary, $\mathcal{G}_{\mathsf{rpRO}}$ first checks whether (sid, x) has been queried before. If not, $\mathcal{G}_{\mathsf{rpRO}}$ stores (sid, x, v) in the query-answer lists. Any honest party can check whether a point has been programmed or not by sending the (ISPROGRAMED, sid, x) to $\mathcal{G}_{\mathsf{rpRO}}$. Thus, in the real world, the programmed points can always be detected. However, in the ideal world, the simulator $\mathcal{S}$ can escape the detection since it can return (ISPROGRAMED, sid, 0) when the adversary invokes (ISPROGRAMED, sid, x) to verify whether a point x has been programmed or not.

The GroRO Model. The GroRO is also modeled as a share functionality $\mathcal{G}_{\mathsf{roRO}}$, and it answers to the queries in the same way as $\mathcal{F}_{\mathsf{RO}}$. The simulator is only granted the restricted observability: some of the queries can be marked as "illegitimate" and potentially disclosed to the simulator. As depicted in Fig. 7, the $\mathcal{G}_{\mathsf{roRO}}$ interacts with a list of ideal functionalities $\bar{\mathcal{F}} = \{\mathcal{F}_1, \ldots, \mathcal{F}_n\}$, where $\mathcal{F}_1, \ldots, \mathcal{F}_n$ are the ideal functionalities for protocols. For any query (sid', x) from any party $P = (\mathsf{pid}, \mathsf{sid})$ where sid' is the content of the SID field, if sid' $\neq$ sid, then this

---

Share Functionality $\mathcal{G}_{\text{rpRO}}$

It interacts with a set of parties $\mathcal{P} = \{P_1, \ldots, P_n\}$ and an adversary $\mathcal{S}$. It is parameterized by the output length $\ell_{\text{out}}(\lambda)$. It maintains two initially empty lists List, Prog.

Query. Upon receiving (QUERY, sid$'$, x) from a party $P_i \in \mathcal{P}$ where $P_i = (\text{pid}, \text{sid})$, or the adversary $\mathcal{S}$:

- Check if $\exists\, v \in \{0,1\}^{\ell_{\text{out}}(\lambda)}$ such that (sid, x, v) $\in$ List. If not, select $v \leftarrow \{0,1\}^{\ell_{\text{out}}(\lambda)}$ and record the tuple (sid$'$, x, v) in List.
- Return (QUERYCONFIRM, sid$'$, v) to the requestor.

Program. Upon receiving (PROGRAM, sid, x, v) with $v \in \{0,1\}^{\ell_{\text{out}}(\lambda)}$ from the adversary $\mathcal{S}$:

- Check if $\exists\, v' \in \{0,1\}^{\ell_{\text{out}}(\lambda)}$ s.t. (sid, x, v') $\in$ List and $v \neq v'$. If so, ignore this input.
- Set List := List $\cup$ $\{(\text{sid}, x, v)\}$ and Prog := Prog $\cup$ $\{(\text{sid}, x)\}$.
- Return (PROGRAMCONFIRM, sid) to $\mathcal{S}$.

IsPrograming. Upon receiving (ISPROGRAMED, sid$'$, x) from a party $P_i \in \mathcal{P}$ where $P_i = (\text{pid}, \text{sid})$, or the adversary $\mathcal{S}$:

- If the input was given by $P_i = (\text{pid}, \text{sid})$ and sid $\neq$ sid$'$, ignore this input.
- If (sid$'$, x) $\in$ Prog, set $b := 1$; otherwise, set $b := 0$.
- Return (ISPROGRAMED, sid$'$, b) to the requester.

Fig. 6. The Global Restricted Programmable Random Oracle Model $\mathcal{G}_{\text{roRO}}$

query is considered "illegitimate". After that, $\mathcal{G}_{\text{roRO}}$ adds the tuple (sid$'$, x, v) to the list of illegitimate queries for SID sid$'$, which we denote as $\mathcal{Q}_{\text{sid}'}$. The illegitimate queries $\mathcal{Q}_{\text{sid}'}$ may be disclosed to an instance of ideal functionality $\mathcal{F} \in \bar{\mathcal{F}}$ whose SID is the one of the illegitimate queries, and the ideal functionality instance $\mathcal{F}$ may leak the illegitimate queries $\mathcal{Q}_{\text{sid}'}$ to the simulator.

Share Functionality $\mathcal{G}_{\text{roRO}}$

It interacts with a set of parties $\mathcal{P} = \{P_1, \ldots, P_n\}$ and an adversary $\mathcal{S}$. It is parameterized by the output length $\ell_{\text{out}}(\lambda)$ and a list of ideal functionalities $\bar{\mathcal{F}} := \{\mathcal{F}_1, \ldots, \mathcal{F}_n\}$. It maintains an initially empty list List.

Query. Upon receiving (QUERY, sid$'$, x) from a party $P_i \in \mathcal{P}$ where $P_i = (\text{pid}, \text{sid})$, or the adversary $\mathcal{S}$, do the same as $\mathcal{G}_{\text{roRO}}$ depicted in Figure 6, except when sid $\neq$ sid$'$, add the tuple (sid$'$, x, v) to the (initially empty) list of illegitimate queries for SID sid$'$, which we denote by $\mathcal{Q}_{\text{sid}'}$.

Observe. Upon receiving a request from an instance of an ideal functionality $\mathcal{F}_i \in \bar{\mathcal{F}}$ with SID sid$'$, return the list of illegitimate queries $\mathcal{Q}_{\text{sid}'}$ for SID sid$'$ to this instance $\mathcal{F}_i$.

Fig. 7. The Global Restricted Observable Random Oracle Model $\mathcal{G}_{\text{roRO}}$

2.4 Building Blocks

In this work, we use the followings as the main building blocks: the Pedersen commitment [39], the ElGamal encryption [20], the Sigma-protocols [15], and the (straight-line extractable) NIZK/NIWH arguments in the RO model [38].

We also use the well-known CDH and DDH assumption [17]. Due to the space limit, here we do not provide the formal descriptions of the building blocks above, and we refer interesting readers to see them in the full version of this paper [41].

3   UC-Secure Endemic OT via Random Oracles

In this section, we provide a new 1-round UC-secure EOT protocol under standard assumptions in the RO model.

We start with the two-round standalone EOT protocol in [13]: in the first round, the sender sends $h := g^s$ using $s \leftarrow \mathbb{Z}_q$; in the second round, the receiver uses sender's message to compute $B := g^r h^b$ based on its choice bit b and its secret randomness $r \leftarrow \mathbb{Z}_q$; finally, the sender computes and outputs $m_0 := \mathcal{F}_{\mathsf{RO}}(B^s)$ and $m_1 := \mathcal{F}_{\mathsf{RO}}((\frac{B}{h})^s)$ while the receiver outputs $m_b := \mathcal{F}_{\mathsf{RO}}(h^r)$. Here we use to notation $y := \mathcal{F}_{\mathsf{RO}}(x)$ to describe the process for querying x to the random oracle $\mathcal{F}_{\mathsf{RO}}$ and obtaining the output y, which aligns with the notation in [11]. Our goals are: (i) reduce the round complexity of this protocol to one simultaneous round; (ii) add new mechanisms to make this protocol UC-secure.

In order to reduce the round complexity, we let the receiver generate h by invoking the RO on a randomly sampled string seed. In this way, the receiver can compute its message without the sender's message, thus only one simultaneous round is needed. This technique can be found in [11]. We then discuss how to provide UC security. The UC-secure EOT protocol requires *extractability*: (i) when the sender is malicious, the simulator should be able to extract the sender's secret randomness, so the simulator can compute both m_0 and m_1; (ii) when the receiver is malicious, the simulator should be able to extract the receiver's choice bit b. In order to extract the sender's secret randomness s, we let the sender additionally generate a straight-line extractable NIZK argument [22,32,38] of s such that $z = g^s$. The straight-line extractability relies on the observability of the RO model. In this way, the simulator can extract the malicious sender's secret randomness. In order to extract the receiver's choice bit b, we let the receiver generate an ElGamal encryption of bit b instead of a Pedersen commitment to bit b, i.e., the receiver computes $(u, v) := (h^r, h^b g^r)$ using $r \leftarrow \mathbb{Z}_q$. We also let the receiver generate a NIZK argument of (b, r) such that $(u, v) = (h^r, h^b g^r)$ to ensure that (u, v) is an ElGamal encryption of a bit b. In this way, the simulator knows $\log_g h$ by making use of the programmability of the RO model, and thus is able to extract b from (u, v).

Let g be the generator of $\mathbb{G}$. Let $\mathcal{F}_{\mathsf{RO1}} : \{0,1\}^* \to \mathbb{G}$ and $\mathcal{F}_{\mathsf{RO2}} : \{0,1\}^* \to \{0,1\}^\lambda$ be random oracles. Let $\mathcal{R}_{\mathsf{ENC}} := \{((g, h, u, v), (r, b)) \mid (b = 0 \wedge (u, v) = (h^r, g^r)) \vee (b = 1 \wedge (u, v) = (h^r, g^r h))\}$ and $\mathcal{R}_{\mathsf{DL}} := \{((g, z), s) \mid z = g^s\}$. We denote by Π_{sleNIZK} the straight-line extractable NIZK argument in the $\mathcal{F}_{\mathsf{RO3}}$-hybrid world. We denote by Π_{NIZK} the NIZK argument in the $\mathcal{F}_{\mathsf{RO4}}$-hybrid world. We note that, the domain and range of $\mathcal{F}_{\mathsf{RO3}}$ and $\mathcal{F}_{\mathsf{RO4}}$ depend on the concrete instantiations of the protocols, for that reason, we do not write them explicitly. Here we assume the synchronous channel $\mathcal{F}_{\mathsf{Syn}}$ is available to the protocol players.

Protocol Description. We present our protocol $\Pi_{\mathsf{EOT\text{-}RO}}$ in Fig. 8; note that, in Fig. 8, we only cover the case where both sender and receiver are honest.

Sender	$\boxed{\mathcal{F}_{\mathrm{RO}i}}$	Receiver$(b \in \{0,1\})$
$s \leftarrow \mathbb{Z}_q; z := g^s$ $\pi_{\mathsf{DL}} \leftarrow \Pi_{\mathsf{sleNIZK}}.\mathsf{Prove}^{\mathcal{F}_{\mathrm{RO3}}}$ $((g,z),s)$ for $\mathcal{R}_{\mathsf{DL}}$	$\xleftarrow{\text{seed}, u, v, \pi_{\mathsf{ENC}}}$ $\xrightarrow{\quad z, \pi_{\mathsf{DL}} \quad}$	seed$\leftarrow \{0,1\}^\lambda; r \leftarrow \mathbb{Z}_q$ $h := \mathcal{F}_{\mathrm{RO1}}(\mathsf{sid}, `R`\|\mathsf{seed})$ $(u,v) := (h^r, h^b g^r)$ $\pi_{\mathsf{ENC}} \leftarrow \Pi_{\mathsf{NIZK}}.\mathsf{Prove}^{\mathcal{F}_{\mathrm{RO4}}}((g,$ $h,u,v),(r,b))$ for $\mathcal{R}_{\mathsf{ENC}}$
$h := \mathcal{F}_{\mathrm{RO1}}(\mathsf{sid}, `R`\|\mathsf{seed})$ Abort if $\Pi_{\mathsf{NIZK}}.\mathsf{Verify}^{\mathcal{F}_{\mathrm{RO4}}}((g,$ $h,u,v),\pi_{\mathsf{ENC}}) = 0$ for $\mathcal{R}_{\mathsf{ENC}}$ Output $m_0 := \mathcal{F}_{\mathrm{RO2}}(\mathsf{sid}, `S`\|v^s)$ $m_1 := \mathcal{F}_{\mathrm{RO2}}(\mathsf{sid}, `S`\|(\frac{v}{h})^s)$		Abort if $\Pi_{\mathsf{sleNIZK}}.\mathsf{Verify}^{\mathcal{F}_{\mathrm{RO3}}}((g,$ $z),\pi_{\mathsf{DL}}) = 0$ for $\mathcal{R}_{\mathsf{DL}}$ Output $m_b := \mathcal{F}_{\mathrm{RO2}}(\mathsf{sid}, `S`\|z^r)$

Fig. 8. 1-round EOT protocol $\Pi_{\mathsf{EOT\text{-}RO}}$ in the $\{\mathcal{F}_{\mathrm{RO}}, \mathcal{F}_{\mathsf{Syn}}\}$-hybrid world, where $\mathcal{F}_{\mathrm{RO}} = \{\mathcal{F}_{\mathrm{RO}i}\}_{i \in [4]}$. Let g be the generator of $\mathbb{G}$. Let $\mathcal{F}_{\mathrm{RO1}} : \{0,1\}^* \to \mathbb{G}$ and $\mathcal{F}_{\mathrm{RO2}} : \{0,1\}^* \to \{0,1\}^\lambda$. Let $\mathcal{R}_{\mathsf{ENC}} := \{((g,h,u,v),(r,b)) \mid (b = 0 \wedge (u,v) = (h^r, g^r)) \vee (b = 1 \wedge (u,v) = (h^r, g^r h))\}$ and $\mathcal{R}_{\mathsf{DL}} := \{((g,z),s) \mid z = g^s\}$.

When sender (resp. receiver) is statically corrupted and receiver (resp. sender) is honest, after sending its message to $\mathcal{F}_{\mathsf{Syn}}$ and waiting for a long time, the honest receiver (resp. sender) will query $\mathcal{F}_{\mathsf{Syn}}$ to obtain the other party's message. If $\mathcal{F}_{\mathsf{Syn}}$ replies the desired message, the honest party will compute and output the local message according to Fig. 8; otherwise, the honest party simply aborts. The security of the protocol has been stated in Theorem 1.

Theorem 1. *Assume the DDH assumption holds in group* $\mathbb{G}$. *Let* $\mathcal{F}_{\mathrm{RO1}} : \{0,1\}^* \to \mathbb{G}$ *and* $\mathcal{F}_{\mathrm{RO2}} : \{0,1\}^* \to \{0,1\}^\lambda$ *be the random oracles. Let* Π_{NIZK} *be an NIZK argument in the* $\mathcal{F}_{\mathrm{RO3}}$-*hybrid world. Let* Π_{sleNIZK} *be a straight-line extractable NIZK argument in the* $\mathcal{F}_{\mathrm{RO4}}$-*hybrid world. The protocol* $\Pi_{\mathsf{EOT\text{-}RO}}$ *depicted in Fig. 8 UC-realizes the functionality* $\mathcal{F}_{\mathsf{EOT}}$ *depicted in Fig. 5 in the* $\{\mathcal{F}_{\mathrm{RO}}, \mathcal{F}_{\mathsf{Syn}}\}$-*hybrid world against static malicious corruption, where* $\mathcal{F}_{\mathrm{RO}} = \{\mathcal{F}_{\mathrm{RO}i}\}_{i \in [4]}$.

Proof. We leave the formal proof in the full version of this paper [41]. $\square$

Instantiation. We instantiate Π_{sleNIZK} for relation $\mathcal{R}_{\mathsf{DL}}$ with the Schnorr's protocol [40] and the *randomized Fischlin transform* [32] which improves the efficiency and applicability of Fischlin transform [22]. We instantiate Π_{NIZK} for relation $\mathcal{R}_{\mathsf{ENC}}$ with the following techniques: we first employ the OR-composition [14] to the Chaum-Pedersen protocols [12] to prove either (g,h,v,u) is a DDH tuple (which means $b = 0$) or $(g,h,\frac{v}{h},u)$ is a DDH tuple (which means $b = 1$), we then apply the the Fiat-Shamir transform [21] to remove the interaction.

Efficiency. Here we compare the efficiency in the amortized setting where the sender and the receiver can reuse some elements for multiple instances of the EOT protocol (in this protocol, the sender can reuse s, π_{DL} while the receiver can reuse the string seed). The amortized setting is also used in [11] for efficiency comparison. By taking the parameters (that achieves 128-bit security) from [32], our protocol requires 18 exponentiations w.r.t. computation and 10 group/field elements w.r.t. communication; while the state-of-the-art 1-round UC-secure RO-based protocol in [34] requires 4 exponentiations w.r.t. computation and 2 group elements w.r.t. communication. Note that, our protocol is based on a standard assumption; whereas the protocol in [34] is based on a non-standard assumption.

4   The Relations Between Endemic OT and Other Primitives

In this section, we first show how to construct a bit commitment protocol via EOT with unconditional security. Subsequently, we complete the picture of OT relations in [34], showing that UOT can be constructed via EOT with unconditional security.

4.1   From Endemic OT to Commitment

Recall that, Brzuska *et al.* proved that bit commitment can be constructed via 1-out-of-2 OT with unconditional security [3]. As remarked in [34], there is a separation between the EOT and OT in the standalone setting: there are no 1-round OT protocols while there are 1-round EOT protocols. Although there is such a separation, we show a surprising fact: bit commitment can also be constructed via a weaker primitive, i.e., EOT, with unconditional security.

We observe that the receiver's message can be viewed as the commitment to the receiver's choice bit b, and the locally computed message m_b together with b can be viewed as the opening. Typically, a commitment protocol requires two properties: hiding and binding. The hiding property comes from the fact: even if the malicious EOT receiver can influence the distribution of m_b, it cannot learn the other message m_{1-b}. The binding property comes from the fact: even if the malicious EOT sender can influence the distributions of both m_0 and m_1, it cannot tell which one is received by the receiver. Furthermore, if we use a UC-secure EOT protocol as the building block, the resulting commitment protocol is also UC-secure. Note that, we only assume authenticated channel $\mathcal{F}_{\mathsf{Auth}}$ is available to the protocol players, and we omit the formal description of the well-known commitment functionality $\mathcal{F}_{\mathsf{Com}}$.

Protocol Description. We present our protocol Π_{Com} in Fig. 9; note that, in Fig. 9 we only cover the case that both committer and receiver are honest. The remaining cases can be found in the full version of this paper [41]. The security of the protocol has been stated in Theorem 2.

Theorem 2. *The protocol Π_{Com} depicted in Fig. 9 UC-realizes the functionality $\mathcal{F}_{\mathsf{Com}}$ with unconditional security in the $\{\mathcal{F}_{\mathsf{EOT}}, \mathcal{F}_{\mathsf{Auth}}\}$-hybrid world against static malicious corruption.*

Proof. We leave the formal proof in the full version of this paper [41].

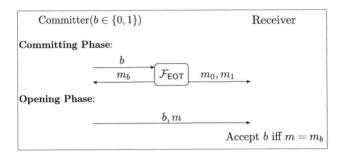

Fig. 9. Bit Commitment Protocol Π_{Com} in the $\{\mathcal{F}_{\mathsf{EOT}}, \mathcal{F}_{\mathsf{Auth}}\}$-Hybrid World

4.2 From Endemic OT to Uniform OT

In [34], the Masny and Rindal showed how to construct UOT with unconditional security in the $\{\mathcal{F}_{\mathsf{EOT}}, \mathcal{F}_{\mathsf{Coin}}, \mathcal{F}_{\mathsf{Auth}}\}$-hybrid world, where $\mathcal{F}_{\mathsf{Coin}}$ is the well-known coin-tossing functionality and we omit the formal description here. We recall the protocol construction in [34] in Fig. 10. However, they only showed how to construct the coin-tossing protocol via UOT. Therefore, whether EOT implies UOT remains an open question.

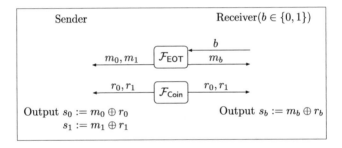

Fig. 10. UOT Protocol Π_{UOT} in the $\{\mathcal{F}_{\mathsf{EOT}}, \mathcal{F}_{\mathsf{Coin}}, \mathcal{F}_{\mathsf{Auth}}\}$-Hybrid World from [34]

Lemma 1 ([34]). *The protocol Π_{UOT} depicted in Fig. 10 UC-realizes $\mathcal{F}_{\mathsf{UOT}}$ depicted in Fig. 4 with unconditional security in the $\{\mathcal{F}_{\mathsf{EOT}}, \mathcal{F}_{\mathsf{Coin}}, \mathcal{F}_{\mathsf{Auth}}\}$-hybrid world against static malicious corruption.*

In this section, we provide a positive answer to this unsolved question. Our solution is as follows: we have already showed that EOT implies commitment in Sect. 4.1, and the coin-tossing protocol can be easily constructed via only commitment; putting things together, we show that EOT implies UOT. Note that, we only assume $\mathcal{F}_{\mathsf{Auth}}$ is available to the protocol players, and we omit the formal description of the well-known coin-tossing functionality $\mathcal{F}_{\mathsf{Coin}}$.

Protocol Description. We present our protocol Π_{Coin} in Fig. 11; note that, in Fig. 11 we only cover the case that both two players are honest. The remaining cases can be found in the full version of this paper [41]. The security of the protocol has been stated in Theorem 3.

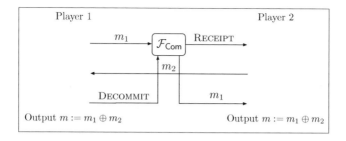

Fig. 11. Coin-Tossing Protocol Π_{Coin} in the $\{\mathcal{F}_{\mathsf{Com}}, \mathcal{F}_{\mathsf{Auth}}\}$-Hybrid World

Theorem 3. *The protocol Π_{Coin} depicted in Fig. 11 UC-realizes the functionality $\mathcal{F}_{\mathsf{Coin}}$ with unconditional security in the $\{\mathcal{F}_{\mathsf{Com}}, \mathcal{F}_{\mathsf{Auth}}\}$-hybrid world against static malicious corruption.*

Proof. We leave the formal proof in the full version of this paper [41].

Formally, we prove that EOT implies UOT through Corollary 1. The security proof of Corollary 1 directly comes from Lemma 1, Theorem 2 and Theorem 3, and thus we omit the trivial proof here.

Corollary 1. *The protocol Π_{UOT} depicted in Fig. 10 UC-realizes $\mathcal{F}_{\mathsf{UOT}}$ depicted in Fig. 4 with unconditional security in the $\{\mathcal{F}_{\mathsf{EOT}}, \mathcal{F}_{\mathsf{Auth}}\}$-hybrid world against static malicious corruption.*

5 GUC-Secure Endemic OT via Global Random Oracles

In this section, we turn to global RO models to seek a stronger variant of UC security, i.e., GUC security. As for the GroRO model, we construct the *first* 1-round GUC-secure EOT protocol under CDH assumption against static adversaries. Basing on that, we propose the *first* 2-round GUC-secure commitment protocol in the GroRO model.

Regarding the GrpRO model, we prove that there exists *no* 1-round GUC-secure EOT protocol in the GrpRO model even with static security. By combining this negative result in the GrpRO model and the positive result in the GroRO model, we reveal a separation between these two models. Furthermore, we construct the *first* 2-round (round-optimal) GUC-secure EOT protocol under DDH assumption in the GrpRO model against adaptive adversaries.

5.1 Feasibility Results in the GroRO Model

Our EOT Protocol. We start with our UC-secure EOT protocol $\Pi_{\text{EOT-RO}}$ depicted in Fig. 8. Recall that, we let the sender send $z := g^s$ using $s \leftarrow \mathbb{Z}_q$, together with a straight-line extractable NIZK argument of s such that $z = g^s$ in $\Pi_{\text{EOT-RO}}$. The straight-line extractable NIZK argument gives the simulator chance of extracting the sender's secret randomness. However, Pass showed that it is impossible to construct NIZK arguments in observable RO model [38], let alone NIZK arguments with straight-line extractability. The good news is that we find that straight-line extractable NIWH argument is sufficient for our purpose, and it is possible in the GroRO model [38]. Therefore, we let the sender generate a straight-line extractable NIWH argument of s such that $z = g^s$. Now let us consider the receiver. In order to extract the receiver's choice bit, we make full use of the programmability of random oracles in $\Pi_{\text{EOT-RO}}$. Since $\mathcal{G}_{\text{roRO}}$ does not permit anyone to program the random oracle, we need to take a different strategy: we let the receiver generate h by invoking the $\mathcal{G}_{\text{roRO}}$ on a randomly sampled string seed, compute a Pedersen commitment to the choice bit $B := g^r h^b$ using $r \leftarrow \mathbb{Z}_q$, and generate a straight-line extractable NIWH argument of (r, b) such that $B = g^r h^b$. Analogously to the sender side, the simulator can extract the malicious receiver's choice bit b.

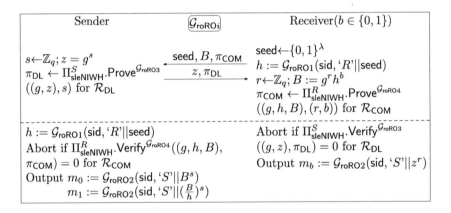

Fig. 12. 1-round EOT protocol $\Pi_{\text{EOT-GroRO}}$ in the $\{\mathcal{G}_{\text{roRO}}, \mathcal{F}_{\text{Syn}}\}$-hybrid world, where $\mathcal{G}_{\text{roRO}} = \{\mathcal{G}_{\text{roRO}i}\}_{i \in [4]}$. Let g be the generator of $\mathbb{G}$. Let $\mathcal{G}_{\text{roRO1}} : \{0,1\}^* \to \mathbb{G}$ and $\mathcal{G}_{\text{roRO2}} : \{0,1\}^* \to \{0,1\}^\lambda$. Let $\mathcal{R}_{\text{Com}} := \{((g,h,B),(r,b)) \mid B = g^r h^b\}$ and $\mathcal{R}_{\text{DL}} := \{((g,z),s) \mid z = g^s\}$.

Let g be the generator of $\mathbb{G}$. Let $\mathcal{G}_{\text{roRO1}} : \{0,1\}^* \to \mathbb{G}$ and $\mathcal{G}_{\text{roRO2}} : \{0,1\}^* \to \{0,1\}^\lambda$. Let $\mathcal{R}_{\text{Com}} := \{((g,h,B),(r,b)) \mid B = g^r h^b\}$ and $\mathcal{R}_{\text{DL}} := \{((g,z),s) \mid z = g^s\}$. We denote by Π_{sleNIWH}^S the straight-line extractable NIWH argument in the $\mathcal{G}_{\text{roRO3}}$-hybrid world which is used for generating the proof by sender. We denote by Π_{sleNIWH}^R the straight-line extractable NIWH argument in the $\mathcal{G}_{\text{roRO4}}$-hybrid world which is used for generating the proof by receiver. We assume synchronous channel $\mathcal{F}_{\mathsf{Syn}}$ is available to the protocol players..

Protocol Description. We present our protocol $\Pi_{\mathsf{EOT\text{-}GroRO}}$ in Fig. 12; note that, in Fig. 12 we only cover the case that both sender and receiver are honest. The remaining cases can be found in the full version of this paper [41]. The security of the protocol has been stated in Theorem 4.

Before giving the theorem, we have to give the transferable EOT functionality $\mathcal{F}_{\mathsf{tEOT}}$ in Fig. 13. The main difference with the traditional EOT functionality is that in $\mathcal{F}_{\mathsf{tEOT}}$, the simulator can request the list of illegitimate queries, which fits the $\mathcal{G}_{\mathsf{roRO}}$ model.

Theorem 4. *Assume the CDH assumption holds in group* $\mathbb{G}$. *Let* $\mathcal{G}_{\mathsf{roRO1}} : \{0,1\}^\lambda \to \mathbb{G}$ *and* $\mathcal{G}_{\mathsf{roRO2}} : \mathbb{G} \to \{0,1\}^\lambda$ *be the random oracles. Let* Π_{sleNIWH}^S *be a straight-line extractable NIWH argument in the* $\mathcal{G}_{\mathsf{roRO3}}$-*hybrid world. Let* Π_{sleNIWH}^R *be a straight-line extractable NIWH argument in the* $\mathcal{G}_{\mathsf{roRO4}}$-*hybrid world. The protocol* $\Pi_{\mathsf{EOT\text{-}GroRO}}$ *depicted in Fig. 12 GUC-realizes the functionality* $\mathcal{F}_{\mathsf{tEOT}}$ *depicted in Fig. 13 in the* $\{\mathcal{G}_{\mathsf{roRO}}, \mathcal{F}_{\mathsf{Syn}}\}$-*hybrid world against static malicious corruption, where* $\mathcal{G}_{\mathsf{roRO}} = \{\mathcal{G}_{\mathsf{roRO}i}\}_{i \in [4]}$.

Proof. We leave the formal proof in the full version of this paper [41].

Functionality $\mathcal{F}_{\mathsf{tEOT}}$

The functionality interacts with two parties S, R and an adversary $\mathcal{S}$.
Transfer/Choose/Process. Same as $\mathcal{F}_{\mathsf{EOT}}$ depicted in Figure 5.

Observe. When asked by the adversary $\mathcal{S}$, obtain from $\mathcal{G}_{\mathsf{roRO}}$ the list of illegitimate queries $\mathcal{Q}_{\mathsf{sid}}$ that pertain to SID sid, and send $\mathcal{Q}_{\mathsf{sid}}$ to the adversary $\mathcal{S}$.

Fig. 13. The Transferable Ideal Functionality $\mathcal{F}_{\mathsf{tEOT}}$ for Endemic Oblivious Transfer

Instantiation. We instantiate Π_{sleNIZK}^S for relation $\mathcal{R}_{\mathsf{DL}}$ with the Schnorr's protocol and the randomized Fischlin transform as in Sect. 3. Note that, although we use the same instantiation as in Sect. 3, we only obtain a straight-line extractable NIWH argument, since here we use a observable RO model [38]. We instantiate Π_{sleNIWH}^R for relation $\mathcal{R}_{\mathsf{Com}}$ with the Okamoto's protocol [37] and the randomized Fischlin transform.

Efficiency. We consider the efficiency of our GUC-secure protocol $\Pi_{\mathsf{EOT\text{-}GroRO}}$ in the amortized setting here, just like we did in Sect. 3. By taking the parameter (that achieves 128-bit security) in [32], our GUC-secure protocol $\Pi_{\mathsf{EOT\text{-}GroRO}}$ requires 53 exponentiations w.r.t. computation and 41 group/field elements w.r.t. communication; while the state-of-the-art 2-round GroRO-based OT protocol in [11] requires 5 exponentiations w.r.t. computation and 2 group elements +

2λ bits string w.r.t. communication. Note that, our protocol only requires CDH assumption, whereas the protocol proposed in [11] requires the DDH assumption, which is stronger.

Our Commitment Protocol. Recall that, we construct a commitment protocol Π_{Com} depicted in Fig. 9 in the $\{\mathcal{F}_{\mathsf{EOT}}, \mathcal{F}_{\mathsf{Auth}}\}$-hybrid world with unconditional security (cf. Sect. 4.1). It is easy to see that if we replace $\mathcal{F}_{\mathsf{EOT}}$ with $\mathcal{F}_{\mathsf{tEOT}}$ and call the resulting protocol Π_{tCom}, then the protocol Π_{tCom} will GUC-realize $\mathcal{F}_{\mathsf{tCom}}$ in the $\{\mathcal{F}_{\mathsf{tEOT}}, \mathcal{F}_{\mathsf{Auth}}\}$-hybrid world with unconditional security, where $\mathcal{F}_{\mathsf{tCom}}$ is the transferable commitment functionality introduced in [9] and here we omit the formal description of $\mathcal{F}_{\mathsf{tCom}}$. Formally, we have the following corollary, and its security proof is analogously to the proof of Theorem 2.

Corollary 2. *The protocol Π_{tCom} GUC-realizes the functionality $\mathcal{F}_{\mathsf{tCom}}$ with unconditional security in the $\{\mathcal{F}_{\mathsf{tEOT}}, \mathcal{F}_{\mathsf{Auth}}\}$-hybrid world against static malicious corruption.*

Instantiation. We instantiate $\mathcal{F}_{\mathsf{tEOT}}$ with our 1-round GUC-secure EOT protocol depicted in Fig. 12. Then we immediate obtain a 2-round GUC-secure commitment protocol Π_{tCom} in the GroRO model; note that, the first round messages are communicated over the synchronous channel $\mathcal{F}_{\mathsf{Syn}}$ and the second round message is communicated over the authenticated channel $\mathcal{F}_{\mathsf{Auth}}$. The security is guaranteed by Theorem 4 and Corollary 2.

Comparison. Our commitment protocol is the *first* 2-round GUC-secure commitment in the GroRO model, while the previous state-of-the-art protocols achieve 3 rounds [36,42]. Note that, Zhou *et al.* proved that it is impossible to construct 2-round GUC-secure commitment protocol in the GroRO model even with static security [42]; but they do not assume $\mathcal{F}_{\mathsf{Syn}}$ is available for protocol players. Our 2-round commitment protocol contains a simultaneous round, so we do not contradict their impossibility result. We also note that, our protocol and protocols in [36,42] are all 3-move static-secure protocols, but ours is the only one whose first two moves can be executed in one simultaneous round; hence, ours is the only one that can achieve 2-round.

5.2   Impossibility and Feasibility Results in the GrpRO Model

Our Impossibility Result. Here we show that there exists *no* 1-round GUC-secure EOT protocol against static adversaries in the GrpRO model.

We prove this impossibility by contradiction. Suppose that there exists such a 1-round GUC-secure EOT protocol. Let us first consider the case where the receiver is corrupted, and the simulator needs to extract the choice bit of the receiver from its message. Recall that, the $\mathcal{G}_{\mathsf{rpRO}}$ only grants the simulator the restricted programmability: although the simulator can program the unqueried points without being detected, the simulator is external to the $\mathcal{G}_{\mathsf{rpRO}}$ and it can not know in real time what queries other parties are sending to $\mathcal{G}_{\mathsf{rpRO}}$. Thus, the simulator needs to program the points in advance and find a way to enforce the corrupt receiver to generate its message on the simulator's programmed points. In that way, the simulator can have the chance of extracting the choice bit of the receiver. However, in a one simultaneous round protocol, the messages between parties have no dependency. Hence the simulator cannot enforce the corrupt receiver to produce its message on the programmed points, and has no advantages over the real world adversary. If the simulator still succeeds to extract the corrupted receiver's choice bit, then distinctions will be revealed when the adversary performs the following attacks. The adversary corrupts the sender, and instructs the sender to run the simulator algorithm above to extract the choice bit from the message sent by the receiver/simulator. However, the receiver/simulator has no idea about the real choice bit, thus with high probability the simulation would fail. Formally, we prove this impossibility through Theorem 5.

Theorem 5. *There exists no terminating 1-round protocol Π that GUC-realizes $\mathcal{F}_{\mathsf{EOT}}$ depicted in Fig. 5 with static security in the $\{\mathcal{G}_{\mathsf{rpRO}}, \mathcal{F}_{\mathsf{Syn}}\}$-hybrid world.*

Proof. We leave the formal proof in the full version of this paper [41].

By combining this negative result in the GrpRO model and the positive result in the GroRO model depicted in Sect. 5.1, we demonstrate a separation between the GroRO and the GrpRO model.

Our EOT Protocol. Theorem 5 rules out the possibility of 1-round GUC-secure EOT protocols in the $\{\mathcal{G}_{\mathsf{rpRO}}, \mathcal{F}_{\mathsf{Syn}}\}$-hybrid world. It makes us wonder if we do not let the sender and the receiver send their messages simultaneously but in a specific order, can we construct a 2-move (also 2-round) GUC-secure protocol?

We start with the UC-secure EOT protocol in the CRS+GrpRO hybrid model proposed by Canetti *et al.* [11]. Their CRS consists of two group elements $g, h \in \mathbb{G}$, and the simulator knows $\log_g h$. They let the receiver generate parameter G, H by invoking the RO on a randomly sampled string seed, and compute two instances of Pedersen commitment to the choice bit $(B_1, B_2) := (g^x G^b, h^x H^b)$ using two sets of different parameters $(g, G), (h, H)$ and the same randomness $x \leftarrow \mathbb{Z}_q$. As for the sender, they let the sender compute $z := g^r h^s$ using randomness $r, s \leftarrow \mathbb{Z}_q$. Finally, the sender outputs $m_0 := \mathcal{G}_{\mathsf{rpRO}}(B_1^r B_2^s)$ and $m_1 := \mathcal{G}_{\mathsf{rpRO}}((\frac{B_1}{G})^r (\frac{B_2}{H})^s)$ while the receiver outputs $m_b := \mathcal{G}_{\mathsf{rpRO}}(z^x)$.

Our goals are: (i) remove the CRS setup of this protocol; (ii) make this protocol GUC-secure in the GrpRO model. To achieve the former goal, we let the sender generate g, h by invoking random oracle on a randomly sampled string seed_1. Then the sender computes $z := g^r h^s$ using $r, s \leftarrow \mathbb{Z}_q$, and sends seed_1, z to the receiver. On the other hand, we let the receiver generate G, H by invoking $\mathcal{G}_{\mathsf{rpRO}}$ on another randomly sampled string seed_2, computes two instances of Pedersen commitment to the choice bit $(B_1, B_2) := (g^x G^b, h^x H^b)$ using the same randomness $x \leftarrow \mathbb{Z}_q$. The local computation is the same as Canetti *et al*'s protocol. In order to show that our modified protocol achieves the latter goal, we show the simulation strategy as follows: when the receiver is malicious, the simulator can extract the receiver's choice bit b by programming the $\mathcal{G}_{\mathsf{rpRO}}$ and knowing α such that $h = g^\alpha$. Then the simulator can extract b by the following strategy: if $B_2 = B_1^\alpha$, it sets $b := 0$; else if $\frac{B_2}{H} = (\frac{B_1}{G})^\alpha$, it sets $b := 1$; else, it sets $b := \bot$. Note that, when B_1, B_2 are not correctly constructed (i.e., the simulator sets $b := \bot$), the malicious receiver cannot compute either m_0 or m_1. When the sender is malicious, the simulator can compute both m_0 and m_1 by programming the $\mathcal{G}_{\text{rpRO}}$ such that (g, h, G, H) is a DDH tuple, i.e., $G = g^t, H = h^t$. In this way, the simulator can compute $m_0 := \mathcal{G}_{\text{rpRO}}(z^x)$ and $m_1 := \mathcal{G}_{\text{rpRO}}(z^{x-t})$.

Sender	$\mathcal{G}_{\text{rpRO}i}$	Receiver($b \in \{0,1\}$)
$\text{seed}_1 \leftarrow \{0,1\}^\lambda$ $(g,h) := \mathcal{G}_{\text{rpRO1}}(\text{sid}, `R'\|\text{seed}_1)$ $r, s \leftarrow \mathbb{Z}_q; z := g^r h^s$	$\xrightarrow{\quad \text{seed}_1, z \quad}$	Abort if seed_1 is programmed $(g,h) := \mathcal{G}_{\text{rpRO1}}(\text{sid}, `R'\|\text{seed}_1)$   $\text{seed}_2 \leftarrow \{0,1\}^\lambda$   $(G,H) := \mathcal{G}_{\text{rpRO1}}(\text{sid}, `R'\|\text{seed}_2)$
	$\xleftarrow{\quad \text{seed}_2, B_1, B_2 \quad}$	$x \leftarrow \mathbb{Z}_q; (B_1, B_2) := (g^x G^b, h^x H^b)$
Abort if seed_2 is programmed $(G,H) := \mathcal{G}_{\text{rpRO1}}(\text{sid}, `R'\|\text{seed}_2)$   Output $m_0 := \mathcal{G}_{\text{rpRO2}}(\text{sid}, `S'\|B_1^r B_2^s)$ $\qquad m_1 := \mathcal{G}_{\text{rpRO2}}(\text{sid}, `S'\|(\frac{B_1}{G})^r(\frac{B_2}{H})^s)$		Output $m_b := \mathcal{G}_{\text{rpRO2}}(\text{sid}, `S'\|z^x)$

Fig. 14. 2-round EOT protocol $\Pi_{\text{EOT-GrpRO}}$ in the $\{\mathcal{G}_{\text{rpRO}}, \mathcal{F}_{\text{Auth}}\}$-hybrid world, where $\mathcal{G}_{\text{rpRO}} = \{\mathcal{G}_{\text{rpRO1}}, \mathcal{G}_{\text{rpRO2}}\}$. Let $\mathcal{G}_{\text{rpRO1}} : \{0,1\}^* \to \mathbb{G} \times \mathbb{G}$ and $\mathcal{G}_{\text{rpRO2}} : \{0,1\}^* \to \{0,1\}^\lambda$.

Let $\mathcal{G}_{\text{rpRO1}} : \{0,1\}^* \to \mathbb{G} \times \mathbb{G}$ and $\mathcal{G}_{\text{rpRO2}} : \{0,1\}^* \to \{0,1\}^\lambda$. Here we assume authenticated channels $\mathcal{F}_{\text{Auth}}$ are available.

Protocol Description. We present our protocol $\Pi_{\text{EOT-GrpRO}}$ in Fig. 14; note that, in Fig. 14 we only cover the case that both sender and receiver are honest. The remaining cases can be found in the full version of this paper [41]. The security of the protocol has been stated in Theorem 6.

Theorem 6. *Assume the DDH assumption holds in group $\mathbb{G}$. Let $\mathcal{G}_{\text{rpRO1}} : \{0,1\}^\lambda \to \mathbb{G} \times \mathbb{G}$ and $\mathcal{G}_{\text{rpRO2}} : \mathbb{G} \to \{0,1\}^\lambda$ be the random oracles. The protocol $\Pi_{\text{EOT-GrpRO}}$ depicted in Fig. 14 GUC-realizes the functionality $\mathcal{F}_{\text{EOT}}$ depicted in Fig. 5 in the $\{\mathcal{G}_{\text{rpRO}}, \mathcal{F}_{\text{Auth}}\}$-hybrid world against adaptive malicious corruption, where $\mathcal{G}_{\text{rpRO}} = \{\mathcal{G}_{\text{rpRO1}}, \mathcal{G}_{\text{rpRO2}}\}$.*

Proof. We leave the formal proof in the full version of this paper [41].

Efficiency. We consider the efficiency of our protocol $\Pi_{\text{EOT-GrpRO}}$ in the amortized setting here, just like we did in Sect. 3. Our protocol requires 5 exponentiations w.r.t. computation and 2 group elements w.r.t. communication; while the state-of-the-art 2-round GrpRO-based OT protocol in [11] requires the same computation and extra 2λ bits string w.r.t. communication compared to our protocol. We emphasize that our protocol achieves GUC security; whereas the protocol proposed in [11] achieves only UC security.

Acknowledgment. We thank anonymous reviewers of Eurocrypt 2023 for their helpful and constructive comments.

References

1. Bellare, M., Micali, S.: Non-interactive oblivious transfer and applications. In: Brassard, G. (ed.) CRYPTO 1989. LNCS, vol. 435, pp. 547–557. Springer, New York (1990). https://doi.org/10.1007/0-387-34805-0_48
2. Bellare, M., Rogaway, P.: Random oracles are practical: a paradigm for designing efficient protocols. In: Denning, D.E., Pyle, R., Ganesan, R., Sandhu, R.S., Ashby, V. (eds.) ACM CCS 93, pp. 62–73. ACM Press, November 1993. https://doi.org/10.1145/168588.168596
3. Brzuska, C., Fischlin, M., Schröder, H., Katzenbeisser, S.: Physically uncloneable functions in the universal composition framework. In: Rogaway, P. (ed.) CRYPTO 2011. LNCS, vol. 6841, pp. 51–70. Springer, Heidelberg (2011). https://doi.org/10.1007/978-3-642-22792-9_4
4. Byali, M., Patra, A., Ravi, D., Sarkar, P.: Fast and universally-composable oblivious transfer and commitment scheme with adaptive security. Cryptology ePrint Archive, Report 2017/1165 (2017). https://eprint.iacr.org/2017/1165
5. Camenisch, J., Drijvers, M., Gagliardoni, T., Lehmann, A., Neven, G.: The wonderful world of global random oracles. In: Nielsen, J.B., Rijmen, V. (eds.) EUROCRYPT 2018. LNCS, vol. 10820, pp. 280–312. Springer, Cham (2018). https://doi.org/10.1007/978-3-319-78381-9_11
6. Canetti, R.: Universally composable security: a new paradigm for cryptographic protocols. In: 42nd FOCS, pp. 136–145. IEEE Computer Society Press, October 2001. https://doi.org/10.1109/SFCS.2001.959888
7. Canetti, R., Dodis, Y., Pass, R., Walfish, S.: Universally composable security with global setup. In: Vadhan, S.P. (ed.) TCC 2007. LNCS, vol. 4392, pp. 61–85. Springer, Heidelberg (2007). https://doi.org/10.1007/978-3-540-70936-7_4
8. Canetti, R., Goldreich, O., Halevi, S.: The random oracle methodology, revisited (preliminary version). In: 30th ACM STOC, pp. 209–218. ACM Press, May 1998. https://doi.org/10.1145/276698.276741
9. Canetti, R., Jain, A., Scafuro, A.: Practical UC security with a global random oracle. In: Ahn, G.J., Yung, M., Li, N. (eds.) ACM CCS 2014, pp. 597–608. ACM Press, November 2014. https://doi.org/10.1145/2660267.2660374
10. Canetti, R., Lindell, Y., Ostrovsky, R., Sahai, A.: Universally composable two-party and multi-party secure computation. In: 34th ACM STOC, pp. 494–503. ACM Press, May 2002. https://doi.org/10.1145/509907.509980
11. Canetti, R., Sarkar, P., Wang, X.: Efficient and round-optimal oblivious transfer and commitment with adaptive security. In: Moriai, S., Wang, H. (eds.) ASIACRYPT 2020. LNCS, vol. 12493, pp. 277–308. Springer, Cham (2020). https://doi.org/10.1007/978-3-030-64840-4_10
12. Chaum, D., Pedersen, T.P.: Wallet databases with observers. In: Brickell, E.F. (ed.) CRYPTO 1992. LNCS, vol. 740, pp. 89–105. Springer, Heidelberg (1993). https://doi.org/10.1007/3-540-48071-4_7

13. Chou, T., Orlandi, C.: The simplest protocol for oblivious transfer. In: Lauter, K., Rodríguez-Henríquez, F. (eds.) LATINCRYPT 2015. LNCS, vol. 9230, pp. 40–58. Springer, Cham (2015). https://doi.org/10.1007/978-3-319-22174-8_3

14. Cramer, R., Damgård, I., Schoenmakers, B.: Proofs of partial knowledge and simplified design of witness hiding protocols. In: Desmedt, Y.G. (ed.) CRYPTO 1994. LNCS, vol. 839, pp. 174–187. Springer, Heidelberg (1994). https://doi.org/10.1007/3-540-48658-5_19

15. Damgård, I.: On Σ-protocols. Lecture Notes, University of Aarhus, Department for Computer Science, p. 84 (2002). https://www.cs.au.dk/ivan/Sigma.pdf

16. David, B., Dowsley, R.: Efficient composable oblivious transfer from CDH in the global random oracle model. In: Krenn, S., Shulman, H., Vaudenay, S. (eds.) CANS 2020. LNCS, vol. 12579, pp. 462–481. Springer, Cham (2020). https://doi.org/10.1007/978-3-030-65411-5_23

17. Diffie, W., Hellman, M.E.: New directions in cryptography. IEEE Trans. Inf. Theory **22**(6), 644–654 (1976)

18. Dodis, Y., Shoup, V., Walfish, S.: Efficient constructions of composable commitments and zero-knowledge proofs. In: Wagner, D. (ed.) CRYPTO 2008. LNCS, vol. 5157, pp. 515–535. Springer, Heidelberg (2008). https://doi.org/10.1007/978-3-540-85174-5_29

19. Doerner, J., Kondi, Y., Lee, E., Shelat, A.: Secure two-party threshold ECDSA from ECDSA assumptions. In: 2018 IEEE Symposium on Security and Privacy, pp. 980–997. IEEE Computer Society Press, May 2018. https://doi.org/10.1109/SP.2018.00036

20. ElGamal, T.: A public key cryptosystem and a signature scheme based on discrete logarithms. In: Blakley, G.R., Chaum, D. (eds.) CRYPTO 1984. LNCS, vol. 196, pp. 10–18. Springer, Heidelberg (1985). https://doi.org/10.1007/3-540-39568-7_2

21. Fiat, A., Shamir, A.: How to prove yourself: practical solutions to identification and signature problems. In: Odlyzko, A.M. (ed.) CRYPTO 1986. LNCS, vol. 263, pp. 186–194. Springer, Heidelberg (1987). https://doi.org/10.1007/3-540-47721-7_12

22. Fischlin, M.: Communication-efficient non-interactive proofs of knowledge with online extractors. In: Shoup, V. (ed.) CRYPTO 2005. LNCS, vol. 3621, pp. 152–168. Springer, Heidelberg (2005). https://doi.org/10.1007/11535218_10

23. Garg, S., Ishai, Y., Srinivasan, A.: Two-round MPC: information-theoretic and black-box. In: Beimel, A., Dziembowski, S. (eds.) TCC 2018. LNCS, vol. 11239, pp. 123–151. Springer, Cham (2018). https://doi.org/10.1007/978-3-030-03807-6_5

24. Garg, S., Ishai, Y., Srinivasan, A.: Two-round MPC: information-theoretic and black-box. Cryptology ePrint Archive, Report 2018/909 (2018). https://eprint.iacr.org/2018/909

25. Garg, S., Srinivasan, A.: Garbled protocols and two-round MPC from bilinear maps. In: Umans, C. (ed.) 58th FOCS, pp. 588–599. IEEE Computer Society Press, October 2017. https://doi.org/10.1109/FOCS.2017.60

26. Genç, Z.A., Iovino, V., Rial, A.: "The simplest protocol for oblivious transfer" revisited. Inf. Process. Lett. **161**, 105975 (2020). https://doi.org/10.1016/j.ipl.2020.105975

27. Goldreich, O., Micali, S., Wigderson, A.: How to play any mental game or a completeness theorem for protocols with honest majority. In: Aho, A. (ed.) 19th ACM STOC, pp. 218–229. ACM Press, May 1987. https://doi.org/10.1145/28395.28420

28. Groth, J., Sahai, A.: Efficient non-interactive proof systems for bilinear groups. In: Smart, N. (ed.) EUROCRYPT 2008. LNCS, vol. 4965, pp. 415–432. Springer, Heidelberg (2008). https://doi.org/10.1007/978-3-540-78967-3_24

29. Hauck, E., Loss, J.: Efficient and universally composable protocols for oblivious transfer from the CDH assumption. Cryptology ePrint Archive, Report 2017/1011 (2017). https://eprint.iacr.org/2017/1011

30. Katz, J.: On achieving the "best of both worlds" in secure multiparty computation. In: Johnson, D.S., Feige, U. (eds.) 39th ACM STOC, pp. 11–20. ACM Press, Jun 2007. https://doi.org/10.1145/1250790.1250793

31. Katz, J., Maurer, U., Tackmann, B., Zikas, V.: Universally composable synchronous computation. In: Sahai, A. (ed.) TCC 2013. LNCS, vol. 7785, pp. 477–498. Springer, Heidelberg (2013). https://doi.org/10.1007/978-3-642-36594-2_27

32. Kondi, Y., Shelat, A.: Improved straight-line extraction in the random oracle model with applications to signature aggregation. In: Agrawal, S., Lin, D. (eds.) ASIACRYPT 2022, pp. 279–309. Springer, Cham (2022). https://doi.org/10.1007/978-3-031-22966-4_10

33. Li, B., Micciancio, D.: Equational security proofs of oblivious transfer protocols. In: Abdalla, M., Dahab, R. (eds.) PKC 2018. LNCS, vol. 10769, pp. 527–553. Springer, Cham (2018). https://doi.org/10.1007/978-3-319-76578-5_18

34. Masny, D., Rindal, P.: Endemic oblivious transfer. In: Cavallaro, L., Kinder, J., Wang, X., Katz, J. (eds.) ACM CCS 2019, pp. 309–326. ACM Press, November 2019. https://doi.org/10.1145/3319535.3354210

35. Masny, D., Rindal, P.: Endemic oblivious transfer. Cryptology ePrint Archive, Report 2019/706 (2019). https://eprint.iacr.org/2019/706

36. Mohassel, P., Rosulek, M., Scafuro, A.: Sublinear zero-knowledge arguments for ram programs. In: Coron, J.-S., Nielsen, J.B. (eds.) EUROCRYPT 2017. LNCS, vol. 10210, pp. 501–531. Springer, Cham (2017). https://doi.org/10.1007/978-3-319-56620-7_18

37. Okamoto, T.: Provably secure and practical identification schemes and corresponding signature schemes. In: Brickell, E.F. (ed.) CRYPTO 1992. LNCS, vol. 740, pp. 31–53. Springer, Heidelberg (1993). https://doi.org/10.1007/3-540-48071-4_3

38. Pass, R.: On deniability in the common reference string and random oracle model. In: Boneh, D. (ed.) CRYPTO 2003. LNCS, vol. 2729, pp. 316–337. Springer, Heidelberg (2003). https://doi.org/10.1007/978-3-540-45146-4_19

39. Pedersen, T.P.: Non-interactive and information-theoretic secure verifiable secret sharing. In: Feigenbaum, J. (ed.) CRYPTO 1991. LNCS, vol. 576, pp. 129–140. Springer, Heidelberg (1992). https://doi.org/10.1007/3-540-46766-1_9

40. Schnorr, C.P.: Efficient identification and signatures for smart cards. In: Brassard, G. (ed.) CRYPTO 1989. LNCS, vol. 435, pp. 239–252. Springer, New York (1990). https://doi.org/10.1007/0-387-34805-0_22

41. Zhou, Z., Zhang, B., Zhou, H.S., Ren, K.: Endemic oblivious transfer via random oracles, revisited. Cryptology ePrint Archive, Paper 2022/1525 (2022). https://eprint.iacr.org/2022/1525

42. Zhou, Z., Zhang, B., Zhou, H.S., Ren, K.: Guc-secure commitments via random oracles: new impossibility and feasibility. In: Agrawal, S., Lin, D. (eds.) ASIACRYPT 2022, pp. 129–158. Springer, Cham (2022). https://doi.org/10.1007/978-3-031-22972-5_5

Half-Tree: Halving the Cost of Tree Expansion in COT and DPF

Xiaojie Guo[1,2] , Kang Yang[1(✉)] , Xiao Wang[3] , Wenhao Zhang[3] ,
Xiang Xie[4,5] , Jiang Zhang[1] , and Zheli Liu[2(✉)]

[1] State Key Laboratory of Cryptology, Beijing, China
yangk@sklc.org
[2] Nankai University, Tianjin, China
xiaojie.guo@mail.nankai.edu.cn, liuzheli@nankai.edu.cn,
jiangzhang09@gmail.com
[3] Northwestern University, Evanston, USA
wangxiao@cs.northwestern.edu, wenhao.zhang@northwestern.edu
[4] Shanghai Qi Zhi Institute, Shanghai, China
xiexiangiscas@gmail.com
[5] PADO Labs, Hong Kong, China

Abstract. GGM tree is widely used in the design of correlated oblivious transfer (COT), subfield vector oblivious linear evaluation (sVOLE), distributed point function (DPF), and distributed comparison function (DCF). Often, the cost associated with GGM tree dominates the computation and communication of these protocols. In this paper, we propose a suite of optimizations that can reduce this cost by half.

- **Halving the cost of COT and sVOLE.** Our COT protocol introduces extra correlation to each level of a GGM tree used by the state-of-the-art COT protocol. As a result, it reduces both the number of AES calls and the communication by half. Extending this idea to sVOLE, we are able to achieve similar improvement with either halved computation or halved communication.
- **Halving the cost of DPF and DCF.** We propose improved two-party protocols for the distributed generation of DPF/DCF keys. Our tree structures behind these protocols lead to more efficient full-domain evaluation and halve the communication and the round complexity of the state-of-the-art DPF/DCF protocols.

All protocols are provably secure in the random-permutation model and can be accelerated based on fixed-key AES-NI. We also improve the state-of-the-art schemes of puncturable pseudorandom function (PPRF), DPF, and DCF, which are of independent interest in dealer-available scenarios.

1 Introduction

The construction of Goldreich-Goldwasser-Micali (GGM) tree [26] yields a pseudorandom function (PRF) family from any length-doubling pseudorandom generator (PRG). In this construction, a PRF key serves as a root and is expanded

The original version of this chapter was revised: this paper showed a wrong target acknowledgement. This now has been corrected. The correction to this chapter is available at https://doi.org/10.1007/978-3-031-30545-0_23

Table 1. Improvements of our protocols in the random-permutation model. Computation is measured as the number of fixed-key AES calls. In sVOLE, communication varies as per two field sizes $|\mathbb{F}|$ and $|\mathbb{K}|$. In DCF protocol, communication varies as per the range size $|\mathcal{R}|$ of comparison functions.

Protocol	Computation	Communication	# Rounds
COT (§4.1)	2×	2×	–
sVOLE (§4.1)	2×	1 ∼ 2×	–
sVOLE (§4.2)	1.33×	2×	–
DPF (§5.2)	1.33×	3×	2×
DCF (§5.3)	1.6×	2 ∼ 3×	2×

into a full binary tree, where each non-leaf node defines two child nodes from its PRG output. The PRF output for an input bit-string is defined as the leaf node labeled by this bit-string. GGM tree has been adapted widely for various cryptographic applications, especially in recent years.

A recent appealing application of GGM tree is to build efficient pseudorandom correlation generators (PCGs) [8,10,12,42,43,46], e.g., correlated oblivious transfer (COT), subfield vector oblivious linear evaluation (sVOLE), etc. In this context, a GGM tree essentially serves as a puncturable pseudorandom function (PPRF). PCGs serve as essential building blocks for secure multi-party computation (MPC) (e.g., [27,33]), zero-knowledge proofs (e.g., [2,21,43]), private set intersection (e.g., [23,40]), etc. Another related application of GGM tree is to build function secret sharing (FSS). In an FSS scheme, a dealer produces two keys, each defining an additive secret sharing of the full-domain evaluation result of some function f without revealing the parameters of f. FSS is very useful even for a simple f, and the dealer can be emulated using an MPC protocol. A distributed point function (DPF) [25] is an FSS scheme for the family of point functions $f^{\bullet}_{\alpha,\beta}(x)$ that output β if $x = \alpha$ and 0 otherwise. DPF has found various applications, including RAM-based secure computation [22], two-server PIR [13,25], private heavy hitters [6], oblivious linear evaluation (OLE) [12], etc. One important variation of DPF is distributed comparison function (DCF), which is an FSS scheme for the family of comparison functions $f^{<}_{\alpha,\beta}(x)$ that output β if $x < \alpha$ and 0 otherwise. DCF has been applied to design mixed-mode MPC [7,14], secure machine-learning inference [30], etc.

In all applications above, the cost associated with GGM tree can often be significant. For example, in the most recent silent OT protocol [18], distributing GGM-tree-related correlations takes more than 70% of the computation and essentially all communication. Similar bottlenecks have also been observed in DPF. For example, in the DPF-based secure RAM computation [22], local expansion of DPF keys takes a majority of the time as well.

1.1 Our Contribution

We propose a suite of *half-trees* as tailored alternatives for several GGM-tree-based protocols, leading to halved computation/communication/round complexity (Table 1, detailed complexity is compared in the sections). Our constructions work in the random-permutation model (RPM) [4,41], which can be efficiently instantiated via, e.g., fixed-key AES-NI.

Correlated GGM Trees for Half-Cost COT and sVOLE. We introduce correlated GGM (cGGM), a tree structure leading to both improved computation and communication in COT. It has an invariant that all same-level nodes sum up to the same global offset. We keep this invariant by setting a left child as the hash of its parent and the associated right child as the parent minus the left child. By plugging this tree into the state-of-the-art COT protocols [18,46], we can prove the security of the whole protocol in the random-permutation model by carefully choosing the hash function. Compared to the optimized GGM tree [28], this tree reduces the number of random-permutation calls and the communication by half.

Using cGGM tree, we can realize sVOLE for any large field and its subfield. This protocol reduces the computation of the prior protocols [10,43] by 2× using a field-based random permutation. However, it only halves the communication when the subfield size is significantly smaller than the field size. Then, we modify our cGGM tree to obtain a pseudorandom correlated GGM (pcGGM) tree, which is similar to a cGGM tree but has pseudorandom leaves. In contrast, pcGGM tree leads to a 2× saving in communication and a 1.33× saving in computation.

Halved communication and round complexity in distributed key generation of DPF and DCF. We introduce another binary tree structure, which adapts our pcGGM tree into a secretly shared form. This tree leads to a new DPF scheme with an improved distributed key generation protocol. This DPF protocol reduces the computation, communication, and round complexity of the prior work roughly by 1.33×, 3×, and 2×, respectively. When the range of point functions is a general ring, this shared tree allows simpler secure computation than the prior works in terms of the last correction word.

We also use an extended version of this shared pcGGM tree to design a new DCF scheme also with an improved distributed key generation protocol. The tree expansion in our DCF is much simpler than the prior work [7], where each parent node has to quadruple in length to produce additional correction words. In our extended shared pcGGM tree, this expansion factor in length is two or three, and the resulting additional correction words are more 2PC-friendly. When used in our DCF protocol with typical parameters, this extended tree leads to about 1.6×, 2 ∼ 3×, and 2× savings in terms of computation, communication, and round complexity in contrast to the prior work.

1.2 Concurrent Work

Recently, Boyle et al. [9] propose two unpredictable punctured functions (UPFs) that can be converted to PPRF with additional $0.5N$ RO calls for N-sized domain. Their first UPF construction needs N RO calls and is provably secure while the second UPF construction needs N RP calls but relies on an ad-hoc conjecture. For m-sized sVOLE tuples, the sVOLE extension protocols based on their proposal either needs $1.5m$ RO calls, or needs m RP calls plus $0.5m$ RO calls. They also propose an sVOLE extension protocol that is based on a stronger variation of UPF and requires m RO calls in total.

In contrast, our protocol is secure in the random-permutation model without any conjecture. Our COT protocol, as a special case of sVOLE protocol, only

Table 2. **Comparison with the concurrent work.** "RO/ROM" (resp., "RP/RPM") is for random oracle (resp., permutation) and the model. P_0 is the sender with a global key, and P_1 is the receiver. Assume weight-t regular LPN noises in sVOLE extension with output length m, field $\mathbb{F}$, and extension field $\mathbb{K}$. Computation is measured by the amount of symmetric-key operations, and there is also LPN-related computation in practice. Communication is measured by assuming P_0 and P_1 have access to random precomputed tuples: (i) [9]: $t \log \frac{m}{t}$ COTs (+ t sVOLEs, for general sVOLE extension), (ii) our COT extension: $t \log \frac{m}{t}$ COTs, (iii) our first sVOLE extension: $t(\log \frac{m}{t} + 1)$ sVOLEs, and (iv) our second sVOLE extension: $t \log \frac{m}{t}$ COTs + t sVOLEs.

	Assump.	Corr.	Computation	Communication (bits)	
				$P_0 \to P_1$	$P_1 \to P_0$
[9]	ROM	sVOLE	m RO calls		
	Ad-hoc^a	sVOLE	m RP calls+ $0.5m$ RO calls	$2t(\log \frac{m}{t} - 1)\lambda$ $+3t \log \|\mathbb{K}\|$	$t \log \|\mathbb{F}\|$
This work	RPM	COT	m RP calls	$t(\log \frac{m}{t} - 1)\lambda + \lambda$	–
		sVOLE	m RP calls	$t(\log \frac{m}{t} - 1) \log \|\mathbb{K}\|$ $+\lambda$	$t(\log \frac{m}{t} + 1) \log \|\mathbb{F}\|$
		sVOLE	$1.5m$ RP calls	$t(\log \frac{m}{t} - 2)\lambda$ $+3t \log \|\mathbb{K}\| + \lambda$	$t \log \|\mathbb{F}\|$

^{a} Security relies on the conjecture that the punctured result of the RPM-based UPF is unpredictable. This UPF uses GGM-style tree expansion $G(x) := \mathsf{H}_0(x) \| \mathsf{H}_1(x)$ for $\mathsf{H}_0(x) := \mathsf{H}(x) \oplus x$ and $\mathsf{H}_1(x) := \mathsf{H}(x) + x \bmod 2^\lambda$.

requires m RP calls and can reduce communication by half; our two sVOLE protocols need m or $1.5m$ RP calls with different levels of communication reduction. More importantly, we also demonstrate how the idea can be applied to DPF/DCF protocols as well.

In Table 2, we compare the cost of sVOLE extension in the two works. The sVOLE extension in both works can be easily turned into the extension of random OTs via the standard transformation [3,10,34]. If we regard one (length-preserving) RO call as two RP calls according to the XOR-based construction of [5], our work also beats the concurrent one in terms of concrete efficiency.

2 Preliminaries

2.1 Notation

Let λ denote the computational security parameter. $n = n(\lambda)$ means that $n \in \mathbb{N}$ is polynomial in λ. Let $\mathsf{negl}(\cdot)$ denote an unspecified negligible function and $\log(\cdot)$ denote the logarithm in base 2. Let $x \leftarrow S$ denote sampling x uniformly at random from a finite set S. Let $[a, b) := \{a, \ldots, b-1\}$ and $[a, b] := \{a, \ldots, b\}$. Let $\mathbb{G}$ (resp., $\mathcal{R}$) denote finite group (resp., ring). We use bold lowercase letters (e.g., $\mathbf{a}$) for vectors. For $i \geq 0$, let $\mathbf{a}^{(i)}$ denote the i-th entry of vector $\mathbf{a}$. Let $\mathsf{unit}_\mathbb{G}(n, \alpha, \beta) \in \mathbb{G}^n$ denote the vector whose α-th entry is β and others are 0. For some field $\mathbb{F}$ and irreducible polynomial $f(X) \in \mathbb{F}[X]$, let $\mathbb{K} = \mathbb{F}[X]/f(X)$ denote an extension field. For some $n \in \mathbb{N}$, we interchangeably use $\mathbb{F}_{2^n}$, $\mathbb{F}_2^n$, and $\{0, 1\}^n$, where $\oplus$ is for bitwise-XOR. For some bit-string $x \in \{0, 1\}^n$, let $\mathsf{lsb}(x)$ denote its least significant bit (LSB), $\mathsf{hb}(x)$ denote its high $n - 1$ bits, and x_i

denote its i-th bit such that x_1 is the most significant one. We use $\|$ for bit-string concatenation and $\circ$ for function composition. Let $\mathsf{Convert}_{\mathbb{G}} : \{0,1\}^* \to \mathbb{G}$ denote a function that maps random strings to pseudorandom $\mathbb{G}$ elements (see Appendix F.1 of the full version [29] for its implementation).

Binary Trees. In an n-level tree, let X_i^j denote the j-th node on its i-level for $i \in [1, n]$ and $j \in [0, 2^i)$. We can write the superscript j into i-bit decomposition, i.e., $X_i^{j_1 \cdots j_i} := X_i^j$. When a node $X_i^j \in \{0,1\}^n$, we can decompose it into a seed $s_i^j := \mathsf{hb}(X_i^j) \in \{0,1\}^{n-1}$ and a control bit $t_i^j := \mathsf{lsb}(X_i^j) \in \{0,1\}$ such that $X_i^j = (s_i^j \| t_i^j)$. We usually omit the superscript j if it is the i-bit prefix of a path $\alpha \in \{0,1\}^n$ of particular interest in a given context. For completeness, let X_0 denote the root. For some $i \in [1, n]$ and $b \in \{0,1\}$, let K_i^b denote the sum of the 2^{i-1} b-side (i.e., left or right) nodes on the i-th level.

Secret Sharings. For some additive Abelian group $\mathbb{G}$ and $x \in \mathbb{G}$, we use $\langle x \rangle^{\mathsf{A}}$ to mean that x is additively shared between two parties and call it a secret for short. For some secret $\langle x \rangle^{\mathsf{A}}$ for $x \in \mathbb{G}$ and party $b \in \{0,1\}$, let $\langle x \rangle_b^{\mathsf{A}} \in \mathbb{G}$ denote the secret share of the party b such that $x = \langle x \rangle_0^{\mathsf{A}} + \langle x \rangle_1^{\mathsf{A}}$. We abbreviate $\langle x \rangle^{\mathsf{A}}$ to $\langle x \rangle$ and $\langle x \rangle_b^{\mathsf{A}}$ to $\langle x \rangle_b$ if $\mathbb{G} = \{0,1\}^n$. For some secret $\langle x \rangle$ for $x \in \{0,1\}^n$ and efficiently computable (possibly non-linear) Boolean circuit $\mathsf{H} : \{0,1\}^n \to \{0,1\}^*$, let $\mathsf{H}(\langle x \rangle)$ denote such a *linear evaluation* that returns a secret $\langle y \rangle$ with share $\langle y \rangle_b := \mathsf{H}(\langle x \rangle_b)$ for each $b \in \{0,1\}$.

2.2   Security Model and Functionalities

We use the *universal composability* (UC) framework [15] to prove security in the presence of a semi-honest, static adversary. We say that a protocol Π *UC-realizes* an ideal functionality $\mathcal{F}$ if for any probabilistic polynomial-time (PPT) adversary $\mathcal{A}$, there exists a PPT adversary (simulator) $\mathcal{S}$ such that for any PPT environment $\mathcal{Z}$ with arbitrary auxiliary input z, the output distribution of $\mathcal{Z}$ in the *real-world* execution where the parties interact with $\mathcal{A}$ and execute Π is computationally indistinguishable from the output distribution of $\mathcal{Z}$ in the *ideal-world* execution where the parties interact with $\mathcal{S}$ and $\mathcal{F}$.

Our protocols use the functionality $\mathcal{F}_{\mathsf{sVOLE}}$ (Fig. 1) of subfield vector oblivious linear evaluation. If $\mathbb{K} = \mathbb{F}_{2^\lambda}$ and $\mathbb{F} = \mathbb{F}_2$, $\mathcal{F}_{\mathsf{sVOLE}}$ degenerates to the COT functionality $\mathcal{F}_{\mathsf{COT}}$ in [46]. If $\mathbb{K} = \mathbb{F}$, $\mathcal{F}_{\mathsf{sVOLE}}$ serves as the VOLE functionality in [8,40,42]. We omit the session IDs and sub-session IDs in the functionalities for simplicity. By convention, we can write sVOLE tuples as two-party *information-theoretic message authentication codes* (IT-MACs) [20,38]. Let $\Delta_b \in \mathbb{K}$ denote the global key of one party P_b. P_b authenticates a value $x \in \mathbb{F}$ of the other party P_{1-b} by sampling a uniform one-time key $\mathsf{K}_b[x] \leftarrow \mathbb{K}$ and giving to P_{1-b} the MAC $\mathsf{M}_{1-b}[x] := \mathsf{K}_b[x] + x \cdot \Delta_b \in \mathbb{K}$. If identity $b \in \{0,1\}$ is clear in a given context, we write Δ, $\mathsf{K}[x]$, and $\mathsf{M}[x]$ for Δ_b, $\mathsf{K}_b[x]$, and $\mathsf{M}_{1-b}[x]$, respectively.

2.3   Circular Correlation Robustness

Circular correlation robustness (CCR) [17,28] is the security notion first introduced for the circuit garbling with Free-XOR optimization [37], where there

---

Functionality $\mathcal{F}_{\mathsf{sVOLE}}$

Parameters: Field $\mathbb{F}$ and its extension field $\mathbb{K}$.

Initialize: Upon receiving (init) from P_0 and P_1, sample $\Delta \leftarrow \mathbb{K}$ if P_0 is honest; otherwise, receive $\Delta \in \mathbb{K}$ from the adversary. Store Δ and send it to P_0. Ignore all subsequent (init) commands.

Extend: This functionality allows polynomially many (extend) commands. Upon receiving (extend, m) from P_0 and P_1:

1. If P_0 is honest, sample $\mathbf{v} \leftarrow \mathbb{K}^m$; otherwise, receive $\mathbf{v} \in \mathbb{K}^m$ from the adversary.
2. If P_1 is honest, sample $\mathbf{u} \leftarrow \mathbb{F}^m$, and compute $\mathbf{w} := \mathbf{v} + \mathbf{u} \cdot \Delta \in \mathbb{K}^m$; otherwise, receive $(\mathbf{u}, \mathbf{w}) \in \mathbb{F}^m \times \mathbb{K}^m$ from the adversary, and recompute $\mathbf{v} := \mathbf{w} - \mathbf{u} \cdot \Delta \in \mathbb{K}^m$.
3. Send $\mathbf{v}$ to P_0 and $(\mathbf{u}, \mathbf{w})$ to P_1.

Global-key queries: If P_1 is corrupted, upon receiving (guess, Δ'), where $\Delta' \in \mathbb{K}$, from the adversary, send (success) to the adversary if $\Delta = \Delta'$; send (fail) to the adversary otherwise.

Fig. 1. Functionality for subfield VOLE.

exists a global key Δ offsetting the inputs and outputs of some function H. [28] showed that a CCR function H can be constructed from a fixed-key block cipher (e.g., AES) modeled as random permutation and a *linear orthomorphism*[1]. In this construction, it takes one block-cipher call to invoke a CCR function.

Definition 1 (Circular Correlation Robustness, [28]). *Let* $\mathsf{H} : \{0,1\}^\lambda \to \{0,1\}^\lambda$, χ *be a distribution on* $\{0,1\}^\lambda$, *and* $\mathcal{O}^{\mathsf{ccr}}_{\mathsf{H},\Delta}(x,b) := \mathsf{H}(x \oplus \Delta) \oplus b \cdot \Delta$ *be an oracle for* $x, \Delta \in \{0,1\}^\lambda$ *and* $b \in \{0,1\}$. H *is* (t,q,ρ,ϵ)-CCR *if, for any distinguisher* $\mathcal{D}$ *running in time at most* t *and making at most* q *queries to* $\mathcal{O}^{\mathsf{ccr}}_{\mathsf{H},\Delta}(\cdot,\cdot)$, *and any* χ *with min-entropy at least* ρ, *it holds that*

$$\left| \Pr_{\Delta \leftarrow \chi} \left[\mathcal{D}^{\mathcal{O}^{\mathsf{ccr}}_{\mathsf{H},\Delta}(\cdot,\cdot)}(1^\lambda) = 1 \right] - \Pr_{f \leftarrow \mathcal{F}_{\lambda+1,\lambda}} \left[\mathcal{D}^{f(\cdot,\cdot)}(1^\lambda) = 1 \right] \right| \le \epsilon,$$

where $\mathcal{D}$ *cannot query both* $(x,0)$ *and* $(x,1)$ *for any* $x \in \{0,1\}^\lambda$.

In this work, $\mathcal{D}$ can only make CCR queries with *restricted* forms, which are reminiscent of those in the Half-Gate garbling scheme [47]. We defer the formal definition of these restricted queries to Appendix A of the full version [29].

---

[1] A mapping $\sigma : \mathbb{G} \to \mathbb{G}$ for an additive Abelian group $\mathbb{G}$ is a linear orthomorphism if (i) σ is a permutation, (ii) $\sigma(x + y) = \sigma(x) + \sigma(y)$ for any $x, y \in \mathbb{G}$, and (iii) $\sigma'(x) := \sigma(x) - x$ is also a permutation. [28] presents two efficient instantiations of σ (with well-defined efficient σ^{-1}, σ', and σ'^{-1}): (i) if $\mathbb{G}$ is a field, $\sigma(x) := c \cdot x$ for some $c \neq 0, 1 \in \mathbb{G}$, and (ii) if $\mathbb{G} = \{0,1\}^n$, $\sigma(x) = \sigma(x_L \| x_R) := (x_L \oplus x_R) \| x_L$ where x_L and x_R are the left and right halves of x. .

2.4   Function Secret Sharing

A function secret sharing (FSS) is a secret sharing scheme where a dealer distributes the shares of a function f to multiple parties, and each party can use its share to *locally* compute the share of $f(x)$ for any *public* x in the domain of f. In this work, we focus on two-party FSS schemes.

Definition 2 (Function Secret Sharing, [7,13]). *For a family $\mathcal{F}_{\mathcal{X},\mathbb{G}}$ of functions with domain $\mathcal{X}$ and range $\mathbb{G}$, where $\mathbb{G}$ is an Abelian group, a two-party FSS scheme with key space $\mathcal{K}_0 \times \mathcal{K}_1$ has the following syntax:*

- $(k_0, k_1) \leftarrow \mathsf{Gen}(1^\lambda, \hat{f})$. *On input 1^λ and the description $\hat{f} \in \{0,1\}^*$ of a function $f \in \mathcal{F}_{\mathcal{X},\mathbb{G}}$, output a key pair $(k_0, k_1) \in \mathcal{K}_0 \times \mathcal{K}_1$.*
- $f_b(x) \leftarrow \mathsf{Eval}(b, k_b, x)$. *On input the party identifier $b \in \{0,1\}$, the party's key $k_b \in \mathcal{K}_b$, and a point $x \in \mathcal{X}$, output the share $f_b(x) \in \mathbb{G}$.*

A two-party FSS scheme $(\mathsf{Gen}, \mathsf{Eval})$ is secure for the function family $\mathcal{F}_{\mathcal{X},\mathbb{G}}$ with leakage $\mathsf{Leak} : \{0,1\}^* \to \{0,1\}^*$ if the following properties hold.

- **Correctness.** *For any function $f \in \mathcal{F}_{\mathcal{X},\mathbb{G}}$ with description $\hat{f}$, and any $x \in \mathcal{X}$,*

$$\Pr\left[(k_0, k_1) \leftarrow \mathsf{Gen}(1^\lambda, \hat{f}) : \textstyle\sum_{b \in \{0,1\}} \mathsf{Eval}(b, k_b, x) = f(x)\right] = 1.$$

- **Security.** *There exists a PPT simulator Sim such that, for any function $f \in \mathcal{F}_{\mathcal{X},\mathbb{G}}$ with the description $\hat{f}$, any $b \in \{0,1\}$, and any PPT adversary $\mathcal{A}$,*

$$\left| \Pr\left[(k_0, k_1) \leftarrow \mathsf{Gen}(1^\lambda, \hat{f}) : \mathcal{A}(1^\lambda, k_b) = 1\right] \right.$$
$$\left. - \Pr\left[k_b \leftarrow \mathsf{Sim}(1^\lambda, b, \mathsf{Leak}(\hat{f})) : \mathcal{A}(1^\lambda, k_b) = 1\right] \right| \leq \mathsf{negl}(\lambda).$$

By default, the leakage $\mathsf{Leak}(\hat{f})$ only involves the domain and the range of f. The following two special FSS schemes have been proposed in [7,13].

Distributed Point Functions (DPFs). A two-party *distributed point function* $(\mathsf{DPF.Gen}, \mathsf{DPF.Eval})$ with domain $\mathcal{X}$ and range $\mathbb{G}$ is a two-party FSS scheme for the function family $\mathcal{F}_{\mathcal{X},\mathbb{G}} = \{f^\bullet_{\alpha,\beta}\}_{\alpha \in \mathcal{X}, \beta \in \mathbb{G}}$ where $f^\bullet_{\alpha,\beta}$ is a *point function* such that $f^\bullet_{\alpha,\beta}(\alpha) = \beta$, and $f^\bullet_{\alpha,\beta}(x) = 0$ for $x \neq \alpha \in \mathcal{X}$.

Distributed Comparison Functions (DCFs). A two-party *distributed comparison function* $(\mathsf{DCF.Gen}, \mathsf{DCF.Eval})$ with domain $\mathcal{X}$ and range $\mathbb{G}$ is a two-party FSS scheme for the function family $\mathcal{F}_{\mathcal{X},\mathbb{G}} = \{f^<_{\alpha,\beta}\}_{\alpha \in \mathcal{X}, \beta \in \mathbb{G}}$ where $f^<_{\alpha,\beta}$ is a *comparison function* such that $f^<_{\alpha,\beta}(x) = \beta$ if $x < \alpha \in \mathcal{X}$, and $f^<_{\alpha,\beta}(x) = 0$ otherwise.

3   Technical Overview

3.1   Improved COT/sVOLE from Correlated GGM Trees

Since COT/sVOLE can be constructed from its "single-point" version using an appropriate LPN assumption, we focus on single-point COT/sVOLE, where the vector $\mathbf{u}$ in a COT/sVOLE tuple $\mathbf{w} = \mathbf{v} + \mathbf{u} \cdot \Delta$ has exactly one non-zero entry.

Correlated OT from Correlated GGM. The core idea behind our single-point COT protocol is that, instead of using a GGM tree with pseudorandom nodes as the state-of-the-art works, our protocol uses a *correlated* GGM (cGGM) tree where *the sum of all same-level nodes equals a global offset* Δ. This invariant can be maintained by using a generalized Davies-Meyer construction with a hash function H: every parent x has left child $H(x)$ and right child $x - H(x)$. cGGM tree leads to two improvements: (i) no additional hash computation is needed for every right child so that the computation is halved, and (ii) if the global offset Δ (i.e., the difference between two first-level nodes) is set up by precomputed random COT tuples, the single-point COT protocol sends only λ bits per level, in contrast to 2λ bits from a standard OT per level in the state-of-the-art works.

To explain our second improvement in detail, we first recall the prior construction from the perspective of GGM tree. In this construction, the sender holds an n-level GGM tree, whose 2^n leaves in $\mathbb{F}_{2^\lambda}$ forms a vector $\mathbf{v} \in \mathbb{F}_{2^\lambda}^{2^n}$. The receiver with a punctured point $\alpha = \alpha_1 \ldots \alpha_n \in \{0,1\}^n$ uses, for each $i \in [1,n]$, a standard OT to select the XOR of all $\overline{\alpha}_i$-side nodes on the i-th level. From these n XORs, the receiver recovers the n off-path GGM-tree nodes just leaving the path α and use these n nodes to recover all leaves except the α-th one, corresponding to a vector $\mathbf{w} \in \mathbb{F}_{2^\lambda}^{2^n}$ with the punctured entry $\mathbf{w}^{(\alpha)}$. The sender samples $\Delta \leftarrow \mathbb{F}_{2^\lambda}$, defines its output as $(\Delta, \mathbf{v})$, and sends $\psi := \Delta \oplus (\oplus_{j \in [0,2^n)} \mathbf{v}^{(j)}) \in \mathbb{F}_{2^\lambda}$ to the receiver. The receiver patches $\mathbf{w}^{(\alpha)} := \psi \oplus (\oplus_{j \neq \alpha} \mathbf{w}^{(j)})$ and defines its output as $(\mathbf{u}, \mathbf{w})$ for $\mathbf{u} = \mathbf{unit}_{\mathbb{F}_2}(2^n, \alpha, 1)$. The computation is dominated by the full GGM-tree expansion while the communication is from n parallel standard OTs, which need n precomputed COT tuples via the standard technique [3,34].

In contrast, our cGGM-tree single-point COT, where the global offset in a cGGM tree coincides with the global key in the n precomputed COT tuples, can directly use these tuples. For each level $i \in [1,n]$, let $M[r_i] = K[r_i] \oplus r_i \cdot \Delta$ be such a tuple where the sender has $(\Delta, K[r_i]) \in \mathbb{F}_{2^\lambda} \times \mathbb{F}_{2^\lambda}$ and the receiver has $(r_i, M[r_i]) \in \mathbb{F}_2 \times \mathbb{F}_{2^\lambda}$, and $K_i^b \in \mathbb{F}_{2^\lambda}$ be the XOR of all b-side nodes for $b \in \{0,1\}$. To select $K_i^{\overline{\alpha}_i}$ as in the prior construction, the receiver sends $\overline{\alpha}_i \oplus r_i$ to the sender, receives back $c_i := K_i^0 \oplus K[r_i] \oplus (\overline{\alpha}_i \oplus r_i) \cdot \Delta$, and computes

$$c_i \oplus M[r_i] = K_i^0 \oplus K[r_i] \oplus (\overline{\alpha}_i \oplus r_i) \cdot \Delta \oplus M[r_i] = K_i^0 \oplus \overline{\alpha}_i \cdot \Delta = K_i^{\overline{\alpha}_i},$$

where the last equality holds since the cGGM tree uses Δ as global offset. For each level, the sender sends λ bits to the receiver, only a half of the 2λ bits in a standard OT. When the point α is random, the message $\overline{\alpha}_i \oplus r_i$ can be avoided as well. The single-point COT outputs are defined as in the prior construction, except that the receiver locally patches $\mathbf{w}^{(\alpha)} := \oplus_{j \neq \alpha} \mathbf{w}^{(j)}$.

The security against the semi-honest sender is straightforward. However, a subtle issue arises in proving the security against the semi-honest receiver. Note that the environment $\mathcal{Z}$ can observe the global key Δ from the honest sender's output and use it to distinguish the two worlds. Let $\{X_i^{\alpha_1 \ldots \alpha_{i-1} \overline{\alpha}_i}\}_{i \in [1,n]}$ be the cGGM-tree off-path nodes recovered by the receiver. In the real world, these off-path nodes satisfy the consistency with Δ: for $j \in [2,n]$, $X_j^{\alpha_1 \ldots \alpha_{j-1} \overline{\alpha}_j}$ equals

$$H\left(\Delta \oplus \bigoplus_{i \in [1,j-1]} X_i^{\alpha_1 \ldots \alpha_{i-1}\overline{\alpha}_i}\right) \oplus \overline{\alpha}_j \cdot \left(\Delta \oplus \bigoplus_{i \in [1,j-1]} X_i^{\alpha_1 \ldots \alpha_{i-1}\overline{\alpha}_i}\right). \quad (1)$$

However, this consistency does not hold in the ideal world where $\{c_i\}_{i \in [1,n]}$ sent by the simulator are sampled at random so that the n off-path nodes will be independently uniform in the ideal world. Thus, $\mathcal{Z}$ can trivially distinguish the two worlds by using the known Δ to check (1). Our security proof addresses this issue by carefully constructing H from a random permutation, allowing global-key queries in the single-point COT functionality, and programming the random permutation and its inverse to keep the consistency. The intuition is that, to distinguish the two worlds, $\mathcal{Z}$ must query the random permutation or its inverse with Δ-related transcripts. Thus, the simulator can observe these queries and extract every potential Δ from them. Using global-key queries, the simulator checks whether an extracted Δ matches that in the single-point COT functionality or not. If so, it immediately programs the two permutation oracles using this Δ so that they are consistent with the simulated $\{c_i\}_{i \in [1,n]}$. Similar proof technique in the random-oracle model have been used in TinyOT [32,38].

Subfield VOLE from Correlated GGM. We further propose a cGGM-based blueprint of single-point sVOLE for field $\mathbb{F}$ and its exponentially large extension $\mathbb{K}$. In this blueprint, we construct an n-level cGGM tree from a hash function $H : \mathbb{K} \to \mathbb{K}$ so that all nodes are in $\mathbb{K}$, and extend the spirit of our single-point COT. The spirit is that the equality $\mathbf{w}^{(\alpha)} = \mathbf{v}^{(\alpha)} \oplus \Delta$ at the punctured point α automatically holds by embedding Δ into a cGGM tree. For single-point sVOLE, we want to likewise keep $\mathbf{w}^{(\alpha)} = \mathbf{v}^{(\alpha)} + \beta \cdot \Delta$ for some $\beta \in \mathbb{F}^*$ and $\Delta \in \mathbb{K}$ at the punctured point α. However, we cannot use $\beta \cdot \Delta$, which is unknown to the sender, as the cGGM-tree global offset. Instead, we can define this offset as the sender's additive share of $\beta \cdot \Delta$ so that the receiver can correct the automatically preserved result at the point α by using its additive share of $\beta \cdot \Delta$.

In detail, the two parties use a random sVOLE tuple $\mathsf{M}[\beta] = \mathsf{K}[\beta] + \beta \cdot \Delta$ for the $\beta \cdot \Delta$ term, where the sender has $(\Delta, \mathsf{K}[\beta]) \in \mathbb{K} \times \mathbb{K}$ and the receiver has $(\beta, \mathsf{M}[\beta]) \in \mathbb{F}^* \times \mathbb{K}$. The sender uses $\mathsf{K}[\beta]$ as the global offset of its cGGM tree, and the receiver selects, for each level i, the sum of all $\overline{\alpha}_i$-side nodes. For the i-th level, let $K_i^b \in \mathbb{K}$ be the sum of all b-side nodes for $b \in \{0,1\}$, and let the two parties have access to a special sVOLE tuple[2] $\mathsf{M}[r_i] = \mathsf{K}[r_i] + r_i \cdot \mathsf{K}[\beta]$, where the sender has $\mathsf{K}[r_i] \in \mathbb{K}$ and the receiver has $(r_i, \mathsf{M}[r_i]) \in \mathbb{F}_2 \times \mathbb{K}$. The sender sends $c_i := \mathsf{K}[r_i] + K_i^0 \in \mathbb{K}$ to the receiver, who defines $\overline{\alpha}_i := r_i$ and can compute

$$(-1)^{r_i} \cdot (-\mathsf{M}[r_i] + c_i) = (-1)^{\overline{\alpha}_i} \cdot (K_i^0 - \overline{\alpha}_i \cdot \mathsf{K}[\beta]) = K_i^{\overline{\alpha}_i},$$

where the last equality holds due to the cGGM invariant. The n selected sums allow the receiver to recover, in a top-down manner, the n off-nodes with respect to α and the 2^n cGGM leaves except the α-th one. The sender defines $\mathbf{v} \in \mathbb{K}^{2^n}$ from its 2^n cGGM-tree leaves, while the receiver defines $\mathbf{w} \in \mathbb{K}^{2^n}$ from the α-exclusive $2^n - 1$ leaves and the locally patched punctured leaf $\mathbf{w}^{(\alpha)} := \mathsf{M}[\beta] -$

---

[2] The special sVOLE tuples for selecting n sums can be obtained from n precomputed random sVOLE tuples by the receiver sending $n \cdot \log |\mathbb{F}|$ bits.

$\sum_{j\neq\alpha} \mathbf{w}^{(j)} = \mathsf{M}[\beta] - (\sum_{j\neq\alpha} \mathbf{w}^{(j)} + \mathbf{v}^{(\alpha)}) + \mathbf{v}^{(\alpha)} = \mathbf{v}^{(\alpha)} + \beta \cdot \Delta$. If the sender defines its output as $(\Delta, \mathbf{v})$ and the receiver defines its output as $(\mathbf{u}, \mathbf{w})$ for $\mathbf{u} := \mathbf{unit}_{\mathbb{F}}(2^n, \alpha, \beta)$, the two parties share a single-point sVOLE correlation.

Our cGGM-based single-point sVOLE protocol also has the issue in proving the security against the semi-honest receiver as the environment $\mathcal{Z}$ sees Δ from the honest sender's output. $\mathcal{Z}$ can compute the cGGM offset $\mathsf{K}[\beta] = \mathsf{M}[\beta] - \beta \cdot \Delta$ and, to distinguish the two worlds, check if the consistency (1) holds for $\mathsf{K}[\beta]$ or not. As in our cGGM-based single-point COT, our simulator addresses this issue by extracting every possible $\mathsf{K}[\beta]$ and the associated $\Delta = \beta^{-1} \cdot (\mathsf{M}[\beta] - \mathsf{K}[\beta])$, querying the single-point sVOLE functionality with Δ, and programming the random permutation and its inverse if the global-key query succeeds.

Subfield VOLE from Pseudorandom Correlated GGM. There is another single-point sVOLE blueprint [10, 43] basing its security on the pseudorandomness of GGM-tree nodes: for some path $\alpha \in \{0, 1\}^n$, the n off-path nodes and the α-th leaf are pseudorandom. Our cGGM tree cannot be used in this blueprint since its same-level nodes are correlated under the global offset. However, we observe that a cGGM tree can be modified into a *pseudorandom* cGGM (pcGGM) tree with the required pseudorandomness.

In an n-level pcGGM tree, we preserve the cGGM invariant for the $\mathbb{F}_{2^\lambda}$ nodes on the first $n - 1$ levels, i.e., using a hash function $\mathsf{H}' : \mathbb{F}_{2^\lambda} \to \mathbb{F}_{2^\lambda}$ and Davies-Meyer construction to keep that all same-level nodes are XORed to a global offset $\Delta \in \mathbb{F}_{2^\lambda}$. Nevertheless, we break the last-level correlation in the pcGGM tree: every parent $x \in \mathbb{F}_{2^\lambda}$ on the $(i-1)$-th level has left child $\mathsf{H}'(x)$ and right child $\mathsf{H}'(x \oplus 1)$. In sVOLE protocols for $\mathbb{K} \neq \mathbb{F}_{2^\lambda}$, the pcGGM leaves will be further converted by the function $\mathsf{Convert}_{\mathbb{K}} : \mathbb{F}_{2^\lambda} \to \mathbb{K}$.

Our core observation for arguing the pseudorandomness of the $n + 1$ pcGGM nodes is that the inputs of the hash function H' are of CCR forms. More specifically, a global $\Delta \in \mathbb{F}_{2^\lambda}$ offsets the two first-level nodes of the pcGGM tree and induces the first $n - 1$ off-path nodes $\{X_i^{\alpha_1 \cdots \alpha_{i-1} \overline{\alpha}_i}\}_{i \in [1,n-1]}$ according to (1) for H'. Meanwhile, the last off-path node $X_n^{\alpha_1 \cdots \alpha_{n-1} \overline{\alpha}_n} \in \mathbb{F}_{2^\lambda}$ and the α-th pcGGM leaf $X_n \in \mathbb{F}_{2^\lambda}$ come from two hash calls of the following form: for $b \in \{0, 1\}$,

$$X_n^{\alpha_1 \cdots \alpha_{n-1} b} = \mathsf{H}'\left(\Delta \oplus (\bigoplus_{i \in [1,n-1]} X_i^{\alpha_1 \cdots \alpha_{i-1} \overline{\alpha}_i}) \oplus b\right).$$

Intuitively, we can use a CCR hash function H' to argue the pseudorandomness of the n off-path nodes and the α-th leaf, which is sufficient for the single-point sVOLE blueprint. The challenge in this security reduction is to show that the CCR queries to H' are legal (i.e., no $(x, 0)$ and $(x, 1)$ for the same x) with overwhelming probability. We address this challenge by resorting to the observation that these inputs are *restricted* so that they are well-structured and are not arbitrarily chosen by the corrupted receiver (the only case where we need the pseudorandomness). Such restricted inputs are reminiscent of the "naturally derived keys" [28, 47] in the Half-Gate garbling scheme so that we can bound the probability similarly. We defer the details to Appendix A of the full version [29]. Note that even if one uses $\mathsf{Convert}_{\mathbb{K}}$ to map the leaves into $\mathbb{K}$, the pseudorandomness of these nodes still holds due to the pseudorandomness of $\mathsf{Convert}_{\mathbb{K}}$.

By plugging our pcGGM tree into the prior single-point sVOLE blueprint, we obtain a more efficient protocol. The improvement owes to the cGGM invariant in its first $n - 1$ levels. In terms of communication, the receiver can use $n - 1$ precomputed random COTs to select the XORs on these levels and recover the first $n - 1$ levels of the sender's pcGGM tree; in contrast, the prior protocols use a standard OT per level due to the two pseudorandom XORs. For the last level in our protocol, the two parties also need a standard OT due to the broken correlation of the two sums. Given the random-permutation-based CCR hash functions in [28], our pcGGM-based single-point sVOLE protocol is secure in the random-permutation model. In particular, this protocol can implement the single-point sVOLE functionality *without* global-key queries since $\Delta \in \mathbb{F}_{2^\lambda}$ is only used in the pcGGM tree and is not included in the sender's output.

3.2   DPF/DCF from Shared Pseudorandom Correlated GGM Trees

DPF Sheme and Protocol. Using a pcGGM-like trick, we present a new DPF scheme, followed by a more efficient distributed protocol. Recall that, in the prior DPF scheme [13], there are two parties sharing an n-level GGM-style tree where the n nodes on some path $\alpha \in \{0,1\}^n$ are pseudorandom with LSB one, and others are zero. Then, the two-party shares of the α-th leaf mask the DPF payload $\beta \in \mathbb{G}$. Our core observation is that we need the pseudorandom α-th leaf to hide β, but the internal pseudorandom on-path nodes are not mandatory. Instead, the two parties can share an n-level pcGGM-style tree (say, spcGGM tree) where (i) the root X_0 and the first $n - 1$ on-path nodes equal a global offset $\Delta \in \mathbb{F}_{2^\lambda}$ with $\mathsf{lsb}(\Delta) = 1$, (ii) the last on-path node (i.e., the α-th leaf) is pseudorandom with LSB one, and (iii) other nodes are zero. As in the prior scheme, the per-party share of this tree is compressed as a key including an XOR share of the root and $n + 1$ public *pseudorandom* correction words.

We explain our construction of these correction words in detail. To keep the invariant (i), the spcGGM tree uses a correction procedure different from the prior one. For each level $i \in [1, n-1]$ with a public correction word $\mathsf{CW}_i \in \mathbb{F}_{2^\lambda}$, and $b \in \{0,1\}$, the b-side secret child of the $(i-1)$-th on-path secret node $\langle X_{i-1} \rangle = \langle s_{i-1} \| t_{i-1} \rangle$ is defined as follows:

$$\langle X_i^{\alpha_1 \ldots \alpha_{i-1} b} \rangle := \mathsf{H}'(\langle X_{i-1} \rangle) \oplus b \cdot \langle X_{i-1} \rangle \oplus \langle t_{i-1} \rangle \cdot \mathsf{CW}_i.$$

Solving this *linear* equation for the *public* CW_i under the constraint (i), we have

$$\mathsf{CW}_i = \mathsf{H}'(\langle X_{i-1} \rangle 0) \oplus \mathsf{H}'(\langle X_{i-1} \rangle 1) \oplus \overline{\alpha}_i \cdot \Delta.$$

As for (ii), we use a public correction word $\mathsf{CW}_n = (\mathsf{HCW}, \mathsf{LCW}^0, \mathsf{LCW}^1) \in \mathbb{F}_{2^{\lambda-1}} \times \mathbb{F}_2 \times \mathbb{F}_2$ to follow the same last-level correction as the prior work. For $b \in \{0,1\}$, define a function $\mathsf{H}'_b(\cdot) := \mathsf{H}'(\cdot \oplus b)$ and the b-side secret child of the $(n-1)$-th on-path secret node $\langle X_{n-1} \rangle = \langle s_{n-1} \| t_{n-1} \rangle$ as follows:

$$\langle X_n^{\alpha_1 \ldots \alpha_{n-1} b} \rangle := \mathsf{H}'_b(\langle X_{n-1} \rangle) \oplus \langle t_{n-1} \rangle \cdot (\mathsf{HCW} \| \mathsf{LCW}^b).$$

Solving this *linear* equation for the *public* CW_n under the constraint (i) and (iii),

$$
\mathsf{HCW} = \mathsf{hb}\Big(\mathsf{H}'_{\overline{\alpha}_n}(\langle X_{n-1}\rangle_0) \oplus \mathsf{H}'_{\overline{\alpha}_n}(\langle X_{n-1}\rangle_1)\Big),
$$
$$
\forall b \in \{0,1\} : \mathsf{LCW}^b = \mathsf{lsb}\Big(\mathsf{H}'_b(\langle X_{n-1}\rangle_0) \oplus \mathsf{H}'_b(\langle X_{n-1}\rangle_1)\Big) \oplus \alpha_n \oplus \overline{b}.
\tag{2}
$$

Note that the n off-path secret nodes $\{\langle X_i^{\alpha_1 \cdots \alpha_{i-1}\overline{\alpha}_i}\rangle\}_{i\in[1,n]}$ are zero secrets according to the above correction procedures. As a result, the two parties hold identical shares of these n off-path nodes and their subtrees, given that the share of a subtree is fully determined by the share of its root (i.e., an off-path node) and the public correction words. This implies the constraint (iii). Finally, the $(n+1)$-th public correction word is defined from the secret α-th leaf $\langle X_n\rangle = \langle s_n \| t_n\rangle$ and the function $\mathsf{Convert}_{\mathbb{G}} : \mathbb{F}_{2^{\lambda-1}} \to \mathbb{G}$ as follows:

$$
\mathsf{CW}_{n+1} = (\langle t_n\rangle_0 - \langle t_n\rangle_1) \cdot \Big(\mathsf{Convert}_{\mathbb{G}}(\langle s_n\rangle_1) - \mathsf{Convert}_{\mathbb{G}}(\langle s_n\rangle_0) + \beta\Big) \in \mathbb{G},
$$

where the DPF payload β is masked by the XOR shares of the α-th leaf.

The DPF security primarily follows from that the first n correction words are of CCR forms, i.e., for $i \in [0, n-1]$, $\langle X_i\rangle_0 \oplus \langle X_i\rangle_1 = X_i = \Delta$ according to the XOR secret sharing scheme and the invariant (i). The Δ-circular correlation in $\mathsf{CW}_1, \ldots, \mathsf{CW}_{n-1}$ is obvious for either corrupted party. In CW_n, the honest party's H' inputs also differ from the corrupted party's H' inputs by Δ. Intuitively, these n correction words use CCR responses as one-time pads, and the underlying CCR queries are as structured as those in the original pcGGM tree. By using a CCR H' and upper bounding the probability of illegal CCR queries, we can prove the pseudorandomness of the first n correction words and the high $\lambda - 1$ bits (i.e., s_n) of the α-th leaf. The pseudorandom $s_n = \langle s_n\rangle_0 \oplus \langle s_n\rangle_1$ and $\mathsf{Convert}_{\mathbb{G}}$ ensure the pseudorandom CW_{n+1} for either corrupted party.

Our DPF scheme enables a more efficient distributed key generation protocol due to the construction of the first $n - 1$ correction words. The insight is that the two parties, who share $\langle \alpha\rangle$ and $\langle \beta\rangle^A$, can use their precomputed COT tuples to set up a secret $\langle \Delta\rangle$ with $\mathsf{lsb}(\Delta) = 1$ and share $\{\langle \overline{\alpha}_i \cdot \Delta\rangle\}_{i\in[1,n]}$ in two rounds, and use the black-box evaluation technique in [22] to locally share each secret $\mathsf{H}'(\langle X_{i-1}\rangle)$. This technique relies on the invariant (iii) so that, for each $i \in [1,n]$, summing the shares of the 2^i nodes on the i-th level returns the share of the i-th level on-path node. Given the two-party shares of $\langle \overline{\alpha}_i \cdot \Delta\rangle$ and $\mathsf{H}'(\langle X_{i-1}\rangle)$, the secure computation of each CW_i only needs one round for revealing $\langle \mathsf{CW}_i\rangle$, leading to $n - 1$ rounds for the first $n - 1$ correction words in total. In contrast, the prior protocol [22] uses (2) for each correction word, and the i-th level HCW depends on $\overline{\alpha}_i$ and should be computed level-by-level. Thus, it securely computes the first $n - 1$ correction words in $2(n - 1)$ rounds: for each level, one round is to share $\langle \mathsf{CW}_i\rangle$ from standard OTs, and another round is to reveal this secret.

We remark that our CW_{n+1} construction uses $\langle t_n\rangle_0 - \langle t_n\rangle_1$ to replace the $(-1)^{\langle t_n\rangle_1}$ term in the prior construction. The correctness is unaffected due to the non-zero LSB (i.e., t_n) of the α-th leaf. However, when $\mathbb{G}$ is a ring, our CW_{n+1} allows the two parties to locally share $\langle t_n\rangle_0 - \langle t_n\rangle_1$ on the ring via the black-box evaluation technique [22]. Thus, the secure computation of CW_{n+1} uses only one secure multiplication of two locally shared ring operands.

DCF Scheme and Protocol. We further show that our spcGGM tree can be extended to realize more efficient DCF scheme and its distributed protocol. Note that comparison function $f_{\alpha,\beta}^<(x)$ can be written as the sum of point function $f_{\alpha,-\alpha_n\cdot\beta}^\bullet(x)$ and a prefix function $V_{\alpha,\beta}(x)$, which returns $\alpha_{h+1}\cdot\beta\in\mathbb{G}$ such that $\alpha_1\dots\alpha_h = x_1\dots x_h$ is the longest common prefix of α and x (for completeness, $\alpha_{n+1} := \alpha_n$). We have shown how to realize the DPF scheme for point function $f_{\alpha,-\alpha_n\cdot\beta}^\bullet(x)$ from spcGGM tree. Then, we want to compute $V_{\alpha,\beta}(x)$ by reusing the prefix information with respect to α and x when traversing the spcGGM tree to evaluate the point function. Following the GGM-style DCF scheme [7], we do this by introducing more nodes to the spcGGM tree and an additional correction procedure to ensure that the sum of the introduced nodes along the path x equals $V_{\alpha,\beta}(x)$. However, our extended spcGGM tree can use less nodes and simpler correction words to compute $V_{\alpha,\beta}(x)$.

To give more details, we first recall how [7] works. It extends a shared GGM tree by replacing its length-doubling PRG with a length-quadrupling PRG so that each secret parent spawns two more secret children in $\mathbb{F}_{2^\lambda}$. For each level $i \in [1,n]$, let $\langle v_i^0\rangle$ and $\langle v_i^1\rangle$ denote such two secret children of the $(i-1)$-th on-path secret parent $\langle X_{i-1}\rangle = \langle s_{i-1} \| t_{i-1}\rangle$, and the two parties correct their additive shares for $V_{\alpha,\beta}(x)$ via the public correction word VCW_i:

$$V_{i-1} := \sum_{b\in\{0,1\}} (-1)^{1-b} \cdot \left(\mathsf{Convert}_\mathbb{G}(\langle v_{i-1}^{\overline{\alpha}_{i-1}}\rangle_b) - \mathsf{Convert}_\mathbb{G}(\langle v_{i-1}^{\alpha_{i-1}}\rangle_b) \right) \in \mathbb{G},$$

$$\mathsf{VCW}_i := (-1)^{\langle t_{i-1}\rangle_1} \cdot \Big(\left(\mathsf{Convert}_\mathbb{G}(\langle v_i^{\overline{\alpha}_i}\rangle_1) - \mathsf{Convert}_\mathbb{G}(\langle v_i^{\overline{\alpha}_i}\rangle_0) \right)$$
$$- V_{i-1} + (\alpha_i - \alpha_{i-1})\cdot\beta \Big) \in \mathbb{G}. \quad (V_0 := 0 \in \mathbb{G}, \alpha_0 = 0)$$

The DCF key per party includes its DPF key for $f_{\alpha,-\alpha_n\cdot\beta}^\bullet(x)$ and $\{\mathsf{VCW}_i\}_{i\in[1,n]}$. The DCF security also requires the pseudorandomness of the n VCW_i's.

In contrast, our DCF scheme shows that it is overkill to introduce two more secret children to each secret parent for the DCF security. For each $i \in [1,n]$, one additional secret child $\langle v_i\rangle = \langle v_i^0\rangle = \langle v_i^1\rangle$ of the secret parent $\langle X_{i-1}\rangle$ suffices, and the pseudorandomness of VCW_i relies on a random $v_i = \langle v_i\rangle_0 \oplus \langle v_i\rangle_1 \in \mathbb{F}_{2^\lambda}$ as $\mathsf{Convert}_\mathbb{G}$ maps random strings to pseudorandom $\mathbb{G}$ elements. We can argue the pseudorandomness of v_i based on the CCR induced by $X_{i-1} = \Delta$, if we use $v_i := \mathsf{H}'(\langle X_{i-1}\rangle_0 \oplus 2) \oplus \mathsf{H}'(\langle X_{i-1}\rangle_1 \oplus 2)$. Collecting all H' inputs for the DPF part and v_i's, we find that these inputs are as structured as those in the original pcGGM tree. The DCF security can follow from a similar hybrid argument.

Our DCF protocol is extended from our DPF protocol with the additional secure computation of $\{\mathsf{VCW}_i\}_{i\in[1,n]}$. Compared with the prior work, our DCF protocol achieves better efficiency due to not only its optimized DPF part but also the structure of each VCW_i. This structure makes the $\mathsf{Convert}_\mathbb{G}$ difference term independent of $\overline{\alpha}_i$. This independence allows the two parties to locally share the $\mathsf{Convert}_\mathbb{G}$ difference via the black-box evaluation technique [22], in contrast to the technique plus OT-based 2PC in the prior protocol. Since there is only one more secret child for each secret parent, the local computation for sharing this difference is halved as well. We can also replace the $(-1)^{\langle t_{i-1}\rangle_1}$ term in the prior VCW_i construction by a linear term $\langle t_{i-1}\rangle_0 - \langle t_{i-1}\rangle_1$, which can be locally shared via the same black-box evaluation technique if $\mathbb{G}$ is a ring. As a result, except the 2PC for sharing $\{\langle \alpha_i \cdot \beta\rangle^{\mathsf{A}}\}_{i\in[1,n]}$, the secure computation of $\{\mathsf{VCW}_i\}_{i\in[1,n]}$ requires n secure multiplications of two shared ring elements. These secure multiplications can run in parallel with that for CW_{n+1}.

In our DCF protocol, each $\langle \alpha_i \cdot \beta\rangle^{\mathsf{A}}$ is secretly shared by carefully reusing the two precomputed COT tuples, which were used to share $\langle \overline{\alpha}_i \cdot \Delta\rangle$, to run a COT-based multiplication between the XOR shared α_i and the additively shared β on the ring. This multiplication generalizes the binary case [1,28] for an XOR shared bit and an XOR shared string by using the well-known arithmetic XOR on the ring: $\langle \alpha_i\rangle_0 \oplus \langle \alpha_i\rangle_1 = \langle \alpha_i\rangle_0 + \langle \alpha_i\rangle_1 - 2 \cdot \langle \alpha_i\rangle_0 \cdot \langle \alpha_i\rangle_1$.

Functionality $\mathcal{F}_{\mathsf{spsVOLE}}$

Parameters: Field $\mathbb{F}$ and its extension field $\mathbb{K}$.

Initialize: Upon receiving (init) from P_0 and P_1, sample $\Delta \leftarrow \mathbb{K}$ if P_0 is honest; otherwise, receive $\Delta \in \mathbb{K}$ from the adversary. Store Δ and send it to P_0. Ignore all subsequent (init) commands.

Extend: This functionality allows polynomially many (extend) commands. Upon receiving (extend, N) from P_0 and P_1:

1. If P_0 is honest, sample $\mathbf{v} \leftarrow \mathbb{K}^N$; otherwise, receive $\mathbf{v} \in \mathbb{K}^N$ from the adversary.
2. If P_1 is honest, sample $\mathbf{u} \leftarrow \mathbb{F}^N$ with exactly one nonzero entry, and compute $\mathbf{w} := \mathbf{v} + \mathbf{u} \cdot \Delta \in \mathbb{K}^N$; otherwise, receive $(\mathbf{u}, \mathbf{w}) \in \mathbb{F}^N \times \mathbb{K}^N$ from the adversary, where $\mathbf{u}$ has at most one nonzero entry, and recompute $\mathbf{v} := \mathbf{w} - \mathbf{u} \cdot \Delta \in \mathbb{K}^N$.
3. Send $\mathbf{v}$ to P_0 and $(\mathbf{u}, \mathbf{w})$ to P_1.

Global-key queries: If P_1 is corrupted, upon receiving (guess, Δ'), where $\Delta' \in \mathbb{K}$, from the adversary, send (success) to the adversary if $\Delta = \Delta'$; send (fail) to the adversary otherwise.

Fig. 2. Functionality for single-point subfield VOLE.

4   Subfield VOLE Extension

Our sVOLE extension follows the blueprint of [10, 42, 43, 46], which uses LPN to locally convert t single-point sVOLE (spsVOLE) tuples output by functionality $\mathcal{F}_{\mathsf{spsVOLE}}$ (Fig. 2) into an sVOLE tuple. We focus on the efficient spsVOLE protocol that UC-realizes $\mathcal{F}_{\mathsf{spsVOLE}}$. Note that the spsVOLE protocol dominates the computation and contributes all communication in sVOLE extension.

$\mathcal{F}_{\mathsf{spsVOLE}}$ is parameterized by a field $\mathbb{F}$ and its extension $\mathbb{K}$, and covers the single-point COT functionality $\mathcal{F}_{\mathsf{spCOT}}$ if $\mathbb{F} = \mathbb{F}_2$ and $\mathbb{K} = \mathbb{F}_{2^\lambda}$. This functionality is the same as that in [43], except that $\mathcal{F}_{\mathsf{spsVOLE}}$ will not abort for an incorrect global-key query. Allowing for global-key queries has been considered in [32,38] and does not weaken the effective security. In the spsVOLE protocol based on pseudorandom correlated GGM, such global-key queries can be removed.

In essence, our spsVOLE protocols work as the PCG protocol [10–12,18] of spsVOLE correlation, although we do not divide the correlation generation into two explicit PCG phases. In Appendix E.1 of the full version [29], we show how to modify one of our spsVOLE protocols to define such two phases, in order to satisfy the "silent property" that a long spsVOLE tuple can be stored as two sublinearly short correlated seeds.

4.1 Single-Point COT and sVOLE from Correlated GGM

In Fig. 3, we present the two evaluation algorithms for our correlated GGM tree, which is defined by two first-level nodes $(k, \Delta - k) \in \mathbb{K}^2$. For every non-leaf node $x \in \mathbb{K}$, its left child is defined as $\mathsf{H}(x) \in \mathbb{K}$ while its right child is defined as $x - \mathsf{H}(x) \in \mathbb{K}$. The following claim is straightforward from an induction.

Parameters: Tree depth $n \in \mathbb{N}$. Field $\mathbb{K}$ with $|\mathbb{K}| \geq 2^\lambda$. Hash function $\mathsf{H} : \mathbb{K} \to \mathbb{K}$.

$\mathsf{cGGM.FullEval}(\Delta, k)$: Given $(\Delta, k) \in \mathbb{K}^2$,

1: $X_1^0 := k \in \mathbb{K}$, $X_1^1 := \Delta - k \in \mathbb{K}$.
2: **for** $i \in [2, n]$, $j \in [0, 2^{i-1})$ **do**
3:     $X_i^{2j} := \mathsf{H}(X_{i-1}^j) \in \mathbb{K}$, $X_i^{2j+1} := X_{i-1}^j - X_i^{2j} \in \mathbb{K}$.
4: $\mathbf{v} := (X_n^0, \ldots, X_n^{2^n-1}) \in \mathbb{K}^{2^n}$.
5: **for** $i \in [1, n]$ **do** $K_i^0 := \sum_{j \in [0, 2^{i-1})} X_i^{2j} \in \mathbb{K}$.
6: **return** $(\mathbf{v}, \{K_i^0\}_{i \in [1,n]})$

$\mathsf{cGGM.PuncFullEval}(\alpha, \{K_i^{\overline{\alpha}_i}\}_{i \in [1,n]})$: Given $(\alpha, \{K_i^{\overline{\alpha}_i}\}_{i \in [1,n]}) \in \{0,1\}^n \times \mathbb{K}^n$,

1: $X_1^{\overline{\alpha}_1} := K_1^{\overline{\alpha}_1} \in \mathbb{K}$.
2: **for** $i \in [2, n]$ **do**
3:     **for** $j \in [0, 2^{i-1})$, $j \neq \alpha_1 \ldots \alpha_{i-1}$ **do**
4:         $X_i^{2j} := \mathsf{H}(X_{i-1}^j) \in \mathbb{K}$, $X_i^{2j+1} := X_{i-1}^j - X_i^{2j} \in \mathbb{K}$.
5:     $X_i^{\alpha_1 \ldots \alpha_{i-1} \overline{\alpha}_i} := K_i^{\overline{\alpha}_i} - \sum_{j \in [0, 2^{i-1}), j \neq \alpha_1 \ldots \alpha_{i-1}} X_i^{2j + \overline{\alpha}_i} \in \mathbb{K}$.
6: $X_n^\alpha := - \sum_{j \in [0, 2^n), j \neq \alpha} X_n^j \in \mathbb{K}$, $\mathbf{w} := (X_n^0, \ldots, X_n^{2^n-1}) \in \mathbb{K}^{2^n}$.
7: **return** $\mathbf{w}$

Fig. 3. Two full-evaluation algorithms for correlated GGM tree.

Claim (Leveled correlation). For any two first-level nodes $(k, \Delta - k) \in \mathbb{K}^2$ and any $i \in [1, n]$, the offset $\Delta \in \mathbb{K}$ equals the sum of all nodes on the i-th level of the correlated GGM tree expanded from $(k, \Delta - k)$ as per $\mathsf{cGGM.FullEval}$.

Corollary 1. *For any $\alpha \in [0, 2^n)$, any $(k, \Delta - k) \in \mathbb{K}^2$, and*

$$(\mathbf{v}, \{K_i^0\}_{i \in [1,n]}) := \mathsf{cGGM.FullEval}(\Delta, k),$$
$$\mathbf{w} := \mathsf{cGGM.PuncFullEval}(\alpha, \{K_i^{\overline{\alpha}_i}\}_{i \in [1,n]}),$$

where $K_i^{\overline{\alpha}_i} := \overline{\alpha}_i \cdot \Delta + (-1)^{\overline{\alpha}_i} \cdot K_i^0$ for $i \in [1, n]$, we have $\mathbf{w}^{(\alpha)} - \mathbf{v}^{(\alpha)} = -\Delta$.

Proof. Claim 4.1 and the definition of cGGM.FullEval imply that $K_i^{\overline{\alpha}_i} \in \mathbb{K}$ in this corollary defines the sum of all $\overline{\alpha}_i$-side nodes on the i-th level of the correlated GGM tree. Then, it follows from the definition of cGGM.PuncFullEval that $\mathbf{v}^{(j)} = \mathbf{w}^{(j)}$ for any $j \neq \alpha \in [0, 2^n)$. Using Claim 4.1 for the last level, we have $\mathbf{w}^{(\alpha)} - \mathbf{v}^{(\alpha)} = -\sum_{j \in [0,2^n), j \neq \alpha} \mathbf{w}^{(j)} - \mathbf{v}^{(\alpha)} = -\sum_{j \in [0,2^n), j \neq \alpha} \mathbf{v}^{(j)} - \mathbf{v}^{(\alpha)} = -\Delta$.

Single-Point COT. Figure 4 describes our single-point COT protocol Π_{spCOT} that runs in the $\mathcal{F}_{\mathsf{COT}}$-hybrid model and uses the cGGM expansion in Fig. 3.

The same Δ in correlated GGM trees. Note that $\mathcal{F}_{\mathsf{spCOT}}$ produces single-point COT tuples with the same global key $\Delta \in \mathbb{F}_{2^\lambda}$ in a number of **Extend** executions. To realize $\mathcal{F}_{\mathsf{spCOT}}$, our protocol Π_{spCOT} proceeds as sketched in Sect. 3.1 but uses the same Δ for the cGGM trees of these executions, each of which samples a fresh $k \leftarrow \mathbb{F}_{2^\lambda}$ for cGGM.FullEval(Δ, k). A merit of using the same Δ in several tree instances is that Π_{spCOT} only invokes one $\mathcal{F}_{\mathsf{COT}}$ instance, and the amortized cost per precomputed COT tuple can be small.

Protocol Π_{spCOT}

Parameters: Field $\mathbb{F}_2$ and its extension field $\mathbb{F}_{2^\lambda}$.

Initialize: This procedure is executed only once.

1. P_0 and P_1 send (init) to $\mathcal{F}_{\mathsf{COT}}$, which returns $\Delta \in \mathbb{F}_{2^\lambda}$ to P_0. P_0 outputs Δ.

Extend: This procedure can be executed many times. P_0 and P_1 input $N = 2^n$ and use cGGM (c.f. Figure 3) for n and $\mathbb{F}_{2^\lambda}$.

2. P_0 and P_1 send (extend, n) to $\mathcal{F}_{\mathsf{COT}}$, which returns $(\mathsf{K}[r_1], \ldots, \mathsf{K}[r_n]) \in \mathbb{F}_{2^\lambda}^n$ to P_0 and $((r_1, \ldots, r_n), (\mathsf{M}[r_1], \ldots, \mathsf{M}[r_n])) \in \mathbb{F}_2^n \times \mathbb{F}_{2^\lambda}^n$ to P_1 such that $\mathsf{M}[r_i] = \mathsf{K}[r_i] \oplus r_i \cdot \Delta$ for $i \in [1, n]$.

3. P_0 samples $c_1 \leftarrow \mathbb{F}_{2^\lambda}$ and sets $k := \mathsf{K}[r_1] \oplus c_1$,

$$(\mathbf{v}, \{K_i^0\}_{i \in [1,n]}) := \mathsf{cGGM.FullEval}(\Delta, k),$$

and $c_i := \mathsf{K}[r_i] \oplus K_i^0$ for $i \in [2, n]$. P_0 sends $(c_1, \ldots, c_n)$ to P_1.

4. P_1 sets $\alpha = \alpha_1 \ldots \alpha_n := \overline{r}_1 \ldots \overline{r}_n \in [0, N)$, $K_i^{\overline{\alpha}_i} := \mathsf{M}[r_i] \oplus c_i$ for $i \in [1, n]$, and

$$\mathbf{u} := \mathbf{unit}_{\mathbb{F}_2}(N, \alpha, 1), \quad \mathbf{w} := \mathsf{cGGM.PuncFullEval}(\alpha, \{K_i^{\overline{\alpha}_i}\}_{i \in [1,n]}).$$

5. P_0 outputs $\mathbf{v}$ and P_1 outputs $(\mathbf{u}, \mathbf{w})$.

Fig. 4. cGGM-based single-point COT protocol in the $\mathcal{F}_{\mathsf{COT}}$-hybrid model.

Security. We prove Theorem 1 by following the sketched intuition in Sect. 3.1 and defer the proof to Appendix B.1 of the full version [29]. Our proof considers polynomially many concurrent **Extend** executions (strictly speaking, subsessions with unique sub-session IDs) that uses the one-time initialized Δ.

Theorem 1. *Given random permutation $\pi : \mathbb{F}_{2^\lambda} \to \mathbb{F}_{2^\lambda}$, efficiently computable linear orthomorphism $\sigma : \mathbb{F}_{2^\lambda} \to \mathbb{F}_{2^\lambda}$ with efficiently computable σ^{-1}, $\sigma'(x) := \sigma(x) \oplus x$, and σ'^{-1} (Footnote 1), and hash function $\mathsf{H}(x) := \pi(\sigma(x)) \oplus \sigma(x)$, protocol Π_{spCOT} (Fig. 4) UC-realizes functionality $\mathcal{F}_{\mathsf{spCOT}}$ (Fig. 2) against any semi-honest adversary in the $\mathcal{F}_{\mathsf{COT}}$-hybrid model and the RPM.*

Communication Optimization. For t concurrent **Extend** executions (e.g., in COT extension), the random c_1's in these executions can be compressed via a PRF $F : \mathbb{F}_{2^\lambda} \times \{0,1\}^* \to \mathbb{F}_{2^\lambda}$. Concretely, P_0 samples a PRF key $k_{\mathsf{prf}} \leftarrow \mathbb{F}_{2^\lambda}$ *after receiving its COT outputs in all executions* and sends this key to P_1. For each execution with sub-session ID ssid, the two parties locally defines the element $c_1 := F(k_{\mathsf{prf}}, \mathsf{ssid})$. This PRF key is only used for the t concurrent executions. The security of this optimization follows from the PRF security and the fact that, in the concurrent executions, the COT messages chosen by the corrupted receiver cannot depend on the PRF key to be sampled by the honest sender.

Complexity Analysis. Consider the complexity per execution when the PRF-based optimization is used in t concurrent **Extend** executions. Π_{spCOT} needs n precomputed COT tuples. P_0 sends $(n-1) \cdot \lambda + \frac{\lambda}{t}$ bits, and P_1 sends nothing. The computation per party comes from the tree expansion with N RP calls.

In the $\mathcal{F}_{\mathsf{COT}}$-hybrid model, the prior single-point COT protocol [46] consumes n precomputed COT tuples. However, P_0 sends $2n \cdot \lambda$ bits. Each party performs about N length-doubling PRG calls, which in turn result in $2N$ RP calls. We can see that our protocol halves both the computation and communication in the prior work. When looking at the whole protocol, the improvement is still huge. For example, the micro benchmark in Silver [18] reported that 70% of the time is spent on GGM-tree-related computation, and thus our protocol will lead to at least 50% of end-to-end computational improvement in COT.

Single-Point sVOLE. We can also realize single-point sVOLE from our cGGM tree by using the high-level idea sketched in Sect. 3.1. This protocol extends Π_{spCOT} by using a cGGM tree whose nodes are in a general *exponentially large* extension field $\mathbb{K}$. The tree expansion therein uses a hash function constructed from a random permutation and a linear orthomorphism over $\mathbb{K}$. We defer the detailed protocol and its security proof to Appendix B.2 of the full version [29].

4.2 Single-Point sVOLE from Pseudorandom Correlated GGM

We can adapt our correlated GGM tree for a *pseudorandom* correlated one with the property that the leaf node at some punctured position α is pseudorandom.

This pseudorandom correlated GGM tree pcGGM is defined in Fig. 5, where the first $n-1$ levels preserve the correlation in Claim 4.1 but all last-level nodes are processed by H_S to break this correlation. The keyed hash function H_S uses some key $S \in \mathbb{F}_{2^\lambda}$, which can be sampled by the receiver in single-point sVOLE and, for simplicity, is assumed to have been sent to the sender before protocol execution. The implementation of H_S is given in Theorem 2. In fact, this pcGGM tree yields PPRF, which is proved in Appendix C of the full version [29].

The pseudorandomness only at the cost of the last-level correlation allows us to follow the single-point sVOLE blueprint in [10,43] but also take advantage of the correlation in the first $n-1$ levels. The protocol is presented in Fig. 6. In this protocol, the sender P_0 only sends λ bits to the receiver P_1 for each of the first $n-1$ levels, given a precomputed COT tuple. For the last level, the two parties use a COT tuple and the standard technique [3,34] to emulate the string OT as in the prior protocols. To amortize the cost per precomputed COT tuple, the pcGGM trees in many **Extend** executions also use the same Δ set by $\mathcal{F}_{\mathsf{COT}}$.

Security. The security against the semi-honest P_0 resorts to the one-time pad s from $\mathcal{F}_{\mathsf{sVOLE}}$. Meanwhile, the security against the semi-honest P_1 relies on that (i)

Parameters: Tree depth $n \in \mathbb{N}$. Field $\mathbb{K}$. Keyed hash function $H_S : \mathbb{F}_{2^\lambda} \to \mathbb{F}_{2^\lambda}$. Function $\mathsf{Convert}_{\mathbb{K}} : \mathbb{F}_{2^\lambda} \to \mathbb{K}$.

pcGGM.FullEval(Δ, k): Given $(\Delta, k) \in \mathbb{F}_{2^\lambda}^2$,
1: $X_1^0 := k \in \mathbb{F}_{2^\lambda}$, $X_1^1 := \Delta \oplus k \in \mathbb{F}_{2^\lambda}$.
2: **for** $i \in [2, n-1]$, $j \in [0, 2^{i-1})$ **do**
3:    $X_i^{2j} := H_S(X_{i-1}^j) \in \mathbb{F}_{2^\lambda}$, $X_i^{2j+1} := X_{i-1}^j \oplus X_i^{2j} \in \mathbb{F}_{2^\lambda}$.
4: **for** $j \in [0, 2^{n-1})$, $b \in \{0, 1\}$ **do** $X_n^{2j+b} := \mathsf{Convert}_{\mathbb{K}}(H_S(X_{n-1}^j \oplus b)) \in \mathbb{K}$.
5: $\mathbf{v} := (X_n^0, \ldots, X_n^{2^n-1}) \in \mathbb{K}^{2^n}$.
6: **for** $i \in [1, n-1]$ **do** $K_i^0 := \oplus_{j \in [0, 2^{i-1})} X_i^{2j} \in \mathbb{F}_{2^\lambda}$.
7: $(K_n^0, K_n^1) := (\sum_{j \in [0, 2^{n-1})} X_n^{2j}, \sum_{j \in [0, 2^{n-1})} X_n^{2j+1}) \in \mathbb{K}^2$.
8: **return** $(\mathbf{v}, \{K_i^0\}_{i \in [1, n-1]}, (K_n^0, K_n^1))$

pcGGM.PuncFullEval$(\alpha, \{K_i^{\overline{\alpha}_i}\}_{i \in [1,n]}, \gamma)$: Given $(\alpha, \{K_i^{\overline{\alpha}_i}\}_i, \gamma) \in \{0, 1\}^n \times \mathbb{K}^n \times \mathbb{K}$,
1: $X_1^{\overline{\alpha}_1} := K_1^{\overline{\alpha}_1} \in \mathbb{F}_{2^\lambda}$.
2: **for** $i \in [2, n-1]$ **do**
3:    **for** $j \in [0, 2^{i-1})$, $j \neq \alpha_1 \ldots \alpha_{i-1}$ **do**
4:       $X_i^{2j} := H_S(X_{i-1}^j) \in \mathbb{F}_{2^\lambda}$, $X_i^{2j+1} := X_{i-1}^j \oplus X_i^{2j} \in \mathbb{F}_{2^\lambda}$.
5:    $X_i^{\alpha_1 \ldots \alpha_{i-1} \overline{\alpha}_i} := K_i^{\overline{\alpha}_i} \oplus (\oplus_{j \in [0, 2^{i-1}), j \neq \alpha_1 \ldots \alpha_{i-1}} X_i^{2j+\overline{\alpha}_i}) \in \mathbb{F}_{2^\lambda}$.
6: **for** $j \in [0, 2^{n-1})$, $j \neq \alpha_1 \ldots \alpha_{n-1}$, $b \in \{0, 1\}$ **do**
7:    $X_n^{2j+b} := \mathsf{Convert}_{\mathbb{K}}(H_S(X_{n-1}^j \oplus b)) \in \mathbb{K}$.
8: $X_n^{\alpha_1 \ldots \alpha_{n-1} \overline{\alpha}_n} := K_n^{\overline{\alpha}_n} - \sum_{j \in [0, 2^{n-1}), j \neq \alpha_1 \ldots \alpha_{n-1}} X_n^{2j+\overline{\alpha}_n} \in \mathbb{K}$.
9: $X_n^\alpha := \gamma - \sum_{j \in [0, 2^n), j \neq \alpha} X_n^j \in \mathbb{K}$, $\mathbf{w} := (X_n^0, \ldots, X_n^{2^n-1}) \in \mathbb{K}^{2^n}$.
10: **return** $\mathbf{w}$

Fig. 5. Two full-evaluation algorithms for pseudorandom correlated GGM tree.

the pcGGM tree with a CCR structure has n pseudorandom off-path nodes and the punctured leaf, giving pseudorandom $c_1, \ldots, c_{n-1}$ and $(c_n^{r_n}, \psi)$, and (ii) the mask of the unselected message $c_n^{\bar{r}_n}$ in the emulated last-level OT is computed by applying $\mathsf{Convert}_\mathbb{K}$ to a CCR response, which is for a legal CCR query with overwhelming probability due to the uniform μ. The proof of Theorem 2 can be found in Appendix B.3 of the full version [29], where we consider polynomially many concurrent **Extend** executions, which use the one-time initialized Δ.

Theorem 2. *Given CCR function* $\mathsf{H} : \mathbb{F}_{2^\lambda} \to \mathbb{F}_{2^\lambda}$, *function* $\mathsf{Convert}_\mathbb{K} : \mathbb{F}_{2^\lambda} \to \mathbb{K}$, *and keyed hash function* $\mathsf{H}_S(x) := \mathsf{H}(S \oplus x)$ *with some key* $S \leftarrow \mathbb{F}_{2^\lambda}$, *protocol* $\Pi_{\mathsf{spsVOLE-pcGGM}}$ *(Fig. 6) UC-realizes functionality* $\mathcal{F}_{\mathsf{spsVOLE}}$ *(Fig. 2) without global-key queries against any semi-honest adversary in the* $(\mathcal{F}_{\mathsf{COT}}, \mathcal{F}_{\mathsf{sVOLE}})$-*hybrid model.*

Communication Optimization. $\Pi_{\mathsf{spsVOLE-pcGGM}}$ can be optimized as follows:

- The two random (c_1, μ) to be sent by the sender in $\Pi_{\mathsf{spsVOLE-pcGGM}}$ can be compressed via the PRF technique for Π_{spCOT}. In t concurrent **Extend** executions, all such random messages can also be compressed in batch.
- The optimization for a large field $\mathbb{F}$ in $\Pi_{\mathsf{spsVOLE-cGGM}}$ also applies.
- If $\mathbb{F} = \mathbb{F}_2$, $\Pi_{\mathsf{spsVOLE-pcGGM}}$ degenerates to single-point COT and can do away with $\mathcal{F}_{\mathsf{sVOLE}}$ so that the receiver need not send a difference $d \in \mathbb{F}$. Instead, the sender locally samples $\Gamma \in \mathbb{K}$ and masks this value with the sum of all last-level nodes in a pcGGM tree. This optimization has been used in [10].

Complexity Analysis. Consider the complexity per execution when the PRF-based optimization is used in t concurrent **Extend** executions. $\Pi_{\mathsf{spsVOLE-pcGGM}}$ uses n precomputed COT tuples and one precomputed sVOLE tuple. P_0 sends $(n-2) \cdot \lambda + 3 \cdot \log |\mathbb{K}| + \frac{\lambda}{t}$ bits, and P_1 sends $\log |\mathbb{F}|$ bits. The computation is dominated by the tree expansion with $1.5N$ RP calls for each party. Compared with the prior works [10,43], our protocol roughly halve the communication, and the reduction in computation is 25%. This computation cost includes no PRG call in $\mathsf{Convert}_\mathbb{K}$, which can be implemented from cheap modulo operations for the field size $|\mathbb{K}|$ considered in many sVOLE applications, e.g., [40,43–45].

Protocol $\Pi_{\mathsf{spsVOLE-pcGGM}}$

Parameters: Field $\mathbb{F}$ and its extension field $\mathbb{K}$.

Initialize: This procedure is executed only once.

1. P_0 and P_1 send (init) to $\mathcal{F}_{\mathsf{COT}}$, which returns $\Delta \in \mathbb{F}_{2^\lambda}$ to P_0.
2. P_0 and P_1 send (init) to $\mathcal{F}_{\mathsf{sVOLE}}$, which returns $\Gamma \in \mathbb{K}$ to P_0. P_0 outputs Γ.

Extend: This procedure can be executed many times. P_0 and P_1 input $N = 2^n$ and use pcGGM (c.f. Figure 5) for n, $\mathbb{K}$, keyed hash function $\mathsf{H}_S : \mathbb{F}_{2^\lambda} \to \mathbb{F}_{2^\lambda}$, and function $\mathsf{Convert}_{\mathbb{K}} : \mathbb{F}_{2^\lambda} \to \mathbb{K}$.

3. P_0 and P_1 send (extend, n) to $\mathcal{F}_{\mathsf{COT}}$, which returns $(\mathsf{K}[r_1], \ldots, \mathsf{K}[r_n]) \in \mathbb{F}_{2^\lambda}^n$ to P_0 and $((r_1, \ldots, r_n), (\mathsf{M}[r_1], \ldots, \mathsf{M}[r_n])) \in \mathbb{F}_2^n \times \mathbb{F}_{2^\lambda}^n$ to P_1 such that $\mathsf{M}[r_i] = \mathsf{K}[r_i] \oplus r_i \cdot \Delta$ for $i \in [1, n]$.
4. P_0 and P_1 send (extend, 1) to $\mathcal{F}_{\mathsf{sVOLE}}$, which returns $\mathsf{K}[s] \in \mathbb{K}$ to P_0 and $(s, \mathsf{M}[s]) \in \mathbb{F} \times \mathbb{K}$ to P_1 such that $\mathsf{M}[s] = \mathsf{K}[s] + s \cdot \Gamma$.
5. P_1 samples $\beta \leftarrow \mathbb{F}^*$, sets $\mathsf{M}[\beta] := \mathsf{M}[s]$, and sends $d := s - \beta \in \mathbb{F}$ to P_0. P_0 sets $\mathsf{K}[\beta] := \mathsf{K}[s] + d \cdot \Gamma$ such that $\mathsf{M}[\beta] = \mathsf{K}[\beta] + \beta \cdot \Gamma$.
6. P_0 samples $(c_1, \mu) \leftarrow \mathbb{F}_{2^\lambda}^2$ and sets $k := \mathsf{K}[r_1] \oplus c_1$,

$$(\mathbf{v}, \{K_i^0\}_{i \in [1, n-1]}, (K_n^0, K_n^1)) := \mathsf{pcGGM.FullEval}(\Delta, k),$$

$c_i := \mathsf{K}[r_i] \oplus K_i^0$ for $i \in [2, n-1]$, $c_n^b := \mathsf{Convert}_{\mathbb{K}}(\mathsf{H}_S(\mu \oplus \mathsf{K}[r_n] \oplus b \cdot \Delta)) + K_n^b$ for $b \in \{0, 1\}$, and $\psi := K_n^0 + K_n^1 - \mathsf{K}[\beta]$.
P_0 sends $(c_1, \ldots, c_{n-1}, \mu, c_n^0, c_n^1, \psi)$ to P_1.
7. P_1 sets $\alpha = \alpha_1 \ldots \alpha_n := \overline{r}_1 \ldots \overline{r}_n \in [0, N)$, $K_i^{\overline{\alpha}_i} := \mathsf{M}[r_i] \oplus c_i$ for $i \in [1, n-1]$, $K_n^{\overline{\alpha}_n} := c_n^{r_n} - \mathsf{Convert}_{\mathbb{K}}(\mathsf{H}_S(\mu \oplus \mathsf{M}[r_n]))$, and

$$\mathbf{u} := \mathbf{unit}_{\mathbb{F}}(N, \alpha, \beta), \quad \mathbf{w} := \mathsf{pcGGM.PuncFullEval}(\alpha, \{K_i^{\overline{\alpha}_i}\}_{i \in [1, n]}, \psi + \mathsf{M}[\beta]).$$

8. P_0 outputs $\mathbf{v}$ and P_1 outputs $(\mathbf{u}, \mathbf{w})$.

Fig. 6. pcGGM-based single-point sVOLE protocol in the $(\mathcal{F}_{\mathsf{COT}}, \mathcal{F}_{\mathsf{sVOLE}})$-hybrid model.

5 DPF and DCF Correlation Generation

We model DPF/DCF correlation generation in functionality $\mathcal{F}_{\mathsf{FSS}}$ (Fig. 7), which includes distributed key generation and local full-domain evaluation. By putting both procedures in the same functionality, we are able to model FSS as an ideal functionality and avoid caveats in the proof. $\mathcal{F}_{\mathsf{FSS}}$ focuses on $N = 2^n$ for $n \in \mathbb{N}$, and we can define a similar functionality for a general $N \in \mathbb{N}$. Using padding, our protocols for $\mathcal{F}_{\mathsf{FSS}}$ also works in this general case.

Functionality $\mathcal{F}_{\mathsf{FSS}}$

Parameters: Ring $\mathcal{R}$. FSS $\in \{\mathsf{DPF}, \mathsf{DCF}\}$ with domain $[0, N)$, where domain size $N = 2^n$ for $n \in \mathbb{N}$, and range $\mathcal{R}$.

Gen: This functionality allows polynomially many (gen) commands. Upon receiving $(\mathsf{gen}, \langle \alpha \rangle_b, \langle \beta \rangle_b^{\mathsf{A}})$ from P_b for each $b \in \{0, 1\}$, where $(\langle \alpha \rangle_b, \langle \beta \rangle_b^{\mathsf{A}}) \in [0, N) \times \mathcal{R}$:

1. Set $\alpha := \langle \alpha \rangle_0 \oplus \langle \alpha \rangle_1 \in [0, N)$, $\beta := \langle \beta \rangle_0^{\mathsf{A}} + \langle \beta \rangle_1^{\mathsf{A}} \in \mathcal{R}$, and $\mathbf{r} \in \mathcal{R}^N$ such that
   - If FSS = DPF, $\mathbf{r}^{(j)} = 0$ for $j \in [0, N)$, $j \neq \alpha$, and $\mathbf{r}^{(\alpha)} = \beta$.
   - If FSS = DCF, $\mathbf{r}^{(j)} = 0$ for $j \in [0, N)$, $j \geq \alpha$, and $\mathbf{r}^{(j)} = \beta$ otherwise.
2. If both parties are honest, sample $\langle \mathbf{r} \rangle_0^{\mathsf{A}}, \langle \mathbf{r} \rangle_1^{\mathsf{A}} \leftarrow \mathcal{R}^N$ such that $\langle \mathbf{r} \rangle_0^{\mathsf{A}} + \langle \mathbf{r} \rangle_1^{\mathsf{A}} = \mathbf{r}$; otherwise (i.e., P_b is corrupted), receive $\langle \mathbf{r} \rangle_b^{\mathsf{A}} \in \mathcal{R}^N$ from the adversary and recompute $\langle \mathbf{r} \rangle_{1-b}^{\mathsf{A}} := \mathbf{r} - \langle \mathbf{r} \rangle_b^{\mathsf{A}} \in \mathcal{R}^N$.
3. Send $\langle \mathbf{r} \rangle_0^{\mathsf{A}}$ to P_0 and $\langle \mathbf{r} \rangle_1^{\mathsf{A}}$ to P_1.

Fig. 7. Functionality for DPF/DCF correlation generation.

One can view $\mathcal{F}_{\mathsf{FSS}}$ as an alternative to the FSS key generation functionality that outputs each FSS key in the key pair to the designated party, who locally uses its key to evaluate its shares of the evaluation results at several points. We note that the full-domain evaluation included in $\mathcal{F}_{\mathsf{FSS}}$ does not complicate its implementation in contrast to the known protocols [7, 22] of the FSS key generation functionality. The reason is that, using the black-box evaluation technique [22], these protocols also perform full-domain evaluation. If FSS correlations are generated for immediate use without long-term storage (e.g., [22]), $\mathcal{F}_{\mathsf{FSS}}$ can be a drop-in replacement of the FSS key generation functionality. However, we also show in Appendix E.2 of the full version [29] that our protocols for $\mathcal{F}_{\mathsf{FSS}}$ can be adapted to realize this key generation functionality.

5.1 DPF and DCF Schemes

Note that DPF/DCF scheme may be used in not only distributed settings (e.g., [22]) but also the scenarios where a trusted dealer is available (e.g., two-server PIR [13, 25]). It would be better for us to present the two schemes alone.

We present in Fig. 8 (resp., Fig. 9) our DPF (resp., DCF) scheme, which is implicitly constructed from a *shared* pseudorandom correlated GGM tree. For simplicity of exposition, we slightly abuse the function $\mathsf{Convert}_{\mathbb{G}} : \{0, 1\}^* \to \mathbb{G}$ so that it can map random strings of either λ or $\lambda - 1$ bits to pseudorandom group elements in $\mathbb{G}$. Our DCF scheme makes *non-black-box* use of our DPF scheme.

Note that our DPF and DCF schemes use a keyed hash function H_S. When there is a trusted dealer, the key S can be uniformly sampled by the dealer. In our DPF and DCF protocols in the upcoming sections, it can be jointly sampled by two parties using one-time public coin-tossing. This hash key can be reused across polynomially many FSS key pairs.

Complexity Analysis. Consider the group $\mathbb{G}$ (e.g., in [7,13,14,22,25]) with the PRG-free implementation of $\mathsf{Convert}_{\mathbb{G}}$ (c.f. Appendix F.1 of the full version [29]).

Our DPF scheme has a full-domain evaluation that takes $1.5N$ RP calls, in contrast to the $2N$ RP calls in the state-of-the-art construction of [13]. Its key generation algorithm uses about $2n + 2$ RP calls while this figure is about $4n$ in the prior work. In our scheme, the key size is $n \cdot \lambda + (\lambda + 1) + \log |\mathbb{G}|$ bits, and the evaluation algorithm takes about n RP calls, both remaining the same complexity as those in the prior work. In our DCF scheme, the full-domain evaluation requires $2.5N$ RP calls, in contrast to $4N$ RP calls in the state-of-the-art construction [7]. Its key generation needs about $4n + 2$ RP calls, in contrast to $8n$ RP calls in the prior work. The key size is $n \cdot \lambda + (\lambda + 1) + (n + 1) \cdot \log |\mathbb{G}|$ bits, and the evaluation requires about $2n$ RP calls, without any improvement.

Parameters: Domain size $N = 2^n$ for $n \in \mathbb{N}$. Group $\mathbb{G}$. Keyed hash function $\mathsf{H}_S : \mathbb{F}_{2^\lambda} \to \mathbb{F}_{2^\lambda}$. Function $\mathsf{Convert}_{\mathbb{G}} : \{0,1\}^* \to \mathbb{G}$.

$\mathsf{DPF.Gen}(1^\lambda, (\alpha, \beta, n, \mathbb{G}))$:

1: Parse $\alpha = \alpha_1 \ldots \alpha_n \in \{0,1\}^n$ and $\beta \in \mathbb{G}$.
2: Sample $\Delta \leftarrow \{0,1\}^\lambda$ such that $\mathsf{lsb}(\Delta) = 1$.
3: Sample $\langle s_0 \| t_0 \rangle_0, \langle s_0 \| t_0 \rangle_1 \leftarrow \{0,1\}^\lambda$ such that $\langle s_0 \| t_0 \rangle_0 \oplus \langle s_0 \| t_0 \rangle_1 = \Delta$.
4: **for** $i \in [1, n-1]$ **do**
5:     $\mathsf{CW}_i := \mathsf{H}_S(\langle s_{i-1} \| t_{i-1} \rangle_0) \oplus \mathsf{H}_S(\langle s_{i-1} \| t_{i-1} \rangle_1) \oplus \overline{\alpha}_i \cdot \Delta$
6:     $\langle s_i \| t_i \rangle_0 := \mathsf{H}_S(\langle s_{i-1} \| t_{i-1} \rangle_0) \oplus \alpha_i \cdot \langle s_{i-1} \| t_{i-1} \rangle_0 \oplus \langle t_{i-1} \rangle_0 \cdot \mathsf{CW}_i$
7:     $\langle s_i \| t_i \rangle_1 := \mathsf{H}_S(\langle s_{i-1} \| t_{i-1} \rangle_1) \oplus \alpha_i \cdot \langle s_{i-1} \| t_{i-1} \rangle_1 \oplus \langle t_{i-1} \rangle_1 \cdot \mathsf{CW}_i$
8: $\langle \mathsf{high}^\sigma \| \mathsf{low}^\sigma \rangle_0 := \mathsf{H}_S(\langle s_{n-1} \| t_{n-1} \rangle_0 \oplus \sigma)$ for $\sigma \in \{0,1\}$
9: $\langle \mathsf{high}^\sigma \| \mathsf{low}^\sigma \rangle_1 := \mathsf{H}_S(\langle s_{n-1} \| t_{n-1} \rangle_1 \oplus \sigma)$ for $\sigma \in \{0,1\}$
10: $\mathsf{HCW} := \langle \mathsf{high}^{\overline{\alpha}_n} \rangle_0 \oplus \langle \mathsf{high}^{\overline{\alpha}_n} \rangle_1$
11: $\mathsf{LCW}^0 := \langle \mathsf{low}^0 \rangle_0 \oplus \langle \mathsf{low}^0 \rangle_1 \oplus \overline{\alpha}_n, \quad \mathsf{LCW}^1 := \langle \mathsf{low}^1 \rangle_0 \oplus \langle \mathsf{low}^1 \rangle_1 \oplus \alpha_n$
12: $\mathsf{CW}_n := (\mathsf{HCW} \| \mathsf{LCW}^0 \| \mathsf{LCW}^1)$
13: $\langle s_n \| t_n \rangle_0 := \langle \mathsf{high}^{\alpha_n} \| \mathsf{low}^{\alpha_n} \rangle_0 \oplus \langle t_{n-1} \rangle_0 \cdot (\mathsf{HCW} \| \mathsf{LCW}^{\alpha_n})$
14: $\langle s_n \| t_n \rangle_1 := \langle \mathsf{high}^{\alpha_n} \| \mathsf{low}^{\alpha_n} \rangle_1 \oplus \langle t_{n-1} \rangle_1 \cdot (\mathsf{HCW} \| \mathsf{LCW}^{\alpha_n})$
15: $\mathsf{CW}_{n+1} := (\langle t_n \rangle_0 - \langle t_n \rangle_1) \cdot (\mathsf{Convert}_{\mathbb{G}}(\langle s_n \rangle_1) - \mathsf{Convert}_{\mathbb{G}}(\langle s_n \rangle_0) + \beta)$
16: $k_b := (\langle s_0 \| t_0 \rangle_b, \{\mathsf{CW}_i\}_{i \in [1, n+1]})$ for $b \in \{0,1\}$
17: **return** (k_0, k_1)

$\mathsf{DPF.Eval}(b, k_b, x)$:

1: Parse $k_b = (\langle s_0^0 \| t_0^0 \rangle_b, \{\mathsf{CW}_i\}_{i \in [1, n+1]})$, $\mathsf{CW}_n = (\mathsf{HCW} \| \mathsf{LCW}^0 \| \mathsf{LCW}^1)$, and $x = x_1 \ldots x_n \in \{0,1\}^n$.
2: **for** $i \in [1, n-1]$ **do**
3:     $\langle s_i^{x_1 \cdots x_i} \| t_i^{x_1 \cdots x_i} \rangle_b := \mathsf{H}_S(\langle s_{i-1}^{x_1 \cdots x_{i-1}} \| t_{i-1}^{x_1 \cdots x_{i-1}} \rangle_b)$
        $\oplus x_i \cdot \langle s_{i-1}^{x_1 \cdots x_{i-1}} \| t_{i-1}^{x_1 \cdots x_{i-1}} \rangle_b \oplus \langle t_{i-1}^{x_1 \cdots x_{i-1}} \rangle_b \cdot \mathsf{CW}_i$
4: $\langle \mathsf{high} \| \mathsf{low} \rangle_b := \mathsf{H}_S(\langle s_{n-1}^{x_1 \cdots x_{n-1}} \| t_{n-1}^{x_1 \cdots x_{n-1}} \rangle_b \oplus x_n)$
5: $\langle s_n^x \| t_n^x \rangle_b := \langle \mathsf{high} \| \mathsf{low} \rangle_b \oplus \langle t_{n-1}^{x_1 \cdots x_{n-1}} \rangle_b \cdot (\mathsf{HCW} \| \mathsf{LCW}^{x_n})$
6: **return** $y_b := (-1)^b \cdot (\mathsf{Convert}_{\mathbb{G}}(\langle s_n^x \rangle_b) + \langle t_n^x \rangle_b \cdot \mathsf{CW}_{n+1})$

Fig. 8. Our DPF scheme with domain $[0, N)$ and range $\mathbb{G}$.

Security. We prove the following theorems in Appendix D.2 and Appendix D.3 of the full version [29]. These theorems turn to the intuition that $\mathsf{CW}_1, \ldots, \mathsf{CW}_n$ are masked by pseudorandom CCR outputs (as the root and the first $n-1$ on-path shared nodes are Δ), and $\mathsf{CW}_{n+1}, \mathsf{VCW}_1, \ldots, \mathsf{VCW}_n$ are masked by some pseudorandom $\mathsf{Convert}_{\mathbb{G}}$ terms taking (pseudo)random CCR outputs as input.

Parameters: Domain size $N = 2^n$ for $n \in \mathbb{N}$. Group $\mathbb{G}$. Keyed hash function $\mathsf{H}_S : \mathbb{F}_{2^\lambda} \to \mathbb{F}_{2^\lambda}$. Function $\mathsf{Convert}_{\mathbb{G}} : \{0,1\}^* \to \mathbb{G}$.

$\mathsf{DCF}.\mathsf{Gen}(1^\lambda, (\alpha, \beta, n, \mathbb{G}))$:

1: Parse $\alpha = \alpha_1 \ldots \alpha_n \in \{0,1\}^n$ and $\beta \in \mathbb{G}$. Let $\alpha_0 := 0$.
2: Run $(k_0', k_1') \leftarrow \mathsf{DPF}.\mathsf{Gen}(1^\lambda, (\alpha, -\alpha_n \cdot \beta, n, \mathbb{G}))$ and store its internal variables.
3: **for** $i \in [1, n]$ **do**
4: $\quad \langle v_i \rangle_0 := \mathsf{H}_S(\langle s_{i-1} \| t_{i-1} \rangle_0 \oplus 2)$
5: $\quad \langle v_i \rangle_1 := \mathsf{H}_S(\langle s_{i-1} \| t_{i-1} \rangle_1 \oplus 2)$
6: $\quad \mathsf{VCW}_i := (\langle t_{i-1} \rangle_0 - \langle t_{i-1} \rangle_1)$
$\qquad\qquad\qquad \cdot (\mathsf{Convert}_{\mathbb{G}}(\langle v_i \rangle_1) - \mathsf{Convert}_{\mathbb{G}}(\langle v_i \rangle_0) + (\alpha_i - \alpha_{i-1}) \cdot \beta)$
7: $k_b := (k_b', \{\mathsf{VCW}_i\}_{i \in [1,n]})$ for $b \in \{0,1\}$
8: **return** (k_0, k_1)

$\mathsf{DCF}.\mathsf{Eval}(b, k_b, x)$:

1: Parse $k_b = (k_b', \{\mathsf{VCW}_i\}_{i \in [1,n]})$. Let $V_b^0 := 0 \in \mathbb{G}$.
2: Run $y_b' := \mathsf{DPF}.\mathsf{Eval}(b, k_b', x)$ and store its internal variables.
3: **for** $i \in [1, n]$ **do**
4: $\quad \langle v_i^{x_1 \ldots x_{i-1}} \rangle_b := \mathsf{H}_S(\langle s_{i-1}^{x_1 \ldots x_{i-1}} \| t_{i-1}^{x_1 \ldots x_{i-1}} \rangle_b \oplus 2)$
5: $\quad V_b^i := V_b^{i-1} + (-1)^b \cdot (\mathsf{Convert}_{\mathbb{G}}(\langle v_i^{x_1 \ldots x_{i-1}} \rangle_b) + \langle t_{i-1}^{x_1 \ldots x_{i-1}} \rangle_b \cdot \mathsf{VCW}_i)$
6: **return** $y_b := y_b' + V_b^n$

Fig. 9. Our DCF scheme with domain $[0, N)$ and range $\mathbb{G}$.

Theorem 3. *Given CCR function* $\mathsf{H} : \mathbb{F}_{2^\lambda} \to \mathbb{F}_{2^\lambda}$, *function* $\mathsf{Convert}_{\mathbb{G}} : \mathbb{F}_{2^{\lambda-1}} \to \mathbb{G}$, *and keyed hash function* $\mathsf{H}_S(x) := \mathsf{H}(S \oplus x)$ *with some key* $S \leftarrow \mathbb{F}_{2^\lambda}$, *Fig. 8 gives a DPF scheme with domain* $[0, N)$ *and range* $\mathbb{G}$.

Theorem 4. *Given CCR function* $\mathsf{H} : \mathbb{F}_{2^\lambda} \to \mathbb{F}_{2^\lambda}$, *function* $\mathsf{Convert}_{\mathbb{G}} : \mathbb{F}_{2^\ell} \to \mathbb{G}$ *with* $\ell \in \{\lambda-1, \lambda\}$, *and keyed hash function* $\mathsf{H}_S(x) := \mathsf{H}(S \oplus x)$ *with some key* $S \leftarrow \mathbb{F}_{2^\lambda}$, *Fig. 9 gives a DCF scheme with domain* $[0, N)$ *and range* $\mathbb{G}$.

5.2 DPF Correlation Generation

We define a leveled evaluation algorithm $\mathsf{DPF}.\mathsf{NextLevel}$ such that, on input a level index $i \in [1, n]$, all nodes on the $(i-1)$-th level of the share of a shared pseudorandom correlated GGM tree, and the public correction word CW_i for the i-th level, outputs all nodes one the i-th level.

Protocol Π_{DPF}

Parameters: Domain size $N = 2^n$ for $n \in \mathbb{N}$. Ring $\mathcal{R}$. Keyed hash function $\mathsf{H}_S : \mathbb{F}_{2^\lambda} \to \mathbb{F}_{2^\lambda}$. Function $\mathsf{Convert}_{\mathcal{R}} : \{0,1\}^* \to \mathcal{R}$. Let $\mathsf{H}' := \mathsf{hb} \circ \mathsf{H}_S$.

DPF Gen: This procedure can be executed many times. For each $b \in \{0,1\}$, P_b inputs $(\langle\alpha\rangle_b, \langle\beta\rangle_b^{\mathsf{A}}) \in [0, N) \times \mathcal{R}$ and proceeds as follows:

1. The two parties run sub-protocol Π_{PREP} (Figure 11), which, for each $b \in \{0,1\}$, returns $\langle\Delta\rangle_b$ and $\{(\mathsf{K}_b[\langle\alpha_i\rangle_{1-b}], \mathsf{M}_b[\langle\alpha_i\rangle_b])\}_{i \in [1,n]}$ to P_b such that $\mathsf{lsb}(\langle\Delta\rangle_0 \oplus \langle\Delta\rangle_1) = 1$, and $\mathsf{M}_b[\langle\alpha_i\rangle_b] = \mathsf{K}_{1-b}[\langle\alpha_i\rangle_b] \oplus \langle\alpha_i\rangle_b \cdot \langle\Delta\rangle_{1-b}$ for $i \in [1,n]$.
2. The two parties send $(\mathsf{sample}, \lambda)$ to $\mathcal{F}_{\mathsf{Rand}}$, which returns $W \in \{0,1\}^\lambda$ to them.
3. P_b computes $\langle s_0^0 \| t_0^0 \rangle_b := \langle\Delta\rangle_b \oplus W$. For $i \in [1, n-1]$, P_b sends to P_{1-b}

$$\langle \mathsf{CW}_i \rangle_b := (\oplus_{j \in [0, 2^{i-1})} \mathsf{H}_S(\langle s_{i-1}^j \| t_{i-1}^j \rangle_b))$$
$$\oplus \overline{\langle\alpha_i\rangle_b} \cdot \langle\Delta\rangle_b \oplus \mathsf{K}_b[\langle\alpha_i\rangle_{1-b}] \oplus \mathsf{M}_b[\langle\alpha_i\rangle_b],$$

   receives $\langle \mathsf{CW}_i \rangle_{1-b}$ from P_{1-b}, and computes $\mathsf{CW}_i := \langle \mathsf{CW}_i \rangle_b \oplus \langle \mathsf{CW}_i \rangle_{1-b}$ and
$$\{\langle s_i^j \| t_i^j \rangle_b\}_{j \in [0, 2^i)} := \mathsf{DPF.NextLevel}(i, \{\langle s_{i-1}^j \| t_{i-1}^j \rangle_b\}_{j \in [0, 2^{i-1})}, \mathsf{CW}_i).$$

4. P_b samples $\mu_b \leftarrow \{0,1\}^\lambda$, computes
$$\langle \mathsf{Xhigh}^\sigma \| \mathsf{Xlow}^\sigma \rangle_b := \oplus_{j \in [0, 2^{n-1})} \mathsf{H}_S(\langle s_{n-1}^j \| t_{n-1}^j \rangle_b \oplus \sigma) \quad \text{for } \sigma \in \{0,1\},$$
$$d_b := \mathsf{H}'(\mu_b \oplus \mathsf{K}_b[\langle\alpha_n\rangle_{1-b}]) \oplus \mathsf{H}'(\mu_b \oplus \mathsf{K}_b[\langle\alpha_n\rangle_{1-b}] \oplus \langle\Delta\rangle_b) \oplus \langle \mathsf{Xhigh}^0 \oplus \mathsf{Xhigh}^1 \rangle_b,$$

   sends (μ_b, d_b) to P_{1-b}, and receives (μ_{1-b}, d_{1-b}) from P_{1-b}. Then, P_b computes
$$\langle \mathsf{HCW} \rangle_b := \langle \mathsf{Xhigh}^{\overline{\langle\alpha_n\rangle_b}} \rangle_b \oplus \mathsf{H}'(\mu_b \oplus \mathsf{K}_b[\langle\alpha_n\rangle_{1-b}])$$
$$\oplus \mathsf{H}'(\mu_{1-b} \oplus \mathsf{M}_b[\langle\alpha_n\rangle_b]) \oplus \langle\alpha_n\rangle_b \cdot d_{1-b},$$
$$\langle \mathsf{LCW}^0 \rangle_b := \langle \mathsf{Xlow}^0 \rangle_b \oplus \langle\alpha_n\rangle_b \oplus b, \qquad \langle \mathsf{LCW}^1 \rangle_b := \langle \mathsf{Xlow}^1 \rangle_b \oplus \langle\alpha_n\rangle_b,$$

   sends $\langle \mathsf{CW}_n \rangle_b := (\langle \mathsf{HCW} \rangle_b \| \langle \mathsf{LCW}^0 \rangle_b \| \langle \mathsf{LCW}^1 \rangle_b)$ to P_{1-b}, receives $\langle \mathsf{CW}_n \rangle_{1-b}$ from P_{1-b}, and computes $\mathsf{CW}_n := \langle \mathsf{CW}_n \rangle_b \oplus \langle \mathsf{CW}_n \rangle_{1-b}$ and
$$\{\langle s_n^j \| t_n^j \rangle_b\}_{j \in [0, N)} := \mathsf{DPF.NextLevel}(n, \{\langle s_{n-1}^j \| t_{n-1}^j \rangle_b\}_{j \in [0, 2^{n-1})}, \mathsf{CW}_n).$$

5. **(Binary field $\mathcal{R} = \mathbb{F}_{2^\ell}$, without $\mathcal{F}_{\mathsf{OLE}}$)**
   P_b computes $\langle \mathsf{CW}_{n+1} \rangle_b^{\mathsf{A}} := (\sum_{j \in [0, N)} \mathsf{Convert}_{\mathcal{R}}(\langle s_n^j \rangle_b)) + \langle\beta\rangle_b^{\mathsf{A}}$.
   (General ring $\mathcal{R}$, using $\mathcal{F}_{\mathsf{OLE}}$)
   The two parties run sub-protocol Π_{MULT} (Figure 12), which, for each $b \in \{0,1\}$, takes as input
$$\langle A \rangle_b^{\mathsf{A}} := (-1)^b \cdot \sum_{j \in [0, N)} \langle t_n^j \rangle_b \in \mathcal{R},$$
$$\langle B \rangle_b^{\mathsf{A}} := (-1)^{1-b} \cdot \sum_{j \in [0, N)} \mathsf{Convert}_{\mathcal{R}}(\langle s_n^j \rangle_b) + \langle\beta\rangle_b^{\mathsf{A}} \in \mathcal{R},$$

   and returns $\langle \mathsf{CW}_{n+1} \rangle_b^{\mathsf{A}}$ to P_b.
   In either case, P_b sends $\langle \mathsf{CW}_{n+1} \rangle_b^{\mathsf{A}}$ to P_{1-b}, receives $\langle \mathsf{CW}_{n+1} \rangle_{1-b}^{\mathsf{A}}$ from P_{1-b}, and computes $\mathsf{CW}_{n+1} := \langle \mathsf{CW}_{n+1} \rangle_b^{\mathsf{A}} + \langle \mathsf{CW}_{n+1} \rangle_{1-b}^{\mathsf{A}}$.
6. P_b computes $k_b := (\langle\Delta\rangle_b \oplus W, \{\mathsf{CW}_i\}_{i \in [1, n+1]})$ and $\langle \mathbf{r}^{(j)} \rangle_b^{\mathsf{A}} := \mathsf{DPF.Eval}(b, k_b, j)$ for $j \in [0, N)$, and outputs $\langle \mathbf{r} \rangle_b^{\mathsf{A}} \in \mathcal{R}^N$.

Fig. 10. DPF correlation generation in the $(\mathcal{F}_{\mathsf{COT}}, \mathcal{F}_{\mathsf{Rand}}, \mathcal{F}_{\mathsf{OLE}})$-hybrid model.

In Fig. 10, we present our DPF correlation generation protocol Π_{DPF}. This protocol operates in the $(\mathcal{F}_{\mathsf{COT}}, \mathcal{F}_{\mathsf{Rand}}, \mathcal{F}_{\mathsf{OLE}})$-hybrid model. $\mathcal{F}_{\mathsf{Rand}}$ is the standard coin-tossing functionality that outputs a uniform string to both parties. $\mathcal{F}_{\mathsf{OLE}}$ is the functionality for oblivious linear evaluation (OLE) on ring $\mathcal{R}$, where P_0 (resp., P_1) is given *random* $(\mathbf{x}_0, \mathbf{z}_0) \in \mathcal{R}^N \times \mathcal{R}^N$ (resp., $(\mathbf{x}_1, \mathbf{z}_1) \in \mathcal{R}^N \times \mathcal{R}^N$) such that $\mathbf{z}_0 + \mathbf{z}_1$ equals the component-wise multiplication $\mathbf{x}_0 \odot \mathbf{x}_1$. We refer readers to Appendix F.2 and Appendix F.3 of the full version [29] for the definitions and instantiations of $\mathcal{F}_{\mathsf{Rand}}$ and $\mathcal{F}_{\mathsf{OLE}}$. If β is a bit-string, Π_{DPF} never uses $\mathcal{F}_{\mathsf{OLE}}$.

Π_{DPF} requires $\mathcal{F}_{\mathsf{Rand}}$ for the following reason. Note that Π_{DPF} uses the same global offset Δ as the roots of polynomially many shared trees, each of which defines a fresh DPF correlation. So, the two shares of this identical root should be "re-randomized" to avoid the identical per-party shares of the defined correlations. The two parties do this re-randomization by calling $\mathcal{F}_{\mathsf{Rand}}$ for a public randomness W and XORing this value to their shares of Δ, respectively.

Protocol Π_{PREP}

Initialize: This procedure is executed only once for each $b \in \{0,1\}$. The two parties send (init) to $\mathcal{F}_{\mathsf{COT}}^b$ with identifier b, which returns $\Delta_b' \in \{0,1\}^\lambda$ to P_b. P_b sends $\mathsf{lsb}(\Delta_b')$ to P_{1-b}, receives $\mathsf{lsb}(\Delta_{1-b}')$ from P_{1-b}, and sets $\langle \Delta \rangle_b := \Delta_b' \oplus (0^{\lambda-1} \| (\mathsf{lsb}(\Delta_{1-b}') \oplus b))$ such that $\mathsf{lsb}(\langle \Delta \rangle_0 \oplus \langle \Delta \rangle_1) = 1$.

For each $b \in \{0,1\}$: P_b inputs $\langle \alpha \rangle_b \in \{0,1\}^n$ and proceeds as follows.

1-1. The two parties send (extend, n) to $\mathcal{F}_{\mathsf{COT}}^b$ with identifier b, which returns $\mathbf{k}_b \in \mathbb{F}_{2^\lambda}^n$ to P_b and $(\mathbf{r}_{1-b}, \mathbf{m}_{1-b}) \in \mathbb{F}_2^n \times \mathbb{F}_{2^\lambda}^n$ to P_{1-b} such that $\mathbf{m}_{1-b} = \mathbf{k}_b \oplus \mathbf{r}_{1-b} \cdot \Delta_b'$.

1-2. P_b sets $\mathbf{g}_b := \langle \alpha \rangle_b \oplus \mathbf{r}_b$, sends $\mathbf{g}_b$ to P_{1-b}, and receives $\mathbf{g}_{1-b}$ from P_{1-b}. For $i \in [1, n]$, P_b sets

$$\mathsf{K}_b[\langle \alpha_i \rangle_{1-b}] := \mathbf{k}_b^{(i)} \oplus \mathbf{g}_{1-b}^{(i)} \cdot \langle \Delta \rangle_b,$$
$$\mathsf{M}_b[\langle \alpha_i \rangle_b] := \mathbf{m}_b^{(i)} \oplus \mathbf{r}_b^{(i)} \cdot (0^{\lambda-1} \| (\mathsf{lsb}(\Delta_b') \oplus (1-b))).$$

1-3. P_b outputs $\langle \Delta \rangle_b$ and $\{(\mathsf{K}_b[\langle \alpha_i \rangle_{1-b}], \mathsf{M}_b[\langle \alpha_i \rangle_b])\}_{i \in [1,n]}$.

Fig. 11. Preprocessing sub-protocol for DPF/DCF correlation generation.

Protocol Π_{MULT}

For each $b \in \{0,1\}$: P_b inputs $(\langle A \rangle_b^{\mathsf{A}}, \langle B \rangle_b^{\mathsf{A}}) \in \mathcal{R}^2$ and proceeds as follows.

1. The two parties send $(\mathsf{extend}, 2)$ to $\mathcal{F}_{\mathsf{OLE}}$, which, for each $b \in \{0,1\}$, returns $(\mathbf{x}_b, \mathbf{z}_b) \in \mathcal{R}^2 \times \mathcal{R}^2$ to P_b such that $\mathbf{z}_0 + \mathbf{z}_1 = \mathbf{x}_0 \cdot \mathbf{x}_1$.

2. P_b computes $(\gamma_b, \zeta_b) := (\langle A \rangle_b^{\mathsf{A}}, \langle B \rangle_b^{\mathsf{A}}) + (\mathbf{x}_b^{(b)}, \mathbf{x}_b^{(1-b)})$, sends (γ_b, ζ_b) to P_{1-b}, and receives $(\gamma_{1-b}, \zeta_{1-b})$ from P_{1-b}.

3. P_b outputs $\langle A \cdot B \rangle_b^{\mathsf{A}} := \langle A \rangle_b^{\mathsf{A}} \cdot \langle B \rangle_b^{\mathsf{A}} + \langle A \rangle_b^{\mathsf{A}} \cdot \zeta_{1-b} - \mathbf{x}_b^{(1-b)} \cdot \gamma_{1-b} + \mathbf{z}_b^{(0)} + \mathbf{z}_b^{(1)}$.

Fig. 12. OLE-based multiplication sub-protocol.

In Π_{DPF}, the key S of the keyed hash function H_S can be produced by one $\mathcal{F}_{\mathsf{Rand}}$ invocation before protocol execution, and we omit this setup for simplicity.

Security. We prove Theorem 5 in Appendix D.4 of the full version [29]. This proof will consider polynomially many concurrent **Gen** executions that uses the one-time initialized Δ. Intuitively, the security primarily follows from the COT-based secure computation of correction words, where the COT tuples are related to the global offset Δ so that the transcripts are masked by CCR responses. In particular, the intermediate transcript d_b is masked by a CCR response coming from a legal CCR query with overwhelming probability due to the uniform μ_b.

Theorem 5. *Given CCR function* $\mathsf{H} : \mathbb{F}_{2^\lambda} \to \mathbb{F}_{2^\lambda}$, *function* $\mathsf{Convert}_\mathcal{R} : \mathbb{F}_{2^{\lambda-1}} \to \mathcal{R}$, *and keyed hash function* $\mathsf{H}_S(x) := \mathsf{H}(S \oplus x)$ *with some key* $S \leftarrow \mathbb{F}_{2^\lambda}$, *protocol* Π_{DPF} *(Fig. 10) UC-realizes functionality* $\mathcal{F}_{\mathsf{DPF}}$ *(Fig. 7) against any semi-honest adversary in the* $(\mathcal{F}_{\mathsf{COT}}, \mathcal{F}_{\mathsf{Rand}}, \mathcal{F}_{\mathsf{OLE}})$-*hybrid model. If* $\mathcal{R} = \mathbb{F}_{2^\ell}$ *for* $\ell \in \mathbb{N}$, *protocol* Π_{DPF} *never invokes* $\mathcal{F}_{\mathsf{OLE}}$.

Table 3. The efficiency of distributed correlation generation for our DPF scheme. All numbers are in milliseconds (*ms*).

		$n = 20$	$n = 22$	$n = 24$	$n = 26$	$n = 28$
$\mathcal{R} = \mathbb{F}_{2^{127}}$	LAN	50	120	397	1501	5920
	WAN	2752	3020	3492	4786	9355
$\mathcal{R} = \mathbb{F}_2$	LAN	29	30	34	52	120
	WAN	2930	3132	3337	3554	3823

Communication Optimization. Π_{DPF} has the following two optimizations:

- For t concurrent **Gen** executions (e.g., in its applications to RAM-based computation [22], FSS-based MPC [7], and OLE extension [12], etc.), each P_b can compress all μ_b's in these executions via a PRF $F : \mathbb{F}_{2^\lambda} \times \{0,1\}^* \to \mathbb{F}_{2^\lambda}$ with a fresh key $k_{\mathsf{prf},b} \leftarrow \mathbb{F}_{2^\lambda}$ sampled *after receiving its COT outputs (from both $\mathcal{F}^b_{\mathsf{COT}}$ and $\mathcal{F}^{1-b}_{\mathsf{COT}}$) in all executions*. For each execution with sub-session ID ssid, the two parties define $\mu_b := F(k_{\mathsf{prf},b}, \mathsf{ssid})$.
- All invocations of $\mathcal{F}_{\mathsf{Rand}}$ can be compressed via another independent PRF key sampled *after the one-time initialization of $\mathcal{F}^b_{\mathsf{COT}}$ and $\mathcal{F}^{1-b}_{\mathsf{COT}}$* so that the root of each P_b's tree is (pseudo)random.
- Another method to save the communication for random μ_b's is to replace H_S by a hash function that meets "CCR for naturally derived keys" [28,47], which can also be implemented in one RP call. Note that μ_b is introduced to prevent the replay attack, which results from the manipulation of COT outputs, against the hashing mask in d_b. The alternative hash function addresses this attack by adding non-repeating tweaks.

Complexity Analysis (Binary Field). Consider the complexity per execution when the first PRF-based optimization is used in t concurrent **Gen** executions. The cost is symmetric. Π_{DPF} uses n COT tuples per party and one $\mathcal{F}_{\mathsf{Rand}}$ call. Each party sends $(n+1)+(n+1)\cdot\lambda+\frac{\lambda}{t}+\log|\mathcal{R}|$ bits. The computation per party is dominated by the tree expansion in n DPF.NextLevel calls, or $1.5N$ RP calls. Π_{DPF} runs in $n+3$ rounds (without counting the one-time setup).

In contrast, the binary-field protocol [22] can be implemented from GMW-style 2PC and n string OTs each with $(\lambda-1)$-bit payloads. One can cast these string OTs into n precomputed COT tuples according to [3,34]. Using these tuples, each party sends $n+n\cdot(3\lambda-1)+\log|\mathcal{R}|$ bits, and the computation per party is dominated by the $2N$ RP calls in GGM tree expansion. This protocol can proceed in $2n+2$ rounds: one for sending n masked choice bits, two for sharing and revealing each of the first n correction words, and one for revealing the $(n+1)$-th correction word. Our savings in computation, communication, and round complexity are about 25%, 66.6%, and 50%, respectively.

We implement Π_{PREP} and Π_{DPF} in C++, and perform benchmarks on a pair of Amazon EC2 R5.xlarge instances. We take binary fields $\mathcal{R}=\mathbb{F}_{2^{127}}$ and $\mathcal{R}=\mathbb{F}_2$ under computational security parameter $\lambda\approx128$. The reported time include both distributed key generation and full-domain evaluation. We set 1Gbps bandwidth with no latency as our LAN setting, and 20Mbps bandwidth with $100ms$ latency as our WAN setting. The results are shown in Table 3. We can see that our protocol is practically efficient, especially for two-server PIR. Although all numbers are reported based on one thread, performing one correlation generation for 2^{28} 127-bit values takes about 6 s, which is about 30% to 40% faster than the performance from a prior implementation in the same threads [22].

Complexity Analysis (General Ring). The two parties additionally need two precomputed OLE tuples for the secure multiplication. Overall, each party sends $(n+1)+(n+1)\cdot\lambda+\frac{\lambda}{t}+3\cdot\log|\mathcal{R}|$ bits, and the protocol runs in $n+4$ rounds.

In contrast, the binary-field protocol [22] can be adapted for the general-ring CW_{n+1} in the DPF scheme [13]. Securely computing this CW_{n+1} consumes two OLE tuples and needs the level-by-level 2PC, which leads to two additional bits in each OT payload per level, to share the last-level control bit $\langle t_n\rangle_1$. Each party sends at most $n+n\cdot(3\lambda+3)+3\cdot\log|\mathcal{R}|$ bits, and the protocol runs in $2n+3$ rounds. The improvement is the same as the binary-field case.

5.3   DCF Correlation Generation

Our DCF protocol Π_{DCF} in Fig. 13 extends Π_{DPF} by also computing n value correction words and defining the evaluation result as per our DCF scheme. If β is a bit-string, the two parties can compute n value correction words without using precomputed OLE tuples. Otherwise, for a general ring element β, these correction words are obtained from OLE-based secure multiplication.

Security. We prove Theorem 6 in Appendix D.5 of the full version [29], where polynomially many concurrent **Gen** executions are considered. The security is also based on the COT- and OLE-based secure computation of the n additional correction words of our DCF scheme. Note that the intermediate y_b^i's are pseudorandom due the masking CCR responses, which are for the legal CCR queries with overwhelming probability in the presence of uniform x_b^i's.

Theorem 6. *Given CCR function* $H : \mathbb{F}_{2^\lambda} \to \mathbb{F}_{2^\lambda}$, *function* $\mathsf{Convert}_{\mathcal{R}} : \mathbb{F}_{2^\ell} \to \mathcal{R}$ *for* $\ell \in \{\lambda - 1, \lambda\}$, *and keyed hash function* $H_S(x) := H(S \oplus x)$ *with some key* $S \leftarrow \mathbb{F}_{2^\lambda}$, *protocol* Π_{DCF} *(Fig. 13) UC-realizes functionality* $\mathcal{F}_{\mathsf{DCF}}$ *(Fig. 7) against any semi-honest adversary in the* $(\mathcal{F}_{\mathsf{COT}}, \mathcal{F}_{\mathsf{Rand}}, \mathcal{F}_{\mathsf{OLE}})$-*hybrid model. If* $\mathcal{R} = \mathbb{F}_{2^\ell}$ *for* $\ell \in \mathbb{N}$, *protocol* Π_{DCF} *never invokes* $\mathcal{F}_{\mathsf{OLE}}$.

Protocol Π_{DCF}

Parameters: Domain size $N = 2^n$ for $n \in \mathbb{N}$. Ring $\mathcal{R}$. Keyed hash function $H_S : \mathbb{F}_{2^\lambda} \to \mathbb{F}_{2^\lambda}$. Function $\mathsf{Convert}_{\mathcal{R}} : \{0,1\}^* \to \mathcal{R}$. Let $H^* := \mathsf{Convert}_{\mathcal{R}} \circ H_S$.

DCF Gen: This procedure can be executed many times. For each $b \in \{0,1\}$, P_b inputs $((\langle\alpha\rangle_b, \langle\beta\rangle_b^{\mathsf{A}}) \in [0, N) \times \mathcal{R}$ and proceeds as in Π_{DPF} (Figure 8), with the same Step 1, 2 and the following modifications to the subsequent steps:

3. Along with $\langle \mathsf{CW}_i \rangle_b$ for $i \in [1, n-1]$, P_b samples $x_b^i \leftarrow \{0,1\}^\lambda$, computes

   $$y_b^i := H^*(x_b^i \oplus K_b[\langle\alpha_i\rangle_{1-b}]) - H^*(x_b^i \oplus K_b[\langle\alpha_i\rangle_{1-b}] \oplus \langle\Delta\rangle_b) + \langle\beta\rangle_b^{\mathsf{A}} - 2 \cdot \langle\alpha_i\rangle_b \cdot \langle\beta\rangle_b^{\mathsf{A}},$$

   sends (x_b^i, y_b^i) to P_{1-b}, receive (x_{1-b}^i, y_{1-b}^i) from P_{1-b}, and computes

   $$\langle\alpha_i \cdot \beta\rangle_b^{\mathsf{A}} := \langle\alpha_i\rangle_b \cdot \langle\beta\rangle_b^{\mathsf{A}} - H^*(x_b^i \oplus K_b[\langle\alpha_i\rangle_{1-b}]) + H^*(x_{1-b}^i \oplus M_b[\langle\alpha_i\rangle_b]) + \langle\alpha_i\rangle_b \cdot y_{1-b}^i.$$

4. Along with $\langle\mathsf{CW}_n\rangle_b$, P_b repeats Step 3 for $i = n$ and computes $\langle\alpha_n \cdot \beta\rangle_b^{\mathsf{A}}$.
5. For $i \in [1, n]$ and $j \in [0, 2^{i-1})$, P_b computes $\langle v_i^j \rangle_b := H_S((s_{i-1}^j \| t_{i-1}^j)_b \oplus 2)$ and $\langle\alpha_0 \cdot \beta\rangle_b^{\mathsf{A}} := 0$. P_b computes $\langle\mathsf{CW}_{n+1}\rangle_b^{\mathsf{A}}$ by using $\langle\alpha_n \cdot \beta\rangle_b^{\mathsf{A}}$ instead of $\langle\beta\rangle_b^{\mathsf{A}}$, and:
   (Binary field $\mathcal{R} = \mathbb{F}_{2^\ell}$, without $\mathcal{F}_{\mathsf{OLE}}$) For $i \in [1, n]$ in parallel:
   P_b computes $\langle\mathsf{VCW}_i\rangle_b^{\mathsf{A}} := (\sum_{j\in[0, 2^{i-1})} \mathsf{Convert}_{\mathcal{R}}(\langle v_i^j \rangle_b)) + \langle\alpha_i \cdot \beta\rangle_b^{\mathsf{A}} - \langle\alpha_{i-1} \cdot \beta\rangle_b^{\mathsf{A}}$
   (General ring $\mathcal{R}$, using $\mathcal{F}_{\mathsf{OLE}}$) For $i \in [1, n]$ in parallel:
   The two parties run sub-protocol Π_{MULT} (Figure 12), which, for each $b \in \{0,1\}$, takes as input

   $$\langle A_i \rangle_b^{\mathsf{A}} := (-1)^b \cdot \sum_{j\in[0, 2^{i-1})} \langle t_{i-1}^j \rangle_b \in \mathcal{R},$$

   $$\langle B_i \rangle_b^{\mathsf{A}} := (-1)^{1-b} \cdot \sum_{j\in[0, 2^{i-1})} \mathsf{Convert}_{\mathcal{R}}(\langle v_i^j \rangle_b) + \langle\alpha_i \cdot \beta\rangle_b^{\mathsf{A}} - \langle\alpha_{i-1} \cdot \beta\rangle_b^{\mathsf{A}} \in \mathcal{R},$$

   and returns $\langle\mathsf{VCW}_i\rangle_b^{\mathsf{A}}$ to P_b.
   In either case, along with $\langle\mathsf{CW}_{n+1}\rangle_b^{\mathsf{A}}$, P_b sends $\langle\mathsf{VCW}_i\rangle_b^{\mathsf{A}}$ to P_{1-b}, receives $\langle\mathsf{VCW}_i\rangle_{1-b}^{\mathsf{A}}$ from P_{1-b}, and computes $\mathsf{VCW}_i := \langle\mathsf{VCW}_i\rangle_b^{\mathsf{A}} + \langle\mathsf{VCW}_i\rangle_{1-b}^{\mathsf{A}}$.
6. P_b computes $k_b := (\langle\Delta\rangle_b \oplus W, \{\mathsf{CW}_i\}_{i\in[1,n+1]}, \{\mathsf{VCW}_i\}_{i\in[1,n]})$ and $\langle\mathbf{r}^{(j)}\rangle_b^{\mathsf{A}} := \mathsf{DCF}.\mathsf{Eval}(b, k_b, j)$ for $j \in [0, N)$, and outputs $\langle\mathbf{r}\rangle_b^{\mathsf{A}} \in \mathcal{R}^N$.

Fig. 13. DCF correlation generation in the $(\mathcal{F}_{\mathsf{COT}}, \mathcal{F}_{\mathsf{Rand}}, \mathcal{F}_{\mathsf{OLE}})$-hybrid model.

Communication Optimization. The optimizations in Sect. 5.2 also applies to the DCF protocol Π_{DCF}. Moreover, the random elements $\{x_b^i\}_{i \in [1,n]}$ in Π_{DCF} can also be compressed using the same technique for the random μ_b's.

Complexity Analysis (Binary Field). Consider the complexity per execution when the first PRF-based optimization is used in t concurrent **Gen** executions. The cost is symmetric. Π_{DCF} consumes n COT tuples per party and one $\mathcal{F}_{\mathsf{Rand}}$ call. Each party sends $(n+1) + (n+1) \cdot \lambda + \frac{\lambda}{t} + (2n+1) \cdot \log |\mathcal{R}|$ bits, and the computation per party comes from the 2.5N RP calls in the tree expansion. Π_{DCF} has round complexity $n + 3$, the same as Π_{DPF} in the binary-field case.

In contrast, the state-of-the-art protocol of [7] requires n string OTs to run GMW-style 2PC. The string OTs consume n precomputed COT tuples and have payloads of $(\lambda - 1) + 2 \cdot \log |\mathcal{R}|$ bits. Using n COT tuples, each party sends $n + n \cdot (3\lambda - 1 + 5 \cdot \log |\mathcal{R}|) + \log |\mathcal{R}|$ bits, and the computation per party is dominated by the 4N RP calls in GGM tree expansion in $2n + 2$ rounds. Our savings in computation and round complexity are 37.5% and 50%, respectively. For a typical ring $\mathcal{R}$ with size $|\mathcal{R}| \approx 2^\lambda$, the communication reduction is about 62.5%. When $\mathcal{R}$ is sufficiently small, this reduction can be 66.6%.

Complexity Analysis (General Ring). Π_{DCF} also works for general $\mathcal{R}$ at the cost of additionally using $2n+2$ precomputed OLE tuples. This general-ring version proceeds in $n + 4$ rounds, and the overall outgoing communication per party is $(n+1) + (n+1) \cdot \lambda + \frac{\lambda}{t} + (4n+3) \cdot \log |\mathcal{R}|$ bits.

In contrast, the OT-based protocol [7] can run in $2n + 3$ rounds. Each party sends at most $n + n \cdot (3\lambda + 3 + 4 \cdot \log |\mathcal{R}|) + (3n + 3) \cdot \log |\mathcal{R}|$ bits and uses $2n + 2$ OLE tuples. Our savings in communication and round complexity are about $50\% \sim 66.6\%$ and 50%, respectively, for typical ring size $|\mathcal{R}| \leq 2^\lambda$.

Acknowledgements. Work of Kang Yang is supported by the National Key Research and Development Program of China (Grant No. 2022YFB2702000), and by the National Natural Science Foundation of China (Grant Nos. 62102037, 61932019). Work of Xiao Wang is supported by DARPA under Contract No. HR001120C0087, NSF award #2016240, #2236819, and research awards from Meta and Google. The views, opinions, and/or findings expressed are those of the author(s) and should not be interpreted as representing the official views or policies of the Department of Defense or the U.S. Government. Work of Jiang Zhang is supported by the National Key Research and Development Program of China (Grant No. 2022YFB2702000), and by the National Natural Science Foundation of China (Grant Nos. 62022018, 61932019). Work of Zheli Liu is supported by the National Natural Science Foundation of China (Grant No. 62032012).

References

1. Asharov, G., Lindell, Y., Schneider, T., Zohner, M.: More efficient oblivious transfer and extensions for faster secure computation. In: Sadeghi, A.R., Gligor, V.D., Yung, M. (eds.) ACM CCS 2013, pp. 535–548. ACM Press (Nov 2013). https://doi.org/10.1145/2508859.2516738

2. Baum, C., Malozemoff, A.J., Rosen, M.B., Scholl, P.: Mac′n′Cheese: zero-knowledge proofs for boolean and arithmetic circuits with nested disjunctions. In: Malkin, T., Peikert, C. (eds.) CRYPTO 2021. LNCS, vol. 12828, pp. 92–122. Springer, Cham (2021). https://doi.org/10.1007/978-3-030-84259-8_4

3. Beaver, D.: Precomputing oblivious transfer. In: Coppersmith, D. (ed.) CRYPTO 1995. LNCS, vol. 963, pp. 97–109. Springer, Heidelberg (1995). https://doi.org/10.1007/3-540-44750-4_8

4. Bellare, M., Hoang, V.T., Keelveedhi, S., Rogaway, P.: Efficient Garbling from a Fixed-Key Blockcipher. In: 2013 IEEE Symposium on Security and Privacy, pp. 478–492. IEEE Computer Society Press (May 2013). https://doi.org/10.1109/SP.2013.39

5. Bhattacharya, S., Nandi, M.: Full indifferentiable security of the Xor of two or more random permutations using the χ^2 method. In: Nielsen, J.B., Rijmen, V. (eds.) EUROCRYPT 2018. LNCS, vol. 10820, pp. 387–412. Springer, Cham (2018). https://doi.org/10.1007/978-3-319-78381-9_15

6. Boneh, D., Boyle, E., Corrigan-Gibbs, H., Gilboa, N., Ishai, Y.: Lightweight Techniques for Private Heavy Hitters. In: 2021 IEEE Symposium on Security and Privacy, pp. 762–776. IEEE Computer Society Press (May 2021). https://doi.org/10.1109/SP40001.2021.00048

7. Boyle, E., et al.: Function secret sharing for mixed-mode and fixed-point secure computation. In: Canteaut, A., Standaert, F.-X. (eds.) EUROCRYPT 2021. LNCS, vol. 12697, pp. 871–900. Springer, Cham (2021). https://doi.org/10.1007/978-3-030-77886-6_30

8. Boyle, E., Couteau, G., Gilboa, N., Ishai, Y.: Compressing Vector OLE. In: Lie, D., Mannan, M., Backes, M., Wang, X. (eds.) ACM CCS 2018. pp. 896–912. ACM Press (Oct 2018). https://doi.org/10.1145/3243734.3243868

9. Boyle, E., et al.: Correlated Pseudorandomness from Expand-Accumulate Codes. In: Dodis, Y., Shrimpton, T. (eds.) CRYPTO 2022, Part II. LNCS, vol. 13508, pp. 603–633. Springer, Heidelberg (Aug 2022). https://doi.org/10.1007/978-3-031-15979-4_21

10. Boyle, E., et al.: Efficient Two-Round OT Extension and Silent Non-Interactive Secure Computation. In: Cavallaro, L., Kinder, J., Wang, X., Katz, J. (eds.) ACM CCS 2019, pp. 291–308. ACM Press (Nov 2019). https://doi.org/10.1145/3319535.3354255

11. Boyle, E., Couteau, G., Gilboa, N., Ishai, Y., Kohl, L., Scholl, P.: Efficient pseudorandom correlation generators: silent OT extension and more. In: Boldyreva, A., Micciancio, D. (eds.) CRYPTO 2019. LNCS, vol. 11694, pp. 489–518. Springer, Cham (2019). https://doi.org/10.1007/978-3-030-26954-8_16

12. Boyle, E., Couteau, G., Gilboa, N., Ishai, Y., Kohl, L., Scholl, P.: Efficient pseudorandom correlation generators from ring-LPN. In: Micciancio, D., Ristenpart, T. (eds.) CRYPTO 2020. LNCS, vol. 12171, pp. 387–416. Springer, Cham (2020). https://doi.org/10.1007/978-3-030-56880-1_14

13. Boyle, E., Gilboa, N., Ishai, Y.: Function Secret Sharing: Improvements and Extensions. In: Weippl, E.R., Katzenbeisser, S., Kruegel, C., Myers, A.C., Halevi, S. (eds.) ACM CCS 2016, pp. 1292–1303. ACM Press (Oct 2016). https://doi.org/10.1145/2976749.2978429

14. Boyle, E., Gilboa, N., Ishai, Y.: Secure computation with preprocessing via function secret sharing. In: Hofheinz, D., Rosen, A. (eds.) TCC 2019. LNCS, vol. 11891, pp. 341–371. Springer, Cham (2019). https://doi.org/10.1007/978-3-030-36030-6_14

15. Canetti, R.: Universally Composable Security: A New Paradigm for Cryptographic Protocols. In: 42nd FOCS, pp. 136–145. IEEE Computer Society Press (Oct 2001). https://doi.org/10.1109/SFCS.2001.959888

16. Chen, S., Steinberger, J.: Tight security bounds for key-alternating ciphers. In: Nguyen, P.Q., Oswald, E. (eds.) EUROCRYPT 2014. LNCS, vol. 8441, pp. 327–350. Springer, Heidelberg (2014). https://doi.org/10.1007/978-3-642-55220-5_19

17. Choi, S.G., Katz, J., Kumaresan, R., Zhou, H.-S.: On the security of the Free-XOR technique. In: Cramer, R. (ed.) TCC 2012. LNCS, vol. 7194, pp. 39–53. Springer, Heidelberg (2012). https://doi.org/10.1007/978-3-642-28914-9_3

18. Couteau, G., Rindal, P., Raghuraman, S.: Silver: silent VOLE and oblivious transfer from hardness of decoding structured LDPC codes. In: Malkin, T., Peikert, C. (eds.) CRYPTO 2021. LNCS, vol. 12827, pp. 502–534. Springer, Cham (2021). https://doi.org/10.1007/978-3-030-84252-9_17

19. Damgård, I., Nielsen, J.B., Nielsen, M., Ranellucci, S.: The tinytable protocol for 2-party secure computation, or: gate-scrambling revisited. In: Katz, J., Shacham, H. (eds.) CRYPTO 2017. LNCS, vol. 10401, pp. 167–187. Springer, Cham (2017). https://doi.org/10.1007/978-3-319-63688-7_6

20. Damgård, I., Pastro, V., Smart, N., Zakarias, S.: Multiparty computation from somewhat homomorphic encryption. In: Safavi-Naini, R., Canetti, R. (eds.) CRYPTO 2012. LNCS, vol. 7417, pp. 643–662. Springer, Heidelberg (2012). https://doi.org/10.1007/978-3-642-32009-5_38

21. Dittmer, S., Ishai, Y., Ostrovsky, R.: Line-Point Zero Knowledge and Its Applications. In: 2nd Conference on Information-Theoretic Cryptography (2021). https://doi.org/10.4230/LIPIcs.ITC.2021.5

22. Doerner, J., shelat, a.: Scaling ORAM for Secure Computation. In: Thuraisingham, B.M., Evans, D., Malkin, T., Xu, D. (eds.) ACM CCS 2017. pp. 523–535. ACM Press (Oct / Nov 2017). https://doi.org/10.1145/3133956.3133967

23. Garimella, G., Pinkas, B., Rosulek, M., Trieu, N., Yanai, A.: Oblivious Key-Value Stores and Amplification for Private Set Intersection. In: Malkin, T., Peikert, C. (eds.) CRYPTO 2021, Part II. LNCS, vol. 12826, pp. 395–425. Springer, Heidelberg, Virtual Event (Aug 2021). https://doi.org/10.1007/978-3-030-84245-1_14

24. Ghosh, S., Nielsen, J.B., Nilges, T.: Maliciously secure oblivious linear function evaluation with constant overhead. In: Takagi, T., Peyrin, T. (eds.) ASIACRYPT 2017. LNCS, vol. 10624, pp. 629–659. Springer, Cham (2017). https://doi.org/10.1007/978-3-319-70694-8_22

25. Gilboa, N., Ishai, Y.: Distributed point functions and their applications. In: Nguyen, P.Q., Oswald, E. (eds.) EUROCRYPT 2014. LNCS, vol. 8441, pp. 640–658. Springer, Heidelberg (2014). https://doi.org/10.1007/978-3-642-55220-5_35

26. Goldreich, O., Goldwasser, S., Micali, S.: How to Construct Random Functions (Extended Abstract). In: 25th FOCS. pp. 464–479. IEEE Computer Society Press (Oct 1984). https://doi.org/10.1109/SFCS.1984.715949

27. Goldreich, O., Micali, S., Wigderson, A.: How to Play any Mental Game or A Completeness Theorem for Protocols with Honest Majority. In: Aho, A. (ed.) 19th ACM STOC. pp. 218–229. ACM Press (May 1987). https://doi.org/10.1145/28395.28420

28. Guo, C., Katz, J., Wang, X., Yu, Y.: Efficient and Secure Multiparty Computation from Fixed-Key Block Ciphers. In: 2020 IEEE Symposium on Security and Privacy, pp. 825–841. IEEE Computer Society Press (May 2020). https://doi.org/10.1109/SP40000.2020.00016

29. Guo, X., et al.: Half-Tree: Halving the Cost of Tree Expansion in COT and DPF. Cryptology ePrint Archive, Report 2022/1431 (2022), https://eprint.iacr.org/2022/1431

30. Gupta, K., Kumaraswamy, D., Chandran, N., Gupta, D.: LLAMA: A Low Latency Math Library for Secure Inference. Privacy Enhancing Technologies Symposium (PETS 2022) (2022). 10.56553/popets-2022-0109

31. Efficient Secure Two-Party Protocols. ISC, Springer, Heidelberg (2010). https://doi.org/10.1007/978-3-642-14303-8

32. Hazay, C., Scholl, P., Soria-Vazquez, E.: Low cost constant round MPC combining BMR and oblivious transfer. In: Takagi, T., Peyrin, T. (eds.) ASIACRYPT 2017. LNCS, vol. 10624, pp. 598–628. Springer, Cham (2017). https://doi.org/10.1007/978-3-319-70694-8_21

33. Heath, D., Kolesnikov, V.: One Hot Garbling. In: Vigna, G., Shi, E. (eds.) ACM CCS 2021, pp. 574–593. ACM Press (Nov 2021). https://doi.org/10.1145/3460120.3484764

34. Ishai, Y., Kilian, J., Nissim, K., Petrank, E.: Extending oblivious transfers efficiently. In: Boneh, D. (ed.) CRYPTO 2003. LNCS, vol. 2729, pp. 145–161. Springer, Heidelberg (2003). https://doi.org/10.1007/978-3-540-45146-4_9

35. Keller, M., Orsini, E., Scholl, P.: MASCOT: Faster Malicious Arithmetic Secure Computation with Oblivious Transfer. In: Weippl, E.R., Katzenbeisser, S., Kruegel, C., Myers, A.C., Halevi, S. (eds.) ACM CCS 2016, pp. 830–842. ACM Press (Oct 2016). https://doi.org/10.1145/2976749.2978357

36. Keller, M., Pastro, V., Rotaru, D.: Overdrive: making SPDZ great again. In: Nielsen, J.B., Rijmen, V. (eds.) EUROCRYPT 2018. LNCS, vol. 10822, pp. 158–189. Springer, Cham (2018). https://doi.org/10.1007/978-3-319-78372-7_6

37. Kolesnikov, V., Schneider, T.: Improved garbled circuit: free xor gates and applications. In: Aceto, L., Damgård, I., Goldberg, L.A., Halldórsson, M.M., Ingólfsdóttir, A., Walukiewicz, I. (eds.) ICALP 2008. LNCS, vol. 5126, pp. 486–498. Springer, Heidelberg (2008). https://doi.org/10.1007/978-3-540-70583-3_40

38. Nielsen, J.B., Nordholt, P.S., Orlandi, C., Burra, S.S.: A new approach to practical active-secure two-party computation. In: Safavi-Naini, R., Canetti, R. (eds.) CRYPTO 2012. LNCS, vol. 7417, pp. 681–700. Springer, Heidelberg (2012). https://doi.org/10.1007/978-3-642-32009-5_40

39. Patarin, J.: The coefficients H technique. In: Avanzi, R.M., Keliher, L., Sica, F. (eds.) SAC 2008. LNCS, vol. 5381, pp. 328–345. Springer, Heidelberg (2009). https://doi.org/10.1007/978-3-642-04159-4_21

40. Rindal, P., Schoppmann, P.: VOLE-PSI: fast OPRF and circuit-PSI from vector-OLE. In: Canteaut, A., Standaert, F.-X. (eds.) EUROCRYPT 2021. LNCS, vol. 12697, pp. 901–930. Springer, Cham (2021). https://doi.org/10.1007/978-3-030-77886-6_31

41. Rogaway, P., Steinberger, J.: Constructing cryptographic hash functions from fixed-key blockciphers. In: Wagner, D. (ed.) CRYPTO 2008. LNCS, vol. 5157, pp. 433–450. Springer, Heidelberg (2008). https://doi.org/10.1007/978-3-540-85174-5_24

42. Schoppmann, P., Gascón, A., Reichert, L., Raykova, M.: Distributed Vector-OLE: Improved Constructions and Implementation. In: Cavallaro, L., Kinder, J., Wang, X., Katz, J. (eds.) ACM CCS 2019, pp. 1055–1072. ACM Press (Nov 2019). https://doi.org/10.1145/3319535.3363228

43. Weng, C., Yang, K., Katz, J., Wang, X.: Wolverine: Fast, Scalable, and Communication-Efficient Zero-Knowledge Proofs for Boolean and Arithmetic Circuits. In: 2021 IEEE Symposium on Security and Privacy. pp. 1074–1091. IEEE Computer Society Press (May 2021). https://doi.org/10.1109/SP40001.2021.00056

44. Weng, C., Yang, K., Xie, X., Katz, J., Wang, X.: Mystique: Efficient Conversions for Zero-Knowledge Proofs with Applications to Machine Learning. In: Bailey, M., Greenstadt, R. (eds.) USENIX Security 2021, pp. 501–518. USENIX Association (Aug 2021)

45. Yang, K., Sarkar, P., Weng, C., Wang, X.: QuickSilver: Efficient and Affordable Zero-Knowledge Proofs for Circuits and Polynomials over Any Field. In: Vigna, G., Shi, E. (eds.) ACM CCS 2021, pp. 2986–3001. ACM Press (Nov 2021). https://doi.org/10.1145/3460120.3484556

46. Yang, K., Weng, C., Lan, X., Zhang, J., Wang, X.: Ferret: Fast Extension for Correlated OT with Small Communication. In: Ligatti, J., Ou, X., Katz, J., Vigna, G. (eds.) ACM CCS 2020, pp. 1607–1626. ACM Press (Nov 2020). https://doi.org/10.1145/3372297.3417276

47. Zahur, S., Rosulek, M., Evans, D.: Two halves make a whole. In: Oswald, E., Fischlin, M. (eds.) EUROCRYPT 2015. LNCS, vol. 9057, pp. 220–250. Springer, Heidelberg (2015). https://doi.org/10.1007/978-3-662-46803-6_8

A New Framework for Quantum Oblivious Transfer

Amit Agarwal[1(✉)], James Bartusek[2], Dakshita Khurana[1], and Nishant Kumar[1]

[1] University of Illinois Urbana-Champaign, Champaign, USA
{amita2,dakshita}@illinois.edu
[2] University of California Berkeley, Berkeley, USA

Abstract. We present a new template for building oblivious transfer from quantum information that we call the "fixed basis" framework. Our framework departs from prior work (e.g., Crepeau and Kilian, FOCS'88) by fixing the *correct* choice of measurement basis used by each player, except for some hidden *trap* qubits that are intentionally measured in a conjugate basis. We instantiate this template in the quantum random oracle model (QROM) to obtain simple protocols that implement, with security against malicious adversaries:

- *Non-interactive* random-input bit OT in a model where parties share EPR pairs a priori.
- Two-round random-input bit OT without setup, obtained by showing that the protocol above remains secure even if the (potentially malicious) OT receiver sets up the EPR pairs.
- Three-round chosen-input string OT from BB84 states without entanglement or setup. This improves upon natural variations of the CK88 template that require at least five rounds.

Along the way, we develop technical tools that may be of independent interest. We prove that natural functions like XOR enable *seedless* randomness extraction from certain quantum sources of entropy. We also use idealized (i.e. extractable and equivocal) bit commitments, which we obtain by proving security of simple and efficient constructions in the QROM.

1 Introduction

Stephen Wiesner's celebrated paper [61] that kickstarted the field of quantum cryptography suggested a way to use quantum information in order to achieve *a means for transmitting two messages either but not both of which may be received.* Later, it was shown that this powerful primitive – named oblivious transfer (OT) [29,54] – serves as the foundation for secure computation [32,43], which is a central goal of modern crytography.

Wiesner's original proposal only required uni-directional communication, from the sender to the receiver. However, it was not proven secure, and succesful attacks on the proposal (given the ability for the receiver to perform multi-qubit measurements) where even discussed in the paper. Later, [20] suggested a way

© International Association for Cryptologic Research 2023
C. Hazay and M. Stam (Eds.): EUROCRYPT 2023, LNCS 14004, pp. 363–394, 2023.
https://doi.org/10.1007/978-3-031-30545-0_13

to use both *interaction* and *bit commitments* (which for example can be instantiated using cryptographic hash functions) to obtain a secure protocol. In this work, we investigate how much interaction is really required to obtain oblivious transfer from quantum information (and hash functions). In particular, we ask

> *Can a sender non-interactively transmit two bits to a receiver*
> *such that the receiver will be able to recover one but not both of the bits?*

In a setting where the sender and receiver share prior EPR pairs, we obtain a positive answer to this question (for random receiver bit). We prove (malicious, simulation-based) security of our protocol in the quantum random oracle model.

Specifically, we consider a setup where the sender and receiver each begin with halves of EPR pairs, which are maximally entangled two-qubit states $\frac{|00\rangle+|11\rangle}{\sqrt{2}}$. These are the simplest type of entangled quantum states, and are likely to be a common shared setup in quantum networks (see e.g. [56] and references therein). They have also attracted much interest as a quantum analogue of the classical common reference string (CRS) model [19,26,44,49]. They have already been shown to be useful for many two-party tasks such as quantum communication via teleportation [10], entanglement-assisted quantum error correction [14], and even cryptographic tasks like key distribution [27] and non-interactive zero-knowledge [19,49].

Non-interactive Bit OT in the EPR Setup Model. We show that once Alice and Bob share a certain (fixed) number of EPR pairs between them, they can realize a *one-shot*[1] bit OT protocol, *securely* implementing an ideal functionality that takes two *bits* m_0, m_1 from Alice and delivers m_b for a uniformly random $b \leftarrow \{0,1\}$ to Bob. We provide an unconditionally secure protocol in the QROM, and view this as a first step towards protocols that rely on concrete properties of hash functions together with entanglement setup.

Furthermore, our result helps understand the power of entanglement as a cryptographic resource. Indeed, non-interactive oblivious transfer is impossible to achieve classically, under any computational assumption, even in the common reference string and/or random oracle model. Thus, the only viable one-message solution is to assume the parties already start with so-called *OT correlations*, where the sender gets random bits x_0, x_1 from a trusted dealer, and the receiver gets x_b for a random bit b. On the other hand, our result shows that OT can be achieved in a one-shot manner just given shared EPR pairs.

We note that an "OT correlations setup" is fundamentally different than an EPR pair setup. First of all, OT correlations are *specific to OT*, while, as desribed above, shared EPR pairs are already known to be broadly useful, and have been widely studied independent of OT. Moreover, an OT correlations setup requires *private* (hidden) randomness, while generating EPR pairs is a

---

[1] We use the terms"one-shot", "one-message", and "non-interactive" interchangably in this work, all referring to a protocol between two parties Alice and Bob that consists only of a single message from Alice to Bob.

deterministic process. In particular, any (even semi-honest) dealer that sets up OT correlations can learn the parties' private inputs by observing the resulting transcript of communication, while this is not necesarily true of an EPR setup by monogamy of entanglement. Furthermore, as we describe next, our OT protocol remains secure even if a *potentially malicious receiver* dishonestly sets up the entanglement.

Two-Message Bit OT without Setup. The notion of two-message oblivious transfer has been extensively studied in the classical setting [2,25,35,51,53] and is of particular theoretical and practical interest. We show that the above protocol remains secure even if the receiver were the one performing the EPR pair setup (as opposed to a trusted dealer / network administrator). That is, we consider a two-message protocol where the receiver first sets up EPR pairs and sends one half of every pair to the sender, following which the sender sends a message to the receiver as before. We show that this protocol also realizes the same bit OT functionality with random receiver choice bit.

This results in the first two-message maliciously-secure variant of OT, without setup, that does not (necessarily) make use of public-key cryptography. However, we remark that we still only obtain the random receiver input functionality in this setting, and leave a construction of two-message chosen-input string OT without public-key cryptography as an intriguing open problem.

Another Perspective: OT Correlations from Entanglement via 1-out-of-2 Deletion. It is well-known that shared halves of EPR pairs can be used to generate shared randomness by having each player measure their halves of EPR pairs in a common basis. But can they also be used to generate OT correlations, where one of the players (say Bob) outputs a random pair of bits, while the other (say Alice) learns only *one* of these (depending on a hidden choice bit), and cannot guess the other bit.[2]

At first, it may seem like the following basic property of EPR pairs gives a candidate solution that requires *no* communication: if Alice and Bob measure their halves in the same basis (say, both computational, hereafter referred to as the $+$ basis), then they will obtain the same random bit r, while if Alice and Bob measure their halves in conjugate bases (say, Alice in the $+$ basis and Bob in the Hadamard basis, hereafter referred to as the $\times$ basis), then they will obtain random and *independent* bits r_A, r_B. Indeed, if Alice and Bob share two EPR pairs, they could agree that Alice measures both of her halves in either the $+$ basis or the $\times$ basis depending on whether her choice bit is 0 or 1, while Bob always measures his first half in the $+$ basis and his second half in the $\times$ basis. Thus, Bob obtains (r_0, r_1), and, depending on her choice b, Alice obtains r_b, while *deleting* information about r_{1-b} by measuring the corresponding register in a conjugate basis.

Of course, there is nothing preventing Alice from simply measuring her first half in the $+$ basis and her second half in the $\times$ basis, obtaining both r_0, r_1

---

[2] While this framing of the problem is different from the previous page, the two turn out to be equivalent thanks to OT reversal and reorientation methods [36].

and rendering this initial candidate completely insecure. However, what if Alice could *prove* to Bob that she indeed measured both qubits in the same basis, *without* revealing to Bob which basis she chose? Then, Bob would be convinced that one of his bits is independent of Alice's view, while the privacy of Alice's choice b would remain intact. We rely on the Random Oracle to implement a cut-and-choose based proof that helps us obtain *maliciously* secure bit OT.

We emphasize that this problem is also interesting in the plain model under computational assumptions. We leave this as an open problem for future work, and discuss it (together other open problems) in Sect. 1.1.

Other Technical Contributions. We make additional technical contributions along the way, that may be of independent interest.

- **Seedless Extraction from Quantum Sources of Entropy.** Randomness extraction has been a crucial component in all quantum OT protocols, and *seeded* randomness extraction from the quantum sources of entropy that arise in such protocols has been extensively studied (see e.g. [13,55]). In our non-interactive and two-message settings, it becomes necessary to extract entropy without relying on the existence of a random seed. As such, we prove the security of *seedless* randomness extractors in this context, which may be of independent interest. In particular, we show that either the XOR function or a random oracle (for better rate) can be used in place of the seeded universal hashing used in prior works. The XOR extractor has been used in subsequent work [9] as a crucial tool in building cryptosystems with certified deletion.
- **Extractable and Equivocal Commitments in the QROM.** We abstract out a notion of (non-interactive) extractable and equivocal bit commitments in the QROM, that we make use of in our OT protocols. We provide a simple construction based on prior work [3,24,63].
- **Three-Message String OT without Entanglement or Setup.** We show that our fixed basis framework makes it possible to eliminate the need for both entanglement and setup with just three messages. The resulting protocol realizes string OT with no entanglement, and only requires one quantum message containing BB84 states followed by two classical messages. Furthermore, it allows both the sender and the receiver to *choose* their inputs to the OT (as opposed to sampling a random input to one of the parties).
  On the other hand, we find that using prior templates [20] necessitates a multi-stage protocol where players have to first exchange basis information in order to establish two channels, resulting in protocols that require at least an extra round of interaction.
- **Concrete Parameter Estimates.** We also estimate the number of EPR pairs/BB84 states required for each of our protocols, and derive concrete security losses incurred by our protocols. This is discussed in the full version [1], where we also provide a table of our estimates. We expect that future work will be able to further study and optimize the concrete efficiency of quantum OT in the QROM, and our work provides a useful starting point.

1.1   Open Problems and Directions for Future Research

Our new frameworks for oblivious transfer raise several fundamental questions of both theoretical and practical interest.

Strengthening Functionality. It would be interesting to obtain non-interactive or two-message variants of non-trivial quantum OT realizing stronger functionality than we obtain in this work[3]. Our work leaves open the following natural questions.

- Does there exist two-message non-trivial quantum *chosen-input* bit OT, that allows both parties to choose inputs?
- Does there exist one- or two-message non-trivial quantum chosen-sender-input *string* OT, with chosen sender strings and random receiver choice bit? Such a string OT may be sufficient to construct non-interactive secure computation (NISC) [37] with chosen sender input and random receiver input.
- Does there exist two-message non-trivial quantum OT without entanglement?
- Can our quantum OT protocols serve as building blocks for other non-interactive functionalities, e.g., by relying on techniques in [31] for one-way secure computation, or [12] for obfuscation?

Strengthening Security. While analyses in this work are restricted to the QROM, our frameworks are of conceptual interest even beyond this specific model. In particular, one could ask the following question.

- Does there exist non-interactive OT with shared EPR pair setup from *any concrete computational hardness assumption*?

One possible direction towards achieving this would be to instantiate our template with post-quantum extractable and equivocal commitments in the CRS model, and then attempt to instantiate the Fiat-Shamir paradigm in this setting based on a concrete hash function (e.g. [15, 16, 41] and numerous followups). Going further, one could even try to instantiate our templates from weak computational hardness including one-way functions (or even pseudorandom states). We imagine that such an OT would find useful applications even beyond MPC, given how two-message classical OT [2, 51] has been shown to imply a variety of useful protocols including two-message proof systems, non-malleable commitments, and beyond [5–7, 39, 40, 42, 52].

Finally, we note that any cryptographic protocol in a broader context typically requires the protocol to satisfy strong composability properties. It would be useful to develop a formal model for UC security with a (global) quantum random oracle, and prove UC security for our OT protocols in this model. Another question is whether one can achieve composably (UC) secure protocols with minimal interaction by building on our frameworks in the CRS model.

---

[3] Here *non-trivial* quantum OT means OT based on assumptions (such as symmetric-key cryptography) or ideal models that are not known to imply classical OT.

Practical Considerations. Our concrete quantum resource requirements and security bounds are computed assuming no transmission errors. On the other hand, actual quantum systems, even those that do not rely on entanglement, are often prone to errors. One approach to reconcile these differences is to employ techniques to first improve fidelity, e.g. of our EPR pair setup via entanglement purification; and then execute our protocol on the resulting states. Another natural approach (following e.g., [11]) could involve directly building error-resilient versions of our protocols that tolerate low fidelity and/or coherence. Another question is whether our games can be improved to reduce resource consumption and security loss, both in the idealized/error-free and error-prone models.

1.2   Related Work

Wiesner [61] suggested the first template for quantum OT, but his work did not contain a security proof (and even discussed some potential attacks). Crepeau and Kilian [20] made progress by demonstrating an approach for basing oblivious transfer on properties of quantum information *plus* a secure"bit commitment" scheme. This led to interest in building bit commitment from quantum information. Unfortunately, it was eventually shown by Mayers, Lo, and Chau [46,47] that bit commitment (and thus oblivious transfer) is *impossible* to build by relying solely on the properties of quantum information.

This is indeed a strong negative result, and rules out the possibility of basing secure computation on quantum information alone. However, it was still apparent to researchers that quantum information must offer *some* advantage in building secure computation systems. One could interpret the Mayers, Lo, Chau impossibility result as indicating that in order to hone in and understand this advantage, it will be necessary to make additional physical, computational, or modeling assumptions beyond the correctness of quantum mechanics. Indeed, much research has been performed in order to tease out the answer to this question, with three lines of work being particularly prominent and relevant[4].

- **Quantum OT from bit commitment.** Although unconditionally-secure bit commitment cannot be constructed using quantum information, [20]'s protocol is still meaningful and points to a fundamental difference between the quantum and classical setting, where bit commitment is not known to imply OT. A long line of work has been devoted to understanding the security of [20]'s proposal: e.g. [11,13,21,48,57,62].
- **Quantum OT in the bounded storage model.** One can also impose physical assumptions in order to recover quantum OT with unconditional security. [22] introduced the *quantum bounded-storage model*, and [60] introduced the more general *quantum noisy-storage model*, and showed how to construct unconditionally-secure quantum OT in these idealized models. There has also been much followup work focused on implementation and efficiency [28,30,38,59].

---

[4] Another line of work studies (unconditional) oblivious transfer with *imperfect* security [17,18,45], which we view as largely orthogonal to our work.

– **Quantum OT from "minicrypt" assumptions.** While [20]'s proposal for obtaining OT from bit commitments suggests that public-key cryptography is not required for building OT in a quantum world, a recent line of work has been interested in identifying the *weakest* concrete assumptions required for quantum OT, with [8,34] showing that the existence of one-way functions suffices and [4,50] showing that the existence of pseudo-random quantum states suffices.

Our work initiates the explicit study of quantum oblivious transfer in the *quantum random oracle model*, a natural model in which to study *unconditionally-secure* quantum oblivious transfer. Any protocol proven secure in the idealized random oracle model immediately gives rise to a natural "real-world" protocol where the oracle is replaced by a cryptographic hash function, such as SHA-256. As long as there continue to exist candidate hash functions with good security against quantum attackers, our protocols remain useful and relevant. On the other hand, the bounded storage model assumes an upper bound on the adversary's quantum storage while noisy storage model assumes that any qubit placed in quantum memory undergoes a certain amount of noise. The quantum communication complexity of these protocols increases with the bounds on storage/noise. It is clear that advances in quantum storage and computing technology will steadily degrade the security and increase the cost of such protocols, whereas protocols in the QROM do not suffer from these drawbacks.

2   Technical Overview

Notation. We will consider the following types of OT protocols.

– $\mathcal{F}_{\mathsf{OT}[k]}$: the *chosen-input string* OT functionality takes as input a bit b from the receiver and two strings $m_0, m_1 \in \{0,1\}^k$ from the sender. It delivers m_b to the receiver.
– $\mathcal{F}_{\mathsf{R-ROT}[1]}$: the *random-receiver-input bit* OT functionality takes as input $\top$ from the receiver and two bits $m_0, m_1 \in \{0,1\}$ from the sender. It samples $b \leftarrow \{0,1\}$ and delivers (b, m_b) to the receiver.
– $\mathcal{F}_{\mathsf{S-ROT}[k]}$: the *random-sender-input string* OT functionality takes as input $\top$ from the sender and (b, m) from the receiver for $b \in \{0,1\}, m \in \{0,1\}^k$. It set $m_b = m$, samples $m_{1-b} \leftarrow \{0,1\}^k$ and delivers (m_0, m_1) to the sender.

2.1   Non-Interactive OT in the Shared EPR Pair Model

As discussed in the introduction, there is a skeleton candidate OT protocol that requires no communication in the shared EPR model that we describe in Fig. 1.

The next step is for Alice to prove that she measured both her qubits in the same basis, without revealing what basis she chose. While it is unclear how Alice could directly prove this, we could hope to rely on the cut-and-choose paradigm to check that she measured "most" out of a *set* of pairs of qubits in the same

- **Setup**: 2 EPR pairs on registers $(\mathcal{A}_0, \mathcal{B}_0)$ and $(\mathcal{A}_1, \mathcal{B}_1)$, where Alice has registers $(\mathcal{A}_0, \mathcal{A}_1)$ and Bob has registers $(\mathcal{B}_0, \mathcal{B}_1)$.
- **Alice's output**: Input $b \in \{0, 1\}$.
  1. If $b = 0$, measure both of $\mathcal{A}_0, \mathcal{A}_1$ in basis $+$ to obtain r_0', r_1'. Output r_0'
  2. If $b = 1$, measure both of $\mathcal{A}_0, \mathcal{A}_1$ in basis $\times$ to obtain r_0', r_1'. Output r_1'.
- **Bob's output**: Measure $\mathcal{B}_0$ in basis $+$ to obtain r_0 and $\mathcal{B}_1$ in basis $\times$ to obtain r_1. Output (r_0, r_1).

Fig. 1. An (insecure) skeleton OT candidate.

basis. Indeed, a cut-and-choose strategy implementing a type of "measurement check" protocol has appeared in the original quantum OT proposal of [20] and many followups. Inspired by these works, we develop such a strategy for our protocol as follows.

Non-interactive Measurement Check. To achieve security, we first modify the protocol so that Alice and Bob use $2n$ EPR pairs, where Alice has one half of every pair and Bob has the other half.

Alice samples a set of n bases $\theta_1, \ldots, \theta_n \leftarrow \{+, \times\}^n$. For each $i \in [n]$, she must measure the ith pair of qubits (each qubit corresponding to a half of an EPR pair) in basis θ_i, obtaining measurement outcomes $(r_{i,0}, r_{i,1})$. Then, she must commit to her bases and outcomes , $(\theta_1, r_{1,0}, r_{1,1}), \ldots, , (\theta_n, r_{n,0}, r_{n,1})$. Once committed, she must *open* commitments corresponding to a randomly chosen (by Bob) $T \subset [n]$ of size k, revealing $\{\theta_i, r_{i,0}, r_{i,1}\}_{i \in T}$. Given these openings, for every $i \in T$, Bob will measure his halves of EPR pairs in bases (θ_i, θ_i) to obtain $(r_{i,0}', r_{i,1}')$. Bob aborts if his outcomes $(r_{i,0}', r_{i,1}')$ do not match Alice's claimed outcomes $(r_{i,0}, r_{i,1})$ for any $i \in T$. If outcomes on all $i \in T$ match, we will say that Bob accepts the measurement check.

Now, suppose Alice passes Bob's check with noticeable probability. Because she did not know the check subset T at the time of committing to her measurement outcomes, we can conjecture that for "most" $i \in [n] \setminus T$, Alice also correctly committed to results of measuring her qubits in bases (θ_i, θ_i). Moreover we can conjecture that the act of committing and passing Bob's check removed from Alice's view information about at least one out of $(r_{i,0}, r_{i,1})$ for most $i \in [n] \setminus T$. We build on techniques for analyzing quantum "cut-and-choose" protocols [13,21] to prove that this is the case.

In fact, we obtain a *non-interactive* instantiation of such a measurement-check by leveraging the random oracle to perform the Fiat-Shamir transform. That is, Alice applies a hash function, modeled as a random oracle, to her set of commitments in order to derive the "check set" T of size k. Then, she can compute openings to the commitments in the set T, and finally send all of her n commitments together with k openings in a single message to Bob. Finally, the unopened positions will be used to derive two strings (t_0, t_1) of $n - k$ bits each, with the guarantee that – as long as Alice passes Bob's check – there exists b such that Alice only has partial information about the string t_{1-b}. We point out that to realize OT, it is not enough for Alice to only have partial information about t_{1-b}, we must in fact ensure that she obtains *no information* about t_{1-b}. We achieve this by developing techniques for *seedless randomness extraction* in this setting, which we discuss later in this overview. The resulting protocol is described in Fig. 2.[5] Security against (malicious) Bob is relatively straightforward in this setting, and essentially reduces to proving that Alice's input bit b remains hidden; this follows due to the hiding of the commitment.

- **Setup:** Random oracle RO and $2n$ EPR pairs on registers $\{\mathcal{A}_{i,b}, \mathcal{B}_{i,b}\}_{i\in[n], b\in\{0,1\}}$, where Alice has register $\mathcal{A} := \{\mathcal{A}_{i,b}\}_{i\in[n], b\in\{0,1\}}$ and Bob has register $\mathcal{B} := \{\mathcal{B}_{i,b}\}_{i\in[n], b\in\{0,1\}}$.
- **Alice's message:** Input $b \in \{0,1\}$.
  1. Sample $\theta_1, \ldots, \theta_n \leftarrow \{+, \times\}^n$ and measure each $\mathcal{A}_{i,0}, \mathcal{A}_{i,1}$ in basis θ_i to obtain $r_{i,0}, r_{i,1}$.
  2. Commit $\mathsf{com}_1, \ldots, \mathsf{com}_n$ to $(\theta_1, r_{1,0}, r_{1,1}), \ldots, (\theta_n, r_{n,0}, r_{n,1})$.
  3. Compute $T = \mathsf{RO}(\mathsf{com}_1, \ldots, \mathsf{com}_n)$, where T is a subset of $[n]$ of size k.
  4. Compute openings $\{u_i\}_{i\in T}$ for $\{\mathsf{com}_i\}_{i\in T}$.
  5. Let $\overline{T} = [n] \setminus T$, and for all $i \in \overline{T}$, set $d_i = b \oplus \theta_i$ (interpreting $+$ as 0 and $\times$ as 1).
  6. Send $\{\mathsf{com}_i\}_{i\in[n]}, T, \{r_{i,0}, r_{i,1}, \theta_i, u_i\}_{i\in T}, \{d_i\}_{i\in\overline{T}}$ to Bob.
- **Alice's output:** $m_b := \mathsf{Extract}(t_b := \{r_{i,\theta_i}\}_{i\in\overline{T}})$.
- **Bob's computation:**
  1. Abort if $T \neq \mathsf{RO}(\mathsf{com}_1, \ldots, \mathsf{com}_n)$ or if verifying any commitment in the set T fails.
  2. For each $i \in T$, measure registers $\mathcal{B}_{i,0}, \mathcal{B}_{i,1}$ in basis θ_i to obtain $r'_{i,0}, r'_{i,1}$, and abort if $r_{i,0} \neq r'_{i,0}$ or $r_{i,1} \neq r'_{i,1}$.
  3. For each $i \in \overline{T}$, measure register $\mathcal{B}_{i,0}$ in the $+$ basis and register $\mathcal{B}_{i,1}$ in the $\times$ basis to obtain $r'_{i,0}, r'_{i,1}$.
- **Bob's output:** $m_0 := \mathsf{Extract}(t_0 := \{r_{i,d_i}\}_{i\in\overline{T}}), m_1 := \mathsf{Extract}(t_1 := \{r_{i,d_i \oplus 1}\}_{i\in\overline{T}})$.

Fig. 2. Non-interactive OT in the shared EPR pair model. Extract is an (unspecified) seedless hash function used for randomness extraction.

To formally prove security against malicious Alice, we build on several recently developed quantum random oracle techniques [23, 24, 63] as well as techniques for analyzing "quantum cut-and-choose" protocols [13, 21]. In particular, we require the random oracle based commitments to be *extractable*, and then take inspiration from [13] to argue that Bob's state on registers $\{\mathcal{B}_{i,0}, \mathcal{B}_{i,1}\}_{i\in\overline{T}}$ is in some sense close to a state described by the information $\{\theta_i, r_{i,0}, r_{i,1}\}_{i\in\overline{T}}$ in

---

[5] Our actual protocol involves an additional step that allows Alice to program any input m_b of her choice, but we suppress this detail in this overview.

Alice's unopened commitments. In more detail, we define a projector Π on registers $\{\mathcal{B}_{i,0}, \mathcal{B}_{i,1}\}_{i \in \overline{T}}$ spanned by all states in the $\{\theta_i\}_{i \in \overline{T}}$ basis that are "close" in Hamming distance to the collection of bits $\{r_{i,0}, r_{i,1}\}_{i \in \overline{T}}$. Since these bits are unopened, defining this projector requires us to run the extractor of the commitment scheme to obtain $\{r_{i,0}, r_{i,1}\}_{i \in \overline{T}}$. We show that, conditioned on Bob not aborting, his left-over state on registers $\{\mathcal{B}_{i,0}, \mathcal{B}_{i,1}\}_{i \in \overline{T}}$ must be negligibly close to the image of Π.

To do so, at a high level, we apply the measure-and-reprogram technique from [23,24], which roughly shows that in this setting, it suffices to consider an *interactive* version of the protocol, where all the commitments are output by Alice *before* T is chosen uniformly at random. At this point, it becomes possible to argue by standard Hoeffding inequalities that Bob's registers must be close to the image of Π (conditioned on Bob not aborting).

Finally, recall that Bob is measuring each $\mathcal{B}_{i,0}$ in the standard basis and each $\mathcal{B}_{i,1}$ in the Hadamard basis (whereas before measurement, as we just determined, most pairs $\mathcal{B}_{i,0}, \mathcal{B}_{i,1}$ were in the image of Π, i.e., "close" to basis states in the same basis). Thus, intuitively, honest Bob's measurements must produce at least some entropy (from Alice's perspective) when performed on any state in Π. Converting this entropy into uniform randomness, as is required by the definition of OT security, turns out to be non-trivial even given prior work on randomness extraction. In the next section, we discuss hurdles and new methods for *extracting uniform randomness* from this entropy.

New Techniques for Randomness Extraction. Note that the arguments above have not yet established a fully secure OT correlation. In particular, Alice may have *some* information about t_{1-b}, whereas OT security would require one of Bob's strings to be completely uniform and independent of Alice's view.

This situation also arises in prior work on quantum OT, and is usually solved via *seeded randomness extraction*. Using this approach, a seed s would be sampled by Bob, and the final OT strings would be defined as $m_0 = \mathsf{Extract}(s, t_0)$ and $m_1 = \mathsf{Extract}(s, t_1)$, where $\mathsf{Extract}$ is a universal hash function. Indeed, quantum privacy amplication [55] states that even given s, $\mathsf{Extract}(s, t_{1-b})$ is uniformly random from Alice's perspective as long as t_{1-b} has sufficient (quantum) min-entropy conditioned on Alice's state.

Unfortunately, this approach would require Bob to transmit the seed s to Alice for Alice to obtain her output $m_b = \mathsf{Extract}(s, t_b)$, making the protocol no longer non-interactive.[6] Instead, we develop techniques for *seedless* extraction that work in our setting, allowing us to make the full description of the hash function used to derive the final strings *public* at the beginning of the protocol.

We provide two instantiations of seedless randomness extraction that work in a setting where the entropy source comes from measuring a state supported on a small superposition of basis vectors in the conjugate basis. More concretely, given

---

[6] One idea would be to sample the seed s as part of the output of the random oracle. However, this does not ensure that s is uniformly random. For example Alice could bias certain bits of s by choosing her commitments in a certain way.

a state on two registers $\mathcal{A}, \mathcal{B}$, where the state on $\mathcal{B}$ is supported on standard basis vectors with small Hamming weight, consider measuring $\mathcal{B}$ in the Hadamard basis to produce x. For what unseeded hash functions Extract does $\mathsf{Extract}(x)$ look uniformly random, even given the state on register $\mathcal{A}$?

- **XOR extractor.** First, we observe that one can obtain a *single* bit of uniform randomness by XORing all of the bits of x together, as long as the superposition on register $\mathcal{B}$ only contains vectors with relative Hamming weight $< 1/2$. This can be used to obtain *bit* OT, where the OT messages m_0, m_1 consist of a single bit. In fact, by adjusting the parameters of the quantum cut-and-choose, the XOR extractor could be used bit-by-bit to extract any number of λ bits. However, this setting would require a number of EPR pairs that grows with λ^3, resulting in a very inefficient protocol.
- **RO extractor.** To obtain a more efficient method of extracting λ bits, we turn to the random oracle model, which has proven to be a useful seedless extractor in the classical setting. Since an adversarial Alice in our protocol has some control over the state on registers $\mathcal{A}, \mathcal{B}$, arguing that $\mathsf{RO}(x)$ looks uniformly random from her perspective requires some notion of *adaptive* reprogramming in the QROM. While some adaptive re-programming theorems have been shown before (e.g. [33,58]), they have all *only considered x sampled from a classical probability distribution*. This is for good reason, since counterexamples in the quantum setting exist, even when x has high min-entropy given the state on register $\mathcal{A}$.[7] In this work, we show that in the special case of x being sampled via measurement in a conjugate basis, one *can* argue that $\mathsf{RO}(x)$ can be replaced with a uniformly random r, without detection by the adversary. Our proof relies on the superposition oracle of [63] and builds on proof techniques in [33]. We leverage our RO extractor to obtain non-interactive λ-bit string OT with a number of EPR pairs that only grows *linearly* in λ.

Differences from the CK88 Template. As mentioned earlier, the original quantum OT proposal [20] and its followups also incorporate a commit-challenge-response measurement-check protocol to enforce honest behavior. However, we point out one key difference in our approach that enables us to completely get rid of interaction. In CK88, parties measure their set of qubits[8] using a *uniformly random* set of basis choices. Then, in order to set up the two channels required for OT, they need to exchange their basis choices with each other (after the measurement check commitments have been prepared and sent). This requires multiple rounds of interaction. In our setting, it is crucial that one of the parties measures (or prepares) qubits in a *fixed* set of bases known to the other party,

---

[7] For example, consider an adversary that, via a single superposition query to the random oracle, sets register $\mathcal{B}$ to be a superposition over all x such that the first bit of $\mathsf{RO}(x)$ is 0. Then, measuring $\mathcal{B}$ in the computational basis will result in an x with high min-entropy, but where $\mathsf{RO}(x)$ is distinguishable from a uniformly random r.

[8] Technically, one party prepares and the other measures BB84 states.

removing the need for a two-way exchange of basis information. In the case of Fig. 2, this party is Bob. Hereafter, we refer to the CK88 template as the *random basis framework*, and our template as the *fixed basis framework*.

Non-interactive OT Reversal. So far, our techniques have shown that, given shared EPR pairs, Alice can send a single message to Bob that results in the following correlations: Alice outputs a bit b and string m_b, while Bob outputs m_0, m_1, thus implementing the $\mathcal{F}_{S-ROT}$ functionality with Bob as the "sender".

However, an arguably more natural functionality would treat Alice as the sender, with some chosen inputs m_0, m_1, and Bob as the receiver, who can recover b, m_b from Alice's message. In fact, for the case that m_0, m_1 are single bits, a "reversed" version of the protocol can already be used to acheive this due to the non-interactive OT reversal of [36]. Let (b, r_b) and (r_0, r_1) be Alice and Bob's output from our protocol, where Alice has chosen b uniformly at random. Then Alice can define $\ell_0 = m_0 \oplus r_b, \ell_1 = m_1 \oplus r_b \oplus b$ and send (ℓ_0, ℓ_1) along with her message to Bob. Bob can then use r_0 to recover m_c from ℓ_c for his "choice bit" $c = r_0 \oplus r_1$. Moreover, since in our protocol the bits r_0, r_1 can be sampled uniformly at random by the functionality, this implies that c is a uniformly random choice bit, unknown to Alice, but unable to be tampered with by Bob. This results in a protocol that satisfies the $\mathcal{F}_{R-ROT[1]}$ functionality, and we have referred to it as our one-shot bit OT protocol in the introduction.

2.2   Two-Message OT Without Trusted Setup

Next, say that we don't want to assume a *trusted* EPR pair setup. In particular, what if we allow Bob to set up the EPR pairs? In this case, a malicious Bob may send any state of his choice to Alice. However, observe that in Fig. 2, Alice's bit b is masked by her random choices of θ_i. These choices remain hidden from Bob due to the hiding of the commitment scheme, plus the fact that they are only used to measure Alice's registers. Regardless of the state that a malicious Bob may send, he will not be able to detect which basis Alice measures her registers in, and thus will not learn any information about b. As a result, we obtain a *two-message* quantum OT protocol in the QROM. As we show in the full version [1], this protocol satisfies the $\mathcal{F}_{S-ROT}$ OT ideal functionality that allows Alice to choose her inputs (b, m), and sends Bob random (m_0, m_1) s.t. $m_b = m$.

Moreover, adding another reorientation message at the end from Bob to Alice – where Bob uses m_0, m_1 as keys to encode his chosen inputs – results in a three-round chosen input string OT protocol realizing the $\mathcal{F}_{OT[k]}$ functionality. However, as we will see in the next section, with three messages, we can *remove the need for entanglement* while still realizing $\mathcal{F}_{OT[k]}$.

Finally, in the case that m_0, m_1 are bits, we can apply the same non-interactive [36] reversal described above to the two-round protocol, resulting in a two-round secure realization of the $\mathcal{F}_{R-ROT[1]}$ ideal functionality. This results in our two-round bit OT protocol as referenced in the introduction.

2.3 Three-Message Chosen-Input OT

We now develop a three-message protocol that realizes the chosen-input string OT functionality $\mathcal{F}_{\mathsf{OT}}$, which takes two strings m_0, m_1 from the sender and a bit b from the receiver, and delivers m_b to the receiver. This protocol will not require entanglement, but still uses the *fixed basis framework*, just like the one discussed in Sect. 2.1.

Recall that in the EPR-based protocol, Bob would obtain (r_0, r_1) by measuring his halves of two EPR pairs in basis $(+, \times)$, while Alice would obtain (r_0, r_1') or (r_0', r_1) respectively by measuring her halves in basis $(+, +)$ or $(\times, \times)$, where (r_0', r_1') are uniform and independent of (r_0, r_1).

Our first observation is that a similar effect is achieved by having Bob send BB84 states polarized in *a fixed basis* instead of sending EPR pairs. That is, Bob samples uniform (r_0, r_1) and sends to Alice the states $|r_0\rangle_+, |r_1\rangle_\times$. Alice would obtain (r_0, r_1') or (r_0', r_1) respectively by measuring these states in basis $(+, +)$ or $(\times, \times)$ respectively, where (r_0', r_1') are uniform and independent of (r_0, r_1). The skeleton protocol is sketched in Fig. 3.

- **Bob's message and output:**
    1. Sample $(r_0, r_1) \leftarrow \{0, 1\}$ and send $|r_0\rangle_+, |r_1\rangle_\times$ in registers $\mathcal{A}_0, \mathcal{A}_1$ to Alice.
    2. Bob's output is (r_0, r_1).
- **Alice's output:** Input $b \in \{0, 1\}$.
    1. If $b = 0$, measure both of $\mathcal{A}_0, \mathcal{A}_1$ in basis $+$ to obtain r_0', r_1'. Output r_0'.
    2. If $b = 1$, measure both of $\mathcal{A}_0, \mathcal{A}_1$ in basis $\times$ to obtain r_0', r_1'. Output r_1'.

Fig. 3. Another (insecure) skeleton OT candidate.

As before, though, there is nothing preventing Alice from retrieving both (r_0, r_1) by measuring the states she obtains in basis $(+, \times)$. Thus, as before, we need a *measurement check* to ensure that Alice measures "most" out of a *set* of pairs of qubits in the same basis. But implementing such a check with BB84 states turns out to be more involved than in the EPR pair protocol.

Non-interactive Measurement Check Without Entanglement. Towards building a measurement check, we first modify the skeleton protocol so that Bob sends $2n$ BB84 qubits $\{|r_{i,0}\rangle_+, |r_{i,1}\rangle_\times\}_{i \in [n]}$ on registers $\{\mathcal{A}_{i,b}\}_{i \in [n], b \in \{0,1\}}$ to Alice (instead of just two qubits). Now Alice is required to sample a set of n bases $\theta_1, \ldots, \theta_n \leftarrow \{+, \times\}^n$. For each $i \in [n]$, she must measure the ith pair of qubits in basis θ_i, obtaining measurement outcomes $(r_{i,0}', r_{i,1}')$. Then, she will commit to her bases and outcomes , $(\theta_1, r_{1,0}', r_{1,1}'), \ldots, (\theta_n, r_{n,0}', r_{n,1}')$. Once committed, she will *open* commitments corresponding to a randomly chosen (by Bob) $T \subset [n]$ of size k, revealing $\{\theta_i, r_{i,0}', r_{i,1}'\}_{i \in T}$.

But Bob cannot check these openings the same way as in the EPR-based protocol. Recall that in the EPR protocol, for every $i \in T$, Bob would measure his halves of EPR pairs in bases (θ_i, θ_i) to obtain $(r_{i,0}, r_{i,1})$, and compare the results against Alice's response. On the other hand, once Bob has sent registers $\{\mathcal{A}_{i,b}\}_{i \in [n], b \in \{0,1\}}$ containing $\{|r_{i,0}\rangle_+, |r_{i,1}\rangle_\times\}_{i \in [n]}$ to Alice, there is no way for him to recover the result of measuring any pair $(\mathcal{A}_{i,0}, \mathcal{A}_{i,1})$ in basis (θ_i, θ_i).

To fix this, we modify the protocol to allow for a (randomly chosen and hidden) set U of "trap" positions. For all $i \in U$, Bob outputs registers $(\mathcal{A}_{i,0}, \mathcal{A}_{i,1})$ containing $|r_{i,0}\rangle_{\vartheta_i}, |r_{i,1}\rangle_{\vartheta_i}$, that is, both qubits are polarized in the same basis $\vartheta_i \leftarrow \{+, \times\}$. All other qubits are sampled the same way as before, i.e. as $|r_{i,0}\rangle_+, |r_{i,1}\rangle_\times$. Alice commits to her measurement outcomes $\{\theta_i, r'_{i,0}, r'_{i,1}\}_{i \in [n]}$, and then reveals commitment openings $\{\theta_i, r'_{i,0}, r'_{i,1}\}_{i \in T}$ for a randomly chosen subset of size T, as before. But Bob can now check Alice on all positions i in the intersection $T \cap U$ where $\vartheta_i = \theta_i$. Specifically, Bob aborts if for any $i \in T \cap U$, $\vartheta_i = \theta_i$ but $(r'_{i,0}, r'_{i,1}) \neq (r_{i,0}, r_{i,1})$. Otherwise, Alice and Bob will use the set $[n] \setminus T \setminus U$ to generate their OT outputs. The resulting protocol is sketched in Fig. 4. Crucially, we make use of a third round in order to allow Bob to transmit his choice of U to Alice, so that they can both agree on the set $[n] \setminus T \setminus U$.

Again, we must argue that any Alice that passes Bob's check with noticeable probability loses information about one out of $r_{i,0}$ and $r_{i,1}$ for "most" $i \in [n] \setminus T \setminus U$. Because she did not know the check subset T or Bob's trap subset U at the time of committing to her measurement outcomes, we can again conjecture that for "most" $i \in [n] \setminus T$, Alice also correctly committed to results of measuring her qubits in bases (θ_i, θ_i). Moreover we can conjecture that the act of committing and passing Bob's check removed from Alice's view information about at least one out of $(r_{i,0}, r_{i,1})$ for most $i \in [n] \setminus T$. This requires carefully formulating and analyzing a quantum sampling strategy that is somewhat more involved than the one in Sect. 2.1. Furthermore, as in Sect. 2.1, we make the measurement check non-interactive by relying on the Fiat-Shamir transform.

2.4   Extractable and Equivocal Commitments

To achieve simulation-based security, our constructions rely on commitments that satisfy *extractability and equivocality*. We model these as classical non-interactive bit commitments that, informally, satisfy the following properties.

- Equivocality: This property ensures that the commitment scheme admits an efficient simulator, let's say $\mathcal{S}_{\mathsf{Equ}}$, that can sample commitment strings that are indistinguishable from commitment strings generated honestly and later, during the opening phase, provide valid openings for either 0 or 1.
- Extractability: This property ensures that the commitment scheme admits an efficient extractor, let's say $\mathcal{S}_{\mathsf{Ext}}$, that, given access to the committer who outputs a commitment string, can output the committed bit.

The need for these two additional properties is not new to our work. Indeed, [21] showed that bit commitment schemes satisfying extraction and equivocation suffice to instantiate the original [11,20] QOT template. [21] called their

- **Inputs:** Bob has inputs m_0, m_1 each in $\{0,1\}^\lambda$, Alice has input $b \in \{0,1\}$.
- **Bob's Message:**
  1. Sample a "large enough" subset $U \subset [n]$, and for every $i \in U$, sample $\vartheta_i \leftarrow \{+, \times\}$.
  2. For every $i \in [n]$, sample $(r_{i,0}, r_{i,1}) \leftarrow \{0,1\}$.
  3. For $i \in U$, set registers $(\mathcal{A}_{i,0}, \mathcal{A}_{i,1})$ to $(|r_{i,0}\rangle_{\vartheta_i}, |r_{i,1}\rangle_{\vartheta_i})$.
  4. For $i \in [n] \setminus U$, set registers $(\mathcal{A}_{i,0}, \mathcal{A}_{i,1})$ to $(|r_{i,0}\rangle_+, |r_{i,0}\rangle_\times)$.
  5. Send $\{\mathcal{A}_{i,0}, \mathcal{A}_{i,1}\}_{i \in [n]}$ to Alice.
- **Alice's message:**
  1. Sample $\theta_1, \ldots, \theta_n \leftarrow \{+, \times\}^n$ and measure each $\mathcal{A}_{i,0}, \mathcal{A}_{i,1}$ in basis θ_i to obtain $r'_{i,0}, r'_{i,1}$.
  2. Compute commitments $\mathsf{com}_1, \ldots, \mathsf{com}_n$ to $(\theta_1, r'_{1,0}, r'_{1,1}), \ldots, (\theta_n, r'_{n,0}, r'_{n,1})$.
  3. Compute $T = \mathsf{RO}(\mathsf{com}_1, \ldots, \mathsf{com}_n)$, where T is parsed as a subset of $[n]$ of size k.
  4. Compute openings $\{u_i\}_{i \in T}$ for $\{\mathsf{com}_i\}_{i \in T}$.
  5. Let $\overline{T} = [n] \setminus T$, and for all $i \in \overline{T}$, set $d_i = b \oplus \theta_i$ (interpreting $+$ as 0 and $\times$ as 1).
  6. Send $\{\mathsf{com}_i\}_{i \in [n]}, T, \{r'_{i,0}, r'_{i,1}, \theta_i, u_i\}_{i \in T}, \{d_i\}_{i \in \overline{T}}$ to Bob.
- **Bob's Message:**
  1. Abort if $T \neq \mathsf{RO}(\mathsf{com}_1, \ldots, \mathsf{com}_n)$ or if verifying any commitment in the set T fails.
  2. If for any $i \in T \cap U$, $r_{i,0} \neq r'_{i,0}$ or $r_{i,1} \neq r'_{i,1}$, abort.
  3. Set $x_0 = m_0 \oplus \mathsf{Extract}(t_0 := \{r_{i,d_i}\}_{i \in [n] \setminus T \setminus U})$ and $x_1 = m_1 \oplus \mathsf{Extract}(t_1 := \{r_{i,d_i \oplus 1}\}_{i \in [n] \setminus T \setminus U})$.
  4. Send (x_0, x_1, U) to Alice.
- **Alice's output:** $m_b := x_b \oplus \mathsf{Extract}(t_b := \{r'_{i,\theta_i}\}_{i \in \overline{T}})$.

Fig. 4. Three-message chosen-input OT without entanglement. Extract is an (unspecified) function used for randomness extraction. Since Bob is sending the final message, we may use a seeded function here.

commitments dual-mode commitments, and provided a construction based on the quantum hardness of the learning with errors (QLWE) assumption. In two recent works [8,34], constructions of such commitment schemes were achieved by relying on just post-quantum one-way functions (and quantum communication).

We show that the most common construction of random-oracle based commitments – where a commitment to bit b is $H(b\|r)$ for uniform r – satisfies both extractability and equivocality in the QROM. Our proof of extractability applies the techniques of [24,63] for on-the-fly simulation with extraction, and our proof of equivocality relies on a one-way-to-hiding lemma from [3].

3   Seedless Extraction from Quantum Sources

In this section, we consider the problem of seedless randomness extraction from a quantum source of entropy. The source of entropy we are interested in comes from applying a Hadamard basis measurement to a state that is in a "small" superposition of computational basis vectors. More concretely, consider an arbitrarily entangled system on registers $\mathcal{A}, \mathcal{X}$, where $\mathcal{X}$ is in a small superposition of computational basis vectors. Then, we want to specify an extractor E such that, if x is obtained by measuring register $\mathcal{X}$ in the Hadamard basis, then $E(x)$ looks uniformly random, even given the "side information" on register $\mathcal{A}$. Note that *seeded* randomness extraction in this setting has been well-studied (e.g. [13,21,55]).

3.1   The XOR Extractor

First, we observe that if E just XORs all the bits of x together, then the resulting bit $E(x)$ is *perfectly* uniform, as long as the original state on $\mathcal{X}$ is only supported on vectors with relative Hamming weight $< 1/2$.

Theorem 1. *Let $\mathcal{X}$ be an n-qubit register, and consider any state $|\gamma\rangle_{\mathcal{A},\mathcal{X}}$ that can be written as*

$$|\gamma\rangle = \sum_{u:\mathcal{HW}(u)<n/2} |\psi_u\rangle_{\mathcal{A}} \otimes |u\rangle_{\mathcal{X}}.$$

Let $\rho_{\mathcal{A},\mathcal{P}}$ be the mixed state that results from measuring $\mathcal{X}$ in the Hadamard basis to produce x, and writing $\bigoplus_{i\in[n]} x_i$ into the single qubit register $\mathcal{P}$. Then

$$\rho_{\mathcal{A},\mathcal{P}} = \mathrm{Tr}_{\mathcal{X}}(|\gamma\rangle\langle\gamma|) \otimes \left(\frac{1}{2}|0\rangle\langle 0| + \frac{1}{2}|1\rangle\langle 1|\right).$$

Proof. First, write the state on $(\mathcal{A}, \mathcal{X}, \mathcal{P})$ that results from applying Hadamard to $\mathcal{X}$ and writing the parity, denoted by $p(x) := \bigoplus_{i\in[n]} x_i$, to $\mathcal{P}$:

$$\frac{1}{2^{n/2}} \sum_{x\in\{0,1\}^n} \left(\sum_{u:\mathcal{HW}(u)<n/2} (-1)^{u\cdot x}|\psi_u\rangle \right) |x\rangle|p(x)\rangle.$$

Then we have that

$$\rho_{\mathcal{A},\mathcal{P}} = \frac{1}{2^n} \sum_{x:p(x)=0} \left(\sum_{u_1,u_2} (-1)^{(u_1 \oplus u_2) \cdot x} |\psi_{u_1}\rangle\langle\psi_{u_2}| \right) \otimes |0\rangle\langle 0|$$

$$+ \frac{1}{2^n} \sum_{x:p(x)=1} \left(\sum_{u_1,u_2} (-1)^{(u_1 \oplus u_2) \cdot x} |\psi_{u_1}\rangle\langle\psi_{u_2}| \right) \otimes |1\rangle\langle 1|$$

$$= \frac{1}{2^n} \sum_{u_1,u_2} |\psi_{u_1}\rangle\langle\psi_{u_2}| \otimes \left(\sum_{x:p(x)=0} (-1)^{(u_1 \oplus u_2) \cdot x} |0\rangle\langle 0| + \sum_{x:p(x)=1} (-1)^{(u_1 \oplus u_2) \cdot x} |1\rangle\langle 1| \right)$$

$$= \frac{1}{2^n} \sum_{u_1,u_2} 2^{n/2} \delta_{u_1=u_2} |\psi_{u_1}\rangle\langle\psi_{u_2}| \otimes (|0\rangle\langle 0| + |1\rangle\langle 1|)$$

$$= \frac{1}{2} \sum_{u:\mathcal{HW}<n/2} |\psi_u\rangle\langle\psi_u| \otimes (|0\rangle\langle 0| + |1\rangle\langle 1|)$$

$$= \mathrm{Tr}_{\mathcal{X}}(|\gamma\rangle\langle\gamma|) \otimes \left(\frac{1}{2}|0\rangle\langle 0| + \frac{1}{2}|1\rangle\langle 1| \right),$$

where the 3rd equality is due to the following claim, plus the observation that $u_1 \oplus u_2 \neq 1^n$ for any u_1, u_2 such that $\mathcal{HW}(u_1), \mathcal{HW}(u_2) < n/2$.

Claim 2. *For any $u \in \{0,1\}^n$ such that $u \notin \{0^n, 1^n\}$, it holds that*

$$\sum_{x:p(x)=0} (-1)^{u \cdot x} = \sum_{x:p(x)=1} (-1)^{u \cdot x} = 0.$$

Proof. For any such $u \notin \{0^n, 1^n\}$, define $S_0 = \{i : u_i = 0\}$ and $S_1 = \{i : u_i = 1\}$. Then, for any $y_0 \in \{0,1\}^{|S_0|}$ and $y_1 \in \{0,1\}^{|S_1|}$, define $x_{y_0,y_1} \in \{0,1\}^n$ to be the n-bit string that is equal to y_0 when restricted to indices in S_0 and equal to y_1 when restricted to indices in S_1. Then,

$$\sum_{x:p(x)=0} (-1)^{u \cdot x} = \sum_{y_1 \in \{0,1\}^{|S_1|}} \sum_{y_0 \in \{0,1\}^{|S_0|}:p(x_{y_0,y_1})=0} (-1)^{u \cdot x_{y_0,y_1}}$$

$$= \sum_{y_1 \in \{0,1\}^{|S_1|}} 2^{|S_0|-1} (-1)^{1^{|S_1|} \cdot y_1} = 2^{|S_0|-1} \sum_{y_1 \in \{0,1\}^{|S_1|}} (-1)^{p(y_1)} = 0,$$

and the same sequence of equalities can be seen to hold for $x : p(x) = 1$.   □

This completes the proof of the theorem.   □

3.2 The Random Oracle Extractor

Next, our goal is to extract multiple bits of randomness from x. To do this, we model E as a *random oracle*. We derive a bound on the advantage any adversary has in distinguishing $E(x)$ from a uniformly random string, based on the number of qubits k in the register $\mathcal{X}$, the number of vectors C in the superposition on register $\mathcal{X}$, and the number of queries q made to the random oracle. In fact, to be as general as possible, we consider a random oracle with input length n, and allow $n - k$ of the bits of the input to the random oracle to be (adaptively) determined by the adversary, while the remaining k bits are sampled by measuring a k-qubit register $\mathcal{X}$.

Theorem 3. *Let $H : \{0,1\}^n \rightarrow \{0,1\}^m$ be a uniformly random function, and let q, C, k be integers. Consider a two-stage oracle algorithm (A_1^H, A_2^H) that combined makes at most q queries to H. Suppose that A_1^H outputs classical strings $(T, \{x_i\}_{i \in T})$, and let $|\gamma\rangle_{\mathcal{A},\mathcal{X}}$ be its left-over quantum state,[9] where $T \subset [n]$ is a set of size $n - k$, each $x_i \in \{0,1\}$, $\mathcal{A}$ is a register of arbitary size, and $\mathcal{X}$ is a register of k qubits. Suppose further that with probability 1 over the sampling of H and the execution of A_1, there exists a set $L \subset \{0,1\}^k$ of size at most C such that $|\gamma\rangle$ may be written as follows:*

$$|\gamma\rangle = \sum_{u \in L} |\psi_u\rangle_{\mathcal{A}} \otimes |u\rangle_{\mathcal{X}}.$$

Now consider the following two games.

- REAL:
    • A_1^H *outputs* $T, \{x_i\}_{i \in T}, |\gamma\rangle_{\mathcal{A},\mathcal{X}}$.
    • $\mathcal{X}$ *is measured in the Hadamard basis to produce a k-bit string which is parsed as $\{x_i\}_{i \in \overline{T}}$, and a left-over state $|\gamma'\rangle_{\mathcal{A}}$ on register $\mathcal{A}$. Define $x = (x_1, \ldots, x_n)$.*
    • A_2^H *is given* $T, \{x_i\}_{i \in T}, |\gamma'\rangle_{\mathcal{A}}, H(x)$, *and outputs a bit.*
- IDEAL:
    • A_1^H *outputs* $T, \{x_i\}_{i \in T}, |\gamma\rangle_{\mathcal{A},\mathcal{X}}$.
    • $r \leftarrow \{0,1\}^m$.
    • A_2^H *is given* $T, \{x_i\}_{i \in T}, \mathrm{Tr}_{\mathcal{X}}(|\gamma\rangle\langle\gamma|), r$, *and outputs a bit.*

Then,

$$|\mathrm{Pr}[\mathsf{REAL} = 1] - \mathrm{Pr}[\mathsf{IDEAL} = 1]| \leq \frac{2\sqrt{q}C + 2q\sqrt{C}}{2^{k/2}} < \frac{4qC}{2^{k/2}}.$$

The proof of this theorem appears in the full version [1].

4   The Fixed Basis Framework: OT from Entanglement

We define (non-interactive) commitments in the quantum random oracle model, and use them to build protocols for OT from shared EPR pairs.

---

[9] That is, consider sampling H, running a purified A_1^H, measuring at the end to obtain $(T, \{x_i\}_{i \in T})$, and then defining $|\gamma\rangle$ to be the left-over state on $\mathcal{A}$'s remaining registers.

Commitments in the Random Oracle Model. A non-interactive commitment scheme with partial opening in the quantum random oracle model consists of classical oracle algorithms (Com, Open, Rec) with the following syntax.

- $\mathsf{Com}^H(1^\lambda, \{m_i\}_{i\in[n]})$: On input the security parameter λ and n messages $\{m_i \in \{0,1\}^k\}_{i\in[n]}$, output n commitments $\{_{,i}\}_{i\in[n]}$ and a state st.
- $\mathsf{Open}^H(\mathsf{st}, T)$: On input a state st and a set $T \subseteq [n]$, output messages $\{m_i\}_{i\in T}$ and openings $\{u_i\}_{i\in T}$.
- $\mathsf{Rec}^H(\{_{,i}\}_{i\in[n]}, T, \{m_i, u_i\}_{i\in T})$: on input n commitments $\{_{,i}\}_{i\in[n]}$, a set T, and a set of message opening pairs $\{m_i, u_i\}_{i\in T}$, output $\{m_i\}_{i\in T}$ or $\perp$.

The commitment scheme is parameterized by $n = n(\lambda)$ which is the number of messages to be committed in parallel, and $k = k(\lambda)$, the length of each message.

In the full version [1], we define correctness, hiding, extractability and equivocality for these commitments. We prove that a natural construction which essentially commits to a bit b as $H(b\|r)$ for $r \leftarrow \{0,1\}^\lambda$, satisfies extractability and equivocality in the QROM. The extractability definition guarantees the existence of a simulator $\mathsf{SimExt} = (\mathsf{SimExt.RO}, \mathsf{SimExt.Ext})$ where $\mathsf{SimExt.RO}$ responds to the adversary's random oracle queries and $\mathsf{SimExt.Sim}$ extracts from the commitment strings output by the adversary.

Theorem 4. *Instantiate Protocol 5 with the* correct, hiding, *and* extractable *non-interactive commitment scheme above. Then the following hold.*

- *When instantiated with the XOR extractor, there exist constants A, B such that Protocol 5 securely realizes $\mathcal{F}_{\mathsf{S-ROT}[1]}$.*
- *When instantiated with the ROM extractor, there exist constants A, B such that Protocol 5 securely realizes $\mathcal{F}_{\mathsf{S-ROT}[\lambda]}$.*

Furthermore, letting λ be the security parameter, q be an upper bound on the total number of random oracle queries made by the adversary, and using the commitment scheme above with security parameter $\lambda_, = 4\lambda$, the following hold.

- *When instantiatied with the XOR extractor and constants $A = 50$, $B = 100$, Protocol 5 securely realizes $\mathcal{F}_{\mathsf{S-ROT}[1]}$ with μ_{R^*}-security against a malicious receiver and μ_{S^*}-security against a malicious sender, where*

$$\mu_{\mathsf{R}^*} = \left(\frac{8q^{3/2}}{2^\lambda} + \frac{3600\lambda q}{2^{2\lambda}} + \frac{148(450\lambda + q + 1)^3 + 1}{2^{4\lambda}}\right), \mu_{\mathsf{S}^*} = \left(\frac{85\lambda^{1/2}q}{2^{2\lambda}}\right).$$

This requires a total of $2(A + B)\lambda = 300\lambda$ EPR pairs.
- *When instantiated with the ROM extractor and constants $A = 1050$, $B = 2160$, Protocol 5 securely realizes $\mathcal{F}_{\mathsf{S-ROT}[\lambda]}$ with μ_{R^*}-security against a malicious receiver and μ_{S^*}-security against a malicious sender, where*

$$\mu_{\mathsf{R}^*} = \left(\frac{8q^{3/2} + 4\lambda}{2^\lambda} + \frac{77040\lambda q}{2^{2\lambda}} + \frac{148(9630\lambda + q + 1)^3 + 1}{2^{4\lambda}}\right), \mu_{\mathsf{S}^*} = \left(\frac{197\lambda^{1/2}q}{2^{2\lambda}}\right).$$

This requires a total of $2(A + B)\lambda = 6420\lambda$ EPR pairs.

Protocol 5

Ingredients and parameters.

- Security parameter λ, and constants A, B. Let $n = (A + B)\lambda$ and $k = A\lambda$.
- A non-interactive extractable commitment scheme $(\mathsf{Com}, \mathsf{Open}, \mathsf{Rec})$, where commitments to 3 bits have size $\ell := \ell(\lambda)$.
- A random oracle $H_{FS} : \{0,1\}^{n\ell} \to \{0,1\}^{\lceil \log \binom{n}{k} \rceil}$.
- An extractor E with domain $\{0,1\}^{n-k}$ which is either
  - The XOR function, so $E(r_1, \ldots, r_{n-k}) = \bigoplus_{i \in [n-k]} r_i$.
  - A random oracle $H_{Ext} : \{0,1\}^{n-k} \to \{0,1\}^\lambda$.

Setup. $2n$ EPR pairs on registers $\{\mathcal{R}_{i,b}, \mathcal{S}_{i,b}\}_{i \in [n], b \in \{0,1\}}$, where the receiver has register $\mathcal{R} := \{\mathcal{R}_{i,b}\}_{i \in [n], b \in \{0,1\}}$ and the sender has register $\mathcal{S} := \{\mathcal{S}_{i,b}\}_{i \in [n], b \in \{0,1\}}$.
Protocol.

- **Receiver message.** R, on input $b \in \{0,1\}$, $m \in \{0,1\}^\lambda$, does the following.
  - **Measurement.** Sample $\theta_1 \theta_2 \ldots \theta_n \leftarrow \{+, \times\}^n$ and for $i \in [n]$, measure registers $\mathcal{R}_{i,0}, \mathcal{R}_{i,1}$ in basis θ_i to obtain $r_{i,0}, r_{i,1}$.
  - **Measurement check.**
    * Compute $(,, \{c_i\}_{i \in [n]}) \leftarrow \mathsf{Com}\left(\{(r_{i,0}, r_{i,1}, \theta_i)\}_{i \in [n]}\right)$.
    * Compute $T = H_{FS}(c_1 \| \ldots \| c_n)$, parse T as a subset of $[n]$ of size k.
    * Compute $\{(r_{i,0}, r_{i,1}, \theta_i), u_i\}_{i \in [T]} \leftarrow \mathsf{Open}(, T)$.
  - **Reorientation.** Let $\overline{T} = [n] \setminus T$, and for all $i \in \overline{T}$, set $d_i = b \oplus \theta_i$ (interpreting $+$ as 0, $\times$ as 1).
  - **Sampling.** Set $x_b = E\left(\{r_{i,\theta_i}\}_{i \in \overline{T}}\right) \oplus m$, and sample $x_{1-b} \leftarrow \{0,1\}^\lambda$.
  - **Message.** Send to S
    $$(x_0, x_1), \{c_i\}_{i \in [n]}, T, \{r_{i,0}, r_{i,1}, \theta_i, u_i\}_{i \in [T]}, \{d_i\}_{i \in \overline{T}}.$$

- **Sender computation.** S does the following.
  - **Check Receiver Message.** Abort if any of the following fails.
    * Check that $T = H_{FS}(c_1 \| \ldots \| c_n)$.
    * Check that $\mathsf{Rec}(\{c_i\}_{i \in T}, \{(r_{i,0}, r_{i,1}, \theta_i), u_i\}_{i \in T}) \neq \bot$.
    * For every $i \in T$, measure the registers $\mathcal{S}_{i,0}, \mathcal{S}_{i,1}$ in basis θ_i to obtain $r'_{i,0}, r'_{i,1}$, and check that $r_{i,0} = r'_{i,0}$ and $r_{i,1} = r'_{i,1}$.
  - **Output.** For all $i \in \overline{T}$, measure the register $\mathcal{S}_{i,0}$ in basis $+$ and the register $\mathcal{S}_{i,1}$ in basis $\times$ to obtain $r'_{i,0}, r'_{i,1}$. Output
    $$m_0 := x_0 \oplus E\left(\{r'_{i,d_i}\}_{i \in \overline{T}}\right), \quad m_1 := x_1 \oplus E\left(\{r'_{i,d_i \oplus 1}\}_{i \in \overline{T}}\right).$$

Fig. 5. Non-interactive random-sender-input OT in the shared EPR pair model.

Then, applying non-interactive bit OT reversal [36] to the protocol that realizes $\mathcal{F}_{\mathsf{S-ROT}[1]}$ immediately gives the following corollary.

Corollary 1. *Given a setup of 300λ shared EPR pairs, there exists a one-message protocol in the QROM that $O\left(\frac{q^{3/2}}{2^\lambda}\right)$-securely realizes $\mathcal{F}_{\mathsf{R-ROT}[1]}$.*

Proof (of Theorem 4**)** Let H_C be the random oracle used by the commitment scheme. We treat H_C and H_{FS} (and H_{Ext} in the case of the random oracle randomness extractor) as separate oracles that the honest parties and adversaries query, which is without loss of generality. We prove security below.

Sender security. First, we show security against a malicious receiver R^*. We will use *on-the-fly* simulation, introduced in [63] as a method of guaranteeing *efficient* simulation of the oracle independent of the number of queries. We will also use the extractor $\mathsf{SimExt} = (\mathsf{SimExt.RO}, \mathsf{SimExt.Sim})$ guaranteed by the commitment scheme. We describe the simulator for our OT protocol against a malicious receiver below.

$\mathsf{Sim}[R^*]$:

- Prepare $2n$ EPR pairs on registers $\mathcal{R}$ and $\mathcal{S}$.
- Initialize R^* with the state on register $\mathcal{R}$. Answer any H_{FS} (and H_{Ext}) queries using an efficient on-the-fly random oracle simulator. Answer H_C queries using $\mathsf{SimExt.RO}$.
- Obtain $(x_0, x_1), \{c_i\}_{i\in[n]}, T, \{(r_{i,0}, r_{i,1}, \theta_i), u_i\}_{i\in T}, \{d_i\}_{i\in\overline{T}}$ from R^* and run

$$\{(r_{i,0}^*, r_{i,1}^*, \theta_i^*)\}_{i\in[n]} \leftarrow \mathsf{SimExt.Ext}(\{c_i\}_{i\in[n]}).$$

- Run the "check receiver message" bullet of the honest sender strategy, except that $\{r_{i,0}^*, r_{i,1}^*\}_{i\in T}$ are used in place of $\{r_{i,0}, r_{i,1}\}_{i\in T}$ for the third check. If any check fails, send **abort** to the ideal functionality, output R^*'s state, and continue to answering the distinguisher's oracle queries.
- Let $b := \mathrm{maj}\{\theta_i^* \oplus d_i\}_{i\in\overline{T}}$. For all $i \in \overline{T}$, measure the register $\mathcal{S}_{i,b\oplus d_i}$ in basis $+$ if $b \oplus d_i = 0$ or basis $\times$ if $b \oplus d_i = 1$ to obtain r_i'. Let $m_b := x_b \oplus E(\{r_i'\}_{i\in\overline{T}})$.
- Send (b, m_b) to the ideal functionality, output R^*'s state, and continue to answering the distinguisher's queries.
- Answer the distinguisher's H_{FS} (and H_{Ext}) queries with the efficient on-the-fly random oracle simulator and H_C queries with $\mathsf{SimExt.RO}$.

Now, given a distinguisher D such that R^* and D make at most q queries combined to H_{FS} and H_C (and H_{Ext}), we consider the following hybrids. The distributions $\Pi[R^*, D, \top]$ and $\widetilde{\Pi}_{\mathcal{F}_{\mathsf{S-ROT}}}[\mathsf{Sim}[R^*], D, \top]$ are formally defined in the full version [1] to be the real and simulated executions of the protocol, respectively.

- Hyb_0: The result of the real interaction between R^* and S. This is a distribution over $\{0,1\}$ described by $\Pi[R^*, D, \top]$.
- Hyb_1: This is identical to Hyb_0, except that all H_C queries of R^* and D are answered via the $\mathsf{SimExt.RO}$ interface, and $\{(r_{i,0}^*, r_{i,1}^*, \theta_i^*)\} \leftarrow \mathsf{Sim.Ext}(\{c_i\}_{i\in[n]})$ is run after R^* outputs its message. The values $\{r_{i,0}^*, r_{i,1}^*\}_{i\in T}$ are used in place of $\{r_{i,0}, r_{i,1}\}_{i\in T}$ for the third sender check.
- Hyb_2: The result of $\mathsf{Sim}[R^*]$ interacting in $\widetilde{\Pi}_{\mathcal{F}_{\mathsf{S-ROT}[1]}}$ (or $\widetilde{\Pi}_{\mathcal{F}_{\mathsf{S-ROT}[\lambda]}}$). This is a distribution over $\{0,1\}$ described by $\widetilde{\Pi}_{\mathcal{F}_{\mathsf{S-ROT}[1]}}[\mathsf{Sim}[R^*], D, \top]$ (or $\widetilde{\Pi}_{\mathcal{F}_{\mathsf{S-ROT}[\lambda]}}[\mathsf{Sim}[R^*], D, \top]$).

The proof of security against a malicious R^* follows by combining the two claims below, Claim 5 and Claim 6.

Claim 5.

$$|\Pr[\mathsf{Hyb}_0 = 1] - \Pr[\mathsf{Hyb}_1 = 1]| \leq \frac{24(A+B)\lambda q}{2^{2\lambda}} + \frac{148(q + 3(A+B)\lambda + 1)^3 + 1}{2^{4\lambda}}.$$

Proof. This follows by a direct reduction to extractability of the commitment scheme, since the only difference is whether or not we simulate the adversary's access to H_C and use the extracted values $\{r^*_{i,0}, r^*_{i,1}\}_{i \in T}$ in place of the opened values $\{r_{i,0}, r_{i,1}\}_{i \in T}$.   □

Claim 6. *For any $q \geq 4$, when E is the XOR extractor and $A = 50, B = 100$, or when E is the ROM extractor and $A = 1050, B = 2160$,*

$$|\Pr[\mathsf{Hyb}_1 = 1] - \Pr[\mathsf{Hyb}_2 = 1]| \leq \frac{8q^{3/2}}{2^{\lambda}}.$$

Proof. First, note that the only difference between these hybrids is that in Hyb_2, the m_{1-b} received by D as part of the sender's output is sampled uniformly at random (by the ideal functionality), where b is defined as $\mathsf{maj}\{\theta^*_i \oplus d_i\}_{i \in \overline{T}}$. Now, we introduce some notation.

- Let $\mathbf{c} := (c_1, \ldots, c_n)$ be the classical commitments.
- Write the classical extracted values $\{(r^*_{i,0}, r^*_{i,1}, \theta^*_i)\}_{i \in [n]}$ as matrices

$$\mathbf{R}^* := \begin{bmatrix} r^*_{1,0} & \cdots & r^*_{n,0} \\ r^*_{1,1} & \cdots & r^*_{n,1} \end{bmatrix}, \boldsymbol{\theta}^* := \begin{bmatrix} \theta^*_1 & \cdots & \theta^*_n \end{bmatrix}.$$

- Given any $\mathbf{R}, \boldsymbol{\theta} \in \{0,1\}^{2 \times n}$, define $|\mathbf{R}_{\boldsymbol{\theta}}\rangle$ as a state on n two-qubit registers, where register i contains the vector $|\mathbf{R}_{i,0}, \mathbf{R}_{i,1}\rangle$ prepared in the $(\boldsymbol{\theta}_i, \boldsymbol{\theta}_i)$-basis.
- Given $\mathbf{R}, \mathbf{R}^* \in \{0,1\}^{2 \times n}$ and a subset $T \subset [n]$, define $\mathbf{R}_T$ to be the columns of $\mathbf{R}$ indexed by T, and define $\Delta(\mathbf{R}_T, \mathbf{R}^*_T)$ as the fraction of columns $i \in T$ such that $(\mathbf{R}_{i,0}, \mathbf{R}_{i,1}) \neq (\mathbf{R}^*_{i,0}, \mathbf{R}^*_{i,1})$. For $T \subset [n]$, let $\overline{T} := [n] \setminus T$.
- Given $\mathbf{R}^*, \boldsymbol{\theta}^* \in \{0,1\}^{2 \times n}$, $T \subseteq [n]$, and $\delta \in (0,1)$, define

$$\Pi^{\mathbf{R}^*, \boldsymbol{\theta}^*, T, \delta} := \sum_{\mathbf{R}: \mathbf{R}_T = \mathbf{R}^*_T, \Delta(\mathbf{R}_{\overline{T}}, \mathbf{R}^*_{\overline{T}}) \geq \delta} |\mathbf{R}_{\boldsymbol{\theta}^*}\rangle\langle\mathbf{R}_{\boldsymbol{\theta}^*}|.$$

Intuitively, this is a projection onto "bad" states as defined by $\mathbf{R}^*, \boldsymbol{\theta}^*, T, \delta$, i.e., states that agree with $\mathbf{R}^*$ on all registers T but are at least δ-"far" from $\mathbf{R}^*$ on registers $\overline{T}$.

Define the following projection, which has hard-coded the description of H_{FS}:

$$\Pi^{\delta}_{\mathsf{bad}} := \sum_{\mathbf{c}, \mathbf{R}^*, \boldsymbol{\theta}^*} |\mathbf{c}\rangle\langle\mathbf{c}|_{\mathcal{C}} \otimes |\mathbf{R}^*, \boldsymbol{\theta}^*\rangle\langle\mathbf{R}^*, \boldsymbol{\theta}^*|_{\mathcal{Z}} \otimes \Pi^{\mathbf{R}^*, \boldsymbol{\theta}^*, H_{FS}(\mathbf{c}), \delta}_{\mathcal{S}},$$

where $\mathcal{C}$ is the register holding the classical commitments, $\mathcal{Z}$ is the register holding the output of SimExt.Ext, and $\mathcal{S}$ is the register holding the sender's halves of EPR pairs. Intuitively, this is a projection onto "bad" states defined by the values $\mathbf{R}^*, \boldsymbol{\theta}^*$, and where the check set T is computed by $H_{FS}(\mathbf{c})$.

We will now prove the following sub-claim, which essentially states that the global state of the system after the malicious receiver outputs their message only has negligible overlap with the "bad" subspace defined above.

SubClaim 7. *Let $\tau := \sum_{H,\mathbf{c},\mathbf{R}^*,\boldsymbol{\theta}^*} p^{(H,\mathbf{c},\mathbf{R}^*,\boldsymbol{\theta}^*)} \tau^{(H,\mathbf{c},\mathbf{R}^*,\boldsymbol{\theta}^*)}$, where*

$$\tau^{(H,\mathbf{c},\mathbf{R}^*,\boldsymbol{\theta}^*)} = |\mathbf{c}\rangle\langle\mathbf{c}|_{\mathcal{C}} \otimes |\mathbf{R}^*,\boldsymbol{\theta}^*\rangle\langle\mathbf{R}^*,\boldsymbol{\theta}^*|_{\mathcal{Z}} \otimes \rho_{\mathcal{S},\mathcal{X}}^{(H,\mathbf{c},\mathbf{R}^*,\boldsymbol{\theta}^*)}$$

be the entire state of the system, including the sender's halves of EPR pairs and the receiver's entire state in Hyb_1 (equivalently also Hyb_2) at the point in the experiment right after R^* outputs its message and SimExt.Ext is run. Here, each $p^{(H,\mathbf{c},\mathbf{R}^*,\boldsymbol{\theta}^*)}$ is the probability that the random oracle H_{FS} is initialized to the function H and the registers $\mathcal{C}, \mathcal{Z}$ hold the classical strings $\mathbf{c}, \mathbf{R}^*, \boldsymbol{\theta}^*$. We also define $\mathcal{S}$ to be the register holding the sender's halves of EPR pairs, and $\mathcal{X}$ to be the register holding the remaining state of the system, which includes the rest of the receiver's classical message and its private state. Then,

- *If $A = 50, B = 100$, then $\mathrm{Tr}(\Pi_{\mathsf{bad}}^{0.25}\tau) \leq \frac{64q^3}{2^{2\lambda}}$.*
- *If $A = 1050, B = 2160$, then $\mathrm{Tr}(\Pi_{\mathsf{bad}}^{0.054}\tau) \leq \frac{64q^3}{2^{2\lambda}}$.*

Proof. Define $\mathsf{Adv}_{\mathsf{R}^*}^{H_{FS}}$ to be the oracle machine that runs Hyb_1 until R^* outputs $\mathbf{c}$ (and the rest of its message), then runs SimExt.Ext to obtain $|\mathbf{R}^*,\boldsymbol{\theta}^*\rangle\langle\mathbf{R}^*,\boldsymbol{\theta}^*|$, and then outputs the remaining state $\rho_{\mathcal{S},\mathcal{X}}$. Consider running the measure-and-reprogram simulator $\mathsf{Sim}[\mathsf{Adv}_{\mathsf{R}^*}]$ [23,24] (described formally in the full version [1]) which simulates H_{FS} queries, measures and outputs $\mathbf{c}$, then receives a uniformly random subset $T \subset [n]$ of size k, and then continues to run $\mathsf{Adv}_{\mathsf{R}^*}$ until it outputs $|\mathbf{R}^*,\boldsymbol{\theta}^*\rangle\langle\mathbf{R}^*,\boldsymbol{\theta}^*|\otimes\rho_{\mathcal{S},\mathcal{X}}$. Letting

$$\Pi_{\mathsf{bad}}^{\delta}[T] := \sum_{\mathbf{c},\mathbf{R}^*,\boldsymbol{\theta}^*} |\mathbf{c}\rangle\langle\mathbf{c}|_{\mathcal{C}} \otimes |\mathbf{R}^*,\boldsymbol{\theta}^*\rangle\langle\mathbf{R}^*,\boldsymbol{\theta}^*|_{\mathcal{Z}} \otimes \Pi_{\mathcal{S}}^{\mathbf{R}^*,\boldsymbol{\theta}^*,T,\delta},$$

for $T \subset [n]$, the measure-and-reprogram theorem [23,24] (also full version [1]) gives

$$\mathrm{Tr}\left(\Pi_{\mathsf{bad}}^{\delta}\tau\right)$$

$$\leq (2q+1)^2 \, \mathbb{E}\left[\mathrm{Tr}\left(\Pi_{\mathsf{bad}}^{\delta}[T]\sigma\right) : \begin{array}{r} (\mathbf{c},\mathsf{st}) \leftarrow \mathsf{Sim}[\mathsf{Adv}_{\mathsf{R}^*}] \\ T \leftarrow S_{n,k} \\ (\mathbf{R}^*,\boldsymbol{\theta}^*,\rho_{\mathcal{S},\mathcal{X}}) \leftarrow \mathsf{Sim}[\mathsf{Adv}_{\mathsf{R}^*}](T,\mathsf{st}) \end{array}\right],$$

where

$$\sigma = |\mathbf{c}\rangle\langle\mathbf{c}|_{\mathcal{C}} \otimes |\mathbf{R}^*,\boldsymbol{\theta}^*\rangle\langle\mathbf{R}^*,\boldsymbol{\theta}^*|_{\mathcal{Z}} \otimes \rho_{\mathcal{S},\mathcal{X}},$$

and $S_{n,k}$ is the set of all subsets of $[n]$ of size k. Crucially, because $\mathsf{Sim}[\mathsf{Adv_{R^*}}]$ is defined to just run $\mathsf{Adv_{R^*}}$ and answer their oracle queries to H_{FS}, it does not touch the sender's registers $\mathcal{S}$ after initializing them with halves of EPR pairs.

Now, recall that the last thing that $\mathsf{Adv_{R^*}}$ does in Hyb_1 is run $\mathsf{SimExt.Ext}$ on $\mathbf{c}$ to obtain $(\mathbf{R}^*, \boldsymbol{\theta}^*)$. Consider instead running $\mathsf{SimExt.Ext}$ on $\mathbf{c}$ immediately after $\mathsf{Sim}[\mathsf{Adv_{R^*}}]$ outputs $\mathbf{c}$. In the full version [1], we show that , has a $\frac{8}{2^{\lambda,/2}}$-commuting simulator, which means that each time we commute the $\mathsf{SimExt.Ext}$ query past a $\mathsf{SimExt.RO}$ query, the overall state of the system changes by at most $\frac{8}{2^{\lambda,/2}}$ in trace distance. Thus, plugging in $\lambda_, = 4\lambda$,

$$\mathrm{Tr}\left(\Pi^\delta_{\mathsf{bad}}\tau\right)$$

$$\leq (2q+1)^2\left(\mathbb{E}\left[\mathrm{Tr}\left(\Pi^\delta_{\mathsf{bad}}[T]\sigma\right) : \begin{array}{c}(\mathbf{c},\mathsf{st}) \leftarrow \mathsf{Sim}[\mathsf{Adv_{R^*}}] \\ (\mathbf{R}^*,\boldsymbol{\theta}^*) \leftarrow \mathsf{SimExt.Ext}(\mathbf{c}) \\ T \leftarrow S_{n,k} \\ \rho_{\mathcal{S},\mathcal{X}} \leftarrow \mathsf{Sim}[\mathsf{Adv_{R^*}}](T,\mathsf{st})\end{array}\right] + \frac{8q}{2^{2\lambda}}\right)$$

$$:= (2q+1)^2\epsilon + \frac{8q(2q+1)^2}{2^{2\lambda}},$$

where

$$\sigma = |\mathbf{c}\rangle\langle\mathbf{c}|_{\mathcal{B}}\otimes|\mathbf{R}^*,\boldsymbol{\theta}^*\rangle\langle\mathbf{R}^*,\boldsymbol{\theta}^*|_{\mathcal{Z}}\otimes\rho_{\mathcal{S},\mathcal{X}},$$

and where we denote the expectation inside the parantheses by ϵ.

Now, since the $\mathcal{S}$ register is not touched by $\mathsf{Sim}[\mathsf{Adv_{R^*}}]$ at any point after $(\mathbf{R}^*, \boldsymbol{\theta}^*)$ are output, we can imagine measuring the $\mathcal{S}$ registers in the $\boldsymbol{\theta}^*$-basis even before T is sampled. Thus, ϵ is at most the probabilty that the following procedure outputs 1, where $\mathbf{R}^*$ represents the matrix output by SimExt, and $\mathbf{R}$ represents the matrix obtained by measuring register $\mathcal{S}$ in the $\boldsymbol{\theta}^*$-basis.

- Let $\mathbf{R}, \mathbf{R}^* \in \{0,1\}^{2\times n}$ be two matrices.
- Sample a uniformly random subset $T \subset [n]$ of size k.
- Output 1 if and only if $(\mathbf{R}_{i,0}, \mathbf{R}_{i,1}) = (\mathbf{R}^*_{i,0}, \mathbf{R}^*_{i,1})$ for all $i \in T$, and $(\mathbf{R}_{i,0}, \mathbf{R}_{i,1}) \neq (\mathbf{R}^*_{i,0}, \mathbf{R}^*_{i,1})$ for at least δ fraction of $i \in \overline{T}$.

In the full version [1], we bound this probability by $2\exp(-2(1 - k/n)^2\delta^2 k)$, using standard Hoeffding inequalities.

- For $\delta = 0.25$, this probability is bounded by

$$2\exp(-2(0.25)^2(1 - A/(A+B))^2A) < 2^{-2\lambda},$$

for $A = 50, B = 100$.
- For $\delta = 0.054$, this probability is bounded by

$$2\exp(-2(0.054)^2(1 - A/(A+B))^2A) < 2^{-2\lambda},$$

for $A = 1050, B = 2160$.

Summarizing, we have that in either case,

$$\mathrm{Tr}\left(\Pi_{\mathsf{bad}}^{\delta}\tau\right) \leq \frac{(2q+1)^2 + 8q(2q+1)^2}{2^{2\lambda}} \leq \frac{64q^3}{2^{2\lambda}},$$

for $q \geq 4$.

□

By the calculations above, and by Gentle Measurement (full version [1]), the τ defined in SubClaim 7 is within $\frac{8q^{3/2}}{2^{\lambda}}$ trace distance of a state τ_{good} in the image of $\mathbb{I} - \Pi_{\mathsf{bad}}^{0.25}$ if $A = 50, B = 100$ and in the image of $\mathbb{I} - \Pi_{\mathsf{bad}}^{0.054}$ if $A = 1050, B = 2160$.

For readability, we note that

$$\mathbb{I} - \Pi_{\mathsf{bad}}^{\delta} = \sum_{\mathbf{c},\mathbf{R}^*,\boldsymbol{\theta}^*} |\mathbf{c}\rangle\langle\mathbf{c}|_{\mathcal{C}} \otimes |\mathbf{R}^*,\boldsymbol{\theta}^*\rangle\langle\mathbf{R}^*,\boldsymbol{\theta}^*|_{\mathcal{Z}} \otimes \left(\mathbb{I} - \Pi^{\mathbf{R}^*,\boldsymbol{\theta}^*,H_{FS}(\mathbf{c}),\delta}\right)_{\mathcal{S}},$$

where for any T,

$$\mathbb{I} - \Pi^{\mathbf{R}^*,\boldsymbol{\theta}^*,T,\delta} = \sum_{\mathbf{R}:(\mathbf{R}_T \neq \mathbf{R}_T^*) \vee (\Delta(\mathbf{R}_{\overline{T}},\mathbf{R}_{\overline{T}}^*) < \delta)} |\mathbf{R}_{\boldsymbol{\theta}^*}\rangle\langle\mathbf{R}_{\boldsymbol{\theta}^*}|.$$

Finally, we show the following two sub-claims to complete the proof of Claim 6.

SubClaim 8. *If E is the XOR extractor, then conditioned on τ being in the image of $\mathbb{I} - \Pi_{\mathsf{bad}}^{0.25}$, it holds that*

$$\Pr[\mathsf{Hyb}_1 = 1] = \Pr[\mathsf{Hyb}_2 = 1].$$

Proof. It suffices to analyze the state τ conditioned on the register that contains T being equal to $H_{FS}(\mathbf{c})$ (otherwise the honest sender/simulator will abort).

If τ is in $\mathbb{I} - \Pi_{\mathsf{bad}}^{0.25}$, it must be the case that the register $\mathcal{S}$ is in the image of $\mathbb{I} - \Pi^{\mathbf{R}^*,\boldsymbol{\theta}^*,T,0.25}$, where $\mathbf{R}^*, \boldsymbol{\theta}^*$ were output by SimExt.Ext. Recall that the sender aborts if the positions measured in T are not equal to $\mathbf{R}_T^*$. Thus, we can condition on the sender not aborting, which, by the definition of $\mathbb{I} - \Pi^{\mathbf{R}^*,\boldsymbol{\theta}^*,T,0.25}$ implies that register $\mathcal{S}_{\overline{T}}$ is supported on vectors $|(\mathbf{R}_{\overline{T}})_{\boldsymbol{\theta}^*}\rangle$ such that $\Delta(\mathbf{R}_{\overline{T}}, \mathbf{R}_{\overline{T}}^*) < 0.25$.

To obtain m_{1-b}, the sender measures register $\mathcal{S}_{i,d_i \oplus b \oplus 1}$ in basis $d_i \oplus b \oplus 1$ for each $i \in \overline{T}$ to obtain a string $r' \in \{0,1\}^{n-k}$. Then, m_{1-b} is set to $E(r')$. Since b is defined as $\mathsf{maj}\{\boldsymbol{\theta}_i^* \oplus d_i\}_{i \in \overline{T}}$ in Hyb_2, at least $(n-k)/2$ of the bits r_i' are obtained by measuring in $1 \oplus \boldsymbol{\theta}_i^*$. Let $M \subset \overline{T}$ be this set of size at least $(n-k)/2$, and define $\mathbf{r}^* \in \{0,1\}^n$ such that $\mathbf{r}_i^* = \mathbf{R}_{i,d_i \oplus b \oplus 1}^*$. We know from above that the register $\mathcal{S}_M$ is supported on vectors $|(\mathbf{r}_M)_{\boldsymbol{\theta}^*}\rangle$ for $\mathbf{r}_M$ such that $\Delta(\mathbf{r}_M, \mathbf{r}_M^*) < 0.5$. Thus, recalling that each of these states is measured in the basis $1 \oplus \boldsymbol{\theta}_i^*$, we can appeal to Theorem 1 (with an appropriate change of basis) to show that m_{1-b} is perfectly uniformly random from R*'s perspective, completing the proof. □

SubClaim 9. *If E is the ROM extractor and $B \geq 326, q \geq 4$, then conditioned on τ being in the image of $\mathbb{I} - \Pi_{\text{bad}}^{0.054}$, it holds that*

$$| \Pr[\text{Hyb}_1 = 1] = \Pr[\text{Hyb}_2 = 1]| \leq \frac{4q}{2^\lambda}.$$

Proof. This follows the same argument as the above sub-claim, until we see that there are $(n-k)/2$ qubits of $\mathcal{S}$ that are measured in basis $1 \oplus \boldsymbol{\theta}_M^*$, and that the state on these qubits is supported on vectors $|(\mathbf{r}_M)_{\boldsymbol{\theta}^*}\rangle$ for $\mathbf{r}_M$ such that $\Delta(\mathbf{r}_M, \mathbf{r}_M^*) < 0.108$. We can then apply Theorem 3 with random oracle input size $n-k$, register $\mathcal{X}$ size $(n-k)/2$, and $|L| \leq 2^{h_b(0.108)(n-k)/2}$. Note that, when applying this theorem, we are fixing any outcome of the $(n-k)/2$ bits of the random oracle input that are measured in $\boldsymbol{\theta}^*$, and setting register $\mathcal{X}$ to contain the $(n-k)/2$ registers that are measured in basis $1 \oplus \boldsymbol{\theta}^*$. This gives a bound of $\frac{4q2^{h_b(0.108)(n-k)/2}}{2^{(n-k)/4}} = \frac{4q}{2^{(n-k)(\frac{1}{4} - \frac{1}{2}h_b(0.108))}} = \frac{4q}{2^{B\lambda(\frac{1}{4} - \frac{1}{2}h_b(0.108))}} \leq \frac{4q}{2^\lambda}$ for $B \geq 326$.   □

This completes the proof of Claim 6.   □

Receiver Security. Next, we show security against a malicious sender S^*. During the proof, we will use an efficient quantum random oracle "wrapper" algorithm $W[(x, z)]$ that provides an interface between any quantum random oracle simulator, such as the on-the-fly simulator, and the machine querying the random oracle. The wrapper will implement a controlled query to the actual random oracle simulator, controlled on the input $\mathcal{X}$ register not being equal to x. Then, it will implement a controlled query to a unitary that maps $|x, y\rangle \rightarrow |x, y \oplus z\rangle$, controlled on the input $\mathcal{X}$ register being equal to x. The effect of this wrapper is that the oracle presented to the machine is the oracle H simulated by the simulator, but with $H(x)$ reprogrammed to z.

$\mathsf{Sim}[\mathsf{S}^*]$:

- Query the ideal functionality with $\perp$ and obtain m_0, m_1.
- Sample T as a uniformly random subset of $[n]$ of size k, sample $d_i \leftarrow \{0, 1\}$ for each $i \in \overline{T}$, and sample $\theta_i \leftarrow \{+, \times\}$ for each $i \in T$.
- For each $i \in [n]$, sample $r_{i,0}, r_{i,1} \leftarrow \{0, 1\}$ and prepare BB84 states $|\psi_{i,0}\rangle, |\psi_{i,1}\rangle$ as follows.
  - If $i \in T$, set $|\psi_{i,0}\rangle = |r_{i,0}\rangle_{\theta_i}, |\psi_{i,1}\rangle = |r_{i,1}\rangle_{\theta_i}$.
  - If $i \in \overline{T}$, set $|\psi_{i,0}\rangle = |r_{i,0}\rangle_+, |\psi_{i,1}\rangle = |r_{i,1}\rangle_\times$.
- For each $i \in T$, let $e_i := (r_{i,0}, r_{i,1}, \theta_i)$ and for each $i \in \overline{T}$, let $e_i := (0, 0, 0)$. Compute $(\mathsf{st}, \{c_i\}_{i \in [n]}) \leftarrow \mathsf{Com}(\{e_i\}_{i \in [n]})$ and $\{u_i\}_{i \in T} \leftarrow \mathsf{Open}(\mathsf{st}, T)$.
- Set $x_0 := E(\{r_{i,d_i}\}_{i \in \overline{T}}) \oplus m_0$ and $x_1 := E(\{r_{i,d_i \oplus 1}\}_{i \in \overline{T}}) \oplus m_1$ (where if E is the ROM extractor, this is accomplished via classical queries to an on-the-fly random oracle simulator for H_{Ext}).
- Run S^* on input $(x_0, x_1), \{c_i\}_{i \in [n]}, T, \{r_{i,0}, r_{i,1}, \theta_i, u_i\}_{i \in T}, \{d_i\}_{i \in \overline{T}}, \{|\psi_{i,b}\rangle\}_{i \in [n], b \in \{0,1\}}$. Answer H_C queries using the on-the-fly random oracle simulator, answer H_{FS} queries using the on-the-fly random oracle simulator wrapped with $W[\{c_i\}_{i \in [n]}, T]$, and if E is the ROM extractor, answer H_{Ext}

queries using the on-the-fly random oracle simulator. Output S^*'s final state and continue to answering the distinguisher's random oracle queries.

Now, given a receiver input $b \in \{0,1\}$, and distinguisher D such that S^* and D make a total of at most q queries combined to H_{FS} and H_C (and H_{Ext}), consider the following sequence of hybrids.

- Hyb_0: The result of the real interaction between $R(b)$ and S^*. This is a distribution over $\{0,1\}$ desrcibed by $\Pi[S^*, D, b]$.
- Hyb_1: This is the same as the previous hybrid except that T is sampled uniformly at random as in the simulator, and H_{FS} queries are answered with the wrapper $W[(\{c_i\}_{i\in[n]}, T)]$.
- Hyb_2: This is the same as the previous hybrid except that the messages $\{(r_{i,0}, r_{i,1}, \theta_i)\}_{i\in\overline{T}}$ are replaced with $(0,0,0)$ inside the commitent.
- Hyb_3: The result of $\mathsf{Sim}[S^*]$ interacting in $\widetilde{\Pi}_{\mathcal{F}_{S-\mathsf{ROT}[1]}}$ (or $\widetilde{\Pi}_{\mathcal{F}_{S-\mathsf{ROT}[\lambda]}}$). This is a distribution over $\{0,1\}$ described by $\widetilde{\Pi}_{\mathcal{F}_{S-\mathsf{ROT}[1]}}[\mathsf{Sim}[S^*], D, b]$ (or $\widetilde{\Pi}_{\mathcal{F}_{S-\mathsf{ROT}[\lambda]}}[\mathsf{Sim}[S^*], D, b]$).

Security against a malicious S^* follows by observing that Hyb_0 and Hyb_1 are identically distributed, since H_{FS} is a random oracle and T is uniformly random in Hyb_1, and the following claims.

Claim 10. $|\Pr[\mathsf{Hyb}_1 = 1] - \Pr[\mathsf{Hyb}_2 = 1]| \leq \frac{4q\sqrt{3(A+B)\lambda}}{2^{2\lambda}}$.

This follows from hiding of the commitments (appropriately parameterized).

Claim 11. $\Pr[\mathsf{Hyb}_2 = 1] = \Pr[\mathsf{Hyb}_3 = 1]$.

Proof. First, note that one difference in how the hybrids are specified is that in Hyb_2, the receiver samples x_{1-b} uniformly at random, while in Hyb_3, x_{1-b} is set to $E(\{r_{i,d_i\oplus b\oplus1}\}_{i\in\overline{T}}) \oplus m_{1-b}$. However, since m_{1-b} is sampled uniformly at random by the functionality, this is an equivalent distribution.

Thus, the only difference between these these hybrids is the basis in which the states on registers $\{S_{i,d_i\oplus b\oplus1}\}_{i\in\overline{T}}$ are prepared (which are the registers $\{S_{i,\theta_i\oplus1}\}_{i\in\overline{T}}$ in Hyb_2). Indeed, note that in Hyb_2, the state on register $S_{i,d_i\oplus b_i\oplus1}$ is prepared by having the receiver measure their corresponding half of an EPR pair (register $\mathcal{R}_{i,d_i\oplus b_i\oplus1}$) in basis $\theta_i = d_i\oplus b$, while in Hyb_3, this state is prepared by sampling a uniformly random bit and encoding it in the basis $d_i \oplus b_i \oplus 1$. However, these sampling procedures both produce a maximally mixed state on register $S_{i,d_i\oplus b\oplus1}$, and thus these hybrids are equivalent. □

This completes the proof. In the full version [1], we also analyze a two-round variant without setup where the receiver sets up entanglement. In addition, we formally describe our 3 round chosen-input OT without entanglement or setup, as well as optimizations of the CK template to minimize round complexity.

Acknowledgments. A. Agarwal, D. Khurana and N. Kumar were supported in part by by NSF CNS-2238718, DARPA SIEVE and a gift from Visa Research. This material is based upon work supported by the Defense Advanced Research Projects Agency through Award HR00112020024.

References

1. Agarwal, A., Bartusek, J., Khurana, D., Kumar, N.: A new framework for quantum oblivious transfer. Cryptology ePrint Archive, Paper 2022/1191 (2022). https://eprint.iacr.org/2022/1191
2. Aiello, B., Ishai, Y., Reingold, O.: Priced oblivious transfer: how to sell digital goods. In: Pfitzmann, B. (ed.) EUROCRYPT 2001. LNCS, vol. 2045, pp. 119–135. Springer, Heidelberg (2001). https://doi.org/10.1007/3-540-44987-6_8
3. Ambainis, A., Hamburg, M., Unruh, D.: Quantum security proofs using semi-classical oracles. In: Boldyreva, A., Micciancio, D. (eds.) CRYPTO 2019. LNCS, vol. 11693, pp. 269–295. Springer, Cham (2019). https://doi.org/10.1007/978-3-030-26951-7_10
4. Ananth, P., Qian, L., Yuen, H.: Cryptography from pseudorandom quantum states. In: Dodis, Y., Shrimpton, T. (eds.) CRYPTO 2022. LNCS, vol. 13507, pp. 208–236. Springer (2022). https://doi.org/10.1007/978-3-031-15802-5_8
5. Badrinarayanan, S., Garg, S., Ishai, Y., Sahai, A., Wadia, A.: Two-message witness indistinguishability and secure computation in the plain model from new assumptions. In: Takagi, T., Peyrin, T. (eds.) ASIACRYPT 2017. LNCS, vol. 10626, pp. 275–303. Springer, Cham (2017). https://doi.org/10.1007/978-3-319-70700-6_10
6. Badrinarayanan, S., Goyal, V., Jain, A., Kalai, Y.T., Khurana, D., Sahai, A.: Promise zero knowledge and its applications to round optimal MPC. In: Shacham, H., Boldyreva, A. (eds.) CRYPTO 2018. LNCS, vol. 10992, pp. 459–487. Springer, Cham (2018). https://doi.org/10.1007/978-3-319-96881-0_16
7. Badrinarayanan, S., Goyal, V., Jain, A., Khurana, D., Sahai, A.: Round optimal concurrent mpc via strong simulation. In: Kalai, Y., Reyzin, L. (eds.) TCC 2017. LNCS, vol. 10677, pp. 743–775. Springer, Cham (2017). https://doi.org/10.1007/978-3-319-70500-2_25
8. Bartusek, J., Coladangelo, A., Khurana, D., Ma, F.: One-way functions imply secure computation in a quantum world. In: Malkin, T., Peikert, C. (eds.) CRYPTO 2021. LNCS, vol. 12825, pp. 467–496. Springer, Cham (2021). https://doi.org/10.1007/978-3-030-84242-0_17
9. Bartusek, J., Khurana, D.: Cryptography with certified deletion. Cryptology ePrint Archive, Paper 2022/1178 (2022). https://eprint.iacr.org/2022/1178
10. Bennett, C.H., Brassard, G., Crépeau, C., Jozsa, R., Peres, A., Wootters, W.K.: Teleporting an unknown quantum state via dual classical and einstein-podolsky-rosen channels. Phys. Rev. Lett. **70**, 1895–1899 (1993). https://doi.org/10.1103/PhysRevLett.70.1895
11. Bennett, C.H., Brassard, G., Crépeau, C., Skubiszewska, M.-H.: Practical quantum oblivious transfer. In: Feigenbaum, J. (ed.) CRYPTO 1991. LNCS, vol. 576, pp. 351–366. Springer, Heidelberg (1992). https://doi.org/10.1007/3-540-46766-1_29
12. Bitansky, N., Vaikuntanathan, V.: A note on perfect correctness by derandomization. In: Coron, J.-S., Nielsen, J.B. (eds.) EUROCRYPT 2017. LNCS, vol. 10211, pp. 592–606. Springer, Cham (2017). https://doi.org/10.1007/978-3-319-56614-6_20
13. Bouman, N.J., Fehr, S.: Sampling in a quantum population, and applications. In: Rabin, T. (ed.) CRYPTO 2010. LNCS, vol. 6223, pp. 724–741. Springer, Heidelberg (2010). https://doi.org/10.1007/978-3-642-14623-7_39
14. Brun, T., Devetak, I., Hsieh, M.H.: Correcting quantum errors with entanglement. Science (New York) **314**, 436–439 (2006). https://doi.org/10.1126/science.1131563

15. Canetti, R., et al.: Fiat-Shamir: from practice to theory. In: Charikar, M., Cohen, E. (eds.) 51st Annual ACM Symposium on Theory of Computing, pp. 1082–1090. ACM Press, Phoenix, AZ, USA (23–26 June, 2019). https://doi.org/10.1145/3313276.3316380
16. Canetti, R., Goldreich, O., Halevi, S.: The random oracle methodology, revisited. J. ACM **51**(4), 557–594 (2004). https://doi.org/10.1145/1008731.1008734
17. Chailloux, A., Gutoski, G., Sikora, J.: Optimal bounds for semi-honest quantum oblivious transfer. Chic. J. Theor. Comput. Sci. **2016** (2016). https://doi.org/10.48550/arXiv.1310.3262
18. Chailloux, A., Kerenidis, I., Sikora, J.: Lower bounds for quantum oblivious transfer. Quantum Info. Comput. **13**(1–2), 158–177 (2013). https://doi.org/10.48550/arXiv.1007.1875
19. Coladangelo, A., Vidick, T., Zhang, T.: Non-interactive zero-knowledge arguments for QMA, with preprocessing. In: Micciancio, D., Ristenpart, T. (eds.) CRYPTO 2020. LNCS, vol. 12172, pp. 799–828. Springer, Cham (2020). https://doi.org/10.1007/978-3-030-56877-1_28
20. Crépeau, C., Kilian, J.: Achieving oblivious transfer using weakened security assumptions (extended abstract). In: 29th Annual Symposium on Foundations of Computer Science, pp. 42–52. IEEE Computer Society Press, White Plains, NY (24–26 Oct 1988). https://doi.org/10.1109/SFCS.1988.21920
21. Damgård, I., Fehr, S., Lunemann, C., Salvail, L., Schaffner, C.: Improving the security of quantum protocols via commit-and-open. In: Halevi, S. (ed.) CRYPTO 2009. LNCS, vol. 5677, pp. 408–427. Springer, Heidelberg (2009). https://doi.org/10.1007/978-3-642-03356-8_24
22. Damgård, I., Fehr, S., Salvail, L., Schaffner, C.: Cryptography in the bounded quantum-storage model. SIAM J. Comput. **37**, 1865–1890 (2008). https://doi.org/10.1137/060651343
23. Don, J., Fehr, S., Majenz, C., Schaffner, C.: Security of the fiat-shamir transformation in the quantum random-oracle model. In: Boldyreva, A., Micciancio, D. (eds.) CRYPTO 2019. LNCS, vol. 11693, pp. 356–383. Springer, Cham (2019). https://doi.org/10.1007/978-3-030-26951-7_13
24. Don, J., Fehr, S., Majenz, C., Schaffner, C.: Online-extractability in the quantum random-oracle model. In: Dunkelman, O., Dziembowski, S. (eds.) EUROCRYPT 2022. LNCS, vol. 13277, pp. 677–706. Springer, Cham (2022). https://doi.org/10.1007/978-3-031-07082-2_24
25. Döttling, N., Garg, S., Hajiabadi, M., Masny, D., Wichs, D.: Two-round oblivious transfer from CDH or LPN. In: Canteaut, A., Ishai, Y. (eds.) EUROCRYPT 2020. LNCS, vol. 12106, pp. 768–797. Springer, Cham (2020). https://doi.org/10.1007/978-3-030-45724-2_26
26. Dupuis, F., Lamontagne, P., Salvail, L.: Fiat-shamir for proofs lacks a proof even in the presence of shared entanglement (2022). https://doi.org/10.48550/ARXIV.2204.02265
27. Ekert, A.K.: Quantum cryptography based on bell's theorem. Phys. Rev. Lett. **67**(6), 661–663 (1991). https://doi.org/10.1103/PhysRevLett.67.661
28. Erven, C., Ng, N., Gigov, N., Laflamme, R., Wehner, S., Weihs, G.: An experimental implementation of oblivious transfer in the noisy storage model. Nat. Commun. **5** (2014). https://doi.org/10.1038/ncomms4418
29. Even, S., Goldreich, O., Lempel, A.: A randomized protocol for signing contracts. Commun. ACM **28**(6), 637–647 (1985). https://doi.org/10.1145/3812.3818

30. Furrer, F., Gehring, T., Schaffner, C., Pacher, C., Schnabel, R., Wehner, S.: Continuous-variable protocol for oblivious transfer in the noisy-storage model. Nat. Commun. **9**(1) (2018). https://doi.org/10.1038/s41467-018-03729-4

31. Garg, S., Ishai, Y., Kushilevitz, E., Ostrovsky, R., Sahai, A.: Cryptography with one-way communication. In: Gennaro, R., Robshaw, M. (eds.) CRYPTO 2015. LNCS, vol. 9216, pp. 191–208. Springer, Heidelberg (2015). https://doi.org/10.1007/978-3-662-48000-7_10

32. Goldreich, O., Micali, S., Wigderson, A.: How to play any mental game or A completeness theorem for protocols with honest majority. In: Aho, A. (ed.) 19th Annual ACM Symposium on Theory of Computing, pp. 218–229. ACM Press, New York City (25–27 May 1987). https://doi.org/10.1145/28395.28420

33. Grilo, A.B., Hövelmanns, K., Hülsing, A., Majenz, C.: Tight adaptive reprogramming in the QROM. In: Tibouchi, M., Wang, H. (eds.) ASIACRYPT 2021. LNCS, vol. 13090, pp. 637–667. Springer, Cham (2021). https://doi.org/10.1007/978-3-030-92062-3_22

34. Grilo, A.B., Lin, H., Song, F., Vaikuntanathan, V.: Oblivious transfer is in MiniQCrypt. In: Canteaut, A., Standaert, F.-X. (eds.) EUROCRYPT 2021. LNCS, vol. 12697, pp. 531–561. Springer, Cham (2021). https://doi.org/10.1007/978-3-030-77886-6_18

35. Halevi, S., Kalai, Y.T.: Smooth projective hashing and two-message oblivious transfer. J. Cryptol. **25**(1), 158–193 (2010). https://doi.org/10.1007/s00145-010-9092-8

36. Ishai, Y., Kilian, J., Nissim, K., Petrank, E.: Extending oblivious transfers efficiently. In: Boneh, D. (ed.) CRYPTO 2003. LNCS, vol. 2729, pp. 145–161. Springer, Heidelberg (2003). https://doi.org/10.1007/978-3-540-45146-4_9

37. Ishai, Y., Kushilevitz, E., Ostrovsky, R., Prabhakaran, M., Sahai, A., Wullschleger, J.: Constant-rate oblivious transfer from noisy channels. In: Rogaway, P. (ed.) CRYPTO 2011. LNCS, vol. 6841, pp. 667–684. Springer, Heidelberg (2011). https://doi.org/10.1007/978-3-642-22792-9_38

38. Ito, T., et al.: Physical implementation of oblivious transfer using optical correlated randomness. Sci. Reports **7**(1) (2017). https://doi.org/10.1038/s41598-017-08229-x

39. Jain, A., Kalai, Y.T., Khurana, D., Rothblum, R.: Distinguisher-dependent simulation in two rounds and its applications. In: Katz, J., Shacham, H. (eds.) CRYPTO 2017. LNCS, vol. 10402, pp. 158–189. Springer, Cham (2017). https://doi.org/10.1007/978-3-319-63715-0_6

40. Kalai, Y.T., Khurana, D., Sahai, A.: Statistical witness indistinguishability (and more) in two messages. In: Nielsen, J.B., Rijmen, V. (eds.) EUROCRYPT 2018. LNCS, vol. 10822, pp. 34–65. Springer, Cham (2018). https://doi.org/10.1007/978-3-319-78372-7_2

41. Kalai, Y.T., Rothblum, G.N., Rothblum, R.D.: From obfuscation to the security of fiat-shamir for proofs. In: Katz, J., Shacham, H. (eds.) CRYPTO 2017. LNCS, vol. 10402, pp. 224–251. Springer, Cham (2017). https://doi.org/10.1007/978-3-319-63715-0_8

42. Khurana, D., Sahai, A.: How to achieve non-malleability in one or two rounds. In: Umans, C. (ed.) 58th Annual Symposium on Foundations of Computer Science, pp. 564–575. IEEE Computer Society Press, Berkeley (15–17 Oct 2017). https://doi.org/10.1109/FOCS.2017.58

43. Kilian, J.: Founding cryptography on oblivious transfer. In: 20th Annual ACM Symposium on Theory of Computing, pp. 20–31. ACM Press, Chicago, IL, USA (2–4 May 1988). https://doi.org/10.1145/62212.62215

44. Kobayashi, H.: Non-interactive quantum perfect and statistical zero-knowledge. In: Ibaraki, T., Katoh, N., Ono, H. (eds.) ISAAC 2003. LNCS, vol. 2906, pp. 178–188. Springer, Heidelberg (2003). https://doi.org/10.1007/978-3-540-24587-2_20

45. Kundu, S., Sikora, J., Tan, E.Y.Z.: A device-independent protocol for xor oblivious transfer. Physics (2020). https://doi.org/10.22331/q-2022-05-30-725, arXiv: Quantum

46. Lo, H.K., Chau, H.F.: Is quantum bit commitment really possible? Phys. Rev. Lett. **78**(17), 3410 (1997). https://doi.org/10.1103/PhysRevLett.78.3410

47. Mayers, D.: Unconditionally secure quantum bit commitment is impossible. Phys. Rev. Lett. **78**(17), 3414 (1997). https://doi.org/10.1103/PhysRevLett.78.3414

48. Mayers, D., Salvail, L.: Quantum oblivious transfer is secure against all individual measurements. In: Proceedings Workshop on Physics and Computation. PhysComp 1994, pp. 69–77. IEEE (1994). https://doi.org/10.1109/PHYCMP.1994.363696

49. Morimae, T., Yamakawa, T.: Classically verifiable NIZK for QMA with preprocessing. In: Agrawal, S., Lin, D. (eds.) ASIACRYPT 2022. LNCS, vol. 13794, pp. 599–627. Springer, Cham (2022). https://doi.org/10.1007/978-3-031-22972-5_21

50. Morimae, T., Yamakawa, T.: Quantum commitments and signatures without one-way functions. In: Dodis, Y., Shrimpton, T. (eds.) CRYPTO 2022. LNCS, vol. 13507, pp. 269–295. Springer, Cham (2022). https://doi.org/10.1007/978-3-031-15802-5_10

51. Naor, M., Pinkas, B.: Efficient oblivious transfer protocols. In: Proceedings of the Twelfth Annual ACM-SIAM Symposium on Discrete Algorithms, SODA 2001, p. 448–457. Society for Industrial and Applied Mathematics, USA (2001). https://dl.acm.org/doi/10.5555/365411.365502

52. Ostrovsky, R., Paskin-Cherniavsky, A., Paskin-Cherniavsky, B.: maliciously circuit-private FHE. In: Garay, J.A., Gennaro, R. (eds.) CRYPTO 2014. LNCS, vol. 8616, pp. 536–553. Springer, Heidelberg (2014). https://doi.org/10.1007/978-3-662-44371-2_30

53. Peikert, C., Vaikuntanathan, V., Waters, B.: A framework for efficient and composable oblivious transfer. In: Wagner, D. (ed.) CRYPTO 2008. LNCS, vol. 5157, pp. 554–571. Springer, Heidelberg (2008). https://doi.org/10.1007/978-3-540-85174-5_31

54. Rabin, M.O.: How to exchange secrets with oblivious transfer. IACR Cryptol. ePrint Arch. **2005**, 187 (2005). https://eprint.iacr.org/2005/187

55. Renner, R., König, R.: Universally composable privacy amplification against quantum adversaries. In: Kilian, J. (ed.) TCC 2005. LNCS, vol. 3378, pp. 407–425. Springer, Heidelberg (2005). https://doi.org/10.1007/978-3-540-30576-7_22

56. Shi, S., Qian, C.: Concurrent entanglement routing for quantum networks: Model and designs. In: Proceedings of the Annual Conference of the ACM Special Interest Group on Data Communication on the Applications, Technologies, Architectures, and Protocols for Computer Communication, SIGCOMM 2020, pp. 62–75. Association for Computing Machinery, New York (2020). https://doi.org/10.1145/3387514.3405853

57. Unruh, D.: Universally composable quantum multi-party computation. In: Gilbert, H. (ed.) EUROCRYPT 2010. LNCS, vol. 6110, pp. 486–505. Springer, Heidelberg (2010). https://doi.org/10.1007/978-3-642-13190-5_25

58. Unruh, D.: Non-interactive zero-knowledge proofs in the quantum random oracle model. In: Oswald, E., Fischlin, M. (eds.) EUROCRYPT 2015. LNCS, vol. 9057, pp. 755–784. Springer, Heidelberg (2015). https://doi.org/10.1007/978-3-662-46803-6_25

59. Wehner, S., Curty, M., Schaffner, C., Lo, H.K.: Implementation of two-party protocols in the noisy-storage model. Phys. Rev. A - Atomic Molecular Opt. Phys. **81**(5) (2010). https://doi.org/10.1103/PhysRevA.81.052336
60. Wehner, S., Schaffner, C., Terhal, B.: Cryptography from noisy storage. Phys. Rev. Lett. **100**, 220502 (2008). https://doi.org/10.1103/PhysRevLett.100.220502
61. Wiesner, S.: Conjugate coding. SIGACT News **15**, 78–88 (1983). https://doi.org/10.1145/1008908.1008920
62. Yao, A.C.C.: Security of quantum protocols against coherent measurements. In: 27th Annual ACM Symposium on Theory of Computing, pp. 67–75. ACM Press, Las Vegas, NV, USA (29 May–1 Jun 1995). https://doi.org/10.1145/225058.225085
63. Zhandry, M.: How to record quantum queries, and applications to quantum indifferentiability. In: Boldyreva, A., Micciancio, D. (eds.) CRYPTO 2019. LNCS, vol. 11693, pp. 239–268. Springer, Cham (2019). https://doi.org/10.1007/978-3-030-26951-7_9

Optimal Single-Server Private Information Retrieval

Mingxun Zhou[1(✉)], Wei-Kai Lin[2], Yiannis Tselekounis[1], and Elaine Shi[1]

[1] Carnegie Mellon University, Pittsburgh, USA
mingxunz@andrew.cmu.edu, tselekounis@sians.org, runting@cs.cmu.edu
[2] Northeastern University, Boston, USA
we.lin@northeastern.edu

Abstract. We construct a single-server pre-processing Private Information Retrieval (PIR) scheme with optimal bandwidth and server computation (up to poly-logarithmic factors), assuming hardness of the Learning With Errors (LWE) problem. Our scheme achieves amortized $\widetilde{O}_\lambda(\sqrt{n})$ server and client computation and $\widetilde{O}_\lambda(1)$ bandwidth per query, completes in a single roundtrip, and requires $\widetilde{O}_\lambda(\sqrt{n})$ client storage. In particular, we achieve a significant reduction in bandwidth over the state-of-the-art scheme by Corrigan-Gibbs, Henzinger, and Kogan (Eurocrypt'22): their scheme requires as much as $\widetilde{O}_\lambda(\sqrt{n})$ bandwidth per query, with comparable computational and storage overhead as ours.

1 Introduction

Imagine that a server holds a large public database DB indexed by $0, 1, \ldots, n-1$, e.g., the repository of DNS entries or a collection of webpages. A client wants to fetch the i-th entry of the database. Although the database is public, the client wants to hide which entry it is interested in. Chor, Goldreich, Kushilevitz, and Sudan [21,22] first formulated this problem as Private Information Retrieval (PIR), and since then, a long line of works have focused on constructing efficient PIR schemes [4,10,11,15,18–20,23–26,28,30,32,35,37–39,42,43,45,46,49,50,53].

The good news is that PIR schemes with *poly-logarithmic* bandwidth are well-known [10,11,15,19,20,28,32,37,38,43,45,49,50,53], either in the single-server or multi-server settings. The bad news is that in the classical PIR setting *without pre-processing*, all known schemes suffer from prohibitive server computation overhead: the server(s) must (in aggregate) perform computation that is linear in the database size n to answer each query. Intuitively, if there is an entry that the server does not look at, it leaks information that the client is not interested in that entry. Beimel, Ishai, and Malkin [7] formalized this intuition into an elegant lower bound, showing that any PIR scheme without pre-processing must incur $\Omega(n)$ server computation per query.

Recognizing this inherent limitation, Beimel et al. [7] introduce a new model for PIR that allows *pre-processing*, and they were the first to show that the

---

W.-K. Lin—The work was done when the author was a post-doctoral researcher at Carnegie Mellon University.

E. Shi—Author ordering is randomized. Full version: https://eprint.iacr.org/2022/609.

© International Association for Cryptologic Research 2023
C. Hazay and M. Stam (Eds.): EUROCRYPT 2023, LNCS 14004, pp. 395–425, 2023.
https://doi.org/10.1007/978-3-031-30545-0_14

linear-computation lower bound can be circumvented with the help of pre-processing. Subsequently, a line of works further explored PIR in the preprocessing model [23,24,52,54], culminating in the recent works by Corrigan-Gibbs, Henzinger, and Kogan [23] and by Shi et al. [54]. Corrigan-Gibbs, Henzinger, and Kogan [23] proved that in the single-server and pre-processing setting, we can construct a PIR scheme with amortized $\widetilde{O}_\lambda(\sqrt{n})$ server and client computation per query, while requiring $\widetilde{O}_\lambda(\sqrt{n})$ client storage. Here, we use $\widetilde{O}_\lambda(\cdot)$ to hide $\mathsf{poly}\,(\lambda, \log n)$ factors, where λ is the security parameter. Corrigan-Gibbs et al. [23] also showed that their scheme achieves optimality up to $\mathsf{poly}\log$ factors in terms of server computation, assuming $\widetilde{O}(\sqrt{n})$ client storage. Unfortunately, their scheme suffers from $\widetilde{O}_\lambda(\sqrt{n})$ bandwidth overhead which is significantly worse than classical PIR schemes without pre-processing. On the other hand, Shi et al. [54] showed that in a setting with two non-colluding servers, we can construct a PIR scheme that incurs only $\widetilde{O}_\lambda(1)$ online bandwidth and $\widetilde{O}_\lambda(\sqrt{n})$ server and client computation per query, while requiring $\widetilde{O}_\lambda(\sqrt{n})$ client storage. Both of these schemes support *unbounded* number of queries after a one-time pre-processing, and the cost of the pre-processing is amortized to each query.

While the two schemes [23,54] achieve similar server and client computation overhead, Shi et al. [54] has the advantage that it achieves $\widetilde{O}_\lambda(1)$ online bandwidth—although unfortunately, this is achieved at the price of requiring two non-colluding servers. Notably, Shi et al.'s scheme is known to be optimal up to $\mathsf{poly}\log$ factors even in the two-server setting, in terms of bandwidth and server computation, assuming that the client can only download roughly $\sqrt{n}$ amount of data during the offline pre-processing phase [24].

Given the state of the art, we ask whether we can achieve the best of both worlds. Specifically, we ask the following natural question—the same open question was also raised by Corrigan-Gibbs et al. in their recent work [23]:

Can we construct a *single-server* pre-processing PIR scheme that achieves (near) *optimality* in both *server computation* and *bandwidth*?

1.1   Our Contributions

We provide an affirmative answer to the aforementioned question by proving the following theorem:

Theorem 1.1. *Assume that the Learning With Errors (LWE) assumption holds. Then, there exists a single-server pre-processing PIR scheme that achieves amortized $\widetilde{O}_\lambda(1)$ bandwidth, $\widetilde{O}_\lambda(\sqrt{n})$ server and client computation per query, and requires $\widetilde{O}_\lambda(\sqrt{n})$ client storage.*

More specifically, in our scheme, there is a one-time pre-processing phase with the same overheads in all dimensions as Corrigan-Gibbs [23] (up to $\mathsf{poly}\log$ factors). During the offline pre-processing, the client and the server engage in $\widetilde{O}_\lambda(\sqrt{n})$ communication, the server performs $\widetilde{O}_\lambda(n)$ computation, and the

Table 1. Comparison of single-server PIR schemes. Q is the batch size for batch PIR, m is the number of clients, n is the database size, and $\epsilon \in (0,1)$ is some suitable constant. "BW" means bandwidth per query. "CRA" means the composite residuosity assumption, ϕ-hiding is a number-theoretic assumption described in [15], "OLDC" means oblivious locally decodable codes, and "VBB" means virtual-blackbox obfuscation.

Scheme	Assumpt.	Adaptive	BW	Per-query time		Extra space	
				Client	Server	Client	Server
Standard [15,19,32]	CRA or ϕ-hiding or LWE	✓	$\widetilde{O}(1)$	$\widetilde{O}(1)$	$O(n)$	0	0
Batch PIR [4,38]	same as above	✗	$\widetilde{O}(1)$	$\widetilde{O}(1)$	$O(\frac{n}{Q})$	0	0
[13,17]	OLDC	✓	n^ϵ	n^ϵ	n^ϵ	$O(1)$	mn
[13]	OLDC, VBB	✓	n^ϵ	n^ϵ	n^ϵ	0	n
[24]	LWE	✓	$\widetilde{O}_\lambda(\sqrt{n})$	$\widetilde{O}_\lambda(\sqrt{n})$	$\widetilde{O}_\lambda(n)$	$\widetilde{O}_\lambda(\sqrt{n})$	0
[23]	LWE	✓	$\widetilde{O}_\lambda(\sqrt{n})$	$\widetilde{O}_\lambda(\sqrt{n})$	$\widetilde{O}_\lambda(\sqrt{n})$	$\widetilde{O}_\lambda(\sqrt{n})$	0
Ours	LWE	✓	$\widetilde{O}_\lambda(1)$	$\widetilde{O}_\lambda(\sqrt{n})$	$\widetilde{O}_\lambda(\sqrt{n})$	$\widetilde{O}_\lambda(\sqrt{n})$	0

client performs $\widetilde{O}_\lambda(\sqrt{n})$ computation. In Theorem 1.1 above, the cost of the pre-processing is *amortized* to the subsequent queries. After the one-time pre-processing, we can support an unbounded number of queries, and for each query, we incur the same costs as stated in Theorem 1.1, in the *worst case*. Our actual construction makes use of two cryptographic primitives: fully homomorphic encryption (FHE) [31,33] and privately programmable pseudorandom functions [10,41,51], both of which have known instantiations assuming LWE.

Near Optimality. Our scheme is optimal up to poly log factors in terms of server computation and bandwidth, in light of the lower bounds proven in recent works [23,24]. Specifically, Corrigan-Gibbs and Kogan [24] showed that for any pre-processing PIR scheme where the server stores only the original database, it must be that $C \cdot T \geq \Omega(n)$ where C is the bandwidth incurred during the offline pre-processing and T is the online server time per query. The recent work of Corrigan-Gibbs, Henzinger, and Kogan [23] proved that for any pre-processing PIR scheme that supports unbounded number of dynamic queries and assuming the server stores only the original database, it must be that $S \cdot T \geq \Omega(n)$ where S is client's storage and T is the online server time per query.

Although in the main body we focus on the special case where the parameters S and T are balanced, in Appendix B of the online full version [56], we discuss how to achieve a smooth tradeoff between S and T. In particular, for any function $f(n) \in [\log^c n, n/\log^c n]$ for some suitable positive constant c, we give a scheme that requires only $\widetilde{O}_\lambda(f(n))$ client space, and achieves $\widetilde{O}_\lambda(n/f(n))$ online server and client time per query, and $\widetilde{O}_\lambda(1)$ bandwidth per query. Therefore, we achieve near optimality for every choice of client space.

Comparison with Prior Schemes. Table 1 compares our scheme against various prior works. We focus on schemes in the *single-server* setting, and for pre-processing PIR schemes, we amortize the pre-processing overhead over an unbounded number of subsequent queries. Among these schemes, batch PIR schemes [4,37,38] must have a large batch size of Q to achieve the stated amortized performance, and fail in the scenario when the queries are generated *adaptively* and arrive one by one. We discuss additional related work in Sect. 1.2.

1.2   Additional Related Work

We now review some additional related work. Besides being first to define PIR with pre-processing, Beimel et al. [7] additionally showed how to construct a preprocessing PIR with polylogarithmic online bandwidth assuming polylogarithmically many non-colluding servers, and poly (n) server storage. Unlike our work as well as the recent works by Corrigan-Gibbs et al. [23,24], the scheme by Beimel et al. [7] employs a *public* pre-processing, where the pre-processing results in no client-side secret state. In fact, in their scheme [7], the server pre-processes the database, resulting in a poly (n)-sized encoding of the database which is then stored by the server. The very recent work of Persiano and Yeo [52] proved that for any PIR scheme with *public* pre-processing, it must be that $T \cdot R \geq \Omega(n\log n)$ where T is the server computation per query and R is size of the additional state computed by the public pre-processing. In comparison, our work considers a *private* pre-processing model, i.e., at the end of the pre-processing, the client stores some secret state not seen by the server. This model matches well with a "subscription model" in practice. For example, every client that needs private DNS service can subscribe with the provider, and during subscription, they perform the one-time pre-processing.

Besides the single-server PIR scheme from FHE mentioned in Table 1, the work of Corrigan-Gibbs and Kogan [24] also propose another scheme assuming only linearly homomorphic encryption, which requires $O(n^{2/3})$ bandwidth and client computation and $O(n)$ server computation per query, as well as $O(n^{2/3})$ client storage. Further, the work of Corrigan-Gibbs, Henzinger, and Kogan [23] additionally suggests a single-server PIR scheme assuming only linearly homomorphic encryption, incurring $O(\sqrt{n})$ bandwidth and client computation, and $O(n^{3/4})$ server computation per query, requiring $O(n^{3/4})$ client storage.

Hamlin et al. [36] suggested a related notion called *private anonymous data access* (PANDA). PANDA is a form of preprocessing PIR which requires an additional *third-party trusted setup* besides the client and the servers; and moreover, the server storage and time grow w.r.t. the number of corrupt clients. In applications (e.g., private DNS) that involve a potentially unbounded number of mutually distrustful clients, PANDA schemes would be unsuitable.

A line of works have explored the concrete efficiency of PIR schemes [4,34,42, 47,48,50]. In particular, the work of Angel et al. [4] relies on batching to amortize the linear server computation over a batch of queries. Kogan and Corrigan-Gibbs [42] gives a practical instantiation of the two-server pre-processing PIR scheme described in their earlier work [24], with a new trick that removes the k-fold parallel repetition. For their private blocklist application, it turns out that the database is somewhat small, and therefore, they are willing to incur $\Theta(n)$ client-side computation per online query, in exchange for logarithmic bandwidth. The work of Patel et al. [50] explores how to rely on a stateful client to improve the concrete performance of PIR schemes. Our work focuses on the asymptotical overhead, and we leave it to future work to consider concretely efficient instantiations that preserve our asymptotical performance.

Some works have considered achieving sublinear server time by relaxing the security definition to differential privacy. Toledo et al. [55] improved the server time to sublinear with this relaxation, assuming a large number of servers are available. Albab et al. [3] also considered the differential privacy notion, and they can achieve sublinear amortized server computation in a batched setting.

Independent Work. Subsequent to our work, Lazaretti and Papamanthou [44] proposed a similar construction. The main difference in their construction is that they claim to rely only on privately *puncturable* PRFs and we rely on privately *programmable* PRFs. However, inside their scheme, they are effectively using rejection sampling to construct a programmable PRF from a puncturable PRF—earlier work has pointed out that this approach will only work if the privately puncturable PRF satisfies rerandomizability [16]. Therefore, for Lazaretti and Papamanthou's scheme [44] to work, they need to rely on a rerandomizable privately puncturable PRF like what Canetti and Chen [16] suggested. Additionally, their privacy proof (in their Eprint version dated 2022-06-23) appears slightly incomplete but likely fixable. In particular, in the inductive argument in their privacy proof in their Section B.1, they argue that the sk part of the client's table is indistinguishable from randomly sampled secret keys (for the hard puncturing key). To prove the PIR scheme secure, they actually need to show that the client's table is indistinguishable form randomly sampled keys, not just for the sk part, but actually for the pair (msk, sk). This is because the server's view actually depends on the msks in the client's table. While it is outside the scope of our paper to complete their proof, we think changing the security definition of their pseudorandom sets to include the msk, and reproving their pseudorandom sets secure under this new definition should lend to fixing this issue.

2   Technical Roadmap

2.1   Starting Point: Optimal 2-Server Scheme by Shi et al.

An Inefficient Toy Scheme. Our starting point is the nearly optimal 2-server scheme by Shi et al. [54], and we will explore how to coalesce the two servers into one. To understand their scheme, it helps to start out with the following toy scheme which is a slight variant of the strawman schemes described in recent works [24,54]. Henceforth, we use the notations Right and Left to denote two non-colluding servers. Let $\mathcal{D}_n$ be some distribution from which we can sample random sets of expected size $\sqrt{n}$—at this moment, the reader need not care what exactly the distribution $\mathcal{D}_n$ is.

Inefficient Toy 2-Server Scheme: Single-Copy Version

Offline preprocessing.   (DB[k] *denotes the k-th bit of the database*)

- Client samples $\sqrt{n}$ sets $S_1, S_2, \ldots, S_{\sqrt{n}} \subseteq \{0, 1, \ldots, n-1\}$ from the distribution $\mathcal{D}_n$.
- Client sends the resulting sets $S_1, \ldots, S_{\sqrt{n}}$ to Left. For each set $j \in [\sqrt{n}]$, Left responds with the parity bit $p_j := \oplus_{k \in S_j} \text{DB}[k]$ of indices in the set.
- Client stores the hint table $T := \{T_j := (S_j, p_j)\}_{j \in [\sqrt{n}]}$.

Online query for index $x \in \{0, 1, \ldots, n-1\}$.

- **Query:** (Client $\Leftrightarrow$ Right)
  1. Find an entry $T_j := (S_j, p_j)$ in its hint table T such that $x \in S_j$. Let $S^* := S_j$ if found, else let S^* be a fresh random set containing x.
  2. Send the set $S := \textbf{ReSamp}(S^*, x)$ to Right, where $\textbf{ReSamp}(S^*, x)$ outputs a set almost identical to S^*, except that the coins used to determine x's membership are re-tossed.
  3. Upon obtaining a response $p := \oplus_{k \in S} \text{DB}[k]$ from Right, output the candidate answer $\beta' := p_j \oplus p$ or $\beta' := 0$ if no such T_j was found earlier.
  4. Client obtains the true answer $\beta := \text{DB}[x]$—the full scheme will repeat this single-copy scheme $k = \omega(\log \lambda)$ times, and β is computed as a majority vote among the k candidate answers, which is guaranteed to be correct except with negligible probability.
- **Refresh** (Client $\Leftrightarrow$ Left)
  1. Client samples a random set S' and sends S' to Left.
  2. Left responds with $p' := \oplus_{k \in S'} \text{DB}[k]$. Let $\widetilde{p} = p' \oplus \beta$ if $x \notin S'$, else let $\widetilde{p} = p'$. If a table entry T_j containing x was found and consumed earlier, Client replaces T_j with $(S' \cup \{x\}, \widetilde{p})$.

In this 2-server toy scheme, during the offline phase, the client samples $\sqrt{n}$ sets each of expected size $\sqrt{n}$ from some distribution $\mathcal{D}_n$. It downloads the parities of all these sets from the Left server. It stores all these sets as well as the parity of each set in a local hint table. During the online phase, to query an index $x \in \{0, 1, \ldots, n-1\}$, the client looks up its hint table and finds a set S^* that contains x, whose parity is p_j. It then resamples the coins that determine whether x is in the set or not. It sends the resampled set to the Right server, which returns the client the parity p'. The client computes $\beta' = p' \oplus p_j$ as the candidate answer. If we choose the distribution $\mathcal{D}_n$ carefully, then, with significant probability, the **ReSamp**(x) will *remove the element x from the set, without adding or removing any other element.* In this case, the candidate answer β' would be correct. If we can ensure that each single copy has $2/3$ correctness probability, then we can amplify the correctness probability to $1 - \mathsf{negl}(\lambda)$ through parallel repetition using $\omega(\log \lambda)$ copies and majority voting. Finally, once we consume a hint from the table, we need to replenish it. To achieve this, the client samples a random set S', and obtains its parity p' from the Left server. The client replaces the consumed entry with the set $S' \cup \{x\}$ and its parity which can be computed knowing p' and $\beta = \mathsf{DB}[x]$.

Privacy. Privacy w.r.t. the Left server is easy to see. Basically, the Left server sees $\sqrt{n}$ random sets sampled from $\mathcal{D}_n$ during the offline phase, and during each online query, it sees an additional random set also sampled from $\mathcal{D}_n$. Privacy w.r.t. the Right server can be proven using an inductive argument. Initially, the client's hint table consists of $\sqrt{n}$ random sets sampled independently from $\mathcal{D}_n$. Suppose that at the end of the i-th query the client's hint table satisfies the above distribution. Then, during the i-th query that requests some index $x \in \{0, 1, \ldots, n - 1\}$, if some hint (S_j, p_j) is matched, i.e., $S_j \ni x$, then, the distribution of S_j is the same as sampling from $\mathcal{D}_n$ subject to containing x. Therefore, the set sent to the Right server, i.e., **ReSamp**(S_j) has the same distribution as sampling at random from $\mathcal{D}_n$. Further, notice that the client replaces the consumed entry with another set sampled at random subject to containing x. Thus, at the end of the i-th query, the client's hint table still has $\sqrt{n}$ independent and identically distributed (i.i.d.) sets sampled from $\mathcal{D}_n$.

Inefficiency of the Toy Scheme. In the toy scheme, both the server and the client perform roughly $\sqrt{n}$ computation per query. However, the online bandwidth to each of the two servers is roughly $\sqrt{n}$, and the client storage is $O(n)$.

Compressing the Bandwidth and Client Storage. *Pseudorandom Sets with Private* **ReSamp**. Shi et al. [54] suggested an idea to improve the efficiency of the toy scheme in the two-server setting. To achieve this, they introduce a cryptographic object called a pseudorandom set (PRSet), allowing us to succinctly represent a pseudorandom set of size roughly $\sqrt{n}$ with a short key of $\mathsf{poly}(\lambda)$ bits. In this way, the client can store a key in place of each set, and send a key to the server in place of the full description of a set. Their PRSet scheme must support the following operations:

- $\mathsf{sk} \leftarrow \mathbf{Gen}(1^\lambda, n)$: samples a key sk that generates a pseudorandom set emulating the distribution $\mathcal{D}_n$;
- $S \leftarrow \mathbf{Set}(\mathsf{sk})$: given a key sk, enumerate the set S;
- $\mathbf{Member}(\mathsf{sk}, x)$: test if an element $x \in \{0, 1, \ldots, n - 1\}$ is in $\mathbf{Set}(\mathsf{sk})$;

- sk$'$ ← **ReSamp**(sk, x): given a key sk, generates a related key sk$'$ that effectively resamples the coins that are used to determine whether x is in the set or not, while preserving all other coins[1];

Designing such a PRSet scheme turns out to be non-trivial, since we need to satisfy the following properties simultaneously.

- *Privacy of* **ReSamp**. The resampled key output by **ReSamp**(sk, x) must hide the point x that is being resampled.
- *Efficient membership test and set enumeration.* The membership test algorithm **Member**(sk, x) must complete in $\widetilde{O}_\lambda(1)$ running time and the set enumeration algorithm **Set**(sk) must complete in $\widetilde{O}_\lambda(\sqrt{n})$ time.

Shi et al. [54] show how to rely on a privately puncturable pseudorandom function [9,14,16] to construct a PRSet scheme that supports a private **ReSamp** operation. Further, to satisfy efficient membership test and efficient set enumeration simultaneously, they carefully crafted a distribution $\mathcal{D}_n$ that the PRSet scheme emulates. Notably, whether two elements are in the set may not be independent in the distribution $\mathcal{D}_n$. Such weak dependence between elements brings additional possibilities of errors. In particular, **ReSamp**(sk, x) *may accidentally remove other elements besides* x. If **ReSamp**(sk, x) either fails to remove x or ends up removing additional elements besides x, the resulting PIR scheme would be incorrect. Shi et al. [54] made sure that the probability of such error is small, such that each single copy of the PIR scheme still has 2/3 correctness.

Optimal 2-Server PIR Scheme. With such a PRSet scheme, we can easily modify the aforementioned toy scheme to compress the client storage and bandwidth [54]. Specifically, during the offline phase, the client sends $\sqrt{n}$ PRSet keys to the Left server. The Left server uses the set enumeration algorithm **Set** to enumerate the sets and sends the client their parity bits. The client now stores a hint table where each entry is of the form (sk_i, p_i), where sk_i is a PRSet key that can be used to generate a set of size roughly $\sqrt{n}$, and p_i is the parity bit as before. During an online query for $x \in \{0, 1, \ldots, n-1\}$, the client finds an sk^* in its hint table such that **Member**(sk^*, x) = 1, and sends the outcome of **ReSamp**(sk^*, x) to the Right server. If such a key is not found, the client simply samples a random sk$'$ ← **Gen**($1^\lambda, n$) and sends it to the server. The client computes the candidate answer the same way as before. What is most interesting is how to perform the refresh operation to replenish the consumed key. This is achieved in the following manner:

- Sample sk$'$ ← **Gen**($1^\lambda, n$) subject to **Member**(sk$', x$) = 1, and send the outcome of **ReSamp**(sk$', x$) to the Left server.
- The Left server enumerates the set using the **Set** algorithm and sends the client the parity bit p'. The client replaces the consumed entry with (sk$', p' \oplus \beta$) where $\beta = \mathsf{DB}[x]$ is the true answer to the current query.

---

[1] Shi et al. [54] referred to **ReSamp** as **Punct** since the operation is implemented by calling the puncturing operation of the underlying privately puncturable PRF.

2.2 Highlights of Our Construction and Proof Techniques

Corrigan-Gibbs and Kogan [24] proposed an FHE-based technique to compile a two-server pre-processing PIR scheme into a single-server scheme, and the technique was further extended by Corrigan-Gibbs, Henzinger, and Kogan [23]—this technique is remotely related to techniques for converting multi-prover proof systems into single-prover proof systems [1,8,27,29,40]. The idea is to get rid of the Left server and redirect the queries originally destined for the Left server instead to the Right server, but now encrypted under a fully homomorphic encryption (FHE) scheme. The server now evaluates the answers to the query through homomorphic evaluation. Unfortunately, this compilation technique is incompatible with Shi et al. [54]. The technicality arises from the fact that FHE evaluation relies on *circuit* as the computation model, whereas the sublinear server computation time of Shi et al. [54] relies on the *RAM* model (since dynamic memory accesses are needed). Recall that every time the server receives a pseudorandom set key, it needs to expand the key to a set of size $\widetilde{O}(\sqrt{n})$, and retrieve the parity of the database bits at precisely these indices. On a RAM, this computation costs $\widetilde{O}(\sqrt{n})$, but now that the key is encrypted under FHE, using a circuit to homomorphically evaluate this computation would require an $\Omega(n)$-sized circuit—this defeats our goal of having sublinear server time.

Fortunately, the following critical observation, first made by Corrigan-Gibbs et al. [23], saves the day.

Observation. Although homomorphically evaluating the parity of a single set takes a linear-sized circuit, we can batch-evaluate the parity bits of $\Theta(\sqrt{n})$ sets in a circuit of size $\widetilde{O}(n)$, leveraging oblivious sort. With batch evaluation, the amortized cost per set is only $\widetilde{O}(\sqrt{n})$.

Idea 1: Batched Refresh Operations. The above batching idea allows us to compile the offline phase of Shi et al. [54] without suffering from the RAM-to-circuit conversion blowup (ignoring poly-logarithmic factors). However, the online phase is problematic, since Shi et al. requires that the client talks to the Left server to perform a refresh operation every time it makes a query.

Our first idea is inspired by Corrigan-Gibbs et al. [23]. Instead of performing refreshes individually, we can group them into $Q = \sqrt{n}$-sized batches. We first consider a bounded scheme that supports only $Q = \sqrt{n}$ queries—in this way, we can hope to front-load all Q refresh operations upfront during the pre-processing phase. It is easy to get an unbounded scheme given a bounded scheme. We can simply rerun the offline setup every Q queries, and amortize the cost of the periodic setup over each query—in fact, it is also not hard to deamortize the periodic setup and spread the work across time.

In summary, through batching the refresh operations, we can hope to achieve $\widetilde{O}_\lambda(\sqrt{n})$ amortized server computation per refresh operation.

Idea 2: A Pseudorandom Set Scheme Supporting **Add** *and* **ReSamp**. If we front-load all Q refresh operations upfront during the offline pre-processing, a new technicality arises. Recall that during a query for $x \in \{0, 1, \ldots, n-1\}$, we must replenish the consumed entry with a set sampled subject to containing the queried element x. During the offline pre-processing, however, we do not have foreknowledge of x. Therefore, we can only hope to sample (pseudo-)random sets (represented by keys) during the offline pre-processing, and add the element x to the set during the online phase.

This means that we need a new PRSet that supports not only **ReSamp**, but also an **Add** operation. Specifically, given a PRSet key sk, the client should be able to call $\mathsf{sk'} \leftarrow \mathbf{Add}(\mathsf{sk}, x)$ and then call $\mathsf{rsk} \leftarrow \mathbf{ReSamp}(\mathsf{sk'}, y)$, and send the resulting rsk to the server. For privacy, the resulting rsk must hide both x and y. To construct such a PRSet scheme, we need a cryptographic primitive called privately programmable pseudorandom functions [10,41,51], which is stronger than the privately puncturable pseudorandom functions employed by Shi et al.

New Proof Techniques. For the optimal two-server scheme of Shi et al. [54], they have a relatively simple privacy proof. In comparison, our privacy proof is much more involved, and we need new techniques to make the privacy proof work.

At a high level, the challenges in the privacy proof arise due to the way the probability analysis is interwined with the cryptography.

Our main new idea in the privacy proof is to introduce a *lazy sampling* technique[2] that provides an alternative way to view how the client generates the key to send to the server—called the "frontend" in our proof. In particular, during the scheme, the client scans through its primary table and checks if each key contains the current query x. Whenever such a check is made and the answer is no, it creates a constraint on the entry, i.e., the entry should not contain x. Whenever an entry is matched during a query x, a constraint is created that the entry should contain x. If the entry was previously promoted from the backup table, these constraints can also be modified accordingly. Thus, we can imagine that the client maintains a set of constraints in this way, and defer the actual sampling of the key to send to the server to the very last moment, subject to the set of constraints that have been maintained on the matching entry. With this lazy sampling view, we can decouple the *frontend* (i.e., how the client interacts with the server) from the *backend* (i.e., how the client maintains its local primary table), and switch their distributions one by one in the subsequent hybrids. In our actual proof later, the frontend and the backend diverge at some point when we switch to the lazy sampling view, and eventually, after switching both the backend and the frontend, they would converge again, i.e., the distribution of the key sent to the server matches the distribution of the matched entry (after some post-processing) again. At this moment, we can undo the lazy sampling view, and continue to complete the proof.

Another technicality in our proof arises from the fact that the form of the standard security definition of privately puncturable PRF is not in a convenient form we can easily use in our proof. For this reason, we introduce a *key technical*

---

[2] Our lazy sampling is remotely reminiscent of the delayed sampling technique of Bartusek and Khurana [5].

lemma (Sect. 6.2) that is closer to the form we want. We repeatedly apply this key technical lemma when making the switches between our hybrid experiments.

To help the reader understand the technicalities of our privacy proof and our new ideas, we give an informal proof roadmap in Sect. 6.1.

3 Preliminaries

3.1 Privately Programmable Pseudorandom Functions

Intuitively, a privately programmable pseudorandom function [10,41,51] is a pseudorandom function (PRF) with one extra capability: it allows one to create a *programmed key* that forces the PRF's outcomes in at most L distinct input points $\{x_i\}$ to be a set of pre-determined values $\{v_i\}$. For security, we want to guarantee the privacy of the programmed inputs. Specifically, if the set of output values $\{v_i\}$ are randomly chosen, then the programmed key should not leak more information about the set of input points programmed. Further, the programmed key should not leak the original PRF's evaluation outcomes at the programmed inputs prior to the programming.

Syntax. Let $\mathcal{X}$ denote the input domain and let $\mathcal{V}$ denote the output range, whose sizes may depend on the security parameter λ. A programmable pseudorandom function is a tuple (**Gen, Eval, Prog, PEval**) of efficient, possibly randomized algorithms with the following syntax:

- **Gen**$(1^\lambda, L)$: given the security parameter λ and an upper bound, L, on the number of programmable inputs, output a master secret key msk.
- **Eval**(msk, x): given the master secret key msk and an input $x \in \mathcal{X}$, output the evaluation result $v \in \mathcal{V}$ on the input x.
- **Prog**$(\text{msk}, P = \{(x_i, v_i)\})$: given the master secret key msk and a set P containing up to L pairs $(x_i, v_i) \in \mathcal{X} \times \mathcal{V}$, where all x_i's must be distinct, output a programmed key sk_P.
- **PEval**(sk_P, x): given a programmed key sk_P and an input $x \in \mathcal{X}$, output the evaluation outcome, $v \in \mathcal{V}$, over the input x.

Correctness of Programming. A programmable function satisfies correctness if for all λ, $L = \text{poly}(\lambda) \in \mathbb{N}$, all sets of up to L pairs $P := \{(x_i, v_i)\} \subseteq \mathcal{X} \times \mathcal{V}$ (with distinct x_is), we have the following:

1. For every $i \in [|P|]$,

$$\Pr\left[\mathbf{PEval}(\text{sk}_P, x_i) \neq v_i \,\middle|\, \begin{array}{l} \text{msk} \leftarrow \mathbf{Gen}(1^\lambda, L) \\ \text{sk}_P \leftarrow \mathbf{Prog}(\text{msk}, P) \end{array}\right] \leq \text{negl}(\lambda), \text{ and}$$

2. For any x' not in P, we have

$$\Pr\left[\mathbf{PEval}(\text{sk}_P, x') \neq \mathbf{Eval}(\text{msk}, x') \,\middle|\, \begin{array}{l} \text{msk} \leftarrow \mathbf{Gen}(1^\lambda, L) \\ \text{sk}_P \leftarrow \mathbf{Prog}(\text{msk}, P) \end{array}\right] \leq \text{negl}(\lambda).$$

We note that Peikert and Shiehian [51] did not define the second correctness condition above, but their proof shows that the second condition also holds.

RealPPRF$_{\mathcal{A}}(1^\lambda, L)$:

  $P := \{(x_i, v_i)\}_{i \in [L']} \leftarrow \mathcal{A}(1^\lambda, L)$

          // require: $L' \leq L$

  msk $\leftarrow$ **Gen**$(1^\lambda, L)$

  sk$_P \leftarrow$ **Prog**(msk, P)

  sk$_P \rightarrow \mathcal{A}$

  repeat

    $x \leftarrow \mathcal{A}$

    Eval(msk, x) $\rightarrow \mathcal{A}$

  until $\mathcal{A}$ halts

IdealPPRF$_{\mathcal{A},\mathsf{Sim}}(1^\lambda, L)$:

  $P := \{(x_i, v_i)\}_{i \in [L']} \leftarrow \mathcal{A}(1^\lambda, L)$

          // require: $L' \leq L$

  sk$_P \leftarrow$ Sim$(1^\lambda, P, L)$

  sk$_P \rightarrow \mathcal{A}$

  repeat

    $x \leftarrow \mathcal{A}$

    If $x \notin \{x_i\}_{i \in [L']}$ then **PEval**(sk$_P$, x) $\rightarrow \mathcal{A}$

    Else $v \xleftarrow{\$} \mathcal{V}, v \rightarrow \mathcal{A}$

  until $\mathcal{A}$ halts

Fig. 1. The real and ideal experiments for simulation security.

RealPPRFPriv$_{\mathcal{A}}(1^\lambda, L)$:

  $\{x_i\}_{i \in [L']} \leftarrow \mathcal{A}(1^\lambda, L)$

          // require: $L' \leq L$

  $\{v_i\}_{i \in [L']} \xleftarrow{\$} \mathcal{V}$

  $P := \{(x_i, v_i)\}_{i \in [L']}$

  msk $\leftarrow$ **Gen**$(1^\lambda, L)$, sk $\leftarrow$ **Prog**(msk, P)

  sk $\rightarrow \mathcal{A}$

IdealPPRFPriv$_{\mathcal{A},\mathsf{Sim}}(1^\lambda, L)$:

  $\{x_i\}_{i \in [L']} \leftarrow \mathcal{A}(1^\lambda, L)$

          // require: $L' \leq L$

  sk $\leftarrow$ Sim$(1^\lambda, L)$

  sk $\rightarrow \mathcal{A}$

Fig. 2. The real and ideal experiments for private programmability.

Security Definitions

Definition 3.1 (Simulation security). *A programmable function is simulation secure, if there is a probabilistic polynomial-time (PPT) simulator* Sim *such that for any PPT adversary $\mathcal{A}$ and any polynomial $L(\lambda)$,*

$$\left\{ \mathsf{RealPPRF}_{\mathcal{A}}(1^\lambda, L) \right\}_{\lambda \in \mathbb{N}} \overset{c}{\approx} \left\{ \mathsf{IdealPPRF}_{\mathcal{A},\mathsf{Sim}}(1^\lambda, L) \right\}_{\lambda \in \mathbb{N}},$$

where RealPPRF *and* IdealPPRF *are the respective views of $\mathcal{A}$ in the executions of Fig. 1 and "$\overset{c}{\approx}$" denotes computational indistinguishability.*

Definition 3.2 (Private programmability). *A programmable function is privately programmable, if there is a PPT simulator* Sim *such that for any PPT adversary $\mathcal{A}$ and any polynomial $L(\lambda)$,*

$$\left\{ \mathsf{RealPPRFPriv}_{\mathcal{A}}(1^\lambda, L) \right\}_{\lambda \in \mathbb{N}} \overset{c}{\approx} \left\{ \mathsf{IdealPPRFPriv}_{\mathcal{A},\mathsf{Sim}}(1^\lambda, L) \right\}_{\lambda \in \mathbb{N}},$$

where RealPPRFPriv *and* IdealPPRFPriv *are the respective views of $\mathcal{A}$ in the executions of Fig. 2.*

Last but not the least, we define an additional security property, i.e., the ordinary pseudorandomness notion for the PRF. We prove that pseudorandomness is implied by private programmability—however, defining this notion explicitly will facilitate our proofs later.

Definition 3.3 (Pseudorandomness). *We say that a programmable pseudorandom function satisfies pseudorandomness iff for every probabilistic polynomial-time adversary $\mathcal{A}$, there exists a negligible function $negl(\cdot)$ such that the following holds:*

$$\left| \Pr[\mathsf{msk} \leftarrow \mathbf{Gen}(1^\lambda, L) : \mathcal{A}^{\mathbf{Eval}(\mathsf{msk}, \cdot)} = 1] - \Pr[\mathsf{rf} \xleftarrow{\$} \mathcal{RF} : \mathcal{A}^{\mathsf{rf}(\cdot)} = 1] \right| \leq negl(\lambda),$$

where $\mathcal{RF}$ denotes the family of random functions that map the input domain $\mathcal{X}$ to the output range $\mathcal{V}$.

Fact 1. *Suppose that a programmable PRF scheme satisfies private programmability, then it also satisfies pseudorandomness.*

Proof. Let q be the maximum number of queries made by the pseudorandomness adversary $\mathcal{A}$. We consider a sequence of hybrids $H_0, H_1, \ldots, H_q$. In H_j where $j \in \{0, 1, \ldots, q\}$, for the first j *distinct* queries made by $\mathcal{A}$, return to $\mathcal{A}$ truly random answers, and for the remaining queries, return the outcomes of the PRF evaluation. If $\mathcal{A}$ makes any repeat query, it always gets the same answer as before.

It suffices to show that no probabilistic polynomial-time $\mathcal{A}$ can distinguish H_i and H_{i+1} for any $i \in \{0, 1, \ldots, q-1\}$. To show this, consider an intermediate hybrid H'_i. In H'_i, the first i distinct queries are answered with true randomness, and the remaining queries are answered using a simulated key generated by $\mathsf{sk} \leftarrow \mathsf{Sim}(1^\lambda, L)$.

We first show that H_{i+1} is computationally indistinguishable from H'_i. Suppose that there is an efficient adversary $\mathcal{A}$ that can distinguish H'_i and H_{i+1}. We can construct an efficient reduction $\mathcal{B}$ that breaks the private programmability of the underlying PRF. $\mathcal{B}$ answers the first i distinct queries from $\mathcal{A}$ using true randomness. When $\mathcal{A}$ submits the $(i+1)$-th distinct query x_{i+1}, $\mathcal{B}$ submits $\{x_{i+1}\}$ to its own challenger. It gets back from its challenger sk. For all remaining queries x_j for $j \in [i+1, q]$, it returns $\mathbf{PEval}(\mathsf{sk}, x_j)$ to answer to $\mathcal{A}$. If $\mathcal{B}$ is playing RealPPRFPriv, then $\mathcal{A}$'s view is statistically indistinguishable from H_{i+1} (where the negligible statistical failure comes from the "correctness of programming" failure probability), else if $\mathcal{B}$ is playing IdealPPRFPriv, then $\mathcal{A}$'s view is identically distributed as H'_i.

Next, we show that H'_i is computationally indistinguishable from H_i. Consider H''_i in which all but the first i queries are answered using a key sk generated as follows: $\mathsf{msk} \leftarrow \mathbf{Gen}(1^\lambda, L)$, $\mathsf{sk} \leftarrow \mathbf{Prog}(\mathsf{msk}, \emptyset)$. H_i is statistically indistinguishable from H''_i due to the correctness of the programmable PRF. H''_i is computationally indistinguishable from H'_i through a straightforward reduction to the private programmability of the PRF.

Summarizing the above, H_i is computationally indistinguishable from H_{i+1} and this suffices for proving the claim.

Construction. In our syntax and security definitions above, we want the programmable PRF to support programming *at most L* inputs. By contrast, Peikert and Shiehian [51] gave a construction of privately programmable PRFs where the **Prog** function must program *exactly L* inputs. Similarly, in their security definitions, the admissible adversary $\mathcal{A}$ is required to satisfy $L' = L$ (as opposed to $L' \leq L$ in our case).

Given a privately programmable PRF construction that programs exactly L inputs, we now show how to construct a new scheme that allows programming *up to* L inputs. In our PIR construction later, we want the PRF's input domain to contain all strings of length up to some parameter $\ell \in \mathbb{N}$. We use the notation $\{0, 1\}^{\leq \ell}$ to denote all strings of length up to ℓ.

Let $\mathsf{PRF}' := (\mathbf{Gen}', \mathbf{Eval}', \mathbf{Prog}', \mathbf{PEval}')$ denote a privately programmable PRF whose input domain is $\mathcal{X}' = \{0, 1\}^{\leq \ell+1}$, i.e., all strings of length up to $\ell + 1$, and whose output range is $\mathcal{V}$, supporting programming exactly L inputs. We now construct a privately programmable PRF scheme denoted PRF whose input domain is $\mathcal{X} = \{0, 1\}^{\leq \ell}$, i.e., all strings of length up to ℓ, and whose output range is $\mathcal{V}$, i.e., the same as that of PRF'.

- $\mathbf{Gen}(1^\lambda, L)$: let $\mathsf{msk} \leftarrow \mathbf{Gen}'(1^\lambda, L)$, and output msk;
- $\mathbf{Eval}(\mathsf{msk}, x)$: output $\mathbf{Eval}'(\mathsf{msk}, x \| 0)$;
- $\mathbf{Prog}(\mathsf{msk}, P = \{(x_i, v_i)\}_{i \in [L']})$:
  - choose $L - L'$ distinct strings of length at most $\ell + 1$ that end with 1, denoted $x'_1, \ldots, x'_{L-L'}$;
  - for $j \in [L - L']$, choose $v_j \xleftarrow{\$} \mathcal{V}$ at random;
  - call $\mathsf{sk} \leftarrow \mathbf{Prog}'(\mathsf{msk}, \{(x_i\|0, v_i)\}_{i \in [L']} \cup \{(x'_j, v_j)\}_{j \in [L-L']})$, and output sk.
- $\mathbf{PEval}(\mathsf{sk}, x)$: let $v \leftarrow \mathbf{PEval}(\mathsf{sk}, x \| 0)$ and output v.

Claim 1. *Suppose that the underlying programmable* PRF' *that maps* $\{0, 1\}^{\ell+1}$ *to* $\mathcal{V}$ *satisfies correctness, simulation security, and private programmability. Then, the above* PRF *which maps* $\{0, 1\}^\ell$ *to* $\mathcal{V}$ *also satisfies correctness, simulation security, and private programmability.*

We defer the proof of the above claim to Appendix E.1 of the online full version [56].

We can use Peikert and Shiehian [51]'s scheme (based on LWE) as our the underlying privately puncturable PRF to instantiate Claim 1. The schem by Boyle et al. [12] is not suitable for our application, since their evaluation time is quasilinear in the input domain size which would lead to super-linear server computation.

3.2   Single-Server Private Information Retrieval

We define a single-server private information retrieval (PIR) scheme in the preprocessing setting. In a single-server PIR scheme, we have two stateful machines called the client and the server. The scheme consists of two phases:

- **Offline setup.** The offline setup phase is run only once upfront. The client receives nothing as input, and the server receives a database $\mathsf{DB} \in \{0,1\}^n$ as input. The client sends a single message to the server, and the server responds with a single message.
- **Online queries.** This phase can be repeated multiple times. Upon receiving an index $x \in \{0, 1, \ldots, n-1\}$, the client sends a single message to the server, and the server responds with a single message. The client performs some computation and outputs an answer $\beta \in \{0, 1\}$.

Correctness. Given a database $\mathsf{DB} \in \{0,1\}^n$, where the bits are indexed $0, 1, \ldots, n-1$, the correct answer for a query $x \in \{0, 1, \ldots, n-1\}$ is the x-th bit of DB.

For correctness, we require that for any q, n, that are polynomially bounded in λ, there is a negligible function $\mathsf{negl}(\cdot)$, such that for any database $\mathsf{DB} \in \{0,1\}^n$, for any sequence of queries $x_1, x_2, \ldots, x_q \in \{0, 1, \ldots, n-1\}$, an honest execution of the PIR scheme with DB and queries $x_1, x_2, \ldots, x_q$, returns all correct answers with probability $1 - \mathsf{negl}(\lambda)$.

Privacy. We say that a single-server PIR scheme satisfies privacy, iff there exists a probabilistic polynomial-time simulator Sim, such that for any probabilistic polynomial-time adversary $\mathcal{A}$ acting as the server, $\mathcal{A}$'s views in the following two experiments are computationally indistinguishable:

- Real: an honest client interacts with $\mathcal{A}$ who acts as the server and may arbitrarily deviate from the prescribed protocol. In every online step t, $\mathcal{A}$ may adaptively choose the next query $x_t \in \{0, 1, \ldots, n-1\}$ for the client, and the client is invoked with x_t;
- Ideal: the simulated client Sim interacts with $\mathcal{A}$ who acts as the server. In every online $\mathcal{A}$ may adaptively choose the next query $x_t \in \{0, 1, \ldots, n-1\}$, and Sim is invoked without receiving x_t.

3.3   The Distribution $\mathcal{D}_n$

For convenience, we often write $x \in \{0, 1, \ldots, n-1\}$ as a binary string, i.e., $x \in \{0, 1\}^{\log n}$.

Our pseudorandom set emulates the same distribution $\mathcal{D}_n$ that was defined earlier in Shi et al. [54]. Specifically, to define the distribution $\mathcal{D}_n$, imagine that we have a random oracle $\mathsf{RO}(\cdot) : \{0, 1\}^* \to \{0, 1\}$ that is sampled at random upfront—our actual PRSet scheme later will replace the RO with a PRF so our construction does not need an RO. Henceforth, let $B := \lceil 2\log\log n \rceil$. An element $x \in \{0, 1\}^{\log n}$ is in the set iff for every $i \in [\frac{\log n}{2} + B]$, $\mathsf{RO}\left((0^B \| x)[i :]\right)$ returns 1— in other words, if hashing every sufficiently long suffix of the string $0^B \| x$ using the random oracle RO gives back 1. Throughout the paper, we write $\log = \log_2$, and assume that $\log n$ is an even integer— this is without loss of generality since we can always round it up to an even number incurring only constant blowup.

Efficient Membership Test and Set Enumeration. One important observation about the distribution $\mathcal{D}_n$ is that the decisions regarding whether two elements x and y are in the set or not can be weakly dependent—as Shi et al. [54] pointed out, this property is important for simultaneously ensuring efficient membership test and efficient set enumeration. Clearly, to test if an element $x \in \{0,1\}^{\log n}$ is in the set or not, we only need to make $\frac{\log n}{2} + B$ calls to the RO.

Enumerating all elements in the set can be accomplished by making roughly $\sqrt{n} \cdot \text{poly} \log n$ calls to RO with at least $1 - o(1)$ probability. Let $\ell \geq \frac{1}{2}\log n + 1$, and let Z_ℓ be the set of all strings z of length exactly ℓ, such that using RO to "hash" all suffixes of z of length at least $\frac{1}{2}\log n + 1$, outputs 1. To enumerate the set generated by RO, we can start with $Z_{\frac{1}{2}\log n + 1}$ which takes at most $2^{\frac{1}{2}\log n + 1}$ calls to generate. Then, for each $\ell := \frac{1}{2}\log n + 2$ to $\log n$, we will generate Z_ℓ from $Z_{\ell-1}$. This can be accomplished by enumerating all elements $z' \in Z_{\ell-1}$, and checking whether $\mathsf{RO}(0||z') = 1$ and $\mathsf{RO}(1||z') = 1$. Finally, for every element $z \in Z_{\log n}$, we check if it is the case that for every $j \in [B]$, $0^j||z$ hashes to 1. If so, the element z is in the set.

Useful Properties of $\mathcal{D}_n$. We will need to use the following useful facts about the distribution $\mathcal{D}_n$ all of which were proven by Shi et al. [54].

Fact 2. *For any fixed $x \in \{0, 1, \ldots, n-1\}$, $\Pr_{S \xleftarrow{\$} \mathcal{D}_n}[x \in S] = \frac{1}{\sqrt{n} \cdot 2^B}$. Moreover,*
$$\mathbb{E}_{S \xleftarrow{\$} \mathcal{D}_n}[|S|] \leq \frac{\sqrt{n}}{log^2 n}.$$

Henceforth, let $\mathcal{D}_n^{+x}$ be the following distribution: sample $S \xleftarrow{\$} \mathcal{D}_n$ subject to $x \in S$. Given $x, y \in \{0,1\}^{\log n}$, we say that x and y are *related*, if they share a common suffix of length at least $\frac{1}{2}\log n + 1$. Given a set $S \subseteq \{0, 1, \ldots, n-1\}$, let $N_{\text{related}}(S, x)$ be the number of elements in S that are related to x.

Fact 3 (Number of related elements in sampled set). *Fix an arbitrary element $x \in \{0, 1, \ldots, n-1\}$. Then,*

$$\mathbb{E}_{S \xleftarrow{\$} \mathcal{D}_n^{+x}}[N_{\text{related}}(S, x)] \leq \frac{1}{log n}$$

Fact 4 (Coverage probability). *Let $m \geq 6\sqrt{n} \cdot log^3 n$. For any fixed $x \in \{0, 1, \ldots, n-1\}$, $\Pr_{S_1, \ldots, S_m \xleftarrow{\$} \mathcal{D}_n^m}[x \notin \cup_{i \in [m]} S_i] \leq 1/n$.*

Henceforth, let $\mathsf{EnumTime}(\mathsf{RO})$ denote the number of RO calls made by the aforementioned set enumeration algorithm to enumerate the set generated by RO.

Fact 5 (Efficient set enumeration). *Suppose that $n \geq 4$. For any fixed $x \in \{0, 1, \ldots, n-1\}$,*

$$\Pr_{\mathsf{RO} \xleftarrow{\$} \mathcal{D}_n^{+x}}\left[\mathsf{EnumTime}(\mathsf{RO}) > 6\sqrt{n}\log^5 n\right] \leq 1/\log n$$

4 Privately Programmable Pseudorandom Set

4.1 Definition

In our Privately Programmable Pseudorandom Set (PRSet) scheme, we can sample a key sk that defines a pseudorandom set. We can support two operations on the key: we can call $\mathbf{Add}(\mathsf{sk}, x)$ to force x to be added to the set, we can also call $\mathbf{ReSamp}(\mathsf{sk}, x)$ to cause the decision whether x is in the set or not to be resampled. The key output by a $\mathbf{ReSamp}$ operation is said to be *final*, i.e., we cannot perform any more operations on it. By contrast, keys output by either $\mathbf{Gen}$ or $\mathbf{Add}$ are said to be *intermediate*, i.e., we can still perform more operations on them. Henceforth, we use the notation rsk to denote a final key and sk to denote an intermediate key. Jumping ahead, later in our PIR scheme, the client always sends to the server a final key during an online query; however, the client locally stores a set of intermediate keys.

- $\mathsf{sk} \leftarrow \mathbf{Gen}(1^\lambda, n)$: given the security parameter 1^λ and the universe size n, samples a secret key sk;
- $S \leftarrow \mathbf{Set}(\mathsf{rsk})$: a deterministic algorithm that outputs a set S given a final secret key rsk;
- $b \leftarrow \mathbf{Member}(\mathsf{sk}, x)$: given an intermediate secret key sk and an element $x \in \{0, 1, \ldots, n-1\}$, output a bit indicating whether $x \in \mathbf{Set}(\mathsf{sk})$;
- $\mathsf{sk}_{+x} \leftarrow \mathbf{Add}(\mathsf{sk}, x)$: given an intermediate secret key sk and an element $x \in \{0, 1, \ldots, n-1\}$, output a secret key sk_{+x} such that $x \in \mathbf{Set}(\mathsf{sk}_{+x})$;
- $\mathsf{rsk}_{-x} \leftarrow \mathbf{ReSamp}(\mathsf{sk}, x)$: given an intermediate secret key sk and an element $x \in \{0, 1, \ldots, n-1\}$, output a final key rsk_{-x} that "resamples" the decision whether x is in the set or not.

We note that a PRSet scheme is parametrized by a family of distributions $\mathcal{D}_n$. The pseudorandom set generated by the PRSet scheme should emulate the distribution $\mathcal{D}_n$—we will define this more formally shortly.

Jumping ahead, later in our application, for each PRSet key sampled using $\mathbf{Gen}$, we perform at most one $\mathbf{Add}$ operation on the key before we perform $\mathbf{ReSamp}$ and obtain a final key.

Efficiency Requirements. Our PRSet scheme samples pseudorandom sets of size roughly $\sqrt{n}$. We want an efficient set enumeration algorithm $\mathbf{Set}(\mathsf{rsk})$ that takes time roughly $\sqrt{n}$ (rather than linear in n). Additionally, we want that the membership test $\mathbf{Member}(\mathsf{sk}, x)$ to complete in polylogarithmic time.

Remark 4.1. We do not give security definitions to our PRSet. Jumping ahead, the privacy proof of our PIR scheme actually opens up the PRSet scheme and relies on the properties of the underlying PRF directly. Nonetheless, abstracting out the PRSet helps to make the description of our PIR scheme conceptually cleaner.

4.2 Construction

We now present our PRSet construction. As mentioned, we assume that for each key sampled through **Gen**, at most one **Add** operation can be performed on the key before we call **ReSamp** which produces a final key.

Intuition for Our PRSet. In our pseudorandom set, we simply replace the RO with a PRF function, such that its description can be compressed using a short key.

Our pseudorandom set supports two additional operations:

– The **Add**(sk, x) operation modifies the secret key sk such that the element $x \in \{0,1\}^{\log n}$ is forced to be in the set. In our construction, this is done in the most naïve way: simply attach the element x to the secret key. This will be fine in our PIR construction since the intermediate key generated by **Add** is stored only on the client side and never sent to the server. Therefore, we do not need the resulting key to hide the point x that is added.

– The **ReSamp**(sk, x) operation takes in an intermediate key that is either the output of **Gen** or the output of a previous **Add** operation, and it resamples the decision whether the element $x \in \{0,1\}^{\log n}$ is in the set or not. In our PIR scheme later, this resampled key will be sent to the server during online queries. Therefore, we want the resulting key to hide not only the element x that is being resampled, but also the element x' that was added earlier should the input key sk be the result of a previous **Add**(_, x') operation.

In our construction, this is accomplished in the following way. First, we sample at random the answers $\{v_i\}_{i \in [\frac{\log n}{2} + B]}$—we want to force the PRF's evaluation at points $\{(0^B || x)[i :]\}_{i \in [\frac{\log n}{2} + B]}$ to be the values $\{v_i\}_{i \in [\frac{\log n}{2} + B]}$. Next, if the input key sk is the result of a previous **Add**(_, x') operation, for any point $(0^B || x')[i :]$ where $i \in [\frac{\log n}{2} + B]$, if $(0^B || x')[i :] \neq (0^B || x)[i :]$, then we want to force the PRF's evaluation on $(0^B || x')[i :]$ to be 1. Finally, we call the underlying PRF's **Prog** function, to force the aforementioned outcomes on all the relevant points. Clearly, the total number of constraints to be forced is at most $L = 2(\frac{\log n}{2} + B)$.

Detailed Construction. We describe our PRSet construction below.

PRSet Scheme

Parameters: $B := \lceil 2 \log \log n \rceil$, $L = 2(\frac{\log n}{2} + B)$.

– sk $\leftarrow$ **Gen**($1^\lambda, n$): call msk $\leftarrow$ PRF.**Gen**($1^\lambda, L$), and output sk := (msk, $\perp$).

– $S \leftarrow$ **Set**(rsk): Same as the set enumeration algorithm in Sect. 3.3, except that the calls to RO($\cdot$) are now replaced with calls to PRF.**PEval**(rsk, $\cdot$).

– $b \leftarrow$ **Member**(sk, x):
  1. Parse sk := (msk', x'). Write $x \in \{0,1\}^{\log n}$ as a binary string and let $z := 0^B || x$. If $x' \neq \perp$, write $x' \in \{0,1\}^{\log n}$ as a binary string and let $z' := 0^B || x'$.

---

2. Output 1 if for every $i \in [\frac{\log n}{2} + B]$, the following holds: either PRF.$\mathbf{Eval}(\mathsf{msk}', z[i :]) = 1$ or $(x' \neq \bot$ and $z[i :] = z'[i :])$. Else, output 0.

- $\mathsf{sk}_{+x} \leftarrow \mathbf{Add}(\mathsf{sk}, x)$: parse $\mathsf{sk} := (\mathsf{msk}', \bot)$, and output $\mathsf{sk}_{+x} := (\mathsf{msk}', x)$.
- $\mathsf{rsk}_{-x} \leftarrow \mathbf{ReSamp}(\mathsf{sk}, x)$:
  1. Parse $\mathsf{sk} := (\mathsf{msk}', x')$, and write $x \in \{0, 1\}^{\log n}$ as a binary string and let $z := 0^B || x$.
  2. Sample uniformly random $v \xleftarrow{\$} \{0, 1\}^{\frac{\log n}{2} + B}$, and let $P := \{(z[i :], v[i])\}_{i \in [\frac{\log n}{2} + B]}$.
  3. If $x' \neq \bot$, do the following. Write $x' \in \{0, 1\}^{\log n}$ as a binary string, and let $z' := 0^B || x'$. For $i \in [\frac{\log n}{2} + B]$, if $z'[i :] \neq z[i :]$, add the constraint $(z'[i :], 1)$ to the set P.
  4. Compute $\mathsf{rsk}_{-x} \leftarrow$ PRF.$\mathbf{Prog}(\mathsf{msk}', P)$, and output rsk_{-x}.

Additional Helpful Notations. In our PIR scheme later, we will only need to call set enumeration for final keys rsk. Therefore, our algorithm description above defines $\mathbf{Set}(\mathsf{rsk})$ only for final keys. However, in our proofs and narratives, it helps to define the set associated with an intermediate key sk as well—however, in this case we need not worry about the running time of $\mathbf{Set}(\mathsf{sk})$. This is defined in the most natural manner:

- If $\mathsf{sk} = (\mathsf{msk}, \bot)$ is the direct output of $\mathbf{Gen}(1^\lambda, n)$, then $\mathbf{Set}(\mathsf{sk})$ is defined just like in Sect. 3.3 except that calls to $\mathsf{RO}(\cdot)$ are replaced with PRF.$\mathbf{Eval}(\mathsf{msk}, \cdot)$;
- If $\mathsf{sk} = (\mathsf{msk}, x)$ is the output of an earlier $\mathbf{Add}$ operation, then $\mathbf{Set}(\mathsf{sk})$ is defined just like in Sect. 3.3 except that calls to $\mathsf{RO}(\cdot)$ are replaced with the following outcomes: 1) we force the outcomes to be 1 at the input points $\{(0^B || x)[i :]\}_{i \in [\frac{\log n}{2} + B]}$; and 2) for all other inputs, we call PRF.$\mathbf{Eval}(\mathsf{msk}, \cdot)$ to obtain the outcome.

Performance Bounds. $\mathbf{Gen}(1^\lambda, n)$ takes $\mathsf{poly}(\lambda, \log n)$ time. Due to Fact 5, $\mathbf{Set}(\mathsf{rsk})$ takes $\sqrt{n} \cdot \mathsf{poly}\log(\lambda, n)$ time with $1 - 1/\log n$ probability. $\mathbf{Member}(\mathsf{sk}, x)$ takes $\mathsf{poly}(\lambda, \log n)$ time. $\mathbf{Add}(\mathsf{sk}, x)$ takes constant time. $\mathbf{ReSamp}(\mathsf{sk}, x)$ takes $\mathsf{poly}(\lambda, \log n)$ time.

Circuit for Set Enumeration. Later in our PIR scheme, during the offline phase, the server needs to perform set enumeration under fully homomorphic encryption. Therefore, we need to describe how to perform set enumeration in circuit. We will describe a circuit construction of size at most $\sqrt{n} \cdot \mathsf{poly}(\lambda, \log n)$ which obtains as input a final key rsk, and outputs a set $S = \{(x_1, b_1), (x_2, b_2), \dots\}$ of size at most $2\sqrt{n}\log^2 n$ with distinct x's, and a bit bSucc indicating success. We want to ensure that if $\mathsf{bSucc} = \mathsf{True}$, then the set generated is correct in the following sense:

- for every $(x, 1) \in S$, x is in the correct set defined by PRF.$\mathbf{PEval}(\mathsf{rsk}, \cdot)$; and
- for every element x in the set defined by PRF.$\mathbf{PEval}(\mathsf{rsk}, \cdot)$, the pair $(x, 1)$ appears in S.

Our circuit construction emulates the set enumeration algorithm of Sect. 3.3.

Our circuit construction works as follows—henceforth we use the term "hash" to mean the computing outcome of PRF.**PEval**(rsk, $\cdot$):

Circuit for set enumeration CSetEnum

1. Let bSucc = True.
2. For every $x \in \{0,1\}^{\frac{1}{2}\log n+1}$, let $b_x = $ PRF.**PEval**(rsk, x). Output an array containing $\{(x, b_x)\}_{x \in \{0,1\}^{\frac{1}{2}\log n+1}}$.
3. Obliviously sort above array such that entries with $b_x = 1$ are moved to the front. Truncate the array at length $2\sqrt{n}\log^2 n$ elements, and if the truncation removes any string that hash to 1, set bSucc = False. Let $Z_{\frac{1}{2}\log n+1}$ be the resulting truncated array, where each entry is of the form (x, b_x).
4. For $\ell = \frac{1}{2}\log n + 2$ to $\log n$, do the following:
   - For each $(x, b_x) \in Z_{\ell-1}$, if $b_x = 1$, write down $(0||x, \mathsf{PRF}.\mathbf{PEval}(\mathsf{rsk}, 0||x))$ and $(1||x, \mathsf{PRF}.\mathbf{PEval}(\mathsf{rsk}, 1||x))$; else write down $(0||x, 0)$ and $(1||x, 0)$.
   - Oblivious sort the resulting array such that all entries marked with 1 move to the front. Truncate the resulting array at length exactly $2\sqrt{n}\log^2 n$. If the truncation removes any string that hash to 1, set bSucc = False. Let Z_ℓ denote the resulting array where each entry is of the form (x, b_x).
5. For every $(x, b_x) \in Z_{\log n}$, check if it is the case that for every $j \in [B]$, PRF.**PEval**(rsk, $0^j || x$) = 1. If so, write down (x, b_x), else, write down $(x, 0)$. Output the resulting array as well as bSucc.

Fact 6. *Using the AKS sorting network [2] or the bitonic sorting network [6] to realize the oblivious sort, the above algorithm can be implemented with a circuit of size $\sqrt{n} \cdot \mathbf{poly}(\lambda, \log n)$.*

Proof. The proof is straightforward given the fact that the AKS sorting circuit has size $O(n'\log n')$ for sorting n' elements, and the bitonic sorting network has size $O(n'\log^2 n')$. Also, note that each **PEval**(rsk, $\cdot$) consumes $\mathsf{poly}(\lambda, \log n)$ gates to implement.

For correctness, we will imagine that the above algorithm is run where PRF.**PEval**(rsk, $\cdot$) is replaced with calls to a random oracle RO— we denote the resulting algorithm as CSetEnum^{RO}. Note that we do not care about the computational model when stating the correctness probability.

Fact 7. *Suppose that $n \geq 4$. For any $x \in \{0, 1, \ldots, n-1\}$,*

$$\Pr_{\mathsf{RO} \overset{\$}{\leftarrow} \mathcal{D}_n^{+x}} \left[\mathsf{CSetEnum}^{\mathsf{RO}} outputs\ \mathsf{bSucc} = \mathsf{True} \right] \geq 1 - 1/\log n,$$

Moreover,

$$\Pr_{\mathsf{RO} \xleftarrow{\$} \mathcal{D}_n} \left[\mathsf{CSetEnum}^{\mathsf{RO}} \, outputs \, \mathsf{bSucc} = \mathsf{True} \right] \geq 1 - 1/\log n$$

Proof. $\mathsf{CSetEnum}^{\mathsf{RO}}$ is a direct implementation of the set enumeration algorithm in Sect. 3.3 except that we truncate each Z_ℓ to size exactly $2\sqrt{n}\log^2 n$. Shi et al. [54] proved that no matter whether RO is sampled from $\mathcal{D}_n^{+x}$ or $\mathcal{D}_n$, with $1 - 1/\log n$ probability, the following good event holds: for all $\ell \in [\frac{\log n}{2} + 1, \log n]$, $|Z_\ell| \leq 2\sqrt{n}\log^2 n$—see the proof of Lemma 6.4 in their paper. The algorithm outputs $\mathsf{bSucc} = 1$ as long as the above good event holds.

5   PIR Scheme

We now describe a PIR scheme that supports a bounded number of queries denoted Q. Given this scheme, we can compile it to a scheme that supports unbounded number of queries by performing the offline setup phase every Q queries, and amortizing this cost over the Q queries.

Intuition. In the offline setup phase, the client chooses $\widetilde{O}(Q)$ keys each of which defines a pseudorandom set of size roughly $\sqrt{n}$. It encrypts these keys under a fully homomorphic encryption (FHE) scheme, and sends the encrypted keys to the server. Through homomorphic evaluation, the server enumerates the sets and computes the encrypted parity (i.e., an encryption of $\oplus_{x \in S} \mathsf{DB}[x]$) for each of these sets S, and returns the encrypted parities to the client. The client decrypts the parities, and stores each set's key as well as its parity. These sets are divided into two parts: the last Q entries are called the *backup* sets or entries, and the remaining are called the *primary* sets or entries. The primary entries are used for answering queries, whereas the backup entries are later promoted to become primary entries as they get consumed. Henceforth, we also use the terms primary table and backup table to refer to the tables that store all primary entries and backup entries, respectively.

In the online phase, whenever the client wants to make a query for the database's value at index $x \in \{0, 1, \ldots, n - 1\}$, it finds the first primary set (sk_i, p_i) such that $\mathbf{Set}(\mathsf{sk}_i)$ contains the query x. It then resamples the decision whether x is in the set or not, and obtains a programmed key. It sends this programmed key to the server, which calls the set enumeration algorithm to enumerate the set S generated by the key. The server then returns the parity p of the set S to the client. The client computes $p_i \oplus p$ as the candidate answer to the query. Since the resampling operation removes the element x from the set with high probability, the candidate answer is correct with high probability. The correctness probability can be further boosted by repeating the same scheme k times and taking the majority vote among the k copies.

Detailed Construction. We describe the detailed construction below.

PIR Scheme for $Q = \sqrt{n}$ queries

Run $k = \omega(\log \lambda)$ parallel copies of the single-copy scheme described below.

Offline phase:

– **Client:**   // let $\mathsf{lenT} := 6\sqrt{n} \cdot \log^3 n$
   • $\mathsf{fsk} \leftarrow \mathsf{FHE.Gen}(1^\lambda)$;
   • For $i \in [k \cdot (\mathsf{lenT} + Q)]$ where $k = \omega(\log \lambda)$, $\mathsf{sk}_i \leftarrow \mathsf{PRSet.Gen}(1^\lambda, n)$, $\overline{\mathsf{sk}}_i \leftarrow \mathsf{FHE.Enc}(\mathsf{fsk}, \mathsf{sk}_i)$;
   • Send $(\overline{\mathsf{sk}}_1, \ldots, \overline{\mathsf{sk}}_{k \cdot (\mathsf{lenT}+Q)})$ to the server.
– **Server:**
   • For $i \in [k \cdot (\mathsf{lenT} + Q)]$, $(\overline{S}_i, \overline{\mathsf{bSucc}}_i) \leftarrow \mathsf{FHE.Eval}(\mathsf{CSetEnum}, \overline{\mathsf{sk}}_i)$;
   • $\{\overline{p}_i\}_{i \in [k \cdot (\mathsf{lenT}+Q)]}$ $\leftarrow$
     $\mathsf{FHE.Eval}(\mathsf{CBatchParity}, \overline{S}_1, \ldots, \overline{S}_{k \cdot (\mathsf{lenT}+Q)})$, where the $\mathsf{CBatchParity}$ circuit is described below. Send $\{\overline{p}_i, \overline{\mathsf{bSucc}}_i\}_{i \in [k \cdot (\mathsf{lenT}+Q)]}$ to the client.
– **Client:**
   • for $i \in [k \cdot (\mathsf{lenT} + Q)]$, $p_i \leftarrow \mathsf{FHE.Dec}(\mathsf{fsk}, \overline{p}_i)$; $\mathsf{bSucc}_i \leftarrow \mathsf{FHE.Dec}(\mathsf{fsk}, \overline{\mathsf{bSucc}}_i)$;
   • choose a subset $I \subseteq [k \cdot (\mathsf{lenT}+Q)]$ of size exactly $\mathsf{lenT} + Q$ such that for any $i \in I$, $\mathsf{bSucc}_i = \mathsf{True}$—if not enough such entries are found, simply abort. Copy $\{(\mathsf{sk}_i, p_i)\}_{i \in I}$ to a table.
   We call the last Q entries of the above table the *backup* table, henceforth renamed to $T^* := \{(\mathsf{sk}_i^*, p_i^*)\}_{i \in [Q]}$. We call the remaining lenT entries the *primary* table, henceforth renamed to $T := \{(\mathsf{sk}_i, p_i)\}_{i \in [\mathsf{lenT}]}$.

Online query for index $x \in \{0, \ldots, n-1\}$:

– **Client:**
   • Sample $\mathsf{sk} \leftarrow \mathsf{PRSet.Gen}(1^\lambda, n)$ subject to $\mathsf{PRSet.Member}(\mathsf{sk}, x) = 1$ and append the entry $(\mathsf{sk}, 0)$ to the table T of primary sets;
   • Find the first entry (sk_i, p_i) in T such that $\mathsf{PRSet.Member}(\mathsf{sk}_i, x) = 1$;
   • Compute $\mathsf{rsk} \leftarrow \mathsf{PRSet.ReSamp}(\mathsf{sk}_i, x)$ and send rsk to the server.
– **Server:** Compute $S \leftarrow \mathsf{PRSet.Set}(\mathsf{rsk})$, and return the parity bit p of the set S to the client. If the set enumeration algorithm has not completed even after making $6\sqrt{n}\log^5 n$ calls to the underlying PRF's $\mathbf{PEval}(\mathsf{rsk}, \cdot)$ function, then return $p = 0$ to the client.
– **Client:** let $\beta' := p \oplus p_i$ be the candidate answer of the current copy, and remove the last entry of T.
   Recall that there are k parallel instances, and let β be the majority vote among the candidate answers of all k copies. Now, let (sk_j^*, p_j^*) denote the next available backup set and perform the following:

- let $\mathsf{sk}' \leftarrow \mathsf{PRSet}.\mathbf{Add}(\mathsf{sk}_j^*, x)$; let $p' := p_j^* \oplus \beta$ if $\mathbf{Member}(\mathsf{sk}_j^*, x) = 0$, else let $p' := p_j^*$;
- let $T_j := (\mathsf{sk}', p')$, and mark the backup entry (sk_j^*, p_j^*) as unavailable.

The Circuit CBatchParity. The circuit CBatchParity takes $S_1, S_2, \ldots, S_{k \cdot (\mathsf{lenT} + Q)}$ as input, where for $j \in [k \cdot (\mathsf{lenT} + Q)]$, S_j contains exactly $2\sqrt{n}\log^2 n$ entries of the form (x, b_x)—specifically, $b_x = \mathsf{True}$ implies that x is the j-th set and $b_x = \mathsf{False}$ implies x is not in the j-th set[3]. The circuit outputs $k \cdot (\mathsf{lenT} + Q)$ parity bits $p_1, \ldots, p_{k \cdot (\mathsf{lenT} + Q)}$ of each of the $k \cdot (\mathsf{lenT} + Q)$ sets.

The circuit can be constructed as follows using oblivious sort:

1. Let $\mathsf{DB} \in \{0, 1\}^n$ be the server's database, let $\mathbf{D} := ((0, \mathsf{DB}[0]), (1, \mathsf{DB}[1]), \ldots, (n - 1, \mathsf{DB}[n - 1]))$.
2. For $j \in [k \cdot (\mathsf{lenT} + Q)]$, let $\mathbf{X}_j = \{(x, b_x, j)\}_{x \in S_j}$
3. Obliviously sort the array $\mathbf{Y} := \mathbf{D} \| \mathbf{X}_1 \| \ldots \| \mathbf{X}_{k \cdot (\mathsf{lenT} + Q)}$, such that each entry of the form $(x, \mathsf{DB}[x])$ is followed by all tuples of the form (x, b_x, j). Henceforth, we call a tuple of the form (x, b_x, j) a consumer.
4. In a linear scan, all consumers receive the $\mathsf{DB}[x]$ they are requesting. At this moment, each consumer entry is updated to $(x, b_x, j, \mathsf{DB}[x])$.
5. Use a circuit that mirrors the oblivious sort circuit in Step 3, and reverse-routes the $\mathsf{DB}[x]$ values back to the position where it came from. As a result, each consumer entry of the form $(x, b_x, j) \in \mathbf{Y}$ receives $\mathsf{DB}[x]$.
6. At this moment, we have an array of the form $\mathbf{X}_1' \| \ldots \| \mathbf{X}_{k \cdot (\mathsf{lenT} + Q)}'$, where each $\mathbf{X}_j'$ contains exactly $2\sqrt{n}\log^2 n$ entries of the form $(x, b_x, j, \mathsf{DB}[x])$. In a linear scan, we can compute for each $j \in [k \cdot (\mathsf{lenT} + Q)]$, the parity bit

$$p_j = \oplus_{(x, b_x, j, \mathsf{DB}[x]) \in \mathbf{X}_j'} (b_x \cdot \mathsf{DB}[x])$$

It is not hard to see that if we instantiate the oblivious sort using either AKS [2] or bitonic sort [6], and given $\mathsf{lenT} = 6\sqrt{n}\log^3 n$ and $Q = \sqrt{n}$, the above circuit has size $O(n \cdot \mathsf{poly} \log n)$.

Performance Bounds. We now analyze the performance bounds of our Q-bounded PIR construction. We may plug in $k = \log^{1.1} n$ since any super-logarithmic function will work. In the analysis below, the k parameter is absorbed in the $\mathsf{poly} \log n$ term, so it does not show up explicitly.

- *Offline phase.* During the offline phase, the client's computation and bandwidth are upper bounded by $\sqrt{n} \cdot \mathsf{poly}(\lambda, \log n)$. The server's computation is upper bounded by $n \cdot \mathsf{poly}(\lambda, \log n)$.
- *Online phase.* The bandwidth is $\mathsf{poly}(\lambda, \log n)$. The client's computation is $\sqrt{n} \cdot \mathsf{poly}(\lambda, \log n)$. The server's computation is also $\sqrt{n} \cdot \mathsf{poly}(\lambda, \log n)$.

---

[3] This input format is inherited from the output format of the circuit CSetEnum.

Supporting Unbounded Number of Queries and Deamortization. To extend the scheme from Q-bounded to supporting an unbounded number of queries, we just need to rerun the offline phase every $Q = \sqrt{n}$ queries. For the scheme with unbounded queries, the amortized bandwidth per query is $\mathsf{poly}\,(\lambda, \log n)$, the amortized client and server computation per query is $\sqrt{n} \cdot \mathsf{poly}\,(\lambda, \log n)$.

This periodic offline setup can be deamortized very easily. Specially, upfront, we perform the offline setup for $2Q$ queries. During the i-th window of Q queries, we perform the offline setup for the $(i + 2)$-th window of Q queries, and so on. This way, when the $(i + 2)$-th window of Q queries starts, the corresponding offline setup will be ready. With deamortization, there is a factor of 2 blowup in storage. There is no additional blowup in terms of amortized computational cost.

6   Privacy Proof

Recall that privacy for a single-server PIR scheme was defined earlier in Sect. 3.2. We now prove that our PIR scheme in Sect. 5, when instantiated with the PRSet scheme in Sect. 4.2, satisfies privacy, as stated in the following theorem.

Theorem 6.1 (Privacy of our PIR scheme). *Suppose that the FHE scheme employed satisfies semantic security, and that the underlying programmable PRF scheme satisfies correctness, private programmability, and simulation security.*

Then, the PIR scheme in Sect. 5, when instantiated with the PRSet scheme in Sect. 4.2, satisfies privacy.

In the remainder of this section, we will prove the above theorem.

6.1   Proof Roadmap

A key insight in our privacy proof is to rely on a *lazy sampling* technique to decompose the *backend* and the *frontend* of a complicated randomized experiment, where the *backend* refers to the primary table stored by the client, and the *frontend* refers to the message the clients sends to the server during each query. Below, we explain the proof intuition, and the formal proofs can be found in Sect. 6.2 and Appendix C.3 of the online full version [56].

We start from the real-world experiment, where the client interacts with the server like in the real-world scheme. First, in Hyb_1, we replace the FHE ciphertexts the client sends to the server in the offline phase with encryptions of 0. Therefore, henceforth we will not be worried about these FHE ciphertexts, and we will focus on what happens in the online phase. In our full proof in Appendix C.3 of the online full version [56], the key is how to get from Hyb_2 to Hyb_6, which are described below.

If we can get to Hyb_6, the rest of the proof can be completed in a similar manner as Shi et al. [54]'s proof. Therefore, the key is how to get from Hyb_2 to Hyb_6. To accomplish this, we introduce a lazy sampling idea to "decouple" the backend and the frontend in our proof.

Table 2. Hyb$_2$ and Hyb$_6$.

Hybrid	Backend	Frontend
	promoted key during query y	during query x
Hyb$_2$	msk $\leftarrow$ **Gen**, sk $:=$ (msk, y)	– find sk $:=$ (msk, y) in T s.t. msk contains x after adding y if $y \neq \perp$
		– program msk s.t. suffixes(x) are resampled and if $y \neq \perp$, suffixes(y)\suffixes(x) forced to 1
Hyb$_6$	msk $\leftarrow$ **Gen** s.t. $y \in$ **Set**(msk)	– find msk in T s.t. $x \in$ **Set**(msk),
		– program msk s.t. suffixes(x) are resampled

Hyb$_3$: *Introduce Lazy Sampling.* We define a hybrid experiment Hyb$_3$ that is an equivalent rewrite of Hyb$_2$ by lazy sampling in the following sense.

1. *Backend: maintain constraints on each entry in T that defines the a-posteriori distribution.* Let $\mathbf{I} = \{i_1, i_2, \ldots, i_q\}$ be the indices of the entries that are matched during each of the $q \leq Q$ queries so far. The client maintains the a-posteriori distribution of each entry of the primary table T conditioned on the local observation $\mathbf{I}$.

   To maintain the a-posteriori distribution, the client maintains a set of constraints of the form $\langle -x \rangle$, $\langle +x \rangle$, $\langle +y : -x \rangle$, or $\langle +y : +x \rangle$ on each entry. A negative constraint of the form $\langle -x \rangle$ means that this entry was not promoted from the backup table, and we have checked that x is not in the set generated by the key, during some query for x. A negative constraint of the form $\langle +y : -x \rangle$ means that this entry was promoted from the backup table during a query for y, and we have checked that after forcing y to be in the set, x is not in the set generated by the key. The positive constraints $\langle +x \rangle$ and $\langle +y : +x \rangle$ are similarly defined but requiring x to be in the set.

   During an online query for some x, the client sequentially scans through the current entries of T. For each entry j, it samples from the a-posteriori distribution to decide if j should be the match. Depending on the decision, it adds either a negative or positive constraint to the current entry.

2. *Frontend: lazy sampling from the a-posteriori distribution.* Whenever the client is about to send a key to the server, it performs lazy sampling of the key based on the a-posteriori distribution on the entry that the client has maintained. More specifically, there are two cases depending on whether the matched entry comes from the backup table or not : 1) it samples a key from the correct a-posteriori distribution, calls **ReSamp** and sends the resulting key to the server; 2) it samples a key from the correct a-posteriori distribution, calls both **Add** and **ReSamp**, and then sends the resulting key to the server.

In our proof, we show that except with negligible probability, the constraints maintained on any entry can be satisfied with inverse polynomial probability for a randomly sampled key.

Hyb_4: *Switch the Backend.* Next, in Hyb_4, we change the backend to be like in Hyb_6, and the client uses the resulting table T to decide which entries are matched during each query, and just like in Hyb_3, the client maintains a set of constraints on each entry of the table, such that the frontend can perform lazy sampling according to the a-posteriori distribution when interacting with the server. Note that this change technically affects the distribution of the matched entries during each query, and thus affects the distribution of the server's view. Fortunately, using the security of the privately programmable PRF, we can prove that even when we make this change on the backend, the server's view remains computationally indistinguishable[4].

Hyb_4 *to* Hyb_6: *Switch the Frontend.* Next, from Hyb_4 to Hyb_6, we change the way the frontend performs the lazy sampling from the method of Hyb_3 to the method of Hyb_6. To complete this proof, we do it in two steps using Hyb_5 as a stepping stone. In Hyb_4, after lazy sampling a key according to the maintained constraints, we program suffixes(x) to be random values and if $y \neq \bot$, we program suffixes$(y)\backslash$suffixes(x) to be 1. In Hyb_5, we remove all the programming and replace it with rejection sampling of simulated keys. In Hyb_6, we introduce back the part of the programming, and we program only suffixes(x) to be random values, while the part suffixes$(y)\backslash$suffixes(x) being forced to be 1 is achieved through rejection sampling. To show that Hyb_4 and Hyb_5 are computationally indistinguishable and that Hyb_5 and Hyb_6 are computationally indistinguishable, we need to make use of the security property of the privately programmable PRF. Some technicalities arise in this proof, since the security definitions of the privately programmable PRF are not in a form that we can use conveniently here. Therefore, as a key stepping stone, we introduce a *key technical lemma* (see Sect. 6.2), that will help us prove the transitions between Hyb_4 and Hyb_5, and between Hyb_5 and Hyb_6 more easily. Further, this key technical lemma can be proven using the security definitions of the privately programmable PRF.

Hyb_6: *Convergence of Backend and Frontend.* One important observation is that in Hyb_b, the frontend and the entry found in the table during each query have the same distribution (modular some post-processing). Therefore, in this step, the backend and the frontend converge again, and this is why we can undo the lazy sampling at this point, and Hyb_6 can be equivalently viewed as in Table 2.

6.2 Technical Lemma for Privately Programmable PRF

We shall consider a programmable PRF whose output range is binary, i.e., $\{0, 1\}$. Henceforth, we use the notation $\mathsf{pred}^X(\mathsf{msk})$ to denote an event that looks at the outputs of PRF.$\mathbf{Eval}(\mathsf{msk}, \cdot)$ at all inputs in X, and outputs either 0 or 1.

---

[4] Note that we need NOT prove that the joint distribution of the backend and the frontend are computationally indistinguishable, we only need to prove that the frontend, i.e., server's view is computationally indistinguishable.

We say that $\mathsf{pred}^X(\cdot)$ is an *admissible* event, iff 1) for a randomly sampled $\mathsf{msk} \leftarrow \mathbf{Gen}(1^\lambda, L)$, it returns 1 with probability at least $1/p(\lambda)$ for some polynomial function $p(\cdot)$; and 2) pred is polynomial-time checkable.

Lemma 6.2 (Strong privacy of programmable PRF). *Let* PRF *be a programmable PRF with a binary output range, and suppose that $L = O(\log \lambda)$. Suppose that* PRF *satisfies private programmability and simulation security. Then, there exists a probabilistic polynomial-time simulator* Sim *such that the following two experiments are computationally indistinguishable to any probabilistic polynomial-time adversary.*

- RealPPRFStrong(1^λ):
  - $X, X', \{v_x\}_{x \in X'}, \mathsf{pred}^{X \cup X'} \leftarrow \mathcal{A}(1^\lambda, L)$ *s.t.* $|X| + |X'| \leq L$, $X \cap X' = \emptyset$, *and* $\mathsf{pred}^{X \cup X'}(\cdot)$ *is admissible;*
  - *for* $x \in X$, *let* $v_x \overset{\$}{\leftarrow} \mathcal{V}$; *let* $P := \{(x, v_x)\}_{x \in X \cup X'}$;
  - *sample* $\mathsf{msk} \leftarrow \mathbf{Gen}(1^\lambda, L)$ *subject to* $\mathsf{pred}^{X \cup X'}(\mathsf{msk}) = 1$, *and let* $\mathsf{sk} \leftarrow \mathbf{Prog}(\mathsf{msk}, P)$;
  - $\mathsf{sk} \to \mathcal{A}$;
- IdealPPRFStrong(1^λ):
  - $X, X', \{v_x\}_{x \in X'}, \mathsf{pred}^{X \cup X'} \leftarrow \mathcal{A}(1^\lambda, L)$ *s.t.* $|X| + |X'| \leq L$, $X \cap X' = \emptyset$, *and* $\mathsf{pred}^{X \cup X'}(\cdot)$ *is admissible;*
  - *sample* $\mathsf{sk} \leftarrow \mathsf{Sim}(1^\lambda, L)$ *subject to the constraint that for any* $x \in X'$, $\mathbf{PEval}(\mathsf{sk}, x) = v_x$;
  - $\mathsf{sk} \to \mathcal{A}$.

In the real experiment RealPPRFStrong, we sample a random key subject to some admissible predicate on X and X', and then program X to be random and program X' to be values of the adversary $\mathcal{A}$'s choice (e.g., all 1s). The lemma states that the real experiment RealPPRFStrong is computationally indistinguishable from an ideal experiment IdealPPRFStrong where we simply sample a random simulated key subject to the set of points X' evaluating to the choices specified by $\mathcal{A}$. Note that in IdealPPRFStrong, we do not perform any programming at all, and replace it with rejection sampling that checks if the set of points in X' evaluate to the choices specified by $\mathcal{A}$.

The intuition is the following. In the real experiment, we sample an msk subject to some predicate pred. The observation is that it does not matter what predicate pred we check, since we eventually reprogram the points in $X \cup X'$, and recall that we require the predicate pred to only look at the PRF's outcomes on $X \cup X'$. Effectively, the reprogramming cancels the effect of the sampling subject to a predicate pred that looks at only $X \cup X'$. In fact, the distribution of the final programmed key is indistinguishable from the ideal experiment, where we simply sample a simulated key that evaluates to adversary-specified values on the set X'.

Deferred Materials

We defer the full privacy proof, the correctness proof of our PIR scheme, how to tune the tradeoff between client storage and the online computation, as well as additional preliminaries to the appendices of the online full version [56].

Acknowledgments. This work is in part supported by a grant from ONR, a gift from Cisco, NSF awards under grant numbers CIF-1705007, 2128519 and 2044679, and a Packard Fellowship. The work is also supported by DARPA SIEVE research program.

References

1. Aiello, W., Bhatt, S., Ostrovsky, R., Rajagopalan, S.R.: Fast verification of any remote procedure call: short witness-indistinguishable one-round proofs for NP. In: Montanari, U., Rolim, J.D.P., Welzl, E. (eds.) ICALP 2000. LNCS, vol. 1853, pp. 463–474. Springer, Heidelberg (2000). https://doi.org/10.1007/3-540-45022-X_39
2. Ajtai, M., Komlós, J., Szemerédi, E.: An $O(n \log n)$ sorting network. In: 15th ACM STOC, pp. 1–9. ACM Press, April 1983. https://doi.org/10.1145/800061.808726
3. Albab, K.D., Issa, R., Varia, M., Graffi, K.: Batched differentially private information retrieval. In: Butler, K.R.B., Thomas, K. (eds.) USENIX Security 2022, pp. 3327–3344. USENIX Association, August 2022
4. Angel, S., Chen, H., Laine, K., Setty, S.T.V.: PIR with compressed queries and amortized query processing. In: 2018 IEEE Symposium on Security and Privacy, pp. 962–979. IEEE Computer Society Press, May 2018. https://doi.org/10.1109/SP.2018.00062
5. Bartusek, J., Khurana, D.: Cryptography with certified deletion. Cryptology ePrint Archive, Report 2022/1178 (2022). https://eprint.iacr.org/2022/1178
6. Batcher, K.E.: Sorting networks and their applications. In: AFIPS (1968). https://doi.org/10.1145/1468075.1468121
7. Beimel, A., Ishai, Y., Malkin, T.: Reducing the servers computation in private information retrieval: PIR with preprocessing. In: Bellare, M. (ed.) CRYPTO 2000. LNCS, vol. 1880, pp. 55–73. Springer, Heidelberg (2000). https://doi.org/10.1007/3-540-44598-6_4
8. Biehl, I., Meyer, B., Wetzel, S.: Ensuring the integrity of agent-based computations by short proofs. In: Rothermel, K., Hohl, F. (eds.) MA 1998. LNCS, vol. 1477, pp. 183–194. Springer, Heidelberg (1998). https://doi.org/10.1007/BFb0057658
9. Boneh, D., Kim, S., Montgomery, H.: Private puncturable PRFs from standard lattice assumptions. In: Coron, J.-S., Nielsen, J.B. (eds.) EUROCRYPT 2017. LNCS, vol. 10210, pp. 415–445. Springer, Cham (2017). https://doi.org/10.1007/978-3-319-56620-7_15
10. Boneh, D., Lewi, K., Wu, D.J.: Constraining pseudorandom functions privately. In: Fehr, S. (ed.) PKC 2017. LNCS, vol. 10175, pp. 494–524. Springer, Heidelberg (2017). https://doi.org/10.1007/978-3-662-54388-7_17
11. Boyle, E., Gilboa, N., Ishai, Y.: Function secret sharing: improvements and extensions. In: Weippl, E.R., Katzenbeisser, S., Kruegel, C., Myers, A.C., Halevi, S. (eds.) ACM CCS 2016, pp. 1292–1303. ACM Press, October 2016. https://doi.org/10.1145/2976749.2978429

12. Boyle, E., Gilboa, N., Ishai, Y., Kolobov, V.I.: Programmable distributed point functions. In: Dodis, Y., Shrimpton, T. (eds.) CRYPTO 2022, Part IV. LNCS, vol. 13510, pp. 121–151. Springer, Heidelberg, August 2022. https://doi.org/10.1007/978-3-031-15985-5_5

13. Boyle, E., Ishai, Y., Pass, R., Wootters, M.: Can we access a database both locally and privately? In: Kalai, Y., Reyzin, L. (eds.) TCC 2017. LNCS, vol. 10678, pp. 662–693. Springer, Cham (2017). https://doi.org/10.1007/978-3-319-70503-3_22

14. Brakerski, Z., Tsabary, R., Vaikuntanathan, V., Wee, H.: Private constrained PRFs (and more) from LWE. In: Kalai, Y., Reyzin, L. (eds.) TCC 2017. LNCS, vol. 10677, pp. 264–302. Springer, Cham (2017). https://doi.org/10.1007/978-3-319-70500-2_10

15. Cachin, C., Micali, S., Stadler, M.: Computationally private information retrieval with polylogarithmic communication. In: Stern, J. (ed.) EUROCRYPT 1999. LNCS, vol. 1592, pp. 402–414. Springer, Heidelberg (1999). https://doi.org/10.1007/3-540-48910-X_28

16. Canetti, R., Chen, Y.: Constraint-hiding constrained PRFs for NC^1 from LWE. In: Coron, J.-S., Nielsen, J.B. (eds.) EUROCRYPT 2017. LNCS, vol. 10210, pp. 446–476. Springer, Cham (2017). https://doi.org/10.1007/978-3-319-56620-7_16

17. Canetti, R., Holmgren, J., Richelson, S.: Towards doubly efficient private information retrieval. In: Kalai, Y., Reyzin, L. (eds.) TCC 2017. LNCS, vol. 10678, pp. 694–726. Springer, Cham (2017). https://doi.org/10.1007/978-3-319-70503-3_23

18. de Castro, L., Polychroniadou, A.: Lightweight, maliciously secure verifiable function secret sharing. In: Dunkelman, O., Dziembowski, S. (eds.) EUROCRYPT 2022, Part I. LNCS, vol. 13275, pp. 150–179. Springer, Heidelberg, May/June 2022. https://doi.org/10.1007/978-3-031-06944-4_6

19. Chang, Y.-C.: Single database private information retrieval with logarithmic communication. In: Wang, H., Pieprzyk, J., Varadharajan, V. (eds.) ACISP 2004. LNCS, vol. 3108, pp. 50–61. Springer, Heidelberg (2004). https://doi.org/10.1007/978-3-540-27800-9_5

20. Chor, B., Gilboa, N.: Computationally private information retrieval (extended abstract). In: 29th ACM STOC, pp. 304–313. ACM Press, May 1997. https://doi.org/10.1145/258533.258609

21. Chor, B., Goldreich, O., Kushilevitz, E., Sudan, M.: Private information retrieval. In: 36th FOCS, pp. 41–50. IEEE Computer Society Press, October 1995. https://doi.org/10.1109/SFCS.1995.492461

22. Chor, B., Kushilevitz, E., Goldreich, O., Sudan, M.: Private information retrieval. J. ACM **45**(6), 965–981 (1998). https://doi.org/10.1145/293347.293350

23. Corrigan-Gibbs, H., Henzinger, A., Kogan, D.: Single-server private information retrieval with sublinear amortized time. In: Dunkelman, O., Dziembowski, S. (eds.) EUROCRYPT 2022, Part II. LNCS, vol. 13276, pp. 3–33. Springer, Heidelberg, May/June 2022. https://doi.org/10.1007/978-3-031-07085-3_1

24. Corrigan-Gibbs, H., Kogan, D.: Private information retrieval with sublinear online time. In: Canteaut, A., Ishai, Y. (eds.) EUROCRYPT 2020. LNCS, vol. 12105, pp. 44–75. Springer, Cham (2020). https://doi.org/10.1007/978-3-030-45721-1_3

25. Demmler, D., Herzberg, A., Schneider, T.: Raid-pir: practical multi-server pir. In: CCSW (2014). https://doi.org/10.1145/2664168.2664181

26. Di Crescenzo, G., Ishai, Y., Ostrovsky, R.: Universal service-providers for database private information retrieval (extended abstract). In: Coan, B.A., Afek, Y. (eds.) 17th ACM PODC, pp. 91–100. ACM, June/July 1998. https://doi.org/10.1145/277697.277713

27. Dodis, Y., Halevi, S., Rothblum, R.D., Wichs, D.: Spooky encryption and its applications. In: Robshaw, M., Katz, J. (eds.) CRYPTO 2016. LNCS, vol. 9816, pp. 93–122. Springer, Heidelberg (2016). https://doi.org/10.1007/978-3-662-53015-3_4

28. Dvir, Z., Gopi, S.: 2-server pir with subpolynomial communication. J. ACM **63**(4) (2016). https://doi.org/10.1145/2968443

29. Dwork, C., Naor, M., Rothblum, G.N.: Spooky interaction and its discontents: compilers for succinct two-message argument systems. In: Robshaw, M., Katz, J. (eds.) CRYPTO 2016. LNCS, vol. 9816, pp. 123–145. Springer, Heidelberg (2016). https://doi.org/10.1007/978-3-662-53015-3_5

30. Gasarch, W.I.: A survey on private information retrieval. Bull. EATCS **82**, 72–107 (2004)

31. Gentry, C.: Fully homomorphic encryption using ideal lattices. In: Mitzenmacher, M. (ed.) 41st ACM STOC, pp. 169–178. ACM Press, May/June 2009. https://doi.org/10.1145/1536414.1536440

32. Gentry, C., Ramzan, Z.: Single-database private information retrieval with constant communication rate. In: Caires, L., Italiano, G.F., Monteiro, L., Palamidessi, C., Yung, M. (eds.) ICALP 2005. LNCS, vol. 3580, pp. 803–815. Springer, Heidelberg (2005). https://doi.org/10.1007/11523468_65

33. Gentry, C., Sahai, A., Waters, B.: Homomorphic encryption from learning with errors: conceptually-simpler, asymptotically-faster, attribute-based. In: Canetti, R., Garay, J.A. (eds.) CRYPTO 2013. LNCS, vol. 8042, pp. 75–92. Springer, Heidelberg (2013). https://doi.org/10.1007/978-3-642-40041-4_5

34. Gilboa, N., Ishai, Y.: Distributed point functions and their applications. In: Nguyen, P.Q., Oswald, E. (eds.) EUROCRYPT 2014. LNCS, vol. 8441, pp. 640–658. Springer, Heidelberg (2014). https://doi.org/10.1007/978-3-642-55220-5_35

35. Hafiz, S.M., Henry, R.: Querying for queries: indexes of queries for efficient and expressive IT-PIR. In: Thuraisingham, B.M., Evans, D., Malkin, T., Xu, D. (eds.) ACM CCS 2017, pp. 1361–1373. ACM Press, October/November 2017. https://doi.org/10.1145/3133956.3134008

36. Hamlin, A., Ostrovsky, R., Weiss, M., Wichs, D.: Private anonymous data access. In: Ishai, Y., Rijmen, V. (eds.) EUROCRYPT 2019. LNCS, vol. 11477, pp. 244–273. Springer, Cham (2019). https://doi.org/10.1007/978-3-030-17656-3_9

37. Henry, R.: Polynomial batch codes for efficient IT-PIR. PoPETs **2016**(4), 202–218 (2016). https://doi.org/10.1515/popets-2016-0036

38. Ishai, Y., Kushilevitz, E., Ostrovsky, R., Sahai, A.: Batch codes and their applications. In: Babai, L. (ed.) 36th ACM STOC, pp. 262–271. ACM Press, June 2004. https://doi.org/10.1145/1007352.1007396

39. Ishai, Y., Kushilevitz, E., Ostrovsky, R., Sahai, A.: Cryptography from anonymity. In: 47th FOCS, pp. 239–248. IEEE Computer Society Press, October 2006. https://doi.org/10.1109/FOCS.2006.25

40. Kalai, Y.T., Raz, R., Rothblum, R.D.: Delegation for bounded space. In: Boneh, D., Roughgarden, T., Feigenbaum, J. (eds.) 45th ACM STOC, pp. 565–574. ACM Press, June 2013. https://doi.org/10.1145/2488608.2488679

41. Kim, S., Wu, D.J.: Watermarking cryptographic functionalities from standard lattice assumptions. J. Cryptol. **34**(3), 1–76 (2021). https://doi.org/10.1007/s00145-021-09391-2

42. Kogan, D., Corrigan-Gibbs, H.: Private blocklist lookups with checklist. In: Bailey, M., Greenstadt, R. (eds.) USENIX Security 2021, pp. 875–892. USENIX Association, August 2021

43. Kushilevitz, E., Ostrovsky, R.: Replication is NOT needed: SINGLE database, computationally-private information retrieval. In: 38th FOCS, pp. 364–373. IEEE Computer Society Press, October 1997. https://doi.org/10.1109/SFCS.1997.646125

44. Lazzaretti, A., Papamanthou, C.: Single server PIR with sublinear amortized time and polylogarithmic bandwidth. Cryptology ePrint Archive, Report 2022/830 (2022). https://eprint.iacr.org/2022/830

45. Lipmaa, H.: First CPIR protocol with data-dependent computation. In: Lee, D., Hong, S. (eds.) ICISC 2009. LNCS, vol. 5984, pp. 193–210. Springer, Heidelberg (2010). https://doi.org/10.1007/978-3-642-14423-3_14

46. Lueks, W., Goldberg, I.: Sublinear scaling for multi-client private information retrieval. In: Böhme, R., Okamoto, T. (eds.) FC 2015. LNCS, vol. 8975, pp. 168–186. Springer, Heidelberg (2015). https://doi.org/10.1007/978-3-662-47854-7_10

47. Menon, S.J., Wu, D.J.: SPIRAL: fast, high-rate single-server PIR via FHE composition. In: 2022 IEEE Symposium on Security and Privacy, pp. 930–947. IEEE Computer Society Press, May 2022. https://doi.org/10.1109/SP46214.2022.9833700

48. Mughees, M.H., Chen, H., Ren, L.: OnionPIR: response efficient single-server PIR. In: Vigna, G., Shi, E. (eds.) ACM CCS 2021, pp. 2292–2306. ACM Press, November 2021. https://doi.org/10.1145/3460120.3485381

49. Ostrovsky, R., Skeith, W.E.: A survey of single-database private information retrieval: techniques and applications. In: Okamoto, T., Wang, X. (eds.) PKC 2007. LNCS, vol. 4450, pp. 393–411. Springer, Heidelberg (2007). https://doi.org/10.1007/978-3-540-71677-8_26

50. Patel, S., Persiano, G., Yeo, K.: Private stateful information retrieval. In: Lie, D., Mannan, M., Backes, M., Wang, X. (eds.) ACM CCS 2018, pp. 1002–1019. ACM Press, October 2018. https://doi.org/10.1145/3243734.3243821

51. Peikert, C., Shiehian, S.: Privately constraining and programming PRFs, the LWE way. In: Abdalla, M., Dahab, R. (eds.) PKC 2018. LNCS, vol. 10770, pp. 675–701. Springer, Cham (2018). https://doi.org/10.1007/978-3-319-76581-5_23

52. Persiano, G., Yeo, K.: Limits of preprocessing for single-server PIR. In: SODA, pp. 2522–2548. SIAM (2022). https://doi.org/10.1137/1.9781611977073.99

53. Pudlák, P., Rödl, V.: Modified ranks of tensors and the size of circuits. In: 25th ACM STOC, pp. 523–531. ACM Press, May 1993. https://doi.org/10.1145/167088.167228

54. Shi, E., Aqeel, W., Chandrasekaran, B., Maggs, B.: Puncturable pseudorandom sets and private information retrieval with near-optimal online bandwidth and time. In: Malkin, T., Peikert, C. (eds.) CRYPTO 2021. LNCS, vol. 12828, pp. 641–669. Springer, Cham (2021). https://doi.org/10.1007/978-3-030-84259-8_22

55. Toledo, R.R., Danezis, G., Goldberg, I.: Lower-cost ε-private information retrieval. PETS (2016). https://doi.org/10.1515/popets-2016-0035

56. Zhou, M., Lin, W.K., Tselekounis, Y., Shi, E.: Optimal single-server private information retrieval. Cryptology ePrint Archive, Paper 2022/609 (2022). https://eprint.iacr.org/2022/609

Weighted Oblivious RAM, with Applications to Searchable Symmetric Encryption

Léonard Assouline[✉] and Brice Minaud

École Normale Supérieure, PSL University, CNRS, Inria, Paris, France
`leonard.assouline@ens.fr`

Abstract. Existing Oblivious RAM protocols do not support the storage of data items of variable size in a non-trivial way. While the study of ORAM for items of variable size is of interest in and of itself, it is also motivated by the need for more performant and more secure Searchable Symmetric Encryption (SSE) schemes.

In this article, we introduce the notion of *weighted* ORAM, which supports the storage of blocks of different sizes. We introduce a framework to build efficient weighted ORAM schemes, based on an underlying standard ORAM satisfying a certain suitability criterion. This criterion is fulfilled by various Tree ORAM schemes, including Simple ORAM and Path ORAM. We deduce several instantiations of weighted ORAM, with very little overhead compared to standard ORAM. As a direct application, we obtain efficient SSE constructions with attractive security properties.

1 Introduction

When sensitive data is stored in an untrusted environment, encryption is not enough. The pattern of memory accesses to encrypted data can reveal a great deal about its contents. In some settings, observing the pattern of memory accesses can allow a honest-but-curious host server to fully reconstruct the contents of an encrypted database [14]; in others, measuring cache misses can enable an attacker to recover secret key material [32]. Untrusted environments where an adversary may be able to observe memory accesses, partially or completely, arise in many common scenarios. These include private information stored in an external cloud service, trusted enclaves running on an untrusted computer, or even public clouds where memory caches are shared across multiple tenants. In all these settings, security requires to hide not only the contents of each data item, but also which item is accessed.

Oblivious RAM (ORAM) protocols provide a powerful tool to fully hide memory access patterns. The notion of ORAM was introduced by Goldreich and Ostrovsky [12], motivated by a scenario where a processor accesses untrusted memory. The processor operates in a RAM model of computation: it wishes to access memory words at arbitrary addresses. Naturally, memory words have a fixed size. In line with its historical motivation, ORAM is normally viewed as storing items of fixed size.

© International Association for Cryptologic Research 2023
C. Hazay and M. Stam (Eds.): EUROCRYPT 2023, LNCS 14004, pp. 426–455, 2023.
https://doi.org/10.1007/978-3-031-30545-0_15

However, in many potential applications of ORAM, it is natural to consider items of variable size. Suppose for instance that a client wishes to store private files on an external cloud storage service. Different files may have different sizes; it may also be the case that the size of a file varies with time. This motivates the idea of ORAM for variable-size items.

Of course, it is possible to generically emulate the storage of variable-size files using a memory allocation scheme for fixed-size items. In our case, using an ORAM for items of fixed size B, the most natural approach is to split each file into chunks of size B. Each chunk is then stored as a separate data item (called a block) within the ORAM, on the server side. To retrieve a file, the client simply queries all chunks corresponding to the desired file.

This simple variable-size-to-fixed-size reduction is not always satisfactory. A first issue relates to padding. Before files can be split into chunks of size B, they must be padded to a multiple of the block size B. If many files are much smaller than the block size, padding becomes expensive. Both motivating applications given below show examples where padding would be prohibitive.

To reduce the cost of padding, it may be tempting to reduce the block size B. However, this increases the ORAM overhead (i.e. the ratio between the communication cost of the ORAM scheme, and the cost of an insecure exchange), since it scales with the number of blocks. For example, an ORAM storing N blocks of size 1 typically has an overhead in polylog N; whereas with N/B blocks of size B, the overhead becomes polylog(N/B). In later applications such as length-hiding ORAM, or zeroSSE in Sect. 6.2, B can be very large, which makes the difference significant. In theory, larger block sizes are also preferable: for instance, Path ORAM achieves optimal $\mathcal{O}(\log n)$ overhead if the block size is $\Omega(\lambda^2)$ bits, but its overhead is $\mathcal{O}(\log^2 n)$ if the block size is $\Theta(\lambda)$ bits (where λ is the security parameter).

In practice, setting the block size to be very small, say a single memory word of 128 bits, has a deeper impact that is easy to overlook, but much more impactful in practice that the asymptotic difference above. Modern computers can only fetch memory from disk at the granularity level of a page, typically 4kB. This is enforced at all levels: by the operating system, in caches, and at the physical disk layer (both for HDDs and SSDs). When fetching many 128-bit words at random locations in the ORAM scheme, the server actually fetches the entire page for each. In each of those pages, only a fraction $1/256$ of the data in the page is actually useful (128 bits out of 4kB). This results in very poor I/O efficiency, which correlates directly with disk throughput [4]. The issue is easy to overlook because it is not reflected in the simple Random-Access Machine model of computation that is used to compute asymptotics, where all memory accesses have unit cost. But it has a very large impact in practice. This is well-known in SSE literature, where an entire branch of the area studies memory efficiency [2,4,23,24]. In ORAM literature, the PHANTOM implementation of Path ORAM uses blocks of size one page, likely for the same reason [21]. Reading many tiny items at random memory locations is extremely inefficient, losing a factor up to B in throughput (when the bottleneck in throughput does not come from bandwidth limitations).

If one thinks of storing entire documents in the context of a private online storage service, having many documents much smaller than the page size is rather unlikely. But in other applications, it is quite realistic. A case in point is the use of ORAM for Searchable Symmetric Encryption (SSE).

Motivating Application 1: Searchable Symmetric Encryption (SSE). The goal of SSE is to enable a client to outsource the storage of an encrypted database to an untrusted server, while being able to securely search the data. At minimum, the client is able to issue search queries asking for all entries that match a given keyword. To realize this functionality, for efficiency reasons, virtually all modern SSE constructions rely a *reverse index*. The reverse index records, for each keyword, the list of identifiers of entries that match the keyword.

The majority of SSE solutions accept to leak the *search pattern* and *access pattern* of the client: that is, they leak to the server the repetition of queries, and the identifiers of documents matched by the queries. This allows those constructions to trade off privacy for efficiency and scalability. Nevertheless, revealing access patterns to the server can be quite damaging, and has led to a number of attacks [7,14]. Those attacks have in turn motivated SSE approaches that rely on ORAM [11,18].

The most natural way to avoid leaking the search pattern is to store the reverse index in an ORAM. In that scenario, the "files" to be stored on an ORAM are actually the list of matches for a given keyword in an SSE scheme. For some databases, there may be many keywords that uniquely identify a file, or that match only a few files. In other words, there may be many lists much smaller than the block size B of the ORAM.

In practice, this is actually a major roadblock. As argued earlier, it is desirable to have a relatively large ORAM block size, at least one memory page. On the other hand, the identifier of an entry can be set to 64 bits, or even less. This means that a single ORAM block is 512 times larger than the minimal list size. If, say, many keywords match less than 10 entries in the database, padding those lists to the block size blows up their storage by a factor more than 50. More generally, if we set p to be the page size, measured in number of identifiers per page, then padding means that server storage grows at least in $\mathcal{O}(pN)$, where N is the size of the plaintext reverse index; whereas we would like to achieve linear storage $\mathcal{O}(N)$. Of course, with $p = 512$ as earlier, the practical difference is quite large.

Addressing that problem is not an easy task. In SSE literature, avoiding the cost of padding to the page size has been the focus of several recent works [4,24]. Those works have motivated the creation of *weighted* memory allocation schemes, that can accommodate items of variable size, including weighted cuckoo hashing [4], and weighted two-choice allocation [24]. However, there is no weighted ORAM. This means that in order to use ORAM with SSE, current options are either to choose a block size much smaller than the page size, or to suffer a prohibitive padding overhead for some data distributions—both of which are undesirable.

Motivating Application 2: Length-Hiding ORAM. Let us go back to the scenario where a client wishes to store private files of various sizes on a honest-but-curious cloud server. As noted earlier, the simplest way to hide access patterns is to store the files in an ORAM. Each file is split into chunks of size B, and each chunk is stored in a separate ORAM block. In order to fetch a file, the client queries all chunks of the file to the ORAM. When a file is queried, the only information leaked to the server is the number of chunks of the file.

In some settings, even that much information may be too much information. For instance, the number of chunks of a file might be enough information to uniquely identify the file [7]. In that case, repeated accesses to the file are leaked to the server. This reveals the access pattern of the client to the files, defeating the purpose of ORAM. More subtly, the length of answers to certain types of database queries can be enough to infer the contents of encrypted data [13]. Traffic analysis attacks are another example of using length information to infer sensitive data [10]. Attacks based on length information can be particularly insidious, because traditional encryption does not attempt to hide length.

If leaking the lengths of the files is judged to be too damaging, the client may wish to use additional mechanisms to protect their privacy. Going back to our running example about private file storage, the simplest and most secure protection is to mandate that, whenever a file is accessed, the client should query as many chunks as the size of the *largest* file. In that case, only the number of chunks of the largest file is leaked to the server—or an upper bound on that number.

Let N be the total size of the files to be stored on the remote server. Let B be the ORAM block size, and let U be an upper bound on the size of the largest file (all quantities are counted in number of memory words). The overhead of ORAM constructions typically scales in $\mathsf{Polylog}(n)$, where n is the number of blocks stored in the ORAM. Setting aside padding issues for a moment, with block size B, we have $n = N/B$. In order to minimize the overhead, it would be attractive the simply set $B = U$. But here again, we would run into padding issues: most files might be much smaller than the largest file. The optimal solution would be a *weighted* ORAM able to accommodate files of arbitrary size up to U, with an overhead $\mathsf{Polylog}(N/U)$, or optimally, $\log(N/U)$.

1.1   Our Contributions

The discussion so far leads to the following question: can we devise a *weighted* ORAM—that is, an ORAM that natively accommodates items of variable size? Beside the motivating applications given in the introduction, the existence of weighted ORAM may be viewed as a natural question: it fits within a long line of work on weighted allocation mechanisms, both within and outside cryptography, such as [2–4,24,28,29].

We will answer the previous question in the affirmative, and build a weighted ORAM. Our construction naturally handles not only items of different sizes, but items whose size varies with time, without the need for padding. To state the result precisely, let us introduce some notation. In the remainder, an atomic item stored within the ORAM is called a *block*. Let B denote an upper bound on the block size. Unlike traditional ORAMs, blocks can take any size in $[1, B]$. We will sometimes call the size of a block its *weight*. Let $w_i \in [1, B]$ denote the weight of the i-th block. Let m be the total number of blocks. Let N be an upper bound on the *total weight* $\sum_{i \leq m} w_i$. We want to build and ORAM that can accommodate *any* vector $\mathbf{w} = (w_i)_{i \leq m}$ of weights, as long as the following two conditions are fulfilled.

Condition 1. Every block w_i has weight at most B;
Condition 2. The total weight $\sum w_i$ is at most N.

For ease of exposition, we will assume that the number of blocks m is fixed, but our constructions can be easily adapted to a variable number of blocks, so long as the previous two conditions continue to hold. The parameters of our ORAM constructions will depend *only* on B and N; crucially, they do not depend on the distribution of the weight vector $\mathbf{w}$.

The interface of our weighted ORAMs is identical to standard ORAM: to retrieve a block, the client queries an identifier of the block (e.g. a virtual memory address). When writing a block, the client also inputs new data for the block. This data need not be of the same size as the data originally associated to the block identifier. The client can freely change the size of a block with every access, so long as Conditions 1 and 2 are respected.

As our main contribution, we build a weighted ORAM in the sense given above. In fact, we show a significantly stronger result. Many standard Tree-based ORAM algorithms admit a natural extension to handle blocks of variable size: at setup, the ORAM is dimensioned as if to accommodate N/B blocks of size B, but instead receives an arbitrary number of blocks of variable size bounded by B, with total size N. These blocks are read and written through the ORAM in essentially the same way as in the original, fixed-block size ORAM, except for minor alterations to reflect the fact that blocks do not have the same size.

The main obstacle with that approach is technical. While Path ORAM is one of the most attractive solutions for practical Tree ORAM [27], its correctness proof is notoriously difficult–prompting the introduction of Simple ORAM as a less efficient variant that allows for a simpler correctness proof [9]. Our main result is to show that the natural weighted extensions of several existing Tree-ORAM schemes, including Path ORAM and Simple ORAM, are in fact correct. For that purpose, we introduce a general framework: we prove that as long as a Tree ORAM fulfills a certain structural property, its weighted extension preserves correctness. The centerpiece of the proof is a Schur-convexity argument, which ultimately reduces the correctness of the weighted extension to that of the original ORAM. (An overview of the proof argument is given in Sect. 4.4, before the formal proof.) Practical experiments show that our weighted ORAM construction behaves in line with the previous analysis.

As an application of weighted ORAM, we build two SSE schemes, ZeroSSE and BlockSSE. Unlike most of SSE literature, both constructions completely hide access patterns. To our knowledge, ZeroSSE is the only construction that leaks neither the access pattern nor the size of retrieved objects, with full correctness. (The only other construction that we are aware of, in [18], pays the price of having a non-negligible correctness failure probability.) BlockSSE hides access pattern, but not the size of retrieved objects. To our knowledge, it is the only ORAM-based SSE with worst-case server storage $\mathcal{O}(N)$, rather than $\mathcal{O}(BN)$, where B is the ORAM block size.

Our main result builds on Tree ORAMs, because of their higher practical efficiency compared to hierarchical ORAMs. This makes tree-based construction currently more attractive for applications such as SSE. Nevertheless, it is worth remarking that the position map of a weighted Tree-based ORAM, as we have built, has blocks of fixed size. Hence, it can be stored using any standard ORAM scheme, not necessarily tree-based. In particular, from a more theoretical perspective, the position map can be stored using an optimal ORAM with logarithmic overhead, following the groundbreaking result of Asharov et al. [1]. This results in a weighted ORAM with logarithmic overhead. The case of building weighted hierarchical ORAM schemes is discussed in the full version.

As another direct application of our construction, setting the block size B of our weighted ORAM to be equal to an upper-bound bound U on the size of the largest item to be stored in the ORAM, we immediately obtain an ORAM with communication overhead $\mathcal{O}(\log^2(N/U))$. If we use an optimal standard ORAM for the position map, as indicated above, we obtain a length-hiding ORAM with communication overhead $\log(N/U)$. This overhead is optimal, since such a goal includes as a special case the setting where all blocks have size U, and is thus subject to known ORAM lower bounds [12,19] for an ORAM storing N/U blocks.

1.2   Related Work

While there is a rich literature on ORAM, surprisingly little of it deals with objects of variable size. To the best of our knowledge, only two articles mention this subdomain of ORAM.

In [26], Roche et al. present the first ORAM that stores objects of variable size. Their goal is to build a remote data structure that satisfies the security requirements of ORAM, and in addition allows for secure deletion of items and history independence. In other words, in the case of a *total leakage of the structure* (such an event is referred to as a *catastrophic attack*):

– Items that have been deleted by the client can never be recovered through leaked data.
– The internal structure does not reveal information about which elements were last accessed.

The data structure is built on top of a weighted ORAM. However, their construction for such an ORAM is limited: obliviousness and correctness (i.e. the client-side stash overflows with negligible probability) can be proven only if the size of the blocks follow a geometric probability distribution. In comparison, although we assume that block sizes are bounded by B, we do not need to assume anything on the distribution of block sizes. In more detail, there are two limitations to the assumptions of [26]. First, many common distributions are not upper-bounded by a geometric distribution, for instance Zipf distributions. Second and more fundamentally, the ORAM user has no reason in general to pick item sizes independently, or to pick them from the same distribution. The construction of [26] was designed with a specific use case in mind; its applicability beyond that use case is limited.

Another construction of ORAM for objects of variable size may be found in [20]. Their construction is also based on Tree ORAMs. The idea is to allow block size to be equal to a multiple of some value s (padding up to a multiple if needed), and to store all "splinters" of size s of a block along the same path from root to leaf. This construction has the strong requirement of a trusted proxy that shuffles blocks during certain operations. Moreover, the construction is flawed (see the full version for further information).

1.3   Organization of the Paper

In Sect. 3 we recall the definitions of ORAM, SSE, and Schur convexity, a tool we will use in our proof. Section 4 is where we state our generic criterion for converting a standard ORAM into one that supports objects of variable size and prove our main result. Concrete examples of known ORAM schemes that we can turn into weighted ORAM are shown in Sect. 5. We discuss applications to the field of SSE in Sect. 6.

2   General Preliminaries

Throughout this work, memory size will be counted as a number of *memory words*. It is assumed that a memory word is large enough to store any address in memory. In practical applications, one may think of 64-bit or 128-bit words. Algorithms will be considered in the RAM model, where accessing an arbitrary memory word costs $O(1)$ operations.

The security parameter is denoted by λ. A quantity is said to be *negligible*, denoted $\mathrm{negl}(\lambda)$, if it is $O(\lambda^{-c})$ for every constant c. A probability is said to be *overwhelming* if it is $1 - \mathrm{negl}(\lambda)$. It is always assumed that the number of blocks N stored in the ORAM satisfies $N \geq \lambda$, so that any quantity $\mathrm{negl}(N)$ is also $\mathrm{negl}(\lambda)$.

When an algorithm A with input x is probabilistic, we may sometimes explicitly write the random coins used by A as an input of A, separated by a semicolon, as in $A(x; r)$.

2.1   Majorization and Schur Convexity

Given a vector $\mathbf{v}$ in $\mathbb{R}^m$, we denote by $\mathbf{v}^{\downarrow} \in \mathbb{R}^m$ the vector with the same components, sorted in decreasing order.

Definition 1 (Majorization order). *Let* $\mathbf{v}$, $\mathbf{w}$ *be two vectors in* $\mathbb{R}^m$ *such that* $\sum_{i=1}^m v_i = \sum_{i=1}^m w_i$. *The vector* $\mathbf{w}$ *is said to* majorize $\mathbf{v}$, *written* $\mathbf{v} \prec \mathbf{w}$, *if:*

$$\forall k \in [1, m], \quad \sum_{i=1}^k v_i^\downarrow \le \sum_{i=1}^k w_i^\downarrow.$$

Definition 2 (Schur convexity). *Let* $f : \mathbb{R}^m \mapsto \mathbb{R}$. *The map* f *is said to be* Schur-convex *if it is non-decreasing for the majorization order. That is, for any two vectors* $\mathbf{v}$, $\mathbf{w}$ *with* $\sum_{i=1}^m v_i = \sum_{i=1}^m w_i$,

$$\mathbf{v} \prec \mathbf{w} \Rightarrow f(\mathbf{v}) \le f(\mathbf{w}).$$

Definition 3 (Convexity). *Let* $f : \mathbb{R}^m \mapsto \mathbb{R}$. *The map* f *is said to be* convex *if for any two vectors* $\mathbf{v}$, $\mathbf{w}$ *in* $\mathbb{R}^m$, *and any* α *in* $[0,1] \subset \mathbb{R}$, *it holds that:*

$$f(\alpha \mathbf{v} + (1 - \alpha)\mathbf{w}) \le \alpha f(\mathbf{v}) + (1 - \alpha)f(\mathbf{w}).$$

Definition 4 (Symmetry). *Let* $f : \mathbb{R}^m \mapsto \mathbb{R}$. *The map* f *is said to be* symmetric *if for any vector* $\mathbf{v} \in \mathbb{R}^m$, *and any permutation matrix* P *over* m *elements,* $f(\mathbf{v}) = f(P\mathbf{v})$.

The link between convexity and Schur convexity is visible in the next lemma.

Lemma 1. *Let* $f : \mathbb{R}^m \mapsto \mathbb{R}$. *If* f *is symmetric and convex, then it is Schur-convex.*

We refer the reader to [22] for a detailed presentation of the theory of majorization, including a proof of Lemma 1.

3   ORAM Preliminaries

3.1   Weighted Oblivious RAM

A weighted ORAM, also written wORAM, is a pair of client-server protocols (Setup, Access), defined as follows.

- Setup(N, B, D) takes as input a number of blocks N, a block size B, and a set D of pairs of the form $(a_i, data_i)$, where the a_i's are pairwise distinct *addresses*, and $data_i$ is arbitrary data of size at least 1 and at most B memory words. Setup outputs an initial client state and initial server state.
- Access(op, a, *data*) takes as input an operation op $\in \{$read, write$\}$, an address a, and some data *data* of size at least 1 and at most B. If op = read, Access outputs the data last written to address a. If op = write, Access replaces the data written at address a by *data*. Access may also update the client and server states.

We say that $\mathtt{Setup}(N, B, D)$ is *legal* if the total amount of data in D (*i.e.* the sum of the sizes of the $data_i$'s) is at most NB. Likewise, we say that $\mathtt{Access}(\mathrm{op}, \mathrm{a}, data)$ is *legal* if address a was defined during setup, and in the case that op = write, if the total amount of data contained in the database after replacing the data at address a by $data$ remains of size at most NB. On the other hand, it is *not* required that the size of $data$ matches the size of the data previously written at a, as long as $data$ is of size at most B, and the total amount of data remains at most NB.

Definition 5 (Correctness). *A wORAM scheme is said to be* correct *if, given a legal setup and any sequence of legal access operations, a read access at address a outputs the data last written at address a, except with negligible probability.*

Definition 6 (Security). *A wORAM scheme is* secure *if, given any two legal sequences of operations* $(\mathtt{Setup}(N, B, D), \mathtt{Access}(\mathrm{op}_1, \mathrm{a}_1, data_1), \dots, \mathtt{Access}$ $(\mathrm{op}_\mathrm{k}, \mathrm{a}_\mathrm{k}, data_k))$ *and* $(\mathtt{Setup}(N, B, D'), \mathtt{Access}(\mathrm{op}'_1, \mathrm{a}'_1, data'_1), \dots, \mathtt{Access}(\mathrm{op}'_\mathrm{k},$ $\mathrm{a}'_\mathrm{k}, data'_k))$ *of the same length, the views of the server arising from each sequence are computationally indistinguishable.*

A few remarks are in order. First, although we have defined $\mathtt{Setup}$ and $\mathtt{Access}$ as general client-server protocols, it is common in ORAM to ask that the server performs behaves like a memory allowing only read and write accesses. That is, the client only ever asks the server to read or write specific data at a specific address: and the server performs no computation if its own. Although this is not required in the previous definition, the wORAM schemes in this work are in that model.

Second, it is assumed that the contents of all memory locations on the server are encrypted using IND-CCA encryption, with a key known only to the client. Whenever the client accesses a memory location, they can reencrypt the data at that location, so that the server cannot learn the contents of any memory location, or whether it was changed during the access. As a result, the only way the server can infer information is by observing which locations the client queries in server memory. That is why the security definition of wORAM (following that of ORAM) focuses only on memory locations.

Finally, note that a standard ORAM scheme is the special case of a wORAM where all addresses store data of the same size B.

3.2 Tree ORAM

We build wORAM by altering standard ORAM schemes following the *Tree ORAM* paradigm. In this section, we provide a high-level algorithmic view of that paradigm. That view is purposefully designed to accommodate several existing Tree ORAM schemes. It will also lay the groundwork for the construction of wORAM in the next section.

Existing Tree ORAM schemes are standard ORAMs, designed to store items of fixed size. In a Tree ORAM, to store N items of size B, the server creates a full binary tree with N leaves. (From now on, we assume N is a power of 2, increasing to the next power of 2 if necessary.) Throughout the article, the root of the tree is viewed as being at the top, and leaves as being at the bottom of the tree. Given a leaf l of the tree, the path from the root to the leaf l is denoted by $\mathcal{P}(l)$.

Each node of the tree, also called a *bucket*, can store up to Z data blocks of size B. Nodes are always padded to be of size ZB before being stored (encrypted) on the server.

In addition to the tree, the server may also store a *stash*, which may contain additional data blocks that could not fit in the tree. In the remainder, we view the stash as a special node directly above the root. This is relevant in two situations. First, there may be cases where a node is full (*i.e* it contains Z items), and where additional items need to be pushed to the parent node; if this happens at the root level, overflowing items are pushed to the stash. Second, whenever we consider the path $\mathcal{P}(l)$ from some leaf l to the root in the tree, we implicitly (and slightly abusively) also consider the stash to be part of the path. The stash is always padded to some upper bound RB, before being stored (encrypted) on the server.

To each item with address a is associated a leaf of the tree $\mathsf{pos}(a)$. The array mapping each address a to the corresponding leaf $\mathsf{pos}(a)$ is called a *position map*. For now, we will assume the position map is stored by the client. By design, Tree ORAMs maintain the following invariant at all times: the item at address a is stored in one of the nodes on the path $\mathcal{P}(\mathsf{pos}(a))$ from the root to leaf $\mathsf{pos}a$ (including the stash, as noted earlier).

During setup, each item with address a is stored in the leaf $\mathsf{pos}(a)$; or if it is full, in the lowest parent of $\mathsf{pos}(a)$ that is not yet full. To access item a, the client retrieves $\mathsf{pos}(a)$ from the position map, then reads the path $\mathcal{P}(\mathsf{pos}(a))$ on the server. Thanks to the invariant, that path contains the item a. Item a is then assigned a new uniformly random leaf. Finally, a special *eviction* procedure is called, which re-inserts item a somewhere on the path to its newly assigned leaf, and may also move other items.

Pseudo-code for the `Evict` procedure is given in Algorithm 1, with additional parameters Z (the number of blocks per bucket, specified by the Tree ORAM scheme; to reflect the fact that Z is an internal parameter of the ORAM construction, and not part of its interface, it is written between brackets), and random coins r. It makes use of the following subroutines:

- `ReadBucket`(*bucket* retrieves a set of pairs $(a_i, data_i)$ from the tree node *bucket*.
- `RemoveBlock`(*bucket, a* removes the item with address a from the tree node *bucket*.
- `ChooseEvictionPath` outputs a path for eviction, which differs depending on the specific Tree ORAM scheme.

Pseudo-code for the `Access` procedure is given in Algorithm 2, with additional parameters Z (the number of blocks per bucket, specified by the Tree ORAM scheme), and random coins r. It makes use of the following subroutines:

Algorithm 1. Access algorithm of a Tree-ORAM.

Access$[Z; r]$(op, a, *newdata*):

1: *leaf* $\leftarrow$ pos[a]
2: pos[a] $\leftarrow$ uniformly random leaf
3: **for** *bucket* in $\mathcal{P}(leaf)$ **do**
4:     **if** $(a, data) \in$ ReadBucket(*bucket*) **then**
5:         RemoveBlock(*bucket*, a)
6: **if** op $=$ write **then**
7:     data $=$ newdata
8: *stash* $\leftarrow$ *stash* $\cup \{(a, data)\}$
9: *path* $\leftarrow$ ChooseEvictionPath(*leaf*)
10: Evict$[Z; r]$(*path*)
11: **return** *data*

– SizeX returns the number of items $|X|$ in X.
– ChooseNextBlock(*stash, bucket, path*) pops an item from the stash, to be stored in the bucket, or outputs $\perp$.
– WriteBucket(*bucket*,X,Z) writes the items in X to the node *bucket*, padding the node to size Z if needed.

Algorithm 2. Generic eviction algorithm.

Evict$[Z; r]$(*path*):

1: Move all blocks in *path* to the stash
2: **for** *bucket* in *path* **do**
3:     $X \leftarrow \varnothing$
4:     **while** Size$(X) < Z$ **do**
5:         *block* $\leftarrow$ ChooseNextBlock(*stash, bucket, path*)
6:         **if** *block* $= \perp$ **then**
7:             break
8:         **else**
9:             $X \leftarrow X \cup \{block\}$
10:     WriteBucket(*bucket*, X, Z)
11: **return**

We will discuss in Sect. 5 how several existing Tree ORAM schemes are captured by the above paradigm.

Correctness of Tree ORAM. Since Tree ORAM is a special case of ORAM, the correctness definition remains the same (Definition 5). However, because of the specificities of Tree ORAM, it can be reformulated in a more convenient manner. That is, the only correctness failure that can occur in a Tree ORAM scheme is that the stash overflows. (The reader familiar with Tree ORAM may object that some Tree ORAM schemes do not use a stash; that case will be handled in Sect. 5).

Recall that the stash is always padded to size RB, *i.e.* it can store up to R items. Hence, correctness amounts to the following statement: at the outcome of any sequence of legal accesses ($\texttt{Setup}, \texttt{Access}_1, \dots, \texttt{Access}_k$), it holds that

$$\Pr[\texttt{Size}(stash) > R] = \text{negl}(\lambda).$$

3.3 ∞-ORAM

Consider a Tree ORAM instantiation $ORAM^Z \leftarrow \texttt{Setup[Z](N, B, D)}$, with bucket capacity Z. If $\mathbf{s}$ is a sequence of accesses, we call $st(ORAM^Z[\mathbf{s}])$ the stash usage, that is, the number of items in the stash at the outcome of the accesses.

In Path ORAM and many Tree ORAM schemes derived from it, the proof of correctness follows similar steps:

- Consider an *infinite* ORAM structure $ORAM^\infty$, which is the same protocol, except buckets have infinite capacity.
- Define a post-processing algorithm G_Z that moves items in the tree produced by running $ORAM^\infty$ (arranging in particular that each tree node contains at most Z items). Denote the stash usage of the post-processed ∞-ORAM by $st^Z(ORAM^\infty[\mathbf{s}])$.
- Prove that $st(ORAM^Z[\mathbf{s}]) = st^Z(ORAM^\infty[\mathbf{s}])$ when using the same random coins on both sides.
- Prove that $\Pr[st^Z(ORAM^\infty[\mathbf{s}]) > R] = \text{negl}(N)$.

The last two points imply that $\Pr[st(ORAM^Z[\mathbf{s}]) > R] = \text{negl}(N)$, *i.e.* the original ORAM scheme is correct. We say that such a protocol admits a *proof via infinite ORAM*.

4   Generic Construction of wORAM from Tree ORAM

4.1   Transformation Overview

Our goal is to give a generic way to transform an existing standard tree ORAM design into one that handles objects of variable size *with no added cost*. To achieve this, we modify the protocols used to interact with the ORAM so that when an object is added to a bucket, it is allowed to "spill out" of it, as long as the size of this spilling out is small. For the correctness proof to hold, we increase the bucket size from Z to $Z+1$ (and $Z=5$). (Practical experiments in Sect. 4.5 suggest that this increase can be heuristically dispensed with.)

4.2   Translation Function

We define a general transform `TransVar` that takes as input a standard Tree ORAM scheme $\mathsf{ORAM}^Z = (\mathsf{Setup}, \mathsf{Access})$ following the framework of Sect. 3.2, and outputs a wORAM scheme $\mathsf{TransVar}(\mathsf{ORAM}^Z) = \mathsf{ORAM}^{*Z} = (\mathsf{Setup}^*, \mathsf{Access}^*)$.

Let us first consider the setup. We say that the starting scheme ORAM^Z has a *regular* setup if its setup procedure is equivalent to creating an empty tree with all items in the stash, then doing repeated evictions towards every leaf in the tree from left to right. Here, by "equivalent" we mean that the output of this process and the output of the normal setup process are identically distributed. In our main theorem, we will require that the starting Tree ORAM ORAM^Z has a regular setup. Although that notion of regularity is unusual, it has the benefit that the behavior of the setup process can be deduced from that of the eviction process. For our purpose, this means it will be enough to explain how to transform the eviction process to handle blocks of variable size.

ORAM^{*Z} is defined in the following way, making only minimal modifications to ORAM^Z to handle items of variable size.

- $\mathsf{Setup}^*(N, B, D)$ initializes a tree with N leaves, whose nodes can hold data of size $(Z+1)B$ bits each, and a stash of the same size RB bits as the standard instance ORAM^Z. It initializes a position map where each address a in D is mapped to a uniformly random leaf. Finally, it performs a *regular* setup: that is, all items in D are placed in the stash, and the Evict^* procedure is called on the path from the root to each leaf, from left to right.
- Access^* is identical to Access, except that it calls the modified subroutine Evict^*.
- Evict^* is identical to Evict, except that it calls the modified subroutines Size^* and $\mathsf{WriteBucket}^*$.
- $\mathsf{Size}^*(X)$ returns the sum of the sizes of all items in X divided by B, instead of the number of items in X.
- $\mathsf{WriteBucket}^*(bucket, X, Z)$ still writes the items in X to node $bucket$, the only difference is that it pads the bucket to size $Z+1$ instead of Z.

4.3   Suitable Tree ORAM Schemes

For a Tree ORAM scheme to be suitable to build wORAM from, it must satisfy certain conditions. This section serves to define those conditions.

Given a sequence of accesses $\mathbf{s}$, some fixed random coins r used during those accesses, and a subset S of nodes in an ∞-ORAM scheme ORAM^*, define the *usage* of S, written $u^S(\mathsf{ORAM}^{*\infty}[\mathbf{s}; r])$, to be the total number of items assigned to the nodes in S. For a wORAM scheme, the usage of S is defined to be the total size of the items assigned to nodes in S, divided by the block size B.

As discussed in Sect. 3.2, a correctness failure for a Tree ORAM scheme ORAM occurs if and only if, at the outcome of a series of accesses $\mathbf{s}$ with random coins r, the stash receives strictly more than R elements. Using the notation from Sect. 3.3, this translates to $st(ORAM^Z[\mathbf{s}; r]) > R$. We say that a subset S of nodes *witnesses* the failure if, in the corresponding ∞-ORAM scheme ORAM* when performing the same sequence of accesses using the same random coins (*viz.* the choices of fresh uniformly random leaves for the position of any accessed item remain the same), $u^S(\mathsf{ORAM}^{*\infty}_L[\mathbf{s}]) > |S| \cdot Z + R$, where $L = \lceil log(N) \rceil$ is the tree height. Intuitively, since the nodes in S can store at most $|S| \cdot Z$ items, it is clear that more than R items must be reassigned to the stash in the original ORAM: that is why we say that S witnesses the failure.

Definition 7 ($F \Rightarrow W, W \Rightarrow F$). *We say that* ORAM *satisfies the $F \Rightarrow W$ property (read: "failure implies witness") with respect to a set $\mathscr{S}$ of subset of nodes, iff for all access sequences $\mathbf{s}$ and all choices of random coins r, $st(ORAM^Z[\mathbf{s}; r]) > R$ implies $\exists S \in \mathscr{S}, u^S(\mathsf{ORAM}^{*\infty}_L[\mathbf{s}]) > |S| \cdot Z + R$. We say that* ORAM *satisfies the $W \Rightarrow F$ (read: "witness implies failure") property if the converse is true.*

Moreover, we say that ORAM *satisfies the $F \Rightarrow W$ (resp. $W \Rightarrow F$) property with union bound if the scheme also satisfies that $\sum_{S \in \mathscr{S}} \Pr[u^S(\mathsf{ORAM}^{*\infty}_L[\mathbf{s}]) > |S| \cdot Z + R] = \mathrm{negl}(\lambda)$. Informally, this means the statement "the probability that a failure witness exists is negligible" can be proved via a union bound over all possible witnesses $S \in \mathscr{S}$.*

The definitions remain the same for a wORAM scheme. In particular, for a wORAM scheme ORAM*, a subset S witnesses a failure if $u^S(\mathsf{ORAM}^{*\infty}_L[\mathbf{s}]) > |S| \cdot Z + R$ (and not $|S| \cdot (Z + 1) + R$, even though, looking forward to our construction of wORAM, we will use buckets of size $(Z + 1)B$).

Definition 8 (Suitable Tree ORAM). *We say that a Tree* ORAM *scheme is suitable if it satisfies the following conditions.*

1. *It admits a proof via infinite ORAM. That is, for all access sequence $\mathbf{s}$ and random coins r, $st(ORAM^Z[\mathbf{s}; r]) > R$ iff $st^Z(ORAM^\infty[\mathbf{s}; r]) > R$.*
2. ORAM *satisfies the $W \Rightarrow F$ property with respect to some set $\mathscr{S}$, with union bound.*
3. $\mathsf{TransVar}($ORAM$)$ *satisfies the $F \Rightarrow W$ property with respect to the same $\mathscr{S}$.*
4. ORAM *allows free evictions. That is, if the client is allowed to trigger evictions on uniformly random leaves at will during a sequence of accesses, correctness still holds.*

Requiring all those properties may seem demanding, but they naturally hold for several existing Tree ORAM schemes, including Path ORAM and Simple ORAM. This will be shown in more detail in Sect. 5. Intuitively, this is because many schemes admit a proof via infinite ORAM, either explicitly (in the case of Path ORAM), or trivially (in the case of Simple ORAM, where the ORAM and its infinite variant are identical up to correctness failures). Similarly, the $F \Rightarrow W$ property is either already known, or trivial; and the *free eviction* property is immediate. The only property that requires some care is to show that $\mathsf{TransVar}($ORAM$)$ satisfies the $F \Rightarrow W$ property. However, it is much more tractable than trying to analyze the correctness of a wORAM scheme directly (even without having to contend with variable size blocks, the correctness analysis of Tree ORAM schemes such as Path ORAM is notoriously complex).

4.4   Main Result

Theorem 1 (Main Theorem). *Let* ORAM *be any suitable Tree ORAM scheme. If* ORAM *is a correct ORAM scheme, then* **TransVar**(ORAM) *is a correct wORAM scheme.*

Before diving into the proof proper, we sketch the underlying approach. Because of the F $\Rightarrow$ W and W $\Rightarrow$ F properties required by the suitability assumption, showing the wORAM scheme is correct essentially amounts to showing that no set $S \in \mathscr{S}$ witnesses a failure. We wish to analyze the function that maps the sizes of items to the usage of S (*i.e.* the sum of sizes of all items in S). Ultimately, we want to show that the probability that the usage of S exceeds $|S| \cdot Z + R$ is negligible, regardless of item sizes.

The proof strategy is to upper-bound the previous probability by a Schur-convex function, and show that this function is negligible. The idea behind this strategy is that if a function of item sizes is Schur-convex, then in order to upper bound the function for *all* possible vectors of item sizes, it is enough to upper-bound it for a set of maximal vectors for the majorization order. Luckily, due to the requirement that item sizes are of size at most B, and that the sum of items sizes are at most NB, a single weight vector majorizes all others, namely the vector $(B, \ldots, B, 0, \ldots, 0)$. Hence, it is enough to upper-bound the function for that specific vector. But this is actually quite easy, because this weight vector essentially amounts to having all items be of the same size, which reduces to the correctness of the original (unweighted) ORAM instance.

Thus, the core of the proof is to find a suitable Schur-convex function. This is done via a first-moment argument (Lemma 2), which allows us to work with expectancies instead of probabilities. Expectancies are much better behaved with respect to convexity (due to the linearity of expectation). Eventually, we massage the upper bound into a suitable Schur-convex function (in the proof, this is the map $\mathbf{w} \mapsto \mathbb{E}[X_{\mathbf{s}, L, S}(\mathbf{w})]$), and show it is convex essentially by showing that it is structured as a composition of convex maps. Using Lemma 1, we deduce that it is Schur-convex.

Proof. First, we show a simple self-contained technical lemma.

Lemma 2. *Let X be an integral random variable defined over $[0, t] \subset \mathbb{N}^+$, with $t \in \mathsf{Poly}(\lambda)$. Then $\Pr[X > R] = \mathsf{negl}(\lambda)$ if and only if $\mathbb{E}(\max(0, X - R)) = \mathsf{negl}(\lambda)$.*

Proof. First, recall that the expectation of a positive integral variable Y can be written as:

$$\mathbb{E}(Y) = \sum_{i \geq 0} \Pr[X > i].$$

As a corollary, for any integral variable Y satisfying $0 \leq Y \leq t$:

$$\Pr[Y > 0] \leq \mathbb{E}(Y) \leq t\Pr[Y > 0]. \tag{1}$$

Observe that the event $X > R$ is equivalent to $\max(0, X - R) > 0$. Using that observation, and applying (1) to the variable $\max(0, X - R)$, we get:

$$\Pr[X > R] \leq \mathbb{E}(\max(0, X - R)) \leq t\Pr[X > R].$$

Since $t \in \mathsf{Poly}(\lambda)$, we are done. ∎

Let ORAM be a suitable and correct Tree ORAM scheme. Let ORAM* ← TransVar(ORAM). Let $\mathbf{s}$ be a legal sequence of accesses for ORAM*. We need to show that $\Pr[st(\mathsf{ORAM}^*[\mathbf{s}]) > R] = \mathsf{negl}(\lambda)$.

Since ORAM satisfies the F ⇒ W property with respect to some set $\mathscr{S}$, it suffices to show that the probability that there exists $S \in \mathscr{S}$ witnessing the failure is negligible, i.e. $\Pr[\exists S \in \mathscr{S}, u^S(\mathsf{ORAM}^*{}_L^{\infty}[\mathbf{s}]) > |S| \cdot (Z + 1) + R]$ is negligible.

Let us fix $S \in \mathscr{S}$. We want to show that $\Pr[u^S(\mathsf{ORAM}^*{}_L^{\infty}[\mathbf{s}]) > |S| \cdot (Z + 1) + R]$ is negligible. (This is not enough to imply that the probability that there *exists* such an S is negligible, since $\mathscr{S}$ may have superpolynomial cardinality; we will come back to this point later.) A crucial observation is that in $\mathsf{ORAM}^*{}_L^{\infty}$, the sizes of data items plays no role. In particular, given an access sequence $\mathbf{s}$ and associated random coins r, the location of each item in the tree is entirely determined *independently of the size of the data items.*

Given an access sequence $\mathbf{s}$ with m items in total, and a *size allocation vector* $\mathbf{w} = (w_i)_{i \leq m} \in [0,1]^m$, define $\mathbf{s}(\mathbf{w})$ to be the access sequence $\mathbf{s}$, modified such that at the outcome of the sequence the i-th item has size w_i. Let Π be the set of permutation matrices of size m. Let $X_{\mathbf{s},L,S}(\mathbf{w}) = \max_{\mathbf{P} \in \Pi}(\max(0, u^S(ORAM^*{}_L^{\infty}[\mathbf{s}(P\mathbf{w})]) - (|S| \cdot Z + R)))$. By Lemma 2, $\mathbb{E}[X_{\mathbf{s},L,S}(\mathbf{w})]$ is an upper bound on $\Pr[u^S(\mathsf{ORAM}^*{}_L^{\infty}[\mathbf{s}]) > |S| \cdot (Z + 1) + R]$, so it is enough to show that $\mathbb{E}[X_{\mathbf{s},L,S}(\mathbf{w})]$ is negligible. This will follow from the next lemma. While the lemma is not difficult to prove, we view it as the core of the argument.

Lemma 3. *Let $\mathbf{s}$ be a legal sequence of accesses, and let $S \in \mathscr{S}$. Then the map $f : \mathbf{w} \mapsto \mathbb{E}[X_{\mathbf{s},L,S}(\mathbf{w})]$ is Schur-convex.*

Proof. First, we show that $X_{\mathbf{s},L,S}$ is convex when the random coins used in the ORAM construction are fixed. Until further notice, we assume that all random coins are fixed. Only $\mathbf{w}$ varies. Let $\lambda \in [0,1]$, and let $\mathbf{v}, \mathbf{w}$ be two size allocation vectors. We begin by observing that the map $g : \mathbf{w} \mapsto u^S(ORAM^*{}_L^{\infty}[\mathbf{s}(P\mathbf{w})])$ is linear. This is because, as already noted, whether an item is stored in a node from S or not is independent of the weight of the items. As a consequence, $g(\mathbf{w})$ is equal to the sum of the weights of items stored in S, i.e. it is a fixed linear combination of w_i's (with binary coefficients). Since g is linear, it is trivially convex.

Now we observe that for any constant C, the map $h : x \mapsto \max(0, x - C)$ is increasing and convex. Since the composition of an increasing convex function with a convex function is convex, we deduce that the map $h \circ g$ is convex. Since $X_{\mathbf{s},L,S}(\mathbf{w}) = \max_{\mathbf{P} \in \Pi} h \circ g(\mathbf{P}\mathbf{w})$, it is a maximum of convex maps, so it is also convex.

On the other hand, $X_{\mathbf{s},L,S}(\mathbf{w})$ is symmetric by construction, since it takes the maximum over all permutations of $\mathbf{w}$. By Lemma 1, since $X_{\mathbf{s},L,S}(\mathbf{w})$ is both symmetric and convex, it is Schur-convex.

It remains to show that Schur convexity still holds when considering the expectation of $X_{\mathbf{s},L,S}(\mathbf{w})$. (From now on, we no longer assume that random coins are fixed.) However, it is easy to see that if a probabilistic map is Schur-convex for every fixed choice of random coins (sometimes called stochastical Schur-convexity), then its expectation is also Schur-convex [22]. We conclude that $\mathbf{w} \mapsto \mathbb{E}[X_{\mathbf{s},L,S}(\mathbf{w})]$ is Schur-convex. ∎

Corollary 1. *Let $\mathbf{s}$ be a legal sequence of accesses with weight vector $\mathbf{w}$, and let $S \in \mathscr{S}$. $\mathbb{E}[X_{\mathbf{s},L,S}(\mathbf{w})]$ is negligible.*

Proof. For an access sequence to be legal, its weight vector $\mathbf{w}$ must satisfy that $w_i \leq B$ for all i, and $\sum w_i \leq NB$. Observe that all such vectors are majorized by the vector $\mathbf{v} = (B, \ldots, B, 0, \ldots, 0)$ containing N initial B's. Since $\mathbb{E}[X_{\mathbf{s},L,S}(\mathbf{w})]$ is Schur-convex, it follows that $\mathbb{E}[X_{\mathbf{s},L,S}(\mathbf{w})] \leq \mathbb{E}[X_{\mathbf{s},L,S}(\mathbf{v})]$: in order to upper bound $\mathbb{E}[X_{\mathbf{s},L,S}(\mathbf{w})]$, it suffices to focus on the weight vector $\mathbf{v}$. (This is the point of using a Schur-convexity argument.)

But in the case of the vector $\mathbf{v}$, all items are of the same size B, or of size 0.[1] In that case, ORAM* behaves exactly like ORAM, except that accesses to items of size 0 translate to evictions without any prior item access. In particular, The usage of S is the same for ORAM* and ORAM. Since we assume that ORAM has the free eviction property, it remains correct when allowing eviction queries by the client. Since it is also assumed to be correct and to satisfy $W \Rightarrow F$, it follows that the usage of S cannot exceed $|S| \cdot Z + R$ except with negligible probability, hence the same holds for ORAM*, and we are done.

So far, we have shown that the probability that any given S witnesses a failure in ORAM* is negligible. To conclude the proof, it remains to show that the probability that there *exists* an $S \in \mathscr{S}$ witnessing a failure is negligible. This does not follow immediately from the previous statement, because $|\mathscr{S}|$ may be superpolynomial. However, looking at the proof of Lemma 2, we see that when switching from expectation to probability and back, we only lose a factor t. In our case, the stash size is a random variable bounded by NB, so we have that for every S,

$$\Pr[u^S(\mathsf{ORAM}^{*\infty}_L[\mathbf{s}(\mathbf{v})]) > |S| \cdot Z + R] \leq NB \Pr[u^S(\mathsf{ORAM}^\infty_L[\mathbf{s}]) > |S| \cdot Z + R].$$

---

[1] The reader may observe that items of size 0 are not technically legal per the earlier definition of wORAM, which asks that items are of size at least 1; however, `TransVar(ORAM)` remains well-defined even for items of size 0, so nothing stops us from using them within the proof—the reason we forbade items of size 0 is that they would allow for an unbounded number of items, which would require a position map of unbounded size, but this is irrelevant for the current line of reasoning.

Since ORAM is assumed to satisfy W $\Rightarrow$ F *with union bound*, and $NB \in \text{poly}(\lambda)$, we know that the sum of the latter quantity over all $S \in \mathscr{S}$ is negligible, hence ORAM* inherits the same union bound property. It follows that the probability that there exists a failure witness S for ORAM* is negligible. Since ORAM* satisfies the F $\Rightarrow$ W property, we conclude that ORAM* is correct.

4.5 Experimental Results

To test empirically the correctness of our weighted ORAM, we implemented a Path ORAM structure and performed simulated accesses. We did two experiments: one with N object of the same size (which simulates the standard case) and one with objects of variable sizes (the sizes are uniformly random, but sum to N). Our results are presented as graphs in Fig. 1.

We took inspiration from the experiment in Sect. 7 of [27]. The experiment went as follows:

- We generated ORAM structures for N objects, with $N = 2^L$ and $L \in \{10, 11, \ldots, 22\}$. The bucket size is $Z \in \{3, 4\}$
- We chose the maximum block size to be $B = 512$.
- For the standard ORAM simulation, all blocks were of size B. For the variable ORAM simulation, blocks were taken uniformly at random in $[B]$, with the total sum of the sizes being $N \cdot B$. The number m of blocks generated is roughly $2 \cdot N$.
- We start with the Path ORAM loaded randomly with the objects at its leaves, and perform between $10 \cdot m$ and $50 \cdot m$ accesses in the order $\{1, 2, \ldots, m, 1, 2, \ldots\}$.

Figure 1 suggests that objects of variable size are even less prone to stash overflows than the standard case. Path ORAM seems to be much more resilient, and able to handle different sets of objects than what the correctness proof shows.

Regarding bucket size, we make an observation similar to that of [27]: even though the correctness of the ORAM was proved for $Z + 1 = 6$, the construction appears resilient enough to work correctly even when $Z + 1 = 4$. In [27], the empirical results suggest that Path ORAM can be used when Z is as low as 4. Thus we have reasons to believe that our method does not lead to a blowup in the server storage.

5 Application to Existing Tree ORAMs

In this section we present several concrete constructions: a weighted Simple ORAM, based on Chung and Pass's Simple ORAM [9], and a weighted Path ORAM, based on the seminal work by Shi *et al.* [27]. The construction for Path-ORAM can be easily adapted to build a weighted *Random-Index ORAM* from the one presented in [16], as the block-holding structure is virtually the same. We also sketch the application to Circuit ORAM [30] and OPRAM [8]. By Theorem 1, in each case, it suffices to show that the scheme is suitable. The weighted variant is then obtained by applying `TransVar`.

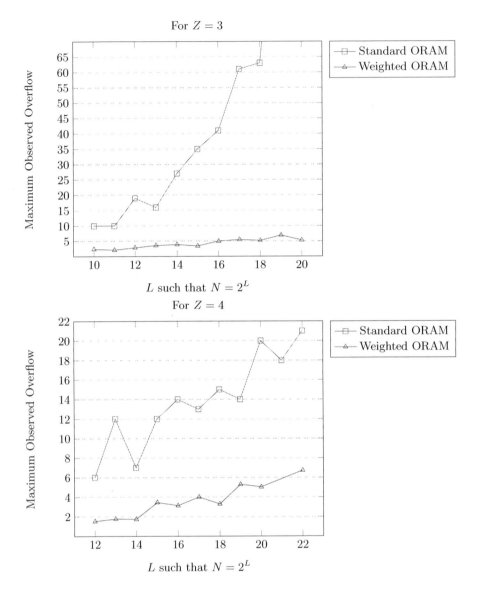

Fig. 1. Experimental results when $Z \in \{3, 4\}$

5.1   Weighted Simple ORAM [9]

Let `SimpleOram` = (`SimpleOram.Setup`, `SimpleOram.Access`) In the original paper, each bucket has a capacity of $Z = O(log(N))$ and the ORAM overflows *iff* there is a bucket with more than Z items: there is no stash. From the perspective of the Tree ORAM framework from Sect. 3.2, a stash does exist, however, it is required that it is empty at the outcome of any (legal) sequence of accesses. That is, we set the stash bound R to 0.

In `SimpleOram`:

- The `ChooseEvictionPath`(*leaf*) method is implemented by choosing a path uniformly at random (the *leaf* argument is ignored).
- The `ChooseNextBlock`(*stash, bucket, path*) method is implemented by returning the first item among items whose position is such that its meet with the current path is exactly *bucket*. (In other words, all items are stored as low as possible along the eviction path.) The correctness of `SimpleOram` relies on the fact that all such items will fit in the current bucket; items are never pushed somewhere else in case a bucket is full.

We want to show that `SimpleOram` is suitable. Define $\mathscr{S}$ to be the set containing the singleton {*bucket*} for each tree node *bucket*. The fact that the correctness of `SimpleOram` is equivalent to the fact that no element of $\mathscr{S}$ witnesses a failure is immediate, since the correctness of `SimpleOram` requires precisely that no node overflows. Hence, `SimpleOram` satisfies W ⇒ F (and F ⇒ W) with respect to $\mathscr{S}$. The fact that TransVar(`SimpleOram`) satisfies F ⇒ W is immediate for the same reason. `SimpleOram` also satisfies the union bound requirement, because its analysis in [9] relies on just such a union bound. The fact that it supports free evictions is also follows directly the analysis in [9] (additional evictions translate to more success chances in the dart game argument at the center of the analysis). We conclude that `SimpleOram` is suitable.

Theorem 2. *TransVar(SimpleOram) is a correct wORAM scheme.*

5.2   Weighted Path ORAM [27]

Let $ORAM_L^Z \leftarrow$ `PathOram.Setup`(N, Z) be an instance of Path ORAM. In `PathOram`, the bucket capacity Z is a small constant (the scheme is proven correct for $Z = 5$, we shall use this value). The stash capacity R is a $O(log(N))$.

In `PathOram`:

- The `ChooseEvictionPath`(*leaf*) method is implemented by returning $\mathcal{P}$(*leaf*).
- The `ChooseNextBlock`(*stash, bucket, path*) method is implemented by returning an item from the buffer such that the its associated position is below *bucket*, and the meet between the position of the item and *path* is lowest among the items in *buffer*. (In other words, the scheme tries to store each item as low as possible along the eviction path.)

Theorem 3. *TransVar(PathOram) is a correct wORAM scheme.*

Proof. Define $\mathscr{S}$ to be the set of all subtrees of the ORAM tree, where a *subtree* is a subset of nodes closed for the *parent* relation (*i.e.* if the set contains a node, it also contains its parent). The analysis of [27] proves that PathOram satisfies both F ⇒ W and W ⇒ F with respect to $\mathscr{S}$, via a union bound. The fact that PathOram supports free evictions also follows from the analysis. In the remainder, we focus on showing that PathOram* ← TransVar(PathOram) satisfies F ⇒ W.

For that purpose, we follow a similar approach to the initial part of the analysis in [27]. Let us define a post-processing algorithm G_Z, which is applied to $ORAM^{*\infty}_L$ after a sequence of accesses. This is an virtual algorithm used only to analyze stash usage, so we can allow it to do things that are not possible within the normal wORAM framework. In particular, we let G_Z "split" any object of size w in two objects of sizes w_1 and w_2 such that $w_1 + w_2 = w$, storing the two chunks at distinct locations. G_Z repeats the following process, as long as there are overfull buckets (*i.e.* whose size is strictly more than Z—to avoid cluttering the notation, all sizes are implicitly divided by the block size B):

1. Select a bucket that has load of more than Z. Let's say that this bucket is at level h on some path P to the root. Remove blocks from the bucket (splitting one if needed) so that it ends up having a load of exactly Z.
2. Find the highest level $i \leq h$ such that the bucket at level i on the path P has a load $< Z$. If such a bucket exists, store as many blocks as possible there until the load is Z (making a split if needed). Keep going upwards, any blocks that remain are stored in the stash.

First, let us prove that the stash usage (i.e. the cumulated size of the objects in the stash) of the post processed ∞-ORAM is greater than the stash usage of $ORAM^{*Z}_L$:

$$st^Z(ORAM^{*\infty}_L[\mathbf{s}]) \geq st(ORAM^{*Z}_L[\mathbf{s}]). \tag{2}$$

Start by noticing that the order in which blocks are processed by G_Z does not matter in the end: the blocks are now "continuous" since we can split them, so the size of the blocks get distributed in the same way towards the same blocks, regardless of origin. So $st^Z(ORAM^{*\infty}_L[\mathbf{s}])$ is unique. We can generalize the argument from [27]: assume that G_Z processes blocks from the bucket β_1 at level l_1 on path p_1, then blocks from the bucket β_2 at level l_2 on path p_2. We want to show that the loads in the buckets in $p_1 \cup p_2$ do not change if we let G_Z process β_2 before β_1 (We can see the stash as being the parent of the root, i.e. at level -1.) Without loss of generality, we can assume that those buckets are siblings (i.e. $l_1 = l_2 = l$), since only $p_1 \cap p_2$ will be affected by a change in the order. Assume that the post-processed blocks from β_1 are of total size W_1, W_2 for those from β_2. G_Z first distributes a "mass" of size W_1 in the buckets from level $l-1$ to -1 in $p_1 \cap p_2$, and then a mass of size W_2 in those same buckets. Before the distribution, let us call V_i the available space in the bucket at level $i \in \{-1, 0, \ldots, l-1\}$ on path $p_1 \cap p_2$. When distributing a mass W, G_Z performs Algorithm 3 (we assume that $V_{-1} = \infty$): The $\{V_i\}$ are the same after a successive application of Algorithm 3 on W_1 then W_2 or after its application on W_2 then W_1.

Algorithm 3. Distribution of mass of blocks

Distribution(W):

1: $i \leftarrow l$
2: **while** $W > 0$ **do**
3:     $i \leftarrow i - 1$
4:     **if** $V_i \geq W$ **then**
5:         $V_i \leftarrow V_i - W$
6:         $W \leftarrow 0$
7:     **else**
8:         $V_i \leftarrow 0$
9:         $W \leftarrow W - V_i$

Remark 1. We wish to attract the reader's attention on one point: in what precedes, we consider for simplicity that blocks are taken in bulk from the buckets, whereas in what follows it is more convenient to assume that G_Z processes them individually. It doesn't make a difference for the same reason that the order doesn't matter.

We can finally prove Statement (2). Informally, we can see that during the accesses, $ORAM^{*Z}_L$ stores blocks in buckets and in the stash in a more lenient way than G_Z, since it allows blocks to "stick out" of the buckets. More precisely, after the accesses of $\mathbf{s}$ in $ORAM^{*\infty}_L[\mathbf{s}]$, there exists a way to move blocks from the buckets they reside in to their final destination from $ORAM^{*Z}_L[\mathbf{s}]$ (in another bucket or the stash). Since the order in which we post-process blocks from the buckets does not matter, we can assume that this particular order is accessed by G_Z. If that is the case, after the processing of each block, G_Z puts that block in the bucket where it belongs according to $ORAM^{*Z}_L[\mathbf{s}]$. However, should a part of the block (or its entirety) stick out of the bucket (i.e. causes the load to become $\geq Z$), this part will be moved to a higher block or the stash. Thus the processing of each block by G_Z causes the stash size to either stay the same or to increase. Thus at the end of the processing, $st^Z(ORAM^{*\infty}_L[\mathbf{s}]) \geq st(ORAM^{*Z}_L[\mathbf{s}])$.

Second, let us prove that the stash usage $st^Z(ORAM^{*\infty}_L[\mathbf{s}])$ in the post-processed ∞-ORAM is $> R$ if and only if there exists a subtree T in $ORAM^{*\infty}_L$ such that $u^T(ORAM^{*\infty}_L[\mathbf{s}]) > n(T) \cdot Z + R$:

$\Longleftarrow$:

If there is such a T, the behavior of G_Z makes it so that the stash must hold more than R objects.

$\Longrightarrow$:

Let us define T to be the maximal subtree that contains all buckets of size at least Z after the post-processing. If a bucket b is not in T, it has an ancestor b' that has a used space of strictly less than Z, so the blocks of b cannot go to the stash. Thus all blocks in the stash came from buckets in T, and thus $u^T(ORAM^{*\infty}_L[\mathbf{s}]) > n(T) \cdot Z + R$.

This shows that PathOram is suitable.   □

5.3   Weighted Oblivious Parallel RAM [8]

Boyle, Chung, and Pass's protocol [8] is based on Simple ORAM. Their framework present ORAM protocols to parallel algorithms, i.e. with multiple processors (clients). The TransVar function is not impacted by the fact that there are several clients: The modifications to the subroutines still capture this case, the correctness analysis holds. The only new component is the broadcast routine, where one of the CPUs broadcasts information about a certain block to the others CPUs. These messages are bounded by the size of the block. That could lead to a leakage, however because of the need to index the blocks, which will take a size of at least $log(m) \geq log(N)$. Thus, we can lower bound the size of the messages by $O(log(N))$: their size will not leak information on the block. This yields a correct weighted OPRAM.

5.4   Weighted Circuit ORAM [30]

Circuit ORAM is a variant of Path ORAM, where the client only needs local space to hold one block. To achieve this, the eviction algorithm is slightly different and the stash is stored by the server (as the parent of the root node) instead of locally.

The correctness analysis of this scheme is based on the same principles as the one for Path ORAM. The function TransVar yields a correct ORAM here too. To prove this, we only need to show how we can adapt for the fact that the stash is stored on top of the tree. Figuring out which way to do this is not obvious since, because of the varying block size, the client cannot simply stream the content of the stash block by block: it would leak block size information. We propose a simple fix, which we also use when dealing with Trivial ORAM:

– We allow the client to store an additional space of size B (the maximal size of a block). This gives the client a local space of at least $2 \cdot B$.
– Whenever the client needs to access the stash, the client streams the content of the stash *chunk by chunk*, where each chunk is of size B. That way, since a block must always reside inside at most 2 chunks (see Fig. 2), the client will read every object at the end of the stash stream.
– When the client wishes to write back a block, it is done locally among two chunks.

This way, the scheme stays correct and secure even with objects of variable size. The application of the generic criterion shows that Circuit ORAM is compatible with blocks of variable size.

6   Searchable Encryption from Weighted ORAM

With Searchable Symmetric Encryption (SSE), a client can delegate the storage of a database to a honest-but-curious server. The client is then able to perform searches on the database by issuing Search queries to the server. In the case

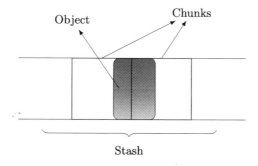

Fig. 2. A block of size $< B$ in 2 chunks

of *dynamic* SSE, the client may also update the database by issuing Update queries to the server. The security goal is that the information leaked to the server during these different operations should be limited, in a sense that will be defined soon.

Here, we focus on the case of single-keyword search. In that setting, the client's database DB consists of a collection of documents, and Search queries ask to retrieve all documents that contain a given keyword. In modern SSE schemes, this functionality is realized efficiently by building a reverse index: For each keyword w, a list of the identifiers of documents matching the keyword, written $DB(w)$, is maintained on the server side in some encrypted form. *Response-revealing* SSE allows the server to learn the list of document identifiers, while response-hiding SSE does not: they are sent back to the client in encrypted form. Once having retrieved the desired document identifiers, the client may perform some additional computation, such as intersecting the results with other queries, or may fetch the documents on the same or a different server. In the case of response-revealing SSE, if the same server stores the reverse index and the documents, the server can immediately send back the documents without the need of an additional roundtrip, at the cost of possibly leaking additional information to the server. We note that the documents could be stored in an ORAM to avoid additional leakage, and that a weighted ORAM would reduce the performance cost of this approach. However, as in most SSE literature, we focus on the reverse index.

For efficiency reasons, SSE typically does not seek to have minimum leakage, but rather to strike a compromise between security and performance by allowing a controlled amount of leakage. In the security model, the leakage allowed by the scheme is expressed by a *leakage function* $\mathcal{L} = \{\mathcal{L}_{\text{Setup}}, \mathcal{L}_{\text{Search}}, \mathcal{L}_{\text{Update}}\}$. The security model asks that during a Setup operation (resp. Search, Update) with input x, the information leaked to the server is included in $\mathcal{L}_{\text{Setup}}(x)$ (resp. $\mathcal{L}_{\text{Search}}(x)$, $\mathcal{L}_{\text{Update}}(x)$). More formally, it is required that there must exist a simulator $\mathcal{S}$ such that the view of the server during Setup(x) (resp. Search(x), Update(x)) should be indistinguishable from $\mathcal{S}(\mathcal{L}_{\text{Setup}}(x))$ (resp. $\mathcal{S}(\mathcal{L}_{\text{Search}}(x))$, $\mathcal{S}(\mathcal{L}_{\text{Update}}(x))$).

Response-revealing SSE schemes leak the *access pattern*: That is, the server learns the identifiers of all documents matched by a query. In some use cases, access pattern leakage can be quite damaging, and allow the server to infer a sizable amount of information about the database [7,14]. Even in the case of response-hiding SSE, the server can typically learn the *query pattern*: that is, the server can learn whenever the client repeats the same query. In many cases, the server can learn the *volume* of the answer: that is, the number of documents matched by the query.

In some use cases, these different types of information leakage can be quite damaging, as shown by so-called *leakage-abuse* attacks [7,15]. To thwart those attacks, recent works have developed various protections: such as volume-hiding SSE [17,25], and the line of work on *leakage suppression* [18]. The strongest form of protection, considered for instance in [11,18,23], involves the use of ORAM, or specialized variants of ORAM. This raises some questions about how to optimize the use of ORAM, in order to preserve the high efficiency goal of SSE. In particular, as discussed *e.g.* in [11], since reverse indexes contain lists that can greatly vary in size, it is not obvious how to fit them into a (fixed-block size) ORAM. Our main point in this section is that weighted construction introduced here fit this setting perfectly. Concretely, we propose two SSE constructions based on weighted ORAM: ZeroSSE and BlockSSE. A brief overview is given Fig. 3. We note that the main point of TWORAM, not reflected in the table, is to reduce the number of roundtrips in the iterative version of Path ORAM, thanks to a clever use of garbled circuits. However garbled circuits add a considerable overhead in practice.

Scheme	client storage	bandwidth overhead
TWORAM [11]	$\mathcal{O}(1)$	$\mathcal{O}(\lambda \log^2 N)$
ZeroSSE	$\mathcal{O}(W)$	$\mathcal{O}(\log(N/U))$
ZeroSSE'	$\mathcal{O}(1)$	$\mathcal{O}(\log^2 W + \log(N/U))$
BlockSSE	$\mathcal{O}(W)$	$\mathcal{O}(\log(N/B))$
BlockSSE'	$\mathcal{O}(1)$	$\mathcal{O}(\log^2 W + \log(N/B))$

Fig. 3. Overhead of ORAM-based SSE constructions. U is an upper bound on the longest list size, $W \leq N$ is the number of keywords, B is the ORAM block size.

6.1 Preliminaries

We follow the standard definition of SSE. A dynamic SSE scheme Σ consists of four protocols, defined as follows.

- $\Sigma.\mathsf{KeyGen}(1^\lambda)$: Takes as input the security parameter λ. Outputs the master secret key K.
- $\Sigma.\mathsf{Setup}(\mathsf{K}, N, \mathsf{DB})$: Takes as input the client secret key K, an upper bound on the database size N, and a database DB. Outputs an encrypted database EDB.

– Σ.Search($\mathsf{K}, w, \mathsf{st}; \mathsf{EDB}$): The client receives as input the secret key K, and keyword w. The server receives as input the encrypted database EDB. Outputs updated encrypted database EDB' for the server.
– Σ.Update($\mathsf{K}, (w, e); \mathsf{EDB}$): The client receives as input the secret key K, and a pair (w, e) of keyword w and document identifier e. The server receives as input the encrypted database EDB. Outputs updated encrypted database EDB' for the server.

The security model expresses that the view of the server can be simulated by an efficient simulator, receiving as input only the output of the leakage function. In more detail, we define two games, SSEReal and SSEIdeal. First, the adversary chooses a database DB. In SSEReal, the encrypted database EDB is generated by Setup($\mathsf{K}, N, \mathsf{DB}$), whereas in SSEIdeal, the encrypted database is simulated by a (stateful) simulator S on input $\mathcal{L}_{\mathsf{Setup}}(\mathsf{DB}, N)$. After receiving EDB, the adversary can issue search and update queries. In SSEReal, queries are answered using the real-world protocol. In SSEIdeal, the Search queries (resp. Update, Setup) on input x are simulated by S on input $\mathcal{L}_{\mathsf{Search}}(x)$ (resp. $\mathcal{L}_{\mathsf{Update}}(x)$, $\mathcal{L}_{\mathsf{Setup}}(x)$). Finally, the adversary outputs a bit b.

The scheme is said to be *$\mathcal{L}$-secure* (*i.e.* secure with respect to the leakage function $\mathcal{L}$) if for all PPT adversaries, there exists a PPT simulator such that the transcripts in the real and ideal world are computationally indistinguishable.

6.2   ZeroSSE

A line of recent work has aimed to hide volume leakage: that is, to hide the number of identifiers matching a given query [17,25]. Hiding volume leakage seems sensible when using ORAM technique to hide the query pattern, since volume leakage reveals information about the repetition of queries. This leads to the question of building on ORAM that also hides volume. For that purpose, an upper bound U is assumed on the volume of the longest list (that is, the longest query answer). As discussed in [11], the first approach one may think of is to use an ORAM with block size U; however, this would require padding all lists to U, which would be prohibitive in many use cases, since the longest list may be several orders of magnitude larger than the average list size. In the worst case, the blowup in storage is $\Omega(U)$, even before considering ORAM overheads. Another approach would be to use a smaller block size, at the cost of a larger ORAM overhead.

The idea of ZeroSSE is simply to use the weighted variant of Path-ORAM, TransVar(PathOram) with U as the upper bound on block size. Relative to the previous two approaches, this minimizes both the overhead due to padding, which is nonexistent since no padding is necessary, and the overhead due to ORAM, since we use the largest block size possible. In fact, since our main result is that Path ORAM can handle items of variable size at essentially no overhead, we contend that this is both the most natural and most efficient solution to build SSE with minimum leakage.

We define ZeroSSE in more details as follows. We note that Setup takes as input additional parameters U, which is an upper bound on the longest list size, and W, and upper bound on the number of keywords.

- ZeroSSE.Setup(K, N, DB, U): Initializes TransVar(PathOram) with block size U and number of leaves $\lceil N/U \rceil$, containing as (variable-size) blocks DB(w) for each keyword w. The position map, of size $\mathcal{O}(W)$ memory words, is stored on the client side.
- ZeroSSE.Search(K, w; EDB): The client queries the ORAM for keyword w to retrieve DB(w).
- ZeroSSE.Update(K, (w, e); EDB): The client queries the ORAM for keyword w to retrieve DB(w), and simply writes back DB(w) $\cup$ $\{e\}$. (Recall that our weighted construction allows modifying the size of blocks on the fly.)

ZeroSSE uses the non-iterative variant of Path-ORAM. This is because a client storage of $\mathcal{O}(W)$, while undesirable in general, is often accepted in forward-secure SSE [6]. Alternatively, we define ZeroSSE′ to use the fully iterative version of Path-ORAM, which reduces the client storage to $\mathcal{O}(1)$ memory words, at the cost of additional roundtrips, and an additional $\mathcal{O}(W \log^2 W)$ bandwidth overhead.

Theorem 4 (Security of ZeroSSE). *Assuming Path-ORAM is a correct and secure ORAM scheme, ZeroSSE is $\mathcal{L}$-secure with respect to the leakage function $\mathcal{L} = \{\mathcal{L}_{Setup}, \mathcal{L}_{Search}, \mathcal{L}_{Update}\}$, with $\mathcal{L}_{Setup} = \{N, U\}$ and $\mathcal{L}_{Search} = \mathcal{L}_{Update} = \varnothing$.*

See the full version for a proof of Theorem 4.

6.3   BlockSSE

An interesting property of ZeroSSE is that updates are indistinguishable from searches. In fact, addition and deletion of an arbitrary number of documents in a list can be performed in a single interaction at no additional cost. However, this also means that adding a single document to a keyword incurs an $\mathcal{O}(U \log^2 U)$ bandwidth cost. If cheaper updates for single documents are desirable, an alternative solution is to use a smaller blocks size. A smaller block size (linearly) reduces the cost of updates, while (logarithmically) increasing the cost of searches. While this is an attractive trade-off in update-heavy use cases, from a security standpoint, the fact that searches and updates are indistinguishable, regardless of the number of documents added or deleted during an update, is lost. BlockSSE also does not support deletions by default, although they can be added generically at some additional cost, as in [5].

An interesting feature of BlockSSE is that we can choose the block size B such that the size of a Path-ORAM tree node ZB is one memory page (or an integral number of memory pages). This optimizes the IO-efficiency of the resulting SSE, as discussed *e.g.* in [4].

To reduce the size of the position map, we use the pointer idea introduced in [31]. Namely, each block belonging to the same list DB(w) contains the position of the previous block. This allows the position map, stored on the client, to only store the position of the last block, resulting in $\mathcal{O}(W)$ storage.

We define BlockSSE in more details as follows. Note that Setup takes as input additional parameters B, which is the desired block size, and W, and upper bound on the number of keywords. Update takes as additional parameter U, which is an upper bound on the longest list size.

- BlockSSE.Setup(K, N, DB, U): Initializes TransVar(PathOram) with block size B and number of leaves $n = \lceil N/B \rceil$. For each keyword w, the list $DB(w)$ is split into $\lceil DB(w)/B \rceil$ chunks of size at most $B - \lceil \log n \rceil$, with no padding. The i-th chunk for keyword w is inserted into the ORAM at a random position, together with the position of the $(i-1)$-th chunk. The position l_w of the last chunk is stored on the client side.
- BlockSSE.Search(K, w, U; EDB): The client queries the ORAM at position l_w, retrieves the last chunk $DB(w)$ together with the position of the penultimate chunk, and iteratively retrieves the position of each previous chunk in the same manner. Each chunk i is assigned a new position uniformly at random, updating the position stored together with the next chunk accordingly.
- BlockSSE.Update($K, (w, e)$; EDB): If l_w is not a multiple of $B - \lceil \log n \rceil$, the client accesses the ORAM at position p_w, adds e to the data, replaces p_w by a new uniformly random position, and updates the ORAM according to this new data and position. If l_w is a multiple of $B - \lceil \log n \rceil$, a new block is inserted at a new uniformly random position, containing as data $\{e\}$ together with the position p_w of the previous last block. On the client side, p_w is updated to the position of the newly inserted block.

Theorem 5 (Security of BlockSSE). BlockSSE *is $\mathcal{L}$-secure with respect to the leakage function* $\mathcal{L} = \{\mathcal{L}_{Setup}, \mathcal{L}_{Search}, \mathcal{L}_{Update}\}$, *with* $\mathcal{L}_{Setup} = \{N, B\}$, $\mathcal{L}_{Search}(w) = \lceil |DB(w)|/B \rceil$, *and* $\mathcal{L}_{Update} = \varnothing$.

See the full version for a proof of Theorem 5. BlockSSE′ is the same as BlockSSE, except the iterative variant of Path-ORAM is used.

Acknowledgments. This work was supported by the ANR project SaFED.

References

1. Asharov, G., Komargodski, I., Lin, W.K., Nayak, K., Peserico, E., Shi, E.: OptORAMa: optimal oblivious RAM. In: Canteaut, A., Ishai, Y. (eds.) EUROCRYPT 2020, Part II. LNCS, vol. 12106, pp. 403–432. Springer, Heidelberg (2020). https://doi.org/10.1007/978-3-030-45724-2_14
2. Asharov, G., Naor, M., Segev, G., Shahaf, I.: Searchable symmetric encryption: optimal locality in linear space via two-dimensional balanced allocations. In: Wichs, D., Mansour, Y. (eds.) 48th ACM STOC, pp. 1101–1114. ACM Press (2016). https://doi.org/10.1145/2897518.2897562
3. Berenbrink, P., Friedetzky, T., Hu, Z., Martin, R.: On weighted balls-into-bins games. Theoret. Comput. Sci. **409**(3), 511–520 (2008)

4. Bossuat, A., Bost, R., Fouque, P.A., Minaud, B., Reichle, M.: SSE and SSD: page-efficient searchable symmetric encryption. In: Malkin, T., Peikert, C. (eds.) CRYPTO 2021, Part III. LNCS, vol. 12827, pp. 157–184. Springer, Heidelberg, Virtual Event, August 2021. https://doi.org/10.1007/978-3-030-84252-9_6

5. Bost, R.: Σοφος: Forward secure searchable encryption. In: Weippl, E.R., Katzenbeisser, S., Kruegel, C., Myers, A.C., Halevi, S. (eds.) ACM CCS 2016, pp. 1143–1154. ACM Press, October 2016. https://doi.org/10.1145/2976749.2978303

6. Bost, R., Fouque, P.A.: Security-efficiency tradeoffs in searchable encryption. PoPETs **2019**(4), 132–151 (2019). https://doi.org/10.2478/popets-2019-0062

7. Cash, D., Grubbs, P., Perry, J., Ristenpart, T.: Leakage-abuse attacks against searchable encryption. In: Ray, I., Li, N., Kruegel, C. (eds.) ACM CCS 2015, pp. 668–679. ACM Press, October 2015. https://doi.org/10.1145/2810103.2813700

8. Chan, T.H.H., Chung, K.M., Shi, E.: On the depth of oblivious parallel RAM. In: Takagi, T., Peyrin, T. (eds.) ASIACRYPT 2017, Part I. LNCS, vol. 10624, pp. 567–597. Springer, Heidelberg, December 2017. https://doi.org/10.1007/978-3-319-70694-8_20

9. Chung, K.M., Pass, R.: A simple ORAM. Cryptology ePrint Archive, Report 2013/243 (2013). https://eprint.iacr.org/2013/243

10. Dyer, K.P., Coull, S.E., Ristenpart, T., Shrimpton, T.: Peek-a-boo, i still see you: why efficient traffic analysis countermeasures fail. In: 2012 IEEE Symposium on Security and Privacy, pp. 332–346. IEEE Computer Society Press, May 2012. https://doi.org/10.1109/SP.2012.28

11. Garg, S., Mohassel, P., Papamanthou, C.: TWORAM: efficient oblivious RAM in two rounds with applications to searchable encryption. In: Robshaw, M., Katz, J. (eds.) CRYPTO 2016, Part III. LNCS, vol. 9816, pp. 563–592. Springer, Heidelberg, August 2016. https://doi.org/10.1007/978-3-662-53015-3_20

12. Goldreich, O., Ostrovsky, R.: Software protection and simulation on oblivious RAMs. J. ACM **43**(3), 431–473 (1996). https://doi.org/10.1145/233551.233553

13. Grubbs, P., Lacharité, M.S., Minaud, B., Paterson, K.G.: Pump up the volume: practical database reconstruction from volume leakage on range queries. In: Lie, D., Mannan, M., Backes, M., Wang, X. (eds.) ACM CCS 2018, pp. 315–331. ACM Press, October 2018. https://doi.org/10.1145/3243734.3243864

14. Grubbs, P., Lacharité, M.S., Minaud, B., Paterson, K.G.: Learning to reconstruct: statistical learning theory and encrypted database attacks. In: 2019 IEEE Symposium on Security and Privacy, pp. 1067–1083. IEEE Computer Society Press, May 2019. https://doi.org/10.1109/SP.2019.00030

15. Grubbs, P., Sekniqi, K., Bindschaedler, V., Naveed, M., Ristenpart, T.: Leakage-abuse attacks against order-revealing encryption. In: 2017 IEEE Symposium on Security and Privacy, pp. 655–672. IEEE Computer Society Press, May 2017. https://doi.org/10.1109/SP.2017.44

16. Halevi, S., Kushilevitz, E.: Random-index oblivious ram. Cryptology ePrint Archive, Paper 2022/982 (2022). https://eprint.iacr.org/2022/982

17. Kamara, S., Moataz, T.: Computationally volume-hiding structured encryption. In: Ishai, Y., Rijmen, V. (eds.) EUROCRYPT 2019, Part II. LNCS, vol. 11477, pp. 183–213. Springer, Heidelberg, May 2019. https://doi.org/10.1007/978-3-030-17656-3_7

18. Kamara, S., Moataz, T., Ohrimenko, O.: Structured encryption and leakage suppression. In: Shacham, H., Boldyreva, A. (eds.) CRYPTO 2018, Part I. LNCS, vol. 10991, pp. 339–370. Springer, Heidelberg, August 2018. https://doi.org/10.1007/978-3-319-96884-1_12

19. Larsen, K.G., Nielsen, J.B.: Yes, there is an oblivious RAM lower bound! In: Shacham, H., Boldyreva, A. (eds.) CRYPTO 2018, Part II. LNCS, vol. 10992, pp. 523–542. Springer, Heidelberg, August 2018. https://doi.org/10.1007/978-3-319-96881-0_18

20. Liu, Z., Huang, Y., Li, J., Cheng, X., Shen, C.: DivORAM: towards a practical oblivious RAM with variable block size. Inf. Sci. **447**, 1–11 (2018). https://doi.org/10.1016/j.ins.2018.02.071, https://www.sciencedirect.com/science/article/pii/S0020025518301427

21. Maas, M., et al.: PHANTOM: practical oblivious computation in a secure processor. In: Sadeghi, A.R., Gligor, V.D., Yung, M. (eds.) ACM CCS 2013, pp. 311–324. ACM Press, November 2013. https://doi.org/10.1145/2508859.2516692

22. Marshall, A.W., Olkin, I., Arnold, B.C.: Inequalities: theory of majorization and its applications, vol. 143. Springer, New York (2010). https://doi.org/10.1007/978-0-387-68276-1

23. Miers, I., Mohassel, P.: IO-DSSE: scaling dynamic searchable encryption to millions of indexes by improving locality. In: NDSS 2017. The Internet Society, February/March 2017

24. Minaud, B., Reichle, M.: Dynamic local searchable symmetric encryption. In: Dodis, Y., Shrimpton, T. (eds) Advances in Cryptology – CRYPTO 2022. CRYPTO 2022. Lecture Notes in Computer Science, vol. 13510. Springer, Cham (2022). https://doi.org/10.1007/978-3-031-15985-5_4

25. Patel, S., Persiano, G., Yeo, K., Yung, M.: Mitigating leakage in secure cloud-hosted data structures: volume-hiding for multi-maps via hashing. In: Cavallaro, L., Kinder, J., Wang, X., Katz, J. (eds.) ACM CCS 2019. pp. 79–93. ACM Press, November 2019. https://doi.org/10.1145/3319535.3354213

26. Roche, D.S., Aviv, A.J., Choi, S.G.: A practical oblivious map data structure with secure deletion and history independence. In: 2016 IEEE Symposium on Security and Privacy, pp. 178–197. IEEE Computer Society Press, May 2016. https://doi.org/10.1109/SP.2016.19

27. Stefanov, E., et al.: Path ORAM: an extremely simple oblivious RAM protocol. In: Sadeghi, A.R., Gligor, V.D., Yung, M. (eds.) ACM CCS 2013, pp. 299–310. ACM Press, November 2013. https://doi.org/10.1145/2508859.2516660

28. Talwar, K., Wieder, U.: Balanced allocations: the weighted case. In: Johnson, D.S., Feige, U. (eds.) 39th ACM STOC, pp. 256–265. ACM Press, June 2007. https://doi.org/10.1145/1250790.1250829

29. Talwar, K., Wieder, U.: Balanced allocations: the weighted case. In: Proceedings of the 39th Annual ACM Symposium on Theory of Computing, pp. 256–265 (2007)

30. Wang, X., Chan, H., Shi, E.: Circuit ORAM: on tightness of the Goldreich-Ostrovsky lower bound. Cryptology ePrint Archive, Report 2014/672 (2014). https://ia.cr/2014/672

31. Wang, X.S., et al.: Oblivious data structures. In: Ahn, G.J., Yung, M., Li, N. (eds.) ACM CCS 2014, pp. 215–226. ACM Press (November 2014). https://doi.org/10.1145/2660267.2660314

32. Weiß, M., Heinz, B., Stumpf, F.: A cache timing attack on AES in virtualization environments. In: Keromytis, A.D. (ed.) FC 2012. LNCS, vol. 7397, pp. 314–328. Springer, Heidelberg (2012). https://doi.org/10.1007/978-3-642-32946-3_23

NanoGRAM: Garbled RAM with $\widetilde{O}(\log N)$ Overhead

Andrew Park[1(✉)], Wei-Kai Lin[2], and Elaine Shi[1]

[1] Carnegie Mellon University, Pittsburgh, USA
ahp2@andrew.cmu.edu, we.lin@northeastern.edu
[2] Northeastern University, Boston, USA
runting@cs.cmu.edu

Abstract. We propose a new garbled RAM construction called NanoGRAM, which achieves an amortized cost of $\widetilde{O}(\lambda \cdot (W \log N + \log^3 N))$ bits per memory access, where λ is the security parameter, W is the block size, and N is the total number of blocks, and $\widetilde{O}(\cdot)$ hides poly log log factors. For sufficiently large blocks where $W = \Omega(\log^2 N)$, our scheme achieves $\widetilde{O}(\lambda \cdot W \log N)$ cost per memory access, where the dependence on N is optimal (barring poly log log factors), in terms of the evaluator's runtime. Our asymptotical performance matches even the *interactive* state-of-the-art (modulo poly log log factors), that is, running Circuit ORAM atop garbled circuit, and yet we remove the logarithmic number of interactions necessary in this baseline. Furthermore, we achieve asymptotical improvement over the recent work of Heath et al. (Eurocrypt '22). Our scheme adopts the same assumptions as the mainstream literature on practical garbled circuits, i.e., circular correlation-robust hashes or a random oracle. We evaluate the concrete performance of NanoGRAM and compare it with a couple of baselines that are asymptotically less efficient. We show that NanoGRAM starts to outperform the naïve linear-scan garbled RAM at a memory size of $N = 2^9$ and starts to outperform the recent construction of Heath et al. at $N = 2^{13}$.

Finally, as a by product, we also show the existence of a garbled RAM scheme assuming only one-way functions, with an amortized cost of $\widetilde{O}(\lambda^2 \cdot (W \log N + \log^3 N))$ per memory access. Again, the dependence on N is nearly optimal for blocks of size $W = \Omega(\log^2 N)$ bits.

1 Introduction

Garbled circuits, originally proposed by Yao [39,40], is a cryptographic technique for two parties to perform secure computation over their private data in two rounds. At a high level, a garbler can garble some computation expressed as a circuit as well as the inputs. An evaluator who obtains the garbled circuit and garbled inputs can securely evaluate the function over the inputs, resulting in garbled outputs that can only be decoded using the garbler's secret key.

Author ordering is randomized. The full version of the paper can be accessed at https://eprint.iacr.org/2022/191.

W-K. Lin—The work was done while the author was a postdoctoral researcher at CMU.

C. Hazay and M. Stam (Eds.): EUROCRYPT 2023, LNCS 14004, pp. 456–486, 2023.
https://doi.org/10.1007/978-3-031-30545-0_16

The evaluator learns nothing about the garbled inputs or outputs. Subsequently, numerous works have focused on making garbled circuits increasingly more practical [1, 10, 21–26, 32, 39, 40, 42]. In practice, however, computations are expressed in the Random Access Machine (RAM) model which is a mismatch for the circuit model. Converting RAM programs to circuits in general incur polynomial overhead in the RAM's space and time, making it prohibitive in practice especially when the computation involves big data. To avoid this expensive RAM-to-circuit conversion overhead, the elegant work of Lu and Ostrovsky [28] suggested a new abstraction called garbled RAM, which aims to garble a RAM program directly without converting it to a circuit. From a theoretical perspective, the goal of garbled RAM is to garble a program incurring only $\mathsf{poly}(\lambda, \log N)$ overhead where λ is the security parameter and N denotes the space of the RAM. Throughout the paper, we often use the metric "amortized cost per memory access" to characterize the performance of a garbled RAM scheme, which is the number of bits that must be communicated per memory access. Since the original work of Lu and Ostrovsky [28], a line of works [14, 17, 24, 29] have focused on improving garbled RAM constructions.

With the exception of the most recent work by Heath et al. [24], prior works on garbled RAM [14, 17, 29] did not care about the poly factor in the $\mathsf{poly}(\lambda, \log N)$ overhead, let alone concrete performance. Nonetheless, since garbled RAM was originally motivated by the need to speed up garbled random-access computation on big data, clearly, our dream is to make garbled RAM practical some day. The very recent work of Heath et al. [24] took a pioneering step towards this dream: they constructed a garbled RAM scheme that achieves $O(\lambda \cdot (W \log^2 N + \log^4 N))$ overhead where W denotes the block size. Specifically, when the block size $W = \Omega(\log^2 N)$, their scheme achieves $O(\lambda \cdot W \cdot \log^2 N)$ overhead. Their scheme assumes the existence of a circular correlation-robust hash or a random oracle — the same assumptions as the mainstream practical garbled circuit literature, including FreeXOR [10, 26] and subsequent improvements [25, 32, 42].

As a baseline of comparison, imagine that we actually allowed interaction. In this case, the state-of-the-art (for moderately large data) is running the Circuit ORAM algorithm [37] on top of an efficient garbled circuit implementation. In this case, the overhead would be $O(\lambda \cdot (W \log N + \log^3 N))$, which is a logarithmic factor smaller than that of Heath et al. [24]. In this paper, we ask the following natural question:

Can we have a (non-interactive) garbled RAM scheme whose asymptotical performance is competitive to the interactive state-of-the-art, that is, running Circuit ORAM on top of garbled circuits?

Our Results and Contributions. We answer the above question affirmatively. Following the elegant work of Heath et al. [24], we take another significant step forward towards the dream of making garbled RAM practical. Concretely, we show a new garbled RAM construction called NanoGRAM, that incurs $\widetilde{O}(\lambda \cdot (W \log N + \log^3 N))$ overhead where $\widetilde{O}(\cdot)$ hides poly log log factors. In comparison with Heath et al. [24], we save almost a logarithmic factor. Our scheme

Table 1: Comparison with prior works, where S_λ denotes the circuit size of the PRF that outputs λ bits, and CCR hash is Circular Correlation-Robust hash. See Appendix G and H of the online full version [30] for details.

	Assumption	Cost per access	Blackbox
Lu and Ostrovsky [28]	Circular GC^a	$O(\lambda S_\lambda W \log^2 N)$	No
Hazay and Lilintal [20]	OWF	$O(\lambda S_\lambda \cdot (W \log N + \lambda \log^2 N + \log^3 N))$	No
Garg et al. [14]	OWF	$O\left(\lambda^2 \cdot (W \log^4 N + \log^6 N)\right)$	Yes
Heath et al. [24]	CCR hashes	$O\left(\lambda \cdot (W \log^2 N + \log^4 N)\right)$	Yes
	OWF^b	$O\left(\lambda^2 \cdot (W \log^2 N + \log^4 N)\right)$	Yes
This work	CCR hashes	$\widetilde{O}\left(\lambda \cdot (W \log N + \log^3 N)\right)$	Yes
	CCR hashes^c	$O\left(\lambda B \cdot (W \log N + \log^3 N)\right)$	Yes
	OWF	$\widetilde{O}\left(\lambda^2 \cdot (W \log N + \log^3 N)\right)$	Yes

a. Circularly secure garbled circuit, see [17].
b. This is not documented in their paper, but it is a standard method to tweak their scheme.
c. Our practically efficient scheme, where B is the statistical security parameter.

makes the same assumptions as Heath et al. [24] as well as the standard literature on efficient garbled circuits [10,25,26,32,42], i.e., either assuming circular correlation-robust hashes or the random oracle model. Further, our garbled RAM construction is *blackbox* in the sense that it does not require garbling the circuit of some cryptographic primitive such as a pseudorandom function (PRF).

Theorem 1 (Garbled RAM from circular correlation-robust hashes).
Assume circular correlation-robust hashes or the random oracle model. There is a blackbox garbled RAM scheme where each memory access incurs an amortized cost of $\widetilde{O}\left(\lambda \cdot (W \log N + \log^3 N)\right)$ where λ is the security parameter, W is the block size, and N is the total number of blocks.
As a direct corollary, if $W = \Omega(\log^2 N)$, then our garbled RAM scheme achieves $\widetilde{O}(\lambda \cdot W \cdot \log N)$ amortized cost per memory access.

Modulo the poly log log factors, we believe that there may be some barriers for further improving our asymptotical results for blackbox garbled RAMs. First, for block sizes $W = \Omega(\log^2 N)$, our scheme has *optimal* dependence on N (barring poly log log factors) due to well-known ORAM lower bounds [18,19,27]. Second, for small block sizes, any further asymptotical improvement would likely imply a *statistically* secure ORAM that breaks the $O(\log^2 N)$ barrier — this is arguably the biggest open problem in the ORAM line of work, and no progress has been made for a long time[1]. Although computationally secure ORAMs [2,31] are a logarithmic factor more efficient than statistically secure ones, so far we do not know how to use computationally secure ORAM techniques in blackbox garbled RAMs, i.e., without having to garble the PRF employed by the ORAM. Third, as mentioned, even when allowing interactions, we do not know any scheme that performs asymptotically better than the Circuit-ORAM-over-garbled-circuit baseline.

---

[1] Garbled RAM only needs an ORAM in a relaxed model where we do not charge the cost of pre-processing, but even in this relaxed model, it remains an open question how to construct a $o(\log^2 N)$ statistical ORAM.

Our work also gives rise to a garbled RAM scheme from OWF but it incurs an extra λ factor in cost, as stated in the following corollary:

Corollary 1 (Garbled RAM from one-way functions). *Assume the existence of one-way functions. There exists a garbled RAM scheme that achieves $\widetilde{O}(\lambda^2 \cdot (\log^3 N + W \log N))$ amortized cost per memory access, where $\widetilde{O}(\cdot)$ hides* poly log log λ *factors.*

In particular, for large enough blocks $W = \Omega(\log^2 N)$, the resulting garbled RAM incurs $\widetilde{O}(\lambda^2 \cdot W \log N))$ amortized cost per memory access.

Compared to Prior Works. Table 1 compares our asymptotical result with prior garbled RAM works. The ealier works (e.g., [14,17,28]) used ORAM as a black-box and did not care about how large the poly log is. Both Heath et al. [24] and our work observe that to optimize the poly log factors, we need to open up the underlying ORAM, and tailor the ORAM's design specifically for garbled RAM. In our paper, a key observation is that the more uncertainty there is regarding which address will be accessed, the more overhead we need to pay to account for the uncertainty. Therefore, one of our main techniques is to localize the uncertainty (of which address is accessed) to polylogarithmically sized regions.

Besides those listed in the table, Gentry et al. [17] also propose a garbled RAM scheme from one-way function and identity-based encryption with poly-logarithmic cost. Additionally, they also propose a garbled RAM scheme from one-way function only but the asymptotical cost is N^ϵ for some constant $\epsilon \in (0,1)$. We did not include it in the table because the result is subsumed by Garg et al. [14]. The table also did not include reusable Garbled RAM [4,5,9] which are based on indistinguishability-based obfuscation (iO). Known reusable garbled RAM constructions can compress the total communication but they do not save the evaluator's runtime.

Concrete Performance. In additional to our main results, we explore the concrete performance. In Appendix A of the online full version [30], we suggest several practical optimizations to our garbled RAM scheme described in Theorem 1. Our practically efficient scheme eliminates constant and poly log log factors while introducing a statistical security parameter, as shown in Table 1. We developed a simulator for our garbled RAM scheme with these suggested optimizations. Our simulation results show that we break even with the naïve linear scan GRAM at about $N = 2^9$ memory size, and we start to outperform the prior work EpiGRAM [24] at about $N = 2^{13}$ memory size.

2 Technical Roadmap

2.1 Background

Encodings. We will use the following forms of encodings.

- *Garbling.* Suppose we choose some secret key $\mathsf{sk} = \Delta = \{0,1\}^\lambda$ where λ is the security parameter. Suppose every wire, which carries one bit, is assigned a *label* (also called a *language*) $L \in \{0,1\}^\lambda$. The *garbling* of a bit $b \in \{0,1\}$ on this wire, denoted $\{\!\{b\}\!\}$, is computed as $\{\!\{b\}\!\} = \Delta \cdot b \oplus L$. This encoding approach was first proposed in the elegant Free XOR work [26]. For a vector of bits $x \in \{0,1\}^k$, we use $\{\!\{x\}\!\}$ to mean the garbling of each bit one by one.
- *Sharing.* For efficiency purposes, we also adopt another form of encodings called *sharings* [24] that support only restricted forms of computation to be elaborated later. Given a random *label* (also called a *language*) $L \in \{0,1\}^k$, we can create a sharing $[\![x]\!]$ of a k bit string $x \in \{0,1\}^k$, that is, $[\![x]\!] = x \oplus L$.

For the time being, the reader may imagine that all encodings are in the form of garblings. We will explain how to use sharings to improve the efficiency later.

The Language Translation Problem. In a garbled circuit scheme, every garbled gate essentially performs some garbled computation over the garbled input wires, the computation result is encoded using the language of the output wires. Since the wiring in a circuit is static, the garbler knows the mapping between each gate's output and input languages a-priori, and can prepare the garbled truth table for each gate accordingly.

As prior works observed [14,17,24,28,29], in a garbled RAM scheme, the key challange is that of a *dynamic* language translation for a memory read or write. Take memory read for example, and henceforth, we also refer to each memory word as a *block*. Suppose that some garbled block resides at some physical location α, and is therefore garbled using a language related to the physical location α. We want to read the block back, but instead encoded using a global-time-dependent label. Only in this way, can we successfully feed this garbled block to the CPU's garbled next-instruction circuit. One can imagine that the garbler prepares a garbled next-instruction circuit for every time step t, and each such garbled circuit speaks a language dependent on the time t. The challenge is that the physical location to read in each time step t is dynamically generated, and cannot be determined statically at garbling time. This means that we need to dynamically translate location-dependent encodings to time-dependent encodings.

Switch: A Minimal Gadget for Dynamic Translation. A garbled switch, proposed in the elegant work of Heath et al. [24], is a basic building block that performs dynamic translation between a parent and two children nodes. Suppose that the parent node receives some garbled data and a garbled direction bit indicating which of the two children should receive the data. The parent node now wants to re-encode the data using a language that the corresponding child recognizes, so the child can receive the data and potentially perform some garbled computation on it. The security requirement says that the evaluator cannot learn anything about the encoded data, but it is allowed to learn the direction bit. Imagine that each node keeps track of some *local time* which corresponds to the number of times the node has been invoked. When garbled data arrives at any node, the input data should be encoded using a label that depends on the node's local time. To garble such a switch, the main challenge comes from the fact that the parent and the two children have different local clocks. When the parent routes garbled data to one of the children, it must re-encode the data using a language that depends on the child's local time. Unfortunately, the garbler cannot statically predict the mapping between the parent's local time and the destination child's local time.

Informally, a garbled switch has the following abstraction:

- **Garble.** The garbler receives an array of input labels denoted **InL**, and two stacks of output labels denoted **OutL**$_0$ and **OutL**$_1$, respectively. Specifically, **InL**$[\tau]$ denotes the language of the τ-th invocation of the parent node, **OutL**$_0[\tau]$ denotes the language of the τ-th invocation of the left child, and **OutL**$_1[\tau]$ denotes the language of the τ-th invocation of the right child. The garbler then outputs some garbled circuitry GC and garbled memory Gmem to be consumed later by the evaluator.
- **Switch.** The evaluator can consume GC and Gmem to perform garbled switch operations described below. In every time step τ (of the parent), the parent receives $\{\!\{b\}\!\}$ and $\{\!\{data\}\!\}$ where $b \in \{0, 1\}$ is a direction bit and data denotes the data to be routed to the b-th child. The evaluator can securely evaluate the following functionality: pop the next unconsumed label L from the b-th stack **OutL**$_b$, re-encode data using the label L, and output the result. We allow the evaluator to learn the direction bit b, however, it should not learn anything about the garbled data data.

Heath et al. [24] proposed an elegant idea that leverages two garbled stacks [24, 38, 42] to realize a garbled switch. Specifically, the garbler initializes two garbled stacks with the encoded contents **OutL**$_0$ and **OutL**$_1$, respectively. Whenever a new request arrives at the parent node, the evaluator makes a real pop from the b-th stack and makes a fake pop from the $(1 - b)$-th stack. The result of the real pop is an encoded label that corresponds to the current local time of the b-th child. The result of the fake pop is simply an encoding of 0. Observe that both popped values are encoded using labels dependent on the parent's local time. Similarly, the input $\{\!\{data\}\!\}$ is also garbled using a label dependent on the parent's local time. This makes it possible for the garbler to prepare a garbled circuit in advance that re-encodes the input $\{\!\{data\}\!\}$ using the popped label instead.

The cost of garbling such a switch is directly related to how many accesses we must provide. Suppose that each of the two children can be visited at most m times, and thus the parent can be visited at most $2m$ times. In this case, the parent's switch would need two garbled stacks each of capacity m. Using existing garbled stack techniques [24, 38, 42], the cost is $O_\lambda(w \cdot m \log m)$ where w is the payload length (i.e., the bit width of data), and we use $O_\lambda(\cdot)$ to hide factors that depend on the security parameter λ. This directly translates to an amortized cost of $O_\lambda(w \cdot \log m)$ per switch operation. Note that later on, we will actually care about minimizing the factors that depend on λ and w; however, for ease of understanding, we ignore these factors for the time being.

Why Heath et al. [24] *is inefficient.* At a very high level, Heath et al. [24] builds upon this minimal switch gadget that is capable of dynamic translation, and eventually obtains a full garbled RAM. Their blueprint is to first use garbled switches to build an *access-revealing one-time memory*, and then upgrade the access-revealing one-time memory to a full-fledged garbled RAM through a hierarchical data structure and recursion techniques. Interestingly, their usage of the hierarchical data structure and recursion is novel and tailored specifically for garbled RAM; it makes use of the fact that the data structure performs shuffling and the garbler is aware of the data shuffling pattern ahead of time, since the garbler is choosing the random coins used in the shuffling.

There are a couple of reasons why the approach of Heath et al. [24] is asymptotically and concretely non-optimal. One of the most important reasons is because their composition of garbled switches in a tree-like fashion is inefficient. To obtain an access-revealing one-time memory of size n, they need to garble a tree of switches with n leaves. The root node must provision for up to n accesses, each of the root's children must provision for $n/2$ accesses, ..., and each leaf must provision for one access. For simplicity, assume $w \geq \log n$. The total cost to garble the tree of switches would therefore be $O_\lambda(w \cdot n \log^2 n)$; which translates to an amortized cost of $O_\lambda(w \cdot \log^2 n)$ for each single request to the one-time memory. This cost is pre-recursion. After applying the full recursion, their asymptotical cost[2] becomes $O_\lambda(W \cdot \log^2 N + \log^4 N)$.

We wish to reduce the cost by roughly a logarithmic factor, that is, we aim for $\widetilde{O}_\lambda(W \cdot \log N)$ *pre-recursion* cost per memory access where $\widetilde{O}(\cdot)$ hides poly log log factors, rather than their $O_\lambda(W \cdot \log^2 N)$ cost.

2.2   Our Approach

As mentioned, with the exception of Heath et al. [24], earlier works on garbled RAM [14,17,28,29] adopt a two-step compilation approach : 1) compile the RAM program to an Oblivious RAM whose memory access patterns are safe to reveal — this approach can rely on off-the-shelf Oblivious RAM algorithms [7,37]; 2) compile an oblivious RAM to a garbled RAM (where the garbling does not shield memory accesses). Each step of the compilation incurs a separate polylogarithmic overhead, and the two sources of overheads are multiplied. Heath et al. [24] suggested a second approach where we work at a lower level of abstraction, and design customized garbled data structures and gadgets and then compose them into a Garbled RAM scheme.

First Attempt. We adopt the second approach. Since a garbled RAM scheme must embed some Oblivious RAM (ORAM) scheme in it, a natural attempt is to

---

[2] Throughout the paper, we use capitalized letters N and W to denote the number of blocks and block size of the final GRAM construction, and we use small letters n, m, and w to denote the size and payload length of building blocks. The reason for this distinction is because we need to instantiate multiple instances of these building blocks with varying parameters in the final scheme.

take a state-of-the-art *statistically* secure ORAM[3] such as Circuit ORAM [7,37], and ask how we can garble such a data structure.

We briefly describe the underlying non-recursive tree-based data structure that underlies Circuit ORAM [7,37]. The full ORAM scheme involves creating logarithmically many such trees through a standard recursion technique [33,35]. The pre-recursion ORAM tree is a binary tree with n leaf nodes, and each non-root node is a bucket of some capacity $O(1)$. The root bucket is super-logarithmic in size for storing overflowing blocks. The main *path invariant* is that every block is assigned to a random path (i.e., a path from the root to a random leaf node), and the choice of this random path is not revealed until the block is next accessed. To fetch a block, one looks up the path where the block resides through recursion, and the path can be identified by a leaf node often denoted leaf — we also call leaf the block's position identifier. Then, one looks up all buckets on the path from the root to the leaf node leaf. When a block with the requested logical address addr is encountered, the block is removed from the corresponding bucket. At this moment, the block is updated if the current operation is a write operation, and a new random path is chosen for the block. The block is then added back to the root bucket tagged with its new position identifier. After every access, we need to perform some maintenance operation that moves blocks closer to the leaf level, such that none of the buckets will overflow except with negligible probability. We may assume that the access patterns of the maintainance operations are a-priori fixed, e.g., using the reverse lexicographical order eviction idea first suggested by Gentry et al. [16].

To garble such a tree-based ORAM, a main challenge is that online phase has dynamic access patterns: every time we request a block, it goes through a random path in the ORAM tree. To solve this challenge, we can potentially rely on the garbled switch data structure. Suppose that every node in the tree has a garbled switch. When a memory access request arrives, it comes with ${addr, leaf}$ where addr is the block's logical address, and leaf is the block's position identifier; further, the request is garbled using a global-time-dependent label which also coincides with the local time of the root switch. Note that the cleartext value of leaf may be safely exposed to the evaluator. Recall that during this access, each bucket on some path will search for a block with the desired logical address addr, and if so, it returns the block's payload; else, it returns 0. We want to make sure that each bucket's fetch result is encoded using some global-time-dependent language, and the collection of all $O(\log n)$ languages are denoted $L_0, \ldots, L_{O(\log n)}$. Let ${L_0, \ldots, L_{O(\log n)}}$ be an encoding of these languages under some global-time-dependent label that is recognized by the root whose local clock coincides with the global clock.

---

[3] Although *computationally* secure ORAMs can achieve asymptotically better overhead in cloud outsourcing scenarios, we currently do not know any way to use computationally secure ORAMs in *blackbox* garbled RAM schemes, without having to securely evaluate the circuits of cryptographic primitives such as pseudo-random functions.

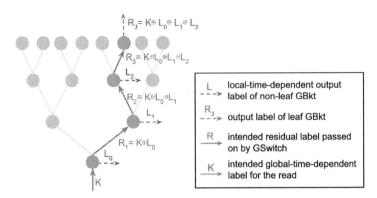

Fig. 1: XOR trick.

Now, imagine that the root receives the information $\{\{addr, leaf, L_0, \ldots, L_{O(\log n)}\}\}$. It uses $b = leaf[0]$ as the direction bit, and wants to route the information it has received to the b-th child. To achieve this, it must first re-encode the pair addr and leaf using a label that is dependent on the local time of the b-th child — and this can be accomplished by the garbled switch. Imagine that every node along the path does the same, and each node uses the next bit in leaf to decide its direction. In this way, each node along the path can receive a fetch instruction garbled using a language that matches its local time, and it can look in its own garbled memory whether a block exists with the desired addr. The fetch result is garbled using the corresponding garbled label which it received as part of the garbled input (i.e., $L_0, \ldots, L_{O(\log n)}$). Finally, some garbled CPU circuit can securely aggregate all $O(\log n)$ fetched results into a final result.

This naïve scheme has two sources of inefficiency. First, the root switch must provision for n accesses, each of the root's children must provision for $n/2 \pm o(n)$ accesses with high probability, and so on. Therefore, the total cost of all the switches is $O_\lambda(w \cdot \log^2 n)$ where w denotes the length of the payload being routed. The second drawback is the fact that the length of the payload w is large, since we need to route $O(\log n)$ labels each of λ bits long.

These two sources of inefficiency each incurs an extra $\log n$ factor that we want to get rid off. Below we discuss how to overcome these two sources of inefficiency. We shall begin with the second problem, which is a little easier than the first one.

Passing a Single Label with an XOR Trick. To overcome the second challenge, we introduce an XOR trick as depicted in Fig. 1. Assume that each node in the tree has a garbled bucket henceforth denoted GBkt and a garbled switch denoted GSwitch. A garbled bucket GBkt supports a Read operation: when given a logical address $\{\{addr\}\}$ garbled under an local-time-dependent input label, it will output the corresponding block's contents $\{\{val\}\}$ if the block is found, or output $\{\!\{0\}\!\}$ if not found. Further, the result is garbled using a local-time-dependent output label. Suppose that we want the final memory fetch result to be encoded under some global-time-dependent label K. Henceforth assume that the root is at level 0 of the tree, and let $\ell_{\max} = O(\log n)$ be the leaf level. As we traverse the path, each non-leaf bucket along the way encodes its result using labels $L_0, L_1, \ldots, L_{\ell_{\max}-1}$, respectively (we abuse notations where $L_0, L_1, \ldots$ are now *local-time-dependent*). Our idea is to pass an encoding of the label $L_{\ell_{\max}} = K \oplus L_0 \oplus \ldots \oplus L_{\ell_{\max}-1}$ to the leaf node, such that the leaf bucket will encode its fetch result using the label $L_{\ell_{\max}}$. This way, all the labels would XOR to K. This means that when we XOR the garbling of all $\ell_{\max} + 1$ fetched results, we obtain a garbling of the fetched result encoded under the label K. To achieve this, we can have each node in a non-leaf level ℓ pass an encoding of the residual label $R_\ell = K \oplus L_0 \oplus \ldots \oplus L_{\ell-1}$ to its child, encoded using a language dependent on the child's local time. The XOR trick saves us one logarithmic factor in cost.

Splitting Switches into Poly-logarithmically Sized Ones. To overcome the first challenge, our idea is to avoid using big switches that must be provisioned with a large number of accesses. Instead, we want to break up the big switches into poly-logarithmically sized ones. To achieve this, we observe that we can leverage ideas from the Bucket ORAM algorithm [13].

Background on Bucket ORAM. At a very high level, Bucket ORAM is a tree-based ORAM but with a hierarchical-style rebuild algorithm.

Let T be the maximum runtime of the RAM program, and let N be its space. In the Bucket ORAM tree, each bucket has size $2\mathsf{B} = O(\log(\frac{T \cdot N}{\delta}))$ where δ is the statistical failure probability. Like in any tree-based ORAM scheme [33], a bucket can store either *filler* blocks denoted $\bot$ or *real* blocks of the format (addr, leaf, data) where addr is the block's logical address, leaf denotes its position identifier, and data denotes its payload. The read phase of the algorithm is also like any tree-based ORAM [7,33,34,37]. To read a block, we first recursively look up its position identifier denoted leaf, we then look up the path from the root leading to leaf for the block requested. The block is removed from the corresponding bucket if found. Besides the tree data structure, there is also a small stash that can store up to B blocks. Any memory request must also search in the stash for the desired block. Moreover, after a block is fetched, it will be added to the stash (possibly with an updated payload string). For the time being, one can imagine that each bucket itself as well as the stash implement small ORAMs [6,8,11] such that they can look up a block in poly log log($\frac{T \cdot N}{\delta}$) time.

Interestingly, the maintainance phase of Bucket ORAM actually resembles a hierarchical ORAM [18,19]. Suppose that n and B are powers of 2. Let root be at level 0, and let $\ell_{\max} = \log_2 \frac{n}{\mathsf{B}}$. Each level i is rebuilt every $2^i \cdot \mathsf{B}$ steps. In particular, at the end of some time step t, if $t + 1$ is a multiple of n, we need to rebuild levels $0, \ldots, \ell_{\max}$ into level $\ell_{\max}$ and empty all remaining levels. Else, if we can express $t + 1$ as $j \cdot 2^\ell$ for some odd integer j, then we need to rebuild

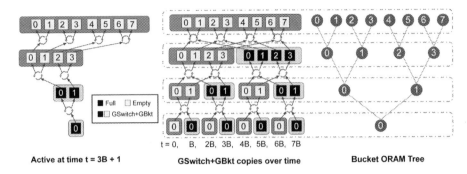

Active at time t = 3B + 1   **GSwitch+GBkt copies over time**   **Bucket ORAM Tree**

Fig. 2: Each node at level ℓ has $T/(\mathsf{B} \cdot 2^\ell)$ copies of GSwitch + GBkt, and at time t, the $\lfloor t/(\mathsf{B} \cdot 2^\ell) \rfloor$-th copy is active. The numbers show which copies of garbled circuitry correspond to which tree node in the same level.

levels $0, \ldots, \ell - 1$ into level ℓ, emptying the levels $0, \ldots, \ell - 1$ in the process. Further, the rebuild process must respect the position identifier each block has chosen. The Bucket ORAM work [13] shows how to accomplish this rebuild using a circuit whose size is *linear* in total number of elements involved in the rebuilding. For the purpose of this work, the details of the rebuild algorithm is not too important. Therefore, we give a brief description below and refer the reader to the Bucket ORAM work [13] for details. At a high level, the Bucket ORAM work suggested that this rebuild can be accomplished through a sequence of MergeSplit operations. In each MergeSplit operation, we take a pair of buckets as inputs and and output a pair of buckets. Each real block in the input buckets will go into one of the output buckets, and the choice depends on the corresponding bit in their leaf label. The MergeSplit operation essentially relies on sorting of objects with 1-bit keys, i.e., compaction [2]. Indeed, if we use a linear-sized compaction circuit to realize each MergeSplit, the total cost of the rebuild would be linear. For our paper, it does not matter to our final asymptotics even if we used bitonic sort to implement the MergeSplit, since this part of the overhead will not be the dominating factor.

Splitting Switches into Poly-Logarithmically Sized Ones. As shown in Fig. 2, each node at level ℓ in the tree has $T/(2^\ell \cdot \mathsf{B})$ instances of GBkt and GSwitch. The instances are indexed from $0, 1, \ldots, T/(2^\ell \cdot \mathsf{B}) - 1$. During time step $t \in [0 : T)$, the garbled instances indexed $\lfloor t/(2^\ell \cdot \mathsf{B}) \rfloor$ are active. Whenever a level is rebuilt, the existing GBkt and GSwitch instances corresponding to all tree nodes in this level finalize, and new instances are initialized.

Due to the rebuild schedule of Bucket ORAM, we know in advance for each instance at some parent node, which instances of its children it must communicate with. In other words, the communication graph between the instances are statically determined.

There are, however, some subtle challenges we need to resolve for this idea to work. Observe that half the switches finalize together with their children — this case is a little easier to handle since the new instances that take over can start fresh. For the other half, when they finalize, their children do not finalize at the same time. However, their children's local clocks have already advanced to some dynamic value which cannot be predicted in advance. In this case, we need to implement an explicit *hand-over* operation such that the new switches can inherit the necessary states from the switches whose jobs they are taking over. To achieve this we need the help of garbled data structures supporting dynamic finalization which we explain below.

Garbled Data Structures with Dynamic Finalization. We adopt a modular framework to present our scheme which makes it easier to verify its correctness and security. A new abstraction we propose is a garbled data structure with a dynamic finalization — we believe that our definitions may be of independent interest in future works on garbled data structures and algorithms.

Consider some data structure that supports some function calls $\mathsf{Func}_1, \ldots,$ Func_c. Additionally, there is a special function called $\mathsf{Finalize}$ which is called at the end of its life cycle to output some final garbled state — for example, the final garbled state can be an encoding of all unvisited blocks stored in the data structure. We assume that except for the $\mathsf{Finalize}$ function, the call schedule for all other functions are fixed a-priori. The $\mathsf{Finalize}$ function, however, may be called at any time t^* within some a-priori known time bound $t_{\max}$. No matter in which local time step t^* the function $\mathsf{Finalize}$ is invoked, the finalized states it outputs must be garbled under some fixed label (that does not depend on t^*). To enforce that the evaluator calls $\mathsf{Finalize}$ at the right time, the $\mathsf{Finalize}$ call has to take in a garbled signal $\{\!\{1\}\!\}$ that explicitly authorizes the call. More specifically, a garbled data structure supporting dynamic finalization has the following abstraction:

- **Garbler.** The garbler takes in some initial memory array **DB**, input and output labels denoted **InL** and **OutL**, and outputs the garbled circuit GC and initial garbled memory Gmem. Specifically, **InL** and **OutL** provide the following labels:

$$\mathbf{InL} := (I_0, \ldots, I_{t_{\max}-1}, C_0, \ldots, C_{t_{\max}-1}, C_{t_{\max}})$$
$$\mathbf{OutL} := (O_0, \ldots, O_{t_{\max}-1}, F)$$

  where for $\tau \in [0 : t_{\max})$, I_τ and O_τ denote the time-dependent labels used to encode the input and the output of the τ-th (non-$\mathsf{Finalize}$) operation, respectively; for $t^* \in [0 : t_{\max}]$, C_{t^*} is the label used to encode the finalization signal should $\mathsf{Finalize}$ be invoked at time step t^*; and F denotes the label used to encode the final state st output by $\mathsf{Finalize}$.
- **Evaluator.**
  1. In each local time step $\tau \in [0 : t_{\max})$, the evaluator can call garbled operations $\{\!\{\mathsf{outp}\}\!\} \leftarrow \mathsf{Func}_{i_\tau}^{\mathsf{GC}}(\mathsf{Gmem}, \{\!\{\mathsf{inp}\}\!\})$ where the call schedule $i_\tau \in$

[c] is fixed a-priori. The inputs and outputs must be garbled under labels dependent on the local time. The operations may cause updates to the internal garbled memory.

2. At some dynamic point of time $t^* \in [0 : t_{\max}]$, the evaluator may call $\widetilde{\mathsf{st}} \leftarrow \mathsf{Finalize}^{\mathsf{GC}}(\mathsf{Gmem}, \widetilde{1})$: The evaluator must input a garbled finalization signal $\widetilde{1}$ (which is garbled under a t^*-dependent label). Intuitively, this signal forces the evaluator to evaluate Finalize in the intended time step t^* and not any other time step. The Finalize algorithm outputs a garbled final state denoted $\widetilde{\mathsf{st}}$, which is garbled under the fixed label F which is *independent* of t^*.

Garbled data structures with dynamic finalization are used in multiple places in our construction. For example,

- Each GBkt instance is visited a dynamic number of times before finalization, and when finalized, it must output the remaining unvisited elements encoded under some fixed label. The results will then be passed to the garbled rebuilder algorithm.
- Each GSwitch instance is also visited a dynamic number of times just like GBkt. As mentioned earlier, for half of the switches, when they finalize, they must pass some internal state to the next switch that takes over, such that the next switch knows the local clocks of the children.
- Finally, some of the building blocks (e.g., garbled stack, access-revealing one-time memory) we use to construct our GBkt and GSwitch are also garbled data structures with dynamic finalization.

We formally define the security for such garbled data structures with dynamic finalization in Sect. 3, and we give efficient instantiations partly relying on a building block called an expiring vault (see Appendix D.1 of the online full version [30]).

The need to support dynamic finalization complicates our construction. In several cases, we cannot use existing building blocks for this reason and have to construct our own variants. For example, in our construction, each GBkt itself is a small garbled dictionary capable of translating a memory fetch result from using a location-based label to using a local-time-dependent label. Since we need a dynamic finalization capability from the GBkt, we cannot directly use prior work such as Heath et al. [24]. Similarly, for other seemingly standard building blocks such as garbled stack, we also have to construct our own variants and prove them secure.

Additional Optimizations. So far, we have explained our ideas assuming that all wires are encoded using garbling. To save a factor of λ, we adopt several ideas suggested by Heath et al. [24]. In particular, we will encode some wires using sharings rather than garblings. Unlike garblings, sharings are space-preserving since the sharing of some string has the same length as the original string. However, sharings can only be involved in restricted computations.

1. a shared bit can be XORed with another shared bit or a constant value known at garbling time that is hard-wired in the garbled circuitry or garbled memory, and the outcome of such an operation is a sharing too, i.e., $(\llbracket x \rrbracket, \llbracket y \rrbracket) \rightarrow \llbracket x \oplus y \rrbracket$;

2. a shared string may be multipled with a garbled bit whose cleartext value is known by the evaluator, and the result of the operation is a sharing, i.e., $(\{\!\{b^E\}\!\}, \llbracket y \rrbracket) \rightarrow \llbracket b \cdot y \rrbracket$ where $y \in \{0,1\}^k$. Throughout the paper, if the evaluator is allowed to know the cleartext of some garbled value $\{\!\{\mathsf{val}\}\!\}$, we often write $\{\!\{\mathsf{val}^E\}\!\}$ to make this explicit.

The elegant work by Heath et al. [24] described techniques to efficiently implement the above operations involving shared bits, assuming the existence of a random oracle. Specifically, the first type of operations require only 1 bit per XOR gate, the second type of operations require only $O(k + \lambda)$ bits to garble a gate that multiply $\{\!\{b^E\}\!\}$ with $\llbracket y \rrbracket$ where k is the bit-width of y.

Later on in our constructions, the data stored in garbled stacks which are part of the garbled switches will be in the form of sharings; furthermore, the labels passed long the tree paths will also be in the form of sharings. These optimizations save us a λ factor in the final costs.

3   Definitions: Garbled Data Structure

Recall that in Sect. 2.1, we defined two types of encodings called *sharings* and *garblings* for garbled circuits. We refer the reader to Appendix B of the online full version [30] for a more detailed review of garbled circuits. We now proceed to define garbled data structures.

Our building blocks involve several garbled data structures. An evaluator can invoke multiple garbled operations of the data structure during its life cycle. Every garbled data structure has a *local time* denoted $\tau \in [0 : t_{\max}]$ where $t_{\max}$ is the maximum number of operations supported. When the τ-th operation is called, we say that the garbled data structure is in local time τ. Unless otherwise stated, our garbled data structures will have the following interface where we use $\widetilde{x}$ to denote an encoding of x which is either a garbling or sharing of x:

- Gmem, GC $\leftarrow$ Garble(1^λ, sk, params, **DB**, **InL**, **OutL**): the algorithm takes in the security parameter, some secret key sk $\in \{0,1\}^\lambda$, parameters params (explained shortly), the initial memory array **DB**, input and output labels denoted **InL** and **OutL** used to encode the garbled inputs and outputs respectively. It outputs the garbled memory Gmem and some garbled circuits denoted GC. Here, the parameters params typically contains the word size often denoted w, the length (often denoted m) of the initial memory array **DB**, and the maximum number of operations denoted $t_{\max}$.
- Gmem$'$, $\widetilde{\mathsf{outp}} \leftarrow \mathsf{Func}_1^{\mathsf{GC}}(\mathsf{Gmem}, \widetilde{\mathsf{inp}})$,

...,

Gmem$'$, $\widetilde{\mathsf{outp}} \leftarrow \mathsf{Func}_c^{\mathsf{GC}}(\mathsf{Gmem}, \widetilde{\mathsf{inp}})$: some functions to be called by the evaluator. We assume that the *call schedule for the functions* $\mathsf{Func}_1, \ldots, \mathsf{Func}_c$ *is known a-priori*, where the call schedule specifies exactly which of these functions will be invoked in each time step $\tau \in [0 : t_{\max})$. For the evaluator to evaluate these functions in a garbled manner, it needs to consume the garbled circuitry GC which we write in the superscript of the procedure. Calling these garbled operations not only outputs some encoded answer $\widetilde{\text{outp}}$, but also may result in updates to the internal encoded memory denoted Gmem'. The inputs $\widetilde{\text{inp}}$ and outputs $\widetilde{\text{outp}}$ are garbled using labels dependent on the data structure's local time.

- $\widetilde{\text{st}} \leftarrow \text{Finalize}^{\text{GC}}(\text{Gmem}, \widetilde{1})$: the Finalize function can be invoked in *any* time step $t^* \in [0 : t_{\max}]$, where t^* also denotes the number of operations invoked prior to calling Finalize. Unless otherwise noted, *exactly when* Finalize *will be invoked is unknown at the time of garbling*. To successfully invoke Finalize, the evaluator must input a garbled finalization signal $\widetilde{1}$ (which is garbled under a t^*-dependent label). Intuitively, this signal forces the evaluator to evaluate Finalize in the intended time step t^* and not any other time step. The Finalize algorithm outputs a garbled final state denoted $\widetilde{\text{st}}$, which is garbled under a fixed label which is *independent* of t^*.

The input/output labels **InL** and **OutL** fed into the Garble algorithm should contain the following:

$$\textbf{InL} := (I_0, \ldots, I_{t_{\max}-1}, C_0, \ldots, C_{t_{\max}-1}, C_{t_{\max}})$$
$$\textbf{OutL} := (O_0, \ldots, O_{t_{\max}-1}, F)$$

where for $\tau \in [0 : t_{\max})$, I_τ and O_τ denote the time-dependent labels used to encode the input inp and the output outp in the τ-th time step, respectively; for $t^* \in [0 : t_{\max}]$, C_{t^*} is the label used to encode the finalization signal should Finalize be invoked at time step t^*; and F denotes the label used to encode the final state st output by Finalize.

Relationship with Garbled Circuits. Garbled circuits can be viewed as a special case of our garbled data structure formulation. Specifically, a garbled circuit can be viewed as a garbled data structure that supports only one operation Func after garbling. For this reason, we do not give a separate definition for garbled circuits. Later on, we will rely on garbled circuits as a building block to construct garbled data structures.

Correctness. Suppose that there is some (insecure) data structure $\mathcal{DS}$ supporting the operations $f_1, \ldots, f_c$ and fin. We say that a garbled data structure scheme correctly implements $\mathcal{DS}$ iff for any $\lambda \in \mathbb{N}$, any $\text{sk} \in \{0,1\}^\lambda$, any params $= (m, w, t_{\max})$, any **DB**, any **InL** and **OutL**, any $1 \leq t^* \leq t_{\max}$, any sequence of function calls $i_0, \ldots, i_{t^*-1} \in [c]$, any input sequence $\text{inp}_0, \ldots, \text{inp}_{t^*-1}$: let $\text{outp}_0, \ldots, \text{outp}_{t^*-1}, \text{st}$ be the correct outcomes when we initialize $\mathcal{DS}$ with **DB** and then make the calls $\{f_{i_\tau}(\text{inp}_\tau)\}_{\tau \in [0:t^*)}$, and fin in sequence, then, the following must be true with probability 1:

- Gmem, GC $\leftarrow \text{Garble}(1^\lambda, \text{sk}, \text{params}, \textbf{DB}, \textbf{InL}, \textbf{OutL})$;

- for $\tau \in [0 : t^*)$: let $\widetilde{\mathsf{inp}_\tau}$ be a correct encoding of inp_τ using label I_τ, let $\mathsf{Gmem}, \widetilde{\mathsf{outp}_\tau} \leftarrow \mathsf{Func}_{i_\tau}^{\mathsf{GC}}(\mathsf{Gmem}, \widetilde{\mathsf{inp}_\tau})$;
- let $\widetilde{1}$ be a correct encoding of the finalization signal 1 under label C_{t^*}, let $\widetilde{\mathsf{st}} \leftarrow \mathsf{Finalize}^{\mathsf{GC}}(\mathsf{Gmem}, \widetilde{1})$;
- then, it must be that $\{\widetilde{\mathsf{outp}_\tau}\}_{\tau \in [0:t^*)}$ and $\widetilde{\mathsf{st}}$ are valid encodings of the correct outputs $\{\mathsf{outp}_\tau\}_{\tau \in [0:t^*)}$ and st, under the labels $\{O_\tau\}_{\tau \in [0:t^*)}$ and F, respectively.

Security. We define the security of garbled data structures below.

Definition 1 (Security of garbled data structures (and garbled circuits)). *We say that a garbled data structure scheme is secure w.r.t. some leakage function* $\mathsf{Leak}(\cdot)$, *iff there exists probabilistic polynomial-time (p.p.t.) simulators* Sim, *such that for for any* $\lambda \in \mathbb{N}$, *any* $\mathsf{params} = (m, w, t_{\max})$, *any* $\mathbf{DB}$, *any* $1 \le t^* \le t_{\max}$, *any sequence of function calls* $i_0, \ldots, i_{t^*-1} \in [c]$, *for any input sequence* $\mathsf{inp}_0, \ldots, \mathsf{inp}_{t^*-1}$, *any output labels* $\mathbf{OutL}$ *of appropriate length, for any subset of inputs* $S \subseteq \{\mathsf{inp}_\tau, 1_\tau\}_{\tau \in [0:t^*)}$ *whose encodings are to be simulated, for any choice of* $\mathbf{InL}[\neg S]$ *where* $\mathbf{InL}[\neg S]$ *denotes the part of* $\mathbf{InL}$ *used to encode the set* $\neg S$, *the outputs of the real and ideal experiments below are computationally indistinguishable:*

Real Experiment. Input: λ, params, $\mathbf{DB}$, t^*, function calls $i_0, \ldots, i_{t^*-1} \in [c]$, input sequence $\mathsf{inp}_0, \ldots, \mathsf{inp}_{t^*-1}$, subset of inputs S, subset of input labels $\mathbf{InL}[\neg S]$, output labels $\mathbf{OutL}$.

1. Sample $\mathsf{sk} \leftarrow \mathsf{Gen}(1^\lambda)$, and sample the remaining unspecified input labels $\mathbf{InL}[S]$ at random;
2. Let $\{\widetilde{S}, \widetilde{\neg S}\} = \{\widetilde{\mathsf{inp}_\tau}, \widetilde{1_\tau}\}_{\tau \in [0:t^*)}$ be correctly encoded inputs and finalization signals using sk and labels $\mathbf{InL}$;
3. Let $\mathsf{Gmem}, \mathsf{GC} \leftarrow \mathsf{Garble}(1^\lambda, \mathsf{sk}, \mathsf{params}, \mathbf{DB}, \mathbf{InL}, \mathbf{OutL})$;
4. Output $\mathsf{Gmem}, \mathsf{GC}, \widetilde{S}$.

Ideal Experiment. Input: λ, params, $\mathbf{DB}$, t^*, function calls $i_0, \ldots, i_{t^*-1} \in [c]$, input sequence $\mathsf{inp}_0, \ldots, \mathsf{inp}_{t^*-1}$, subset of inputs S, subset of input labels $\mathbf{InL}[\neg S]$, output labels $\mathbf{OutL}$.

1. Sample $\mathsf{sk} \leftarrow \mathsf{Gen}(1^\lambda)$;
2. Let $\widetilde{\neg S}$ be correctly encoded inputs in subset $\neg S$ using sk and labels $\mathbf{InL}[\neg S]$;
3. Run the ideal functionality using the given $\mathbf{DB}$, function calls $f_{i_0}, \ldots, f_{i_{t^*-1}}$, and input sequence $\mathsf{inp}_0, \ldots, \mathsf{inp}_{t^*-1}$, and finally, run fin. Let $\mathsf{outp}_0, \ldots, \mathsf{outp}_{t^*-1}$ and st be the results correspondingly;
4. Let $\{\widetilde{\mathsf{outp}_\tau}\}_{\tau \in [0:t^*)}$ and $\widetilde{\mathsf{st}}$ be correctly encoded outputs and finalized state using sk and labels $\mathbf{OutL}$;
5. Run the simulator

$$\mathsf{Sim}\left(1^\lambda, \mathsf{params}, t^*, \{i_\tau, \widetilde{\mathsf{outp}_\tau}\}_{\tau \in [0:t^*)}, \widetilde{\mathsf{st}}, \widetilde{\neg S}, \mathsf{Leak}(\{i_\tau, \mathsf{inp}_\tau\}_{\tau \in [0:t^*)})\right)$$

and output the result.

Note that when $\neg S = \emptyset$, then the above notion is a direct adaptation of the standard security definition for garbled circuits to garbled data structures. Therefore, the above definition can be viewed as a generalization of standard garbled circuit security. In particular, this generalization allows us to fix the encodings of a subset of the inputs denoted $\neg S$, feed these encodings $\widetilde{\neg S}$ to the simulator, and have the simulator simulate the the rest of the garbled inputs $\widetilde{S}$, along with the garbled circuitry GC and garbled memory Gmem. We sometimes refer to the set of inputs $\neg S$ whose input labels have been fixed as the *fixed set*, and the set of inputs S whose input labels are not fixed as the *free set*. We make this generalization for convenience later. Jumping ahead, when we write our garbled algorithms, we often allow *garbled input sharing*, that is, the same garbled input wire is fed into two or more garbled components. In this case, we will need to use the generalized security definition in our proofs.

As mentioned earlier, we have two forms of encodings, garblings and sharings. Later in our constructions, in fact only *garbled* wires (as opposed to shared wires) can be input to multiple garbled components. Therefore, we additionally impose the following constraints to Definition 1:

- The fixed set $\neg S$ must contain only *garbled* inputs variables;
- Any *shared* input must be in the free set S.

Existing constructions of garbled circuits [1,10,25,26,32,39,40,42], including the techniques needed from Heath et al. [24] naturally satisfy the above generalized notion too.

Encoding Cleartext Outputs. Later in our construction, sometimes we also have a garbled circuit or garbled data structure output cleartext rather than encoded outputs. Our above formulation actually also captures cleartext outputs if we use the encoding scheme described in Appendix B.1 of the online full version [30], and thus we can adopt this formulation without loss of generality. In particular, a cleartext output bit can be expressed as either a sharing whose label is 0, or a garbling whose label ends with a 0 bit. In particular, we will follow the approach mentioned in prior work [24,42], where we choose Δ at random subject to the last bit being 1. In this way, as long as the label of a garbling ends with a 0 bit, the last bit of the encoding will be the cleartext value of the bit.

Performance Metric. In this paper, we measure cost by the size of the garbled program, in terms of the number of bits. We often use the metric "cost per access" where we amortize the total cost over the number of memory accesses.

Remark 1. Unless otherwise noted, we assume the above syntax and conventions for any garbled data structure we define. There is one slight exception, which is the data structure GSwitch defined in Sect. 4.2 — in fact, this is the critical data structure for handling the non-determinism of memory accesses. Jumping ahead a little, GSwitch is initialized with two stacks of output labels denoted $\mathbf{OutL}_0$ and $\mathbf{OutL}_1$, and every operation, one label is popped from a stack of choice, and this popped label will be used as the output label.

Remark 2. Known garbled circuits constructions [1, 10, 21–26, 32, 39, 40, 42] also satisfy the following notion of simulation — our proofs also make use of this simulation notion. There exists a simulator Sim′, such that for any output labels **OutL**,

$$\mathsf{GC} \stackrel{c}{\equiv} \mathsf{Sim}'(1^\lambda, C)$$

where GC is the honest garbling of the circuit C using randomly generated input labels as well as **OutL**, and $\stackrel{c}{\equiv}$ means computational indistinguishability. This notion says we can simulate the garbled circuitry without knowing the (encoded) outputs, if we do not have to also simulate the active encoded inputs.

3.1   Notational Conventions

Omitting Gmem *and* GC*without risking ambiguity.* In the above, we use Gmem to denote a garbled data structure's internal encoded memory. Since the external caller of the data structure need not worry about Gmem, when we write our algorithms, we often omit writing the Gmem term explicitly. Moreover, we also omit writing the GC in the superscript of the garbled function calls without risking ambiguity. For example, suppose we use GDataStruct to denote some instance of a garbled data structure, we often write $\widetilde{\mathsf{outp}} \leftarrow \mathsf{GDataStruct.Func}_i(\widetilde{\mathsf{inp}})$, omitting the Gmem as well as the GC-superscript. This means that this function call is consuming the Gmem and GC of the GDataStruct instance.

Implicit Label Matching Convention. We often rely on an implicit label matching convention to describe our garbled data structures. For example, if we write the following statements as part of the evaluator's algorithm:

$$\mathsf{GDataStruct}_0.\mathsf{Func}(\{\!\{x\}\!\}):$$
$$\{\!\{y\}\!\} \leftarrow \mathsf{GDataStruct}_1.\mathsf{Foo}(\{\!\{x\}\!\});$$
$$\{\!\{z\}\!\} \leftarrow \mathsf{GDataStruct}_2.\mathsf{Bar}(\{\!\{y\}\!\});$$
$$\text{output } \{\!\{z\}\!\};$$

Assuming that $\mathsf{GDataStruct}_1$ and $\mathsf{GDataStruct}_2$ are not called anywhere else, then the above implies that

- the input label of the τ-th call to $\mathsf{GDataStruct}_0.\mathsf{Func}$ should match the the input label of the τ-th call to $\mathsf{GDataStruct}_1.\mathsf{Foo}$;
- the output label of the τ-th call to $\mathsf{GDataStruct}_1.\mathsf{Foo}$ should match the the input label of the τ-th call to $\mathsf{GDataStruct}_2.\mathsf{Bar}$;
- the output label of the τ-th call to $\mathsf{GDataStruct}_0.\mathsf{Func}$ should match the the output label of the τ-th call to $\mathsf{GDataStruct}_2.\mathsf{Bar}$;

Unless otherwise noted, the labels for all variables are randomly selected subject to such implicit matching constraints (which can always be unambiguously implied by our algorithm description).

4   Building Blocks for Garbled Memory

4.1   Stack (GStack)

Definition. A garbled stack GStack is initialized with some initial memory array denoted **DB**, and it supports Pop operations controlled by a flag denoted $b \in \{0, 1\}$. If $b = 0$, nothing will be popped, and if $b = 1$ an element will be popped from the stack. In our application later, it is actually safe to reveal the control flag b. For GStack, we let params $= (m, w, t_{\max})$, where m is the number of entries in the initial **DB**, w is the bit-width of each entry, and $t_{\max}$ is the maximum number of Pop operations. It is promised that at most m number of Pop calls will have the flag b set to 1, i.e., the stack will never deplete. We shall assume that m is a power of 2, and moreover, $m \geq 16$.

- Gmem, GC $\leftarrow$ Garble(1^λ, sk, params, **DB**, **InL**, **OutL**): takes in the security parameter λ, the parameters params, the initial stack elements **DB** containing m elements each of size w, and the input/output garbling labels denoted **InL** and **OutL** respectively, and outputs some internal garbled memory Gmem and garbled circuitry GC.
- Gmem$'$, $[\![\mathsf{res}]\!] \leftarrow \mathsf{Pop}^{\mathsf{GC}}(\mathsf{Gmem}, \{\!\{b^E\}\!\})$: depending on the flag b, either pop an element from the stack or do nothing. Correctness requires that 1) if $b = 1$, then the result $\mathsf{res} = \mathbf{DB}[\mathsf{cnt}_\tau]$ where τ is the current time step, and cnt_τ denotes the total number of Pop operations so far (not counting the current one) where the flag $b = 1$; and 2) if $b = 0$, then the result $\mathsf{res} = 0$. Moreover, it must be that $\mathsf{Lbl}([\![\mathsf{res}]\!])$ is the τ-th output label contained in **OutL**.
- $\{\!\{\mathsf{ucnt}\}\!\} \leftarrow \mathsf{Finalize}^{\mathsf{GC}}(\mathsf{Gmem}, \{\!\{1\}\!\})$: upon receiving a garbled signal $\{\!\{1\}\!\}$ indicating that the data structure should be finalized in this time step, output a garbling of ucnt, the total number of elements popped expressed in a unary format and prepended with 0s to a length of m. Correctness also requires that $\mathsf{Lbl}(\{\!\{\mathsf{ucnt}\}\!\})$ is the finalization label contained in **OutL**.

Construction. Although efficient garbled stacks have been proposed in earlier works [24,38,41,42], we need a variant that supports dynamic finalization. To support this new feature, we propose a new abstraction called a garbled vault denoted GVault in Appendix D.1 of the online full version [30]. We use GVault to construct a new garbled stack with dynamic finalization in Appendix D.2 of the online full version [30].

4.2   Switch (GSwitch)

A switch is a two-way router. Imagine that the switch receives some message $\mathsf{msg} := (\mathsf{leaf}, \mathsf{addr}, L)$. The first bit of leaf, that is, $\mathsf{leaf}[0]$, is used to determine whether the message is supposed to be forwarded to its left child or right child. The switch has a hard-wired array denoted **RdL** of length $t_{\max}$, where $t_{\max}$ is the maximum number of times that the switch can be invoked. The switch wants to route the transformed message $(\mathsf{leaf}[1:], \mathsf{addr}, L \oplus \mathbf{RdL}[\tau])$ to the child selected by leaf[0], where τ is the switch's local time step, i.e., how many times it has been invoked before (not including the current invocation). Later on, every node in the ORAM tree will employ such a switch to pass on information to one of its two children during an ORAM fetch operation.[4] Altogether, this allows us to read and remove a block along a path from the root to some leaf node. In particular, each node consumes the next bit in the leaf identifier to determine the routing direction. The term $\mathbf{RdL}[\tau]$ is the local-time-dependent output label used by the garbled bucket paired with the switch, and we want to xor the incoming label L with $\mathbf{RdL}[\tau]$ before passing it on — see Sect. 2.2 for a more detailed explanation.

When we want to garble a switch, the main challenge is that of *label translation*: the input $\widetilde{\mathsf{msg}} = (\{\!\!\{\mathsf{leaf}, \mathsf{addr}\}\!\!\}_\tau, [\![L]\!]_\tau)$ is encoded using a local-time-dependent label where τ denotes the local time of the switch. The switch needs to re-encode the transformed message $(\mathsf{leaf}[1:], \mathsf{addr}, L \oplus \mathbf{RdL}[\tau])$ under a label that is dependent on the child's local time. However, the child's local time cannot be predicted at the garble time, since it depends on the actual inputs leaf which are chosen dynamically online. We adapt an elegant idea proposed by Heath et al. [24] to solve this problem. Suppose that we are promised that each child will be invoked at most $t'_{\max}$ number of times. We will create two garbled stacks each containing $t'_{\max}$ labels (denoted $\mathbf{OutL_0}$ and $\mathbf{OutL_1}$, respectively), corresponding to the languages of the left and right children each time they are invoked. Given the direction bit $b := \mathsf{leaf}[0]$, we securely pop the next label from b-th stack, and we use this popped label to re-encode the output message to be routed to the corresponding child. Later in our application, we are actually allowed to leak the leaf part of the input which is related to the memory access patterns. More specifically, leaf actually corresponds to a path in the Bucket ORAM tree [13], and since its choice is random, it is safe to reveal leaf.

Definition. For GSwitch, we define params = $(B, \mathbf{w})$ where 2B is the maximum number of times Switch can be invoked, and $\mathbf{w}$ records the lengths of of the inputs to Switch, including the lengths of leaf, addr, and L. The lengths of all other variables will be determined by λ, $\mathbf{w}$, and B. Specifically, $\mathbf{RdL}$ contains 2B entries each of $|L|$ bits long; $\mathbf{InL}$ contains 2B entries each of $\lambda(|\mathsf{leaf}| + |\mathsf{addr}|) + |L|$ bits long; for $b \in \{0, 1\}$, $\mathbf{OutL}_b$ contains 2B entries each of $|\mathbf{InL}|$ bits long; and FinL contains 2B entries each of $2B\lambda$ bits long if $\mathbf{InitL} = \emptyset$, else it contains 2B entries each of 2λ bits long.

For each $b \in \{0, 1\}$, it is promised that Switch will only be invoked at most B times with the direction bit leaf[0] = b. Later in our application, in fact, we guarantee that in expectation, Switch is invoked only B times, and the probability that there will be 2B or more invocations is negligibly small. A garbled switch GSwitch consists of the following possibly randomized algorithms:

- Gmem, GC $\leftarrow$ Garble(1^λ, sk, params, $\mathbf{RdL}$, $\mathbf{InL}$, $\mathbf{OutL_0}$, $\mathbf{OutL_1}$, $\mathbf{FinL}$): the Garble algorithm takes in the security parameter 1^λ, the secret key sk, parameters params a list of labels $\mathbf{RdL}$ to be consumed in each time step (by the

---

[4] Using switches of arity-2 is the most efficient with our current techniques.

associated garbled bucket), the input labels **InL**, two lists of output labels **OutL$_0$** and **OutL$_1$**, as well as labels denoted FinL used to encode the output of Finalize. It outputs the garbled circuits GC and the initial garbled memory Gmem.

We often write **InL** := (**InitL**, **ReqL**, **CtrlL**) where the part **InitL** is consumed by Init, the part **ReqL** is consumed by Switch, and the part **CtrlL** is used to garble the finalization signals for all time steps.

- Gmem$'$ ← Init^{GC}(Gmem, $\{\!\{\text{st}^E\}\!\}$): this function may be called at most once upfront before any invocation of Switch. Specifically, if we parse **InL** := (**InitL**, _, _) where **InL** was passed to Garble, Init should be invoked if **InitL** $\neq \emptyset$; else it will not be invoked.

- Gmem$'$, $\{\!\{\text{leaf}'\}\!\}$, $\{\!\{\text{addr}'\}\!\}$, $[\![L']\!]$ ← Switch^{GC}(Gmem, $\{\!\{\text{leaf}^E\}\!\}$, $\{\!\{\text{addr}\}\!\}$, $[\![L]\!]$): for correctness, the outputs must satisfy: leaf$'$ = leaf[1 :], addr$'$ = addr, L' = $L \oplus \textbf{RdL}[\tau]$ where τ is the current local time step. Moreover, let $b = $ leaf[0], and let cnt$_b$ be the number of times Switch has been invoked with direction bit leaf[0] = b (not counting the current one); then, it must be that Lbl($\{\!\{\text{leaf}'\}\!\}$, $\{\!\{\text{addr}'\}\!\}$, $[\![L']\!]$) is the first $|\textbf{InL}| - \lambda$ bits of **OutL$_b$**[cnt$_b$] — the last λ bits are reserved for garbling the finalization signal.

- $\{\!\{\text{st}\}\!\}$ or $\{\!\{1_L, 1_R\}\!\}$ ← Finalize(Gmem, $\{\!\{1\}\!\}$) :
  - If **InitL** $\neq \emptyset$, the output should be of the form $\{\!\{1_L, 1_R\}\!\}$, where Lbl($\{\!\{1_L\}\!\}$) is the last 2λ bits of **OutL$_0$**[cnt$_0$] and Lbl($\{\!\{1_R\}\!\}$) is the last 2λ bits of **OutL$_1$**[cnt$_1$]. Here, we use the subscripts "L" and "R" are used to differentiate the two 1 bits;
  - Else if **InitL** $= \emptyset$ the output should be of the form $\{\!\{\text{st}\}\!\}$; furthermore, st is of the form st := (st$_0$, st$_1$), such that for $b \in \{0, 1\}$, each st$_b$ is a bit vector containing exactly cnt$_b$ and padded with 0s to a length of exactly B, where cnt$_b$ is the total number of times Switch has been invoked a direction bit leaf[0] = b; and moreover, Lbl($\{\!\{\text{st}\}\!\}$) = **FinL**.

Remark 3. (Two types of GSwitch*es depending on whether* **InitL** $= \emptyset$*).* Later on in our construction (see also Fig. 2), there will be two types of garbled switches, those that correspond to *empty* buckets of the Bucket ORAM (i.e., where **InitL** $= \emptyset$) and those that correspond to *full* buckets (i.e., where **InitL** $\neq \emptyset$). For the latter type (**InitL** $\neq \emptyset$), when the switch first becomes active, its children switches have been operating for a while, and this is why we need to call its Init procedure to synchronize its state with its children. The input to the Init is passed down from the previous parent of their children, i.e., the garbled switch whose role it is taking over. The former type (**InitL** $= \emptyset$) need not perform initialization, since their children switches are fresh when they first become active. When the latter type (**InitL** $\neq \emptyset$) finalizes, its children need to be "rebuilt" as well; this is why it needs to pass the authenticated finalization signals $\{\!\{1_L, 1_R\}\!\}$ to its children.

Construction. Although Heath et al. [24] describe a garbled switch scheme for constructing an access-revealing garbled one-time memory, again we need a

Evaluator   **Garbler**

– $\mathsf{Init}(\{\!\{\mathsf{st}_\emptyset^E\}\!\})$: // *called when* $\mathbf{InitL} \neq \emptyset$

   1. parse $\{\!\{\mathsf{st}_\emptyset^E\}\!\} :=$ $\{\!\{\beta_{b,i}\}\!\}_{b\in\{0,1\},i\in[0:2B)}$;

   2. for $b \in \{0,1\}$, $i \in [0:2B)$, call $\mathsf{GStack}_b.\mathsf{Pop}(\{\!\{\beta_{b,i}\}\!\})$;

– $\mathsf{Switch}(\{\!\{\mathsf{leaf}^E\}\!\}, \{\!\{\mathsf{addr}\}\!\}, \llbracket L\rrbracket)$:

   1. Call $\{\!\{\beta_0 = \mathsf{leaf}[0]\}\!\}$, $\{\!\{\beta_1 = 1 - \beta_0\}\!\}$, $\{\!\{\mathsf{leaf}' = \mathsf{leaf}[1:]\}\!\}$, $\{\!\{\mathsf{addr}' = \mathsf{addr}\}\!\}$, $\llbracket L' = L \oplus \mathbf{RdL}[\tau]\rrbracket \leftarrow$ $\mathsf{GCSw}_\tau(\{\!\{\mathsf{leaf}\}\!\}, \{\!\{\mathsf{addr}\}\!\}, \llbracket L\rrbracket, \llbracket\mathbf{RdL}[\tau]\rrbracket)$;

   2. For $b \in \{0,1\}$, $\llbracket K_b, \_\,\rrbracket \leftarrow \mathsf{GStack}_b.\mathsf{Pop}(\{\!\{\beta_b\}\!\})$; // *here* $\_$ *means ignore the last* 2λ *bits*

   3. Output $(\{\!\{\mathsf{leaf}'\}\!\}, \{\!\{\mathsf{addr}'\}\!\}, \llbracket L'\rrbracket) \oplus$ $\llbracket K_0\rrbracket \oplus \llbracket K_1\rrbracket \oplus \mathsf{TrL}_\tau$.

– $\mathsf{Finalize}(\{\!\{1\}\!\})$:

   1. If $\mathbf{InitL} \neq \emptyset$, call:
- $\{\!\{1_L, 1_R\}\!\} \leftarrow \mathsf{Dec}_{\{1\}}(\mathsf{ct}_\tau)$;
- $\llbracket\_, K_0'\rrbracket \leftarrow \mathsf{GStack}_0.\mathsf{Pop}(\{\!\{1_L\}\!\})$;
- $\llbracket\_, K_1'\rrbracket \leftarrow \mathsf{GStack}_1.\mathsf{Pop}(\{\!\{1_R\}\!\})$;
- $\{\!\{1_L'\}\!\} := \{\!\{1\}\!\} \oplus \llbracket K_0'\rrbracket \oplus \mathsf{TrL}_{0,\tau}'$;
- $\{\!\{1_R'\}\!\} := \{\!\{1\}\!\} \oplus \llbracket K_1'\rrbracket \oplus \mathsf{TrL}_{1,\tau}'$;

     and output $\{\!\{1_L', 1_R'\}\!\}$.

   2. Else, call
- $\{\!\{\mathsf{st}_0\}\!\} \leftarrow \mathsf{GStack}_0.\mathsf{Finalize}(\{\!\{1\}\!\})$,
- $\{\!\{\mathsf{st}_1\}\!\} \leftarrow \mathsf{GStack}_1.\mathsf{Finalize}(\{\!\{1\}\!\})$,

     and output $\{\!\{\mathsf{st}_0, \mathsf{st}_1\}\!\}$.

Create two garbled stacks GStack_0 and GStack_1 as explained in a separate subroutine;

For each $\tau \in [0:2B)$, create the sharing $\llbracket\mathbf{RdL}[\tau]\rrbracket$, and garble the GCSw_τ circuit (whose functionality is defined on the left);

For each $\tau \in [0:2B)$, compute the translation label $\mathsf{TrL}_\tau := \mathsf{Lbl}(\llbracket K_0\rrbracket_\tau) \oplus \mathsf{Lbl}(\llbracket K_1\rrbracket_\tau) \oplus \mathsf{Lbl}(\{\!\{\mathsf{leaf}', \mathsf{addr}'\}\!\}_\tau, \llbracket L'\rrbracket_\tau)$;

If $\mathbf{InitL} \neq \emptyset$, then, for each $\tau \in [0:2B)$, create the ciphertext $\mathsf{ct}_\tau = \mathsf{Enc}_{\{1\}_\tau}(\{\!\{1_L, 1_R\}\!\}_\tau)$, and compute $\mathsf{TrL}_{0,\tau}' := \mathsf{Lbl}(\llbracket K_0'\rrbracket_\tau) \oplus \mathsf{Lbl}(\{\!\{1\}\!\}_\tau)$ and $\mathsf{TrL}_{1,\tau}' := \mathsf{Lbl}(\llbracket K_1'\rrbracket_\tau) \oplus \mathsf{Lbl}(\{\!\{1\}\!\}_\tau)$.

Fig. 3: GSwitch algorithm.

new variant that supports 1) dynamic finalization; and 2) the XOR trick. We therefore describe a new variant supporting these features. Our construction is explained in Fig. 3 which calls the following subroutine for creating the garbled stacks. Note that when $\mathbf{InitL} \neq \emptyset$, we are using the variant of GStack that does not have a Finalize call (see Appendix D.2 of the online full version [30]).

Subroutine for creating garbled stacks

– Let $m = 2B$ and let $w = |\mathbf{OutL}_0[0]|$. Parse $\mathbf{InL} := (\mathbf{InitL}, \_, \_)$.

– If $\mathbf{InitL} \neq \emptyset$, then: let $t_{\max} = 4B + 1$; parse $\mathbf{InitL} := (\mathbf{InitL}_0, \mathbf{InitL}_1)$, and let $\mathbf{ctrlL} \xleftarrow{\$} \{0,1\}^\lambda$. For $b \in \{0,1\}$, let $\mathbf{IL}_b = \mathbf{InitL}_b||\mathsf{rand}()||\mathbf{ctrlL} \in \{0,1\}^{m\cdot\lambda + 2t_{\max}\cdot\lambda}$; let $\mathbf{OL}_b \xleftarrow{\$} \{0,1\}^{t_{\max}\cdot(w+\lambda)}$.

- Else, let $t_{\max} = 2B$; let $\mathbf{ctrlL} \overset{\$}{\leftarrow} \{0,1\}^\lambda$, for $b \in \{0,1\}$, let $\mathbf{IL}_b = \mathrm{rand}()\|$ $\mathbf{ctrlL} \in \{0,1\}^{2t_{\max}\cdot\lambda}$; let $\mathbf{OL}_b = \mathrm{rand}()\|\mathbf{FinL} \in \{0,1\}^{t_{\max}\cdot w + m\cdot\lambda}$. // GStack$_0$ and GStack$_1$ share the same finalization signal labels for all time steps
- For $b \in \{0,1\}$: call (GStack$_b$.Gmem, GStack$_b$.GC) $\leftarrow$ GStack$_b$.Garble(1^λ, sk, params $= (m, w, t_{\max})$, $\mathbf{DB} = \mathbf{OutL}_b$, $\mathbf{IL}_b$, $\mathbf{OL}_b$).

In Fig. 3, when we write the evaluator's algorithm, we do not explicitly write the time step τ, however, keep in mind that the inputs and outputs of Switch as well as the inputs to Finalize are actually encoded using τ-dependent labels. When we write the garbler's algorithm, since the garbler must create some garbled circuitry per time step τ, we explicitly write out the current time step τ in subscript, e.g., $\{\!\!\{ \mathrm{var} \}\!\!\}_\tau$ means the variable garbled under a τ-dependent label.

The cost of GSwitch is dominated by the garbled stacks which take $O(\log B)$ overhead. Thus, the construction in Fig. 3 costs $O\left(B \cdot (\lambda \cdot w_1 + w_2) \cdot \log B\right)$ bits, where $w_1 = |\mathsf{leaf}| + |\mathsf{addr}|$ and $w_2 = |L|$.

Security Proofs. We defer the security proofs for GSwitch to Appendix D.3 of the online full version [30].

Leaf Switches (GLeafSwitch) We need a special (but simpler) type of switches for the leaf level. We defer the detailed description of the leaf switches to Appendix D.4 of the online full version [30].

5   Non-Recursive Garbled Memory (**NRGRAM**)

5.1   Definition

A non-recursive garbled memory (NRGRAM) is almost an entire garbled memory, except that to access each logical addr, one has to provide a position identifier (both garbled and in cleartext) henceforth denoted $\{\!\!\{\mathsf{leaf}^E\}\!\!\}$, which specifies a path in the Bucket ORAM tree that the requested block resides on. More specifically, let params $= (n, w, T)$ where n denotes the total number of blocks stored in the NRGRAM, w denotes the bit-width of each block's payload (not including metadata fields such as addr and leaf), and T denotes the maximum number of time steps. The call schedule is fixed a-priori: it must be a sequence of alternating requests ReadRm, Add, ReadRm, Add, ..., and in total there are T number of ReadRm operations and T number of Add operations.

A non-recursive garbled memory (NRGRAM) provides the following interface:

- Gmem, GC $\leftarrow$ Garble(1^λ, sk, params, $\mathbf{InL}^R$, $\mathbf{InL}^A$, $\mathbf{OutL}$): upon receiving the input labels $\mathbf{InL}^R$ for all the ReadRm calls and the input labels $\mathbf{InL}^A$ for all the Add calls, as well as the output labels $\mathbf{OutL}$ for the ReadRm calls, output GC and the initial Gmem;

- Gmem$'$, $\{\!\{$rdata$\}\!\}$ $\leftarrow$ ReadRm^{GC}(Gmem, $\{\!\{$addr, leaf$^E\}\!\}$): upon receiving $\{\!\{$addr, leaf$^E\}\!\}$, output $\{\!\{$rdata$\}\!\}$. If addr exists in the data structure and provided that $\{\!\{$leaf$^E\}\!\}$ is a correct position identifier garbled under $\mathbf{InL}^R[t]$ where t denotes the local time, then rdata should be the value of the block at logical address addr; else if addr is not found, then rdata $= \perp$. In either case, Lbl(rdata) should match $\mathbf{OutL}[t]$.
- Gmem$'$ $\leftarrow$ Add^{GC}(Gmem, $\{\!\{$addr, leaf, data$\}\!\}$): upon receiving a garbled block $\{\!\{$addr, leaf, data$\}\!\}$, add it to the data structure. Henceforth, before addr is requested again, the block should reside on the path corresponding to leaf.

The local time t of a NRGRAM data structure is the number of times Add has been invoked (not counting the current invocation we are currently inside an Add call). Later in our full garbled RAM scheme, in every RAM step, each NRGRAM's ReadRM and Add functions will be each invoked once. Therefore, each NRGRAM's local time t coincides with the global time t of the garbled RAM, and each NRGRAM must support T calls which is the same as the RAM's maximum runtime. For this reason, we use the letter t to denote the NRGRAM's local time, and use T to denote the maximum number of time steps that must be supported.

Remark 4. We assume the first bit of the data field is used to encode whether the block is $\perp$. Specifically, if the first bit is 0, then the block is treated as $\perp$. We assume that when the honest evaluator calls Add($\{\!\{$addr, leaf, data$\}\!\}$), the first bit of data is set to 1.

5.2 Data Structures and Labels

Without loss of generality, we may assume the capacity of the non-recursive ORAM tree n, the bucket capacity B, and the RAM's runtime T are all powers of 2. Let root be at level 0, and leaf be at level $\ell_{\max} := \log_2 \frac{n}{B}$. We assume that the RAM program starts at time $t = 0$, and every time step the clock t increments by 1. Since in every RAM step, each non-recursive bucket ORAM is invoked once, the global time t also coincides with the non-recursive ORAM tree's local time step.

Additional Building Blocks. To construct our NRGRAM, we need a few additional building blocks, namely, garbled buckets denoted GBkt, garbled level rebuilder GRebuild, and garbled stash GStash. Their functionalities are roughly summarized below.

- GStash supports functions Read, Add, and Finalize, and it is parameterized by the maximum number of operations GStash.m and the word size GStash.w.
- GBkt is parameterized by the number of entries m, the maximum number of operations $t_{\max}$, and the bit-width of each entry w. It supports Init($\{\!\{\mathbf{DB}\}\!\}$) which initializes the bucket with the list $\mathbf{DB}$, Read($\{\!\{$addr$\}\!\}$) which looks up the entry addr, and Finalize. Similar to GSwitch, we write the input labels as $(\mathbf{InitL}, \mathbf{ReqL}, \mathbf{CtrlL})$ for (Init, Read, Finalize) correspondingly, and the output labels of Read and Finalize are written as $(\mathbf{RdL}, \mathbf{FinL})$.

– GRebuild is parameterized by the time t and a corresponding level $\ell \in [0, \ell_{\max}]$ that depends on t. It takes in the stash the and the levels from 0 to ℓ, and then it outputs a new stash and new levels from 0 to $\min(\ell + 1, \ell_{\max})$.

We defer the description of these building blocks to Appendix D.7, D.6, and C.1 of the online full version [30].

Garbled Circuit Inventory. All of the following garbled circuits are prepared by the garbler upfront in one shot. Each node at level ℓ in the tree has $T/(2^\ell \cdot \mathsf{B})$ instances (i.e., copies) of the following garbled circuitry: 1) GSwitch or GLeafSwitch, and 2) GBkt. The instances are indexed from $0, 1, \ldots, T/(2^\ell \cdot \mathsf{B}) - 1$. During the fetch phase of time step $t \in [0 : T)$, the garbled instance indexed $\lfloor t/(2^\ell \cdot \mathsf{B}) \rfloor$ will be active.

During time step $t \in [0 : T - 2]$, if $(t + 1) \mod n = j \cdot (\mathsf{B} \cdot 2^\ell)$ where j is an odd integer, then there is some garbled circuitry that rebuilds levels $0, 1, \ldots, \ell$. In particular, if $\ell = \ell_{\max}$, then the rebuild takes as input garbled levels $0, 1, \ldots, \ell$ and outputs new garbled levels $0, 1, \ldots, \ell$; else, it takes garbled levels $0, 1, \ldots, \ell - 1$ and outputs new garbled levels $0, 1, \ldots, \ell$.

There are in total T/B instances of GStash, indexed by $0, 1, \ldots, T/\mathsf{B} - 1$. During time step t, the $\lfloor t/\mathsf{B} \rfloor$-th GStash instance is active.

Terminology. We shall use the notation GStash^t to denote the the GStash instance active at time t. We use the notation $\mathsf{GSwitch}^{V,t}$, $\mathsf{GLeafSwitch}^{V,t}$ or $\mathsf{GBkt}^{V,t}$ to denote the GSwitch, GLeafSwitch, or GBkt instance associated with tree node V and active at time t. Sometimes we represent a tree node $V = (i, j)$ which refers to the the j-th tree node in the i-th level. Using this notation, the same GStash, GSwitch, or GBkt instance *may have multiple aliases*. Similarly, we use $\mathsf{GRebuild}^t$ to denote the GRebulid instance to be invoked at the end of time step t.

We say that $\mathsf{GSwitch}^{V,t}$ is the parent of $\mathsf{GSwitch}^{U,t}$ (or $\mathsf{GLeafSwitch}^{U,t}$) if V is a parent of U in the bucket ORAM tree; in this case, we also say that $\mathsf{GSwitch}^{U,t}$ or $\mathsf{GLeafSwitch}^{U,t}$ is a (left or right) child of $\mathsf{GSwitch}^{V,t}$. Note that these two GSwitch instances must be active at the same time for them to have a parent/child relationship. We often say that a switch instance $\mathsf{GSwitch}^{V,t}$ (or $\mathsf{GLeafSwitch}^{V,t}$) and a bucket instance $\mathsf{GBkt}^{V,t}$ are *paired* with each other — note that they are active at the same time t and belonging to the same tree node V.

Choosing Labels. For each GStash, GSwitch, GLeafSwitch, and GBkt instance, the garbler chooses all of the labels (needed by the Garble procedures) at random, subject to the following constraints:

– $\mathsf{GSwitch}^{V,t}$ and its paired $\mathsf{GBkt}^{V,t}$ share the same address labels (for the $\{\!\{\mathsf{addr}\}\!\}$ inputs to the Read or Switch procedures) and finalization signal labels in all time steps. Moreover, $\mathsf{GBkt}^{V,t}.\mathbf{RdL} = \mathsf{GSwitch}^{V,t}.\mathbf{RdL}$ (or $\mathsf{GBkt}^{V,t}.\mathbf{RdL} = \mathsf{GLeafSwitch}^{V,t} = \mathbf{RdL}$ for the leaf level).

– The call at time t to $\mathsf{GSwitch}^{\mathrm{root},t}$ should adopt the input labels $\mathbf{InL}^R[t]$ (of the NRGRAM); further, GStash^t, $\mathsf{GBkt}^{\mathrm{root},t}$, and $\mathsf{GSwitch}^{\mathrm{root},t}$ share the same address labels (for the $\{\!\{\mathsf{addr}\}\!\}$ inputs to the Read or Switch procedure) in all time steps. Further, the call at time t to $\mathsf{GStash}^t.\mathsf{Add}$ should adopt the input labels $\mathbf{InL}^A[t]$ (of the NRGRAM);

– If non-leaf switches $\mathsf{GSwitch}_0$ and $\mathsf{GSwitch}_1$ are the left and right children of $\mathsf{GSwitch}$, then, for each $\tau \in [0:2B]$, let

$$\mathsf{GSwitch}.\mathbf{OutL}_0[\tau] := \mathsf{GSwitch}_0.\mathbf{ReqL}[\tau]\|\mathsf{GSwitch}_0.\mathbf{CtrlL}[\tau]$$
$$\mathsf{GSwitch}.\mathbf{OutL}_1[\tau] := \mathsf{GSwitch}_1.\mathbf{ReqL}[\tau]\|\mathsf{GSwitch}_1.\mathbf{CtrlL}[\tau]$$

If leaf switches $\mathsf{GLeafSwitch}_0$ and $\mathsf{GLeafSwitch}_1$ are the left and right children of $\mathsf{GSwitch}$, and moreover, GBkt_0 and GBkt_1 are the two buckets associated with $\mathsf{GLeafSwitch}_0$ and $\mathsf{GLeafSwitch}_1$, respectively, then, for all $\tau \in [0:2B]$, let[5]

$$\mathsf{GSwitch}.\mathbf{OutL}_0[\tau] := \mathsf{GBkt}_0.\mathbf{ReqL}[\tau]\|\mathsf{GLeafSwitch}_0.\mathbf{InL}[\tau]\|\mathsf{GBkt}_0.\mathbf{CtrlL}[\tau]$$
$$\mathsf{GSwitch}.\mathbf{OutL}_1[\tau] := \mathsf{GBkt}_1.\mathbf{ReqL}[\tau]\|\mathsf{GLeafSwitch}_1.\mathbf{InL}[\tau]\|\mathsf{GBkt}_1.\mathbf{CtrlL}[\tau]$$

– If $\mathsf{GSwitch}^{V,t}$ and $\mathsf{GSwitch}^{V,t+1}$ are not the same instance and they have the same children, then, let $\mathsf{GSwitch}^{V,t}.\mathbf{FinL} = \mathsf{GSwitch}^{V,t+1}.\mathbf{InitL}$ and let $\mathsf{GSwitch}^{V,t}.\mathbf{InitL} = \emptyset$ — in this case, our algorithm will not call $\mathsf{GSwitch}^{V,t}.\mathsf{Init}$ but will call $\mathsf{GSwitch}^{V,t+1}.\mathsf{Init}$.

For each level rebuilder instance denoted $\mathsf{GRebuild}^t$, let t be the time step at the end of which this rebuilder instance $\mathsf{GRebuild}^t$ is invoked — it must be that $(t+1) \mod n$ is an odd multiple of 2^ℓ. Suppose $\ell \neq \ell_{\max}$, i.e., the rebuild takes in levels $0, 1, \ldots, \ell-1$ and rebuilds levels $0, 1, \ldots, \ell$ — the case where $\ell = \ell_{\max}$ is similar. The garbler chooses the input and output labels of $\mathsf{GRebuild}^t$ as follows. For $i \in [0:\ell)$, let $\mathsf{GBkt}^{(i,0),t}, \ldots, \mathsf{GBkt}^{(i,2^i-1),t}$ be the garbled bucket instances active in level i at time t, and let GStash^t be the garbled stash active at time t; then, $\mathsf{GRebuild}.\mathbf{InL} = \mathsf{GStash}^t.\mathbf{FinL}\|\{\mathsf{GBkt}^{(i,j),t}.\mathbf{FinL}\}_{i\in[0:\ell),j\in[0:2^i)}$. For $i \in [0:\ell]$, let $\mathsf{GBkt}^{(i,0),t+1}, \ldots, \mathsf{GBkt}^{(i,2^i-1),t+1}$ be the garbled bucket instances active in level i at time $t+1$, and let GStash^{t+1} be the garbled stash instance active at time $t+1$. Then, $\mathsf{GRebuild}^t.\mathbf{OutL} := \{\mathsf{GBkt}^{(i,j),t+1}.\mathbf{InitL}\}_{i\in[0:\ell],j\in[2^i]}$.

5.3   Construction

We describe our NRGRAM construction in Fig. 4, where the relevant data structures and how to choose the encoding labels were explained earlier in Sect. 5.2. In the step marked $(\diamondsuit)$, the same variables $\{\!\{\mathsf{leaf}\}\!\}, \{\!\{\mathsf{addr}\}\!\}, [\![L]\!]$ are overwritten by the outcome of the call to $\mathsf{GSwitch}^{V,t}.\mathsf{Switch}(\{\!\{\mathsf{leaf}\}\!\}, \{\!\{\mathsf{addr}\}\!\}, [\![L]\!])$; keep in mind that the output variables do not have the same labels as the input variables, although the notation is the same.

---

[5]   The leaf switches take no $\{\!\{\mathsf{addr}\}\!\}$ nor Finalize, and hence the parent $\mathsf{GSwitch}$ outputs $\{\!\{\mathsf{addr}\}\!\}$ or Finalize only to the children buckets (Fig. 4).

Evaluator	Garbler

Evaluator

ReadRm $\left(\{\!\{ addr, leaf^E \}\!\} \right)$:

- if $t = 0$, then for every tree node V, call
  GBkt^{V,0}.Init($\{\!\{ bkt_V^\emptyset \}\!\}$);
- $\_, \{\!\{ rdata_s \}\!\} \leftarrow$ GStash^t.Read($\{\!\{ addr \}\!\}$);
- $[\![L]\!] := [\![\mathbf{L}^*[t]]\!]$;
- For each node V in the tree from the root to leaf,
  - If V is not a leaf: let $\{\!\{ leaf \}\!\}, \{\!\{ addr \}\!\}, [\![L]\!] \leftarrow$
    GSwitch^{V,t}.Switch($\{\!\{ leaf \}\!\}, \{\!\{ addr \}\!\}, [\![L]\!]$); ($\diamond$)
  - Else: TrL $\leftarrow$ GLeafSwitch^{V,t}.Switch($[\![L]\!]$);
  - $\{\!\{ rdata_\ell \}\!\} \leftarrow$ GBkt^{V,t}.Read($\{\!\{ addr \}\!\}$) where ℓ
    denotes the level of V;
- Let $\{\!\{ rdata \}\!\} := TrL \oplus \{\!\{ rdata_s \}\!\} \oplus \left(\oplus_{\ell=0}^{\ell_{max}} \{\!\{ rdata_\ell \}\!\} \right)$
  and output $\{\!\{ rdata \}\!\}$.

Add ($\{\!\{ addr, leaf, data \}\!\}$):

- If $t + 1 = T$, return; else continue with the following.
- Call GStash^t.Add($\{\!\{ addr, leaf, data \}\!\}$);
- If $(t + 1)$ is a multiple of n: invoke the garbled
  rebuilding algorithm similar to the case below
  marked $(\star)$, except that here, we shuffle levels
  $0, \ldots, \ell_{max}$ into levels $0, \ldots, \ell_{max}$;
- Else if $(t + 1) \mod n = j \cdot (B \cdot 2^\ell)$ for some odd
  integer j and some integer ℓ: $(\star)$
  - Let $\{\!\{ stash \}\!\} \leftarrow$ GStash^t.Finalize();
  - Call RecFinalize(root, $\{\!\{ 1^* \}\!\}_t, \ell$) described
    below;
  - For each level $i \in [0 : \ell)$, let
    $\{\!\{ level_i \}\!\} := \cup_{j \in [0:2^i]} \{\!\{ bkt_{i,j} \}\!\}$ where the
    variables $\{\!\{ bkt_{i,j} \}\!\}$ are output inside the
    RecFinalize call;
  - $\{\!\{ level_i \}\!\}_{i \in [0:\ell]} \leftarrow$
    GRebuild^t($\{\!\{ stash \}\!\} \{\!\{ level_i \}\!\}_{i \in [0:\ell-1]}$);
  - For $i \in [0 : \ell]$, parse
    $\{\!\{ level_i \}\!\} := \{\!\{ bkt'_{i,j} \}\!\}_{j \in [0:2^i]}$; for $j \in [0 : 2^i)$,
    call GBkt$^{(i,j),t+1}$.Init($\{\!\{ bkt'_{i,j} \}\!\}$);

RecFinalize($V, \{\!\{ 1 \}\!\}, \ell$)

- $\{\!\{ bkt_V \}\!\} \leftarrow$ GBkt^{V,t}.Finalize($\{\!\{ 1 \}\!\}$);
- If ℓ the leaf level, then return; else let $\{\!\{ st \}\!\}$
  or $\{\!\{ 1_L, 1_R \}\!\} \leftarrow$ GSwitch^{V,t}.Finalize($\{\!\{ 1 \}\!\}$); if
  GSwitch$^{V,t+1}$ has the same children switches as
  GSwitch^{V,t}, call GSwitch$^{V,t+1}$.Init($\{\!\{ st \}\!\}$);
- Let U_L, U_R be the children of V, if the level of U_L
  and U_R is at most ℓ, call RecFinalize($U_L, \{\!\{ 1_L \}\!\}, \ell$),
  RecFinalize($U_R, \{\!\{ 1_R \}\!\}, \ell$).

Garbler

for every tree node V, let bkt$_V^\emptyset$ be an array
of 0s of appropriate length, create garbled
state $\{\!\{ bkt_V^\emptyset \}\!\}$;
for $t \in [0 : T)$, let $\mathbf{L}^*[t] =$
$\mathbf{OutL}[t] \oplus$ GStash^t.$\mathbf{OutL}[t \mod B]$;
create sharings $[\![\mathbf{L}^*]\!] := \{ \mathbf{L}^*[t] \oplus$
$K_t \}_{t \in [0:T)}$ where K_t should match the
part of GSwitch^{root,t}.$\mathbf{InL}$ that is used for
encoding the input $[\![L]\!]$ at time t;

call GSwitch.Garble for all GSwitch
instances; call GLeafSwitch.Garble for all
GLeafSwitch instances;

call GBkt.Garble for all GBkt instances;

call GStash.Garble for all GStash instances;

for every $t \in [0 : T)$ such that $t + 1$
is a multiple of B, create a garbled
finalization signal $\{\!\{ 1^* \}\!\}_t$ using the label
GSwitch^{root,t}.$\mathbf{CtrlL}[B]$;

call GRebuild.Garble for all GRebuild
instances;

Fig. 4: Non-Recursive Garbled RAM (NRGRAM) construction.

The garbled data structures adopt the following parameters (see the supplementary for the parameters of GStash, GLeafSwitch, and GBkt):

- For each GStash instance, the maximum number of operations GStash.$m = B$, and the word size GStash.$w = w + \log_2 n$;
- For each GSwitch instance at level ℓ of the tree, let GSwitch.$B = B$, and the addr field has bit width $\log_2 n$, the leaf field has bit width $\log_2 n - \ell$, the bit width of the L field has width $\lambda \cdot w$;
- Each GLeafSwitch instance is parametrized with the maximum number of invocations GLeafSwitch.$t_{\max}$ = GLeafSwitch.m = $2B$ and the element bit-width GLeafSwitch.$w = \lambda \cdot w$;
- Each GBkt instance adopts the parameters GBkt.m = GBkt.$t_{\max}$ = $2B$, and the bit widths of the addr and val fields are $\log_2 n$ and w, respectively.

We now analyze the asymptotic performance of our NRGRAM scheme. One can easily verify that the dominating cost is incurred by the GBkt instances. The total cost of our NRGRAM is

$$O(1) \cdot \frac{T}{B} \cdot \log n \cdot B \cdot \lambda \cdot \left(w \cdot \log^2 B + \log n \cdot \log^3 B + \log^4 B \right)$$
$$= O \left(T \cdot \log n \cdot \lambda \cdot (w + \log n \log B + \log^2 B) \cdot \log^2 B \right)$$

Proof of Security. We defer the proof of security for our NRGRAM to Appendix E of the online full version [30].

6   Final Garbled RAM (**GRAM**) and Concrete Performance

Full Garbled RAM Construction. Our final garbled RAM scheme is obtained by applying the standard recursion technique [33, 35] to the NRGRAM. The idea is to recursively store the position map in a smaller NRGRAM, and then store the position map of the position map in an even smaller NRGRAM, and do on. The recursion will stop in logarithmically many iterations as long as the block size is at least $C \log N$ for some appropriate constant C. We defer the detailed construction and proofs to Appendix F of the online full version [30].

Practical Optimizations and Concrete Performance. In Appendix A.1 of the online full version [30], we propose several practical optimizations for our garbled RAM scheme.

We also developed a simulator to evaluate the concrete performance of our scheme. We defer the detailed explanation of the simulator and our experimental methology to Appendix A.2 of the online full version [30]. In Fig. 5a, we compared the performance of NanoGRAM with that of the naïve linear-scan GRAM as well as EpiGRAM [24], where the word size $W = 128$ bits. Here, we use a standard platform-independent performance metric, i.e., *the garbled circuit size amortized to each memory access*, that is used in this line of work [24, 32].

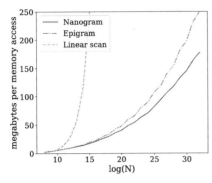
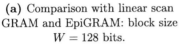

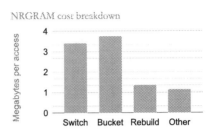

(a) Comparison with linear scan GRAM and EpiGRAM: block size $W = 128$ bits.

(b) Cost breakdown of NRGRAM$_D$, $W = 128$ bits, $N = 2^{15}$.

Fig. 5: Concrete performance of NanoGRAM. The y-axis is the size of the garbled RAM program amortized to each memory access.

Given the circuit size, we can estimate the runtime on typical computers using the results of earlier works [32]. In NanoGRAM, since the parameter B (i.e., average load per bucket) has to be at least 64 or 128 to get a reasonable statistical security parameter, the smallest N we used in our experiment is 2^8. Just like EpiGRAM, we start to outperform the naïve linear-scan GRAM at about $N = 2^9$. Our concrete performance is on par with EpiGRAM at small choices of N, but at about $N = 2^{13}$, we start to outperform EpiGRAM, and as shown in the figure, the improvement is of an asymptotical nature — the larger the N, the greater our speedup.

Figure 5b shows the cost breakdown for the NRGRAM for the final data level. The breakdown suggests that the garbled buckets are the most costly, whereas the garbled switches closely follow. This plot also shows the motivation for our optimizations — had we not performed these optimizations, the total garbled bucket cost would be more than 2× higher than the total garbled switch cost.

Acknowledgments. This work is in part supported by a DARPA SIEVE grant, a Packard Fellowship, NSF awards under the grant numbers 2128519 and 2044679, and a grant from ONR. We gratefully acknowledge Wenting Zheng for helpful technical discussions during an early phase of the project.

References

1. Applebaum, B.: Garbling xor gates "for free" in the standard model. In: TCC (2013). https://doi.org/10.1007/978-3-642-36594-2_10
2. Asharov, G., Komargodski, I., Lin, W.K., Nayak, K., Peserico, E., Shi, E.: OptORAMa: Optimal Oblivious RAM. In: Eurocrypt (2020). https://doi.org/10.1007/978-3-030-45724-2_14

3. Batcher, K.E.: Sorting networks and their applications. In: American Federation of Information Processing Societies: AFIPS Conference Proceedings (1968). https://doi.org/10.1145/1468075.1468121

4. Canetti, R., Chen, Y., Holmgren, J., Raykova, M.: Adaptive succinct garbled RAM or: How to delegate your database. In: TCC (2016). https://doi.org/10.1007/978-3-662-53644-5_3

5. Canetti, R., Holmgren, J.: Fully succinct garbled RAM. In: ITCS, pp. 169–178. ACM (2016). https://doi.org/10.1145/2840728.2840765

6. Chan, T.H., Nayak, K., Shi, E.: Perfectly secure oblivious parallel RAM. In: TCC (2018). https://doi.org/10.1007/978-3-030-03810-6_23

7. Chan, T.H., Shi, E.: Circuit OPRAM: unifying statistically and computationally secure orams and oprams. In: TCC (2017). https://doi.org/10.1007/978-3-319-70503-3_3

8. Chan, T.H., Shi, E., Lin, W., Nayak, K.: Perfectly oblivious (parallel) RAM revisited, and improved constructions. In: ITC (2021). https://doi.org/10.4230/LIPIcs.ITC.2021.8

9. Chen, Y., Chow, S.S.M., Chung, K., Lai, R.W.F., Lin, W., Zhou, H.: Cryptography for parallel RAM from indistinguishability obfuscation. In: ITCS. pp. 179–190. ACM (2016). https://doi.org/10.1145/2840728.2840769

10. Choi, S.G., Katz, J., Kumaresan, R., Zhou, H.S.: On the security of the "free-xor" technique. In: TCC (2012). https://doi.org/10.1007/978-3-642-28914-9_3

11. Damgård, I., Meldgaard, S., Nielsen, J.B.: Perfectly secure oblivious RAM without random oracles. In: TCC, pp. 144–163 (2011). https://doi.org/10.1007/978-3-642-19571-6_10

12. Fincher, D.: The curious case of benjamin button, film (2008)

13. Fletcher, C., Naveed, M., Ren, L., Shi, E., Stefanov, E.: Bucket ORAM: Single online roundtrip, constant bandwidth Oblivious RAM. Cryptology ePrint Archive, Report 2015/1065 (2015)

14. Garg, S., Lu, S., Ostrovsky, R.: Black-box garbled RAM. In: FOCS (2015). https://doi.org/10.1109/FOCS.2015.22

15. Garg, S., Lu, S., Ostrovsky, R., Scafuro, A.: Garbled ram from one-way functions. STOC (2015). https://doi.org/10.1145/2746539.2746593

16. Gentry, C., Goldman, K.A., Halevi, S., Jutla, C.S., Raykova, M., Wichs, D.: Optimizing ORAM and using it efficiently for secure computation. In: PETS (2013). https://doi.org/10.1007/978-3-642-39077-7_1

17. Gentry, C., Halevi, S., Lu, S., Ostrovsky, R., Raykova, M., Wichs, D.: Garbled ram revisited. In: EUROCRYPT (2014)

18. Goldreich, O.: Towards a theory of software protection and simulation by oblivious RAMs. In: STOC (1987). https://doi.org/10.1145/28395.28416

19. Goldreich, O., Ostrovsky, R.: Software protection and simulation on oblivious RAMs. J. ACM (1996). https://doi.org/10.1145/233551.233553

20. Hazay, C., Lilintal, M.: Gradual gram and secure computation for ram programs. In: Security and Cryptography for Networks (2020). https://doi.org/10.1007/978-3-030-57990-6_12

21. Heath, D., Kolesnikov, V.: Stacked garbling. In: Micciancio, D., Ristenpart, T. (eds.) CRYPTO 2020. LNCS, vol. 12171, pp. 763–792. Springer, Cham (2020). https://doi.org/10.1007/978-3-030-56880-1_27

22. Heath, D., Kolesnikov, V.: Logstack: Stacked garbling with O(b log b) computation. In: EUROCRYPT (2021). https://doi.org/10.1007/978-3-030-77883-5_1

23. Heath, D., Kolesnikov, V.: One hot garbling. In: CCS (2021). https://doi.org/10.1145/3460120.3484764

24. Heath, D., Kolesnikov, V., Ostrovsky, R.: Epigram: Practical garbled ram. In: EUROCRYPT (2022). https://doi.org/10.1007/978-3-031-06944-4_1

25. Kolesnikov, V., Mohassel, P., Rosulek, M.: FleXOR: flexible garbling for xor gates that beats free-XOR. In: Garay, J.A., Gennaro, R. (eds.) CRYPTO 2014. LNCS, vol. 8617, pp. 440–457. Springer, Heidelberg (2014). https://doi.org/10.1007/978-3-662-44381-1_25

26. Kolesnikov, V., Schneider, T.: Improved Garbled Circuit: Free XOR Gates and Applications. In: ICALP (2008). https://doi.org/10.1007/978-3-540-70583-3_40

27. Larsen, K.G., Nielsen, J.B.: Yes, there is an oblivious ram lower bound! In: Shacham, H., Boldyreva, A. (eds.) CRYPTO 2018. LNCS, vol. 10992, pp. 523–542. Springer, Cham (2018). https://doi.org/10.1007/978-3-319-96881-0_18

28. Lu, S., Ostrovsky, R.: How to Garble RAM programs? In: Johansson, T., Nguyen, P.Q. (eds.) EUROCRYPT 2013. LNCS, vol. 7881, pp. 719–734. Springer, Heidelberg (2013). https://doi.org/10.1007/978-3-642-38348-9_42

29. Lu, S., Ostrovsky, R.: Black-box parallel garbled RAM. In: CRYPTO (2017)

30. Park, A., Lin, W.K., Shi, E.: NanoGRAM: Garbled RAM with $\widetilde{O}(\log N)$ overhead. Cryptology ePrint Archive, Paper 2022/191 (2022). https://eprint.iacr.org/2022/191

31. Patel, S., Persiano, G., Raykova, M., Yeo, K.: Panorama: Oblivious ram with logarithmic overhead. In: FOCS (2018). https://doi.org/10.1109/FOCS.2018.00087

32. Rosulek, M., Roy, L.: Three halves make a whole? beating the half-gates lower bound for garbled circuits. In: Malkin, T., Peikert, C. (eds.) CRYPTO 2021. LNCS, vol. 12825, pp. 94–124. Springer, Cham (2021). https://doi.org/10.1007/978-3-030-84242-0_5

33. Shi, E., Chan, T.-H.H., Stefanov, E., Li, M.: Oblivious RAM with $O((\log N)^3)$ Worst-Case Cost. In: Lee, D.H., Wang, X. (eds.) ASIACRYPT 2011. LNCS, vol. 7073, pp. 197–214. Springer, Heidelberg (2011). https://doi.org/10.1007/978-3-642-25385-0_11

34. Stefanov, E., et al.: Path ORAM - an extremely simple oblivious ram protocol. In: CCS (2013). https://doi.org/10.1145/2508859.2516660

35. Stefanov, E., Shi, E., Song, D.: Towards practical oblivious RAM. In: Network and Distributed System Security Symposium (NDSS) (2012)

36. Waksman, A.: A permutation network. J. ACM 15(1), 159–163 (jan 1968). https://doi.org/10.1145/321439.321449

37. Wang, X.S., Chan, T.H.H., Shi, E.: Circuit ORAM: On Tightness of the Goldreich-Ostrovsky Lower Bound. In: CCS (2015). https://doi.org/10.1145/2810103.2813634

38. Wang, X.S., et al.: Oblivious Data Structures. In: CCS (2014). https://doi.org/10.1145/2660267.2660314

39. Yao, A.C.C.: Protocols for secure computations (extended abstract). In: FOCS (1982). https://doi.org/10.5555/1382436.1382751

40. Yao, A.C.C.: How to generate and exchange secrets. In: FOCS (1986). https://doi.org/10.1109/SFCS.1986.25

41. Zahur, S., Evans, D.: Circuit Structures for Improving Efficiency of Security and Privacy Tools. In: IEEE S & P (2013). https://doi.org/10.1109/SP.2013.40

42. Zahur, S., Rosulek, M., Evans, D.: Two halves make a whole. In: Oswald, E., Fischlin, M. (eds.) EUROCRYPT 2015. LNCS, vol. 9057, pp. 220–250. Springer, Heidelberg (2015). https://doi.org/10.1007/978-3-662-46803-6_8

Lower Bound Framework for Differentially Private and Oblivious Data Structures

Giuseppe Persiano[1] and Kevin Yeo[2(✉)]

[1] Universitá di Salerno and Google, Fisciano, Italy
[2] Google and Columbia University, New York, USA
kwlyeo@google.com

Abstract. In recent years, there has been significant work in studying data structures that provide privacy for the operations that are executed. These primitives aim to guarantee that observable access patterns to physical memory do not reveal substantial information about the queries and updates executed on the data structure. Multiple recent works, including Larsen and Nielsen [Crypto'18], Persiano and Yeo [Eurocrypt'19], Hubáček *et al.* [TCC'19] and Komargodski and Lin [Crypto'21], have shown that logarithmic overhead is required to support even basic RAM (array) operations for various privacy notions including obliviousness and differential privacy as well as different choices of sizes for RAM blocks b and memory cells ω.

We continue along this line of work and present the first logarithmic lower bounds for differentially private RAMs (DPRAMs) that apply regardless of the sizes of blocks b and cells ω. This is the first logarithmic lower bounds for DPRAMs when blocks are significantly smaller than cells, that is $b \ll \omega$. Furthermore, we present new logarithmic lower bounds for differentially private variants of classical data structure problems including sets, predecessor (successor) and disjoint sets (union-find) for which sub-logarithmic plaintext constructions are known. All our lower bounds extend to the multiple non-colluding servers setting.

We also address an unfortunate issue with this rich line of work where the lower bound techniques are difficult to use and require customization for each new result. To make the techniques more accessible, we generalize our proofs into a framework that reduces proving logarithmic lower bounds to showing that a specific problem satisfies two simple, minimal conditions. We show our framework is easy-to-use as all the lower bounds in our paper utilize the framework and hope our framework will spur more usage of these lower bound techniques.

1 Introduction

In this work, we will study *privacy-preserving data structures* in the setting where a client outsources the storage of data to one or more potentially untrusted servers (such as a cloud provider). Even though the client delegates the storage to the server, the client may need to perform operations on the outsourced data

---

The full version of this paper may be found at [39].

© International Association for Cryptologic Research 2023
C. Hazay and M. Stam (Eds.): EUROCRYPT 2023, LNCS 14004, pp. 487–517, 2023.
https://doi.org/10.1007/978-3-031-30545-0_17

in an efficient manner. In terms of privacy, the client wishes to maintain the confidentiality of the outsourced data. A straightforward first attempt is for the client to encrypt all data locally before transferring to the server. While guaranteeing that the server cannot see the data in plaintext, this technique does not address the leakage of access patterns that the server observes when the client performs operations on the outsourced data. For example, the server may observe the exact memory locations that are retrieved or modified. Therefore, it is integral to protect the patterns of data access to also maintain privacy for the actions performed over the outsourced data.

Oblivious RAMs. Oblivious RAMs (ORAMs), introduced by Goldreich and Ostrovsky [17], are one cryptographic primitive that may be leveraged to hide access patterns. At a high level, ORAMs can be viewed as a data structure that enables maintenance of a dynamic array where the client either query or update any entry. The obliviousness privacy guarantee of ORAMs ensures that any adversary given two candidate equal-length operational sequences and observes the access pattern incurred by the execution of one of the sequences still cannot determine the identity of the executed operational sequence. In recent years, ORAMs have been studied extensively to try and determine the optimal overhead (see [5,9,10,14,17–19,25,30,32,40,43] and references therein). For b-bit entries on machines with memory cell (word) size of ω bits, the best known constructions obtain logarithmic overhead $O((1 + b/\omega) \cdot \log n)$ [1]. This ends up being optimal as it matches the lower bounds of $\Omega((b/\omega) \cdot \log n)$ by Larsen and Nielsen [28] and $\Omega(\log n/(1+\log(\omega/b)))$ by Komargodski and Lin [23] up to logarithmic factors in b and ω for all choices of b and ω. Due to their strong privacy guarantees, ORAMs have seen usage in many applications such as multi-party computation [4,15,47] and secure cloud storage systems [3,42].

Differentially Private RAMs. In various practical applications, the guarantees provided by obliviousness end up being unnecessarily strong. For example, we can consider the problem of privacy-preserving data analysis where the goal is to reveal statistics about a data set, but still maintain the privacy of each individual. An algorithm is considered *differentially private* if the probability distribution of the output of the algorithm for two data sets that differ in only one record will not differ significantly. Therefore, if the adversary observes the disclosure of the algorithm, it may not learn information about whether an individual was a member of the input data set. Consider the problem of privacy-preserving data analysis over a data set outsourced to an untrusted server. For any accesses to the data set, we could use an ORAM to completely hide any subset of records accessed from the data set. However, this may be stronger privacy than needed as the differentially private disclosure only provides privacy for individuals.

Instead, we turn to differentially private RAMs (DPRAMs) whose privacy guarantees align closer to the ones used in privacy-preserving data analysis. DPRAMs aim to provide privacy for individual operations, but may reveal information about a sequence consisting of many operations. In more detail, if an adversary receives two candidate equal-length operational sequences that differ in one operation and the access pattern incurred by the execution of one of the two sequences, the adversary should not be able to guess the identity of the executed sequence with too high probability. Due to the weaker guarantees, there is hope to obtain sub-logarithmic overhead smaller than ORAMs. For example, sub-logarithmic constructions have been shown for differentially private Turing machines, stacks and queues [24] whereas logarithmic overhead is required for their oblivious counterparts [21,24]. Unfortunately, the $\Omega(b/\omega \cdot \log n)$ lower bound for DPRAMs by Persiano and Yeo [37] showed that this is impossible when $b = \Omega(\omega)$. However, no such lower bound is known when blocks are significantly smaller than cells, $b \ll \omega$, leading to the following question that was also posed as an open problem in [23]:

> *What is the optimal overhead for differentially private RAMs for the setting when blocks are much smaller than cells, $b \ll \omega$?*

We resolve this by proving a logarithmic lower bound for all choices of b and ω.

Framework for Cell Probe Lower Bounds. Starting from the seminal work of Larsen and Nielsen [28] that introduced the usage of cell probe techniques for oblivious RAMs, there has been a significant amount of work for proving cell probe lower bounds for various data structure problems and privacy guarantees. Previous works have considered lower bounds for different privacy notions beyond obliviousness and differential privacy including obliviousness without adversarial knowledge of operational boundaries [20], obliviousness in the multiple non-colluding server setting [29] and searchable encryption leakage functions [34]. Lower bounds have also been proven for other oblivious data structure problems beyond RAMs including stacks, queues, deques, heaps and search trees [21] as well as near-neighbor search [27].

Unfortunately, the lower bounds end up being very technical and customized to each specific setting. To date, if one wished to prove lower bounds for a specific data structure with certain privacy guarantees, one would have to understand all the various techniques and modify them accordingly to obtain the desired lower bound. Ideally, we would like to encapsulate the re-usable portions of the proofs into a blackbox framework that enables future users to prove lower bounds by only modifying parts that need to be customized for the specific data structure problem and/or privacy notion. This leads us to the following natural question:

> *Is it possible to generalize the techniques into a framework that enables easier lower bound proofs for future works?*

To address this, we present a framework that reduces proving logarithmic lower bounds for privacy-preserving data structures to showing that the data structure problem and privacy notion satisfy two simple (and seemingly minimal) conditions. Furthermore, we show that our framework is widely applicable by proving logarithmic lower bounds for a whole set of new data structure problems for which sub-logarithmic upper bounds are known with no privacy guarantees.

1.1   Our Contributions

We summarize our results below. All our lower bounds are proven in the cell probe model where overhead refers to the required number of probes into server memory cells. If one restricts the server to be passive (i.e., may not perform any computation), then our results become communication lower bounds.

Differentially Private RAMs (DPRAMs). For our first result, we present new lower bounds for DPRAMs. Informally speaking, a RAM is (ϵ, δ)-*differentially private* if, for any two sequences of operations O_1 and O_2 that differ in one operation and for any PPT adversary $\mathcal{A}$, we have that $p_1^{\mathcal{A}} \le e^{\epsilon} \cdot p_2^{\mathcal{A}} + \delta$, where $p_\eta^{\mathcal{A}}$ is the probability that $\mathcal{A}$ outputs 1 on input the transcript of the RAM executing sequence O_η. We look at in the setting where blocks are significantly smaller than the word size, $b \ll \omega$ and show that DPRAMs must still have logarithmic overhead regardless of the parameter settings for b and ω. In our work, we will prove the following theorem. Throughout this section, we ignore $O(\log \log \log n)$ factors to avoid being overburdensome. See Theorem 5 for a more precise statement.

Theorem 1 (Informal). *Any* (ϵ, δ)-*DP RAM for* n *b-bit entries with constant* $\epsilon > 0$, *sufficiently small, constant* $\delta > 0$ *and client storage of* c *bits has overhead:*

$$\Omega\left(\frac{\log(nb/c)}{1 + \log(\omega/b)}\right).$$

To interpret the lower bound, we note that our lower bound is the same as the one proved in [37] for DPRAMs in the case $b = \Theta(\omega)$. However, for the case when $b \ll \omega$, our lower bound ends up peaking a lot higher. For example, consider the case where $b = \Theta(1)$ and $\omega = \Theta(\log n)$. Then, our lower bound ends being $\tilde{\Omega}(\log n)$ while the lower bound in [37] becomes trivial at $\Omega(1)$. In other words, our result ends up proving logarithmic lower bounds for all reasonable choices of block and cell sizes $b = \log^{O(1)}(n)$ and $\omega = \log^{O(1)}(n)$. In such regimes, our lower bound is tight up to $O(\log \log n)$ factors with the best known ORAM constructions [1].

Additionally, we show that we can extend our lower bound to the multiple server setting improving previous multi-server ORAM lower bounds by Larsen et al. [29]. These are the first logarithmic lower bounds for DPRAMs in the multi-server setting (regardless of the choice of b and ω).

General Framework. To make these techniques more accessible, we develop a framework that abstracts out the necessary properties of a cryptographic data structure for which logarithmic lower bounds may be obtained. We modularize the proof such that the lower bound techniques leverage properties of either the data structure problem or privacy in exactly two points. Then, we identify the two properties needed to prove logarithmic lower bounds:

1. *Large Information Retrieval:* For any data structure problem P, one must find a random sequence of n updates $\mathbf{U} = (\mathbf{u}_1, \ldots, \mathbf{u}_n)$ such that for any consecutive sequence of ℓ updates $\mathbf{u}_a, \ldots, \mathbf{u}_{a+\ell-1}$, there exists a set Q of $O(\ell)$ queries

whose answers have high entropy with respect to updates $\mathbf{u}_a, \ldots, \mathbf{u}_{a+\ell-1}$. If we let $\mathbf{A}(\mathbf{U}, Q)$ be the answers of all queries $q \in Q$ immediately executed after $\mathbf{U}$, then we must have that the average contribution to the entropy for each of the $O(\ell)$ queries is at least $\Omega(v)$ bits:

$$H(\mathbf{A}(\mathbf{U}, Q) \mid \mathbf{u}_1, \ldots, \mathbf{u}_{a-1}, \mathbf{u}_{a+\ell}, \ldots, \mathbf{u}_n)/\ell = \Omega(v).$$

2. *Event Probability Transfer*: Consider the setting with $k \geq 1$ server(s) where at most one server is compromised by the adversary. Let $E_i(U, q)$ be any event that is observable by a PPT adversary that compromises the i-th server when executing the update sequence $\mathbf{U}$ from above and a query q. Furthermore, suppose that the probability of the event satisfies $\Pr[E_i(\mathbf{U}, q)] \geq \zeta/k$ for some constant $\zeta > 0$. Then, the same event must occur with similar probability for any other query q':

$$\Pr[E_i(\mathbf{U}, q')] = \Omega(\Pr[E_i(\mathbf{U}, q)]).$$

The first property requires that the data structure problem is "complex" enough to enable retrieving updates with queries. For example, this rules out contrived data structures whose queries may not return any information about updates. The second property acts as a proxy for leveraging the privacy guarantees. For any data structure problem and associated privacy guarantees that can satisfy the above two properties, we immediately get the following theorem (see Theorem 3 for a formal statement).

Theorem 2 (Informal). *Let P be a data structure problem satisfying the above two properties with query outputs of b bits. Any data structure DS solving P using at most client storage of c bits must have overhead:*

$$\Omega \left(\frac{b}{v} \cdot \frac{\log(nb/c)}{1 + \log(\omega/b)} \right).$$

As a result, we believe that we have made the lower bound techniques more accessible as one can reduce the problem of proving logarithmic lower bounds to simply showing that the data structure problem satisfies the two properties above. Furthermore, we identify that a key metric is the ratio between the size of the query output b and the amount of information gained per query v.

New Data Structure Lower Bounds. We show that our framework is widely applicable by proving logarithmic lower bounds for many data structure problems where lower bounds are not known with respect to any privacy guarantees. In our applications, we target data structure problems where $o(\log n)$ upper bounds are known when no privacy guarantees are required. By plugging these data structure problems into our framework, we obtain $\tilde{\Omega}(\log n)$ lower bounds showing that the differentially private versions of these data structures inherently require more overhead compared to the non-private versions. In particular, we prove logarithmic lower bounds for the following data structure problems:

- *Set Membership*: In this problem, the data structure maintains a subset $S \subseteq [n]$. A query for $i \in [n]$ returns a bit indicating whether $i \in S$. This is a natural problem where the output is a single bit and the cell size ω is much larger. Without privacy, one can solve this problem using a bit vector of length n and answer queries in constant time. Using our framework, we show that DP versions would, instead, require $\Omega(\log(n/c)/\log \omega)$ overhead.
- *Predecessor and Successor*: Predecessor (successor) aim to maintain a subset $S \subseteq U$ of size at most n. A query for some $i \in U$ returns the largest (smallest) item in S that is no larger (smaller) than the query input i. Without privacy requirements, one can solve predecessor in $O(\log \log n)$ overhead using van Emde Boas trees [45] when $|U| = n^{O(1)}$. When DP guarantees are required, we show that the overhead must be $\Omega(\log(n/c)/\log(\omega/\log n))$.
- *Disjoint Sets (Union-Find)*: Finally, we consider the disjoint sets data structure that maintains a set of sets over n elements. The union operation takes two elements and joins their corresponding sets. The find operation takes an element and returns a set representation of the input element. For any two elements in the same set, the find operation will return the same set representation. The classical algorithm achieves overhead $O(\alpha(n))$ where $\alpha(n)$ is the inverse Ackermann function that is essentially constant in all practical settings. We show that the DP version requires overhead $\Omega(\log(n/c)/\log(\omega/\log n))$.

One result of our new framework is that we can prove lower bounds for natural data structures that do not enable writing of random blocks of data. Most prior works [20, 21, 23, 27–29, 37] considered "key-value" data structures where the values could be b-bit random blocks to derive enough entropy for lower bounds. The above data structure problems do not enable storing random b-bit blocks, but our framework is still able to prove logarithmic lower bounds. Finally, our framework may handle other privacy guarantees besides differential privacy and obliviousness. For example, our framework may prove lower bounds for leakage functions common in searchable encryption extending [34].

Separation Result for Oblivious Stacks (and Queues). Finally, we consider the generality of our framework. For example, one may question whether there exist data structures that do not satisfy our framework's two required properties, but could still have a logarithmic lower bound. We provide evidence that our framework is quite general and tight by studying stacks and queues, two data structures that do not satisfy the first condition of large information retrieval. For oblivious stacks and queues, Jacob, Larsen and Nielsen [21] proved an $\Omega(b/\omega \cdot \log(nb/c))$ lower bound. For differentially private stacks and queues, Komargodski and Shi [24] showed an upper bound of $O((1 + b/\omega) \cdot \log \log n)$. The correct overhead is unknown for oblivious stacks and queues when $b \ll \omega$.

We present constructions of oblivious stacks and queues with $O(b/\omega \cdot \log(nb/c))$ amortized overhead. So, one may obtain sub-logarithmic overhead when $b \ll \omega$. If $b = O(1)$ and $\omega = \Theta(\log n)$, then our construction uses $O(1)$ amortized overhead. Furthermore, our result can obtain even sub-constant amortized times. When $b = O(1)$ and $\omega = \Theta(\log^2 n)$, our construction requires

$O(1/\log n)$ overhead meaning that, on average, only one operation amongst $\log n$ operations require interacting with the server. To our knowledge, this is the first separation between an online oblivious data structure and ORAMs when $b \ll \omega$.

Re-framing this result with respect to our framework, it becomes clear that oblivious stacks and queues should not satisfy the properties of our framework. Therefore, we believe that if one can prove logarithmic lower bounds for a differentially private version of a data structure problem P for all choices of b and ω, then one should be able to do so using our framework by showing that P satisfies the two necessary properties.

1.2 Related Works

Balls-and-Bins Lower Bounds. The first logarithmic lower bounds were proven by Goldreich and Ostrovsky [17] of the form $\Omega((b/\omega)\cdot(\log n/\log c))$ where the client has storage of c bits. Boyle and Naor [6] pointed out that these lower bounds only existed in the balls-and-bins model with a non-encoding assumption on the underlying blocks. Lower bounds of the form $\Omega(b/\omega \cdot (\log n/\log c))$ for DPRAMs were proven in [33]. Cash, Drucker and Hoover [7] proved lower bounds showing that one-round ORAMs must have $\Omega(\sqrt{n})$ overhead or client storage in the balls-and-bins model. Lower bounds for PIR were proven in similar models including for public preprocessing [2,38] and private preprocessing [11,12,50].

Cell Probe Lower Bounds. The cell probe model is a computational model where only probes into memory are charged cost. Everything else such as computation or randomness generation can be done for free. Therefore, proving cell probe lower bounds is the holy grail as these lower bounds will apply to any realistic computational model. Although, proving cell probe lower bounds ends up being difficult for this reason as the highest static lower bounds are $\tilde{\Omega}(\log n)$ [31] and the highest dynamic lower bounds are $\tilde{\Omega}(\log^2 n)$ [26]. For privacy-preserving data structures, the first cell probe lower bounds were proven by Larsen and Nielsen [28] for ORAMs. Further works have proven lower bounds for other oblivious data structures [21] and near-neighbor search [27]. Other works have also considered various privacy notions including differentially private RAMs [37], ORAMs where adversaries do not know the boundaries of operations [20], ORAMs with multiple servers [29] and searchable encryption [34].

Lower Bound Barriers. Boyle and Naor [6] showed that proving unconditional lower bounds for offline ORAMs (that is, all operations are provided at one time) would imply currently unknown circuit lower bounds. Extending this result, Weiss and Wichs [49] showed that lower bounds for read-only online ORAMs would result in new lower bounds for either locally decodable codes or circuits.

Constructions. As mentioned early, there has been a long line of work attempting to construct ORAMs efficiently such as [1,14,17,18,25,32,40,43] as well as in various settings including statistical security [10], multi-party computation [15,47], multiple non-colluding servers [19,30] and parallel access [5,9] to list some examples. Beyond ORAMs, other works have considered construction oblivious variants of other data structures [22,41,48]. Previous works also presented constructions for differentially private RAMs [33,46], search trees [8], Turing machines, stacks and queues [24].

2   Technical Overview

Reviewing the Information Transfer Tree. We start with the information transfer tree technique of Pătrașcu and Demaine [35] used first by Larsen and Nielsen [28] to prove ORAM cell probe lower bounds. Komargodski and Lin [23] extended the technique to enable proving logarithmic lower bounds for ORAMs even when blocks are smaller than cells ($b < \omega$). At a high level, the information transfer tree technique arranges n operations into a tree with arity $\chi \geq 2$ where each of the n operations are uniquely assigned to a leaf node based on the execution order. Each cell read is uniquely assigned to an internal node as the lowest common ancestor of the leaf nodes associated to the operation performing the cell read and the last operation to overwrite the read cell. For internal node v, the totality of information that is read by queries in the right subtree rooted at v from updates in the left subtree of v exists in the contents of cells in the set of probes assigned to v. For any subtree rooted at v with ℓ leaf nodes, the number of assigned probes is maximized at $\Omega(\ell)$ when right subtree reads blocks overwritten in the left subtree. As the adversary may also compute the information transfer tree, it must be that each internal node is assigned its maximum. Otherwise, the adversary can determine that the worst case sequence was not executed. Summing the worst case across all internal nodes obtains the lower bound.

Unfortunately, the information transfer technique seems to inherently require a strong privacy condition, like obliviousness, for sequences differing in $\tilde{\Omega}(n)$ operations as the worst-case sequences for each internal node differ drastically. This is incompatible with differential privacy as the privacy guarantees degrade exponentially in the number of different operations. We note that Patel *et al.* [34] investigated weaker leakage guarantees for encrypted search using information transfer, but still leveraged privacy for sequences differing in $\tilde{\Omega}(n)$ operations.

Previous Chronogram Approach. To prove lower bounds for differentially private RAMs, Persiano and Yeo [37] adapted the chronogram (introduced by Fredman and Saks [16]). The chronogram considers hard sequences of $\Theta(n)$ updates followed by a single query. The n updates are divided into $K = \tilde{O}(\log n)$ epochs that decay exponentially by a factor of $r \geq 2$. Epochs are numbered in reverse order, so that the i-th epoch has r^i updates. The main idea is as follows. For any epoch i, the information stored about updates occuring in the i-th epoch must appear in updates following the i-th epoch. Since we chose epochs to decay exponentially, the total size of epochs $\{1, \ldots, i-1\}$ is strictly smaller than the i-th epoch. As a result, future update operations cannot encode all the information written in the i-th epoch as long as r is chosen sufficiently large. Consider the final query to randomly retrieve information from written in the i-th epoch. If the data structure answers queries correctly, then, intuitively, the query must directly probe cells last overwritten in the i-th epoch with high probability. Finally, differential privacy guarantees require that the query probes a similar number of cells last overwritten from all K epochs to hide the identity of the epoch from which information is retrieved. We highlight privacy is only needed for sequences differing in the final query.

The crux of the above technique is an efficient communication protocol built using a too-good-to-be-true data structure. In this communication game, Alice and Bob both receives updates in all but the i-th epoch. Alice also receives the answers to queries in the i-th epoch that it wishes to encode to Bob. To do this, Alice and Bob will jointly execute the data structure with Alice helping Bob to fill in the i-th epoch. For all updates before epoch i, Alice and Bob can individually execute the updates. Alice will execute the i-th epoch of updates and keep track of all cell writes. For updates in following epochs, Alice will record any reads to cells (both locations and contents) last overwritten in epoch i. Finally, Alice will also execute all queries relevant to the i-th epoch and record all reads to cell last overwritten in epoch i. The set of all cell locations and contents that are read during operations following epoch i are encoded to Bob. So, Bob executes the data structure identically to Alice and retrieves query outputs to the i-th epoch.

There are two key observations to complete the proof. First, the encoding of cells and locations of all updates following epoch i is too small to encode everything about epoch i. Therefore, the information needed to retrieve a query must be encoded in cells last overwritten in the i-th epoch. Since queries output b bits, one can use an averaging argument to show that $\Omega(b/\omega)$ cells must be probed by random queries to retrieve b bits of information from the i-th epoch.

A New Chronogram Approach for Small Blocks. Unfortunately, the above approach suffers from an b/ω factor that seems inherent in the specific communication protocol. When $b < \omega$, there is nothing ruling out the data structure from storing the answers for $\Theta(\omega/b)$ queries in a single cell.

Our paper introduces a more efficient communication protocol than the one in [37] to handle these settings. If our goal is to prove logarithmic lower bounds, then we must show that random queries must probe $\Omega(1)$ cell last overwritten in epoch i regardless of the choices of b and ω. This is impossible if we rely on trying to encode the contents of cells probed by a query since cell sizes ω are larger than the output of the query b. Instead, we make the observation that the outputs of queries are actually smaller than contents of cells. In other words, it is more efficient for Alice to simply encode the answers to queries instead of encoding the contents of even a single cell probed by a query. However, Alice cannot simply encode the answers of all queries to Bob as this would not enable deriving any meaningful lower bound on query time. So, we also need another method to further compress Alice's encoding. The second idea is for Alice to identify queries that do not need to be encoded at all. For example, consider a query that does not probe any cell last overwritten by the i-th epoch. These queries may be executed correctly by Bob for free without any additional information from Alice. However, the frequency of these free queries is unclear. If no free queries exist, we would obtain a trivial encoding of simply sending all the query's outputs. In fact, a contrived data structure could simply force every query retrieving updates from the i-th epoch to simply probe a cell last overwritten in the i-th epoch to guarantee that there are no free queries at all. By increasing the update overhead by a single probe, each update in the i-th epoch can write to one additional cell that will be read by the corresponding subsequent query ensuring no free queries.

Taking a closer look, the above approach by a contrived data structure only succeeds because the epoch structure is fixed ahead of time. Instead, we consider a randomized epoch structure that cannot be leveraged by the data structure. To do this, we pick a random number of updates from $\{n/2, \ldots, n\}$ followed by a single query. The structure of $K = \tilde{O}(\log n)$ epochs is built over the final $n/2$ updates. Consider any data structure that probes at most $K/100$ cells during queries. As the epochs are randomly placed, we can show that if the data structure can answer a query regarding a block written in the i-th epoch then it will have to probe a cell last overwritten in the i-th epoch with some constant probability, of approximately $1/100$. In other words, we just showed that around $(99/100)$-fraction of queries that retrieve information from the i-th epoch end up being free queries in Alice's encoding. As a result, we obtain a very efficient communication protocol that allows us to prove that queries must probe $\Omega(1)$ cells from all K epochs.

We note that the lower bound in [37] also used randomized epoch structures, but did so to remove $\log \log n$ factors from the lower bound. Their work would still obtain an $\Omega(\log n / \log \log n)$ lower bound without random epochs. In our work, we leverage random query locations in a vastly different way to prove the existence of many free queries. Without this, we cannot prove anything more than a trivial $\Omega(1)$ lower bound.

Comparison with [36]. We note that Pătrașcu and Tarniță [36] also studied the setting of proving chronogram lower bounds when blocks were smaller than memory cells. However, they only considered data structures without any privacy requirements. Instead, they had to leverage properties of the underlying data structure problems. One can view our work as an extension of [36] where we prove chronogram lower bounds for easier data structure problems, but heavily rely on the privacy requirements of the data structure. In fact, all problems studied in our paper are known to have sub-logarithmic upper bounds without privacy requirements. As a result, we had to develop new techniques (especially in the efficient communication protocol) to be able to utilize differential privacy to prove lower bounds for these easier data structure problems.

3   Lower Bound Model

We prove our lower bounds in a variant of the cell probe model that were introduced by Larsen and Nielsen [28]. At a high level, the cell probe model only charges data structures for probes into memory cells. All other operations are free of charge (such as computation and randomness generation). To enable lower bounds for cryptographic data structures, we use the cell probe model that adapts the setting to multiple parties representing the client and $k \geq 1$ server(s). We assume that the client has at most c bits of storage. Each server's storage consists of memory cells (words) of ω bits. In this variant of the cell probe model, the only operation that is charged cost is to probe a cell in any of the server's memory. In our model, all accesses into client memory are free of charge. Additionally, we assume there exists an arbitrarily long, but finite, random string $\mathcal{R}$ that is available to both parties without any cost to access. One can view $\mathcal{R}$ as a random oracle, so our lower bounds apply even if one assumes random oracles exists.

In our work, we will consider dynamic data structure problems. By dynamic, we refer to the fact that the data structure enables operations that allow its users to update the information stored by the data structure. Furthermore, dynamic data structures are allowed to update its memory representation during each operation. We present a formal definition of dynamic data structures below:

Definition 1 (Dynamic Data Structure Problem). *A dynamic data structure consists of the tuple (U_u, U_q) where U_u is the universe of update operations and U_q is the universe of query operations. The error probability is at most α if for every sequence of updates $u_1, \ldots, u_n \in (U_u)^n$ and every query $q \in U_q$, the probability that the query $q(u_1, \ldots, u_n)$ produces the wrong answer is at most α.*

Next, we consider the view of the adversarial server(s) in this model. In particular, each of the $k \geq 1$ servers will receive a transcript consisting of everything that each server observes while processing operations that are executed by the client. For any sequence of operations $O \in (U_u \cup U_q)^{|O|}$, we denote by $\mathbb{V}_i(O)$ the view of the i-th server when processing the operational sequence O. The transcript $\mathbb{V}_i(O)$ will consist of the contents of all memory cells stored on the i-th server as well as sequences of probes to cells that occur for each of the operations in the sequence O. We note that $\mathbb{V}_i(O)$ also contains information denoting the boundaries of when each operation starts and ends[1]. If the adversary compromises the i-th server, the adversary will receive $\mathbb{V}_i(O)$. We use $\mathcal{T}_{\mathsf{DS}}(O)$ to denote the entire transcript seen by the adversary for all compromised servers. Note that our definition assumes that the adversarial server(s) are honest-but-curious. As we are proving lower bounds, assuming that the adversary is weaker makes our result stronger as our lower bounds immediately also apply to more stronger adversaries such as those that are malicious.

Using the above definition, one can now formulate privacy notions for data structures. For example, obliviousness guarantees that any efficient adversary $\mathcal{A}$ should not be able to distinguish between $\mathbb{V}_i(O_1)$ and $\mathbb{V}_i(O_2)$ for any two equal-length sequences O_1 and O_2. In our work, we will consider two weaker notions: differential privacy and privacy with respect to leakage functions. As our framework does not make assumptions on any specific privacy notion, we delay formal definitions of these notions until Sect. 5.

---

[1] We note that Hubáček *et al.* [20] proved a logarithmic lower bound for ORAMs even when the adversary does not learn operational boundaries. We leave it as future work to adapt their techniques to work with our proof.

4   Framework for Lower Bounds

In this section, we present a formal framework for proving lower bounds. In particular, we will only assume certain properties of the data structure problem (that we will describe later) and then we show that for any problems that satisfy these properties, one can immediately utilize our framework to prove lower bounds. Later, we will show that one can utilize our framework for many settings with different privacy guarantees and/or data structure functionalities.

Consider a data structure problem $P = (U_u, U_q)$. For any sequence of U of update operations and for any query operation $q \in U_q$, we denote by $A(U, q)$ the *correct answer* to q when it is executed following the update operations in U. We abuse notation and, for a sequence $Q = (q_1, \ldots, q_\ell)$ of queries, we denote by $A(U, Q)$ the sequence of the *correct* answers for queries $q_i \in Q$ obtained by executing each query directly after the update sequence U. We re-iterate that this set consists of all the correct answers and not the answers returned by a potentially randomized data structure with non-zero error probabilities. We will abuse notation and use $\mathbf{A}(\mathbf{U}, Q)$ for distribution $\mathbf{U}$ over update sequences to denote the distribution over the sequences of correct answers with respect to a update sequence distributed according $\mathbf{U}$. When $\mathbf{U}$ and Q are clear from context, we will drop the arguments and simply use $\mathbf{A}$.

We are now ready to formally define the required properties.

Definition 2 (Large Information Retrieval). *We say that a data structure problem P has the* Large Information Retrieval *property with parameter v if there exists a distribution $\mathbf{U} = (\mathbf{u}_1, \ldots, \mathbf{u}_n)$ over sequences of n update operations such that for any subsequence $(\mathbf{u}_a, \ldots, \mathbf{u}_{a+\ell-1})$ of $\ell \geq \sqrt{n}$ update operations, there exists a sequence Q of length $\ell \leq |Q| \leq c \cdot \ell$, for some constant $c \geq 1$, such that*

$$H(\mathbf{A}(\mathbf{U}, Q) \mid \mathbf{u}_1, \ldots, \mathbf{u}_{a-1}, \mathbf{u}_{a+\ell}, \ldots, \mathbf{u}_n) \geq \ell \cdot v.$$

Definition 3 (Event Probability Transfer). *Consider a data structure* DS *for the problem P. For any update sequence U and query q, let $E(U, q)$ be some event that can be checked whether to have occurred by a PPT adversary such that $\Pr[E(U, q)] \geq \zeta$ for some constant $\zeta > 0$. We say that P has the* Event Probability Transfer *if for every* DS *and for any two queries q and q', it must be that*

$$\Pr[E(U, q')] = \Omega(\Pr[E(U, q)])$$

where the probability is over the internal randomness of DS.

Next, we present the main theorem of our framework.

Theorem 3. *Consider a data structure problem P that allows* update *and* query *operations such that query outputs are b bits and $b = n^{O(1)}$.[2] Let* DS *be any data structure for P with expected update and query overhead t_u and t_q*

---

[2] For most natural problems, the output size is $b = O(\log n)$. For generality, we picked the largest upper bound as possible for b without affecting our lower bound.

respectively, client storage c and error probability $\alpha \leq v/(b \log^2 n)$ *in the cell probe model with* $\omega \geq 1$ *cell size. If P enjoys the Large Information Retrieval property with parameter* v *and Event Probability Transfer property then*

$$t_u + t_q = \Omega \left(\frac{v}{b} \cdot \frac{\log(nv/c)}{1 + \log((\omega + \log\log n)/b)} \right).$$

We dedicate the remainder of this section to proving this theorem. Later, we will show how to apply our framework to prove lower bounds in various settings.

Discussion about b and v. In the above theorem, b is the number of bits to describe the output of each query. On the other hand, v is the amount of information that is retrieved about the random updates with each query. In general, we know that $v \leq b$ as we cannot learn more information that the query output's size. Prior works have made the assumption that $b = v$ such as for array maintenance. By generalizing this, we illuminate the importance of this ratio for lower bounds in cryptographic data structures. In later sections when we prove lower bounds for specific problems, we will convert natural problems to artificial variants with the goal of maximizing the ratio v/b to prove higher lower bounds.

We point out that this b/v factor is distinctly different from the b/ω factor that appears in prior lower bounds. The b/v factor characterizes the average information retrieved per bit in the query output. In contrast, the b/ω factor characterizes the number (or fraction) of cells needed to represent the answer of a single query. For the case when cell size is larger than the query output $\omega > b$, our lower bound is better than the previous one of $\Omega(b/\omega \log(nb/c))$ [37] as it only loses $1/(1 + \log((\omega + \log\log n)/b))$ factor.

Comparison with [23]. We note that our lower bound is slightly lower than the one proved by Komargodski and Lin [23]. They proved a lower bound of the form $\Omega(\log(nb/c)/\log(\omega/b))$ but, to our knowledge, may be only applied to strong oblivious guarantees. On the other hand, we prove a lower bound of the form $\Omega(\log(nb/c)/\log((\omega + \log\log n)/b))$, but it is applicable to a wider range of possibly weaker privacy guarantees and data structure functionalities. We note the gap is very small and only exists in very restricted settings. When $\omega = \Omega(\log\log n)$, both lower bounds are asymptotically identical. Furthermore, if $b = \Omega(\omega)$, we can use the original $\Omega(b/\omega \cdot \log(nb/c))$ lower bounds such as [28]. Therefore, a gap between the lower bounds exists only when $\omega = o(\log\log n)$ and $b = o(\omega)$. It is not hard to see that the gap is at most $O(\log\log\log n)$.

Discussion about Error Probability. We note that one can obtain a slightly stronger theorem for constant error probability α if one is willing to make additional assumptions about the data structure DS. In particular, if one assumes that $v = \Theta(b)$, then one can prove lower bounds that hold also for data structures that err with constant probability. For convenience and the ability to handle general data structures, we consider weaker error probabilities of $O(1/\log^2 n)$. This is still much larger than the negligible error required for cryptographic primitives.

Weaker Large Information Retrieval. In our definitions, we assumed that every subsequence of at least $\sqrt{n}$ updates enabled a query sequence whose outputs had high entropy. A weaker definition would have sufficed for our lower bound where only a certain fraction of the subsequences admit this property (such as if a random subsequence satisfied this property with constant probability). However, we chose the stronger definition as it was sufficient for all applications of our lower bound framework and enabled simpler proofs.

4.1   An Efficient Communication Protocol

In this section, we show that a data structure for any problem P with error probability at most α emits a public coin one-way communication protocol for the problem where Alice wishes to efficiently encode the correct answers for all queries in a query set to Bob. In particular, this protocol efficiently encodes the output of queries even if the query output of b bits is significantly smaller than the cell size ω. We describe the problem below:

Communication Problem. Let $U = (u_1, \ldots, u_m)$ be a sequence of update operations. In the communication problem, Alice and Bob will receive the same sub-sequence of update operations $U' = (u_1, \ldots, u_{a-1}, u_{a+\ell}, \ldots, u_m)$ where the consecutive ℓ operations $u_a, \ldots, u_{a+\ell-1}$ are omitted, along with a set of queries Q and a random string $\mathcal{R}$. Additionally, Alice will receive sequence $A(U, Q)$; that is, the set of correct answers for all $q \in Q$ where each query is executed immediately after U. The goal of Alice will be to encode $A(U, Q)$ to Bob. In particular, Alice's encoding will have to account for the fact that Bob is missing ℓ update operations while ensuring Bob receives the correct answers.

Random Variables. Next, we denote some additional random variables that will be used to bound the total communication of our protocol. In particular, these variables will measure the number of probes by future updates and queries into the group of updates that are missing in Bob's input.

- $\mathbf{X}_u^{\geq a+\ell}$ denotes the number of probes perform by the update operations $(u_{a+\ell}, \ldots, u_m)$ into a cell last overwritten by an update in the missing group $(u_a, \ldots, u_{a+\ell-1})$.
- $\mathbf{X}_Q$ denotes the number of probes performed by all queries $q \in Q$ into a cell last overwritten by an update in the missing group $(u_a, \ldots, u_{a+\ell-1})$.
- $\mathbf{T}_u^{\geq a+\ell}$ denotes the total number of probes performed by all update operations starting from and including $u_{a+\ell}$.

Lemma 1. *If there exists a data structure* DS *for problem P that has error probability $0 < \alpha < 1$, then there is a public coin one-way communication protocol solving the above problem using expected communication at most*

$$\mathbb{E}\left[\mathbf{X}_u^{\geq a+\ell}\right]\left(\omega + \log \frac{t_u(m-a-\ell+1)}{\mathbb{E}[\mathbf{X}_u^{\geq a+\ell}]}\right) + \mathbb{E}\left[\mathbf{X}_Q\right]\cdot\left(b + \log \frac{1}{\mathbb{E}[\mathbf{X}_Q]}\right) + \alpha \cdot |Q| \cdot \left(b + \log \frac{1}{\alpha}\right).$$

Proof. We start by presenting our communication protocol below followed an analysis of correctness and the encoding length.

Alice's Encoding. We describe the procedure used by Alice to encode the correct answers $A(U, Q)$. Recall that Alice and Bob share the update sequence U' as well as public randomness $\mathcal{R}$. The encoding consists of five phases.

1. Alice reconstructs the missing ℓ update operations $u_a, \ldots, u_{a+\ell-1}$ by trying all possible update operations until finding the sequence that matches the answers in the set $A(U, Q)$.
2. Alice runs the data structure, using shared random string $\mathcal{R}$, and executes all the update operations $(u_1, \ldots, u_{a-1})$. That is, Alice executes all updates until the ones missing from Bob's input.
3. Alice executes the missing update operations $(u_a, \ldots, u_{a+\ell-1})$ that are not part of Bob's input. At the end of this phase, Alice appends the c bits found in client memory after the last update operation $u_{a+\ell-1}$.
4. Alice executes all updates in the remaining update operations known to both parties $(u_{a+\ell}, \ldots, u_m)$ using the shared random string $\mathcal{R}$.
   In this phase, Alice keeps a list of all the *special* probes of this phase. A probe is *special* if it is a probe to a cell last overwritten by an update in the missing group. For this purpose, the probes of this phase are indexed with the integers $0, 1, 2$ and so forth. At the end of this phase, Alice appends an encoding of the set of indices of the special probes along with the ordered sequence of all the cell contents read by these probes.
5. Alice executes each query q from the query set Q. All queries are executed starting from the state of the data structure at the end of update u_m (that is, after the last update operation). In this phase, Alice keeps two lists: a list of the *non-free* queries that include a probe to a cell last overwritten in epoch i and a list of the *wrong* queries for which the data structure returns the wrong answer. At the end of this phase, Alice appends an encoding of the subset of queries that are either non-free or wrong along with the ordered sequence of the correct answers of the non-free and wrong queries.

Bob's Decoding. We describe Bob's decoding algorithm to recover the correct answers in $A(U, Q)$. Recall that Bob receives the subsequence of update operations $U' = (u_1, \ldots, u_{a-1}, u_{a+\ell-1}, \ldots, a_m)$ and the random string $\mathcal{R}$.

1. Bob executes the updates $u_1, \ldots, u_{a-1}$ using the shared random string $\mathcal{R}$.
2. Bob skips the missing updates $u_a, \ldots, u_{a+\ell-1}$ and reads the content of the client memory at the end of update $u_{a+\ell-1}$ found in the encoding. Bob keeps the server memory in the state at the end of update operation u_{a-1}.
3. Bob executes the remaining updates $u_{a+\ell}, \ldots, a_m$ using the shared random string $\mathcal{R}$. Before performing a probe as requested by the data structure, Bob checks if the probe is in the list of the special probes as found in the encoding. If the probe is special, Bob uses the cell contents found in the encoding. Otherwise, Bob performs the probe using the current snapshot of the server memory.
4. Bob takes a snapshot of the server and client memory at the end of update u_m and uses it as a starting state for all the queries $q \in Q$. For each query q, Bob first checks whether the query is non-free or wrong. If so, the answer of the query is read from the encoding. Otherwise, the answer of the query is obtained by executing the data structure's query algorithm.

Correctness. As Alice and Bob share the same random string $\mathcal{R}$ and updates outside of the missing group $u_a, \ldots, u_{a+\ell-1}$, their executions of the data structure are identical up to update operation u_{a-1}. For all updates $u_{a+\ell}$ and afterwards, every probe to a cell last overwritten by an update in the missing group $u_a, \ldots, u_{a+\ell-1}$ (thus, the cell contents are unknown to Bob) are encoded by Alice. Therefore, all cells overwritten in update operation $u_{a+\ell}$ and after are correct and identical to Alice's execution. Finally, for the $|Q|$ queries, we note that Bob can get the correct answer whenever the query is correct and does not probe any cell last overwritten by the missing group. As Alice encodes the answer for all queries not satisfying the above two conditions, Bob will always retrieve the correct answers for every query $q \in Q$.

Expected Length of the Encoding. We now bound the expected length of the encoding produced by Alice in each phase.

1. Alice does not produce any encoding in phase 1 and phase 2.
2. In phase 3, Alice encodes client memory for a total of c bits.
3. Phase 4 contributes the encoding of the subset of special probes along with contents of the cells probed by a special probe. In other words, a subset of $X_u^{\geq a+\ell}$ probes of the set of total probes performed during the updates $u_{a+\ell}, \ldots, u_m$ after the missing group along with ω bits for each of the $X_u^{\geq a+\ell}$ probes. Therefore, phase 3 contributes at most:

$$
\mathbb{E}\left[\log\binom{\mathbf{T}_u^{\geq a+\ell}}{\mathbf{X}_u^{\geq a+\ell}} + \omega \cdot \mathbf{X}_u^{\geq a+\ell}\right]
$$

$$
\leq \mathbb{E}\left[\mathbf{X}_u^{\geq a+\ell} \log \frac{\mathbf{T}_u^{\geq a+\ell}}{\mathbf{X}_u^{\geq a+\ell}}\right] + \omega \cdot \mathbb{E}\left[\mathbf{X}_u^{\geq a+\ell}\right] \quad \left(\text{by } \log\binom{n}{k} \leq k\log(n/k)\right)
$$

$$
\leq \mathbb{E}\left[\mathbf{X}_u^{\geq a+\ell}\right] \log \frac{\mathbb{E}[\mathbf{T}_u^{\geq a+\ell}]}{\mathbb{E}[\mathbf{X}_u^{\geq a+\ell}]} + \omega \cdot \mathbb{E}\left[\mathbf{X}_u^{\geq a+\ell}\right] \quad \text{(by concavity)}
$$

$$
\leq \mathbb{E}\left[\mathbf{X}_u^{\geq a+\ell}\right]\left(\omega + \log \frac{t_u(m-a-\ell+1)}{\mathbb{E}[\mathbf{X}_u^{\geq a+\ell}]}\right). \quad \left(\text{by } \mathbb{E}[\mathbf{T}_u^{\geq a+\ell}] \leq t_u(m-a-\ell)\right)
$$

4. Phase 5 contributes the encoding of the set of non-free and wrong queries. If the data structure has probability of error $0 \leq \alpha < 1$, then the expected number of wrong queries is $\alpha \cdot |Q|$ queries and b bits are added to the encoding for each wrong query. Similarly, for the non-free queries, the encoding of a subset of size P_Q^i of a set of size ℓ_i followed by $b \cdot P_Q^i$ bits. Therefore, phase 4 contributes at most the following expected number of bits to the encoding.

$$
\mathbb{E}\left[\log\binom{|Q|}{\alpha \cdot |Q|}\right] + \alpha b |Q| + \mathbb{E}\left[\log\binom{|Q|}{\mathbf{X}_Q}\right] + b \cdot \mathbb{E}[\mathbf{X}_Q]
$$

$$
\leq \alpha |Q|(b + \log 1/\alpha) + \mathbb{E}\left[\mathbf{X}_Q \cdot \log \frac{|Q|}{\mathbf{X}_Q}\right] + b \cdot \mathbb{E}[\mathbf{X}_Q]
$$

$$
\leq \alpha |Q|(b + \log 1/\alpha) + \mathbb{E}[\mathbf{X}_Q] \cdot \left(b + \log \frac{|Q|}{\mathbb{E}[\mathbf{X}_Q]}\right).
$$

This completes the proof of our public coin one-way communication protocol. $\square$

4.2   The Hard Distribution

We now describe the distribution of updates and queries that we will use to prove our lower bound. We then show how to organize the updates into epochs so to utilize the protocol of the previous section. At a high level, by looking at the components of the communication cost of Lemma 1, we notice that the first component is due to the reconstruction of the necessary information for future updates occurring after the missing updates. The second component takes into account the amount of information for queries that were embedded during the missing update operations. Note that the first component depends only on the update time while the second component depends only on the query time. We organize our updates into epochs so that the two components are balanced and we can obtain a lower bound on the sum of query and update times.

Our hard distribution will make use of the random update sequence $\mathbf{U} = (\mathbf{u}_1, \ldots, \mathbf{u}_n)$ that we will assume exists for the data structure problem P. We define our hard distribution denoted by $\mathcal{U}$ as follows:

1. Pick m uniformly at random from $\{n/2 + 1, n/2 + 1, \ldots, n\}$.
2. Output sequence of operations $U = (\mathbf{u}_1, \ldots, \mathbf{u}_m)$.

In other words, we are picking a random prefix of length between $n/2$ and n from the random update sequence $\mathbf{U}$. For any query q, we denote by $\mathcal{Q}(q)$ the distribution over the sequences $Q(q) = (U, q)$ obtained by selecting U according to $\mathcal{U}$. Additionally, we will consider $\mathcal{Q}(Q)$ with respect to a set of queries Q. In this case, $\mathcal{Q}(Q)$ consists of a random update sequence drawn from $\mathcal{U}$ as well as a uniformly random query drawn from Q. Our final hard distribution will be $\mathcal{Q}(q)$ for some query q.

Definition of Epochs. Let $U = (u_1, \ldots, u_m)$ be a sequence of operations in the support of $\mathcal{U}$. Define r to be the multiplicative decay between each future epoch. We will choose a correct value of r later, but we will ensure that $r \geq 2$. We partition the operations of U into epochs of exponentially increasing sizes $\ell_1 := r, \ell_2 := r^2, \ldots$ with epochs starting from u_m and growing backward to u_1. That is, epoch 1 consists of operations $u_m, u_{m-1}, \ldots, u_{m-r+1}$, epoch 2 of operations $u_{m-r}, \ldots, u_{m-r-r^2+1}$ and so on. We define $s_i := \sum_{j=1}^{i} \ell_j$ to be the number of the operations in epochs $1, \ldots, i$. Another way to view s_i is that it is the total number of operations that occur after epoch $i + 1$. We will denote U_i to be the set of all updates in epoch i. We will also denote U_{-i} to be the set of all updates except for those that are updated in the i-th epoch. The index of the starting update operation of the i-th epoch will be denoted by p_i.

We say that an epoch is *large* if $\ell_i \geq \max\{8c/v, \sqrt{n}\}$ and we denote by K the number of large epochs. Note that the number of large epochs is $K = \Theta(\log_r(m/\ell_i)) = \Theta(\log_r(nv/c))$.

The organization of updates into epochs formalizes the intuition provided in the previous section. For any large epoch i with ℓ_i updates, we note that the number of update operations following it is at most $2\ell_i/r$. In other words, the future updates are a little bit smaller than the total number of updates within the i-th epoch. So, we can balance the two components of the communication cost in the one-way protocol from the prior section to prove our lower bound.

Important Notions of Information. Finally, we will introduce two more variables that will aim to capture the notion of information that will be utilized throughout our work. In particular, these will look very similar to the communication cost of the one-way protocol from the prior section. However, they will be used specifically with respect to our epoch organization. We denote $\mathbf{X}_u^{\geq p_i-1}$ to be the number of probes performed by updates occurring after the i-th epoch (that is, in epochs $i-1, \ldots, 0$) that access a cell last overwritten in the i-th epoch. We denote $\mathbf{X}_Q^i$ to be the number of probes performed by all queries $q \in Q$ to cells last overwritten in the i-th epoch. We denote $\mathbf{X}_q^i$ to the number of probes performed by a single query $q \in Q$ to cells last overwritten in the i-th epoch.

We denote by $\mathcal{Z}(i, Q)$ the quantity defined as follows:

$$\mathcal{Z}(i, Q) = \min \left\{ |Q| \cdot v, \mathbb{E}\left[\mathbf{X}_u^{\geq p_i-1}\right](\omega + \log \log n) + b \cdot \mathbb{E}\left[\mathbf{X}_Q^i\right] \right\}.$$

This captures the total amount of information needed to answer all queries $q \in Q$. Note, this matches the communication cost of our one-way communication protocol in Lemma 1 by plugging in the i-th epoch as the missing group of updates. We use the minimum as we know the information transferred is at most $|Q| \cdot v$ bits as v bits are learned on average from each $|Q|$ queries. For a single query $q \in Q$, we can similarly define $\mathcal{Z}(i, q)$:

$$\mathcal{Z}(i, q) = \min \left\{ v, \frac{\mathbb{E}[\mathbf{X}_u^{\geq p_i-1}](\omega + \log \log n)}{|Q|} + b \cdot \mathbb{E}\left[\mathbf{X}_q^i\right] \right\}.$$

We use minimum as the average information in a single query is v bits. We will utilize $\mathcal{Z}(i, Q)$ and $\mathcal{Z}(i, q)$ later as the events that can be viewed by an adversary.

4.3 Bounding Query and Update Times

Finally, we will finish the proof of Theorem 3 in this section. In particular, we will leverage the epoch organization as well as our one-way communication protocol to prove lower bounds on the query and update times. To do this, we start by showing that the cost of the one-way communication protocol can be directly related to the entropy of the correct answers of the query set.

Lemma 2. *Consider a data structure* DS *with error probability* $\alpha \leq v/(b \log^2 n)$ *for a data structure problem* P *that satisfies the Large Information Retrieval property. Then for every large epoch* i *such that* $\mathbb{E}[\mathbf{X}_u^{p_i-1}] = O(t_u \ell_i/(rK))$, *there exists a sequence* Q_i *of at least* ℓ_i *queries such that*

$$\mathcal{Z}(i, Q_i) = \Omega(\ell_i \cdot v).$$

Proof. We remind the reader that a large epoch i consists of $\ell_i \geq \sqrt{n}$ update operations. Therefore, if we consider a sequence $\mathbf{U}$ of n updates and the subsequence of the ℓ_i updates of the i-th epoch then, by the Large Information Retrieval property, there exists a sequence Q_i of queries such that

$$H(\mathbf{A}(\mathbf{U}, Q_i) \mid \mathbf{U}_{-i}) \geq \ell_i v,$$

where $\mathbf{U}_{-i}$ is the sequence of updates obtained from $\mathbf{U}$ by removing the updates of epoch i. Since Q_i has at least ℓ_i queries, it suffices to focus on the second argument of the minimum of the definition of $\mathcal{Z}(i)$.

Next, we utilize query set Q_i in the context of the one-way communication protocol of Lemma 1, where Alice and Bob receive the updates $\mathbf{U}_{-i}$. By Shannon's source coding theorem, the expected length of Alice's encoding of $\mathbf{A}(\mathbf{U}, Q)$ must be at least the entropy of $\mathbf{A}(\mathbf{U}, Q)$ conditioned on the shared information $\mathbf{U}_{-i}$ and $\mathcal{R}$. Moreover, observe that $\mathcal{R}$ is chosen independently from $\mathbf{U}$ and Q and thus the expected length of the encoding must be at least

$$H(\mathbf{A}(\mathbf{U}, Q), \mid \mathbf{U}_{-i}, \mathcal{R}) = H(\mathbf{A}(\mathbf{U}, Q) \mid \mathbf{U}_{-i}) \geq \ell_i v.$$

In other words, the expected communication cost must be $\Omega(\ell_i \cdot v)$.

Recall that we use p_i to denote the position of the first operation of the i-th epoch and s_{i-1} is the number of update operations in epochs $1, 2, \ldots, i-1$. Furthermore, we use $\mathbf{X}_{Q_i}^i$ to denote the number of probes by queries $q \in Q_i$ into cells last overwritten by updates $\mathbf{U}_i$ in the i-th epoch. Therefore, by Lemma 1,

$$c + \mathbb{E}\left[\mathbf{X}_u^{\geq p_{i-1}}\right]\left(w + \log \frac{t_u s_{i-1}}{\mathbb{E}[\mathbf{X}_u^{\geq p_{i-1}}]}\right) + \mathbb{E}\left[\mathbf{X}_{Q_i}^i\right]\left(b + \log \frac{|Q_i|}{\mathbb{E}[\mathbf{X}_{Q_i}^i]}\right) + \alpha \cdot |Q_i| \cdot \left(b + \log \frac{1}{\alpha}\right) \geq \ell_i v.$$

Note, that $\alpha \leq v/(b \log^2 n)$, so we get that the last addend is at most $|Q_i| v / \log^2 n \cdot (1 + \log(bn/v))$. As $b = n^{O(1)}$ and $|Q_i| = O(\ell_i)$, we get that this is at most $\ell_i v \cdot O(1/\log n) \leq \ell_i v/8$ for sufficiently large n. For a large epoch, we also have $c \leq \ell_i v/8$. Therefore,

$$\mathbb{E}\left[\mathbf{X}_u^{\geq p_{i-1}}\right]\left(w + \log \frac{t_u s_{i-1}}{\mathbb{E}[\mathbf{X}_u^{\geq p_{i-1}}]}\right) + \mathbb{E}\left[\mathbf{X}_{Q_i}^i\right]\left(b + \log \frac{|Q_i|}{\mathbb{E}[\mathbf{X}_Q^i]}\right) \geq \frac{3}{4} \cdot \ell_i v.$$

Consider two cases. If $\mathbb{E}\left[\mathbf{X}_Q^i\right] \leq |Q_i|/16$, then $\log \frac{|Q_i|}{\mathbb{E}[\mathbf{X}_{Q_i}^i]} \leq 4$. Therefore,

$$\mathbb{E}\left[\mathbf{X}_u^{\geq p_{i-1}}\right]\left(w + \log \frac{t_u s_{i-1}}{\mathbb{E}[\mathbf{X}_u^{\geq p_{i-1}}]}\right) + b \cdot \mathbb{E}\left[\mathbf{X}_{Q_i}^i\right] \geq \frac{1}{2} \cdot \ell_i v$$

as $|Q_i| \geq \ell_i$. Finally, we use the fact that $\mathbb{E}[\mathbf{X}_u^{p_{i-1}}] = O(t_u \ell_i/(rK))$ and plug it into the above to obtain the following inequality:

$$\mathbb{E}\left[\mathbf{X}_u^{\geq p_{i-1}}\right](w + \log \log n) + b \cdot \mathbb{E}\left[\mathbf{X}_{Q_i}^i\right] = \Omega(\ell_i v)$$

where we used the fact that $s_{i-1}/\ell_i \leq 2/r$ and $K = O(\log n)$ by our epoch construction. This completes the proof for the case of $\mathbb{E}\left[\mathbf{X}_{Q_i}^i\right] \leq |Q_i|/16$. For the other case when $\mathbb{E}\left[\mathbf{X}_{Q_i}^i\right] \geq |Q_i|/16$, we can see that the result is trivially obtained by plugging the value into $\mathcal{Z}(i)$ since $|Q_i| \geq \ell_i$. $\qquad\square$

The lemma above tells us that, for every large epoch, there exists one set of queries with a large value of $\mathcal{Z}$. The set of "expensive" queries depends on the epoch and different epochs might have different bad queries. Conversely, a query q might be "expensive" for one epoch but not for the others. Next, we show that the Adversarially Observable Event implies that there exists one query that is "expensive" for all epochs.

Using the Adversarially Observable Event. As we shall see later, this property is guaranteed by the security notions (differential privacy, obliviousness) that we will consider for the specific data structure problems for which we will derive lower bounds. We note that quantity $\mathcal{Z}(i, q)$ only depends on the data structure probes and thus it can be efficiently computed by an adversary even without knowing the executed query q. Therefore, by the Adversarially Observable Event property, its value should not "vary too much" with q.

To formalize this, we define the event $\mathbf{E}_q^i$ to be a binary random variable that checks whether $\mathcal{Z}(i, q)$ is above a certain threshold. In particular, we denote

$$\mathbf{E}_q^i = 1 \iff \frac{\mathbf{X}_u^{\geq p_{i-1}}}{|Q|} (\omega + \log\log n) + b \cdot \mathbf{X}_q^i \geq \beta v$$

for some constant $\beta > 0$ that we will choose later. Note, the above formula is the second argument of $\mathcal{Z}(i, q)$. We will also use $\mathbf{E}_Q^i$ as a binary random variable with respect to the second argument of $\mathcal{Z}(i, Q)$ as follows:

$$\mathbf{E}_Q^i = 1 \iff \mathbf{X}_u^{\geq p_{i-1}} (\omega + \log\log n) + b \cdot \mathbf{X}_Q^i \geq |Q|\beta v$$

We show that there exists a single query q such that $\Pr[\mathbf{E}_q^i = 1] \geq p$ for some constant probability $p > 0$ for all large epochs i. We prove this next:

Lemma 3. *Consider a data structure* DS *for a data structure problem* P *satisfying the Large Information Retrieval and the Event Probability Transfer properties. Then, there exists a query q and a constant $0 < p \leq 1$ such that for all large epochs i where $\mathbb{E}[\mathbf{X}_u^{p_{i-1}}] = O(t_u \ell_i/(rK))$, $\Pr[\mathbf{E}_q^i = 1] \geq p$.*

Proof. By Lemma 2, we know that for each large epoch i, it must be that the following holds for some constant $0 < \gamma < 1$:

$$\mathcal{Z}(i, Q) = \min\left\{\ell_i \cdot v, \mathbb{E}\left[\mathbf{X}_u^{\geq p_{i-1}}\right] (\omega + \log\log n) + b \cdot \mathbb{E}\left[\mathbf{X}_Q^i\right]\right\} \geq \gamma \cdot |Q| \cdot v$$

as $|Q| = O(\ell_i)$. We set the value β from the definition of the events $\mathbf{E}_Q^i$ and $\mathbf{E}_q^i$ equal to $\beta := \gamma/2$. For each large epoch i where $\mathbb{E}[\mathbf{X}_u^{p_{i-1}}] = O(t_u \ell_i/(rK))$, we will show there exists some query $q_i \in Q$ such that $\Pr[\mathbf{E}_{q_i}^i = 1] > p'$ for some constant positive probability p'. Suppose this is false and $\Pr[\exists q \in Q, \mathbf{E}_q^i = 1] = o(1)$. Then, we get that with probability at least $1 - o(1)$, the following is true:

$$\sum_{q \in Q} \mathcal{Z}(i, q) = \sum_{q \in Q} \frac{\mathbf{X}_u^{\geq p_{i-1}}}{|Q|} (\omega + \log\log n) + b \cdot \mathbf{X}_q^i \leq \gamma/2 \cdot |Q| \cdot v$$

where we can always use the second argument of $\mathcal{Z}(i,q)$ by our assumption that $\mathbf{E}_q^i \neq 1$. Let $p_q^i = \Pr[\exists q \in Q, \mathbf{E}_q^i = 1]$. Next, we bound the expectation of $\mathcal{Z}(i,Q)$:

$$\mathbb{E}[\mathcal{Z}(i,Q)] \leq (1 - p_q^i) \sum_{q \in Q} \left(\frac{\mathbf{X}_u^{\geq p_{i-1}}}{|Q|} (\omega + \log\log n) + b \cdot \mathbf{X}_q^i \right) + p_q^i \cdot (|Q| \cdot v)$$

$$\leq \gamma/2 \cdot |Q| \cdot v + o(|Q|v) < \gamma \cdot |Q| \cdot v.$$

To understand this inequality, we consider the two cases. We can always bound the value of $\mathcal{Z}(i,Q)$ by $|Q| \cdot v$ as we do when $\exists q \in Q$ such that $\mathbf{E}_q^i = 1$. For the other case, note that $\mathcal{Z}(i,q) < v$ so we can replace it with the second argument of $\mathcal{Z}(i,q)$ and apply linearity of expectation. Note that the last derived inequality contradicts with the first inequality from Lemma 2. Therefore, for some probability $p' > 0$, for each large epoch i such that $\mathbb{E}[\mathbf{X}_u^{p_{i-1}}] = O(t_u \ell_i/(rK))$, there exists $q_i \in Q$ and $\Pr[\mathbf{E}_{q_i}^i = 1] > p'$.

Since the value of $\mathbf{E}_q^i$ can be efficiently computed, the Event Probability Transfer property gives that there exists a query q such that $\Pr[\mathbf{E}_q^i = 1] = p$ for some constant $p > 0$ and for all large epochs i.   □

The above lemma shows that there must exist one "expensive" query q for which $\mathcal{Z}(i,q)$ is large for all large epochs i for which the expected value of $\mathbf{X}_u^{p_{i-1}}$ is not too large. We next show that these extra conditions holds for all large epochs. In particular, we show that the average number of probes to cells last overwritten in each of the ℓ_i update operations is at most $O(t_u/r)$.

Lemma 4. $\sum_i \mathbb{E}[\mathbf{X}_u^{\geq p_{i-1}}]/\ell_i = O(t_u/r)$ over all large epochs i.

Proof. We start by identifying which probes contribute to $\mathbf{X}_u^{\geq p_{i-1}}$ for all large epochs i. Let us consider a probe occurring as part of the β-th update operation and denote by γ the index of the operation that last overwrote the same cell. We index operations according to the time they were performed so that updates occurring in epoch 1 have the largest index. In other words, update operations are numbered from left to right and we remind the reader that epochs are numbered from right to left. Therefore we have $\beta > \gamma$ and we let x denote the epoch satisfying the inequality $s_{x-1} \leq \beta - \gamma < s_x$. Note that this x is unique as s_i grows as i grows. We break down the analysis into two different cases.

Case I: $i < x$. The probe does not contribute to $\mathbf{X}_u^{\geq p_{i-1}}$ for $i < x$ regardless of the location of the query operation. First, suppose that the query operation occurs immediately after the β-th operation; that is, the β-th update operation is part of epoch 1. Since $\beta - \gamma \geq s_{x-1}$, the γ-th operation takes place after epoch $x - 1$ has finished and, since $i < x$, this implies that epoch i begins after the γ-th update has been performed. If instead the query operation does not occur immediately following the β-th operation then i-th epoch will begin even later and thus it is still after the γ-th update operation has been performed.

Case II: $i \geq x$. First of all observe that epoch $i - 1$ must start between γ and β and thus there at most $\beta - \gamma < s_x$ good positions. Moreover, observe that epoch

$i-1$ cannot start before $\beta - s_{i-1} + 1$, for otherwise operation β would take place before operation 1 which is clearly a contradiction. We thus have at most s_{i-1} good positions. Therefore the probability that a probe performed as part of the β-th update contributes to $\mathbf{X}_u^{\geq p_{i-1}}$ is at most $2/n \cdot \min\{s_{i-1}, s_x\}$.

Now a probe associated with x contributes to $\mathbf{X}_u^{\geq p_{i-1}}$, for randomly chosen epoch i, for at most $2/(nK) \cdot \min\{s_{i-1}, s_x\}$, for $i \geq x$. By summing over all $i \geq x$, we can bound the contribution of one probe to a random epoch by $\sum_{i \geq x} \frac{2\min\{s_{i-1}, s_x\}}{n} \frac{1}{K} \leq \frac{4\ell_i}{rnK}$. As we have at most $n \cdot t_u$ probes, we conclude that $\sum_i \mathbb{E}[\mathbf{X}_u^{\geq p_{i-1}}]/\ell_i \leq 4t_u/r$. $\square$

Finally, we are ready to prove our main theorem.

Proof of Theorem 3. We start from Lemma 2. For every large epoch i such that $\mathbb{E}[\mathbf{X}_u^{\geq p_{i-1}}] = O(t_u\ell_i/(rK))$, we have $\Pr[\mathcal{Z}(i, q) = \Omega(v)] \geq p$ for some constant $p > 0$ for every query q. In other words, we know that by linearity of expectation:

$$\frac{\mathbb{E}[\mathbf{X}_u^{\geq p_{i-1}}]}{|Q|}(\omega + \log\log n) + b \cdot \mathbb{E}\left[\mathbf{X}_q^i\right] = \Omega(v).$$

First, we do the easier task of bounding $\mathbb{E}[\mathbf{X}_q^i]$. Note that the expected query time is $\sum_i \mathbb{E}[\mathbf{X}_q^i] \leq t_q$ where we only iterate over all large epochs i. Consider the experiment of picking a random epoch $\mathbf{i}$. Then, know that $\mathbb{E}[\mathbf{X}_q^{\mathbf{i}}] \leq t_q/K$ where K is the number of large epochs. By Markov's inequality, we know that $\Pr_{\mathbf{i}}[\mathbb{E}[\mathbf{X}_q^{\mathbf{i}}] \leq 100t_q/K] \geq 99/100$.

By Lemma 4, we know that $\sum_i \mathbb{E}[\mathbf{X}_u^{\geq p_{i-1}}]/\ell_i \leq \gamma t_u/r$ for some constant $\gamma > 0$ over all large epochs i. Again, we can show that for a random index $\mathbf{i}$, that $\Pr_{\mathbf{i}}[\mathbb{E}[\mathbf{X}_u^{\geq p_{i-1}}] \leq 100\gamma\ell_i t_u/(rK)] \geq 99/100$ as there are K large epochs. Then,

$$\Pr_{\mathbf{i}}\left[\mathbb{E}[\mathbf{X}_u^{\geq p_{i-1}}] \leq \frac{100\gamma\ell_i t_u}{rK} \wedge \mathbb{E}[\mathbf{X}_q^{\mathbf{i}}] \leq \frac{100t_q}{K}\right] \geq 98/100.$$

We pick any such i satisfying the above two inequalities for the rest of the proof. By plugging the above bounds into the inequality and using $|Q| = \Theta(\ell_i)$,

$$\frac{t_u}{rK}\left(\omega + \log\frac{s_{i-1}}{\ell_i}rK\right) + \frac{t_q}{K}b = \Omega(v).$$

By using the fact that $s_{i-1}/\ell_i \leq 2/r$ and $K = O(\log n)$ as $r \geq 2$, we obtain

$$\frac{t_u}{rK}(\omega + \log\log n) + \frac{t_q}{K}b = \Omega(v).$$

Finally by substituting $r = 2 + (\omega + \log\log n)/b$ and $K = \Theta(\log_r(nv/c))$,

$$t_u + t_q = \Omega\left(\frac{v}{b} \cdot K\right) = \Omega\left(\frac{v}{b} \cdot \frac{\log(nv/c)}{1 + \log((\omega + \log\log n)/b)}\right)$$

that completes our proof. $\square$

4.4   Extension to Multiple Non-colluding Servers

In this section, we show that our framework may also be extended to the multiple non-colluding server setting. We assume there are k servers and the PPT adversary has compromised exactly one server. Our lower bound immediately applies to settings where the adversary compromises multiple (or even all) servers. First, we define the equivalent of the Event Probability Transfer property for k servers.

Definition 4 (k-Event Probability Transfer). *For any update sequence U and query q, let $E_i(U, q)$ be some event that can be checked whether to have occurred by a PPT adversary that compromised the i-th server. Suppose that $\Pr[E_i(U, q)] \geq \zeta/k$ for some constant $\zeta > 0$. Then, we say that a data structure enjoys the k-Event Probability Transfer property if for any query q', it holds that*

$$\Pr[E_i(U, q')] = \Omega(\Pr[E_i(U, q)])$$

where the probability is over the internal randomness of the data structure.

We present our theorem below and defer the proof to the full version that adapts some ideas from [29] for our proof technique.

Theorem 4. *Consider a data structure problem P that allows* update *and* query *operations such that query outputs are b bits and $b = n^{O(1)}$. Consider a data structure* DS *that implements problem P over k servers with expected update and query overhead t_u and t_q respectively, client storage c and error probability $\alpha \leq v/(b \log^2 n)$ in the cell probe model with $\omega \geq 1$ cell size. If P enjoys the Large Information Retrieval property and the Event Probability Transfer property then*

$$t_u + t_q = \Omega\left(\frac{v}{b} \cdot \frac{\log(nv/c)}{1 + \log((\omega + \log\log n)/b)}\right).$$

The above lower bound holds even for $k = n^{O(1)}$ servers. In particular, the above can be used to show lower bound that even if a PPT adversary compromises only one of $k = n^{O(1)}$ servers under certain privacy properties. See Sect. 5.1 for some further discussion.

5   Lower Bounds

In this section, we show that our framework may be used to derive a whole new set of logarithmic lower bounds for differentially private (and, thus, oblivious) versions of data structure problems.

We start by applying our framework to prove our main result of logarithmic lower bounds for DP RAMs in the setting of $b \ll \omega$. To show that our framework may handle various privacy guarantees, we show that we can extend the searchable encryption lower bounds in [34] for the setting of $b \ll \omega$. We also consider a suite of classical data structures where $o(\log n)$ overhead is known without any privacy guarantees. Through our framework, we show that these data structures require logarithmic overhead as soon as privacy requirements are enforced. All missing proofs are deferred to the full version.

5.1 Differentially Private RAMs

As the first application of our framework, we will prove logarithmic lower bounds for differentially private (DP) RAMs. As a reminder, a prior lower bound of $\Omega(b/\omega \cdot \log(nb/c))$ was proved in [37]. However, this does not preclude sub-logarithmic overhead when $b \ll \omega$. For example, if $b = O(1)$ and $\omega = \Theta(\log n)$, the above lower bound becomes trivial at $\Omega(1)$. In this section, we show that this lower bound remains logarithmic even in the case when $b \ll \omega$.

We start by defining $(\epsilon, \delta, 1, k)$-DP for k-server data structures for which the view of an adversary that corrupts 1 of the k servers is (ϵ, δ)-DP, following the definition in [37] where neighboring sequences of operations are those that differ in exactly one operation. As a note, this definition uses computational differential privacy with respect to efficient adversaries.

Definition 5. *A data structure* DS *is* $(\epsilon, \delta, 1, k)$-DP *(differentially private) if for any pair of operational sequences* O_1 *and* O_2 *that differ in at most one operation and any PPT adversary* $\mathcal{A}$ *that compromises one of the* k *servers,*

$$\Pr[\mathcal{A}(\mathcal{T}_{\mathsf{DS}}(O_1)) = 1] \leq e^\epsilon \Pr[\mathcal{A}(\mathcal{T}_{\mathsf{DS}}(O_2)) = 1] + \delta$$

where $\mathcal{T}_{\mathsf{DS}}(O)$ *is the transcript seen by the adversary across all compromised servers when the operational sequence* O *is executed by* DS.

We show that our lower bound framework enables proving logarithmic lower bound for DP RAMs as follows. See the proof in the full version.

Theorem 5. *Any* $(\epsilon, \delta, 1, k)$-DP *data structure* DS *that solves the dynamic array maintenance problem for* n b-*bit entries with constant* $\epsilon > 0$ *and* $\delta < \beta/k$, *for a sufficiently small constant* $\beta > 0$, *expected update and query time* t_u *and* t_q, *client storage* c *and error probability* $\alpha \leq 1/\log^2 n$ *in the cell probe model with* $\omega \geq 1$ *cell size must satisfy the following:*

$$t_u + t_q = \Omega \left(\frac{\log(nb/c)}{1 + \log((\omega + \log\log n)/b)} \right).$$

Discussion about k and δ. We note that for the setting of $k \geq 2$ servers and one compromised server, we can only prove non-trivial lower bounds when $\delta < 1/k$. To see this, note that there is a trivial algorithm that picks one of the random k servers and performs a plaintext data structure. An adversary will only see anything with probability at most $1/k$. Therefore, this is a $(0, 1/k)$-DP data structure. Our lower bound shows that anything with stronger security parameters results in the identical lower bound as the single-server model. As an extreme example, if $k = n^{O(1)}$ and $\delta = \mathsf{negl}(n)$, our lower bound still holds.

5.2 Set Membership

Next, we move onto proving lower bounds for other data structures. In general, previous lower bounds have focused on "key-value" types of data structures.

For example, RAMs are essentially arrays with keys from $[n]$ and b-bit values. Prior lower bounds relied upon the fact that the b-bit value is truly random.

We show that our lower bound framework can also used to prove lower bounds for data structures without associated values. For the first such problem, we will consider the simple dynamic set data structure that maintains a subset $S \subseteq [n]$ that enables the following two operations:

1. add(i): Adds item $i \in U$ into subset S.
2. query(i): Returns 1 if $i \in S$ and 0 otherwise.

Note that the set problem is a natural problem where the query output size is only a single bit that will most likely be much smaller than the word size ω.

In the non-oblivious setting, it is clear that the dynamic set problem over the universe $[n]$ can be solved with $O(1)$ time using a bit vector of length n. Using our framework, we will show that the dynamic set membership problem with differential privacy requires logarithmic overhead. The proof may be found in the full version.

Theorem 6. *Any $(\epsilon, \delta, 1, k)$-DP data structure* DS *that solves the dynamic set problem over $[n]$ with constant $\epsilon > 0$ and $\delta < \beta/k$ for a sufficiently small constant $\beta > 0$, expected update and query time t_u and t_q, client storage c and error probability $\alpha \leq 1/\log^2 n$ in the cell probe model with $\omega \geq 1$ cell size must satisfy:*

$$t_u + t_q = \Omega \left(\frac{\log(n/c)}{1 + \log(\omega + \log\log n)} \right).$$

5.3 Predecessor and Successor

We consider another classic data structure for which sub-logarithmic overhead constructions are known without any privacy requirements. In this section, we will prove lower bounds for the predecessor and successor problem. The predecessor data structure stores subset $S \subseteq U$ of size at most n with the following:

– add(i): Adds item $i \in U$ into subset S.
– query(i): Returns the value $\max\{s \in S : s \leq i\}$. That is, the largest value that is not strictly larger than the value of i.

In the non-oblivious setting, there exists dynamic predecessor and successor data structures with overhead $O(\log\log |U|)$ using van Emde Boas trees [45]. For standard settings of $|U| = n^{O(1)}$, this becomes $O(\log\log n)$. With differentially privacy, the overhead must be logarithmic. See the proof in the full version.

Theorem 7. *Any $(\epsilon, \delta, 1, k)$-DP data structure* DS *that solves the dynamic predecessor (successor) problem over universe U storing at most n items with constant $\epsilon > 0$ and $\delta < \beta/k$ for a sufficiently small constant $\beta > 0$, expected update and query time t_u and t_q, client storage c and error probability $\alpha \leq 1/\log^2 n$ in the cell probe model with $\omega \geq 1$ cell size must satisfy the following:*

$$t_u + t_q = \Omega \left(\frac{\log(n \log(|U|/n)/c)}{1 + \log((\omega + \log\log n)/\log(|U|/n))} \right).$$

5.4   Disjoint Sets (Union-Find)

Another classic data structure that has very efficient (sub-logarithmic) overhead is the disjoint sets (union-find) data structure. At a high level, the disjoint sets data structure must maintain n items that may be arranged into disjoint sets. Initially, the n items are assumed to be in n individual different sets. Afterwards, the following operations may be performed:

– union(a, b): Given $a, b \in [n]$, merge the two sets containing a and b.
– find(a): Given an item $a \in [n]$, return the identity of the set containing a.

For correctness, it is required that if two items $a, b \in [n]$ are in the same set, then find(a) should be equal to find(b). Also, if a and b are not in the same set, then find(a) should be different from find(b). We will assume that set representations are integers from the set $[n^{O(1)}]$ as done by classic constructions. Thus, the query output size is $O(\log n)$ bits.

There are classic constructions [44] that require only $O(\alpha(n))$ overhead where $\alpha(n)$ is the inverse Ackermann function. In all reasonable settings, $\alpha(n)$ is practically constant. If we enforce differentially privacy, we leverage our framework to prove a logarithmic lower bound. See the proof in the full version.

Theorem 8. *Any $(\epsilon, \delta, 1, k)$-DP data structure* DS *that solves the dynamic disjoint set problem over at most n items with constant $\epsilon > 0$ and $\delta < \beta/k$ for a sufficiently small constant $\beta > 0$, expected update and query time t_u and t_q, client storage c and error probability $\alpha = O(1/\log^2 n)$ in the cell probe model with $\omega \geq 1$ cell size must satisfy the following:*

$$t_u + t_q = \Omega\left(\frac{\log(n/c)}{1 + \log(\omega/\log n)}\right).$$

5.5   Searchable Encryption (Encrypted Multi-maps)

Finally, we show that our framework can also be used to prove logarithmic lower bounds for other privacy notions beyond differential privacy and obliviousness. In this section, we consider lower bounds for data structures that provide guarantees on upper bounds on leakage functions. We note this is a standard approach to proving privacy for searchable encryption schemes [13].

Patel *et al.* [34] proved lower bounds for encrypted multi-maps that guarantee leakage at most the *decoupled key-equality leakage* pattern $\mathcal{L}_{\mathsf{DecKeyEq}}$. This leakage reveals whether two queries (or two updates) operations occur for the same key. However, this leakage does not reveal whether a query and an update operation occur on the same key. In particular, they showed such data structures must have overhead $\Omega(b/\omega \cdot \log(nb/c))$ for multi-maps that can store values of b bits. Once again, there remains the possibility that sub-logarithmic overhead is possible when $b \ll \omega$. Using our framework, we show that logarithmic overhead is still required. We refer to $(\mathcal{L}, \epsilon, 1, k)$-secure as a data structure with leakage at most $\mathcal{L}$, adversarial advantage at most ϵ for a PPT adversary that compromises one of k servers. Formal definitions and the proof may be found in the full version.

Theorem 9. *Any* $(\mathcal{L}_{\mathsf{DecKeyEq}}, \beta/k, 1, k)$-*secure data structure* DS *that solves the dynamic multi-map problem for* n *b-bit entries for a sufficiently small constant* $\beta > 0$, *expected update and query time* t_u *and* t_q, *client storage* c *and error probability* $\alpha \leq 1/\log^2 n$ *in the cell probe model with* $\omega \geq 1$ *cell size must satisfy:*

$$t_u + t_q = \Omega \left(\frac{\log(nb/c)}{1 + \log((\omega + \log \log n)/b)} \right).$$

$\mathcal{L}_{\mathsf{DecKeyEq}}$ **Lower Bounds.** Similar to differential privacy, we can prove a generic result for $\mathcal{L}_{\mathsf{DecKeyEq}}$ leakage with respect to the Event Transfer Probability property. See the full version for more details. As a result, we can prove lower bounds for $\mathcal{L}_{\mathsf{DecKeyEq}}$-secure versions for sets, predecessor and union-find. We omit further details as they follow as straightforward applications of our framework.

6 Constructions for Oblivious Stacks and Queues

We show that it is possible to construct an oblivious stack (queue) with sublogarithmic overhead. by showing one can speed up oblivious stacks (queues) by a multiplicative b/ω factor. This gives a separation result showing that, when $b \ll \omega$, oblivious stacks (queues) are inherently faster than ORAMs. Our construction will match the $\Omega(b/\omega \cdot \log(nb/c))$ lower bound in [21].

Construction. We now describe our oblivious stack construction. It can be modified in a straightforward manner to also obtain oblivious queues or deques. Our construction of an oblivious stack of at most n elements of size b with a server with word size ω will make black-box use of any ORAM Π with blocks of length $b' = \omega$. The ORAM will store at most $N = O(n \cdot (b/\omega))$ blocks each containing $L := \omega/b$ stack elements. We can now consider two settings depending on the values of b and ω. When $b < \omega$, $L > 1$ signifies that each ORAM block stores multiple stack elements. For $b \geq \omega$, $L \leq 1$ signifies that a stack element is spread over one or more ORAM blocks. Assuming one-way functions, there exist ORAMs with $O(\log(Nb'/c)) = O(\log(nb/c))$ query overhead and $O(c)$ client storage when the block size is equal to the word size [1].

At a high level, the client will store an integer counter C describing the total number of blocks currently stored in the stack to keep track of the location of the stack top. For the case when $b \geq \omega$, we can directly use the above ORAM as an oblivious stack and each stack operation will involve b/ω ORAM operations. The value of C keeps a pointer to where these operation must occur.

Let us now focus on the case when $b < \omega$ and each ORAM block thus contains $L = \omega/b$ stack blocks. The idea is to break up stack operations into groups of L operations. To locally handle the L operations of a group, we make sure that, at the start of a group of operations, the client local memory contains the L elements at the top of the stack. As it is easily seen, this is all the information needed to perform a group of L operations and at the end of a group, the local client memory holds at most $2L$ stack elements (this happens if all L operations are push operations). The client thus performs the write of at most $2L$ stack elements back to the ORAM. Since each ORAM block contains $L = \omega/b$ blocks, this can be accomplished by 3 ORAM write operations, as $2L$ stack elements could spread over 3 ORAM blocks. Not to break obliviousness, the client performs 3 writes even if the stack elements found in client memory at the end of a group happen to belong to fewer ORAM blocks. Following this and to prepare for the next group, the client reads the top L elements of the stack from the ORAM and this can be accomplished by reading 2 ORAM blocks. A formal description and proof may be found in the full version.

Theorem 10. *Assuming one-way functions, the above construction is an oblivious stack for block size $b \geq 1$ and word size $\omega \geq 1$ with client storage $c = O(\omega + \log n)$ bits, server storage $O(n \cdot b)$ bits and amortized overhead $O(b/\omega \cdot \log(nb/c))$.*

7   Conclusions

In this work, we present logarithmic lower bounds for differentially private data structures for all parameter settings of block sizes b and cell sizes ω. This improves upon the prior lower bounds proved in [37] for the setting of $b \ll \omega$ and answers an open question posed in [23]. Our lower bounds apply for differentially private RAMs, sets, predecessor and disjoint sets (union-find).

Additionally, we present a framework that can be re-used for different data structure problems and privacy guarantees. To try and make our techniques more accessible, we identify two simple, minimal conditions that are required to prove lower bounds in our framework. We reduce proving logarithmic lower bounds to showing that a specific data structure problem and privacy guarantee satisfy the two conditions of our framework. We hope our framework will make it easier to prove lower bounds without unnecessarily customizing techniques.

Acknowledgements. This research was supported in part by the Algorand Centres of Excellence programme managed by Algorand Foundation. Any opinions, findings, and conclusions or recommendations expressed in this material are solely those of the authors.

References

1. Asharov, G., Komargodski, I., Lin, W.-K., Nayak, K., Peserico, E., Shi, E.: OptORAMa: Optimal oblivious RAM. In: Canteaut, A., Ishai, Y. (eds.) EURO-CRYPT 2020. Part II, volume 12106 of LNCS, pp. 403–432. Springer, Heidelberg (2020). https://doi.org/10.1007/978-3-030-45724-2_14

2. Beimel, A., Ishai, Y., Malkin, T.: Reducing the servers' computation in private information retrieval: PIR with preprocessing. J. Cryptol. **17**(2), 125–151 (2004)

3. Bindschaedler, V., Naveed, M., Pan, X., Wang, X.F., Huang, Y.: Practicing oblivious access on cloud storage: the gap, the fallacy, and the new way forward. In: Ray, I., Li, N., Kruegel, C. (eds.) ACM CCS 2015, pp. 837–849. ACM Press, October 2015

4. Boyle, E., Chung, K.-M., Pass, R.: Large-scale secure computation: multi-party computation for (parallel) RAM programs. In: Gennaro, R., Robshaw, M. (eds.) CRYPTO 2015. LNCS, vol. 9216, pp. 742–762. Springer, Heidelberg (2015). https://doi.org/10.1007/978-3-662-48000-7_36

5. Boyle, E., Chung, K.-M., Pass, R.: Oblivious parallel RAM and applications. In: Kushilevitz, E., Malkin, T. (eds.) TCC 2016. LNCS, vol. 9563, pp. 175–204. Springer, Heidelberg (2016). https://doi.org/10.1007/978-3-662-49099-0_7

6. Boyle, E., Naor, M.: Is there an oblivious RAM lower bound? In: Sudan, M. (eds.) ITCS 2016, pp. 357–368. ACM, January 2016

7. Cash, D., Drucker, A., Hoover, A.: A lower bound for one-round oblivious RAM. In: Pass, R., Pietrzak, K. (eds.) TCC 2020. LNCS, vol. 12550, pp. 457–485. Springer, Cham (2020). https://doi.org/10.1007/978-3-030-64375-1_16

8. Hubert Chan, T.-H., Chung, K.-M., Maggs, B.M., Shi, E.: Foundations of differentially oblivious algorithms. In: Chan, T.M. (eds.) 30th SODA, pp. 2448–2467. ACM-SIAM, January 2019

9. Chen, B., Lin, H., Tessaro, S.: Oblivious parallel RAM: improved efficiency and generic constructions. In: Kushilevitz, E., Malkin, T. (eds.) TCC 2016. LNCS, vol. 9563, pp. 205–234. Springer, Heidelberg (2016). https://doi.org/10.1007/978-3-662-49099-0_8

10. Chung, K.-M., Liu, Z., Pass, R.: Statistically-secure ORAM with $\tilde{O}(\log^2 n)$ overhead. In: Sarkar, P., Iwata, T. (eds.) ASIACRYPT 2014. LNCS, vol. 8874, pp. 62–81. Springer, Heidelberg (2014). https://doi.org/10.1007/978-3-662-45608-8_4

11. Corrigan-Gibbs, H., Henzinger, A., Kogan, D.: Single-server private information retrieval with sublinear amortized time. In: Dunkelman, O., Dziembowski, S. (eds.) Advances in Cryptology – EUROCRYPT 2022. EUROCRYPT 2022. Lecture Notes in Computer Science, vol 13276 (2022). Springer, Cham. https://doi.org/10.1007/978-3-031-07085-3_1

12. Corrigan-Gibbs, H., Kogan, D.: Private information retrieval with sublinear online time. In: Canteaut, A., Ishai, Y. (eds.) EUROCRYPT 2020. LNCS, vol. 12105, pp. 44–75. Springer, Cham (2020). https://doi.org/10.1007/978-3-030-45721-1_3

13. Curtmola, R., Garay, J.A., Kamara, S., Ostrovsky, R.: Searchable symmetric encryption: improved definitions and efficient constructions. In: Juels, A., Wright, R.N., De Capitani di Vimercati, S. (eds.) ACM CCS 2006, pp. 79–88. ACM Press, October/November 2006

14. Devadas, S., van Dijk, M., Fletcher, C.W., Ren, L., Shi, E., Wichs, D.: Onion ORAM: a constant bandwidth blowup oblivious RAM. In: Kushilevitz, E., Malkin, T. (eds.) TCC 2016. LNCS, vol. 9563, pp. 145–174. Springer, Heidelberg (2016). https://doi.org/10.1007/978-3-662-49099-0_6

15. Doerner, J., Shelat, A.: Scaling ORAM for secure computation. In: Thuraisingham, B.M., Evans, D., Malkin, T., Xu, D. (eds.) ACM CCS 2017, pp. 523–535. ACM Press, October/November 2017

16. Fredman, M.L., Saks, M.E.: The cell probe complexity of dynamic data structures. In: 21st ACM STOC, pp. 345–354. ACM Press, May 1989

17. Goldreich, O., Ostrovsky, R.: Software protection and simulation on oblivious rams. J. ACM (JACM) (1996)

18. Goodrich, M.T., Mitzenmacher, M., Ohrimenko, O., Tamassia, R.: Privacy-preserving group data access via stateless oblivious RAM simulation. In: Rabani, Y. (ed.) 23rd SODA, pp. 157–167. ACM-SIAM, January 2012

19. Gordon, S.D., Katz, J., Wang, X.: Simple and efficient two-server ORAM. In: Peyrin, T., Galbraith, S. (eds.) ASIACRYPT 2018. LNCS, vol. 11274, pp. 141–157. Springer, Cham (2018). https://doi.org/10.1007/978-3-030-03332-3_6

20. Hubáček, P., Koucký, M., Král, K., Slívová, V.: Stronger lower bounds for online ORAM. In: Hofheinz, D., Rosen, A. (eds.) TCC 2019. LNCS, vol. 11892, pp. 264–284. Springer, Cham (2019). https://doi.org/10.1007/978-3-030-36033-7_10
21. Jacob, R., Larsen, K.G., Nielsen, J.B.: Lower bounds for oblivious data structures. In: Chan, T.M. (ed.) 30th SODA, pp. 2439–2447. ACM-SIAM, January 2019
22. Jafargholi, Z., Larsen, K.G., Simkin, M.: Optimal oblivious priority queues. In: Marx, D. (ed.) 32nd SODA, pp. 2366–2383. ACM-SIAM, January 2021
23. Komargodski, I., Lin, W.-K.: A logarithmic lower bound for oblivious RAM (for all parameters). In: Malkin, T., Peikert, C. (eds.) CRYPTO 2021. LNCS, vol. 12828, pp. 579–609. Springer, Cham (2021). https://doi.org/10.1007/978-3-030-84259-8_20
24. Komargodski, I., Shi, E.: Differentially oblivious turing machines. In: Lee, J.R. (ed.) ITCS 2021, vol. 185, pp. 68:1–68:19. LIPIcs, January 2021
25. Kushilevitz, E., Lu, S., Ostrovsky, R.: On the (in)security of hash-based oblivious RAM and a new balancing scheme. In: Rabani, Y. (ed.) 23rd SODA, pp. 143–156. ACM-SIAM, January 2012
26. Larsen, K.G.: The cell probe complexity of dynamic range counting. In: Karloff, H.J., Pitassi, T. (eds.) 44th ACM STOC, pp. 85–94. ACM Press, May 2012
27. Larsen, K.G., Malkin, T., Weinstein, O., Yeo, K.: Lower bounds for oblivious near-neighbor search. In: Chawla, S. (ed.) 31st SODA, pp. 1116–1134. ACM-SIAM, January 2020
28. Larsen, K.G., Nielsen, J.B.: Yes, there is an oblivious RAM lower bound! In: Shacham, H., Boldyreva, A. (eds.) CRYPTO 2018. LNCS, vol. 10992, pp. 523–542. Springer, Cham (2018). https://doi.org/10.1007/978-3-319-96881-0_18
29. Larsen, K.G., Simkin, M., Yeo, K.: Lower bounds for multi-server oblivious RAMs. In: Pass, R., Pietrzak, K. (eds.) TCC 2020. LNCS, vol. 12550, pp. 486–503. Springer, Cham (2020). https://doi.org/10.1007/978-3-030-64375-1_17
30. Lu, S., Ostrovsky, R.: Distributed oblivious RAM for secure two-party computation. In: Sahai, A. (ed.) TCC 2013. LNCS, vol. 7785, pp. 377–396. Springer, Heidelberg (2013). https://doi.org/10.1007/978-3-642-36594-2_22
31. Panigrahy, R., Talwar, K., Wieder, U.: Lower bounds on near neighbor search via metric expansion. In: 51st FOCS, pp. 805–814. IEEE Computer Society Press, October 2010
32. Patel, S., Persiano, G., Raykova, M., Yeo, K.: PanORAMa: oblivious RAM with logarithmic overhead. In: Thorup, M. (ed.) 59th FOCS, pp. 871–882. IEEE Computer Society Press, October 2018
33. Patel, S., Persiano, G., Yeo, K.: What storage access privacy is achievable with small overhead? In: ACM PODS (2019)
34. Patel, S., Persiano, G., Yeo, K.: Lower bounds for encrypted multi-maps and searchable encryption in the leakage cell probe model. In: Micciancio, D., Ristenpart, T. (eds.) CRYPTO 2020. LNCS, vol. 12170, pp. 433–463. Springer, Cham (2020). https://doi.org/10.1007/978-3-030-56784-2_15
35. Patrascu, M., Demaine, E.D.: Logarithmic lower bounds in the cell-probe model. SIAM J. Comput. (2006)
36. Pătraşcu, M., Tarniţă, C.E.: On dynamic bit-probe complexity. Theoret. Comput. Sci. 380(1–2), 127–142 (2007)
37. Persiano, G., Yeo, K.: Lower bounds for differentially private RAMs. In: Ishai, Y., Rijmen, V. (eds.) EUROCRYPT 2019. LNCS, vol. 11476, pp. 404–434. Springer, Cham (2019). https://doi.org/10.1007/978-3-030-17653-2_14
38. Persiano, G., Yeo, K.: Limits of preprocessing for single-server PIR. In: Annual ACM-SIAM Symposium on Discrete Algorithms (2022)

39. Persiano, G., Yeo, K.: Lower bound framework for differentially private and oblivious data structures. Cryptology ePrint Archive, Paper 2022/1553 (2022). https://eprint.iacr.org/2022/1553

40. Ren, L., et al.: Constants count: practical improvements to oblivious RAM. In: Jung, J., Holz, T. (eds.) USENIX Security 2015, pp. 415–430. USENIX Association, August 2015

41. Elaine Shi. Path oblivious heap: Optimal and practical oblivious priority queue. In 2020 IEEE Symposium on Security and Privacy, pages 842–858. IEEE Computer Society Press, May 2020

42. Stefanov, E., Shi, E.: ObliviStore: high performance oblivious cloud storage. In: 2013 IEEE Symposium on Security and Privacy, pp. 253–267. IEEE Computer Society Press, May 2013

43. Stefanov, E., et al.: Path ORAM: an extremely simple oblivious RAM protocol. In: Sadeghi, A.-R., Gligor, V.D., Yung, M. (eds.) ACM CCS 2013, pp. 299–310. ACM Press, November 2013

44. Tarjan, R.E., Van Leeuwen, J.: Worst-case analysis of set union algorithms. J. ACM (JACM) (1984)

45. van Emde Boas, P.: Preserving order in a forest in less than logarithmic time. In: Symposium on Foundations of Computer Science (1975)

46. Wagh, S., Cuff, P., Mittal, P.: Differentially private oblivious ram. In: Proceedings on Privacy Enhancing Technologies (2018)

47. Wang, X.S., Huang, Y., Hubert Chan, T.-H., Shelat, A., Shi, E.: SCORAM: oblivious RAM for secure computation. In: Ahn, G.-J., Yung, M., Li, N. (eds.) ACM CCS 2014, pp. 191–202. ACM Press, November 2014

48. Wang, X.S., et al.: Oblivious data structures. In: Ahn, G.-J., Yung, M., Li, N. (eds.) ACM CCS 2014, pp. 215–226. ACM Press, November 2014

49. Weiss, M., Wichs, D.: Is there an oblivious RAM lower bound for online reads? In: Beimel, A., Dziembowski, S. (eds.) TCC 2018. LNCS, vol. 11240, pp. 603–635. Springer, Cham (2018). https://doi.org/10.1007/978-3-030-03810-6_22

50. Yeo, K.: Lower bounds for (batch) pir with private preprocessing. In: Eurocrypt 2023 (2023, to appear)

Lower Bounds for (Batch) PIR
with Private Preprocessing

Kevin Yeo[(✉)]

Google and Columbia University, New York, USA
kwlyeo@google.com

Abstract. In this paper, we study *(batch) private information retrieval with private preprocessing*. Private information retrieval (PIR) is the problem where one or more servers hold a database of n bits and a client wishes to retrieve the i-th bit in the database from the server(s). In *PIR with private preprocessing* (also known as offline-online PIR), the client is able to compute a private r-bit hint in an offline stage that may be leveraged to perform retrievals accessing at most t entries. For privacy, the client wishes to hide index i from an adversary that has compromised some of the servers. In the *batch PIR* setting, the client performs queries to retrieve the contents of multiple entries simultaneously.

We present a tight characterization for the trade-offs between hint size r and number of accessed entries t during queries. For any PIR scheme that enables clients to perform batch retrievals of k entries, we prove a lower bound of $tr = \Omega(nk)$ when $r \geq k$. When $r < k$, we prove that $t = \Omega(n)$. Our lower bounds hold when the scheme errs with probability at most $1/15$ and against PPT adversaries that only compromise one out of ℓ servers for any $\ell = O(1)$. Our work also closes the multiplicative logarithmic gap for the single query setting ($k = 1$) as our lower bound matches known constructions. Our lower bounds hold in the model where each database entry is stored without modification but each entry may be replicated arbitrarily.

Finally, we show connections between PIR and the online matrix-vector (OMV) conjecture from fine-grained complexity. We present barriers for proving lower bounds for two-server PIR schemes in general computational models as they would immediately imply the OMV conjecture.

1 Introduction

Private information retrieval (also known as PIR) is a powerful cryptographic primitive that enables privacy-preserving retrieval of entries from a database held by one or more servers where a subset of the servers may be untrusted and colluding. For a database with n entries uniquely indexed by integers from $[n]$, PIR enables a client to retrieve the i-th entry of the database without revealing

---

The full version of this paper may be found at [71].

C. Hazay and M. Stam (Eds.): EUROCRYPT 2023, LNCS 14004, pp. 518–550, 2023.
https://doi.org/10.1007/978-3-031-30545-0_18

the query index i to the subset of colluding adversarial servers. The primitive of PIR was first introduced by Chor, Kushilevitz, Goldreich and Sudan [20] in the multi-server information-theoretic setting where the adversary compromises a strict subset of the servers with many follow-up work in this area (see [4,7,9,19, 31,32,70] and references therein). Kushilevitz and Ostrovsky [51] first studied PIR in the single-server setting against computationally bounded adversaries. Many further works have also studied single-server PIR including [2,3,5,8,16, 28,34,35,52,58,59] to list some examples.

PIR is an important cryptographic tool due to its endless implications to real-world settings. PIR has been used as a critical component in the design of many practical privacy-preserving applications such as advertising [38,66], communication [6,57], friend discovery [11], media consumption [40] and publish-subscribe systems [18] to list some examples.

Despite the potential applicability of PIR, the computational overhead of PIR remains a significant bottleneck that hinders wide spread usage of PIR in large-scale real-world settings. Beimel, Ishai and Malkin [10] proved that linear server computation is always required even in the multi-server setting where only a strict subset of servers is compromised.

In an attempt to surpass this barrier, many prior works have considered variants of PIR that have successfully overcome the linear server computation obstacle. We present two of these successful variants in PIR with preprocessing and batch PIR below.

PIR with Preprocessing. Beimel, Ishai and Malkin [10] introduced the notion of PIR with preprocessing where the server may compute a public r-bit hint in an offline, preprocessing stage. During query time, the server will aim to leverage the hint to answer PIR queries with sub-linear computational time t. We will denote this the *public preprocessing* setting as the hint is made available to the adversary's view. For this model, Beimel, Ishai and Malkin [10] presented constructions that had $O(n^{1/2+\epsilon})$ server time during queries but required polynomial $n^{O(1)}$ sized hints. On the other hand, Beimel, Ishai and Malkin [10] proved a $tr = \Omega(n)$ lower bound that was further improved to $tr = \Omega(n \log n)$ in [64]. This model has also been studied under the name of public-key doubly-efficient PIR [15]. There remains a large gap between the best upper and lower bounds for sub-linear server time $t = o(n)$ as the best upper bounds still require $tr = n^{O(1)}$.

As an analog, one can also consider the *private preprocessing* setting (also known as offline-online PIR) where the r-bit private client hint H is computed and stored by the client hidden from the adversary's view. This model has been studied in many works including [14,15,17,27,41,60,67]. Corrigan-Gibbs and Kogan [24] presented an upper bound of $tr = O(n)$. For example, this means that one can obtain sub-linear server time such as $t = \tilde{O}(\sqrt{n})$ using a $\tilde{O}(\sqrt{n})$-bit hint. The same work also proves a lower bound of $tr = \tilde{\Omega}(n)$. We note that there remains a multiplicative logarithmic gap between known constructions and lower bounds leading to the following question:

What is the optimal trade-off between hint size and server computation for PIR with private preprocessing?

Batch PIR. Another approach to obtain sub-linear server computation for PIR is to consider *batch queries*. In this setting, the client knows a batch of k entries that it wishes to retrieve ahead of time. The goal is to obtain amortized sub-linear server time across all k queries to beat the naive approach of executing k independent queries that results in $t = O(nk)$. Batch PIR has been studied in a large number of works including [5,6,10,39,43,47,56,62]. Excitingly, it has been shown that one can execute batch PIR queries with minimal overhead compared to single-query PIR. Ishai, Kushilevitz, Ostrovsky and Sahai [47] showed the existence of a batch PIR that uses total server time $t = \tilde{O}(n)$ when retrieving k entries simultaneously. Therefore, the amortized time per query is $\tilde{O}(n/k)$ that is sub-linear for sufficiently large k.

Combining Batching and Preprocessing. An intriguing idea to further improve the computational overhead of PIR would be to combine the techniques from batching and private preprocessing. First, we can take a look at what seems possible. As stated earlier, one can perform batch PIR queries with almost no overhead compared to single-query PIR. The dream would be to obtain the same result when performing batch queries for state-of-the-art PIR with private preprocessing schemes. In more detail, this dream construction would enable performing batch queries to k entries while maintaining the trade-off $tr = \tilde{O}(n)$ that results in amortized sub-linear query time $\tilde{O}(n/(rk))$ when using r-bit hints.

On the other hand, we can consider the efficiency achieved by straightforward approaches. The simplest construction is to execute k queries in parallel by storing k hints and performing k query algorithms resulting in $tr = \tilde{O}(nk^2)$. Another option is to perform k queries in sequence using a construction that enables multiple queries for a single preprocessing stage (such as the two-server schemes in [24,67]). This results in $tr = \tilde{O}(nk)$ but requires k rounds of client-server interaction. There remains a gap between the potential dream construction and the straightforward approaches. This leads to the following interesting question:

> *What is the optimal efficiency achievable by PIR schemes*
> *that utilize both batch queries and private prepocessing?*

In this work, we address this question by providing a tight characterization of the trade-offs between the hint size and online server query time. We show that the dream construction is not possible and known approaches already achieve the optimal trade-off.

1.1   Our Contributions

In this paper, we will prove a tight characterization of the trade-offs between the hint size and the number of accessed (probed) entries during query time for PIR schemes that aim to combine batching and offline private preprocessing techniques. Note that any lower bound on number of probed entries is also a lower bound on server query time. We will present a lower bound that encompasses a wide range of constructions and matches the overhead of prior works.

Lower Bound. As our main result, we will prove a trade-off between the size of the private hint, r, computed in the offline preprocessing stage and the number of entries accessed (probed) by the server during online query execution, t, that also acts as a lower bound on the server time during queries. For a scheme that enables batches of k queries, we will show that $tr = \Omega(nk)$. To enable wider applicability of our result, we prove our lower bound for constructions with potentially multiple rounds of interaction during queries, non-zero error probabilities and/or inefficient preprocessing algorithms. Additionally, we consider weak PPT adversaries that only compromise one server. The following lower bounds are proven where the server(s) store the database is an unencoded manner, but may arbitrarily replicate entries (see Sect. 2.2 for more details).

Theorem 1 (Informal). *For any $\ell = O(1)$ and any k-query, ℓ-server batch PIR with private preprocessing scheme that errs with probability at most $1/15$ and is secure against a PPT adversary that compromises one server, it must be that $tr = \Omega(nk)$ when $k \leq r \leq n/400$. If $r < k$, it must be that $t = \Omega(n)$.*

The condition that $k \leq r \leq n/400$ is necessary to rule out trivial edge cases. There is a trivial setting where the entire database is stored in the hint using $r = n$. This would require $t = 0$ server time to retrieve any entries circumventing our lower bound. We avoid this edge case by enforcing that $r \leq n/400$. The choice of $n/400$ was for convenience and one may re-do our proofs to prove the same result for $r \leq n/c$ for constant $c \leq 400$. In the case that $r < k$, one can ignore the hint and execute a k-query batch PIR in $\tilde{O}(n)$ time matching our lower bound.

As our lower bound is for multiple servers, it immediately applies to the single server setting. Additionally, our result also applies to more powerful adversaries that compromise multiple (or all) servers or use infinite computational power.

We note that our lower bound immediately applies to the single-query setting where $k = 1$. As an immediate corollary, we get that:

Theorem 2 (Informal). *For any $\ell = O(1)$ and any ℓ-server, single-query PIR with private preprocessing scheme that errs with probability at most $1/15$ and is secure against a PPT adversary that compromises one server, it must be that $tr = \Omega(n)$ when $r \leq n/400$.*

This improves upon the previous known single query lower bounds [24] by multiplicative logarithmic factors closing the gap for single-query setting (for example, see Appendix A of [64] for a concrete matching instantiation). Our batch lower bound also improves upon the batch lower bounds from a concurrent work [22] by multiplicative logarithmic factors.

Finally, we note that our lower bounds may be directly applied to PIR with public preprocessing. The server may arbitrary store a r-bit hint encoding of the database. Then, our work proves a $tr = \Omega(n)$ lower bound. However, we note that better lower bounds of $tr = \Omega(n \log n)$ were proven in [64].

Upper Bound. In terms of constructions, we note that our lower bound has already shown that one of the straightforward approaches of performing k sequential queries is already optimal (up to logarithmic factors). However, this construction requires k rounds of interaction between the client and the server. To obtain a single-round optimal construction, one can use the pipelined queries property of prior works [24,49,67] where each client query is independent of server responses and the client can issue multiple queries simultaneously. We refer readers to the full version for a more detailed description.

For completeness, we show that there also exists a blackbox reduction from single-query to batch PIR with private preprocessing without requiring the pipelined query property. Our reduction maintains a single round, but increases the overhead by additional logarithmic factors (unlike the pipelined query approach described above).

Theorem 3 (Informal). *Assuming the existence of a single-query, ℓ-server PIR with private preprocessing with* $tr = f(n)$, *there exists a k-query batch, ℓ-server PIR with private preprocessing scheme with a single-round query such that* $tr = \tilde{O}(k \cdot f(n))$.

Barriers to General Lower Bounds. Finally, we also study PIR lower bounds in general computational models without any restrictions on database storage. To do this, we present connections between PIR and the online matrix-vector OMV conjecture [45] from fine-grained complexity. We show a barrier to proving lower bounds for PIR schemes in general models. If one is able to prove a slightly weaker variant of our standard PIR model lower bounds in general models, it would immediately imply the online matrix-vector OMV conjecture.

Theorem 4 (Informal). *For any constant $\epsilon > 0$, suppose there exists no single-query, two-server PIR with private preprocessing with* $tr = O(n^{1-\epsilon})$. *Then, the online matrix-vector OMV conjecture is true.*

1.2 Technical Overview

Lower Bound. As our main result, we will lower bound the product of the private client hint size and the number of probed entries during query time. The core idea starts from considering any batch PIR with private preprocessing scheme that probes a sub-linear number of entries in the database. For simplicity, we will focus on the single-server setting with an information-theoretic adversary. Consider any scheme Π that only probes at most half the database (that is, $t \leq n/2$). For a database $D \in \{0,1\}^n$, consider a batch query $q \subseteq [n]$ to a random subset of k entries and the subset of entries that are probed when executing q, denoted by P. Note that the adversary sees the set of probed entries P. In the information-theoretic setting, it must be that the probed set P must be independent of the query q. As a result, we should expect that only half of the k random entries in q will also be probed (i.e., $|P \cap q| \leq k/2$). We show similar ideas still hold in the multi-server setting against PPT adversaries.

The above statement ends up providing a powerful way to compress the database. By probing and knowing the contents of at most t entries, the execution of query q will enable learning the contents of approximately $k/2$ entries for free.

In other words, we are able to design a compression algorithm for database D using Π whose compression performance directly relates to the query time of Π. As the query time t decreases, the rate of compression of our above algorithm increases. If we take D to be a uniformly random n-bit string, we can immediately get lower bounds on query time t and the hint size r as our algorithm should not be able to compress D beyond the information-theoretic minimum.

Finally, we note that there is a technical obstacle in designing the compression algorithm as described. The above description showed that one can compress using a single query to get the contents of $k/2$ entries for free. To get a strong compression rate, we need that each query recovers $\Theta(k)$ *new* entries for free. In other words, these discovered-for-free entries must not have been probed or queried by previous queries used by the compression algorithm. To overcome this obstacle, we show that picking uniformly random queries will enable discovery of $\Theta(k)$ new entries that were not previously probed or queried. As a result, it suffices for the compression algorithm to try a set of random queries to find the necessary query sequence that enables strong compression.

Comparison with [24] and [22] . We highlight the improvements in our proof techniques compared to the single-query lower bound in [24] and batch lower bound in [22] that enable logarithmically higher lower bounds. Our lower bound works directly with (batch) PIR whereas the prior works [22,24] uses abstractions through Yao's box problem. Therefore, we are able to prove stronger properties about (batch) PIR itself without worrying whether these properties also apply to the abstracted problem. Prior works [22,24] focus on Yao's box problem without utilizing any privacy properties of PIR. In particular, there is a mismatch between the requirements of Yao's box problem and the guarantees from PIR protocols. In the former, the querier is forbidden from directly probing boxes that are queried. For the latter, it is possible that all queried entries are probed directly but the probability must be small (see Lemma 3). Both prior works first prove lower bounds on Yao's box problem with some error probability and translate it to PIR later which results in losing logarithmic factors. In contrast, our work combines error probability directly with privacy properties of PIR enabling us to prove stronger lower bounds for (batch) PIR with private preprocessing.

Secondly, our paper proves stronger aggregate properties for multiple batch PIR queries. We show that there exists a set of multiple batch PIR queries such that at least $k/5$ probes performed by each query were not probed by any other batch PIR query in the set. As a result, we avoid unnecessarily encoding batch PIR queries that do not provide a significant number of free entries in our compression algorithms (see Step 5(b)ii in Fig. 2). In contrast, [22] only proves properties of probed entries overlapping with queried entries for a single query in the multi-box extension of Yao's box problem (roughly corresponding to a single batch PIR query). Afterwards, the compression algorithm of [22] uses a greedy approach by adding the multi-box queries that probe the most new entries. Unlike our proof, this does not guarantee that queries with a small number of free entries are not encoded.

Upper Bound. For our single-round construction, we will leverage batch codes (introduced by Ishai, Kushilevitz, Ostrovsky and Sahai [47]) and any single-query PIR with private preprocessing scheme. At a high level, our construction uses batch codes to split up the database D into m buckets and perform a single-query PIR to each of the m buckets. We note this is a standard technique done in the past (see [5,6,47] as some examples). Batch codes guarantee that for any batch query $q = \{i_1, \ldots, i_k\} \subseteq [n]$, each of the i_j-th entries may be found in one of the m buckets. We will execute m parallel instances of single-query PIR with private preprocessing scheme for each of the m buckets where each instance uses (r/m)-bit hints. As the queries are done in parallel, we note our query algorithm uses a single-round of interaction. By plugging in a state-of-the-art batch code construction and single-query PIR with private preprocessing scheme, we obtain a single-round construction such that $tr = \tilde{O}(n)$ matching our lower bound.

Connection to Online Matrix-Vector Conjecture. Finally, we show barriers to proving lower bounds in general models of computation. To do this, we present a reduction from the online matrix-vector OMV conjecture [45] to PIR with private preprocessing. To do this, we start from the simple two-server, information-theoretic PIR with $O(\sqrt{n})$ communication [20] where the database is represented as a $\sqrt{n} \times \sqrt{n}$ matrix M. During query time, the client uploads vectors $a, b \in \{0, 1\}^{\sqrt{n}}$ to each server respectively and the servers respond with matrix-vector multiplications Ma and Mb. We show that if there exists an efficient algorithm for solving OMV, each server can use the same algorithm to also provide answers for PIR with similar overhead. As a result, similar lower bounds that we have already proven for PIR with private preprocessing in general computational models would immediately imply that the OMV conjecture is true. In other words, this is a barrier as the OMV conjecture is a well-studied open problem and a core conjecture in fine-grained complexity.

1.3   Related Works

Private Information Retrieval. PIR is a heavily studied cryptographic primitive first introduced by Chor, Kushilevitz, Goldreich and Sudan [20] in the multi-server setting where it is assumed only a strict subset of servers are compromised and colluding. Many follow-up works have worked on improving the communication efficiency of multi-server PIR in the information-theoretic setting including [4,7,9,32,70]. The most communication-efficient scheme is by Dvir and Gopi [31] using matching vector codes [30]. Similar work has been done for computationally-secure multi-server PIR [12,19,36] where the most efficient constructions utilize function secret sharing techniques [13]. Single-server PIR was introduced by Kushilevitz and Ostrovsky [51] with many follow-up works including [8,16,28,35,52,59] aiming to improve efficiency or utilize different assumptions. Recent work has focused on optimizing the concrete efficiency of single-server schemes using lattice-based homomorphic encryption [2,3,5,34,58].

PIR with Preprocessing. PIR with public preprocessing was first introduced by Beimel, Ishai and Malkin [10] where the hint is public and studied in several follow-up works [15,64]. The PIR with private preprocessing model has been studied in many works and under many different names including doubly-efficient PIR [14,15,17], private stateful information retrieval [60], private anonymous data access [41] and offline-online PIR [24,67]. For private preprocessing, Corrigan-Gibbs and Kogan [24] presented a construction with optimal trade-offs $tr = \tilde{O}(n)$ that was later extended to handle blocklist lookups efficiently [49]. Shi, Aqeel, Chandrasekaran and Maggs [67] presented logarithmic communication two-server schemes with optimal trade-offs. Further follow-up works have aimed to improve the efficiency in various dimensions [25,44].

Batch PIR. Several prior works have studied batch PIR to obtain efficient constructions using matrix multiplication [10,56], batch codes [42,47,62], the ϕ-hiding assumption [39] and list-decoding algorithms [43]. Recent works have considered practical constructions that utilize *probabilistic batch codes* [5,6] with error rates that are experimentally analyzed. These works obtain asymptotically optimal batch code parameters, but err on a subset of potential batch queries.

PIR Lower Bounds. Lower bounds for PIR have been studied for a variety of different complexity measures. Beimel, Ishai and Malkin [10] showed that server computation must be linear without any preprocessing even in the multi-server setting. Prior works have proven communication lower bounds for PIR [37,69].

In the public preprocessing setting, Beimel, Ishai and Malkin [10] showed that $tr = \Omega(n)$ that was improved to $tr = \Omega(n \log n)$ by Persiano and Yeo [64]. This is the highest lower bound possible for PIR with public preprocessing without implying higher lower bounds for branching programs (see [10,15]). For the private preprocessing model, Corrigan-Gibbs and Kogan [24] proved a lower bound $tr = \tilde{\Omega}(n)$ for a single query.

Compression Proofs. In our proof, we will use the incompressibility technique that has been used widely in the past. These were also used in prior PIR lower bounds [64]. To list some examples outside of PIR, incompressibility has been used in the studies of generic cryptographic constructions [33], one-way functions and PRGs [26], proofs of space [1], random oracles [21,29,68], the discrete logarithm problem [23] and oblivious data structures [46,48,50,54,61,63,65].

2 Definitions

2.1 Batch PIR with Private Preprocessing

We start by defining batch PIR with private preprocessing (also known as batch offline-online PIR). We present our formal definition:

Definition 1 (Batch PIR with Private Preprocessing). *A k-query batch PIR with private preprocessing scheme Π is a triplet of efficient algorithms $\Pi = (\Pi.\mathsf{Preprocess}, \Pi.\mathsf{Encode}, \Pi.\mathsf{Query})$ such that*

1. *$H \leftarrow \Pi.\mathsf{Preprocess}(R_H; D)$: The preprocessing algorithm is executed by the client and the server(s). The client receives the coin tosses R_H as input and the server(s) receives the database D as input to compute a preprocessed r-bit hint H. The hint H is privately stored by the client.*

2. $E \leftarrow \Pi.\mathsf{Encode}(D)$: *The encoding algorithm is executed by each server. Each server receives the database D and computes an encoding of the database E.*
3. $\mathsf{res} \leftarrow \Pi.\mathsf{Query}(q, H, R; E)$: *The query algorithm is jointly executed by the client and the server(s). The client receives as input the batch query of k entries $q = \{i_1, \ldots, i_k\} \subseteq [n]$, the hint H and coin tosses R while the server(s) receives the encoded database E as input. Once the query algorithm is complete, the client receives res, the algorithm's attempted response to query q.*

In the above definition, the query algorithm may be interactive and use multiple client-server roundtrips. We will prove our lower bound for query algorithms with unbounded round complexity to encompass more constructions. For our upper bounds, we will focus on single-round schemes for better efficiency.

Definition 2 (Standard PIR Model with Replications). *A k-query batch PIR with private preprocessing scheme $\Pi = (\Pi.\mathsf{Preprocess}, \Pi.\mathsf{Encode}, \Pi.\mathsf{Query})$ is in the standard PIR model if it satisfies Definition 1 and $\Pi.\mathsf{Encode}$ may replicate entries arbitraily and store a permutation of the replicated entries.*

Constructions in the above model ensure that the server stores each database entry without encoding. Additionally, the server can replicate entries arbitrarily and store a permutation of the copies thereafter. We will use the standard PIR model with replications for our lower bound (see Sect. 2.2 for more details).

Next, we will define the correctness of constructions. We define a query as correct if the query algorithm returns the correct contents for all k queried entries. If the contents of any of the k queried entries is incorrect, the answer is deemed incorrect. The error probability is defined as follows:

Definition 3 (Correctness). *A batch PIR with private preprocessing scheme Π errs with probability at most ϵ if, for every database $D \in \{0,1\}^n$ and query $q \subseteq [n]$, it holds that*

$$\Pr_{\mathbf{R}_H, \mathbf{R}}[\Pi.\mathsf{Query}(q, \mathbf{H}, \mathbf{R}; E) \neq (D_i)_{i \in q} \mid \mathbf{H}] \leq \epsilon$$

where $E \leftarrow \Pi.\mathsf{Encode}(D)$ and $\mathbf{H} \leftarrow \Pi.\mathsf{Preprocess}(\mathbf{R}_H; D)$.

We move on to formally defining the security of batch PIR with private preprocessing schemes. We consider adversaries $\mathcal{A}$ that compromise $1 \leq \ell_{\mathcal{A}} \leq \ell$ out of the ℓ total servers. When a server is compromised, the adversary $\mathcal{A}$ sees the request sent to the server as well as operations performed by the server. For the i-th server, we denote the adversary's view by transcript $\mathcal{T}_i$. We define security using the game in Fig. 1. We denote $p_{\mathcal{A}}^\eta(D)$ as the probability that the adversary $\mathcal{A}$ outputs 1 in the game $\mathsf{IndGame}_{\mathcal{A}}^\eta(D)$ that is taken over the randomness of coin tosses R_H and R as well as any internal randomness of the adversary $\mathcal{A}$. Using this we define security as:

Definition 4 ($(\delta, \ell_{\mathcal{A}}, \ell)$-Security). *A ℓ-server batch PIR with private preprocessing scheme is computationally $(\delta, \ell_{\mathcal{A}}, \ell)$-secure if for all probabilistically polynomial time (PPT) adversaries $\mathcal{A}$ that compromise at most $\ell_{\mathcal{A}}$ servers and all sufficiently large databases D, the following holds:*

$$|p_{\mathcal{A}}^0 - p_{\mathcal{A}}^1| \leq \delta(|D|).$$

$\mathsf{IndGame}_{\mathcal{A}}^{\eta}(D)$:

1. The challenger $\mathcal{C}$ runs $E \leftarrow \Pi.\mathsf{Encode}(D)$.
2. The adversary $(q^0, q^1, S) \leftarrow \mathcal{A}(D, E)$ on input the database D and encoded database E outputs two batch queries q^0 and q^1 as well as subset $S \subseteq [\ell]$ of the $\ell_{\mathcal{A}}$ servers to compromise as the challenge.
3. The challenger $\mathcal{C}$ executes $H \leftarrow \Pi.\mathsf{Preprocess}(R_H; D)$ to obtain hint H using random coin tosses R_H and records transcripts $\mathcal{T}_1^p, \ldots, \mathcal{T}_{\ell}^p$.
4. The challenger $\mathcal{C}$ executes $\Pi.\mathsf{Query}(q^{\eta}, H, R; E)$ using random coin tosses R and records transcripts $\mathcal{T}_1, \ldots, \mathcal{T}_{\ell}$.
5. The challenger $\mathcal{C}$ sends transcripts for all compromised servers, $\{\mathcal{T}_i^p, \mathcal{T}_i\}_{i \in S}$, to the adversary $\mathcal{A}$.
6. The adversary $\mathcal{A}(\{\mathcal{T}_i^p, \mathcal{T}_i\}_{i \in S})$ outputs a bit b.

Fig. 1. Security game for PIR with private preprocessing.

The above may be modified to consider statistical security by considering all computationally unbounded adversaries $\mathcal{A}$. We note that the *private* preprocessing is reflected by the fact that the adversary $\mathcal{A}$ does not receive the hint H as input and only the server's view of the interaction during the preprocessing phase. In contrast, the adversary would receive the hint H as input in the *public* preprocessing setting (see the definitions in [10,64]).

Finally, we define the efficiency of batch PIR with private preprocessing schemes. We will consider worst-case notions for all costs as follows:

Definition 5 ((r, t)-Efficiency). *A batch PIR with private preprocessing scheme is (r, t)-efficient if the following two properties hold:*

1. *For all databases $D \in \{0, 1\}^n$ and coin tosses R_H, the hint H produced by $\Pi.\mathsf{Preprocess}(R_H; D)$ is at most r bits.*
2. *For all databases $D \in \{0, 1\}^n$, queries $q \subseteq [n]$, random coin tosses R_H and R, the running time of $\Pi.\mathsf{Query}(q, H, R; E)$ is at most t where $H \leftarrow \Pi.\mathsf{Preprocess}(R_H; D)$ and $E \leftarrow \Pi.\mathsf{Encode}(D)$.*

2.2   Lower Bound Model

Standard PIR Model with Replications. The standard PIR model has been used to prove PIR lower bounds in prior works [10,24,64]. In the standard PIR model, the database is stored by the server(s) without any encoding. In our work, we will consider an extension where the server(s) may store an encoding of the database that consists of replicating various entries. We will refer to this extension as the *standard PIR model with replications*. For example, the database may permute the database a polynomial number of times and store a permutation thereafter. This covers replications of databases over multiple servers and the usage of systematic batch codes (see Sect. 4).

In our model, the client is able to store a r-bit hint that is computed in an preprocessing stage before the query. When measuring query time, the only cost is the number of entries that are probed or accessed. All other operations during query time can be performed free of charge including computation, accessing and generating randomness and accessing the hint. We only measure costs using server operations. So, our model enables clients to do all operations free of charge. We also note that our model does not account for the computational time needed to compute the hint. Therefore, our model applies to constructions even if their preprocessing algorithm is very computationally expensive. In terms of adversaries, we will only consider PPT adversaries that compromise one server. As we consider weak adversaries, our lower bound immediately implies to more powerful adversaries that may compromise multiple servers or use unbounded computational resources.

To our knowledge, the above model captures the most efficient constructions in many different categories. For example, the standard PIR model with replications is utilized by the most concretely efficient computational single-server PIR constructions using leveled FHE [2,3,5,58], two-server PIR constructions using function secret sharing [12,13], batch PIR [5,6,10,39,43,47,56,62] and all PIR with private preprocessing schemes [22,24,67]. Therefore, proving lower bounds in this model is important to understand the limitations of current techniques.

Barriers to General Models. We note that more expressive models are currently unable to prove high lower bounds for PIR. For example, we could consider the cell probe model that enables arbitrary encoding. Unfortunately, the highest lower bounds in the cell probe model peak at $\tilde{\Omega}(\log^2 n)$ [53] that are too low to prove meaningful lower bounds for PIR currently. We also note there are several barriers to proving similar lower bounds as ours with arbitrary server encoding. For example, such lower bounds would be one way to rule out the existence of some variants of program obfuscation. The constructions of Boyle, Ishai, Pass and Wootters [15] utilize server encoding and obfuscation to obtain sub-linear query time without any client storage and, thus, would beat our lower bound. In Sect. 5, we show that lower bounds in general models would also imply the online matrix-vector conjecture that is a core pillar of fine-grained complexity.

3   Lower Bound

In this section, we prove our lower bound for batch PIR with private preprocessing that characterizes the trade-offs between hint size and online query time for the server(s). We will prove the following theorem:

Theorem 5. *Let Π be a k-batch, ℓ-server PIR with private preprocessing scheme in the standard PIR model with replications that uses r-bit hints and probes at most t entries during online query time for any $\ell = O(1)$. Furthermore, suppose Π is computationally $(\delta, 1, \ell)$-secure for $\delta \leq 1/(25\ell)$ and Π errs with probability at most $\epsilon \leq 1/15$. If $k \leq r \leq n/400$, then $tr = \Omega(nk)$. Otherwise when $r < k$, then $t = \Omega(n)$.*

In our proof, we will assume that $k \leq r \leq n/400$. For the case when $r < k$, we will arbitrarily pad the hint until $r = k$. Even with this padding, note that the lower bound of $tr = \Omega(nk)$ immediately implies a lower bound of $t = \Omega(n)$. We note our lower bound applies for protocols with any number of round-trips. Additionally, we note that the choice of $\delta \leq 1/(25\ell)$ and $\epsilon \leq 1/15$ was for convenience. One can re-do our proofs for different constants. Our assumption of $\delta \leq (1/25\ell)$ being a constant is to improve our lower bound as it also applies to standard settings of negligible advantage for adversaries. Also, our results directly imply lower bounds against stronger adversaries that may compromise more than one server. Finally, we note that the assumption $r \leq n/400$ is necessary to rule out the trivial case where the entire database is stored in the hint and online queries do not need to probe any entries (i.e., $t = 0$). One can also re-do our proofs to also encompass larger choices of $r \leq n/c$ for smaller constant $1 < c < 400$.

To prove our main result, we will actually prove a variant of the theorem. Here, we will assume that the number of queries in each batch is larger than some constant and no larger than $n/10$. We formalize this in the following theorem:

Theorem 6. *Let Π be a k-batch, ℓ-server PIR with private preprocessing scheme in the standard PIR model with replications that uses r-bit hints and probes at most t entries during online query time where $\ell = O(1)$ and $k_c \leq k \leq n/10$ for some constant k_c. Furthermore, suppose Π is computationally $(\delta, 1, \ell)$-secure for $\delta \leq 1/(25\ell)$ and Π errs with probability at most $\epsilon \leq 1/15$. If $k \leq r \leq n/400$, then $tr = \Omega(nk)$. Otherwise when $r < k$, then $t = \Omega(n)$.*

It turns out this immediately implies our main theorem for any $k \geq 1$. In particular, we show that Theorem 6 immediately implies Theorem 5.

Proof of Theorem 5. To prove this, we show a reduction that any protocol Π for any $k \geq 1$ can be converted into a protocol Π' where $k_c \leq k' \leq n/10$ without any asymptotic overhead. Suppose there exists Π that beats Theorem 5. If $k_c \leq k \leq n/10$, we are already done.

If $k < k_c$, we can construct Π' for $k' = k_c$ from Π by executing $O(k_c/k)$ queries in parallel. This means storing $O(k_c/k)$ hints and running the query algorithm $O(k_c/k)$ times for each hint. As a result, $t' = t \cdot O(k_c/k)$ and $r' = r \cdot O(k_c/k)$. As $k \geq 1$ and $k_c = O(1)$, we know that $O(k_c/k) = O(1)$ and get that $t'r' = O(tr)$ with no additional asymptotic overhead to contradict Theorem 6.

When $n/10 < k \leq n$, we construct Π' for $k' = n/10$ from Π by arbitrarily padding queried entries that will be ignored. Then, execute a single query using Π. Note, this results in $t'r' = O(tr)$ with no additional asymptotic overhead as $k = \Theta(k')$ to contradict Theorem 6. $\qquad\square$

Proof Overview. The rest of this section will be devoted to prove Theorem 6. Our proof of Theorem 6 will proceed in three steps:

1. First, we will characterize the relationship between queried and probed entries. Our goal is to show that not all queried entries can also be probed by leveraging the privacy requirements of PIR (Sect. 3.1).

2. Secondly, we show that random coin tosses and random batch queries allow for great compression by enabling to determine the contents of entries without ever requiring to probe the entry directly (Sect. 3.2).
3. Finally, we present an impossible compression scheme leveraging the above two facts that contradicts Shannon's source coding theorem to complete the proof (Sect. 3.3).

Additional Notation. For convenience, we will introduce additional notation that will be used throughout our proof. We will denote the set of entries probed by the set $\Pi.\mathsf{Probes}(q, D, H, R) \subseteq [n]$ for a batch query q, database D, hint H and coin tosses R. That is, $i \in \Pi.\mathsf{Probes}(q, D, H, R)$ if and only if the i-th entry of D is probed by at least one of the ℓ servers. Secondly, we will use $\mathbf{H}$ to represent a hint that is randomly generated by the preprocessing stage. That is, $\mathbf{H} \leftarrow \Pi.\mathsf{Preprocess}(D, \mathbf{R}_H)$ where $\mathbf{R}_H$ are uniformly random coin tosses. We will frequently write probabilities of the form $\Pr_{\mathbf{H},\mathbf{R}}[i \in \Pi.\mathsf{Probes}(q, D, \mathbf{H}, \mathbf{R})]$ that denotes whether the i-th entry is probed on any of the ℓ servers over the probabilities of randomly generated hints and coin tosses. In particular, this will be shorthand for the formal probability statement:

$$\Pr_{\mathbf{H},\mathbf{R}}[i \in \Pi.\mathsf{Probes}(q, D, \mathbf{H}, \mathbf{R})] = \Pr_{\mathbf{R}_H,\mathbf{R}}[i \in \Pi.\mathsf{Probes}(q, D, \mathbf{H}, \mathbf{R}) \mid \mathbf{H}]$$

where $\mathbf{H} \leftarrow \Pi.\mathsf{Preprocess}(\mathbf{R}_H; D)$. Additionally, we will use similar shorthand when analyzing error probabilities:

$$\Pr_{\mathbf{H},\mathbf{R}}[\Pi.\mathsf{Query}(q, \mathbf{H}, \mathbf{R}; D) \neq (D_i)_{i \in q}] = \Pr_{\mathbf{R}_H,\mathbf{R}}[\Pi.\mathsf{Query}(q, \mathbf{H}, \mathbf{R}; D) \neq (D_i)_{i \in q} \mid \mathbf{H}]$$

where $\mathbf{H} \leftarrow \Pi.\mathsf{Preprocess}(\mathbf{R}_H; D)$. In general, we will use $\mathbf{H}$ to represent a hint generated by providing random coin tosses $\mathbf{R}_H$ to $\Pi.\mathsf{Preprocess}(\mathbf{R}_H; D)$.

3.1   Characterizing Queried and Probed Entries

The main goal in this section is to characterize the set of probed entries and their relationship with the batch of k queried entries. At a high level, consider any Π that does not probe every entry in the database. For simplicity, suppose that Π probes only half the entries. Is it possible that the set of probed entries can be heavily correlated with the original set of k queries? For example, is it possible that Π can probe the entries corresponding to all k queries without being detected by an adversary? We resolve these questions here by providing a formal characterization between queried and probed entries.

To do this we start by making the following assumption:

$$t \leq n/(100\ell). \tag{1}$$

This is without loss of generality as otherwise our proof will already be complete as $t > n/(100\ell)$ immediately implies $tr = \Omega(nk)$ since $r \geq k$ and ℓ is constant.

Consider the t probed entries across all ℓ servers. For any of the n entries in the database, we will consider the i-th entry to be probed if the entry is probed by at least one of the ℓ servers. Therefore, we know that at most $n/(100\ell)$ unique entries are probed for each online query. Intuitively, there should be a large fraction of the n entries that are probed only with $1/(100\ell)$ probability. We formalize this for a fixed k-batch query as follows:

Lemma 1. *Let $D \in \{0,1\}^n$ be any database. Fix k-batch query $\{1,\ldots,k\} \subseteq [n]$. Then, there exists a subset $S \subseteq [n]$ such that $|S| \geq n/2$ and for all $i \in S$, then*

$$\Pr_{\mathbf{H},\mathbf{R}}[i \in \varPi.\mathsf{Probes}(\{1,\ldots,k\}, D, \mathbf{H}, \mathbf{R})] \leq \frac{1}{50\ell}.$$

Proof. Towards a contradiction, suppose that this is false. That means, there exists strictly more than $n/2$ entries that are probed with probability at least $1/(50\ell)$. Then, we get that

$$t = \mathbb{E}_{\mathbf{H},\mathbf{R}}[|\varPi.\mathsf{Probes}(\{1,\ldots,k\}, D, \mathbf{H}, \mathbf{R})|] > \frac{n}{2} \cdot \frac{1}{50\ell} = \frac{n}{100\ell}.$$

This is a contradiction as we had assumed $t \leq n/(100\ell)$ in Eq. 1. $\qquad\square$

Next, we construct a polynomial time adversary $\mathcal{A}$ to distinguish queries to $\{1,\ldots,k\}$ and any other batch query. More formally, we construct a family of adversaries $\mathcal{A}_{i,q}$, for all $i \in [n]$ and $q \subseteq [n]$ below.

Adversary $\mathcal{A}_{i,q}$:

- **Challenge Phase $\mathcal{A}_{i,q}(D)$:**
  1. Return $(\{1,\ldots,k\}, q, \{x\})$ for uniformly random x from $[\ell]$.
- **Output Phase $\mathcal{A}_{i,q}(\mathcal{T}_x^p, \mathcal{T}_x)$:**
  1. Retrieve $\varPi.\mathsf{Probes}$ from $\mathcal{T}_x$ specifying all entries probed on the compromised server.
  2. Return 1 if and only if $i \in \varPi.\mathsf{Probes}$.

In other words, $\mathcal{A}_{i,q}$ is defined such that it compromises one of the ℓ servers uniformly at random, picks challenge queries q and $\{1,\ldots,k\}$ and returns 1 if and only if the i-th entry is probed. We prove the following lemma using $\mathcal{A}_{i,q}$.

Lemma 2. *Suppose that $\varPi$ is computationally $(\delta, 1, \ell)$-secure. Fix any k-batch query $q \subseteq [n]$ and database $D \in \{0,1\}^n$. Let $S \subseteq [n]$ be as stated in Lemma 1 and suppose index $i \in S$. If $\delta \leq 1/(25\ell)$, then*

$$\Pr_{\mathbf{H},\mathbf{R}}[i \in \varPi.\mathsf{Probes}(q, D, \mathbf{H}, \mathbf{R})] \leq \frac{1}{25}.$$

Proof. Towards a contradiction, suppose that the statement is false. Consider adversary $\mathcal{A}_{i,q}$. For query $\{1,\ldots,k\}$, we know that $\mathcal{A}_{i,q}$ outputs 1 with probability at most $1/(50\ell)$ by Lemma 1 as $i \in S$. On the other hand, consider the probed entries on any query q. We know the probability that i is probed on at least one of the ℓ servers is strictly larger than $1/25$. As $\mathcal{A}_{i,q}$ compromises one server at random, we know that $\mathcal{A}_{i,q}$ observes that the i-th entry is probed with probability strictly greater than $1/(25\ell)$. Therefore, $\mathcal{A}_{i,q}$ outputs 1 with probability strictly greater than $1/(25\ell)$. This contradicts the fact that any computational adversary has distinguishing advantage at most $\delta \leq 1/(25\ell)$ as the advantage is strictly greater than $1/(25\ell) - 1/(50\ell) = 1/(25\ell)$ to derive our contradiction. $\square$

Finally, we use the above lemma to prove our main characterization of probed entries in relation to the set of entries that are queried. In particular, we will prove an upper bound on the number of queried entries that are also probed.

Lemma 3. *Fix any database $D \in \{0,1\}^n$ and any k-batch query $q \subseteq [n]$. Let $S \subseteq [n]$ be as defined in Lemma 1. Then,*

$$\Pr_{\mathbf{H,R}}\left[\left|q \cap S \cap \Pi.\mathsf{Probes}(q, D, \mathbf{H}, \mathbf{R})\right| \leq \frac{|q \cap S|}{5}\right] \geq \frac{4}{5}.$$

Proof. Let $q = \{i_1, \ldots, i_k\}$ be the query to k indices $i_1, \ldots, i_k$. By Lemma 2,

$$\Pr_{\mathbf{H,R}}[i_j \in \Pi.\mathsf{Probes}(q, D, \mathbf{H}, \mathbf{R})] \leq \frac{1}{25}$$

whenever $i_j \in S$. Let $X_j = 1$ if and only if $i_j \in S \cap \Pi.\mathsf{Probes}(q, D, \mathbf{H}, \mathbf{R})$ and 0 otherwise. Note that $\mathbb{E}_{\mathbf{H,R}}[X_j \mid i_j \in S] \leq 1/25$. If we let X be the total number of queried entries of S that are also probed, that is $X = |q \cap S \cap \Pi.\mathsf{Probes}(q, D, \mathbf{H}, \mathbf{R})|$, then we know that $\mathbb{E}_{\mathbf{H,R}}[X] \leq |q \cap S|/25$ by linearity of expectation as $X = X_1 + \ldots + X_j$. By Markov's inequality, we get that

$$\Pr_{\mathbf{H,R}}\left[\left|q \cap S \cap \Pi.\mathsf{Probes}(q, D, \mathbf{H}, \mathbf{R})\right| \geq \frac{|q \cap S|}{5}\right]$$

$$= \Pr_{\mathbf{H,R}}\left[X \geq \frac{|q \cap S|}{5}\right] = \Pr_{\mathbf{H,R}}\left[X \geq 5 \cdot \frac{|q \cap S|}{25}\right] \leq \frac{1}{5}$$

since $\mathbb{E}_{\mathbf{H,R}}[X] \leq |q \cap S|/25$ to complete the proof. $\square$

The above lemma formally shows that at most $(1/5)$-fraction of queried entries that appear in S will also be probed with high probability.

Discussion about Model. For our lower bound, we design an adversary that must detect whether the i-th entry of the database is probed. This is possible in the standard PIR model with replications as the adversary knows the relationship between each probed entry and its original index in the database. If the database is encoded arbitrarily, this adversarial strategy is no longer possible. This is the main challenge in extending our result to general models.

3.2   Discovering Good Batch Queries

In this section, we will prove results about finding batch queries that will enable good compression of the database. At a high level, these *good* batch queries $q = \{i_1, \ldots, i_k\} \subseteq [n]$ are ones that enable computing a large fraction of queried entries, D_{i_j}, without probing the i_j-th entry directly. That is, $i_j \notin \Pi.\text{Probes}(q, D, H, R)$ for the used hint H and coin tosses R.

To formalize the above, we will aim to identify *good* sets for various entities. We start by defining the notion of goodness for sets of queries and randomness. We start by saying that a triplet of a k-batch query $q \subseteq [n]$, hint H and coin tosses R are *good* if and only if the following two properties hold:

1. (**Correctness.**) $\Pi.\text{Query}(q, H, R; D) = (D_i)_{i \in q}$.
2. (**Discovery.**) $|q \cap \Pi.\text{Probes}(q, D, H, R)| \leq 4k/5$.

We denote a triplet being good by $E^q(q, H, R) = 1$ if the above two conditions holds for the given triplet (q, H, R). Otherwise, we say $E^q(q, H, R) = 0$. Note, that the first property ensures correctness of retrieving the contents of all queried entries. The second property enables discovery. That is, at least $k/5$ of the queried entries are not probed directly during query execution.

Next, we move onto pairs of hints H and coin tosses R. In particular, we are interested in finding pairs (H, R) that enable the above properties for most queries. For this, we will focus on the query set Q that consists of all k-batch queries that aim to retrieve k distinct entries. We will denote $\mathbf{q}$ as the random variable that draws a query uniformly at random from Q. We say that pair of hint and coin toss H and R are good if and only if the following condition holds:

$$\Pr_{\mathbf{q}}[E^q(\mathbf{q}, H, R) = 1] \geq \frac{1}{30}.$$

We denote a pair H and R to be good by $E^R(H, R) = 1$ and $E^R(H, R) = 0$ for when it is not good. In other words, we say that a hint H and coin tosses R are good if and only if $(1/30)$-th of the queries $q \in Q$ exists such that q returns the correct answer and at most $(4/5)$-th of queried entries are probed when using the fixed hint H and coin toss R. In the next lemma, we show that a large fraction of pairs (H, R) are good and satisfy the above property.

Lemma 4. *Fix any database D. Then, we get that*

$$\Pr_{\mathbf{H}, \mathbf{R}}[E^R(\mathbf{H}, \mathbf{R}) = 1] \geq \frac{1}{50}.$$

Proof. Throughout the proof, we will denote $\mathbf{q}$ as being drawn uniformly from the query set Q. As Π errs with probability at most $\epsilon \leq 1/15$, we know that

$$\Pr_{\mathbf{q}, \mathbf{H}, \mathbf{R}}[\Pi.\text{Query}(\mathbf{q}, \mathbf{H}, \mathbf{R}; D) \neq (D_i)_{i \in \mathbf{q}}] = \epsilon \leq \frac{1}{15}.$$

By Lemma 3, we know that

$$\Pr_{\mathbf{q}, \mathbf{H}, \mathbf{R}}\left[|\mathbf{q} \cap S \cap \Pi.\text{Probes}(\mathbf{q}, D, \mathbf{H}, \mathbf{R})| \leq \frac{|\mathbf{q} \cap S|}{5}\right] \geq \frac{4}{5}.$$

We can bound the intersection size of q and S as follows. Let X be the number of indices in $q \setminus S$. As we know that $\mathbf{q}$ is chosen as a random k subset of $[n]$ and $|S| \geq n/2$, we get that $\mathbb{E}[X] \leq k/2$. By Markov's inequality, we know that $Pr[X \geq 3k/4] = \Pr[X \geq 3/2 \cdot k/2] \leq 2/3$. Therefore, we get that

$$\Pr_{\mathbf{q}}\left[|\mathbf{q} \cap S| \geq \frac{k}{4}\right] = 1 - \Pr_{\mathbf{q}}\left[X \geq \frac{3k}{4}\right] \geq \frac{1}{3}.$$

Then, we can see that if $|q \cap S| \geq k/4$ and $|q \cap S \cap \Pi.\text{Probes}(q, D, H, R)| \leq |q \cap S|/5$, this immediately implies that $|q \cap \Pi.\text{Probes}(q, D, H, R)| \leq |q \setminus S| + |q \cap S|/5 \leq 3k/4 + k/20 = 4k/5$. Therefore, we get that

$$\Pr_{\mathbf{q},\mathbf{H},\mathbf{R}}\left[|\mathbf{q} \cap \Pi.\text{Probes}(\mathbf{q}, D, \mathbf{H}, \mathbf{R})| \leq \frac{4k}{5}\right]$$

$$\geq \Pr_{\mathbf{q},\mathbf{H},\mathbf{R}}\left[|\mathbf{q} \cap S| \geq \frac{k}{4} \wedge |\mathbf{q} \cap \Pi.\text{Probes}(\mathbf{q}, D, \mathbf{H}, \mathbf{R})| \leq \frac{|q \cap S|}{5}\right]$$

$$\geq \Pr_{\mathbf{q},\mathbf{H},\mathbf{R}}\left[|\mathbf{q} \cap S| \geq \frac{k}{4}\right] - \Pr_{\mathbf{q},\mathbf{H},\mathbf{R}}\left[|\mathbf{q} \cap \Pi.\text{Probes}(\mathbf{q}, D, \mathbf{H}, \mathbf{R})| > \frac{|q \cap S|}{5}\right]$$

$$= \frac{1}{3} - \frac{1}{5} = \frac{2}{15}.$$

Then, we get that

$$\Pr_{\mathbf{q},\mathbf{H},\mathbf{R}}[E^q(\mathbf{q}, \mathbf{R}, \mathbf{H}) = 1]$$

$$\geq \Pr_{\mathbf{q},\mathbf{H},\mathbf{R}}\left[|\mathbf{q} \cap \Pi.\text{Probes}(\mathbf{q}, D, \mathbf{H}, \mathbf{R})| \leq \frac{4k}{5}\right] - \Pr_{\mathbf{q},\mathbf{H},\mathbf{R}}[\Pi.\text{Query}(\mathbf{q}, \mathbf{H}, \mathbf{R}; D) \neq (D_i)_{i \in \mathbf{q}}]$$

$$\geq \frac{1}{15}.$$

Towards a contradiction, suppose that $\Pr_{\mathbf{H},\mathbf{R}}[E(\mathbf{H}, \mathbf{R}) = 1] < 1/50$. This contradicts the prior inequality as we get that:

$$\Pr_{\mathbf{q},\mathbf{H},\mathbf{R}}[E^q(\mathbf{q}, \mathbf{H}, \mathbf{R}) = 1]$$

$$\leq \sum_{x \in \{0,1\}} \Pr_{\mathbf{H},\mathbf{R}}[E^H(\mathbf{H}, \mathbf{R}) = x] \Pr_{\mathbf{q},\mathbf{H},\mathbf{R}}[E^q(\mathbf{q}, \mathbf{H}, \mathbf{R}) = 1 \mid E^H(\mathbf{H}, \mathbf{R}) = x]$$

$$< \frac{1}{50} + \left(\frac{49}{50} \cdot \Pr_{\mathbf{q},\mathbf{H},\mathbf{R}}[E^q(\mathbf{q}, \mathbf{H}, \mathbf{R}) = 1 \mid E^H(\mathbf{H}, \mathbf{R}) = 0]\right)$$

$$< \frac{1}{50} + \frac{49}{50} \cdot \frac{1}{30} < \frac{1}{15}.$$

As a result, we know that $\Pr_{\mathbf{H},\mathbf{R}}[E(\mathbf{H}, \mathbf{R}) = 1] \geq 1/50$. $\qquad\square$

Next, we will consider the intersection of a random query with an arbitrary subset X of at most $n/100$ entries. In particular, we expect that if we pick a random k-batch query from Q, then approximately $(1/100)$-th fraction of the chosen queries would also appear in X. Later, we will use X to model previously probed and queried entries. In other words, we are aiming to show that a random query will not query too many entries that have been previously probed or queried. We formalize this in the following lemma:

Lemma 5. *For any subset $X \subset [n]$ such that $|X| \leq n/100$,*

$$\Pr_{\mathbf{q}} \left[|\mathbf{q} \cap X| > \frac{k}{10} \right] \leq \frac{1}{60}$$

where $\mathbf{q}$ is drawn uniformly at random from Q.

Proof. Note that we can model the choice of $\mathbf{q}$ as picking a random subset of size k from $[n]$. For any fixed $X \subset [n]$, we can see that

$$\Pr[|\mathbf{q} \cap X| > k/10] \leq \frac{\binom{n/100}{k/10} \cdot \binom{n}{9k/10}}{\binom{n}{k}} \leq \frac{\left(\frac{en}{10k}\right)^{k/10} \cdot \left(\frac{10n}{9k}\right)^{9k/10}}{\left(\frac{n}{k}\right)^{k}}$$

$$\leq \left(\frac{e}{10} \cdot \left(\frac{10}{9} \right)^{9} \right)^{k/10} \leq \frac{1}{60}$$

where we use Stirling's approximation of binomial coefficients $(a/b)^b \leq \binom{a}{b} \leq (ea/b)^b$ and assuming that k is a sufficiently large constant $\qquad\square$

3.3   An Impossible Encoding

Next, we use the characterization of probe probabilities from the prior two sections to construct an impossible compression for databases drawn from our hard distribution that we define below:

> **Hard Distribution.** Our hard distribution for databases, that we denote by $\mathbf{D}$, will be a uniformly random n-bit string. In other words, each of the n entries will be a uniformly random bit.

At a high level, our compression algorithm will leverage Π to efficiently recover as many queried entries without needing to probe the corresponding physical entry. We are able to do this by leveraging the formal characterization of Lemma 3 that shows that only a constant fraction of queried entries will also be probed with reasonably high probability. Then, we will leverage Lemmata 4 and 5 to find these *good* queries amongst random queries. In more detail, the compression algorithm will perform in rounds. In each round, the goal is to find a good k-batch query amongst a set of random k-batch queries such that a large portion of the contents of queried entries are unknown and will not be probed. Before going into more detail, we start by formalizing the model for presenting our compression scheme.

One-Way Communication Protocols. To formally prove our lower bound, we will consider a one-way communication protocol between parties Alice (the encoder) and Bob (the decoder). Alice will receive the input database. The goal of Alice is to send a single message to Bob that will enable Bob to always successfully decode the input database. Additionally, Alice and Bob will also receive the same shared randomness as input that will be used to help encode and decode the input database. In particular, the shared randomness will consist of the random coin tosses $\mathbf{R_{shared}}$ needed to execute Π and will be independent of the input database D.

Next, we prove a lemma that shows that the length of Alice's encoding cannot be much smaller than the minimum number of random bits stored in a database drawn from the hard distribution. We will consider prefix-free encodings where one possible message is not a prefix of another possible message.

Lemma 6. *For any one-way communication protocol where Alice's encodings are prefix-free and Bob is always able to decode the database D, it must be that*

$$\mathbb{E}[\|\mathsf{Enc}(\mathbf{D})\|] \geq n$$

where the randomness is over the hard distribution of databases $\mathbf{D}$, the shared random coin tosses $\mathbf{R_{shared}}$ and internal randomness of Alice's encoding algorithm.

Proof. To prove this lemma, we will utilize Shannon's source coding theorem that states the expected length of any prefix-free encoding scheme must be at least the entropy of the input conditioned on any shared inputs. In other words,

$$\mathbb{E}[\|\mathsf{Enc}(\mathbf{D})\|] \geq H(\mathbf{D} \mid \mathbf{R_{shared}}) = H(\mathbf{D}) = n.$$

The first equality is from the fact $\mathbf{R_{shared}}$ are random coin tosses independent of $\mathbf{D}$. The second equality uses that $\mathbf{D}$ is a uniformly random n-bit string.   □

Discussion about Errors. In Lemma 6, we require that the encoding enables perfect decoding. However, this does not mean that we only prove lower bounds for schemes with zero error probability. In fact, we will utilize constructions that may err with probability as high $\epsilon \leq 1/15$ to build a perfect encoding scheme. To do this, our encoding will only rely on the PIR scheme for correct queries.

Encoding and Decoding Algorithms. We now formally present the encoding and decoding algorithms for our one-way communication protocol. Note that there are no computational bounds on the encoding and decoding algorithms. In particular, we will only care that Alice's encoding length is short in expectation and Bob is always able to decode the database.

First, we will formally describe the shared randomness $\mathbf{R_{shared}}$. In particular, $\mathbf{R_{shared}}$ will be broken into two parts. The first part will consist of random coin tosses $\mathbf{R}$ to execute a query. The second part will consist of uniformly random queries chosen from the query set Q. In particular, the second part will look of the form $(\mathbf{q}_1, \ldots, \mathbf{q}_s)$ where $s = 20n/(t + k/10)$. In other words, there will

Alice's Encoding: Alice receives database D and randomness $R_{shared} = (R, q_1, \ldots, q_s)$ where $s = 20n/(t + k/10)$.

1. Set $H \leftarrow \Pi.\text{Preprocess}(R_H; D)$ using random coin tosses R_H.
2. Set $A \leftarrow \emptyset$ to keep track of probed and queried entries.
3. Set P to be an empty string recording probed entries.
4. Set $S \leftarrow \emptyset$ to keep track of indices of successful query sets.
5. For $i = 1, \ldots, s$:
   (a) If $|S| \geq s/2000$:
      i. Terminate loop.
   (b) Check if q_i satisfies the following properties:
      i. (**Correctness.**) $\Pi.\text{Query}(q_i, H, R; D) = (D_x)_{x \in q_i}$.
      ii. (**Overlap with Known Entries.**) $|q_i \cap A| \leq k/10$.
      iii. (**Overlap with Probes.**) $|q_i \cap \Pi.\text{Probes}(q_i, D, H, R)| \leq 4k/5$.
   (c) If q_i does satisfies the above:
      i. Set $U \leftarrow \Pi.\text{Probes}(q_i, D, H, R) \setminus A$ to be all probed entries that were not previously probed or queried in the order they were first probed.
      ii. If $|U| < t$, add entries in $[n] \setminus U$ to U in increasing index order until U contains t entries.
      iii. Set $S \leftarrow S \cup \{i\}$.
      iv. Set $P \leftarrow (P, (D_u)_{u \in U})$. That is, all entries in U in the order they were first probed followed by added entries in increasing order.
      v. Set $A \leftarrow A \cup U$.
      vi. Add the smallest $k/10$ indexed entries in $q_i \setminus A$ to A.
6. If $|S| < s/2000$, return the encoding $(0, D)$ as a 0-bit followed by a trivial n-bit encoding of D.
7. Set $\text{Enc} \leftarrow (1, H, S, P)$ to be a 1-bit, the hint H using r bits and set S of successful query indices and P from the above loop. Note S requires $\log \binom{s}{s/2000}$ bits and P requires $ts/2$ bits to encode.
8. Set $\text{Enc} \leftarrow (\text{Enc}, \{D_x\}_{x \in [n] \setminus A})$. That is, the contents of all entries with indices in $[n] \setminus A$ in increasing index order. Note, each of the $s/2000$ successful queries adds exactly $t + k/10$ entries into A. So, the size of A at the end is $s/2000 \cdot (t + k/10) = n/100$ and this step requires $99n/100$ bits.
9. Return Enc.

Fig. 2. Description of Alice's encoding algorithm.

Bob's Decoding: Bob receives Alice's encoding and randomness $R_{\text{shared}} = (R, q_1, \ldots, q_s)$ where $s = 20n/(t + k/10)$.

1. If the encoding starts with a 0-bit, decode D trivially and return D.
2. Decode H using the next r bits.
3. Decode $S \subseteq [s]$ using the next $\log \binom{s}{s/2000}$ bits.
4. Decode P using the next $st/2$ bits.
5. Set B to be the decoded database.
6. Set $A \leftarrow \emptyset$ to keep track of all indices that have been either probed or queried.
7. For $i \in S$ in increasing order:
   (a) Execute $\Pi.\mathsf{Query}(q_i, H, R; D)$. Even though Bob does not know the database entirely, Bob can complete this execution using Alice's encoding in the following way:
   (b) If Bob attempts to probe an entry $x \notin A$:
      i. Bob will use the next bit of P to decode D_x.
      ii. Set $B[x] \leftarrow D_x$.
      iii. Set $A \leftarrow A \cup \{x\}$.
   (c) If Bob attempts to probe an entry $x \in A$:
      i. Use $B[x]$ as the contents of the entry.
   (d) Set $B[x]$ to be the answer given by $\Pi.\mathsf{Query}(q_i, H, R; D)$ for $x \in q_i$.
   (e) If Bob probes less than $a < t$ entries outside of A, Bob uses the next $t - a$ bits in P to decode the smallest $t - a$ indexed entries outside of A. Then, Bob adds their contents into B and their indices in A.
   (f) Add the smallest $k/10$ indexed entries in $q_i \setminus A$ to A.
8. Decode $\{D_x\}_{x \in [n] \setminus A}$. Set $B[x] \leftarrow D_x$ for all $x \in [n] \setminus A$.
9. Return B.

Fig. 3. Description of Bob's decoding algorithm.

be s random batch queries from Q. Note that all of this shared randomness is independent of the database D.

Next, we describe Alice's encoding algorithm. The main goal of Alice is to compress the database D using Π. Alice will go through the random queries q_i with the goal of finding a query in the set that enables extracting entries in D without ever probing them. To do this, Alice aims to find queries that are correct with the caveat that the queried entries should not have been previously discovered and they will not be probed by the query itself when using random coin tosses R_H and R. When Alice finds such a *good* query that enables a high discovery rate, Alice will encode the identity of these queries and all necessary probed entries to let Bob simulate the queries as well. To do this, Alice will only encode contents of entries that were not previously discovered. Once Alice is able to find enough queries to encode at least $n/100$ of the entries in D, Alice will complete the encoding by sending the remaining undiscovered entries in D trivially. Alice's encoding algorithm is provided in Fig. 2.

Next, we describe Bob's decoding algorithm. The goal of Bob is to simulate queries identically to Alice. To do this, Bob keeps track of all entries whose contents have been discovered. For each query encoded by Alice, Bob will aim to execute the query without knowing the input database D. To do this, Bob performs probes one at a time. For any entries whose contents are known to Bob, Bob can simply use their contents and continue executing. For any probed entry that is unknown to Bob, Bob will use Alice's encoding to determine the contents. As we ensure Alice and Bob use the same hint H coin tosses R, it can be guaranteed that Alice and Bob execute queries identically. After executing all queries, Bob will simply decode all remaining unknown entries using the trivial encoding sent by Alice. Bob's decoding algorithm is provided in Fig. 3.

Correctness. To see that the one-way communication protocol always enables Bob to decode the database, we will show that Alice and Bob simulate queries in the exact same way. In particular, Bob will only execute queries q_i that satisfy the conditions that are checked by Alice. For each of these queries, Bob will execute them identically to Alice as they use the same hint H and coin tosses R and any entries that are not known to Bob will be encoded by Alice. As a result, Alice and Bob will execute all of these queries identically. Furthermore, Alice and Bob will maintain identical sets A throughout the execution of their entire algorithms and Bob will be able to get the contents of all entries in A. Finally, as all entries outside of A are encoded trivially, we get that Bob is able to decode the database successfully.

Prefix-Free Encoding. Note any encoding starting with a 0-bit cannot be a prefix of an encoding starting with a 1-bit and vice versa. Therefore, it suffices to show the set of 0-bit encodings and 1-bit encodings are prefix-free independently. All encodings starting with a 0-bit are the same length of $1 + n$ and, thus, prefix-free. Similarly, all encodings prefixed with a 1-bit are the same length of $1 + r + \log \binom{s}{s/2000} + st/2000 + 99n/100$ bits and, also, prefix-free.

Encoding Length. Next, we analyze the length of Alice's encoding in bits. Our goal is to prove an upper bound on the expected encoding length. We break this down into two cases. The first case is when Alice's encoding starts with a 0-bit. In this case, Alice's encoding uses $1 + n$ bits. Next, we upper bound the probability that Alice's encoding starts with a 0-bit. This only occurs when $|S| < s/2000$. Consider any set of random queries $\mathbf{q}_1, \ldots, \mathbf{q}_s$. For each single query $\mathbf{q}_i$, we note that the probability that $\mathbf{q}_i$ satisfies the conditions of Step 5b of Alice's algorithm is at least

$$\Pr_{\mathbf{q}_i}[E^q(\mathbf{q}_i, H, R) = 1] - \Pr_{\mathbf{q}_i}[|\mathbf{q}_i \cap A| > k/10].$$

If we assume that the input $\mathbf{R}_H$ and $\mathbf{R}$ satisfy property that $E^R(\mathbf{H}, \mathbf{R}) = 1$ where $\mathbf{H} = \Pi.\mathsf{Preprocess}(D, \mathbf{R}_H)$, then we get that $\mathbf{q}_i$ satisfies the conditions of Step 5b of Alice's algorithm with probability at least

$$\Pr_{\mathbf{q}_i}[E^q(\mathbf{q}_i, H, R) = 1 \mid E^R(H, R) = 1] - \Pr_{\mathbf{q}_i}[|\mathbf{q}_i \cap A| > k/10] \geq \frac{1}{30} - \frac{1}{60} = \frac{1}{60}$$

by using Lemma 5 and the definition of $E^R(\mathbf{H}, \mathbf{R}) = 1$. Therefore, the probability that $\mathbf{q}_i$ satisfies the conditions of Step 5b is at least $1/60$. Then, we know that

$\mathbb{E}[|S|] \geq s/60$. Denote the probability of less than $s/2000$ queries succeeding by f, then

$$f = \Pr\left[|S| < \frac{s}{2000} \mid E^R(H, R) = 1\right]$$
$$= \Pr\left[|S| < \left(1 - \frac{97}{100}\right) \cdot \frac{s}{60} \mid E^R(H, R) = 1\right] \leq e^{-\frac{(97)^2}{(100)^2 60^2} \frac{s}{}} < \frac{4}{5}$$

using Chernoff's bound, $s \geq 1000$ and the fact that the failure of each query set is an independent event. We get that $s \geq 1000$ by our assumptions that $t \leq n/(100\ell) \leq n/100$ as $\ell \geq 1$ and $k \leq n/10$ implying that $t + k/10 \leq n/50$. Therefore, Alice's encoding starts with a 0-bit with probability at most

$$\Pr_{\mathbf{H,R}}[E^R(\mathbf{H,R}) = 0] + \Pr_{\mathbf{H,R}}[E^R(\mathbf{H,R}) = 1] \cdot \Pr[|S| < s/2000 \mid E^R(\mathbf{H,R}) = 1]$$
$$\leq \frac{49}{50} + \frac{1}{50} \cdot f < 1$$

where we use Lemma 4 to bound $\Pr_{\mathbf{H,R}}[E^R(\mathbf{H,R}) = 0] \leq 49/50$.

Next, we will analyze the case when Alice's encoding starts with a 1-bit. First, we show that it is always guaranteed that the condition $|A| = n/100$ will be true once Alice reaches the end of the encoding algorithm. Note that each successful query increases A by $t + k/10$ entries. Furthermore, Alice executes exactly $s/2000 = n/(100(t + k/10))$ queries. So, $|A| = s(t + k/10)/2 = n/100$.

All successful queries encode t probed entries. Encoding the indices of successful queries requires $\log \binom{s}{s/2000}$. Then, the encoding length is at most

$$1 + r + \log\binom{s}{s/2000} + \frac{st}{2000} + (n - |A|) \leq 1 + r + \frac{s\log(2000e)}{2000} + \frac{st}{2000} + (n - |A|)$$
$$\leq 1 + r + \frac{n}{100} \cdot \frac{t + \log(2000e)}{t + k/10} + \frac{99n}{100}$$

using the fact that $\binom{a}{b} \leq (ea/b)^b$. Then, we get that Alice's expected encoding length is at most

$$1 + fn + (1 - f) \cdot \left(r + \frac{n}{100} \cdot \frac{t + \log(2000e)}{t + k/10} + \frac{99n}{100}\right).$$

Completing the Proof. Finally, we complete the proof by combining the above analysis of Alice's expected encoding length combined with Lemma 6.

Proof of Theorem 6. By Lemma 6, we know that Alice's expected encoding length must be at least n bits. Therefore, we get the inequality

$$1 + fn + (1 - f) \cdot \left(r + \frac{n}{100} \cdot \frac{t + \log(2000e)}{t + k/10} + \frac{99n}{100}\right) \geq n$$
$$\iff (1 - f) \cdot \left(r + \frac{n}{100} \cdot \frac{t + \log(2000e)}{t + k/10} + \frac{99n}{100}\right) \geq (1 - f)n - 1$$

$$\Longleftrightarrow r + \frac{n}{100} \cdot \frac{t + \log(2000e)}{t + k/10} \geq \frac{n}{100} - O(1)$$

$$\Longleftrightarrow r(t + k/10) \geq \frac{nk}{2000} - O(t + k)$$

$$\Longleftrightarrow rt \geq \frac{nk}{2000} - O(t + k) - \frac{rk}{10}$$

where we will assume that $k \geq 20 \log(2000e)$ and use the fact that $1/(1 - f) = O(1)$ as $f < 4/5$. We use that $r \leq n/400$ to see that $rk/10 \leq nk/4000$ and get

$$(r + \Theta(1))(t + \Theta(1)) \geq \frac{nk}{4000}$$

where we also use that $r \geq k \geq k_c$ for some sufficiently large but constant k_c. We assume that n is sufficiently large to get that $tr = \Omega(nk)$. $\square$

4 Upper Bound

In this section, we present upper bounds for batch PIR with private preprocessing. As a reminder, we recall two ways to obtain optimal constructions matching our lower bound. First, one can execute k queries in sequence with any known single-query scheme [24,67] that uses k-rounds. Another option is to use pipelined queries approach utilizing a specific property of previous constructions [24,49,67] where client queries do not depend on server responses. In other words, clients may issue k queries simultaneously (see the full version for more details). In this section, we show that one can construct blackbox reductions from single-query to batch PIR without assuming any other properties of the single-query scheme.

4.1 Blackbox Single-Query to Batch Reduction

In the rest of this section, we will present constructions with single-round query algorithms. Our schemes will make blackbox usages of batch codes and single-query PIR with private preprocessing schemes. We note our described constructions make standard usage of batch codes for enabling batch PIR (see [5,6,47] for example) from any single-query PIR protocol. Our main adaptation is replacing the single-query PIR protocol with any single-query PIR with private preprocessing protocol.

Batch Codes. Batch codes are a primitive first introduced by Ishai, Kushilevitz, Ostrovsky and Sahai [47] that studies the problem of distributing a database of n bits into m buckets. The goal of the distribution is to enable any user to retrieve any batch of k entries by only querying at most t bits from each of the m buckets. Typically, the goal of batch codes is to minimize the total size of the encoding denoted by N.

There are several variants of batch codes that have been studied in the past. For our construction, we will focus on systematic batch codes that handle non-multiset queries. Systematic batch codes require that each symbol of the codeword to be an entry in the original database. Note, this ensures that our construction uses the same conditions as our lower model. Some batch codes handle the more difficult setting of multiset queries where the same entry may be retrieved multiple times. For our protocol, we only require handling queries that retrieve k distinct entries. It is straightforward to handle batch PIR queries with duplicate entries using only non-multiset queries.

Additionally, we will only use systematic batch codes with $t = 1$. This means that only a single symbol in each bucket will be accessed. In other words, the decoding algorithm A is trivial as it will simply read one of the k desired entries from each of the m buckets. These codes have been referred to as replication-based batch codes [47] or combinatorial batch codes [62] in the past. Furthermore, we will assume that the decoding algorithm can obtain correct buckets and entries within the bucket without needing the database. This is a feature that is used for most usages of batch codes for batch PIR (such as [5,6,47]).

Definition 6 ([62]). *A $(n, N, k, m, 1)$ combinatorial batch code C is a set system $(X, \mathcal{B})$ where X is a set of n elements, $\mathcal{B} = (B_1, \ldots, B_m)$ is a collection of m subsets of X and a decoding algorithm C_A such that:*

1. *$N = \sum_{i \in [m]} |B_i|$. That is, the total length of all m subsets is at most N (where the length of each bucket is independent of x).*
2. *For each subset $\{x_1, \ldots, x_k\} \subseteq X$, $C_A(\{x_1, \ldots, x_k\}) = ((i_1, j_1), \ldots, (i_k, j_k))$ such that x_a is the j_a-the entry of B_{i_a} for all $a \in [k]$ and all of $(i_1, \ldots, i_k)$ are distinct.*

Protocol. We will formally present our single-round protocol in this section. At a high level, we will assume the existence of a $(n, N, k, m, 1)$ combinatorial batch code C that can handle non-multiset queries. Additionally, we will assume the existence of a single-query PIR with private preprocessing scheme that uses r-bit hints and t online query time. We will use both C and Π in a blackbox manner to construct our protocol.

Our protocol will first apply the batch code C to split up the database $D \in \{0, 1\}^n$ into m buckets to get $C(D) = (B_1, \ldots, B_m)$ where each bucket contains a subset of entries from D, $B_j \subseteq D$, since C is systematic. By the guarantees of batch codes, we know that for every subset $\{i_1, \ldots, i_k\} \subseteq [n]$, there exists a subset $\{j_1, \ldots, j_k\} \subseteq [m]$ such that $D_{i_x} \in B_{j_x}$ for all $x \in [k]$. Next, instantiate m parallel instances of Π on each of the m buckets, $B_1, \ldots, B_m$, using hint lengths of r/m bits for all m instances. During query time for batch query $\{i_1, \ldots, i_k\} \subseteq [n]$, use the batch code to identify the subset $\{j_1, \ldots, j_k\} \subseteq [m]$ such that $D_{i_x} \in B_{j_x}$ for all $x \in [k]$. For each of these k buckets, perform a query to retrieve D_{i_x}. For the remaining $m - k$ buckets, retrieve any arbitrary entry. For the formal construction and proof, we refer readers to the full version.

Theorem 7. *Let C be a systematic $(n, N, k, m, 1)$ batch code and Π be a single-query PIR with private preprocessing scheme that is (δ, ℓ_A, ℓ)-secure with error probability ϵ and uses r-bit hints and online query time $t(n, r)$. Then, there exists a k-query batch PIR with private preprocessing scheme that is $(m\delta, \ell_A, \ell)$-secure with error probability $k\epsilon$. If this construction uses r'-bit hints, then*

$$t'(n, r') = O(t(N_1, r'/m) + \ldots + t(N_m, r'/m))$$

where N_i is the number of bits in the i-th bucket of the encoding by C.

Relation to Lower Bound Model. Note that our lower bound model assumes that there is no encoding of the database beyond arbitrary replication. As systematic batch codes only require replication, the construction is compatible with our lower bound model.

Instantiations. Next, we pick different options for batch codes C and single-query PIR with private preprocessing Π to instantiate our construction. In this case, we do not require the feature that a single preprocessing stage handles multiple queries. As a result, we can use either any of the constructions in [24,67] to get the following constructions from batch codes.

Theorem 8. *Assuming the existence of a systematic $(n, N, k, m, 1)$ batch code and a single-query PIR with private preprocessing scheme that is $(\delta, 1, \ell)$-secure where δ is negligible and $\ell \in \{1, 2\}$ such that $tr = \tilde{O}(n)$ and is correct except with negligible probability, then there exists a single-round, k-query batch PIR with private preprocessing that is $(\delta, 1, \ell)$-secure where δ is negligible and $\ell \in \{1, 2\}$, uses r-bit hints and online query time t such that $tr = \tilde{O}(N \cdot m)$ and returns the correct answer except with negligible probability.*

For instantiating batch codes, many prior works (see [5,6,42,47,62] and references therein) have studied batch codes that may be used with PIR. For our purposes, we can use the $(n, O(n \log n), k, O(k), 1)$ batch code presented by Ishai, Kushilevitz, Ostrovsky and Sahai [47] that is built from unbalanced expanders. Using this batch code, we get the a construction with $tr = \tilde{O}(nk)$ that matches our lower bound (up to logarithmic factors).

Non-explicit vs Explicit Batch Codes. As a caveat, the above used batch code is non-explicit. One can plug-in other explicit batch codes or explicit constructions of unbalanced expanders into the Ishai, Kushilevitz, Ostrovsky and Sahai [47] batch code to obtain an explicit batch PIR with private preprocessing. However, these explicit constructions will result in worse parameters.

5   Barriers for General Lower Bounds

In the prior sections, we prove all our lower bounds in the standard PIR model as done in prior works (such as [10,24,64]). Recall that in the standard PIR model, the database of n entries must be stored without any modification. A more ambitious goal would be to prove lower bounds without restrictions on the underlying PIR algorithms. For example, a natural goal is to extend the above lower bounds to the case where the PIR algorithm may encode and store the database of n entries arbitrarily but using only a bounded amount of preprocessing time such as polynomial $n^{O(1)}$ time. We denote this the *general PIR model* where the PIR construction may store the database of n entries in any encoded manner. During query time, we denote the online time as the total amount of online computation performed by the server to process client queries. See the full version for more details on the general PIR model.

We will study connections between PIR and the online matrix-vector OMV conjecture from fine-grained complexity. We show barriers for proving lower bounds in general models as we show that such lower bounds would immediately imply the OMV conjecture that is a well-studied open problem in the theoretical computer science community and a core pillar of fine-grained complexity.

5.1   Online Matrix-Vector OMV Conjecture

At a high level, the OMV problem receives a single matrix $n \times n$ matrix M as input that may be preprocessed in polynomial time. Afterwards, n vectors $v_1, \ldots, v_n$ will be given in an online fashion such that the multiplication fo Mv_i must be output before receiving the next vector in the stream. We formally define the online matrix-vector problem below:

Definition 7 (Online Matrix-Vector Multiplication). *The online matrix-vector multiplication problem* OMV *takes as input a matrix* $M \in \{0,1\}^{n \times n}$ *and a stream of vectors* $v_1, \ldots, v_n \in \{0,1\}^n$. *The goal is to output* Mv_i *over* $\mathbb{F}_2$ *before seeing any input vectors* $v_{i+1}, \ldots, v_n$.

As matrix-vector multiplication is a fundamental problem in algorithms, the problem has been well-studied. A trivial algorithm would be to perform no preprocessing and simply answer each Mv_i naively requiring $O(n^3)$ total time. To date, the best known algorithm requires total time $n^3/2^{\Omega(\sqrt{\log n})}$ by Larsen and Williams [55]. However, this algorithm specifically requires using properties of the Boolean semiring. To our knowledge, there remains no better algorithm for OMV over any field including $\mathbb{F}_2$. Due to lack of progress, it has been conjectured [45] that there is no algorithm for solving the OMV problem in truly sub-cubic $O(n^{3-\epsilon})$ time. We formally present the OMV conjecture below:

Definition 8 (Online Matrix-Vector Conjecture [45]). *For any constant* $\epsilon > 0$, *there does not exist any algorithm with total online query time* $O(n^{3-\epsilon})$ *that can solve the online matrix-vector multiplication problem with error probability at most* $1/3$ *even with* $n^{O(1)}$ *preprocessing time of the matrix* M.

The online matrix-vector OMV conjecture is a very important conjecture in the area of fine-grained complexity that aim to quantify hardness within P along with other important conjectures such as the strong exponential time hypothesis (SETH), the 3SUM conjecture and the all-pairs shortest path (APSP) problem. The OMV conjecture has been used to prove the tight conditional lower bounds for several dynamic data structure problems including reachability and single-source shortest paths in directed graphs [45].

Boolean Semiring vs. $\mathbb{F}_2$. The standard definition of OMV is defined over the Boolean semiring where addition and multiplication are replaced by Boolean OR and AND operations (see [45,55] for example). In our work, we focus on the matrix-vector multiplication over $\mathbb{F}_2$. However, we note that the Boolean semiring variant of OMV is not easier than the $\mathbb{F}_2$ version of OMV. In the full version, we present a reduction showing that any algorithm solving OMV over $\mathbb{F}_2$ may be used to solve OMV over the Boolean semiring for completeness.

5.2   Barriers for General PIR Lower Bounds

We start by showing that we can construct efficient PIR constructions using efficient algorithms for online matrix-vector multiplication OMV. The result of this reduction is a barrier to proving lower bounds for PIR in more general bounds. In particular, we show that if one were able to prove lower bounds of $tr = \Omega(n)$ from Sect. 3 without the restrictions of the standard PIR model, this would immediately imply that the online matrix-vector conjecture is true.

We present a reduction from OMV that enables constructing efficient two-server PIR with public preprocessing schemes. Note that we had only focused on private preprocessing schemes. The main difference is that public preprocessing enables the adversary to view the execution and output of the preprocessing algorithm. We highlight that any lower bound for PIR with private preprocessing immediately implies the identical lower bound for public preprocessing. See the full version for formal definitions.

Theorem 9. *If an online matrix-vector multiplication algorithm running in total time $t(n)$ with $p(n)$ preprocessing time and error probability at most $\epsilon(n)$, then there exists a single-round, perfectly-secure, two-server PIR with public preprocessing with $O(p(n))$ preprocessing time, $O(t(\sqrt{n})/\sqrt{n})$ amortized online time over $\sqrt{n}$ queries, $O(\sqrt{n})$ communication and error probability at most $\epsilon(n)$.*

Proof. For this reduction, we start from a slight adaptation of the $O(\sqrt{n})$ communication two-server PIR scheme [20]. We arrange the database of n entries into a $\sqrt{n} \times \sqrt{n}$ matrix M. Suppose that we wish to query for an entry (i, j) in the i-th row and j-th column of M. The client will generate a uniformly random vector $a \in \{0, 1\}^{\sqrt{n}}$ where each entry is either 0 or 1 with probability $1/2$. Next, the client will compute $b = a \oplus 1_j$ that flips the bit in the j-th entry of a. The vector a is sent to the first server and the vector b is sent to the second server. Afterwards, each server will compute the matrix-vector multiplication $a' = Ma$ and $b' = Mb$ over $\mathbb{F}_2$. Note that $a'[i] \oplus b'[i] = M[i][j]$ and, thus, the client can retrieve the desired entry. For privacy, note that each vector a and b are identical to uniformly random vectors meaning the scheme is perfectly-secure.

Now, suppose that we have an algorithm $\mathcal{A}$ for the OMV problem with total time $t(n)$ over n queries and preprocessing time $p(n)$. We instantiate $\mathcal{A}$ with the $\sqrt{n} \times \sqrt{n}$ matrix M representing the n entries of the database in each of the two servers requiring $2p(n)$ preprocessing time. When responding to queries, each server will utilize $\mathcal{A}$ to compute the matrix-vector multiplication. Therefore, the total time to answer $\sqrt{n}$ queries is $2 \cdot t(\sqrt{n})$ and, thus, the amortized time is $O(t(\sqrt{n})/\sqrt{n})$. Note, the client is unable to retrieve the desired entry only when at least one of the responses from the server is not correct. By parallel repetition and taking the majority answer, we can drive down the error probability to be at most $\epsilon(n)$ without affecting the overall overhead except by constant factors. Finally, the query algorithm requires a single round completing the proof.   □

Next, we present the corollary of the above theorem showing that lower bounds for PIR with private preprocessing would immediately prove that the OMV conjecture is true. See the full version for the proof.

Corollary 1. *For any constant $\epsilon > 0$, suppose there does not exist any two-server computationally-secure PIR with private preprocessing scheme in the general model that uses $n^{O(1)}$ preprocessing time, r-bit hints, amortized online time t over $\sqrt{n}$ queries and error probability at most $1/3$ such that $tr = O(n^{1-\epsilon})$. Then, the online matrix-vector OMV conjecture is true.*

We note that the above was presented to focus on PIR with private preprocessing. One can generalize the above theorem in several ways. First, the above corollary still holds even if we only considered PIR with public preprocessing time with truly sub-linear $t = O(n^{1-\epsilon})$ time. Secondly, the result still holds even if the lower bound applied only to perfectly-secure two-server PIR schemes. Finally, the result also holds for any k-server scheme where $k \geq 2$.

Discussion about Public Preprocessing. Prior works have also proven lower bounds for public preprocessing including [10,64]. All these lower bounds are also proven in the standard PIR model. The results in this section also show that proving lower bounds for PIR with public preprocessing in more general models would immediately imply that the OMV conjecture is true.

6   Conclusions and Open Problems

In this paper, we present a tight characterization of the trade-offs between the hint size and online query time for batch PIR with private preprocessing. In particular, we present a $tr = \Omega(nk)$ lower bound when retrieving k entries. On the other hand, we show the existence of a $tr = \tilde{O}(nk)$ single-round query construction. In other words, our results show that one can only reap the benefits of the techniques from one of batch PIR or PIR with private preprocessing. When ignoring private preprocessing (i.e. $r < k$), we can apply known batch PIR techniques and get that $t = \tilde{\Theta}(n)$. For optimal PIR with private preprocessing schemes with $tr = \tilde{\Theta}(n)$ and $r \geq k$, one cannot beat the efficiency of the naive approach of performing k queries sequentially to get $tr = \tilde{\Theta}(nk)$. Additionally, we show the same efficiency may be achieved with a single-round query algorithm using batch codes. We leave the following high-level open question:

What techniques may be combined with private preprocessing to further improve the efficiency of PIR?

In this work, we ruled out using batch PIR techniques to further speed up PIR with private preprocessing. One way to improve PIR efficiency may be use more complex encodings of databases beyond replication.

Acknowledgements. The author would like to thank Chengyu Lin, Zeyu Liu and Tal Malkin for initial discussions and feedback on earlier versions of this paper, Giuseppe Persiano for reading an early draft and helpful suggestions for improving the paper, Henry Corrigan-Gibbs, Alexandra Henzinger and Dmitry Kogan for discussion about the pipelined queries approach and Josh Alman for discussion on the online matrix-vector conjecture. This research was supported in part by the Algorand Centres of Excellence programme managed by Algorand Foundation. Any opinions, findings, and conclusions or recommendations expressed in this material are solely those of the authors.

References

1. Abusalah, H., Alwen, J., Cohen, B., Khilko, D., Pietrzak, K., Reyzin, L.: Beyond Hellman's time-memory trade-offs with applications to proofs of space. In: Takagi, T., Peyrin, T. (eds.) ASIACRYPT 2017. LNCS, vol. 10625, pp. 357–379. Springer, Cham (2017). https://doi.org/10.1007/978-3-319-70697-9_13
2. Aguilar-Melchor, C., Barrier, J., Fousse, L., Killijian, M.-O.: XPIR: private information retrieval for everyone. In: PoPETS (2016)
3. Ali, A., Lepoint, T., Patel, S., Raykova, M., Schoppmann, P., Seth, K., Yeo, K.: Communication-computation trade-offs in PIR. In: USENIX Security (2021)
4. Ambainis, A.: Upper bound on the communication complexity of private information retrieval. In: Degano, P., Gorrieri, R., Marchetti-Spaccamela, A. (eds.) ICALP 1997. LNCS, vol. 1256, pp. 401–407. Springer, Heidelberg (1997). https://doi.org/10.1007/3-540-63165-8_196
5. Angel, S., Chen, H., Laine, K., Setty, S.: PIR with compressed queries and amortized query processing. In: IEEE Symposium on Security and Privacy (2018)
6. Angel, S., Setty, S.: Unobservable communication over fully untrusted infrastructure. In: USENIX OSDI (2016)
7. Beimel, A., Ishai, Y.: Information-theoretic private information retrieval: a unified construction. In: Orejas, F., Spirakis, P.G., van Leeuwen, J. (eds.) ICALP 2001. LNCS, vol. 2076, pp. 912–926. Springer, Heidelberg (2001). https://doi.org/10.1007/3-540-48224-5_74
8. Beimel, A., Ishai, Y., Kushilevitz, E., Malkin, T.: One-way functions are essential for single-server private information retrieval. In: ACM STOC (1999)
9. Beimel, A., Ishai, Y., Kushilevitz, E., Raymond, J.-F.: Breaking the $O(n^{1/(2k-1)})$ barrier for information-theoretic private information retrieval. In: FOCS (2002)
10. Beimel, A., Ishai, Y., Malkin, T.: Reducing the servers' computation in private information retrieval: PIR with preprocessing. J. Cryptol. (2004)
11. Borisov, N., Danezis, G., Goldberg, I.: DP5: a private presence service. In: Proceedings on Privacy Enhancing Technologies (2015)
12. Boyle, E., Gilboa, N., Ishai, Y.: Function secret sharing. In: Oswald, E., Fischlin, M. (eds.) EUROCRYPT 2015. LNCS, vol. 9057, pp. 337–367. Springer, Heidelberg (2015). https://doi.org/10.1007/978-3-662-46803-6_12
13. Boyle, E., Gilboa, N., Ishai. Y.: Function secret sharing: improvements and extensions. In: ACM SIGSAC CCS (2016)
14. Boyle, E., Holmgren, J., Weiss, M.: Permuted puzzles and cryptographic hardness. In: Hofheinz, D., Rosen, A. (eds.) TCC 2019. LNCS, vol. 11892, pp. 465–493. Springer, Cham (2019). https://doi.org/10.1007/978-3-030-36033-7_18
15. Boyle, E., Ishai, Y., Pass, R., Wootters, M.: Can we access a database both locally and privately? In: Kalai, Y., Reyzin, L. (eds.) TCC 2017. LNCS, vol. 10678, pp. 662–693. Springer, Cham (2017). https://doi.org/10.1007/978-3-319-70503-3_22
16. Cachin, C., Micali, S., Stadler, M.: Computationally private information retrieval with polylogarithmic communication. In: Stern, J. (ed.) EUROCRYPT 1999. LNCS, vol. 1592, pp. 402–414. Springer, Heidelberg (1999). https://doi.org/10.1007/3-540-48910-X_28
17. Canetti, R., Holmgren, J., Richelson, S.: Towards doubly efficient private information retrieval. In: Kalai, Y., Reyzin, L. (eds.) TCC 2017. LNCS, vol. 10678, pp. 694–726. Springer, Cham (2017). https://doi.org/10.1007/978-3-319-70503-3_23
18. Cheng, R., Scott, W., Parno, B., Zhang, I., Krishnamurthy, A., Anderson, T.: Talek: a private publish-subscribe protocol. Technical report (2016)

19. Chor, B., Gilboa, N.: Computationally private information retrieval. In: STOC (1997)
20. Chor, B., Kushilevitz, E., Goldreich, O., Sudan, M.: Private information retrieval. J. ACM (1998)
21. Coretti, S., Dodis, Y., Guo, S., Steinberger, J.: Random Oracles and non-uniformity. In: Nielsen, J.B., Rijmen, V. (eds.) EUROCRYPT 2018. LNCS, vol. 10820, pp. 227–258. Springer, Cham (2018). https://doi.org/10.1007/978-3-319-78381-9_9
22. Corrigan-Gibbs, H., Henzinger, A., Kogan, D.: Single-server private information retrieval with sublinear amortized time. In: Dunkelman, O., Dziembowski, S. (eds.) Advances in Cryptology – EUROCRYPT 2022. EUROCRYPT 2022. Lecture Notes in Computer Science, vol 13276. Springer, Cham (2022). https://doi.org/10.1007/978-3-031-07085-3_1
23. Corrigan-Gibbs, H., Kogan, D.: The discrete-logarithm problem with preprocessing. In: Nielsen, J.B., Rijmen, V. (eds.) EUROCRYPT 2018. LNCS, vol. 10821, pp. 415–447. Springer, Cham (2018). https://doi.org/10.1007/978-3-319-78375-8_14
24. Corrigan-Gibbs, H., Kogan, D.: Private information retrieval with sublinear online time. In: Canteaut, A., Ishai, Y. (eds.) EUROCRYPT 2020. LNCS, vol. 12105, pp. 44–75. Springer, Cham (2020). https://doi.org/10.1007/978-3-030-45721-1_3
25. Davidson, A., Pestana, G., Celi, S.: Frodopir: simple, scalable, single-server private information retrieval. In: PETS (2023)
26. De, A., Trevisan, L., Tulsiani, M.: Time space tradeoffs for attacks against one-way functions and PRGs. In: Rabin, T. (ed.) CRYPTO 2010. LNCS, vol. 6223, pp. 649–665. Springer, Heidelberg (2010). https://doi.org/10.1007/978-3-642-14623-7_35
27. Di Crescenzo, G., Ishai, Y., Ostrovsky, R.: Universal service-providers for private information retrieval. J. Cryptol. (2001)
28. Di Crescenzo, G., Malkin, T., Ostrovsky, R.: Single database private information retrieval implies oblivious transfer. In: Preneel, B. (ed.) EUROCRYPT 2000. LNCS, vol. 1807, pp. 122–138. Springer, Heidelberg (2000). https://doi.org/10.1007/3-540-45539-6_10
29. Dodis, Y., Guo, S., Katz, J.: Fixing cracks in the concrete: random oracles with auxiliary input, revisited. In: Coron, J.-S., Nielsen, J.B. (eds.) EUROCRYPT 2017. LNCS, vol. 10211, pp. 473–495. Springer, Cham (2017). https://doi.org/10.1007/978-3-319-56614-6_16
30. Dvir, Z., Gopalan, P., Yekhanin, S.: Matching vector codes. In: FOCS (2010)
31. Dvir, Z., Gopi, S.: 2-server PIR with subpolynomial communication. JACM (2016)
32. Efremenko, K.: 3-query locally decodable codes of subexponential length. SIAM J. Comput. (2012)
33. Gennaro, R., Gertner, Y., Katz, J., Trevisan, L.: Bounds on the efficiency of generic cryptographic constructions. SIAM J. Comput. (2005)
34. Gentry, C., Halevi, S.: Compressible FHE with applications to PIR. In: TCC (2019)
35. Gentry, C., Ramzan, Z.: Single-database private information retrieval with constant communication rate. In: Caires, L., Italiano, G.F., Monteiro, L., Palamidessi, C., Yung, M. (eds.) ICALP 2005. LNCS, vol. 3580, pp. 803–815. Springer, Heidelberg (2005). https://doi.org/10.1007/11523468_65
36. Gilboa, N., Ishai, Y.: Distributed point functions and their applications. In: Nguyen, P.Q., Oswald, E. (eds.) EUROCRYPT 2014. LNCS, vol. 8441, pp. 640–658. Springer, Heidelberg (2014). https://doi.org/10.1007/978-3-642-55220-5_35
37. Goldreich, O., Karloff, H., Schulman, L.J., Trevisan, L.: Lower bounds for linear locally decodable codes and private information retrieval. In: CCC (2002)

38. Green, M., Ladd, W., Miers, I.: A protocol for privately reporting ad impressions at scale. In: ACM SIGSAC CCS (2016)
39. Groth, J., Kiayias, A., Lipmaa, H.: Multi-query computationally-private information retrieval with constant communication rate. In: Nguyen, P.Q., Pointcheval, D. (eds.) PKC 2010. LNCS, vol. 6056, pp. 107–123. Springer, Heidelberg (2010). https://doi.org/10.1007/978-3-642-13013-7_7
40. Gupta, T., Crooks, N., Mulhern, W., Setty, S., Alvisi, L., Walfish, M.: Scalable and private media consumption with Popcorn. In: USENIX NSDI (2016)
41. Hamlin, A., Ostrovsky, R., Weiss, M., Wichs, D.: Private anonymous data access. In: Ishai, Y., Rijmen, V. (eds.) EUROCRYPT 2019. LNCS, vol. 11477, pp. 244–273. Springer, Cham (2019). https://doi.org/10.1007/978-3-030-17656-3_9
42. Henry, R.: Polynomial batch codes for efficient IT-PIR. In: PoPETS (2016)
43. Henry, R., Huang, Y., Goldberg, I.: One (block) size fits all: PIR and SPIR with variable-length records via multi-block queries. In: NDSS (2013)
44. Henzinger, A., Hong, M.M., Corrigan-Gibbs, H., Meiklejohn, S., Vaikuntanathan, V.: One server for the price of two: simple and fast single-server private information retrieval. In: USENIX Security (2023)
45. Henzinger, M., Krinninger, S., Nanongkai, D., Saranurak, T.: Unifying and strengthening hardness for dynamic problems via the online matrix-vector multiplication conjecture. In: STOC (2015)
46. Hubáček, P., Koucký, M., Král, K., Slívová, V.: Stronger lower bounds for online ORAM. In: TCC (2019)
47. Ishai, Y., Kushilevitz, E., Ostrovsky, R., Sahai, A.: Batch codes and their applications. In: ACM Symposium on Theory of Computing (2004)
48. Jacob, R., Larsen, K.G., Nielsen, J.B.: Lower bounds for oblivious data structures. In: SODA (2019)
49. Kogan, D., Corrigan-Gibbs, H.: Private blocklist lookups with checklist. In: USENIX Security (2021)
50. Komargodski, I., Lin, W.-K.: A logarithmic lower bound for oblivious RAM (for all parameters). In: Malkin, T., Peikert, C. (eds.) CRYPTO 2021. LNCS, vol. 12828, pp. 579–609. Springer, Cham (2021). https://doi.org/10.1007/978-3-030-84259-8_20
51. Kushilevitz, E., Ostrovsky, R.: Replication is not needed: single database, computationally-private information retrieval. In: FOCS (1997)
52. Kushilevitz, E., Ostrovsky, R.: One-way trapdoor permutations are sufficient for non-trivial single-server private information retrieval. In: Preneel, B. (ed.) EUROCRYPT 2000. LNCS, vol. 1807, pp. 104–121. Springer, Heidelberg (2000). https://doi.org/10.1007/3-540-45539-6_9
53. Larsen, K.G.: The cell probe complexity of dynamic range counting. In: STOC (2012)
54. Larsen, K.G., Nielsen, J.B.: Yes, there is an oblivious RAM lower bound! In: Shacham, H., Boldyreva, A. (eds.) CRYPTO 2018. LNCS, vol. 10992, pp. 523–542. Springer, Cham (2018). https://doi.org/10.1007/978-3-319-96881-0_18
55. Larsen, K.G., Williams, R.: Faster online matrix-vector multiplication. In: SODA (2017)
56. Lueks, W., Goldberg, I.: Sublinear scaling for multi-client private information retrieval. In: Böhme, R., Okamoto, T. (eds.) FC 2015. LNCS, vol. 8975, pp. 168–186. Springer, Heidelberg (2015). https://doi.org/10.1007/978-3-662-47854-7_10
57. Mittal, P., Olumofin, F., Troncoso, C., Borisov, N., Goldberg, I.: PIR-Tor: scalable anonymous communication using private information retrieval. In: USENIX Security Symposium (2011)

58. Mughees, M.H., Chen, H., Ren, L.: OnionPIR: response efficient single-server PIR. In: ACM SIGSAC CCS (2021)

59. Ostrovsky, R., Skeith, W.E.: A survey of single-database private information retrieval: techniques and applications. In: Okamoto, T., Wang, X. (eds.) PKC 2007. LNCS, vol. 4450, pp. 393–411. Springer, Heidelberg (2007). https://doi.org/10.1007/978-3-540-71677-8_26

60. Patel, S., Persiano, G., Yeo, K.: Private stateful information retrieval. In: ACM SIGSAC CCS (2018)

61. Patel, S., Persiano, G., Yeo, K.: Lower bounds for encrypted multi-maps and searchable encryption in the leakage cell probe model. In: Micciancio, D., Ristenpart, T. (eds.) CRYPTO 2020. LNCS, vol. 12170, pp. 433–463. Springer, Cham (2020). https://doi.org/10.1007/978-3-030-56784-2_15

62. Paterson, M.B., Stinson, D.R., Wei, R.: Combinatorial batch codes. Adv. Math. Commun. (2009)

63. Persiano, G., Yeo, K.: Lower bounds for differentially private RAMs. In: Ishai, Y., Rijmen, V. (eds.) EUROCRYPT 2019. LNCS, vol. 11476, pp. 404–434. Springer, Cham (2019). https://doi.org/10.1007/978-3-030-17653-2_14

64. Persiano, G., Yeo, K.: Limits of preprocessing for single-server PIR. In: Annual ACM-SIAM Symposium on Discrete Algorithms (2022)

65. Persiano, G., Yeo, K.: Lower bound framework for differentially private and oblivious data structures. In: Hazay, C., Stam, M. (eds.) EUROCRYPT 2023, LNCS 14004, pp. xx–yy, 2023. Springer, Heidelberg (2023)

66. Servan-Schreiber, S., Hogan, K., Devadas, S.: Adveil: a private targeted-advertising ecosystem. Cryptology ePrint Archive (2021)

67. Shi, E., Aqeel, W., Chandrasekaran, B., Maggs, B.: Puncturable pseudorandom sets and private information retrieval with near-optimal online bandwidth and time. In: Malkin, T., Peikert, C. (eds.) CRYPTO 2021. LNCS, vol. 12828, pp. 641–669. Springer, Cham (2021). https://doi.org/10.1007/978-3-030-84259-8_22

68. Unruh, D.: Random Oracles and auxiliary input. In: Menezes, A. (ed.) CRYPTO 2007. LNCS, vol. 4622, pp. 205–223. Springer, Heidelberg (2007). https://doi.org/10.1007/978-3-540-74143-5_12

69. Wehner, S., de Wolf, R.: Improved lower bounds for locally decodable codes and private information retrieval. In: Caires, L., Italiano, G.F., Monteiro, L., Palamidessi, C., Yung, M. (eds.) ICALP 2005. LNCS, vol. 3580, pp. 1424–1436. Springer, Heidelberg (2005). https://doi.org/10.1007/11523468_115

70. Yekhanin, S.: Towards 3-query locally decodable codes of subexponential length. J. ACM (2008)

71. Yeo, K.: Lower bounds for (batch) pir with private preprocessing. Cryptology ePrint Archive, Paper 2022/828 (2022). https://eprint.iacr.org/2022/828

How to Compress Encrypted Data

Nils Fleischhacker[1]($\boxtimes$) , Kasper Green Larsen[2] , and Mark Simkin[3]

[1] Ruhr University Bochum, Bochum, Germany
mail@nilsfleischhacker.de
[2] Aarhus University, Aarhus, Denmark
larsen@cs.au.dk
[3] Ethereum Foundation, Aarhus, Denmark
mark.simkin@ethereum.org

Abstract. We study the task of obliviously compressing a vector comprised of n ciphertexts of size ξ bits each, where at most t of the corresponding plaintexts are non-zero. This problem commonly features in applications involving encrypted outsourced storages, such as searchable encryption or oblivious message retrieval. We present two new algorithms with provable worst-case guarantees, solving this problem by using only homomorphic additions and multiplications by constants. Both of our new constructions improve upon the state of the art asymptotically and concretely.

Our first construction, based on sparse polynomials, is perfectly correct and the first to achieve an asymptotically optimal compression rate by compressing the input vector into $\mathcal{O}(t\xi)$ bits. Compression can be performed homomorphically by performing $\mathcal{O}(n \log n)$ homomorphic additions and multiplications by constants. The main drawback of this construction is a decoding complexity of $\Omega(\sqrt{n})$.

Our second construction is based on a novel variant of invertible bloom lookup tables and is correct with probability $1 - 2^{-\kappa}$. It has a slightly worse compression rate compared to our first construction as it compresses the input vector into $\mathcal{O}(\xi\kappa t/\log t)$ bits, where $\kappa \geq \log t$. In exchange, both compression and decompression of this construction are highly efficient. The compression complexity is dominated by $\mathcal{O}(n\kappa/\log t)$ homomorphic additions and multiplications by constants. The decompression complexity is dominated by $\mathcal{O}(\kappa t/\log t)$ decryption operations and equally many inversions of a pseudorandom permutation.

1 Introduction

It is well known that in general encrypted data cannot be compressed. In this work, we study the task of compressing encrypted data, when a small amount

N. Fleischhacker—Funded by the Deutsche Forschungsgemeinschaft (DFG, German Research Foundation) under Germany's Excellence Strategy - EXC 2092 CASA - 390781972.
K. G. Larsen—Supported by Independent Research Fund Denmark (DFF) Sapere Aude Research Leader grant No. 9064-00068B.

C. Hazay and M. Stam (Eds.): EUROCRYPT 2023, LNCS 14004, pp. 551–577, 2023.
https://doi.org/10.1007/978-3-031-30545-0_19

of knowledge about the structure of the underlying plaintexts is known. More concretely, we consider encryptions of vectors $\boldsymbol{m} = (m_1, \ldots, m_n)$ where at most t distinct coordinates in $\boldsymbol{m}$ are non-zero. In the context of outsourced storage applications the task of compressing such vectors appears naturally.

In searchable encryption [3,26], we have a client Charlie, who holds a vector $(m_1, \ldots, m_n)$ of data elements and wants to store it remotely on server Sally. To hide the contents of the data elements, Charlie encrypts the data vector under a secret key only she knows before sending it to Sally. Later on, Charlie may want to search through the vector and retrieve all elements that match some secret keyword. A series of recent works [1,6–8,18,27] have shown how to construct searchable encryption schemes from fully homomorphic encryption [12,22] with reasonable concrete efficiency. Conceptually, these approaches are comprised of two major steps. First Charlie sends a short keyword-dependent hint to the server, who uses it to obliviously transform the vector of ciphertexts $(c_1, \ldots, c_n)$ into a new vector $\tilde{\boldsymbol{c}} = (\tilde{c}_1, \ldots, \tilde{c}_n)$, where for $i \in \{1, \ldots, n\}$ the ciphertext $\tilde{c}_i$ is either an encryption of the original message m_i in c_i or zero, depending on whether m_i was matching the keyword of Charlie or not. In the second step, the server obliviously compresses the vector $\tilde{\boldsymbol{c}}$ under the assumption that no more than t ciphertexts were matching the keyword and sends it back to Charlie. If the assumption about the sparsity of the vector $\tilde{\boldsymbol{c}}$ was correct, then Charlie successfully decodes the vector and obtains the desired result. If the assumption was not correct, then Charlie may not be able to retrieve the output.

The best compression algorithm used in this context is due to Choi et al. [8], which compresses $\tilde{\boldsymbol{c}}$ into a bit string of length $\Omega(t\xi(\kappa + \log n))$, where ξ is the length of one ciphertext entry. Under the assumption that the plaintext messages are of a specific form[1], the authors show that Charlie can correctly decode the vector with probability $1 - 2^{-\kappa}$. Both compressing and decoding are computationally concretely efficient.

In the oblivious message retrieval setting, recently introduced by Liu and Tromer [19], we have a server Sally, who keeps a public bulletin board, and multiple clients Charlie, Chucky, and Chris. Each of the clients can post encrypted messages for any of the other clients on the bulletin board, but would like to hide who is the recipient of which message. At some point, for example, Chucky may want to retrieve all messages that are intended for him. Naively, he could simply download all contents from Sally's bulletin board, but this would incur a large bandwidth overhead that is linear in the total number of messages stored by Sally. Instead, the idea behind oblivious message retrieval is to let Chucky generate a short identity-dependent hint that can be used by Sally to obliviously generate a short message that contains all relevant encrypted messages for Chucky. Conceptually, the construction of Liu and Tromer follows the exact same blueprint as the searchable encryption scheme outlined above. First Sally obliviously filters her vector with the hint provided by Chucky and then she

---

[1] This assumption can be removed at the cost of doubling the size of the compressed vector and additionally assuming that one is not only given $\tilde{c}$, but also some auxiliary vector $\hat{c}$ as the output of the first step of their protocol.

obliviously compresses the filtered vector under the assumption that not too many messages are addressed to Chucky.

From an efficiency perspective, the solution of Liu and Tromer is rather expensive. To compress, Sally performs $\Omega(tn + \kappa t \log t)$ homomorphic additions and $\Omega(tn)$ homomorphic multiplications by constants, where κ is the correctness error defined as in the searchable encryption example. Sally's message to Chucky is $\Omega(\xi t + \xi \kappa t \log t)$ bits long. To decode the result from Sally's message, Chucky needs to perform gaussian elimination on a matrix of size $\mathcal{O}(t) \times \mathcal{O}(t)$, which incurs a computational overhead of $\Omega(t^3)$. The authors provide heuristic optimizations of their constructions that improve their performance significantly, but unfortunately these come without asymptotic bounds or provable correctness guarantees.

Taking a step back and looking at the two applications described above from a more abstract point of view, one can recognize that both follow a very similar blueprint. In the first step, both apply some vastly different techniques to convert a vector of ciphertexts into a sparse vector containing only the desired entries. In the second step, both works solve the identical problem. They both need to compress a sparse homomorphically encrypted vector with nothing but the knowledge of how many entries are non-zero, and in particular without any knowledge about which entries are zero and which ones are not. How to compress such a sparse encrypted vector is the topic of this work.

1.1   Our Contribution

We present two new algorithms, one based on polynomials and one based on algorithmic hashing, for compressing sparse encrypted vectors, which both improve upon the prior state of the art in terms of compression rate. Our algorithms only rely on homomorphic additions and homomorphic multiplications by constants. Both of our constructions have provable worst-case bounds for all their parameters.

Compressing via Polynomials. Our first construction (Sect. 4) is perfectly correct and is based on the concept of sparse polynomial interpolation. Its compression rate has an asymptotically optimal dependence on t, as the compressed vector is merely $\mathcal{O}(\xi \cdot t)$ bits large. During compression one needs to perform $\mathcal{O}(n \log n)$ homomorphic additions and equally many homomorphic multiplications by constants. The main bottleneck of this solution is the decompression complexity of $\tilde{\mathcal{O}}(t \cdot \sqrt{n})$, which depends on the length n of the original vector. Although the compression rate is much better than that of previous works, such as those Choi et al. [8] and that of Liu and Tromer [19], this construction suffers from a slower decompression time.

Compressing via Hashing. Our second construction (Sect. 5) is a randomized hashing based solution, which is correct with probability $1 - 2^{-\kappa}$, where the probability is taken over the random coins of the compression algorithm. We develop a novel data structure that is heavily inspired by the invertible bloom lookup tables of Goodrich and Mitzenmacher [14], but can be applied efficiently to encrypted data. Both compression and decompression are highly efficient. During compression one needs to perform $\mathcal{O}(n\kappa/\log t)$ homomorphic additions and multiplications by constants, where $\kappa \geq \log t$. During decompression the main costs come from $\mathcal{O}(\kappa t/\log t)$ many decryptions and equally many evaluations of a pseudorandom permutation. In contrast to our polynomial based solution, however, the compressed vector is $\mathcal{O}(\xi\kappa t/\log t)$ bits large. Nevertheless, this construction outperforms all prior works in terms of compression rate, while having either superior or comparable compression and decompression complexities.

1.2   Strawman Approach

When the sparse vector is encrypted using a fully homomorphic encryption scheme, conceptually simple solutions to the compression problem exist. For instance, Sally could just homomorphically sort all entries in the vector and then only send back the t largest entries. Such solutions, however, require her to perform multiplications of encrypted values. This is problematic for multiple reasons. Multiplications of encrypted values are much more computationally expensive than homomorphic additions or multiplications by constants. Since Sally may potentially store a very large database, we would like to minimize her computational overhead. Furthermore, if the data is encrypted using a somewhat homomorphic encryption scheme, then the multiplicative depth of the circuit that can be executed on the vector by Sally is bounded. Ideally, we would like the compression step to be concretely efficient and not require the use of any multiplications of encrypted values. For these reasons, we only focus on compression algorithms that require homomorphic additions and multiplications by constants in this work.

1.3   Additional Related Works

In addition to what has already been discussed above, there are several other works that are related to ours. Johnson, Wagner, and Ramchandran [16] showed that, assuming messages from a source with bounded entropy, it is possible to compress one-time pad encryptions without knowledge of the encryption key through a clever application of Slepian-Wolf coding [24]. Their result only applied to linear stream ciphers but was later extended to block ciphers using certain chaining modes by Klinc et al. [17]. These result do not apply to our setting, where we focus on compressing vectors encrypted using more complex homomorphic public-key encryption schemes.

In the context of fully homomorphic encryption, multiple works [4,20,25] have studied the question of how to optimize the encryption rate, i.e., the size of the ciphertext relative to the size of the plaintext, by packing multiple plaintexts into one ciphertext. These results are related, but do not allow for obliviously "removing" irrelevant encryptions of zero.

Another line of works [5,11,13] studies the compressed sensing problem, where the task is to design a matrix A such that it is possible to recover, possibly high-dimensional, but sparse vectors x from a vector of measurements Ax of small dimension. In general these works aim to recover an approximation of x even when given somewhat noisy measurements. In our case, we are interested in the simpler problem of exact recovery of a sparse vector. Our construction based on polynomials can be seen as a matrix-vector multiplication. Looking ahead, our matrix A will be a carefully chosen Vandermonde matrix that allows for very efficient matrix vector multiplication. The server will multiply this public matrix with the encrypted vector and send back the result that can be decoded by the client. Our second construction, based on hashing, does not fall into this category of algorithms.

2 Preliminaries

Notation. Given a possibly randomized function $f : X \to Y$, we will sometimes abuse notation and write $f(\boldsymbol{x}) := (f(x_1), \ldots, f(x_n))$ for $\boldsymbol{x} \in X^n$. For a set X, we write $x \leftarrow X$ to denote the process of sampling a uniformly random element $x \in X$. For a vector $\boldsymbol{v} \in X^n$, we write v_i to denote its i-th component. For a matrix $M \in X^{n \times m}$, we write $M[i, j]$ to denote the cell in the i-th row and j-th column. We write $[n]$ to denote the set $\{1, \ldots, n\}$. For a set X^n, we define the scissor operator $\gg\!\!<(X^n) := \{(x_1, \ldots, x_n) \in X^n \mid x_i \neq x_j \ \forall i, j \in [n]\}$ to denote the subset of X^n consisting only of those vectors with unique entries.

Definition 1 (Sparse Vector Representation). *Let $\mathbb{F}_q$ be a field and let $\boldsymbol{a} \in \mathbb{F}_q^n$ be a vector. The sparse representation of $\boldsymbol{a}$ is the set $\mathsf{sparse}(\boldsymbol{a}) := \{(i, a_i) \mid a_i \neq 0\}$.*

2.1 Homomorphic Encryption

Informally, a homomorphic encryption scheme allows for computing an encryption of $f(\boldsymbol{m})$, when only given the description of f and an encryption of message vector $\boldsymbol{m}$. Throughout the paper, we assume that functions are represented as circuits composed of addition and multiplication gates.

Definition 2. *A homomorphic encryption scheme $\mathcal{E}$ is defined by a tuple of PPT algorithms* (Gen, Enc, Eval, Dec) *that work as follows:*

Gen(1^λ): *The key generation algorithm takes the security parameter 1^λ as input and returns a secret key* sk *and public key* pk. *The public key implicitly defines a message space $\mathcal{M}$ and ciphertext space $\mathcal{C}$. We denote the set of all public keys as $\mathcal{P}$.*

Enc(pk, m): *The encryption algorithm takes the public key* pk *and message $m \in \mathcal{M}$ as input and returns a ciphertext $c \in \mathcal{C}$.*

Eval(pk, f, $\boldsymbol{c}$): *The evaluation algorithm takes the public key* pk, *a function $f : \mathcal{M}^n \to \mathcal{M}^m$, and a vector $\boldsymbol{c} \in \mathcal{C}^n$ of ciphertexts as input and returns a new vector of ciphertexts $\tilde{\boldsymbol{c}} \in \mathcal{C}^m$.*

Dec(sk, c): *The deterministic decryption algorithm takes the secret key* sk *and ciphertext* $c \in \mathcal{C}$ *as input and returns a message* $m \in \mathcal{M} \cup \{\bot\}$.

Throughout the paper we assume that the ciphertext size is fixed and does not increase through the use of the homomorphic evaluation algorithm. We extend the definition of Enc and Dec to vectors and matrices of messages and ciphertexts respectively, by applying them componentwise, i.e., for any matrix $M \in \mathcal{M}^{n \times m}$, we have $\mathsf{Enc}(\mathsf{pk}, M) = C$ with $C \in \mathcal{C}^{n \times m}$ and $C[i, j] = \mathsf{Enc}(\mathsf{pk}, M[i, j])$ and equivalently $\mathsf{Dec}(\mathsf{sk}, C) = M'$ with $M' \in \mathcal{M}^{n \times m}$ and $M'[i, j] = \mathsf{Dec}(\mathsf{sk}, C[i, j])$. Let $\mathcal{E}$ be an additively homomorphic encryption scheme with message space $\mathcal{M} = \mathbb{F}_q$ for some prime power q. And let $f : \mathbb{F}_q^2 \to \mathbb{F}_q$, $f(a, b) := a + b$ and let $g_\alpha : \mathbb{F}_q \to \mathbb{F}_q$, $g(a) := \alpha \cdot a$ for any constant $\alpha \in \mathbb{F}_q$. For notational convenience we write $\mathsf{Eval}(\mathsf{pk}, f, (c_1, c_2)^\mathsf{T})$ as $c_1 \boxplus c_2$ and $\mathsf{Eval}(\mathsf{pk}, g_\alpha, c)$ as $\alpha \boxdot c$ with pk being inferrable from context. For the sake of simplicity we restrict ourselves to homomorphic encryption schemes with unique secret keys, i.e. for a given pk, there exists at most one sk, such that $(\mathsf{sk}, \mathsf{pk}) \leftarrow \mathsf{Gen}(1^\lambda)$. We write $\mathsf{Gen}^{-1}(\mathsf{pk})$ to denote the – not efficiently computable – unique secret key.

Later on in the paper, it will be convenient for us to talk about ciphertexts that may not be fresh encryptions, but still allow for some homomorphic operations to be performed on them.

Definition 3 ($\mathcal{Z}$-Validity). *Let* (Gen, Enc, Eval, Dec) *be a homomorphic encryption scheme, let* $\mathcal{Z}$ *be a class of circuits, and let* pk *be a public key. A vector* c *of ciphertexts is* $\mathcal{Z}$-valid *for* pk, *iff for all functions* $f \in \mathcal{Z}$ *it holds that* $\bot \notin \mathsf{Dec}(\mathsf{Gen}^{-1}(\mathsf{pk}), c)$ *and* $\mathsf{Dec}(\mathsf{Gen}^{-1}(\mathsf{pk}), \mathsf{Eval}(\mathsf{pk}, f, c)) = f(\mathsf{Dec}(\mathsf{sk}, c))$. *We denote by* $\mathsf{vld}(\mathcal{Z}, \mathsf{pk})$ *the set of ciphertext vectors* $\mathcal{Z}$-valid *for* pk.

2.2 Polynomial Kung Fu

Let $f(x) = \sum_{i=0}^{d} a_i \cdot x^i \in \mathbb{F}_q[x]$ be a polynomial with coefficients from a finite field $\mathbb{F}_q$. The degree of f is defined as the largest exponent in any monomial with a non-zero coefficient. We say that f is s-sparse, if the number of non-zero monomials is at most s or more formally if $|\{a_i \mid a_i \neq 0 \wedge i \in [n]\}| \leq s$. It is well-known that any polynomial of degree at most d can be interpolated from $d+1$ evaluation points. In this work, we will make use of the less well-known fact that sparse polynomials can be interpolated from a number of evaluation points that is linear in the polynomial's sparsity. The first algorithms for interpolating sparse univariate and multivariate polynomials were presented by Prony [21] and Ben-Or and Tiwari [2] respectively. We will make use of the following result by Huang and Gao [15] for sparse interpolation of univariate polynomials over finite fields:

Theorem 4 ([15]). *Let* $f \in \mathbb{F}_q[x]$ *be an* s-sparse univariate polynomial of degree at most d with coefficients from a finite field $\mathbb{F}_q$. Let $\omega \in \mathbb{F}_q$ be a primitive $2(s + 1)$-th root of unity. There exists an algorithm Interpolate that takes evaluations $f(\omega^0), \ldots, f(\omega^{2s+1})$ as input and returns the coefficients of f in sparse representation in time $\tilde{\mathcal{O}}(s \cdot \sqrt{d})$.*

The algorithm of Huang and Gao relies on a subroutine for finding discrete logarithms. Using Shank's algorithm [23] for this step, we obtain the computational complexity stated in the above theorem with deterministic performance guarantees.

Another tool we will use is the Fast Fourier Transform, (re-)discovered by Cooley and Tukey [9] which allows for evaluating a degree d polynomial given as a list of coefficients at $\ell \leq d$ evaluation points simultaneously in time $\mathcal{O}(d \log d)$. More precisely, for a fixed set of evaluation points $(\omega^0, \ldots, \omega^\ell)$, one can represent the circuit taking the polynomial coefficients $(a_0, \ldots, a_d)$ as input and returning $(f(\omega^0), \ldots, f(\omega^\ell))$ as a series of $\mathcal{O}(\log d)$ alternating layers of $\mathcal{O}(d)$ addition or multiplication by constants gates respectively.

Theorem 5 [Fast Fourier Transform]. *Let $d, \ell \in \mathbb{N}$ with $d \geq \ell$. Let $f = \sum_{i=0}^{d} a_i \cdot x^i \in \mathbb{F}_q[x]$ be a polynomial of degree at most d with coefficients from a finite field $\mathbb{F}_q$. Let $\omega \in \mathbb{F}_q$ be a primitive ℓ-th root of unity. There exists an arithmetic circuit FFT comprised of a series of $\mathcal{O}(\log d)$ alternating layers of $\mathcal{O}(d)$ addition or multiplication by constants gates respectively that takes $(a_0, \ldots, a_d)$ as well as $(\omega^0, \ldots, \omega^\ell)$ as input and returns $(f(\omega^0), \ldots, f(\omega^\ell))$.*

2.3 Invertible Bloom Lookup Tables

An invertible Bloom lookup table (IBLT) is a data structure first introduced by Goodrich and Mitzenmacher [14] that supports three operations called Insert, Peel, and List. The insertion operations adds elements to the data structure, the deletion operations removes them[2] and the list operation recovers all currently present elements with high probability, if not too many elements are present.

The data structure consists of two $\gamma \times 8t$ matrices C, the count matrix and V the valueSum matrix. It further requires t-wise independent hash functions $h_i : \{0,1\}^* \to [8t]$ for $i \in [\gamma]$. Initially all values are set to 0. To insert an element x into the data structure, we locate the cells $C_{i,h_i(x)}$ and $V_{i,h_i(x)}$ for $i \in [\gamma]$ and add 1 to each counter and x to each valueSum. To remove an element, we perform the inverse operations. To list all elements currently present in (C, V), we repeatedly perform a peeling operation until (C, V) is empty. The peeling operation finds a cell with counter 1, adds that corresponding valueSum value to the output list and deletes the element from (C, V). The only way the list operation may fail is if (C, V) is not empty, but the peeling operation cannot find any cell with counter 1. It has been shown by Goodrich and Mitzenmacher that this probability decreases exponentially in $\gamma \log t$. We formally describe the algorithms in Fig. 1.

Theorem 6 ([14]). *Let $h_1, \ldots, h_\gamma$ be t-wise independent hash functions, then for any $X = \{x_1, \ldots, x_t\}$ it holds that*

$$\Pr\left[B := \mathsf{Insert}((0^2)^{\gamma \times 8t}, X) : \mathsf{List}(B) \neq X\right] \leq \mathcal{O}(2^{-(\gamma-2)\log t}),$$

---

[2] For the present discussion, we assume that only previously inserted elements are deleted.

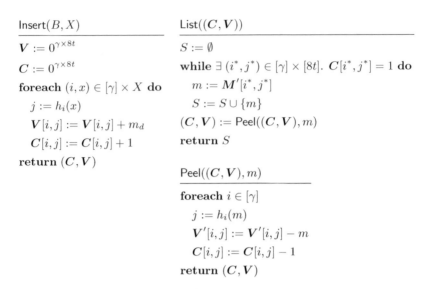

Fig. 1. An invertible Bloom lookup table

where the probability is taken over the random choices of $h_1, \ldots, h_\gamma$.

Remark 1. The construction of an IBLT can be modified to store tuples of values, by maintaining multiple valueSum matrices, one for each component. As long as one of the components remains unique among all inserted values, it is sufficient to use this component as input to the has functions, without affecting Theorem 6. We will make use of this in our construction in Sect. 5.

3   Ciphertext Compression

In this section we formally define the concept of a ciphertext compression scheme (Compress, Decompress). Intuitively, the compression algorithm takes the public encryption key pk as well as a vector of ciphertexts c from some family $\mathcal{F}_{pk}$ of ciphertext vectors as input and returns some compressed representation thereof. The decompression algorithm gets the compressed representation as well as the secret decryption key as input and should return the decryption of c.

Definition 7 (Ciphertext Compression Scheme). *Let $\mathcal{E} = (\mathsf{Gen}, \mathsf{Enc}, \mathsf{Eval}, \mathsf{Dec})$ be a homomorphic public key encryption scheme with ciphertext size $\xi = \xi(\lambda)$. Let $\mathcal{P}$ be the public key space of $\mathcal{E}$. For each $\mathsf{pk} \in \mathcal{P}$ let $\mathcal{F}_{pk}$ be a set of ciphertext vectors. A δ-compressing, $(1 - \epsilon)$-correct ciphertext compression scheme for the family $\mathcal{F} := \{\mathcal{F}_{pk} \mid \mathsf{pk} \in \mathcal{P}\}$ is a pair of PPT algorithms (Compress, Decompress), such that for any $(\mathsf{sk}, \mathsf{pk}) \leftarrow \mathsf{Gen}(1^\lambda)$ and any $c \in \mathcal{F}_{pk}$ the output length of $\mathsf{Compress}(\mathsf{pk}, c)$ is at most $\delta\xi|c|$ and it holds that*

$$\Pr[\mathsf{Decompress}(\mathsf{sk}, \mathsf{Compress}(\mathsf{pk}, c)) = \mathsf{sparse}(\mathsf{Dec}(\mathsf{sk}, c))] = 1 - \epsilon(\lambda),$$

where the probability is taken over the random coins of the compression and decompression algorithms.

Remark 2. Note, that a ciphertext compression scheme gives no guarantee whatsoever in the case where $c \notin \mathcal{F}_{\mathsf{pk}}$.

4 Compression via Sparse Polynomials

In this section we present our first construction, which is based on the idea of interpolating sparse polynomials. Given the right building blocks, the construction is conceptually very simple. We simply view the sparse encrypted vector $(c_1, \ldots, c_n)$ as the coefficient representation of sparse polynomial. Using the Fast Fourier Transform, we homomorphically evaluate this polynomial efficiently at some sufficient number of points. These encrypted evaluations will constitute the compression of the vector. To obtain the original vector during decompression, we simply decrypt the evaluation points and interpolate the corresponding sparse polynomial.

Definition 8 (Fast Fourier Functions). *The class of fast fourier functions is the set of functions* $\mathcal{Z}_{\mathsf{FFT}}^{\ell} = \{f_x^{\ell} \mid x \in \mathbb{F}_q^{\ell}\}$ *with*

$$f_x^{\ell} : \mathbb{F}_q^n \to \mathbb{F}_q^{\ell}, \quad f_x(a) := \mathsf{FFT}(a, x).$$

Definition 9. ($\mathcal{Z}_{\mathsf{FFT}}^{2(t+1)}$**-Valid Low Hamming Weight Ciphertext Vectors).** *Let* $\mathcal{E} = (\mathsf{Gen}, \mathsf{Enc}, \mathsf{Eval}, \mathsf{Dec})$ *be a homomorphic public key encryption scheme. For any* $\mathsf{pk} \in \mathcal{P}$, *let*

$$\mathcal{F}_{t,\mathsf{pk}}^{\mathsf{FFT}} := \big\{ c \in \mathsf{vld}(\mathcal{Z}_{\mathsf{FFT}}^{2(t+1)}, \mathsf{pk}) \mid \mathsf{hw}(\mathsf{Dec}(\mathsf{Gen}^{-1}(\mathsf{pk}), c)) < t \big\}.$$

We then define the family of $\mathcal{Z}_{\mathsf{FFT}}^{2(t+1)}$*-valid ciphertext vectors with low hamming weight as* $\mathcal{F}_t^{\mathsf{FFT}} := \{\mathcal{F}_{t,\mathsf{pk}}^{\mathsf{FFT}} \mid \mathsf{pk} \in \mathcal{P}\}$.

Compress(pk, c)	Decompress($\mathsf{sk}, \tilde{c}$)
$\tilde{c} \leftarrow \mathsf{Eval}\big(\mathsf{pk}, \mathsf{FFT}(\cdot, (\omega^0, \ldots, \omega^{2t+1})), c\big)$	$m \leftarrow \mathsf{Dec}(\mathsf{sk}, \tilde{c})$
return $\tilde{c}$	$S \leftarrow \mathsf{Interpolate}(m)$
	return S

Fig. 2. A ciphertext compression scheme for $\mathcal{F}_t^{\mathsf{FFT}}$ based on sparse polynomials. Here $\mathsf{FFT}(\cdot, (\omega^0, \ldots, \omega^{2t+1}))$ refers to the circuit of the function $f_{(\omega^0, \ldots, \omega^{2t+1})}$ from Definition 8, i.e., the FFT circuit with the hardcoded second input $(\omega^0, \ldots, \omega^{2t+1})$.

Theorem 10. *Let* $\mathcal{E} = (\mathsf{Gen}, \mathsf{Enc}, \mathsf{Eval}, \mathsf{Dec})$ *be an additively homomorphic encryption scheme with message space* $\mathcal{M} = \mathbb{F}_q$ *with ciphertext size* $\xi = \xi(\lambda)$. *Let* $n, t \in \mathbb{N}$ *be integers such that* $n < q$ *and let* $\omega \in \mathbb{F}_q$ *be a* $2(t+1)$-*th primitive root of unity. Then* $(\mathsf{Compress}, \mathsf{Decompress})$ *from Fig. 2 is a* $2(t+1)/n$-*compressing perfectly correct ciphertext compression scheme for family* $\mathcal{F}_t^{\mathsf{FFT}}$.

Proof. Let $\boldsymbol{c}$ be an arbitrary, but fixed $\mathcal{Z}_{\mathsf{FFT}}^{2(t+1)}$-valid ciphertext vector and let S be an arbitrary vector in sparse representation. Due to the validity condition on $\boldsymbol{c}$ we know that

$$
\Pr \left[
\begin{array}{r}
\tilde{\boldsymbol{c}} \leftarrow \mathsf{Eval}\left(\mathsf{pk}, \mathsf{FFT}\left(\cdot, (\omega^0, \ldots, \omega^{2t+1})\right), \boldsymbol{c}\right) \\
\boldsymbol{m} \leftarrow \mathsf{Dec}(\mathsf{sk}, \tilde{\boldsymbol{c}}) \\
S = \mathsf{Interpolate}(\boldsymbol{m})
\end{array}
\right]
$$

$$
= \Pr \left[
\begin{array}{r}
\boldsymbol{m} \leftarrow \mathsf{Dec}(\mathsf{sk}, \boldsymbol{c}) \\
\boldsymbol{m}' \leftarrow \mathsf{FFT}\left(\boldsymbol{m}, (\omega^0, \ldots, \omega^{2t+1})\right) \\
S = \mathsf{Interpolate}(\boldsymbol{m}')
\end{array}
\right].
$$

Furthermore, the $\mathcal{Z}_{\mathsf{FFT}}^{2(t+1)}$-validity of $\boldsymbol{c}$ tells us that $\mathsf{Dec}(\mathsf{sk}, \boldsymbol{c})$ is a vector of hamming weight at most t or, when viewed as a polynomial in coefficient representation, a t-sparse polynomial of degree at most n. From Theorem 4 it follows this sparse polynomial can be correctly interpolated from its $2(t+1)$ evaluations produced by $\mathsf{FFT}(\mathsf{Dec}(\mathsf{sk}, \boldsymbol{c}), (\omega^0, \ldots, \omega^{2t+1}))$ and therefore

$$
\mathsf{Interpolate}(\mathsf{FFT}(\mathsf{Dec}(\mathsf{sk}, \boldsymbol{c}), (\omega^0, \ldots, \omega^{2t+1}))) = \mathsf{sparse}(\mathsf{Dec}(\mathsf{sk}, \boldsymbol{c})).
$$

The output of $\mathsf{Compress}$ is a vector of $2(t+1)$ ciphertexts of size ξ and thus the scheme is $2(t+1)/n$ compressing. □

5   Compression via IBLTs

In this section we present our second construction, which is on a variant of invertible Bloom lookup tables. Given a vector of ciphertexts $\boldsymbol{c}$ the idea is to homomorphically insert the corresponding non-zero plaintexts into an (encrypted) IBLT. The encrypted IBLT would then constitute the compression of the vector.

This approach encounters two problems: First, the insertion operation of an IBLT requires hashing the value to choose the cells to insert it in, which we cannot do because we do not have access to the plaintext. Second, since we do not *know* which of the ciphertexts correspond to a non-zero it is unclear how to only insert those.

The first problem can be solved using Remark 1 by actually storing pairs (d, m_d). Since the index d is both publically known and unique, we can rely on only hashing d to derive the positions to insert the values.

The second problem is a bit trickier to solve. To build some intuition, we can first consider an easier compression problem where in addition to $\boldsymbol{c}$ we are given an additional vector of ciphertexts $\boldsymbol{h}$ containing "zero hints". I.e., h_d decrypts to 0 if c_i decrypts to 0 and h_d decrypts to 1, if c_d decrypts to anything else.

The IBLT then gets initialized as three matrices, a count matrix $\boldsymbol{C}$ and two valueSum matrices $\boldsymbol{M}$ and $\boldsymbol{D}$ with each cell containing an encryption of zero. To insert the content of ciphertext c_d into the IBLT, we can then for $i \in [\gamma]$ compute $j := h_i(d)$ and insert the value by setting $\boldsymbol{C}[i,j] := \boldsymbol{C} \boxplus h_d$, $\boldsymbol{M}[i,j] := \boldsymbol{M} \boxplus c_d$, and $\boldsymbol{D}[i,j] := \boldsymbol{D} \boxplus (d \boxdot h_d)$.

Note that for any ciphertext corresponding to zero, this results in zero being added to all entries, which is equivalent to not inserting the value at all. Decompressing then involves decrypting all three matrices and using the List algorithm to extract pairs (d, m_d) giving us a sparse representation of the plaintext vector corresponding to $\boldsymbol{c}$. By the correctness guarantee of an IBLT, this works as long as not too many ciphertexts decrypt to a non-zero value.

However, actually getting such "zero hint" ciphertexts may not be feasible in all scenarios, especially if the encryption scheme is *only* additively homomorphic. This means we need to somehow simulate having a count matrix without these zero hints.

The trick that we use is to choose a vector of random values $\boldsymbol{k}$ that we will use to "recognize" cells that only contain a single message. We will still initialize two matrices $\boldsymbol{M}$ and $\boldsymbol{K}$ but inserting into the IBLT is now done by setting $\boldsymbol{M}[i,j] := \boldsymbol{M} \boxplus c_d$, and $\boldsymbol{K}[i,j] := \boldsymbol{K} \boxplus (k_d \boxdot c_d)$. Note now, that after decryption, for any cell (i,j) that only contains a single value m_d, we have that $\boldsymbol{M}[i,j] = m_d$ and $\boldsymbol{K}[i,j] = k_d \cdot m_d$. By checking if $\boldsymbol{K}[i,j]/\boldsymbol{M}[i,j]$ corresponds to one of the values in $\boldsymbol{k}$, we can thus recognize which cells contain only a single value and which index it corresponds to, allowing us to peel the message from the IBLT. In section we prove in a helpful lemma in Sect. 5.2 we prove that we can bound the probability that this recognition procedure produces false positives.

There still remains the problem that simply using a random vector $\boldsymbol{k}$ and storing it, which would require $\mathcal{O}(n)$ storage and $\mathcal{O}(n)$ computation to recognize the entries. To solve this issue we introduce the concept of wunderbar pseudorandom vectors in Sect. 5.1, which allows us to store a compact $\mathcal{O}(\lambda)$ representation of a pseudorandom vector $\boldsymbol{k}$ and recognition of vector entries in time $\mathcal{O}(\mathsf{polylog}(n))$.

5.1   Wunderbar Pseudorandom Vectors

The concept of a pseudorandom vector is conceptually similar to that of pseudorandom sets introduced in [10], except that we do not require puncturability. The idea is that it allows us to sample a short description of a long vector, which is indistinguishable from a random vector with unique entries. Importantly, we require that there exists an efficient algorithm that can recover the position of a given entry in the vector in time independent of the vector length. Naively one can always find the position in linear time in the vector length. This is, however, not good enough for our application, which is why we require the pseudorandom vector to be "wunderbar". In particular, we want the description length of the vector to be in $\mathcal{O}(\lambda)$ and getting individual entries as well as index recovery should be possible in $\mathcal{O}(\mathsf{polylog}(n))$.

Definition 11. *A pseudorandom vector with index recovery for an efficiently sampleable universe $K = K(\lambda)$ consists of a triple of ppt algorithms* (Sample, Entry, Index) *such that*

Sample$(1^\lambda, n)$: *The sampling algorithm takes as input the security parameter λ and the vector length n in unary and outputs the description of a pseudorandom vector s.*

Entry(s, i): *The deterministic retrieving algorithm takes as input a description s and an index $i \in [n]$ and outputs a value $k_i \in K$.*

Index(s, k): *The deterministic index recovery algorithm takes as input a description s and a value k and outputs either an index $i \in [n]$ or $\perp$.*

A pseudorandom vector with index recovery is correct*, if for all vector lengths $n = \mathsf{poly}(\lambda)$ and all seeds $s \leftarrow \mathsf{Gen}(1^\lambda, 1^n)$ it holds that:*

1. *For all indices $i \in [n]$ it holds that* Index$(s, \mathsf{Entry}(s, i)) = i$.
2. *For all all $k^* \notin \{\mathsf{Entry}(s, i) \mid i \in [n]\}$ it holds that* Index$(s, k^*) = \perp$.

The pseudorandom vector is wunderbar *if the description of a vector has length $\mathcal{O}(\lambda)$ and the runtime of* Entry *and* Index *is $\mathcal{O}(\mathsf{polylog}(n))$. A pseudorandom vector is* secure*, if for all $n = \mathsf{poly}(\lambda)$ and all ppt algorithms $\mathcal{A}$*

$$\left| \Pr \left[\begin{array}{l} s \leftarrow \mathsf{Sample}(1^\lambda, 1^n), \\ \boldsymbol{k} := \begin{pmatrix} \mathsf{Entry}(s, 1) \\ \vdots \\ \mathsf{Entry}(s, n) \end{pmatrix} : \mathcal{A}(\boldsymbol{k}) \end{array} \right] - \Pr[\boldsymbol{k} \leftarrow \mathcal{K}(K^n) : \mathcal{A}(\boldsymbol{k})] \right| \leq \mathsf{negl}(\lambda)$$

Remark 3. For ease of notation we define two algorithms DummySample and DummyIndex that represent a dummy version of a pseudorandom vector with index recovery. I.e., DummySample$(1^\lambda, n)$ simply samples $\boldsymbol{k} \leftarrow \mathcal{K}(K^n)$ and DummyIndex$(\boldsymbol{k}, k)$ performs an exhaustive search and returns i iff $k_i = k$ and $\perp$ if none of them match. Using this notation, the above security definition can be rewritten as

$$\left| \Pr \left[\begin{array}{l} s \leftarrow \mathsf{Sample}(1^\lambda, 1^n), \\ \boldsymbol{k} := \begin{pmatrix} \mathsf{Entry}(s, 1) \\ \vdots \\ \mathsf{Entry}(s, n) \end{pmatrix} : \mathcal{A}(\boldsymbol{k}) \end{array} \right] - \Pr[\boldsymbol{k} \leftarrow \mathsf{DummySample}(1^\lambda, n) : \mathcal{A}(\boldsymbol{k})] \right|$$
$$\leq \mathsf{negl}(\lambda)$$

Wunderbar Pseudorandom Vectors from Pseudorandom Permuations. Let $\mathbb{F}_{p^m}$ be a field such that $m \cdot \lfloor \log p \rfloor \geq \lambda$. We construct wunderbar pseudorandom vectors over a subset $K \subseteq \mathbb{F}_{p^m}$ from an arbitrary family of pseudorandom permutations over $\mathbb{F}_2^\lambda$. To do so we need an efficiently computable and efficiently invertible injective function binToField mapping from $\mathbb{F}_2^\lambda$ to $\mathbb{F}_{p^m}$. The exact function is irrelevant, but for concreteness, we specify it in the following. Let $\{0,1\} : [q] \to \mathbb{F}_2^{\lceil \log q \rceil}$ denote the function that maps an integer to its canonical binary representation and let $\mathsf{proj} : \mathbb{F}_2^{\lceil \log q \rceil} \to [q]$ be its inverse. Then we specify

$$\mathsf{binToField} : \mathbb{F}_2^\lambda \to \mathbb{F}_{p^m} \quad \mathsf{binToField}((b_1, \ldots, b_\lambda)) := \sum_{i=0}^{m-1} c_i x^i$$

where

$$c_i := \sum_{j=1}^{\min\{\lceil \frac{\lambda}{m} \rceil, \lambda - i \lceil \frac{\lambda}{m} \rceil\}} 2^{j-1} b_{i\lceil \frac{\lambda}{m} \rceil + j}.$$

We further specify the inverse function as

$$\mathsf{fieldToBin} : \mathbb{F}_{p^m} \to \mathbb{F}_2^\lambda \cup \{\bot\}$$

$$\mathsf{fieldToBin}(\sum_{i=0}^{m-1} c_i x^i) := \begin{cases} \bot & \text{if } \exists c_i.\ c_i \geq 2^{\min\{\lceil \frac{\lambda}{m} \rceil, \lambda - i \lceil \frac{\lambda}{m} \rceil\}} \\ (b_1, \ldots, b_\lambda) & \text{otherwise} \end{cases}$$

where

$$b_i := \mathsf{bin}\left(c_{\lfloor i/\lceil \lambda/m \rceil \rfloor}\right)_{i - \lfloor i/\lceil \lambda/m \rceil \rfloor \cdot \lceil \lambda/m \rceil}.$$

Sample$(1^\lambda, 1^n)$	Entry$((s,n), i)$	Index$((s,n), k)$
$s \leftarrow \mathbb{F}_2^\lambda$	$\boldsymbol{b} := \mathsf{bin}(i)$	$\boldsymbol{b}' := \mathsf{fieldToBin}(k)$
return (s,n)	$\boldsymbol{b}' := \mathsf{PRP}(s, \boldsymbol{b})$	**if** $\boldsymbol{b}' \neq \bot$
	return $\mathsf{binToField}(\boldsymbol{b}')$	$\quad \boldsymbol{b} := \mathsf{PRP}^{-1}(s, \boldsymbol{b}')$
		$\quad$ **if** $\mathsf{proj}(\boldsymbol{b}) \in [n]$
		$\quad\quad$ **return** $\mathsf{proj}(\boldsymbol{b})$
		return $\bot$

Fig. 3. A wunderbar pseudorandom vector for $K \subseteq \mathbb{F}_{p^m}$ constructed from a family of pseudorandom permuations over $\mathbb{F}_2^\lambda$.

Theorem 12. *Let* PRP *be a secure family of pseudorandom permuations over some* $\mathbb{F}_2^\lambda$. *Then* $(\mathsf{Sample}, \mathsf{Entry}, \mathsf{Index})$ *as described in Fig. 3 is a secure wunderbar pseudorandom vector with index recovery for universe* $K = \{\mathsf{binToField}(\boldsymbol{b}) \mid \boldsymbol{b} \in \mathbb{F}_2^\lambda\}$.

Proof. We need to establish that the construction is correct, wunderbar, and secure. It is simple to see that the construction is correct:

$$
\begin{aligned}
&\mathsf{Index}((s,n), \mathsf{Entry}((s,n),i)) \\
&= \mathsf{Index}((s,n), \mathsf{binToField}(\mathsf{PRP}(s,\mathsf{bin}(i)))) &&\text{(Def. of Entry)} \\
&= \mathsf{proj}(\mathsf{PRP}^{-1}(s, \mathsf{fieldToBin}(\mathsf{binToField}(\mathsf{PRP}(s,\mathsf{bin}(i)))))) &&\text{(Def. of Index)} \\
&= \mathsf{proj}(\mathsf{PRP}^{-1}(s, \mathsf{PRP}(s,\mathsf{bin}(i)))) \\
&= \mathsf{proj}(\mathsf{bin}(i)) \\
&= i.
\end{aligned}
$$

Similarly, it is easy to see that the construction is wunderbar: the description consists of $s \in \mathbb{F}_2^\lambda$ and $n = \mathsf{poly}(\lambda) \le \lambda^c$ for some constant c. Therefore, it has size at most $\lambda + c \cdot \log \lambda \in \mathcal{O}(\lambda)$. The runtime of Entry is in fact independent of n and thus trivially in $\mathcal{O}(\mathsf{polylog}(n))$ and the only computation in Index that depends on n, is the membership check $\mathsf{proj}(\boldsymbol{b}) \in [n]$ which can be performed in time $\mathcal{O}(\log n) \subset \mathcal{O}(\mathsf{polylog}(n))$.

It remains to show that the construction is secure. Let $n = n(\lambda) = \mathsf{poly}(\lambda)$ and let $\mathcal{A}$ be an arbitrary PPT algorithm, such that We construct an adversary $\mathcal{B}$ against the pseudorandomness of as follows. $\mathcal{B}$ takes as input the security parameter λ and is given access to an oracle. For each $i \in [n]$, query $\mathsf{bin}(i)$ to the oracle, receiving back $\boldsymbol{b}_i'$ and compute $k_i := \mathsf{binToField}(\boldsymbol{b}_i')$. Invoke $\mathcal{A}(\boldsymbol{k})$ and output whatever $\mathcal{A}$ outputs. Clearly, $\mathcal{B}$ is also PPT, needing a runtime overhead of just n oracle queries over simply running $\mathcal{A}$. We now consider two cases: if, on the one hand, the oracle is $\mathsf{PRP}(s,\cdot)$, then for all $i \in [n]$ $k_i = \mathsf{binToField}(\mathsf{PRP}(s,\mathsf{bin}(i))) = \mathsf{Entry}((s,n),i)$. I.e., we have

$$
\begin{aligned}
&\Pr[s \leftarrow \mathbb{F}_2^\lambda : \mathcal{B}^{\mathsf{PRP}(s,\cdot)} = 1] \\
&= \Pr[s \leftarrow \mathsf{Sample}(1^\lambda, 1^n), \boldsymbol{k} := (\mathsf{Entry}(s,1), \dots, \mathsf{Entry}(s,n))^\mathsf{T}) : \mathcal{A}(\boldsymbol{k})].
\end{aligned}
\tag{1}
$$

If, on the other hand, the oracle is a truly random permutation g, then for all $i \in [n]$ it holds that $k_i = \mathsf{binToField}(g(\mathsf{bin}(i)))$ and therefore

$$
\begin{aligned}
&\Pr[g \leftarrow \Pi(\mathbb{F}_2^\lambda) : \mathcal{B}^{g(\cdot)} = 1] \\
&= \Pr[g \leftarrow \Pi(\mathbb{F}_2^\lambda); \forall i \in [n].\, k_i = \mathsf{binToField}(g(\mathsf{bin}(i))) : \mathcal{A}(\boldsymbol{k})] &&(2) \\
&= \Pr[(\boldsymbol{b}_1', \dots, \boldsymbol{b}_n') \leftarrow \mathord{\gg\!\!\!\!\ll}((\mathbb{F}_2^\lambda)^n); \boldsymbol{k} = (\mathsf{binToField}(\boldsymbol{b}_i'))_{i \in [n]} : \mathcal{A}(\boldsymbol{k})] &&(3) \\
&= \Pr[\boldsymbol{k} \leftarrow \mathord{\gg\!\!\!\!\ll}(K^n) : \mathcal{A}(\boldsymbol{k})]. &&(4)
\end{aligned}
$$

Here, Eq. 3 holds because g is a uniformly chosen random permutation and therefore the values $g(\mathsf{bin}(i))$ are uniformly distributed conditioned on not being duplicates and Eq. 4 holds because $\mathsf{binToField}$ is an injective function into K.

Combining Eq. 1 and Eq. 4 we get

$$\left| \Pr \left[\begin{array}{l} s \leftarrow \mathsf{Sample}(1^\lambda, 1^n), \\ k := \begin{pmatrix} \mathsf{Entry}(s,1) \\ \vdots \\ \mathsf{Entry}(s,n) \end{pmatrix} \end{array} : \mathcal{A}(k) \right] - \Pr[k \leftarrow \mathcal{K}(K^n) : \mathcal{A}(k)] \right|$$

$$= \left| \Pr[s \leftarrow \mathbb{F}_2^\lambda : \mathcal{B}^{\mathsf{PRP}(s,\cdot)} = 1] - \Pr[g \leftarrow \{f : \mathbb{F}_2^\lambda \to \mathbb{F}_2^\lambda\} : \mathcal{B}^{g(\cdot)} = 1] \right|$$

$$\leq \mathsf{negl}(\lambda)$$

where the last inequality follows from the fact that PRP is pseudorandom. $\square$

5.2 A Helpful Lemma

We prove a helpful lemma which allows to bound the probability of false positives when attempting to detect cells with only a single entry in the IBLT. Recall, that we have two matrices M and K, where the cells of M contain sums of messages m_d and the cells of K contain sums of $k_d \cdot m_d$ for a random vector k. We check for cells containing only a single message, i.e. cells that can be peeled, by checking whether $K[i,j]/M[i,j]$ corresponds to one of the values in k. A false positive could occur, if for some set of at least two non-zero messages corresponding to indices $I \subseteq [n]$ it happens to hold that

$$k_j = \frac{\sum_{i \in I} k_i m_i}{\sum_{i \in I} m_i}$$

for some $j \in [n]$. The lemma states that we can bound the probability of this occuring by choosing the entries of k from a large enough space.

Lemma 13. *Let $K \subseteq \mathbb{F}_q$, $(m_1, \ldots, m_n) \in \mathbb{F}_q^n$ and $I \subseteq [n]$ be arbitrary such that $\sum_{i \in I} m_i \neq 0$ and there exist $i, i' \in I$ with $0 \notin \{m_i, m_{i'}\}$. It holds that*

$$\Pr \left[k \leftarrow K^n : \exists j \in [n]. k_j = \frac{\sum_{i \in I} k_i m_i}{\sum_{i \in I} m_i} \right] \leq \frac{n}{|K|}$$

Proof. Using a union bound we have

$$\Pr \left[k \leftarrow K^n : \exists j \in [n]. k_j = \frac{\sum_{i \in I} k_i m_i}{\sum_{i \in I} m_i} \right]$$

$$\leq \sum_{j \in [n]} \Pr \left[k \leftarrow K^n : k_j = \frac{\sum_{i \in I} k_i m_i}{\sum_{i \in I} m_i} \right]. \tag{5}$$

It thus remains to bound the above probability for individual j. Let $j \in [n]$ be arbitrary but fixed and let $\xi = 1$ if $j \in I$ and $\xi = 0$ otherwise. It then holds that

$$\Pr\left[\boldsymbol{k} \leftarrow K^n : k_j = \frac{\sum_{i \in I} k_i m_i}{\sum_{i \in I} m_i}\right]$$

$$= \Pr\left[\boldsymbol{k} \leftarrow K^n : k_j \cdot \sum_{i \in I} m_i = \sum_{i \in I} k_i m_i\right]$$

$$= \Pr\left[\boldsymbol{k} \leftarrow K^n : k_j \cdot \left(\sum_{i \in I} m_i - \xi m_j\right) = \sum_{i \in I} k_i m_i - k_j \xi m_j\right]$$

$$= \Pr\left[\boldsymbol{k} \leftarrow K^n : k_j \cdot \sum_{i \in I \setminus \{j\}} m_i = \sum_{i \in I \setminus \{j\}} k_i m_i\right]$$

We now consider two cases. If $\sum_{i \in I \setminus \{j\}} = 0$, let $j' \in I \setminus \{j\}$ be an index, such that $m_{j'} \neq 0$. Note that such an index always exists by the condition on I. We then have

$$\Pr\left[\boldsymbol{k} \leftarrow K^n : k_j \cdot \overbrace{\sum_{i \in I \setminus \{j\}} m_i}^{=0} = \sum_{i \in I \setminus \{j\}} k_i m_i\right]$$

$$= \Pr\left[\boldsymbol{k} \leftarrow K^n : 0 = \sum_{i \in I \setminus \{j\}} k_i m_i\right]$$

$$= \Pr\left[\boldsymbol{k} \leftarrow K^n : k_{j'} = \frac{\sum_{i \in I \setminus \{j, j'\}} k_i m_i}{-m_{j'}}\right]$$

where $(-m_{j'})^{-1}$ is always defined by the condition that $m_{j'} \neq 0$. Since the right hand side of the equality is independent of $k_{j'}$, the probability that the equality holds is at most $1/|K|$ for any choice of k_i, $i \neq j'$. Thus, in this case

$$\Pr\left[\boldsymbol{k} \leftarrow K^n : k_j = \frac{\sum_{i \in I} k_i m_i}{\sum_{i \in I} m_i}\right] \leq \frac{1}{|K|}. \tag{6}$$

In the other case, i.e., if $\sum_{i \in I \setminus \{j\}} \neq 0$, $(\sum_{i \in I \setminus \{j\}})^{-1}$ is well defined and we have

$$\Pr\left[\boldsymbol{k} \leftarrow K^n : k_j \cdot \sum_{i \in I \setminus \{j\}} m_i = \sum_{i \in I \setminus \{j\}} k_i m_i\right] = \Pr\left[\boldsymbol{k} \leftarrow K^n : k_j = \frac{\sum_{i \in I \setminus \{j\}} k_i m_i}{\sum_{i \in I \setminus \{j\}} m_i}\right].$$

Here again, the right hand side of the equality is independent of k_j. Thus, the probability that the equality holds is at most $1/|K|$ for any choice of k_i, $i \neq j$ and also in this case it holds that

$$\Pr\left[\boldsymbol{k} \leftarrow K^n : k_j = \frac{\sum_{i \in I} k_i m_i}{\sum_{i \in I} m_i}\right] \leq \frac{1}{|K|} \tag{7}$$

Finally, combining Eq. 5 with Eq. 6 and Eq. 7, we get

$$\Pr\left[\boldsymbol{k} \leftarrow K^n : \exists j \in [n]. k_j = \frac{\sum_{i \in I} k_i m_i}{\sum_{i \in I} m_i}\right] \leq \frac{n}{|K|} \qquad \square$$

By observing that the statistical distance betweem K^n and $\varkappa(K^n))$ is at most $n^2/|K|$ due to the birthday bound, we obtain the following corollary.

Corollary 14. *Let $K \subseteq \mathbb{F}_q$, $(m_1, \ldots, m_n) \in \mathbb{F}_q^n$ and $I \subseteq [n]$ be arbitrary such that $\sum_{i \in I} m_i \neq 0$ and there exist $i, i' \in I$ with $0 \notin \{m_i, m_{i'}\}$. It holds that*

$$\Pr\left[\boldsymbol{k} \leftarrow \varkappa(K^n) : \exists j \in [n]. \, k_j = \frac{\sum_{i \in I} k_i m_i}{\sum_{i \in I} m_i}\right] \leq \frac{n^2 + n}{|K|}$$

5.3 Construction of Ciphertext-Compression from IBLTs

Populating the IBLT involves homomorphically evaluating an inner product between the encrypted vector and a plain vector. Therefore, the compression scheme can only work for ciphertext vectors that allow the evaluation of inner product functions defined in the following.

Definition 15 (Inner Product Functions). *The class of inner product functions is the set of functions $\mathcal{Z}_{\mathsf{ip}} = \{f_{\boldsymbol{a}} \mid \boldsymbol{a} \in \mathbb{F}_q^n\}$ with*

$$f_{\boldsymbol{a}} : \mathbb{F}_q^n \to \mathbb{F}_q, \quad f_{\boldsymbol{a}}(\boldsymbol{x}) := \langle \boldsymbol{a}, \boldsymbol{x} \rangle.$$

The family of ciphertext vectors the construction is applicable to is then exactly those ciphertext vectors with low hamming weight and allow the evaluation of inner product functions. We define this family as follows.

Definition 16. ($\mathcal{Z}_{\mathsf{ip}}$-Valid Low Hamming Weight Ciphertext Vectors). *Let $\mathcal{E} = (\mathsf{Gen}, \mathsf{Enc}, \mathsf{Eval}, \mathsf{Dec})$ be a homomorphic public key encryption scheme. For any $\mathsf{pk} \in \mathcal{P}$, let*

$$\mathcal{F}_{t,\mathsf{pk}}^{\mathsf{ip}} := \left\{\boldsymbol{c} \in \mathsf{vld}(\mathcal{Z}_{\mathsf{ip}}, \mathsf{pk}) \mid \mathsf{hw}(\mathsf{Dec}(\mathsf{Gen}^{-1}(\mathsf{pk}), \boldsymbol{c})) < t\right\}.$$

We then define the family of $\mathcal{Z}_{\mathsf{ip}}$-valid ciphertext vectors with low hamming weight as $\mathcal{F}_t^{\mathsf{ip}} := \{\mathcal{F}_{t,\mathsf{pk}} \mid \mathsf{pk} \in \mathcal{P}\}$.

Theorem 17. *Let $\mathcal{E} = (\mathsf{Gen}, \mathsf{Enc}, \mathsf{Eval}, \mathsf{Dec})$ be an additively homomorphic encryption scheme with message space $\mathcal{M} = \mathbb{F}_q$ for some prime power q with ciphertext size $\xi = \xi(\lambda)$. Let $\lambda, \kappa, t, n \in \mathbb{N}$ be integers and let $\gamma := \lceil \frac{\kappa}{\log t} \rceil + 2$. Let PRF be a family of pseudorandom functions $\mathsf{PRF} : [\gamma] \times [2^\lambda] \to [8t]$ and let $(\mathsf{Sample}, \mathsf{Entry}, \mathsf{Index})$ be a wunderbar pseudorandom vector with index recovery for a universe $K = K(\lambda) \subseteq \mathbb{F}_q$ with $|K| \geq 2^\kappa (8t\gamma)(n^3 + n^2)$. Then $(\mathsf{Compress}, \mathsf{Decompress})$ from Fig. 4 is a $(\mathcal{O}(\lambda) + 16t\gamma\xi)/(n\xi)$-compressing $(1 - \mathcal{O}(2^{-\kappa}) - \mathsf{negl}(\lambda))$-correct ciphertext compression scheme for family $\mathcal{F}_t^{\mathsf{ip}}$.*

Proof. The output of the compression algorithm consists of a s_1, s_2 and $16t\gamma$ ciphertexts. Since the pseudorandom vector is wunderbar, it holds that $|s_1| = \mathcal{O}(\lambda)$ and s_2 is chosen as a λ-bit string. Therefore, it is easy to see that the scheme is $(\mathcal{O}(\lambda) + 16t\gamma\xi)/(n\xi)$-compressing. It remains to prove that it is correct. To do so we define a series of six hybrid schemes in Figs. 5 through 9.

Compress(pk, c)	Decompress(sk, (s_1, s_2, M, K))
$s_1 \leftarrow$ Sample$(1^\lambda, n)$	$S := \emptyset$
$s_2 \leftarrow \{0, 1\}^\lambda$	$M' :=$ Dec(sk, M)
$M :=$ Enc(pk, $0)^{\gamma \times 8t}$	$K' :=$ Dec(sk, K)
$K :=$ Enc(pk, $0)^{\gamma \times 8t}$	$D' :=$ Initialize()
foreach $(i, d) \in [\gamma] \times [n]$ do	while $\exists\, (i^*, j^*) \in [\gamma] \times [8t].\ D'[i^*, j^*] \neq \perp$ do
$\quad j :=$ PRF$(s_2, (i, d))$	$\quad (d, k, m) := (D'[i^*, j^*], K'[i^*, j^*], M'[i^*, j^*])$
$\quad M[i, j] := M[i, j] \boxplus c_d$	$\quad S := S \cup \{(d, m)\}$
$\quad k :=$ Entry(s_1, d)	$\quad$ Update(d, k, m)
$\quad K[i, j] := K[i, j] \boxplus (k \boxdot c_d)$	return S
return (s_1, s_2, M, K)	

Initialize()	Update(d, k, m)
$D' := \perp^{\gamma \times 8t}$	foreach $i \in [\gamma]$ do
foreach $(i, j) \in [\gamma] \times [8t]$ do	$\quad j :=$ PRF$(s_2, (i, d))$
$\quad$ if $M'[i, j] \neq 0$	$\quad M'[i, j] := M'[i, j] - m$
$\quad\quad D'[i, j] :=$ Index$\left(s_1, \frac{K'[i,j]}{M'[i,j]}\right)$	$\quad K'[i, j] := K'[i, j] - k$
return D'	$\quad$ if $M'[i, j] \neq 0$
	$\quad\quad D'[i, j] :=$ Index$\left(s_1, \frac{K'[i,j]}{M'[i,j]}\right)$
	$\quad$ else
	$\quad\quad D'[i, j] := \perp$

Fig. 4. A ciphertext compression scheme based on invertible bloom lookup tables and wunder pseudorandom vectors.

Claim 18. *For any $\mathcal{Z}_{\mathsf{ip}}$-valid vector of ciphertexts it holds that*

$$\Pr[\text{Decompress}(\text{sk}, \text{Compress}(\text{pk}, c)) = \text{sparse}(\text{Dec}(\text{sk}, c))]$$
$$= \Pr[\text{Decompress}_1(\text{Compress}_1(\text{Dec}(\text{sk}, c))) = \text{sparse}(\text{Dec}(\text{sk}, c))]$$

Proof. Following Definition 15 we denote by f_a the inner product function $f_a :$ $\mathbb{F}_q^n \rightarrow \mathbb{F}_q$, $f_a(x) := \langle a, x \rangle$. Further, we denote

$$v_{i,j} := \begin{pmatrix} \delta_{j, \text{PRF}(s_2, (i, 1))} \\ \vdots \\ \delta_{j, \text{PRF}(s_2, (i, n))} \end{pmatrix} \qquad w_{i,j} := \begin{pmatrix} \text{Entry}(s_1, 1) \cdot \delta_{j, \text{PRF}(s_2, (i, 1))} \\ \vdots \\ \text{Entry}(s_1, n) \cdot \delta_{j, \text{PRF}(s_2, (i, n))} \end{pmatrix}$$

Now, let M_0, K_0, M_0', K_0' and M_1, K_1, M_1', K_1' denote the relevant matrices in the actual scheme and hybrid 1 respectively. We note, that since c is $\mathcal{Z}_{\mathsf{ip}}$-valid,

$\text{Compress}_1(m)$	$\text{Decompress}_1((s_1, s_2, M, K))$
$s_1 \leftarrow \text{Sample}(1^\lambda, n)$	$S := \emptyset$
$s_2 \leftarrow \{0,1\}^\lambda$	$M' := M$
$M := 0^{\gamma \times 8t}$	$K' := K$
$K := 0^{\gamma \times 8t}$	$D' := \text{Initialize}()$
$\textbf{foreach } (i,d) \in [\gamma] \times [n] \textbf{ do}$	$\textbf{while } \exists\, (i^*, j^*) \in [\gamma] \times [8t].\ D'[i^*, j^*] \neq \bot \textbf{ do}$
$\quad j := \text{PRF}(s_2, (i,d))$	$\quad (d, k, m) := (D'[i^*, j^*], K'[i^*, j^*], M'[i^*, j^*])$
$\quad M[i,j] := M[i,j] + m_d$	$\quad S := S \cup \{(d, m)\}$
$\quad k := \text{Entry}(s_1, d)$	$\quad \text{Update}(d, k, m)$
$\quad K[i,j] := K[i,j] + (k \cdot m_d)$	$\textbf{return } S$
$\textbf{return } (s_1, s_2, M, K)$	

Fig. 5. The first hybrid scheme works exactly as the actual ciphertext compression scheme, except that it operates on *plaintext* messages instead of encrypted messages. I.e., ciphertexts are now decrypted before compression instead of between compression and decompression.

it holds for all $(i, j) \in [\gamma] \times [8t]$ that

$$
\begin{aligned}
M'_0[i,j] &= \text{Dec}(\text{sk}, M_0[i,j]) & \text{(Definition 3)}\\
&= \text{Dec}(\text{sk}, \bigboxplus_{d \in \{[n]\,|\,\text{PRF}(s_2,(i,d))=j\}} c_d)\\
&= \text{Dec}(\text{Eval}(\text{pk}, f_{v_{i,j}}, c))\\
&= f_{v_{i,j}}(\text{Dec}(\text{sk}, c))\\
&= \sum_{d \in \{[n]\,|\,\text{PRF}(s_2,(i,d))=j\}} \text{Dec}(\text{sk}, c_d) = M'_1[i,j]
\end{aligned}
$$

as well as

$$
\begin{aligned}
K'_0[i,j] &= \text{Dec}(\text{sk}, K_0[i,j]) & \text{(Definition 3)}\\
&= \text{Dec}(\text{sk}, \bigboxplus_{d \in \{[n]\,|\,\text{PRF}(s_2,(i,d))=j\}} c_d \cdot \text{Entry}(s_1, d))\\
&= \text{Dec}(\text{Eval}(\text{pk}, f_{w_{i,j}}, c))\\
&= f_{w_{i,j}}(\text{Dec}(\text{sk}, c))\\
&= \sum_{d \in \{[n]\,|\,\text{PRF}(s_2,(i,d))=j\}} \text{Dec}(\text{sk}, c_d) \cdot \text{Entry}(s_1, d) = K'_1[i,j]
\end{aligned}
$$

Since the computation on M', K' is otherwise identical between the two hybrids, the claim immediately follows. $\qquad\square$

$\mathsf{Compress}_2(\boldsymbol{m})$	$\mathsf{Decompress}_2((\boldsymbol{k}, s_2, \boldsymbol{M}, \boldsymbol{K}))$
$\boldsymbol{k} \leftarrow \mathsf{DummySample}(1^\lambda, n)$	$S := \emptyset$
$s_2 \leftarrow \{0,1\}^\lambda$	$\boldsymbol{M}' := \boldsymbol{M}$
$\boldsymbol{M} := 0^{\gamma \times 8t}$	$\boldsymbol{K}' := \boldsymbol{K}$
$\boldsymbol{K} := 0^{\gamma \times 8t}$	$\boldsymbol{D}' := \mathsf{Initialize}_2()$
$\textbf{foreach } (i,d) \in [\gamma] \times [n] \textbf{ do}$	$\textbf{while } \exists\, (i^*, j^*) \in [\gamma] \times [8t].\ \boldsymbol{D}'[i^*, j^*] \neq \bot \textbf{ do}$
$\quad j := \mathsf{PRF}(s_2, (i,d))$	$\quad (d, k, m) := (\boldsymbol{D}'[i^*, j^*], \boldsymbol{K}'[i^*, j^*], \boldsymbol{M}'[i^*, j^*])$
$\quad \boldsymbol{M}[i,j] := \boldsymbol{M}[i,j] + m_d$	$\quad S := S \cup \{(d, m)\}$
$\quad k := k_d$	$\quad \mathsf{Update}_2(d, k, m)$
$\quad \boldsymbol{K}[i,j] := \boldsymbol{K}[i,j] + (k \cdot m_d)$	$\textbf{return } S$
$\textbf{return } (\boldsymbol{k}, s_2, \boldsymbol{M}, \boldsymbol{K})$	

$\mathsf{Initialize}_2()$	$\mathsf{Update}_2(d, k, m)$
$\boldsymbol{D}' := \bot^{\gamma \times 8t}$	$\textbf{foreach } i \in [\gamma] \textbf{ do}$
$\textbf{foreach } (i,j) \in [\gamma] \times [8t] \textbf{ do}$	$\quad j := \mathsf{PRF}(s_2, (i,d))$
$\quad \textbf{if } \boldsymbol{M}'[i,j] \neq 0$	$\quad \boldsymbol{M}'[i,j] := \boldsymbol{M}'[i,j] - m$
$\quad\quad \boldsymbol{D}'[i,j] := \mathsf{DummyIndex}\left(\boldsymbol{k}, \frac{\boldsymbol{K}'[i,j]}{\boldsymbol{M}'[i,j]}\right)$	$\quad \boldsymbol{K}'[i,j] := \boldsymbol{K}'[i,j] - k$
$\textbf{return } \boldsymbol{D}'$	$\quad \textbf{if } \boldsymbol{M}'[i,j] \neq 0$
	$\quad\quad \boldsymbol{D}'[i,j] := \mathsf{DummyIndex}\left(\boldsymbol{k}, \frac{\boldsymbol{K}'[i,j]}{\boldsymbol{M}'[i,j]}\right)$
	$\quad \textbf{else}$
	$\quad\quad \boldsymbol{D}'[i,j] := \bot$

Fig. 6. The second hybrid scheme works exactly as the first hybrid scheme, except that instead of using the wunder pseudorandom vector it uses the dummy sampler and the dummy index recovery to work with a uniformly random vector $\boldsymbol{k} \in \mathcal{K}^n$.

Claim 19. *If* (Sample, Entry, Index) *is a secure pseudorandom vector, it holds for any key pair* (sk, pk) *and any vector* $\boldsymbol{c}$ *that*

$$\left| \begin{array}{l} \Pr[\mathsf{Decompress}_1(\mathsf{Compress}_1(\mathsf{Dec}(\mathsf{sk}, \boldsymbol{c}))) = \mathsf{sparse}(\mathsf{Dec}(\mathsf{sk}, \boldsymbol{c}))] \\ - \Pr[\mathsf{Decompress}_2(\mathsf{Compress}_2(\mathsf{Dec}(\mathsf{sk}, \boldsymbol{c}))) = \mathsf{sparse}(\mathsf{Dec}(\mathsf{sk}, \boldsymbol{c}))] \end{array} \right| \leq \mathsf{negl}(\lambda).$$

Proof. We construct an attacker $\mathcal{A}$ against security of the pseudorandom vector as follows. On input $\boldsymbol{k}$, $\mathcal{A}$ executes $\mathsf{Decompress}_2(\mathsf{Compress}_2(\mathsf{Dec}(\mathsf{sk}, \boldsymbol{c})))$, except that it uses its input $\boldsymbol{k}$ instead of sampling a fresh one. If $\boldsymbol{k}$ was chosen using $\boldsymbol{k} \leftarrow \mathsf{DummySample}(1^\lambda, n)$, this is identical to a regular execution of $\mathsf{Decompress}_2(\mathsf{Compress}_2(\mathsf{Dec}(\mathsf{sk}, \boldsymbol{c})))$. If on the other hand $\boldsymbol{k}$ was chosen by sampling $s_2 \leftarrow \mathsf{Sample}(1^\lambda, n)$ and setting $\boldsymbol{k} := (\mathsf{Entry}(s, 1), \dots, \mathsf{Entry}(s, n))^\mathsf{T}$, this is identical to a regular execution of $\mathsf{Decompress}_1(\mathsf{Compress}_1(\mathsf{Dec}(\mathsf{sk}, \boldsymbol{c})))$. Therefore, by the security of the pseudorandom vector

$\text{Compress}_3(\boldsymbol{m})$

$k \leftarrow \text{DummySample}(1^\lambda, n)$

$s_2 \leftarrow \{0,1\}^\lambda$

$\boldsymbol{M} := 0^{\gamma \times 8t}$

$\boldsymbol{K} := 0^{\gamma \times 8t}$

$\boldsymbol{C} := 0^{\gamma \times 8t}$

foreach $(i,d) \in [\gamma] \times [n]$ **do**

$\quad j := \text{PRF}(s_2, (i,d))$

$\quad \boldsymbol{M}[i,j] := \boldsymbol{M}[i,j] + m_d$

$\quad k := k_d$

$\quad \boldsymbol{K}[i,j] := \boldsymbol{K}[i,j] + (k \cdot m_d)$

$\quad$ **if** $m_d \neq 0$ **do**

$\quad\quad \boldsymbol{C}[i,j] := \boldsymbol{C}[i,j] + 1$

return $(k, s_2, \boldsymbol{M}, \boldsymbol{K}, \boldsymbol{C})$

$\text{Decompress}_3((k, s_2, \boldsymbol{M}, \boldsymbol{K}, \boldsymbol{C}))$

$S := \emptyset$

$\boldsymbol{M}' := \boldsymbol{M}$

$\boldsymbol{K}' := \boldsymbol{K}$

$\boldsymbol{D}' := \text{Initialize}_2()$

while $\exists\, (i^*, j^*) \in [\gamma] \times [8t].\ \boldsymbol{C}[i^*, j^*] = 1$ **do**

$\quad (d, k, m) := (\boldsymbol{D}'[i^*, j^*], \boldsymbol{K}'[i^*, j^*], \boldsymbol{M}'[i^*, j^*])$

$\quad S := S \cup \{(d, m)\}$

$\quad \text{Update}_3(d, k, m)$

return S

$\text{Update}_3(d, k, m)$

---

foreach $i \in [\gamma]$ **do**

$\quad j := \text{PRF}(s_2, (i,d))$

$\quad \boldsymbol{M}'[i,j] := \boldsymbol{M}'[i,j] - m$

$\quad \boldsymbol{K}'[i,j] := \boldsymbol{K}'[i,j] - k$

$\quad \boldsymbol{C}[i,j] := \boldsymbol{C}[i,j] - 1$

$\quad$ **if** $\boldsymbol{M}'[i,j] \neq 0$

$\quad\quad \boldsymbol{D}'[i,j] := \text{DummyIndex}\left(k, \frac{\boldsymbol{K}'[i,j]}{\boldsymbol{M}'[i,j]}\right)$

$\quad$ **else**

$\quad\quad \boldsymbol{D}'[i,j] := \bot$

Fig. 7. The third hybrid scheme works exactly as the second hybrid scheme, except that it maintains a matrix counting how many non-zero messages are mapped to each individual cell and deciding which messages to peel based on these exact counts instead of relying on the matrix $\boldsymbol{K}$.

$$
\begin{aligned}
\text{negl}(\lambda) \geq\ & \left| \Pr\left[s \leftarrow \text{Sample}(1^\lambda, n), \boldsymbol{k} := \begin{pmatrix} (\text{Entry}(s,1) \\ \vdots \\ \text{Entry}(s,n) \end{pmatrix} : \mathcal{A}(\boldsymbol{k}) \right] \right. \\
& \left. - \Pr[\boldsymbol{k} \leftarrow \text{DummySample}(1^\lambda, n) : \mathcal{A}(\boldsymbol{k})] \right| \\
=\ & \left| \Pr[\text{Decompress}_1(\text{sk}, \text{Compress}_1(\text{pk}, c)) = \text{sparse}(\text{Dec}(\text{sk}, c))] \right. \\
& \left. - \Pr[\text{Decompress}_2(\text{Compress}_2(\text{Dec}(\text{sk}, c))) = \text{sparse}(\text{Dec}(\text{sk}, c))] \right|
\end{aligned}
$$

$\square$

Claim 20. *It holds that*

$$\left| \begin{array}{l} \Pr[\mathsf{Decompress}_2(\mathsf{Compress}_2(\mathsf{Dec}(\mathsf{sk}, c))) = \mathsf{sparse}(\mathsf{Dec}(\mathsf{sk}, c))] \\ - \Pr[\mathsf{Decompress}_3(\mathsf{Compress}_3(\mathsf{Dec}(\mathsf{sk}, c))) = \mathsf{sparse}(\mathsf{Dec}(\mathsf{sk}, c))] \end{array} \right| \le 2^{-\kappa}.$$

Proof. We first note two things

1. Whenever a correct element (m, d) is peeled, the resulting matrices (C', M', K', D) are identical to the scenario where $m_d = \mathsf{Dec}(\mathsf{sk}, c_d) = 0$ and all other mesages are unchanged.
2. In the third hybrid scheme only correct elements are peeled.

The first observation follows because a correct peeling removes a message from the relevant cells by subtracting the corresponding values, which is equivalent to not adding them in the first place, which is exactly what happens if the message is zero. The second observation follows because we correctly keep track of the number of non-zero elements in each cell and only peel those, where a single non-zero element remains. By these observations, at any point during the execution of the decompression loop, there exists a vector $m' \in \mathbb{F}_q^n$, such that for all (i, j)

$$K'[i, j] := \begin{cases} d & \text{if } \frac{\sum_{\iota \in I_i} k_\iota m_\iota}{\sum_{\iota \in I_i} m_\iota} = k_d \\ \bot & \text{otherwise} \end{cases}$$

where $I_i = \{\iota \in [n] \mid \mathsf{PRF}(s_1, (i, \iota)) = j\}$.

We denote by $E_{r,i,j}$ the event that before the r-th iteration of the main loop of $\mathsf{Decompress}_4$, it holds that $C[i, j] > 1$ but $K[i, j] \ne \bot$. Note that $\mathsf{Decompress}_4$ and $\mathsf{Decompress}_3$ behave identically unless at least one of $E_{r,i,j}$ for $(r, i, j) \in [n] \times [\gamma] \times [8t]$ occurs.

Therefore by a union bound and Corollary 14

$$\left| \begin{array}{l} \Pr[\mathsf{Decompress}_3(\mathsf{sk}, \mathsf{Compress}_3(\mathsf{pk}, c)) = \mathsf{sparse}(\mathsf{Dec}(\mathsf{sk}, c))] \\ - \Pr[\mathsf{Decompress}_4(\mathsf{Compress}_4(\mathsf{Dec}(\mathsf{sk}, c))) = \mathsf{sparse}(\mathsf{Dec}(\mathsf{sk}, c))] \end{array} \right|$$

$$\le \sum_{(r,i,j) \in [n] \times [\gamma] \times [8t]} \Pr[E_{r,i,j}]$$

$$\le \sum_{(r,i,j) \in [n] \times [\gamma] \times [8t]} \frac{n^2 + n}{|K|}$$

$$= \frac{(8t\gamma)(n^3 + n^2)}{|K|} \le \frac{(8t\gamma)(n^3 + n^2)}{2^\kappa \cdot (8t\gamma)(n^3 + n^2)} \le 2^{-\kappa}$$

$\square$

Claim 21. *It holds that*

$$\left| \begin{array}{l} \Pr[\mathsf{Decompress}_3(\mathsf{Compress}_3(\mathsf{Dec}(\mathsf{sk}, c))) = \mathsf{sparse}(\mathsf{Dec}(\mathsf{sk}, c))] \\ = \Pr[\mathsf{Decompress}_4(\mathsf{Compress}_4(\mathsf{Dec}(\mathsf{sk}, c))) = \mathsf{sparse}(\mathsf{Dec}(\mathsf{sk}, c))] \end{array} \right|.$$

$\mathsf{Compress}_4(m)$	$\mathsf{Decompress}_4((k, s_2, M, K, C, D))$
$k \leftarrow \mathsf{DummySample}(1^\lambda, n)$	$S := \emptyset$
$s_2 \leftarrow \{0,1\}^\lambda$	$M' := M$
$M := 0^{\gamma \times 8t}$	$K' := K$
$K := 0^{\gamma \times 8t}$	$D' := D$
$C := 0^{\gamma \times 8t}$	$\textbf{while } \exists\, (i^*, j^*) \in [\gamma] \times [8t].\ C[i^*, j^*] = 1 \textbf{ do}$
$D := 0^{\gamma \times 8t}$	$\quad (d, k, m) := (D'[i^*, j^*], K'[i^*, j^*], M'[i^*, j^*])$
$\textbf{foreach } (i, d) \in [\gamma] \times [n] \textbf{ do}$	$\quad S := S \cup \{(d, m)\}$
$\quad j := \mathsf{PRF}(s_2, (i, d))$	$\quad \mathsf{Update}_4(d, k, m)$
$\quad M[i, j] := M[i, j] + m_d$	$\textbf{return } S$
$\quad k := k_d$	
$\quad K[i, j] := K[i, j] + (k \cdot m_d)$	$\mathsf{Update}_4(d, k, m)$
$\quad \textbf{if } m_d \neq 0 \textbf{ do}$	
$\quad\quad C[i, j] := C[i, j] + 1$	$\textbf{foreach } i \in [\gamma] \textbf{ do}$
$\quad\quad D[i, j] := D[i, j] + d$	$\quad j := \mathsf{PRF}(s_2, (i, d))$
$\textbf{return } (k, s_2, M, K, C, D)$	$\quad M'[i, j] := M'[i, j] - m$
	$\quad K'[i, j] := K'[i, j] - k$
	$\quad C[i, j] := C[i, j] - 1$
	$\quad D'[i, j] := D'[i, j] - d$

Fig. 8. The fourth hybrid scheme works exactly as the third hybrid scheme, except that the matrix D which before contained the indices of the messages *if* it could be inferred from the matrix K is now maintained with a sum of the indices of all messages mapped to the cell. This means that whenever $C[i, j] = 1$, $D[i, j]$ contains the index of the single non-zero message mapped to cell (i, j).

Proof. The only difference between the two hybrids could occur, if when peeling a message from cell (i, j), the content of $D[i, j]$ would differ between the two hybrids. However, this is not possible, since in hybrid three we have

$$D[i, j] = \mathsf{DummyIndex}(k, \frac{K[i, j]}{M[i, j]})$$

$$= \mathsf{DummyIndex}(k, \frac{k_d \cdot m_d}{m_d}) = \mathsf{DummyIndex}(k, k_d) = d$$

just as in hybrid four. □

The fifth hybrid is identical to the fourth hybrid except that the now unnecessary matrix K is removed. The following claim trivially follows from the fact that K is not used in either hybrids.

Claim 22. *It holds that*

$$\left| \begin{array}{l} \Pr[\mathsf{Decompress}_4(\mathsf{Compress}_4(\mathsf{Dec}(\mathsf{sk}, c))) = \mathsf{sparse}(\mathsf{Dec}(\mathsf{sk}, c))] \\ = \Pr[\mathsf{Decompress}_5(\mathsf{Compress}_5(\mathsf{Dec}(\mathsf{sk}, c))) = \mathsf{sparse}(\mathsf{Dec}(\mathsf{sk}, c))] \end{array} \right| .$$

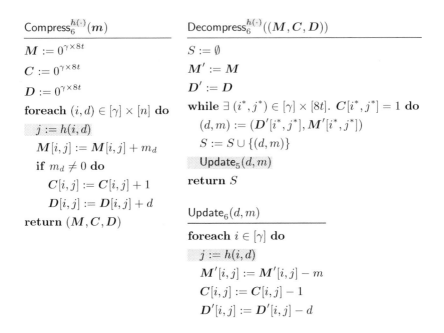

$\mathsf{Compress}_6^{h(\cdot)}(m)$

$M := 0^{\gamma \times 8t}$

$C := 0^{\gamma \times 8t}$

$D := 0^{\gamma \times 8t}$

foreach $(i, d) \in [\gamma] \times [n]$ **do**

    $j := h(i, d)$

    $M[i, j] := M[i, j] + m_d$

    if $m_d \neq 0$ **do**

        $C[i, j] := C[i, j] + 1$

        $D[i, j] := D[i, j] + d$

return (M, C, D)

$\mathsf{Decompress}_6^{h(\cdot)}((M, C, D))$

$S := \emptyset$

$M' := M$

$D' := D$

while $\exists\, (i^*, j^*) \in [\gamma] \times [8t].\ C[i^*, j^*] = 1$ **do**

    $(d, m) := (D'[i^*, j^*], M'[i^*, j^*])$

    $S := S \cup \{(d, m)\}$

    $\mathsf{Update}_5(d, m)$

return S

$\mathsf{Update}_6(d, m)$

---

foreach $i \in [\gamma]$ **do**

    $j := h(i, d)$

    $M'[i, j] := M'[i, j] - m$

    $C[i, j] := C[i, j] - 1$

    $D'[i, j] := D'[i, j] - d$

Fig. 9. The sixth hybrid scheme works exactly as the fifth hybrid scheme, except that instead of using a pseudorandom function to derive j from (i, d), it uses a truly random function h given as an oracle.

Claim 23. *If* PRF *is a secure pseudorandom function then it holds that*

$$\left| \begin{array}{l} \Pr[\mathsf{Decompress}_5(\mathsf{Compress}_5(\mathsf{Dec}(\mathsf{sk}, c))) = \mathsf{sparse}(\mathsf{Dec}(\mathsf{sk}, c))] \\ - \Pr[\mathsf{Decompress}_6^{h(\cdot,\cdot)}(\mathsf{Compress}_6^{h(\cdot,\cdot)}(\mathsf{Dec}(\mathsf{sk}, c))) = \mathsf{sparse}(\mathsf{Dec}(\mathsf{sk}, c))] \end{array} \right|$$
$$\leq \mathsf{negl}(\lambda).$$

Proof. The only difference between the two hybrids is the use of the function $\mathsf{PRF}(s_2, \cdot, \cdot)$ in the fifth hybrid and $h(\cdot, \cdot)$ in the sixth hybrid. Thus, the claim follows from a straightforward reduction that, given access to an oracle o, executes $\mathsf{Decompress}_6^{o(\cdot,\cdot)}(\mathsf{Compress}_6^{o(\cdot,\cdot)}(\mathsf{Dec}(\mathsf{sk}, c)))$ and outputs 0 if the result equals $\mathsf{sparse}(\mathsf{Dec}(\mathsf{sk}, c))$ and 1 otherwise. $\qquad\square$

Claim 24. *It holds for any vector of ciphertexts with hamming weight at most t that*

$$\Pr[\mathsf{Decompress}_6(\mathsf{Compress}_6(\mathsf{Dec}(\mathsf{sk}, c))) = \mathsf{sparse}(\mathsf{Dec}(\mathsf{sk}, c))] \leq \mathcal{O}(2^{-\kappa})$$

Proof. Denote $m := \mathsf{Dec}(\mathsf{sk}, c)$, $S := \{(d, m') \mid m' = m_d\}$ and $S_{\neq 0} := \{(d, m') \in S \mid m' \neq 0\} = \mathsf{sparse}(m)$. Since c has Hamming weight at most t, we have that $|S_{\neq 0}| \leq t$.

Comparing hybrid six with the definition of an IBLT in Fig. 1, and keeping in mind Remark 1 we can observe, that what $\mathsf{Compress}_6$ actually outputs is simply an IBLT for pairs containing all elements of $S_{\neq 0}$ using hash functions $h(i, \cdot)$. Further, $\mathsf{Decompress}_6$ is in fact the same as List with Update_6 being identical to Peel. And since $|S_{\neq 0}| \leq t$ and random functions are t-wise independent, it thus holds by Theorem 6 that

$$\Pr[\mathsf{Decompress}_6(\mathsf{Compress}_6(m)) = \mathsf{sparse}(m)]$$
$$= \Pr[\mathsf{List}(\mathsf{Insert}(B_0, S_{\neq 0})) = S_{\neq 0}] \geq 1 - \mathcal{O}(2^{-(\gamma-2)\log t}) \geq 1 - \mathcal{O}(2^{-\kappa})$$

$\square$

By combining all of the above claims and using the triangle inequality it follows that

$$\Pr[\mathsf{Decompress}(\mathsf{sk}, \mathsf{Compress}(\mathsf{pk}, c)) = \mathsf{sparse}(\mathsf{Dec}(\mathsf{sk}, c))]$$
$$\geq 1 - \mathcal{O}(2^{-\kappa}) - \mathsf{negl}(\lambda)$$

as claimed. $\square$

References

1. Akavia, A., Feldman, D., Shaul, H.: Secure search on encrypted data via multi-ring sketch. In: Lie, D., Mannan, M., Backes, M., Wang, X. (eds.) ACM CCS 2018: 25th Conference on Computer and Communications Security, pp. 985–1001. ACM Press, Toronto (2018). https://doi.org/10.1145/3243734.3243810
2. Ben-Or, M., Tiwari, P.: A deterministic algorithm for sparse multivariate poly-nominal interpolation (extended abstract). In: 20th Annual ACM Symposium on Theory of Computing, pp. 301–309. ACM Press, Chicago (1988). https://doi.org/10.1145/62212.62241
3. Boneh, D., Di Crescenzo, G., Ostrovsky, R., Persiano, G.: Public key encryption with keyword search. In: Cachin, C., Camenisch, J.L. (eds.) EUROCRYPT 2004. LNCS, vol. 3027, pp. 506–522. Springer, Heidelberg (2004). https://doi.org/10.1007/978-3-540-24676-3_30
4. Brakerski, Z., Gentry, C., Halevi, S.: Packed ciphertexts in LWE-based homomorphic encryption. In: Kurosawa, K., Hanaoka, G. (eds.) PKC 2013. LNCS, vol. 7778, pp. 1–13. Springer, Heidelberg (2013). https://doi.org/10.1007/978-3-642-36362-7_1
5. Candès, E.J., Romberg, J., Tao, T.: Robust uncertainty principles: Exact signal reconstruction from highly incomplete frequency information. IEEE Trans. Inf. Theory **52**(2), 489–509 (2006). https://doi.org/10.1109/TIT.2005.862083

6. Cheon, J.H., Kim, M., Kim, M.: Optimized search-and-compute circuits and their application to query evaluation on encrypted data. IEEE Trans. Inf. Forens. Secur. **11**(1), 188–199 (2016). https://doi.org/10.1109/TIFS.2015.2483486

7. Cheon, J.H., Kim, M., Lauter, K.: Homomorphic computation of edit distance. In: Brenner, M., Christin, N., Johnson, B., Rohloff, K. (eds.) FC 2015. LNCS, vol. 8976, pp. 194–212. Springer, Heidelberg (2015). https://doi.org/10.1007/978-3-662-48051-9_15

8. Choi, S.G., Dachman-Soled, D., Gordon, S.D., Liu, L., Yerukhimovich, A.: Compressed oblivious encoding for homomorphically encrypted search. In: Vigna, G., Shi, E. (eds.) ACM CCS 2021: 28th Conference on Computer and Communications Security. pp. 2277–2291. ACM Press, Virtual Event (2021). https://doi.org/10.1145/3460120.3484792

9. Cooley, J.W., Tukey, J.W.: An algorithm for the machine calculation of complex Fourier series. Math. Comput. **19**(90), 297–301 (1965)

10. Corrigan-Gibbs, H., Kogan, D.: Private information retrieval with sublinear online time. In: Canteaut, A., Ishai, Y. (eds.) EUROCRYPT 2020. LNCS, vol. 12105, pp. 44–75. Springer, Cham (2020). https://doi.org/10.1007/978-3-030-45721-1_3

11. Donoho, D.L.: Compressed sensing. IEEE Trans. Inf. Theory **52**(4), 1289–1306 (2006). https://doi.org/10.1109/TIT.2006.871582

12. Gentry, C.: A Fully Homomorphic Encryption Scheme. Ph.D. thesis, Stanford, CA, USA (2009)

13. Gilbert, A., Indyk, P.: Sparse recovery using sparse matrices. Proc. IEEE **98**(6), 937–947 (2010). https://doi.org/10.1109/JPROC.2010.2045092

14. Goodrich, M.T., Mitzenmacher, M.: Invertible bloom lookup tables. In: 49th Annual Allerton Conference on Communication, Control, and Computing (Allerton), pp. 792–799. IEEE Computer Society Press (2011). https://doi.org/10.1109/Allerton.2011.6120248

15. Huang, Q.L., Gao, X.S.: Revisit sparse polynomial interpolation based on randomized kronecker substitution. In: England, M., Koepf, W., Sadykov, T.M., Seiler, W.M., Vorozhtsov, E.V. (eds.) CASC 2019: 21st International Workshop on Computer Algebra in Scientific Computing, vol. 11661, pp. 215–235. Springer, Heidelberg (2019). https://doi.org/10.1007/978-3-030-26831-2_15

16. Johnson, M., Wagner, D., Ramchandran, K.: On compressing encrypted data without the encryption key. In: Naor, M. (ed.) TCC 2004. LNCS, vol. 2951, pp. 491–504. Springer, Heidelberg (2004). https://doi.org/10.1007/978-3-540-24638-1_27

17. Klinc, D., Hazay, C., Jagmohan, A., Krawczyk, H., Rabin, T.: On compression of data encrypted with block ciphers. In: Storer, J.A., Marcellin, M.W. (eds.) DCC 2009: 19th Data Compression Conference. pp. 213–222. IEEE Computer Society Press, Snowbird (2009). https://doi.org/10.1109/DCC.2009.71

18. Lauter, K., López-Alt, A., Naehrig, M.: Private computation on encrypted genomic data. In: Aranha, D.F., Menezes, A. (eds.) LATINCRYPT 2014. LNCS, vol. 8895, pp. 3–27. Springer, Cham (2015). https://doi.org/10.1007/978-3-319-16295-9_1

19. Liu, Z., Tromer, E.: Oblivious message retrieval. In: Dodis, Y., Shrimpton, T. (eds.) Advances in Cryptology - CRYPTO 2022, Part I. LNCS, vol. 13507, pp. 753–783. Springer, Heidelberg (2022). https://doi.org/10.1007/978-3-031-15802-5_26

20. Peikert, C., Vaikuntanathan, V., Waters, B.: A framework for efficient and composable oblivious transfer. In: Wagner, D. (ed.) CRYPTO 2008. LNCS, vol. 5157, pp. 554–571. Springer, Heidelberg (2008). https://doi.org/10.1007/978-3-540-85174-5_31

21. de Prony, G.: Essai expérimental et analytique sur les lois de la dilatabilité des fluides élastiques et sur celles de la force expansive de la vapeur de l'eau et de la vapeur de l'alcool à différentes températures. J. l'École Polytech. **1**(22), 24–76 (1795)

22. Rivest, R.L., Adleman, L., Dertouzos, M.L.: On data banks and privacy homomorphisms. In: DeMillo, R.A., Lipton, R.J., Dobkin, D.P., Jones, A.K. (eds.) Foundations of Secure Computation, pp. 169–179. Academic Press (1978)

23. Shanks, D.: Class number, a theory of factorization, and genera. In: Lewis, D.J. (ed.) 1969 Number Theory Institute. Proceedings of Symposia in Pure Mathematics, vol. 20, pp. 415–440. American Mathematical Society (1971)

24. Slepian, D., Wolf, J.: Noiseless coding of correlated information sources. IEEE Trans. Inf. Theory **19**(4), 471–480 (1973). https://doi.org/10.1109/TIT.1973.1055037

25. Smart, N.P., Vercauteren, F.: Fully homomorphic SIMD operations. Designs Codes Cryptogr. **71**(1), 57–81 (2012). https://doi.org/10.1007/s10623-012-9720-4

26. Song, D.X., Wagner, D., Perrig, A.: Practical techniques for searches on encrypted data. In: 2000 IEEE Symposium on Security and Privacy, pp. 44–55. IEEE Computer Society Press, Oakland (2000). https://doi.org/10.1109/SECPRI.2000.848445

27. Yasuda, M., Shimoyama, T., Kogure, J., Yokoyama, K., Koshiba, T.: Secure pattern matching using somewhat homomorphic encryption. In: Juel, A., Parno, B. (eds.) CCSW 2013: The ACM Cloud Computing Security Workshop, pp. 65–76. ACM Press, Berlin (2013). https://doi.org/10.1145/2517488.2517497

Quantum Cryptography

Public Key Encryption with Secure Key Leasing

Shweta Agrawal[1], Fuyuki Kitagawa[2], Ryo Nishimaki[2], Shota Yamada[3], and Takashi Yamakawa[2(✉)]

[1] IIT Madras, Chennai, India
[2] NTT Social Informatics Laboratories, Tokyo, Japan
takashi.yamakawa@ntt.com
[3] National Institute of Advanced Industrial Science and Technology (AIST), Tokyo, Japan

Abstract. We introduce the notion of public key encryption with secure key leasing (PKE-SKL). Our notion supports the leasing of decryption keys so that a leased key achieves the decryption functionality but comes with the guarantee that if the quantum decryption key returned by a user passes a validity test, then the user has lost the ability to decrypt. Our notion is similar in spirit to the notion of secure software leasing (SSL) introduced by Ananth and La Placa (Eurocrypt 2021) but captures significantly more general adversarial strategies. (In more detail, our adversary is not restricted to use an honest evaluation algorithm to run pirated software.) Our results can be summarized as follows:

1. *Definitions:* We introduce the definition of PKE with secure key leasing and formalize a security notion that we call indistinguishability against key leasing attacks (IND-KLA security). We also define a one-wayness notion for PKE-SKL that we call OW-KLA security and show that an OW-KLA secure PKE-SKL scheme can be lifted to an IND-KLA secure one by using the (quantum) Goldreich-Levin lemma.

2. *Constructing IND-KLA PKE with Secure Key Leasing:* We provide a construction of OW-KLA secure PKE-SKL (which implies IND-KLA secure PKE-SKL as discussed above) by leveraging a PKE scheme that satisfies a new security notion that we call *consistent or inconsistent security against key leasing attacks (CoIC-KLA security)*. We then construct a CoIC-KLA secure PKE scheme using 1-key Ciphertext-Policy Functional Encryption (CPFE) that in turn can be based on any IND-CPA secure PKE scheme.

3. *Identity Based Encryption, Attribute Based Encryption and Functional Encryption with Secure Key Leasing:* We provide definitions of secure key leasing in the context of advanced encryption schemes such as identity based encryption (IBE), attribute-based encryption (ABE) and functional encryption (FE). Then we provide constructions by combining the above PKE-SKL with standard IBE, ABE and FE schemes.

Notably, our definitions allow the adversary to request *distinguishing* keys in the security game, namely, keys that distinguish the

C. Hazay and M. Stam (Eds.): EUROCRYPT 2023, LNCS 14004, pp. 581–610, 2023.
https://doi.org/10.1007/978-3-031-30545-0_20

challenge bit by simply decrypting the challenge ciphertext, as long as it returns them (and they pass the validity test) before it sees the challenge ciphertext. All our constructions satisfy this stronger definition, albeit with the restriction that only a bounded number of such keys is allowed to the adversary in the IBE and ABE (but not FE) security games.

Prior to our work, the notion of single decryptor encryption (SDE) has been studied in the context of PKE (Georgiou and Zhandry, Eprint 2020) and FE (Kitigawa and Nishimaki, Asiacrypt 2022) but all their constructions rely on strong assumptions including indistinguishability obfuscation. In contrast, our constructions do not require any additional assumptions, showing that PKE/IBE/ABE/FE can be upgraded to support secure key leasing for free.

1   Introduction

Recent years have seen amazing advances in cryptography by leveraging the power of quantum computation. Several novel primitives such as perfectly secure key agreement [11], quantum money [35], quantum copy protection [1], one shot signatures [5] and such others, which are not known to exist in the classical world, can be constructed in the quantum setting, significantly advancing cryptographic capabilities.

In this work, we continue to study harnessing quantum powers to protect against software piracy. The quantum no-cloning principle intuitively suggests applicability to anti-piracy, an approach which was first investigated in the seminal work of Aaronson [1], who introduced the notion of quantum copy protection. At a high level, quantum copy protection prevents users from copying software in the sense that it guarantees that when an adversary is given a copy protected circuit for computing some function f, it cannot create two (possibly entangled) quantum states, both of which can compute f. While interesting in its own right for preventing software piracy, quantum copy protection (for some class of circuits) also has the amazing application of public-key quantum money [2]. Perhaps unsurprisingly, constructions of quantum copy protection schemes from standard cryptographic assumptions have remained largely elusive. This motivates the study of primitives weaker than quantum copy protection, which nevertheless offer meaningful guarantees for anti-piracy.

Secure software leasing (SSL), introduced by Ananth and La Placa [9], is such a primitive, which while being weaker than quantum copy-protection, is nevertheless still meaningful for software anti-piracy. Intuitively, this notion allows to encode software into a version which may be leased or rented out, for some specific term at some given cost. Once the lease expires, the lessee returns the software and the lessor can run an efficient procedure to verify its validity. If the software passes the test, we have the guarantee that the lessee is no longer able to run the software (using the honest evaluation algorithm).

In this work, we explore the possibility of equipping public key encryption (PKE) with a key leasing capability. The benefits of such a capability are indisputable – in the real world, decryption keys of users often need to be revoked, for instance, when a user leaves an organization. In the classical setting, nothing prevents the user from maintaining a copy of her decryption key and misusing its power. Revocation mechanisms have been designed to prevent such attacks, but these are often cumbersome in practice. Typically, such a mechanism entails the revoked key being included in a Certificate Revocation List (CRL) or Certificate Revocation Trees (CRT), or some database which is publicly available, so that other users are warned against its usage. However, the challenges of effective certificate revocation are well acknowledged in public key infrastructure – please see [12] for a detailed discussion. If the decryption keys of a PKE could be encoded as quantum states and allow for verifiable leasing, this would constitute a natural and well-fitting solution to the challenge of key revocation.

1.1   Prior Work

In this section, we discuss prior work related to public key encryption (PKE) and public key functional encryption (PKFE), where decryption keys are encoded into quantum states to benefit from uncloneability. For a broader discussion on prior work related to quantum copy protection and secure software leasing, we refer the reader to Sect. 1.4.

Georgiou and Zhandry [20] introduced the notion of single decryptor encryption (SDE), where the decryption keys are unclonable quantum objects. They showed how to use one-shot signatures together with extractable witness encryption with quantum auxiliary information to achieve public key SDE. Subsequently, Coladangelo, Liu, Liu, and Zhandry [17] achieved SDE assuming iO and extractable witness encryption or assuming subexponential iO, subexponential OWF, LWE and a strong monogamy property (which was subsequently shown to be true [19]). Very recently, Kitagawa and Nishimaki [27] introduced the notion of single-decryptor functional encryption (SDFE), where each functional decryption key is copy protected and provided collusion-resistant single decryptor PKFE for P/poly from the subexponential hardness of iO and LWE.

It is well-known [3,9] that copy protection is a stronger notion than SSL[1] – intuitively, if an adversary can generate two copies of a program, then it can return one of them while keeping the other for later use. Thus, constructions of single decryptor encryption [17,20,27] imply our notion of PKE with secure key leasing from their respective assumptions, which all include at least the assumption of iO (see Appendix A of the full version for the detail). Additionally, in the context of public key FE, the only prior work by Kitagawa and Nishimaki [27] considers the restricted single-key setting where an adversary is given a single decryption key that can be used to detect the challenge bit. In contrast, we consider the more powerful multi-key setting, which makes our definition of FE-SKL incomparable to the SDFE considered by [27]. For the primitives of IBE and ABE, there has been no prior work achieving any notion of key leasing to the best of our knowledge. We also note that Aaronson et al. [3] studied

---

[1] The informed reader may observe that this implication may not always be true due to some subtleties, but we ignore these for the purpose of the overview.

the notion of "copy-detection", which is a weaker form of copy protection, for any "watermarkable" functionalities based on iO and OWF. In particular, by instantiating the construction with the watermarkable PKE of [22], they obtain PKE with copy-detection from iO + PKE.

Overall, all previous works that imply PKE-SKL are designed to achieve the stronger goal of copy protection (or the incomparable goal of copy detection) and rely at least on the strong assumption of iO. In this work, our goal is to achieve the weaker goal of PKE-SKL from standard assumptions.

1.2   Our Results

In this work, we initiate the study of public key encryption with secure key leasing. Our results can be summarized as follows:

1. *Definitions:* We introduce the definition of PKE with secure key leasing (PKE-SKL) to formalize the arguably natural requirement that decryption keys of a PKE scheme is encoded into a leased version so that the leased key continues to achieve the decryption functionality but now comes with an additional "returnability" guarantee. In more detail, the security of PKE-SKL requires that if the quantum decryption key returned by a user passes a validity test, then the user has lost the ability to decrypt. To capture this intuition, we formalize a security notion that we call indistinguishability against key leasing attacks (IND-KLA security). We also define a one-wayness notion for PKE-SKL that we call OW-KLA security and show that an OW-KLA secure PKE-SKL scheme can be lifted to an IND-KLA secure one by using the (quantum) Goldreich-Levin lemma.

2. *Constructing IND-KLA PKE with Secure Key Leasing:* We provide a construction of OW-KLA secure PKE-SKL (which imples IND-KLA PKE-SKL as discussed above) by leveraging a PKE scheme that satisfies a new security notion that we call *consistent or inconsistent security against key leasing attacks (CoIC-KLA security)*. We then construct a CoIC-KLA secure PKE scheme using 1-key Ciphertext-Policy Functional Encryption (CPFE) that in turn can be based on any IND-CPA secure PKE scheme.

3. *Identity Based Encryption, Attribute Based Encryption and Functional Encryption with Secure Key Leasing:* We provide definitions of secure key leasing in the context of advanced encryption schemes such as identity based encryption (IBE), attribute-based encryption (ABE) and functional encryption (FE). Then we provide constructions by combining the above PKE-SKL with standard IBE, ABE and FE schemes.

   Notably, our definitions allow the adversary to request *distinguishing* keys in the security game, namely, keys that distinguish the challenge bit by simply decrypting the challenge ciphertext. Recall that this was not permitted in the classical setting to avoid trivializing the security definition. However, in the quantum setting, we consider a stronger definition where the adversary can request such keys so long as it returns them (and they pass the validity test) before it sees the challenge ciphertext. All our constructions satisfy this stronger definition, albeit with the restriction that only a bounded number of such keys be allowed to the adversary in the IBE and ABE (but not FE) security games. We emphasize that this restriction is a result of our techniques and could potentially be removed in future work.

We note that, in general, secure software leasing (SSL) only ensures a notion of security where the adversary is forced to use an honest evaluation algorithm for the software. However, our definition (and hence constructions) of PKE/ABE/FE SKL do not suffer from this limitation. Our constructions do not require any additional assumptions, showing that PKE/IBE/ABE/FE can be upgraded to support secure key leasing for free.

1.3 Technical Overview

We proceed to give a technical overview of this work.

Definition of PKE with Secure Key Leasing. We first introduce the definition of PKE with secure key leasing (PKE-SKL). A PKE-SKL scheme SKL consists of four algorithms ($\mathcal{KG}$, Enc, $\mathcal{Dec}$, $\mathcal{Vrfy}$), where the first three algorithms form a standard PKE scheme except the following differences on $\mathcal{KG}$.[2]

- $\mathcal{KG}$ outputs a quantum decryption key $d\!k$ instead of a classical decryption key.
- $\mathcal{KG}$ outputs a (secret) verification key vk, together with a public encryption key and quantum decryption key.

The verification algorithm $\mathcal{Vrfy}$ takes as input a verification key and a quantum decryption key, and outputs $\top$ or $\bot$. In addition to decryption correctness, SKL should satisfy verification correctness that states that $\mathcal{Vrfy}(\mathsf{vk}, d\!k) = \top$ holds, where $(\mathsf{ek}, d\!k, \mathsf{vk}) \leftarrow \mathcal{KG}(1^\lambda)$.

The security of PKE-SKL requires that once a user holding a quantum decryption key returns the key correctly, the user can no longer use the key and lose the ability to decrypt. We formalize this as a security notion that we call indistinguishability against key leasing attacks (IND-KLA security). It is defined by using the following security game.

1. First, the challenger generates $(\mathsf{ek}, d\!k, \mathsf{vk}) \leftarrow \mathcal{KG}(1^\lambda)$ and sends ek and $d\!k$ to an adversary $\mathcal{A}$.
2. $\mathcal{A}$ sends two challenge plaintexts $(\mathsf{m}_0^*, \mathsf{m}_1^*)$ and a quantum state $\widetilde{d\!k}$ that is supposed to be a correct decryption key. The challenger checks if $\mathcal{Vrfy}(\mathsf{vk}, \widetilde{d\!k}) = \top$ holds. If not, $\mathcal{A}$ is regarded as invalid and the game ends here. Otherwise, the game goes to the next step.[3]

---

[2] In this paper, standard math or sans serif font stands for classical algorithms and classical variables. The calligraphic font stands for quantum algorithms and the calligraphic font and/or the bracket notation for (mixed) quantum states.

[3] We also consider a slightly stronger definition where the adversary can get access to a verification oracle many times, and the adversary is regarded as valid if the answer to at least one query $\widetilde{d\!k}$ is $\top$. In this overview, we focus on the "1-query" security for simplicity.

3. The challenger generates $\mathsf{ct}^* \leftarrow \mathsf{Enc}(\mathsf{ek}, \mathsf{m}^*_{\mathsf{coin}})$ and sends it to $\mathcal{A}$, where $\mathsf{coin} \leftarrow \{0,1\}$.
4. $\mathcal{A}$ outputs coin'.

IND-KLA security guarantees that any QPT $\mathcal{A}$ cannot guess coin correctly significantly better than random guessing, conditioned on $\mathcal{A}$ being valid. In more detail, for any QPT adversary $\mathcal{A}$ that passes the verification with a non-negligible probability, we have $\left| \Pr[\mathsf{coin}' = \mathsf{coin} \mid \mathcal{V}\!\mathit{rfy}(\mathsf{vk}, \widetilde{dk}) = \top] - 1/2 \right| = \mathsf{negl}(\lambda)$.

One-Wayness to Indistinguishability. It is natural to define a one-wayness notion for PKE-SKL, which we call OW-KLA security, by modifying the above definition so that the adversary is required to recover entire bits of a randomly chosen message from its ciphertext. Similarly to standard PKE, we can transform a OW-KLA secure PKE-SKL scheme into an IND-KLA secure one by using (quantum) Goldreich-Levin lemma [4,17]. Hence, though our goal is to construct an IND-KLA secure scheme, it suffices to construct an OW-KLA secure one.

Basic Idea for OW-KLA Secure Scheme. Towards realizing a OW-KLA secure PKE-SKL scheme, we construct an intermediate scheme $\mathsf{Basic} = (\mathsf{Basic}.\mathcal{KG}, \mathsf{Basic}.\mathsf{Enc}, \mathsf{Basic}.\mathcal{Dec}, \mathsf{Basic}.\mathcal{V}\!\mathit{rfy})$ using two instances of a standard PKE scheme, with parallel repetition. Let $\mathsf{PKE} = (\mathsf{PKE}.\mathsf{KG}, \mathsf{PKE}.\mathsf{Enc}, \mathsf{PKE}.\mathsf{Dec})$ be a standard PKE scheme. $\mathsf{Basic}.\mathcal{KG}$ generates two key pairs $(\mathsf{ek}_0, \mathsf{dk}_0)$ and $(\mathsf{ek}_1, \mathsf{dk}_1)$ using $\mathsf{PKE}.\mathsf{KG}$ and outputs $\mathsf{ek} := (\mathsf{ek}_0, \mathsf{ek}_1)$, $dk := 1/\sqrt{2}(|0\rangle\,|\mathsf{dk}_0\rangle + |1\rangle\,|\mathsf{dk}_1\rangle)$, and $\mathsf{vk} := (\mathsf{dk}_0, \mathsf{dk}_1)$. Given m and ek, $\mathsf{Basic}.\mathsf{Enc}$ generates $\mathsf{ct}_0 \leftarrow \mathsf{PKE}.\mathsf{Enc}(\mathsf{ek}_0, \mathsf{m})$ and $\mathsf{ct}_1 \leftarrow \mathsf{PKE}.\mathsf{Enc}(\mathsf{ek}_1, \mathsf{m})$ and outputs $\mathsf{ct} := (\mathsf{ct}_0, \mathsf{ct}_1)$. $\mathsf{Basic}.\mathcal{Dec}$ can decrypt this ciphertext using the decryption keys dk_0 and dk_1, respectively, in superposition. Since both decryptions result in the same message m, we can decrypt ciphertexts without collapsing dk. Finally, $\mathsf{Basic}.\mathcal{V}\!\mathit{rfy}$ checks if the input decryption key is an equal-weight superposition of dk_0 and dk_1. Concretely, it applies a binary outcome measurement w.r.t. a projection $\Pi_{\mathrm{vrfy}} := \frac{1}{2}\left(|0\rangle\,|\mathsf{dk}_0\rangle + |1\rangle\,|\mathsf{dk}_1\rangle\right)\left(\langle 0|\,\langle \mathsf{dk}_0| + \langle 1|\,\langle \mathsf{dk}_1|\right)$, and returns $\top$ if and only if the state is projected onto Π_{vrfy}.

Intuitively, if the adversary has returned the correct decryption key, then it no longer has the capability to decrypt since the decryption key cannot be cloned. However, this scheme does not satisfy OW-KLA because an adversary can pass the verification with probability $1/2$ simply by measuring the decryption key and returning the collapsed decryption key. Such an adversary can keep the decryption capability even after passing verification because the decryption key collapses to a classical string, which can be easily copied. Nonetheless, it is reasonable to expect that this attack strategy is optimal because there appears to be no obvious way to attack with a better advantage. That said, it is unclear how to turn this intuition into a formal proof assuming only IND-CPA security of the underlying PKE. To address this gap, we introduce a new security notion for PKE, that we call *consistent or inconsistent security against key leasing attacks (CoIC-KLA security)*. Using this, we can prove that the aforementioned adversarial strategy is optimal and Basic satisfies 1/2-OW-KLA security.

By being 1/2-OW-KLA secure, we mean that the probability that an adversary can correctly return a decryption key and recover the challenge plaintext simultaneously is at most $1/2 + \mathsf{negl}(\lambda)$. Below, we introduce the definition of CoIC-KLA security and how to prove 1/2-OW-KLA security of Basic using CoIC-KLA security. Then, we explain how to achieve a full OW-KLA secure scheme by applying parallel amplification to Basic.

Definition of CoIC-KLA security. CoIC-KLA security is defined by using the following game.

1. The challenger generates $(\mathsf{ek}_0, \mathsf{dk}_0)$ and $(\mathsf{ek}_1, \mathsf{dk}_1)$ using PKE.KG, and generates $d\!k := 1/\sqrt{2}(|0\rangle\,|\mathsf{dk}_0\rangle + |1\rangle\,|\mathsf{dk}_1\rangle)$. The challenger sends ek_0, ek_1, and $d\!k$ to an adversary $\mathcal{A}$. In this game, $\mathcal{A}$ can access the verification oracle only once, where the oracle is given a quantum state and returns the outcome of the projective measurement $(\Pi_{\mathrm{vrfy}}, I - \Pi_{\mathrm{vrfy}})$.
2. $\mathcal{A}$ sends two plaintexts $(\mathsf{m}_0^*, \mathsf{m}_1^*)$ to the challenger. The challenger picks random bits a, b and generates $\mathsf{ct}_0 = \mathsf{Enc}(\mathsf{ek}_0, \mathsf{m}_a)$ and $\mathsf{ct}_1 = \mathsf{Enc}(\mathsf{ek}_1, \mathsf{m}_{a \oplus b})$. Then, the challenger sends ct_0 and ct_1 to $\mathcal{A}$.
3. $\mathcal{A}$ outputs a bit b'.

Then, CoIC-KLA security requires that any QPT $\mathcal{A}$ cannot guess b significantly better than random guessing. In the above game, if $b = 0$, ct_0 and ct_1 are ciphertexts of the same plaintext m_a^*. On the other hand, if $b = 1$, ct_0 and ct_1 are ciphertexts of the different plaintexts m_a^* and $\mathsf{m}_{1 \oplus a}^*$. Thus, we call this security notion consistent or inconsistent security.

1/2-OW-KLA security of Basic. We explain how to prove 1/2-OW-KLA security of Basic based on CoIC-KLA security of PKE. The OW-KLA security game for Basic is as follows.

1. The challenger generates $(\mathsf{ek}_0, \mathsf{dk}_0)$ and $(\mathsf{ek}_1, \mathsf{dk}_1)$ using PKE.KG, sets $\mathsf{ek} := (\mathsf{ek}_0, \mathsf{ek}_1)$ and $d\!k := 1/\sqrt{2}(|0\rangle\,|\mathsf{dk}_0\rangle + |1\rangle\,|\mathsf{dk}_1\rangle)$, and sends ek and $d\!k$ to an adversary $\mathcal{A}$.
2. The adversary returns a quantum state $\widetilde{dk}$ that is supposed to be a correct decryption key. The challenger checks if the result of applying Π_{vrfy} defined above to $\widetilde{dk}$ is 1. If not, $\mathcal{A}$ is regarded as invalid and the game ends here. Otherwise, the game goes to the next step.
3. The challenger generates random plaintext m^* and two ciphertexts $\mathsf{ct}_0 \leftarrow \mathsf{PKE.Enc}(\mathsf{ek}_0, \mathsf{m}^*)$ and $\mathsf{ct}_1 \leftarrow \mathsf{PKE.Enc}(\mathsf{ek}_1, \mathsf{m}^*)$, and sends $\mathsf{ct} := (\mathsf{ct}_0, \mathsf{ct}_1)$ to $\mathcal{A}$.
4. $\mathcal{A}$ outputs m'.

In this game, we say that $\mathcal{A}$ wins if (a) $\widetilde{dk}$ passes the verification, that is, the result of applying Π_{vrfy} to $\widetilde{dk}$ is 1, and (b) $\mathsf{m}' = \mathsf{m}^*$ holds. $\mathcal{A}$ can win this game with probability at least $1/2$ by just measuring $1/\sqrt{2}(|0\rangle\,|\mathsf{dk}_0\rangle + |1\rangle\,|\mathsf{dk}_1\rangle)$, returns collapsed key, and decrypt the challenge ciphertext with the key. As stated above, we can prove that this is the optimal strategy for $\mathcal{A}$, that is, we can bound the advantage of $\mathcal{A}$ by $1/2 + \mathsf{negl}(\lambda)$. The proof can be done by using game sequences. We denote the probability that $\mathcal{A}$ wins in Game i as $\Pr[S_i]$.

Game 0: This is exactly the above game.

Game 1: We defer the verification of the returned key $\widetilde{dk}$ after $\mathcal{A}$ outputs m'.

From the deferred measurement principle, we have $\Pr[S_0] = \Pr[S_1]$.

Game 2: We change $\mathcal{A}$'s winning condition (b). Concretely, we replace (b) with (b') m' $\in \{m^*, \tilde{m}\}$ holds, where $\tilde{m}$ is a random plaintext.

Since we relaxed $\mathcal{A}$'s winning condition, we have $\Pr[S_1] \leq \Pr[S_2]$.

Game 3: We generate ct_1 as $ct_1 \leftarrow$ PKE.Enc($ek_1, \tilde{m}$) instead of $ct_1 \leftarrow$ PKE.Enc (ek_1, m^*).

The only difference between Game 2 and 3 is that ct_0 and ct_1 are ciphertexts of the same plaintext in Game 2, but they are ciphertexts of different plaintexts in Game 3. Thus, we obtain $|\Pr[S_2] - \Pr[S_3]| = \mathsf{negl}(\lambda)$ using CoIC security of PKE.

We complete the proof by showing that $\Pr[S_3] \leq 1/2 + \mathsf{negl}(\lambda)$ holds if PKE satisfies one-wayness (that is implied by CoIC-KLA security). To show it, we use the following Fact 1.

Fact 1: Assume PKE satisfies one-wayness. Then, given $1/\sqrt{2}(|0\rangle\,|dk_0\rangle + |1\rangle\,|dk_1\rangle)$, PKE.Enc($ek_0, m^*$), and PKE.Enc($ek_1, \tilde{m}$), no adversary can obtain ($dk_0, \tilde{m}$) or (dk_1, m^*) with non-negligible probability.

This can be proved by using the fact that even if we measure $1/\sqrt{2}(|0\rangle\,|dk_0\rangle + |1\rangle\,|dk_1\rangle)$ in the computational basis before giving it to the adversary, the adversary still has success probability at least $\epsilon/2$, where ϵ is the success probability of the original experiment [13, Lemma 2.1].

Suppose $\Pr[S_3] = 1/2 + 1/\mathsf{poly}(\lambda)$ for some polynomial poly. This means that conditioned that m' $\in \{m^*, \tilde{m}\}$, $\widetilde{dk}$ returned by $\mathcal{A}$ passes the verification with probability significantly greater than $1/2$. Thus, if we measure $\widetilde{dk}$ in the computational basis, we obtain dk_0 with some inverse polynomial probability and also dk_1 with some inverse polynomial probability. (If either one is obtained with overwhelming probability, $\widetilde{dk}$ cannot pass the verification with probability significantly greater than $1/2$.) This means that using $\mathcal{A}$, we can obtain either one pair of ($dk_0, \tilde{m}$) or (dk_1, m^*) with inverse polynomial probability, which contradicts Fact 1. Thus, we obtain $\Pr[S_3] \leq 1/2 + \mathsf{negl}(\lambda)$.

From the above discussions, we can conclude that if PKE satisfies CoIC-KLA security, Basic satisfies 1/2-OW-KLA security.

Full OW-KLA Security by Parallel Repetition. To achieve a fully OW-KLA secure scheme, we apply parallel amplification to Basic in the following way. When generating a key tuple, we generate λ key tuples ($ek_i, \widetilde{dk_i}, vk_i$) of Basic and set $ek' := (ek_i)_{i \in [\lambda]}$, $\widetilde{dk}' := (\widetilde{dk_i})_{i \in [\lambda]}$, and $vk' := (vk_i)_{i \in [\lambda]}$. When encrypting a plaintext m, we divide it into λ pieces $m_1, \cdots, m_\lambda$, and encrypt each m_i using ek_i. Then decryption and verification are performed naturally by running the underlying procedures in Basic for every $i \in [\lambda]$. We can prove the full OW-KLA security of this construction using a strategy analogous to that used to achieve 1/2-OW-KLA security of Basic. We remark that it is unclear whether we can amplify 1/2-OW-KLA security to full OW-KLA security in a black box way and our security proof relies on the specific structure of our scheme.

Constructing CoIC-KLA Secure PKE Scheme. In the rest of this overview, we mainly explain how to construct CoIC-KLA secure PKE scheme. We construct it using 1-key Ciphertext-Policy Functional Encryption (CPFE) that in turn can be based on any IND-CPA secure PKE scheme.

We first review the definition of 1-key CPFE scheme. A 1-key CPFE scheme CPFE consists of four algorithms (FE.Setup, FE.KG, FE.Enc, FE.Dec). Given a security parameter, FE.Setup outputs a master public key mpk and a master secret key msk. FE.KG takes as input msk and a string x and outputs a decryption key sk_x tied to the string x. FE.Enc takes as input mpk and a description of a circuit C and outputs a ciphertext ct. If we decrypt this ciphertext ct with sk_x using FE.Dec, we can obtain $C(x)$. The security of it states that ciphertexts of two circuits C_0 and C_1 are computationally indistinguishable for an adversary who has decryption key sk_x for x of its choice, as long as $C_0(x) = C_1(x)$ holds.

Letting CPFE = (FE.Setup, FE.KG, FE.Enc, FE.Dec) be a 1-key CPFE scheme, we construct a CoIC secure PKE scheme PKE = (PKE.KG, PKE.Enc, PKE.Dec) as follows. PKE.KG generates (mpk, msk) $\leftarrow$ CPFE.Setup(1^λ) and a decryption key $sk_x \leftarrow$ CPFE.KG(msk, x) for random string x, and outputs an encryption key ek := mpk and the corresponding decryption key dk := sk_x. Given ek = mpk and m, PKE.Enc outputs FE.Enc(mpk, $C[m]$), where $C[m]$ is the constant circuit that outputs msg on any input. Given dk = sk_x and ct, PKE.Dec simply outputs CPFE.Dec(sk_x, ct). We see that PKE satisfies decryption correctness from that of CPFE.

Before proving CoIC-KLA security of PKE, we explain a nice tracing property of PKE that plays an important role in the proof. It says that if there exists a decoder that can distinguish PKE.Enc(ek, m_0^*) and PKE.Enc(ek, m_1^*) with probability $1/2 + 1/\text{poly}(\lambda)$ for some plaintexts m_0^*, m_1^* and polynomial poly, we can extract the string x tied to the decryption key from the decoder. Concretely, the following fact holds.

Fact 2: Consider the following experiment. The challenger generates (ek := mpk, dk := sk_x) using PKE.KG and sends them to an adversary $\mathcal{A}$. $\mathcal{A}$ outputs a decoder D together with m_0^*, m_1^* that can predict random bit b from PKE.Enc(ek, m_b^*) with probability $1/2 + 1/\text{poly}(\lambda)$ for some polynomial poly. Then, we can extract x from D with inverse polynomial probability.

In fact, if the decoder D is a classical decoder, we can extract x from D with a probability close to 1 as follows. Let $\tilde{C}[b, m_0, m_1, i]$ be the circuit that is given x as an input and outputs $m_{b \oplus x[i]}$, where $x[i]$ is the i-th bit of x. Then, suppose we generate many random $(b, \text{FE.Enc}(\text{mpk}, \tilde{C}[b, m_0^*, m_1^*, i]))$ and estimate the probability that the decoder D outputs b given FE.Enc(mpk, $\tilde{C}[b, m_0^*, m_1^*, i]$) as an input. By the CPFE's security, FE.Enc(mpk, $\tilde{C}[b, m_0^*, m_1^*, i]$) is indistinguishable from a correctly generated ciphertext of $m^*_{b \oplus x_i}$, that is, $\mathsf{PKE.Enc}(\mathsf{ek}, m^*_{b \oplus x_i}) = \mathsf{FE.Enc}(\mathsf{mpk}, C[m^*_{b \oplus x_i}])$ from the view of $\mathcal{A}$ and D who has sk_x, since $\tilde{C}[b, m^*_0, m^*_1, i](x) = C[m^*_{b \oplus x_i}](x) = m^*_{b \oplus x_i}$. Then, the result of the estimation should be as follows.

- In the case of $x[i] = 0$, each sample used for the estimation looks $(b, \mathsf{PKE.Enc}(\mathsf{ek}, m_b))$ from the view of D. Thus, the result of the estimation should be greater than $1/2$ from the fact that D correctly predicts random bit b from $\mathsf{PKE.Enc}(\mathsf{ek}, m_b)$ with probability $1/2 + 1/\mathrm{poly}(\lambda)$.
- In the case of $x[i] = 1$, each sample used for the estimation looks $(b, \mathsf{PKE.Enc}(\mathsf{ek}, m_{1 \oplus b}))$ from the view of D. Thus, the result of the estimation should be smaller than $1/2$ since D outputs $1 \oplus b$ given $\mathsf{PKE.Enc}(\mathsf{ek}, m_{1 \oplus b})$ with probability $1/2 + 1/\mathrm{poly}(\lambda)$.

Therefore, by checking if the result of the estimation is greater than $1/2$ or not, we can extract $x[i]$. By doing this for every i, we can extract entire bits of x.

The above extraction technique is a direct application of that used by Kitagawa and Nishimaki [28] to realize watermarking scheme secure against quantum adversaries. By using their technique, even if the decoder is a quantum decoder $\mathcal{D}$ that consists of a unitary and an initial quantum state, we can extract x from $\mathcal{D}$ with inverse polynomial probability, as long as $\mathcal{D}$ has a high distinguishing advantage. Roughly speaking, this is done by performing the above estimation using (approximate) projective implementation proposed by Zhandry [37] that is based on the technique by Marriott and Watrous [30]. By extending the above extraction technique, we can obtain the following fact.

Fact 3: Consider the following experiment. The challenger generates $(\mathsf{ek}_0 := \mathsf{mpk}_0, \mathsf{dk}_0 := \mathsf{sk}_{x_0})$ and $(\mathsf{ek}_1 := \mathsf{mpk}_1, \mathsf{dk}_1 := \mathsf{sk}_{x_1})$ using $\mathsf{PKE.KG}$, and sends ek_0, ek_1, and $1/\sqrt{2}(|0\rangle |\mathsf{dk}_0\rangle + |1\rangle |\mathsf{dk}_1\rangle) = 1/\sqrt{2}(|0\rangle |\mathsf{sk}_{x_0}\rangle + |1\rangle |\mathsf{sk}_{x_1}\rangle)$ to an adversary $\mathcal{A}$. $\mathcal{A}$ outputs a quantum decoder $\mathcal{D}$ together with (m^*_0, m^*_1) that can predict b from $\mathsf{PKE.Enc}(\mathsf{ek}_0, m_a)$ and $\mathsf{PKE.Enc}(\mathsf{ek}_1, m_{a \oplus b})$ with probability $1/2 + 1/\mathrm{poly}(\lambda)$ for some polynomial poly. Then, we can extract both x_0 and x_1 from $\mathcal{D}$ with inverse polynomial probability.

We now explain how we can prove CoIC-KLA security of PKE using Fact 3. To this end, we introduce one more fact.

Fact 4: Given mpk_0, mpk_1, and $1/\sqrt{2}(|0\rangle |\mathsf{sk}_{x_0}\rangle + |1\rangle |\mathsf{sk}_{x_1}\rangle)$, where $(\mathsf{mpk}_0, \mathsf{sk}_{x_0})$ and $(\mathsf{mpk}_1, \mathsf{sk}_{x_1})$ are generated as in $\mathsf{PKE.KG}$, no adversary can compute both x_0 and x_1 with non-negligible probability.

Similarly to Fact 1, we can prove this from the fact that even if we measure $1/\sqrt{2}(|0\rangle |\mathsf{sk}_{x_0}\rangle + |1\rangle |\mathsf{sk}_{x_1}\rangle)$ in the computational basis before giving it to the adversary, the adversary still has success probability at least $\epsilon/2$, where ϵ is the success probability of the original experiment [13, Lemma 2.1].

Suppose there exists a QPT adversary $\mathcal{A}$ that breaks CoIC-KLA security of PKE. We consider the following adversary $\mathcal{B}$ using $\mathcal{A}$. Given mpk_0, mpk_1, and $1/\sqrt{2}(|0\rangle |\mathsf{sk}_{x_0}\rangle + |1\rangle |\mathsf{sk}_{x_1}\rangle)$, $\mathcal{B}$ simulates CoIC-KLA security game for $\mathcal{A}$ by setting $\mathsf{ek}_0 := \mathsf{mpk}_0$, $\mathsf{ek}_1 := \mathsf{mpk}_1$, and $d\!k := 1/\sqrt{2}(|0\rangle\,|\mathsf{sk}_{x_0}\rangle + |1\rangle\,|\mathsf{sk}_{x_1}\rangle)$ until $\mathcal{A}$ outputs two plaintexts $(\mathsf{m}_0^*, \mathsf{m}_1^*)$. When $\mathcal{A}$ makes a verification query, $\mathcal{B}$ just returns a random bit. Let U be the unitary that performs the rest of $\mathcal{A}$'s actions given the challenge ciphertexts. Also, let q be the internal state of $\mathcal{A}$ at this point. Then, from the averaging argument and the fact that $\mathcal{B}$ correctly answers to $\mathcal{A}$'s verification query with probability $1/2$, with some inverse polynomial probability, the quantum decoder $\mathcal{D} = (U, q)$ is a decoder that can predict b from $\mathsf{PKE.Enc}(\mathsf{ek}_0, \mathsf{m}_a^*)$ and $\mathsf{PKE.Enc}(\mathsf{ek}_1, \mathsf{m}_{a\oplus b}^*)$ with probability $1/2 + 1/\mathrm{poly}(\lambda)$ for some polynomial poly. Thus, by using the extractor that is guaranteed to exist by Fact 3, $\mathcal{B}$ can obtain both x_0 and x_1 with some inverse polynomial probability, which contradicts Fact 4. This means that PKE satisfies CoIC-KLA security.

Extension to Advanced Encryption Systems with Secure Key Leasing. We also provide constructions of advanced encryption schemes such as ABE and FE with secure key leasing. We do not focus on IBE in this paper since IBE is a special case of ABE and our transformation preserves the underlying function class.[4] We construct these schemes by carefully combining standard ABE (resp. FE) with PKE-SKL in the way that each decryption key of the resulting ABE-SKL (resp. FE-SKL) scheme includes a decryption key of the underlying PKE-SKL scheme and a ciphertext of the ABE-SKL (resp. FE-SKL) scheme cannot be decrypted without the decryption key of the underlying PKE-SKL scheme. By doing so, our ABE-SKL and FE-SKL take over the secure key leasing security from the underlying PKE-SKL. Moreover, since PKE-SKL can be based on any PKE, our ABE-SKL and FE-SKL can be based on any standard ABE and FE, respectively.

ABE-SKL. Here, we provide an overview of ABE with secure key leasing. Let us start with the definition of plain ABE (without key leasing). An ABE scheme ABE consists of four algorithms (ABE.Setup, ABE.KG, ABE.Enc, ABE.Dec) and is associated with a relation R. Given a security parameter, ABE.Setup outputs a master public key mpk and a master secret key msk. ABE.KG takes as input msk and a key attribute y and outputs a user secret key sk_y tied to the attribute y. ABE.Enc takes as input mpk, a ciphertext attribute x, and a message msg and outputs a ciphertext ct. The decryption of the ciphertext is possible only when $R(x, y) = 1$. For this reason, we call a user secret key for attribute y satisfying $R(x, y) = 1$ a decrypting key (for a ciphertext associated with x). As for the security, we require that $\mathsf{ABE.Enc}(x^*, \mathsf{m}_0^*)$ should be computationally indistinguishable from $\mathsf{ABE.Enc}(x^*, \mathsf{m}_1^*)$ as long as an adversary is only given non-decrypting keys for the ciphertext (i.e., user secret keys for y satisfying $R(x^*, y) = 0$).

We now define the notion of ABE with secure key leasing (ABE-SKL) by extending the syntax of ABE. The difference from the above is that the key

---

[4] Although ABE is a special case of FE, we need stronger assumptions for (collusion-resistant) FE to instantiate them. In addition, the security level of FE-SKL that we can achieve is different from that of ABE-SKL. Hence, we consider both ABE and FE.

generation algorithm is now quantum and it outputs user secret key usk_y along with verification key vk. We also additionally introduce a verification algorithm that takes vk and a quantum state usk' and outputs $\top$ if it judges that the user secret key corresponding to vk is correctly returned and $\bot$ otherwise. As for the security, we require that $\mathsf{ABE.Enc}(x^*, m_0)$ should be computationally indistinguishable from $\mathsf{ABE.Enc}(x^*, m_1)$ if the adversary returns all decrypting keys before it is given the challenge ciphertext. Here, we say the adversary returns the key if the adversary provides the challenger with a quantum state that makes the verification algorithm output $\top$.

For the construction, the basic idea is to use ABE for access control and PKE-SKL for obtaining security against key leasing attacks. To enable this idea, we encrypt a message m for an attribute x so that the decryptor recovers PKE-SKL ciphertext $\mathsf{skl.ct} = \mathsf{SKL.Enc}(\mathsf{skl.ek}, m)$ if it has decrypting key and nothing otherwise, where skl.ek is an individual encryption key corresponding to the user. The user is given the corresponding decryption key skl.dk and can recover the message by decrypting skl.ct. Roughly speaking, the security follows since (1) a user with a non-decrypting key cannot obtain any information and (2) even a user with a decrypting key cannot recover the message from skl.ct once it returns skl.dk due to the security of SKL.

The generation of user individual SKL ciphertext is somewhat non-trivial since ABE can only encrypt a single message. In order to achieve this, we use an idea similar to [23,32] that combines encryption with the garbled circuits. In particular, we garble the encryption circuit of SKL that hardwires a message and encrypt the labels by ABE. We then provide a secret key of ABE for a user only for the positions corresponding to skl.ek. This allows a user with decrypting key to recover the labels corresponding to skl.ek and then run the garbled circuit on input the labels to recover skl.ct.

Unfortunately, the introduction of the garbled circuits in the construction poses some limitations on the security of the scheme. In particular, once the adversary obtains two decrypting user secret keys, the message can be revealed from the garbled circuit in the ciphertext since the security of garbled circuits is compromised when labels for two different inputs are revealed. Therefore, we are only able to prove 1-bounded distinguishing key security,[5] where the adversary can make a single decrypting key query and should return the key before the challenge ciphertext is given. We note that the adversary can make an arbitrary number of non-decrypting key queries throughout the game, unlike bounded collusion ABE [21,26] and only the number of decrypting keys is bounded.

Ideally, we would like to have a scheme without restriction on the number of decrypting keys. However, we do not know how to achieve it without strong assumptions like functional encryption or indistinguishability obfuscation. Instead, we achieve intermediate security notion that we call q-bounded

---

[5] When we consider the security game for ABE-SKL, a decrypting key can be used for distinguishing the challenge bit by decrypting the challenge ciphertext (if it is not returned). Therefore, we use the term "decrypting key" and "distinguishing key" interchangeably.

distinguishing key security without introducing additional assumption, where the number of decrypting keys is bounded by some pre-determined polynomial. To do so, we use the same idea as [26], which converts single bounded collusion ABE into q-bounded collusion ABE. The construction is based on the balls and bins idea, where we prepare multiple "bins", each of which consists of multiple instances of 1-bounded distinguishing key secure ABE-SKL 1ABE. The key generation algorithm chooses a single instance from each bin randomly and generates a user secret key for each of them. The encryption algorithm secret shares the message and encrypts them using the instances of the 1ABE so that the same share is encrypted by the instances in the same bin. By careful choices of the parameters and analysis, in the security proof, we can argue that there exists a bin such that 1ABE instances used for generating decrypting keys in that bin are all distinct. This means that for every 1ABE instance in that bin, only a single decrypting key is generated and thus, we can use 1-bounded distinguishing key security for each of them. While this overall proof strategy is the same as [26], our proof is a little bit more complex than theirs because the adversary is allowed to make an unbounded number of (non-decrypting) key queries.

PKFE-SKL. We move to the overview of PKFE-SKL. In this work, we focus on Key-Policy FE (KPFE) with secure key leasing. We start with the definition of plain FE (without key leasing). An FE scheme FE consists of four algorithms (FE.Setup, FE.KG, FE.Enc, FE.Dec) and is associated with a function class $\mathcal{F}$. Given a security parameter, FE.Setup outputs a public key pk and a master secret key msk. FE.KG takes as input msk and a function $f \in \mathcal{F}$ and outputs a functional decryption key sk_f tied to the function f. FE.Enc takes as input pk and a plaintext x and outputs a ciphertext ct. The decryption result is $f(x)$. For security, we require that $\mathsf{FE.Enc}(\mathsf{pk}, x_0)$ should be computationally indistinguishable from $\mathsf{FE.Enc}(\mathsf{pk}, x_1)$ as long as an adversary is only given functional decryption keys for $\{f_i\}_i$ such that $f_i(x_0) = f_i(x_1)$ for all i.

We define the notion of FE with secure key leasing (FE-SKL) by extending the syntax of FE like ABE-SKL. The key generation algorithm is now quantum and it outputs functional decryption key $\widetilde{\mathsf{sk}}_f$ along with verification key vk. We also introduce a verification algorithm that takes vk and a quantum state $\widetilde{\mathsf{sk}}'$ and outputs $\top$ if it judges that the functional decryption key corresponding to vk is correctly returned and $\bot$ otherwise.

In the security game of PKFE-SKL, the adversary can send a *distinguishing* key query f such that $f(x_0^*) \neq f(x_1^*)$ where (x_0^*, x_1^*) are the challenge plaintexts *as long as it returns a valid functional decryption key for f.* We consider a security game where the adversary can send unbounded polynomially many distinguishing and non-distinguishing (that is, $f(x_0^*) = f(x_1^*)$) key queries and tries to distinguish $\mathsf{FE.Enc}(\mathsf{pk}, x_0)$ from $\mathsf{FE.Enc}(\mathsf{pk}, x_1)$.

We transform a (classical) PKFE scheme into a PKFE scheme with secure key leasing by using the power of PKE-SKL. The basic idea is as follows. When we generate a functional decryption key for function f, we generate a key triple of PKE-SKL and a functional decryption key of the classical PKFE for a function W that computes a PKE-SKL ciphertext of $f(x)$. That is, we wrap $f(x)$ by

PKE-SKL encryption. A decryption key of PKE-SKL is appended to fe.sk$_W$, which is the functional decryption key for W. Hence, we can decrypt the PKE-SKL ciphertext and obtain $f(x)$. The PKE-SKL decryption key for f is useless for another function g since we use different key triples of PKE-SKL for each function.

More specifically, we generate PKE-SKL keys (skl.ek, skl.$s\!k$, skl.vk) and a PKFE functional decryption key fe.sk$_W$ $\leftarrow$ FE.KG(fe.msk, $W[f, \text{skl.ek}]$), where function $W[f, \text{skl.ek}]$ takes as input x and outputs a PKE-SKL ciphertext SKL.Enc(skl.ek, $f(x)$).[6] A functional decryption key for f consists of (fe.sk$_W$, skl.$s\!k$). A ciphertext of x is a (classical) PKFE ciphertext FE.Enc(fe.pk, x). If we return skl.$s\!k$ for f (verified by skl.vk) before we obtain FE.Enc(fe.pk, x), we cannot obtain $f(x)$ from SKL.Enc(skl.ek, $f(x)$) by the security of PKE-SKL.

We need to prove security against an adversary that obtains a functional decryption key for f such that $f(x_0^*) \neq f(x_1^*)$ where (x_0^*, x_1^*) is a pair of challenge plaintexts if the adversary returns the functional decryption key. To handle this issue, we rely on IND-KLA security and need to embed a challenge ciphertext of PKE-SKL into a PKFE ciphertext. We use the trapdoor method of FE (a.k.a. Trojan method) [6,14] for this purpose. We embed an SKFE functional decryption key and ciphertext in a PKFE functional decryption key and ciphertext, respectively. We use these SKFE functional decryption key and ciphertext for the trapdoor mode of PKFE. We gradually change SKFE ciphertexts and keys so that we can embed a PKE-SKL challenge ciphertext by using the adaptively single-ciphertext function privacy of SKFE. Once we succeed in embedding a PKE-SKL challenge ciphertext, we can change a ciphertext of x_0^* into a ciphertext of x_1^* such that $f(x_0^*) \neq f(x_1^*)$ as long as the functional decryption key $s\!k_f = $ (fe.sk$_W$, skl.$s\!k$) for f is returned. This is because skl.$s\!k$ is returned and we can use IND-KLA security under skl.ek.

1.4 Other Related Work

Quantum Copy Protection. Aaronson [1] introduced the notion of quantum copy protection and constructed a quantum copy protection scheme for arbitrary unlearnable Boolean functions relative to a quantum oracle. He also provided two heuristic copy-protection schemes for point functions in the standard model. Coladangelo et al. [18] provided a quantum copy-protection scheme for a class of evasive functions in the QROM. Subsequently, Aaronson et al. [3] constructed a quantum copy protection scheme for unlearnable functions relative to classical oracles. By instantiating the oracle with post-quantum candidate obfuscation schemes, they obtained a heuristic construction of copy protection. Coladangelo et al. [17] provided a copy-protection scheme for pseudorandom functions in the plain model assuming iO, OWF and extractable witness encryption, or assuming subexponential iO, subexponential OWF, LWE and a strong "monogamy

---

[6] We ignore the issue of encryption randomness here. In our construction, we use (puncturable) PRFs to generate encryption randomness.

property" (which was was proven to be true in a follow-up work [19]). Ananth et al. [7,8] also constructed copy protection for point functions, which in turn can be transformed into copy protection for compute-and-compare programs. Sattath and Wyborski [33] studied unclonable decryptors, which are an extension of SDE. Their unclonable decryptors scheme is *secret key* encryption and can be instantiated with iO and OWF, or quantum oracles.

Secure Software Leasing. Secure software leasing (SSL) was introduced by Ananth and La Placa [9], where they also provided the first SSL scheme supporting a subclass of "evasive" functions by relying on the existence of public key quantum money and the learning with errors assumption. Evasive functions is a class of functions for which it is hard to find an accepting input given only black-box access to the function. Their construction achieves a strong security notion called *infinite term security*. They also demonstrate that there exists an unlearnable function class such that it is impossible to achieve an SSL scheme for that function class, even in the CRS model. Later, Coladangelo et al. [18] improved the security notion achieved by [9] by relying on the QROM, for the same class of evasive functions. Additionally, Kitagawa, Nishimaki and Yamakawa [29] provided a finite term secure SSL scheme for pseudorandom functions (PRFs) in the CRS model by assuming the hardness of the LWE problem against polynomial time quantum adversaries. Additionally, this work achieves classical communication. Further, Broadbent et al. [16] showed that SSL is achievable for the aforementioned evasive circuits without any setup or computational assumptions that were required by previous work, but with finite term security, quantum communication and correctness based on a distribution. The notion of secure leasing for the powerful primitive of functional encryption was studied by Kitagawa and Nishimaki [27], who introduced the notion of *secret key* functional encryption (SKFE) with secure key leasing and provided a transformation from standard SKFE into SKFE with secure key leasing without relying on any additional assumptions.

Certified Deletion. Broadbent and Islam [15] introduced the notion of quantum encryption with certified deletion, where we can generate a (classical) certificate to ensure that *a ciphertext* is deleted. They constructed a one-time SKE scheme with certified deletion without computational assumptions. After that, many works presented various quantum encryption primitives (PKE, ABE, FE and so on) with certified deletion [10,24,25,31]. The root of quantum encryption with certified deletion is revocable quantum time-released encryption by Unruh [34]. It is an extension of time-released encryption where a sender can revoke quantum encrypted data before a pre-determined time. If the revocation succeeds, the receiver cannot obtain the plaintext information.

2   Preliminaries

Notations and Conventions. In this paper, standard math or sans serif font stands for classical algorithms (e.g., C or Gen) and classical variables (e.g., x or pk). Calligraphic font stands for quantum algorithms (e.g., $\mathcal{G}en$) and calligraphic font and/or the bracket notation for (mixed) quantum states (e.g., q or $|\psi\rangle$).

Let $[\ell]$ denote the set of integers $\{1, \cdots, \ell\}$, λ denote a security parameter, and $y := z$ denote that y is set, defined, or substituted by z. For a finite set X and a distribution D, $x \leftarrow X$ denotes selecting an element from X uniformly at random, $x \leftarrow D$ denotes sampling an element x according to D. Let $y \leftarrow \mathsf{A}(x)$ and $y \leftarrow \mathcal{A}(\chi)$ denote assigning to y the output of a probabilistic or deterministic algorithm A and a quantum algorithm $\mathcal{A}$ on an input x and χ, respectively. When we explicitly show that A uses randomness r, we write $y \leftarrow \mathsf{A}(x; r)$. PPT and QPT algorithms stand for probabilistic polynomial-time algorithms and polynomial-time quantum algorithms, respectively. Let negl denote a negligible function. For strings $x, y \in \{0, 1\}^n$, $x \cdot y$ denotes $\bigoplus_{i \in [n]} x_i y_i$ where x_i and y_i denote the ith bit of x and y, respectively.

Standard Cryptographic Tools. We omit the definitions of standard cryptographic tools including SKE, PKE, ABE, FE, puncturable PRFs, and garbling schemes. See Sect. 2.1 of the full version for their definitions.

3   Public Key Encryption with Secure Key Leasing

We define PKE-SKL and its security notions and show a relationship between them.

Definition 3.1 (PKE with Secure Key Leasing). *A PKE-SKL scheme* SKL *is a tuple of four algorithms* $(\mathcal{KG}, \mathsf{Enc}, \mathcal{D}ec, \mathcal{V}rfy)$. *Below, let* $\mathcal{X}$ *be the message space of* SKL.

$\mathcal{KG}(1^\lambda) \to (\mathsf{ek}, d\!k, \mathsf{vk})$: *The key generation algorithm takes a security parameter* 1^λ, *and outputs an encryption key* ek, *a decryption key* $d\!k$, *and a verification key* vk.

$\mathsf{Enc}(\mathsf{ek}, \mathsf{m}) \to \mathsf{ct}$: *The encryption algorithm takes an encryption key* ek *and a message* $\mathsf{m} \in \mathcal{X}$, *and outputs a ciphertext* ct.

$\mathcal{D}ec(d\!k, \mathsf{ct}) \to \tilde{\mathsf{m}}$: *The decryption algorithm takes a decryption key* $d\!k$ *and a ciphertext* ct, *and outputs a value* $\tilde{\mathsf{m}}$.

$\mathcal{V}rfy(\mathsf{vk}, \widetilde{d\!k}) \to \top / \bot$: *The verification algorithm takes a verification key* vk *and a (possibly malformed) decryption key* $\widetilde{d\!k}$, *and outputs* $\top$ *or* $\bot$.

Decryption correctness: *For every* $\mathsf{m} \in \mathcal{X}$, *we have*

$$\Pr\left[\mathcal{D}ec(d\!k, \mathsf{ct}) = \mathsf{m} \;\middle|\; \begin{array}{l} (\mathsf{ek}, d\!k, \mathsf{vk}) \leftarrow \mathcal{KG}(1^\lambda) \\ \mathsf{ct} \leftarrow \mathsf{Enc}(\mathsf{ek}, \mathsf{m}) \end{array}\right] = 1 - \mathsf{negl}(\lambda).$$

Verification correctness: *We have*

$$\Pr\left[\mathcal{V}rfy(\mathsf{vk}, d\!k) = \top \;\middle|\; (\mathsf{ek}, d\!k, \mathsf{vk}) \leftarrow \mathcal{KG}(1^\lambda)\right] = 1 - \mathsf{negl}(\lambda).$$

Remark 3.1. We can assume without loss of generality that a decryption key of a PKE-SKL scheme is reusable, i.e., it can be reused to decrypt (polynomially) many ciphertexts. In particular, we can asusme that for honestly generated ct and $d\!k$, if we decrypt ct by using $d\!k$, the state of the decryption key after the decryption is negligibly close to that before the decryption in terms of trace distance. This is because the output of the decryption is almost deterministic by decryption correctness, and thus such an operation can be done without almost disturbing the input state by the gentle measurement lemma [36]. A similar remark applies to all variants of PKE-SKL (IBE, ABE, and FE with SKL) defined in this paper.

Remark 3.2. Though we are the first to define PKE with secure key leasing, SKFE with secure key leasing was already defined by Kitagawa and Nishimaki [27]. The above definition is a natural adaptation of their definition with the important difference that we do not require classical certificate of deletion.

We define two security definitions for PKE-SKL, IND-KLA and OW-KLA security.

Definition 3.2 (IND-KLA Security). *We say that a PKE-SKL scheme* SKL *with the message space* $\mathcal{X}$ *is IND-KLA secure, if it satisfies the following requirement, formalized from the experiment* $\mathsf{Exp}^{\mathsf{ind\text{-}kla}}_{\mathsf{SKL},\mathcal{A}}(1^\lambda, \mathsf{coin})$ *between an adversary* $\mathcal{A}$ *and a challenger* $\mathcal{C}$:

1. $\mathcal{C}$ *runs* $(\mathsf{ek}, \widetilde{dk}, \mathsf{vk}) \leftarrow \mathcal{KG}(1^\lambda)$ *and sends* ek *and* $\widetilde{dk}$ *to* $\mathcal{A}$.
2. *Throughout the experiment,* $\mathcal{A}$ *can access the following (stateful) verification oracle* $O_{\mathcal{V}rfy}$ *where* V *is initialized to be* $\perp$:

   $O_{\mathcal{V}rfy}(\widetilde{dk})$: *It runs* $d \leftarrow \mathsf{Vrfy}(\mathsf{vk}, \widetilde{dk})$ *and returns* d. *If* $V = \perp$ *and* $d = \top$, *it updates* $V := \top$.
3. $\mathcal{A}$ *sends* $(\mathsf{m}_0^*, \mathsf{m}_1^*) \in \mathcal{X}^2$ *to* $\mathcal{C}$. *If* $V = \perp$, $\mathcal{C}$ *output* 0 *as the final output of this experiment. Otherwise,* $\mathcal{C}$ *generates* $\mathsf{ct}^* \leftarrow \mathsf{Enc}(\mathsf{ek}, \mathsf{m}_{\mathsf{coin}}^*)$ *and sends* ct^* *to* $\mathcal{A}$.
4. $\mathcal{A}$ *outputs a guess* coin' *for* coin. $\mathcal{C}$ *outputs* coin' *as the final output of the experiment.*

For any QPT $\mathcal{A}$, *it holds that*

$$\mathsf{Adv}^{\mathsf{ind\text{-}kla}}_{\mathsf{SKL},\mathcal{A}}(\lambda) := \left| \Pr[\mathsf{Exp}^{\mathsf{ind\text{-}kla}}_{\mathsf{SKL},\mathcal{A}}(1^\lambda, 0) \to 1] - \Pr[\mathsf{Exp}^{\mathsf{ind\text{-}kla}}_{\mathsf{SKL},\mathcal{A}}(1^\lambda, 1) \to 1] \right| \leq \mathsf{negl}(\lambda).$$

We say that SKL *is 1-query IND-KLA secure if the above holds for any QPT* $\mathcal{A}$ *that makes at most one query to* $O_{\mathcal{V}rfy}$.

Remark 3.3. When we consider a 1-query adversary, we can assume that its query is made before receiving the challenge ciphertext ct^* without loss of generality. This is because otherwise the experiment always outputs 0.

Remark 3.4. By a standard hybrid argument, one can show that IND-KLA security implies multi-challenge IND-KLA security where the adversary is allowed to request arbitrarily many challenge ciphertexts. Thus, if we have an IND-KLA secure PKE-SKL scheme for single-bit messages, we can extend the plaintext length to an arbitrary polynomial by bit-by-bit encryption.

Definition 3.3 (OW-KLA Security). *We say that a PKE-SKL scheme* SKL *with the message space* $\mathcal{X}$ *is OW-KLA secure, if it satisfies the following requirement, formalized from the experiment* $\mathsf{Exp}^{\mathsf{ow\text{-}kla}}_{\mathsf{SKL},\mathcal{A}}(1^\lambda)$ *between an adversary* $\mathcal{A}$ *and a challenger* $\mathcal{C}$:

1. $\mathcal{C}$ *runs* $(\mathsf{ek}, \widetilde{\mathit{dk}}, \mathsf{vk}) \leftarrow \mathcal{KG}(1^\lambda)$ *and sends* ek *and* $\widetilde{\mathit{dk}}$ *to* $\mathcal{A}$.
2. *Throughout the experiment,* $\mathcal{A}$ *can access the following (stateful) verification oracle* O_{Vrfy} *where* V *is initialized to be* $\bot$:

   $O_{\mathit{Vrfy}}(\widetilde{\mathit{dk}})$: *It runs* $d \leftarrow \mathsf{Vrfy}(\mathsf{vk}, \widetilde{\mathit{dk}})$ *and returns* d. *If* $V = \bot$ *and* $d = \top$, *it updates* $V := \top$.
3. $\mathcal{A}$ *sends* RequestChallenge *to* $\mathcal{C}$. *If* $V = \bot$, $\mathcal{C}$ *outputs* 0 *as the final output of this experiment. Otherwise,* $\mathcal{C}$ *chooses* $\mathsf{m}^* \leftarrow \mathcal{X}$, *generates* $\mathsf{ct}^* \leftarrow \mathsf{Enc}(\mathsf{ek}, \mathsf{m}^*)$ *and sends* ct^* *to* $\mathcal{A}$.
4. $\mathcal{A}$ *outputs* m. $\mathcal{C}$ *outputs* 1 *if* $\mathsf{m} = \mathsf{m}^*$ *and otherwise outputs* 0 *as the final output of the experiment.*

For any QPT $\mathcal{A}$, *it holds that*

$$\mathsf{Adv}^{\mathsf{ow\text{-}kla}}_{\mathsf{SKL},\mathcal{A}}(\lambda) := \Pr[\mathsf{Exp}^{\mathsf{ow\text{-}kla}}_{\mathsf{SKL},\mathcal{A}}(1^\lambda) \rightarrow 1] \leq \mathsf{negl}(\lambda).$$

We say that SKL *is 1-query OW-KLA secure if the above holds for any QPT* $\mathcal{A}$ *that makes at most one query to* O_{Vrfy}.

We show the following theorem.

Theorem 3.1 *If there exists a 1-query OW-KLA secure PKE-SKL scheme, there exists an IND-KLA secure PKE-SKL scheme.*

Thus, it suffices to construct 1-query OW-KLA secure scheme for constructing IND-KLA secure scheme. The proof is based on quantum Goldreich-Levin lemma with quantum auxiliar inputs [4,17] and goes through an additional security notion called one-more unreturnability (OMUR). See Sect. 3.2 of the full version for the proof.

4   Public Key Encryption with CoIC-KLA Security

We introduce a new security notion called CoIC-KLA security for PKE, and construct a PKE scheme that satisfies it based on any IND-CPA secure PKE scheme. Looking ahead, it is used as a building block of our construction of PKE-SKL in Sec. 5.

4.1   Definition

Definition 4.1 (CoIC-KLA Security). *We say that a PKE scheme* PKE *with the message space* $\mathcal{X}$ *is CoIC-KLA secure, if it satisfies the following requirement, formalized from the experiment* $\mathsf{Exp}^{\mathsf{coic\text{-}kla}}_{\mathsf{PKE},\mathcal{A}}(1^\lambda)$ *between an adversary* $\mathcal{A}$ *and a challenger* $\mathcal{C}$:

1. C runs $(\mathsf{ek}_0, \mathsf{dk}_0) \leftarrow \mathsf{KG}(1^\lambda)$ and $(\mathsf{ek}_1, \mathsf{dk}_1) \leftarrow \mathsf{KG}(1^\lambda)$, and generates $\widetilde{dk} := \frac{1}{\sqrt{2}}(|0\rangle\,|\mathsf{dk}_0\rangle + |1\rangle\,|\mathsf{dk}_1\rangle)$. C sends ek_0, ek_1, and $\widetilde{dk}$ to $\mathcal{A}$. $\mathcal{A}$ can get access to the following oracle only once.

   $\mathcal{O}(\widetilde{dk})$: On input a possibly malformed decryption key $\widetilde{dk}$, it applies a binary-outcome measurement $(\boldsymbol{I} - \Pi_{\mathrm{vrfy}}, \Pi_{\mathrm{vrfy}})$, where Π_{vrfy} is the projection to the right decryption key, i.e.,

   $$\Pi_{\mathrm{vrfy}} := \left(\frac{1}{\sqrt{2}}\left(|0\rangle\,|\mathsf{dk}_0\rangle + |1\rangle\,|\mathsf{dk}_1\rangle\right)\right)\left(\frac{1}{\sqrt{2}}\left(\langle 0|\,\langle \mathsf{dk}_0| + \langle 1|\,\langle \mathsf{dk}_1|\right)\right).$$

   It returns the measurement outcome (indicating whether the state was projected onto Π_{vrfy} or not).
2. $\mathcal{A}$ sends $(\mathsf{m}_0^*, \mathsf{m}_1^*) \in \mathcal{X}^2$ to C. C generates $a, b \leftarrow \{0, 1\}$ and generates $\mathsf{ct}_0^* \leftarrow \mathsf{Enc}(\mathsf{ek}_0, \mathsf{m}_a^*)$ and $\mathsf{ct}_1^* \leftarrow \mathsf{Enc}(\mathsf{ek}_1, \mathsf{m}_{a \oplus b}^*)$. C sends ct_0^* and ct_1^* to $\mathcal{A}$.
3. $\mathcal{A}$ outputs a guess b' for b. C outputs 1 if $b = b'$ and 0 otherwise as the final output of the experiment.

For any QPT $\mathcal{A}$, it holds that

$$\mathsf{Adv}_{\mathsf{PKE},\mathcal{A}}^{\mathsf{coic\text{-}kla}}(\lambda) := 2 \cdot \left|\Pr[\mathsf{Exp}_{\mathsf{PKE},\mathcal{A}}^{\mathsf{coic\text{-}kla}}(1^\lambda) \to 1] - \frac{1}{2}\right| \le \mathsf{negl}(\lambda).$$

4.2   Construction

We construct a CoIC-KLA secure PKE $\mathsf{PKE} = (\mathsf{Gen}, \mathsf{Enc}, \mathsf{Dec})$ using a 1-key CPFE scheme $\mathsf{CPFE} = (\mathsf{CPFE.Setup}, \mathsf{CPFE.KG}, \mathsf{CPFE.Enc}, \mathsf{CPFE.Dec})$ as a building block.

$\mathsf{Gen}(1^\lambda)$:
 – Generate $(\mathsf{MPK}, \mathsf{MSK}) \leftarrow \mathsf{CPFE.Setup}(1^\lambda)$.
 – Generate $x \leftarrow \{0, 1\}^\lambda$ and $\mathsf{sk}_x \leftarrow \mathsf{CPFE.KG}(\mathsf{MSK}, x)$.
 – Output $\mathsf{ek} := \mathsf{MPK}$ and $\mathsf{dk} := \mathsf{sk}_x$.
$\mathsf{Enc}(\mathsf{ek}, \mathsf{m})$:
 – Parse $\mathsf{ek} = \mathsf{MPK}$.
 – Let $C[\mathsf{m}]$ be a constant circuit that outputs m on any input. C is padded so that it has the same size as the circuit C^* appeared in the security proof.
 – Output $\mathsf{ct} \leftarrow \mathsf{CPFE.Enc}(\mathsf{MPK}, C[\mathsf{m}])$.
$\mathsf{Dec}(\mathsf{dk}, \mathsf{ct})$:
 – Parse $\mathsf{dk} = \mathsf{sk}_x$.
 – Output $\mathsf{m}' \leftarrow \mathsf{CPFE.Dec}(\mathsf{sk}_x, \mathsf{ct})$.

The decryption correctness of PKE follows from that of CPFE. We show the following theorem.

Theorem 4.1. *If* CPFE *is 1-key secure, then* PKE *is CoIC-KLA secure.*

In the full version, we actually prove that PKE satisfies a security notion called strong CoIC-KLA security, which implies CoIC-KLA security. See Sect. 4.3 of the full version for the proof.

Since 1-key CPFE exists if IND-CPA secure PKE exists, the above theorem implies the following theorem.

Theorem 4.2. *If there is an IND-CPA secure PKE scheme, then there is a CoIC-KLA secure PKE scheme.*

5   Construction of PKE-SKL

Let cPKE = (cPKE.KG, cPKE.Enc, cPKE.Dec) be a PKE scheme satisfying CoIC-KLA security with message space $\{0,1\}^\ell$ where $\ell = \omega(\log \lambda)$. Then, we construct a PKE-SKL scheme (SKL.$\mathcal{KG}$, SKL.Enc, SKL.$\mathcal{Dec}$, SKL.$\mathcal{Vrfy}$) with message space $\{0,1\}^{\lambda\ell}$ as follows.

SKL.$\mathcal{KG}(1^\lambda)$:
- Generate (cPKE.ek$_{i,b}$, cPKE.dk$_{i,b}$) ← cPKE.KG(1^λ) for $i \in [\lambda]$ and $b \in \{0,1\}$.
- Output an encryption key

$$\mathsf{ek} := \{\mathsf{cPKE.ek}_{i,b}\}_{i\in[\lambda],b\in\{0,1\}},$$

  a decryption key

$$d\!k := \bigotimes_{i\in[\lambda]} \frac{1}{\sqrt{2}}\left(|0\rangle\,|\mathsf{cPKE.dk}_{i,0}\rangle + |1\rangle\,|\mathsf{cPKE.dk}_{i,1}\rangle\right),$$

  and a verification key

$$\mathsf{vk} := \{\mathsf{cPKE.dk}_{i,b}\}_{i\in[\lambda],b\in\{0,1\}}.$$

SKL.Enc(ek, m):
- Parse ek = $\{\mathsf{cPKE.ek}_{i,b}\}_{i\in[\lambda],b\in\{0,1\}}$ and m = $m_1\|\dots\|m_\lambda$ where $m_i \in \{0,1\}^\ell$ for each $i \in [\lambda]$.
- Generate cPKE.ct$_{i,b}$ ← cPKE.Enc(cPKE.ek$_{i,b}$, m$_i$) for $i \in [\lambda]$ and $b \in \{0,1\}$.
- Output ct := $\{\mathsf{cPKE.ct}_{i,b}\}_{i\in[\lambda],b\in\{0,1\}}$.

SKL.$\mathcal{Dec}(d\!k, \mathsf{ct})$:
- Parse $d\!k = \bigotimes_{i\in[\lambda]} d\!k_i$ and ct = $\{\mathsf{cPKE.ct}_{i,b}\}_{i\in[\lambda],b\in\{0,1\}}$.
- Let U_{dec} be a unitary such that for all cPKE.dk′, cPKE.ct′$_0$, and cPKE.ct′$_1$:

$$|b\rangle\,|\mathsf{cPKE.dk}'\rangle\,|\mathsf{cPKE.ct}'_0, \mathsf{cPKE.ct}'_1\rangle\,|0\rangle$$

$$\xrightarrow{U_{\mathrm{dec}}} |b\rangle\,|\mathsf{cPKE.dk}'\rangle\,|\mathsf{cPKE.ct}'_0, \mathsf{cPKE.ct}'_1\rangle\,|\mathsf{cPKE.Dec}(\mathsf{cPKE.dk}', \mathsf{cPKE.ct}'_b)\rangle$$

Note that such a unitary can be computed in quantum polynomial-time since we assume that cPKE.Dec is a deterministic classical polynomial-time algorithm.

– For all $i \in [\lambda]$, generate

$$U_{\text{dec}} \left(\widetilde{dk}_i \otimes |\text{cPKE.ct}_{i,0}, \text{cPKE.ct}_{i,1}\rangle \langle \text{cPKE.ct}_{i,0}, \text{cPKE.ct}_{i,1}| \otimes |0\rangle \langle 0| \right) U_{\text{dec}}^\dagger,$$

measure the rightmost register, and let m'_i be the measurement outcome.

– Output $\mathsf{m}' := \mathsf{m}'_1 \| \ldots \| \mathsf{m}'_\lambda$.

SKL.$\mathcal{V}$rfy(vk, $\widetilde{dk}$):

– Parse $\mathsf{vk} = \{\text{cPKE.dk}_{i,b}\}_{i \in [\lambda], b \in \{0,1\}}$.

– Apply a binary-outcome measurement $(\boldsymbol{I} - \Pi_{\text{vrfy}}^{\text{vk}}, \Pi_{\text{vrfy}}^{\text{vk}})$ on $\widetilde{dk}$ where $\Pi_{\text{vrfy}}^{\text{vk}}$ is the projection onto the right decryption key, i.e.,

$$\Pi_{\text{vrfy}}^{\text{vk}} := \bigotimes_{i \in [\lambda]} \left(\frac{1}{\sqrt{2}} \left(|0\rangle |\text{cPKE.dk}_{i,0}\rangle + |1\rangle |\text{cPKE.dk}_{i,1}\rangle \right) \right)$$
$$\left(\frac{1}{\sqrt{2}} \left(\langle 0| \langle \text{cPKE.dk}_{i,0}| + \langle 1| \langle \text{cPKE.dk}_{i,1}| \right) \right).$$

If the measurement outcome is 1 (indicating that the state was projected onto $\Pi_{\text{vrfy}}^{\text{vk}}$), output $\top$ and otherwise output $\bot$.

The correctness of SKL easily follows from that of cPKE. Below, we show that SKL is 1-query OW-KLA secure.

Theorem 5.1. *If* cPKE *is CoIC-KLA secure, then* SKL *is 1-query OW-KLA secure.*

See Sect. 5 of the full version for the proof.

By combining Theorems 3.1, 4.2 and 5.1, we obtain the following theorem.

Theorem 5.2. *If there is an IND-CPA secure PKE scheme, then there is an IND-KLA secure PKE-SKL scheme.*

6   Attribute-based Encryption with Secure Key Leasing

6.1   Definitions

The syntax of ABE-SKL and its security are defined as follows.

Definition 6.1 (ABE with Secure Key Leasing). *An ABE-SKL scheme* ABE-SKL *is a tuple of six algorithms* (Setup, $\mathcal{KG}$, Enc, $\mathcal{D}ec$, $\mathcal{C}ert$, Vrfy). *Below, let* $\mathcal{X} = \{\mathcal{X}_\lambda\}_\lambda$, $\mathcal{Y} = \{\mathcal{Y}_\lambda\}_\lambda$, *and* $R = \{R_\lambda : \mathcal{X}_\lambda \times \mathcal{Y}_\lambda \to \{0,1\}\}_\lambda$ *be the ciphertext space, the key attribute space, and the associated relation of* ABE-SKL, *respectively.*

Setup(1^λ) $\to$ (pk, msk): *The setup algorithm takes a security parameter* 1^λ, *and outputs a public key* pk *and master secret key* msk.

$\mathcal{KG}$(msk, y) $\to$ (usk, vk): *The key generation algorithm takes a master secret key* msk *and a key attribute* $y \in \mathcal{Y}$, *and outputs a user secret key* usk *and a verification key* vk.

$\mathsf{Enc}(\mathsf{pk}, x, m) \rightarrow \mathsf{ct}$: *The encryption algorithm takes a public key* pk, *a ciphertext attribute* $x \in \mathcal{X}$, *and a plaintext* m, *and outputs a ciphertext* ct.

$\mathcal{D}ec(\mathit{usk}, x, \mathsf{ct}) \rightarrow z$: *The decryption algorithm takes a user secret key* usk, *a ciphertext attribute* x, *and a ciphertext* ct *and outputs a value* $z \in \{\perp\} \cup \{0,1\}^{\ell}$.

$\mathcal{V}rfy(\mathsf{vk}, \mathit{usk}') \rightarrow \top/\perp$: *The verification algorithm takes a verification key* vk *and a quantum state* usk', *and outputs* $\top$ *or* $\perp$.

Decryption correctness: *For every* $x \in \mathcal{X}$ *and* $y \in \mathcal{Y}$ *satisfying* $R(x, y) = 1$, *we have*

$$\Pr\left[\mathcal{D}ec(\mathit{usk}, x, \mathsf{ct}) = m \;\middle|\; \begin{array}{l} (\mathsf{pk}, \mathsf{msk}) \leftarrow \mathsf{Setup}(1^{\lambda}) \\ (\mathit{usk}, \mathsf{vk}) \leftarrow \mathcal{KG}(\mathsf{msk}, y) \\ \mathsf{ct} \leftarrow \mathsf{Enc}(\mathsf{pk}, x, m) \end{array}\right] = 1 - \mathsf{negl}(\lambda).$$

Verification correctness: *For every* $y \in \mathcal{Y}$, *we have*

$$\Pr\left[\mathcal{V}rfy(\mathsf{vk}, \mathit{usk}) = \top \;\middle|\; \begin{array}{l} (\mathsf{pk}, \mathsf{msk}) \leftarrow \mathsf{Setup}(1^{\lambda}) \\ (\mathit{usk}, \mathsf{vk}) \leftarrow \mathcal{KG}(\mathsf{msk}, y) \end{array}\right] = 1 - \mathsf{negl}(\lambda).$$

Definition 6.2 (Adaptive/Selective Indistinguishability against Key Leasing Attacks). *We say that an ABE-SKL scheme* ABE-SKL *for relation* $R : \mathcal{X} \times \mathcal{Y} \rightarrow \{0,1\}$ *is secure against adaptive indistinguishability against key leasing attacks (Ada-IND-KLA), if it satisfies the following requirement, formalized from the experiment* $\mathsf{Exp}^{\mathsf{ada\text{-}ind\text{-}kla}}_{\mathcal{A},\mathsf{ABE\text{-}SKL}}(1^{\lambda}, \mathsf{coin})$ *between an adversary* $\mathcal{A}$ *and a challenger:*

1. *At the beginning, the challenger runs* $(\mathsf{pk}, \mathsf{msk}) \leftarrow \mathsf{Setup}(1^{\lambda})$ *and initialize the list* $L_{\mathcal{KG}}$ *to be an empty set. Throughout the experiment,* $\mathcal{A}$ *can access the following oracles.*

   $O_{\mathcal{KG}}(y)$: *Given* y, *it finds an entry of the form* (y, vk, V) *from* $L_{\mathcal{KG}}$. *If there is such an entry, it returns* $\perp$. *Otherwise, it generates* $(\mathit{usk}, \mathsf{vk}) \leftarrow \mathcal{KG}(\mathsf{msk}, y)$, *sends* usk *to* $\mathcal{A}$, *and adds* $(y, \mathsf{vk}, \perp)$ *to* $L_{\mathcal{KG}}$.

   $O_{\mathcal{V}rfy}(y, \mathit{usk}')$: *Given* (y, usk'), *it finds an entry* (y, vk, V) *from* $L_{\mathcal{KG}}$. *(If there is no such entry, it returns* $\perp$.) *It then runs* $d := \mathcal{V}rfy(\mathsf{vk}, \mathit{usk}')$ *and returns* d *to* $\mathcal{A}$. *If* $V = \perp$, *it updates the entry into* (y, vk, d).

2. *When* $\mathcal{A}$ *sends* (x^*, m_0, m_1) *to the challenger, the challenger checks if for any entry* (y, vk, V) *in* $L_{\mathcal{KG}}$ *such that* $R(x^*, y) = 1$, *it holds that* $V = \top$. *If so, the challenger generates* $\mathsf{ct}^* \leftarrow \mathsf{Enc}(\mathsf{pk}, x^*, m_{\mathsf{coin}})$ *and sends* ct^* *to* $\mathcal{A}$. *Otherwise, the challenger outputs* 0.

3. $\mathcal{A}$ *continues to make queries to* $O_{\mathcal{KG}}(\cdot)$ *and* $O_{\mathcal{V}rfy}(\cdot, \cdot)$. *However,* $\mathcal{A}$ *is not allowed to send a key attribute* y *such that* $R(x^*, y) = 1$ *to* $O_{\mathcal{KG}}$.

4. $\mathcal{A}$ *outputs a guess* coin' *for* coin. *The challenger outputs* coin' *as the final output of the experiment.*

For any QPT $\mathcal{A}$, *it holds that*

$$\mathsf{Adv}^{\mathsf{ada\text{-}lessor}}_{\mathsf{PKFE\text{-}SKL},\mathcal{A}}(\lambda) := \left| \Pr[\mathsf{Exp}^{\mathsf{ada\text{-}lessor}}_{\mathsf{ABE\text{-}SKL},\mathcal{A}}(1^{\lambda}, 0) \rightarrow 1] - \Pr[\mathsf{Exp}^{\mathsf{ada\text{-}lessor}}_{\mathsf{ABE\text{-}SKL},\mathcal{A}}(1^{\lambda}, 1) \rightarrow 1] \right|$$
$$\leq \mathsf{negl}(\lambda).$$

We say that ABE-SKL *is secure against selective indistinguishability against key leasing attacks (Sel-IND-KLA) if the above holds for all QPT adversaries that declare* x^* *at the beginning of the experiment.*

Remark 6.1. In Deftinition 6.2, the key generation oracle returns $\perp$ if the same y is queried more than once. To handle the situation where multiple keys for the same attribute y are generated, we need to manage indices for y such as $(y, 1, vk_1, V_1), (y, 2, vk_2, V_2)$. Although we can reflect the index management in the definition, it complicates the definition and prevents readers from understanding the essential idea.Thus, we use the simplified definition above.

We also consider the following security notion where we introduce additional restriction that the number of distinguishing keys that are issued (and eventually returned) before ct^* is generated is bounded by some predetermined parameter q. Here, distinguishing key refers to a key that can decrypt the challenge ciphertext if it is not returned.

Definition 6.3 (Bounded Distinguishing Key Ada-IND-KLA/Sel-IND-KLA for ABE). *For defining bounded distinguishing key Ada-IND-KLA security, we consider the same security game as that for Ada-IND-KLA (i.e.,* $\mathsf{Exp}^{\mathsf{ada\text{-}ind\text{-}kla}}_{\mathcal{A},\mathsf{ABE\text{-}SKL}}(1^\lambda, \mathsf{coin})$) *except that we change the step 2. in Definition 6.2 with the following:*

2' When $\mathcal{A}$ sends (x^*, m_0, m_1) to the challenger, the challenger checks if there are at most q entries (y, vk, V) in $L_{\mathcal{KG}}$ such that $R(x^*, y) = 1$ and for all these entries, $V = \top$. If so, the challenger generates $ct^* \leftarrow \mathsf{Enc}(\mathsf{pk}, x^*, m_{\mathsf{coin}})$ and sends ct^* to $\mathcal{A}$. Otherwise, the challenger outputs 0.

We then define the advantage $\mathsf{Adv}^{\mathsf{ada\text{-}ind\text{-}kla}}_{\mathsf{ABE\text{-}SKL},\mathcal{A},q}(\lambda)$ *similarly to* $\mathsf{Adv}^{\mathsf{ada\text{-}ind\text{-}kla}}_{\mathsf{ABE\text{-}SKL},\mathcal{A}}(\lambda)$. *We say* ABE-SKL *is q-bounded distinguishing key Ada-IND-KLA secure if for any QPT adversary $\mathcal{A}$,* $\mathsf{Adv}^{\mathsf{ada\text{-}ind\text{-}kla}}_{\mathsf{ABE\text{-}SKL},\mathcal{A},q}(\lambda)$ *is negligible. We also define q-bounded distinguishing key Sel-IND-KLA security analogously by enforcing the adversary to output its target x^* at the beginning of the game.*

We emphasize that while the number of distinguishing keys that the adversary can obtain in the game is bounded by a fixed polynomial, the number of non-distinguishing keys (i.e., keys for y with $R(x^*, y) = 0$) can be unbounded.

6.2   1-Bounded Distinguishing Key Construction

We construct an ABE-SKL scheme 1ABE $=$ (Setup, $\mathcal{KG}$, Enc, $\mathcal{Dec}$, $\mathcal{Vrfy}$) for relation $R : \mathcal{X} \times \mathcal{Y} \to \{0,1\}$ with 1-bounded distinguishing key Ada-IND-KLA/Sel-IND-KLA security whose message space is $\{0,1\}^\ell$ by using the following building blocks.

- IND-KLA secure PKE-SKL SKL.($\mathcal{KG}$, Enc, $\mathcal{Dec}$, $\mathcal{Vrfy}$). Without loss of generality, we assume that skl.ek $\in \{0,1\}^{\ell_{\mathsf{ek}}}$ and the randomness space used by SKL.Enc is $\{0,1\}^{\ell_{\mathsf{rand}}}$ for some $\ell_{\mathsf{ek}}(\lambda)$ and $\ell_{\mathsf{rand}}(\lambda)$. We also assume that the message space of SKL is $\{0,1\}^\ell$.
- Adaptively/Selectively secure ABE ABE.(Setup, KG, Enc, Dec) for relation R with message space $\{0,1\}^\lambda$.

- A garbling scheme GC = (Grbl, GCEval). Without loss of generality, we assume that the labels of GC are in $\{0,1\}^\lambda$.

Setup(1^λ):
- For $i \in [\ell_{\mathsf{ek}}]$ and $b \in \{0,1\}$, run (abe.pk$_{i,b}$, abe.msk$_{i,b}$) ← ABE.Setup(1^λ).
- Output (pk, msk) := ($\{$abe.pk$_{i,b}\}_{i \in [\ell_{\mathsf{ek}}], b \in \{0,1\}}$, $\{$abe.msk$_{i,b}\}_{i \in [\ell_{\mathsf{ek}}], b \in \{0,1\}}$).

$\mathcal{KG}$(msk, y):
- Generate (skl.ek, skl.dk, skl.vk) ← SKL.$\mathcal{KG}$(1^λ).
- Run abe.sk$_i$ ← ABE.KG(ABE.msk$_{i,\mathsf{skl.ek}[i]}$, y) for $i \in [\ell_{\mathsf{ek}}]$, where skl.ek[$i$] denotes the i-th bit of the binary string skl.ek.
- Output usk := ($\{$abe.sk$_i\}_{i \in [\ell_{\mathsf{ek}}]}$, skl.ek, skl.$\mathit{dk}$) and vk := skl.vk.

Enc(pk, x, m):
- Choose R ← $\{0,1\}^{\ell_{\mathsf{rand}}}$.
- Construct circuit $E[m, \mathsf{R}]$, which is a circuit that takes as input an encryption key skl.ek of SKL and outputs SKL.Enc(skl.ek, m; R).
- Compute ($\{$lab$_{i,b}\}_{i \in [\ell_{\mathsf{ek}}], b \in \{0,1\}}$, $\widetilde{E}$) ← Grbl(1^λ, $E[m, \mathsf{R}]$).
- Run abe.ct$_{i,b}$ ← ABE.Enc(abe.pk$_{i,b}$, x, lab$_{i,b}$) for $i \in [\ell_{\mathsf{ek}}]$ and $b \in \{0,1\}$.
- Output ct := ($\{$abe.ct$_{i,b}\}_{i \in [\ell_{\mathsf{ek}}], b \in \{0,1\}}$, $\widetilde{E}$).

$\mathcal{Dec}$(usk, x, ct):
- Parse usk = ($\{$abe.sk$_i\}_{i \in [\ell_{\mathsf{ek}}]}$, skl.ek, skl.$\mathit{dk}$) and ct = ($\{$abe.ct$_{i,b}\}_{i \in [\ell_{\mathsf{ek}}], b \in \{0,1\}}$, $\widetilde{E}$).
- Compute lab$_i$ ← ABE.Dec(ABE.sk$_i$, x, abe.ct$_{i,\mathsf{skl.ek}[i]}$) for $i \in [\ell_{\mathsf{ek}}]$.
- Compute skl.ct = GCEval($\widetilde{E}$, $\{$lab$_i\}_{i \in [\ell_{\mathsf{ek}}]}$).
- Compute and output m' ← SKL.$\mathcal{Dec}$(skl.dk, skl.ct).

$\mathcal{Vrfy}$(vk, usk'):
- Parse vk = skl.vk and usk' = ($\{$abe.sk$_i\}_{i \in [\ell_{\mathsf{ek}}]}$, skl.ek$'$, skl.$\mathit{dk}'$).
- Compute and output SKL.$\mathcal{Vrfy}$(skl.vk, skl.dk').

We show that the scheme satisfies decryption correctness. To see this, we first observe that the decryption algorithm correctly recovers labels of $\widetilde{E}$ corresponding to the input skl.ek by the correctness of ABE. Therefore, skl.ct recovered by the garbled circuit evaluation equals to SKL.Enc(skl.ek, m; R) by the correctness of GC. Then, the message m is recovered in the last step by the correctness of SKL. We can also see that the verification correctness follows from that of SKL.

Theorem 6.1. *If ABE is adaptively (resp., selectively) secure, GC is secure, and SKL is IND-KLA secure, then 1ABE above is 1-bounded distinguishing key Ada-IND-KLA (resp., Sel-IND-KLA) secure.*

See Sect. 6.2 of the full version for the proof.

6.3 Q-Bounded Distinguishing Key Construction

By using the technique of [26], we can upgrade 1-bounded distinguishing key security to Q-bounded distinguishing key security for any polynomial $Q = Q(\lambda)$. Then we obtain the following theorem.

Theorem 6.2. *If there exists an adaptively (resp., selectively) secure an ABE scheme for relation R, then for any polynomial $Q = Q(\lambda)$, there is a Q-bounded distinguishing key Ada-IND-KLA (resp., Sel-IND-KLA) secure ABE scheme for relation R.*

See Sect. 6.3 of the full version for the proof.   We remark that Theorem 6.2 preserves the relation R. Thus, this in particular gives a compiler that upgrades (selectively or adaptively secure) normal IBE into IBE-SKL.

7 Functional Encryption with Secure Key Leasing

7.1 Definitions

The syntax of FE-SKL is defined as follows.

Definition 7.1 (PKFE with Secure Key Leasing). *A PKFE-SKL scheme* PKFE-SKL *is a tuple of six algorithms* (Setup, $\mathcal{KG}$, Enc, $\mathcal{Dec}$, Cert, Vrfy). *Below, let $\mathcal{X}$, $\mathcal{Y}$, and $\mathcal{F}$ be the plaintext, output, and function spaces of* PKFE-SKL, *respectively.*

Setup(1^λ) $\rightarrow$ (pk, msk): *The setup algorithm takes a security parameter 1^λ, and outputs a public key* pk *and master secret key* msk.

$\mathcal{KG}$(msk, f) $\rightarrow$ (fsk, vk): *The key generation algorithm takes a master secret key* msk *and a function $f \in \mathcal{F}$, and outputs a functional decryption key fsk and a verification key* vk.

Enc(pk, x) $\rightarrow$ ct: *The encryption algorithm takes a public key* pk *and a plaintext $x \in \mathcal{X}$, and outputs a ciphertext* ct.

$\mathcal{Dec}$(fsk, ct) $\rightarrow$ $\widetilde{x}$: *The decryption algorithm takes a functional decryption key fsk and a ciphertext* ct, *and outputs a value $\tilde{x}$.*

$\mathcal{Vrfy}$(vk, fsk') $\rightarrow$ $\top/\bot$: *The verification algorithm takes a verification key* vk *and a quantum state fsk', and outputs $\top$ or $\bot$.*

Decryption correctness: *For every $x \in \mathcal{X}$ and $f \in \mathcal{F}$, we have*

$$\Pr\left[\mathcal{Dec}(\mathit{fsk}, \mathsf{ct}) = f(x) \,\middle|\, \begin{array}{l} (\mathsf{pk}, \mathsf{msk}) \leftarrow \mathsf{Setup}(1^\lambda) \\ (\mathit{fsk}, \mathsf{vk}) \leftarrow \mathcal{KG}(\mathsf{msk}, f) \\ \mathsf{ct} \leftarrow \mathsf{Enc}(\mathsf{pk}, x) \end{array}\right] = 1 - \mathsf{negl}(\lambda).$$

Verification correctness: *For every $f \in \mathcal{F}$, we have*

$$\Pr\left[\mathcal{Vrfy}(\mathsf{vk}, \mathit{fsk}) = \top \,\middle|\, \begin{array}{l} (\mathsf{pk}, \mathsf{msk}) \leftarrow \mathsf{Setup}(1^\lambda) \\ (\mathit{fsk}, \mathsf{vk}) \leftarrow \mathcal{KG}(\mathsf{msk}, f) \end{array}\right] = 1 - \mathsf{negl}(\lambda).$$

Remark 7.1. Although Kitagawa and Nishimaki [27] require SKFE-SKL to have classical certificate generation algorithm for deletion, we do not since it is optional.If there exists a PKE-SKL scheme that has a classical certificate generation algorithm, our PKFE-SKL scheme also has a classical certificate generation algorithm.

Definition 7.2 (Adaptive Indistinguishability against Key Leasing Attacks). *We say that a PKFE-SKL scheme* PKFE-SKL *for* $\mathcal{X}, \mathcal{Y}$, *and* $\mathcal{F}$ *is an adaptively indistinguishable secure against key leasing attacks (Ada-IND-KLA), if it satisfies the following requirement, formalized from the experiment* $\mathsf{Exp}^{\mathsf{ada-ind-kla}}_{\mathcal{A},\mathsf{PKFE-SKL}}(1^{\lambda}, \mathsf{coin})$ *between an adversary* $\mathcal{A}$ *and a challenger:*

1. *At the beginning, the challenger runs* $(\mathsf{pk}, \mathsf{msk}) \leftarrow \mathsf{Setup}(1^{\lambda})$. *Throughout the experiment,* $\mathcal{A}$ *can access the following oracles.*

   $O_{\mathcal{KG}}(f)$: *Given* f, *it finds an entry* (f, vk, V) *from* $L_{\mathcal{KG}}$. *If there is such an entry, it returns* $\perp$. *Otherwise, it generates* $(\mathit{fsk}, \mathsf{vk}) \leftarrow \mathcal{KG}(\mathsf{msk}, f)$, *sends* fsk *to* $\mathcal{A}$, *and adds* $(f, \mathsf{vk}, \perp)$ *to* $L_{\mathcal{KG}}$.

   $O_{\mathcal{Vrfy}}(f, \mathit{fsk}')$: *Given* (f, fsk'), *it finds an entry* (f, vk, V) *from* $L_{\mathcal{KG}}$. *(If there is no such entry, it returns* $\perp$.*) It computes* $d \leftarrow \mathcal{Vrfy}(\mathsf{vk}, \mathit{fsk}')$ *and sends* d *to* $\mathcal{A}$. *If* $V = \top$, *it does not update* $L_{\mathcal{KG}}$. *Else if* $V = \perp$, *it updates the entry by setting* $V := d$.

2. *When* $\mathcal{A}$ *sends* (x_0^*, x_1^*) *to the challenger, the challenger checks if for any entry* (f, vk, V) *in* $L_{\mathcal{KG}}$ *such that* $f(x_0^*) \neq f(x_1^*)$, *it holds that* $V = \top$. *If so, the challenger generates* $\mathsf{ct}^* \leftarrow \mathsf{Enc}(\mathsf{pk}, x_{\mathsf{coin}}^*)$ *and sends* ct^* *to* $\mathcal{A}$. *Otherwise, the challenger outputs* 0. *Hereafter,* $\mathcal{A}$ *is not allowed to send a function* f *such that* $f(x_0^*) \neq f(x_1^*)$ *to* $O_{\mathcal{KG}}$.

3. $\mathcal{A}$ *outputs a guess* coin' *for* coin. *The challenger outputs* coin' *as the final output of the experiment.*

For any QPT $\mathcal{A}$, *it holds that*

$$\mathsf{Adv}^{\mathsf{ada-ind-kla}}_{\mathsf{PKFE-SKL},\mathcal{A}}(\lambda) := \left| \Pr[\mathsf{Exp}^{\mathsf{ada-ind-kla}}_{\mathsf{PKFE-SKL},\mathcal{A}}(1^{\lambda}, 0) \to 1] - \Pr[\mathsf{Exp}^{\mathsf{ada-ind-kla}}_{\mathsf{PKFE-SKL},\mathcal{A}}(1^{\lambda}, 1) \to 1] \right|$$
$$\leq \mathsf{negl}(\lambda).$$

Remark 7.2. Definition 7.2 assumes that the adversary does not get more than one decryption key for the same f for simplification as Remark 6.1.

7.2 Constructions

We describe our PKFE-SKL scheme in this section. We construct a PKFE-SKL scheme PKFE-SKL = $(\mathsf{Setup}, \mathcal{KG}, \mathsf{Enc}, \mathcal{Dec}, \mathcal{Vrfy})$ by using the following building blocks.

- IND-KLA secure PKE-SKL SKL = $\mathsf{SKL}.(\mathcal{KG}, \mathsf{Enc}, \mathcal{Dec}, \mathcal{Vrfy})$.
- Adaptively secure PKFE FE = $\mathsf{FE}.(\mathsf{Setup}, \mathsf{KG}, \mathsf{Enc}, \mathsf{Dec})$.
- Adaptively single-ciphertext function private SKFE SKFE = $\mathsf{SKFE}.(\mathsf{Setup}, \mathsf{KG}, \mathsf{Enc}, \mathsf{Dec})$.
- Pseudorandom-secure SKE SKE = $\mathsf{SKE}.(\mathsf{Enc}, \mathsf{Dec})$.
- Puncturable PRF PRF = $(\mathsf{PRF.Gen}, \mathsf{F}, \mathsf{Puncture})$.

We set $\ell_{\mathsf{pad}} := |\mathsf{skfe.ct}| - |x|$ and $\ell_{\mathsf{ske}} := |\mathsf{ske.ct}|$, where $|x|$ is the input length of PKFE-SKL, $|\mathsf{skfe.ct}|$ is the ciphertext length of SKFE, and $|\mathsf{ske.ct}|$ is the ciphertext length of SKE.

Setup(1^λ):
- Generate (fe.pk, fe.msk) $\leftarrow$ FE.Setup(1^λ).
- Output (pk, msk) := (fe.pk, fe.msk).

$\mathcal{KG}$(msk, f):
- Generate (skl.ek, skl.$s\mathcal{k}$, skl.vk) $\leftarrow$ SKL.$\mathcal{KG}$(1^λ).
- Choose ske.ct $\leftarrow \{0,1\}^{\ell_{\mathsf{ske}}}$.
- Construct a circuit $W[f, \mathsf{skl.ek}, \mathsf{ske.ct}]$, which is described in Fig. 1.
- Generate fe.sk$_W \leftarrow$ FE.KG(fe.msk, $W[f, \mathsf{skl.ek}, \mathsf{ske.ct}]$).
- Output fsk := (fe.sk$_W$, skl.$s\mathcal{k}$) and vk := skl.vk.

Enc(pk, x):
- Choose K $\leftarrow$ PRF.Gen(1^λ).
- Compute fe.ct $\leftarrow$ FE.Enc(fe.pk, $(x\|0^{\ell_{\mathsf{pad}}}, \bot, \mathsf{K})$).
- Output ct := fe.ct.

$\mathcal{Dec}$(fsk, ct):
- Parse fsk = (fe.sk, skl.$s\mathcal{k}$) and ct = fe.ct.
- Compute skl.ct $\leftarrow$ FE.Dec(fe.sk, fe.ct).
- Compute and output $y \leftarrow$ SKL.$\mathcal{Dec}$(skl.$s\mathcal{k}$, skl.ct).

$\mathcal{Vrfy}$(vk, fsk'):
- Parse vk = skl.vk and fsk' = (fe.sk$'$, skl.$s\mathcal{k}'$).
- Compute and output SKL.$\mathcal{Vrfy}$(skl.vk, skl.$s\mathcal{k}'$).

Function $W[f, \mathsf{skl.ek}, \mathsf{ske.ct}](x', \mathsf{ske.sk}, \mathsf{K})$

Constants: Function f, PKE-SKL encryption key skl.ek, SKE ciphertext ske.ct.
Input: Plaintext x', SKE key ske.sk, PRF key K.

1. If ske.sk $= \bot$, do the following:
   - Parse $x' = x\|\bar{x}$ such that $|\bar{x}| = \ell_{\mathsf{pad}}$.
   - Compute and output skl.ct := SKL.Enc(skl.ek, $f(x)$; $\mathsf{F}_\mathsf{K}(\mathsf{skl.ek})$).
2. If ske.sk $\neq \bot$, do the following:
   - Compute skfe.sk $\leftarrow$ SKE.Dec(ske.sk, ske.ct).
   - Compute and output z := SKFE.Dec(skfe.sk, x').

Fig. 1. The description of $W[f, \mathsf{skl.ek}, \mathsf{ske.ct}]$

The decryption correctness of PKFE-SKL follows from the correctness of FE and the decryption correctness of SKL. The verification correcntess of PKFE-SKL follows from the verification correcntess of SKL. We prove the security of PKFE-SKL.

Theorem 7.1. *If* PKFE *is adaptively secure,* SKFE *is adaptively single-ciphertext function private,* PRF *is a secure punctured PRF, and* SKE *has the ciphertext pseudorandomness, then* PKFE-SKL *above is Ada-IND-KLA.*

Theorem 7.2. *If* PKFE *is q-bounded adaptively secure,* SKFE *is adaptively single-ciphertext function private,* PRF *is a secure punctured PRF, and* SKE *has the ciphertext pseudorandomness, then* PKFE-SKL *above is q-bounded Ada-IND-KLA.*

The poofs are given in Sect. 7.3 of the full version.

Acknowledgement. This work was supported in part by the DST "Swarnajayanti" fellowship, Cybersecurity Center of Excellence, IIT Madras, National Blockchain Project and the Algorand Centres of Excellence programme managed by Algorand Foundation. Any opinions, findings, and conclusions or recommendations expressed in this material are those of the author(s) and do not necessarily reflect the views of sponsors. The fourth author was partially supported by JST AIP Acceleration Research JPMJCR22U5 and JSPS KAKENHI Grant Number 19H01109, Japan.

References

1. Aaronson, S.: Quantum copy-protection and quantum money. In: 2009 24th Annual IEEE Conference on Computational Complexity, pp. 229–242. IEEE (2009). https://doi.org/10.1109/ccc.2009.42

2. Aaronson, S., Christiano, P.: Quantum money from hidden subspaces. In: Karloff, H.J., Pitassi, T. (eds.) 44th ACM STOC, pp. 41–60. ACM Press (2012). https://doi.org/10.1145/2213977.2213983

3. Aaronson, S., Liu, J., Liu, Q., Zhandry, M., Zhang, R.: New approaches for quantum copy-protection. In: Malkin, T., Peikert, C. (eds.) CRYPTO 2021, Part I. LNCS, vol. 12825, pp. 526–555. Springer, Heidelberg, Virtual Event (2021). https://doi.org/10.1007/978-3-030-84242-0_19

4. Adcock, M., Cleve, R.: A quantum Goldreich-Levin theorem with cryptographic applications. In: Alt, H., Ferreira, A. (eds.) STACS 2002. LNCS, vol. 2285, pp. 323–334. Springer, Heidelberg (2002). https://doi.org/10.1007/3-540-45841-7_26

5. Amos, R., Georgiou, M., Kiayias, A., Zhandry, M.: One-shot signatures and applications to hybrid quantum/classical authentication. In: Makarychev, K., Makarychev, Y., Tulsiani, M., Kamath, G., Chuzhoy, J. (eds.) 52nd ACM STOC, pp. 255–268. ACM Press (2020). https://doi.org/10.1145/3357713.3384304

6. Ananth, P., Brakerski, Z., Segev, G., Vaikuntanathan, V.: From selective to adaptive security in functional encryption. In: Gennaro, R., Robshaw, M.J.B. (eds.) CRYPTO 2015, Part II. LNCS, vol. 9216, pp. 657–677. Springer, Heidelberg (2015). https://doi.org/10.1007/978-3-662-48000-7_32

7. Ananth, P., Kaleoglu, F.: Unclonable encryption, revisited. In: Nissim, K., Waters, B. (eds.) TCC 2021, Part I. LNCS, vol. 13042, pp. 299–329. Springer, Heidelberg (2021). https://doi.org/10.1007/978-3-030-90459-3_11

8. Ananth, P., Kaleoglu, F., Li, X., Liu, Q., Zhandry, M.: On the feasibility of unclonable encryption, and more. In: Dodis, Y., Shrimpton, T. (eds.) CRYPTO 2022, Part II. LNCS, vol. 13508, pp. 212–241. Springer, Heidelberg (2022). https://doi.org/10.1007/978-3-031-15979-4_8

9. Ananth, P., La Placa, R.L.: Secure software leasing. In: Canteaut, A., Standaert, F.X. (eds.) EUROCRYPT 2021, Part II. LNCS, vol. 12697, pp. 501–530. Springer, Heidelberg (2021). https://doi.org/10.1007/978-3-030-77886-6_17

10. Bartusek, J., Khurana, D.: Cryptography with certified deletion. Cryptology ePrint Archive, Report 2022/1178 (2022), https://eprint.iacr.org/2022/1178

11. Bennett, C.H., Brassard, G.: Quantum cryptography: Public key distribution and coin tossing. arXiv preprint arXiv:2003.06557 (2020). https://doi.org/10.1016/j.tcs.2014.05.025

12. Boneh, D., Ding, X., Tsudik, G., Wong, C.M.: A method for fast revocation of public key certificates and security capabilities. In: Wallach, D.S. (ed.) USENIX Security 2001. USENIX Association (2001)

13. Boneh, D., Zhandry, M.: Secure signatures and chosen ciphertext security in a quantum computing world. In: Canetti, R., Garay, J.A. (eds.) CRYPTO 2013, Part II. LNCS, vol. 8043, pp. 361–379. Springer, Heidelberg (2013). https://doi.org/10.1007/978-3-642-40084-1_21

14. Brakerski, Z., Segev, G.: Function-private functional encryption in the private-key setting. J. Cryptol. 31(1), 202–225 (2017). https://doi.org/10.1007/s00145-017-9255-y

15. Broadbent, A., Islam, R.: Quantum encryption with certified deletion. In: Pass, R., Pietrzak, K. (eds.) TCC 2020, Part III. LNCS, vol. 12552, pp. 92–122. Springer, Heidelberg (2020). https://doi.org/10.1007/978-3-030-64381-2_4

16. Broadbent, A., Jeffery, S., Lord, S., Podder, S., Sundaram, A.: Secure software leasing without assumptions. In: Nissim, K., Waters, B. (eds.) TCC 2021, Part I. LNCS, vol. 13042, pp. 90–120. Springer, Heidelberg (2021). https://doi.org/10.1007/978-3-030-90459-3_4

17. Coladangelo, A., Liu, J., Liu, Q., Zhandry, M.: Hidden cosets and applications to unclonable cryptography. In: Malkin, T., Peikert, C. (eds.) CRYPTO 2021, Part I. LNCS, vol. 12825, pp. 556–584. Springer, Heidelberg, Virtual Event (2021). https://doi.org/10.1007/978-3-030-84242-0_20

18. Coladangelo, A., Majenz, C., Poremba, A.: Quantum copy-protection of compute-and-compare programs in the quantum random oracle model. arXiv:2009.13865 (2020)

19. Culf, E., Vidick, T.: A monogamy-of-entanglement game for subspace coset states. Quantum 6, 791 (2022). https://doi.org/10.22331/q-2022-09-01-791

20. Georgiou, M., Zhandry, M.: Unclonable decryption keys. Cryptology ePrint Archive, Report 2020/877 (2020). https://eprint.iacr.org/2020/877

21. Gorbunov, S., Vaikuntanathan, V., Wee, H.: Functional encryption with bounded collusions via multi-party computation. In: Safavi-Naini, R., Canetti, R. (eds.) CRYPTO 2012. LNCS, vol. 7417, pp. 162–179. Springer, Heidelberg (2012). https://doi.org/10.1007/978-3-642-32009-5_11

22. Goyal, R., Kim, S., Manohar, N., Waters, B., Wu, D.J.: Watermarking public-key cryptographic primitives. In: Boldyreva, A., Micciancio, D. (eds.) CRYPTO 2019, Part III. LNCS, vol. 11694, pp. 367–398. Springer, Heidelberg (2019). https://doi.org/10.1007/978-3-030-26954-8_12

23. Goyal, R., Koppula, V., Waters, B.: Semi-adaptive security and bundling function-alities made generic and easy. In: Hirt, M., Smith, A.D. (eds.) TCC 2016-B, Part II. LNCS, vol. 9986, pp. 361–388. Springer, Heidelberg (2016). https://doi.org/10.1007/978-3-662-53644-5_14

24. Hiroka, T., Morimae, T., Nishimaki, R., Yamakawa, T.: Quantum encryption with certified deletion, revisited: Public key, attribute-based, and classical communication. In: Tibouchi, M., Wang, H. (eds.) ASIACRYPT 2021, Part I. LNCS, vol. 13090, pp. 606–636. Springer, Heidelberg (2021). https://doi.org/10.1007/978-3-030-92062-3_21

25. Hiroka, T., Morimae, T., Nishimaki, R., Yamakawa, T.: Certified everlasting functional encryption. Cryptology ePrint Archive, Report 2022/969 (2022). https://eprint.iacr.org/2022/969

26. Itkis, G., Shen, E., Varia, M., Wilson, D., Yerukhimovich, A.: Bounded-collusion attribute-based encryption from minimal assumptions. In: Fehr, S. (ed.) PKC 2017, Part II. LNCS, vol. 10175, pp. 67–87. Springer, Heidelberg (2017). https://doi.org/10.1007/978-3-662-54388-7_3

27. Kitagawa, F., Nishimaki, R.: Functional encryption with secure key leasing. Asiacrypt 2022 (to appear) (2022)

28. Kitagawa, F., Nishimaki, R.: Watermarking PRFs against quantum adversaries. In: Dunkelman, O., Dziembowski, S. (eds.) EUROCRYPT 2022, Part III. LNCS, vol. 13277, pp. 488–518. Springer, Heidelberg (2022). https://doi.org/10.1007/978-3-031-07082-2_18

29. Kitagawa, F., Nishimaki, R., Yamakawa, T.: Secure software leasing from standard assumptions. In: Nissim, K., Waters, B. (eds.) TCC 2021, Part I. LNCS, vol. 13042, pp. 31–61. Springer, Heidelberg (2021). https://doi.org/10.1007/978-3-030-90459-3_2

30. Marriott, C., Watrous, J.: Quantum arthur-merlin games. Comput. Complex. **14**(2), 122–152 (2005). https://doi.org/10.1007/s00037-005-0194-x

31. Poremba, A.: Quantum proofs of deletion for learning with errors. In: Kalai, Y.T. (ed.) 14th Innovations in Theoretical Computer Science Conference, ITCS 2023, January 10–13, 2023, MIT, Cambridge, Massachusetts, USA. LIPIcs, vol. 251, pp. 90:1–90:14. Schloss Dagstuhl - Leibniz-Zentrum für Informatik (2023). https://doi.org/10.4230/LIPIcs.ITCS.2023.90

32. Sahai, A., Seyalioglu, H.: Worry-free encryption: functional encryption with public keys. In: Al-Shaer, E., Keromytis, A.D., Shmatikov, V. (eds.) ACM CCS 2010. pp. 463–472. ACM Press (2010). https://doi.org/10.1145/1866307.1866359

33. Sattath, O., Wyborski, S.: Uncloneable decryptors from quantum copy-protection. arxiv:2203.05866 (2022)

34. Unruh, D.: Revocable quantum timed-release encryption. J. ACM **62**(6), 49:1–49:76 (2015)

35. Wiesner, S.: Conjugate coding. ACM Sigact News **15**(1), 78–88 (1983). https://doi.org/10.1145/1008908.1008920

36. Winter, A.J.: Coding theorem and strong converse for quantum channels. IEEE Trans. Inf. Theory **45**(7), 2481–2485 (1999). https://doi.org/10.1109/18.796385

37. Zhandry, M.: Schrödinger's pirate: How to trace a quantum decoder. In: Pass, R., Pietrzak, K. (eds.) TCC 2020, Part III. LNCS, vol. 12552, pp. 61–91. Springer, Heidelberg (2020). https://doi.org/10.1007/978-3-030-64381-2_3

Another Round of Breaking and Making Quantum Money:
How to Not Build It from Lattices, and More

Jiahui Liu[1]([⊠]) [iD], Hart Montgomery[2] [iD], and Mark Zhandry[3] [iD]

[1] University of Texas at Austin, Austin, USA
jiahui@cs.utexas.edu
[2] Linux Foundation, San Francisco, USA
hmontgomery@linuxfoundation.org
[3] NTT and Princeton University, Princeton, USA

Abstract. This work provides both negative and positive results for publicly verifiable quantum money.

- In the first part, we give a general theorem, showing that a certain natural class of quantum money schemes from lattices cannot be secure. We use this theorem to break the recent quantum money proposal of Khesin, Lu, and Shor ([KLS22]).
- In the second part, we propose a framework for building quantum money and quantum lightning we call *invariant money* which abstracts and formalizes some ideas of quantum money from knots [FGH+12] and its precedent work [LAF+10]. In addition to formalizing this framework, we provide concrete hard computational problems loosely inspired by classical knowledge-of-exponent assumptions, whose hardness would imply the security of *quantum lightning*, a strengthening of quantum money where not even the bank can duplicate banknotes.
- We discuss potential instantiations of our framework, including an oracle construction using cryptographic group actions and instantiations from rerandomizable functional encryption, isogenies over elliptic curves, and knots.

1 Introduction

1.1 Motivation

Quantum information promises to revolutionize cryptography. In particular, the no cloning theorem of quantum mechanics opens the door to *quantum cryptography*: cryptographic applications that are simply impossible classically. The progenitor of this field, due to Wiesner [Wie83], is quantum money: quantum digital currency that cannot be counterfeited due to the laws of physics. Since Wiesner's proposal, many applications of quantum information to cryptography have been proposed, including quantum key distribution (QKD) [BB87], randomness expansion [Col09, CY14, BCM+18], quantum copy protection [Aar09, AL21, ALL+21, CLLZ21], quantum one-time programs [BGS13], and much more.

© International Association for Cryptologic Research 2023
C. Hazay and M. Stam (Eds.): EUROCRYPT 2023, LNCS 14004, pp. 611–638, 2023.
https://doi.org/10.1007/978-3-031-30545-0_21

Throughout the development of quantum cryptography, quantum money has remained a central object, at least implicitly. Indeed, the techniques used for quantum money are closely related to those used in other applications. For example, the first message in the BB84 quantum QKD protocol [BB87] is exactly a banknote in Wiesner's scheme. The techniques used by [BCM+18] to prove quantumness using classical communication have been used to construct quantum money with classical communication [RS19]. The subspace states used by [AC12] to construct quantum money were recently used to build quantum copy protection [ALL+21].

The Public Verification Barrier. Wiesner's scheme is only privately verifiable, meaning that the mint is needed to verify. This results in numerous weaknesses. Improper verification opens the scheme to active attacks [Lut10]. Moreover, private verification is not scalable, as the mint would be required to participate in every single transaction. Wiesner's scheme also requires essentially perfect quantum storage, since otherwise banknotes in Wiesner's scheme will quickly decohere and be lost.

All these problems are readily solved with *publicly verifiable* quantum money[1], where anyone can verify, despite the mint being the sole entity that can mint notes. Public verification immediately eliminates active attacks, and solves the scaling problem since the transacting users can verify the money for themselves. Aaronson and Christiano [AC12] also explain that public verifiability allows for also correcting any decoherence, so users can keep their banknotes alive indefinitely.

Unfortunately, constructing convincing publicly verifiable quantum money has become a notoriously hard open question. Firstly, some natural modifications to Wiesner's quantum money scheme will not give security under public verification [FGH+10]. Aaronson [Aar09], and later Aaronson and Christiano [AC12] gave publicly verifiable quantum money relative to quantum and classical oracles, respectively. Such oracle constructions have the advantage of provable security, but it is often unclear how to instantiate them in the real world[2]: in both [Aar09] and [AC12], "candidate" instantiations were proposed, but were later broken [LAF+10, CPDDF+19]. Another candidate by Zhandry [Zha19] was broken by Roberts [Rob21]. Other candidates have been proposed [FGH+12, Kan18, KSS21], but they all rely on new, untested assumptions that have received little cryptanalysis effort. The one exception, suggested by [BDS16] and proved by [Zha19], uses indistinguishability obfuscation (iO) to instantiate Aaronson and Christiano's scheme [AC12]. Unfortunately, the post-quantum security of iO remains poorly understood, with all known constructions of post-quantum iO [GGH15, BGMZ18, BDGM20, WW21] being best labeled as candidates, lacking justification under widely studied assumptions.

Thus, it remains a major open question to construct publicly verifiable quantum money from standard cryptographic tools. Two such post-quantum tools we

---

[1] Sometimes it is also referred to as public-key quantum money. We may use the two terms interchangeably.

[2] Quantum oracles are quantum circuits accessible only as a black-box unitary. They are generally considered as strong relativizing tools when used in proofs. Classical oracles are black-box classical circuits, a much weaker tool.

will investigate in this work are the two most influential and well-studied: lattices and isogenies over elliptic curves.

This public verification barrier is inherited by many proposed applications of quantum cryptography. For example, quantum copy protection for any function whose outputs can be verified immediately implies a publicly verifiable quantum money scheme. As such, all such constructions in the standard model [ALL+21, CLLZ21] require at a minimum a computational assumption that implies quantum money.[3]

Quantum Money Decentralized: Quantum Lightning. An even more ambitious goal is a publicly verifiable quantum money where the bank/mint itself should *not* be capable of duplicating money states. To guarantee unclonability, the scheme should have a "collision-resistant" flavor: no one can (efficiently) generate two valid money states with the same serial number. This notion of quantum money appeared as early in [LAF+10]; the name "quantum lightning" was given in [Zha19].

Quantum lightning has broader and more exciting applications: as discussed in [Zha19, Col19, CS20, AGKZ20], it can be leveraged as verifiable min-entropy, useful building blocks to enhance blockchain/smart contract protocols and moreover, it could lead to decentralized cryptocurrency without a blockchain.

Quantum money has a provably secure construction from iO, a strong cryptographic hammer but still a widely used assumption. On the other hand, quantum lightning from even *relatively standard-looking* assumptions remains open. Some existing constructions [Kan18, KSS21] use strong oracles such as quantum oracles, with conjectured instantiations that did not go through too much cryptanalysis. [FGH+12] is another candidate built from conjectures in knot theory. But a correctness proof and security reduction are not provided in their paper.

Collapsing vs. Non-collapsing. With a close relationship to quantum money, collapsing functions [Unr16] are a central concept in quantum cryptography. A collapsing function f says that one should not be able to distinguish a superposition of pre-images $\frac{|x_1\rangle + |x_2\rangle \cdots |x_k\rangle}{\sqrt{k}}$, from a measured pre-image $|x_i\rangle, i \in [k]$ for some image $y = f(x_i)$, for all $i \in [k]$.

While collapsing functions give rise to secure post-quantum cryptography like commitment schemes, its precise opposite is necessary for quantum money: if no verification can distinguish a money state in a superposition of many supports from its measured state, a simple forgery comes ahead. Hence, investigating the collapsing/non-collapsing properties of hash functions from lattices and isogenies will provide a win-win insight into quantum money and post-quantum security of existing cryptographic primitives.

---

[3] This holds true even for certain weaker versions such as copy *detection*, also known as infinite term secure software leasing.

2   Our Results

In this work, we give both negative and positive results for publicly verifiable quantum money.

Breaking Quantum Money. Very recent work by Khesin, Lu, and Shor [KLS22] claims to construct publicly verifiable quantum money from the hardness of worst-case lattice problems, a standard assumption. Our first contribution is to identify a fatal flaw in their security proof, and moreover show how to exploit this flaw to forge unlimited money. After communicating this flaw and attack, the authors of [KLS22] have retracted their paper.[4]

More importantly, we show that a general class of *natural* money schemes based on lattices *cannot* be both secure and publicly verifiable. We consider protocols where the public key is a short wide matrix $\mathbf{A}^T$, and a banknote with serial number $\mathbf{u}$ is a superposition of "short" vectors $\mathbf{y}$ such that $\mathbf{A}^T \cdot \mathbf{y} = \mathbf{u} \bmod q$. Our attack works whenever $\mathbf{A}^T$ is uniformly random. We also generalize this to handle the case where $\mathbf{A}^T$ is uniform conditioned on having a few public short vectors in its kernel. This generalization includes the Khesin-Lu-Shor scheme as a special case. Our result provides a significant barrier to constructing quantum money from lattices.

Along the way, we prove that the SIS hash function is *collapsing* [Unr16] for all moduli, resolving an important open question in the security of post-quantum hash functions.[5]

Invariant Money/Lightning. To complement our negative result, we propose a new framework for building quantum money, based on invariants. Our framework abstracts some of the ideas behind the candidate quantum money from knots in [FGH+12] and behind [LAF+10]. Our main contributions here are two-fold:

- We propose a (classical) oracle construction that implements our framework assuming the existence of a quantum-secure cryptographic group action and a relatively modest assumption about *generic* cryptographic group actions. We then give proposals for instantiating our invariant framework on more concrete assumptions. The first is based on isogenies over elliptic curves[6]; the second is based on rerandomizable functional encryption with certain properties; finally, we also discuss the quantum money from knots construction in [FGH+12] with some modifications.
- In order to gain confidence in our proposals, we for the first time formalize abstract properties of the invariant money under which security can be proved. Concretely, we prove that a certain mixing condition is sufficient to characterize the states accepted by the verifier, and in particular prove

---

[4] We thank the authors of [KLS22] for patiently answering our numerous questions about their work, which was instrumental in helping us identify the flaw.

[5] Previously, [LZ19] showed that SIS was collapsing for a super-polynomial modulus.

[6] The recent attacks [CD22, MM22, Rob22] on SIDH do not apply to the isogeny building blocks we need. We will elaborate in the full version.

correctness[7]. We also propose "knowledge of path" security properties for abstract invariant structures which would be sufficient to justify security. These knowledge of path assumptions are analogs of the "knowledge of exponent" assumption on groups proposed by Damgård [Dam92]. Under these assumptions, we are even able to show that the invariants give quantum *lightning* [LAF+10, Zha19], the aforementioned strengthening of quantum money that is known to have additional applications.

Note that the knowledge of exponent assumption in groups is quantumly broken on groups due to the discrete logarithm being easy. However, for many of our assumptions, which are at least conjectured to be quantum-secure, the analogous knowledge of path assumption appears plausible, though certainly more cryptanalysis is needed to gain confidence. The main advantage of our proposed knowledge of path assumption is that it provides a concrete cryptographic property that cryptographers can study and analyze with a well-studied classical analog.

3   Technical Overview

3.1   How to Not Build Quantum Money from Lattices

We first describe a natural attempt to construct quantum money from lattices, which was folklore but first outlined by Zhandry [Zha19]. The public key will contain a random tall matrix $\mathbf{A} \in \mathbb{Z}_q^{m \times n}, m \gg n$. To mint a banknote, first generate a superposition $|\psi\rangle = \sum_{\mathbf{y}} \alpha_{\mathbf{y}} |\mathbf{y}\rangle$ of short vectors $\mathbf{y} \in \mathbb{Z}^m$, such that $|\mathbf{y}| \ll q$. A natural $|\psi\rangle$ is the discrete-Gaussian-weighted state, where $\alpha_{\mathbf{y}} \propto \sqrt{e^{-\pi|\mathbf{y}|^2/\sigma^2}}$ for a width parameter σ. Then compute in superposition and measure the output of the map $\mathbf{y} \mapsto \mathbf{A}^T \cdot \mathbf{y} \bmod q$, obtaining $\mathbf{u} \in \mathbb{Z}_q^n$. The state collapses to:

$$|\psi_{\mathbf{u}}\rangle \propto \sum_{\mathbf{y}:\mathbf{A}^T\cdot\mathbf{y}=\mathbf{u}} \alpha_{\mathbf{y}} |\mathbf{y}\rangle .$$

This will be the money state, and $\mathbf{u}$ will be the serial number. This state can presumably not be copied: if one could construct two copies of $|\psi_{\mathbf{u}}\rangle$, then one could measure both, obtaining two short vectors $\mathbf{y}, \mathbf{y}'$ with the same coset $\mathbf{u}$. As $|\psi_{\mathbf{u}}\rangle$ is a superposition of many vectors (since $m \gg n$), with high probability $\mathbf{y} \neq \mathbf{y}'$. Subtracting gives a short vector $\mathbf{y} - \mathbf{y}'$ such that $\mathbf{A}^T \cdot (\mathbf{y} - \mathbf{y}') = 0$, solving the Short Integer Solution (SIS) problem. SIS is presumably hard, and this hardness can be justified based on the hardness of worst-case lattice problems such as the approximate Shortest Vector Problem (SVP).

The challenge is: how to verify $|\psi_{\mathbf{u}}\rangle$? Certainly, one can verify that the support of a state is only short vectors $\mathbf{y}$ such that $\mathbf{A}^T \cdot \mathbf{y} = \mathbf{u}$. But this alone is not enough: one can fool such a verification by any *classical* $\mathbf{y}$ in the support of

---

[7] [FGH+12] did not analyze correctness of their knot-based proposal, nor analyze the states accepted by their verifier and formalize the property needed for a security proof. [LAF+10] had informal correctness analysis on their proposal, but also did not analyze the security property needed.

$|\psi_{\mathbf{u}}\rangle$. To forge then, an adversary simply measures $|\psi_{\mathbf{u}}\rangle$ to obtain $\mathbf{y}$, and then copies $\mathbf{y}$ as many times as it likes.

To get the scheme to work, then, one needs a verifier that can distinguish classical $\mathbf{y}$ from superpositions. This is a typical challenge in designing publicly verifiable money schemes. A typical approach is to perform the quantum Fourier transform (QFT): the QFT of $\mathbf{y}$ will result in a uniform string, whereas the QFT of $|\psi_{\mathbf{u}}\rangle$ will presumably have structure. Indeed, if $|\psi_{\mathbf{u}}\rangle$ is the Gaussian superposition, following ideas of Regev [Reg05], the QFT of $|\psi_{\mathbf{u}}\rangle$ will be statistically close to a superposition of samples $\mathbf{A} \cdot \mathbf{r} + \mathbf{e}$, where $\mathbf{r}$ is uniform in $\mathbb{Z}_q^n$, and $\mathbf{e} \in \mathbb{Z}_q^m$ is another discrete Gaussian of width q/σ. The goal then is to distinguish such samples from uniform.

Unfortunately, such distinguishing is likely hard, as this task is the famous (decisional) Learning with Errors (LWE) problem. LWE is presumably hard, which can be justified based on the hardness of the same worst-case lattice problems as with SIS, namely SVP. So either LWE is hard, or the quantum money scheme is insecure in the first place.

Nevertheless, this leaves open a number of possible strategies for designing quantum money from lattices, including:

1. What if non-Gaussian $|\psi\rangle$ is chosen?
2. What if distinguishing is not done via the QFT but some other quantum process?
3. What if we somehow make LWE easy?

The first significant barrier beyond the hardness of LWE is due to Liu and Zhandry [LZ19]. They show that, if the modulus q is super-polynomial, then the map $\mathbf{y} \mapsto \mathbf{A}^T \cdot \mathbf{y}$ for a random $\mathbf{A}$ is *collapsing* [Unr16]: that is, for *any* starting state $|\psi_{\mathbf{u}}\rangle$ of short vectors, distinguishing $|\psi_{\mathbf{u}}\rangle$ from $\mathbf{y}$ is infeasible for *any* efficient verification process. Collapsing is the preferred notion of post-quantum security for hash functions, as it is known that collision resistance is often not sufficient for applications when quantum adversaries are considered.

The result of [LZ19] follows from the hardness of LWE (which is quantumly equivalent to SIS [Reg05]), albeit with a noise rate super-polynomially smaller than q/σ which is a stronger assumption than the hardness with rate q/σ. Moreover, their result requires q to be super-polynomially larger than σ. In practice, one usually wants q to be polynomial, and the result of [LZ19] leaves open the possibility of building quantum money in such a setting.

What about making LWE easy (while SIS remains hard)? The usual approach in the lattice literature to making decisional LWE easy is to output a short vector $\mathbf{s}$ in the kernel of $\mathbf{A}^T$. If $|\mathbf{s}| \ll (q/\sigma)$, this allows for distinguishing LWE samples from uniform, since $\mathbf{s} \cdot (\mathbf{A} \cdot \mathbf{r} + \mathbf{e}) = \mathbf{s} \cdot \mathbf{e}$, which will be small relative to q, while $\mathbf{s} \cdot \mathbf{x}$ for uniform $\mathbf{x}$ will be uniform in $\mathbb{Z}_q$. Unfortunately, adding such short vectors breaks the security proof, since $\mathbf{s}$ is a SIS solution, solving SIS is trivially easy by outputting $\mathbf{s}$. To revive the security, one can try reducing to the 1-SIS problem, which is to find a short SIS solution that is linearly independent of $\mathbf{s}$. 1-SIS can be proved hard based on the same worst-case lattice problems as SIS [BF11]. However, in the scheme above, it is not clear if measuring two forgeries and taking the difference should result in a vector linearly independent of $\mathbf{s}$.

The Recent Work of [KLS22]. Very recently, Khesin, Lu, and Shor [KLS22] attempt to provide a quantum money scheme based on lattices. Their scheme has some similarities to the blueprint discussed above, taking advantage of each of the strategies 1, 2 and 3. But there are other differences as well: the state $|\psi\rangle$ is created as a superposition over a lattice rather than the integers, and the measurement of $\mathbf{u}$ is replaced with a move complex general positive operator-value measurement (POVM). [KLS22] claims to prove security under the hardness of finding a second short vector in a random lattice when already given a short vector. This problem is closely related to 1-SIS, and follows also from the hardness of worst-case lattice problems.

Our Results. First, we show an alternative view of [KLS22] which shows that it does, indeed, fall in the above framework. That is, there is a way to view their scheme as starting from $|\psi\rangle$ that is a non-Gaussian superposition of short integer vectors $\mathbf{y}$. The minting process in our alternate view then measures $\mathbf{A}^T \cdot \mathbf{y}$, where $\mathbf{A}$ is part of the public key, and is chosen to be uniform except that it is orthogonal to 3 short vectors $\mathbf{s}_0, \mathbf{s}_1, \mathbf{s}_2$. These vectors play a role in verification, as they make the QFT non-uniform. Using this alternative view, we also demonstrate a flaw in the security proof of [KLS22], showing that forged money states actually do not yield new short vectors in the lattice. See Section D of the full version for details.

We then go on (Sect. 5) to show an explicit attack against their money scheme. More generally, we show an attack on a wide class of instantiations of the above framework. Our attack works in two steps:

- First, we extend the collapsing result of [LZ19] to also handle the case of polynomial modulus, and in particular, we only need LWE to be hard for noise rate that is slightly smaller than q/σ. This resolves an important open by showing that SIS is collapsing for all moduli.
  Our proof requires a novel reduction that exploits a more delicate analysis of the quantum states produced in the proof of [LZ19]. We also extend the result in a meaningful way to the case where several short kernel vectors $\mathbf{s}_0, \mathbf{s}_1, \ldots$ are provided. We show that instead of just using $\mathbf{y}$ as a forgery (which can be distinguished using the short vectors $\mathbf{s}_i$), a particular superposition over vectors of the form $\mathbf{y} + \sum_i c_i \mathbf{s}_i$ can fool any efficient verification. Fooling verification requires the hardness a certain "k-LWE" problem, which we show follows from worst-case lattice problems in many settings (see Section E). This requires us to extend the known results on k-LWE hardness, which may be of independent interest.
- Then we show how to construct such a superposition efficiently given only $\mathbf{y}$ and the $\mathbf{s}_i$, in many natural settings. Our settings include as a special case the setting of [KLS22]. Along the way, we explain how to construct Gaussian superpositions over lattices, when given a short basis. The algorithm is a coherent version of the classical discrete Gaussian sampling algorithm [GPV08]. In general, it is not possible to take a classical distribution and run it on a superposition of random coins to get a superposition with

weights determined by the distribution. This is because the random coins themselves will be left behind and entangled with the resulting state. We show how to implement the classical algorithm coherently in a way that does not leave the random coins behind or any other entangled bits. Such an algorithm was previously folklore (e.g. it was claimed to exist without justification by [KLS22]), but we take care to actually write out the algorithm.

After communicating this flaw and attack to the authors of [KLS22], they have retracted their paper.[8]

3.2   Quantum Money from Walkable Invariants

In the second part of the paper, we describe a general framework for instantiating publicly verifiable quantum money from invariants satisfying certain conditions. This framework abstracts the ideas behind the construction of quantum money from knots [FGH+12] and its precedent [LAF+10].

At a high level, we start from a set X, which is partitioned into many disjoint sets $O \subseteq X$. There is a collection of efficiently computable (and efficiently invertible) permutations on X, such that for every permutation in the collection and every O in the partition, the permutation maps elements of O to O. Such a set of permutations allows one to take an element $x \in O$, and perform a walk through O. We additionally assume an invariant $I : X \to Y$ on X, such that I is constant on each element O of the partition. In other words, I is invariant under action by the collection of permutations.

In the case of [FGH+12], X is essentially the set of knot diagrams[9], the permutations are Reidemeister moves, and the invariant is the Alexander polynomial.

An honest quantum money state will essentially be a uniform superposition over O[10]. Such a state is constructed by first constructing the uniform superposition over X, and then measuring the invariant I. Applying a permutation from the collection will not affect such a state. Thus, verification attempts to test whether the state is preserved under action by permutations in the collection by performing an analog of a swap test, and only accepts if the test passes.

In [FGH+12], it is explained why certain attack strategies are likely to be incapable of duplicating banknotes. However, no security proof is given under widely believed hard computational assumptions. To make matters worse, [FGH+12] do not analyze what types of states are accepted by the verifier. It could be, for example, that duplicating a banknote perfectly is computationally infeasible, but there are fake banknotes that pass verification that can be duplicated; this is exactly what happens in the lattice-based schemes analyzed

---

[8] We once again want to emphasize that the authors of [KLS22] were exceptionally helpful and we thank them for their time spent helping us understand their work.

[9] Due to certain concerns about security, [FGH+12] actually sets X to contain extra information beyond a knot diagram.

[10] Technically, it is a uniform superposition over the pre-images of some y in the image of I. If multiple O have the same y, then the superposition will be over all such O.

above in Sect. 3.1. Given the complexities of their scheme, there have been limited efforts to understand the security of the scheme. This is problematic, since there have been many candidates for public key quantum money that were later found to be insecure.

Generally, a fundamental issue with public key quantum money schemes is that, while quantum money schemes rely on the no-cloning principle, the no-cloning theorem is information-theoretic, whereas publicly verifiable quantum money is always information-theoretically clonable. So unclonability crucially relies on the adversary being computationally efficient. Such computational unclonability is far less understood than traditional computational tasks. Indeed, while there have been a number of candidate post-quantum hard computational tasks, there are very few quantum money schemes still standing. The challenge is in understanding if and how quantum information combines with computational bounds to give computational unclonability.

To overcome this challenge, the security analysis should be broken into two parts: one part that relies on *information-theoretic* no-cloning, and another part that relies on a computational hardness assumption. Of course, the security of the scheme itself could be such an assumption, so we want to make the assumption have nothing to do with cloning. One way to accomplish this is to have the assumption have classical inputs and outputs (which we will call "classically meaningful"), so that it could in principle be falsified by a classical algorithm, which are obviously not subject to quantum unclonability. Separating out the quantum information from the computational aspects would hopefully give a clearer understanding of why the scheme should be unclonable, hopefully allow for higher confidence in security. Moreover, as essentially all widely studied assumptions are classically meaningful, any attempt to prove security under a widely studied assumptions would have to follow this blueprint, and indeed the proof of quantum money from obfuscation [Zha19] is of this form.

Our Results. In this work, we make progress towards justifying invariant-based quantum money.

- First, we prove that if a random walk induced by the collection of permutations mixes, then we can completely characterize the states accepted by verification. The states are exactly the uniform superpositions over O^{11}. Unfortunately, it is unclear if the knot construction actually mixes, and any formal proof of mixing seems likely to advance knot theory[12].
- Second, we provide concrete security properties under which we can prove security. These properties, while still not well-studied, at least have no obvious connection to cloning, and are meaningful even classically. Under these

---

[11] Or more generally, if multiple O have the same y, then accepting states are exactly those that place equal weight on elements of each O, but the weights may be different across different O.

[12] Nevertheless we provide a discussion on the knot money instantiation in the knot instantiation section of the full version.

assumptions, we can even prove that the schemes are in fact quantum lightning, the aforementioned strengthening of quantum money where not even the mint can create two banknotes of the same serial number.

Our Hardness Assumptions. We rely on two hardness assumptions in our invariant money scheme for a provably secure: the *path-finding* assumption and *knowledge of path finding* assumption.

Informally speaking, the path-finding assumption states that, given some adversarially sampled x from a set of elements X and given a set of "permutations" Σ, it is hard for any efficient adversary, given a random $z \in X$, where there exists some $\sigma \in \Sigma$ such that $\sigma(x) = z$, to find such a σ. One can observe that it is similar to a "discrete logarithm" style of problem. Even though we cannot use discrete logarithm due to its quantum insecurity, we have similar hard problems in certain isogenies over ellitic curves, abstracted as "group action discrete logarithm" problems [ADMP20].

Our Knowledge of Path Assumptions. The main novel assumption we use is a "knowledge of path" assumption. This roughly says that if an algorithm outputs two elements x, z in the same O, then it must "know" a path between them: a list of permutations from the collection that, when composed, would take x to z. While such a knowledge of path assumption is undoubtedly a strong assumption, it seems plausible in a number of relevant contexts (e.g. elliptic curve isogenies that have no known non-trivial attacks or "generic" group actions).

Formalizing the knowledge of path assumption is non-trivial. The obvious *classical* way to define knowledge of path is to say that for any adversary, there is an extractor that can compute the path between x and z. Importantly, the extractor must be given the same random coins as the adversary, so that it can compute x and z for itself and moreover know what random choices the adversary made that lead to x, z. Essentially, by also giving the random coins, we would be effectively making the adversary deterministic, which is crucial for the extractor's output to be related to the adversary's output.

Unfortunately, quantumly the above argument does not make much sense, as quantum algorithms can have randomness without having explicit random coins. In fact, there are quantum procedures that are *inherently probabilistic*, in the sense that the process is efficient, but there is no way to run the process twice and get the same outcome both times. This is actually crucial to our setting: we are targeting the stronger quantum lightning, which means that even the mint cannot create two banknotes with the same serial number. This means that the minting process is inherently probabilistic. The adversary could, for example, run the minting process, but with its own minting key. Such an adversary would then be inherently probabilistic and we absolutely would need a definition that can handle such adversaries.

Our solution is to exploit the fact that quantum algorithms can always be implemented *reversibly*. We then observe that with a classical reversible adversary, an equivalent way to define knowledge assumptions would be to just feed the entire *final* state of the adversary (including output) into the extractor.

By reversibility, this is equivalent to giving the input, coins included, to the extractor. But this alternate extraction notion actually *does* make sense quantumly. Thus our knowledge of path assumption is defined as giving the extractor the entire final (quantum) state of the reversible adversary, and asking that the extractor can find a path between x and z. This assumption allows us to bypass the issue of inherently probabilistic algorithms, and is sufficient for us to prove security.

Instantiations of Invariant Quantum Money and Lightning. After we provide the characterization of security needed for invariant money, we discuss four candidate instantiations[13]:

- We show a construction from structured oracles and generic cryptographic group actions. Notably, while we do not know how to instantiate these oracles, we can prove that this construction is secure assuming the existence of a cryptographic group action and the assumption that the knowledge of path assumption holds over a generic cryptographic group action.[14]
- We explain how re-randomizable functional encryption, a type of functional encryption with special properties that seem reasonable, can be used to build another candidate quantum lightning. We don't currently have a provably secure construction from standard cryptographic assumptions for this special re-randomizable functional encryption, but we provide a candidate construction based on some relatively well-studied primitives.
- Elliptic curve isogenies are our final new candidate instantiation. We outline how, given some assumptions about sampling certain superpositions of elliptic curves, it may be possible to build quantum lightning from isogeny-based assumptions.
- Finally, we analyze the construction of quantum money from knots in [FGH+12] in our framework.

For all these three constructions, we show that their corresponding *path-finding* problem between two elements x, z in the same O is relatively straightforward to study (reducible to reasonably well-founded assumptions). Nevertheless, we need the knowledge of path assumptions to show that we can extract these paths from a (unitary) adversary. We believe that one may show a knowledge-of-path property when replacing some plain model components in the above candidates with (quantum accessible) *classical* oracles, thus giving the possibility for a first quantum lightning scheme relative to only classical oracles and widely studied assumptions.

4   Preliminaries

In this section we explain some background material needed for our work.

---

[13] Throughout the sections on invariant quantum money framework and construction in the full verison, we will sometimes interchangeably use "money" or "lightning". But in fact the proposed candidates are all candidates for quantum lightning.

[14] This seems like a very plausible assumption to us: classically, the knowledge of exponent would almost trivially hold over generic groups.

For quantum notations, we denote $|\cdot\rangle$ as the notation for a pure state and $|\cdot\rangle\langle\cdot|$ for its density matrix. ρ denotes a general mixed state.

We will go over some fundamental lattice facts and then move to quantum money definitions. Due to the restriction of space, we leave some additional lattice basics, hardness theorems and necessary quantum background (in particular related to lattices) to Appendix preliminaries section of the full version.

4.1   Lattice Basics

We say a distribution $\mathcal{D}$ is (B, δ)-bounded if the probability that $\mathcal{D}$ outputs a value larger than B is less than δ. We extend this to distributions that output vectors in an entry-by-entry way. Given a set of vectors $\mathbf{B} = \{\mathbf{b}_1, ..., \mathbf{b}_n\}$, we define the norm of $\mathbf{B}$, denoted $||\mathbf{B}||$, as the length of the longest vector in $\mathbf{B}$, so $||\mathbf{B}|| = \max_i ||\mathbf{b}_i||$. For any lattice Λ, we define the minimum distance (or first successive minimum) $\lambda_1(\Lambda)$ as the length of the shortest nonzero lattice vector in Λ.

We next define discrete Gaussians formally. Since we later use their lemmas, our definition is loosely based on that of [BLP+13].

Definition 1. *For any $\sigma > 0$, the n-dimensional Gaussian function $\rho_\sigma : \mathbb{R}^n \to [0, 1]$ is defined as*

$$\rho_r(\mathbf{x}) = e^{-\pi \frac{\mathbf{x}^2}{\sigma^2}}$$

We define the discrete Gaussian function *with parameter σ at point $\mathbf{p} \in \mathbb{R}^n$, which we usually denote $\mathcal{D}_{\mathbf{\Psi}_\sigma}$ or just $\mathbf{\Psi}_\sigma$ when the context is clear, as the function over all of the integers $\mathbf{y} \in \mathbb{Z}^n$ such that the probability mass of any $\mathbf{y}$ is proportional to*

$$e^{-\pi \frac{(\mathbf{p}-\mathbf{y})^2}{\sigma^2}}.$$

We can also define more complicated discrete Gaussians over lattices. In this case, let $\mathbf{\Sigma}$ be a matrix in $\mathbb{R}^{n \times n}$. The discrete Gaussian over a lattice Λ with center $\mathbf{p}$ and "skew" parameter Σ is the function over all lattice points in Λ such that the probability mass of any $\mathbf{y}$ is proportional to

$$e^{-\pi(\mathbf{p}-\mathbf{y})^T(\mathbf{\Sigma}\mathbf{\Sigma}^T)^{-1}(\mathbf{p}-\mathbf{y})},$$

very similar to as before. We usually denote this type of discrete Gaussian as $\mathbf{\Psi}_{\Lambda, \mathbf{\Sigma}, \mathbf{p}}$ or $\mathcal{D}_{\mathbf{\Psi}_{\Lambda, \Sigma, \mathbf{p}}}$, where we sometimes substitute σ for Σ when $\mathbf{\Sigma} = \sigma \cdot \mathbf{I}_n$, where $\mathbf{I}_n$ is the $n \times n$ identity matrix. We also sometimes omit parameters when they are obvious (e.g. 0) in context.

We will explain how to efficiently sample discrete Gaussians quantumly in B.3 of the full version.

4.2   General LWE Definition

In this section we define basic LWE with an eye towards eventually defining k-LWE. We note that, while equivalent to the standard definitions, our definitions here are presented a little bit differently than usual in lattice cryptography. This is so that we can keep the notation more consistent with the typical quantum money and quantum algorithms presentation styles. We first provide a properly parameterized definition of the LWE problem [Reg05].

Definition 2 *Learning with Errors (LWE) Problem: Let n, m, and q be integers, let $\mathcal{D}_\mathbf{A}$ and $\mathcal{D}_\mathbf{r}$ be distributions over $\mathbb{Z}_q^n$, and let $\mathcal{D}_\Psi$ be a distribution over $\mathbb{Z}_q^m$. Let $\mathbf{A} \in \mathbb{Z}_q^{m \times n}$ be a matrix where each row is sampled from $\mathcal{D}_\mathbf{A}$, let $\mathbf{r} \in \mathbb{Z}_q^n$ be a vector sampled from $\mathcal{D}_\mathbf{r}$, and let $\mathbf{e} \in \mathbb{Z}_q^m$ be a vector sampled from $\mathcal{D}_\Psi$. Finally, let $\mathbf{t} \in \mathbb{Z}_q^m$ be a uniformly random vector.*

The $(n, m, q, \mathcal{D}_\mathbf{A}, \mathcal{D}_\mathbf{r}, \mathcal{D}_\Psi)$-LWE problem is defined to be distinguishing between the following distributions:

$$(\mathbf{A}, \mathbf{A} \cdot \mathbf{r} + \mathbf{e}) \quad and \quad (\mathbf{A}, \mathbf{t}).$$

4.3   Quantum Money and Quantum Lightning

Here, we define public key quantum money and quantum lightning. Following Aaronson and Christiano [AC12], we will only consider so-called "mini-schemes", where there is only a single banknote.

Both quantum money and quantum lightning share the same syntax and correctness requirements. There are two quantum polynomial-time algorithms Gen, Ver such that:

- Gen(1^λ) samples a classical serial number σ and a quantum state $|\psi\rangle$.
- Ver($\sigma, |\psi\rangle$) outputs a bit 0 or 1.

Correctness. We require that there exists a negligible function negl such that $\Pr[\mathsf{Ver}(\mathsf{Gen}(1^\lambda))] \geq 1 - \mathsf{negl}(\lambda)$.

Security. Where public key quantum money and quantum lightning differ is in security. The differences are analogous to the differences between one-way functions and collision resistance.

Definition 3 (Quantum Money Unforgeability). (Gen, Ver) *is secure public key quantum money if, for all quantum polynomial-time A, there exists a negligible negl such that A wins the following game with probability at most negl:*

- *The challenger runs $(\sigma, |\psi\rangle) \leftarrow \mathsf{Gen}(1^\lambda)$, and gives $\sigma, |\psi\rangle$ to A.*
- *A produces a potentially entangled joint state $\rho_{1,2}$ over two quantum registers. Let ρ_1, ρ_2 be the states of the two registers. A sends $\rho_{1,2}$ to the challenger.*
- *The challenger runs $b_1 \leftarrow \mathsf{Ver}(\sigma, \rho_1)$ and $b_2 \leftarrow \mathsf{Ver}(\sigma, \rho_2)$. A wins if $b_1 = b_2 = 1$.*

Definition 4 (Quantum Lightning Unforgeability). $(\mathsf{Gen}, \mathsf{Ver})$ *is secure quantum lightning if, for all quantum polynomial-time A, there exists a negligible* negl *such that A wins the following game with probability at most* negl*:*

- *A, on input 1^λ, produces and sends to the challenger σ and $\rho_{1,2}$, where $\rho_{1,2}$ is a potentially entangled joint state over two quantum registers.*
- *The challenger runs $b_1 \leftarrow \mathsf{Ver}(\sigma, \rho_1)$ and $b_2 \leftarrow \mathsf{Ver}(\sigma, \rho_2)$. A wins if $b_1 = b_2 = 1$.*

The difference between quantum lightning and quantum money is therefore that in quantum lightning, unclonability holds, even for adversarially constructed states.

Note that, as with classical collision resistance, quantum lightning does not exist against non-uniform adversaries. Like in the case of collision resistance, we can update the syntax and security definition to utilize a common reference string (crs), which case non-uniform security can hold. For this paper, to keep the discussion simple, we will largely ignore the issue of non-uniform security.

5   Our General Attack on a Class of Quantum Money

Due to limitation of space, we leave a detailed discussion of the [KLS22] money scheme and its flaw in of the full version.

Now, we show that a natural class of schemes, including the equivalent view on [KLS22] demonstrated in the full version, cannot possibly give secure quantum money schemes, regardless of how the verifier works.

5.1   The General Scheme

Here, we describe a general scheme which captures the alternate view above. Here, we use somewhat more standard notation from the lattice literature. Here we give a table describing how the symbols from section C map to this section:

This Section	Section C.3
q	P
n	1
m	$d' = d + 2$
$\mathbf{A}$	$\mathbf{v}'$ as a column vector
$|\psi\rangle$	$|\phi'\rangle$
$\mathbf{u}$	T
W	$k + \sqrt{m} \times \sigma \times \omega(\sqrt{\log(\lambda)})$

Setup. Let q be a super-polynomial, which may or may not be prime. Sample from some distribution several short vectors $\mathbf{s}_1, \ldots, \mathbf{s}_\ell \in \mathbb{Z}_q^m$ for a constant ℓ, and assemble them as a matrix $\mathbf{S} \in \mathbb{Z}_q^{m \times \ell}$. Then generate a random matrix $\mathbf{A} \in \mathbb{Z}_q^{m \times n}$ such that $\mathbf{A}^T \cdot \mathbf{S} = 0 \bmod q$.

Minting. Create some superposition $|\psi\rangle$ of vectors in $\mathbf{y} \in \mathbb{Z}_q^m$ such that an all but negligible fraction of the support of $|\psi\rangle$ are on vectors with norm W. Let $\alpha_{\mathbf{y}}$ be the amplitude of $\mathbf{y}$ in $|\psi\rangle$.

Then apply the following map to $|\psi\rangle$:

$$|\mathbf{y}\rangle \to |\mathbf{y}, \mathbf{A}^T \cdot \mathbf{y} \bmod q\rangle$$

Finally, measure the second register to obtain $\mathbf{u} \in \mathbb{Z}_q^n$. This is the serial number, and the note is $|\psi_{\mathbf{u}}\rangle$, whatever remains of the first register, which is a superposition over short vectors $\mathbf{y}$ such that $\mathbf{A}^T \cdot \mathbf{y} = \mathbf{u}$.

Verification. We do not specify verification. Indeed, in the following we will show that the money scheme is insecure, for *any* efficient verification scheme.

5.2 Attacking the General Scheme

We now show how to attack the general scheme. Let $\mathbf{C}$ be a matrix whose columns span the space orthogonal to the columns of $\mathcal{S}$. Let $|\psi_{\mathbf{u}}'\rangle$ be the state sampled from $|\psi_{\mathbf{u}}\rangle$ by measuring $\mathbf{y} \mapsto \mathbf{C}^T \cdot \mathbf{y}$, and letting $|\psi_{\mathbf{u}}'\rangle$ be whatever is left over.

Our attack will consist of two parts:

- Showing that $|\psi_{\mathbf{u}}'\rangle$ is indistinguishable from $|\psi_{\mathbf{u}}\rangle$, for *any* efficient verification procedure. We show (Sect. 5.3) that this follows from a certain "k-LWE" assumption, which depends on the parameters of the scheme (k, n, m, q, etc.). In Section D of the full version, we justify the assumption in certain general cases, based on the assumed hardness of worst-case lattice problems. Note that these lattice problems are essentially (up to small differences in parameters) the same assumptions we would expect are needed to show security for the money scheme in the first place. As such, if k-LWE does not hold for these special cases, most likely the quantum money scheme is insecure anyway. Our cases include the case of [KLS22].
- Showing that $|\psi_{\mathbf{u}}'\rangle$ can be cloned. Our attack first measures $|\psi_{\mathbf{u}}'\rangle$ to obtain a single vector $\mathbf{y}$ in it's support. To complete the attack, it remains to construct $|\psi_{\mathbf{u}}'\rangle$ from $\mathbf{y}$; by repeating such a process many times on the same $\mathbf{y}$, we successfully clone. We show (Sect. 5.4) that in certain general cases how to perform such a construction. Our cases include the case of [KLS22].

Taken together, our attack shows that not only is [KLS22] insecure, but that it quite unlikely that any tweak to the scheme will fix it.

5.3 Indistinguishability of $|\psi_{\mathbf{u}}'\rangle$

Here, we show that our fake quantum money state $|\psi_{\mathbf{u}}'\rangle$ passes verification, despite being a very different state that $|\psi_{\mathbf{u}}\rangle$. We claim that, from the perspective of any efficient verification algorithm, $|\psi_{\mathbf{u}}'\rangle$ and $|\psi_{\mathbf{u}}\rangle$ are indistinguishable. This would mean our attack succeeds.

Toward this end, let $\mathbf{C} \in \mathbb{Z}_q^{m \times (m-\ell)}$ be a matrix whose rows span the space orthogonal to $\mathbf{S}$: $\mathbf{C}^T \cdot \mathbf{S} = 0$. Notice that the state $|\psi_{\mathbf{u}}'\rangle$ can be equivalently constructed by applying the partial measurement of $\mathbf{C}^T \cdot \mathbf{y}$ to $|\psi_{\mathbf{u}}\rangle$.

Consider the following problem, which is closely related to "k-LWE" (Definition 4 in the full version):

Problem 1. Let n, m, q, Σ be functions of the security parameter, and D a distribution over $\mathbf{S}$. The $(n, m, q, \Sigma, \ell, D)$-LWE problem is to efficiently distinguish the following two distributions:

$$(\mathbf{A}, \mathbf{A} \cdot \mathbf{r} + \mathbf{e}) \quad \text{and} \quad (\mathbf{A}, \mathbf{C} \cdot \mathbf{r}' + \mathbf{e}) ,$$

Where $\mathbf{r}$ is uniform in $\mathbb{Z}_q^n$, $\mathbf{r}'$ is uniform in $\mathbb{Z}_q^{m-\ell}$, and $\mathbf{e}$ is Gaussian of width Σ. We say the problem is *hard* if, for all polynomial time quantum algorithms, the distinguishing advantage is negligible.

In Section D of the full version, we explain that in many parameter settings, including importantly the setting of [KLS22], that the hardness of Problem 1 is true (assuming standard lattice assumptions).

With the hardness of Problem 1, we can show the following, which is a generalization of a result of [LZ19] that showed that the SIS hash function is collapsing for super-polynomial modulus:

Theorem 1. *Consider sampling* $\mathbf{A}, \mathbf{S}$ *as above, and consider any efficient algorithm that, given* $\mathbf{A}, \mathbf{S}$, *samples a* $\mathbf{u}$ *and a state* $|\phi_{\mathbf{u}}\rangle$ *with the guarantee that all the support of* $|\phi_{\mathbf{u}}\rangle$ *is on vectors* $\mathbf{y}$ *such that (1)* $\mathbf{A}^T \cdot \mathbf{y} = \mathbf{u} \bmod q$ *and (2)* $|\mathbf{y}|_2 \leq W$.

Now suppose $|\phi_{\mathbf{u}}\rangle$ *is sampled according to this process, and then either (A)* $|\phi_{\mathbf{u}}\rangle$ *is produced, or (B)* $|\phi_{\mathbf{u}}'\rangle$ *is produced, where* $|\phi_{\mathbf{u}}'\rangle$ *is the result of applying the partial measurement of* $\mathbf{C}^T \cdot \mathbf{y}$ *to the state* $|\phi_{\mathbf{u}}\rangle$.

Suppose there exists Σ *such that* $q/W\Sigma = \omega(\sqrt{\log \lambda})$ *such that* $(n, m, q, \Sigma, \ell, D)$-LWE *is hard. Then cases (A) and (B) are computationally indistinguishable.*

Note that an interesting consequence of Theorem 1 in the case $\ell = 0$ is that it shows that the SIS hash function is collapsing for any modulus, under an appropriate (plain) LWE distribution. This improves upon [LZ19], who showed the same but only for super-polynomial modulus. We now give the proof of Theorem 1:

Proof. For an integer t, let $\lfloor \cdot \rceil_t$ denote the function that maps a point $x \in \mathbb{Z}_q$ to the $z \in \{0, \lfloor q/t \rfloor, \lfloor 2q/t \rfloor, \cdot, \lfloor (t-1)q/t \rfloor\}$ that minimizes $|z - x|$. Here, $|z - x|$ is the smallest a such that $z = x \pm a \bmod q$. In other words, $\lfloor \cdot \rceil_t$ is a course rounding function that rounds an $x \in \mathbb{Z}_q$ to one of t points that are evenly spread out in $\mathbb{Z}_q$.

Let ρ be a mixed quantum state, whose support is guaranteed to be on $\mathbf{y}$ such that (1) $\mathbf{A}^T \cdot \mathbf{y} = \mathbf{u} \bmod q$ and (2) $|\mathbf{y}|_2 \leq W$. For a quantum process M acting on ρ, let $M(\rho)$ be the mixed state produced by applying M_i to ρ. We will consider a few types of procedures applied to on quantum states.

M_0: Given $\mathbf{A}$, M_0 is just the partial measurement of $\mathbf{y} \mapsto \mathbf{C}^T \cdot \mathbf{y}$.

M_1^t: Given $\mathbf{A}$, to apply this measurement, first sample an LWE sample $\mathbf{b} = \mathbf{A} \cdot \mathbf{r} + \mathbf{e}$. Then apply the measurement $\mathbf{y} \mapsto \lfloor \mathbf{b} \cdot \mathbf{y} \rceil_t$. Discard the measurement outcome, and output the remaining state.

Lemma 1. *For any constants t, d, $M_1^t(\rho)$ is statistically close to $\frac{1}{d} M_1^{t \times d}(\rho) + \left(1 - \frac{1}{d}\right) \rho$*

Note that Lemma 1 means that M_1^t can be realized by the mixture of two measurements: $M_1^{t \times d}$ with probability $1/t^2$, and the identity with probability $\left(1 - \frac{1}{d}\right)$. We now give the proof.

Proof. Consider the action of M_1^t on $|\mathbf{y}\rangle\langle\mathbf{y}'|$, for a constant t. First, an LWE sample $\mathbf{b} = \mathbf{A} \cdot \mathbf{r} + \mathbf{e}$ is chosen. Then conditioned on this sample, if $\lfloor \mathbf{b} \cdot \mathbf{y} \rceil_t = \lfloor \mathbf{b} \cdot \mathbf{y}' \rceil_t$, the output is $|\mathbf{y}\rangle\langle\mathbf{y}'|$. Otherwise the output is 0. Averaging over all $\mathbf{b}$, we have that

$$M_1^t(|\mathbf{y}\rangle\langle\mathbf{y}'|) = \Pr_{\mathbf{b}}[\lfloor \mathbf{b} \cdot \mathbf{y} \rceil_t = \lfloor \mathbf{b} \cdot \mathbf{y}' \rceil_t]$$

where the probability is over $\mathbf{b}$ sampled as $\mathbf{b} = \mathbf{A} \cdot \mathbf{r} + \mathbf{e}$. Recalling that $\mathbf{u} = \mathbf{A}^T \cdot \mathbf{y} = \mathbf{A}^T \cdot \mathbf{y}'$, we have that:

$$\mathbf{b} \cdot \mathbf{y} = \mathbf{r} \cdot \mathbf{u} + \mathbf{e} \cdot \mathbf{y}$$
$$\mathbf{b} \cdot \mathbf{y}' = \mathbf{r} \cdot \mathbf{u} + \mathbf{e} \cdot \mathbf{y}'$$

Now, by our choice of Σ, $|\mathbf{e} \cdot (\mathbf{y} - \mathbf{y}')| < q/t$ for any constant t, except with negligible probability. We will therefore assume this is the case, incurring only a negligible error.

Note that $\mathbf{z} := \mathbf{r} \cdot \mathbf{u}$ is uniform in $\mathbb{Z}_q$ and independent of $\mathbf{e} \cdot \mathbf{y}, \mathbf{e} \cdot \mathbf{y}'$. So measuring $\lfloor \mathbf{b} \cdot \mathbf{y} \rceil_t$ is identical to measuring the result of rounding $\mathbf{e} \cdot \mathbf{y}$, except that the rounding boundaries are rotated by a random $\mathbf{z} \in \mathbb{Z}_q$. Since the rounding boundaries are q/t apart, at most a single rounding boundary can be between $\mathbf{e} \cdot \mathbf{y}$ and $\mathbf{e} \cdot \mathbf{y}'$, where "between" means lying in the shorter of the two intervals (of length $|\mathbf{e} \cdot (\mathbf{y} - \mathbf{y}')|$) resulting by cutting the circle $\mathbb{Z}_q$ at the points $\mathbf{e} \cdot \mathbf{y}$ and $\mathbf{e} \cdot \mathbf{y}'$. $\lfloor \mathbf{b} \cdot \mathbf{y} \rceil_t = \lfloor \mathbf{b} \cdot \mathbf{y}' \rceil_t$ if and only if no rounding boundary is between them.

Since the cyclic shift $\mathbf{z}$ is uniform each rounding boundary is uniform. Since there are t rounding boundaries and no two of them can between $\mathbf{e} \cdot \mathbf{y}$ and $\mathbf{e} \cdot \mathbf{y}'$, we have that, conditioned on $\mathbf{e}$, the probability $\lfloor \mathbf{b} \cdot \mathbf{y} \rceil_t \neq \lfloor \mathbf{b} \cdot \mathbf{y}' \rceil_t$ is therefore $\frac{t}{q} |\mathbf{e} \cdot (\mathbf{y} - \mathbf{y}')|$. Averaging over all $\mathbf{e}$, we have that, up to negligible error:

$$M_1^t(|\mathbf{y}\rangle\langle\mathbf{y}'|) = \left(1 - \frac{t}{q} \mathop{\mathbb{E}}_{\mathbf{e}}[|\mathbf{e} \cdot (\mathbf{y} - \mathbf{y}')|]\right) |\mathbf{y}\rangle\langle\mathbf{y}'|$$

Notice then that $M_1^t(|\mathbf{y}\rangle\langle\mathbf{y}'|) = \frac{1}{d} M_1^{t \times d}(|\mathbf{y}\rangle\langle\mathbf{y}'|) + \left(1 - \frac{1}{d}\right) |\mathbf{y}\rangle\langle\mathbf{y}'|$. By linearity, we therefore prove Lemma 1.   □

Note that the proof of Lemma 1 also demonstrates that M_0 and M_1^t commute, since their action on density matrices is just component-wise multiplication by a fixed matrix.

M_2^t: Given $\mathbf{A}$, to apply this measurement, first sample an LWE sample $\mathbf{b} = \mathbf{C} \cdot \mathbf{r}' + \mathbf{e}$. Then apply the measurement $\mathbf{y} \mapsto \lfloor \mathbf{b} \cdot \mathbf{y} \rceil_t$. Let p_t be the probability that $\lfloor x \rceil_t = \lfloor y \rceil_t$ for uniformly random $x, y \in \mathbb{Z}_q$. Note that for any constant t, $p_t \leq t^{-1} + O(q^{-1})$.

Lemma 2. *For any constant t, $M_2^t(\rho)$ is statistically close to $M_0(M_1^t(\rho)) + p_t(\rho - M_0(\rho))$.*

Note that unlike Lemma 1, the expression in Lemma 2 does not correspond to a mixture of measurements applied to ρ. However, we will later see how to combine Lemma 2 with Lemma 1 to obtain such a mixture.

Proof. The proof proceeds similarly to Lemma 1. We consider the action of M_2^t on $|\mathbf{y}\rangle\langle\mathbf{y}'|$, and conclude that

$$M_2^t(|\mathbf{y}\rangle\langle\mathbf{y}'|) = \Pr_{\mathbf{b}}[\lfloor \mathbf{b} \cdot \mathbf{y} \rceil_t = \lfloor \mathbf{b} \cdot \mathbf{y}' \rceil_t]$$

where the probability is over $\mathbf{b} = \mathbf{C} \cdot \mathbf{r}' + \mathbf{e}$. But now we have that

$$\mathbf{b} \cdot \mathbf{y} = \mathbf{r}'^T \cdot \mathbf{C}^T \mathbf{y} + \mathbf{e} \cdot \mathbf{y}$$
$$\mathbf{b} \cdot \mathbf{y}' = \mathbf{r}'^T \cdot \mathbf{C}^T \mathbf{y} + \mathbf{e} \cdot \mathbf{y}'$$

We consider two cases:

- $\mathbf{C}^T \cdot \mathbf{y} = \mathbf{C}^T \cdot \mathbf{y}'$. This case is essentially identical to the proof of Lemma 1, and we conclude that $\Pr_{\mathbf{b}}[\lfloor \mathbf{b} \cdot \mathbf{y} \rceil_t = \lfloor \mathbf{b} \cdot \mathbf{y}' \rceil_t] = 1 - \frac{t}{q} \mathbb{E}_{\mathbf{e}}[|\mathbf{e} \cdot (\mathbf{y} - \mathbf{y}')|]$. Note that for such $\mathbf{y}, \mathbf{y}'$, we also have

  $$M_0(M_1^t(|\mathbf{y}\rangle\langle\mathbf{y}'|)) + p_t(|\mathbf{y}\rangle\langle\mathbf{y}'| - M_0(|\mathbf{y}\rangle\langle\mathbf{y}'|)) = M_1^t(M_0(|\mathbf{y}\rangle\langle\mathbf{y}'|)) + p_t \times 0 = 1 - \frac{t}{q} \mathbb{E}_{\mathbf{e}}[|\mathbf{e} \cdot (\mathbf{y} - \mathbf{y}')|] \ ,$$

  since M_0 is the identity on such $|\mathbf{y}\rangle\langle\mathbf{y}'|$. Thus, we have the desired equality for $\rho = |\mathbf{y}\rangle\langle\mathbf{y}'|$.
- $\mathbf{C}^T \cdot \mathbf{y} \neq \mathbf{C}_T \cdot \mathbf{y}'$. In this case, $\mathbf{b} \cdot \mathbf{y}$ and $\mathbf{b} \cdot \mathbf{y}'$ are independent and uniform over $\mathbb{Z}_p$. Therefore, $\Pr_{\mathbf{b}}[\lfloor \mathbf{b} \cdot \mathbf{y} \rceil_t = \lfloor \mathbf{b} \cdot \mathbf{y}' \rceil_t] = p_t$. Note that for such $\mathbf{y}, \mathbf{y}'$, we also have

  $$M_0(M_1^t(|\mathbf{y}\rangle\langle\mathbf{y}'|)) + p_t(|\mathbf{y}\rangle\langle\mathbf{y}'| - M_0(|\mathbf{y}\rangle\langle\mathbf{y}'|)) = 0 + p_t|\mathbf{y}\rangle\langle\mathbf{y}'|,$$

  since $M_0(|\mathbf{y}\rangle\langle\mathbf{y}'|) = 0$ in this case.

Thus for each $|\mathbf{y}\rangle\langle\mathbf{y}'|$, we have the desired equality. By linearity, this thus extends to all ρ. □

Combining Lemmas 1 and 2, we obtain:

Corollary 1. *For any constants t, d, $M_2^t(\rho)$ is statistically close to $\frac{1}{d} M_0(M_1^{t \times d}(\rho)) + \left(1 - \frac{1}{d} - p_t\right) M_0(\rho) + p_t \rho$.*

For d such that $1 - \frac{1}{d} - p_t \geq 0$, this represents a mixture of measurements $M_0 \circ M_1^{t \times d}$, M_0, and the identity.

We are now ready to prove Theorem 1. Suppose there is an algorithm A that constructs a mixed state ρ, and then can distinguish ρ from $M_0(\rho)$ with (signed) advantage ϵ. Let d be a positive integer, to be chosen later. Let $\rho_0 = \rho$, and $\rho_i = M_1^{t \times d}(\rho_{i-1})$. Note that for any polynomial i, ρ_i can be efficiently constructed. Let $\epsilon_0 = \epsilon$, and ϵ_i be the (signed) distinguishing advantage of A when given ρ_i vs $M_0(\rho_i)$.

Let δ_i be the (signed) distinguishing advantage of A for $M_2^t(\rho_i)$ and $M_1^t(\rho_i)$. Write $g = 1 - \frac{1}{d} - p_t$. Invoking Lemma 1 and Corollary 1 with d, we have that

$$\delta_i = \frac{1}{d}\epsilon_{i+1} + g\epsilon_i$$

Now, we note that δ_i must be negligible, by the assumed hardness of $(n, m, q, \Sigma, \ell, D)$-LWE. Solving the recursion gives:

$$\epsilon_i(-dg)^{-i} = \epsilon - \frac{1}{d}\sum_{j=0}^{i-1}(-dg)^{-j}\delta_{j+1}$$

Next, assume d is chosen so that dg is a constant greater than 1. Define $T = \sum_{j=0}^{\lambda-1}(dg)^{-j} = \frac{dg}{dg-1} - 2^{-O(\lambda)}$. Consider the adversary A' for $(n, m, q, \Sigma, \ell, D)$-LWE, which does the following:

- On input $\mathbf{A}, \mathbf{S}, \mathbf{b}$, where $\mathbf{b} = \mathbf{A} \cdot \mathbf{r} + \mathbf{e}$ or $\mathbf{b} = \mathbf{C} \cdot \mathbf{r}' + \mathbf{e}$, it chooses $j \in [0, \lambda - 1]$ with probability $(dg)^{-j}/T$
- Then it constructs ρ according to A.
- Next, A' computes ρ_j by applying $M_1^{t \times d}$ to ρ for j times.
- Now A' applies the measurement $\mathbf{y} \mapsto \lfloor \mathbf{b} \cdot \mathbf{y} \rceil_t$ to ρ_j, obtaining ρ_j'.
- A' runs the distinguisher for A, obtaining a bit b
- A' outputs b if j is even, $1 - b$ if j is odd.

Note that if $\mathbf{b}$ is $\mathbf{A} \cdot \mathbf{r} + \mathbf{e}$, then $\rho' = M_1^t(\rho_i)$, and if $\mathbf{b}$ is $\mathbf{C} \cdot \mathbf{r}' + \mathbf{e}$, then $\rho' = M_2^t(\rho_i)$. Therefore, the distinguishing advantage of A' is:

$$\delta = \frac{1}{T}\sum_{j=0}^{\lambda-1}(-dg)^{-j}\delta_{j+1}$$

Thus, we have that

$$\epsilon_\lambda(-dg)^{-\lambda} = \epsilon - \frac{T}{d}\delta ,$$

Noting that ϵ_λ must trivially be in $[-1/2, 1/2]$, we have that:

$$|\delta| \geq \frac{d}{T}\left(|\epsilon| - \frac{1}{2}(dg)^{-\lambda}\right) \geq d\left(1 - \frac{1}{dg}\right)|\epsilon| - 2^{-O(\lambda)}$$

Thus, if A has non-negligible distinguishing advantage, so does A', breaking the $(n, m, q, \Sigma, \ell, D)$-LWE assumption. This completes the proof of Theorem 1. $\square$

5.4   Constructing $|\psi'_\mathbf{u}\rangle$

Here, we explain how to construct $|\psi'_\mathbf{u}\rangle$, given just the vector $\mathbf{y}$ that resulted from measuring it. We first observe that, since $|\psi'_\mathbf{u}\rangle$ has support only on vectors that differ from $\mathbf{y}$ by multiples of the columns of $\mathbf{S}$, we can write:

$$|\psi'_\mathbf{u}\rangle \propto \sum_\mathbf{t} \alpha_{\mathbf{y}+\mathbf{S}\cdot\mathbf{t}}|\mathbf{y} + \mathbf{S}\cdot\mathbf{t}\rangle$$

Where $\alpha_\mathbf{y}$ is the amplitude of $\mathbf{y}$ in $|\psi\rangle$. This gives a hint as to how to construct $|\psi'_\mathbf{u}\rangle$: create a superposition over short linear combinations of $\mathbf{S}$, and then use linear algebra to transition to a superposition over $\mathbf{y} + \mathbf{S}\cdot\mathbf{t}$, weighted according to α. The problem of course is that α may be arbitrary except for having support only on short vectors. Therefore, we do not expect to be able to construct $|\psi'_\mathbf{u}\rangle$ in full generality, and instead focus on special (but natural) cases, which suffice for our use.

Wide Gaussian Distributed. Suppose the initial state $|\psi\rangle$ is the discrete Gaussian over the integers: $|\psi\rangle = |\mathbf{\Psi}_{\mathbb{Z}^m,\Sigma,\mathbf{c}}\rangle$ for some center $\mathbf{c}$ and covariance matrix Σ. Then $|\psi'_\mathbf{u}\rangle$ is simply

$$|\mathbf{\Psi}_{\mathcal{L}+\mathbf{y},\Sigma,\mathbf{c}}\rangle$$

Here, $\mathcal{L}$ is the integer lattice generated by the columns of $\mathbf{S}$, and $\mathcal{L} + \mathbf{y}$ is the lattice $\mathcal{L}$ shifted by $\mathbf{y}$. We can construct the state $|\mathbf{\Psi}_{\mathcal{L}+\mathbf{y},\Sigma,\mathbf{c}}\rangle$ by first constructing $|\mathbf{\Psi}_{\mathcal{L},\Sigma,\mathbf{c}-\mathbf{y}}\rangle$, and then adding $\mathbf{y}$ to the superposition. Thus, as long as $\mathbf{s}_i^T \cdot \Sigma^{-1} \cdot \mathbf{s}_i \leq 1/\omega(\sqrt{\log\lambda})$ for all i, we can construct the necessary state.

Constant Dimension, Hyper-ellipsoid Bounded. Here, we restrict $\mathcal{L}$ to having a constant number of columns, but greatly generalize the distributions that can be handled.

A hyper-ellipsoid is specified by a positive definite matrix Σ, which defines the set $E_{\Sigma,\mathbf{c}} = \{\mathbf{y} : (\mathbf{y} - \mathbf{c})^T \cdot \mathbf{M} \cdot (\mathbf{y} - \mathbf{c}) \leq 1\}$.

Definition 5 (Good Hyper-ellipsoid). *A* good hyper-ellipsoid *for $|\psi\rangle$ is an $E_{\Sigma,\mathbf{c}}$ such that there exists a function $\eta(\lambda)$ and polynomials $p(\lambda), q(\lambda)$ such that, if $|\psi\rangle$ is measured to get a vector $\mathbf{y}$, then each of the following are true except with negligible probability:*

- *$\mathbf{y} \in E_{\Sigma,\mathbf{c}}$. In other words, $E_{\Sigma,\mathbf{c}}$ contains essentially all the mass of $|\psi\rangle$.*
- *$|\alpha_\mathbf{x}|^2 \leq \eta(\lambda)$. In other words, η is an approximate upper bound on $\alpha_\mathbf{x}$.*
- *If a random vector $\mathbf{x}$ is chosen from $E_{\Sigma,\mathbf{c}} \cap \{\mathbf{y} + \mathbf{S}\cdot\mathbf{t} : \mathbf{t} \in \mathbb{Z}^\ell\}$, then with probability at least $1/p(\lambda)$, $|\alpha_\mathbf{x}|^2 \geq \eta/q(\lambda)$. In other words, $E_{\Sigma,\mathbf{c}}$ doesn't contain too many points with mass too much lower than η.*

Taken together, a good hyper-ellipsoid is one that fits reasonably well around the $|\psi\rangle$. It must contain essentially all the support of $|\psi\rangle$, but can over-approximate it by a polynomial factor.

Lemma 3. *Suppose there is a good hyper-ellipsoid for $|\psi\rangle$, and that $\alpha_\mathbf{y}$ can be efficiently computed given any vector $\mathbf{y}$. Then there is a polynomial-time algorithm which constructs $|\psi'_\mathbf{u}\rangle$ from $\mathbf{y}$*

Proof. Let $E_{\Sigma,\mathbf{c}}$ be the good hyper-ellipsoid. Let $\mathcal{L}$ be the lattice generated by the columns of $\mathbf{S}$. By assumption, with overwhelming probability if we measure $|\psi\rangle$ to get $\mathbf{y}$, we have $\mathbf{y} \in E_{\Sigma,\mathbf{c}}$. Let $E_{\Sigma',\mathbf{c}'}$ be the ellipsoid that is the intersection of $E_{\Sigma,\mathbf{c}}$ and the affine space $\{\mathbf{y} + \mathbf{S} \cdot \mathbf{t} : \mathbf{t} \in \mathbb{R}^\ell\}$.

Claim. There is PPT algorithm which, given $\mathbf{S}, \Sigma'$, computes $\mathbf{T} = \{\mathbf{r}_1, \cdots, \mathbf{r}_{\ell'}\}$ such that:

- $\mathbf{r}_i^T \cdot (\Sigma')^{-1} \cdot \mathbf{r}_i \leq 2$ for all $i \in [\ell']$, and
- $E_{\Sigma',\mathbf{c}'} \cap \{\mathbf{y} + \mathbf{T} \cdot \mathbf{t} : \mathbf{t} \in \mathbb{Z}^{\ell'}\} = E_{\Sigma',\mathbf{c}'} \cap \{\mathbf{y} + \mathbf{S} \cdot \mathbf{t} : \mathbf{t} \in \mathbb{Z}^\ell\}$.

Proof. Write $(\Sigma')^{-1}$ as $(\Sigma')^{-1} = \mathbf{U}^T \cdot \mathbf{U}$. Let $\mathbf{S}' = \{\mathbf{s}'_1 = \mathbf{U} \cdot \mathbf{s}_1, \ldots, \mathbf{s}'_\ell = \mathbf{U} \cdot \mathbf{s}_n\}$, and let $\mathcal{L}'$ be the lattice generated by $\mathbf{S}'$. Since ℓ is constant, we can find shortest vectors in $\mathcal{L}'$ in polynomial time. Therefore, compute $\mathbf{r}'_1, \ldots, \mathbf{r}'_\ell$ such that $\mathbf{r}'_i$ is the shortest vector in $\mathcal{L}'$ that is linearly independent from $\{\mathbf{r}'_1, \ldots, \mathbf{r}'_{i-1}\}$. Then let ℓ' be such that $|\mathbf{r}'_{\ell'}|^2 \leq 2$, but $|\mathbf{r}'_{\ell'+1}|^2 > 2$, or $\ell' = \ell$ if no such ℓ' exists.

Finally, let $\mathbf{r}_i = \mathbf{U}^{-1} \cdot \mathbf{r}'_i$. Clearly, we have that $\mathbf{r}_i^T \cdot (\Sigma')^{-1} \cdot \mathbf{r}_i \leq 2$. It remains to show that $E_{\Sigma',\mathbf{c}'} \cap \{\mathbf{y} + \mathbf{T} \cdot \mathbf{t} : \mathbf{t} \in \mathbb{Z}^{\ell'}\} = E_{\Sigma',\mathbf{c}'} \cap \{\mathbf{y} + \mathbf{S} \cdot \mathbf{t} : \mathbf{t} \in \mathbb{Z}^\ell\}$. First, we notice that the lattice $\mathcal{L}(\mathbf{T})$ spanned by $\mathbf{T}$ is a sub-lattice of $\mathcal{L}(\mathbf{S})$ spanned by $\mathbf{S}$. So one containment is trivial. Now assume toward contradiction that there is a $\mathbf{x} \in E_{\Sigma',\mathbf{c}'} \cap \{\mathbf{y} + \mathbf{S} \cdot \mathbf{t} : \mathbf{t} \in \mathbb{Z}^\ell\}$ that is not in $E_{\Sigma',\mathbf{c}'} \cap \{\mathbf{y} + \mathbf{T} \cdot \mathbf{t} : \mathbf{t} \in \mathbb{Z}^{\ell'}\}$. This means $\mathbf{x} - \mathbf{y}$ is in $\mathcal{L}(\mathbf{S})$. We also have that $(\mathbf{y} - \mathbf{c}')^T \cdot (\Sigma')^{-1} \cdot (\mathbf{y} - \mathbf{c}') \leq 1$ (since and $(\mathbf{x} - \mathbf{c}')^T \cdot (\Sigma')^{-1} \cdot (\mathbf{x} - \mathbf{c}') \leq 1$. By the triangle inequality, we have therefore that $(\mathbf{x} - \mathbf{y})^T \cdot (\Sigma')^{-1} \cdot (\mathbf{x} - \mathbf{y}) \leq 2$.

But then we have that $\mathbf{U} \cdot (\mathbf{x} - \mathbf{y})$ has norm at most 2, lies in $\mathcal{L}'$, and is linearly independent of $\{\mathbf{r}'_1, \ldots, \mathbf{r}'_{\ell'}\}$. This contradicts that $\mathbf{r}'_{\ell'+1}$ (which has norm squared strictly greater than 2) is a shortest vector linearly independent of $\{\mathbf{r}'_1, \ldots, \mathbf{r}'_{\ell'}\}$. This completes the proof of the claim. □

We now return to proving Lemma 3. Let $\beta = \omega(\log \lambda)$. We construct $|\psi'_\mathbf{u}\rangle$ in three steps:

- We first construct a state negligibly close to $|\Psi_{\mathcal{L}+\mathbf{y},\beta\Sigma',\mathbf{c}'}\rangle$, as we did in the Gaussian-distributed case above.
- We then construct the state $|E\rangle$, defined as the uniform superposition over the intersection of $\mathcal{L} + \mathbf{y}$ and $E_{\Sigma',\mathbf{c}'}$. $|E\rangle$ will be obtained from $|\Psi_{\mathcal{L}+\mathbf{y},\beta\Sigma',\mathbf{c}'}\rangle$ via a measurement.
- Construct $|\psi'_\mathbf{u}\rangle$ from $|E\rangle$. This also will be obtained via a measurement.

We now describe the two measurements. We start from the second. Let η, p, q be the values guaranteed by the goodness of $E_{\Sigma,\mathbf{c}}$. Define $\eta_\mathbf{x} = 1/\eta$ if $|\alpha_\mathbf{x}|^2 \leq \eta$, and otherwise $\eta_\mathbf{x} = 1/|\alpha_\mathbf{x}|^2$. To obtain $|\psi'_\mathbf{u}\rangle$ from $|E\rangle$, we apply the following map in superposition and measure the second register:

$$|\mathbf{x}\rangle \mapsto |\mathbf{x}\rangle \left(\sqrt{\eta_\mathbf{x}} \alpha_\mathbf{x} |0\rangle + \sqrt{1 - |\eta_\mathbf{x} \alpha_\mathbf{x}|^2} |1\rangle \right)$$

Suppose for the moment that $\eta_{\mathbf{x}} = 1/\eta$ for all $\mathbf{x}$. Then conditioned on the measurement outcome being 0, the resulting state is exactly $|\psi'_{\mathbf{u}}\rangle$. By the guarantee that $E_{\Sigma,\mathbf{c}}$ is good, we have that except with negligible probability over the choice of $\mathbf{y}$, all but a negligible fraction of the support of $|\psi'_{\mathbf{u}}\rangle$ satisfies $\eta_{\mathbf{x}} = 1/\eta$. Therefore, we will assume (with negligible error) this is the case. The probability the measurement is 0 (over the choice of $\mathbf{y}$ as well) is $\mathbb{E}_{\mathbf{x} \leftarrow E_{\Sigma',\mathbf{c}'}}[\alpha_{\mathbf{x}}^2/\eta]$, which, with probability at least $1/p$ over the choice of $\mathbf{y}$, is at least $1/q$. Thus, the overall probability of outputting 0 is inverse polynomial, and in this case we produce a state negligibly close to $|\psi'_{\mathbf{u}}\rangle$.

It remains to construct $|E\rangle$ from $|\Psi_{\mathcal{L}+\mathbf{y},\beta\Sigma',\mathbf{c}'}\rangle$. This follows a very similar rejection-sampling argument. Let

$$\gamma_{\mathbf{x}} = \begin{cases} e^{-\pi/\beta} \times \sqrt{e^{\pi(\mathbf{x}-\mathbf{c}')^T \cdot (\beta\Sigma')^{-1} \cdot (\mathbf{x}-\mathbf{c}')}} & \text{if } (\mathbf{x} - \mathbf{c}')^T \cdot (\Sigma')^{-1} \cdot (\mathbf{x} - \mathbf{c}') \leq 1 \\ 0 & \text{otherwise} \end{cases}$$

Note that $0 \leq \gamma_{\mathbf{x}} \leq 1$. Now apply to $|\Psi_{\mathcal{L}+\mathbf{y},\beta\Sigma',\mathbf{c}'}\rangle$ the map $|\mathbf{x}\rangle \mapsto |\mathbf{x}\rangle(\gamma_{\mathbf{x}}|0\rangle + \sqrt{1-\gamma_{\mathbf{x}}^2}|1\rangle)$, and measure the second coordinate. If the measurement outcome is 0, then the resulting state is exactly $|E\rangle$. For $\mathbf{x} \in E_{\Sigma',\mathbf{c}'}$, we have $\gamma_{\mathbf{x}} \geq e^{-\pi/\beta} \geq 1-o(1)$. Therefore, the probability the measurement outputs 0 is at least $1-o(1)$ times the probability measuring $\Psi_{\mathcal{L}+\mathbf{y},\beta\Sigma',\mathbf{c}'}$ produces an $\mathbf{x} \in E_{\Sigma',\mathbf{c}'}$. This latter probability is $O_\ell(\beta^{-\ell/2})$, where the constant hidden by the big O depends on ℓ. Since ℓ is constant and β is polynomial (in fact, sub-polynomial), the overall probability is polynomial. This completes the construction of $|\psi'_{\mathbf{u}}\rangle$ and the proof of Lemma 3. □

Applying to [KLS22]: To avoid confusion, we first refer the readers to our alternate view on [KLS22] scheme in section C.3 and then we will see how to apply our attack onto their scheme in section C.5 of the full version.

6 Invariant Money

From this section on, we discuss our positive results on quantum money/lightning.

We now describe our framework for instantiating quantum money using invariants, or more precisely what we call *walkable* invariants.

Let X, Y be sets, and $I : X \to Y$ an efficiently computable function from X to Y. I will be called the "invariant." We will additionally assume a collection of permutations $\sigma_i : X \to X$ indexed by $i \in [r]$ for some integer r, with the property that the permutations respect the invariant:

$$I(\sigma_i(x)) = I(x), \forall i \in [r]$$

In other words, action by each σ_i preserves the value of the invariant. We require that σ_i is efficiently computable given i. r may be polynomial or may be exponential. To make the formalism below simpler, we will be implicitly assuming that there exists a perfect matching between the σ_i such that for any matched $\sigma_i, \sigma_{i'}$, we have $\sigma_{i'} = \sigma_i^{-1}$. Moreover, i' can be found given i. This can be relaxed somewhat to just requiring that σ_i^{-1} can be efficiently computed given i, but requires a slightly more complicated set of definitions.

Given a point x, the orbit of x, denoted $O_x \subseteq X$, is the set of all z such that there exists a non-negative integer k and $i_1, \ldots, i_k \in [r]$ such that $z = \sigma_{i_k}(\sigma_{i_{k-1}}(\cdots \sigma_{i_1}(x)\cdot))$. In other words, O_x is the set of all z "reachable" from x by applying some sequence of permutations. Note that $I(z) = y$ for any $z \in O_x$. We will therefore somewhat abuse notation, and define $I(O_x) = y$. We also let P_y be the set of pre-images of y: $P_y = \{x \in X : I(x) = y\}$.

We will additionally require a couple properties, which will be necessary for the quantum money scheme to compile:

- **Efficient Generation of Superpositions:** It is possible to construct the uniform superposition over X: $|X\rangle := \frac{1}{\sqrt{|X|}} \sum_{x \in X} |x\rangle$.
- **Mixing Walks:** For an orbit O, with a slight abuse of notation let $\sigma_{O,i}$ be the (possibly exponentially large) permutation matrix associated with the action by σ_i on O. Then let $M_O = \frac{1}{r} \sum_{i \in [r]} \sigma_{O,i}$ be the component-wise average of the matrices. Let $\lambda_1(O), \lambda_2(O)$ be the largest two eigenvalues by absolute value[15], counting multiplicities. Note that $\lambda_1(O) = 1$, with corresponding eigenvector the all-1's vector. We need that there is an inverse polynomial δ such that, for every orbit O, $\lambda_2(O) \leq 1 - \delta$. This is basically just a way of saying that a random walk on the orbit using the σ_i mixes in polynomial time.

We call such a structure above a walkable invariant.

6.1 Quantum Money from Walkable Invariants

We now describe the basic quantum money scheme.

Minting. To mint a note, first construct the uniform superposition $|X\rangle$ over X. Then apply the invariant I in superposition and measure, obtaining a string y, and the state collapsing to:

$$|P_y\rangle := \frac{1}{\sqrt{|P_y|}} \sum_{x \in P_y} |x\rangle$$

This is the quantum money state, with serial number y.

Verification. To verify a supposed quantum money state $|\phi\rangle$ with serial number y, we do the following.

- First check that the support of $|\phi\rangle$ is contained in P_y. This is done by simply applying the invariant I in superposition, and measuring if the output is y. If the check fails immediately reject.

---

[15] They are real-valued, since M_O is symmetric, owing to the fact that we assumed the σ_i are perfectly matched into pairs that are inverses of each other.

- Then apply the projective measurement given by the projection $\sum_{O \subseteq P_y} |O\rangle\langle O|$, where O ranges over the orbits contained in P_y, and $|O\rangle := \frac{1}{\sqrt{|O|}} \sum_{x \in O} |x\rangle$. In other words, project onto states where, for each orbit, the weights of x in that orbit are all identical; weights between different orbits are allowed to be different.

  We cannot perform this measurement exactly, but we can perform it approximately using the fact that $\lambda_2(O) \leq 1 - \delta$. This is described in Sect. 6.2 below. Outside of Sect. 6.2, we will assume for simplicity that the measurement is provided exactly.

  If the projection rejects, reject the quantum money state. Otherwise accept.

It is hopefully clear that honestly-generated money states pass verification. Certainly their support will be contained in P_y, and they apply equal weight to each element in an orbit (and in fact, equal weight across orbits).

6.2 Approximate Verification

Here, we explain how to approximately perform the verification projection $V = \sum_{O \subseteq P_y} |O\rangle\langle O|$, using the fact that $\lambda_2(0) \leq 1 - \delta$ for all O. The algorithm we provide is an abstraction of the verification procedure of [FGH+12], except that work presented the algorithm without any analysis. We prove that the algorithm is statistically close to the projection V, provided the mixing condition $\lambda_2(0) \leq 1 - \delta$ is met.

Theorem 2. *Assume $\lambda_2(0) \leq 1 - \delta$ for all O, for some inverse-polynomial δ. Then there is a QPT algorithm $\tilde{V}$ such that, for any state $|\psi\rangle$, if we let $|\psi'\rangle$ be the un-normalized post-measurement state from applying $\tilde{V}$ to $|\psi\rangle$ in the case $\tilde{V}$ accepts, then $|\psi'\rangle$ is negligibly close to $V|\psi\rangle$.*

We refer the readers to section E.1 of the full version for the proof due to restriction on the space.

6.3 Hardness Assumptions

We rely on two hardness assumptions in our inviant money scheme: the *path-finding assumpion* and the *knowledge of path* assumption. Due to space constraints, we refer the readers to E.2 for the presentation on our hardness assumptions needed.

Informally speaking, the path-finding assumption states that, given some adversarially sampled x in a set X, it is hard for any efficient adversary, given a random $x' \in X$ such that there exists some σ such that $\sigma(x) = x'$, to find such a σ.

The knowledge of path assumption can be thought of as a quantum analogue to the (classical) knowledge of exponent assumption. We define two different versions of the knowledge of path assumption to account for the fact that some of our invariants could be invertible.

6.4   Security

Theorem 3. *Assuming the Path-Finding assumption and the Knowledge of Path Assumption, the scheme above is secure quantum lightning. If the invariant is invertible, then assuming the Path-Finding assumption, the Knowledge of Path Assumption for Invertible Invariants, and the Inversion Inverting assumption, the scheme above is secure quantum lightning.*

We refer the readers to E.3 of the full version for the formal statements of the above assumptions and the proof on the above theorem.

References

[Aar09]   Aaronson, S.: Quantum copy-protection and quantum money. In: Proceedings of the 2009 24th Annual IEEE Conference on Computational Complexity, CCC 2009, pp. 229–242, Washington, DC, USA, 2009. IEEE Computer Society (2009)

[AC12]   Aaronson, S., Christiano, P.: Quantum money from hidden subspaces. In: Karloff, H.J., Pitassi, T. (eds.) 44th Annual ACM Symposium on Theory of Computing, pp. 41–60, New York, NY, USA, 19–22 May 2012. ACM Press (2012)

[ADMP20]   Alamati, N., De Feo, L., Montgomery, H., Patranabis, S.: Cryptographic group actions and applications. In: Moriai, S., Wang, H. (eds.) ASIACRYPT 2020. LNCS, vol. 12492, pp. 411–439. Springer, Cham (2020). https://doi.org/10.1007/978-3-030-64834-3_14

[AGKZ20]   Amos, R., Georgiou, M., Kiayias, A., Zhandry, M.: One-shot signatures and applications to hybrid quantum/classical authentication. In: Proceedings of the 52nd Annual ACM SIGACT Symposium on Theory of Computing, pp. 255–268 (2020)

[AL21]   Ananth, P., La Placa, R.L.: Secure software leasing. In: Canteaut, A., Standaert, F.-X. (eds.) EUROCRYPT 2021. LNCS, vol. 12697, pp. 501–530. Springer, Cham (2021). https://doi.org/10.1007/978-3-030-77886-6_17

[ALL+21]   Aaronson, S., Liu, J., Liu, Q., Zhandry, M., Zhang, R.: New approaches for quantum copy-protection. In: Malkin, T., Peikert, C. (eds.) CRYPTO 2021. LNCS, vol. 12825, pp. 526–555. Springer, Cham (2021). https://doi.org/10.1007/978-3-030-84242-0_19

[BB87]   Bennett, C.H., Brassard, G.: Quantum public key distribution reinvented. SIGACT News **18**(4), 51–53 (1987)

[BCM+18]   Brakerski, Z., Christiano, P., Mahadev, U., Vazirani, U.V., Vidick, T.: A cryptographic test of quantumness and certifiable randomness from a single quantum device. In: Thorup, M. (ed.) 59th Annual Symposium on Foundations of Computer Science, pp. 320–331, Paris, France, 7–9 October 2018. IEEE Computer Society Press (2018)

[BDGM20]   Brakerski, Z., Döttling, N., Garg, S., Malavolta, G.: Factoring and pairings are not necessary for IO: circular-secure LWE suffices. Cryptology ePrint Archive, Report 2020/1024 (2020). https://eprint.iacr.org/2020/1024

[BDS16]   Ben-David, S., Sattath, O.: Quantum tokens for digital signatures (2016). https://arxiv.org/abs/1609.09047

[BF11]   Boneh, D., Freeman, D.M.: Linearly homomorphic signatures over binary fields and new tools for lattice-based signatures. In: Catalano, D., Fazio, N., Gennaro, R., Nicolosi, A. (eds.) PKC 2011. LNCS, vol. 6571, pp. 1–16. Springer, Heidelberg (2011). https://doi.org/10.1007/978-3-642-19379-8_1

[BGMZ18] Bartusek, J., Guan, J., Ma, F., Zhandry, M.: Return of GGH15: provable security against zeroizing attacks. In: Beimel, A., Dziembowski, S. (eds.) TCC 2018. LNCS, vol. 11240, pp. 544–574. Springer, Cham (2018). https://doi.org/10.1007/978-3-030-03810-6_20

[BGS13]   Broadbent, A., Gutoski, G., Stebila, D.: Quantum one-time programs. In: Canetti, R., Garay, J.A. (eds.) CRYPTO 2013. LNCS, vol. 8043, pp. 344–360. Springer, Heidelberg (2013). https://doi.org/10.1007/978-3-642-40084-1_20

[BLP+13] Brakerski, Z., Langlois, A., Peikert, C., Regev, O., Stehlé, D.: Classical hardness of learning with errors. In: Boneh, D., Roughgarden, T., Feigenbaum, J. (eds.) 45th Annual ACM Symposium on Theory of Computing, pp. 575–584, Palo Alto, CA, USA, 1–4 June 2013. ACM Press (2013)

[CD22]   Castryck, W., Decru, T.: An efficient key recovery attack on SIDH (preliminary version). Cryptology ePrint Archive (2022)

[CLLZ21] Coladangelo, A., Liu, J., Liu, Q., Zhandry, M.: Hidden Cosets and applications to unclonable cryptography. In: Malkin, T., Peikert, C. (eds.) CRYPTO 2021. LNCS, vol. 12825, pp. 556–584. Springer, Cham (2021). https://doi.org/10.1007/978-3-030-84242-0_20

[Col09]   Colbeck, R.: Quantum and relativistic protocols for secure multi-party computation (2009)

[Col19]   Coladangelo, A.: Smart contracts meet quantum cryptography (2019)

[CPDDF+19] Pena, M.C., Díaz, R.D., Faugère, J.C., Encinas, L.H., Perret, L.: Non-quantum cryptanalysis of the noisy version of Aaronson-Christiano's quantum money scheme. IET Inf. Secur. **13**(4), 362–366 (2019)

[CS20]   Coladangelo, A., Sattath, O.: A quantum money solution to the blockchain scalability problem. Quantum **4**, 297 (2020)

[CY14]   Coudron, M., Yuen, H.: Infinite randomness expansion with a constant number of devices. In: Shmoys, D.B. (ed.) 46th Annual ACM Symposium on Theory of Computing, pp. 427–436, New York, NY, USA, 31 May–3 June 2014. ACM Press (2014)

[Dam92]   Damgård, I.: Towards practical public key systems secure against chosen ciphertext attacks. In: Feigenbaum, J. (ed.) CRYPTO 1991. LNCS, vol. 576, pp. 445–456. Springer, Heidelberg (1992). https://doi.org/10.1007/3-540-46766-1_36

[FGH+10] Farhi, E., Gosset, D., Hassidim, A., Lutomirski, A., Nagaj, D., Shor, P.: Quantum state restoration and single-copy tomography for ground states of Hamiltonians. Phys. Rev. Lett. **105**(19), 190503 (2010)

[FGH+12] Farhi, E., Gosset, D., Hassidim, A., Lutomirski, A., Shor, P.W.: Quantum money from knots. In: Goldwasser, S. (ed.) ITCS 2012: 3rd Innovations in Theoretical Computer Science, pp. 276–289, Cambridge, MA, USA, 8–10 January 2012. Association for Computing Machinery (2012)

[GGH15] Gentry, C., Gorbunov, S., Halevi, S.: Graph-induced multilinear maps from lattices. In: Dodis, Y., Nielsen, J.B. (eds.) TCC 2015. LNCS, vol. 9015, pp. 498–527. Springer, Heidelberg (2015). https://doi.org/10.1007/978-3-662-46497-7_20

[GPV08] Gentry, C., Peikert, C., Vaikuntanathan, V.: Trapdoors for hard lattices and new cryptographic constructions. In: Ladner, R.E., Dwork, C. (eds.) 40th Annual ACM Symposium on Theory of Computing, pp. 197–206, Victoria, BC, Canada, 17–20 May 2008. ACM Press (2008)

[Kan18] Kane, D.M.: Quantum money from modular forms (2018). https://arxiv.org/abs/1809.05925

[KLS22] Khesin, A.B., Lu, J.Z., Shor, P.W.: Publicly verifiable quantum money from random lattices (2022). https://arxiv.org/abs/2207.13135v2

[KSS21] Kane, D.M., Sharif, S., Silverberg, A.: Quantum money from quaternion algebras. Cryptology ePrint Archive, Report 2021/1294 (2021). https://eprint.iacr.org/2021/1294

[LAF+10] Lutomirski, A., et al.: Breaking and making quantum money: toward a new quantum cryptographic protocol. In: Yao, A.C.-C. (ed.) ICS 2010: 1st Innovations in Computer Science, pp. 20–31, Tsinghua University, Beijing, China, 5–7 January 2010. Tsinghua University Press (2010)

[Lut10] Lutomirski, A.: An online attack against Wiesner's quantum money (2010). https://arxiv.org/abs/1010.0256

[LZ19] Liu, Q., Zhandry, M.: Revisiting post-quantum Fiat-Shamir. In: Boldyreva, A., Micciancio, D. (eds.) CRYPTO 2019. LNCS, vol. 11693, pp. 326–355. Springer, Cham (2019). https://doi.org/10.1007/978-3-030-26951-7_12

[MM22] Maino, L., Martindale, C.: An attack on SIDH with arbitrary starting curve. Cryptology ePrint Archive (2022)

[Reg05] Regev, O.: On lattices, learning with errors, random linear codes, and cryptography. In: Gabow, H.N., Fagin, R. (eds.) 37th Annual ACM Symposium on Theory of Computing, pp. 84–93, Baltimore, MA, USA, 22–24 May 2005. ACM Press (2005)

[Rob21] Roberts, B.: Security analysis of quantum lightning. In: Canteaut, A., Standaert, F.-X. (eds.) EUROCRYPT 2021. LNCS, vol. 12697, pp. 562–567. Springer, Cham (2021). https://doi.org/10.1007/978-3-030-77886-6_19

[Rob22] Robert, D.: Breaking SIDH in polynomial time. Cryptology ePrint Archive (2022)

[RS19] Radian, R., Sattath, O.: Semi-quantum money. In: Proceedings of the 1st ACM Conference on Advances in Financial Technologies, AFT 2019, pp. 132–146, New York, NY, USA. Association for Computing Machinery (2019)

[Unr16] Unruh, D.: Computationally binding quantum commitments. In: Fischlin, M., Coron, J.-S. (eds.) EUROCRYPT 2016. LNCS, vol. 9666, pp. 497–527. Springer, Heidelberg (2016). https://doi.org/10.1007/978-3-662-49896-5_18

[Wie83] Wiesner, S.: Conjugate coding. SIGACT News **15**(1), 78–88 (1983)

[WW21] Wee, H., Wichs, D.: Candidate obfuscation via oblivious LWE sampling. In: Canteaut, A., Standaert, F.-X. (eds.) EUROCRYPT 2021. LNCS, vol. 12698, pp. 127–156. Springer, Cham (2021). https://doi.org/10.1007/978-3-030-77883-5_5

[Zha19] Zhandry, M.: Quantum lightning never strikes the same state twice. In: Ishai, Y., Rijmen, V. (eds.) EUROCRYPT 2019. LNCS, vol. 11478, pp. 408–438. Springer, Cham (2019). https://doi.org/10.1007/978-3-030-17659-4_14

From the Hardness of Detecting Superpositions to Cryptography: Quantum Public Key Encryption and Commitments

Minki Hhan[1], Tomoyuki Morimae[2], and Takashi Yamakawa[2,3(✉)]

[1] KIAS, Seoul, Republic of Korea
[2] Yukawa Institute for Theoretical Physics, Kyoto University, Kyoto, Japan
[3] NTT Social Informatics Laboratories, Tokyo, Japan
takashi.yamakawa@ntt.com

Abstract. Recently, Aaronson et al. (arXiv:2009.07450) showed that detecting interference between two orthogonal states is as hard as swapping these states. While their original motivation was from quantum gravity, we show its applications in quantum cryptography.

1. We construct the first public key encryption scheme from cryptographic *non-abelian* group actions. Interestingly, the ciphertexts of our scheme are quantum even if messages are classical. This resolves an open question posed by Ji et al. (TCC '19). We construct the scheme through a new abstraction called swap-trapdoor function pairs, which may be of independent interest.

2. We give a simple and efficient compiler that converts the flavor of quantum bit commitments. More precisely, for any prefix X, Y ∈ {computationally, statistically, perfectly}, if the base scheme is X-hiding and Y-binding, then the resulting scheme is Y-hiding and X-binding. Our compiler calls the base scheme only once. Previously, all known compilers call the base schemes polynomially many times (Crépeau et al., Eurocrypt '01 and Yan, Asiacrypt '22). For the security proof of the conversion, we generalize the result of Aaronson et al. by considering quantum auxiliary inputs.

1 Introduction

When can we efficiently distinguish a superposition of two orthogonal states from their probabilistic mix? A folklore answer to this question was that we can efficiently distinguish them whenever we can efficiently map one of the states to the other. Recently, Aaronson, Atia and, Susskind [1] gave a complete answer to the question. They confirmed that the folklore was almost correct but what actually characterizes the distinguishability is the ability to *swap* the two states rather than the ability to map one of the states to the other.[1]

We explain their result in more detail by using the example of Schrödinger's cat following [1]. Let |Alive⟩ and |Dead⟩ be orthogonal states, which can be understood as the states of alive and dead cats in Schrödinger's cat experiment.

---

[1] We remark that the meaning of "swap" here is different from that of the SWAP gate as explained below.

© International Association for Cryptologic Research 2023
C. Hazay and M. Stam (Eds.): EUROCRYPT 2023, LNCS 14004, pp. 639–667, 2023.
https://doi.org/10.1007/978-3-031-30545-0_22

Then, the authors showed that one can efficiently swap $|\text{Alive}\rangle$ and $|\text{Dead}\rangle$ (i.e., there is an efficiently computable unitary U such that $U|\text{Dead}\rangle = |\text{Alive}\rangle$ and $U|\text{Alive}\rangle = |\text{Dead}\rangle$) if and only if there is an efficient distinguisher that distinguishes $\frac{|\text{Alive}\rangle + |\text{Dead}\rangle}{\sqrt{2}}$ and $\frac{|\text{Alive}\rangle - |\text{Dead}\rangle}{\sqrt{2}}$ with certainty. Note that distinguishing $\frac{|\text{Alive}\rangle + |\text{Dead}\rangle}{\sqrt{2}}$ and $\frac{|\text{Alive}\rangle - |\text{Dead}\rangle}{\sqrt{2}}$ is equivalent to distinguishing $\frac{|\text{Alive}\rangle + |\text{Dead}\rangle}{\sqrt{2}}$ and the uniform probabilistic mix of $|\text{Alive}\rangle$ and $|\text{Dead}\rangle$.[2] Moreover, they showed that the equivalence is robust in the sense that a partial ability to swap $|\text{Alive}\rangle$ and $|\text{Dead}\rangle$, i.e., $|\langle\text{Dead}|U|\text{Alive}\rangle + \langle\text{Alive}|U|\text{Dead}\rangle| = \Gamma$ for some $\Gamma > 0$ is equivalent to distinguishability of $\frac{|\text{Alive}\rangle + |\text{Dead}\rangle}{\sqrt{2}}$ and $\frac{|\text{Alive}\rangle - |\text{Dead}\rangle}{\sqrt{2}}$ with advantage $\Delta = \Gamma/2$. They gave an interpretation of their result that observing interference between alive and dead cats is "necromancy-hard", i.e., at least as hard as bringing a dead cat back to life.

While their original motivation was from quantum gravity, we find their result interesting from cryptographic perspective. Roughly speaking, the task of swapping $|\text{Alive}\rangle$ and $|\text{Dead}\rangle$ can be thought of as a kind of search problem where one is given $|\text{Alive}\rangle$ (resp. $|\text{Dead}\rangle$) and asked to "search" for $|\text{Dead}\rangle$ (resp. $|\text{Alive}\rangle$). On the other hand, the task of distinguishing $\frac{|\text{Alive}\rangle + |\text{Dead}\rangle}{\sqrt{2}}$ and $\frac{|\text{Alive}\rangle - |\text{Dead}\rangle}{\sqrt{2}}$ is apparently a decision problem. From this perspective, we can view their result as a "search-to-decision" reduction. Search-to-decision reductions have been playing the central role in cryptography, e.g., the celebrated Goldreich-Levin theorem [20]. Based on this observation, we tackle the following two problems in quantum cryptography.[3]

Public Key Encryption from Non-abelian Group Actions. Brassard and Yung [8] initiated the study of cryptographic group actions. We say that a group G acts on a set S by an action $\star : G \times S \to S$ if the following are satisfied:

1. For the identity element $e \in G$ and any $s \in S$, we have $e \star s = s$.
2. For any $g, h \in G$ and any $s \in S$, we have $(gh) \star s = g \star (h \star s)$.

For a cryptographic purpose, we assume (at least) that the group action is one-way, i.e., it is hard to find g' such that $g' \star s = g \star s$ given s and $g \star s$. The work of [8] proposed instantiations of such cryptographic group actions based on the hardness of discrete logarithm, factoring, or graph isomorphism problems.

Cryptographic group actions are recently gaining a renewed attention from the perspective of *post-quantum* cryptography. Ji et al. [25] proposed new instantiations based on general linear group actions on tensors. Alamati et al. [2]

---

[2] The distinguishing advantage is (necessarily) halved. This can be seen by the following equality:

$$\frac{1}{2}\left(|\text{Alive}\rangle\langle\text{Alive}| + |\text{Dead}\rangle\langle\text{Dead}|\right)$$
$$= \frac{1}{2}\left(\left(\frac{|\text{Alive}\rangle + |\text{Dead}\rangle}{\sqrt{2}}\right)\left(\frac{\langle\text{Alive}| + \langle\text{Dead}|}{\sqrt{2}}\right) + \left(\frac{|\text{Alive}\rangle - |\text{Dead}\rangle}{\sqrt{2}}\right)\left(\frac{\langle\text{Alive}| - \langle\text{Dead}|}{\sqrt{2}}\right)\right).$$

[3] It may be a priori unclear why these problems are related to [1]. This will become clearer in the technical overview in Sect. 2.

proposed isogeny-based instantiations based on earlier works [10,13,32]. Both of them are believed to be secure against quantum adversaries.

An important difference between the instantiations in [25] and [2] is that the former considers *non-abelian* groups whereas the latter considers *abelian* groups. Abelian group actions are particularly useful because they give rise to a non-interactive key exchange protocol similar to Diffie-Hellman key exchange [15]. Namely, suppose that $s \in S$ is published as a public parameter, Alice publishes $g_A \star s$ as a public key while keeping g_A as her secret key, and Bob publishes $g_B \star s$ as a public key while keeping g_B as his secret key. Then, they can establish a shared key $g_A \star (g_B \star s) = g_B \star (g_A \star s)$. On the other hand, an eavesdropper Eve cannot know the shared key since she cannot know g_A or g_B by the one-wayness of the group action.[4] This also naturally gives a public key encryption (PKE) scheme similar to ElGamal encryption [17]. On the other hand, the above construction does not work if G is a non-abelian group. Indeed, cryptographic applications given in [25] are limited to *Minicrypt* primitives [24], i.e., those that do not imply PKE in a black-box manner. Thus, [25] raised the following open question:[5]

Question 1: *Can we construct PKE from non-abelian group actions?*

Flavor Conversion for Quantum Bit Commitments. Commitments are one of the most important primitives in cryptography. It enables one to "commit" to a (classical) bit[6] in such a way that the committed bit is hidden from other parties before the committer reveals it, which is called the *hiding* property, and the committer cannot change the committed bit after sending the commitment, which is called the *binding* property. One can easily see that it is impossible for *classical* commitments to achieve both hiding and binding properties against unbounded-time adversaries. It is known to be impossible even with *quantum* communication [26,28]. Thus, it is a common practice in cryptography to relax either of them to hold only against computationally bounded adversaries. We say that a commitment scheme is computationally (resp. statistically) binding/hiding, if it holds against (classical or quantum depending on the context) polynomial-time (resp. unbounded-time) adversaries. Then, there are the following two *flavors* of commitments: One is computationally hiding

---

[4] For the actual security proof, we need a stronger assumption than the one-wayness. This is similar to the necessity of decisional Diffie-Hellman assumption, which is stronger than the mere hardness of the discrete logarithm problem, for proving security of Diffie-Hellman key exchange.

[5] The statement of the open problem in [25] is quoted as follows: *"Finally, it is an important open problem to build quantum-secure public-key encryption schemes based on hard problems about GLAT or its close variations."* Here, GLAT stands for General Linear Action on Tensors, which is their instantiation of non-abelian group action. Thus, **Question 1** is slightly more general than what they actually ask. .

[6] We can also consider commitments for multi-bit strings. But we focus on *bit* commitments in this paper.

and statistically binding, and the other is computationally binding and statistically hiding.[7] In the following, whenever we require statistical hiding or binding, the other one should be understood as computational since it is impossible to statistically achieve both of them as already explained.

In classical cryptography, though commitments of both flavors are known to be equivalent to the existence of one-way functions [22,23,30], there is no known direct conversion between them that preserves efficiency or the number of interactions. Thus, their constructions have been studied separately.

Recently, Yan [35], based on an earlier work by Crépeau, Légaré, and Salvail [14], showed that the situation is completely different for quantum bit commitments, which rely on quantum communication between the sender and receiver. First, he showed a round-collapsing theorem, which means that any interactive quantum bit commitments can be converted into non-interactive ones. Then he gave a conversion that converts the flavor of any non-interactive quantum bit commitments using the round-collapsing theorem.

Though Yan's conversion gives a beautiful equivalence theorem, a disadvantage of the conversion is that it does not preserve the efficiency. Specifically, it calls the base scheme polynomially many times (i.e., $\Omega(\lambda^2)$ times for the security parameter λ). Then, it is natural to ask the following question:

Question 2: *Is there an efficiency-preserving flavor conversion for quantum bit commitments?*

1.1   Our Results

We answer both questions affirmatively using (a generalization of) the result of [1].

For **Question 1**, we construct a PKE scheme with quantum ciphertexts based on non-abelian group actions. This resolves the open problem posed by [25].[8] Our main construction only supports classical one-bit messages, but we can convert it into one that supports quantum multi-qubit messages by hybrid encryption with quantum one-time pad as showin in [9]. Interestingly, ciphertexts of our scheme are quantum even if messages are classical. We show that our scheme is IND-CPA secure if the group action satisfies *pseudorandomness*, which is a stronger assumption than the one-wayness introduced in [25]. In addition, we show a "win-win" result similar in spirit to [37]. We show that if the group action is one-way, then our PKE scheme is IND-CPA secure *or* we can use the group action to construct one-shot signatures [3].[9] Note that constructing

---

[7] Of course, we can also consider computationally hiding and computationally binding one, which is weaker than both flavors.

[8] The statement of their open problem (quoted in Footnote 5) does not specify if we are allowed to use quantum ciphertexts. Thus, we claim to resolve the problem even though we rely on quantum ciphertexts. If they mean *post-quantum* PKE (which has classical ciphertexts), this is still open.

[9] This is a simplified claim and some subtle issues about uniformness of the adversary and "infinitely-often security" are omitted here. See Lemma 2 for the formal statement.

one-shot signatures has been thought to be a very difficult task. The only known construction is relative to a classical oracle and there is no known construction in the standard model. Even for its significantly weaker variant called tokenized signatures [5], the only known construction in the standard model is based on indistinguishability obfuscation [12]. Given the difficulty of constructing tokenized signatures, let alone one-shot signatures, it is reasonable to conjecture that our PKE scheme is IND-CPA secure if we built it on "natural" one-way group actions. Our PKE scheme is constructed through an abstraction called *swap-trapdoor function pairs* (STFs), which may be of independent interest.

For **Question 2**, We give a new conversion between the two flavors of quantum commitments. That is, for $X, Y \in$ {computationally,statistically,perfectly}, if the base scheme is X-hiding and Y-binding, then the resulting scheme is Y-hiding and X-binding. Our conversion calls the base scheme only once in superposition. Specifically, if Q_b is the unitary applied by the sender when committing to $b \in \{0, 1\}$ in the base scheme, the committing procedure of the resulting scheme consists of a single call to Q_0 or Q_1 controlled by an additional qubit (i.e., application of a unitary such that $|b\rangle |\psi\rangle \mapsto |b\rangle (Q_b |\psi\rangle)$) and additional constant number of gates. For the security proof of our conversion, we develop a generalization of the result of [1] where we consider auxiliary quantum inputs.

We show several applications of our conversion. We remark that our conversion does not give any new feasibility results since similar conversions with worse efficiency were already known [14,35]. However, our conversion gives schemes with better efficiency in terms of the number of calls to the building blocks.

2 Technical Overview

We give a technical overview of our results. In the overview, we assume that the reader has read the informal explanation of the result of [1] at the beginning of Sect. 1.

2.1 Part I: PKE from Group Actions

Suppose that a (not necessarily abelian) group G acts on a finite set S by a group action $\star : G \times S \to S$. Suppose that it is one-way, i.e., it is hard to find g' such that $g' \star s = g \star s$ given s and $g \star s$.[10]

Our starting point is the observation made in [8] that one-way group actions give claw-free function pairs as follows. Let s_0 and $s_1 := g \star s_0$ be public parameters where $s_0 \in S$ and $g \in G$ are uniformly chosen. Then if we define a function $f_b : G \to S$ by $f_b(h) := h \star s_b$ for $b \in \{0, 1\}$, the pair (f_0, f_1) is claw-free, i.e., it is hard to find h_0 and h_1 such that $f_0(h_0) = f_1(h_1)$. This is because if one can find such h_0 and h_1, then one can break the one-wayness of the group action by outputting $h_1^{-1} h_0$, since $f_0(h_0) = f_1(h_1)$ implies $(h_1^{-1} h_0) \star s_0 = s_1$.

---

[10] We will eventually need pseudorandomness, which is stronger than one-wayness, for the security proof of our PKE scheme. We defer the introduction of pseudorandomness for readability.

Unfortunately, claw-free function pairs are not known to imply PKE. The reason of the difficulty of constructing PKE is that claw-free function pairs do not have trapdoors. Indeed, it is unclear if there is a trapdoor that enables us to invert f_0 and f_1 for the above group-action-based construction. Our first observation is that the above construction actually has a weak form of a trapdoor: If we know g as a trapdoor, then we can find h_1 such that $f_0(h_0) = f_1(h_1)$ from h_0 by simply setting $h_1 := h_0 g^{-1}$ and vice versa. Though this trapdoor g does not give the power to invert f_0 or f_1, this enables us to break claw-freeness in a strong sense. We formalize such function pairs as swap-trapdoor function pairs (STFs).[11] For the details of STFs, see Sect. 4.1.

Next, we explain our construction of a PKE scheme with quantum ciphertexts. Though it is a generic construction based on STFs with certain properties, we here focus on the group-action-based instantiation for simplicity. (For the generic construction based on STFs, see Sect. 4.2.) A public key of our PKE scheme consists of s_0 and $s_1 = g \star s_0$ and a secret key is g. For encrypting a bit b, the ciphertext is set to be

$$ct_b := \frac{1}{\sqrt{2}} \left(|0\rangle \, |f_0^{-1}(y)\rangle + (-1)^b \, |1\rangle \, |f_1^{-1}(y)\rangle \right) \tag{1}$$

for a random $y \in S$.[12] Here, $|f_{b'}^{-1}(y)\rangle$ is the uniform superposition over $f_{b'}^{-1}(y) := \{h \in G : f_{b'}(h) = y\}$ for $b' \in \{0,1\}$. The above state can be generated by a standard technique similar to [7,27]. Specifically, we first prepare

$$\frac{1}{\sqrt{2}}(|0\rangle + (-1)^b \, |1\rangle) \otimes \frac{1}{\sqrt{|G|}} \sum_{h \in G} |h\rangle \,,$$

compute a group action by h in the second register on s_0 or s_1 controlled by the first register to get

$$\frac{1}{\sqrt{2|G|}} \left(\sum_{h \in G} |0\rangle \, |h\rangle \, |h \star s_0\rangle + (-1)^b \sum_{h \in G} |1\rangle \, |h\rangle \, |h \star s_1\rangle \right),$$

and measure the third register to get $y \in S$. At this point, the first and second registers collapse to the state in Eq. (1).[13] Decryption can be done as follows. Given a ciphertext ct_b, we apply a unitary $|h\rangle \to |hg\rangle$ on the second register controlled on the first register. Observe that the unitary maps $|f_1^{-1}(y)\rangle$ to $|f_0^{-1}(y)\rangle$. Then, the resulting state is $\frac{1}{\sqrt{2}} \left(|0\rangle \, |f_0^{-1}(y)\rangle + (-1)^b \, |1\rangle \, |f_0^{-1}(y)\rangle \right)$. Thus, measuring the first register in the Hadamard basis results in message b.

Next, we discuss how to prove security. Our goal is to prove that the scheme is IND-CPA secure, i.e., ct_0 and ct_1 are computationally indistinguishable. Here, we rely on the result of [1]. According to their result, one can distinguish ct_0 and ct_1 if and only if one can swap $|0\rangle \, |f_0^{-1}(y)\rangle$ and $|1\rangle \, |f_1^{-1}(y)\rangle$. Thus, it suffices

---

[11] The intuition of the name is that one can "swap" h_0 and h_1 given a trapdoor.

[12] Precisely, y is distributed as $h \star s_0$ for uniformly random $h \in G$.

[13] Note that $|f_0^{-1}(y)| = |f_1^{-1}(y)|$ for all $y \in S$.

to prove the hardness of swapping $|0\rangle |f_0^{-1}(y)\rangle$ and $|1\rangle |f_1^{-1}(y)\rangle$ with a non-negligible advantage.[14] Unfortunately, we do not know how to prove this solely assuming the claw-freeness of (f_0, f_1). Thus, we introduce a new assumption called *conversion hardness*, which requires that one cannot find h_1 such that $f_1(h_1) = y$ given $|f_0^{-1}(y)\rangle$ with a non-negligible probability. Assuming it, the required hardness of swapping follows straightforwardly since if one can swap $|0\rangle |f_0^{-1}(y)\rangle$ and $|1\rangle |f_1^{-1}(y)\rangle$, then one can break the conversion hardness by first mapping $|0\rangle |f_0^{-1}(y)\rangle$ to $|1\rangle |f_1^{-1}(y)\rangle$ and then measuring the second register.

The remaining issue is how to prove conversion hardness based on a reasonable assumption on the group action. We show that pseudorandomness introduced in [25] suffices for this purpose. Pseudorandomness requires the following two properties:

1. The probability that there exists $g \in G$ such that $g \star s_0 = s_1$ is negligible where $s_0, s_1 \in S$ are uniformly random.
2. The distribution of $(s_0, s_1 := g \star s_0)$ where $s_0 \in S$ and $g \in G$ are uniformly random is computationally indistinguishable from the uniform distribution over S^2.

Note that we require Item 1 because otherwise Item 2 may unconditionally hold, in which case there is no useful cryptographic application. We argue that pseudorandomness implies conversion hardness as follows. By Item 2, the attack against the conversion hardness should still succeed with almost the same probability even if we replace s_1 with a uniformly random element of S. However, then there should exist no solution by Item 1. Thus, the original success probability should be negligible.

While [25] gave justification of pseudorandomness of their instantiation of group actions, it is a stronger assumption than one-wayness. Thus, it is more desirable to get PKE scheme solely from one-wayness. Toward this direction, we show the following "win-win" result inspired by [37]. If (f_0, f_1) is claw-free but not conversion hard, then we can construct a one-shot signatures. Roughly one-shot signatures are a quantum primitive which enables us to generate a classical verification key vk along with a quantum signing key sk in such a way that one can use sk to generate a signature for whichever message of one's choice, but cannot generate signatures for different messages simultaneously. For simplicity, suppose that (f_0, f_1) is claw-free but its conversion hardness is totally broken. That is, we assume that we can efficiently find h_1 such that $f_1(h_1) = y$ given $|f_0^{-1}(y)\rangle$. Our idea is to set $|f_0^{-1}(y)\rangle$ to be the secret key and y to be the corresponding verification key. For signing to 0, the signer simply measures $|f_0^{-1}(y)\rangle$ to get $h_0 \in f_0^{-1}(y)$ and set h_0 to be the signature for the message 0. For signing to 1, the signer runs the adversary against conversion hardness to get h_1 such that $f_1(h_1) = y$ and set h_1 to be the signature for the message 1. If one can generate signatures to 0 and 1 simultaneously, we can break claw-freeness since $f_0(h_0) = f_1(h_1) = y$. Thus, the above one-shot signature is secure if (f_0, f_1) is claw-free. In the general case where the conversion hardness is not

---

[14] See Theorem 1 for the precise meaning of the advantage for swapping.

necessarily completely broken, our idea is to amplify the probability of finding h_1 from $|f_0^{-1}(y)\rangle$ by a parallel repetition. Based on this result, we can see that if the group action is one-way, then our PKE scheme is IND-CPA secure or we can construct one-shot signatures.

2.2 Part II: Flavor Conversion for Commitments

Definition of Quantum Bit Commitments. First, we recall the definition of quantum bit commitments as formalized by Yan [35]. He (based on earlier works [11,18,36]) showed that any (possibly interactive) quantum bit commitment scheme can be written in the following (non-interactive) canonical form. A canonical quantum bit commitment scheme is characterized by a pair of unitaries (Q_0, Q_1) over two registers **C** (called the commitment register) and **R** (called the reveal register) and works as follows.

Commit phase: For committing to a bit $b \in \{0, 1\}$, the sender generates the state $Q_b |0\rangle_{\mathbf{C}, \mathbf{R}}$ and sends **C** to the receiver while keeping **R** on its side.[15]

Reveal phase: For revealing the committed bit, the sender sends **R** along with the committed bit b to the receiver. Then, the receiver applies $Q_b^\dagger$ to **C** and **R** and measures both registers. If the measurement outcome is $0 \ldots 0$, the receiver accepts and otherwise rejects.

We require a canonical quantum bit commitment scheme to satisfy the following hiding and binding properties. The hiding property is defined analogously to that of classical commitments. That is, the computational (resp. statistical) hiding property requires that quantum polynomial-time (resp. unbounded-time) receiver (possibly with quantum advice) cannot distinguish commitments to 0 and 1 if only given **C**.

On the other hand, the binding property is formalized in a somewhat different way from the classical case. The reason is that a canonical quantum commitment scheme cannot satisfy the binding property in the classical sense. The classical binding property roughly requires that a malicious sender can open a commitment to either of 0 or 1 except for a negligible probability. On the other hand, in canonical quantum bit commitment schemes, if the sender generates a uniform superposition of commitments to 0 and 1, it can open the commitment to 0 and 1 with probability 1/2 for each.[16] Thus, we require a weaker binding property called the honest-binding property, which intuitively requires that it is difficult to map an honestly generated commitment of 0 to that of 1 without touching **C**. More formally, the computational (resp. statistical) honest-binding property requires that for any polynomial-time computable (resp. unbounded-time computable) unitary U over **R** and an additional register **Z** and an auxiliary state $|\tau\rangle_{\mathbf{Z}}$, we have

---

[15] We write $|0\rangle$ to mean $|0 \ldots 0\rangle$ for simplicity.

[16] A recent work by Bitansky and Brakerski [6] showed that a quantum commitment scheme may satisfy the classical binding property if the receiver performs a measurement in the commit phase. However, such a measurement is not allowed for canonical quantum bit commitments.

$$\left\| (Q_1 |0\rangle \langle 0| Q_1^\dagger)_{\mathbf{C},\mathbf{R}} (I_{\mathbf{C}} \otimes U_{\mathbf{R},\mathbf{Z}})((Q_0 |0\rangle)_{\mathbf{C},\mathbf{R}} |\tau\rangle_{\mathbf{Z}}) \right\| = \mathsf{negl}(\lambda).$$

One may think that honest-binding is too weak because it only considers honestly generated commitments. However, somewhat surprisingly, [35] proved that it is equivalent to another binding notion called the *sum-binding* [16].[17] The sum-binding property requires that the sum of probabilities that any (quantum polynomial-time, in the case of computational binding) *malicious* sender can open a commitment to 0 and 1 is at most $1 + \mathsf{negl}(\lambda)$. In addition, it has been shown that the honest-binding property is sufficient for cryptographic applications including zero-knowledge proofs/arguments (of knowledge), oblivious transfers, and multi-party computation [18,29,34,36]. In this paper, we refer to honest-binding if we simply write binding.

Our Conversion. We propose an efficiency-preserving flavor conversion for quantum bit commitments inspired by the result of [1]. Our key observation is that the swapping ability and distinguishability look somewhat similar to breaking binding and hiding of quantum commitments, respectively. The correspondence between distinguishability and breaking hiding is easier to see: The hiding property directly requires that distinguishing commitments to 0 and 1 is hard. The correspondence between the swapping ability and breaking binding is less clear, but one can find similarities by recalling the definition of (honest-)binding for quantum commitments: Roughly, the binding property requires that it is difficult to map the commitment to 0 to that to 1. Technically, a binding adversary does not necessarily give the ability to swap commitments to 0 and 1 since it may map the commitment to 1 to an arbitrary state instead of to the commitment to 0. But ignoring this issue (which we revisit later), breaking binding property somewhat corresponds to swapping.

However, an important difference between security notions of quantum commitments and the setting of the theorem of [1] is that the former put some restrictions on registers the adversary can touch: For hiding, the adversary cannot touch the reveal register $\mathbf{R}$, and for binding, the adversary cannot touch the commitment register $\mathbf{C}$. To deal with this issue, we make another key observation that the equivalence between swapping and distinguishing shown in [1] preserves *locality*. That is, if the swapping unitary does not touch some qubits of $|\text{Alive}\rangle$ or $|\text{Dead}\rangle$, then the corresponding distinguisher does not touch those qubits either, and vice versa.

The above observations suggest the following conversion. Let $\{Q_0, Q_1\}$ be a canonical quantum bit commitment scheme. Then, we construct another scheme $\{Q_0', Q_1'\}$ as follows:

- The roles of commitment and reveal registers are swapped from $\{Q_0, Q_1\}$ and the commitment register is augmented by an additional one-qubit register. That is, if $\mathbf{C}$ and $\mathbf{R}$ are the commitment and reveal registers of $\{Q_0, Q_1\}$, then

---

[17] The term "sum-binding" is taken from [33].

the commitment and reveal registers of $\{Q'_0, Q'_1\}$ are defined as $\mathbf{C}' := (\mathbf{R}, \mathbf{D})$ and $\mathbf{R}' := \mathbf{C}$ where $\mathbf{D}$ is a one-qubit register.

- For $b \in \{0, 1\}$, the unitary Q'_b is defined as follows:

$$Q'_b |0\rangle_{\mathbf{C},\mathbf{R}} |0\rangle_{\mathbf{D}} := \frac{1}{\sqrt{2}} \left((Q_0 |0\rangle)_{\mathbf{C},\mathbf{R}} |0\rangle_{\mathbf{D}} + (-1)^b (Q_1 |0\rangle)_{\mathbf{C},\mathbf{R}} |1\rangle_{\mathbf{D}}\right), \quad (2)$$

where $(\mathbf{C}', \mathbf{R}')$ is rearranged as $(\mathbf{C}, \mathbf{R}, \mathbf{D})$.[18]

One can see that $\{Q'_0, Q'_1\}$ is almost as efficient as $\{Q_0, Q_1\}$: For generating, $Q'_b |0\rangle_{\mathbf{C},\mathbf{R}} |0\rangle_{\mathbf{D}}$ one can first prepare $|0\rangle_{\mathbf{C},\mathbf{R}} (|0\rangle + (-1)^b |1\rangle)_{\mathbf{D}}$ and then apply Q_0 or Q_1 to $(\mathbf{C}, \mathbf{R})$ controlled by $\mathbf{D}$. We prove that the hiding and binding properties of $\{Q_0, Q_1\}$ imply binding and hiding properties of $\{Q'_0, Q'_1\}$, respectively. Moreover, the reduction preserves all three types of computational/statistical/perfect security. Thus, this gives a conversion between different flavors of quantum bit commitments.

Security Proof. At an intuitive level, the theorem of [1] with the above "locality-preserving" observation seems to easily give a reduction from security of $\{Q'_0, Q'_1\}$ to that of $\{Q_0, Q_1\}$: If we can break the hiding property of $\{Q'_0, Q'_1\}$, then we can distinguish $Q'_b |0\rangle_{\mathbf{C},\mathbf{R}} |0\rangle_{\mathbf{D}}$ without touching $\mathbf{R}' = \mathbf{C}$. Then, their theorem with the above observation gives a swapping algorithm that swaps $(Q_0 |0\rangle_{\mathbf{C},\mathbf{R}}) |0\rangle_{\mathbf{D}}$ and $(Q_1 |0\rangle_{\mathbf{C},\mathbf{R}}) |1\rangle_{\mathbf{D}}$ without touching $\mathbf{R}' = \mathbf{C}$, which clearly breaks the binding property of $\{Q_0, Q_1\}$. One may expect that the reduction from binding to hiding works analogously. However, it is not as easy as one would expect due to the following reasons.

1. An adversary that breaks the binding property is weaker than a "partial" swapping unitary that swaps $Q'_0 |0\rangle_{\mathbf{C}',\mathbf{R}'}$ and $Q'_1 |0\rangle_{\mathbf{C}',\mathbf{R}'}$ needed for [1]. For example, suppose that we have a unitary U such that $UQ'_0 |0\rangle_{\mathbf{C}',\mathbf{R}'} = Q'_1 |0\rangle_{\mathbf{C}',\mathbf{R}'}$ and $UQ'_1 |0\rangle_{\mathbf{C}',\mathbf{R}'} = -Q'_0 |0\rangle_{\mathbf{C}',\mathbf{R}'}$. Clearly, this completely breaks the binding property of $\{Q'_0, Q'_1\}$. However, this is not sufficient for applying [1] since $| \langle 0| Q_1'^\dagger U Q'_0 |0\rangle + \langle 0| Q_0'^\dagger U Q'_1 |0\rangle | = 0$.
2. For security of quantum bit commitments, we have to consider adversaries with quantum advice, or at least those with ancilla qubits even for security against uniform adversaries. However, the theorem of [1] does not consider any ancilla qubits.

Both issues are already mentioned in [1]. In particular, Item 1 is an essential issue. They prove the existence of a pair of orthogonal states $|\text{Alive}\rangle$ and $|\text{Dead}\rangle$ such that we can map $|\text{Alive}\rangle$ to $|\text{Dead}\rangle$ by an efficient unitary, but $| \langle\text{Dead}| U |\text{Alive}\rangle + \langle\text{Alive}| U |\text{Dead}\rangle | \approx 0$ for all efficient unitaries U [1, Theorem 3]. For Item 2, they (with acknowledgment to Daniel Gottesman) observe that the conversion from a distinguisher to a swapping unitary works even with any quantum advice, but the other direction does not work if there are ancilla qubits [1, Footnote 2].

---

[18] We only present how Q'_b works on $|0\rangle_{\mathbf{C},\mathbf{R}} |0\rangle_{\mathbf{D}}$ for simplicity. Its definition on general states can be found in Theorem 7.

One can see that the above issues are actually not relevant to the reduction from the hiding of $\{Q'_0, Q'_1\}$ to the binding of $\{Q_0, Q_1\}$. However, for the reduction from the binding of $\{Q'_0, Q'_1\}$ to the hiding of $\{Q_0, Q_1\}$, both issues are non-trivial. Below, we show how to resolve those issues.

Solution to Item 1. By the result of [1, Theorem 3] as already explained, this issue cannot be resolved if we think of $Q'_0 |0\rangle_{\mathbf{C'},\mathbf{R'}}$ and $Q'_1 |0\rangle_{\mathbf{C'},\mathbf{R'}}$ as general orthogonal states. Thus, we look into the actual form of them presented in Eq. (2). Then, we observe that an adversary against the binding property does not touch $\mathbf{D}$ since that is part of the commitment register $\mathbf{C'}$ of $\{Q'_0, Q'_1\}$. Therefore, he cannot cause any interference between $(Q_0 |0\rangle)_{\mathbf{C},\mathbf{R}} |0\rangle_{\mathbf{D}}$ and $(Q_1 |0\rangle)_{\mathbf{C},\mathbf{R}} |1\rangle_{\mathbf{D}}$. Therefore, if it maps

$$\frac{1}{\sqrt{2}} \left((Q_0 |0\rangle)_{\mathbf{C},\mathbf{R}} |0\rangle_{\mathbf{D}} + (Q_1 |0\rangle)_{\mathbf{C},\mathbf{R}} |1\rangle_{\mathbf{D}} \right) \mapsto \frac{1}{\sqrt{2}} \left((Q_0 |0\rangle)_{\mathbf{C},\mathbf{R}} |0\rangle_{\mathbf{D}} - (Q_1 |0\rangle)_{\mathbf{C},\mathbf{R}} |1\rangle_{\mathbf{D}} \right),$$

then it should also map

$$\frac{1}{\sqrt{2}} \left((Q_0 |0\rangle)_{\mathbf{C},\mathbf{R}} |0\rangle_{\mathbf{D}} - (Q_1 |0\rangle)_{\mathbf{C},\mathbf{R}} |1\rangle_{\mathbf{D}} \right) \mapsto \frac{1}{\sqrt{2}} \left((Q_0 |0\rangle)_{\mathbf{C},\mathbf{R}} |0\rangle_{\mathbf{D}} + (Q_1 |0\rangle)_{\mathbf{C},\mathbf{R}} |1\rangle_{\mathbf{D}} \right).$$

Thus, the ability to map $Q'_0 |0\rangle_{\mathbf{C'},\mathbf{R'}}$ to $Q'_1 |0\rangle_{\mathbf{C'},\mathbf{R'}}$ is equivalent to swapping them for this particular construction when one is not allowed to touch $\mathbf{D}$. A similar observation extends to the imperfect case as well. Therefore, Item 1 is not an issue for the security proof of this construction.

Solution to Item 2. To better understand the issue, we review how the conversion from a swapping unitary to a distinguisher works. For simplicity, we focus on the perfect case here, i.e., we assume that there is a unitary U such that $U |\text{Dead}\rangle = |\text{Alive}\rangle$ and $U |\text{Alive}\rangle = |\text{Dead}\rangle$ for orthogonal states $|\text{Alive}\rangle$ and $|\text{Dead}\rangle$. Then, we can construct a distinguisher $\mathcal{A}$ that distinguishes $\frac{|\text{Alive}\rangle + |\text{Dead}\rangle}{\sqrt{2}}$ and $\frac{|\text{Alive}\rangle - |\text{Dead}\rangle}{\sqrt{2}}$ as follows: Given a state $|\eta\rangle$, which is either of the above two states $\frac{|\text{Alive}\rangle + |\text{Dead}\rangle}{\sqrt{2}}$ or $\frac{|\text{Alive}\rangle - |\text{Dead}\rangle}{\sqrt{2}}$, it prepares $\frac{|0\rangle + |1\rangle}{\sqrt{2}}$ in an ancilla qubit, applies U controlled by the ancilla, and measures the ancilla in Hadamard basis. An easy calculation shows that the measurement outcome is 1 with probability 1 if $|\eta\rangle = \frac{|\text{Alive}\rangle + |\text{Dead}\rangle}{\sqrt{2}}$ and 0 with probability 1 if $|\eta\rangle = \frac{|\text{Alive}\rangle - |\text{Dead}\rangle}{\sqrt{2}}$.

Then, let us consider what happens if the swapping unitary uses ancilla qubits. That is, suppose that we have $U |\text{Dead}\rangle |\tau\rangle = |\text{Alive}\rangle |\tau'\rangle$ and $U |\text{Alive}\rangle |\tau\rangle = |\text{Dead}\rangle |\tau'\rangle$ for some ancilla states $|\tau\rangle$ and $|\tau'\rangle$. When $|\tau\rangle$ and $|\tau'\rangle$ are orthogonal, the above distinguisher does not work because there does not occur interference between states with 0 and 1 in the control qubit. To resolve this issue, our idea is to "uncompute" the ancilla state. A naive idea to do so is to apply $U^\dagger$, but then this is meaningless since it just goes back to the original state. Instead, we prepare a "dummy" register that is initialized to be $\frac{|\text{Alive}\rangle + |\text{Dead}\rangle}{\sqrt{2}}$. Then, we add an application of $U^\dagger$ to the ancilla qubits and the dummy register controlled by the control qubit. Then, the ancilla qubit goes back to $|\tau\rangle$ while the state in the dummy register does not change because it is invariant under the swapping of $|\text{Alive}\rangle$ and $|\text{Dead}\rangle$. Then, we can see that this modified distinguisher distinguishes $\frac{|\text{Alive}\rangle + |\text{Dead}\rangle}{\sqrt{2}}$ and $\frac{|\text{Alive}\rangle - |\text{Dead}\rangle}{\sqrt{2}}$ with advantage 1.

Unfortunately, when the swapping ability is imperfect, the above distinguisher does not work. However, we show that the following slight variant of the above works: Instead of preparing $\frac{|\text{Alive}\rangle + |\text{Dead}\rangle}{\sqrt{2}}$, it prepares $\frac{|\text{Alive}\rangle|0\rangle + |\text{Dead}\rangle|1\rangle}{\sqrt{2}}$. After the controlled application of $U^\dagger$, it flips the rightmost register (i.e., apply Pauli X to it). In the perfect case, this variant also works with advantage 1 since the state in the dummy register becomes $\frac{|\text{Dead}\rangle|0\rangle + |\text{Alive}\rangle|1\rangle}{\sqrt{2}}$ after the application of the controlled $U^\dagger$, which goes back to the original state $\frac{|\text{Alive}\rangle|0\rangle + |\text{Dead}\rangle|1\rangle}{\sqrt{2}}$ by the flip. Our calculation shows that this version is robust, i.e., it works even for the imperfect case.

There are several caveats for the above. First, it requires the distinguisher to take an additional quantum advice $\frac{|\text{Alive}\rangle|0\rangle + |\text{Dead}\rangle|1\rangle}{\sqrt{2}}$, which is not necessarily efficiently generatable in general.[19] Second, there occurs a quadratic reduction loss unlike the original theorem in [1] without ancilla qubits. Nonetheless, they are not a problem for our purpose.

3   Preliminaries

Notations used throughout the paper and definitions of basic cryptographic primitives are given in the full version.

3.1   Canonical Quantum Bit Commitments

We define *canonical* quantum bit commitments as defined in [35].

Definition 1 (Canonical quantum bit commitments). *A canonical quantum bit commitment scheme is represented by a family* $\{Q_0(\lambda), Q_1(\lambda)\}_{\lambda \in \mathbb{N}}$ *of polynomial-time computable unitaries over two registers* **C** *(called the* commitment *register) and* **R** *(called the* reveal *register). In the rest of the paper, we often omit* λ *and simply write* Q_0 *and* Q_1 *to mean* $Q_0(\lambda)$ *and* $Q_1(\lambda)$.

Remark 1. Canonical quantum bit commitments are supposed to be used as follows. In the commit phase, to commit to a bit $b \in \{0, 1\}$, the sender generates a state $Q_b |0\rangle_{\mathbf{C},\mathbf{R}}$ and sends **C** to the receiver while keeping **R**. In the reveal phase, the sender sends b and **R** to the receiver. The receiver projects the state on $(\mathbf{C}, \mathbf{R})$ onto $Q_b |0\rangle_{\mathbf{C},\mathbf{R}}$, and accepts if it succeeds and otherwise rejects.

Definition 2 (Hiding). *We say that a canonical quantum bit commitment scheme* $\{Q_0, Q_1\}$ *is computationally (rep. statistically) hiding if* $\text{Tr}_{\mathbf{R}}(Q_0(|0\rangle\langle 0|)_{\mathbf{C},\mathbf{R}} Q_0^\dagger)$ *is computationally (resp. statistically) indistinguishable from* $\text{Tr}_{\mathbf{R}}(Q_1(|0\rangle\langle 0|)_{\mathbf{C},\mathbf{R}} Q_1^\dagger)$. *We say that it is perfectly hiding if they are identical states.*

---

[19] We remark that they are efficiently generatable in our application where $|\text{Alive}\rangle$ and $|\text{Dead}\rangle$ correspond to commitments to 0 and 1.

Definition 3 (Binding). *We say that a canonical quantum bit commitment scheme $\{Q_0, Q_1\}$ is computationally (rep. statistically) binding if for any polynomial-time computable (resp. unbounded-time) unitary U over $\mathbf{R}$ and an additional register $\mathbf{Z}$ and any polynomial-size state $|\tau\rangle_{\mathbf{Z}}$, it holds that*

$$\left\| (Q_1 |0\rangle \langle 0| Q_1^\dagger)_{\mathbf{C},\mathbf{R}} (I_\mathbf{C} \otimes U_{\mathbf{R},\mathbf{Z}})((Q_0 |0\rangle)_{\mathbf{C},\mathbf{R}} |\tau\rangle_{\mathbf{Z}}) \right\| = \mathsf{negl}(\lambda).$$

We say that it is perfectly binding if the LHS is 0 for all unbounded-time unitary U.

3.2 Equivalence Between Swapping and Distinguishing

The following theorem was proven in [1].

Theorem 1 ([1, Theorem 2]).

1. *Let $|x\rangle, |y\rangle$ be orthogonal n-qubit states. Let U be a polynomial-time computable unitary over n-qubit states and define Γ as*

$$\Gamma := |\langle y| U |x\rangle + \langle x| U |y\rangle|.$$

   Then, there exists a QPT distinguisher $\mathcal{A}$ that makes a single black-box access to controlled-U and distinguishes $|\psi\rangle := \frac{|x\rangle + |y\rangle}{\sqrt{2}}$ and $|\phi\rangle := \frac{|x\rangle - |y\rangle}{\sqrt{2}}$ with advantage $\frac{\Gamma}{2}$. Moreover, if U does not act on some qubits, then $\mathcal{A}$ also does not act on those qubits.

2. *Let $|\psi\rangle, |\phi\rangle$ be orthogonal n-qubit states, and suppose that a QPT distinguisher $\mathcal{A}$ distinguishes $|\psi\rangle$ and $|\phi\rangle$ with advantage Δ without using any ancilla qubits. Then, there exists a polynomial-time computable unitary U over n-qubit states such that*

$$\frac{|\langle y| U |x\rangle + \langle x| U |y\rangle|}{2} = \Delta$$

   where $|x\rangle := \frac{|\psi\rangle + |\phi\rangle}{\sqrt{2}}$ and $|y\rangle := \frac{|\psi\rangle - |\phi\rangle}{\sqrt{2}}$. Moreover, if $\mathcal{A}$ does not act on some qubits, then U also does not act on those qubits.

Remark 2 (Descriptions of quantum circuits.). For the reader's convenience, we give the concrete descriptions of quantum circuits for the above theorem, which are presented in [1].

For Item 1, let $\widetilde{U} := e^{i\theta} U$ for θ such that

$$\mathrm{Re}(\langle y| \widetilde{U} |x\rangle + \langle x| \widetilde{U} |y\rangle) = |\langle y| U |x\rangle + \langle x| U |y\rangle|.$$

Then, $\mathcal{A}$ is described in Fig. 1.

For Item 2, let $V_\mathcal{A}$ be a unitary such that

$$V_\mathcal{A} |\psi\rangle = \sqrt{p} |1\rangle |\psi_1\rangle + \sqrt{1-p} |0\rangle |\psi_0\rangle$$
$$V_\mathcal{A} |\phi\rangle = \sqrt{1-p+\Delta} |0\rangle |\phi_0\rangle + \sqrt{p-\Delta} |1\rangle |\phi_1\rangle$$

for some $|\psi_0\rangle$, $|\psi_1\rangle$, $|\phi_0\rangle$, and $|\phi_1\rangle$. That is, $V_\mathcal{A}$ is the unitary part of $\mathcal{A}$. Then, U is described in Fig. 2.

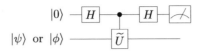

Fig. 1. Quantum circuit for $\mathcal{A}$ in Item 1 of Theorem 1.

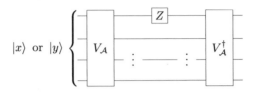

Fig. 2. Quantum circuit for U in Item 2 of Theorem 1.

Remark 3. Though the final requirement in both items ("Moreover,...") is not explicitly stated in [1, Theorem 2], it is easy to see from Figs. 1 and 2. This observation is important for our application to commitments and PKE.

4   Quantum-Ciphertext Public Key Encryption

In Sect. 4.1, we introduce a notion of swap-trapdoor function pairs, which can be seen as a variant of trapdoor claw-free function pairs [21]. In Sect. 4.2, we define quantum-ciphertext PKE and construct it based on STFs. In Sect. 4.3, we construct STFs based on group actions.

4.1   Swap-Trapdoor Function Pairs

We introduce a notion of swap-trapdoor function pairs (STFs). Similarly to trapdoor claw-free function pairs, a STF consists of two functions $f_0, f_1 : \mathcal{X} \to \mathcal{Y}$. We require that there is a trapdoor which enables us to "swap" preimages under f_0 and f_1, i.e., given x_b, we can find $x_{b\oplus 1}$ such that $f_{b\oplus 1}(x_{b\oplus 1}) = f_b(x_b)$. The formal definition of STFs is given below.

Definition 4 (Swap-trapdoor function pair). *A* swap-trapdoor function pair (STF) *consists of algorithms* (Setup, Eval, Swap).

Setup(1^λ) $\to$ (pp, td)**:** *This is a PPT algorithm that takes the security parameter* 1^λ *as input, and outputs a public parameter* pp *and a trapdoor* td*. The public parameter* pp *specifies functions* $f_b^{(\mathrm{pp})} : \mathcal{X} \to \mathcal{Y}$ *for each* $b \in \{0, 1\}$*. We often omit the dependence on* pp *and simply write* f_b *when it is clear from the context.*

Eval(pp, b, x) $\to y$**:** *This is a deterministic classical polynomial-time algorithm that takes a public parameter* pp*, a bit* $b \in \{0, 1\}$*, and an element* $x \in \mathcal{X}$ *as input, and outputs* $y \in \mathcal{Y}$*.*

Swap(td, b, x) → x': *This is a deterministic classical polynomial-time algorithm that takes a trapdoor* td, *a bit* $b \in \{0,1\}$, *and an element* $x \in \mathcal{X}$ *as input, and outputs* $x' \in \mathcal{X}$.

We require a STF to satisfy the following:

Evaluation Correctness. *For any* (pp, td) ← Setup(1^λ), $b \in \{0,1\}$, *and* $x \in \mathcal{X}$, *we have* Eval(pp, b, x) = $f_b(x)$.

Swapping Correctness. *For any* (pp, td) ← Setup(1^λ), $b \in \{0,1\}$, *and* $x \in \mathcal{X}$, *if we let* $x' \leftarrow$ Swap(td, b, x), *then we have* $f_{b \oplus 1}(x') = f_b(x)$ *and* Swap(td, $b \oplus 1, x'$) $= x$. *In particular,* Swap(td, $b, \cdot$) *induces an efficiently computable and invertible one-to-one mapping between* $f_0^{-1}(y)$ *and* $f_1^{-1}(y)$ *for any* $y \in \mathcal{Y}$.

Efficient Random Sampling over $\mathcal{X}$. *There is a PPT algorithm that samples an almost uniform element of* $\mathcal{X}$ *(i.e., the distribution of the sample is statistically close to the uniform distribution).*

Efficient Superposition over $\mathcal{X}$. *There is a QPT algorithm that generates a state whose trace distance from* $|\mathcal{X}\rangle = \frac{1}{\sqrt{|\mathcal{X}|}} \sum_{x \in \mathcal{X}} |x\rangle$ *is* negl(λ).

Remark 4 (A convention on "Efficient random sampling over $\mathcal{X}$*" and "Efficient superposition over* $\mathcal{X}$*" properties).* In the rest of this paper, we assume that we can sample elements from *exactly* the uniform distribution of $\mathcal{X}$. Similarly, we assume that we can *exactly* generate $|\mathcal{X}\rangle$ in QPT. They are just for simplifying the presentations of our results, and all the results hold with the above imperfect version with additive negligible loss for security or correctness.

We define two security notions for STFs which we call *claw-freeness* and *conversion hardness*. Looking ahead, what we need in our construction of quantum-ciphertext PKE in Sect. 4.2 is only conversion hardness. However, since there are interesting relations between them as we show later, we define both of them here.

Definition 5 (Claw-freeness). *We say that a STF* (Setup, Eval, Swap) *satisfies claw-freeness if for any non-uniform QPT algorithm* $\mathcal{A}$, *we have*

$$\Pr[f_0(x_0) = f_1(x_1) : (\text{pp}, \text{td}) \leftarrow \text{Setup}(1^\lambda), (x_0, x_1) \leftarrow \mathcal{A}(\text{pp})] = \text{negl}(\lambda).$$

Definition 6 (Conversion hardness). *We say that a STF* (Setup, Eval, Swap) *satisfies conversion hardness if for any non-uniform QPT algorithm* $\mathcal{A}$, *we have*

$$\Pr[f_1(x_1) = y : (\text{pp}, \text{td}) \leftarrow \text{Setup}(1^\lambda), x_0 \leftarrow \mathcal{X}, y := f_0(x_0), x_1 \leftarrow \mathcal{A}(\text{pp}, |f_0^{-1}(y)\rangle)] = \text{negl}(\lambda)$$

where we remind that $|f_0^{-1}(y)\rangle := \frac{1}{\sqrt{|f_0^{-1}(y)|}} \sum_{x \in f_0^{-1}(y)} |x\rangle$.

Remark 5 (On asymmetry of f_0 and f_1). Conversion hardness requires that it is hard to find x_1 such that $f_1(x_1) = y$ given $|f_0^{-1}(y)\rangle$. We could define it in the other way, i.e., it is hard to find x_0 such that $f_0(x_0) = y$ given $|f_1^{-1}(y)\rangle$. These two definitions do not seem to be equivalent. However, it is easy to see that if there is a STF that satisfies one of them, then it can be modified to satisfy the other one by just swapping the roles of f_0 and f_1. In this sense, the choice of the definition from these two versions is arbitrary.

We show several lemmas on the relationship between claw-freeness and conversion hardness.

First, we show that claw-freeness implies conversion hardness if f_0 is collapsing.

Lemma 1 (Claw-free and collapsing → Conversion hard). *If f_0 is collapsing, then claw-freeness implies conversion hardness.*

We defer the proof to the full version.

As a special case of Lemma 1, claw-freeness implies conversion hardness when f_0 is *injective* (in which case f_1 is also injective). This is because any injective function is trivially collapsing.

We remark that a conversion hard STF is not necessarily claw-free, because a claw can be augmented in STF without hurting the conversion hardness.

Next, we show a "win-win" result inspired from [37]. We roughly show that a claw-free but non-conversion-hard STF can be used to construct one-shot signatures [3]. Roughly one-shot signatures are a genuinely quantum primitive which enables us to generate a classical verification key vk along with a quantum signing key sk in such a way that one can use sk to generate a signature for whichever message of one's choice, but cannot generate signatures for different messages simultaneously. The only known construction of one-shot signatures is relative to a classical oracle and there is no known construction in the standard model. Even for its weaker variant called tokenized signatures [5], the only known construction in the standard model is based on indistinguishability obfuscation [12]. Given the difficulty of constructing tokenized signatures, let alone one-shot signatures, it is reasonable to conjecture that natural candidate constructions of STFs satisfy conversion hardness if it satisfies claw-freeness. This is useful because claw-freeness often follows from weaker assumptions than conversion hardness, which is indeed the case for the group action-based construction in Sect. 4.3.

Before stating the lemma, we remark some subtlety about the lemma. Actually, we need to assume a STF that is claw-free but not *infinitely-often uniform* conversion hard. Here, "infinitely-often" means that it only requires the security to hold for infinitely many security parameters rather than all security parameters. (See [37, Sect. 4.1] for more explanations about infinitely-often security.) The "uniform" means that security is required to hold only against uniform adversaries as opposed to non-uniform ones. Alternatively, we can weaken the assumption to a STF that is claw-free but not uniform conversion hard if we weaken the goal to be *infinitely-often* one-shot signatures. We remark that similar limitations also exist for the "win-win" result in [37].

Then, the lemma is given below.

Lemma 2 (Claw-free and non-conversion hard STF → One-shot signatures). *Let* (Setup, Eval, Swap) *be a STF that satisfies claw-freeness. Then, the following statements hold:*

1. *If* (Setup, Eval, Swap) *is not infinitely-often uniform conversion hard, then we can use it to construct one-shot signatures.*
2. *If* (Setup, Eval, Swap) *is not uniform conversion hard, then we can use it to construct infinitely-often one-shot signatures.*

We defer the proof to the full version since the idea is already explained in Sect. 2.1.

Instantiations. Our main instantiation of STFs is based on group actions, which is given in Sect. 4.3.

A lattice-based instantiation is also possible if we relax the requirements to allow some "noises" similarly to [7]. The noisy version is sufficient for our construction of quantum-ciphertext PKE given in Sect. 4.2. However, since lattice-based (classical) PKE schemes are already known [19,31], we do not try to capture lattice-based instantiations in the definition of STFs.

4.2 Quantum-Ciphertext Public Key Encryption

In this section, we define quantum-ciphertext PKE and construct it based on STFs.

Definition. We define quantum-ciphertext PKE for one-bit messages for simplicity. The multi-bit message version can be defined analogously, and a simple parallel repetition works to expand the message length. Moreover, we can further extend the message space to quantum states by a hybrid encryption with quantum one-time pad as in [9], i.e., we encrypt a quantum message by a quantum one-time pad, and then encrypt the key of the quantum one-time pad by quantum PKE for classical messages.

Definition 7 (Quantum-ciphertext public key encryption). *A quantum-ciphertext public key encryption (quantum-ciphertext PKE) scheme (with single-bit messages) consists of algorithms* (KeyGen, Enc, Dec).

KeyGen(1^λ) $\to$ (pk, sk): *This is a PPT algorithm that takes the security parameter 1^λ as input, and outputs a classical public key* pk *and a classical secret key* sk.

Enc(pk, b) $\to$ ct: *This is a QPT algorithm that takes a public key* pk *and a message $b \in \{0,1\}$ as input, and outputs a quantum ciphertext* ct.

Dec(sk, ct) $\to$ $b'/\bot$: *This is a QPT algorithm that takes a secret key* sk *and a ciphertext* ct *as input, and outputs a message $b' \in \{0,1\}$ or $\bot$.*

It must satisfy correctness as defined below:
Correctness. *For any $m \in \{0,1\}$, we have*

$$\Pr[m' = m : (\text{pk}, \text{sk}) \leftarrow \text{KeyGen}(1^\lambda), ct \leftarrow \text{Enc}(\text{pk}, m), m' \leftarrow \text{Dec}(\text{sk}, ct)] = 1 - \text{negl}(\lambda).$$

$\square$

We define IND-CPA security for quantum-ciphertext PKE similarly to that for classical PKE as follows.

Definition 8 (IND-CPA security). *We say that a quantum-ciphertext PKE scheme* (KeyGen, Enc, Dec) *is* IND-CPA *secure if for any non-uniform QPT adversary $\mathcal{A}$, we have*

$$|\Pr[\mathcal{A}(\text{pk}, ct_0) = 1] - \Pr[\mathcal{A}(\text{pk}, ct_1) = 1]| = \text{negl}(\lambda),$$

where (pk, sk) $\leftarrow$ KeyGen(1^λ), $ct_0 \leftarrow$ Enc(pk, 0), *and* $ct_1 \leftarrow$ Enc(pk, 1).

Construction. Let (Setup, Eval, Swap) be a STF. We construct a quantum-ciphertext PKE scheme (KeyGen, Enc, Dec) as follows.

KeyGen(1^λ): Generate (pp, td) $\leftarrow$ Setup(1^λ) and output pk := pp and sk := td.
Enc(pk, $b \in \{0, 1\}$): Parse pk = pp. Prepare two registers **D** and **X**. Generate the state

$$\frac{1}{\sqrt{2}}(|0\rangle + (-1)^b |1\rangle)_{\mathbf{D}} |\mathcal{X}\rangle_{\mathbf{X}} = \frac{1}{\sqrt{2|\mathcal{X}|}}(|0\rangle + (-1)^b |1\rangle)_{\mathbf{D}} \sum_{x \in \mathcal{X}} |x\rangle_{\mathbf{X}}.$$

Prepare another register **Y**, coherently compute f_0 or f_1 into **Y** controlled by **D** to get

$$\sum_{x \in \mathcal{X}} \frac{1}{\sqrt{2|\mathcal{X}|}}(|0\rangle_{\mathbf{D}} |x\rangle_{\mathbf{X}} |f_0(x)\rangle_{\mathbf{Y}} + (-1)^b |1\rangle_{\mathbf{D}} |x\rangle_{\mathbf{X}} |f_1(x)\rangle_{\mathbf{Y}}),$$

and measure **Y** to get $y \in \mathcal{Y}$. At this point, **D** and **X** collapse to the following state:[20]

$$\frac{1}{\sqrt{2}}(|0\rangle_{\mathbf{D}} |f_0^{-1}(y)\rangle_{\mathbf{X}} + (-1)^b |1\rangle_{\mathbf{D}} |f_1^{-1}(y)\rangle_{\mathbf{X}}).$$

The above state is set to be ct.[21]
Dec(sk, ct): Parse sk = td. Let U_{td} be a unitary over **D** and **X** such that[22]

$$U_{\mathsf{td}} |0\rangle_{\mathbf{D}} |x\rangle_{\mathbf{X}} = |0\rangle_{\mathbf{D}} |x\rangle_{\mathbf{X}},$$
$$U_{\mathsf{td}} |1\rangle_{\mathbf{D}} |x\rangle_{\mathbf{X}} = |1\rangle_{\mathbf{D}} |\mathsf{Swap}(\mathsf{td}, 1, x)\rangle_{\mathbf{X}}.$$

Apply U_{td} on the register (**D**, **X**) and measure **D** in the Hadamard basis and output the measurement outcome $b' \in \{0, 1\}$.

Correctness.

Theorem 2. (KeyGen, Enc, Dec) *satisfies correctness.*

Proof. An honestly generated ciphertext ct is of the form

$$\frac{1}{\sqrt{2}}(|0\rangle_{\mathbf{D}} |f_0^{-1}(y)\rangle_{\mathbf{X}} + (-1)^b |1\rangle_{\mathbf{D}} |f_1^{-1}(y)\rangle_{\mathbf{X}}).$$

By the definition of U_{td} and the swapping correctness, it is easy to see that we have

$$U_{\mathsf{td}} |0\rangle_{\mathbf{D}} |f_0^{-1}(y)\rangle_{\mathbf{X}} = |0\rangle_{\mathbf{D}} |f_0^{-1}(y)\rangle_{\mathbf{X}},$$
$$U_{\mathsf{td}} |1\rangle_{\mathbf{D}} |f_1^{-1}(y)\rangle_{\mathbf{X}} = |1\rangle_{\mathbf{D}} |f_0^{-1}(y)\rangle_{\mathbf{X}}.$$

---

[20] Note that the swapping correctness implies that $|f_0^{-1}(y)| = |f_1^{-1}(y)|$ for any $y \in \mathcal{Y}$.
[21] Remark that one does not need to include y in the ciphertext.
[22] Note that the second operation is possible because $\mathsf{Swap}(\mathsf{td}, 0, \mathsf{Swap}(\mathsf{td}, 1, x)) = x$.

Thus, applying U_{td} on ct results in the following state:

$$\frac{1}{\sqrt{2}}(|0\rangle_{\mathbf{D}}|f_0^{-1}(y)\rangle_{\mathbf{X}} + (-1)^b|1\rangle_{\mathbf{D}}|f_0^{-1}(y)\rangle_{\mathbf{X}}) = \frac{1}{\sqrt{2}}(|0\rangle_{\mathbf{D}} + (-1)^b|1\rangle_{\mathbf{D}}) \otimes |f_0^{-1}(y)\rangle_{\mathbf{X}}.$$

The measurement of $\mathbf{D}$ in the Hadamard basis therefore results in b.   □

Security.

Theorem 3. *If* (Setup, Eval, Swap) *satisfies conversion hardness,* (KeyGen, Enc, Dec) *is IND-CPA secure.*

We can prove Theorem 3 by using Item 2 of Theorem 1. We defer the proof to the full version since the idea is already explained in Sect. 2.1.

4.3   Instantiation from Group Actions

We review basic definitions about cryptographic group actions and their one-wayness and pseudorandomness following [25]. Then, we construct a STF based on it.

Basic Definitions.

Definition 9 (Group actions). *Let G be a (not necessarily abelian) group, S be a set, and $\star : G \times S \to S$ be a function where we write $g \star s$ to mean $\star(g, s)$. We say that $(G, S, \star)$ is a* group action *if it satisfies the following:*

1. *For the identity element $e \in G$ and any $s \in S$, we have $e \star s = s$.*
2. *For any $g, h \in G$ and any $s \in S$, we have $(gh) \star s = g \star (h \star s)$.*

To be useful for cryptography, we have to at least assume that basic operations about $(G, S, \star)$ have efficient algorithms. We require the following efficient algorithms similarly to [25].

Definition 10 (Group actions with efficient algorithms). *We say that a group action $(G, S, \star)$ has* efficient algorithms *if it satisfies the following:*[23]

Unique representations: *Each element of G and S can be represented as a bit string of length $\text{poly}(\lambda)$ in a unique manner. Thus, we identify these elements and their representations.*
Group operations: *There are classical deterministic polynomial-time algorithms that compute gh from $g \in G$ and $h \in G$ and g^{-1} from $g \in G$.*
Group action: *There is a classical deterministic polynomial-time algorithm that computes $g \star s$ from $g \in G$ and $s \in S$.*

---

[23] Strictly speaking, we have to consider a family $\{(G_\lambda, S_\lambda, \star_\lambda)\}_{\lambda \in \mathbb{N}}$ of group actions parameterized by the security parameter to meaningfully define the efficiency requirements. We omit the dependence on λ for notational simplicity throughout the paper.

Efficient recognizability: *There are classical deterministic polynomial-time algorithms that decide if a given bit string represents an element of G or S, respectively.*

Random sampling: *There are PPT algorithms that sample almost uniform elements of G or S (i.e., the distribution of the sample is statistically close to the uniform distribution), respectively.*

Superposition over G: *There is a QPT algorithm that generates a state whose trace distance from $|G\rangle$ is $\mathsf{negl}(\lambda)$.*

Remark 6 (A convention on "Random sampling" and "Superposition over G" properties). In the rest of this paper, we assume that we can sample elements from *exactly* uniform distributions of G and S. Similarly, we assume that we can *exactly* generate $|G\rangle$ in QPT. They are just for simplifying the presentations of our results, and all the results hold with the above imperfect version with additive negligible loss for security or correctness.

The above requirements are identical to those in [25] except for the "superposition over G" property. We remark that all candidate constructions proposed in [25] satisfy this property as explained later.

Assumptions. We define one-wayness and pseudorandomness following [25].

Definition 11 (One-wayness). *We say that a group action $(G, S, \star)$ with efficient algorithms is* one-way *if for any non-uniform QPT adversary $\mathcal{A}$, we have*

$$\Pr\left[g' \star s = g \star s : s \leftarrow S, g \leftarrow G, g' \leftarrow \mathcal{A}(s, g \star s)\right] = \mathsf{negl}(\lambda).$$

Definition 12 (Pseudorandomness). *We say that a group action $(G, S, \star)$ with efficient algorithms is* pseudorandom *if it satisfies the following:*

1. We have

$$\Pr[\exists g \in G \ s.t. \ g \star s = t : s, t \leftarrow S] = \mathsf{negl}(\lambda).$$

2. For any non-uniform QPT adversary $\mathcal{A}$, we have

$$|\Pr\left[1 \leftarrow \mathcal{A}(s, t) : s \leftarrow S, g \leftarrow G, t := g \star s\right] - \Pr\left[1 \leftarrow \mathcal{A}(s, t) : s, t \leftarrow S\right]| = \mathsf{negl}(\lambda).$$

Remark 7 (On Item 1). We require Item 1 to make Item 2 non-trivial. For example, if $(G, S, \star)$ is transitive, i.e., for any $s, t \in S$, there is $g \in G$ such that $g \star s = t$, Item 2 trivially holds because the distributions of $t = g \star s$ is uniformly distributed over S for any fixed s and random $g \leftarrow G$.

Remark 8 (Pseudorandom $\rightarrow$ One-way). We remark that the pseudorandomness immediately implies the one-wayness as noted in [25].

Instantiations. Ji et al. [25] gave several candidate constructions of one-way and pseudorandom group actions with efficient algorithms based on general linear group actions on tensors. We briefly describe one of their candidates below. Let $\mathbb{F}$ be a finite field, and $k, d_1, d_2..., d_k$ be positive integers (which are typically set as $k = 3$ and $d_1 = d_2 = d_3$). We set $G := \prod_{j=1}^{k} GL_{d_j}(\mathbb{F})$, $S := \bigotimes_{j=1}^{k} \mathbb{F}^{d_j}$, and define the group action by the matrix-vector multiplication as

$$(M_j)_{j \in [k]} \star T := \left(\bigotimes_{j=1}^{k} M_j \right) T$$

for $(M_j)_{j \in [k]} \in \prod_{j=1}^{k} GL_{d_j}(\mathbb{F})$ and $T \in \bigotimes_{j=1}^{k} \mathbb{F}^{d_j}$. See [25] for attempts of cryptanalysis and justification of the one-wayness and pseudorandomness. We remark that we introduced an additional requirement of the "superposition over G" property in Definition 10, but their candidates satisfy this property. In their candidates, the group G is a direct product of general linear groups over finite fields (or symmetric groups for one of the candidates), and a uniformly random matrix over finite fields is invertible with overwhelming probability for appropriate parameters.

Construction of STF. We construct a STF based on group actions. Let $(G, S, \star)$ be a group action with efficient algorithms (as defined in Definition 10). Then, we construct a STF as follows.

$\mathsf{Setup}(1^\lambda)$: Generate $s_0 \leftarrow S$ and $g \leftarrow G$, set $s_1 := g \star s_0$, and output $\mathsf{pp} := (s_0, s_1)$ and $\mathsf{td} := g$. For $b \in \{0, 1\}$, we define $f_b : G \to S$ by $f_b(h) := h \star s_b$.
$\mathsf{Eval}(\mathsf{pp} = (s_0, s_1), b, h)$: Output $f_b(h) = h \star s_b$.
$\mathsf{Swap}(\mathsf{td} = g, b, h)$: If $b = 0$, output hg^{-1}. If $b = 1$, output hg.

The evaluation correctness is trivial. The swapping correctness can be seen as follows: For any $h \in G$, $f_1(\mathsf{Swap}(\mathsf{td}, 0, h)) = f_1(hg^{-1}) = (hg^{-1}) \star s_1 = h \star s_0 = f_0(h)$. Similarly, for any $h \in G$, $f_0(\mathsf{Swap}(\mathsf{td}, 1, h)) = f_0(hg) = (hg) \star s_0 = h \star s_1 = f_1(h)$. For any $h \in G$, $\mathsf{Swap}(\mathsf{td}, 1, \mathsf{Swap}(\mathsf{td}, 0, h)) = \mathsf{Swap}(\mathsf{td}, 1, hg^{-1}) = (hg^{-1})g = h$.

The efficient sampling and efficient superposition properties directly follow from the corresponding properties of the group action.

We prove the following theorem.

Theorem 4. *The following hold:*

1. *If $(G, S, \star)$ is one-way, then $(\mathsf{Setup}, \mathsf{Eval}, \mathsf{Swap})$ is claw-free.*
2. *If $(G, S, \star)$ is pseudorandom, then $(\mathsf{Setup}, \mathsf{Eval}, \mathsf{Swap})$ is conversion hard.*

We defer the proof to the full version because it is easy.

Quantum-Ciphertext PKE from Group Actions. Recall that conversion hard STFs suffice for constructing IND-CPA secure quantum ciphertext PKE (Theorem 3). Then, by Lemmata 1 and 2 and Theorem 4, we obtain the following corollaries.

Corollary 1. *If there exists a pseudorandom group action with efficient algorithms, there exists an IND-CPA secure quantum-ciphertext PKE.*

Remark 9 (Lossy encryption). Actually, we can show that the quantum-ciphertext PKE constructed from a pseudorandom group action is lossy encryption [4], which is stronger than IND-CPA secure one. We omit the detail since our focus is on constructing IND-CPA secure schemes.

Corollary 2. *If there exists a one-way group action with efficient algorithms such that f_0 is collapsing,*[24] *there exists a uniform IND-CPA secure quantum-ciphertext PKE scheme.*

Corollary 3. *If there exists a one-way group action with efficient algorithms, there exists a uniform IND-CPA secure quantum-ciphertext PKE scheme or infinitely-often one-shot signatures.*[25]

5   Equivalence Between Swapping and Distinguishing with Auxiliary States

For our application to conversion for commitments, we need a generalization of Theorem 1 that considers auxiliary quantum states. While it is straightforward to generalize Item 2 to such a setting,[26] a generalization of Item 1 is non-trivial. The problems is that the unitary U may not preserve the auxiliary state when it "swaps" $|x\rangle$ and $|y\rangle$.[27] Intuitively, we overcome this issue by "uncomputing" the auxiliary state in a certain sense.

Theorem 5 (Generalization of Theorem 1 with auxiliary states)

1. *Let $|x\rangle, |y\rangle$ be orthogonal n-qubit states and $|\tau\rangle$ be an m-qubit state. Let U be a polynomial-time computable unitary over $(n+m)$-qubit states and define Γ as*

$$\Gamma := \left\| (\langle y| \otimes I^{\otimes m})U |x\rangle |\tau\rangle + (\langle x| \otimes I^{\otimes m})U |y\rangle |\tau\rangle \right\|.$$

   Then, there exists a non-uniform QPT distinguisher $\mathcal{A}$ with advice $|\tau'\rangle = |\tau\rangle \otimes \frac{|x\rangle|0\rangle + |y\rangle|1\rangle}{\sqrt{2}}$ that distinguishes $|\psi\rangle = \frac{|x\rangle + |y\rangle}{\sqrt{2}}$ and $|\phi\rangle = \frac{|x\rangle - |y\rangle}{\sqrt{2}}$ with advantage $\frac{\Gamma^2}{4}$. Moreover, if U does not act on some qubits, then $\mathcal{A}$ also does not act on those qubits.

2. *Let $|\psi\rangle, |\phi\rangle$ be orthogonal n-qubit states, and suppose that a non-uniform QPT distinguisher $\mathcal{A}$ with an m-qubit advice $|\tau\rangle$ distinguishes $|\psi\rangle$ and $|\phi\rangle$ with advantage Δ without using additional ancilla qubits besides $|\tau\rangle$.*

---

[24] We currently have no candidate of such a one-way group action.

[25] The uniform IND-CPA security is defined similarly to the IND-CPA security in Definition 8 except that the adversary is restricted to be *uniform* QPT.

[26] Indeed, such a generalization of Item 2 is already implicitly used in the proof of Theorem 3.

[27] This is also observed in [1, Footnote 2].

Then, there exists a polynomial-time computable unitary U over $(n + m)$-qubit states such that

$$\frac{|\langle y| \langle \tau| U |x\rangle |\tau\rangle + \langle x| \langle \tau| U |y\rangle |\tau\rangle |}{2} = \Delta$$

where $|x\rangle := \frac{|\psi\rangle + |\phi\rangle}{\sqrt{2}}$ and $|y\rangle := \frac{|\psi\rangle - |\phi\rangle}{\sqrt{2}}$. Moreover, if $\mathcal{A}$ does not act on some qubits, then U also does not act on those qubits.

Remark 10. We remark that Item 1 does *not* preserve the auxiliary state unlike Item 2. Though this does not capture the intuition that "one can distinguish $|\psi\rangle$ and $|\phi\rangle$ whenever he can swap $|x\rangle$ and $|y\rangle$", this is good enough for our purpose. We also remark that there is a quadratic reduction loss in Item 1. We do not know if it is tight while both items of Theorem 1 is shown to be tight in [1].

Proof of Theorem 5. Item 2 directly follows from Item 2 of Theorem 1 by considering $|x\rangle |\tau\rangle$ and $|y\rangle |\tau\rangle$ as $|x\rangle$ and $|y\rangle$ in Theorem 1. We prove Item 1 below.

Proof of Item 1. Let $\mathbf{A}$ and $\mathbf{A}'$ be n-qubit registers, $\mathbf{Z}$ be an m-qubit register, and $\mathbf{B}$ be a 1-qubit register. We define a unitary $\widetilde{U}$ over $(\mathbf{A}, \mathbf{Z}, \mathbf{A}', \mathbf{B})$ as follows:

$$\widetilde{U} := X_{\mathbf{B}} U_{\mathbf{A}', \mathbf{Z}}^{\dagger} U_{\mathbf{A}, \mathbf{Z}} \tag{3}$$

where $X_{\mathbf{B}}$ is the Pauli X operator on $\mathbf{B}$ and $U_{\mathbf{A}', \mathbf{Z}}^{\dagger}$ means the inverse of $U_{\mathbf{A}', \mathbf{Z}}$, which works similarly to $U_{\mathbf{A}, \mathbf{Z}}$ except that it acts on $\mathbf{A}'$ instead of on $\mathbf{A}$.

Then, we prove the following claim.

Claim 6. *Let $|x\rangle, |y\rangle, |\tau\rangle$, and Γ be as in Item 1 of Theorem 5, $\widetilde{U}$ be as defined in Eq. (3), and $|\sigma\rangle_{\mathbf{A}', \mathbf{B}}$ be the state over $(\mathbf{A}', \mathbf{B})$ defined as follows:*

$$|\sigma\rangle_{\mathbf{A}', \mathbf{B}} := \frac{|x\rangle_{\mathbf{A}'} |0\rangle_{\mathbf{B}} + |y\rangle_{\mathbf{A}'} |1\rangle_{\mathbf{B}}}{\sqrt{2}}. \tag{4}$$

Then, it holds that

$$\left| \langle y|_{\mathbf{A}} \langle \tau|_{\mathbf{Z}} \langle \sigma|_{\mathbf{A}', \mathbf{B}} \widetilde{U} |x\rangle_{\mathbf{A}} |\tau\rangle_{\mathbf{Z}} |\sigma\rangle_{\mathbf{A}', \mathbf{B}} + \langle x|_{\mathbf{A}} \langle \tau|_{\mathbf{Z}} \langle \sigma|_{\mathbf{A}', \mathbf{B}} \widetilde{U} |y\rangle_{\mathbf{A}} |\tau\rangle_{\mathbf{Z}} |\sigma\rangle_{\mathbf{A}', \mathbf{B}} \right| = \frac{\Gamma^2}{2}.$$

We first finish the proof of Item 1 assuming that Claim 6 is correct. By Item 1 of Theorem 1, Claim 6 implies that there is a QPT distinguisher $\widetilde{\mathcal{A}}$ that distinguishes

$$|\widetilde{\psi}\rangle = \frac{(|x\rangle + |y\rangle)_{\mathbf{A}} |\tau\rangle_{\mathbf{Z}} |\sigma\rangle_{\mathbf{A}', \mathbf{B}}}{\sqrt{2}}$$

and

$$|\widetilde{\phi}\rangle = \frac{(|x\rangle - |y\rangle)_{\mathbf{A}} |\tau\rangle_{\mathbf{Z}} |\sigma\rangle_{\mathbf{A}', \mathbf{B}}}{\sqrt{2}}$$

with advantage $\frac{\Gamma^2}{4}$. Moreover, $\widetilde{\mathcal{A}}$ does not act on qubits on which $\widetilde{U}$ does not act. In particular, $\widetilde{\mathcal{A}}$ does not act on qubits of $\mathbf{A}$ and $\mathbf{Z}$ on which $U_{\mathbf{A},\mathbf{Z}}$ does not act since $\widetilde{U}$ acts on $\mathbf{A}$ and $\mathbf{Z}$ only through $U_{\mathbf{A},\mathbf{Z}}$ and $U_{\mathbf{A}',\mathbf{Z}}^{\dagger}$. Thus, by considering $\widetilde{\mathcal{A}}$ as a distinguisher $\mathcal{A}$ with advice $|\tau'\rangle = |\tau\rangle_{\mathbf{Z}} |\sigma\rangle_{\mathbf{A}',\mathbf{B}}$ that distinguishes $|\psi\rangle = \frac{|x\rangle + |y\rangle}{\sqrt{2}}$ and $|\phi\rangle = \frac{|x\rangle - |y\rangle}{\sqrt{2}}$, Item 1 is proven. Below, we prove Claim 6.

Proof of Claim 6. For $(a,b) \in \{(x,x),(x,y),(y,x),(y,y)\}$, we define

$$|\tau'_{ab}\rangle_{\mathbf{Z}} := (\langle b|_{\mathbf{A}} \otimes I_{\mathbf{Z}}) U_{\mathbf{A},\mathbf{Z}} |a\rangle_{\mathbf{A}} |\tau\rangle_{\mathbf{Z}} .$$

Then, we have

$$\Gamma = \left\| |\tau'_{xy}\rangle_{\mathbf{Z}} + |\tau'_{yx}\rangle_{\mathbf{Z}} \right\| \tag{5}$$

and

$$U_{\mathbf{A},\mathbf{Z}} |x\rangle_{\mathbf{A}} |\tau\rangle_{\mathbf{Z}} = |x\rangle_{\mathbf{A}} |\tau'_{xx}\rangle_{\mathbf{Z}} + |y\rangle_{\mathbf{A}} |\tau'_{xy}\rangle_{\mathbf{Z}} + |\text{garbage}_x\rangle_{\mathbf{A},\mathbf{Z}} \tag{6}$$

$$U_{\mathbf{A},\mathbf{Z}} |y\rangle_{\mathbf{A}} |\tau\rangle_{\mathbf{Z}} = |x\rangle_{\mathbf{A}} |\tau'_{yx}\rangle_{\mathbf{Z}} + |y\rangle_{\mathbf{A}} |\tau'_{yy}\rangle_{\mathbf{Z}} + |\text{garbage}_y\rangle_{\mathbf{A},\mathbf{Z}} \tag{7}$$

where $|\text{garbage}_x\rangle_{\mathbf{A},\mathbf{Z}}$ and $|\text{garbage}_y\rangle_{\mathbf{A},\mathbf{Z}}$ are (not necessarily normalized) states such that

$$(\langle x|_{\mathbf{A}} \otimes I_{\mathbf{Z}}) |\text{garbage}_x\rangle_{\mathbf{A},\mathbf{Z}} = (\langle y|_{\mathbf{A}} \otimes I_{\mathbf{Z}}) |\text{garbage}_x\rangle_{\mathbf{A},\mathbf{Z}} = 0, \tag{8}$$

$$(\langle x|_{\mathbf{A}} \otimes I_{\mathbf{Z}}) |\text{garbage}_y\rangle_{\mathbf{A},\mathbf{Z}} = (\langle y|_{\mathbf{A}} \otimes I_{\mathbf{Z}}) |\text{garbage}_y\rangle_{\mathbf{A},\mathbf{Z}} = 0. \tag{9}$$

Then,

$$\langle y|_{\mathbf{A}} \langle \tau|_{\mathbf{Z}} \langle \sigma|_{\mathbf{A}',\mathbf{B}} \widetilde{U} |x\rangle_{\mathbf{A}} |\tau\rangle_{\mathbf{Z}} |\sigma\rangle_{\mathbf{A}',\mathbf{B}}$$
$$= \langle y|_{\mathbf{A}} \langle \tau|_{\mathbf{Z}} \langle \sigma|_{\mathbf{A}',\mathbf{B}} X_{\mathbf{B}} U_{\mathbf{A}',\mathbf{Z}}^{\dagger} (|x\rangle_{\mathbf{A}} |\tau'_{xx}\rangle_{\mathbf{Z}} + |y\rangle_{\mathbf{A}} |\tau'_{xy}\rangle_{\mathbf{Z}} + |\text{garbage}_x\rangle_{\mathbf{A},\mathbf{Z}}) |\sigma\rangle_{\mathbf{A}',\mathbf{B}}$$
$$= \langle \tau|_{\mathbf{Z}} \langle \sigma|_{\mathbf{A}',\mathbf{B}} X_{\mathbf{B}} U_{\mathbf{A}',\mathbf{Z}}^{\dagger} |\tau'_{xy}\rangle_{\mathbf{Z}} |\sigma\rangle_{\mathbf{A}',\mathbf{B}} \tag{10}$$

where the first equality follows from Eq. (6) and the second equality follows from Eq. (8) and the assumption that $|x\rangle$ and $|y\rangle$ are orthogonal. By Eqs. (4), (6) and (7), it holds that

$$U_{\mathbf{A}',\mathbf{Z}} X_{\mathbf{B}} |\tau\rangle_{\mathbf{Z}} |\sigma\rangle_{\mathbf{A}',\mathbf{B}}$$
$$= U_{\mathbf{A}',\mathbf{Z}} \frac{|\tau\rangle_{\mathbf{Z}} ((|x\rangle_{\mathbf{A}'} |1\rangle_{\mathbf{B}} + |y\rangle_{\mathbf{A}'} |0\rangle_{\mathbf{B}})}{\sqrt{2}}$$
$$= \frac{1}{\sqrt{2}} \left(\begin{array}{c} \left(|x\rangle_{\mathbf{A}'} |\tau'_{xx}\rangle_{\mathbf{Z}} + |y\rangle_{\mathbf{A}'} |\tau'_{xy}\rangle_{\mathbf{Z}} + |\text{garbage}_x\rangle_{\mathbf{A}',\mathbf{Z}} \right) |1\rangle_{\mathbf{B}} \\ + \left(|x\rangle_{\mathbf{A}'} |\tau'_{yx}\rangle_{\mathbf{Z}} + |y\rangle_{\mathbf{A}'} |\tau'_{yy}\rangle_{\mathbf{Z}} + |\text{garbage}_y\rangle_{\mathbf{A}',\mathbf{Z}} \right) |0\rangle_{\mathbf{B}} \end{array} \right). \tag{11}$$

Then, it holds that

$$\langle\tau|_{\mathbf{Z}}\,\langle\sigma|_{\mathbf{A'},\mathbf{B}}\,X_{\mathbf{B}}U_{\mathbf{A'},\mathbf{Z}}^{\dagger}\,|\tau'_{xy}\rangle_{\mathbf{Z}}\,|\sigma\rangle_{\mathbf{A'},\mathbf{B}}$$

$$=\frac{1}{2}\left(\begin{array}{l}\left(\langle x|_{\mathbf{A'}}\,\langle\tau'_{xx}|_{\mathbf{Z}}+\langle y|_{\mathbf{A'}}\,\langle\tau'_{xy}|_{\mathbf{Z}}+\langle\mathrm{garbage}_{x}|_{\mathbf{A'},\mathbf{Z}}\right)\langle 1|_{\mathbf{B}}\\ +\left(\langle x|_{\mathbf{A'}}\,\langle\tau'_{yx}|_{\mathbf{Z}}+\langle y|_{\mathbf{A'}}\,\langle\tau'_{yy}|_{\mathbf{Z}}+\langle\mathrm{garbage}_{y}|_{\mathbf{A'},\mathbf{Z}}\right)\langle 0|_{\mathbf{B}}\end{array}\right)\left(|x\rangle_{\mathbf{A'}}\,|0\rangle_{\mathbf{B}}+|y\rangle_{\mathbf{A'}}\,|1\rangle_{\mathbf{B}}\right)|\tau'_{xy}\rangle_{\mathbf{Z}}$$

$$=\frac{1}{2}((\langle\tau'_{xy}|+\langle\tau'_{yx}|)_{\mathbf{Z}}\,|\tau'_{xy}\rangle_{\mathbf{Z}}\,,$$

(12)

where the first equality follows from Eqs. (4) and (11) and the second equality follows from Eqs. (8), (9) and the assumption that $|x\rangle$ and $|y\rangle$ are orthogonal.

By Eqs. (10) and (12), we have

$$\langle y|_{\mathbf{A}}\,\langle\tau|_{\mathbf{Z}}\,\langle\sigma|_{\mathbf{A'},\mathbf{B}}\,\widetilde{U}\,|x\rangle_{\mathbf{A}}\,|\tau\rangle_{\mathbf{Z}}\,|\sigma\rangle_{\mathbf{A'},\mathbf{B}}=\frac{1}{2}((\langle\tau'_{xy}|+\langle\tau'_{yx}|)_{\mathbf{Z}}\,|\tau'_{xy}\rangle_{\mathbf{Z}}\,.$$

(13)

By a similar calculation, we have

$$\langle x|_{\mathbf{A}}\,\langle\tau|_{\mathbf{Z}}\,\langle\sigma|_{\mathbf{A'},\mathbf{B}}\,\widetilde{U}\,|y\rangle_{\mathbf{A}}\,|\tau\rangle_{\mathbf{Z}}\,|\sigma\rangle_{\mathbf{A'},\mathbf{B}}=\frac{1}{2}((\langle\tau'_{xy}|+\langle\tau'_{yx}|)_{\mathbf{Z}}\,|\tau'_{yx}\rangle_{\mathbf{Z}}\,.$$

(14)

By Eqs. (13) and (14), we have

$$\langle y|_{\mathbf{A}}\,\langle\tau|_{\mathbf{Z}}\,\langle\sigma|_{\mathbf{A'},\mathbf{B}}\,\widetilde{U}\,|x\rangle_{\mathbf{A}}\,|\tau\rangle_{\mathbf{Z}}\,|\sigma\rangle_{\mathbf{A'},\mathbf{B}}+\langle x|_{\mathbf{A}}\,\langle\tau|_{\mathbf{Z}}\,\langle\sigma|_{\mathbf{A'},\mathbf{B}}\,\widetilde{U}\,|y\rangle_{\mathbf{A}}\,|\tau\rangle_{\mathbf{Z}}\,|\sigma\rangle_{\mathbf{A'},\mathbf{B}}$$

$$=\frac{1}{2}\left\||\tau'_{xy}\rangle_{\mathbf{Z}}+|\tau'_{yx}\rangle_{\mathbf{Z}}\right\|^{2}.$$

By combining the above with Eq. (5), we complete the proof of Claim 6. □

This completes the proof of Theorem 5. □

6   Our Conversion for Commitments

In this section, we give a conversion for canonical quantum bit commitments that converts the flavors of security using Theorem 5.

Theorem 7 (Converting Flavors). *Let $\{Q_0, Q_1\}$ be a canonical quantum bit commitment scheme. Let $\{Q'_0, Q'_1\}$ be a canonical quantum bit commitment scheme described as follows:*

- *The roles of commitment and reveal registers are swapped from $\{Q_0, Q_1\}$ and the commitment register is augmented by an additional one-qubit register. That is, if $\mathbf{C}$ and $\mathbf{R}$ are the commitment and reveal registers of $\{Q_0, Q_1\}$, then the commitment and reveal registers of $\{Q'_0, Q'_1\}$ are defined as $\mathbf{C'} := (\mathbf{R}, \mathbf{D})$ and $\mathbf{R'} := \mathbf{C}$ where $\mathbf{D}$ is a one-qubit register.*
- *For $b \in \{0, 1\}$, the unitary Q'_b is defined as follows:*

$$Q'_b := (Q_0 \otimes |0\rangle\langle 0|_{\mathbf{D}} + Q_1 \otimes |1\rangle\langle 1|_{\mathbf{D}})\left(I_{\mathbf{R},\mathbf{C}} \otimes Z_{\mathbf{D}}^b H_{\mathbf{D}}\right)$$

where $Z_{\mathbf{D}}$ and $H_{\mathbf{D}}$ denote the Pauli Z and the Hadamard operators on $\mathbf{D}$.

Then, the following hold for $X, Y \in \{computationally, statistically, perfectly\}$:

1. *If* $\{Q_0, Q_1\}$ *is* X *hiding, then* $\{Q_0', Q_1'\}$ *is* X *binding.*
2. *If* $\{Q_0, Q_1\}$ *is* Y *binding, then* $\{Q_0', Q_1'\}$ *is* Y *hiding.*

Note that we have

$$Q_b' \left|0\right\rangle_{\mathbf{C'}, \mathbf{R'}} = \frac{1}{\sqrt{2}} \left((Q_0 \left|0\right\rangle)_{\mathbf{C}, \mathbf{R}} \left|0\right\rangle_{\mathbf{D}} + (-1)^b (Q_1 \left|0\right\rangle)_{\mathbf{C}, \mathbf{R}} \left|1\right\rangle_{\mathbf{D}} \right)$$

for $b \in \{0, 1\}$ where $(\mathbf{C'}, \mathbf{R'})$ is rearranged as $(\mathbf{C}, \mathbf{R}, \mathbf{D})$.

We defer the proof of Theorem 7 to the full version since it easily follows from Theorem 5 as explained in Sect. 2.2.

Applications. We give applications of Theorem 7 in the full version.

Acknowledgements. MH is supported by a KIAS Individual Grant QP089801. TM is supported by JST Moonshot R&D JPMJMS2061-5-1-1, JST FOREST, MEXT QLEAP, the Grant-in-Aid for Scientific Research (B) No.JP19H04066, the Grant-in Aid for Transformative Research Areas (A) 21H05183, and the Grant-in-Aid for Scientific Research (A) No.22H00522.

References

1. Aaronson, S., Atia, Y., Susskind, L.: On the hardness of detecting macroscopic superpositions. Electron. Colloquium Comput. Complex., 146 (2020)
2. Alamati, N., De Feo, L., Montgomery, H., Patranabis, S.: Cryptographic group actions and applications. In: Moriai, S., Wang, H. (eds.) ASIACRYPT 2020. LNCS, vol. 12492, pp. 411–439. Springer, Cham (2020). https://doi.org/10.1007/978-3-030-64834-3_14
3. Amos, R., Georgiou, M., Kiayias, A., Zhandry, M.: One-shot signatures and applications to hybrid quantum/classical authentication. In: Makarychev, K., Makarychev, Y., Tulsiani, M., Kamath, G., Chuzhoy, J. (eds.) 52nd ACM STOC, pp. 255–268. ACM Press, June 2020. https://doi.org/10.1145/3357713.3384304
4. Bellare, M., Hofheinz, D., Yilek, S.: Possibility and impossibility results for encryption and commitment secure under selective opening. In: Joux, A. (ed.) EUROCRYPT 2009. LNCS, vol. 5479, pp. 1–35. Springer, Heidelberg (2009). https://doi.org/10.1007/978-3-642-01001-9_1
5. Ben-David, S., Sattath, O.: Quantum tokens for digital signatures. Cryptology ePrint Archive, Paper 2017/094 (2017). https://eprint.iacr.org/2017/094
6. Bitansky, N., Brakerski, Z.: Classical binding for quantum commitments. In: Nissim, K., Waters, B. (eds.) TCC 2021. LNCS, vol. 13042, pp. 273–298. Springer, Cham (2021). https://doi.org/10.1007/978-3-030-90459-3_10
7. Brakerski, Z., Christiano, P., Mahadev, U., Vazirani, U.V., Vidick, T.: A cryptographic test of quantumness and certifiable randomness from a single quantum device. In: Thorup, M. (ed.) 59th FOCS, pp. 320–331. IEEE Computer Society Press, October 2018. https://doi.org/10.1109/FOCS.2018.00038
8. Brassard, G., Yung, M.: One-way group actions. In: Menezes, A.J., Vanstone, S.A. (eds.) CRYPTO 1990. LNCS, vol. 537, pp. 94–107. Springer, Heidelberg (1991). https://doi.org/10.1007/3-540-38424-3_7

9. Broadbent, A., Jeffery, S.: Quantum homomorphic encryption for circuits of low T-gate complexity. In: Gennaro, R., Robshaw, M. (eds.) CRYPTO 2015. LNCS, vol. 9216, pp. 609–629. Springer, Heidelberg (2015). https://doi.org/10.1007/978-3-662-48000-7_30

10. Castryck, W., Lange, T., Martindale, C., Panny, L., Renes, J.: CSIDH: an efficient post-quantum commutative group action. In: Peyrin, T., Galbraith, S. (eds.) ASIACRYPT 2018. LNCS, vol. 11274, pp. 395–427. Springer, Cham (2018). https://doi.org/10.1007/978-3-030-03332-3_15

11. Chailloux, A., Kerenidis, I., Rosgen, B.: Quantum commitments from complexity assumptions. In: Aceto, L., Henzinger, M., Sgall, J. (eds.) ICALP 2011. LNCS, vol. 6755, pp. 73–85. Springer, Heidelberg (2011). https://doi.org/10.1007/978-3-642-22006-7_7

12. Coladangelo, A., Liu, J., Liu, Q., Zhandry, M.: Hidden cosets and applications to unclonable cryptography. In: Malkin, T., Peikert, C. (eds.) CRYPTO 2021. LNCS, vol. 12825, pp. 556–584. Springer, Cham (2021). https://doi.org/10.1007/978-3-030-84242-0_20

13. Couveignes, J.M.: Hard homogeneous spaces. Cryptology ePrint Archive, Paper 2006/291 (2006). https://eprint.iacr.org/2006/291

14. Crépeau, C., Légaré, F., Salvail, L.: How to convert the flavor of a quantum bit commitment. In: Pfitzmann, B. (ed.) EUROCRYPT 2001. LNCS, vol. 2045, pp. 60–77. Springer, Heidelberg (2001). https://doi.org/10.1007/3-540-44987-6_5

15. Diffie, W., Hellman, M.E.: New directions in cryptography. IEEE Trans. Inf. Theor. **22**(6), 644–654 (1976). https://doi.org/10.1109/TIT.1976.1055638

16. Dumais, P., Mayers, D., Salvail, L.: Perfectly concealing quantum bit commitment from any quantum one-way permutation. In: Preneel, B. (ed.) EUROCRYPT 2000. LNCS, vol. 1807, pp. 300–315. Springer, Heidelberg (2000). https://doi.org/10.1007/3-540-45539-6_21

17. ElGamal, T.: A public key cryptosystem and a signature scheme based on discrete logarithms. IEEE Trans. Inf. Theor. **31**, 469–472 (1985)

18. Fang, J., Unruh, D., Yan, J., Zhou, D.: How to base security on the perfect/statistical binding property of quantum bit commitment? In: Bae, S.W., Park, H. (eds.) 33rd International Symposium on Algorithms and Computation, ISAAC 2022, December 19–21, 2022, Seoul, Korea. LIPIcs, vol. 248, pp. 26:1–26:12. Schloss Dagstuhl - Leibniz-Zentrum für Informatik (2022). https://doi.org/10.4230/LIPIcs.ISAAC.2022.26

19. Gentry, C., Peikert, C., Vaikuntanathan, V.: Trapdoors for hard lattices and new cryptographic constructions. In: Ladner, R.E., Dwork, C. (eds.) 40th ACM STOC, pp. 197–206. ACM Press, May 2008. https://doi.org/10.1145/1374376.1374407

20. Goldreich, O., Levin, L.A.: A hard-core predicate for all one-way functions. In: 21st ACM STOC, pp. 25–32. ACM Press, May 1989. https://doi.org/10.1145/73007.73010

21. Goldwasser, S., Micali, S., Rivest, R.L.: A "paradoxical" solution to the signature problem (extended abstract). In: 25th FOCS, pp. 441–448. IEEE Computer Society Press, October 1984. https://doi.org/10.1109/SFCS.1984.715946

22. Haitner, I., Reingold, O.: Statistically-hiding commitment from any one-way function. In: Johnson, D.S., Feige, U. (eds.) 39th ACM STOC, pp. 1–10. ACM Press, June 2007. https://doi.org/10.1145/1250790.1250792

23. Håstad, J., Impagliazzo, R., Levin, L.A., Luby, M.: A pseudorandom generator from any one-way function. SIAM J. Comput. **28**(4), 1364–1396 (1999). https://doi.org/10.1137/S0097539793244708

24. Impagliazzo, R.: A personal view of average-case complexity. In: Proceedings of the 10th Annual Structure in Complexity Theory Conference, Minneapolis, Minnesota, USA, 19–22 June 1995, pp. 134–147. IEEE Computer Society (1995). https://doi.org/10.1109/SCT.1995.514853

25. Ji, Z., Qiao, Y., Song, F., Yun, A.: General linear group action on tensors: a candidate for post-quantum cryptography. In: Hofheinz, D., Rosen, A. (eds.) TCC 2019. LNCS, vol. 11891, pp. 251–281. Springer, Cham (2019). https://doi.org/10.1007/978-3-030-36030-6_11

26. Lo, H.K., Chau, H.F.: Is quantum bit commitment really possible? Phys. Rev. Lett. **78**(17), 3410 (1997). https://doi.org/10.1103/physrevlett.78.3410

27. Mahadev, U.: Classical homomorphic encryption for quantum circuits. In: Thorup, M. (ed.) 59th FOCS, pp. 332–338. IEEE Computer Society Press, October 2018. https://doi.org/10.1109/FOCS.2018.00039

28. Mayers, D.: Unconditionally secure quantum bit commitment is impossible. Phys. Rev. Lett. **78**(17), 3414 (1997). https://doi.org/10.1103/physrevlett.78.3414

29. Morimae, T., Yamakawa, T.: Quantum commitments and signatures without one-way functions. In: Dodis, Y., Shrimpton, T. (eds.) CRYPTO 2022, Part I. LNCS, vol. 13507, pp. 269–295. Springer, Heidelberg, August 2022. https://doi.org/10.1007/978-3-031-15802-5_10

30. Naor, M.: Bit commitment using pseudorandomness. J. Cryptol. **4**(2), 151–158 (1991). https://doi.org/10.1007/BF00196774

31. Regev, O.: On lattices, learning with errors, random linear codes, and cryptography. J. ACM **56**(6), 34:1–34:40 (2009). https://doi.org/10.1145/1568318.1568324

32. Rostovtsev, A., Stolbunov, A.: Public-key cryptosystem based on isogenies. Cryptology ePrint Archive, Paper 2006/145 (2006). https://eprint.iacr.org/2006/145

33. Unruh, D.: Computationally binding quantum commitments. In: Fischlin, M., Coron, J.-S. (eds.) EUROCRYPT 2016. LNCS, vol. 9666, pp. 497–527. Springer, Heidelberg (2016). https://doi.org/10.1007/978-3-662-49896-5_18

34. Yan, J.: Quantum computationally predicate-binding commitments with application in quantum zero-knowledge arguments for NP. In: Tibouchi, M., Wang, H. (eds.) ASIACRYPT 2021. LNCS, vol. 13090, pp. 575–605. Springer, Cham (2021). https://doi.org/10.1007/978-3-030-92062-3_20

35. Yan, J.: General properties of quantum bit commitments (extended abstract). In: Agrawal, S., Lin, D. (eds.) Advances in Cryptology - ASIACRYPT 2022–28th International Conference on the Theory and Application of Cryptology and Information Security, Taipei, Taiwan, 5–9 December, 2022, Proceedings, Part IV. Lecture Notes in Computer Science, vol. 13794, pp. 628–657. Springer, Heidelberg (2022). https://doi.org/10.1007/978-3-031-22972-5_22

36. Yan, J., Weng, J., Lin, D., Quan, Y.: Quantum bit commitment with application in quantum zero-knowledge proof (extended abstract). In: Elbassioni, K.M., Makino, K. (eds.) Algorithms and Computation - 26th International Symposium, ISAAC 2015, Nagoya, Japan, 9–11 December, 2015, Proceedings. Lecture Notes in Computer Science, vol. 9472, pp. 555–565. Springer, Heidelberg (2015). https://doi.org/10.1007/978-3-662-48971-0_47
37. Zhandry, M.: Quantum lightning never strikes the same state twice. In: Ishai, Y., Rijmen, V. (eds.) EUROCRYPT 2019, Part III. LNCS, vol. 11478, pp. 408–438. Springer, Heidelberg, May 2019. https://doi.org/10.1007/978-3-030-17659-4_14

Correction to: Half-Tree: Halving the Cost of Tree Expansion in COT and DPF

Xiaojie Guo⬤, Kang Yang⬤, Xiao Wang⬤, Wenhao Zhang⬤,
Xiang Xie⬤, Jiang Zhang⬤, and Zheli Liu⬤

Correction to:
Chapter "Half-Tree: Halving the Cost of Tree
Expansionin COT and DPF" in: C. Hazay and M. Stam (Eds.):
EUROCRYPT 2023, LNCS 14004,
https://doi.org/10.1007/978-3-031-30545-0_12

In the original publication, the target acknowledgement was not correct. This has now been corrected.

The updated original version of this chapter can be found at
https://doi.org/10.1007/978-3-031-30545-0_12

Author Index

C. Hazay and M. Stam (Eds.): EUROCRYPT 2023, LNCS 14004, pp. 669–670, 2023.
https://doi.org/10.1007/978-3-031-30545-0

Printed in the United States
by Baker & Taylor Publisher Services